TRACTATUS DE SIGNIS

THE SEMIOTIC OF JOHN POINSOT

Pero con mas desseo de que su mano de V. R. los emiende y perficcione en todo.

Magis autem desidero, ut libri sub manibus [tuis] ad ultimam et omnimodam perfectionem eleventur.

My great hope is that the books in your hands will reach their highest and fullest perfection.

Juan de S. Thomas
3 July 1635
Alcalá

TRACTATUS DE SIGNIS

THE SEMIOTIC OF JOHN POINSOT

Interpretive Arrangement by

JOHN N. DEELY

in consultation with

RALPH AUSTIN POWELL,

from the 1930 Reiser edition (emended second impression)

of the *Ars Logica,*

itself comprising the first two parts of the five part

Cursus Philosophicus of 1631–1635,

by the same author.

First Published at

ALCALÁ DE HENARES

(Complutum), Iberia,

1632.

IN BILINGUAL FORMAT

FIRST EDITION

1985

UNIVERSITY OF CALIFORNIA PRESS

BERKELEY · LOS ANGELES · LONDON

University of California Press
Berkeley and Los Angeles, California

University of California Press, Ltd.
London, England

Manufactured in the United States of America

Cataloging in Publication Data for Libraries

Poinsot, John ("Joannes a Sancto Thoma"), 1589-1644.
Tractatus de Signis.
Bilingual edition of early,
perhaps earliest, fully systematized treatise in semiotic,
originally published at Alcalá de Henares (Complutum), Iberia, 1632,
as part of the *Ars Logica* of the same author,
itself comprising the first two parts
of the five-part *Cursus Philosophicus* of 1631-1635.
Bibliography: p. 587.
Including five indices.
1. Semiotics. 2. Logic—early works before 1800.
3. Signs and symbols.
I. Deely, John N. II. Powell, Ralph Austin. III. Title.
BC60.J5724 1985 160 82-17658
ISBN 0-520-04252-2

ACKNOWLEDGMENTS and DEDICATION

In the spring of 1970 this work was undertaken because of, and later sustained by, the vision of Thomas A. Sebeok.

Yet the work would not have reached its fulfillment without the learned assistance and patient counsel of Ralph Austin Powell, a graduate of Poinsot's own alma mater and his brother in religious life. His subtle mastery of philosophical traditions—the Greek, the Latin, the German, and the French—was an improbable resource made priceless by being put at my disposal throughout the project.

Translation finally of the inscrutable Latin of Poinsot's "Word to the Reader" of 1631 and 1640 was owing to J. Kenneth Downing. Archaic usage was much reduced through detailed suggestions of Bert Mahoney. Editorial assistance in point of organization came from Heinz Schmitz, and in point of grammar from Brooke Williams, who also mastered Spanish Round Gothic script for the frontispiece. The task of getting the notes on the text into presentable typescript was executed with admirable fidelity and steadiness by Claire Levy, as were many related tasks performed by my student Felicia Kruse. Carl Lenhart contributed help with proofreading.

The aim for the *Treatise* text proper was to produce matching linguistic columns, beginning and ending within the same line of text on every page. The extent to which this goal has been realized is due to the involvement and consummate skill in typesetting of Bud MacFarlane, Production Manager of Composition Specialists.

Jack Miles of the University of California Press pursued contractual arrangements for this work with understanding, vision, and respect for detail. Chet Grycz of the same press stands out in the work's actual production by his distinct commitment to its being realized in the integrity of its design. His was not the first press to try to see how this might be possible, a fact which provides the reader an intimation of the exceptional talent Mr. Grycz brings to bear on his work.

A subsidy for publishing in bi-lingual format was provided from three sources, the American Midwest Province of Saint Albert the Great, the DeRance Publication Fund of the ACPA in response to a proposal initiated under the presidency of Desmond FitzGerald, and Mr. Jerome Powell. Free time along with typing and copying facilities for an initial draft of this work was provided by Mortimer J. Adler.

This work is dedicated to the memory of J. Eris Powell (1875-1949), whose concept of Public Life in the end made this work possible, and to the memory of his wife, Mary Conroy Powell (1888-1960). It is dedicated also to the memory of a monk of the abbey of Solesmes, with the hope that his work will be somehow continued—Dom Boissard, who produced the magnificent five volumes of the Solesmes edition of Poinsot's theological *Cursus* according to standards the present little work has sought to realize in its own order. His death in December of 1979 robbed humane culture for the second time (the first was Père Combefis' death in 1679) of a completed edition worthy of its proper merits.

CONTENTS

Σημιωτική

The Third Branch may be called Σημιωτική, or *the Doctrine of Signs;* the most usual whereof being Words, it is aptly enough termed also Λογική, Logick; the business whereof, is to consider the Nature of Signs, the Mind makes use of for the understanding of Things, or conveying its Knowledge to others.

And, perhaps, if they were distinctly weighed, and duly considered, they would afford us another sort of Logick and Critick, than what we have been hitherto acquainted with.

John Locke,
''Of the Division of the Sciences
[beyond the Speculative and the Practical],''
1690

ABBREVIATIONS

Aristotle is cited according to the page, column (a, b), and line of the Berlin edition (following Reiser 1930, XVII-XVIII: see Index Aristotelicus, p. 517 below).

Le = the Roman Leonine Edition of the works of St. Thomas Aquinas, 1882 ssq. (following Reiser, loc. cit.: see Index Thomisticus, p. 518 below).

Pa = the Parma edition of the works of St. Thomas Aquinas, 1852-1873 (following Reiser, loc. cit.: see Index Thomisticus, p. 518 below).

P.L. = *Patrologiae Cursus Completus*, ed. J.-P. Migne, *Series Latina*, Vols. 1-162, Paris: 1878-1889.

Poinsot is cross-referenced according to the Parts of the original publication of the *Cursus Philosophicus*, specifically: *Artis Logicae Prima Pars* = Logica 1. p. = 1631, *Artis Logicae Secunda Pars* = Logica 2. p. = 1632, *Naturalis Philosophiae Prima Pars* = Phil. nat. 1. p. = 1633, *Naturalis Philosophiae Tertia Pars* = Phil. nat. 3. p. = 1634, *Naturalis Philosophiae Quarta Pars* = Phil. nat. 4. p. = 1635), followed by the Question (q.), Article (art.), and, where necessary, also by specific volume (I, II, III), page, column (a, b), and line references to Reiser's edition of the whole (Turin: Marietti, 1930-1937). The *Naturalis Philosophiae Secunda Pars*, on astronomy, was suppressed in the year of scheduled publication (1634, the year of Galileo's condemnation in Rome) by Poinsot himself, and there is no extant text of this Part known at the present time: see discussion in the "Editorial Afterword" following the text of the *Treatise*.

Reiser's own footnotes from his edition of the *Cursus* are incorporated into this edition of the *Treatise on Signs*, those referring to the works of Aristotle, St. Thomas, or any other author with punctuation, spacing, and capitalization unchanged.

To the Reader of This Edition:

The semiotic of John Poinsot here presented autonomously for the first time was disengaged from a larger work entitled the *Ars Logica*, itself but the first two parts of a five-part *Cursus Philosophicus*. Since this work has a considerable historical interest in its own right, and in order to minimize the violence of editing the *tractatus de signis* into a whole independent of that original context, we have settled on the following manner of presentation.

Putting ourselves in the position of a reader coming to the *Ars Logica* for the first time and interested only in Poinsot's discussion of signs, we asked ourselves: What sections of the work would this hypothetical reader have to look at in order to appreciate that discussion both in its own terms and in terms of the whole of which it originally formed a part? To what extent are these separable philosophically?

The pages that follow make up our solution to this problem. We have left Poinsot's text stand virtually entirely according to the order he proposed for it within the *Ars Logica* as a whole. To make this order clear, we have included title pages, and all *general statements* Poinsot set down concerning the whole (and therefore the *Treatise* as part), inserting where appropriate and to bridge necessary jumps a series of brief comments designated "semiotic markers," designed to show the reader how the rationale of all editing is derived from the original author's own intentions; and second, we have included all and only those sections of the whole which have a direct bearing on understanding the doctrine proposed in the *Treatise on Signs* proper, as the semiotic markers make clear.

In other words, we have tried to provide the reader with a guided tour of the *Ars Logica* that leads directly to an understanding of the doctrine of signs contained in that work, but does so by enabling him or her to appreciate the historical origin of the account in the context of its author's own understanding of previous logical and philosophical traditions. We have chosen this format as the one best suited, so far as we could judge, to exhibit the unique mediating status Poinsot's *Treatise* occupies "archeologically," as it were, in the Western tradition between the ontological concerns of ancient, medieval, and renaissance philosophy, and the epistemological concerns of modern and contemporary thought.

At the end of the work, the reader will find a lengthy "Editorial Afterword" explaining the entire work and giving its background and prospectus, much the sort of materials commonly given in an Introduction to a translated

work. The device of the semiotic markers made it possible in this case to bypass the need for lengthy introductory materials enabling the reader to grasp the editorial structure of the whole, yet without of course obviating the need for detailed discussions somewhere of the principles of the English text, and of the historical situation of the author and his work. Thus we have been able to enter simply and directly into the doctrinal content of the main text, without cluttering its entrance with more than a very few lines of contemporary origin.

The reader will also find at the end of the work a complete series of indices to this entire edition, both to its main text (which indices are explained at length in the ''Afterword'' just mentioned) and to its accompanying editorial materials, followed by a comprehensive list of bibliographical references. Bibliographical references not complete in the markers or in the notes on the text will be found there. All indexical references to the *Treatise* itself with its attendant parts (i.e., to the bi-lingual portions of this edition) are by page and line numbers, thus providing the reader with the exact place of each reference in this English edition of Poinsot's text and, at the same time, the almost exact place in the parallel column of the Latin original. Similarly, all cross-references to other parts of Poinsot's *Cursus Philosophicus*, as in the running heads of the present edition, are according to the pages, columns (a, b), and lines of the Reiser edition, as set out in the ''Abbreviations'' immediately preceding this preface.

From the
First and Second Parts
of the

ARS LOGICA

The Excerpts Which Exhibit
the Rationale
of the
Treatise on Signs
and the
Manner of Its Derivation

SPAIN

1631–1632

LECTORI:[1]

Brevitatem sectantes otiosum videbitur morosa praefatione diffundi, vel ipsa Spiritus Sancti sententia id praedamnante: «Stultum est ante historiam diffluere, in ipsa vero historia succingi»[2]. Ne ergo taedium et onus lectori in ipso limine iniciamus, tantum admonuerim studii nostri scopum eo collimasse, ut ad brevem et concisam methodum pro viribus Logicae et Philosophiae disciplinam iuxta S. Thomae sensum redigeremus. Idcirco non solum visum est eius solidam sequi et imitari doctrinam, sed ordinem, brevitatem modestiamque aemulari.

Ut methodum ordinemque sequeremur, in operis fronte Logicam in duas partes dividimus. *Prima* dialecticas disputationes, quas Summulas vocant, complectitur et circa formam logicalem versatur. *Secunda,* circa praedicabilia et praedicamenta ac libros Posteriorum, tractat de instrumentis logicalibus ex parte materiae et posterioristicae resolutionis, ut abundantius in initio huius libri adnotamus.

Ut brevitatem imitaremur, immensam inextricabilium quaestionum silvam et spinosa sophismatum dumeta excidere curavimus, quae audientium mentibus onerosae et pungentes utilitatis nihil, dispendii non parum afferebant. Ad haec metaphysicas difficultates pluresque alias ex libris de Anima, quae disputantium ardore in ipsa Summularum cunabula irruperant, suo loco amandavimus et tractatum de signis et notitiis[3] in Logica super librum Perihermenias expedimus. Quidquid autem in tractatu de termino et aliis locis ad Logicam remittimus, ibidem etiam loca adnotamus. Nec tamen omnino evadere potuimus, quin aliqua libaremus ex praecipuis magisque necessariis difficultatibus, quae et docentibus et discentibus ad logicales quaestiones explicandas conducebant. Curabit autem lector, ut viso aliquo textus capitulo difficultates illi correspondentes inquirat in quaestionibus; sic enim omnes, quae occurrerint,

To the Reader of 1631:[1]

It is useless to put off with a wordy preface those who appreciate brevity—in the words of the Spirit: "There would be no sense in expanding the preface to the history and curtailing the history itself."[2] In order therefore to avoid wearying the reader, let me say only this concerning the scope of my work, that I have adopted, for the sake of brief and concise exposition, a method suited to the vigor of a Logic and Philosophy developed according to the mind of St. Thomas Aquinas. Accordingly, my plan has been not only to follow and represent his assured doctrine, but to emulate as well his order, brevity, and modesty.

Following his method and organization, I have divided the whole of Logic into two parts. The *first part*, which is called the *Summulae* books, comprises dialectical disputations and treats of formal logic. The *second part*, which concerns the predicables, categories, and the books of Posterior Analytics, treats of logical tools from the standpoint of analysis of content, as I explain more fully where those books are taken up.

To imitate the brevity of St. Thomas, I have taken care to cut out of the *Summulae* books a vast forest of intractable questions and a thorny thicket of sophisms which serve only to burden and abrade the minds of students, causing no little damage in the past. The metaphysical and other difficulties from the books On the Soul which the ardor of disputants has caused to intrude into the very beginning of the *Summulae* books, I have removed to their proper place, locating a *treatise on signs and notices* or *modes of awareness*[3] in Logic relative to the book On Interpretation. Whatever I have removed to the second part of Logic from the discussion of the term or other *Summulae* topics, I have so noted at the appropriate place. Even so, I have not been able to postpone discussion of all difficulties, but have taken up in the first part some of the principal and more necessary questions that conduce to an understanding of logical questions for teachers and students alike. The reader will therefore take care, when he has completed a chapter of the *Summulae* text, to look into the corresponding difficulties discussed in the disputed questions which follow the *Summulae*

---

[1] *Auctoris in universam Logicam praefatio.* Author's preface to the entire *Ars Logica.*

[2] 2. Machab. 2, 33.

[3] As the term "awareness" is not usually used in the plural as an English word, I have used the expression "modes of awareness," analogous to Norman Kemp Smith's translation of *Erkenntnisse* as "modes of knowledge" (cf. *Immanuel Kant's Critique of Pure Reason,* trans. Norman Kemp Smith [New York: St. Martin's Press, 1963], p. 42, note 1). Given the level of awareness under discussion in the context of our *Treatise,* "notices" would also be an appropriate rendering.

in the first part of Logic; for in this way the reader will be able more easily to perceive and overcome all the difficulties that arise.

Finally, to engrave modesty (one of the more gracious of the holy Doctor's angelic virtues) upon this brevity, I have adopted the policy of abstaining from lengthy citations and lists of names in referring —whether favorably or adversely—to the positions of various authors (for I do not publish this work for the sake of contention or for promotion of partisan rivalries, but to advance inquiry into truth, which concerns doctrine and not persons). This policy is also calculated to better dispose readers, in whom knowledge is instilled the more easily when it is studied not so much in terms of the contention of authors and authorities as in terms of the struggle for truth alone. My fullest wish, cultured reader, is that you may attain truth with increased profit from this fragile but dedicated pen. Farewell.

Alcalá, Spain, 1631

difficultates facilius percipiet et evincere poterit.

Ut denique modestiam (gratiorem inter angelicas S. Doctoris virtutes gemmam) brevi huic annulo exculperemus, placuit sic diversorum auctorum placita aut referre aut impugnare aut sequi, ut plerumque a prolixa citatione et publicatione nominum abstineremus (nec enim haec nostra evulgamus aut contentioni aut aemulationis zelo obsecundantes, sed veritatis inquisitioni servientes, quae doctrinam respicit, non personas); et ut audientium commodo prospiceremus, quibus facilius instillatur doctrina, si non tam auctorum et auctoritatum concertationi quam veritatis solius luctae studeatur. Quam ut multiplicato foenore assequi possis, humanissime lector, tenui hoc, sed affectuoso calamo plenissime peroptamus. Vale.

Alcalá, Spain, 1631

First Semiotic Marker

This "Word to the Reader" of 1631 includes Poinsot's public announcement of his forthcoming *Treatise on Signs*. Though that *Treatise* is to be issued as a part of the much larger work on Logic, the *Ars Logica* that he here introduces, it is clear from the way he singles out the *Treatise* that it occupies a position of special importance in his understanding of the whole.

Moreover, the relationship of the *Treatise* to his *Summulae*, or introductory, texts on logic is clear: it covers the same material as the opening chapters of the introductory texts, but at a deeper level and reorganized according to a different point of view, one for which Poinsot himself has no specific name, but which exactly corresponds to the viewpoint Locke will suggest and label *semiotic* fifty-nine years later and without knowledge of Poinsot's groundbreaking work.

Finally, in asserting that the "proper place" for the *Treatise* is under the traditional heading of "Interpretation," Poinsot implies a critique of the entire tradition of Latin Aristotelianism which had developed a logic exclusively of terms and propositions, and arguments made from these, whereas in fact "interpretation" is a much broader activity coextensive with the entire life of the mind, what Peirce, developing Locke's suggestion, will label in our own day *semiosis*. This critique will become much sharper and more explicit when Poinsot reaches the point in his survey of the whole of logic traditionally conceived where the Aristotelian books on interpretation would normally be considered, as we shall see.

But in the meantime, the lines to be followed for disengaging the *Treatise on Signs* from the larger whole of the *Ars Logica* have already been clearly drawn in all essentials: the reader should have a look at the opening *Summulae* texts which germinate in terminist perspective (the perspective of a logic of terms, propositions, and arguments) the problems reduced to their proper unity in the *Treatise on Signs*; then turn to the section of the second part of Poinsot's Logic concerning the Aristotelian treatment of "Interpretation" where one will find the *Treatise on Signs* proper. Additionally, since the *Treatise* was originally embedded in the second part of the larger whole of the *Ars Logica*, Poinsot's "Introduction to the Entire Work," explaining its style and organization, would pertain equally to an understanding of the independent *Treatise*, as would the "Word to the Reader" Poinsot added in 1640 to a republication of the *Artis Logicae Secunda Pars*, inasmuch as this second part was the original matrix of the *Treatise on Signs*. We take up each of these texts therefore in their proper order.

PROLOGUS TOTIUS DIALECTICAE

in Duobus Praeludiis

INTRODUCTION TO THE ENTIRE WORK

in Two Prologues

[3a1-b7]

First Prologue

[on the style of the work]

Wherein Is Set Forth the Exercise and Practice of Dialectical Disputation

Praeludium Primum

Quo Proponitur Dialecticae Disputationis Exercitium et Praxis

At the very beginning of the dialectic art that we modestly set out to explain, it seemed best to show beginners the form and procedure of disputation in actual use and practice. It can be briefly described as follows.

In any disputation, the first concern of *the one arguing* should be to propose an argument *entirely reduced to form*. That is to say, having stripped away everything superfluous, whether ambiguous words or lengthy declarations, the one arguing should succinctly and distinctly propose a syllogism or an enthymeme. A *syllogism* contains three propositions, which are called the *major* premise, the *minor* premise, and the conclusion or *consequent*, connected by the sign of illation, which is the particle ''therefore.'' The *connection itself*, however, is called the illation or *consequence*. An *enthymeme* contains two propositions, of which the first is called an *antecedent*, the second a *consequent*, also connected by an illation. For example, if I want to prove that one ought not embrace a life of voluptuousness, I form a syllogism thus: ''Whatever opposes true human virtue ought not to be embraced; a voluptuous life opposes true human virtue; therefore it ought not to be embraced.'' Or, if I wish to form an enthymeme of antecedent and consequent, I form it thus: ''A voluptuous life is opposed to the arduousness of virtue; therefore it ought not to be embraced.''

In ipsa fronte artis Dialecticae, quam pro exiguitate nostra explicare aggredimur, formam modumque disputationis tironibus in ipso exercitio et praxi proponere visum est, quae sic breviter explicari potest.

Igitur in quacumque disputatione primo loco arguens proponere curet **argumentum**, omnino ad formam redactum, omnibus aliis, sive verborum ambagibus sive longis declarationibus amputatis, succincteque ac distincte syllogismum vel enthymema proponat.* Et syllogismus continet tres propositiones, quae dicuntur maior et minor et conclusio seu consequens, per notam illationis, quae est particula ,, ergo '', connexas; ipsa autem connexio vocatur illatio vel consequentia. Enthymema autem continet duas propositiones, quarum prima vocatur antecedens, secunda consequens, eodem etiam modo connexas. V. g. intendo probare, quod vita voluptuosa non sit amplectenda, formo sic syllogismum: « Quidquid honestati virtutis repugnat, non est amplectendum; vita voluptuosa honestati virtutis repugnat; ergo non est amplectenda ». Vel si volo formare enthymema ex antecedente et consequente, sic formo: « Vita voluptuosa opponitur arduitati virtutis; ergo non est amplectenda ».

---

* Cf. p. 456 for explanation of typographic conventions used in the text.

Hearing the formulation of the argument, *the one responding* should attend to nothing except to repeat integrally and faithfully the argument proposed, and meanwhile, while he repeats the argument, he should consider carefully whether each premise is true, and to be granted, or false, and to be denied, or doubtful or equivocal, and to be distinguished. He should likewise consider whether the consequence or illation is valid or invalid. Having repeated the argument once without saying anything by way of response, the one responding then should repeat and respond to the propositions of the argument taken singly, in this order: If there were *three propositions* and he thinks the *first* to be *true*, he should say: ''*I grant the major* premise.'' If he thinks it *false*, he should say: ''*I deny the major*.'' If he thinks it *does not matter for the conclusion* that ought to be inferred or drawn, he should say: ''*Let the major pass*,'' although this formula should be used modestly and rarely,[1] and not unless it is *clearly* the case that the proposition is irrelevant. If he thinks the major is *doubtful* or *equivocal*, he should say: ''*I distinguish the major*,'' and make the distinction with few and clear words, based on the term in which there is an equivocation. Having made the distinction, he should not immediately explain it, unless either the opponent asks for an explanation, or [he himself sees how] it was not expressed clearly enough, in which case he should explain it as briefly as he can. Especially at the beginning of a disputation he should not use up time explaining distinctions, but should in no wise depart from the form itself of his argument. When the major has been granted or explained under a distinction, he proceeds to the minor premise and observes the same procedures in denying or conceding or distinguishing that we have set out for the major premise. Then, coming to the conclusion, if it must be *conceded*, he says: ''*I grant the consequence*.'' If it must be *denied*, he says, ''*I deny the consequence*.'' But if the conclusion must be *distinguished*, he should *not* say, ''I distinguish the *consequence*,'' but rather, ''I distinguish the *consequent*;'' *for since the consequence consists in the illation itself, but not in an assertion of truth, it can be a valid or an invalid illation*, and so can be granted or denied as valid or invalid, *but it cannot be distinguished, because a distinction falls upon* an equivocation or ambiguity in a proposition so far as the proposition has *diverse senses in signifying a truth, not upon the correctness itself of an illation*. The *consequent*, however, is the illated [or inferred] *proposition*, which can be *certain* or

Audita propositione argumenti **defendens** ad nihil aliud attendat, quam ut integre ac fideliter propositum argumentum repetat et interim, dum argumentum resumit, perpendat, an aliqua praemissarum sit vera, ut concedatur, vel falsa, ut negetur, an dubia vel aequivoca, ut distinguatur; item consequentia seu illatio an sit bona vel mala. Resumpto semel argumento et nihil ad illud respondens, secundo repetat et ad singulas propositiones respondeat hoc ordine. Si fuerint tres propositiones et primam videat esse veram, dicat: «Concedo maiorem». Si videat esse falsam, dicat: «Nego maiorem». Si videat non pertinere ad conclusionem inferendam, dicat: «Transeat maior», quamquam hoc verbo modeste et parce utendum est,[1] nec nisi clare constet propositionem impertinenter se habere. Si videat maiorem esse dubiam aut aequivocam, dicat: «Distinguo maiorem», et super terminum, in quo est aequivocatio, faciat distinctionem brevibus verbis, et non confusis. Data autem distinctione non statim illam explicet, nisi vel impugnator id petat, vel non satis clare fuerit prolata, et tunc brevissime illam explicet. Praesertim autem in initio disputationis non consumat tempus in explicandis distinctionibus, sed ab ipsa forma nullatenus recedat. Concessa maiore vel sub distinctione explicata procedat ad minorem et idem observet in negando vel concedendo aut distinguendo, sicut diximus de maiori. Deinde ad conclusionem deveniendo, si est concedenda, dicat: «Concedo consequentiam», si neganda, dicat: «Nego consequentiam». Si autem est distinguenda, non dicat: «Distinguo consequentiam», sed «distinguo consequens»; consequentia enim cum consistat in ipsa illatione, non vero in assertione veritatis, potest esse bona vel mala illatio, et sic concedi aut negari ut bona vel mala, sed non distingui, quia distinctio cadit super aequivocationem aut ambiguitatem propositionis, quatenus habet diversos sensus in significando veritatem, non super ipsam convenientiam illationis. Ipsum autem consequens est propositio illata, quae potest esse certa aut

[1] In fact, Poinsot uses this expression only once in his *Treatise*, at 144/11 (=*660a48*).

equivocal or *ambiguous*; whence, when it is equivocal, it is distinguished, and so one does not say "I distinguish the consequence," but "I distinguish the consequent." Yet if the consequent is to be conceded or denied, since this cannot be done except by conceding or denying the consequence itself, it suffices to say "I deny (or I grant) the consequence," but not to say "I deny (or I grant) the consequent."

When a distinction has been made respecting some proposition, that same distinction should be applied as many times as the same equivocation occurs. One should not subdistinguish the sense of a distinction once that distinction has been granted unless *another* equivocation plainly appears which cannot be removed by the prior distinction. It is safer to deny whatever is false and not permit it to pass, unless it is certainly a case of an invalid consequence. If the one responding does not grasp the sense of the proposition, and so is unable to discern truth or falsity or equivocation, he should ask the one propounding the argument to explain its sense, and then he should repeat the explanation.

Finally, the one responding should take care to answer with few words, and to be bound only by the form of the argument. Nor should he give a reason for everything he says, unless a reason is asked of him. He should rather leave to the one arguing the entire burden of proof; for in this way the force of the argument becomes more formally clear, and it is the more quickly dispatched.

It is part of the task of *the one presenting the argument*: *First*, not to lay down many presuppositions, nor to introduce many middle terms, nor to propose excessively long or intricate propositions, but to hold succinctly and stringently to form, not by asking many questions, but rather by setting forth proofs, except when the force of the argument devolves upon this, that he is asked a reason for the things said, or when the state of the disputation and the point of the difficulty have not yet been made sufficiently clear. *Second*, to proceed always with the same middle term through its causes and principles, or in deducing an inconsistency, but not to switch to another middle term, or to repeat a proof already proposed either in the same or in other words, because both are unduly wordy and tedious. *Finally*, he should not always use a syllogism, but sometimes an enthymeme, which proceeds more briefly and concisely and manifests less force of hidden illation, and for this reason presents a greater difficulty to the one responding.

aequivoca aut ambigua, unde quando aequivoca est, distinguitur, et sic non dicitur « distinguo consequentiam », sed « distinguo consequens ». Si tamen concedendum aut negandum est consequens, quia id fieri non potest, nisi concedendo aut negando ipsam consequentiam, sufficit dicere, nego vel concedo consequentiam, non vero consequens.

Facta distinctione super aliqua propositione, quoties occurrat eadem aequivocatio, adhibeat eandem distinctionem. Non subdistinguat sensum distinctionis semel concessum, nisi evidenter alia aequivocatio appareat, quae priori distinctione tolli non potuit. Quodcumque falsum, tutius est negare, nec permittere ut transeat, nisi certo constet de malitia consequentiae. Si sensum propositionis non percipiat, ut veritatem aut falsitatem vel aequivocationem discernat, petat ab arguente, ut eius sensum explicet, et tunc resumat.

Denique curet pauca respondere et solum alligari formae argumenti, nec de omnibus, quae dicit, velit rationem reddere, nisi ab ipso petatur, sed totum onus probandi arguenti relinquat; sic enim et argumenti vis formalius innotescit et citius expeditur.

Ad munus **argumentatoris** pertinet: P r i m o, non praemittere plures praesuppositiones, nec inculcare plura media, nec propositiones nimis longas aut intricatas proponere, sed succincte ad formam se astringere, non pluribus interrogationibus utendo, sed magis probationes urgendo, nisi quando vis argumenti ad hoc devolvitur, ut petatur ratio dictorum, vel quando status disputationis et punctus difficultatis nondum est sufficienter declaratus. S e c u n d o, prosequatur semper idem medium per suas causas et principia, vel ad inconveniens deducendo, non vero divertat ad aliud medium, nec repetat probationem semel propositam aut eisdem aut aliis verbis, quia utrumque valde prolixum et taediosum est. D e n i q u e non semper utatur syllogismo, sed quandoque enthymemate, quod brevius et concisius procedit minusque manifestat vim latentis illationis ideoque maiorem respondenti incutit difficultatem.

It is, finally, *the task of the Moderator* of the dialectical exercise:[2] *First,* to comprehend attentively the entire progress of the argument and disputation. *Second,* to see to it that the form of arguing and responding is fully observed. *Third,* not to assume or preempt the function of the one responding, much less that of the one arguing, but to suggest prudently according to the perceived need of the one responding a denial, a concession, or a distinction within some proposition. *Finally,* to render a judgment briefly at the end of the disputation and to clear up any obscurities.

Ad munus tandem **Patroni** seu **Praesidentis** spectat:[2] Primo, attente totum progressum argumenti et disputationis comprehendere. Secundo, providere, ut forma arguendi et respondendi omnino servetur. Tertio, officium respondentis non assumere vel praevenire, et multo minus impugnatoris, sed provide iuxta quod viderit indigere respondentem, suggerere negationem, concessionem aut distinctionem propositionis. Tandem, in fine iudicium de disputatione breviter ferre et obscura declarare.

[2] This, in effect, is the task that falls to the reader of the *Treatise on Signs*.

[5a4-43]

Second Prologue

The Division of the Logical Art, Its Order and Necessity

Praeludium Secundum

Artis Logicae Divisio, Ordo, Necessitas

In any art, thought must be given principally to two things, namely, the matter in which the art works, and the form drawn out of that matter. For example, houses are made from stones and wood, but their form is *a composition,* because these particular beams and stones are coordinated among themselves in the single figure and structure of a house. The architect does not supply the material, but presupposes its reality; what he does supply and draw out is the form, which, because it was properly educed by art, is simultaneously principally intended by that art, as being something produced by it. But Logic is "a kind of art which has as its function the direction of reason, lest it err in the paths of discoursing and knowing," just as the art of the builder directs the worker, lest he err in the building of the house. And therefore Logic is called a *rational art,* not only because it exists in the reasoning mind as in a subject, just as do all arts, but because the materials it directs are themselves works of human understanding.

Now since reason proceeds analytically in developing opinions and making judgments, that is to say, in deducing its principles and discerning proofs by which reason is manifested, the preservation of reason from error is identical with enabling it to resolve rightly and properly the reasonings to which it applies itself. For this reason, Aristotle called the parts of Logic dealing with the making sure of judgments "analytics," that is, resolutory, because they teach the right resolution of reasonings and the avoidance of errors. But

In omni arte duo sunt praecipue considerandа, scilicet materia, in qua ars operatur, et forma, quae in tali materia inducitur, sicut in facienda domo materia sunt lapides et ligna, forma autem est compositio, quia ista inter se coordinantur in una figura et structura domus. Materiam artifex non facit, sed praesupponit, formam vero inducit, quae quia proprie educitur ab arte, est etiam principaliter intenta ab illa, utpote factura eius. Est autem Logica « ars quaedam, cuius munus est dirigere rationem, ne in modo discurrendi et cognoscendi erret », sicut ars aedificatoria dirigit artificem, ne erret in facienda domo. Et ideo Logica dicitur ars rationalis, non solum quia est in ratione ut in subiecto, sicut aliae artes, sed quia materia, quam dirigit, sunt ipsa opera rationis.

Et quia ratio ad discurrendum et ferendum iudicium procedit per modum resolutionis, hoc est, in sua principia deducendo et probationes, quibus manifestatur, discernendo, idem est Logicam dirigere rationem, ne erret, ac dirigere, ut recte et debite resolvat. Unde Aristoteles partes Logicae, quae docent certum praebere iudicium, vocavit analyticas, id est resolutorias, quia docent recte et sine errore resolvere. Fit au-

right resolution of reasonings comes about owing both to the requirements of the form and to the certitude of the matter. "Materials" here signifies the things or objects we wish to rightly objectify or come to know. But form is the very mode or disposition whereby the objects known are connected in a pattern according to which they may be properly expressed and cognized, for without such connection no truth is conceived, nor does any discourse, or illation of one truth from another, develop. Now resolution (analysis) on the side of the form is said to pertain to *prior analytics*, but resolution on the side of the materials, in terms of certainty and requisite conditions, pertains to *posterior analytics*, because the consideration of a form created by art (the *methodology* or *technique*) is *prior* to the consideration of materials in any art.

Hence we *divide* the art of Logic into two parts. In the first part, we treat of all that pertains to the form of logical art and to prioristic analysis, the subjects treated by Aristotle in the books On Interpretation and in the books of the Prior Analytics. These are also the subjects customarily treated in the *Summulae* books for beginning students. In the second part, we treat of what pertains to the content of the reasoning or to posterioristic analysis, especially in the matter of demonstrations, at which Logic aims above all.[1]

And in that first part—the *Summulae* textbooks—we provide brief summaries as the first thing students must learn; then, for advanced students, we dispute more difficult questions. In the second part, by contrast, we submit to dispute more useful and weighty questions, following an ordered summary of the texts of Porphyry and of Aristotle.

tem recta resolutio tum ex debita forma, tum ex certitudine materiae. Materia sunt res seu obiecta, quae volumus recte cognoscere. Forma autem est ipse modus seu dispositio, qua connectuntur obiecta cognita, ut debite discurratur et cognoscatur, quia sine connexione nec veritas aliqua concipitur, nec ex una veritate ad aliam fit discursus et illatio. Et resolutio ex parte formae dicitur pertinere ad priorem resolutionem, ex parte vero materiae secundum certitudinem et conditiones debitas ad posteriorem resolutionem, eo quod consideratio formae artificiosae est prior in aliqua arte, quam consideratio materiae.

Hinc ergo sumimus **divisionem** artis Logicae et facimus duas partes: In prima agemus de omnibus his, quae pertinent ad formam artis Logicae et ad prioristicam resolutionem, de quibus egit Philosophus in libris Perihermenias et in libris Priorum Analyticorum, et in Summulis tradi solent tironibus. In secunda vero parte agemus de his, quae pertinent ad materiam logicalem seu ad posterioristicam resolutionem, maxime in demonstratione, ad quam praecipue ordinatur Logica.[1]

Et in hac prima parte formamus brevem textum pro discipulis primum erudiendis, deinde pro provectioribus quaestiones difficiliores disputamus. In secunda vero parte iuxta textum Porphyrii et Aristotelis summatim positum utiliores et graviores subiciemus disputationes.

[1] Poinsot's own distribution of the materials in this traditional coverage is represented in the following schema:

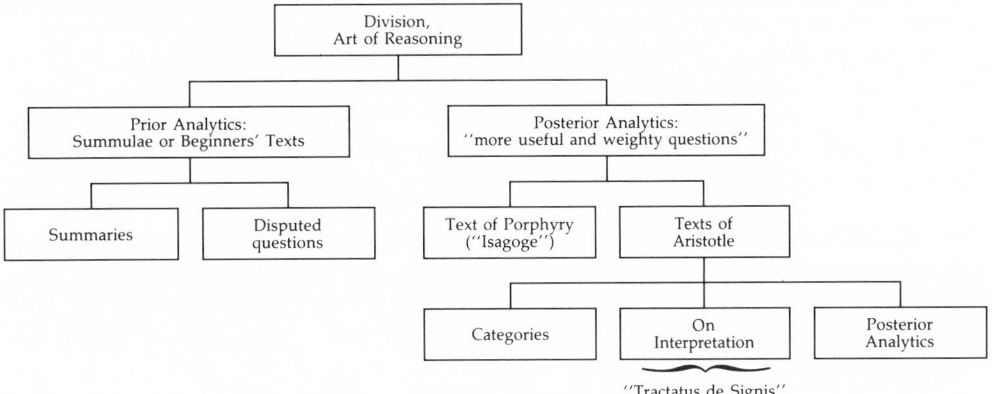

The Order of Treatment.—Since Logic provides the means of reasoning rightly, and since there are three acts of reason, which pass into one another, as St. Thomas teaches in the first reading of the first book of his *Commentary on the Posterior Analytics,*[2] there is no better order to follow than that of treating Logic in terms of these three operations. The first operation of our understanding is called simple apprehension or awareness—as when I think of a man without making any judgments concerning him. The second is composition or division, when to wit I know a thing in such a way as to attribute or deny something to it, as when I say a man is white or deny he is a stone. The third operation is discourse, as when I infer and gather from some known truth another not so known; for example, from the truth of the proposition "man is rational" I infer that "he is therefore capable of learning through experience." The first thing I apprehend therefore are terms, then I compose from them a proposition, and finally I make of propositions discourse.

Hence we separate *this first part* into three books: A first for treating of whatever pertains to the first operation, and it is here that we discuss simple terms. A second for the second operation, where we treat of speaking and of the proposition and its properties. A third book for the third operation, where we treat of the ways of discoursing and of forming syllogisms and induction and all else that pertains to the domain of things to be reasoned.

In the *second part* of the Logic we treat of what pertains to the matter of such operations, especially as they are ordered to the forming of certain judgments derived from necessary truths, which comes about through demonstration. Now necessary truths depend upon essential predicates, of the sort organized in the categories, and these in turn derive from the predicables, which express the modes of predicating, as will be explained more fully at the beginning of the Second Part of the Logic. Nor is it redundant for simple terms and what pertains to the first operation to be treated twice in Logic, because, as St. Thomas says in the first reading of his *Commentary* on the first book of Aristotle's *On Interpretation,*[3] simple terms are treated from one point of view in the book of *Categories*, namely, as signifying simple essences, from another point of view in the book *On Interpretation*, namely, as they are parts of an enunciation,

Ordo agendi. — Cum Logica dirigat modum recte ratiocinandi et sint tres actus rationis, in quibus de uno proceditur ad alium, ut docet S. Thomas 1. Poster. lect. 1.[2], non potest melior ordo observari, quam ut tractatum Logicae per has tres operationes distribuamus. Prima operatio nostri intellectus vocatur simplex apprehensio, ut cum intelligo hominem nihil de illo affirmando vel negando. Secunda est compositio aut divisio, cum videlicet ita cognosco rem, ut illi aliquid attribuam vel negem, ut cum dico hominem album aut nego hominem esse lapidem. Tertia operatio est discursus, ut cum ex aliqua veritate nota infero et colligo aliam non ita notam, ut cum ex ista veritate « homo est rationalis » infero « ergo est disciplinabilis ». Primum ergo apprehendo terminos, deinde compono ex illis propositionem, denique formo ex propositionibus discursum.

Sic ergo **in hac prima parte** distribuemus tres libros: Primum pro his, quae pertinent ad primam operationem, ubi agemus de simplicibus terminis. Secundum pro secunda operatione, ubi agemus de oratione et propositione eiusque proprietatibus. Tertium pro tertia, ubi agemus de modo discurrendi et formandi syllogismos et inductionem ceteraque pertinentia ad ratiocinandum.

In secunda autem parte Logicae agemus de his, quae pertinent ad materiam talium operationum, praecipue ut ordinatur ad formandum certum iudicium ex veritatibus necessariis, quod fit per demonstrationem. Veritates autem necessario pendent ex praedicatis essentialibus, quae coordinantur in praedicamentis, et haec ex praedicabilibus, quae dicunt modos praedicandi, ut latius initio secundae partis Logicae explicabitur. Nec est inconveniens, quod de simplicibus et his, quae pertinent ad primam operationem, agatur in Logica bis, quia, ut notat S. Thomas 1. Periherm. lect. 1.[3], de dictionibus simplicibus sub alia consideratione agitur in Praedicamentis, scilicet ut significant simplices essentias, sub alia in libro Perihermenias, scilicet ut sunt partes enuntiationis,

[2] *Le* I. 138. n. 4.
[3] *Le* I. 8. n. 5.

and from yet another viewpoint in the books of *Prior Analytics*, namely, as they constitute a syllogistic order.

Finally, since it is possible in discourse to arrive at a judgment in three different ways—namely, certainly, through demonstration; topically, through opinion; and erroneously, through sophisms—Aristotle treats of opinion in the *Topics* and of sophistic syllogisms in the *Refutations* after treating of demonstration and knowledge in the books of *Posterior Analytics*.

There is the greatest *need for this art*, both for the general reason that man requires arts to direct his works rightly and without error, and for the specific reason that Logic directs the works of human understanding on which all discourse and reasoning depend for being right, free of error, and orderly—something very necessary for a man making use of reason. But more of this in the opening question of the second part of the Logic.

sub alia in libris Priorum, scilicet ut constituunt ordinem syllogisticum.

Denique, quia in discursu procedi potest tripliciter ad formandum iudicium, scilicet certo per demonstrationem, topice per opinionem, erronee per sophismata, ideo Aristoteles postquam in libris Posteriorum egit de demonstratione et scientia, agit in Topicis de opinativo et in Elenchis de sophistico syllogismo.

Necessitas huius artis maxima est, tum generali ratione omnium artium, quae necessariae sunt, ut homo in suis operibus recte et sine errore dirigatur, tum specialiter, quia Logica dirigit opera rationis, ex quibus omnis discursus et ratiocinatio pendet, ut recta sit et sine errore et ordinate procedens, quod utique valde necessarium est homini ratione utenti. Sed de hoc amplius q. 1. prooem. secundae partis Logicae.

Second Semiotic Marker

The importance of this second prologue to appreciating the interest of Poinsot's *Treatise on Signs* lies in seeing the extent of the tradition which Poinsot undertakes to dominate in writing his *Ars Logica.* The *Isagoge* (or "Introduction") of Porphyry, along with the *Categories* and other of Aristotle's logical tracts, was introduced to the Latin West in the sixth century through the translations and commentaries of Boethius. Though the creative period of Scholastic logic did not begin until around the middle of the twelfth century (Bochenski, 1961: 149), the kind of problematic presented by Aristotle in his Prior Analytics and focused on by the Scholastics in their textbooks of logic, together with the works of Porphyry and Boethius, formed the center of logical discussion for the whole of Latin thought up to the dawn of modern times. Thus Poinsot, coming at the very end of Latin philosophy and Aristotelianism, but without seeing that work and time as at an end, sought to situate his *Treatise on Signs* relative to the whole Latin past of the philosophical tradition, and was more concerned with clarifying the tradition than he was with marking out a new beginning. Nothing could put him in sharper contrast with his contemporary, René Descartes, who wanted to begin anew at the expense of tradition. Nonetheless, Poinsot's *Treatise,* as we shall see, essays a new beginning able to incorporate and redistribute the entire medieval and renaissance heritage of philosophical discourse, while at the same time opening it to the central epistemological concerns that come to the fore in classical modern philosophy, precisely by putting the heritage of the past into what we now call a semiotic perspective.

Yet, as a Professor in the great Spanish university at Alcalá, charged particularly with preserving and elaborating the philosophical heritage of St. Thomas Aquinas, Poinsot did not think that the introductory course in logic, which in that university milieu was the point of entry into the whole of philosophical thought, was the proper place to lay the foundations of a new beginning. Hence, explicitly aware, as already indicated in his "Word to the Reader," that the semiotic point of view is *interruptive* of the then traditional terminist treatment of introductory logical questions—called *Summulae* in the wake of the overwhelming success of the thirteenth-century introductory text, the *Summulae Logicales* of Peter of Spain (cf. Simonin, 1930: 143), a man born in Poinsot's native Lisbon—and also *foundational* to it, Poinsot is careful to reserve the full discussion of signs to the second part of his Logic, which part is neither introductory nor properly restricted to concern with logical form. He is fur-

ther careful to situate the full discussion within that second part at a point where the students following his *Cursus Philosophicus* will have already become familiar with those notions in the Latin tradition to which the semiotician can most fruitfully refer for the purpose of making intelligible and effective the new beginning in philosophy that the doctrine of signs requires. We will see this explicitly put in Poinsot's "Remarks on Aristotle's books On Interpretation" (pp. 38-39 below), which spell out the relation of the *Treatise* to the Aristotelian tradition, its philosophical justification, and its presuppositions.

But in this second prologue, together with the "Word to the Reader" of the *Ars Logica* already examined (pp. 4-6 above), the sense in which the *Treatise on Signs* constitutes a new beginning is already clear. In the first place, it covers the very materials that make up the opening three chapters of the *Summulae* books. In the second place, and more fundamentally, these opening materials of the *Summulae* books concern *the simplest elements of the primary form of cognitive life*: nothing less than the role of the sign at the origins and foundations of awareness is what Poinsot undertakes to envisage in removing the discussion from the traditional terminist perspective and recasting it in a unity and perspective proper to it. The *Treatise*, then, for all Poinsot's conservative concerns and commitment to tradition in the very sense that post-Cartesian Europe will reject, is of its very nature a radical work: it takes up again the then traditional point of entry into philosophical study, and reshapes that point of departure according to a semiotic understanding of the fundamental activity of mind—namely, awareness as such. We have here nothing less than the doctrinal beginnings of the semiotic revolution, which has become an intellectual movement only in our century.

Prima Pars

ARTIS LOGICAE

SUMMULARUM

Liber Primus

De His, Quae Spectant Ad Primam Operationem Intellectus

João Poinsot

Complutum
(Alcalá)

1631

The First Part of the

ART OF LOGIC

BOOKS FOR BEGINNERS
[Preliminary Texts on the Doctrine of Signs]

The First of the *Summulae* Books
Covering Matters Which Pertain to the
First Operation of the Understanding

João Poinsot

Complutum
(Alcalá)

1631

Chapter 1

The Definition of Term

Authors think differently about the definition of a term,[1] according as they consider in it diverse respects or functions: that of a part entering into the composition of a sentence in whatever manner; or that of a principal part in the mode of an extreme only, whether an extreme terminating the analysis of a proposition and argument, or an extreme in the mode of a predicate and of a subject.

Certainly all these considerations are legitimate and have a place in the discussion of terms, but *one must see which among them more suitably expresses the nature of a term for purposes of the present discussion*. Our minds proceed analytically in matters of knowledge, and particularly in Logic (which is called "Analytics" by Aristotle,[2] because it is resolutory). There must, therefore, be an element or term of this analysis designatable as final, beyond which resolution by logical art cannot proceed (just as also in natural generation prime matter is the ultimate principle of resolution). If this were not the case, either the resolution would proceed to infinity, or there would not be a complete resolution. And since the completion of an analysis and the starting point of synthesis are the same, that which is the last element into which logical composites are resolved or analyzed

Caput Primum

Definitio Termini

Varie de definitione termini[1] sentiunt auctores, secundum quod considerant in eo diversos respectus vel officia, sive partis componentis orationem quomodocumque, sive partis principalis et per modum extremi tantum, sive per modum terminantis resolutionem propositionis et syllogismi, sive per modum praedicati et subiecti.

Et quidem considerationes istae verae sunt et omnes in termino locum habent, sed oportet videre, quaenam convenientius explicet naturam termini, ut pertinet ad praesens. Cum enim mens nostra in scientiis resolutorie procedat, et praesertim in Logica, quae Analytica ab Aristotele[2] dicitur, quia resolutoria, oportet, quod sit designabile ultimum elementum seu terminus huius resolutionis, ultra quod non fiat resolutio ab arte, sicut etiam in naturali generatione materia prima est ultimum principium resolutionis, alioquin vel procedetur in infinitum, vel non fiet perfecta resolutio. Et quia idem est terminus resolutionis et principium compositionis, id quod fuerit ultimum elementum, in quod composita logicalia resolvun-

---

[1] The 1663 Lyons text adds: "*id est simplicis dictionis, ut homo, Petrus, lapis*"—"that is, of a simple expression, such as 'man,' 'Peter,' 'stone.' "

[2] Rhet. I. c. 4. (1359 b 10).

will also be the first element out of which the others are composed.

With this in mind, our concern in the present discussion is with the term understood as the last element into which every logical composite—even the proposition itself and a statement—is resolved; because from this term, as from something first and simple, it is proper to begin. And although Aristotle, in his *Prior Analytics*, Book I, chap. 1,[3] would define the term as that "into which a proposition is resolved as into a predicate and a subject," nevertheless, he has not yet there defined the term in its entire extent, but restrictively, as it serves for syllogistic construction and composition. A syllogism is established from three terms inasmuch as they are extremes in propositions and take on the order or character of a syllogistic, i.e., illative, part. In other passages, Aristotle has considered the term under a more universal rationale as it is also common to noun and verb (not called "term," but "expression" or "diction"), as the noun or the verb functions in a sentence, rather than in an inference. Whence St. Thomas, in Book I, reading 8, n. 17, of his *Commentary on Aristotle's Treatise on Interpretation*,[4] explaining Aristotle's statement that "a noun and a verb only will be an expression,"[5] says: "And it is clear from the context that Aristotle himself would have used this name ["expression": *dictio*] for signifying the parts of a sentence." According to Aristotle and St. Thomas, therefore, there is some rationale common to the parts of a sentence, which the Philosopher calls "an expression" (or "diction") and which we are calling "a term," on the grounds that in it all analysis is terminated, not only of the syllogism, but even of a sentence, which is composed of simple expressions and consequently resolved into them. And in reading 5, n. 15, of the same work,[6] St. Thomas says that sometimes "name" is understood according as it signifies generally any expression whatever, including even the verb. And at the beginning of his *Summa of the Whole Logic of Aristotle*,[7] he calls terms the "parts of a sentence." We say, therefore, that one should begin from this most general acceptation of "term" as from the final element of the whole of logical analysis, and that one should define "term" accordingly.

tur, dicetur etiam primum, ex quo cetera componuntur.

Hoc igitur attendentes dicimus nos agere in praesenti de termino sub conceptu ultimi elementi, in quod terminatur omnis resolutio compositionis logicae, etiam ipsius propositionis et orationis, quia ab hoc ut a primo et simpliciori convenit incipere. Et licet Aristoteles in 1. Priorum[3] definierit terminum per id, «in quod resolvitur propositio ut in praedicatum et subiectum», tamen ibi non definivit terminum in tota sua latitudine, sed contracte, ut deservit ad fabricam et compositionem syllogisticam, in qua syllogismus constat ex tribus terminis, quatenus sunt extrema in propositionibus et induunt habitudinem partis syllogisticae, id est illativae. Ceterum alibi consideravit Aristoteles terminum sub universaliori ratione, ut etiam est communis nomini et verbo, et non sub vocabulo termini, sed sub vocabulo dictionis, ut induit ordinem componentis enuntiationem, non habitudinem inferentis in syllogismo. Unde D. Thomas 1. Periherm. lect. 8. § *Excludit*[4] exponens illud verbum Aristotelis: «Nomen ergo et verbum dictio sit sola»,[5] inquit: «Et videtur ex modo loquendi, quod ipse imposuerit hoc nomen ad significandum partes enuntiationis». Datur ergo secundum Aristotelem et D. Thomam aliqua ratio communis partibus enuntiationis, quam Philosophus dictionem, nos terminum vocamus, quia in ipso omnis resolutio terminatur, non solum syllogismi, sed etiam enuntiationis, quae ex simplicibus componitur et consequenter in illa resolvitur. Et ibidem lect. 5. § *Ostendit*[6] dicit S. Thomas, quod aliquando nomen sumitur, prout communiter significat quamlibet dictionem, etiam ipsum verbum. Et in opusc. 48. in initio[7] vocat terminos ,,partes enuntiationis''. Ab hac ergo communissima acceptione termini tamquam ab ultimo elemento totius resolutionis logicae dicimus esse incipiendum et de illo tradendam definitionem.

[3] c. 1. (24 b 16).
[4] *Le* I. 39. n. 17.
[5] Periherm. c. 5. (17 a 17).
[6] *Le* I. 26. n. 15.
[7] Summa tot. Log. Arist. Prooem. (*Pa* XVII. 54 a).

And so an expression ("diction") or *term is defined* not through the extremes of a proposition only, or through predicate and subject, but through something more general, namely, "that out of which a simple proposition is made;" or rather, following Aristotle, who defined noun, verb, and statement as spoken words (because they are the signs more known to us), the term is defined: "A vocal expression significative by stipulation, from which a simple proposition or sentence is constructed."[8] But in order to include the mental and the written term, it will be defined: "A sign out of which a simple proposition is constructed."

It is called a sign or significant sound in order to exclude sounds without significance, e.g., "blitiri," just as Aristotle excludes them in the case of the noun and the verb; and since every term is a noun, a verb, or an adverb, if none of these is a sound without significance, no sound without significance is a term, as I will show more at length in the question concerning this matter. It is said to be by stipulation, in order to exclude sounds naturally significant, e.g., a groan. It is said to be that from which a simple proposition is made, in order to rule out the proposition or statement itself, which is not the elementary component, but is something composite as a whole; and if it is sometimes a component, it is a component not of a simple but of a hypothetical proposition.

Whether a term outside of a proposition is a part in act as regards the essence and character of a part, even though not functioning as a component, I will discuss in this first part of Logic in Art. 3 of Q. 1, "Concerning Terms."

Et sic **definitur terminus** seu dictio non per extremum propositionis tantum aut per praedicatum et subiectum, sed per aliquid communius, scilicet « id, ex quo simplex conficitur propositio »; vel potius imitantes Aristotelem, qui nomen, verbum et orationem per voces definit, quia sunt signa nobis notiora, definitur: « Vox significativa ad placitum, ex qua simplex conficitur propositio vel oratio ».[8] Ut autem comprehendit mentalem terminum et scriptum, definietur: « Signum, ex quo simplex conficitur propositio ».

Dicitur *signum vel vox significativa* ad excludendum voces non significativas, ut blitiri, sicut illas exclusit Aristoteles in nomine et verbo; et cum omnis terminus sit nomen, verbum vel adverbium, si nihil horum est vox non significativa, non est terminus, ut latius in quaestione de hac re ostendam. Dicitur *ad placitum* ad excludendas voces significativas naturaliter, ut gemitus. Dicitur *ex qua simplex conficitur propositio* ad excludendam ipsam propositionem seu orationem, quae non est primum elementum componens, sed est aliquid compositum ut totum, et si aliquando componit, non simplicem, sed hypotheticam propositionem componit.

An vero terminus sit extra propositionem actu pars, quantum ad essentiam et habitudinem partis, licet non quoad exercitium componendi, dicemus infra q. 1. de Termino, art. 3.

[8] cf. Periherm. c. 2. (16 a 19); c. 4. (16 b 26).

Chapter 2

The Definition and Division of Signs

Caput Secundum

Definitio et Divisio Signi

A term, no less than a statement and a proposition, and any other logical instrument, is defined by means of signification. This is due to the fact that the understanding knows by means of the signification of concepts, and expresses what it knows by means of the signification of sounds, so that, without exception, all the instruments which we use for knowing and speaking are signs. Therefore, if the student of logic is to know his tools—namely, terms and statements—in an exact manner, it is necessary that he should also know what a sign is. *The sign*, therefore, *admits of the following general definition*: "That which represents something other than itself to a cognitive power."[1]

To better understand this definition, one must consider that there is a fourfold cause of knowledge namely, a productive, objective, formal, and instrumental cause.[2] The productive or efficient cause is the power itself which elicits an act of knowledge, for example, the eye, the ear, the understanding. The object is the thing which stimulates or toward which a cognition tends,

Quia ergo tam terminus quam oratio et propositio et reliqua instrumenta logicalia per significationem definiuntur, eo quod intellectus cognoscit per conceptus significativos et loquitur per voces significativas, et in universum omnia instrumenta, quibus ad cognoscendum et loquendum utimur, signa sunt, ideo ut logicus exacte cognoscat instrumenta sua, scilicet terminos et orationes, oportet, quod etiam cognoscat, quid sit signum. **Signum** ergo **definitur** in communi: «Id, quod potentiae cognoscitivae aliquid aliud a se repraesentat».[1]

Quae definitio ut melius innotescat, oportet considerare, quod est quadruplex causa cognitionis, scilicet efficiens, obiectiva, formalis et instrumentalis.[2] Efficiens est ipsa potentia, quae elicit cognitionem, sicut oculus, auditus, intellectus. Obiectum est res, quae movet vel ad quam tendit cognitio,

[1] The 1663 Lyons text adds: "*Ita tradimus definitionem signi, ut complectatur omnia signa, tam formalia quam instrumentalia. Definitio enim quae communiter circumfertur: 'Signum est, quod praeter species, quas ingerit sensui, aliud facit in cognitionem venire,' solum instrumentali signo competit.*"—"We formulate the definition of a sign thus so that it embraces all signs, formal as well as instrumental. For the definition which is commonly circulated: 'A sign is anything that, besides the impressions it conveys to sense, makes another come into cognition,' applies only to an instrumental sign." See further Book I, Question 1, 116/1-13, Question 5, 199/33-201/27, the Sequel to Book I, 216/7-217/27; and note 17 below. Also Book II, Question 1, 225/11-228/47.

[2] See Book II, Question 4, 262/5-263/22.

as when I see a stone or a man.[3] The formal cause is the awareness itself whereby a power is rendered cognizant, as the sight itself of the stone or of the man.[4] The instrumental cause is the means by which the object is represented to the power, as a picture of Caesar represents Caesar.[5] The object is threefold, to wit, stimulative only, terminative only, both stimulative and terminative at once. An object that is only a stimulus is one that arouses a power to form an awareness not of the stimulating object itself, but of another object, as, for example, the picture of the emperor, which moves the power to know the emperor.[6] An object that is terminative only is a thing known through an awareness produced by some other object, for example, the emperor known through the picture.[7] An object that is simultaneously terminative and stimulative is one that arouses a power to form a cognition of the very object stimulating, as when the wall is seen in itself.

Thus, "making cognizant" has wider extension than does "representing,"[8] and "representing" more than "signifying."[9] For *to make cognizant* is said of every cause concurring in the production of knowledge; and so it is said in *four* ways, namely, effectively, objectively, formally, and instrumentally. *Effectively*, as of the power itself eliciting cognition and of the causes concurring in that production, as of God moving, the understanding acting or producing specifying forms, the inclinations of habit, etc. *Objectively*, as of the very thing which is known. For example, if I know a man, the man as an object makes himself known by presenting himself to the power. *Formally*, as of the awareness itself, which, as a form, makes the power know. *Instrumentally*, as of the very medium or means bearing object to power, as the picture of the emperor conveys the emperor to the understanding as a medium,[10] and this means we call the instrument.[11] *To represent* is said of each factor which makes anything become present to a power, and so is said in *three* ways, namely, *objectively*, *formally*, and *instrumentally*. For an object

ut cum video lapidem vel hominem.[3] Formalis est ipsa notitia, qua redditur potentia cognoscens, ut visio ipsa lapidis vel hominis.[4] Instrumentalis est medium, per quod obiectum repraesentatur potentiae, sicut imago exterior Caesaris repraesentat Caesarem.[5] Obiectum est triplex, scilicet motivum tantum, terminativum tantum, motivum et terminativum simul. Motivum tantum est, quod movet potentiam ad formandam notitiam non sui, sed alterius, sicut imperatoris imago, quae movet ad cognoscendum imperatorem.[6] Terminativum tantum est res cognita per notitiam ab alio obiecto productam, sicut imperator cognitus per imaginem.[7] Terminativum et motivum simul, quod movet potentiam ad formandam cognitionem sui, sicut quando paries in se videtur.

Igitur facere cognoscere latius patet quam repraesentare,[8] et repraesentare quam significare.[9] Nam *facere cognoscere* dicitur de omni concurrente ad cognitionem; et sic dicitur quadrupliciter, scilicet effective, obiective, formaliter et instrumentaliter. Effective, ut de ipsa potentia eliciente cognitionem et de causis ad eam concurrentibus, ut de Deo movente, intellectu agente seu producente species, habitu adiuvante etc. Obiective, ut de ipsa re, quae cognoscitur. V. g. si cognosco hominem, homo ut obiectum facit cognoscere seipsum praesentando se potentiae. Formaliter, ut de ipsa notitia, quae tamquam forma reddit cognoscentem. Instrumentaliter, ut de ipso medio deferente obiectum ad potentiam, ut imago imperatoris defert imperatorem ad intellectum quasi medium,[10] et hoc medium vocamus instrumentum.[11] *Repraesentare* dicitur de omni eo, quo aliquid fit praesens potentiae, et sic dicitur tripliciter, scilicet obiective, formaliter et instrumentaliter. Obiectum enim reprae-

[3] See Book I, Question 4, 166/4-168/48, 180/10-181/14.
[4] See Book II, Question 1, 223/7-224/19, 224/29-225/10; and Question 2, 240/1 ff.
[5] See Book I, Question 2, 135/7-11; Question 5, 201/28-203/32.
[6] See esp. Book I, Question 4, 169/1-173/38, esp. 172/44-46; and 181/15-185/29.
[7] See esp. Book I, Question 4, 173/39-180/7, 185/30-192/14.
[8] See Book I, Question 1, 124/19-39.
[9] See Book I, Question 1, 116/23-117/17, 122/16-124/18; and the Sequel to Book I, 219/29-48.
[10] See Book I, Question 1, esp. 124/42-127/6, and note 25, p. 125; and 128/7-131/7.
[11] See Book I, Question 5, 203/15-32.

such as the wall represents itself objectively, an awareness represents formally, a footprint[12] instrumentally. *To signify* is said of that by which something distinct from itself becomes present, and so is said in only *two* ways, namely, formally and instrumentally.

Hence arises the twofold *division of the sign*. For insofar as signs are ordered *to a power*, they are divided into formal and instrumental signs;[13] but insofar as signs are ordered *to something signified*, they are divided according to the cause of that ordering into natural and stipulative and customary.[14] A formal sign[15] is the formal awareness which represents of itself, not by means of another. An instrumental sign[16] is one that represents something other than itself from a pre-existing cognition of itself as an object, as the footprint of an ox represents an ox. And this definition is usually given for signs generally.[17] A natural sign[18] is one that represents from the nature of a thing, independently of any stipulation and custom whatever,[19] and so it represents the same for all,[20] as smoke signifies a fire burning. A stipulated sign[21] is one that represents something owing to an imposition by the will of a community,[22] like the linguistic expression "man." A customary sign is one that represents from use alone without any public imposition, as napkins upon the table signify a meal.[23] We will treat at length all of these matters pertaining to the nature and division of signs in the first two Books of our Treatise on Signs.[24]

sentat se obiective, ut paries, notitia repraesentat formaliter, vestigium[12] instrumentaliter. *Significare* dicitur de eo, quo fit praesens aliquid distinctum a se, et sic solum dicitur dupliciter, scilicet formaliter et instrumentaliter.

Hinc nascitur duplex **divisio signi.** Nam qua parte signum ordinatur ad potentiam, dividitur in signum formale et instrumentale;[13] quatenus vero ordinatur ad signatum, dividitur penes causam ordinantem illud in naturale et ad placitum et ex consuetudine.[14] Signum formale[15] est formalis notitia, quae seipsa, non mediante alio, repraesentat. Signum instrumentale[16] est, quod ex praeexistente cognitione sui aliquid aliud a se repraesentat, sicut vestigium bovis repraesentat bovem. Et haec definitio solet tradi communiter de signo.[17] Signum naturale[18] est, quod ex natura rei repraesentat quavis impositione et consuetudine remota;[19] et sic repraesentat idem apud omnes,[20] ut fumus ignem. Signum ad placitum,[21] quod repraesentat aliquid ex impositione voluntatis per publicam auctoritatem,[22] ut vox homo. Signum ex consuetudine, quod ex solo usu repraesentat sine publica impositione, sicut mappae supra mensam significant prandium.[23] De his omnibus, quae ad naturam et divisionem signorum spectant, late agimus in Tractatu de Signis, Libro Primo et Secundo.[24]

---

[12] The 1663 Lyons text adds: "*vel imago*" — "or an image."

[13] The basis of this division is not as straightforward as first here appears: see Book I, Question 2, 145/10-28 with 143/8-20, Question 3, 161/45-162/21 with 163/12-164/12, Question 5, 202/19-22 with 201/28-202/8; Book II, Question 1, 238/28-45 with 235/15-25, and 229/24-38.

[14] See esp. Book II, Questions 5 and 6.

[15] See Book II, Question 2, and references in notes 4, 10, and 13 above.

[16] See references in notes 5, 10, 11, and 13 above; also Book I, Question 4, 172/44-6, 172/49-173/28.

[17] The 1663 Lyons text adds: "*sed non convenit nisi signo instrumentali*" — "but it applies only to an instrumental sign."

[18] See esp. Book I, Question 2, 133/13ff., and Question 6, 205/35-209/32, 210/36-215/5.

[19] See esp. Book III, Question 4, 335/23-39.

[20] See Book II, Question 6, 283/23-32.

[21] See esp. Book II, Questions 5 and 6.

[22] Poinsot nowhere explicitly develops this notion of "public authority" ("will of a community"), but it seems to involve in the end nothing more than the acceptance by another person of one person's usage of a sign for given purposes. Thus *any* stipulation is public *in principle*, and becomes public *in fact* through the mere tacit sanction of its use in given contexts. "Public authority," thus, could be rendered as "a socially structured human intention." Cf. Book II, Questions 5 and 6.

[23] See esp. Book II, Question 6, 278/1ff.

[24] The original text reads here: ". . . in Logica q. 21. et 22."

Chapter 3

Some Divisions of Terms

Caput Tertium

De Quibusdam Divisionibus Terminorum

The *first division* of terms is into mental, vocal, and written terms. A mental term is the awareness or concept from which a simple proposition is made.[1] A vocal term was defined in chapter 1 above.[2] A written term is a mark signifying by stipulation, from which a simple proposition is made.

The *mental term,* if we attend to its various essential kinds, is divided according to the objects which differentiate the modes of awareness. And so in the present discussion we are not treating of the division of those essential kinds of term, but only of certain general conditions of apprehensions or of concepts whereby various ways of knowing are distinguished. And note that it is simple awareness that is divided here, that is, awareness pertaining only to the first operation of the mind; for we are treating of the division of mental terms, but a term looks to the first operation. Whence in this division of awareness, any awareness pertaining to discourse or to composition is not included; for none of these is a term or simple apprehension. And similarly,

Prima divisio termini est in mentalem, vocalem et scriptum. Mentalis est notitia seu conceptus, ex quo simplex conficitur propositio.[1] Vocalis supra est definitus cap. 1.[2] Scriptus est scriptura ad placitum significans, ex qua simplex conficitur propositio.

Terminus mentalis, si attendamus ad diversas species essentiales eius, dividitur penes obiecta, a quibus species notitiarum sumitur. Et sic non agimus de divisione illorum in praesenti, sed solum agimus de quibusdam generalibus conditionibus notitiarum seu conceptuum, quibus distinguuntur varii modi cognoscendi. Et nota, dividi hic notitiam simplicem, id est pertinentem tantum ad primam operationem; agimus enim de divisione termini mentalis, terminus autem ad primam operationem spectat. Unde in hac divisione notitiarum non includitur aliqua notitia pertinens ad discursum aut ad compositionem; nulla enim istarum est terminus vel simplex apprehensio. Et similiter

---

[1] The 1663 Lyons text adds: "*Conceptus est illa imago, quam intra nos formamus, cum aliquid intelligimus*"—"A concept is that image which we form within ourselves when we understand something." See, in the *Treatise on Signs* proper, esp. Book I, Question 1, 132/47-133/12, Question 3, 164/13-165/8; and Book II, Question 2, esp. notes 17 and 27.

[2] at 24/8-9, as "a sound that signifies through stipulation."

all practical awareness, and all awareness bespeaking an order to the will, is removed, because the will is not moved by the simple apprehension of a term, but by a composition or judgment concerning the appropriateness of a thing, as we will say in the books *Concerning the Soul*.[3]

Therefore awareness, which is a simple apprehension, or the mental term, is divided first into *intuitive and abstractive* awareness.[4] This division includes not only intellective awareness, but also the awareness of the external senses, which is always intuitive, and of the internal senses, which is sometimes intuitive, sometimes abstractive. An intuitive awareness is the awareness of a thing physically present. And I say "of a thing physically present," not "of a thing presented to a given cognitive power"; for "to be physically present" pertains to a thing in itself as it is independent of the cognitive power, whereas "to be presented" pertains to the thing as it is the object of the very power, which is something common to every awareness. An abstractive awareness is an awareness of an absent thing, which is understood in a way oposed to an intuitive awareness.

Apprehension is divided second, on the side of the concept, into *ultimate and nonultimate* concepts.[5] An ultimate concept is a concept of a thing signified by means of a term; for example, the thing which is a man is signified by means of the linguistic expression "man." A nonultimate or mediative concept is the concept of a term itself as signifying, for example, the concept of this term "man."

Third, concepts are divided into *direct and reflexive*.[6] A reflexive concept is one by which we know ourselves knowing, and thus has for an object some act or concept or capacity within us. A direct concept is one by which we know any object independent of our concept, yet without reflecting on our cognition, as when a [particular] stone or man is known.

removetur omnis notitia practica et quae dicit ordinem ad voluntatem, quia voluntas non movetur a simplici apprehensione termini, sed a compositione seu iudicio de convenientia rei, ut dicemus in libro de Anima.[3]

Igitur notitia, quae est simplex apprehensio, seu terminus mentalis PRIMO dividitur in notitiam intuitivam et abstractivam.[4] Quae divisio non solum amplectitur notitiam intellectivam, sed etiam sensuum externorum, quae semper sunt notitiae intuitivae, et internorum, quae aliquando sunt intuitivae, aliquando abstractivae. Notitia intuitiva est notitia rei praesentis. Et dico rei praesentis, non praesentatae ipsi potentiae; esse enim praesens pertinet ad rem in seipsa, ut est extra potentiam, esse praesentatam convenit rei, ut obiectae ipsi potentiae, quod omni notitiae commune est. Notitia abstractiva est notitia rei absentis, quae opposito modo intelligitur ad intuitivam.

SECUNDO dividitur notitia ex parte conceptus in conceptum ultimatum et non ultimatum.[5] Conceptus ultimatus est conceptus rei significatae per terminum, ut res, quae est homo, est significata per vocem, „homo". Conceptus non ultimatus seu medius est conceptus ipsius termini ut significantis, ut conceptus huius termini „homo".

TERTIO dividitur conceptus in directum et reflexum.[6] Reflexus est, quo cognoscimus nos cognoscere, atque ita habet pro obiecto aliquem actum vel conceptum aut potentiam intra nos. Directus est, quo cognoscimus aliquod obiectum extra conceptum nostrum, nec reflectimus supra cognitionem nostram, ut cum cognoscitur lapis vel homo.

[3] Phil. nat. 4. p. q. 12. art. 1. et 2.

[4] This distinction forms the subject matter for Book III, Questions 1 and 2 of the *Treatise on Signs*.

[5] This is the subject matter of Book III, Question 4, of the *Treatise* proper.

[6] This is the subject of Book III, Question 3.

Third Semiotic Marker

These opening two and a half chapters of the first of the introductory logic or *Summulae* books contain all the terms that form the subject of the discussion in the *Treatise on Signs* to follow in the Second Part of the Logic. This illustrates how literally exact was Poinsot's observation "To the Reader" above that the problems of the semiotic foundations of the simplest awareness are latent in the very beginning of logical and philosophical study.

Hewing to tradition at the level of introductory discussion, Poinsot writes the *Summulae* from the terminist point of view, but with awareness of the semiotic foundations, thus:

First *Summulae* Book, chapters 1-3:

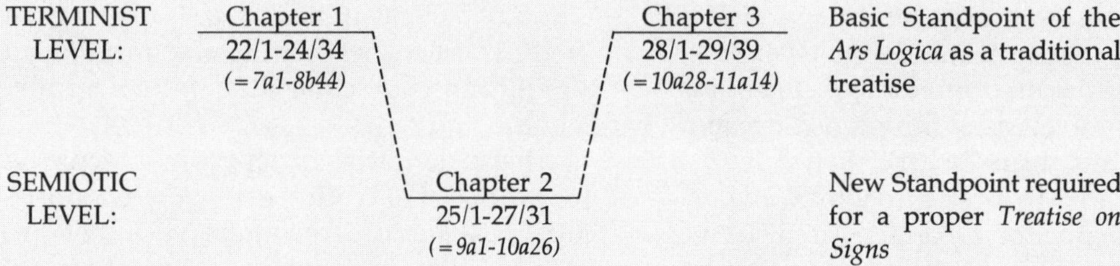

Here the semiotic view is *interruptive* rather than continuative, and nothing shows this more plainly than the tedious, recondite list of 25/14-27/6, wherein are enumerated the complex of terms involved in the germination of the "definitio signi" demurely proposed (25/11-13) to replace the definition that has served as the principal basis of semiotic discussion in the Latin world since the fifth century, namely, the definition proposed by St. Augustine (27/14-18, along with note on text from the first Lyons edition of 1663). This last point, the need for a new definition at the base of semiotic understanding, indeed, will become the point of departure for the *Treatise on Signs* proper (see below, Book I, 116/1-13). Here again the revolutionary character of his thought breaks through Poinsot's own conservative designs, as the standpoint of his *Treatise*—the semiotic standpoint—for the second time compels him to criticize in its entirety the Latin tradition of philosophical understanding he seeks to preserve and extend.

ARTIS
LOGICAE

SECVNDA PARS,

IN PRÆDICABILIA, PRÆDICAMENTA
Libros Perihermenias,& Posteriorum.

AVTHORE P. M. Fr. IOANNE DE S. THOMA, LISBONIENSI, ORDINIS Prædicatorum, Supremi Senatus fidei Quæsitore, in Complutensi Academia publico Theologiæ professore in Cathedra Vespertina,& insignis Collegij S. Thomæ Regente.

Edictio quarta ab Authore reuisa,& emendata.

64.

CVM PRIVILEGIO.

MATRITI, Ex Officina CAROLI SANCHEZ
Anno M.DC.XXXX.

A costa de Esperança Francisca, viuda de Francisco Redon.

Title page from the 1640 Madrid edition of the Second Part of the *Ars Logica*, containing the *Treatise on Signs*. This was the last edition issued in Poinsot's lifetime, and it is here that he singles out the Treatise as an independent whole and gives it its title. See discussions below, pp. 404–411, 445–446. Photograph courtesy of Norma Elia Cantú.

Secunda Pars

ARTIS LOGICAE

In *Isagogen* Porphirii,
Aristotelis
Categorias
et
Libros Perihermenias
et
Posteriorum

João Poinsot

Complutum
(Alcalá)

1632

The Second Part of the

ART OF LOGIC

Covering the *Isagoge* of Porphyry,
of Aristotle
the *Categories*
and
Books on Interpretation
and
Posterior Analytics

João Poinsot

Complutum
(Alcalá)

1632

Lectori:[1]

Oppignoratam fidem meam in emittenda secunda Logicae parte, editione hac libero, legentium utilitati felicius obstrictam, avidius vinculatam. Certe quod in me fuit, addiscentium commodo intentus, quibus in longum disputatae quaestiones non parum impedimento sunt et taedio, fateor sic me ista tractasse, ut accuratioribus oculis haud quaquam praeluxisse praesumam, at nec tardioribus offudisse caliginem, illud perpetuo curans, ut quanta brevitate fieri possit, quid tenendum sit, aperiatur, ne variis ambagibus disputationem terendo dum aliorum placita displicent, sententiam propriam suspendamus. Optime enim admonuit Ambrosius praefatione in Psalmos[2] «faciliora esse, quae brevius explicantur». Praecipuam autem scriptoris intentionem praesertim in istis prioribus scientiis enucleandis in eo sitam arbitror, ut facilitatem potius exhibeat quam eruditionem et multiplicem doctrinae paraturam.

Quod in prima Logicae parte promisimus de quaestionibus pluribus, quae ibi tractari solent, hic expediendis, plane solvimus, excepto quod iustis de causis tractatum de signis, pluribus nec vulgaribus difficultatibus scaturientem, ne hic iniectus aut sparsus gravaret tractatus alio satis per se graves, seorsum edendum duximus loco commentarii in libros Perihermenias simul cum quaestionibus in libros Posteriorum, et pro commodiori libri usu a tractatu Praedicamentorum seiunximus.

Quod reliquum Philosophiae naturalis pro integro artium cursu complendo desideratur, simili stilo ac labore in diem evulgandum eadem fide iterum obligata devovemus. Vale.

Madrid, Spain
1640

To the Reader of 1640:[1]

With the appearance of this book I fulfill the pledge I gave of publishing the second part of Logic, an event made the more pleasant by its ties to the advantage of the readers. Aiming at the advantage of those who are learners and find prolix disputation of questions tedious and no small hindrance, I claim to have so handled the subject that I would by no means presume to have anticipated those of quicker perception, but for the slower wits I have not raised a fog. I strive always to disclose with what brevity I can the viewpoint to be held, lest we tiresomely hold forth on obscure opinions we do not consider sound while leaving in ambiguity what we do think is the case. Ambrose counsels well in his preface to the Psalms[2] when he says that ''matters become easier when they are explained in brief.'' Especially in these beginning courses of study, I think the chief intention of a writer should be more to disclose the ease of the matter than the learning and complex fabric of his field.

We have now covered as we promised the several questions traditionally dealt with in the first part of Logic, except that, for good reasons, the treatise on signs, swarming with so many and extraordinary difficulties, and in order to free the introductory texts of the pervasive presence of its uncommon difficulties, we have decided to publish separately in place of a commentary on the books *On Interpretation* and together with questions on the books of *Posterior Analytics*; and for the more convenient use of the work, we have separated the treatise on signs from the discussion of the *Categories*.

What remains to be discussed of natural philosophy in order to complete the course of studies in the Arts we pledge ourselves to treat in the same style and manner. Farewell.

Madrid, Spain
1640

---

[1] *Auctoris praefatio in 4. editionem secundae partis artis Logicae*. Author's preface to the 4th edition of the Second Part of the *Ars Logica* (Madrid, 1640).

[2] Migne P.L. XIV. 967 B.

Fourth Semiotic Marker

This "Word to the Reader," entitling the *Treatise* as a single tractate, was added by Poinsot to the fourth separate edition of the second part of his Logic published in Madrid in 1640, eight years after the first publication of this part at Alcalá in 1632. It reiterates in even stronger terms the claim of special importance and novelty made for the *Treatise on Signs* in the original "Word to the Reader" of 1631 that announced the work as forthcoming. This retrospect of 1640 thus amounts to a historical reissuing of the earlier claim for the unity of the *Tractatus de signis* as something *new* in the entire Latin West, as we now see, the first systematic semiotic.

It reaffirms, in short, in as clear terms as one could wish, the virtual autonomy the *Treatise* enjoys relative to the other parts of the Logic and *Cursus Philosophicus*, of which the Logic comprises but two of the five original volumes issued between 1631 and 1635, and all written, as Poinsot here troubles to note, "in the same style and manner" and as part of "a complete course of philosophical study in the Faculty of Arts." For of all the many parts comprising the five volumes of the *Cursus Philosophicus*, it is certainly striking that the *Treatise* is the only part that Poinsot, who does not indulge in wordy advertising, expressly singles out for mention as unique and "published separately" in his otherwise quite traditional selection of materials and arrangement of topics.

The virtual autonomy tacitly claimed here for the *Treatise* by its author is precisely what the present editor and translator claims to have realized in the present edition, the first edition of the work so constructed in the long history of the *Ars Logica*, the second part of which has undergone ten Latin publications since its original appearance in 1632. (The 1640 Madrid edition, the fourth of these ten printings, was the last before its author's death.)

It is worthy of note historically that Poinsot places the *Treatise* on a footing of at least equal importance to the discussion of the *Posterior Analytics*, a work which, though generally neglected in the modern and contemporary developments of logic, was keenly investigated and developed in the medieval-renaissance traditions of logic and philosophy which were Poinsot's privileged heritage as a major professor in a major center of the Iberian university world of the early seventeenth century.

Perhaps most important to note, however, is the fact that Poinsot identifies the subject of semiotic as lying at the heart and foundation of the problematic of formal logic, that kind of problematic presented in the Prior Analytics and, according to Bochenski (1961: 2-4), the constant central problematic of Logic

throughout all its phases in the ages of Western thought down to the present time. No observation could better bring out again the revolutionary import with which the semiotic perspective first systematically essayed by Poinsot is pregnant. The merit of Poinsot's treatment, moreover, is to make clear that semiotic lies at the foundations of logic precisely because and inasmuch as logic constitutes a mode of knowledge (*cognitio*), for it is the foundations of knowledge as such and in its entirety—simple awareness—that are the first province of semiotic and its unique vantage for grasping the unity of the life of the mind.

We arrive now at last at Poinsot's introduction to the *Treatise on Signs* proper.

Super Libros PERIHERMENIAS[1]

Remarks on Aristotle's *Books on Interpretation*, Explaining the Relation of the *Treatise on Signs* to the Aristotelian Tradition, Its Philosophical Justification, and Its Presuppositions within the *Ars Logica*

The title *Perihermenias* is best translated "On Interpretation." In these books, Aristotle treats principally of the statement and proposition. To this end, it was found necessary to treat first of their parts, which are the noun and the verb, and then of their properties, such as opposition, equivalence, contingency, possibility, and the like. These matters we have covered in the *Summulae* books; for all of them are ordered and pertain to Prior Analytics [i.e., the analysis of discourse in terms of its logical elements and their interrelation].

Nevertheless, because these matters are all treated in those books by way of interpretation and signification, since indeed the universal instrument of Logic is the *sign*, from which all its instruments are constituted, therefore, lest the foundation of the expositions of logical form go unexamined, the project of the present work is to treat of these things which were introduced in the *Summulae* books for explaining the nature and divisions of signs, but which have been set aside for special treatment here. For the grasp of beginners is not proportioned to these questions about signs. Now, however, in this work, they may be authentically introduced, following a

Libri Perihermenias sic vocantur quasi dicas ,,de Interpretatione''. In his agit Aristoteles de oratione et propositione principaliter. Ad quod necesse fuit prius agere de earum partibus, quae sunt nomen et verbum. Deinde de earum proprietatibus, quales sunt oppositio, aequipollentia, contingentia, possibilitas et alia similia. De his egimus in libris Summularum; haec enim omnia ordinantur et pertinent ad prioristicam resolutionem.

Sed tamen, quia haec omnia tractantur in his libris per modum interpretationis et significationis, commune siquidem Logicae instrumentum est *signum*, quo omnia eius instrumenta constant, idcirco visum est in praesenti pro doctrina horum librorum ea tradere, quae ad explicandam naturam et divisiones signorum in Summulis insinuata, huc vero reservata sunt. Nec enim tironum captui quaestiones istae de signis proportionatae sunt. Nunc autem in hoc loco genuine introducuntur, post notitiam habi-

---

[1] The two Greek words, "περὶ ἑρμηνείας," were early conflated by the Latins into a single word (Zigliara, 1882), as we see instanced here. Conversely, Aristotle's work itself of this title, which is a single book in the Greek, was commonly divided by the Latin interpreters into two books, the first comprising chapters 1-9, the second chapters 10-15 (Spiazzi, 1955: xi). A great deal of philosophical history pertinent to semiotics in the Latin age is signaled by these seeming vagaries: see my "The Relation of Logic to Semiotics," *Semiotica* 35—3/4 (1981), esp. note 23.

consideration of mind-dependent being[2] and of the category of relation,[3] on which considerations this inquiry concerning the nature and definable essence of signs principally depends.[4]

That the inquiry into signs might be the more clearly and fruitfully conducted, it seemed best to devote to it a separate treatise, rather than to include it in the discussion of the category of relation, in order to avoid making the discussion of relation prolix and tedious through the inclusion of extraneous matter, and also to avoid a confused and over-brief consideration of the sign.

Concerning the rationale proper to signs, therefore, two things present themselves as the principal objects of controversy. The *first* concerns the nature and definition of a sign in general; the *second* concerns its division, and each divided member in particular. In Book I[5] of this *Treatise* we put in order the first of these matters, the second we put in order in Books II and III.[6]

tam de ente rationis[2] et praedicamento relationis,[3] a quibus principaliter dependet inquisitio ista de natura et quidditate signorum.[4]

Ut autem clarius et uberius tractaretur, visum est seorsum de hoc edere tractatum, nec solum ad praedicamentum relationis illud reducere, tum ne illius praedicamenti disputatio extraneo hoc tractatu prolixior redderetur et taediosior, tum ne istius consideratio confusior esset et brevior.

Igitur circa ipsam rationem signorum duo principalia occurrunt disputanda: *Primum* de natura et definitione signi in communi, *secundum* de divisione eius et de quolibet in particulari. Et primum expediemus in hoc libro,[5] secundum in sequenti.[6]

---

[2] Included here as the First Preamble to the *Treatise*.

[3] Included here as the Second Preamble to the *Treatise*.

[4] Why the discussion of signs principally depends upon the prior notions of mind-dependent being and of relation, and particularly upon that of relation—i.e., what is the implicit content of 38/21-39/8—I have set forth at some length in '' 'Semiotic' as the Doctrine of Signs,'' *Ars Semeiotica* 1/3 (1977), 41-68.

[5] In the original Latin: ''in hac quaestione,'' i.e., Logica 2. p. q. 21.

[6] Book III of the *Treatise* should be regarded (as Reiser has suggested in his ''*Tabula Synoptica Totius Logicae*,'' p. XVII) as an extended treatment of the working of the formal sign defined and defended in the opening Questions of Book II. See Appendix B below. Hence the addition of ''et notitiis'' to ''tractatum de signis'' in the 1631 Word to the Reader above; and the reference in the Latin here (''. . . in sequenti'') to Books II and III as a unit.

Fifth Semiotic Marker

These remarks are in effect Poinsot's Foreword to the *Treatise on Signs* proper. They confirm what we have already gathered from the "Words to the Reader" of 1631 and 1640; in particular they confirm the foundational character of the *Treatise* relative to the logical tradition already inferred from the Second Prologue above.

But in addition, these remarks expressly identify those other parts of the *Ars Logica* required for understanding the doctrine of signs Poinsot undertakes to establish—namely, the parts discussing mind-dependent being and relation as a category, type, or "kind" of mind-independent being. Moreover, of the two discussions presupposed, Poinsot makes it clear that the discussion of relation as a distinct variety of being is the more crucial one, from the fact that he considered incorporating the discussion of the sign into his discussion of relation (39/6-11). This inference is confirmed by the discovery the careful reader makes that the possibility of mind-dependent being is owing to the very same unique feature of relation as that upon which Poinsot ultimately bases his account of signifying, namely, the indifference of relation to the subjective ground or cause of its existence. It is because relation alone of the varieties of mind-independent existence is essentially unaffected when it is transferred into a state of dependency upon knowledge and cognitive life that such a thing as mind-dependent being of any sort is possible in the first place, and it is this same fact that ultimately accounts for the possibility of semiosis. Thus, the understanding of signifying in Poinsot's doctrine depends upon an adequate understanding of mind-dependent being *and* relation, but the understanding of mind-dependent being in turn depends upon the understanding of relation. It is in the theory of relative being, therefore, that Poinsot ultimately locates the foundations of semiotic, as the opening question of the *Treatise* proper will make abundantly clear.

The relevant portions of Poinsot's prior discussion first of mind-dependent being and then of relation comprise all that is necessary to translate the virtual autonomy of the *Treatise on Signs* from the *Cursus Philosophicus* into an actual independence. Accordingly, we here include the necessary parts from those prior discussions as the First and Second Preambles, respectively, in this first independent edition of the *Treatise on Signs*. This completes the series of comments sufficient to show the reader how the rationale of all editing in this first edition derives from Poinsot's own intentions, and does violence neither to the original *Ars Logica* nor to the now freed *Treatise on Signs* originally embedded therein. Reserving the main discussion of editing and translation to the end of the work, we are now in a position to let Poinsot begin the exposition of his *doctrina signorum* proper.

From the Second Part of the

ARS LOGICA

The

TRACTATUS DE SIGNIS

Proper

In Two Preambles and Three books,
with Appendices

Praeambulum Primum:

DE ENTE RATIONIS*

First Preamble:

ON MIND-DEPENDENT BEING*

*In the original Latin: "*Quaestio II. De Ente Rationis Logico, Quod Est Secunda Intentio.*" Logica 2. p.: "Question 2. On Logical Mind-Dependent Being, Which Second Intention Is."

Order of the Preamble

Ordo Praeambuli[1]

In beginning to treat of Logic, pedagogy requires us to start from more universal considerations. We begin the discussion with being as existing dependently upon apprehension, not indeed precisely according as it is opposed to being as existing independently of apprehension and is something common to all mind-dependent beings (for this sense pertains to the metaphysician[2]) but as dependence upon apprehension is

Ut obiectum seu materiam Logicae tractare incipiamus, ipso ordine doctrinae oportet ab universalioribus incipere. Et sic disputationem inchoamus ab ente rationis, non quidem prout praecise opponitur enti reali et est commune omnibus entibus rationis, sic enim pertinet ad metaphysicum,[2] sed ut est commune

---

[1] These two preliminary paragraphs have no separate title in Reiser's edition.

[2] Here is the opening occasion to comment on a conflict among the school philosophers of the seventeenth century that is of the first importance to the doctrine of signs, not only theoretically, but historically as well.

Theoretically, the issue may be sharply drawn in terms of the opposed writings of Poinsot and the great Latin master of seventeenth-century philosophy, Francis Suarez (d. 1617). Suarez begins with a thesis fairly classical among the Aristotelians of medieval and renaissance times: " . . . *diximus, objectum adaequatum et directum metaphysicae non esse ens commune ad reale et rationis, sed ad reale tantum*" (*Disputationes Metaphysicae*, disp. 47, sect. 3, par. 3: "We categorically assert that the adequate and direct object of metaphysics is not being common to the mind-independent and mind-dependent orders, but being restricted to the mind-independent order entirely"). But he construes this thesis in a sense so strong as to be inimical to—indeed, entirely destructive of—the possibility of a foundational doctrine of signifying: "*Ostendimus enim ens non solum non esse univocum ad ens reale et rationis, verum etiam non habere unum conceptum communem illis, etiam analogum, sed vel esse aequivocum, vel ad summum, analogum analogia proportionalitis*" (ibid.: "For we will show not only that being is not univocal to the mind-independent and mind-dependent orders, but also that there is *no* concept common to the two, not even an analogous one; rather, any allegedly common concept is either equivocal, or, at the most, analogous by an analogy of proportionality"). Considering that, as Poinsot shows, it is *precisely* the essential univocity of relation in the two orders that creates, first, the very possibility of a mind-dependent order of being, and, consequently, the ground of semiosis among the higher animals, this view of Suarez as it applies to the particular case of relations removes entirely the possibility of working out a doctrine of signs: "*Cum ergo relationes rationis non sint entia realia, et consequenter nec vera entia, . . . Addo praeterea, non posse habere univocam convenientiam cum relationibus realibus, si supponamus illas esse vera entia realia. . . . Ratio autem est, quia cum ens rationis nihil sit, non potest habere veram similitudinem ac convenientiam cum ente reali, in qua convenientia fundari solet univocatio et unitas conceptus; ergo non potest aliquis verus conceptus et essentialis esse communis enti reali et rationis. Et ideo merito Soncin., 4 Metaph., q. 5 et 6. approbat dictum Hervaei (quanquam errore typographi tribuatur Henrico), Quodl. 3, q. 1, articulo primo, in fine, non magis posse ens esse univocum ad ens reale et rationis, quam sit homo ad hominem vivum et mortuum. Habet autem hoc dictum eamdem rationem veritatis in communi, et in tali ente, scilicet, relatione, quia sicut ens rationis non est verum ens, sed fictum, sic relatio rationis non est vera relatio, sed ficta* . . ."—"Since therefore mind-dependent relations are not beings independently of being

common only to second intentions, which intentions pertain to the logician.[3]

Here, there are three considerations: *First*, what is this mind-dependent being?[4] *Second*, how many such are there?[5] *Third*, by what cause is it formed?[6] Prior to these considerations, however, to establish at least a rudimentary notion of mind-dependent being in its opposition to mind-independent being [i.e., as it pertains to Metaphysics], some features of the order of mind-dependent being as such must be examined.[7]

solis secundis intentionibus, quae ad logicum spectant.[3]

Circa quod tria consideranda occurrunt: *Primum*, quodnam sit hoc ens rationis;[4] *secundum*, quotuplex sit;[5] *tertium*, per quam causam formetur.[6] *Prius* tamen, ut aliqua saltem imperfecta notitia entis rationis in communi habeatur, aliqua de ipso genere entis rationis praelibanda sunt.[7]

---

known, and consequently not true beings, . . . I state further that they cannot coincide univocally with mind-independent relations, if we suppose these latter to be true mind-independent beings. . . . The reason for this is that, since mind-dependent being is nothing, it cannot have a true similitude and coincidence with mind-independent being, on which coincidence the univocity and unity of a concept is customarily founded; therefore there can be no true and essential concept common to mind-independent and mind-dependent being. Thus Soncinus, in his *Metaphysical Questions*, qq. 5 and 6, rightly approves the saying of Hervaeus (although the saying is attributed to Henricus because of a printer's error) in the third of his *Questions at Random*, toward the end of Article 1, that being can no more be univocal to mind-independent and mind-dependent being, than man can be univocal to a living man and a dead man. Yet this dictum has the same ground of truth in the case of common being [*ens commune*: being as such] and in this particular case or kind of being, namely, relation, because, just as mind-dependent being is not true but constructed or fictive being, so a mind-dependent relation is not a true but a fictive relation . . ." (*Disputationes Metaphysicae*, disp. 47, sect. 3, par. 3. Cf. Poinsot, Second Preamble, Article 2, esp. 93/17-96/32).

This view forecloses the possibility of a doctrine of signs, for, as Poinsot remarks (Book I, Question 1, 117/28-118/18, 119/40-48), the fundamental problem for the semiotician is precisely that of finding a category and vocabulary for explaining the coming together in signification of the distinct orders of what is and what is not independent of human understanding. And it is precisely the essential univocity of relations in these two orders, so far as awareness is concerned, that makes such an account possible (see esp. Book I, Question 2, 149/41-151/21, Question 4, 187/28-190/24, and notes 13, 33, and 35 thereto; Book II, Question 1, 235/36-236/46, Question 5, esp. 270/37-271/21 and the Second Preamble, Article 2, 93/17-96/36). Cf. Doyle, 1983, for details of Suarez's view in this regard.

The historical importance of Poinsot's and Suarez's opposition on this point of doctrine lies in the fact that it was the teaching of Suarez in the *Disputationes Metaphysicae* that became the *philosophia recepta* so far as Latin Aristotelianism was to be imbibed into the newly forming national language traditions of modern philosophy, particularly in France, the Netherlands, and Germany. Quite simply: a coherent doctrine of signs is impossible along the theoretical lines laid down by Suarez and essentially followed on the subject of relations, as Weinberg (1965) has shown, without exception by Hobbes, Locke, Berkeley, Hume, Descartes, Spinoza, Leibniz, and Kant, i.e., by modern thought up to Hegel, who again introduces an understanding of relation compatible with semiotics (and semiosis!). Because of this striking fact, and the historical juxtaposition of Poinsot's and Suarez's opposed accounts of relation in the milieu of the seventeenth century, I will cite at strategic points throughout the *Treatise* the doctrinal conflict between these two figures so far as concerns the foundations of semiotic in the relative, to facilitate not only a grasp of the doctrine Poinsot adumbrates, but also, and especially, future research into the early Latin roots of modern thought as the reconstruction of philosophy along semiotic lines goes forward. Suffice it to add that these notes are heuristic in design only, and in no sense substitute for a complete, detailed examination of the full ramifications of the differing accounts of relative being afforded by these two thinkers as it affects all that concerns the doctrine of signs and its prospective significance for reconstructing the history of philosophy. For example, the interested reader should compare Suarez's disp. 54, "*De entibus rationis*," with the present Preamble to see how completely one's account of mind-dependent being is affected by one's account of relative being, whereas my notes will be restricted to the latter, foundational differences.

[3] Logica 2. p. q. 27 "*De unitate et distinctione scientiarum*" ("On the unity and distinction of the sciences"), art. 1., Reiser ed. Vol. I 826b28-40: ". . . *Logica, sumit suam unitatem ab abstractione, quam habet similem quidem Metaphysicae, sed diversam ab ea, quia est solum abstractio negativa. Versatur enim circa intentiones rationis, quatenus instrumenta sunt speculandi; quae abstractio est entis rationis, non prout praecise opponitur enti reali in communi, sic enim secundario pertinet ad Metaphysicam, sed prout fundatur in rebus intellectis, et a tali esse cognito rerum accipit abstractionem.*"—"Logic derives its unity from the abstraction which it has similar indeed to that of Metaphysics, but different therefrom by the fact that it is only a negative abstraction. For it treats of intentions of reason to the extent they are instruments of speculative thought; which abstraction is of mind-dependent being not precisely according as it is opposed to mind-independent being in general, for in that sense it pertains secondarily to Metaphysics, but according as it is founded on things understood, and it is from such a *cognized* being of things that Logic takes abstraction." See further ibid., 824b45-825b35, esp. 825b6-21; and Deely, 1981, 1982, Winance, 1985, for general discussion.

[4] 58/1-61/30, esp. 60/7-11.

[5] 61/31-64/14, esp. 61/37-42 and 63/9-64/14.

[6] 65/1-76/45, esp. 71/20-29, 66/47-51 and 73/17-74/4, 75/1-21.

[7] 48/1-57/48.

Sixth Semiotic Marker

The reader should carefully note, for purposes of understanding Poinsot's *Treatise*, the contrast between the opening paragraph and the concluding sentence of Poinsot's explanation here of the "Order of the First Preamble." There are few sharper examples of the care demanded on a reader's part by the elliptical style in which Poinsot characteristically expresses developments in his doctrine.

The opening paragraph, speaking strictly from the point of view of the *Ars Logica* as a traditional logical tract, makes the point that the full consideration of mind-dependent being does not fall within the purview of logic, since there are many types of mind-dependent being besides the one constituting the subject of formal logical studies. But Poinsot recurs in his final remark, the second sentence of the second paragraph, to the broader perspective of metaphysics already implicit in his opening remark (the first sentence of the first paragraph), by making the further, strictly foundational point that the sort of mind-dependent being of concern to the logician cannot be properly understood except as a contraction or specification of the complete notion, and therefore he devotes the entire First Article following to an exposé of mind-dependent being in its full amplitude, i.e., in what is common to the entire order of what exists dependently upon being apprehended in its opposition to what exists independently of being apprehended ("ens reale"). It is mind-dependent being in this complete sense that is of import to the doctrine of signs, as well as in the more restricted, logical sense which will become the principal focus of the Second Article following.

Hence the three steps indicated in the sentence beginning the second paragraph of the *Ordo Praeambuli* here do not at all correspond to the three Articles of the Preamble, as a casual reading of the opening paragraph might suggest. Rather, all three steps refer only to the *last two* of the Articles, and only indicate Poinsot's order of treatment as it covers mind-dependent being in the narrower sense, i.e., as it is proper to a tract in (then) traditional logic.

The last of the three Articles comprising this First Preamble, it should be further noted, though within the perspective of the special treatment of Article 2 as concerned to set off the mind-dependent being of logic, functions also semiotically as an amplification of the general (metaphysical) perspective of Article 1. The reason for this is that, in order to explain the cause of the mind-dependent being constituting the object of logic as a science, which being is but a specific one among other varieties of mind-dependent being, Poinsot

has to explain in general the contrast between mind-dependent being ''materially'' and ''formally'' considered, and this contrast proves to be nothing less than the contrast between mind-dependent being as it exists and functions zoösemiotically—that is, at the perceptual level common to men and beasts—and mind-dependent being as it is able to be precised uniquely at the level of human understanding. The point is so fundamental for establishing the horizon and perspectives of the doctrine of signs that it must be underscored here at the very entrance to the doctrine's perhaps earliest systematic exposition.

The ''perceptual level common to men and the higher animals,'' in Poinsot's tradition, is explained by the doctrine of internal and external sense (Poinsot, 1635: Qq. IV-IX, incorporated into the textual notes arranged throughout the later parts of the *Treatise*, as explained in the ''Editorial Afterword,'' pp. 456, 466 n. 107, and 481-485; see also Deely, 1971a: 55-83); so that, in Article 3 of this Preamble, as in Book II, Question 2, of the *Treatise*, whatever is said about the cognitive constructions or products of internal sense as such—i.e., as these powers function in their own right, and not merely (as in human experience) as ordered to and permeated by the further constructions of intellectual apprehension—applies equally to all animals capable of perception. It is, thus, because internal sense knows through formal signs (Book II, Question 2) and forms ''materially'' mind-dependent beings (First Preamble, Article 3) that animals besides human beings develop social structures based on custom (Book I, Question 6; Book II, Question 6). By contrast, the restricted variety or species of mind-dependent being identified in Article 2 of this Preamble as ''second intentions,'' as a formal variety of mind-dependent being—by no means the only such variety, but the only one directly concerning traditional logic—is found only in intellectual apprehension as it is proper to human beings, owing to their species-specific power of reason or ''understanding''; yet internal-sense powers apprehend and employ for practical purposes (e.g., deception among animals) many varieties of mind-dependent being, in perfect indifference to the fact that such employments have no status (are *non ens*) in the world as it is independently of apprehension, as Poinsot's analysis so skillfully and repeatedly shows over the course of this third Article. In short, everything that is there said about mind-dependent being as formed by and functioning within the purview of internal sense must be taken zoosemiotically, as applying to all animals capable of perception, and not just anthroposemiotically, as is demanded by the narrower remarks on the ''second intentions'' of formal logic found in Article 2.

Article 1

What in General a Mind-Dependent Being Is, and How Many Kinds There Are

Articulus Primus

Quid Sit Ens Rationis in Communi et Quotuplex

If we attend to the signification of the name taken in its fullest extent, ''mind-dependent being'' expresses that which depends on the mind in any way. But something can so depend either as an effect depends on a cause, or as an object depends on the one knowing.

In the first way, something can be found to depend on the mind as an effect upon a cause in two senses: either because it is from the mind as from an efficient cause, the way that works of art [or technology] are devised and come to be by virtue of the mind; or because it is in the mind as in a subject and material cause, the way that acts and habits are in the understanding. But each of these senses pertains to the order of mind-independent being, because a being referred to in either of these two senses has a true and physical existence [i.e., an existence which does not wholly consist in being known], though one dependent upon understanding.

That which depends on the understanding in the second way, however, namely, as an object, is properly called a mind-dependent or mental being, so far as is pertinent to present concerns, because it has *no* existence outside of the mind, but is said to exist only objectively within apprehension, and so is opposed to mind-independent or physical being. That there is being in this sense, to be sure, has been denied by some, yet it is affirmed by the general consensus of theologians and philosophers, since they all distinguish mind-independent being from constructed, fictive, or mind-dependent being, by the fact that the former exists in the world of nature, while the latter does not have an existence in nature but is only known and constructed. Quite apart from any expert

Ens rationis in omni sua latitudine, si nominis significationem attendamus, dicit id, quod dependet aliquo modo a ratione. Potest autem dependere vel ut effectus a causa vel ut obiectum a cognoscente.

Primo modo invenitur aliquid dupliciter dependere a ratione, vel quia est ab ipsa ut ab efficiente, sicut opera artis, quae per rationem excogitantur et fiunt, vel quia est in ipsa ut in subiecto et causa materiali, sicut actus et habitus sunt in intellectu. Sed uterque iste modus pertinet ad ens reale, quia ens sic dictum habet veram et realem existentiam, dependentem tamen ab intellectu.

Quod autem secundo modo ab intellectu dependet, scilicet ut obiectum, dicitur proprie ens rationis, ut pertinet ad praesens, quia nullum esse habet extra rationem, sed solum obiective dicitur esse in ipsa, et sic opponitur enti reali. Quod quidem licet aliqui negaverint, communi tamen theologorum et philosophorum consensu dari constat, cum omnes distinguant ens reale ab ente ficto seu rationis, quia illud existit in rerum natura, hoc non habet existentiam in re, sed solum cognoscitur et fingitur. Imo

opinion, experience itself sufficiently proves that there is such a thing as being whose entire existence depends on the mind, since we witness ourselves imagining and knowing many things which are entirely impossible, and such are the constructed or fictive beings. They are beings, certainly, because they are known in the way being is known; but they are constructs or fictions, because no true being on the side of physical nature corresponds to them.

From these observations a **general definition** or explication of mind-dependent being can be drawn, namely, that it is "being having existence objectively in the mind, to which no being in the physical world corresponds." This formulation is taken from the following works of St. Thomas: *On Being and Essence*, chap. 1;[1] the *Commentary on the Metaphysics of Aristotle*, Book V, lect. 9;[2] and the *Summa theologica*, I, q. 16, art. 3, reply to obj. 2. In these works, it is said that that being is called mind-dependent or mental which, while it posits nothing in the physical world and in itself is not a being, is nevertheless formed or understood as a being in the mind. This way of explaining mind-dependent being is the more suitable in view of the fact that, since being is denominated from the act of being and in terms of an order to existence, just as mind-independent being is defined in terms of the order to the existence that it has truly and in the world of physical nature, so mind-dependent being, which is opposed to physical being, must be explained in the opposite way, namely, as that which does not have an existence in the world of nature and does have existence objectively in cognition.

The view taken by some, however, such as Durandus (in his *Commentary on the Sentences of Peter Lombard*, Book I, dist. 19, q. 5, n. 7), that mind-dependent being consists in the extrinsic denomination whereby a thing is said to be "cognized" or "known," is made doubtful in the first place because, as we shall soon see, whether an extrinsic denomination is formally a mind-dependent being is a point strongly disputed among the experts. In the second place, it is false that mind-dependent being universally speaking consists as such in the mere denomination of something as cognized or known. For this denomination either is the form constituting a mind-dependent being, or it is that which receives the formation of a mind-dependent being. The first alternative cannot be the case, because the denomination in question can also fall upon the mind-independent beings which are denominated cognized (known), yet are not formed by this denomination into mind-dependent beings, because they are not rendered constructs or fictions. If we consider the second alternative, we find it is true that an extrinsic denomination is apprehended as a mind-dependent being, yet not only extrinsic denomination, but other non-beings as well, such as negations, privations, etc.

ipsa experientia sufficienter id probat, cum videamus multa nos imaginari et cognoscere, quae omnino impossibilia sunt, et talia sunt entia ficta. Entia quidem, quia cognoscuntur ad modum entis, ficta vero, quia non correspondet illis aliquod esse verum a parte rei.

Ex quibus elici potest **definitio** seu explicatio entis rationis in communi, scilicet quod sit «ens habens esse obiective in ratione, cui nullum esse correspondet in re». Quod sumitur ex D. Thoma libro de Ente et Essentia cap. 1.[1] et 5. Metaph. lect. 9.[2] et 1. p. q. 16. art. 3. ad 2. dicente, quod ens rationis dicitur, quod cum in re nihil ponat et in se non sit ens, formatur tamen seu accipitur ut ens in ratione. Qui modus explicandi convenientior est, quia cum ens dicatur ab essendo et per ordinem ad existentiam, sicut ens reale definitur per ordinem ad esse, quod vere habet et in re, ita ens rationis, quod illi opponitur, oportet, quod opposito modo explicetur, scilicet quod non habet esse in re et habet illud in cognitione obiective.

Quod vero aliqui dicunt ens rationis consistere in denominatione extrinseca, qua res dicitur cognita, ut Durandus in 1. dist. 19. q. 5. n. 7., imprimis dubium assumitur, cum inter auctores valde controversum sit, an denominatio extrinseca formaliter sit ens rationis, ut statim dicemus. Deinde falsum est universaliter loquendo ens rationis ut sic consistere in sola denominatione cogniti. Nam ista denominatio vel est forma constituens ens rationis, vel est id, quod suscipit formationem entis rationis. Primum esse non potest, cum denominatio ista etiam cadere possit super entia realia, quae denominantur cognita, nec tamen hac denominatione formantur in entia rationis, quia ficta non redduntur. Si secundum, verum est denominationem extrinsecam apprehendi ut ens rationis, sed non solum denominatio extrinseca, sed alia etiam non entia, ut negationes, privationes etc.

[1] *Pa* XVI. 330 a.
[2] *Pa* XX. 402 a.

But if you should ask, What is it to have being in cognition?, the response is that this depends on what we shall have to say shortly [in Article 3] concerning the cause of a mind-dependent being and the act by which it is formed. Meanwhile, suffice it to listen to St. Thomas when he says, in his *Commentary on the Metaphysics of Aristotle*, Book IV, reading 1,[3] n. 540: ''We say of any things that they exist in the mind from the fact that the mind, during the time it affirms or denies anything of them, deals with them as if with some beings.'' This statement must not be understood as saying that a mind-dependent being is formed only by a proposition that denies or affirms, but as saying that the formation of a proposition concerning an object that does not have a physical existence in the world of nature is a sign that the object in question is grasped by the understanding in the way a being is grasped, because the copula that signifies the act of being is applied to it.

And so the very act of understanding, attaining—in just the way it would attain an extramental being—an object that does not exist extramentally, has two aspects: not only does it, insofar as it is a cognition, render something known, and in this respect posit in the object only the extrinsic denomination of being known; but it also renders that object known on the pattern (that is, in the likeness or guise) of a being, while in fact it is not a being (that is, does not exist extramentally), and this is to give the object a mind-dependent, constructed, or fictive existence. And so St. Thomas, in his *Treatise on the Nature of a Genus*, chap. 1,[4] says that a mind-dependent being is produced whenever the understanding attempts to apprehend that which does not exist, and therefore construes that which is not as if it were a being. And in his *Commentary on the Sentences of Peter Lombard*, Book I, dist. 2, q. 1, art. 3,[5] he says that a mind-dependent being results as a consequence of the manner of understanding reality that exists independently of the human mind, and that the intentions that our understanding introduces are of this sort. In this passage from the *Commentary on the Sentences*, St. Thomas reckons ''to be effected by,'' ''to be introduced by,'' ''to be apprehended by,'' and ''to be consequent upon'' the manner or way of the understanding, as equivalent expressions as far as concerns mind-dependent being. And thus, as we will say below, a mind-dependent being does not have a formally fictive or objective existence from this, that it is rendered known as *that which* is known; for in this respect it is already supposed to have a being or some rationale upon which the denomination of ''known thing'' falls. But that act, which respects a non-being under the rationale and guise

Si autem quaeras, quid sit habere esse in cognitione, *respondetur* hoc pendere ex his, quae postea dicenda sunt de causa et actu, quo formatur ens rationis. Interim sufficit audire D. Thomam 4. Metaph. lect. 1,[3] ubi inquit: «Dicimus aliqua in ratione esse, quia ratio de eis negotiatur quasi de quibusdam entibus, dum de eis aliquid affirmat vel negat». Quod non est intelligendum, quasi ens rationis solum formetur per propositionem, quae negat vel affirmat, sed quia formatio propositionis circa obiectum, quod non habet esse a parte rei, est signum, quod ad modum entis ab intellectu accipitur, quia ei applicatur copula, quae significat esse.

Itaque ipse actus intellectus attingens obiectum ad modum entis, quod extra intellectum non est, habet duo: et in quantum cognitio reddit cognitum, et sic in obiecto solum ponit denominationem extrinsecam cogniti, et in quantum ad instar entis reddit tale obiectum cognitum, cum in re non sit ens, et hoc est dare esse rationis seu esse fictum. Et sic D. Thomas opusc. 42. cap. 1.[4] dicit, quod tunc efficitur ens rationis, quando intellectus nititur apprehendere, quod non est, et ideo fingit illud ac si esset ens. Et in 1. Sentent. dist. 2. q. 1. art. 3.[5] inquit, quod ens rationis consequitur ex modo intelligendi rem, quae est extra animam, et huiusmodi sunt intentiones, quas intellectus noster adinvenit. Ubi S. Thomas pro eodem reputat in ente rationis effici, adinveniri, apprehendi et consequi ex modo intelligendi. Et ita, ut infra dicemus, ens rationis non habet formaliter esse fictum seu obiectivum per hoc, quod reddatur cognitum ut *quod*; sic enim iam supponitur habere esse seu rationem aliquam, supra quam cadat denominatio cogniti. Sed ille actus, qui respicit non ens sub ratione et

[3] *Pa* XX. 343 a.
[4] De natura generis (*Pa* XVII. 8 a).
[5] *Pa* VI. 23 b.

of a being, is said to construct or to form the mind-dependent being, and not just to denominate. And in this consists the having of being [exclusively] objectively in the understanding, to wit, that that which is not a being is, by the very method of cognizing, constructed apprehensively as being, i.e., constructed by way of being known as a being.

You might say: If that is so, then every object that is conceived by the understanding otherwise than as it is in the physical world is a mind-dependent being. But the consequent is false; for we conceive many mind-independent beings—such as God and pure spirits and those things which we have not experienced—after the pattern of some other physical being, and not as they are in themselves.

The consequence is denied, because such mind-independent beings as lie outside our direct experience and are conceived by us, are supposed to be true physical beings existing in fact. Whence the rationale of being is not attributed to them from the process of cognizing; but because they are not attained in a mode proper and special to themselves, they are said to be attained after the pattern of another. Yet the fact of being cognized on the pattern of another does not suffice for them to be denominated beings formed absolutely by the mind in the rationale of being, but they are denominated cognized or known by way of an alien nature, not by way of their proper being, and they receive thence in their known being a connotation relative to that on whose pattern they are known.

Having now a general notion of mind-dependent being, it remains also to establish briefly how many kinds of mind-dependent being there are. Now the task of working out a scheme that divides mind-dependent being in its entire extent does not fall to the logician, who treats only of logical mind-dependent being, which is one of the members of the division. But nevertheless, that it might be known to which member of the division logical mind-dependent being pertains, we mention briefly that St. Thomas, in his *Disputed Questions on Truth*, q. 21, art. 1,[6] exhaustively divides mind-dependent being understood in the most general way into two members, namely, into *negation* and mind-dependent *relation*. There are, he says, only two possible kinds of mind-dependent being, namely, a negation or some relation; "for every absolute use of a word signifies something existing in the nature of things." Under negation, however, he also includes privation. For privation is a kind of negation or lack of a form in a subject suited for receiving the opposite form, whereas negation is a lack of a form in a subject unsuited for that form. For example: the lack of a visual capacity in a stone is a

modo entis, dicitur fingere seu formare ens rationis, et non solum denominare. Et in hoc consistit habere esse obiective in intellectu, id est ex ipso modo cognoscendi affici apprehensive ut ens, quod non est ens.

Dices: Ergo omne obiectum, quod aliter ab intellectu concipitur quam sit in re, est ens rationis. Consequens est falsum; nam plura entia realia cognoscimus ad instar alterius, et non sicut sunt in se, sicut Deum et angelos et ea, quae non sumus experti.

Negatur consequentia, quia talia entia supponuntur in re esse vera entia realia. Unde ex modo cognoscendi non attribuitur illis ratio entis, sed quia modo proprio et speciali suo non attinguntur, dicuntur attingi ad instar alterius. Quod tamen non sufficit, ut denominentur entia formata a ratione absolute in ratione entis, sed denominantur modo alienae naturae, non propriae esse cognita, et connotationem inde recipiunt in suo cognosci ad id, ad cuius modum cognoscuntur.

Habita notitia entis rationis in communi, restat etiam breviter attingere, **quotuplex sit ens rationis**. De divisione ergo, quae ens rationis in tota sua latitudine dividit, non pertinet agere ad logicum, qui solum tractat de ente rationis logico, quod est unum ex membris dividentibus. Sed tamen ut sciatur, ad quod membrum divisionis pertineat, breviter dicimus D. Thomam in q. 21. de Veritate art. 1.[6] dividere ens rationis communissime sumptum in duo membra adaequate dividentia, scilicet in *negationem* et *relationem* rationis. Id, inquit, quod est rationis, non potest esse nisi duplex, scilicet negatio vel aliqua relatio; «omnis enim positio absoluta aliquid in rerum natura existens significat». Sub negatione autem etiam privationem includit. Nam privatio est quaedam negatio seu carentia formae in subiecto apto ad recipiendam formam oppositam, negatio autem est carentia in subiecto repugnante formae, sicut negatio poten-

[6] *Pa* IX. 304 a et b.

negation; in a man, it is a privation. Relation too has something proper by virtue of its concept, which is being toward another, that can be found in apprehension alone and not in physical reality—when, specifically, it so bears toward another that it is not in anything, as St. Thomas shows in the *Summa theologica*, I, q. 28, art. 1.

Not all admit the sufficiency of this division, however, because some think that being as it exists dependently upon the mind ought first to be divided into that which has a foundation in mind-independent being and that which does not; and the former is called a reasoned mind-dependent being, the latter a mind-dependent being of reasoning. But only that mind-dependent being which is reasoned is, they say, divided into negation and relation, whereas that mind-dependent being which is of the mind reasoning they think is found in all the categories. See Serna's *Commentary on the Logic of Aristotle*, disp. 1, sect. 4, q. 2, art. 3; Cabero's *Digest of Logic*, "Concerning Universals," disp. 1, dub. 3; and Merinero's *Commentary on the Whole of Aristotle's Dialectical Works according to the Mind of John Duns Scotus*, disp. 3, q. 2.

Others espouse the view that there are no determinate kinds of mind-dependent being, but every incompatibility or every thing impossible and involving a contradiction, they say, is a kind of mind-dependent being, because everything of that sort is a constructed or fictional being. This is the position Martinez takes in *The Syllogistic Art of Aristotle*, disp. 2, "prologue" to q. 1.

Others assign other kinds of mind-dependent being arbitrarily, but there is no need to consider seriously such views.

Taking all these differences of opinion into account, it must yet be said that **this division of mind-dependent being into negations and relations is the best and is exhaustive, and is the one more directly suited to mind-dependent being in general.**

For in the case of a mind-dependent being we can consider three factors or elements: The first is the subject to which it is attributed; the second is the very rationale which is conceived and attributed to another; the third is that on the pattern of which the mind-dependent being is conceived and apprehended.

On the side of the subject to which the mental construct is attributed, sometimes there is a foundation in fact for something's being attributed to that subject in such or such a way, sometimes not. And the distinction between a mind-dependent being with a foundation in fact and one without such a foundation is drawn in terms of this difference; for the distinction in question is understood respectively to that subject to which a given mind-dependent being or mental construct is attributed.

Similarly *on the side of that on whose pattern* a mind-dependent being is conceived, it is not contradictory to find in-

tiae visivae in lapide est negatio, in homine privatio. Relatio etiam habet proprium ex vi sui conceptus, qui est ad alterum, quod possit inveniri in sola apprehensione et non in re, quando scilicet ita se habet ad aliud, quod non est in aliquo, ut D. Thomas ostendit 1. p. q. 28. art. 1.

Huius autem divisionis sufficientiam NON OMNES ADMITTUNT, quia existimant aliqui prius esse dividendum ens rationis in illud, quod habet fundamentum in re et quod non habet; et primum vocatur rationis ratiocinatae, secundum rationis ratiocinantis. Solum autem illud, quod est rationis ratiocinatae, dicunt dividi in negationem et relationem, quod vero est rationis ratiocinantis per omnia genera putant divagari. Videatur Serna in Logica disp. 1. sect. 4. q. 2. art. 3., Mag. Cabero de Universalibus disp. 1. dub. 3., Merinero disp. 3. q. 2.

Alii existimant nullam dari speciem determinatam entis rationis, sed omnem repugnantiam seu omne impossibile et contradictionem implicans dicunt esse speciem entis rationis, quia omne illud est ens fictum. Ita Martinez disp. 2. prologi q. 1.

Alii alias species pro libito assignant, de quibus non est curandum.

DICENDUM NIHILOMINUS EST **optimam et adaequatam esse hanc divisionem et magis directe conveniens enti rationis in communi.**

Nam in ente rationis TRIA possumus considerare: *Primum* est subiectum cui attribuitur; *secundum* est ratio ipsa, quae concipitur et attribuitur alteri; *tertium* est id, ad cuius instar concipitur et apprehenditur.

Ex parte subiecti, cui attribuitur, aliquando invenitur fundamentum, ut tali vel tali modo aliquid ei attribuatur, aliquando non. Et ita respectu huius sumitur illa distinctio entis rationis cum fundamento vel sine fundamento in re; accipitur enim hoc respective ad id, cui attribuitur tale ens rationis.

Similiter ex parte eius, ad cuius instar concipitur ens rationis, non

stances in all the categories, because sometimes a mental construct or being can be constructed and apprehended after the pattern of substance (a chimera, for example, or a golden mountain), sometimes after the pattern of quantity (a vacuum, for instance), sometimes after the pattern of quality (as, for instance, if death or blindness were conceived as a blackness or a kind of dark form, etc.).[7]

But indeed if we consider mind-dependent being *on the side of the thing conceived*, or on the side of that which, even though it is not a being in the physical world, is knowable in the way a physical being is knowable, then mind-dependent or mental being is exhaustively divided into these two members as into the primary kinds of mind-dependent being, namely, into negation and relation, under which many negations and relations are subdivided. And because this is the formal element that is attained in a mind-dependent being, therefore this division is the direct and formal one, though yet other divisions can also be admitted, but as based on the conditions for mind-dependent being, not as based on mind-dependent being directly.

This division is, moreover, exhaustive, because the very rationale of mental or mind-dependent being formally consists in an opposition to physical or mind-independent being, specifically, the rationale of a mind-dependent being consists in the fact that it is not susceptible of a mind-independent existence. But this mental being is either something positive or nonpositive. If nonpositive, it is a negation, that is, something not positing but removing a form. If positive, it can only be a relation, because every positive absolute, since it is not conceived in terms of another, but in terms of itself, is either a substance in itself or an accident in another. Wherefore no positive absolute can be understood as a mind-dependent being, because through the very concept of being in itself or in another it imports something of physical (or mind-independent) reality. But relation alone,[8] because it bespeaks not only the concept of "being in," but also the concept of "being toward" (by reason of which precisely relation does not bespeak an existence in terms of itself, but the extrinsic attainment of a terminus), can therefore without contradiction be conceived without anything of mind-independent reality—and therefore as a mind-dependent being—by a conceiving of that relational being not as in another or as in itself, but as toward another with the negation of an existence in another.

But you may object on two counts: First, in order to prove that privations and negations are not rightly said

repugnat per omnia genera divagari, quia aliquando potest fingi et apprehendi aliquid ad instar substantiae, ut chimaera, mons aureus, aliquando ad instar quantitatis, ut vacuum, aliquando ad instar qualitatis, ut si mors vel caecitas concipiatur tamquam nigredo vel forma quaedam obscura etc.[7]

At vero si consideremus ens rationis ex parte rei conceptae seu ex parte eius, quod ad modum entis realis cognoscibile est, cum in re non sit ens, adaequate dividitur in illa duo membra tamquam in prima genera entis rationis, scilicet in *negationem* et *relationem*, sub quibus plures negationes et relationes subdividuntur. Et quia hoc est formale, quod attingitur in ente rationis, ideo haec divisio est directa et formalis, cum tamen aliae divisiones etiam possint admitti, sed quasi desumptae ex conditionibus entis rationis, non quasi directe sub illo positae.

Est autem adaequata haec divisio, quia ratio ipsa entis rationis formaliter consistit in oppositione ad ens reale, scilicet quod non sit capax existentiae. Hoc autem vel est aliquid positivum vel non positivum. Si non positivum, est negatio, id est non ponens, sed tollens formam. Si positivum, solum potest esse relatio, quia omne positivum absolutum, cum non concipiatur ad aliud, sed in se, vel in se est substantia vel accidens in alio. Quare non potest aliquid positivum absolutum sumi ut ens rationis, cum per ipsum conceptum essendi in se vel in alio realitatem aliquam importet. Sola vero relatio,[8] quia non dicit solum conceptum ,,in'', sed etiam conceptum ,,ad'', ratione cuius praecise non dicit existentiam in se, sed extrinsecam termini attingentiam, ideo non repugnat concipi sine realitate, atque adeo ut ens rationis, concipiendo illud non ut in alio vel ut in se, sed ut ad aliud cum negatione existentiae in aliquo.

Sed obicies duo: Primo ad probandum non recte dici privationem et nega-

---

[7] But see the Second Preamble, Article 2, 95/18-96/36.

[8] See Article 3 of this Preamble, 69/13-69/40, and in the Second Preamble see Article 2, 94/24-96/36, esp. 95/18ff.

to be mind-dependent beings. For privation and negation bespeak a lack of a form and denominate a subject deficient apart from any mind's considering; therefore they are not fictive deficiencies nor constructed (mind-dependent) beings.

The consequent is clear from the fact that mind-dependent being depends upon cognition in order to be and in order to confer its formal effect; therefore if prior to cognition a privation or a negation gives its denomination to things, negation is not a mind-dependent being. And the same argument applies to an extrinsic denomination such as being seen or being known, namely, that, apart from any consideration of the understanding, through this alone, that there is a seeing of the wall in the eye, the wall is denominated seen, and similarly, prior to the resultance of a mind-dependent being, a nature can be denominated superior and inferior, predicate or subject, etc.

This is confirmed by the fact that an extrinsic denomination follows on a mind-independent form existing in some subject; therefore the denomination itself is a mind-independent form. The consequent is clear from the fact that, just as the denomination that follows on a substantial form is substantial, and one that follows on an accidental form is accidental, so one that follows on a mind-independent form must be mind-independent.

The response to this[9] is that negation, as bespeaking the lack of a form, is given on the side of mind-independent being negatively, because the form itself is not in the thing. Yet it is not called a mind-dependent being for this reason, but because, while in the physical world it is not a being, but the absence of a form, it is understood by the mind after the manner of a being, and so prior to the consideration of the understanding it denominates a deficient subject. But this deficiency or lack is not properly a formal effect, nor is to remove a form some form, but the deficiency is understood in the manner of a formal effect, inasmuch as it is understood in the mode of a form, and consequently after the pattern of a formal effect, while in fact the deficiency or lack in question is not a formal effect, but the removal of that effect. And similarly there is an extrinsic denomination on the part of mind-independent being as regards the denominating form. But because its application to the thing denominated is not mind-independently in the very thing denominated, therefore to conceive that form as

tionem esse entia rationis. Nam privatio et negatio nullo intellectu considerante dicunt carentiam formae et denominant subiectum carens; ergo non sunt carentiae fictae nec entia rationis.

Patet *consequens*, quia ens rationis dependet a cognitione, ut sit et ut conferat suum effectum formalem; ergo si ante cognitionem dat suam denominationem rebus, negatio non est ens rationis. Et idem argumentum fit de denominatione extrinseca, v. g. esse visum, esse cognitum, quod nullo intellectu considerante per hoc solum, quod detur visio parietis in oculo, denominatur paries visus, et similiter ante resultantiam entis rationis potest denominari natura superior et inferior, praedicatum vel subiectum etc.

Et confirmatur, quia denominatio extrinseca sequitur ad formam realem existentem in aliquo subiecto; ergo est forma realis. *Consequens* patet, quia, sicut denominatio, quae sequitur ad formam substantialem, est substantialis, et quae sequitur ad accidentalem, est accidentalis, ita quae sequitur ad formam realem, debet esse realis.

RESPONDETUR[9] negationem, ut dicit carentiam formae, dari a parte rei negative, quia ipsa forma in re non est. Non tamen ex hoc dicitur ens rationis, sed quia cum in re non sit ens, sed carentia formae, accipitur ab intellectu per modum entis, et ita ante considerationem intellectus denominat subiectum carens. Sed ista carentia proprie non est effectus formalis, nec tollere formam est aliqua forma, sed per modum effectus formalis accipitur ab intellectu, quatenus per modum formae accipitur, et consequenter ad modum effectus formalis, cum in re illa carentia non sit effectus formalis, sed ablatio illius. Et similiter denominatio extrinseca a parte rei datur quantum ad formam denominantem. Sed quia applicatio eius ad rem denominatam non est realiter in ipsa re denominata, ideo concipere illam formam ut

[9] i.e., to 53/46-54/19.

adjoining and applied to the very thing denominated is something mind-dependent. But to be a predicate and subject, superior and inferior, is found prior to the awareness of understanding only fundamentally, not formally under the concept of relation, as will be explained at greater length in treating of universals.

To the confirmation[10] the response is that some hold absolutely that an extrinsic denomination is something mind-dependent—Vazquez, for example, in his *Commentary on the Summa theologica*, I, disp. 115, chap. 2, n. 2, and I-II, disp. 95, chap. 10. But *others* think that absolutely it is something physical or mind-independent, though by an extrinsic, not an intrinsic, mind-independence, that produces its effect without anything superadded by the mind: thus Suarez, in the last of his *Metaphysical Disputations*, sect. 2, and others. But it seems truer that in the denomination in question two factors concur, namely, the form itself as the denominating rationale, and its adjacency or application to the thing denominated as the condition. And as regards the form itself, it is manifest that it is something mind-independent or physical, as the sight, by which the wall is denominated *seen*, is a form in the eye independent of being itself apprehended objectively; yet the application of the form as it touches the denominated subject is not something mind-independent, because it posits nothing in the wall itself. Every nonphysical apprehended thing is, however, something mind-dependent, and so, from the side of the application, an extrinsic denomination is something mind-dependent in the denominated form. The subject [extrinsically] denominated is nevertheless said to be denominated prior to the operation of the understanding, not by reason of that which the understanding posits in the denominated subject, but by reason of that which the understanding supposes besides that subject, because in itself an extrinsic denomination is a mind-independent form, but it does not exist mind-independently in that which it denominates. Whence by reason of nonexistence it is taken as a mind-dependent being, yet by reason of the pre-existence in another from which it respects the denominated thing it is said to denominate prior to the operation of the understanding.

And if it should be asked to which member of this division an extrinsic denomination pertains when it is conceived as a mind-dependent being, the response is that it pertains to relation, because it is not conceived as affecting by negating and removing a form, but by ordering and depending on that whence the denomination is taken, or on that toward which it is imposed and destined through cognition.

adiacentem et applicatam ipsi rei denominatae, aliquid rationis est. Esse autem praedicatum et subiectum, superius et inferius, ante cognitionem intellectus solum invenitur fundamentaliter, non formaliter sub conceptu relationis, ut latius dicetur agendo de universalibus.

Ad confirmationem[10] respondetur *aliquos* absolute sentire, quod denominatio extrinseca est aliquid rationis, ut P. Vazquez 1. p. disp. 115. cap. 2. n. 2. et 1. 2. disp. 95. cap. 10. *Alii* vero, quod absolute est aliquid reale, realitate tamen extrinseca, non intrinseca, quae sine aliquo rationis superaddito praebet suum effectum. Ita Suarez disp. ult. Metaph. sect. 2. et alii. *Sed verius videtur*, quod in denominatione ista concurrunt duo, scilicet ipsa forma ut ratio denominans, et adiacentia seu applicatio eius ad denominatum ut conditio. Et quantum ad ipsam formam, manifestum est esse aliquid reale, sicut visio, qua paries denominatur visus, realis forma est in oculo; applicatio tamen eius, ut tangit subiectum denominatum, non est aliquid reale, quia nihil in ipso pariete ponit. Omne autem non reale apprehensum est quid rationis, et sic ex parte applicationis in forma denominata aliquid rationis est denominatio extrinseca. Dicitur tamen denominatum subiectum ante operationem intellectus, non ratione eius, quod in illo ponit, sed ratione eius, quod extra illud supponit, quia in se est forma realis, sed non realiter existit in eo, quod denominat. Unde ratione non existentiae sumitur ut ens rationis, ratione autem praeexistentiae in alio, a quo respicit rem denominatam, dicitur denominare ante operationem intellectus.

Et si inquiratur, ad quod membrum huius divisionis pertineat denominatio extrinseca, quando concipitur ut ens rationis, *respondetur* pertinere ad relationem, quia non concipitur ut afficiens negando et tollendo formam, sed ordinando et dependendo ab eo, unde sumitur denominatio, vel ad id, ad quod imponitur et destinatur per cognitionem.

10 54/20-28.

A second objection is offered to prove that the division is not exhaustive. For a mind-dependent unity of the sort given to a universal by the understanding is something made by the mind, and neither a relation nor a negation. It is not a relation, because unity is said absolutely, not respectively. It is not a negation, both because unity bespeaks something positive and not pure negation, as St. Thomas says in the *Summa theologica*, I, q. 11, art. 1; and because if it were a negation, it would have to be conceived in the manner of a mind-dependent being, and thus would not be called a mind-dependent unity—that is, plurality negated by the mind—but a being of the mind (a mind-dependent being) absolutely. And similarly, a mind-dependent duality or distinction is not a negation, since it rather removes the negation of unity; nor is it a relation, because the relation of the distinguished terms is founded upon a distinction or duality; therefore it is something of another kind.

This is confirmed in the case of things that are purely figments, such as a chimera, a golden mountain, and the like. For these are not negations nor relations, but various substances synthesized by the mind out of antithetical parts. And similarly there can be a mind-dependent quality or quantity—for example, if a vacuum is understood in the manner of a quantity, or darkness in the manner of a quality. Therefore not all mind-dependent beings reduce to negation and relation.

Some have responded[11] by saying that a unity that is only mental is taken from the unity of a concept, and that a mind-dependent or mental distinction is taken from a plurality of concepts, which is certainly true on the part of the cause producing or causing mind-dependent being. But the present inquiry is not about the efficient cause of mind-dependent being, but about the objective or fundamental cause. Whence my own response[12] is that a mind-dependent unity on the side of the object pertains formally to negation or privation, because it is nothing other than a segregation of that in which there is coincidence or agreement from the several making a difference. And to the first reason assigned for the contrary view[13] the response is that, according to St. Thomas in the passage cited, unity materially and entitatively is something positive, but formally it is the negation of a division. And to the second reason[14] my response is that it

Secundo obicitur ad probandum, quod non sit divisio adaequate. Nam unitas rationis, qualis attribuitur universali ab intellectu, est aliquid rationis, et non relatio neque negatio. Non relatio, quia unitas dicitur absolute, non respective. Non negatio, tum quia unitas dicit aliquid positivum et non puram negationem, ut dicit S. Thomas 1. p. q. 11. art. 1.; tum quia, si esset negatio, deberet concipi per modum entis rationis, et sic non diceretur unitas rationis, id est negatio rationis, sed ens rationis absolute. Et similiter dualitas seu distinctio rationis non est negatio, cum potius tollat negationem unitatis, nec relatio, quia super distinctionem seu dualitatem fundatur relatio distinctorum; ergo est altera species.

Confirmatur in his, quae sunt pure figmenta, ut chimaera, mons aureus et similia. Haec enim non sunt negationes nec relationes, sed plures substantiae ab intellectu adunatae ex partibus inter se repugnantibus. Et similiter potest dari qualitas vel quantitas rationis, ut si vacuum accipiatur per modum quantitatis vel tenebrae per modum qualitatis. Ergo non omnia entia rationis ad illa duo reducuntur.

RESPONDETUR[11] aliquos existimare, quod unitas rationis tantum sumitur ex unitate conceptus, et distinctio ex pluralitate, quod quidem verum est ex parte causae efficientis seu causantis ens rationis, quam in praesenti non inquirimus, sed de obiectiva seu fundamentali. Unde respondemus,[12] quod unitas rationis ex parte obiecti pro formali pertinet ad negationem seu privationem, quia nihil aliud est quam segregatio eius, in quo est convenientia a pluribus facientibus differentiam. Et ad *primam* impugnationem[13] respondetur, quod secundum D. Thomam in illo loco unitas materialiter et entitative est aliquid positivum, sed formaliter est negatio divisionis. Et ad *secundam*[14] respondetur, quod

[11] to 56/1-19.
[12] to 56/1-19.
[13] 56/7-9.
[14] 56/9-14.

is not contradictory for this mind-dependent unity to be also a mind-dependent being, since indeed the very negation or separation of plurality and difference is understood in the fashion of a being. And to the added remark concerning a mind-dependent duality or distinction,[15] my response is that a mind-dependent distinction is formally a mental relation, and is the very relation itself of the distinguished terms, whose distinction is a kind of relation by the very fact that they are only distinguished mind-dependently, even though the distinguished extremes are themselves sometimes conceived on the pattern of absolute things, as, for example, after the pattern of two substances, etc. But this relation of the distinction is founded not on another distinction formally understood, but fundamentally, that is, on a virtual plurality that obtains on the side of the object as subjected to a plurality of concepts.

To the confirmation[16] the response is that all the figments in question are mind-dependent beings which are negation; not indeed that there is a mind-dependent substance or a mind-dependent quantity, because that which is formed by the understanding on the pattern of a mind-independent being is not a substance or a quantity, but negations of substance or of quantity conceived on the pattern of a substance or of a quantity. That on whose pattern something is conceived is not said to be a mind-dependent being, however, but that object which, while it is not in itself a being, is conceived after the pattern of a being. Concerning this, see further Article 2 of the Second Preamble[17] on Relation.[18]

From this it follows that in the case of the metaphysical universal, which expresses only a nature abstracted and conceived in the manner of a unity (as we will say in the following Question), there is already found something mind-dependent, namely, that which, owing to an abstraction, belongs to the nature represented or known, to wit, the unity, whether aptitude or nonimpossibility for being in many. For these negations are something mind-dependent, but are not formally second intentions, which consist in a relation founded on the natures thus abstracted. But the universal thus abstracted is called metaphysical, not logical, because not every mind-dependent being formally and directly pertains to Logic, but second intention, as we have shown with the help of St. Thomas in Article 3 of the preceding Question. But a second intention is a mind-dependent relation, not a negation like unity, and yet it belongs to a thing abstracted and one.

non repugnat, quod ista unitas rationis sit etiam ens rationis; siquidem ipsa negatio seu separatio pluralitatis et differentiae per modum entis accipitur ab intellectu. Et ad id, quod additur de dualitate seu distinctione rationis,[15] respondetur, quod distinctio rationis formaliter relatio rationis est, et est ipsamet relatio distinctorum, quae hoc ipso, quod sola ratione distinguuntur, eorum distinctio relatio quaedam est, licet ipsa extrema ad instar absolutorum aliquando distincta concipiantur, v. g. ad modum duplicis substantiae etc. Fundatur autem relatio ista distinctionis non super alia distinctione formaliter accepta, sed fundamentaliter, id est in pluralitate virtuali, quae tenet se ex parte obiecti, ut pluralitati conceptuum subicitur.

Ad confirmationem[16] respondetur omnia illa figmenta esse entia rationis, quae sunt negatio; non vero dari substantiam rationis vel quantitatem rationis, quia non est substantia vel quantitas id, quod per rationem formatur ad instar entis realis, sed negationes substantiae vel quantitatis ad instar substantiae vel quantitatis concipiuntur. Non dicitur autem ens rationis id, ad cuius instar aliquid concipitur, sed id, quod concipitur ad instar entis, cum non sit in se ens. De hoc vide latius infra Praeambulum Secundum[17] de Relatione art. 2.[18]

Ex hoc sequitur, quod in universali metaphysico, quod solum dicit naturam abstractam et per modum unius conceptam, ut seq. quaest. dicemus, iam invenitur aliquid rationis, scilicet id, quod ex vi abstractionis convenit naturae repraesentatae seu cognitae, id est unitas sive aptitudo aut non repugnantia ad essendum in pluribus. Istae enim negationes aliquid rationis sunt, sed non sunt formaliter secundae intentiones, quae in relatione consistunt fundata in naturis sic abstractis. Dicitur autem universale sic abstractum metaphysicum, non logicum, quia non omne ens rationis formaliter et directe pertinet ad Logicam, sed secunda intentio, ut ex D. Thoma ostendimus quaest. praec. art. 3. Haec autem est relatio rationis, non negatio, ut unitas, et tamen convenit rei abstractae et uni.

[15] 56/14-19.
[16] 56/20-29.
[17] In the original Latin: "q. 17."
[18] esp. 96/1-36.

[290b22-291a7]

Article 2

What Is the Second Intention and Logical Mind-Dependent Relation and How Many Kinds Are There

Articulus Secundus

Quid Sit Secunda Intentio et Relatio Rationis Logica et Quotuplex

This is the mind-dependent being of which the logician properly treats, inasmuch as the specific type of relation which is considered by a logician is brought about as a result of an ordination of concepts. Thus St. Thomas says, in Book IV of his *Commentary on the Metaphysics of Aristotle*, reading 4,[1] that ''mind-dependent objective being is properly the name of those intentions which the understanding brings about within or introduces into considered things, such as, for example, the intention of a genus, species, and the like,'' and mind-dependent objective being of this [restricted] kind is properly the subject of Logic.

Supposed here therefore are the things which we said about terms of the first and second intention in the first of the *Summulae* books.[2] And ''intention'' is used in the present context not according as it expresses the act of the will respecting an end as distinguished from [the act of] choice [of means to realize that objective], but as standing for or supposing the act or conception of the understanding, which is said to be an intention in a general way, because it tends toward another, to wit, toward an object. And so just as the concept in one mode is formal, in another mode objective (that is to say, is the very cognition or thing

Hoc ens rationis est, de quo proprie agit logicus, quatenus ex ordinatione conceptuum adinvenitur talis relatio, quae a logico consideratur. Et ita D. Thomas in 4. Metaph. lect. 4.[1] inquit, quod «ens rationis dicitur proprie de illis intentionibus, quas ratio adinvenit in rebus consideratis, sicut intentio generis, speciei et similium», et huiusmodi ens rationis est proprie subiectum Logicae.

Supponenda ergo sunt, quae de terminis primae et secundae intentionis diximus in 1. libro Summularum.[2] Et sumitur intentio in praesenti, non prout dicit actum voluntatis, qui distinguitur ab electione et respicit finem, sed pro actu seu conceptu intellectus, qui dicitur intentio generali modo, quia tendit in aliud, scilicet in obiectum. Et ita sicut conceptus alius est formalis, alius obiectivus, scilicet ipsa cognitio vel res

[1] *Pa* XX. 349 a et b.

[2] Logica 1. p. lib. 1. c. 4, 12b49-13a19: ''*Terminus* primae intentionis *est, qui significat aliquid secundum id, quod habet in re vel in suo proprio statu, id est secluso statu, quem habet in intellectu et prout conceptum, sicut album, homo ut in re. Terminus* secundae intentionis *est, qui significat aliquid secundum id, quod habet per conceptum mentis et in statu intellectus, sicut species, genus, et alia similia, quae logicus tractat. Et dicuntur ista primae et secundae intentionis, quia id, quod convenit alicui secundum se, est quasi primum in illo et status proprius; quod vero convenit alicui, secundum quod est intellectum,*

known), so is a formal intention one mode, an objective intention another. The very mind-dependent relation which is attributed to a thing cognized is called an objective intention; but the very concept by means of which an objective intention is formed is called a formal intention. For example, when we conceive "animal" as superior to its inferiors, the very universality obtaining on the side of animal conceived is called an objective or passive intention, but the concept itself by which animal is so conceived is called a formal intention. And so a formal intention as distinguished against an objective intention is one relation, [but] the formality of a second intention as it obtains on the side of the object cognized is something else again; for the formality of a second intention is always something mind-dependent, as being something resulting from cognition, but a formal intention is an act whose being does not depend on itself being cognized.

But this formality of a second intention is called "second intention" according to the difference from a first intention, as if a second state or condition of an object were being expressed. For an object can be considered in two states: *First,* as it is in itself, whether as regards existence or as regards definable structure. *Second,* as it is in apprehension, and this state of existing in cognition is second in respect of the state of existing in itself, which is first, because just as knowability follows on entity, so being known follows on that being which an object has in itself. Those affections or formalities, therefore, belonging to a thing according as it is in it-

cognita, ita alia est intentio formalis, alia obiectiva. Obiectiva dicitur ipsa relatio rationis, quae attribuitur rei cognitae; formalis vero ipse conceptus, per quem formatur. Sicut quando concipimus animal tamquam superius ad sua inferiora, ipsa universalitas ex parte animalis se tenens dicitur intentio obiectiva seu passiva, ipse vero conceptus, quo sic concipitur animal, dicitur intentio formalis. Et sic aliud est formalis intentio, ut distinguitur contra obiectivam, aliud formalitas intentionis secundae, ut tenet se ex parte obiecti cogniti; haec enim semper est aliquid rationis, utpote ex cognitione resultans, illa vero est actus realis.

Vocatur vero secunda intentio ista secundum differentiam a prima, quasi dicatur secundus status seu conditio obiecti. Potest enim obiectum considerari in duplici statu: *Primo,* secundum quod est in se, sive quantum ad existentiam sive quantum ad quidditatem. *Secundo,* ut est in apprehensione, et status iste essendi in cognitione est secundus respectu status essendi in se, qui est primus, quia sicut cognoscibilitas sequitur ad entitatem, ita esse cognitum est post illud esse, quod habet in se. Illae ergo affectiones seu formalitates, quae conveniunt rei prout in

est quasi secundum et secundus status superveniens primo, et ideo vocatur secundae intentionis, quasi secundi status."—"A term of the *first intention* is one that signifies something according to that which the signified has in reality (independently of its being known) or in its own proper condition, that is to say, apart from the condition or status it has in the understanding and according as it is conceived, such as a white thing, or a man, as existing independently of cognition. A term of the *second intention* is one that signifies something according to that which the signified has owing to a concept of the mind and in the condition or state of the understanding, such as species, genus, and things of like kind that logicians treat. And these are said to be of first and second intention, because that which belongs to anything according to its own being is, as it were, primary in that thing and its own condition or state; but that which belongs to anything according as it is understood is as it were secondary and a second condition or state supervening upon the first, and for this reason it is called 'of second intention,' as of the second status."

The reader should note, however, that, as Poinsot puts it (Logica 2. p. q. 12. art. 1., Reiser ed. 464b24-28): "*. . . etiam in entibus rationis potest inveniri prima intentio, sicut sunt multae negationes et privationes et denominationes extrinsecae*"—"a first intention can also be found in the case of mind-dependent beings, as are many negations and privations and extrinsic denominations." Thus, social and cultural roles and personality structure, though mind-dependent creations, *yet belong to the order of first intention*: e.g., see 60/15-35 in this Article, and Book I, Question 2, 141/28-142/13, and note 32 p. 150, at the end. Also (ibid., 464b28-33): "*Potest etiam una secunda intentio materialiter substerni et denominari accidentaliter ab alia secunda intentione, et sic induit quasi modum primae intentionis respectu eius, cui substernitur.*"—"One second intention can even be materially subtended and accidentally denominated by another second intention, and so a second intention assumes the manner of a first intention in respect of the second intention to which it is subtended." See 61/31ff. below.

self, are called first intentions; those belonging to the thing according as it is known are called second intentions. And because it is the task of Logic to order things as they exist in apprehension, therefore of itself Logic considers second intentions, the intentions which coincide with things as known.

From which it follows first that **not every mind-dependent objective relation is a second intention, but, nevertheless, every second intention taken formally, and not only fundamentally, is a mind-dependent objective relation, not a mind-independent form, nor an extrinsic denomination, as some erroneously think**.

The first part of this[3] is manifestly the case, because even though every mind-dependent relation results from cognition, yet not every such relation denominates a thing only in the state of a cognized being, which is a second state, but some also do so in the state of an existence independent of cognition, as, for example, the relations of Creator and Lord do not denominate God known in himself, but God existing, and similarly being a doctor, being a judge. For the existing man, not the man as cognized, is a doctor or a judge, and so those mind-dependent relations [being a doctor, judge, teacher, etc.] denominate a state of existence.[4]

Here *note this difference*: even though cognition is the cause from which a mind-dependent relation results (as it is the cause of all mind-dependent being), and thus, as the mind-dependent relation belongs to and denominates some subject, it necessarily requires cognition, yet cognition does not always render *the object itself apt* and congruous for the reception of such a denomination, so that the denomination belongs to that object *only in cognized being*, for this happens only in second intentions. And thus the relations of Creator and Lord, judge and doctor, as they denominate a subject, require cognition, which causes such relations, but does not render the subject capable in cognized or known being of receiving that denomination. But indeed the being of a genus or species not only supposes cognition causing such relations, but also supposes a cognition which renders the subject abstracted from individuals, and upon the thing so abstracted falls that denomination [i.e., the denomination by a second intention].

The second part of the conclusion[5] is expressly that of St. Thomas in his work, *On the Nature of Genus*, chap. 12,[6] where he says that second intentions are properties

se, vocantur primae intentiones, quae conveniunt rei prout cognita, vocantur secundae. Et quia pertinet ad Logicam dirigere res, secundum quod sunt in apprehensione, ideo per se considerat Logica intentiones secundas, quae conveniunt rebus ut cognitis.

EX QUO DEDUCITUR PRIMO, **quod non omnis relatio rationis est secunda intentio, omnis tamen secunda intentio formaliter sumpta, et non solum fundamentaliter, est relatio rationis, non forma realis, non denominatio extrinseca, ut male aliqui putant.**

Prima pars[3] constat manifeste, quia licet omnis relatio rationis resultet ex cognitione, non tamen omnis ista relatio denominat rem solum in statu cogniti, qui est status secundus, sed etiam in statu existentiae extra cognitionem, sicut relatio Creatoris et Domini non denominat Deum in se cognitum, sed Deum existentem, et similiter esse doctorem, esse iudicem. Neque enim homo ut cognitus est doctor aut iudex, sed homo existens, et ita denominant illae relationes pro statu existentiae.[4]

Ubi discerne, quod licet cognitio sit causa, ex qua resultat relatio rationis (quod omni enti rationis commune est), et ita ut conveniat et denominet relatio rationis aliquod subiectum, necessario exigat cognitionem, non tamen semper cognitio reddit ipsum obiectum aptum et congruum susceptivum talis denominationis, ita ut solum conveniat illi in esse cognito, sed solum hoc contingit in intentionibus secundis. Et ita relatio Creatoris et Domini, iudicis et doctoris, ut denominet subiectum, requirit cognitionem, quae talem relationem causet, sed non quae constituat subiectum in esse cognito capax, ut denominationem illam suscipiat. At vero esse genus vel speciem non solum supponit cognitionem causantem tales relationes, sed etiam supponit cognitionem, quae reddat subiectum abstractum ab inferioribus, et super rem sic abstractam cadit illa denominatio.

Secunda vero pars[5] est expresse D. Thomae in opusc. 42. cap. 12.,[6] ubi dicit, quod secundae intentiones sunt proprie-

[3] 60/7-8.
[4] Cf. Book I, Question 2, 141/12-142/13, esp. 141/37-142/8.
[5] 60/9-13.
[6] De natura generis (*Pa* XVII. 17 a).

belonging to things as a result of their having being in understanding; and the *Disputed Questions on the Power of God*, q. 7, art. 9,[7] says that "they [i.e., second intentions] follow upon the mode of understanding"; and the *Commentary on the Metaphysics of Aristotle*, Book IV, reading 4,[8] says that second intentions belong to things as cognized or known by the understanding. They are therefore not mind-independent objective forms, but mind-dependent ones.

And this is the case, both because the rationale of genus and of species and of *any other universals* [i.e., formal universals] consists in a relation of superiors [e.g., classes] to inferiors [e.g., instances], which relations cannot be mind-independent (for otherwise there would be given a universal formally existing in the order of mind-independent being), and also because these intentions suppose for a fundament a known being, as for example a genus supposes a thing's being abstracted from inferiors and belongs to that thing by reason of the abstraction. Therefore a second intention supposes the extrinsic denomination of a thing cognized and abstracted, but it is not formally the extrinsic denomination itself, and much less are second intentions mind-independent forms; for in that case they would descend to the singular things themselves in which they would be found mind-independently existing, and not only in what is abstracted from singulars. But the very act of understanding is a kind of act independent of being itself apprehended, yet it is not the objective second intention itself of which we now treat, but the formal intention from which this objective [second] intention results.

It follows secondly that although a first intention absolutely taken must be something mind-independent or belonging to something in the state of being independent of objective apprehension (for otherwise it would not be simply first, because that which is mind-independent always precedes and is prior to that which is mind-dependent), yet nevertheless **it is not contradictory that one second intention should be founded on another. In such a case, the founding second intention takes on as it were the condition of a first intention in respect of the other or founded intention, not because it is simply first, but because it is prior to that intention which it founds.**

For since the understanding is reflexive upon its own acts, it can know reflexively the second intention itself and found upon that cognized intention another second intention; for example, the intention of a genus which is attributed to animal, can as cognized again found the second intention of species, inasmuch as the intention of genus

tates convenientes rebus ex eo, quod sunt in intellectu; et q. 7. de Potentia art. 9.,[7] quod «sequuntur modum intelligendi»; et 4. Metaph. lect. 4.,[8] quod conveniunt rebus prout cognitae ab intellectu. Non ergo reales formae sunt, sed rationis.

Et constat hoc, *tum* quia ratio generis et speciei et reliquorum universalium consistit in relatione superiorum ad inferiora, quae non possunt esse relationes reales, alias daretur universale formaliter a parte rei. *Tum* etiam, quia istae intentiones supponunt pro fundamento esse cognitum, sicut genus supponit rem esse abstractam ab inferioribus et ratione abstractionis ei convenit. Ergo supponit denominationem extrinsecam cogniti et abstracti, non vero formaliter est ipsa denominatio extrinseca, et multo minus sunt formae reales; sic enim descenderent ad ipsa singularia, in quibus realiter invenirentur, et non solum in abstracto a singularibus. Ipse autem actus intellectus est quidam actus realis, sed non est ipsa intentio secunda obiectiva, de qua nunc agimus, sed formalis, ex qua ista obiectiva resultat.

SECUNDO SEQUITUR, quod licet prima intentio absolute sumpta debeat esse aliquid reale vel conveniens alicui in statu realitatis, alias non esset simpliciter prima, quia semper id, quod est reale, praecedit et prius est eo, quod est rationis, nihilominus tamen **non repugnat etiam in ipsa secunda intentione aliam secundam intentionem fundari, et tunc secunda intentio fundans induit quasi conditionem primae intentionis respectu alterius fundatae, non quia sit simpliciter prima, sed quia est prior illa, quam fundat.**

Nam cum intellectus sit reflexivus supra suos actus, potest ipsam secundam intentionem reflexe cognoscere et super ipsam cognitam fundare aliam secundam intentionem; sicut intentio generis, quae tribuitur animali, iterum ut cognita potest fundare secundam intentionem speciei, quatenus intentio generis est quaedam species praedicabilis. Et tunc secunda ista

[7] *Pa* VIII. 163 a.
[8] *Pa* XX. 349 b.

is a kind of predicable species. And then this founded second intention denominates the founding second intention as prior, by reason of which circumstance it is said that the genus formally is a genus and denominatively is a species. This is something that frequently happens in these second intentions, to wit, that one of them is in itself formally of a certain type, but is of another type as known denominatively. Nevertheless these are all said to be second intentions, even though the one second intention is founded on another second intention, and there is not said to be a third or a fourth intention, because they all belong to (or coincide with) the object as known, but being known is always a second state for a thing. And because one second intention as it founds another takes on as it were the condition of a first intention in respect of that other founded on it, so even that intention which is founded is always said to be second.

You may say: A second intention respects a first intention as something correlative, because second is spoken of in view of the first, therefore the second intention does not respect the first intention as a fundament, but as a terminus. Again: A second intention is predicated of its fundament, for example: "Man is a species"; but a second intention is not predicated of a first, for this is false: "A first intention is a second intention"; therefore a second intention is not founded on a first intention.

The response to the first argument[9] is that the second intention does not respect the first as something correlative in the manner of a terminus, but as a subject to which it is attributed and which it denominates or on which it is founded. And so it is expressed through an order to a first intention as to a subject, not as to a terminus; just as a relation is expressed through an order to an absolute as to a subject or fundament, but not as to a correlative, unless it takes on the rationale of a terminus, and then it will be something respective or correlative, not as a subject, as we will say in [treating] the category of relation. And similarly the formal correlative of a second intention always is some second intention, as genus to species and vice versa.

To the second argument[10] it is said that a second intention is predicated of a first intention in the concrete, as white of a man, but not in the abstract; and for this reason it is true that man is a species, and false that a first intention is a second intention. For second

intentio fundata denominat priorem fundantem, ratione cuius dicitur, quod genus formaliter est genus et denominative species. Quod frequenter contingit in istis secundis intentionibus, quod secundum se una formaliter sit talis, et denominative ut cognita sit alia. Et nihilominus omnes istae dicuntur secundae intentiones, licet una fundetur super aliam, non tertia vel quarta intentio, quia omnes conveniunt obiecto ut cognito, esse autem cognitum est semper status secundus rei. Et quia una intentio ut fundat aliam, induit quasi conditionem primae respectu illius, et sic illa, quae fundatur, semper dicitur secunda.

DICES: Secunda intentio respicit primam ut correlativum, quia secunda dicitur per respectum ad primam, ergo non ut fundamentum, sed ut terminum. *Item:* Secunda intentio praedicatur de suo fundamento, ut «Homo est species»; sed secunda intentio non praedicatur de prima, nam haec est falsa: «Prima intentio est secunda intentio»; ergo non fundatur in illa.

Respondetur *ad primum*[9] secundam intentionem non respicere primam ut correlativum per modum termini, sed per modum subiecti, cui attribuitur et quod denominat vel in quo fundatur. Et sic dicitur per ordinem ad primam ut ad subiectum, non ut ad terminum; sicut relatio dicitur per ordinem ad absolutum ut ad subiectum vel fundamentum, non vero ut ad correlativum, nisi induat rationem termini, et tunc erit aliquid respectivum seu correlativum, non ut subiectum, ut dicemus in praedicamento relationis. Et similiter correlativum formale secundae intentionis semper est aliqua secunda intentio, ut genus ad speciem et e contra.

Ad secundum[10] dicitur, quod secunda intentio praedicatur de prima in concreto, sicut album de homine, sed non in abstracto; et ideo est verum, quod homo est species, et falsum, quod prima intentio sit secunda intentio. Nam etiam secundae

---

[9] 62/19-23.
[10] 62/23-28.

intentions can also be signified by an abstract name, in general by this name, ''second intention,'' as well as in particular, as by the name, ''universality,'' ''generality,'' and the like, which imply only a form of understanding in the abstract, but do not signify the subject or thing on which they are founded directly, but indirectly; just as whiteness in the abstract implies a body indirectly, because it is a quality of a body.

If you ask, how many types of second intention are there and how are they divided, the answer is that all relations are divided by reason of their proximate fundament or rationale of founding, as we will say in [our treatment of] the category of relation.[11] Whence also the mind-dependent relation, which is formed on the pattern of mind-independent relation, is rightly divided by means of its fundaments. But because the fundament of a second intention is a thing as known and as it is subjected to the state of apprehension, the division of second intention is also drawn according to the diverse orders of the known (for whose ordination the second intention is formed). Whence, because the first operation of the understanding is ordered and directed in one way, the second operation in another way, and the third in yet another, therefore second intentions may be divided in different ways according to the diverse ordinations of these operations, and in each operation there will be different intentions according to different orders of directability.

As, for example, in the first operation the intention of the term which is ordered as a part of an enunciation and syllogism is one order of directability, under which the diverse intentions of a part are contained, such as the rationale of a name, the rationale of a copula, and of the other terms; another order of directability is the intention of universality in the mode of a higher predicable (which is also divided into the various modes of universality, such as genus, species, etc.), to which corresponds the intention of subjectability, as it is found in the individual and in the other lower predicates.

In the second operation, however, is found the intention of a statement, which order of directability is divided through the various modes of perfect and imperfect statement. Again the proposition, which is one of the perfect forms of statement, is divided into the affirmative and the negative and the other divisions which we have explained in the second of

intentiones nomine abstracto significari possunt, tam in communi per hoc nomen ,,secunda intentio'' quam in particulari, ut hoc nomine ,,universalitas, genereitas'' et similia, quae solum important formam rationis in abstracto, subiectum autem seu rem, in qua fundantur, non significant directe, sed in obliquo; sicut albedo in abstracto importat corpus in obliquo, quia est qualitas corporis.

Si quaeras, quotuplex sit secunda intentio et quomodo dividatur, respondetur omnem relationem dividi ratione sui fundamenti proximi seu rationis fundandi, ut dicemus in praedicamento relationis.[11] Unde similiter relatio rationis, quae ad instar relationis realis formatur, recte dividetur per sua fundamenta. Cum autem fundamentum secundae intentionis sit res ut cognita et ut subest statui apprehensionis, iuxta diversum ordinem cogniti, ad cuius ordinationem secunda intentio formatur, sumetur quoque divisio secundae intentionis. Unde, quia aliter ordinatur et dirigitur prima operatio intellectus, aliter secunda et aliter tertia, ideo penes diversas ordinationes istarum operationum dividetur secunda intentio, et in qualibet operatione secundum diversum ordinem dirigibilitatis erit diversa intentio.

Sicut *in prima* operatione alia est intentio termini, quae ordinatur ut pars enuntiationis et syllogismi, sub qua diversae intentiones partis continentur, sicut ratio nominis, ratio verbi et aliorum terminorum; alia est intentio universalitatis per modum superioris praedicabilis, quae etiam dividitur in varios modos universalitatis, ut genus, species etc., cui correspondet intentio subicibilitatis, sicut invenitur in individuo et aliis inferioribus praedicatis.

In secunda autem operatione invenitur intentio orationis, quae dividitur per varios modos orationis perfectae et imperfectae. Rursus propositio, quae est una ex orationibus perfectis, dividitur per affirmativam et negativam et alias divisiones,

---

[11] q. 17. art. 3., i.e., in the present work, Second Preamble, Article 3, esp. 101/11-26.

the *Summulae* books.[12] And again the proposition founds other second intentions, which are the properties of a proposition, such as opposition and conversion, which pertain to the whole proposition, and supposition and extension, predicate and subject, and the like, which are properties of the parts of a proposition, as was explained in the same book.[13]

Finally in the third operation is the intention of the consequence or of argumentation, which order of directability is divided through induction and syllogism; and induction through ascent from singulars to universals and descent from universals to singulars,[14] the syllogism through the various modes and figures, which are explained in the same book.[15]

quas libro 2. Summularum explicavimus.[12] Et rursus propositio fundat alias secundas intentiones, quae sunt proprietates propositionis, ut oppositio et conversio, quae pertinent ad totam propositionem, et suppositio et ampliatio, praedicatum et subiectum aliaque similia, quae sunt proprietates partium propositionis, ut in eodem libro explicatum est.[13]

Denique *in tertia* operatione est intentio consequentiae seu argumentationis, quae dividitur per inductionem et syllogismum; et illa per ascensum et descensum,[14] hic per varios modos et figuras, de quibus ibidem dictum est.[15]

---

[12] Logica 1. p. lib. 2. c. 7.

[13] Logica 1. p. lib. 2. c. 9-19. incl.

[14] Poinsot here remarks in passing a point of fundamental import for semiotic which was recognized but underdeveloped by the scholastics, then forgotten wholly by the moderns. In discussing this point in *Introducing Semiotic* (Deely 1982: 67-75), thus, I remarked (pp. 71, 72-73): ". . . it would seem that the most fertile development for semiotics in this area of logic comes with the re-discovery by C. S. Peirce around 1866 that the notion of induction is heterogeneous, comprising not one but two distinct species of movement: the movement of the mind whereby we form an hypothesis on the basis of sensory experience, which Peirce called *abduction* (sometimes "hypothesis," also "retroduction"), and the movement back whereby we confirm or infirm our hypothesis with reference to the sensory, for which movement Peirce retained the name *induction*. . . .

"In this way of understanding the matter, a simplistic 'contrast of opposite directions in the reasoning process between the same two points' (cf. Eco 1976: 131-133) is replaced rather by the phenomenological contrast between thought in its interaction with the realm of material things outside itself, on the one hand—which interaction moreover is of a twofold character; and thought considered in its internal development according to the relations which are proper to its own realm. Thus we have the three irreducibly distinct movements recognized in common by Peirce and some among the older Latin authors grounded in the integral treatment of the *Organon*:

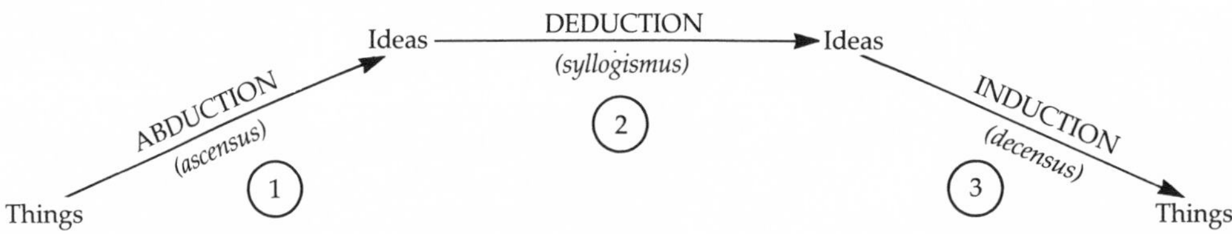

[15] Logica 1. p. lib. 3. c. 2., 3., 5., 6.

Article 3[1]

By What Powers and Through Which Acts Do Mind-Dependent Beings Come About

Articulus Tertius[1]

Per Quam Potentiam et Per Quos Actus Fiant Entia Rationis

There is no doubt that the powers by which [objectively] mind-dependent being is produced must be powers that work immanently; for powers that work transitively, it is clear, produce something existing independently of understanding. But some immanent powers are cognitive, others are appetitive. And as regards those which are appetitive, some have said that mind-dependent beings can result from the will [as well as from the understanding]—Scotus, for example, against whom Cajetan argues in his *Commentary on the Summa theologica*, I, q. 28, art. 1. It must be noted, however, that Scotus, in his *Commentary on the Sentences of Peter Lombard*, Book III, dist. 26, q. 2 [which is the passage Cajetan refers to], seems to have been speaking of mind-dependent being not strictly, but as the name "mind" includes both the understanding and the will in its signification. Moreover, there are some who extend this capacity to produce mind-dependent being to any power whatever from which there results in an object an extrinsic denomination, on the basis of the view that mind-dependent being consists in an extrinsic denomination, which view we have discussed already.[2] As regards the cognitive powers, however, there is room for wondering whether at least the internal senses—the imaginative or fantasizing power, for example—do not produce mind-dependent beings, because the internal senses construct and imagine many objects that are beings entirely fictive.

Constat potentias, quibus fit ens rationis, debere esse potentias operantes immanenter; nam quae transeunter operantur, patet facere aliquid extra intellectum existens. Potentiae autem immanentes aliae sunt cognoscitavae, aliae appetitivae. Et de *appetitivis* aliqui dixerunt etiam ex voluntate resultare entia rationis, ut Scotus, contra quem agit Caietanus 1. p. q. 28. art. 1. Quamvis Scotus loqui videatur de ente rationis non stricte, sed prout hoc nomen ,,ratio'' comprehendit intellectum et voluntatem, in 3. dist. 26. q. 2. § *Resp.* Imo aliqui hoc extendunt ad quamlibet potentiam, unde resultat in obiecto extrinseca denominatio, eo quod existimant ens rationis in denominatione extrinseca consistere, de quibus diximus praec. art.[2] De potentiis vero *cognoscitivis* dubitari potest, saltem de sensibus internis, ut de imaginativa vel phantasia, quia multa fingunt et imaginantur, quae sunt entia omnino ficta.

---

[1] "Articulus IV" in the original Latin.
[2] esp. 49/29-51/7, and 54/29-55/49.

Turning from the questions concerning the powers that produce mind-dependent beings to questions concerning the act itself forming a mind-dependent being, we find again room for doubt on two points. *First*, there is the question whether a mind-dependent being can be formed by an absolute act, such as a simple operation is, or does the production of a mind-dependent being require some comparative or compositive act? *Second*, there is the question whether a mind-dependent being requires, in order to exist, a reflexive act whereby it would be known from the very mental being formed as from the object known; or indeed does a direct act suffice, an act whereby something which is not a being is known on the pattern of a being?

Taking up each of these four doubtful points in turn, I say first: **Neither the will nor the external senses form mind-dependent beings, in the sense that by virtue neither of an act of the will as such nor of an act of external sense as such would mind-dependent beings have existence.**

The conclusion is certain and is PROVED BY ONE SINGLE REASON, because the will and the external senses alike do not form their object, but presuppose an object formed outside of themselves. Therefore they do not construct anything within themselves, but if they apprehend a constructed or fictive object, they presuppose that it was constructed and formed by some other power.

The antecedent is clearly verified in the case of the will, which supposes an object proposed by cognition, whether that object be true or apparent; therefore the will itself does not produce an object, but is borne to a proposed object. The external senses, on the other hand, are borne to objects posited outside of, not within, themselves; but whatever has an existence outside or independent of a cognitive power is not a mind-dependent being.

Nor does it matter that the senses are deceived in many cases, and therefore know only fictively. For the external senses are not deceived in themselves, but are occasionally said to be deceived from the fact that they provide the understanding with an occasion for being deceived—as sight, for example, on seeing fool's gold, is not deceived by judging that it is gold: rather does this judgment pertain to the understanding. Sight, for its part, apprehends only that colored outward appearance of the fool's gold, in which there is not falsity or fiction.

I say secondly: **The internal senses do not form mind-dependent beings formally speaking, although materially they are able to represent that on whose pattern some fictive entity is formed, which is to form mind-dependent beings materially.**

De actu vero formante ens rationis in duobus etiam potest esse dubium: *Primo*, an possit fieri per actum absolutum, qualis est operatio simplex, an requirat aliquem comparativum vel compositivum. *Secundo*, an requirat actum reflexum, quo cognoscatur de ipso ente rationis formato tamquam de obiecto cognito, ad hoc ut existat; an vero sufficiat actus directus, quo cognoscatur aliquid, quod non est ens, ad instar entis.

DICO PRIMO: **Neque voluntas neque sensus externi formant entia rationis, ita quod ex vi actuum eorum habeant esse.**

Conclusio est certa et probatur unica RATIONE, quia tam voluntas quam sensus externi non formant suum obiectum, sed extra se supponunt formatum. Ergo non fingunt aliquid intra se, sed si respiciunt obiectum fictum, ab alio supponunt esse fictum et formatum.

Antecedens patet in voluntate, quae supponit obiectum propositum per cognitionem, sive sit verum sive apparens; ergo ipsa non facit obiectum, sed in obiectum propositum fertur. Sensus vero externi feruntur in obiecta extra se posita, non intra se; quidquid autem habet esse extra potentiam cognoscentem, non est ens rationis.

Nec obstat, quod sensus falli videatur in multis, atque adeo ficte cognoscere. Non enim fallitur sensus externus in se, sed occasionaliter dicitur falli, quia praebet occasionem intellectui, ut fallatur, sicut visus videns aurichalcum non fallitur iudicando, quod sit aurum, sed hoc iudicium pertinet ad intellectum. Visus autem solum apprehendit illam apparentiam coloris aurichalci, in quo falsitas aut fictio non est.

DICO SECUNDO: **Sensus interni non formant entia rationis formaliter loquendo, licet materialiter repraesentare possint id, ad cuius instar formatur aliquod ens fictum, quod est materialiter formare entia rationis.**

We say that the internal senses "formally speaking" do not form mind-dependent beings, that is, they do not form them by discriminating between mind-dependent being and physical being, and by conceiving that which is not a being after the pattern of physical being. Materially, however, to cognize a mind-dependent being is to attain the very appearance of a being physically real, but not to discriminate between that which is of the mind and that which is of the physical world.[3] For example, the imaginative power can form a gold mountain, and similarly it can construct an animal composed of a she-goat, a lion, and a serpent, which is the Chimera [of Greek mythology]. But in these constructions the imagination itself attains only that which is sensible or representable to sense. Yet internal sense does not attain the fact that objects so known have a condition relative to non-being, and from this relationship condition are said to be constructed, fictive, mind-dependent, or mental—which is formally to discriminate between being and non-being.

The REASON seems clear: internal sense cannot refer to anything except under a sensible rationale; but the fact that that which is represented to it as sensible happens to be opposed to physical being, does not pertain to internal sense to judge, because internal sense does not

Dicimus ,,formaliter loquendo'' non formare illa, id est discernendo inter ens rationis et ens reale, et concipiendo id, quod non est ens, ad instar entis realis. Materialiter autem cognoscere ens rationis est ipsam apparentiam realis entis attingere, sed non discernere inter id, quod rationis et realitatis est.[3] V. g. imaginativa potest formare montem aureum et similiter animal compositum ex capra, leone et serpente, quod est chimaera. Sed in istis solum attingit id, quod sensibile seu quoad sensum repraesentabile est. Quod autem habeant habitudinem ad non ens et ex ista habitudine entia ficta seu rationis dicantur, quod est formaliter discernere inter ens et non ens, sensus internus non attingit.

RATIO videtur manifesta, quia sensus internus non potest ferri in aliquid nisi sub ratione sensibilis; quod autem id, quod sibi repraesentatur ut sensibile, opponatur enti reali, ad ipsum non pertinet iudicare, quia non concipit ens sub ra-

[3] Phil. nat. 4. p. q. 8. art. 3., Reiser ed., III. 263b41-264a11, and 269b47-270a14: "*Et non est necesse, quod omnia, quae cognoscuntur in intellectu vel sensu interno, sint cognita per sensum externum, sed sufficit, quod in specie, quae emittitur ab obiecto et deinde a sensu, virtualiter contineantur illa omnia et explicari possint in potentia superiori. Et sic dicit D. Thomas 1. p. q. 78. art. 4. ad 4., 'quod licet operatio intellectus oriatur a sensu, tamen in re apprehensa per sensum intellectus multa cognoscit, quae sensus percipere non potest, et similiter aestimativa, licet inferiori modo.' Itaque bene potest cognosci per sensum internum aliquid, quod directe et formaliter a sensu externo non cognoscatur, sed sit modus aliquis seu respectus fundatus in illis sensibilibus et in eis virtualiter contentus.*"—"It is not necessary that everything known in the understanding or cognized by internal sense should be apprehended by the external senses. It is enough if all those things are virtually contained in the formal specification that is emitted by the object and then by sense, and can be unfolded in the higher power. Thus St. Thomas says in the *Summa theologica*, I, q. 78, art. 4, reply to objection 4, that 'although the operation of the understanding arises out of sense, the understanding yet cognizes many facets of the thing apprehended through sense that sense cannot perceive, and the same holds for the estimative power, although to a lesser extent.' It can well be, therefore, that something can be known through internal sense that is not known directly and formally by external sense, but is some modality or respect founded on those sensibles and virtually contained in them." (See Book II, Question 2, p. 243 note 8.) "*. . . non colligi, quod potentia sensitiva sit reflexiva, ex eo quod formet idolum et mediante illo cognoscat obiectum repraesentatum in illo, dummodo non cognoscat ipsum verbum in actu signato et tamquam obiectum cognitum, sed ut medium cognoscendi. Sicut etiam non reflectit supra ipsum actum, licet utatur illo tamquam medio cognoscente et tendente ad obiectum, sic utitur idolo formato ut repraesentante sibi obiectum extra tamquam termino producto ad repraesentandum aliud, non ut sentiatur in se, quod requirebatur ad reflexionem.*"—"It is not to be gathered that the sensitive power [i.e., internal sense] is reflexive from the fact that it forms an icon and by means of that icon knows the object represented therein, while it does not know the word itself [i.e., the icon] as a significate, but as the means of the knowing. Just as sense does not reflect upon the act itself of knowing, even though it uses that activity as the means of cognizing and tending toward the object, so too does it use the icon formed as representing to itself an external object as a term produced for representing another, not as something sensed within itself, which would be required for reflexion." (See below, note 17 and 71/20-72/17; Book II, Questions 1 and 2, esp. note 8 of Question 2, p. 243; and Book III, Question 3.)

conceive of being under the rationale of being. The fact, however, of anything's being regarded as a constructed or fictive being formally consists in this, that it is known to have nothing of entitative reality in the physical world, and yet is attained or grasped on the pattern of a physical entity; otherwise, no discrimination is made between mind-independent being and constructed or fictive being, but only that is attained on whose pattern a mind-dependent being is formed. When this object is something sensible, there is no reason why it cannot be known by sense. But sense attains only that which is sensible in an object, whereas the condition relative to the non-being in whose place the object is surrogated and whence it fictively has being, does not pertain to sense. For this reason, sense does not differentiate a constructed being, under the formal rationale of being a construct, from a true being.

But that sense is able to know fictive being *materially* is manifestly the case. Not, indeed, from the fact that even external sense can, for example, cognize a fictive color or appearance, because this color, even though it is the color [of a given object] only apparently, is nevertheless not a fictive being, but one true and physical, that is to say, it is something resulting from light. But that sense grasps mind-dependent beings is proved by this fact, that internal sense synthesizes many things which outside itself in no way are or can be. Sense therefore knows something which is in itself a constructed or fictive being, although the fiction itself sense does not apprehend, but only that which, in the fictive being, offers itself as sensible. But sense does not perceive a privation of a proper object—darkness, for example—by constructing it in the manner of a being, but by not eliciting an act of seeing.

I say thirdly: **The understanding needs some comparative act in order that mind-dependent beings might be formed and be said to exist formally and not only fundamentally.**

This conclusion is taken FROM ST. THOMAS's *Commentary* on the first Book of Aristotle's treatise *On Interpretation*, reading 10,[4] where he says that "the understanding forms intentions of this sort"—he was discussing universals—"according as it compares them to the things that occur independently of the mind." And in his *Disputed Questions on the Power of God*, q. 7, art. 11,[5] he says that the mental relations that the understanding invents and attributes to the things understood are one thing, but the mental relations that result from the mode of understand-

tione entis. Quod autem aliquid accipiatur tamquam ens fictum, formaliter consistit in hoc, quod cognoscatur nihil entitatis habere in re, et tamen ad instar entis attingi; alioquin non discernitur inter ens reale et ens fictum, sed solum attingitur illud, ad cuius instar formatur ens rationis. Quod quando est aliquid sensibile, non repugnat a sensu cognosci, sed ad sensum solum pertinet id, quod in illo de sensibilitate est attingere, habitudinem vero ad non ens, cuius loco subrogatur et unde ficte habet esse, ad sensum non pertinet, et ideo ens fictum sub formali ratione ficti ab ente vero non discernit.

Quod vero ens fictum materialiter possit cognoscere sensus, constat manifeste. Non quidem, quia sensus etiam externus potest v. g. cognoscere colorem fictum seu apparentem, quia iste color, licet apparenter sit color, non tamen est ens fictum, sed verum et reale, scilicet aliquid ex luce resultans. Sed ex eo probatur, quia sensus internus multa ad invicem componit, quae extra se nullo modo sunt aut esse possunt. Cognoscit ergo aliquid, quod in se est ens fictum, licet ipsam fictionem non apprehendat, sed solum id, quod in illo ente ficto tamquam sensibile se offert. Privationem autem proprii obiecti, ut tenebras, sensus non percipit fingendo illas ad modum entis, sed actum videndi non eliciendo.

DICO TERTIO: **Intellectus indiget aliquo actu comparativo, ut entia rationis formentur et dicantur formaliter esse et non solum fundamentaliter.**

Haec conclusio sumitur ex Divo Thoma 1. Periherm. lect. 10.,[4] ubi inquit, quod «huiusmodi intentiones (de universalibus loquebatur) intellectus format, secundum quod comparat eas ad res, quae fiunt extra animam». Et q. 7. de Potentia art. 11.[5] inquit, quod relationes rationis aliae sunt, quas intellectus invenit et attribuit rebus intellectis, aliae vero,

[4] *Le* I. 48. n. 9.
[5] *Pa* VIII. 166 b.

ing are quite another, although the understanding does not devise that mode, but proceeds in conformity with it. And relations of the first sort the mind indeed brings about by considering the ordering of that which is in the understanding to the things which are independent thereof, or also by considering the ordering of the things understood [as such] among themselves; but the other relations result from the fact that the understanding understands one thing in an order to another. Therefore St. Thomas thinks that all [mind-dependent] intentions are formed by some act of comparing or relating.

THE REASON FOR THIS CONCLUSION is the fact that every mind-dependent being is either a relation or a negation. If a relation, it must be apprehended comparatively to a term. If a negation, it must be conceived positively on the pattern of being, which is to be conceived comparatively to another. If this negation is conceived absolutely, it is not conceived positively, since in itself it is nothing positive. It must therefore be conceived on the pattern of a being [i.e., comparatively], not only because, on the side of the principle of the knowing, it has to be conceived through a physical specification, but also because, on the side of the term known, it must be grasped on the pattern of a being. And this requires some comparative awareness, as, for example, when I conceive the city of Rome on the pattern of Toledo, I conceive Rome comparatively and not absolutely, because I conceive it connotatively and respectively to another. So too when I conceive a negation on the pattern of being, I conceive it, not absolutely, but respectively and comparatively. A mind-dependent *relation*, however, because it is of itself expressed positively and not negatively, requires a comparative cognition on other grounds, specifically, because a relation is a kind of comparison to a term, and again because it is conceived after the pattern of a physical relation, even though it is in itself positively expressed.[6]

By the phrase "a comparative act," however, we understand not only a compositive, in the sense of a judicative, comparison (which pertains to the second operation of the mind), but any cognition whatever that conceives [its object] with a connotation of and an ordering to another—something that can also occur outside of the second operation of the mind, as, for example, when we apprehend a relation through the order to a terminus.

quae consequuntur modum intelligendi, licet illum modum intellectus non adinveniat, sed ex modo intelligendi consequatur. Et primas quidem relationes ratio adinvenit considerando ordinem eius, quod est in intellectu, ad res, quae sunt extra, vel etiam ordinem intellectum ad invicem; aliae vero consequuntur ex eo, quod intellectus intelligit unum in ordine ad aliud. Ergo omnes intentiones existimat D. Thomas formari per aliquem actum comparantem.

ET RATIO conclusionis est, quia omne ens rationis vel est relatio vel aliqua negatio. Si relatio, debet comparative apprehendi ad terminum. Si negatio, debet concipi positive ad instar entis, quod est comparative ad alterum. Quae *negatio* si concipitur absolute, non concipitur positive, cum in se nihil positivum sit. Debet ergo concipi ad modum entis, non solum quia ex parte principii cognoscendi per speciem realem concipi debet, sed etiam quia ex parte termini cogniti debet accipi ad instar entis. Et hoc exigit aliquam notitiam comparativam, sicut quando concipio Romam ad instar Toleti, comparative concipio Romam et non absolute, quia connotative et respective ad aliud. Ita quando negationem concipio ad instar entis, non absolute, sed respective et comparative concipio illud. *Relatio* autem rationis quia positive de se dicitur et non negative, aliunde indiget comparativa cognitione, scilicet quia relatio comparatio quaedam est ad terminum, et rursus quia ad instar relationis realis concipitur, licet in se positive dicatur.[6]

Nomine autem *actus comparativi* non solum intelligimus comparationem compositivam vel iudicativam, quae pertinet ad secundam operationem, sed quamcumque cognitionem, quae cum connotatione et ordine ad aliud concipit, quod etiam extra secundam operationem fieri potest, ut quando apprehendimus relationem per ordinem ad terminum.

[6] See Article 1 of this Preamble, 53/8-45, and in the Second Preamble, Article 2, esp. 96/1-36, in connection with this entire passage (69/13-40).

A mind-dependent being can also come about as the result of a compositive or of a discursive comparison. Indeed, because the understanding affirms that there is such a thing as blindness, the Philosopher, in his *Metaphysics*, Book V, and St. Thomas in his *Commentary* thereon (reading 9, n. 896[7]) as well as in numerous other places, proves that blindness is a mind-dependent being. Through that enunciation, therefore, whereby something is affirmed of a non-being, non-being is conceived positively as if it were a being, specifically, through the connotation of the verb "is."

And I have said in this third conclusion[8] that the understanding requires a comparative act "in order that mind-dependent beings might be said to exist formally and not just fundamentally." For the fundament of a mental relation does not require this comparison, as appears in the case when a nature is divested of individuating conditions by a simple abstraction, and yet in such a case there is not an act of comparison, but only a precision from particular instances. But then the universal is not a logical universal formally, but a metaphysical universal, which is the fundament for a logical intention, as will be explained in Q. 4 below, "On the Cause of a Universal Concept."

From this you can gather that, in the case of mind-dependent relations, there comes about a denomination even before the relation itself is known in act through a comparison, owing solely to this: that the fundament is posited. For example, a nature is denominated universal by the very fact that it is abstracted, even before it is actually related or compared [to its instances]; and the letters in a closed book are a sign, even if the relation of the sign, which is mind-dependent, is not actually considered;[9] and God is denominated Lord, even if the relation of a lord is not actually considered, but by reason of dominative power.[10] *In this, mind-dependent or mental relations differ from mind-independent or physical relations,*[11] because mind-independent relations do not denominate unless they exist, as, for example, someone is not said to be a father unless he actually has a relation to a son; nor is one thing said to be similar to another unless it has a similarity, even though it might have the fundament for a similarity. The *reason for this difference* is that in the case of mind-dependent relations, their actual existence consists in actually being cognized objectively, which is something that does not take its origin

Potest etiam fieri ens rationis per comparationem compositivam aut discursivam. Imo quia de caecitate intellectus affirmat, quod est, probat Philosophus et D. Thomas 5. Metaph. lect. 9.[7] et alibi saepe, quod caecitas est ens rationis. Per illam ergo enuntiationem, qua de non ente affirmatur aliquid, positive concipitur ac si esset ens, scilicet per connotationem ad verbum ,,est''.

Et dixi in conclusione,[8] «ut entia rationis dicantur formaliter esse et non solum fundamentaliter». Nam fundamentum relationis rationis non requirit istam comparationem, ut patet, quando simplici abstractione denudatur natura a conditionibus individuantibus, et tamen ibi non est actus comparationis, sed sola praecisio ab inferioribus. Sed tunc universale non est universale logicum formaliter, sed metaphysicum, quod est fundamentum intentionis logicae, ut infra q. 4. dicetur.

Unde colliges, quod in relationibus rationis contingit fieri denominationem, etiam antequam actu cognoscatur per comparationem ipsa relatio, solum per hoc, quod ponatur fundamentum. V. g. natura denominatur universalis hoc ipso, quod abstrahitur, etiam antequam actu comparetur; et litterae in libro clauso sunt signum, etiamsi actu non consideretur relatio signi, quae est rationis,[9] et Deus denominatur Dominus, etiamsi actu non consideretur relatio domini, sed ratione potentiae dominativae.[10] In quo differunt relationes rationis a realibus,[11] quia reales non denominant nisi existant, sicut non dicitur aliquis pater, nisi actu habeat relationem ad filium, nec similis, nisi habeat similitudinem, etiamsi habeat fundamentum. *Cuius ratio est*, quia in relationibus rationis esse actuale ipsarum consistit in actualiter cognosci obiective, quod non provenit ex fundamento et ter-

[7] *Pa* XX. 402 b.

[8] at 68/35-38.

[9] See Book I, Question 1, 127/7-131/18, esp. 127/43-128/6 and 130/10-43; Book II, Question 5, 275/8-29.

[10] Ibid., esp. 275/25-29.

[11] Cf. Second Preamble, Article 2, 90/41-91/29, and Book II, Question 5, 275/8-41.

from the fundament and terminus, but from the understanding.[12] Whence many things could be said of a subject by reason of a fundament without the resultance of a relation, because this does not follow upon the fundament itself and the terminus, but upon cognition. But in the case of physical relations, since the relation naturally results from the fundament and the terminus, nothing belongs in an order to a terminus by virtue of a fundament, except by the medium of a relation. We understand, however, that this denomination arises from the proximate fundament absolutely speaking, but not in every way, because not under that formality by which it is denominated by the relation as known and existing; for God is denominated "Lord" but is not related before the relation. This is something that does not occur in cases of physical relations, because when the relations do not exist, their fundaments in no way denominate in an order to a terminus.

I say fourthly and finally: **The cognition forming a mind-dependent being is not a reflexive cognition respecting that being as a thing cognized as the object which [is known], but rather that direct cognition which denominates the very non-mind-independent being (or being that is not relative independently of mind) "known" on the pattern of a mind-independent being or relation is said to form a mind-dependent being. It is from that direct cognition that a mind-dependent being results.**

The REASON FOR THIS CONCLUSION is clear: such a cognition, whereby a mind-dependent being itself is denominated cognized reflexively and as the "object which," supposes the [already] formed mind-dependent being, since indeed the cognition is borne upon that being as upon the terminus cognized. Therefore such a reflexive cognition does not initially form that mind-dependent being, but supposes its having been formed and, as it were, examines that objective construct. Whence a [subjective] denomination in the one cognizing does not come about from the intentions thus reflexively cognized, as when a pure spirit or when God perceives intellectually that a man is syllogizing or forming a proposition, God is not on that account said to syllogize or to express the proposition, and yet he understands as if in a reflexive and signified act the very syllogism and proposition and logical intentions. And it is the same when anyone understands these intentions by examining their nature; for then the very intentions examined

mino, sed ex intellectu.[12] Unde multa poterunt ratione fundamenti dici de subiecto sine resultantia relationis, quia haec non sequitur ipsum fundamentum et terminum, sed cognitionem. In relationibus vero realibus cum relatio naturaliter resultet ex fundamento et termino, nihil convenit ex vi fundamenti in ordine ad terminum nisi media relatione. Intelligimus autem convenire denominationem hanc ratione fundamenti proximi absolute loquendo, sed non omni modo, quia non sub illa formalitate, qua denominatur a relatione ut cognita et existente; denominatur enim Deus ante relationem Dominus, sed non relatus. Quod in relationibus realibus non contingit, quia non existente relatione nullo modo denominant in ordine ad terminum.

DICO ULTIMO: **Cognitio formans ens rationis non est reflexa respiciens ipsum tamquam rem cognitam ut quod, sed illa cognitio directa, quae ipsum non ens reale vel quod realiter relativum non est, denominat cognitum ad instar entis vel relationis realis, dicitur formare vel ex illa resultare ens rationis.**

RATIO est manifesta, quia talis cognitio, qua ipsum ens rationis denominatur cognitum reflexe et tamquam *quod*, supponit ens rationis formatum, siquidem super ipsum fertur tamquam super terminum cognitum. Ergo talis cognitio reflexa non primo format ipsum, sed supponit formatum et quasi speculatur ipsum ens rationis. Unde ab intentionibus sic reflexe cognitis non fit denominatio in cognoscentem, sicut quando angelus vel Deus intelligit hominem syllogizare aut propositionem formare, non propterea dicitur Deus syllogizare vel enuntiare, et tamen intelligit quasi in actu reflexo et signato ipsum syllogismum et propositionem et intentiones logicas. Et idem est, quando aliquis intelligit istas intentiones speculando naturam earum; tunc enim non forman-

[12] See, however, Book I, Question 6, 212/21-34, and above in the present Article, 66/47-68/34, esp. 67/5-9.

are not formed, but upon them others are founded, inasmuch as they are cognized in general or by way of predication, etc. And so St. Thomas says, in chapter 3 of his *Treatise on the Nature of a Genus*,[13] that a mental construct or being is effected precisely when the understanding attempts to apprehend something that is not, and for this reason constructs that non-being as if it were a being. And in Book I of his *Commentary on the Sentences of Peter Lombard*, dist. 2, q. 1, art. 3,[14] he says that intentions result "from the mode of understanding extramental reality." What formally and essentially forms initially mind-dependent being is not, therefore, the reflexive cognition whereby precisely a mind-dependent being is denominated cognized as being mind-dependent, but the cognition whereby that which is not is denominated cognized on the pattern of that which is.

Resolution of Counter-Arguments

First, it is argued: Many other powers besides the understanding are concerned with non-beings by attaining and ordering them on the pattern of physical being; therefore these other powers will also form mind-dependent beings.

The antecedent is proved in the case of the will and of internal sense. For the will reaches out toward an apparent good which is not a good in fact; it also orders one good to another as means to end, which sometimes is not truly a means nor truly ordered. Therefore it compares one object to another by a relation not existing in fact, which is to form a mind-dependent being.

Similarly sense, especially internal sense, compares one object to another by forming propositions and discourse concerning singulars, and, out of diverse kinds of things, sense forms a fictive or constructed being, such as, for example, a gold mountain out of gold and a mountain, as St. Thomas teaches in the *Summa theologica*, I, q. 12, art. 9, reply to obj. 2. Therefore sense apprehends constructed or fictive beings. And, generally, from each sense follows the extrinsic denomination of being known, which is a mind-dependent being.

The response to this argument is: I deny the antecedent. To the proof,[15] the response is that the will, since it bears on an apprehended object, does not know that object formally, nor does the will give it being through

tur ipsae intentiones speculatae, sed super ipsas fundantur aliae, quatenus cognoscuntur in universali vel per modum praedicationis etc. Et ita dicit S. Thomas opusc. 42. cap. 3.,[13] quod tunc efficitur ens rationis, quando intellectus nititur apprehendere, quod non est, et ideo fingit illud, ac si ens esset. Et in 1. Sentent. dist. 2. q. 1. art. 3.[14] dicit, quod intentiones consequuntur «ex modo intelligendi rem extra animam». Non ergo cognitio reflexa, qua praecise ens rationis denominatur cognitum ut quod, sed qua denominatur cognitum ad instar entis id, quod non est, formaliter et per se primo format ens rationis.

Solvuntur argumenta.

Primo arguitur: Nam multae aliae potentiae praeter intellectum versantur circa non entia, attingendo illa et ordinando ad instar entis realis; ergo etiam formabunt entia rationis.

Antecedens probatur in voluntate et sensu interno. Nam *voluntas* tendit appetendo in bonum apparens, quod non est bonum in re; ordinat etiam unum ad aliud ut medium in finem, quod aliquando vere non est medium nec vere ordinatur. Ergo comparat unum alteri comparatione non existente in re, quod est formare ens rationis.

Similiter *sensus*, praesertim internus, comparat unum alteri, formando propositiones et discursus circa singularia, et ex speciebus diversis format ens fictum, ut ex auro et monte montem aureum, ut docet D. Thomas 1. p. q. 12. art. 9. ad 2. Ergo cognoscit entia ficta. Et generaliter ex omni sensu consequitur denominatio extrinseca cogniti, quae est ens rationis.

Respondetur: Negatur antecedens. Ad probationem[15] respondetur, quod *voluntas* cum feratur in obiectum cognitum et apprehensum, formaliter non cognoscit illud nec dat illi esse per ra-

[13] De natura generis (*Pa* XVII. 10 a).
[14] *Pa* VI. 23 b.
[15] 72/25-32.

the mind, but that which results from the act of the appetite is rather a kind of extrinsic denomination, which is indeed a mind-dependent being fundamentally; but only when it is actually known after the pattern of a mind-independent form or relation does it exist in act [i.e., formally]. The will itself therefore does not construct the apparent good, but supposes an object known and proposed to itself, and so does not form the object. But the ordination of a means to an end is also proposed to the will by the understanding. The will effects that ordination only by desiring, not by perceiving. Such an ordination certainly posits an extrinsic denomination in the thing ordinately willed, but it does not formally render the mind-dependent being known.

To that which is added concerning sense,[16] the response is that internal sense so compares or relates one thing to another by forming a proposition and discourse, that the sense does not formally cognize the very ordination of predicate and of subject and of antecedent to consequent by distinguishing a fictive from a physical relation.[17] And similarly, sense cognizes a gold mountain as regards that which is sensible in those represented parts of gold and a mountain, not as regards the rationale of the construction or fiction as distinguished from a mind-independent

tionem, sed solum id, quod resultat ex actu appetitus, est aliqua denominatio extrinseca, quae quidem est ens rationis fundamentaliter; quando autem actu cognoscitur ad instar formae seu relationis realis, tunc existit actu. Bonum ergo apparens voluntas ipsa non fingit, sed cognitum et sibi propositum supponit, et sic non format ipsum. Ordinatio autem medii ad finem etiam sibi proponitur ab intellectu, ipsa vero solum appetendo ordinat, non agnoscendo. Talis autem ordinatio ponit quidem denominationem extrinsecam in re ordinate volita, non formaliter reddit ens rationis cognitum.

Ad id, quod additur *de sensu*,[16] respondetur, quod sensus internus ita comparat unum alteri formando propositionem et discursum, quod ipsam ordinationem praedicati et subiecti, et antecedentis ad consequens formaliter non cognoscit discernendo relationem fictam a reali.[17] Et similiter montem aureum cognoscit quantum ad id, quod sensibile est in illis partibus repraesentatis auri et montis, non quantum ad rationem fictionis, ut distin-

---

[16] 72/33-43.

[17] Phil. nat. 4. p. q. 8. art. 3., Reiser ed. III. 263b13-41: ". . . *non cognosci relationes a sensu interno sub proprio modo relationis, scilicet cum comparatione ad terminum vel discursu neque in universali, sed ut se tenent ex parte fundamenti seu ut exercentur in illo, non ut in actu signato et secundum se relatio potest apprehendi. Fundamentum autem est res ipsa sensibilis prout convenientiam vel disconvenientiam fundat. Sic autem non sentitur a sensu externo, quia illud fundare convenientiam vel disconvenientiam non est color vel sonum aut odor vel aliquid, quod sensu externo percipitur, ipsa tamen relatio ut condistincta a fundamento et ut comparative accepta ad terminum non attingitur per aestimativam sine collatione. Et cum dicitur, quod tales relationes non sunt aliquo modo sensibiles per se vel per accidens, respondetur, quod directe non sunt aliquod tale sensibile nec formaliter, bene tamen fundamentaliter, quatenus in illis fundantur, sicut in natura et qualitatibus lupi fundatur contrarietas ad ovem.*"—"Relations are not known by internal sense under the modality proper to relation, that is to say, with a comparison to a term or by discourse, nor are they known in general, but as they obtain on the side of the fundament or as they are exercised therein, not as relation can be apprehended as an actual significate and according to its own being. But the foundation of the relations knowable by internal sense [e.g., 263a38-39, 265b21: aversion, friendliness, offspring, hostility, parents, etc.] is the sensible thing itself according as it founds harmony [utility] or disharmony [harmfulness]. But the sensible thing is not sensed in this way by external sense, because that founding of harmony or discord is not color or sound or smell or anything that is perceived by external sense, yet the relation itself as contrasted to [counterdistinguished from] the fundament and as understood comparatively to the terminus is not attained in perceptual evaluation without collation [i.e., the sort of comparison that is possible only consequent on the capacity for understanding the related things as existing independently of the interests of the perceiving organism]. And when it is said that relations of the sorts in question are not in any way sensible directly or indirectly, the answer is that directly they are not anything thus sensible nor are they formally sensible, but they are indeed sensible fundamentally, insofar as they are founded in those sensible individuals, as, for example, inimicality-to-a-sheep is founded in the nature and qualities of a wolf." See further note 3 above, and Book II, Question 2, notes 3, 8, and 27.

reality. To cognize in this regard is to cognize not formally that which is constructed in the rationale of a being, but materially that on whose pattern is constructed that which in itself is not. But the extrinsic denomination that follows on the cognition of sense, insofar as an extrinsic denomination is not a mind-dependent relation formally but fundamentally, is then a mind-dependent relation formally when it is cognized on the pattern of a [mind-independent] relation.

Second, it is argued: A simple apprehension of the understanding does not compare or distinguish the rationale of fictive or constructed being from the rationale of true being. If it did, it would not be a simple apprehension, but one comparative or compositive with another. Therefore the understanding, when it simply apprehends, does not form a mind-dependent being formally speaking, as neither do the internal senses.

This is confirmed by the fact that a simple apprehension is not a construct nor a fiction; for a construct may be false, whereas a simple apprehension is always true, precisely because it represents a thing as it is in itself or as it is proposed to the apprehension. Therefore the object of a simple apprehension is not a constructed or fictive being, and consequently is not a mind-dependent being.

The response to this argument[18] is that simple apprehension does not compare one thing to another by affirming or denying, but it does indeed compare by differentiating one thing from another and by attaining the order of one thing to another, just as it knows things that are relative and attains the definition of a thing, the congruity of terms, and the distinction of categories. Whence in discussing the categories, according to the Philosopher, one treats of simple apprehension, as St. Thomas says in his *Commentary* on the first Book of Aristotle's treatise *On Interpretation*, reading 1.[19] Simple apprehension, therefore, has enough comparison for forming a mind-dependent being. Moreover, we do not deny to internal sense the formation of a mind-dependent being on the grounds of the absence of comparison, but on the grounds of the absence of a knowing of universality, because sense does not cognize the more universal rationales by discriminating between true being and constructed or fictive being, which is something that simple apprehension does do; for simple apprehension discriminates between categorial things and those things that are not in a category of mind-independent being.

guitur a realitate. Quod est cognoscere non formaliter id, quod in ratione entis fingitur, sed materialiter id, ad cuius instar fingitur, quod in se non est. Denominatio autem extrinseca, quae sequitur ad cognitionem sensus, in quantum denominatio extrinseca non est formaliter relatio rationis, sed fundamentaliter, tunc autem est formaliter, quando ad instar relationis cognoscitur.

Secundo arguitur: Simplex apprehensio intellectus etiam non comparat neque discernit rationem ficti a ratione entis veri, quia alias non esset simplex apprehensio, sed comparativa seu compositiva cum altero. Ergo non format ens rationis formaliter loquendo, sicut neque sensus interni.

Et confirmatur, quia simplex apprehensio non est fictio; fictio enim falsitati subiecta est, simplex autem apprehensio semper est vera, quia praecise repraesentat rem, ut est in se seu ut proponitur sibi. Ergo eius obiectum non est ens fictum, et consequenter neque ens rationis.

RESPONDETUR,[18] quod *simplex apprehensio* non comparat unum alteri affirmando vel negando, bene tamen discernendo unum ab alio et ordinem unius ad alterum attingendo, sicut cognoscit relativa et attingit definitionem rei et congruitatem terminorum ac praedicamentorum distinctionem. Unde in praedicamentis secundum Philosophum agitur de simplici apprehensione, ut dicit S. Thomas 1. Periherm. lect. 1.[19] Habet ergo sufficientem comparationem ad formandum ens rationis. *Sensui autem interiori* non negamus formationem entis rationis ex defectu comparationis, sed ex defectu universalitatis cognoscendi, quia non cognoscit universaliores rationes discernendo inter ens verum et fictum, quod tamen facit simplex apprehensio; discernit enim praedicamenta ab iis, quae in praedicamento non sunt.

---

[18] 74/10-18.

[19] *Le* I. 7. n. 2. et 8. n. 5.

To the confirmation[20] I answer that a simple apprehension is not a construction (or fiction) in the way of an enunciation by affirming or denying, in which consists the construction (or fiction) that is a deception or falsity; but a simple apprehension can well be a construction (or fiction) in the way of formation, by apprehending something which is not in fact, or by apprehending something impossible after the manner of a being and differentiating that impossible thing from a true and physical being. Whence simple apprehension does not always apprehend a thing as it is in itself, in the sense of never apprehending one thing on the pattern of another, because we apprehend many things not through proper concepts but through connotative ones; but simple apprehension does apprehend a thing as it is in itself in the sense of apprehending it without the addition of a composition, by reason of which it is also said that simple apprehension is not false, because formally it does not judge nor enunciate, in which alone consists formal truth or falsity. But simple apprehension can very well apprehend something that is not on the pattern of that which is, without affirming or denying.

Finally, it is argued: A mind-dependent being can exist even without a comparative act, therefore it can also be formed without a comparative act.

The antecedent is proved: In the first place, when in the very exercise some proposition or syllogism is formed, a second intention results and the proposition itself is denominated being, and yet a relation is not then known comparatively to its term or on the pattern of a mind-independent relation. Likewise, when a mind-dependent being is itself said to be known reflexively, it has existence through this being known, since indeed it objectively terminates the cognition, which is what it is to exist objectively. Nor is there any reason why a mind-independent or physical nature conceived and known in general should be said to exist objectively, but a mind-dependent being known in general should not be said to exist objectively. A mind-dependent being is known in general, however, when it is reflexively rendered known and expressed in act. Finally, the Philosopher, in the fifth book of his *Metaphysics*,[21] and St. Thomas, in his *Commentary* thereon, reading 9,[22] say that blindness and any mind-dependent being whatever is said to be from this, that the proposition is true whereby we say, "Blindness exists." But when this proposition is formed, privation is not considered on the pattern of a being, nor does that comparative act [i.e., the act of cognitively comparing a non-being to a being] occur; there-

Ad confirmationem[20] dicitur, quod simplex apprehensio non est fictio per modum enuntiationis affirmando vel negando, in quo consistit fictio, quae est deceptio seu falsitas; sed bene potest esse fictio per modum formationis, apprehendendo aliquid, quod in re non est, seu rem impossibilem ad modum entis et discernendo ipsum ab ente vero et reali. Unde non semper apprehendit rem, ut est in se, quasi numquam ad instar alterius, cum plura apprehendamus non per proprios conceptus, sed per connotativos; sed apprehendit, ut est in se, id est sine additione compositionis, ratione cuius dicitur etiam, quod simplex apprehensio non est falsa, quia formaliter non iudicat neque enuntiat, in quo solum consistit veritas vel falsitas formalis. Bene tamen potest aliquid, quod non est, apprehendere ad instar eius, quod est, sine hoc, quod affirmet vel neget.

Ultimo arguitur: Nam ens rationis etiam sine actu comparativo potest existere, ergo et formari.

Antecedens probatur: Nam *imprimis* quando in ipso exercitio formatur aliqua propositio vel syllogismus, resultat secunda intentio et ipsa propositio denominatur esse, et tamen tunc non cognoscitur comparative relatio ad suum terminum vel ad instar relationis realis. *Item* quando ipsum ens rationis reflexe dicitur cognitum, per hoc cognosci habet esse, siquidem obiective terminat cognitionem, quod est obiective existere. Nec est aliqua ratio, cur natura realis in communi concepta et cognita dicatur esse obiective, ens autem rationis cognitum in communi non dicatur existere obiective. Cognoscitur autem in communi, quando reflexe et in actu signato redditur cognitum. *Denique* Philosophus in 5. Metaph.[21] et Divus Thomas ibi lect. 9.[22] dicunt, quod caecitas et quodlibet ens rationis dicitur esse ex hoc, quod vera est propositio, qua dicimus: «Caecitas est». Sed quando formatur haec propositio, non consideratur privatio ad instar en-

[20] 74/19-26.
[21] c. 7. (1017 a 31).
[22] *Pa* XX. 402 a.

fore without such an act a mind-dependent being exists formally.

The response to this is: I deny the antecedent. To the first proof[23] it is said that when a proposition is formed, there is not yet the second intention of the proposition formally, but fundamentally proximately; just as when a universal nature is abstracted from singulars, there is not yet an intention of universality, but its fundament. Nevertheless the proposition and syllogism is denominated by the very fact that it is formed in exercise, just as something is denominated a metaphysical universal by the very fact that it is abstracted. For, as we have said above,[24] the denomination of a mind-dependent form can be had even from the proximate fundament itself, before the mind-dependent form is formally cognized and existing.

To the second proof[25] it is said that when a mind-dependent being is cognized reflexively, it exists objectively as denominated extrinsically in cognized being, not as initially formed. But to terminate cognition as if extrinsically and as that upon which cognition falls, is not to be formed in a rationale of being [mind-dependent or mind-independent], but to be supposed as formed, and, thus presupposed, to be denominated by a reflexive cognition, which is as second, not first, in respect of the mind-dependent being. But when mind-dependent being is cognized in general, it is not said to be formed, because it is supposed as formed already; but the very universality or community under which it is cognized is formed. A mind-independent or physical nature, likewise, when it is cognized in general, is not that which is formed, but its universality, which is then first taken on the pattern of relation, when the object is cognized relatively to its instances.

To the final proof[26] the answer is that when that proposition, ''Blindness exists,'' is formed, blindness is considered in the very exercise as existing, and therefore on the pattern of a mind-independent being, and so it is then a mind-dependent being formally, and is then cognized comparatively as much in respect of its predicate as in respect of that on whose pattern it is conceived as existing.[27]

tis nec fit actus comparativus; ergo sine tali actu existit formaliter ens rationis.

RESPONDETUR: Negatur antecedens. Ad primam probationem[23] dicitur, quod quando formatur propositio, non est adhuc formaliter secunda intentio propositionis, sed fundamentaliter proxime; sicut quando abstrahitur natura universalis a singularibus, nondum est intentio universalitatis, sed fundamentum eius. Denominatur tamen propositio et syllogismus hoc ipso, quod formatur in exercitio, sicut denominatur aliquid universale metaphysicum hoc ipso, quod abstrahitur. Nam, ut supra[24] diximus, denominatio formae rationis etiam ex ipso fundamento proximo potest haberi, antequam formaliter cognoscatur et existat forma rationis.

Ad secundam probationem[25] dicitur, quod ens rationis quando cognoscitur reflexe, existit obiective, ut denominatum extrinsece in esse cogniti, non ut primo formatum. Terminare autem cognitionem quasi extrinsece et tamquam id, super quod cadit cognitio, non est formari in ratione entis, sed formatum supponi, et sic praesuppositum denominari a cognitione reflexa, quae est quasi secunda, non prima respectu entis rationis. Quando autem cognoscitur ens rationis in communi, non dicitur formari, quia iam formatum supponitur; sed formatur ipsa universalitas seu communitas, sub qua cognoscitur. Natura autem realis quando cognoscitur in universali, non ipsa est, quae formatur, sed universalitas eius, quae tunc primo ad instar relationis accipitur, cum obiectum relative cognoscitur ad inferiora.

Ad ultimam probationem[26] dicitur, quod quando formatur illa propositio: «Caecitas est», in ipso exercitio consideratur caecitas ut existens, atque adeo ad instar entis realis, et sic formaliter tunc est ens rationis, et tunc cognoscitur comparative tam respectu sui praedicati quam respectu eius, ad cuius instar concipitur ut existens.[27]

---

[23] 75/25-30.

[24] 70/24-71/19, and Article 1, esp. 54/31-55/2.

[25] 75/30-39.

[26] 75/40-76/2.

[27] The 1663 Lyons text adds: ''*et per hoc constituitur ens rationis*''—''and it is through this that it is constituted a mind-dependent being.''

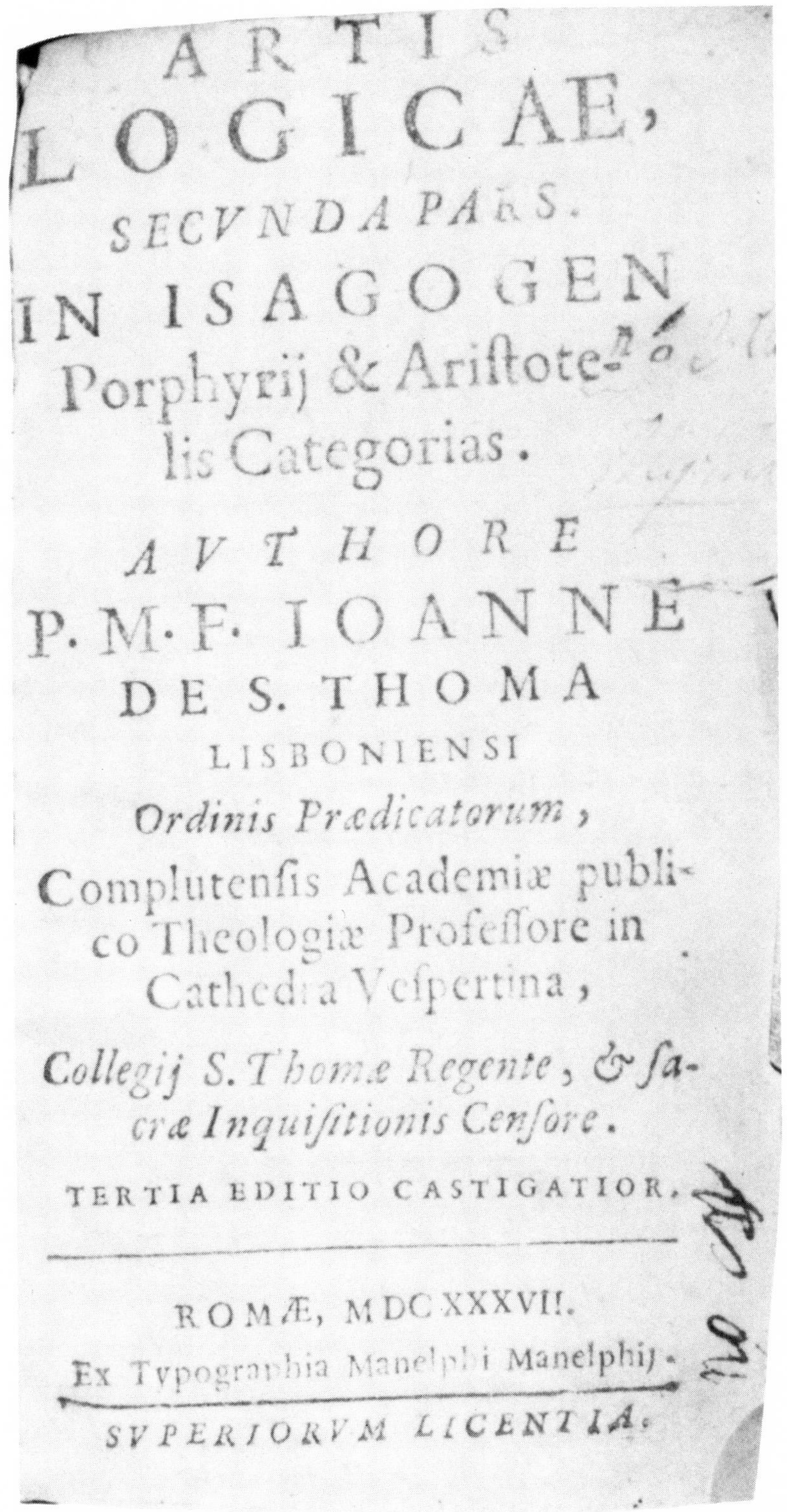

ARTIS
LOGICAE,
SECVNDA PARS.
IN ISAGOGEN
Porphyrij & Ariſtote-
lis Categorias.
AVTHORE
P. M. F. IOANNE
DE S. THOMA
LISBONIENSI
Ordinis Prædicatorum,
Complutenſis Academiæ publi-
co Theologiæ Profeſſore in
Cathedra Veſpertina,
*Collegij S. Thomæ Regente, & ſa-
cræ Inquiſitionis Cenſore.*
TERTIA EDITIO CASTIGATIOR.

ROMÆ, MDCXXXVII.
Ex Typographia Manelphi Manelphij.

SVPERIORVM LICENTIA.

Title page from the 1637 Rome edition of the Second Part of the *Ars Logica*. This is actually the fourth edition containing the *Prima Pars* of the *Ars Logica* (see p. 113 below), but only the second edition of the *Secunda Pars* as such. The volume was issued as part of the first general edition of Poinsot's completed *Cursus Philosophicus*, and it is from the general title given to the volumes of the Natural Philosophy in this edition that the *Cursus Philosophicus* gets it most proper name. Discussion in note 5, p. 396 below. Photograph courtesy of Norma Elia Cantú.

Praeambulum Secundum:

DE RELATIONE*

Second Preamble:

ON RELATION*

* In the original Latin: "*Quaestio XVII. De Praedicamento Relationis.*" Logica 2. p.: "Question 17. On the Category of Relation."

Article 1

Whether There Exist on the Side of Mind-Independent Being Intrinsic Forms Which Are Relations

Articulus Primus

Utrum a Parte Rei Dentur Relationes, Quae Sint Formae Intrinsecae

When speaking of relation in its entire latitude, as it comprehends transcendental and categorial, according to the way being must be expressed in discourse and according to the way relation has being, I find no one who completely denies all relation. For even the ancient philosophers did not deny relations according to the way being must be expressed in discourse, as is clear from the text of the chapter on ''Relation'' in Aristotle's *Categories*, although in the same chapter Aristotle established against those ancients the categorial relation, which differs entirely from an absolute being.[1]

Speaking therefore of relations in *this* sense, which applies to relations only according to the way they have being as distinguished from every subjective or ''absolute'' entity, some have thought that relations are nothing but either extrinsic denominations or something mind-dependent; which view is customarily attributed to the Nominalists and to those who do not distinguish mind-independent relations from a fundament. But these last speak in a far different sense, as we will see below when we treat the difficulty. Finally, some think that relations do not belong to things except according to objective being, and are only intentional affections or conditions by which we compare one thing to another. Whence they constitute relations [i.e., make them consist] not in a respect, but in

Loquendo de relatione in tota sua latitudine, ut comprehendit transcendentalem et praedicamentalem, secundum dici et secundum esse, non invenio, qui absolute negaverit omnem relationem. Nam etiam antiqui philosophi non negabant relationes secundum dici, ut ex textu cap. ,,Ad aliquid'' constat, licet praedicamentalem relationem, quae omnino ab absoluto ente differat Aristoteles contra illos ibidem statuerit.[1]

Loquendo ergo de relationibus in hac sententia prout distinguuntur ab omni entitate absoluta quod solum convenit relationibus secundum esse, aliqui existimaverunt nihil aliud esse quam vel denominationes extrinsecas vel aliquid rationis; quod Nominalibus attribui solet et illis, qui relationes reales a fundamento non distinguunt. Sed isti ultimi in sensu longe diverso loquuntur, ut infra videbimus tractando difficultatem. Denique alii existimant relationes non convenire rebus nisi secundum esse obiectivum et solum esse intentionales affectiones, quibus rem unam alteri comparamus. Unde non in respectu, sed in comparatione relationes con-

[1] Categ. c. 7. (6 a 36 - 8 b 24).

a comparison; in the order of physical being, in contrast to objective being, however, all relations are according to the way being must be expressed in discourse, because a related thing is nothing but an independent or absolute thing known through a comparison to another. And they want this to be the opinion of Aristotle in the chapter on "Relation" in the *Categories*, and in Book V of the *Metaphysics*, chap. 15.[2] And others cite St. Thomas's *Summa theologica*, I-II, q. 7, art. 2, reply to obj. 1, where he teaches that something is denominated relative not only from that which is in it, but also from that which touches it from the outside.

However, that we may start our own consideration from this last point, in no way can this opinion be ascribed to the Philosopher, because in the chapter on "Relation" he manifestly rejects the definition of the ancients, who defined relatives only according to the way being must be expressed in discourse, by the fact that it followed from their definition that even substance, along with any being whatever that is expressed with a dependence on and a comparison to another, is something relative. But Aristotle in defining relatives says that "they are those things whose entire being consists in bearing toward another." But in the opinion of those who posit relations only according to the way being must be expressed in discourse, the whole being of relatives does not bear toward another, since indeed the being which they have independently of mind is absolute, but they have a respect only because they are cognized comparatively to another. Therefore Aristotle's definition of relations as things whose whole being exists toward another does not apply to such relatives. Whence in vain would Aristotle have emended the definition of the ancients, had he posited relations only according to the way being must be expressed in discourse; for the ancients did not deny them, nor that they are cognized comparatively to another. And therefore Cajetan well noted in his *Commentary* on this chapter, "Relation," that in this definition, the Philosopher has defined relation according to the nature which it has, not according to that which is cognized or expressed, and therefore he said "are a relation to something" but not "are expressed in relation to something"; but in the definition of the ancients it was said "are expressed in relation to something." Therefore the Philosopher posited mind-independent relations distinct from relations according to the way being must be expressed in discourse.

There can be no doubt what THE OPINION OF ST. THOMAS is, for he expressly argues against those who said that relation is not a thing of nature, but something of the mind. See the *Summa theologica* I, q. 13, art. 7; q. 28,

stituunt; in re autem omnes relationes esse secundum dici, quia nihil aliud est relatum quam res absoluta cognita per comparationem ad aliud. Et volunt hanc esse Aristotelis sententiam in isto cap. Ad aliquid et 5. Metaph. cap. 15.[2] Et alii citant D. Thomam 1. 2. q. 7. art. 2. ad 1., ubi docet relatum denominari aliquid non solum ab eo, quod inest, sed etiam ab eo, quod extrinsecus adiacet.

Ceterum, ut ab hoc ultimo incipiamus, nullatenus potest haec sententia Philosopho adscribi, cum manifeste in cap. Ad aliquid reiciat definitionem antiquorum, qui solum definierunt relativa secundum dici, eo quod ex eorum definitione sequebatur etiam substantiam esse relatam et quodcumque ens, quod cum dependentia et comparatione ad alterum dicitur. Aristoteles vero definiens relata dicit, «quod sunt illa, quorum totum suum esse se habet ad aliud». Sed in sententia eorum, qui solum ponunt relationes secundum dici, non totum esse relatorum se habet ad aliud, siquidem esse, quod habent in re, est absolutum, solum vero habent respectum, quia cognoscuntur comparative ad aliud. Ergo talibus relatis non convenit definitio Aristotelis, quorum totum esse se habet ad aliud. Unde frustra Aristoteles emendaret definitionem antiquorum, si solum poneret relationes secundum dici; eas enim non negabant antiqui, neque quod comparative ad aliud cognoscerentur. Et ideo bene notavit Caietanus in Comment. huius cap. Ad aliquid, quod in hac definitione Philosophus definivit relationem secundum naturam, quam habet, non secundum quod cognoscitur vel dicitur, et ideo dixit ,,ad aliquid sunt" non vero ,,ad aliquid dicuntur"; in definitione vero antiquorum dicebatur ,, ad aliquid dicuntur". Ergo Philosophus relationes reales posuit distinctas a relationibus secundum dici.

De mente S. Thomae nullatenus dubitari potest, cum ex professo impugnet eos, qui dicebant relationem non esse rem naturae, sed aliquid rationis. Videatur 1. p. q. 13. art. 7. et q. 28. art. 2. et q. 39. art.

[2] 1020 b 26.

art. 2; and q. 39, art. 1. See also the *Summa contra gentiles,* Book II, chap. 12; the *Disputed Questions on the Power of God,* q. 7, arts. 8 and 9,[3] and q. 8, art. 2.[4] And in a thousand other passages, but particularly in these, St. Thomas clearly affirms that **relation is something mind-independent and an inhering accident**.

THE FOUNDATION OF THIS VIEW is the fact that relations according to the way being must be expressed in discourse have an absolute being and are not totally toward another; mind-dependent relations do not exist except in an apprehension of the understanding, from which they have an objective act of being; but apart from any consideration of the mind, some things are encountered in reality which have no being other than a being toward another. Therefore physical relations are encountered, which are not according to the way being must be expressed in discourse, and so can constitute a category apart from [the categories of] "absolute" mind-independent beings.

The antecedent[5] is proved, because, apart from the mind's consideration, there are encountered in reality some things to which can be assigned no relatively independent or absolute being. For order is encountered—for example, an army on parade, the ordered physical universe; similitude, dependence, parenthood, and other like things are encountered, which cannot be explained by any absolute being, and the whole content or being in these things possesses itself relative to another. The sign of this is the fact that when the terminus becomes nonexistent, the similitude or parenthood disappears. But if the being of those things were something absolute, it would not disappear solely in consequence of the disappearance of the term. But to deny that these things are given in the order of mind-independent being when no finite intelligence is forming and constructing them, is to deny that which even the most unlearned of men recognize in nature.

This reason is often used by St. Thomas, and he indicates another in the first Book of the *Commentary on the Sentences Written for Annibald,* dist. 26, q. 2, art. 1,[6] culled from the believed fact of there being divine relations, which, insofar as they are mutually distinguished, are given independently of the finite mind, for otherwise the relative persons would not be distinguished independently of the finite mind, which would be a heretical assertion. But the divine relations are not distinguished except as pure relations are according to the way they have their being. For if they were distinguished other than in a pure relation, there would be

1., et 2. Contra Gent. cap. 12. et q. 7. de Potentia art. 8. et 9.[3] et q. 8. de Potentia art. 2.[4] Et mille aliis locis, sed praecipue in istis clare **affirmat relationem esse aliquid reale et accidens inhaerens.**

FUNDAMENTUM EST, quia relationes secundum dici habent esse absolutum et non totum sunt ad aliud; relationes rationis non sunt nisi in intellectu apprehendente, a quo habent esse obiectivum; sed in re nullo intellectu considerante inveniuntur aliqua non habentia aliud esse quam ad aliud. Ergo inveniuntur relationes reales, quae non sunt secundum dici et sic praedicamentum seorsum a rebus absolutis possunt constituere.

Antecedens[5] probatur, quia nullo intellectu considerante inveniuntur in re aliqua, quibus nullum esse absolutum assignari potest. Invenitur enim ordo, ut exercitus ordinatus, universum ordinatum; invenitur similitudo, dependentia, paternitas et alia similia, quae nullo esse absoluto explicari possunt, et totum esse in eis se habet ad alterum. Cuius signum est, quia non existente termino deficit similitudo aut paternitas. Si autem esse illorum esset quid absolutum, non deficeret ex solo defectu termini. Negare vero, quod ista in re dentur nullo intellectu formante et fingente illa, est negare id, quod vel rusticissimi homines in re dari cognoscunt.

Hac ratione utitur saepe D. Thomas aliamque indicat in 1. ad Annibaldum dist. 26. q. 2. art. 1.[6] petitam ex relationibus divinis, quae in quantum distinguuntur inter se realiter, a parte rei dantur, alioquin non distinguerentur realiter personae relativae, quod esset haereticum. Non distinguuntur autem, nisi ut purae relationes sunt secundum esse. Si enim in alio quam in pura relatione distinguerentur, non solum relativa, sed etiam absoluta dividerentur in Deo. Ergo dantur

---

[3] *Pa* VIII. 161-164.
[4] *Pa* VIII. 170-172.
[5] 82/12-14.
[6] *Pa* XXII. 76 a.

not only relative things divided in God, but absolute ones also [which is impossible]. Therefore there exist in God relations independent of all finite minds, although on account of the supreme divine simplicity they are identified with substance. Why therefore should there be any reluctance to acknowledge a mind-independent existence of relations among created things, relations which are neither substance nor infinite?

Finally, how does the understanding form pure respects, if it has only absolute things or relations according to the way being must be expressed in discourse, as the pattern on which to form them? Relations formed by the understanding therefore will be mere figments, because they do not have in the order of being independent of cognition pure and true relations on whose pattern they are formed.[7]

Nor can it be said that these relations are indeed given independently of cognized being, but as *extrinsic denominations*, not as intrinsic forms. For against this is the fact that every extrinsic denomination takes its origin from some real (i.e., independent of being itself apprehended) form existing in another subject, just as being seen or known originates from a cognition existing in an apprehending subject. Therefore if relation is an extrinsic denomination, it takes its origin from some form existing in another subject. Therefore that form in itself is either a relation or an absolute entity. If it is a relation, there is already given an intrinsic relative form, and so, just as it is given in that subject, it could likewise be given in another. But if it is an absolute form, yet extrinsically informing, how can a relative denomination arise from that form? For a relative formal effect does not emanate from an absolute form, neither intrinsically nor extrinsically; just as being seen is not the denomination of a relation in the wall, but of termination. Although it is conceived by us in the mode of a relation, in fact it is not a relation.

Finally, those holding this opinion will find it most difficult to explain how there are three relative persons in the divine processions constituted and distinct independently of every finite mind, if relations are extrinsic denominations. They will likewise find it very difficult to explain from which absolute form such denominations derive. But if in God relations are not extrinsic denominations, but intrinsic forms, although substantial and identified with the divine substance, why would we say that such an order of relative being, although not identified with substance, is impossible in creatures? Created things have rather more the fundament of such a relation, because they are more dependent and ordered or subordinated to another.

in Deo reales relationes, licet propter summam simplicitatem divinam identificatae cum substantia. Cur ergo in creatis repugnabit dari tales relationes, quae nec substantia sint nec infinitae?

Denique quomodo intellectus puros respectus format, si non habet nisi res absolutas seu relationes secundum dici, ad quarum instar eas formet? Erunt ergo mera figmenta relationes ab intellectu formatae, cum non habeant in re puras et veras relationes, ad quarum instar formentur.[7]

Nec dici potest dari quidem in re istas relationes, sed per modum *denominationis extrinsecae*, non intrinsecae formae. Sed contra est, quia omnis extrinseca denominatio provenit ex forma aliqua reali existente in alio subiecto, sicut esse visum aut cognitum ex cognitione existente in cognoscente. Ergo si relatio est denominatio extrinseca, provenit ex aliqua forma existente in alio subiecto. Ergo vel illa forma in se est relatio vel absoluta entitas. Si est relatio, iam datur forma relativa intrinseca, et sic sicut datur in illo subiecto, ita poterit dari in alio. Si autem est forma absoluta, extrinsece tamen informans, quomodo potest ab illa provenire denominatio relativa? A forma enim absoluta non emanat effectus formalis relativus, neque intrinsece nec extrinsece; sicut esse visum in pariete non est denominatio relationis, sed terminationis, quamvis a nobis per modum relationis concipiatur, sed in re relatio non est.

Denique durissime explicabit haec sententia, quomodo sunt tres personae relativae in divinis realiter constitutae et distinctae, si sunt denominationes extrinsecae, et a qua forma absoluta tales denominationes proveniunt. Si autem in Deo extrinsecae denominationes non sunt, sed formae intrinsecae, licet substantiales et identificatae cum divina substantia, cur dicemus repugnare in creaturis tale genus entis relativi, licet non identificatum cum substantia, cum potius res creatae magis habeant fundamentum talis relationis, quia magis sunt dependentes et ordinatae vel subordinatae ad aliud.

[7] Cf. First Preamble, Article 1, 57/26-29 and below, Article 2, 96/3-8.

Resolution of Counter-Arguments

You object first: A relation posits nothing mind-independent in a subject beyond the extrinsic denomination of coexisting extremes. For it is not apparent how this mode, which is called relation, contradistinguished from the remaining absolute forms, comes to a thing without an intrinsic change of that thing, if the relation is its intrinsic mode, nor does it appear how a relation would be caused anew from the sole positing of a term at whatever distance; as, for example, if something white is produced in the Indies when I am existing in Spain, that relation [of similarity] results from such a distant term, nor is it produced now by the agent which had produced the whiteness here in Spain, because such an agent has often already ceased to be at the time when the relation results, therefore it cannot then act.

Second, because it seems to increase to infinity the multitude of relations in the same subject to all the things which are similar, equal, agents, patients, etc., in respect of that subject. And especially because one relation can also found other relations, since two relations are not less similar than are two absolute things, and so the number of relations will increase to infinity.

Finally, because there seems to be no necessity for multiplying these relative entities by distinguishing them from absolute ones. For by the very fact that two white things are posited, they will be similar without another entity or mode; and by the very fact that someone generates, he will be a father without another additional entity. Since therefore there is no experiential evidence for these relations, and since the other argument for their existence is satisfied merely by the positing of two extremes, it is not proved on any solid grounds that these relations are intrinsic forms. Whence St. Thomas says, in the *Summa of the Whole Logic of Aristotle*, chap. 3,[8] that a relation does not differ from a fundament except by reason of an extrinsic term. And in the passage cited above from the *Summa theologica*, I-II, q. 7, art. 2, reply to obj. 1, he teaches that a thing is denominated relative not only from that which is in it, but also from that which comes to it from without.

To the first objection,[9] I answer that a relation accrues to a subject without any change that is directly and immediately terminated at the relation, but not without a change that is teminated mediately

Solvuntur argumenta.

Obicies primo: Relatio nihil reale ponit in subiecto praeter extrinsecam denominationem extremorum coexistentium. Nam iste modus, qui dicitur relatio, condistinctus a reliquis formis absolutis non apparet, quomodo adveniat rei sine intrinseca eius mutatione, si intrinsecus eius modus est, nec quomodo de novo causetur ex sola positione termini in quacumque distantia; ut si aliquod album producitur in India me existente in Hispania, resultat illa relatio ab illo termino ita distanti, neque producitur nunc ab agente, qui produxit albedinem hic, quia tale agens saepe iam desiit, quando relatio resultat, ergo tunc non potest agere.

Secundo, quia videtur in infinitum crescere multitudo relationum in eodem subiecto ad omnia, quae sunt sibi similia, aequalia, agentia, patientia etc. Et praesertim, quia etiam una relatio potest alias fundare, cum non minus sint similes duae relationes quam duo absoluta, et sic in infinitum crescet numerus relationum.

Denique, quia nulla videtur necessitas multiplicandi istas entitates relativas, distinguendo illas ab absolutis. Nam hoc ipso, quod ponantur duo alba, sine alia entitate vel modo erunt similia, et hoc ipso, quod quis genuit, sine alia additione entitatis erit pater. Cum ergo nulla detur experientia istarum relationum, et alius discursus, quo probantur dari, sufficienter salvatur sola positione duorum extremorum, non videtur solido fundamento probari, quod istae relationes sint formae intrinsecae. Unde D. Thomas opusc. 48. tract. de Ad aliquid cap. 3.[8] dicit relationem non differre a fundamento nisi ratione termini extrinseci. Et loco supra cit. ex 1. 2. q. 7. art. 2. ad 1. docet relatum denominari non solum ab eo, quod inest, sed etiam ab eo, quod extrinsecus adiacet.

Ad primum[9] **respondetur**, quod relatio advenit subiecto sine aliqua mutatione, quae directe et immediate terminetur ad relationem, non tamen sine mutatione, quae

[8] Summa tot. Log. Arist. (*Pa* XVII. 74 a).
[9] 84/2-17.

and indirectly at that relation. Just as risibility results from the same action by which a man is produced, so from the production of a white thing is produced similitude to another existing white thing. But if another white thing did not exist, by virtue of the generation of the first white thing, that similitude and any other relation that would result from the positing of its terminus would remain in a virtual state. Whence distance neither conduces to nor obstructs the resultance of a pure relation, because these relations do not depend upon a local situation; for far or near, a son is in the same way the son of his father. Nor is the relation in the other extreme produced by the terminus itself through some emission of power when it is brought into existence. Rather is the existence of the terminus the condition for a relation's resulting from an already existing fundament by virtue of the original generation whereby that fundament was brought into being as inclining toward any terminus of such a fundament. Whence even though the generating has now ceased, it yet remains in its effect or power, inasmuch as it leaves a fundament sufficient for a relation to result, just as there remains from the efficient cause of something heavy a capacity in the physical object to be moved downward when an obstacle is removed.

And when one insists that Aristotle often teaches that a relation is not the terminus of a change, I answer that it is not the terminus of a physical change essentially and directly; yet the Philosopher does not deny that it is the terminus of a change incidentally (by reason of a concomitant attribute, that is, through another—namely, its fundament) and secondarily. Whence St. Thomas, in his *Commentary* on Book V of the *Physics*, reading 3,[10] expressly teaches that a physical change takes place in mind-independent relations, namely, some new determination according to which what was in the fundament is drawn into act. And in his *Commentary* on the *Metaphysics*, Book XI, reading 12,[11] he says that "in being toward something there is no movement except incidentally."

To the second objection,[12] I answer that it is not incongruous for these relations to be multiplied as often as fundaments and termini are multiplied, although the position St. Thomas takes greatly moderates the number of relations, for he states in the *Summa theologica*, III, q. 35, art. 5, that the numerically same relation can be referred to numerically diverse terms. But

mediate et indirecte terminetur ad illam. Sicut eadem actione, qua producitur homo, dimanat risibilitas, sic ad productionem albi producitur similitudo ad aliud album, quod existit. Si autem non existit, manet ex vi generationis albi quasi in virtute illa similitudo et quaecumque alia relatio, ut resultet posito suo termino. Unde ad hoc nihil conducit vel obstat distantia, quia relationes istae non dependent a locali situatione; eodem enim modo est filius sui patris filius distans et indistans. Neque enim ab ipso termino, quando ponitur per aliquam emissionem virtutis, producitur relatio in alio extremo, sed positio termini est conditio, ut ex fundamento antea posito resultet relatio ex vi primae generationis, qua positum est in rerum natura ut petens respicere quemcumque terminum talis fundamenti. Unde licet generans iam desierit, remanet tamen in sua virtute, quatenus relinquit sufficiens fundamentum, ut resultet relatio, sicut remanet virtute in gravi, ut moveatur deorsum a generante remoto obstaculo.

Et quando fit *instantia*, quod Aristoteles saepe docet relationem non esse terminum mutationis, *respondetur* non esse terminum mutationis physicae per se et directe; non tamen negat Philosophus esse terminum mutationis per accidens, id est per aliud et secundario. Unde D. Thomas in 5. Phys. lect. 3.[10] expresse docet mutationem realem fieri in relationibus realibus, scilicet aliquam novam determinationem, secundum quam explicatur in actu, quod erat in fundamento. Et 11. Metaph. lect. 12.[11] dicit, «quod in ad aliquid non est motus nisi per accidens».

Ad secundum[12] respondetur nullum esse inconveniens, quod multiplicentur istae relationes, quoties multiplicantur fundamenta et termini. Praesertim vero in sententia D. Thomae multo minor est numerus relationum, quia ponit unam relationem numero posse ad diversos terminos numero referri 3. p. q. 35. art. 5. Unam vero

[10] *Le* II. 237. n. 7.
[11] *Pa* XX. 617 b.
[12] 84/18-25.

he categorically denies that one relation is founded on another relation, as we will show below at length.[13] See the *Disputed Questions on the Power of God*, q. 7, art. 9, reply to obj. 2,[14] and the *Summa theologica*, I, q. 42, art. 1, reply to obj. 4.

To the third objection:[15] there is as much need to posit this category of relation as an ontological rationale as there is to posit a category of quantity or quality. We know there are forms of quantity and quality from seeing their effects. In the same way, from seeing in the world of nature the effect of some things ordered and having a condition relative to other things, such as similitude, paternity, order, etc.; and from seeing that in these things this effect of respecting is without admixture of any absolute rationale, that their whole being consists in a respect; it is from seeing this, I say, that we best gather that there is this pure sort of relative being, just as we gather from absolute effects that there are absolute entities. Nor is greater experience needed for this than in the case of other accidental forms where we experience the effects, to be sure, but not their distinction from substance.[16] But were God to let two white things exist without the resultance of a relation, they would remain similar fundamentally, not formally.

relationem fundari in alia omnino negat D. Thomas, quod infra latius ostendemus.[13] Et videri potest q. 7. de Potentia art. 9. ad 2.[14] et 1. p. q. 42. art. 1. ad 4.

Ad tertium[15] dicitur, quod non est minor necessitas ponendi hoc genus entitatis relativae quam genus quantitatis vel qualitatis. Quia enim videmus effectus quantitatis et qualitatis, inde tales formas dari colligimus. Sic etiam quia videmus dari hunc effectum in rerum natura, scilicet ordinari aliqua et habitudinem habere ad alia, sicut similitudo, paternitas, ordo etc., et in istis non est iste effectus respiciendi mixtus cum ratione absoluta, sed totum esse eorum consistit in respectu, inde optime colligimus dari hoc genus entitatis relativae, sicut ex effectibus absolutis entitates absolutas. Nec est necessaria ad hoc maior experientia quam in aliis formis accidentalibus, in quibus experimur quidem effectus, sed non earum distinctionem a substantia.[16] Quodsi Deus relinqueret duo alba sine resultantia relationis, manerent similia fundamentaliter, non formaliter.

---

[13] In Article 3 of this Preamble, 102/36-105/13, esp. 104/42-105/6. Further in Logica 2. p. q. 17. art. 5. 600a19-25, and Appendix C of the present work esp. 380/10ff., notably 386/20-21 and 387/17ff.

[14] *Pa* VIII. 163 b.

[15] 84/26-44.

[16] The reader should advert here to the *entirely experiential claim* Poinsot is making for his affirmation of relation as among the furnishings of the physical world. Note too that he is saying that the modes of being classified as ''accidents'' in the Aristotelian scheme of ''categories'' (see below, Book I, Question 1, note 10) are not what sense attains, as opposed to ''substance,'' but are *analyzed out of* what sense directly attains: ''*cognitio externa propter sui imperfectionem et materialitatem non potest seipsam attingere neque accidentia, quae in se sunt, sed obiecta corporeo modo sibi applicata*'' (Phil. nat. 4. p. q. 6. art. 4., Reiser ed. III. 195b21-25).—''External sense cognition, on account of its imperfection and materiality, can attain neither itself nor [even] the accidents that are independent of sensation, but only objects as here and now physically acting upon the sense.'' There are thus for Poinsot two levels at work in Aristotle's categorial scheme: the effects of the diverse ''accidental'' characteristics of bodies which are directly given in experience without any distinction from the individuals (''substances'') possessing those characteristics, and in which direct experience is given the contrast between two different sorts of relativity; and a *second level* on which we distinguish by a further analysis between the characteristics directly given in experience and the individuals as such *possessing* those characteristics. It is only on this second level of analysis, once removed from the directly givens of experience, that we can speak of a contrast between ''substance'' and ''accidents.'' See further (*inter alia*) ibid.: 116a26-117b20, esp. 117a24-27.

The importance of this for the doctrine of signs is considerable, for it means that semiotic analysis begins at a point *prior* to the classical ontology of ''substance'' and ''accident'' (cf. Poinsot, Phil. nat. 1. p. q. 1. art. 3., Reiser ed. II. 20a1-33b8; discussion in Powell 1983: 28-29), with the immediately experienced contrast of subjective and intersubjective elements of experience, wherein ''substance'' is only implied. We do not experience the distinction of substance from accidents, whence substance is not known by experience as a distinct reality; but we *do* directly experience relations *secundum dici* and *secundum esse*, whence substance and the scheme of ac-

As regards the interpretation of the texts cited from St. Thomas: to the first one[17] from the *Summa of the Whole Logic of Aristotle,*[18] the response is that the sense of the passage is that a relation differs from its fundament by reason of an extrinsic terminus—that is, it takes distinction from the terminus; but the passage does not deny that the relation in itself is an intrinsic form, a fact that St. Thomas affirms many times. And that it is specifically an inhering accident, he teaches in q. 7 of the *Disputed Questions on the Power of God*, art. 9, reply to obj. 7.[19] But in the second passage from the *Summa theologica*, I-II,[20] St. Thomas teaches only that relation takes denomination not only from that which is intrinsic, that is to say, insofar as it is inhering, but from that which concerns it from without, that is, from the terminus or from the order to that terminus, which does not remove, but supposes, that the relation is inhering, which is St. Thomas's own exposition in the passage cited from the *Disputed Questions on the Power of God*, and in the *Summa theologica*, I, q. 28, art. 2.[21]

Ad loca D. Thomae: Ad primum[17] ex opusc. 48.[18] respondetur sensum esse, quod relatio differt ratione termini extrinseci, id est sumit distinctionem a termino; non vero negat, quod in se sit forma intrinseca, quod toties affirmat D. Thomas. Et specialiter quod sit accidens inhaerens, docet q. 7. de Potentia art. 9. ad 7.[19] In secundo autem loco ex 1. 2.[20] solum docet D. Thomas, quod relatio denominationem sumit non solum ex eo, quod inest, id est in quantum inhaerens, sed eo, quod extrinsecus adiacet, id est ex termino seu ex ordine ad illum, quod non tollit, sed supponit, quod sit inhaerens, quae est expositio ipsius in cit. loco de Potentia et 1. p. q. 28. art. 2.[21]

---

cidents are alike derived by further analysis. Hence the two "categories" fundamental to the doctrine of signs—the starting point of the *Treatise* (Book I, Question 1, 117/18-23)—include all reality that can be directly experienced in what *will be* called 'accidents' once substance has been rationally, i.e., analytically, *further* distinguished among the *secundum dici* relatives. What is decisive here is that this way of conceptualizing the matter affords in effect and in principle an alternative categorial scheme to Aristotle's own, equally comprehensive of all reality, but more fundamental, being—unlike Aristotle's scheme, wherein the most basic reality, substance, is not directly experienced or experienceable as such, but only as characterized thus and so (i.e., in its accidents)—entirely reducible to what can be directly experienced, namely, the contrast between what is and what is not *purely* relative, the relative *secundum esse* (order among elements or units making up a system) and the relative *secundum dici* (the elements or units ordered).

Concerned as he was to fit an understanding of signs into the then traditional ontological system of philosophy, Poinsot will continue to use throughout—particularly, for example, in the closing discussions of Book III, Question 2, 313/1-323/35—the traditional terminology of the substance-accident scheme; but the reader who failed to see that the fundamental thrust of the semiotic he essays is independent of, because ultimately foundational to, *any* such scheme (see my " 'Semiotic' as the Doctrine of Signs," *Ars Semeiotica* 1/3 [1977], 41-68), and who failed to adjust the understanding of the apparently "traditional" terminology accordingly, would be bound to misunderstand entirely the *doctrina* Poinsot is essaying. The novelty of these two "categories" as Poinsot construes them is the key to the system. Further discussion in Deely 1982: n. 9, pp. 168-179.

[17] 84/37-40.

[18] Summa tot. Log. Arist. (*Pa* XVII. 74 a).

[19] *Pa* VIII. 164 a.

[20] 84/40-44.

[21] This discussion is expanded in detail in Appendix C, pp. 377-389 below. Note particularly the distinction Poinsot implies between an "intrinsic" form which is *inherent* (i.e., "accidental" or *subjective* in character) and an intrinsic form which is yet *not as such* in what is proper to it—as distinct from what is casual of it—an *inhering* form, namely, categorial relation (i.e., *intersubjective* being), and therefore also any objective connections as such (i.e., ontological relations, even when dependent upon being cognized. See Book II, Question 5, 272/25-45, *inter alia*.

[577b6-44]

Article 2

What is Required for a Categorial Relation

Articulus Secundum

Quid Requiratur, ut Aliqua Relatio Sit Praedicamentalis

To see why relation must be included in a categorial scheme of the modes or ways in which mind-independent subjects differ in being, one must see how relation in nature differs both from mind-dependent objective relation and from transcendental relation, which also is customarily called relation according to the way being must be expressed in discourse.

The better to perceive this difference, let us start from the common teaching that in this category of being which is called relation, three factors must concur, namely, a subject, a fundament, and a terminus. The subject, which is a factor common to every accident, is that which is formed and denominated by the relation. The fundament is required as the rationale and cause whence these relations obtain an entitative being and existence. The terminus is required as that toward which this respect tends and at which it rests. And though a cause is required for every entity and form, yet in a special sense a fundament is said to be required for a relation, because other forms require a cause only in order to be produced in being and exist, whereas relation—owing to its minimal entitative character and because in terms of its proper concept it is toward another—requires a fundament not only in order to exist but also in order to be able to remain in existence, that is, in order to be a mind-independent rationale of physical being. And thus St. Thomas said, in Book I of the *Commentary on the Sentences Written for Annibald*, dist. 30, q. 1,

Ad cognoscendam relationem praedicamentalem oportet discernere illam et a relatione rationis et a relatione transcendentali, quae etiam appellari solet relatio secundum dici.

Ut autem hoc possit melius percipi, SUPPONENDA est communis doctrina, quod in hoc genere entis, quod vocatur relatio, tria debent concurrere, scilicet subiectum, fundamentum et terminus. Subiectum, quod est commune omni accidenti, est illud, quod formatur et denominatur a relatione. Fundamentum requiritur tamquam ratio et causa, unde relationes istae sortiuntur entitatem et esse. Terminus tamquam id, ad quod tendit et in quo sistit iste respectus. Et licet ad omnem entitatem et formam requiratur causa, specialiter tamen ad relationem dicitur requiri fundamentum, quia aliae formae solum requirunt causam, ut producantur in esse et existant, relatio autem propter suam minimam entitatem et quia ex proprio conceptu est ad aliud, requirit fundamentum non solum ut existat, sed etiam ut sit capax existendi, id est ut sit entitas realis. Et ita dixit D. Thomas in 1. ad Annibaldum dist. 30. quaest. unica

art. 1,[1] that "relation is nothing other than the bearing of one thing toward another; whence according to its proper rationale it need not be anything in that of which it is predicated, although it sometimes is this owing to the cause of the relative condition." And practically the same notion is expressed in Book I, dist. 26, q. 2, art. 1 of St. Thomas's *Commentary on the Sentences of Peter Lombard*,[2] and in the *Summa theologica*, I, q. 28, art. 1, where he says that "those things which are said to be toward something signify according to their proper rationale only a respect toward another. This respect sometimes indeed is in the nature of things, as when some things are ordered among themselves according to their nature." And the reason for this is that relation, on account of its minimal entitative character, does not depend on a subject in precisely the same way as the other absolute forms, but stands rather as a third kind of being consisting in and resulting from the coordination [in time] of two extremes; and therefore, in order to exist in the nature of things, a relation *continuously* depends on the fundament coordinating it with a term, and not *only* on a subject and productive cause.

From these familiar distinctions it will not be difficult to point out the difference between relations according to the way being must be expressed in discourse and relations according to the way some things have being, mind-independent and mind-dependent. For things which are relative according to the way they have being, and things which are relative according to the way their being requires expression, are distinguished in the very way that relativity is exercised, because, in the case of things relative according to the way they have being, the whole rationale or exercise is to respect, and for that reason they are said to respect a terminus in the rationale of a pure terminus. But the exercise or rationale of a relation according to the way something must be expressed in discourse is not purely to respect a terminus, but to exercise something else whence a relation could follow; and for this reason St. Thomas put it well in Book 2, dist. 1, q. 1, art. 5, reply to obj. 8, of his *Commentary on the Sentences of Peter Lombard*,[3] when he wrote that these relatives involve a fundament *and* a relation, whereas things relative according to the way they have being express *only* a relation, because it is easy to see that things relative according to the way they must be expressed in discourse bear on a terminus rather by founding a relation than by actually respecting, and for that reason they do not respect the terminus in question in the rationale of a pure terminus, but according to some other rationale—that of a cause, say, or of an effect, or of an object, or of some such. So a relation according to the way being must

art. 1.,[1] «quod relatio non est aliud quam habitudo unius ad alterum; unde secundum propriam rationem non habet, quod sit aliquid in eo, de quo dicitur, sed hoc aliquando habet ex habitudinis causa». Et idem fere habet in 1. dist. 26. q. 2. art. 1.[2] et 1. p. q. 28. art. 1., ubi inquit, quod «ea, quae dicuntur ad aliquid, significant secundum propriam rationem solum respectum ad aliud. Qui quidem respectus aliquando est in rerum natura, utpote quando aliquae res secundum naturam suam ad invicem ordinatae sunt». Et hoc ideo est, quia relatio propter suam minimam entitatem non praecise dependet a subiecto sicut aliae formae absolutae, sed se habet ut entitas tertia ex coordinatione duorum extremorum consistens et resultans, ideoque ut sit in rerum natura debet dependere a fundamento coordinante illam ad terminum, et non solum a subiecto et causa productiva.

Ex his non erit difficile discernere inter relationes secundum dici et secundum esse, reales et rationis. Relativa enim SECUNDUM ESSE et SECUNDUM DICI discriminantur ex ipso exercitio, quia in relativis secundum esse tota ratio seu exercitium est respicere, et ideo dicuntur respicere terminum in ratione puri termini. Exercitium vero seu ratio relationis secundum dici non est pure respicere terminum, sed aliquid aliud exercere, unde sequatur relatio; ideoque dixit bene S. Thomas in 2. dist. 1. q. 1. art. 5. ad 8. primo loco positum,[3] quod ista relativa important fundamentum et relationem, relativa vero secundum esse tantum relationem dicunt, quia videlicet relativa secundum dici potius erga terminum se habent fundando relationem quam actu respiciendo, et ideo non in ratione puri termini ipsum respiciunt, sed secundum aliam rationem, puta causae vel effectus aut obiecti aut quid simile. Quapropter relatio secundum dici

[1] *Pa* XXII. 84 b.
[2] *Pa* VI. 219 b.
[3] *Pa* VI. 393 b.

be expressed in discourse is constantly distinguished, in the writings of St. Thomas, from relation according to the way relation has being, in that the principal significate of an expression expressing a relation according to the way a subject must be expressed in discourse is not a relation, but something else, upon which a relation follows. But when the principal significate of any expression is the relation itself, and not anything absolute, then there is a relation according to the way the thing signified has being, as is clear from the *Summa theologica*, I, q. 13, art. 7; the *Commentary on the Sentences of Peter Lombard*, Book I, dist. 30, q. 1, art. 2;[4] and from chap. 1 of the Tractate concerning the category of relation in the *Summa of the Whole Logic of Aristotle*,[5] where St. Thomas clearly teaches this.

The establishing of this difference also establishes that an expression expressing a transcendental relation—which is nothing else than a relation according to the way subjective being must be expressed in discourse—does not convey relation from its principal significate, but something absolute, upon which some relation follows or could follow. For if it does not convey an absolute, it will not be transcendental, that is, ranging through diverse categories, but will look to one category only. Whence a transcendental relation is not a form adventitious to a subject or absolute thing, but one assimilated to it, yet connoting something extrinsic upon which the subject depends or with which it is engaged, as, for example, matter relative to form, a head relative to the headed, a creature relative to God; and so transcendental relation coincides with relation according to the way being must be expressed in discourse. Some erroneously divide relation according to the way it has being into transcendental and categorial.[6] This is a wrong division, because a transcendental relation is in the absolute entity itself and does not differ from its [subjective] being, and so its whole being is not toward another, which is required for a relation to be ontological, i.e., a relation according to the way it has being. But whether the transcendental relation imports some imperfection and dependency and must for that reason be excluded from God is a question for the metaphysicians and theologians.

But mind-independent and mind-dependent relations, which division is found in relation only according to the

in hoc perpetuo distinguitur a relatione secundum esse ex D. Thoma, quod principale significatum relationis secundum dici non est relatio, sed aliquid aliud, ad quod sequitur relatio. Quando autem principale significatum alicuius est relatio ipsa et non aliquid absolutum, tunc est relatio secundum esse, ut constat ex 1. p. q. 13. art. 7. et in 1. dist. 30. q. 1. art. 2.[4] et opusc. 48. tract. de praedicamento Ad aliquid cap. 1.,[5] ubi manifeste hoc docet.

Ex quo etiam constat, quod *relatio transcendentalis*, quae non est alia a relatione secundum dici, non importat ex principali significato relationem, sed aliquid absolutum, ad quod sequitur vel sequi potest aliqua relatio. Nam si absolutum non importat, transcendentalis non erit, id est vagans per diversa genera, sed ad unum praedicamentum tantum spectabit. Unde relatio transcendentalis non est forma adveniens subiecto seu rei absolutae, sed illi imbibita, connotans tamen aliquid extrinsecum, a quo pendet vel circa quod versatur, ut materia ad formam, caput ad capitatum, creatura ad Deum, sicque relatio transcendentalis coincidit cum relatione secundum dici. Et male ab aliquibus relatio secundum esse dividitur in transcendentalem et praedicamentalem,[6] cum transcendentalis sit in ipsa entitate absoluta nec ab eius esse differat, et sic non sit totum suum esse ad aliud, quod requiritur ad relationem secundum esse. An vero transcendentalis relatio imperfectionem aliquam et dependentiam importet ideoque a Deo releganda sit, ad metaphysicos et theologos spectat.

RELATIONES AUTEM REALES ET RATIONIS, quae divisio solum in relatione

[4] *Pa* VI. 245 b.

[5] Summa tot. Log. Arist. (*Pa* XVII. 73 a).

[6] Principal among the "some" Poinsot has in mind here was certainly Suarez: "*Tertio ac praecipue dividitur relatio realis et secundum esse, in transcendentalem et praedicamentalem . . .*"—"Thirdly and principally is real and ontological relation divided into transcendental and categorial . . .": *Disputationes Metaphysicae*, disp. 47, sect. 3, par. 10. "*. . . relationes autem quae tantum sunt secundum dici, proprie et in rigore sumptas, distingui ab omnibus relationibus secundum esse, sive transcendentales sint, sive praedicamentales*"—". . . relations which, taken in a proper and strict sense, are only according to the way being must be expressed in discourse, are distinguished from all ontological relations, whether transcendental or categorial": ibid, par. 9.

way relation has being, are seen to be different owing principally to the absence of any of the conditions required for the relations to be mind-independent. Now five such conditions are required by St. Thomas in the first chapter of the Tractate on the category of relation in the *Summa of the Whole Logic of Aristotle,*[7] two on the side of the subject of the relation, two on the side of the terminus of the relation, and one on the part of the things related. On the side of the subject, the two conditions are that the subject of the relation be a mind-independent being and that it be a fundament, that is to say, that the subject of the relation have the rationale of the founding independently of that rationale's being known. On the side of the terminus, the conditions are that the terminus of the relation be something mind-independent and mind-independently existing, and second, that it be mind-independently distinct from the other extreme [i.e., the subject of the relation]. But on the part of the relatives, i.e., of the subjective things related, the condition is that they be of the same order, for want of which condition there is not a mind-independent relation of God to a creature, nor of a measure to the measured, if the measure is of a different order from that of measured. This doctrine accords with what St. Thomas teaches in the *Commentary on the Sentences of Peter Lombard*, Book I, dist. 26, q. 2, art. 1,[8] and in the *Summa theologica*, I, q. 28, art. 1. Yet formally and principally the whole difference between a mind-independent relation and a mind-dependent one comes down to this, that a physical relation has a mind-independent fundament with a coexistent terminus, while a mental relation lacks such a fundament,[9] as St. Thomas explains in the *Commentary on the Sentences Written for Annibald*, Book I, dist. 30, q. 1, art. 1.[10]

Taking these differences as established, I say by way of resolution: **In order for any relation to be categorial, it must have those conditions by which it is distinguished both from a mind-dependent relation and from a transcendental relation, i.e., a relation according to the way being must be expressed in discourse; and therefore categorial relation is defined as a mind-independent form whose whole being is toward another.**

By the first part of this conclusion categorial relation is distinguished from mental relation, which is not a mind-independent form; by the second part of the conclusion categorial relation is distinguished from transcendental relation and anything abso-

secundum esse invenitur, discriminantur penes carentiam alicuius ex conditionibus requisitis ad relationes reales. Requiruntur autem quinque conditiones a D. Thoma opusc. 48. tract. de Relativis cap. 1.,[7] duae ex parte subiecti, duae ex parte termini, una ex parte relatorum. Ex parte *subiecti*, quod subiectum sit ens reale et fundamentum seu rationem fundandi realem habeat. Ex parte *termini*, quod terminus sit res aliqua realis et realiter existens, et secundo, quod sit distincta realiter ab alio extremo. Ex parte vero *relativorum*, quod sint eiusdem ordinis, defectu cuius Dei ad creaturam non est relatio realis nec mensurae ad mensuratum, si sit diversi ordinis. Quae doctrina concordat his, quae docet in 1. dist. 26. q. 2. art. 1.[8] et 1. p. q. 28. art. 1. Formaliter tamen et principaliter reducitur tota differentia inter relationem realem et rationis, quod relatio realis habet fundamentum reale cum coexistentia termini, relatio rationis caret fundamento,[9] ut ex D. Thoma sumitur 1. ad Annibaldum dist. 30. quaest. unica art. 1.[10]

His suppositis resolutorie dico: **Ad hoc ut relatio aliqua sit praedicamentalis, requiritur, quod habeat illas conditiones, quibus distinguatur a relatione rationis et transcendentali sive secundum dici, ideoque definitur relatio praedicamentalis, quod sit forma realis, cuius totum esse est ad aliud.**

Per primam particulam distinguitur a relatione rationis, quae realis forma non est, per secundam a relatione transcendentali et quolibet absoluto,

[7] Summa tot. Log. Arist. (*Pa* XVII. 73 a, b).

[8] *Pa* VI. 219 b.

[9] This is the "formal and principal difference" from the point of view of the fundament as cause of the being of the relationship. Since, however, in the case of mind-dependent relations the fundament is not the cause of the relation's being, it is also possible to discriminate the two cases "formally and principally" from the point of view of the different ways the fundaments function in the denomination of a subject as relative: see the First Preamble, Article 3, 70/24-71/19. This latter point of view is the one that is proximately crucial for the notion of the sign as *ontologically* relative, i.e., relative in its proper being without regard for the subjective ground whence springs its being-toward: see Book I, Question 1, 125/31-39.

[10] *Pa* XXII. 84 b.

lute the whole being of which is not toward another, since in itself it is also something absolute.

In fact the three conditions of a categorial relation are implied in this conclusion: First, that it be an ontological relation, that is, a relation according to the way it has being; second, that it be mind-independent, where we include all the conditions required[11] for mind-independent relation; third, that it be finite. (Scotus adds a fourth condition, to wit, that the relation be intrinsically adventitious, that is to say, that it be a relation which immediately arises without any further change when the fundament and the term are posited; but relations extrinsically adventitious he limits to the last six categories, which do not result immediately and as if from within when a fundament and term are given, but need some extrinsic change in order to result. But in treating of the last six categories in Q. 19 we will show that these extrinsically advenient modes are not relations.)

By the first of these conditions for a categorial relation are excluded all relations according to the expressibility of subjective being in discourse, i.e., all transcendental relations; by the second are excluded all mind-dependent relations; by the third all divine relations, which fall outside a category, since they are pure acts.

But you might ask concerning that condition[12] of a mind-independent and categorial relation, namely, that the extremes be mind-independently distinct, whether it is required that they be distinct on the part of the things, that is, of the extremes materially, or whether it is required that they be distinct not only materially but also on the part of the rationale of their foundation, so that the proximate fundament of the relation is also mind-independently distinct from the relation.

The response to this inquiry is that in this lies the difference between the schools of St. Thomas and of Scotus. For Scotus, in Book I of his *Commentary on the Sentences of Peter Lombard*, dist. 31, q. 1, requires only a distinction between the things which are the extremes, not between the rationales of founding. St. Thomas requires both, as is clear in the *Summa theologica*, I, q. 42, art. 1, where on this ground he denies that there is an ontological relation of similarity and equality between the divine persons independently of our minds, because the foundation [of relations of similarity and equality] is the same in each of the persons, to wit, the divine essence, by reason of which they are alike; it would be the same if one whiteness existed in two

cuius totum esse non est ad aliud, cum in se etiam absolutum aliquid sit.

Colliguntur vero *tres conditiones relationis praedicamentalis*: Prima, quod sit relatio secundum esse; secunda, quod sit realis, ubi includimus omnes conditiones requisitas[11] ad relationem realem; tertia, quod sit finita. Scotus quartam addit conditionem, scilicet quod sit relatio intrinsecus adveniens, id est quae sine ulla mutatione, posito fundamento et termino statim consurgit; relationes vero extrinsecus advenientes reicit ad sex ultima praedicamenta, quae posito fundamento et termino non immediate et quasi ab intrinseco resultant, sed extrinseca aliqua mutatione indigent, ut resultent. Sed q. 19. agendo de sex ultimis praedicamentis ostendemus non esse relationes istas extrinsecus advenientes.

Ex prima ergo conditione relationis praedicamentalis excluduntur omnes relationes secundum dici sive transcendentales, ex secunda eiciuntur omnes relationes rationis, ex tertia omnes relationes divinae, quae e praedicamento exulant, cum sint actus puri.

SED INQUIRES circa illam conditionem[12] relationis realis et praedicamentalis, scilicet quod extrema sint distincta realiter, an requiratur, quod sint distincta solum ex parte rerum seu extremorum materialiter, an etiam ex parte rationis fundandi, ita ut fundamentum proximum sit etiam realiter distinctum.

Respondetur in hoc esse differentiam inter scholam D. Thomae et Scoti. Scotus enim in 1. dist. 31. quaest. unica requirit solum distinctionem inter res, quae sunt extrema, non inter rationes fundandi. D. Thomas utrumque requirit, ut patet 1. p. q. 42. art. 1., ubi ex eo negat inter divinas personas dari relationem realem similitudinis et aequalitatis, quia fundamentum est idem in omnibus personis, scilicet divina essentia, ratione cuius assimilantur, et idem esset, si poneretur una albedo in duobus lapidi-

[11] at 91/3-20.
[12] 91/12-16.

stones. The reason for this is taken from Cajetan and the other interpreters commenting on q. 42, art. 1, because in these relatives [i.e., in the case of ontological relatives that are reciprocal] the material extremes are referred because the rationales themselves of the founding are referred; for it is because the whitenesses are similar that the white things are similar. Whence if, on the contrary, the whitenesses are not similar, because there is only one whiteness, the white things themselves could not be *similar* in whiteness, because they are the same, since by hypothesis there is only one and the same whiteness. But if they are similar, it will be in something else, not in the formal rationale itself of a white thing. But it is enough to have insinuated this concerning this difficulty, for it is a difficulty that looks more to the theologians and the metaphysicians.

bus. Cuius ratio sumitur ex Caietano ibi, et aliis interpretibus, quia in his relativis ex eo referuntur extrema materialia, quia ipsae rationes fundandi referuntur; quia enim albedines sunt similes, res albae sunt similes. Unde e contra si albedines similes non sunt, quia est unica albedo, ipsa alba similia esse non possunt in albedine, sed sunt idem, utpote cum sit unica tantum et eadem albedo. Si vero sunt similia, erit in aliquo alio, non in ipsa ratione formali albi. Sed de hac difficultate hoc insinuasse sufficiat, magis enim spectat ad theologos et metaphysicos.

Resolution of Counter-Arguments

A problem arises first from that well-known but difficult passage in the *Summa theologica*, I, q. 28, art. 1, where St. Thomas says that only in the case of the things that are a being toward something are there instances that conform both to the order of mind-independent being and to the order of mind-dependent being. The statement has been a source of difficulties for many. For St. Thomas is speaking either of categorial relation or of relation as it abstracts from the division into mind-independent and mind-dependent. If he is speaking in the first way, it is false that mind-dependent relations are found among the categorial relations, or else we have falsely asserted that for a categorial relation a mind-independent exercise of being-toward is required. If he is speaking in the second way, it is true that in relation conceived apart from the difference between being mind-independent and mind-dependent both terms of the division are found, but it is false to say that this way of considering being is found to be possible only if the being considered is itself a relation. For even in the case of substance something can be conceived fictively, which would be called a substance having its being from the mind, as are a chimera, a goat-deer, and similar mythical creatures. In the case of quantity, an imaginary arrangement of parts outside of parts can be conceived; and similarly in the other categories. Therefore something objectively mind-dependent is not found in the case of relation alone. And Cajetan's response to this difficulty in his *Commentary* on the passage in question serves only to increase the difficulty, for he says, in his *Commentary on the Summa theologica*, I, q. 28, art. 1, that relation has this unique property, that for it to exist dependently on the mind is not a condition diminishing its rationale, because that relation which is mind-dependent is a true relation. This increases the difficulty, for it is certain that if a mental relation were a true relation, it would make a subject refer truly, not fictively, and therefore not through apprehension alone, but physically.

This difficulty has provided the occasion for many of

Solvuntur argumenta.

Primo arguitur loco illo D. Thomae satis noto, sed difficili, 1. p. q. 28. art. 1., ubi dicit, quod solum in his, quae sunt ad aliquid, inveniuntur aliqua secundum rem et aliqua secundum rationem. Quae verba multis difficilia visa sunt. Nam vel loquitur D. Thomas de relatione praedicamentali vel de relatione, prout abstrahit a reali et rationis. Si primo modo, falsum est in relatione praedicamentali inveniri relationes rationis, vel falso diximus ad relationem praedicamentalem requiri, quod sit realis. Si secundo modo, verum est in relatione sic abstracta utramque reperiri, scilicet realem et rationis, sed falsum est hoc solum reperiri in relatione. Nam etiam in substantia potest aliquid ficte concipi, quod dicetur substantia rationis, sicut chimaera, hircocervus et similia, et in quantitate spatium imaginarium et similia in aliis generibus. Ergo non in sola relatione invenitur aliquid rationis. Et auget difficultatem responsio Caietani ibidem, quod relatio peculiariter hoc habet, quod esse in ratione non est conditio diminuens, sed est vera relatio illa, quae est rationis; constat enim, quod si esset vera relatio, vere faceret referre subiectum et non ficte, atque adeo neque per apprehensionem, sed realiter.

Haec difficultas occasionem praebuit multis sinistre intelligendi Divum

understanding St. Thomas in a twisted way, as it has also been the occasion of much poor philosophizing about relation. For some think that physical relation divides into two concepts, namely, the concept of an accident, which they call "being in," and the concept of a respect, which they call "being toward," and that the first is something mind-independent, while the second is either dependent upon mind or else abstracts from the mind-independent and the mind-dependent. Others think that St. Thomas wished only to assert that something can be fabricated by human understanding on the pattern of a categorial relation.[13] Others, finally, think that he is speaking of relation as it abstracts from, i.e., is conceived apart from, the difference between being independent of or dependent upon mind.

But the proponents of the first interpretation[14] exclude true mind-independence from the category of relation, if that which is proper to such a category—namely, the respect and rationale of being toward—is not instantiated independently of mind. But proponents of the second interpretation[15] do not speak of anything peculiar to relation, as St. Thomas posits, because some mind-dependent beings can also be formed on the pattern of the other categories of mind-independent being, as, for example, on the pattern of substance and of quantity, etc.

Wherefore the third interpretation[16] is the truest as regards one point, namely, that St. Thomas is speaking of relation in its entire latitude, as it abstracts from being independent of or dependent upon mind. For he did not say that in the category of being-toward-something are found some things conformed to the order of mind-dependent being, but he said unqualifiedly, "in the case of these things, which are a being toward something," in order to indicate that he is not speaking of relation as it is a category determinately of mind-independent being, but according to itself absolutely—to which point some who read St. Thomas less carefully ought to pay attention. St. Thomas, therefore, in the passage in question, is speaking of relation under the most formal concept of a being-toward, and he asserts that from that content by which the relation is considered toward a terminus, it both exists positively, and *is not determinately a mind-independent form*, but is indifferent to the exercise of a mind-independent or a mind-dependent act of existence, even though a categorial exercise of being-toward would also be mind-independently founded. And thus St. Thomas did not wish to point out which relation would be mind-independent or which mind-dependent, but [rather] the rationale or content owing to which relation is [*peculiarly*] able to be mind-independent or mind-

Thomam aut minus bene philosophandi de relatione. Quidam enim existimant relationem realem partiri in duos conceptus, scilicet in conceptum accidentis, quem vocant *in*, et respectum, quem vocant *ad*; et primum esse realem, secundum rationis vel abstrahere a reali et rationis. Alii existimant solum voluisse D. Thomam significare, quod potest aliquid excogitari per rationem ad instar relationis praedicamentalis.[13] Alii denique, quod loquitur de relatione, ut abstrahit a reali et rationis.

Sed primi[14] excludunt veram realitatem in praedicamento relationis, si id, quod est proprium talis praedicamenti, scilicet respectus et ratio *ad*, non realizatur. Secundi[15] vero non dicunt aliquid peculiare relationis, ut S. Thomas ponit, quia etiam possunt aliqua entia rationis formari ad similitudinem aliorum generum, v. g. ad instar substantiae et quantitatis etc.

Quare tertia expositio[16] quantum ad unum verissima est, scilicet quod D. Thomas loquitur de relatione in tota sua latitudine, ut abstrahit a reali et rationis. Neque enim dixit S. Doctor, quod in praedicamento Ad aliquid inveniuntur aliqua secundum rationem, sed absolute dixit ,,in his, quae sunt ad aliquid", ut significaret se non loqui de relatione, ut determinate est genus, sed absolute secundum se. Quod deberent aliqui attendere, qui minus sollicite legunt S. Doctorem. Itaque loquitur Divus Thomas de relatione sub formalissimo conceptu *ad* et significat, quod ex illa parte, qua consideratur ad terminum, et positive se habet et non est determinate realis forma, sed permittit, quod sit ens reale vel rationis; licet *ad* praedicamentale et fundatum reale sit. Et ita non voluit D. Thomas significare, quae relatio sit realis vel quae rationis, sed ex qua parte habet relatio, quod possit esse realis vel ratio-

[13] This is the interpretation settled on by Suarez in the *Disputationes Metaphysicae*, disp. 47, sect. 3, par. 5. He discusses the view of Cajetan in par. 2.

[14] 94/3-8.

[15] 94/9-11.

[16] 94/11-14.

dependent, namely, the rationale or content whereby it is toward a terminus; for even though it can have a mind-independent existence there, yet it does not have a mind-independent existence *from* there. St. Thomas makes this point expressly in his *Commentary on the Sentences Written for Annibald*, Book I, dist. 26, q. 2, art. 1,[17] where he says that "relation can be considered in two ways. In one way, as regards that toward which it is said to be [i.e., its terminus], from which it has the rationale of a relation, and as regards this it need not posit anything, although too it need not for this reason be nothing; for there are certain respects which are something in the order of being as it exists independently of mind, but certain others which are nothing in the order of mind-independent being. In another way, relation can be considered as regards that in which it is, and so when it has existence in a subject, it is in the subject independently of mind." Thus St. Thomas.

But *how this is peculiar to the case of relation* and is not found in the other categories, we say is owing to the fact that in the other categories their proper and most formal rationale cannot be understood positively unless it is also understood entitatively, because their positive rationale is toward themselves only and subjective, and for this reason is not understood positively unless also entitatively; for that which is toward itself is an entity. Only relation has [both] to be being and toward being, and from that content by which it is toward being, it exists positively, yet it does not have thence the rationale of being mind-independent. But a mind-independent existence comes to relation from one source, namely, from a [mind-independent] fundament, the positive rationale of toward from elsewhere, namely, from the terminus, from which the relation does not have to be being, but toward being, although that toward is truly mind-independent when it is founded. That therefore something can be considered positively, even if it does not exist entitatively independently of mind, is proper to relation. And this is all that Cajetan wished to say in his *Commentary* on the passage in question from the *Summa theologica*, when he said that a mind-dependent relation is a true relation, not by the truth of an entity and of an informing form, but by the truth of an objective and positive tendency toward a term.[18] Nor did Cajetan say that in the case of a categorial relation, the very toward is something constructed; for he says expressly that it is truly instantiated mind-independently.

nis, scilicet ex parte, qua est ad terminum; licet enim ibi realitatem habere possit, non tamen inde. Quod expressit S. Doctor in 1. ad Annibaldum dist. 26. q. 2. art. 1.[17] dicens, «quod relatio potest dupliciter considerari, uno modo quantum ad id, ad quod dicitur, ex quo rationem relationis habet, et quantum ad hoc non habet, quod ponat aliquid, quamvis etiam ex hoc non habeat, quod nihil sit; sunt enim quidam respectus, qui sunt aliquid secundum rem, quidam vero, qui nihil. Alio modo quantum ad id, in quo est, et sic quando habet eam in subiecto, realiter inest». Sic D. Thomas.

Quomodo autem hoc sit peculiare in relatione et in aliis generibus non inveniatur, dicimus ex eo esse, quia in aliis generibus ratio propria et formalissima eorum non potest positive intelligi, nisi entitative etiam intelligatur, quia positiva eorum ratio est ad se tantum et absoluta, et ideo non intelligitur positive nisi etiam entitative, quod enim est ad se, entitas est. Sola relatio habet esse ens et ad ens, et pro ea parte, qua se habet ad ens, positive se habet, nec tamen inde habet entitatem realem. Sed aliunde relationi provenit realitas, scilicet a fundamento, aliunde positiva ratio *ad*, scilicet ex termino, ex quo non habet esse ens, sed ad ens, licet illud *ad* vere reale sit, quando fundatum est. Quod ergo aliquid possit considerari positive, etiamsi non entitative realiter, proprium relationis est. Et hoc solum voluit dicere Caietanus cit. loco, cum dixit relationem rationis esse veram relationem, non veritate entitatis et formae informantis, sed veritate obiectivae et positivae tendentiae ad terminum.[18] Neque Caietanus dixit, quod in relatione praedicamentali ipsum *ad* est aliquid rationis; expresse enim dicit, quod vere realizatur.

---

[17] *Pa* XXII. 76 a.

[18] Poinsot's exegesis of Cajetan on this central point of St. Thomas's understanding of relation is nicely confirmed and summarized by the following remark from Cajetan's *Commentary* (1507 publication date) on the *Summa theologica*, I, q. 28, art. 1, par. 9: "*relatio est tale ens, cui additum* esse in ratione *non est conditio diminuens, sicut in aliis. Rosa enim secundum rationem, non est rosa; neque Homerus in opinione, est Homerus; relatio autem in ratione, est vera relatio. . . . Nec distinctio rosae*

When one insists that, as a matter of fact, other kinds of being too can in this way be said to be something mind-dependent—as a mind-dependent substance will be a chimera, a mind-dependent quantity an imaginary space, and so on for the other categories: *The response is* that, as was explained in our First Preamble on mind-dependent being,[19] that on whose pattern a mind-dependent being is formed is not called mind-dependent; for mind-dependent being is formed on the pattern of mind-independent being, but that unreal being which is conceived on the pattern of a mind-independent being is called a mind-dependent being. There is not therefore mind-dependent substance nor mind-dependent quantity, because even though some non-being may be conceived on the pattern of a substance—for example, the chimera—and some on the pattern of quantity—for example, imaginary space—yet neither substance itself nor any rationale of subjectivity is conceived by the understanding and formed in being on the pattern of some *other* mind-independent being. And for this reason that negation or chimerical non-being and that non-being of an imaginary space will be said to be a mind-dependent being. But this [i.e., any unreal object whatever conceived as being a subject or a subjective modification of being] is the mind-dependent being which is called negation, yet it will not be a mind-dependent substance, because substance itself is not conceived as a mind-dependent being patterned after some mind-independent being—rather, negations or non-beings are conceived on the pattern of substance and quantity. But in the case of relatives, indeed, not only is there some non-being conceived on the pattern of relation, but also the very relation conceived on the part of the respect toward, while it does not exist in the mind-independent order, is conceived or formed on the pattern of a mind-independent relation, and so that which is formed in being, and not only that after whose pattern it is formed, is a relation, and by reason of this there are in fact mind-dependent relations, but not mind-dependent substances.[20]

Quando vero instatur, quod etiam alia genera possunt hoc modo dici aliquid rationis, sicut substantia rationis erit chimaera, quantitas rationis spatium imaginarium, et sic de aliis: *Respondetur*, quod, ut supra dictum est [in] Praeambulo Primo art. 1.,[19] non dicitur ens rationis illud, ad cuius instar formatur; formatur enim ens rationis ad instar entis realis, sed dicitur ens rationis illud non reale, quod ad instar realis entis concipitur. Non datur ergo substantia rationis nec quantitas rationis, quia licet aliquod non ens concipiatur ad instar substantiae, v. g. chimaera, et aliquid ad instar quantitatis, v. g. spatium imaginarium, non tamen ipsa substantia vel aliqua substantiae ratio concipitur per rationem et formatur in esse ad instar alterius entis realis. Et ideo illa negatio seu non ens chimaerae, et illud non ens spatii imaginarii dicetur ens rationis. Sed hoc est ens rationis, quod vocatur negatio, non autem erit substantia rationis, cum non ipsa substantia ut ens rationis ad instar alicuius realis concipiatur, sed negationes seu non entia ad instar substantiae et quantitatis. At vero in relativis non solum aliquod non ens concipitur ad instar relationis, sed etiam ipsa relatio ex parte respectus ad, cum non existit in re, concipitur seu formatur ad instar relationis realis, et sic est, quod formatur in esse, et non solum id, ad cuius instar formatur, et ratione huius datur relatio rationis, non substantia rationis.[20]

---

in esse naturae et esse rationis, est distinctio diversarum quidditatum, quarum una sit ens reale, et altera sit ens rationis, ut in relatione contingere diximus: sed est distinctio unius et eiusdem secundum diversos modos essendi, scilicet simpliciter vel secundum quid."—"Relation is the sort of being for which the qualification *existing in the mind* does not detract from what is proper to it, as it does detract from what is proper to all other sorts of being. For a rose formed by thought is not a rose, nor is Homer in the mind's consideration Homer; but a relation formed by the mind is a true relation . . . . Nor is the distinction between a rose in natural existence and in mental existence a distinction of two diverse things, of which the one is a mind-independent being and the other a mind-dependent being, as we have said happens in the case of relation: but it is a distinction of one and the same thing according to different modes of existing, namely, absolutely or relatively." The interested reader is well advised to read this entire article of Cajetan's *Commentary* on this point so essential for semiotic.

[19] In the original Latin: "q. 12. art. 1," which would seem to be an error, since the reference does fit q. 2 (i.e., our First Preamble), art. 1, 57/26-30, but does not fit anything discussed in art. 1 of q. 12 of the Logic (q. 12: "*De accidente quinto praedicabili*"—"On the fifth predicable accident"; art. 1: "*Utrum definitiones et divisiones accidentis recte sint traditae a Porphyrio*"—"Whether the definitions and divisions of accident are rightly treated by Porphyry").

[20] Cf. above, the First Preamble, Article 3, 69/13-40.

It is argued secondly: the supreme genus of this category is a true mind-independent relation, and yet this genus does not have a terminus distinct from itself, which it respects; therefore we have falsely said that this is required for a real categorial relation.

The minor is proved by the fact that the terminus in question is something relative or something absolute. It is not absolute because (as we will ourselves say below[21]) the formal terminus of a relation is not something absolute, but relative. Besides which, that absolute cannot be anything mind-independent existing in the singular; for relation in general cannot respect something determinately singular as terminus, for thus all relations would respect that determinate thing. But if it is something abstracted from singulars, that something cannot terminate a physical relation, because it is not given

Secundo arguitur: Supremum genus huius praedicamenti est vera relatio realis, et tamen non habet terminum distinctum a se, quem respiciat; ergo falso diximus hoc requiri ad relationem realem praedicamentalem.

Minor probatur, quia vel ille terminus est aliquid relativum vel absolutum. Non absolutum, quia, ut infra[21] dicemus, formalis terminus relationis non est aliquid absolutum, sed relativum. Praeterquam quod illud absolutum non potest esse aliquid reale existens in singulari; nec enim relatio in communi potest respicere pro termino aliquid singulare determinate, sic enim omnes relationes illum respicerent. Si autem est aliquid abstractum a singularibus, illud non potest terminare

---

[21] Logica 2. p. q. 17. art. 5., "*Utrum relatio formaliter terminetur ad absolutum vel ad relativum*" ("Whether a relation is formally terminated at something absolute or at something relative"), Reiser ed., I. 596a43-b36: "*Dico primo: Ratio formalis termini relativi, ut terminus est, non potest esse aliquid omnino absolutum et ad se.*

"*Ratio est duplex: Prima, quia terminus in quantum terminus formaliter alicuius est terminus; nihil enim terminat nisi alterum. Ergo terminus relationis est aliquid relationis; ergo si est relatio praedicamentalis, terminus illius est pure terminus, id est non habet aliud quam terminare seu opponi relationi et esse aliquid ipsius ut respicientis. In quo differt a fundamento, quia fundamentum oportet, quod det esse relationi secundum inhaerentiam, in quo esse convenit cum accidente absoluto. Terminus autem non dat esse relationi, sed oppositionem terminationis. Ergo formalitas termini non est aliquid absolutum.*

"*Secunda ratio est, quia, ut constat ex D. Thoma 1. ad Annibaldum dist. 30. quaest. unica art. 1. ad 3* [*Pa* XXII. 84 b.], *terminus non potest intelligi nisi sub opposita habitudine. Et 2. Contra Gent. cap. 11. dicit, quod 'non potest intelligi aliquid relative dici ad alterum, nisi e converso illud relative dicatur ad ipsum.' Et ratio est, quia relatio ut relatio oppositionem habet non minus quam contrarietas vel privatio; non habet autem oppositionem nisi ad suum terminum; ergo terminus ut terminus est oppositus ei relative. Sicut ergo non potest intelligi relatio nisi ut habens oppositionem ad terminum, ita neque terminus formaliter intelligitur nisi ut oppositus; sed illa oppositio est relativa; ergo in quantum terminus est aliquid relativum.*" —"I say first: the formal character of the terminus of a relative, as it is a terminus, cannot be something entirely absolute and existing in itself.

"The reason is twofold. In the first place, a terminus, insofar as it is such formally, is the terminus of something; for nothing terminates unless it terminates another. Therefore the terminus of a relation is something, i.e., a part, of the relation; therefore if the relation is categorial, its terminus is purely such, that is, it does not have other than to terminate or to be opposed to the relation and to be something of that relation as of a respecting. In this the terminus differs from the fundament, because it is necessary for the fundament to give existence to the relation according to inherence, in which existence the relation comes together with an absolute accident. But the terminus does not give existence to the relation, but the opposition of termination. Therefore the formality of the terminus is not something absolute.

"In the second place, as is clear from Book I, dist. 30, q. 1, art. 1, reply to objection 3 of St. Thomas's *Commentary on the Sentences Written for Annibald*, a terminus cannot be understood except under a condition of opposition. And in Book 2, chapter 11, of the *Summa contra gentiles*, St. Thomas says that 'one thing spoken of relative to another thing cannot be understood unless that other thing is spoken of conversely as relative to the first.' And the reason is that a relation as a relation has an opposition no less than does contrariety or privation; but it does not have an opposition except to its terminus; therefore the terminus as terminus is opposed to it relatively. Just therefore as relation cannot be understood except as having an opposition to a terminus, so neither can a terminus be understood formally except as something opposed; but that opposition is something relative; therefore a terminus of a relation is something relative insofar as it is a terminus."

on the side of mind-independent being. But if it is something relative, either it is equal to that supreme genus or inferior. If equal, two genera of relations are given. If inferior, it would be respected by relation in general as that of which relation is predicated, not as that at which relation is terminated essentially as relation, but as something universal.

The response to this[22] is that relation in general does not respect a terminus in act and in exercise, but is only conceived as the rationale and definable essence of relation itself and as a superior grade by which individual relations are constituted for respecting, not [as] that which exertively respects, for relation [generically considered] has this through its inferiors; just as first substance taken vaguely and in general is that by which accidents are supported, not that which exertively supports them. And the reason for this is that relation generically taken is not the concept of relation as opposed, but as uniting by a common rationale the nature of relation. Whence in that concept both relatives and correlatives come together, they do not have therein an opposition; but a relation is not *exercised* toward a terminus except under a relative opposition. And thus relation conceived under a generic concept is stripped of a state of opposition and only explicates the concept in which all relations agree, but not the exercise of respecting a terminus, even though it is the rationale of respecting that in its inferiors. And even in the opinion that the terminus of a relation is something absolute, terminus in general cannot be understood univocally, because according to this opinion a terminus of a relation is found in whatever category, nor can one terminus which is respected by relation as such come about from all the categories; but a determinate terminus it does not respect, since it is generic relation.

It is argued thirdly: Transcendental relations also have their whole being toward another. For example, the whole essence of matter is relative to form, the whole essence of habit and of act is relative to an object; for thence they have their entire specific rationale. But a categorial relation, on the contrary, does not have its whole being toward another, because it is also an inhering accident, and so has being in, not toward, the subject of the relation.

relationem realem, cum non detur a parte rei. Si autem est aliquid relativum, vel est illi aequale vel inferius. Si aequale, dabuntur duo genera relationum. Si inferius, respicietur a relatione in communi ut id, de quo praedicatur, non ut id, ad quod terminatur per se ut relatio, sed ut universale.

RESPONDETUR,[22] quod relatio in communi non respicit terminum in actu et in exercitio, sed solum concipitur ut ratio et quidditas ipsius relationis et ut gradus superior, quo relationes inferiores constituuntur ad respiciendum, non id, quod exercite respicit, id enim habet per sua inferiora; sicut substantia prima vage et in communi accepta est id, quo substatur accidentibus, non id, quod exercite illis substat. Et huius ratio est, quia relatio generice sumpta non est conceptus relationis ut oppositae, sed ut unientis ratione communi naturam relationis. Unde in illo conveniunt tam relativa quam correlativa, non in illo oppositionem habent; relatio autem non exercetur ad terminum nisi sub oppositione relativa. Et ita relatio concepta sub conceptu generico exuit statum oppositionis et tantum explicat conceptum, in quo conveniunt omnes relationes, non autem exercitium respiciendi terminum, licet sit ratio respiciendi illum in suis inferioribus. Et etiam in sententia, quod terminus relationis sit aliquid absolutum, non tamen potest accipi terminus in communi tamquam aliquid unum, quia secundum hanc sententiam in quocumque genere invenitur terminus relationis nec potest ex omnibus generibus unus terminus fieri, qui respiciatur a relatione ut sic; determinatum autem terminum non respicit, cum sit generica relatio.

Tertio arguitur: Relationes transcendentales etiam habent totum suum esse ad aliud, sicut tota essentia materiae est ad formam, tota essentia habitus et actus ad obiectum; inde enim habent totam speciem. E contra vero relatio praedicamentalis non totum suum esse habet ad aliud, cum etiam sit accidens inhaerens, et sic habet esse in subiecto, non ad subiectum.

---

[22] to 97/1-98/8.

This is confirmed by the fact that a transcendental relation too depends upon its terminus, just as does an ontological relation. There is, therefore, no reason why a transcendental relation could be terminated at something nonexistent, but not a categorial relation.

The response to this[23] is that a transcendental relation is not primarily and essentially toward another in the way a categorial relation is, for, even though the entire specific rationale and essence of transcendental relations derives from or depends on another, it is nevertheless not toward another. For example, matter depends on form, and act on object, as upon causes from which they have existence and specification. And from this it results that they respect that other as a terminus. But that it be primarily and essentially toward another as toward a terminus is proper to categorial relation. And for this reason it is said that categorial relation respects a terminus purely as a terminus, that is, only as toward another, not as from another or concerning another or by any other mode of causality whatever, in the way that transcendental relation respects a terminus not purely but by reason of some mode of causality. But the fact that a categorial relation is said to be in a subject does not take away from the fact that its whole being is toward another—"whole," I say, that is, the being proper and peculiar to itself, in which it differs from other absolute categories or subjective kinds of being; yet by supposing the common rationale of an accident, namely, to be in something, by reason of which rationale an accident does not have to be toward another, but does not exclude it either.

To the confirmation[24] the response is that a transcendental relation is not primarily and essentially toward another, as has been said, but from another or concerning another, as a dependency or a causality or something of the kind; which can sometimes be verified not by that which is the case in fact but by that which could be the case or that which is required for something's being the case. But a categorial relation, because it has its whole being toward another, does not arise except from the positing in fact of the extremes. Whence if either is lacking, the categorial relation itself ceases to be.

Confirmatur, quia relatio transcendentalis etiam dependet a suo termino sicut relatio secundum esse. Ergo non est ratio, cur transcendentalis possit terminari ad non existens, non vero praedicamentalis.

RESPONDETUR,[23] quod relatio transcendentalis non est primo et per se ad aliud sicut praedicamentalis, quia licet tota earum species et essentia sumatur ab alio vel dependeat ab alio, non tamen ad aliud, sicut materia dependet a forma et actus ab obiecto sicut a causis, a quibus habent esse et specificationem. Et ex hoc consequitur, quod respiciunt illud ut terminum. Sed quod primo et per se sit ad aliud ut ad terminum, est proprium relationis praedicamentalis. Et ideo dicitur, quod respicit terminum ut pure terminum, id est tantum ut ad aliud, non ut ab alio vel circa aliud vel quocumque alio causalitatis modo sicut transcendentalis. Quod vero relatio praedicamentalis dicitur esse in subiecto, non tollit, quin totum suum esse sit ad aliud, totum, inquam, id est proprium et peculiare ipsius esse, in quo differt ab aliis generibus absolutis; supponendo tamen rationem communem accidentis, scilicet esse in aliquo, ratione cuius non habet esse ad aliud, sed nec id excludit.

Ad confirmationem[24] respondetur, quod transcendentalis relatio non est primo et per se ad aliud, ut dictum est, sed ab alio vel circa aliud, ut dependentia vel causalitas aut aliquid simile; quod aliquando salvari potest non per id, quod de facto est sed per id, quod convenire potest, vel postulat, ut conveniat. Relatio autem praedicamentalis, quia totum suum esse habet ad aliud, non consurgit nisi ex positione extremorum. Unde altero illorum deficiente deficit.

---

[23] to 98/40-99/5.
[24] 99/1-5.

Article 3

What Are the Divisions of Categorial Relation and What Are Its Essential Types

In divisions of categorial relation we can consider two lines of dividing, one according to conditions incidental to the relation, another according to its specific and essential differences.

In the first line, relation is divided in two ways. First, into reciprocal and nonreciprocal relations.[1] Second, reciprocal relations are divided into symmetrical and asymmetrical relations. A relation is reciprocal, when there is on the side of each extreme a relation of the same order or rationale of being—that is to say: if a reciprocal relation is in its being independent of being cognized (mind-independent) , then it is so on the side of both extremes; if it is mind-dependent, then both extremes are dependent upon being known. For example: father and son are referred reciprocally. Nor is it sufficient that they are mutually converted, because even nonreciprocal things are converted, that is, one respects and the other is respected. A nonreciprocal relation, conversely, exists when there is a true and proper relation in one extreme only, as, for example, a creature in relation to God, knowledge in relation to the knowable. A symmetrical relation is a reciprocal relation of the same rationale or denomination, as, for example, a relation of similarity and a relation of equality: both extremes denominate something "similar" or "equal." An asymmetrical relation is a relation which denominates differently in each terminus or sub-

Articulus Tertius

Quae Sint Divisiones Relationis Praedicamentalis et Eius Species

In divisionibus relationis praedicamentalis possumus considerare DUPLICEM LINEAM DIVIDENDI: Prima penes conditiones accidentales relationis, secunda penes species et essentiales differentias.

Primo modo dividitur relatio dupliciter: *Primo* in relationes mutuas et non mutuas.[1] Et *secundo* relatio mutua dividitur in relationem aequiparantiae et disquiparantiae. Relatio mutua est, quando ex parte utriusque extremi datur ad invicem relatio eiusdem ordinis seu entitatis, id est, si sit relatio realis, quod ex parte utriusque extremi realis sit, si sit rationis, quod utraque sit rationis; v. g. pater et filius mutuo referuntur. Nec sufficit quod mutuo convertantur, quia etiam non mutua convertuntur, id est unum respicit et aliud respicitur. Relatio non mutua est e converso, quando tantum in uno extremo est relatio vera et propria, sicut in creatura ad Deum, in scientia ad scibile. Relatio aequiparantiae est relatio mutua eiusdem rationis seu denominationis, sicut relatio similitudinis et relatio aequalitatis utrumque extremum denominat simile vel aequale. Relatio disquiparantiae est diversae denominationis in utro-

---

[1] or: "bilateral and unilateral."

ject, as father is said relative to son, not to father, and a master to a servant, not to another master. And these divisions are called incidental (based on concomitant attributes of relations rather than on relations as such), because the rationales of the reciprocal and of the nonreciprocal, the symmetrical and the asymmetrical, are not understood directly according to their fundaments and termini but as consequent upon a relation's mode of touching a given terminus and fundament, from which two factors the essential type of a relation is derived.

In the second line of division, relation is divided into essential types according to the fundaments of relation, to which fundaments must also correspond diverse formal termini. Now the Philosopher, in his *Metaphysics*, Book 5, chap. 15[2] (reading 17 of St. Thomas's *Commentary*[3]), proposes three fundaments by which relation in general is divided. The first fundament is that of subjects relative according to unity and number. On unity and number are founded relations of similarity and dissimilarity, agreement and disagreement, etc. The second fundament is that of subjects relative according to action and reception. For example, it is in this way that all effects and causes are relative. The third fundament is in subjects relative by being one a measure and the other measurable, as cognitive powers are measured by the objects which properly specify them.

The sufficiency of this division St. Thomas establishes in the passage of his *Commentary on the Metaphysics of Aristotle* cited above.[4] To understand the *Commentary* at this point, one must bear in mind that, although every absolute category of mind-independent being can be the subject of a relation as materially receiving and denominated by the given relation, yet only those characteristics of subjects which have the rationale of ordering one subject to another can have the rationale of a fundament. Whence it happens that, as St. Thomas says in his *Disputed Questions on the Power of God*, q. 7, art. 8,[5] through "substance" and "quality," according to their proper concepts, a thing is not ordered to anything but itself otherwise than incidentally, inasmuch as a quality or a substantial form or matter possesses the rationale of an active or a passive energy, or according as some rationale of quantity—namely, unity (identity) or number [nonidentity]—is considered in them. Wherefore those things alone which induce a rationale of ordering one thing to another are foundations for re-

que extremo, sicut pater dicitur ad filium, non ad patrem, et dominus ad servum, non ad alium dominum. Et istae divisiones dicuntur *accidentales*, quia ratio mutui et non mutui, aequiparantiae vel disquiparantiae, non sumuntur directe penes fundamenta et terminos, sed consequuntur relationem secundum modum tangendi talem terminum et fundamentum, a quibus species relationis sumitur.

Secundo modo sumitur divisio relationis in species essentiales penes fundamenta relationum, quibus etiam debent correspondere diversi termini formales. Proposuit autem Philosophus 5. Metaph.,[2] lect. 17. apud D. Thomam,[3] tria fundamenta, quibus generaliter dividitur relatio. *Primum* fundamentum est penes unitatem et numerum, in quibus fundantur relationes similitudinis et dissimilitudinis, convenientiae et disconvenientiae etc. *Secundum* fundamentum est penes actionem et passionem sicut omnes effectus et causae. *Tertium* penes mensuram et mensurabile, sicut potentiae mensurantur a suis obiectis, a quibus specificantur.

SUFFICIENTIAM huius divisionis colligit S. Thomas loco cit.[4] Quae ut intelligatur, est advertendum, quod licet omne praedicamentum absolutum possit esse subiectum relationis, quasi materialiter recipiens illam et denominatum ab illa, non tamen potest habere rationem fundamenti nisi id, quod habet rationem ordinandi unum ad aliud. Ex quo fit, quod, ut dicit S. Thomas q. 7. de Potentia art. 8.,[5] per substantiam et qualitatem secundum suos proprios conceptus non ordinatur aliquid nisi ad seipsum, non ad alterum, nisi per accidens, secundum quod qualitas vel forma substantialis aut materia habet rationem virtutis activae vel passivae, aut in eis consideratur aliqua ratio quantitatis, id est unitas seu identitas aut numerus. Quare solum erunt fundamenta relationum illa, quae inducunt rationem ordinandi unum ad aliud. Omne

[2] c. 15. (1020 b 26).
[3] *Pa* XX. 420 a.
[4] 101/14-17.
[5] *Pa* VIII. 161 b.

lations. But every thing which is ordered to another is ordered either according to being, or according to operation—or power to operate, or according to proportion, that is to say, number and agreement. If it is ordered to another according to being, it is a fundament for relations of measure and measurable, because those things are measured which receive being and specification dependently from another. If according to operation and power, it is a fundament according to action and reception. If according to proportion and agreement, which the Philosopher calls according to quantity (that is, unity or number), it is a fundament for relations of unity and diversity, agreement and disagreement. But there is no fourth rationale habilitating and ordering one thing to another which cannot be reduced to one of these three.

Many of the customarily disputed points concerning the foundations of ontological relations pertain to Metaphysics. But the disputed points must be at least partially brought to resolution here, because without at least some awareness of these points, the rationale of the categorial relation cannot be perfectly isolated by the understanding. And the points of difficulty are reduced to three. First, whether mind-independent relations themselves, precisely as such, are able to found other relations. Second, whether each of these three fundaments truly founds categorial relations, or only relations according to the way being must be expressed in discourse. Third, whether relations of the second type [action (causing) and reception (being caused)] have for their immediate fundament the very action and reception, or the active and receptive dispositions. The explanation of the proper rationale and nature of the three fundaments will come out in the course of explaining these three points of basic difficulty.

The First Difficulty

Concerning the first difficulty,[6] there is dissention between the school of St. Thomas and the school of Scotus. For Scotus thinks that it is indeed possible for one categorial relation to be founded on another such relation. The principal ground for this opinion is the absence of any reason why we should say that all the other natures which agree and differ among themselves—whether they are substantial or accidental —found a relation of identity and agreement, but that two relations—for example, two paternities or two filiations—cannot found such relations, since they truly have agreement between themselves and disagreement from others. Now the argument that relations are of themselves relative forms

autem, quod ordinatur ad aliud, vel ordinatur secundum esse vel secundum operationem seu virtutem vel secundum proportionem seu numerum et convenientiam. Si secundum esse, est fundamentum mensurae et mensurabilis, quia ea mensurantur, quae accipiunt esse et specificationem ab alio. Si secundum operationem et virtutem, est fundamentum secundum actionem et passionem. Si secundum proportionem et convenientiam, quod Philosophus vocat secundum quantitatem, id est unitatem vel numerum, est fundamentum unitatis et diversitatis, convenientiae et disconvenientiae. Nulla autem alia ratio datur habilitans et ordinans unum ad alterum, quae ad istas non reducatur.

Plura autem solent circa ista fundamenta controverti, quae ad Metaphysicam spectant. Sed quia sine aliqua saltem eorum notitia non potest relationis praedicamentalis ratio perfecte dignosci, ideo saltem aliqua delibanda sunt. Et reducuntur ad TRES DIFFICULTATES: Prima, an ipsaemet relationes reales possint fundare alias. Secunda, an revera omnia ista tria fundamenta fundent relationes praedicamentales, an solum secundum dici. Tertia, an relationes secundi generis habeant pro fundamento immediato ipsam actionem et passionem, an potentiam activam et passivam. In quibus difficultatibus explicandis obiter explicabitur propria ratio et natura talium fundamentorum.

Prima difficultas.

Circa primam difficultatem[6] est dissensio inter scholam D. Thomae et Scoti. Nam Scotus putat super relationem posse etiam fundari aliam relationem praedicamentalem. Cuius praecipua ratio est, quia non est, unde dicamus, quod omnes aliae naturae, sive substantiales sive accidentales, quae conveniunt et differunt inter se, fundent relationem identitatis et convenientiae, duae autem relationes, v. g. duae paternitates vel duae filiationes, id non possint fundare, cum vere habeant convenientiam inter se et disconvenientiam ab aliis. Quod vero relationes sint formae relativae seipsis ideoque

[6] 102/23-25.

and for this reason do not seem to need other relations in order to be similar or dissimilar, is a futile argument, because paternity, for example, is a form of being related in the nature of father, not in the nature of similar or dissimilar; therefore it will need other relative forms in order to be similar or dissimilar.

And this is confirmed by the fact that proportionality is defined (according to Euclid[7]) as a similarity of two proportions. Therefore upon proportions, which are relations, is founded another relation, namely, one of similarity.

Nevertheless, ST. THOMAS EXPRESSLY HOLDS THE OPPOSITE, in the *Summa theologica*, I, q. 42, art. 1, reply to obj. 4. And generally many authors agree. The FOUNDATION FOR THIS OPINION is the fact that a progression into infinity among relations would follow. For if paternity, for example, founds a relation of similarity to another paternity, it will also found a relation of dissimilarity to filiation or to any other relation. And again that relation of dissimilarity will found another of similarity to a similar type of relation, and the relation of similarity will found a dissimilarity to any other type. And so, by alternating into infinity, a relation of similarity will found a relation of dissimilarity to another and the relation of dissimilarity will found a relation of similarity to the similar. But for there to be an infinity of relations is antinomic, both for the general reason against positing an actual infinite—about which we speak in discussing Book 3 of Aristotle's *Physics*[8]—and for a special reason, because in causes with respect to effects there cannot be a progression into infinity because the infinite is not traversible, neither by motion nor by causality. For there will not be an assignable final effect, if infinite causalities and effects precede. But the fundaments of relations are the causes or principles from which the relations result; therefore there is not an infinite regress in them.

A twofold solution is usually assigned to this argument. The first solution admits a progression into infinity among relations, in the way that the division of a continuum into undesignatable parts is infinite. Others stop the progression with relations that are referred according to the same rationale; in this way, for example, two paternities found a relation of identity, yet the relation of identity so founded does not found another relation of

non videantur indigere aliis relationibus, ut sint similes vel dissimiles, futile est, quia paternitas v. g. est forma referendi in ratione patris, non in ratione similis vel dissimilis, ergo indigebit aliis formis relativis, ut sint similes vel dissimiles.

Et confirmatur, quia proportionalitas secundum Euclidem[7] definitur similitudo duarum proportionum. Ergo super proportiones, quae sunt relationes, fundatur alia relatio, quae est similitudinis.

Nihilominus oppositum tenet expresse S. Thomas 1. p. q. 42. art. 1. ad 4. Et communiter multi auctores sequuntur. FUNDAMENTUM EST, quia sequeretur processus in infinitum in relationibus. Nam si paternitas v. g. fundat relationem similitudinis ad aliam paternitatem, etiam fundabit relationem dissimilitudinis ad filiationem vel ad aliam relationem. Et rursus illa relatio dissimilitudinis fundabit aliam similitudinis ad similem speciem relationis, et relatio similitudinis fundabit dissimilitudinem ad aliam speciem. Et sic alternando in infinitum similitudo fundabit dissimilitudinem ad aliud et dissimilitudo ad simile. Dari autem infinitas relationes est inconveniens tum propter generalem rationem ponendi infinitum in actu, de quo dicemus 3. Phys.,[8] tum propter specialem rationem, quia in causis respectu effectuum non potest dari processus in infinitum, quia infinitum non est pertransibile neque per motum neque per causalitatem. Non enim erit assignabilis ultimus effectus, si infinitae causalitates et effectus praecedunt. Fundamenta autem relationum sunt causae seu principia, ex quibus resultant; ergo in illis non datur processus in infinitum.

DUPLEX SOLUTIO assignari solet huic argumento. Prima admittit processum in infinitum in relationibus, sicut divisio continui in partes indesignabiles infinita est. Alii sistunt processum in relationibus, quae referuntur secundum eandem rationem; sicut duae paternitates fundant relationem identitatis, tamen relatio identitatis sic fundata non fundat aliam relationem

[7] Element. (1. 5.) defin. 3., 4., 7.
[8] Phil. nat. 1. p. q. 15.

similarity and identity, but by itself respects all identity.

But the first solution admits a progression into infinity in causes, which is rejected by the Philosopher in Book II, chap. 2, of the *Metaphysics*,[9] and which clearly calls for rejection, because if for one effect infinite concourses or causalities are required, it is never possible to designate a final effect, because there is no assignable final concourse [of causes]. Moreover, even though in the case of the absolute power of God there is room for doubt whether there can be an actual infinite, yet no one doubts that it cannot be given naturally, as is proved in my discussion of Book III of the *Physics*.[10] There is therefore no infinite progression in the causation of relations. The example of the division of the continuum is not to the point, because that infinity is not one of actually divided parts, but is a quantity divisible potentially and syncategorematically; but the relations in our case are actually infinite.

The second solution, on the other hand, is excluded by the reason given above.[11] For we do not say that on one relation is founded only a relation of similarity which, by itself in all cases and not through a superadded relation, will have a similarity to others, but we also say[12] that that one relation founds a relation of dissimilarity, just as it founds one of similarity. And then by alternating, the infinite progression follows, because upon the relation of similarity we found one of dissimilarity, and upon the relation of dissimilarity we found one of similarity. And again by commutating we find always a new relation and a procession into infinity, which argument the second solution does not render void, speaking as it does only of a relation of one rationale.

The response to the basis of the opposed argument[13] is that relations of the same type indeed have a similarity and agreement that is quasi-transcendental [i.e., according to the way they must be expressed in discourse], but not a categorial relative, for otherwise an infinite progression would result, as has been said. But we can investigate a-priori the reason for this, in terms of the feebleness of relation, which has so minimal a rationale of entitative being that it is not sufficient to found a mind-independent relation; for in fact every fundament must

similitudinis et identitatis, sed seipsa respicit omnem identitatem.

Sed prima solutio admittit processum in infinitum in causis, qui a Philosopho reprobatur in 2. Metaph.[9] et ex se patet, quia si ad unum effectum requiruntur infiniti concursus seu causalitates, numquam potest signari ultimus effectus, quia non est designabilis ultimus concursus. Et praeterea, licet de potentia absoluta vertatur in dubium, an possit dari infinitum in actu, tamen naturaliter nullus dubitat dari non posse, ut 3. Phys. probatur.[10] Non ergo datur processus in infinitum in causatione relationum. Exemplum autem de divisione continui non est ad rem, quia illa infinitas non est partium actu divisarum, sed est quantitas divisibilis in potentia et syncategorematice; relationes autem in nostro casu sunt infinitae actu.

Secunda vero solutio ex ratione supra posita[11] exclusa est. Non enim dicimus in una relatione solum fundari relationem similitudinis, quae utique seipsa, et non per relationem superadditam, similitudinem habebit ad alias, sed etiam dicimus[12] unam relationem fundare relationem dissimilitudinis, sicut fundat similitudinis. Et tunc alternando sequitur processus in infinitum, cum super relationem similitudinis fundamus dissimilitudinem et super relationem dissimilitudinis fundamus similitudinem. Et iterum commutando invenimus semper novam relationem et processum in infinitum. Quod solutio ista non evacuat, quae solum loquitur de relatione unius rationis.

AD OPPOSITUM VERO FUNDAMENTUM[13] respondetur, quod relationes eiusdem speciei habent quidem similitudinem et convenientiam quasi transcendentalem, non relativam praedicamentalem, ne sequatur processus in infinitum, ut dictum est. A priori autem possumus investigare rationem huius ex debilitate relationis, quae tam minimae entitatis est, ut non sufficiat ad fundandam relationem realem; omne quippe

[9] c. 2. (994 a 1); S. Thom. lect. 2. (*Pa* XX. 300 b, 301).
[10] Phil. nat. 1. p. q. 15. art. 1. et 2.
[11] at 103/15-27.
[12] 103/17-27.
[13] 102/39-48.

be more perfect than that which is founded, just as one accident cannot substand another by sustaining that other, as we said in q. 15,[14] because it does not have a more perfect mode of being. Thus, since all relations are equal in the mode of being relative, one cannot be the fundament of another.

To the confirmation[15] the response is as follows. Admitting Euclid's definition of proportionality, it remains for Scotus to prove that the similarity or equality of proportions in question is a relation distinct from and founded upon the relations of the proportions; for it suffices for that equality to be transcendental.

The Second Difficulty

Concerning the second difficulty,[16] some have said that relations of the first and third type are not categorial. But some think that all relations of the first type are mind-dependent, because their fundament supposes something produced by the mind, namely, a formal or essential unity common to many, otherwise a relation of the first type will not be founded on unity.

Others think that relations of the first type are transcendental, because unity and number, upon which these relations are founded, are something transcendental and found in every category. For there is not any reason why we should say that a relation of unity and number is restricted only to quantitative number, since a relation of similarity and difference is found even in the case of pure spirits.

Finally, some exclude relations of the first type from the category of mind-independent relation, since they think relations of this type are extrinsic denominations, both because the multitude of relative entities will otherwise be immensely multiplied, since the combinations of agreement and disagreement are practically infinite; and because paternity and filiation in the case of the divine Persons do not found mind-independent relations of similarity and diversity, therefore these relations are not of themselves mind-independent; and because coexistence or distance bespeak extrinsic denomination, as does the rationale of a right-hand side in a column. Therefore diversity and similarity will likewise be extrinsic denominations.

fundamentum debet esse perfectius eo, quod fundatur, sicut unum accidens non potest substare alteri sustentando illud, ut diximus q. 15.,[14] quia non habet perfectiorem modum essendi. Sic cum omnes relationes sint aequales in modo essendi relativo, una non potest esse fundamentum alterius.

Ad confirmationem[15] respondetur admittendo definitionem Euclidis de proportionalitate. Sed restat probandum Scoto, quod ista similitudo seu aequalitas proportionum sit relatio distincta et fundata super relationibus proportionum; sufficit enim, quod sit transcendentalis illa aequalitas.

Secunda difficultas.

Circa secundum[16] aliqui dixerunt RELATIONES PRIMI ET TERTII GENERIS non esse praedicamentales. Sed quidam existimant esse rationis, quia fundamentum relationum primi generis supponit aliquid rationis, id est unitatem formalem vel essentialem, communem multis, alias non poterit fundari super unitatem.

Alii existimant esse transcendentales, quia unitas et numerus, super quod fundantur istae relationes, sunt aliquid transcendentale et in omni genere inventum. Nec enim est aliqua ratio, cur dicamus relationem unitatis et numeri solum restringi ad numerum quantitativum. Cum etiam in angelis inveniatur relatio similitudinis et differentiae.

Denique alii excludunt RELATIONES PRIMI GENERIS a praedicamento relationis, quia putant esse denominationes extrinsecas, *tum* quia alias multiplicabitur in immensum multitudo entitatum relativarum, cum sint fere infinitae combinationes convenientiae et disconvenientiae; *tum* quia paternitas et filiatio in divinis non fundant relationes reales similitudinis et diversitatis, ergo ex se istae relationes reales non sunt; *tum* quia coexistentia vel distantia dicunt extrinsecam denominationem, sicut ratio dextri in columna. Ergo similiter diversitas et similitudo erunt denominationes extrinsecae.

---

[14] Logica 2. p. q. 15. art. 2.
[15] 103/7-11.
[16] 102/25-28.

Turning to relations of the third type, some exclude these from the category of mind-independent relation, because they place them among the transcendentals. For it seems superfluous that in the case of knowledge relative to the knowable there should be [both] a categorial relation and a transcendental relation of the sort that remains in knowledge when the knowable is destroyed. Others think that relations of the third type are extrinsic denominations, because even though knowledge founds a categorial relation to the knowable, nevertheless, that relation is not a relation of this third type, but of the first or of the second type. On the other hand, Aristotle does not count the relation of knowledge to knowable or of measured to measure in this third type, but, on the contrary, the relation of the knowable to knowledge and of the measure to the measured, as is clear in Book V of the *Metaphysics*, chap. 15;[17] but a relation of measure to measured is not a mind-independent relation.

Nevertheless, **it must be asserted, as common opinion holds, that relations of both the first and the third type are categorial,** which is the view shared by Aristotle and St. Thomas and Scotus.

And the sole reason is that all the factors required for a categorial relation concur in the case of these relations,[18] no less than in relations of the second type. For in these are found mind-independent correlatives mind-independently distinct, namely, those things between which there is similarity or diversity, mensuration and measure. There is also found an existing terminus, as I now suppose; for if the existence of the terminus is wanting, the categorial relation will perish, even as in the case of relations of the second type. There is similarly a mind-independent fundament [i.e., a fundament which does not depend for its being on being known objectively] in relations of the third type, indeed, one of dependence in specification upon the object, just as in relations of the second type the physical foundation of the relations is the dependence of effect upon cause; and the fundament is distinct from the relation itself of the second type, because, as St. Thomas well notes in his *Commentary on the Metaphysics of Aristotle*, Book V, reading 17,[19] the fundament of the third type of relation is the commensuration to the specifying object, not a proportion or unity, as in the first type, or an action and efficiency, as in the second. Similarly in relations of the first type, the fundament is something mind-independent, not indeed some

Relationes autem tertii generis quidam excludunt a praedicamento relationis, quia reiciunt illas ad transcendentales. Videtur enim superfluum, quod in scientia ad scibile detur relatio praedicamentalis et transcendentalis, qualis est, quae remanet in scientia destructo scibili. Alii existimant esse denominationes extrinsecas, quia licet scientia fundet relationem praedicamentalem ad scibile, tamen illa non est relatio huius tertii generis, sed primi vel secundi. In hoc autem tertio genere Aristoteles non numerat relationem scientiae ad scibile vel mensurati ad mensuram, sed e converso scibilis ad scientiam et mensurae ad mensuratum, ut patet in 5. Metaph. cap. 15.;[17] mensurae autem non est relatio realis.

Nihilominus **cum communi sententia asserendum est utrumque genus relationum, primum et tertium, esse praedicamentale**, ut cum Aristotele et D. Thoma et Scoto tenetur communiter.

Et ratio unica est, quia concurrunt in istis relationibus omnia, quae ad relationem praedicamentalem requiruntur,[18] non minus quam in relationibus secundi generis. Nam in istis inveniuntur correlativa realia realiter distincta, scilicet illa, inter quae est similitudo aut diversitas, mensuratio et mensura. Invenitur etiam terminus existens, ut nunc suppono; nam si existentia termini deficiat, peribit relatio, sicut etiam in relationibus secundi generis. Similiter datur fundamentum reale, in relationibus quidem tertii generis dependentiae in specificatione ab obiecto, sicut in relationibus secundi generis dependentiae effectus a causa; et distinctum est fundamentum ab ipsa relatione secundi generis, quia, ut bene notat D. Thomas 5. Metaph. lect. 17.,[19] fundamentum tertii generis est commensuratio ad obiectum specificans, non proportio seu unitas, ut in primo, vel actio et efficientia, ut in secundo. Similiter in relationibus primi generis fundamentum est aliquid reale, non quidem unitas aliqua communis exis-

---

[17] 1020 b 30.
[18] Cf. 91/3-20.
[19] *Pa* XX. 421 a, b.

common unity existing in many, but an agreement or conformity of the sort that is in distinct subjects, as, for example, on the side of physical nature Peter and Paul are alike, Peter and a horse are not alike. The rationale of the categorial relation, therefore, is found no less in relations of the first and third type than in relations of the second type.

You may say: In relations of the first type, the rationale of founding, namely, unity or agreement, is not found distinct from the subject, as in relations of the second type action is distinguished from the power to act. But in the first place this is false in the case of a relation of accidental similarity. Second, in the case of an essential similarity, why must the rationale of founding be distinguished from the subject? For there is required a mind-independent distinction only between the extremes of relations, but why is a mind-independent distinction necessary between the subject and the rationale of founding? And if it is legitimate to argue from divine to created things, one finds there a rationale of founding not distinct from the Father, namely, generative power, and yet it founds a mind-independent relation.

Nor again does it matter that among these relations of the first and of the third type are sometimes found transcendental relations, as between knowledge and the knowable, and sometimes between similar extremes. For in the first place, if this were an obstacle, even relations of the second type would be obliterated, because between a cause and an effect there is a transcendental relation, as, for example, the transcendental relation of a creature to God, because an effect respects not only under the rationale of a pure terminus but under the rationale of a cause. Second, in the case of relations of similarity and difference, we see that when the term is destroyed the relation of similarity ceases; therefore there was not only a transcendental relation, because this relation does not perish when the term perishes, but there is also a categorial relation. And this appears much more clearly in the case of a relation of accidental similarity, which is founded on something superadded, but does not transcend.

To the foundations of the arguments opposed to relations of the first type being categorial:[20] To the first argument,[21] the response is that these relations are not said to be founded on unity according as unity bespeaks indivision (since a relation requires rather divided and distinct extremes), but on unity according as it bespeaks an agreement and conform-

tens in multis, sed convenientia vel conformitas, qualis est in distinctis subiectis, sicut a parte rei Petrus et Paulus conveniunt, Petrus et equus disconveniunt. Nihil ergo minus invenitur ratio praedicamentalis relationis in istis quam in secundo genere.

Dices: Non invenitur in relationibus primi generis ratio fundandi distincta a subiecto, scilicet unitas seu convenientia, sicut in relationibus secundi generis actio distinguitur a potentia. Sed *imprimis* hoc est falsum in relatione similitudinis accidentalis. *Deinde* in similitudine essentiali cur requiritur, quod ratio fundandi distinguatur a subiecto? Solum enim requiritur distinctio realis inter extrema relationum, inter subiectum autem et rationem fundandi cur est necessaria? Et si a divinis ad creata fas est argumentari, ibi invenitur ratio fundandi, v. g. potentia generativa indistincta a Patre, et tamen fundat relationem realem.

Nec iterum obstat, quod in his aliquando inveniuntur relationes transcendentales, ut inter scientiam et scibile, et aliquando inter extrema similia. Nam *imprimis*, si hoc obstaret, etiam relationes secundi generis essent ablegandae, quia inter effectum et causam datur transcendentalis relatio, ut creaturae ad Deum, quia non solum sub ratione puri termini, sed sub ratione causae respicit effectus. *Deinde* in relationibus similitudinis et diversitatis videmus, quod destructo termino deficit relatio similitudinis; ergo non solum erat transcendentalis relatio, quia haec non perit pereunte termino, sed est praedicamentalis. Et multo melius id apparet in relatione similitudinis accidentalis, quae fundatur in aliquo superaddito, non autem transcendit.

Ad fundamenta opposita:[20] *Ad primum,*[21] contra relationes primi generis, respondetur, quod istae relationes non dicuntur fundari in unitate, prout unitas dicit indivisionem, cum potius relatio divisa et distincta extrema requirat, sed in unitate, prout dicit convenientiam et conformitatem, quae

---

[20] 105/18-47.
[21] 105/18-23.

ity which is in several subjects. A formal unity made by the mind and positively undivided, therefore, is not needed.

To the second argument[22] it is said that the fundament of this relation is found materially in all the categories of mind-independent being, but formally it is always one thing, namely, agreement or unity, in whatever class or category it is found. And this argument applies in the same way against relations of the second type. For action and reception, cause and effect, are also found in diverse categories of mind-independent being; for all things are effects of God, many are also causes, at least material or formal causes [if not productive ones].

To the third argument against admitting that there are categorial relations founded on unity and number[23] the response is that that multitude of relations[24] in no way frightens us into denying that there are such relations; for howsoever great, it is finite. Moreover, by holding with St. Thomas that one relation is terminated by several numerically distinct terms, the multitude of relations is sufficiently moderated. Concerning the case of the divine Persons,[25] we say that there is another reason why paternity and filiation do not found mind-independent relations of similarity and diversity, namely, because (as was said above) mind-independent relations are not founded on other relations. But no argument that there cannot be mind-independent relations of similarity or diversity among created absolute things follows thence. Concerning coexistence and distance,[26] I say that nothing prevents their being mind-independent relations just as are similarity and difference. Nor is it like the case of a right and a left side, which is found physically only in an animal in which there is a heart or other organs from which the right part draws strength and energies, which is not found in a column, but a column is said to be on the right denominatively by the juxtaposition of an animal.

To the arguments raised against relations of the third type being categorial:[27] To the first argument[28] the response is that even if there is a transcendental relation, a categorial relation is not superfluous; nay rather, a categorial relation is frequently founded on a transcendental relation, as in the case of a relation to a cause founded on an effect. And the transcendental relation too serves a

in pluribus subiectis est. Non est ergo expectanda unitas formalis facta per rationem et positive indivisa.

Ad secundum[22] dicitur, quod fundamentum huius relationis materialiter divagatur per omnia genera, sed formaliter semper est unum, scilicet convenientia seu unitas, in quocumque genere seu praedicamento inveniatur. Et eodem modo procedit hoc argumentum contra relationes secundi generis. Nam etiam actio et passio, causa et effectus in diversis praedicamentis reperitur; omnia enim effectus sunt Dei, plura etiam sunt causae saltem materiales aut formales.

Ad tertium[23] respondetur, quod illa multitudo relationum[24] nullo modo nos terret, ut negemus dari tales relationes; quantumcumque enim grandis, finita est, praeterquam quod in sententia D. Thomae ponentis, unam relationem ad plures terminos numero distinctos terminari, satis moderata est relationum mulititudo. De relationibus[25] dicimus esse aliam rationem, quia, ut supra dictum est, relationes reales non fundantur in aliis relationibus. Inde tamen non fit argumentum, quod in rebus creatis absolutis non possit dari relatio realis similitudinis vel diversitatis. De coexistentia et distantia[26] dico nihil prohibere, quod sint relationes reales sicut similitudo et differentia. Nec est simile de dextro et sinistro, quod solum invenitur realiter in animali, in quo est cor vel alia organa, a quibus dextera pars trahit robur et vires, quod in columna non invenitur, sed dicitur dextera denominative a iuxtapositione animalis.

Ad ea, quae obiciuntur contra relationes tertii generis:[27] *Ad primam partem*[28] respondetur non esse superfluam relationem praedicamentalem, etiamsi detur transcendentalis, imo plerumque praedicamentalis in transcendentali; fundatur, ut in effectu relatio ad causam. Et deservit etiam

[22] 105/24-32.
[23] 105/33-47.
[24] 105/36-39.
[25] 105/40-43.
[26] 105/44-46.
[27] 106/1-18.
[28] 106/1-7.

purpose, because even when the terminus is removed and destroyed, the transcendental order remains, but not the categorial one.

To the second argument[29] the response is that the meaning of the Philosopher's text must be taken from where he first posited a relation on the part of measurable to measure, saying:[30] "Other relatives are related as measurable to measure." Then he gives the example: "as the knowable to knowledge, the sensible to sense," in order to show that these relations are not reciprocal, a point which he had made more explicitly when he was explaining those extremes [namely, the termini of relations of the third type] on whose part there is no relation, but which are denominated [relative] by other extremes [that is, the subjects of the relations] in which there are true relations, not extrinsic denominations.

The reason why the relations of this third type are not reciprocal is given by St. Thomas in the *Summa theologica*, I, q. 13, art. 7, and in his *Disputed Questions on the Power of God*, q. 7, art. 10.[31] It is that the extremes are not of the same order, but one depends upon and is subordinated to the other, not conversely, because, as is plain, one is measure, the other measurable, one perfecting, the other perfectible; but something perfecting as perfecting does not depend on the perfectible, but the reverse. Whence they are not ordered reciprocally, but only the one is [categorially] ordered to the other. And thus God is independent of the order of creatures, the sensible is independent of sense, the intelligible is independent of understanding, because all these act or specify without change of themselves, and so they belong to another order, that is to say, they are outside or independent of the change of their correlatives, as they do not depend on one another nor are they reciprocally referred.

The Third Difficulty

Authors preoccupy themselves with the third point,[32] and some anxiously enough. But the matter does not seem to me of great moment. All agree that an action is required at least as a condition, and also that a proximate and radical principle of action is required. But Scotus, in his *Commentary on the Sentences of Peter Lombard*, Book IV, dist. 6, q. 10, and in his *Commentary on the Metaphysics of Aristotle*, Book V, chap. 14, says that since the action passes and the relation endures, the action cannot be the fundament of the relation, because when a fundament is removed, the relation which adheres to or is identified

transcendentalis, quia adhuc remoto et destructo termino manet transcendentalis ordo, non praedicamentalis.

Ad secundam partem[29] respondetur sensum Philosophi ex littera desumi, ubi prius posuit relationem ex parte mensurabilis ad mensuram dicens:[30] «Alia relativa se habent ut mensurabile ad mensuram». Deinde subdit exemplum, «ut scibile ad scientiam, sensibile ad sensum», ut ostenderet has relationes mutuas non esse, quod expressius fiebat explicando illa extrema, ex parte quorum relatio non datur, sed ab altero extremo denominantur, in quo relationes verae sunt, non denominationes extrinsecae.

Cur autem relationes istius tertii generis mutuae non sint, rationem reddit D. Thomas 1. p. q. 13. art. 7. et q. 7. de Potentia art. 10.,[31] quia extrema non sunt eiusdem ordinis, sed unum dependet et subordinatur alteri, non e converso, quia videlicet unum est mensura, alterum mensurabile, unum perficiens, alterum perfectibile; perficiens autem ut perficiens non pendet a perfectibili, sed e converso. Unde non mutuo ordinantur, sed unum tantum ordinatur ad aliud. Et sic Deus est extra ordinem creaturae, sensibile extra sensum, intelligibile extra intellectum, quia haec omnia sine mutatione sui agunt aut specificant, et ita sunt extra ordinem, id est extra mutationem suorum correlativorum, ut non mutuo pendeant nec referantur.

Tertia difficultas.

Circa tertium punctum[32] decertant AUCTORES, et aliqui satis anxie. Mihi vero videtur res non tanti momenti. Conveniunt omnes requiri actionem saltem ut conditionem, requiri etiam principium actionis proximum et radicale. Sed Scotus in 4. dist. 6. q. 10. et 5. Metaph. cap. 14. inquit, quod cum actio transeat et relatio duret, non potest actio esse fundamentum relationis, quia sublato fundamento concidit relatio, quae ei adhaeret vel identificatur.

---

29 106/8-18.
30 1020 b 30.
31 *Pa* VIII. 165 a, b.
32 102/28-34.

with it is destroyed. Action is required therefore for the founding of a relation as a condition in the order of becoming, [but] not for keeping the relation in being as is the fundament.

Others, such as Suarez in his *Metaphysical Disputations*, disp. 47, sect. 12, n. 5, the better to provide for the conservation of the relation, say that it is founded neither on the action nor on the proximate power, but on the radical or root power, that is, on the substance itself, because a father has an actual relation of paternity not only after the action passes, but even if the power of generating is lost; therefore this relation cannot be founded on the proximate power. For if the power itself were the fundament, the very fact of the power's being destroyed would put an end to the relation; for when the fundament is removed, a relation does not remain. This argument recommends itself to those who distinguish proximate from root powers; for they are bound to say that, if a relation is founded on a power, and if when the fundament passes the relation does not remain, then, when the proximate power is destroyed, the relation of an action does not remain if it was founded on that power; whence if it does remain, it must be founded on the root power. But Scotus, who does not distinguish proximate from root powers, consequently does not admit that a proximate power is lost unless the substance is destroyed, although the power's action would be blocked if the organ upon which it depends were destroyed.

Nevertheless, THE OPINION OF ST. THOMAS holds that these **relations of the second type are founded upon action and reception as on the proper fundament, and not only as a requisite condition.** For action and reception are required generally as a condition for any and every relation, because, as St. Thomas says in his *Commentary on the Sentences of Peter Lombard*, Book I, dist. 9,[33] a new relation cannot arise in anything mind-independently except through a movement, specifically, one mediately terminated at the very relation, immediately at the fundament or terminus. And we do not doubt that some relations are founded immediately upon an active power itself, as a power of heating respects something able to be heated; for the power has this relation antecedently to an action, since indeed this relation is not to an effect, but to an object able to be affected insofar as it is an object of that power,

Requiritur ergo actio ad fundandam relationem quasi in fieri ut conditio, non ad conservandum in esse tamquam fundamentum.

Alii, ut P. Suarez disp. 47. Metaph. sect. 12. n. 5., ut melius provideant conservationi relationis, dicunt eam neque in actione neque in potentia proxima fundari, sed in radicali, id est in ipsa substantia, quia pater relationem paternitatis in actu habet, non solum postquam transit actio, sed etiam si potentia generandi amittatur; ergo non potest relatio ista fundari in potentia proxima. Si enim ipsa esset fundamentum, hoc ipso quod destrueretur, desineret esse relatio; fundamento enim sublato relatio non manet. Quod argumentum urget in sententia distinguentium potentias proximas a radicalibus; tenentur enim dicere, quod si relatio fundatur in potentia et transeunte fundamento non manet relatio, quod destructa potentia proxima relatio actionis non manet, si in illa fundatur, unde si manet, fundari debet in radicali potentia. Sed Scotus, qui non distinguit potentias proximas a radicalibus, consequenter non admittit, quod tollatur potentia proxima nisi destructa substantia, licet possit impediri, ne agat, si destruatur organum, a quo potentia dependet.

NIHILOMINUS **sententia D. Thomae tenet relationes istas secundi generis fundari supra actionem et passionem tamquam supra fundamentum proprium, et non solum tamquam conditionem requisitam.** Hoc enim generaliter requiritur ad omnem relationem, quia, ut dicit D. Thomas in 1. dist. 9. in exposit. litterae,[33] non potest relatio nova nasci realiter in aliquo nisi per motum, scilicet mediate terminatum ad ipsam relationem, immediate ad fundamentum vel terminum. Et non dubitamus aliquas relationes fundari immediate super ipsam potentiam activam, sicut calefactivum respicit calefactibile; hoc enim antecedenter habet ad actionem, siquidem ista relatio non est ad effectum, sed ad obiectum factibile, in quantum obiectum est illius potentiae,

[33] *Pa* VI. 88 b.

and is therefore reduced to a relation of the third type rather [than of the second type], because it is in the mode of a commensuration, as is gathered from St. Thomas's *Commentary on the Metaphysics of Aristotle*, Book V, reading 17.[34]

But when speaking of a relation of the second type, because it is not to the affectable, but to the affected or effect, St. Thomas always teaches that it is founded upon action or reception, as is clear in the *Summa theologica*, I, q. 28, art. 4, the *Summa of the Whole Logic of Aristotle*, chap. 4 of the Tractate on the category of relation,[35] and the *Summa contra gentiles*, Book IV, chap. 24. But more explicitly and better in the *Commentary on the Sentences of Peter Lombard*, Book III, dist. 8, q. 1, art. 5,[36] where, after having said that these relations are founded on action and reception, St. Thomas adds: "It must likewise be considered that certain relations do not arise from acts according as they are in act, but rather according as they were, as, for example, someone is called a father after a pregnancy follows from an act of sexual intercourse, and such relations are founded upon that which is left in the agent from the action, whether it be a disposition or a habit or some right and power or whatever else is of this kind." From these words it is clear that actions are not said to found relations according as the actions are producing but according as they have in fact produced,[37] and therefore actions leave on the side of the effect the production of that effect, indeed, but on the side of the cause they leave some determination to the past effect, whether through habit or through disposition or right or anything of the kind. For that there is such a determination or change left in the cause, even when the action is over, is clear from the fact that a created cause, when its action is over and an effect produced, respects this effect otherwise than it had formerly respected it. For formerly it had respected that effect as something producible by itself; but after it has produced, it no longer respects that effect as producible by itself, whether this be extrinsically or intrinsically, because a created cause cannot produce the numerically same effect twice. Therefore that relation or transcending order to the effect formerly possible for itself, is different from the order to the effect no longer so possible, the reason for which fact is that the cause respects that [latter] effect as produced, and so some determina-

ideoque potius reducitur ad relationem tertii generis, quia est per modum commensurationis, ut ex D. Thoma colligitur 5. Metaph. lect. 17.[34]

Loquendo autem de relatione secundi generis, quia non est ad factibile, sed ad factum seu effectum, semper docet D. Thomas fundari supra actionem vel passionem, ut patet 1. p. q. 28. art. 4. et opusc. 48. tract. de Relatione cap. 4.[35] et 4. Contra Gent. cap. 24. Sed expressius et melius in 3. dist. 8. q. 1. art. 5.,[36] ubi postquam dixit fundari relationes istas in actione et passione, subdit: «Item considerandum est, quod quaedam relationes non innascuntur ex actibus, secundum quod sunt in actu, sed magis secundum quod fuerunt, sicut aliquis dicitur pater, postquam ex actione est effectus consecutus, et tales relationes fundantur super id, quod in agente ex actione relinquitur, sive sit dispositio sive habitus sive aliquod ius et potestas vel quidquid aliud est huiusmodi». Ex quibus verbis constat, quod actiones non dicuntur fundare relationes, secundum quod sunt in fieri, sed secundum quod in facto esse,[37] atque adeo relinquunt ex parte quidem effectus productionem illius, ex parte vero causae determinationem aliquam ad effectum praeteritum, sive per habitum sive per dispositionem aut ius vel aliquid simile. Quod enim talis determinatio seu mutatio detur in causa, etiam transacta actione, manifestum relinquitur, quia causa creata transacta actione et effectu producto aliter respicit hunc effectum quam antea respiciebat. Antea enim respiciebat illum ut factibilem a se; postquam autem produxit, non amplius respicit illum ut factibilem a se, sive hoc sit ab extrinseco sive ab intrinseco, quia causa creata non potest reproducere eundem numero effectum. Variatur ergo relatio illa seu ordo transcendens ad effectum antea sibi possibilem, iam sibi non possibilem, quod ideo est, quia respicit illum ut factum, et sic relinquitur deter-

---

[34] *Pa* XX. 421 a, b.

[35] Summa tot. Log. Arist. (*Pa* XVII. 74).

[36] *Pa* VII. 103 a.

[37] i.e., actions found relations not as the actions pertain to the order of becoming but as they are absorbed into the order of being.

tion or change or ordination to the produced effect is left in the cause, by reason of which it is ordered to that effect as to something produced and no longer as to something possible, which is not the case for God, who, even after he has produced an effect once, is able to produce that selfsame effect again a second time. We have therefore the explanation of how a relation of the second type is founded when the action is over, to wit, it is not founded upon the bare power, but on the power as determined by the action, even when the action itself is over, and so it is truly founded upon the action, not as on a becoming, but on the determination it leaves in the cause.

Whence the answer to the foundation of the opposed argument[38] is that when a fundament is removed a relation is removed. But the fundament of the relation in question is not a radical or proximate principle considered without qualification; for so considered, a principle bespeaks only the relation of something able to act, not of something acting, for one who is able to procreate is not called a father, but one who procreates. Whence these relations of the second type must have for the specifying fundament, and not only for a necessary condition, an action as such and not only the power. For the specific rationale of these relations is not according to some ability to act, but according to action. But that from which the specification is taken functions as the fundament and not as a condition; yet a relation of this second type is not founded on an action inasmuch as the action briefly endures in act, but inasmuch as it leaves its determination in the power, not only proximate, but also radical; which determination is not removed as long as the radical or root principle endures, even if the action passes or the proximate power is destroyed.

minatio aliqua seu immutatio aut ordinatio in causa ad effectum productum, ratione cuius ordinatur ad illum ut ad factum et non amplius ut possibilem, quod non est in Deo, qui etiam postquam produxit effectum, potest reproducere. Habemus ergo transacta actione quomodo fundetur relatio, scilicet non super nuda potentia, sed determinata ab actione, etiam actione ipsa transacta, et sic vere super actione fundatur, non ut in fieri, sed ut in sua determinatione manet in causa.

UNDE AD OPPOSITUM FUNDAMENTUM[38] respondetur, quod remoto fundamento removetur relatio. Sed fundamentum in hac relatione non est radicale vel proximum principium nude sumptum; sic enim solum dicit relationem potentis agere, non agentis, neque enim dicitur pater, qui potest generare, sed qui generavit. Unde relationes istae secundi generis debent habere pro fundamento specificante, et non solum pro conditione requisita, ipsam actionem et non solum potentiam. Species enim harum relationum non est secundum posse agere, sed secundum agere. Illud autem, a quo sumitur specificatio, ut fundamentum se habet et non ut conditio, nec tamen fundatur in actione, quatenus brevi durat in actu, sed quatenus determinationem sui derelinquit in potentia, non solum proxima, sed etiam radicali; quae determinatio non tollitur, quamdiu radicale principium durat, etiamsi actio transeat vel potentia proxima destruatur.

---

[38] 109/45-110/1, 110/14-16, 110/21-22.

ARTIS LOGICAE, PRIMA PARS. DE DIALECTICIS INSTITVTIONIBVS, QVAS SVMMVLAS VOCANT.

AVTHORE P. M. F. IOANNE DE S. Thoma Lusitano Ordinis Prædicatorum, insignis Collegij S. Thom. Regente, & in Complutensi Academia publico Theologiæ Professore in Cathedra Vespertina.

EDITIO SECVNDA CASTIGATIOR.

Anno 1634

CVM PRIVILEGIO.

Compluti, Apud ANTONIVM VAZQVEZ, Typographum Vniuersitatis.

LECTORI.

BReuitatem se[c]tantes ociosum videbitur moro sa præfatione diffundi, vel ipsa Spiritus Sancti sententia id prædamnante 2. Macha. 2. *Stultum est ante historiam diffluere, in ipsa verò historia succingi*. Ne ergo tædium, & onus Lectori in ipso limine inijciamus, tantum admonuerim, studij nostri scopũ eo collimasse, vt ad breuem, & concissam methodum pro viribus, Logicæ, & Philosophiæ disciplinam iuxta S. Thomæ sensum redigeremus. Id circò non solum visum est eius solidam sequi, & imitari doctrinam, sed ordinem, breuitatem, modestiamque æmulari.

Vt methodum, ordinemque sequeremur, in ipsa operis fronte Logicam in duas partes diuidimus. Prima, dialecticas disputationes, quas summulas vocant, complectitur, & circa formam logicalem versatur. Secunda, circa prædicabilia, & prædicamenta, ac libros Posteriorum tractat de instrumẽtis logicalibus ex parte materiæ, & posterioristicæ resolutionis, vt abundantius in initio huius libri adnotamus.

Vt breuitatem imitaremur, immensam inextricabilium quæstionum syluam, & spinosa Sophismatum dumeta excidere curauimus, quæ audientium mentibus onerosa, & pungentes, vtilitatis nihil, dispendij non parum afferebant. Ad hæc, metaphysicas difficultates, pluresque alias ex libris de Anima, quæ disputantium ardore in ipsa summularũ cunabula irrumperant, suo loco amandauimus, & tractatum de signis ac notitijs, in Logica super librũ Peri-

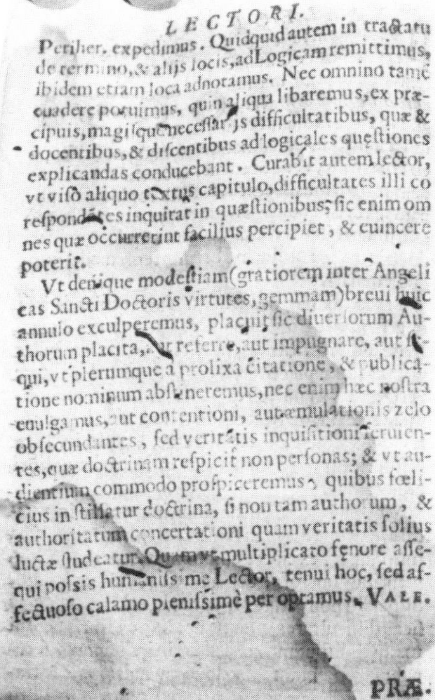

LECTORI.

Periher. expedimus. Quidquid autem in tractatu de termino, & alijs locis, ad Logicam remittimus, ibidem etiam loca adnotamus. Nec omnino tamẽ euadere potuimus, quin aliqua libaremus, ex præcipuis, magisque necessarijs difficultatibus, quæ & docentibus, & discentibus ad logicales quęstiones explicandas conducebant. Curabit autem lector, vt viso aliquo textus capitulo, difficultates illi correspondẽtes inquirat in quæstionibus; sic enim omnes quæ occurrerint facilius percipiet, & euincere poterit.

Vt denique modestiam (gratiorem inter Angelicas Sancti Doctoris virtutes, gemmam) breui huic annulo exculperemus, placuit sic diuersorum Authorum placita, aut referre, aut impugnare, aut sequi, vt plerumque a prolixa citatione, & publicatione nominum abstineremus, nec enim hæc nostra euulgamus, aut contentioni, aut æmulationis zelo obsecundantes, sed veritatis inquisitioni seruientes, quæ doctrinam respicit non personas; & vt audientium commodo prospiceremus, quibus fœlicius instillatur doctrina, si non tam authorum, & authoritatum concertationi quam veritatis solius lucta studeatur. Quam vt multiplicato fęnore assequi possis humanissime Lector, tenui hoc, sed affectuoso calamo plenissimè per optamus. VALE.

PRÆ.

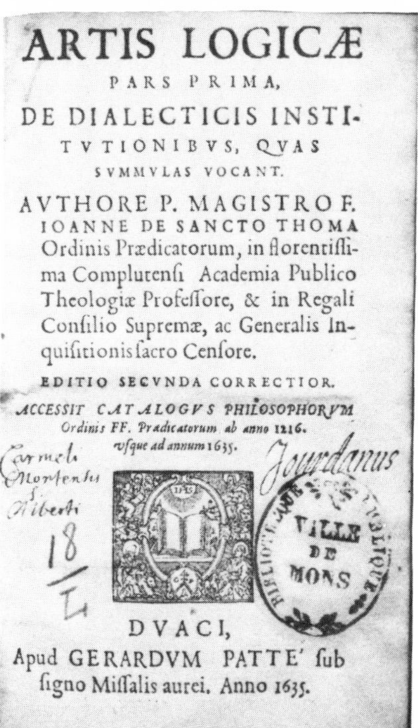

ARTIS LOGICÆ

PARS PRIMA,

DE DIALECTICIS INSTITVTIONIBVS, QVAS SVMMVLAS VOCANT.

AVTHORE P. MAGISTRO F. IOANNE DE SANCTO THOMA Ordinis Prædicatorum, in florentissima Complutensi Academia Publico Theologiæ Professore, & in Regali Consilio Supremæ, ac Generalis Inquisitionis sacro Censore.

EDITIO SECVNDA CORRECTIOR.

ACCESSIT CATALOGVS PHILOSOPHORVM Ordinis FF. Prædicatorum ab anno 1216. vsque ad annum 1635.

DVACI,

Apud GERARDVM PATTE' sub signo Missalis aurei. Anno 1635.

Panels 1–3 are the title page and "Word to the Reader" (translated pp. 5–6) from the second edition (1634) of the lost exemplar of the 1631 First Part of the *Ars Logica,* announcing the Treatise on Signs as something new in philosophy. Discussion p. 7 above, pp, 405–406, 446 esp. n. 75 below. Panel 4 is the title page from the 1635 Douai edition, thought by the publisher to be the second, but in fact the third, edition of this part. Discussion pp. 405–406, esp. note 12, p. 446 note 75, below. Photographs from 1634 edition courtesy of Norma Elia Cantú; from 1635, courtesy of Christiane Pierard.

Liber Primus

DE SIGNO SECUNDUM SE*

Book I

CONCERNING THE SIGN IN ITS PROPER BEING*

* In the original Latin: "*Quaestio XXI. De Signo Secundum Se.*" Logica 2. p.: "Question 21. Concerning the Sign in Its Proper Being."

Question 1[1]

Whether a Sign Is in the Order of Relation

Quaestio Prima[1]

Utrum Signum Sit in Genere Relationis

The present discussion turns on the definition of sign given in the first of the *Summulae* books, chap. 2,[2] namely, that a sign is ''that which represents something other than itself to a knowing power.'' We have settled on a definition formulated in this general way, so as to include all the kinds of signs, both formal and instrumental. For the usual definition accepted as a matter of course by the theologians in their commentaries on the opening of Book IV of *The Sentences of Peter Lombard,*[3] the one taken from Augustine[4]—''A sign is something which, besides the impressions that it conveys to sense, makes something come into cognition'' —applies only to the instrumental sign.

In our definition, therefore, two things concur to constitute the general rationale of a sign. The first is the rationale of something manifestative or representative. The second is an order to another, specifically, on the one hand, to the thing which is represented (which must be other than the sign, for nothing is a sign of itself nor signifies itself), and, on the other hand, to the cognitive power to which the sign manifests and represents the thing distinct from itself.

To be sure, something manifestative *as such* need not bespeak a relation, both because the manifestative

Supponenda est definitio signi, quae lib. 1. Summul. cap. 2.[2] tradita est, scilicet quod signum est «id, quod repraesentat aliud a se potentiae cognoscenti». Quam definitionem ita communiter tradidimus, ut complecteremur omnia signorum genera, et formale et instrumentale. Nam vulgaris definitio, quae circumferri solet apud theologos in initio 4. Sentent.[3] ex Augustino[4]: «Signum est, quod praeter species, quas ingerit sensui, aliquid facit in cognitionem venire», instrumentali signo solum convenit.

In nostra ergo definitione ad rationem signi in communi duo concurrunt: Primum est ratio manifestativi seu repraesentativi. Secundum ordo ad alterum, scilicet ad rem, quae repraesentatur, quae debet esse diversa a signo, nihil enim est signum sui nec significat se, et ad potentiam, cui manifestat et repraesentat rem a se distinctam.

Et quidem manifestativum *ut sic* constat non dicere relationem, tum quia potest sal-

---

[1] In the original Latin: ''Articulus Primus.'' Each ''Question'' of each ''Book'' of the *Treatise on Signs* is an ''Articulus'' in the original Latin. Accordingly, since the change is noted here as a systematic affair, it will not be further noted at the head of each ''Question.'' See the ''Editorial Afterword,'' Section III.A.

[2] Logica 1. p. lib. 1. c. 2., 25/12-13 above (Reiser's text here reads incorrectly: ''cap. 4.'').

[3] dist. 1. q. 1. art. 1. quaestiunc. 2. (*Pa* VII. 454 a).

[4] De doctrina christiana II. c. 1. n. 1. (Migne P.L. XXXIV. 35).

can be verified in an order to itself and without respect to another—as when light manifests itself, when an object represents itself in perception, etc.—and because one thing can manifest another without a dependence on that other, but rather through a dependence of the other on the one manifesting, as, for example, principles manifest conclusions, light manifests colors, or the vision of God manifests creatures, as the more expert theologians explain the *Summa theologica*, I, qq. 12 and 14. In such cases, an illustration and manifestation of another takes place without a dependence upon and subordination to the thing manifested.

But indeed the manifestative element *of a sign* is found both with an order to another, because nothing signifies itself, although something can represent itself, and with a dependence on that other to which it is ordered, because a sign is always less than what it signifies and is dependent thereon as on a measure.[5]

We ask therefore whether this formal rationale of a sign consists, primarily and essentially, in a relation according to the way it has being (*an ontological relation*) **or in a relation according to the way being must be expressed in discourse** (*a transcendental relation*), *that is to say,*[6] **in something** *subjective* **which founds an ontological relation.**

What a relation is according to the way being must be expressed in discourse and according to the way it has being, what a transcendental relation is and what a categorial relation is, has been explained in our Second Preamble[7] concerning Relation.[8] And we speak here of ontological rela-

vari in ordine ad se et sine respectu ad alterum, ut quando lux manifestat seipsam, quando obiectum repraesentat se, ut videatur, etc.; tum quia potest aliquid manifestare alterum sine dependentia ab ipso, sed potius per dependentiam alterius a se, sicut principia manifestant conclusiones, lux colores, Deus visus creaturas, ut peritiores theologi docent 1. p. q. 12. et 14. In quibus illustratio et manifestatio alterius sine dependentia et subordinatione ad rem manifestatam fit.

At vero manifestativum *signi* invenitur et cum ordine ad alterum, quia nihil seipsum significat, licet se repraesentare possit, et cum dependentia, quia signum semper est minus significato et ab ipso ut a mensura dependens.[5]

QUAERIMUS ERGO, an formalis ista ratio signi consistat in relatione secundum esse primo et per se, an in relatione secundum dici seu[6] in aliquo absoluto, quod fundet talem relationem.

Quid sit autem relatio secundum dici et secundum esse, relatio transcendentalis et praedicamentalis, dictum est in Praeambulo Secundo[7] de Relatione.[8] Et

---

[5] The systematic contrast between *representation* and *signification* (or between the sign as a representation and the sign as such, the representative [or manifestative] and the significative aspects of a sign), which runs throughout the *Treatise*, is most fully explained at 122/17-123/25 and 132/16-46.

[6] *Seu* in classical Latin usage introduces an alternative condition or a disjunction. This has led even careful scholars (e.g., Yves R. Simon, John J. Glanville, and G. Donald Hollenhorst, *The Material Logic of John of St. Thomas* [Chicago: The University of Chicago Press, 1955], p. 389) into a most serious misreading of Poinsot at this point—most serious, because it involves as a consequence nothing less than total misunderstanding of the point of departure for the doctrine of signs. Their rendering of this passage reads: "We propose to determine whether the formal notion of the sign consists, primarily and essentially, (a) in a relation according to existence or (b) in a relation according to expression or (c) in a thing absolute which would ground the relation that the sign implies." This is not a correct reading of the text.

What Poinsot envisages here, as Ralph Powell has shown (see my "What's in a Name?" *Semiotica* 22:1-2 [1978], 159-163, esp. note 8, pp. 175-176), and as is clear from the first two Articles of the Second Preamble above, are not three alternatives for the being proper to signs, but only two. The *seu* here, thus, expresses neither an alternative condition nor a disjunction, but an *explication only*. Poinsot is using "*seu*" *not* in the classical but rather in line with the novel medieval sense cited by Du Cange, *Glossarium Mediae et Infimae Latinitatis* (orig. publ. 1883-1887; Graz, Austria: Akademische Druck— u. Verlagsanstalt, 1954, VII: 461: "Seu, pro *Et*, conjunctiva. Occurrit passim" (see also the entry for *sive*, p. 499). In other words, the *seu* here adds something further but not opposed to the preceding *secundum dici*, namely, its explication *aliis verbis*. *Secundum esse* and *secundum dici* are exclusive and exhaustive *secundum rem*, so that the *seu* here adds to *secundum dici* something *secundum verba tantum*—a *verbal* alternative that is *conceptually equivalent*. Note the parallel construction in Poinsot's text shortly below at 118/21-24; and see the Second Preamble, Article 1, note 16, p. 86 above, and Article 2, 89/21-91/29, esp. 90/15-37.

[7] In the original Latin: "q. 17."

[8] Articles 1 and 2.

tion—of relation according to the way it has being—not of categorial relation, because we are discussing the sign in general, as it includes equally the natural and the social sign, in which general discussion even the signs which are mental artifacts[9]—namely, stipulated signs as such—are involved. And for this reason, the rationale *common* to signs cannot be that of a categorial being, nor a categorial relation,[10] although it *could* be an ontological relation, according to the point made by St. Thomas in the *Summa theologica*, I, q. 28, art. 1, and explained in our Preamble[11] on Relation—to wit, that only in the case of these things which exist toward another is found some mind-independent relation and some mind-dependent relation,[12] which latter relation plainly is not categorial, but is called a relation according to the way relation has being (an ontological relation), because it is purely a relation and does not import anything absolute.

Some authors think that the general rationale of a sign does not consist in a respect according to the way it has being toward a thing signified and toward a power, but in a respect according to the way being must be expressed in discourse, that is to say, in something absolute founding that ontological relation. And they assign for the rationale of a sign this: to be something leading cognition to another. That this is the fundament of the sign seems to follow from St. Thomas's remark in Book IV, dist. 4, q. 1, art. 1, of his *Commentary on the Sentences of Peter Lombard*,[13] where he says that the rationale of a sign in the sacramental character is founded in something, because a sign, besides the impressions which it conveys to sense, makes known something other. A sign, therefore, does not formally consist in a relation, but in the

loquimur hic de relatione secundum esse, non de relatione praedicamentali, qui loquimur de signo in communi, prout includit tam signum naturale quam ad placitum, in quo involvitur etiam signum, quod est aliquid rationis,[9] scilicet signum ad placitum. Et ideo praedicamentale ens esse non potest nec relatio praedicamentalis,[10] licet possit esse relatio secundum esse iuxta doctrinam D. Thomae 1. p. q. 28. art. 1. explicatam [in] eodem Praeambulo,[11] quod solum in his, quae sunt ad aliquid, invenitur aliqua relatio realis et aliqua rationis,[12] quae relatio manifestum est, quod non sit praedicamentalis, sed vocatur relatio secundum esse, quia pure relatio est et non aliquid absolutum importat.

Igitur ALIQUI AUCTORES existimant rationem signi in communi non consistere in respectu secundum esse ad rem significatam et ad potentiam, sed in respectu secundum dici seu in aliquo absoluto fundante illam relationem. Et assignant pro ratione signi hoc, quod est esse ductivum cognitionis ad aliud. Hoc enim esse fundamentum signi videtur deduci ex D. Thoma in 4. dist. 4. q. 1. art. 1.[13] dicente, quod ratio signi in charactere fundatur in aliquo, quia signum praeter species, quas ingerit sensibus, aliquid aliud facit in cognitionem venire. Non ergo signum formaliter in relatione con-

---

[9] i.e., which are mind-dependent beings.

[10] See Logica 2. p. q. 14. art. 1., "*Quid sit praedicamentum et quid requiratur ut aliquid sit in praedicamento*" ("What a category is and what are the conditions for anything's belonging to a category"), Reiser ed., 500b36-501a2: "*Et quia praedicamentorum distinctio ad hoc introducta est, ut diversarum naturarum ordines et classes proponerentur, ad quae omnia, quae naturam aliquam participant, reducerentur, ideo imprimis secludendum est ab omni praedicamento ens rationis, quia non habet naturam neque entitatem veram, sed fictam, ideoque neque ad praedicamentum verum, sed fictum reici debet. Unde D. Thomas q. 7. de Potentia art. 9. tantum res extra animam dicit pertinere ad praedicamenta.*"—"Since the distinction of the categories was introduced for this, that the orders and classes of diverse natures might be set forth, to which all the things that participate some nature might be reduced, the very first thing to be excluded from *every* category is mind-dependent being, for being that depends for its existence on being cognized (mind-dependent being) has not a nature nor a true entity, but a constructed one, and therefore must be relegated not to a true category, but to a constructed one. Whence St. Thomas says (in q. 7, art. 9 of his *Disputed Questions on the Power of God*) that only a thing independent of the mind pertains to the categories." See above, Second Preamble, Article 1, note 16, p. 86.

[11] In the original Latin: "eadem q. 17."

[12] See the Second Preamble, Article 2, esp. 93/17-96/36, but also 89/21-91/28. See further the First Preamble, Article 1, 51/37-52/6, 53/32-45, Article 2, 60/7-44, Article 3, 70/24-71/19.

[13] *Pa* VII. 506 a.

fundament of a relation. And this leading to another to be known is nothing else than the representative or manifestative rationale itself, not, indeed, in its entire latitude, as including self-representation, but as it is restricted to being manifestative of another. This indeed respects a power in the way an object does, and in the same order and line as an object; but an object does not consist in a categorial relation to a power, nor in a dependence on that power.

My own answer to the question before us is this: **the rationale of a sign formally speaking does not consist in a relation according to the way being must be expressed in discourse [a transcendental relation], but in a relation according to the way relation has being [an ontological relation].**

I have said "formally speaking," because materially and presuppositively the sign bespeaks the rationale of something manifestative or representative of another, which doubtless does not imply only a relation according to the way relation has being, as we will show shortly. Formally, however, the rationale of a sign does not bespeak the mere rationale of something representative of another, since it is well known that many things represent or manifest another, and not in the mode of a sign, as, for example, God represents creatures, and every cause an effect, and principles manifest conclusions, and light manifests colors: yet these do not have the rationale of a sign. Therefore, to represent another is indeed required for a sign, but a sign does not consist in this alone; for *a sign adds something beyond representing, and formally bespeaks representing another deficiently or dependently upon the very thing signified, and by substituting in the capacity of that thing*. And thus a sign respects a significate not as something purely self-manifested and self-illuminated, but as the principal knowable and the measure of the sign, something in whose place the sign is surrogated and whose vicegerent the sign is in bringing that knowable thing to a cognitive power.

We add in conclusion that the rationale of a sign consists in a relation according to the way relation has being, prescinding now from the question whether that ontological relation is mind-independent (physical) or mind-dependent (objective only); for we take this up in the following question. And thus we employ a designation [ontological] common to both kinds of relation, and do not deal with only the mind-independent or the mind-dependent relation determinately.

So explained, the conclusion is drawn initially FROM THE TEACHING OF ST. THOMAS. For St. Thomas expressly posits that a sign is an instance of a relation founded

sistit, sed in fundamento relationis. Et hoc ductivum ad alterum cognoscendum nihil aliud est, quam ipsa ratio repraesentativi seu manifestativi, non quidem in tota sua latitudine, ut etiam comprehendit repraesentare se, sed prout restringitur ad manifestativum alterius, quod quidem respicit potentiam sicut obiectum, et in eodem ordine et linea, qua obiectum; obiectum autem non consistit in relatione praedicamentali ad potentiam nec in dependentia ab illa.

SIT ERGO UNICA CONCLUSIO: **Ratio signi formaliter loquendo non consistit in relatione secundum dici, sed secundum esse.**

Dixi ,,formaliter loquendo'', quia materialiter et praesuppositive dicit rationem manifestativi seu repraesentativi alterius, quod sine dubio non importat solam relationem secundum esse, ut statim ostendemus. Formaliter autem ratio signi non dicit solam rationem repraesentativi alterius, cum constet multa repraesentare aliud seu manifestare, et non per modum signi, sicut Deus repraesentat creaturas, et omnis causa effectus, et principia manifestant conclusiones, et lux colores; nec tamen habent rationem signi. Igitur repraesentare aliud requiritur quidem ad signum, sed non in hoc solo consistit; addit autem supra repraesentare, et formaliter dicit repraesentare aliud deficienter vel dependenter ab ipsa re significata, et quasi vice illius substituendo. Et ita respicit significatum non ut pure manifestatum et illuminatum a se, sed ut principale cognoscibile et mensuram sui, cuius loco subrogatur et cuius vices gerit in deducendo ad potentiam.

Addimus in conclusione consistere in relatione secundum esse, abstrahendo nunc an sit relatio realis vel rationis; de hoc enim art. seq. agemus. Et ita utimur vocabulo communi utrique relationi, et non solum agimus de relatione reali vel rationis determinate.

Sic explicata conclusio deducitur primo EX DOCTRINA D. THOMAE. Nam D. Thomas expresse ponit, quod signum est

on something other. But a relation founded on something other is a relation according to the way it has being, and, if it is physical, belongs to the category of a mind-independent being-toward something. Therefore, a sign consists in a relation according to the way it has being, an ontological relation.

The consequence is valid. The minor premise is taken from Book IV of St. Thomas's *Commentary on the Sentences Written for Annibald*, dist. 4, q. 1, art. 1,[14] where he says that "the nature of relation is to be founded always on some other kind of being." Therefore, relation founded on something other is condistinguished from the other kinds of being on which it can be founded, and consequently it is distinguished from a relation transcendental and according to the way being must be expressed in discourse, because these relations are not distinguished from the other kinds of being, as was shown in our Preamble[15] on Relation.[16] For transcendental relations are not pure respects, but absolute entities [intrinsically] ordered or dependent with regard to another, as we have proved more at length in our Preamble[17] on Relation.[18] Therefore a relation founded on some other kind of being is always a relation according to the way relation has being, and if it is mind-independent, it will be categorial.

The major premise, on the other hand, is established explicitly by St. Thomas himself, both in the work cited just above, and in his *Commentary on the Sentences of Peter Lombard*, Book IV, dist. 4, q. 1, art. 1,[19] and again in the *Summa theologica*, III, q. 63, art. 2, reply to obj. 3, where, having given the argument: the sign is an instance of relation, therefore the sacramental character is an instance of relation, since a sacrament is a sign; he responds that sign implies a relation founded on something, and since the sign-relation of the sacramental character cannot be founded immediately on the essence of the soul, it must be founded on some superadded quality, and the sacramental character consists in this quality antecedently to the relation of sign. St. Thomas therefore is of the view that a sign-relation is a relation founded on something other. And if it were only a relation according to the way being must be expressed in discourse, that is, a transcendental relation, he would not deny that the sacramental character consists in such a relation, because a quality can well be

in genere relationis fundatae in aliquo alio. Sed relatio fundata in aliquo alio est relatio secundum esse et de praedicamento ad aliquid, si realis sit. Ergo signum consistit in relatione secundum esse.

Consequentia est legitima. Et minor sumitur ex doctrina D. Thomae in 4. ad Annibaldum dist. 4. quest. unica, art. 1.[14] dicente, «quod natura relationis est, ut semper fundetur in aliquo alio genere entis». Ergo relatio fundata in aliquo alio condistinguitur ab aliis generibus entis, in quibus potest fundari, et consequenter distinguitur a relatione transcendentali et secundum dici, quia istae relationes non distinguuntur ab aliis generibus entis, ut in Praeambulo[15] de Relatione ostensum est.[16] Nec enim sunt puri respectus, sed entitates absolutae circa aliud ordinatae vel dependentes, ut latius probavimus in Praeambulo nostro[17] de Relatione.[18] Ergo relatio fundata in aliquo alio genere entis semper est relatio secundum esse, et si sit realis, erit praedicamentalis.

Maior vero probatur aperte ex ipso D. Thoma, tum in loco nuper cit., tum in 4. dist. 4. q. 1. art. 1.[19] et 3. p. q. 63. art. 2. ad 3., ubi cum possuisset argumentum, quod signum est in genere relationis, ergo character est in genere relationis, cum sit signum, respondet, quod signum importat relationem fundatam in aliquo, et cum non possit relatio signi characteris fundari immediate in essentia animae, debet fundari in aliqua qualitate superaddita, et in hac qualitate consistit character antecedenter ad relationem signi. Sentit ergo D. Thomas, quod relatio signi est relatio fundata in aliquo alio. Et si solum esset relatio secundum dici seu transcendentalis, non negaret D. Thomas characterem in tali relatione consistere, quia qualitas bene potest esse

[14] *Pa* XXII. 335 b.
[15] In the original Latin: "quaest."
[16] Article 2, 90/15-30.
[17] In the original Latin: "q. 17."
[18] Esp. Article 2, 89/21-90/37.
[19] *Pa* VII. 506 a.

a relation according to the way being must be expressed in discourse, as knowledge exists relative to an object and every act or habit to that by which it is specified. When therefore St. Thomas identifies the sacramental character with a quality and rules out identifying it with relation, he definitively rules out any identification of the sacramental character with a relation categorial and according to the way it has being, that is, he excludes it from the category of relation; for by placing it in the category of quality he had not sufficiently excluded its identification with a relation according to the way being must be expressed in discourse, since even in the category of quality is found relation according to the way being must be expressed in discourse. But St. Thomas identifies the rationale of a sign with that relation from which he excludes the sacramental character. Therefore it is manifest that he constitutes the rationale of sign in a relation according to the way relation has being or in a categorial relation.

And THE FOUNDATION FOR THIS CONCLUSION is taken from the very nature and defining feature of a sign, because the rationale of a sign does not consist only in representing or manifesting another than itself, but in that specific mode of manifesting by which one thing represents another as modally subordinate thereto, as the less to the more principal, as the measured to its measure, as something substituted and vicegerent to that for which it is substituted, and in whose capacity it functions. But a relation of measured to measure and of one substituting for its principal is a categorial relation. Therefore the relation of sign to signified is categorial.

The minor premise of the argument is clear from the fact that a relation of measured to measure is a relation of the third of the three types of relation in the category of relation, as was proved in our Preamble on relation,[20] Article 3.[21] The major premise, on the other hand, is clear from the fact that the relation of a sign insofar as it is a sign directly respects the significate as the principal thing to be known, to which the sign leads the power. For the function of a sign is to be a means and something substituting in the place of a thing signified, which the sign manifests intentionally to a cognitive power, since the thing does not become known by means of itself, but through a substitute. Whence if a thing is manifest in itself, the rationale and office of sign ceases. A sign therefore is something respecting a significate as substituting for it, and something subordinate and ministerial to it and measured by it; for the more closely a sign is related to the significate in itself, the better it signifies. Nor is this

relatio secundum dici, ut scientia se habet ad obiectum et omnis actus seu habitus ad id, a quo specificatur. Cum ergo ponit characterem in qualitate et reicit a relatione, utique a relatione praedicamentali et secundum esse reicit, id est a praedicamento relationis; nam a relatione secundum dici non sufficienter reiciebat ponens illum in praedicamento qualitatis, cum in hoc etiam inveniatur relatio secundum dici. Sed in illa relatione ponit D. Thomas rationem signi, a qua reicit characterem. Ergo manifestum est, quod in relatione secundum esse seu praedicamentali constituit rationem signi.

Et sumitur FUNDAMENTUM huius conclusionis ex ipsa natura et quidditate signi, quia ratio signi non consistit tantum in hoc, quod est repraesentare seu manifestare aliud a se, sed in tali modo manifestandi, quod est repraesentare aliud tamquam inferiori modo ad illud, ut minus principale ad magis principale, ut mensuratum ad suam mensuram, ut substitutum et vices gerens ad id, pro quo substituitur et cuius gerit vices. Sed relatio mensurati ad mensuram et substituentis ad suum principale est relatio praedicamentalis. Ergo relatio signi ad signatum praedicamentalis est.

M i n o r constat, cum relatio mensurati ad mensuram sit relatio tertii generis in praedicamento relationis, ut supra [in] Praeambulo Secundo[20] probatum est.[21] M a i o r autem est manifesta, quia relatio signi in quamtum signum directe respicit signatum tamquam principale cognoscendum, ad quod ducit potentiam. Ad hoc enim deservit signum, ut sit medium et substituens loco signati, quod intendit manifestare potentiae, eo quod res per seipsam non innotescit, sed per tale medium. Unde si res seipsa manifestatur, cessat ratio et officium signi. Est ergo signum respiciens signatum ut subrogatum vice ipsius et aliquid deserviens et ministrans ipsi et mensuratum per ipsum; tanto enim melius signum significat, quanto propinquius se habet ad signatum in se. Neque hoc suffi-

[20] In the original Latin: "q. 17."

[21] Article 3, esp. 101/11-102/15, and 105/15-109/34.

sufficiently explained by a transcendental relation, inasmuch as a sign bespeaks some connection with a signified and by its very nature manifests that signified thing; for this is required, but it is not sufficient. For just as a son (although he is an effect of a father, and under the rationale of an effect respects that father transcendentally, yet in the rationale of son, as that rationale bespeaks likeness to another by reason of origin) does not express a transcendental relation, but one categorial and according to the way relation has being; so a sign (although in the rationale of something manifestative and representative it respects a significate transcendentally, yet as it expresses the rationale of something measured and substituted for a significate, and, as it were, ministerial to it as to what is principal), respects the significate by an ontological relation, a relation according to the way it has being.

From this can be seen the difference between the rationale of something *manifestative* and of something *significative*. That which is manifestative principally respects a power as the terminus toward which it tends or which it stimulates, and similarly, to represent something to a power is accomplished only by rendering the something in question present to the power as knowable. This, according to St. Thomas, in q. 7 of the *Disputed Questions on Truth*, art. 5, reply to obj. 2,[22] is but [for the power] to contain a similitude of the [represented] other. This containing of a similitude, however, can occur without there being any relation which is a relation according to the way relation has being: in the first place, because such a containing can be a perfection simply and without any dependence on the thing represented, as God represents creatures in [the divine] ideas; in the second place, because this containing [i.e., this being similar] is conserved and exercised even when the [represented] term does not exist, and consequently even without a categorial relation, as is clear in a representation of a future or of a past thing; in the third place, finally, because this representation pertains to the rationale of something stimulating or arousing the power to which an object is rendered present by means of the representation. Whence it pertains essentially and directly to the object itself to be represented; but the object does not consist in an ontological relation to the power—on the contrary, an object, essentially speaking, does not respect a power or depend on it, but power on object; for a power takes [its] specification from an object. Therefore to represent and to manifest do not consist in an ontological relation [i.e., neither a representation nor a manifestation is a relation according to the way it has being].

cienter explicatur relatione transcendentali, quatenus signum connexionem aliquam dicit cum signato et ratione ipsius manifestat illud; hoc enim requiritur, sed non sufficit. Sicut enim filius, licet sit effectus patris, et sub ratione effectus transcendentaliter ipsum respiciat, tamen in ratione filii, ut dicit simile alteri in ratione processionis, non dicit relationem transcendentalem, sed praedicamentalem et secundum esse; ita signum, licet in ratione manifestativi et repraesentativi respiciat signatum transcendentaliter, tamen ut dicit rationem mensurati et substituti respectu signati, et quasi ministrans ipsi ut principali, respicit ipsum relatione secundum esse.

Et hinc discernitur differentia inter rationem manifestativi et significativi, quod *manifestativum* principaliter respicit potentiam ut terminum, ad quem tendit vel quem movet, et similiter repraesentare aliquid potentiae solum perficitur per hoc, quod reddat aliquid praesens potentiae cognoscibiliter, quod secundum D. Thomam, q. 7. de Veritate art. 5. ad. 2.,[22] non est aliud quam similitudinem alterius continere. Ista autem continentia similitudinis sine aliqua relatione dari potest, quae sit relatio secundum esse: *Tum* quia talis continentia potest esse perfectio simpliciter et sine ulla dependentia a re repraesentata, sicut Deus repraesentat creaturas in ideis. *Tum* quia conservatur ista continentia et exercetur etiam non existente termino, et consequenter etiam sine relatione praedicamentali, ut constat in repraesentatione rei futurae vel praeteritae. *Tum* denique quia repraesentatio ista pertinet ad rationem movendi potentiam, cui redditur praesens obiectum per repraesentationem. Unde ipsi obiecto per se et directe convenit repraesentari; obiectum autem non consistit in relatione secundum esse ad potentiam, imo per se loquendo non respicit potentiam aut ab ea dependet, sed potentia ab ipso; ab eo enim specificationem sumit. Non ergo repraesentare et manifestare in relatione secundum esse consistunt.

---

[22] *Pa* IX. 108 b.

But to signify or to be significative is understood directly through an order to a significate for which it substitutes and in whose capacity it functions as the means by which the significate is brought to a power. For a sign ministers to and subserves the significate itself in this, that the sign brings and presents that significate to the power as the sign's principal content capable of being presented. In just the same way too we consider two aspects in a minister and substitute for another, namely, subjection to that other whose place is taken as to the principal, and the effect which he is commissioned by his principal to achieve. In this way, therefore, a sign, even though in representing it respects a power in order to manifest thereto what is signified (because a sign is destined and used for this effect), and in this precise consideration relative to a power need not consist in a relation according to the way relation has being, yet in the subordination to what is signified, inasmuch as it respects that signified as what is principal and as the measure of itself, a sign must necessarily consist in [an ontological] relation thereto, just as a servant bespeaks a relation to a master and [as] a minister or instrument [bespeaks a relation] to its principal.

You might say: a sign does not respect a signifiable as a pure terminus, but as the object of its signification; therefore a sign does not consist in a pure respect, but in a transcendental order, just as a cognitive power and knowledge respect an object, and yet the object measures the knowledge and the power.

But against this is the fact that a sign does not respect a significate as an object or subject matter with which it is precisely concerned, as a cognitive power and knowledge respect their objects, but rather as a substitute and vicegerent of the significate and surrogated in its place of representing to a power. And because a sign directly implies this substitution for and surrogation to another, it is therefore formally something relative to that for which it substitutes. A cognitive power and knowledge, by contrast, do not imply this relation to an object, but imply the rationale of a principle and an aptitude concerning something of the one operating [i.e., an agent's aptitude], which does not pertain to relation formally speaking; for it does not pertain to relation to be operative, but to be subject and substituted does pertain to relation. And thus knowledge and cognitive power, act and habit, respect an object as their measure fundamentally, not in a formally relative manner as does a sign, which is

At vero *significare* seu *significativum esse* directe sumitur per ordinem ad signatum, pro quo substituit et cuius vices gerit tamquam medium, quo signatum ducitur ad potentiam. In hoc enim ministrat et deservit signum ipsi signato, quod defert illud et praesentat potentiae tamquam suum principale repraesentabile; sicut etiam in ministro et substituto alterius duo consideramus, scilicet subiectionem ad alterum, cuius gerit vices, ut ad principale, et effectum, pro quo ministrat et vices eius gerit. Sic ergo signum, licet in repraesentando respiciat potentiam, ut ei manifestet signatum, quia ad hunc effectum destinatur et assumitur, et in hac praecisa consideratione ad potentiam non petat consistere in relatione secundum esse, tamen in subordinatione ad signatum, quatenus respicit ipsum ut principale et ut mensuram sui, necessario debet in relatione ad ipsum consistere, sicut servus dicit relationem ad dominum et minister seu instrumentum ad suum principale.

DICES: Signum non respicit significabile ut purum terminum, sed ut obiectum suae significationis, ergo non consistit in puro respectu, sed in ordine transcendentali, sicut potentia et scientia respiciunt obiectum, et tamen obiectum mensurat scientiam et potentiam.

Sed contra est, quia signum non respicit signatum ut obiectum seu materiam, circa quam versetur praecise, sicut potentia et scientia sua obiecta respiciunt, sed tamquam substitutum et vices signati gerens et loco eius subrogatum in repraesentando potentiae. Et quia directe signum importat hanc substitutionem et subrogationem ad alterum, ideo formaliter est quid relativum ad id, pro quo substituit. Potentia autem et scientia non important hanc relationem ad obiectum, sed important rationem principii et virtutis circa aliquid operantis, quod non est relationis formaliter loquendo; operari enim relationi non convenit, esse autem subiectum et substitutum relationis est. Et ita scientia et potentia, actus et habitus respiciunt obiectum ut mensuram sui fundamentaliter, non relative formaliter sicut signum, quod forma-

formally something subordinated and subsidiary to a signified, that is to say, is its vicegerent. This is the point of St. Thomas's teaching in the *Summa theologica*, I, q. 13, art. 7, reply to obj. 1, where he says that "some relative words are imposed to signify the relative condition or state itself, as, for example, 'master' and 'servant,' 'father' and 'son,' and the like; and these words are said to be relative according to the way relation has being. But some relative words are imposed to signify the things which certain relations are consequent upon, such words as 'mover' and 'moved,' 'head' and 'that which has a head,' which are said to be relative according to the way being must be expressed in discourse." Wherefore "knowledge" and "power" signify the very thing and principle upon which follows a relation to whatever objects, but "sign" directly signifies the respect toward the significate to which the sign is subordinated as a vicar to its principal.

And from this you learn the *basis for distinguishing between a power* or light (which is the vitality of the power), *and a specifying form* or specifier,[23] both of which to be sure—power and specifier—concern an object, but a specifier as vicegerent of the object and containing it as its substitute, the power as tending toward the object as a thing to be apprehended. Whence between power and object it is sufficient that there be a proportion of acquiring something and of tending toward the terminus which is acquired, which is the proportion of the principle of a motion to the terminus. But a specifying form must have a proportion to an object as of something substituting for and acting on behalf of that object. And so, if it is perfectly and adequately vicegerent of the object, there is required an altogether exact proportion in representable being, by reason of which a corporeal representation cannot be the specifier of a spiritual object, nor can a created representation be the specifier for an uncreated object. But if an uncreated representation is posited, the entity of the specifier will also be uncreated.

Resolution of Counter-Arguments

The main basis for the opinion opposed [to the view that a sign is a relation according to the way it has being] is the case when a sign formally signifies a nonexisting thing, as when the footprint of an ox signifies a nonexisting ox, or a statue of an emperor signifies a dead emperor. In such cases there is formally a sign; for a well-made inference from act to potency holds: "It signifies, therefore it is a sign," and yet formally there

liter est quid subordinatum et inferius signato seu vices eius gerens. Et pro hoc servit doctrina S. Thomae 1. p. q. 13. art. 7. ad. 1., ubi inquit, «quod relativa quaedam sunt imposita ad significandum ipsam habitudinem relativam, ut dominus et servus, pater et filius et huiusmodi, et haec dicuntur relativa secundum esse. Quaedam vero sunt imposita ad significandum res, quas consequuntur quaedam habitudines, sicut movens et motum, caput et capitatum, quae dicuntur relativa secundum dici». Quare scientia et potentia significant rem ipsam et principium, ad quod sequitur habitudo ad talia obiecta, signum autem directe significat respectum ad signatum, cui subordinatur ut vicarium suo principali.

Et hinc disces fundamentum ad discernendum inter potentiam seu lumen, quod est virtus potentiae, et speciem,[23] quod utraque quidem versantur circa obiectum, sed species ut vices gerens obiecti et ipsum continens quasi eius substitutum, virtus autem potentiae ut tendens ad obiectum apprehendendum. Unde inter potentiam et obiectum sufficit proportio acquirentis aliquid et tendentis ad terminum, qui acquiritur, quae est proportio principii motus ad terminum. At vero species debet habere proportionem ad obiectum tamquam substituentis et vices eius gerentis. Et ita si perfecte et adaequate vices eius gerat, requiritur omnimoda proportio in esse repraesentabili, ratione cuius nec corporea repraesentatio potest esse species spiritualis obiecti nec creata repraesentatio species obiecto increato. Si autem ponitur increata repraesentatio, etiam et entitas speciei increata erit.

Solvuntur argumenta.

Praecipuum fundamentum sententiae oppositae est, qui signum rem non existentem formaliter significat, ut vestigium bovis bovem non existentem, imago imperatoris mortuum imperatorem. Ergo formaliter est signum; ab actu enim ad potentiam bene valet: «Significat, ergo est signum», et tamen formaliter non est relatio, quia

[23] See Book II, Questions 2 and 3, esp. 242/3-245/4, and 254/1-255/15.

is not a relation, because there is no categorial relation to a nonexisting term. Therefore, a sign does not formally consist in a relation.

This is confirmed by the fact that the formal rationale of a sign is sustained by this, that it be something truly and formally leading a cognitive power to what it signifies. But to lead a power to a significate does not come about by means of a relation, but by means of the proportion and connection which obtains between the sign and the signified, which is the fundament of a relation. Therefore a sign does not formally consist in a relation, but in the fundament of a relation. The major premise follows from the definition of sign. If a sign is "that which represents something to a knowing power," then it is accordingly something leading the power to an object signified. The minor premise is proved by the fact that for a sign to represent to me, it is not necessary that I should be aware of its relation. For example, a countryman knows an animal by its tracks, not by thinking of a relation, and brute animals make use of signs (as will be explained below), and do not know the relation, but only the significate precisely as it is known in the sign. Therefore, if the relation is not known, the relation does not lead, and so does not pertain to the formal rationale of the sign.

In response to this, the first thing to be said is that the argument [24] has no force in the eyes of those who think that a sign-relation is always mind-dependent or mental, even in the case of natural signs, because they think the sign-relation is founded upon the apprehensibility of the things which are signs. But given that the relation of a natural sign to its significate is mind-independent, the response to the foregoing argument is that when an emperor dies his statue does not remain a sign formally, but virtually and fundamentally. Yet a sign arouses or stimulates a cognitive power by reason of its fundament, not by reason of its relation, just as a father begets not by reason of a relation, but by reason of a generative power, and yet being a father consists formally in a relation.[25]

ad terminum non existentem non datur relatio praedicamentalis. Ergo signum formaliter in relatione non consistit.

Confirmatur, quia formalis ratio signi salvatur per hoc, quod sit vere et formaliter ductivum potentiae ad suum signatum. Sed ducere potentiam ad signatum non fit media relatione, sed media proportione et connexione, quae est inter signum et signatum, quae est fundamentum relationis. Ergo signum formaliter non consistit in relatione, sed in fundamento relationis. *Maior* constat ex definitione signi «quod repraesentat aliquid potentiae cognoscenti», ergo est ductivum potentiae ad signatum. *Minor* probatur, quia ut signum mihi repraesentet, non est necesse, quod cognoscam relationem eius, sicut rusticus ex vestigio cognoscit animal non cogitando de relatione, et bruta utuntur signis, ut infra dicetur, nec relationem cognoscunt, sed solum signatum, prout cognoscitur in signo. Ergo si relatio non cognoscitur, relatio non ducit, et sic non pertinet ad formalem rationem signi.

RESPONDETUR imprimis illud argumentum[24] carere vi in opinione eorum, qui existimant relationem signi semper esse rationis, etiam in signis naturalibus, quia existimant fundari in eorum apprehensibilitate. Sed dato, quod relatio signi naturalis realis sit, respondetur, quod mortuo imperatore non manet signum formaliter, sed virtualiter et fundamentaliter. Signum autem ratione sui fundamenti movet potentiam, non ratione suae relationis, sicut pater non ratione relationis generat, sed ratione potentiae generativae, et tamen formaliter consistit in relatione.[25]

---

[24] 124/42-125/3.

[25] In the immediately preceding and following lines, Poinsot might seem to be thinking in the perspective only of instrumental signs. This, however, is not the case, as he expressly recurs to these passages in his Phil. nat. 4. p. q. 6. art. 3: "*licet species seu similitudo, ut habeat relationem realem praedicamentalem ad obiectum, requirat existentiam illius, tamen ut sit repraesentativum eius et exerceat repraesentationem ad potentiam, sufficit transcendentalis ordo ad obiectum, qui remanet etiam non existente obiecto, et est fundamentum illius relationis, sicut mortuo imperatore potest imago eius repraesentare ipsum, licet non respicere realiter ipsum. Et sic diximus in Logica q. 21. art. 1., quod licet signum consistat in relatione secundum esse, tamen exercitium repraesentandi non fit per relationem ipsam, sed per fundamentum eius, quod est esse repraesentativum, sicut pater licet relatione sit pater, non tamen relatione generat, sed fundamento relationis, quae est potentia generativa*" (Reiser ed., III. 191a4-25).—"Although a specifier or similitude requires the existence of an object in order to have a mind-independent categorial relation thereto, nevertheless, for it to be representative

And to the proof:[26] "It signifies formally, i.e., in act, therefore it is formally a sign," the consequence is flatly denied, because it suffices to be a sign virtually in order to signify in act. This can be readily seen in an example: X in act causes and produces an effect, therefore it is in act really a cause; for when the cause in question no longer exists in itself, through the virtuality or efficacy it leaves behind, it causes and causes formally, because the effect is then formally produced. Just so, when a sign exists and by a virtual signification formally leads the mind to something signified [which no longer exists in fact], it is nevertheless not a sign formally, but virtually and fundamentally. For since the rationale of moving or stimulating the mind remains, which comes about through the sign insofar as it is something representative, even if the relation of substitution for the signified does not remain, the sign is able to exercise the functions of substituting without the relation, just as a servant or minister can perform the operations of his ministry even when the master, to whom he bespeaks a relation, and in which relation the rationale of servant and minister formally consists, has died.

To the confirmation[27] the response is that in the rationale of something conductive or leading, there are two elements to be considered, to wit, the capacity or rationale of exercising the very representation of the thing to be conveyed, and the relation of subjection to or substitution for that on whose behalf it exercises the representation, just as in the case of a master, both a power of governing or coercing subjects and a relation to them are considered, and in the case of a servant, both a power of obeying and a relation of subjection. As regards the capacity to lead representatively, we grant that it is not a relation according to the way relation has being, but the fundament of [such] a relation; specifically, it is that proportion and connection with the thing signified; but as regards the formality of sign, which is not any pro-

Et ad probationem:[26] «Formaliter, id est actu significat, ergo formaliter est signum», negatur liquide consequentia, quia sufficit virtualiter esse signum, ut actu significet. Et instatur manifeste in hac: B actu causat et producit effectum, ergo actu in re est causa; nam ipsa causa non existens in se, per virtutem a se relictam causat et formaliter causat, quia effectus tunc formaliter producitur. Sic existente signo et significatione virtuali formaliter ducit potentiam ad signatum, et tamen formaliter non est signum, sed virtualiter et fundamentaliter. Cum enim maneat ratio movendi potentia, quod fit per signum, in quantum repraesentativum est, etiamsi non maneat relatio substitutionis ad signatum, potest exercere functiones substituentis sine relatione, sicut servus vel minister potest exercere operationes sui ministerii etiam mortuo domino, ad quem dicit relationem, et in qua formaliter consistit ratio servi et ministri.

Ad confirmationem[27] respondetur, quod in ratione ductivi est duo considerare, scilicet vim seu rationem exercendi ipsam repraesentationem ducendi, et relationem subiectionis seu substitutionis ad id, pro quo eam exercet, sicut in domino et consideratur potestas gubernandi seu coercendi subditos et relatio ad illos, et in servo potestas obediendi et relatio subiectionis. Quantum ad vim ducendi repraesentative, fatemur non esse relationem secundum esse, sed fundamentum relationis, scilicet illa proportio et connexio cum signato; sed quantum ad formalitatem signi, quae non

of that object and exercise representation to the cognitive power, a transcendental order to the object suffices. And this order remains even when the object does not exist, and it is the fundament of that relation, just as when the emperor dies his image can represent him, even though it cannot mind-independently respect him. And so we said in the Logic, q. 21, art. 1, that although a sign consists in an ontological relation, yet the exercise of representing does not come about through the relation itself, but through its fundament, which is to be representative, just as a father, even though he is a father by a relation, yet does not generate by the relation, but by the fundament of the relation, which is the generative power." On this last point, crucial to the doctrine of signs, see particularly the First Preamble, Article 2, 60/26-44, Article 3, 70/24-71/19; Second Preamble, Article 1, 84/45-84/40, Article 2, 88/14-27, 89/13-20, 95/25-36, Article 3, 110/39-42; Book I, Question 2, 141/12-142/13, Question 3, 165/9-16, Question 5, note 21, p. 201, and 201/28-202/27; Book II, Question 5, 275/7-29; and in this Question the responses to the second counterargument below, 128/7-131/18.

[26] esp. 124/47-125/3.

[27] 125/4-25.

portion and representation, but one subserving and substituted for what is signified, it consists formally in the relation of a *substituted* representative, just as being a servant or being a master are formally relations, and yet the right of coercing and of obeying are not relations according to the way they have being.

A second argument against the view that a sign consists in the very relation to what is signified, rather than in the fundament of any such relation, is as follows: A sign formally consists in this, that it is something able to lead a cognitive power to a significate; for it is through this that anything has signification, which is the form of [i.e., which constitutes] a sign, and it is through this that the definition of a sign—namely, what represents to a knowing power something other than itself—applies to it. But a sign has this ability to lead to a signified even as a means and instrument, through a transcendental relation. Therefore, it is in that relation that a sign formally consists.

The minor premise is proved: For a sign has the ability to lead a power as the means to something signified, through that from which it has the ability to manifest the significate to a power. It has this manifestative ability, however, not by reason of a categorial relation, but by reason of a transcendental relation, because when a transcendental relation of cause or of effect or of image is known, or when any connection of two things is known, the terminus of the relation or connection is immediately attained. Therefore there is no need for any categorial relation in order that a sign might lead to a signified or be able to so lead, since a transcendental relation sufficiently exercises the requisite ability. Nor will it do to say that that transcendental relation is the fundament of the sign-relation, because what is only fundamentally of a given character cannot bring about the formal effect, just as a generative power cannot formally constitute a father, nor a quality a resemblance, even though they are the fundaments of these relations. Therefore, if a transcendental relation only founds the sign-relation, it would not provide formally the formal effect of the sign or its exercise.

This is confirmed by the fact that it is incongruous to say that in the case of stipulated signs, they do not continue to be signs formally when they are not here and now related to what they signify, as in the case of a closed book: The sign—the printing within—is not seen, and so does not have in act the relation which, since it is mind-dependent, depends here and now upon an actual cognition. Therefore a sign cannot consist formally in a relation according to the way relation has

est quaelibet proportio et repraesentatio, sed subserviens et substituta signato, consistit formaliter in relatione substituti repraesentativi, sicut esse servum vel esse dominum formaliter relationes sunt, et tamen ius coercendi et obediendi relationes secundum esse non sunt.

Secundo arguitur: Signum formaliter consistit in hoc, quod est posse ducere potentiam ad signatum; per hoc enim habet significationem, quae est forma signi, et per hoc convenit illi definitio signi, scilicet repraesentativum alterius a se potentiae cognoscenti. Sed hoc, quod est posse ducere ad signatum etiam tamquam medium et instrumentum, habet per relationem transcendentalem; ergo in illa consistit signum formaliter.

Minor probatur: Nam per id habet signum ducere potentiam ad signatum ut medium, per quod habet manifestare potentiae signatum. Hoc autem habet non ratione relationis praedicamentalis, sed transcendentalis, quia cognita relatione transcendentali causae vel effectus vel imaginis vel quacumque connexione duorum, attingitur statim terminus. Ergo non requiritur aliqua relatio praedicamentalis, ut signum ducat ad signatum vel possit ducere, cum transcendentalis id sufficienter exerceat. Nec valet dicere, quod illa transcendentalis relatio est fundamentum relationis signi, quia quod solum est tale fundamentaliter, non potest dare effectum formalem, sicut potentia generativa non potest formaliter constituere patrem nec qualitas simile, licet sint fundamenta istarum relationum. Ergo si relatio transcendentalis solum fundat relationem signi, formaliter non praebet effectum formalem signi aut eius exercitium.

Et confirmatur, quia inconveniens est in signis ad placitum, quod non maneant signa formaliter, quando actu non respiciunt suum signatum, ut in libro clauso, in quo non cognoscitur signum illud seu litterae ibi scriptae, et sic actu non habent relationem, quae cum sit rationis, ab actuali cognitione dependet. Ergo non potest consistere signum formaliter in relatione secundum

being.[28] The antecedent is proved by the fact that a sign in a closed book retains its imposition [i.e., its stipulated character and status], therefore also its signification, which can be reduced to act by opening the book. Therefore it is formally and actually a sign, because it retains in act a signification.[29]

In response, it must be said that nothing more is proved by this second argument[30] than by the preceding argument,[31] and therefore we say that the formal rationale of a sign consists in this, that it can lead someone to the knowledge of a significate, not by an ability [to lead] in any way whatever, but in one subjected to and substituting for the signified and subsidiary thereto in the rationale of sign. And therefore, in a sign, both the capacity for moving or arousing the power and the order of substituting relative to that on whose behalf it stimulates or moves, are considered. And the first is a transcendental relation; the second, a categorial one. And it is in the second that the sign consists, not in the first, because the first, namely, to manifest another, also belongs to things which are not signs, as we have remarked in the example of light manifesting colors, of an object representing itself, of God representing creatures. The fact therefore that when an effect is perceived a cause is known, or that when an image is perceived the archetype is cognized, does not formally constitute the rationale of sign, unless we add the peculiar relation of a substituting representative, etc., which is to say, a relation according to the way relation has being.

And to the further argument,[32] the response is that the fundament of a sign does not formally constitute the rationale of the sign as regards that which formally belongs to subjection and substitution, but as regards that which belongs to the capacity for arousing or moving,[33] just as a generative power constitutes the capacity for generating in a father, not the formal relation of [being] a father, which consists in the rationale of an assimilating principle [a principle of likeness] and of having an authority relative to the son.

As regards the confirmation of the second argument,[34] opinions differ widely on how it must be answered, in-

esse.[28] *Antecedens* autem probatur, quia signum in libro clauso retinet suam impositionem, ergo et suam significationem, quae potest reduci ad actum aperiendo librum. Ergo est formaliter et actu signum, quia actu retinet significationem.[29]

Respondetur illo argumento[30] nihil magis probari quam praecedenti,[31] et ideo dicimus, quod formalis ratio signi consistit in hoc, quod est posse ducere aliquem in cognitionem signati, non potentia quomodocumque, sed subiecta et substituente pro signato et illi inferiori in ratione signi. Et ideo consideratur in signo et vis movens potentiam et ordo substituentis ad id, pro quo movet. Et primum est relatio transcendentalis, secundum praedicamentalis. Et in secunda consistit signum, non in prima, quia prima, scilicet manifestare alterum, etiam illis convenit, quae signa non sunt, sicut diximus de luce manifestante colores, obiecto se repraesentante, Deo repraesentante creaturas. Quod ergo viso effectu cognoscatur causa vel visa imagine archetypus, non constituit formaliter rationem signi, nisi addamus peculiarem relationem repraesentativi substituentis etc., quod relationem secundum esse dicit.

Et ad impugnationem[32] respondetur, quod fundamentum signi non constituit formaliter rationem signi, quantum ad id, quod formaliter est subiectionis et substitutionis, sed quantum ad id, quod est virtutis movendi,[33] sicut potentia generativa constituit virtutem generandi in patre, non formalem relationem patris, quae consistit in ratione principii assimilantis et auctoritatem habentis in ordine ad filium.

Ad confirmationem[34] respondetur varie aliquos sentire in hac parte de signis ad placitum, eo quod in illis relatio signi

---

[28] In addition to Poinsot's formal response to this at line 7 ff. immediately below, see the First Preamble, Article 3, above, 70/24-71/19; and Book II, Question 5, 275/8-29, below.

[29] The 1663 Lyons text adds: "*Et ideo non consistit in pura relatione, quia haec non reducitur ad actum, sed semper respicit actu suum terminum, si est vera relatio.*"— "And therefore it does not consist in a pure relation, because this is not reduced to act, but always respects in act its term, if it is a true relation."

[30] 127/7-20.

[31] 124/42-125/25.

[32] 127/34-42.

[33] Cf. 125/31-39 above, and Question 5, 200/27-201/27 below.

[34] 127/43-128/6.

asmuch as it concerns stipulated signs, owing to the fact that in the case of such signs the sign-relation (if there is one) is acknowledged by all to be not mind-independent, but mind-dependent.

And there are some who think that mind-dependent relation not only denominates, but also exists by the existence of its fundament, at least imperfectly and inchoately, and so denominates even before it is actually apprehended. But this response leaves unresolved the very two points of difficulty which are to be explained. The first point of difficulty is that even such an existence will not denominate the sign in question as a sign perfectly and simply, but only inchoately and imperfectly; and thus a sign in a closed book, or a sign uttered vocally but not actually apprehended in a relation [to what it signifies], will not be a sign perfectly, but inchoately and imperfectly, yet it would acquire the perfect rationale of a sign when it is actually apprehended. The same difficulty to which this position was proposed as a solution, therefore, remains outstanding, namely, how can the sign in a closed book, or in a vocal utterance not apprehended relatively, perfectly signify and lead to a significate? For the linguistic mark or sound "man" does not represent its significate less perfectly if its relation is apprehended than if it is not apprehended, for it retains imposition and perfect signification in the same way [in either case]. Therefore it will be a sign prior to the relation perfectly and consummately and not only inchoately, because equally perfectly it signifies and is a sign prior to that relation.[35]—The second point of difficulty turns on the fact that the imperfect and inchoate existence in question is either only fundamental and virtual in respect of the sign, or actual as well. If it is only fundamental, this is to say that only the fundament of the sign exists, not the sign itself formally. If actual, it is very difficult to see how a mind-independent physical existence of the sort exercised by the fundament should, prior to an actual apprehension, render actually existing that which is a mind-dependent being possessed only of an objective existence. For in that case it will not be a purely mind-dependent being, since it will be capable of a physical existence as well, albeit an imperfect and inchoate one.

Others are of the opinion that a stipulated sign is formally a sign even prior to the formal existence of the

(si datur) secundum omnium consensum realis non est, sed rationis.

Et sunt, qui putant relationem rationis non solum denominare, sed etiam existere existentia sui fundamenti, saltem imperfecte et inchoate, et sic denominare etiam, antequam actu apprehendatur. Sed restant huic responsioni duo difficilia explicanda. Primum, quod etiam talis existentia non denominabit perfecte et simpliciter tale sed solum inchoate et imperfecte; et sic signum in libro clauso vel in voce prolatum, sed non actu apprehensa relatione, non erit signum perfecte, sed inchoate et imperfecte, acquiret vero perfectam rationem signi, quando actu apprehenditur. Restat ergo eadem difficultas, quae in hanc cogit solutionem, scilicet quomodo signum in libro clauso vel in voce prolatum, sed non apprehensum relative, possit perfecte significare et ducere in signatum. Nec enim minus perfecte repraesentat ly homo suum significatum, si apprehendatur relatio eius, quam si non apprehendatur, retinet enim eodem modo impositionem et perfectam significationem. Ergo erit perfecte et consummate signum et non solum inchoate ante relationem, quia aeque perfecte significat et est signum ante illam.[35] — Secunda difficultas est, quia illa imperfecta existentia et inchoata vel est solum fundamentalis et virtualis respectu signi vel etiam actualis. Si fundamentalis tantum, hoc est dicere, quod solum existit fundamentum signi, non formaliter ipsum signum. Si actualis, difficile valde est, quod existentia realis, qualis est fundamenti, ante actualem apprehensionem reddat actualiter existens id, quod est ens rationis et solum habens esse obiectivum. Sic enim non erit pure ens rationis, cum sit capax etiam realis existentiae, licet imperfectae et inchoatae.

Alii existimant formaliter esse signum etiam ante formalem existentiam relationis

---

[35] The 1663 Lyons text adds: "*Aut saltem dignosceremus illam imperfectam significationem ex defectu apprehensionis relationis provenientem, aut posita relatione crescentem, quod nullus experitur. Si autem aeque perfecte ducit ante illam relationem, aeque perfecte significat et aeque perfecte est signum, ergo non solum imperfecte et inchoate existit.*"—"Or at least we should distinguish that imperfect signification arising from want of apprehension, or increasing when the relation is posited, which no one experiences. But if it leads equally perfectly prior to that relation, it equally perfectly signifies and is equally perfectly a sign, therefore it does not only imperfectly and inchoately exist."

relation of the sign. Others deem it to be a sign only in a moral way, because the imposition [the social institution of its meaning] is said to remain in a moral way. But the difficulty is whether this would be a sign-existence in act or not. For to speak of a sign being in act ''morally'' is to employ a mitigating particle, as if one were to say in act ''fundamentally,'' or in act ''virtually''; for that ''morality'' of the enduring imposition [namely, social usage] is the fundament of a relation.

Wherefore, it ought to be said simply that the imposition or stipulation of something to be a sign of such or such a thing is only the fundament of the relation of the sign, because it gives to the sign a connection with a given thing and a substitution for it for the purpose of signifying, not naturally, but according to the intention of the one imposing, just as the abstraction of a nature is the fundament of universality. Whence just as a natural sign exercises signification by reason of its fundament, even when it does not have a relation in act to what is signified owing to the nonexistence of that particular significate—for example, the statue of the emperor when the emperor himself is dead;[36] so a linguistic sound or mark, even when the relation is not conceived in act and consequently does not exist by means of a concept, still signifies and represents by reason of the imposition once made. This imposition does not create the sign formally, but fundamentally and proximately, as we will explain in Book II,[37] Question[38] 5.[39] And there is nothing particularly puzzling or incongruous about the fact that, in the case of these mind-dependent relatives, when the actual cognition of some pattern ceases, the formal existence of that pattern and the formal denomination originating from such an existence should also cease, and arise again when there is another actual cognition, as long as the fundamental denomination remains constant — the sort of denomination that remains in a universal when it is removed from comparison and relation and posited alone in abstraction; for it continues to be something universal metaphysically, not logically. So a stipulated sign without a cognized relation continues to be a sign morally and fundamentally and (as it were) metaphysically, that is to say, it remains in an order to the effect of representing; but it does not continue to be a sign formally and (as it were) logically or as regards the intention of the relation.[40]

You will press the point: That passive imposition of a sign leaves nothing mind-independent or physical in the sign, therefore it cannot move the cognitive power nor

signi. *Alii* solum morali modo censeri signum, quia morali modo dicitur manere impositio. Sed an hoc sit actu esse signum vel non, est difficultas. Nam actu moraliter est particula diminuens, perinde ac si dicatur actu fundamentaliter vel actu virtualiter; moralitas enim illa impositionis durantis est fundamentum relationis.

Quare simpliciter dicendum est, quod impositio seu destinatio alicuius, ut sit signum talis vel talis rei, solum est fundamentum relationis signi, quia dat illi connexionem cum tali re et subrogationem pro illa ad significandum non naturaliter, sed secundum placitum imponentis, sicut abstractio naturae est fundamentum universalitatis. Unde sicut signum naturale ratione sui fundamenti exercet significationem, etiamsi non habeat relationem actu ad signatum, quia tale signatum non existit, ut imago imperatoris ipso mortuo;[36] ita vox vel scriptura, etiamsi actu non concipiatur relatio et consequenter non existat mediante conceptu, adhuc significat et repraesentat ratione impositionis semel factae, quae non reddit formaliter signum, sed fundamentaliter proxime, ut dicemus [in] libro[37] seq. q.[38] 5.[39] Et non est ullum inconveniens in his relativis rationis, quod cessante cognitione actuali alicuius formae cesset formalis existentia illius et formalis denominatio a tali existentia proveniens, et rursus posita cognitione consurgat, manente semper fundamentali denominatione, qualis manet in universali remota comparatione et relatione positaque sola abstractione; manet enim universale metaphysice, non logice. Sic signum ad placitum sine relatione cognita manet signum moraliter et fundamentaliter et quasi metaphysice, id est in ordine ad effectum repraesentandi, non formaliter et quasi logice seu quoad intentionem relationis.[40]

Instabis: Illa impositio passiva signi nihil reale in eo relinquit, ergo nequit

[36] 125/26-126/22 above, esp. note 25.
[37] In the original Latin: ''quaest.''
[38] In the original Latin: ''art.''
[39] esp. at 275/9-41. See also the First Preamble, Article 3, 70/11-71/19.
[40] See also Book II, Question 5, 273/22-275/41.

lead that power to a significate, because a power cannot be moved by that which is nothing; for an object stimulating actuates and perfects a power, which the imposition in question cannot do. Therefore [a linguistic mark in a closed book or a linguistic sound heard but not understood] does not remain a sign fundamentally, [for] this [i.e., the fundamental being of a sign] consists in a stimulating and representing.

I answer that the entire argument so stated also applies to the case of the stipulated sign when it exists in act and completely; for it is always true of this genre of sign that it is something produced by the mind. And therefore we say that a stipulated sign moves (acts) by reason of the imposition, not as knowable immediately and by reason of itself, but mediately and through another, just as any other unreal beings; and thus we say, presupposing that its knowability is got by borrowing, a stipulated sign takes on the rationale of something moving and representing, just as it also takes on the rationale of something knowable.[41]

A third argument: the genus of sign is [defined by] the rationale of something representative together with the rationale of a knowable object, knowable not terminally, as what is signified, but instrumentally or mediately. But the rationale of something representative and the rationale of an object do not express the rationale of an ontological relation, but of a transcendental relation; what is more, the formality of something knowable as such is not being formally, but presuppositively, since it is a coincident property of being and consequently not the determinate kind of being that relation is; therefore neither is the sign the kind of being that relation is.

The consequence of this argument is clear, for if the genus does not fall within the pattern of something relative, how can the specific kinds of signs pertain to relation? The minor premise of the argument we grant. The major premise follows from the definition of the sign as what represents to a cognizing power; therefore being something representative and being an object or knowable thing belong to a sign essentially. For something cannot lead to the cognition of a signified except by objectifying and representing itself to a cognitive power; but "representing" cannot be predicated of a sign essentially as species or difference, since it also belongs to other things. Therefore it must be predicated as the genus.

This is confirmed: If sign in general cannot consist in a relation, then absolutely a sign is not a relation. The antecedent is proved in two ways. First, because the condition of being a sign is common to the formal and the instrumental sign; a formal sign, however, is not a relation, but a quality, since it is an awareness or concept, as is said

movere potentiam nec ducere illam ad signatum, quia potentia nequit moveri ab eo, quod est nihil; obiectum enim movens actuat et perficit potentiam, quod illa impositio non potest. Ergo non manet fundamentaliter signum, hoc est vis movens et repraesentans.

Respondetur totum hoc procedere etiam in signo ipso ad placitum existente actu et complete; semper enim aliquid rationis est. Et ideo dicimus, quod movet ratione impositionis, non ut cognoscibilis immediate et ratione sui, sed mediate et per aliud, sicut reliqua entia non realia, et sic supposita eius cognoscibilitate emendicata induit rationem moventis et repraesentantis sicut et cognoscibilis.[41]

Tertio arguitur: Genus signi est ratio repraesentativi et ratio obiecti cognoscibilis, non ultimi, ut signatum, sed medii. Sed ratio repraesentativi et obiecti non dicunt rationem relationis secundum esse, sed transcendentalis; imo et formalitas cognoscibilis ut sic non est ens formaliter, sed praesuppositive, cum sit passio entis et consequenter nec determinatum ens, quod est relatio; ergo neque signum.

Consequentia patet, quia si genus non est in ratione relativi, quomodo species ad relationem potest pertinere? *Minor* a nobis admittitur. *Maior* ex definitione signi constat, quod potentiae cognoscitivae repraesentativum est; ergo repraesentativum et ratio obiecti seu cognoscibilis signo essentialiter convenit. Non enim aliter ducere potest in cognitionem signati nisi obiciendo et repraesentando se potentiae; repraesentativum autem non potest essentialiter dici de signo ut species vel differentia, cum etiam aliis conveniat, ergo ut genus.

Confirmatur: Signum in communi non potest consistere in relatione, ergo absolute signum non est relatio. *Antecedens* probatur, *tum* quia signum est commune ad signum formale et instrumentale; formale autem non est relatio, sed qualitas, cum sit notitia vel conceptus, ut infra dicetur. *Tum* quia est com-

[41] See Question 4 below, 189/8-190/3 and esp. note 35 p. 190.

below. Second, because the condition of being a sign is common to the stipulated and the natural sign; there is, however, no relation common to both except relation abstracting from the mind-independent and the mind-dependent, in the opinion of those who say that the relation of a natural sign is mind-independent. But the relation of a sign is more determinate and contracted than that which abstracts from the mind-independent and the mind-dependent. Therefore the sign in general does not bespeak a relation according to the way it has being; for it would have to be placed determinately in some member of ontological relation, either in the physical or in the mental. [Yet if it were placed in one of these determinately, the condition of being a sign could not be common to both stipulated and natural signs.]

The response to this third argument[42] is that being representative is not the genus of sign, but the fundament, just as generative power is not the genus of paternity, but the fundament; nor is the fundament of sign the representative alone—for by itself the representative bears only remotely on a sign to be founded—but a definite sort of representative factor, namely, one substituting for a signified and subordinated to it in representing and leading it to a cognitive power. And representing is posited in the definition of the sign as the fundament which pertains to relation; for the sign as an instance of relation depends essentially on a fundament. And if the relation is of some cause or effect or operation, the entirety of its reality comes about through the fundament; for a relation has no other reality than to respect, if it is an ontological relation, just as a father generates by reason of a fundament, a master commands by reason of a fundament, a minister substitutes and operates by reason of a fundament, a sign represents by reason of a fundament. And this follows from the fact that the rationale of object or of a thing which can be represented is in a sign first in respect of itself; for it objectifies itself to the cognitive power, and insofar as it is an object it directly respects the power as measure of the power. All of which is not the genus of sign; for a sign more principally respects the significate to which it subordinates the very rationale of representing. Whence a sign begins to consist in a substitutive relation to a signified; a representative, however, as connecting itself substitutively with a signified, founds that relation, and that connection is the substitution fundamentally.

To the first part of the confirmation[43], the response is that awareness and a concept have the rationale of

mune ad signum ad placitum et naturale; nulla autem relatio utrique communis est nisi relatio abstrahens a reali et rationis, in sententia affirmante, quod relatio signi naturalis est realis. Relatio autem signi est magis determinata et contracta quam illa, quae abstrahit a reali et rationis. Ergo signum in communi non dicit relationem secundum esse; deberet enim poni in aliquo membro determinate, vel reali vel rationis.

Respondetur,[42] quod repraesentativum non est genus signi, sed fundamentum, sicut generativum non est genus paternitatis, sed fundamentum; nec repraesentativum tantum, sic enim solum remote se habet ad signum fundandum, sed repraesentativum tale, id est substituens pro signato eique subordinatum in repraesentando et ducendo ad potentiam. Et ponitur in definitione signi sicut fundamentum, quod pertinet ad relationem; dependet enim essentialiter a fundamento. Et si relatio sit alicuius causae vel effectus vel exercitii, totum ipsum exercitium fit per fundamentum; relatio enim aliud exercitium non habet quam respicere, si sit relatio secundum esse, sicut pater ratione fundamenti generat, dominus ratione fundamenti imperat, minister ratione fundamenti substituit et operatur, signum ratione fundamenti repraesentat. Et constat hoc, quia ratio obiecti seu repraesentabilis in signo primum est respectu sui; se enim obicit potentiae, et in quantum obiectum directe respicit potentiam ut mensura eiusdem. Quod totum non est genus signi; signum enim principalius respicit signatum, cui subordinat rationem ipsam repraesentandi. Unde in relatione substitutiva ad signatum incipit consistere; repraesentativum autem, ut connectens se substitutive cum signato, fundat illam relationem, et illa connexio est substitutio fundamentaliter.

Ad confirmationem[43] respondetur, quod notitia et conceptus habent ra-

[42] 131/19-43.
[43] 132/47-133/12.

a quality as they are an act or an image of an object, upon which likeness is founded the relation of the formal sign, in which relation the sign essentially consists, insofar as it is through it that awareness and concepts substitute for an object.[44] Just as the sacramental character is called by St. Thomas (in the passages cited above) a sign fundamentally, since in itself it is a quality, yet a quality founding a sign-relation: so a concept and an awareness are qualities which signify informatively, not objectively, but they found the relation constitutive of a formal sign, that is, the relation of the sign whose representation and exercise of signifying is brought about by the fact that it is informing.

And to the other part of the confirmation[45] the response is that sign in general bespeaks a relation more determinate than relation in general, whether a sign is a transcendental relation or an ontological relation. For that argument[46] bears on a point which every position [i.e., any theory of signs] must give an account of, to wit, how is it that the sign in general is a determinate kind of being and inferior to being as such, and yet is divided into the mind-independent or physical and the mind-dependent or purely objective? Indeed, even if a sign is a transcendental relation, in the case of a natural sign that relation will be mind-independent and in the case of a stipulated sign mind-dependent. This part of the argument, therefore, does not offer any special difficulty for our assertion that the sign-relation is ontological, that is, a relation according to the way relation has being. Wherefore it must be said that there is nothing to prevent inferior [less universal] things from being clothed in an analogous concept and divided in a manner analogical to, although more restricted than, superior [more universal] things. And according as analogues of a more restricted analogy are referred to a more universal analogous concept, they are not placed under a determinate and univocal member of a division of the more universal analogy, but relate analogously both among themselves in the restricted analogy and to the members of the more universal analogy. A familiar example is in this name "wisdom." For wisdom is a concept more determinate than being, and yet it is neither created nor uncreated determinately, but can be divided into both, because it can be understood analogically. But if "wisdom" were understood univocally, then it will be determinately created or determinately uncreated. In the same way, the name "man," if likewise understood as it abstracts from the differences between a true man and a pictured man, a living man and a dead man, is something inferior to [less universal than] being, but not in a determinate

tionem qualitatis, ut sunt actus vel imago obiecti, super quod fundatur relatio signi formalis, in qua essentialiter signum consistit, quatenus sic substituunt pro obiecto.[44] Sicut character dicitur a Divo Thoma locis supra citatis signum fundamentaliter, cum in se qualitas sit, fundans tamen relationem signi: sic conceptus et notitia qualitates sunt informative, non obiective significantes, fundant autem relationem signi formalis, id est cuius repraesentatio et exercitium significandi informando fit.

Et ad alteram partem argumenti[45] respondetur, quod signum in communi dicit relationem magis determinatam quam relatio in communi, sive transcendentalis sit sive relatio secundum esse. Nam illud argumentum[46] in omni opinione currit, quomodo scilicet signum in communi sit ens determinatum et inferius ad ens ut sic, et tamen dividatur in reale et rationis; siquidem si relatio transcendentalis est, in signo naturali realis erit et in signo ad placitum rationis. Non ergo specialem difficultatem affert contra nostram assertionem de relatione signi secundum esse. Quare dicendum est nullum esse inconveniens, quod res inferiores induant conceptum analogum et dividantur modo analogico sicut superiora, licet magis restricto. Et prout subsunt conceptui analogo, non ponuntur sub determinato et univoco membro divisionis superioris, sed ad utrumque analogice pertinent. Exemplum vulgare est in hoc nomine ,,Sapientia''. Est enim conceptus magis determinatus quam ens, et tamen nec est determinate creata nec increata, sed potest dividi in utramque, quia potest sumi analogice. Si vero sumatur univoca sapientia, sic erit determinate creata vel determinate increata. Eodem modo homo, si sumatur etiam ut abstrahit a vero et picto, vivo et mortuo, aliquid inferius est ad ens, sed non in determinato membro, quia analogice

[44] See Question 3 below, 164/13-165/8, and the Sequel to Book I, 219/29-48.
[45] 132/1-15.
[46] at ibid.

member of some division of being, because it is understood analogically, and consequently not as determinately one nor determinately in one member. Thus the state of being a sign, as something common to the natural and the stipulated, is analogous, just as if it were common to a true sign and a pictured sign, a mind-independent sign and a mind-dependent sign, and, accordingly, the sign as such is not in a determinate division of being or of relation, but each of its inferiors, i.e., each of its particular instances, will be in a determinate order or class according to its kind.[47]

sumitur, et consequenter non ut determinate unum nec determinate in uno membro. Sic signum ut commune ad naturale et ad placitum est analogum veluti ad signum verum et pictum, reale et rationis, et prout sic non est in determinato membro entis vel relationis, sed quodlibet suorum inferiorum secundum se erit in determinato genere.[47]

---

[47] Cf. Book II, Question 1, 235/46-236/46.

Question 2

Whether the Sign-Relation in the Case of Natural Signs Is Mind-Independent or Mind-Dependent

Quaestio Secunda

Utrum in Signo Naturali Relatio Sit Realis vel Rationis

To get to the point of difficulty, it is necessary to distinguish the several relations which can concur in a sign. There is no doubt that some of these relations could exist in a natural sign independently of mind, yet they are not the formal and definitive relation of sign. A sign by its definition is "that which represents something to a knowing power." If the sign is outside the cognitive power, in order to represent another it must have in itself the rationale of an object knowable in itself, so that the cognitive power might arrive at another by knowing the sign.[1] If, on the other hand, the sign is a formal sign and within the power, in order to represent another it must be an intentional representation independent of being itself known objectively, which in the physical order is a kind of quality, yet one with a relation of similitude to that of which it is a representation, and with an order to the power.[2]

Similarly, for a sign to be said to represent this rather than that, there has to be in it some congruence or proportion and connection with the given significate. This proportion or congruence can take several forms. Sometimes it is one of an effect to a cause or of cause to effect, as, for example, smoke

Ut attingatur punctus difficultatis, oportet discernere plures relationes, quae in signo concurrere possunt. Et de aliquibus non est dubium, quod in signo naturali possint esse reales, non tamen illae sunt ipsa formalis et quidditativa relatio signi. Cum enim signum iuxta suam definitionem dicatur «id, quod repraesentat aliquid potentiae cognoscenti», oportet, quod in signo, ut repraesentet aliud, si sit signum extra potentiam, habeat rationem obiecti cognoscibilis in se, ut eo cognito ad aliud potentia deveniat;[1] si vero sit signum formale et intra potentia, quod sit realis et intentionalis repraesentatio, quae in re qualitas quaedam est, cum relatione tamen similitudinis ad id, cuius est repraesentatio, et ordine ad potentiam.[2]

Similiter habet inveniri in signo aliqua convenientia seu proportio et connexio cum tali significato, ut dicatur repraesentare hoc potius quam illud. Quae proportio seu convenientia varia est. Aliquando enim est effectus ad causam vel causae ad effectum,

---

[1] See Question 3 below, 163/12-36, esp. note 11; Book II, Question 1, 224/13-19, and Question 2, note 27, p. 249, citation from Poinsot's Phil. nat. 4 p. q. 11, art. 2.

[2] See above, Question 1, 132/47-134/10; and below, Book II, Question 1, 227/9-49, 231/45-233/2, Question 2, 250/7-39.

as an effect signifies fire, clouds or wind as a cause signify rain. Sometimes it is one of similitude or of an image or of whatever other proportion. But in the case of stipulated signs, it is the imposition and appointment, the acceptance, by common usage. In a word: since a sign functions relative to a significate and to a cognitive power, the respects or rationales which habilitate it to the power or those which habilitate it to the signified can precede the forming of the rationale of a sign. But the formal and definitive rationale of a sign does not consist in these, nor does its relation to the thing signified (although the Jesuit school of Aristotelian commentary associated with the university of Coimbra, Portugal, the so-called "Conimbricenses," holds the opposite opinion in Book I, q. 1, art. 2 of their Commentary on the *Perihermenias* books), since indeed they can be separated and found apart from the rationale of a sign. For the rationale of an object is found without the rationale of a sign; and the rationale of an effect or cause or similitude or image can also be found apart from the rationale of a sign. Again because a relation to some thing bespeaks diverse fundaments and formal rationales, as, for example: the relation to an effect or a cause, which is founded on an action; or the relation of an image, which is founded on a similarity of imitation without an order to a cognitive power; or the relation of a sign, which is founded on the measured's being relative to its measure in the mode of a representative substituting for another in an order to a cognitive power, which the other relations do not respect.

We ask, therefore, whether that formal and most proper sign-relation, which is found in addition to or as arising from all those involved in the habilitation of a sign to its significate or to a cognitive power, is a mind-independent relation in the case of physical or natural signs. And we certainly acknowledge that the relation of object to power, which precedes the sign-relation in the case of the instrumental sign, whether by way of stimulating or of terminating, is not a mind-independent relation, because an object does not respect a power by a relation that is mind-independent according to the way it has being, but rather the power respects the object and depends upon and is specified by it. And supposing that the relation of object to power were mind-independent, and that the object reciprocally respects the power in just the way that the power respects the object (which is certainly an assumption contrary to fact, since the object is the measure and the power the measured), this relation still would not be the relation nor the rationale of the sign, because the rationale of an object formally and directly respects or is respected by the power in such a way that the respect between the two is im-

sicut fumus significat ignem ut effectus, nubes vel ventus significat pluviam ut causa. Aliquando est similitudinis vel imaginis vel cuiuscumque alterius proportionis; in signis autem ad placitum est impositio et destinatio a republica. Et unico verbo: Cum signum se habeat ad signatum et ad potentiam, possunt praecedere ad construendam rationem signi vel respectus seu rationes, quae habilitent ipsum ad potentiam vel ad signatum. Sed in istis non consistit formalis et quidditativa ratio signi nec relatio eius ad rem significatam, licet oppositum sentiant Conimbric. 1. Periherm. q. 1. art. 2.; siquidem possunt separari et inveniri sine ratione signi. Nam ratio obiecti sine ratione signi invenitur, ratio etiam effectus vel causae vel similitudinis aut imaginis sine ratione signi possunt reperiri. Item quia diversum fundamentum et rationem formalem dicit relatio ad rem aliquam, ut ad effectum vel causam, quod fundatur in actione, vel imaginis, quod fundatur in similitudine imitationis sine ordine ad potentiam, vel signi, quod fundatur in mensurato ad mensuram per modum repraesentativi substituentis pro alio in ordine ad potentiam, quam non respiciunt aliae relationes.

Quaerimus ergo, an illa formalis et propriissima relatio signi, quae praeter istas omnes reperitur aut ex illis consurgit, realis relatio sit in signis realibus vel naturalibus. Et quidem fatemur, quod relatio obiecti ad potentiam, quae praecedit in signo instrumentali sive per modum moventis sive terminantis, realis relatio non est, quia obiectum non respicit potentiam relatione reali secundum esse, sed potius potentia respicit obiectum et ab eo dependet et specificatur. Et dato, quod relatio obiecti ad potentiam realis esset, et mutuo respiceret obiectum potentiam, sicut potentia obiectum (quod constat esse falsum, cum obiectum sit mensura et potentia mensuratum), tamen non est relatio neque ratio signi, quia ratio obiecti formaliter et directe respicit vel respicitur a potentia ita, quod immediatus respectus est

mediate; but the rationale of a sign directly respects a signified and a power indirectly, because it respects the thing signified as that which is to be manifested to a cognitive power.[3] Therefore there is a different line and order of respecting in an object inasmuch as it is an object, and in a sign inasmuch as it is a sign, although for it to be a sign, an object must be supposed.[4]

I answer the question before us therefore by saying: **The relation of a natural sign to its significate by which the sign is constituted in being as a sign, is mind-independent and not mind-dependent, considered in itself and by virtue of its fundament and presupposing the existence of the terminus and the other conditions for a mind-independent or physical relation.**

This seems to be the view more in conformity with THE THINKING OF ST. THOMAS, principally because he teaches that the sign-relation in the sacramental character is founded on a quality superadded to the soul, which quality is a physical fundament, as is clear from the *Summa theologica*, III, q. 63, art. 2, reply to obj. 3, and in the *Commentary on the Sentences of Peter Lombard*, Book IV, dist. 4, q. 1, art. 1.[5] And he is speaking of the proximate fundament, because he opposes those who have said that this relation is founded immediately upon the soul, and

inter ipsa; ratio autem signi directe respicit signatum et in obliquo potentia, quia respicit signatum ut manifestandum potentiae.[3] Diversa ergo linea et ordo respiciendi est in obiecto quatenus obiectum, et in signo quatenus signum, licet ut signum sit, obiectum supponi debeat.[4]

RESPONDEO ERGO ET DICO: **Relatio signi naturalis ad suum signatum, qua constituitur in esse signi, realis est, et non rationis, quantum est ex se et vi sui fundamenti et supponendo existentiam termini ceterasque conditiones relationis realis.**

Haec videtur conformior menti S. Thomae. Primo, quia docet relationem signi characteris fundari in qualitate superaddita animae, quae reale fundamentum est, ut patet 3. p. q. 63. art. 2. ad 3. et in 4. dist. 4. q. 1. art. 1.[5] Et loquitur de fundamento proximo, quia impugnat eos, qui dicebant fundari hanc relationem immediate super animam, et

---

[3] The Lyons text of 1663 adds: "*Unde distinctio et varietas signorum non sumitur ex ordine ad potentiam vel ex diverso modo immutandi illam sicut obiectum, sed ex diversitate rei significatae. Licet enim eodem modo immutet potentiam vestigium bovis et fumus, tamen differunt in ratione signi propter diversum respectum ad signatum, non ad potentiam.*"—"Whence the distinction and variety of signs is not taken from the order to a power or from diverse ways of affecting that power as an object, but from a diversity of the thing signified. For even though a cow's footprint and smoke affect a cognitive power in the same way, they nevertheless differ in the rationale of sign on account of diverse respects to the signified, not to the power." Cf. this Question below, 145/10-28; and Book II, Question 1, 238/28-45.

[4] The Lyons text of 1663 adds: "*Similiter relationes illae, quibus signum proportionare potest ad signatum, diversae sunt formaliter a relatione ipsa signi, e.g. relatio effectus vel causae, similitudinis vel imaginis etc., licet aliqui recentes confundant relationem signi cum istis relationibus, sed immerito: tum quia diversum exercitium est in signo significare vel causari aut similem esse. In significando enim exercetur substitutio principalis signati, ut manifestetur potentiae, in ratione vero causae aut effectus nihil de ordine ad potentiam includitur; quare distincta fundamenta sunt, et sic distinctas relationes postulant. Et praeterea separari possunt relationes istae a relatione signi, sicut filius est similis patri et effectus eius et imago, non tamen signum. Addit ergo relatio signi super illas relationes, quas supponit aut praerequirit, ut habilitetur et proportionetur huic signato potius quam illi.*"—"Similarly, those relations by which a sign can be proportioned to a signified are formally other than the sign-relation itself, e.g., the relation of effect to cause, of similitude or image, etc., even though some recent authors confound the sign-relation with these relations, but unwarrantably: because to signify or to be caused or to be similar are diverse exercises in a sign. For in signifying, a substitution for the principal significate is exercised, that that principal may be manifested to a power, but in the rationale of a cause or an effect is included nothing of an order to a cognitive power; wherefore they are distinct fundaments, and so postulate distinct relations. These relations, moreover, can be separated from the sign-relation, just as a son is similar to the father and his effect and image, but not a sign. The sign-relation therefore adds to these relations, which it supposes or prerequires in order to be habilitated and proportioned to this significate rather than to that one." See Book I, Question 3 below, 160/10-21, and the discussion in note 13 of that same Question, pp. 163-164.

[5] *Pa* VII. 506 a.

he teaches that there must be something else to mediate, upon which the sign-relation of the sacramental character is founded, namely, the quality of the character; he is speaking therefore of the proximate fundament. And in the *Summa theologica*, I, q. 16, art. 6, he says that while health does not reside in urine and in medicine, "there is nevertheless something in both, on account of which the latter indeed produces and the former signifies health." Therefore the sign-relation in the case of a natural sign is founded on something independent of mind, some physical characteristic or quality of the sort that founds the relation of urine to health, namely, something that possesses intrinsically the power of signifying, just as medicine possesses intrinsically the power of effecting health.

THE FOUNDATION OF THE CONCLUSION is taken from the very nature and definable structure of the sign, which consists in this, that it be something more known by which is represented and manifested something more unknown, as St. Thomas well notes in his *Disputed Questions on Truth*, q. 9, art. 4, reply to obj. 5,[6] and in his *Commentary on the Sentences*, Book IV, dist. 1, q. 1, art. 1, quaestiunc. 1, reply to obj. 5, and quaestiunc. 2.[7] But for something to be more known than another and render that other knowable and representable, it is required that the knowability of the former should be more capable of arousing or stimulating a cognitive power, and determined or conditioned to the specific significate, in order that it should arouse [the power] to [an awareness of] that significate rather than some other one, whether this arousal and representation comes about formally or objectively. But that a thing is knowable in itself cannot be something produced by the mind; and that it is more knowable relatively to another and renders that other represented, is also something mind-independent in the case of natural signs. Therefore the sign-relation in the case of a natural sign is mind-independent.

The minor premise here has two parts, to wit, that a thing in itself is knowable independently of mind, and also that relatively to another it renders that other represented and knowable independently of mind.

The first part of the minor premise is proved by the fact that a thing is knowable prior to any operation of the understanding. For if it were rendered knowable by the operation of the understanding, it would be knowable through being known and so would not be knowable prior to cognition, which contradicts the fact that cognition in us is taken from what is knowable; but

docet debere mediare aliud, super quod fundetur relatio characteristici signi, scilicet qualitatem characteris; loquitur ergo de fundamento proximo. Et 1. p. q. 16. art. 6. dicit, quod licet in urina et medicina non sit sanitas, «est tamen aliquid in utroque, per quod hoc quidem facit, illud vero significat sanitatem». Ergo in aliquo reali fundatur relatio signi naturalis, qualis est urinae ad sanitatem, nempe in aliquo, quod habet in se, ut significet, sicut medicina habet, ut efficiat.

ET FUNDAMENTUM conclusionis deducitur ex ipsa natura et quidditate signi, quae in eo consistit, quod sit aliquid magis notum, quo repraesentetur et manifestetur ignotius, ut bene notat S. Thomas q. 9. de Veritate art. 4. ad 5.[6] et in 4. dist. 1. q. 1. art. 1. quaestiunc. 1. ad 5., quaestiunc. 2.[7] Ad hoc autem, quod aliquid sit notius altero illudque reddat cognoscibile et repraesentabile, requiritur, quod cognoscibilitas istius sit habilior altera ad movendum potentiam, et determinata seu affecta ad tale signatum, ut ad illud potius moveat quam ad aliud, sive ista motio et repraesentatio fiat formaliter sive obiective. Sed quod aliquid in seipso sit cognoscibile, non potest esse aliquid rationis; quod vero relate ad alterum sit cognoscibilius et reddens ipsum repraesentatum, aliquid etiam reale est in signis naturalibus. Ergo relatio signi naturalis realis est.

Minor habet duas partes, scil. quod res in seipsa sit cognoscibilis realiter, et quod etiam relate ad alterum reddat realiter aliud repraesentatum et cognoscibile.

Et quoad primam partem probatur, quia ante omnem operationem intellectus res est cognoscibilis. Si enim per operationem intellectus cognoscibilis redderetur, esset cognoscibilis per esse cognitum, et sic non esset cognoscibilis ante cognitionem, quod repugnat, quia cognitio sumitur in nobis a cognoscibili,

[6] *Pa* IX. 151 b.
[7] *Pa* VII. 455 b.

if the knowable is rendered such by the mind or by knowledge, then knowledge is prior to knowability, and consequently knowledge is not taken from knowability as from an object.

Nor does it matter that the cognizable or the object does not respect the cognitive power by a mind-independent relation, but by a mind-dependent relation, because the very mind-independence of knowability is proven the more strongly by this fact. For it is because the power depends on the object, and not the object on the power, that the object respects the power by a mind-dependent relation; and the object exists as measure, the power, however, as measured, which pertains to relations of the third type[8] in which the measured is dependent and therefore respects physically, but the measure does not depend on the measured and so respects it only through the mind. But nevertheless this fact itself argues for the greater reality in the very rationale of measure, inasmuch as it is the less dependent and consequently the less reality is in [its] relation [to the measured] just as, for example, the fact that God is a lord relatively is something mental, but potestatively it is something physical. And similarly a free act is physically free in God and by a much greater independence of our mind, because only by our mind is it referred to the free object, while physically it does not depend on it. Therefore the knowable in physical objects is absolutely and in itself something mind-independent, but relatively to a cognitive power it is something mind-dependent. But that knowability is greater or more manifest in one thing than in another, is not taken from the mind-dependent relation to a power, which is found in every object, but from the greater force and efficacy of arousing or stimulating and manifesting, which in itself is something independent of mind.

The second part of the minor premise[9] is shown by the fact that although the knowable is something mind-dependent in its order to a power, nevertheless it is in itself something mind-independently knowable. Therefore, in order for a natural sign to be knowable not only in itself and with respect to itself, but also with respect to another in whose capacity it functions and for which it substitutes in knowability and presentation, a relation must intervene independently of mind. The consequence is clear from the fact that the substitutive relation in the case of natural signs is founded on the physical cognizability and mind-independent connection of the sign with a specific significate, in order that the sign

si autem per rationem seu per cognitionem redditur cognoscibile, prior est cognitio quam cognoscibilitas, et consequenter ab illa ut ab obiecto non sumitur.

Neque obstat, quod cognoscibile seu obiectum non reali relatione respicit potentiam, sed relatione rationis, quia potius ex hoc realitas ipsa cognoscibilitatis probatur. Ideo enim respicit potentiam relatione rationis, quia potentia pendet ab obiecto, non obiectum a potentia; et se habet obiectum ut mensura, potentia autem ut mensuratum, quod pertinet ad relationes tertii ordinis,[8] in quibus mensuratum est dependens ideoque realiter respicit, mensura vero non pendet a mensurato et sic solum per rationem respicit illud. Sed tamen hoc ipsum arguit maiorem realitatem in ipsa ratione mensurae, quanto est minus dependens et consequenter minor realitas est in relatione, sicut Deum esse dominum relative est aliquid rationis, sed potestative est aliquid reale. Et similiter actus liber realiter est liber in Deo et multo maiori realitati, quia solum per rationem refertur ad obiectum liberum, realiter autem ab eo non pendet. Sic ergo cognoscibile in obiectis realibus absolute et in se aliquid reale est, sed relative ad potentiam aliquid rationis. Quod autem cognoscibilitas in uno sit maior aut manifestior altera, non sumitur ex relatione rationis ad potentiam, quae in omni obiecto invenitur, sed ex maiori vi et efficacia movendi et manifestandi, quae in se aliquid reale est.

Secunda vero pars illius minoris[9] ostenditur, quia licet cognoscibile per ordinem ad potentiam sit aliquid rationis, tamen in se realiter cognoscibile est. Ergo ut non solum sit cognoscibile in se et respectu sui, sed etiam respectu alterius, cuius vices gerit et pro quo substituit in cognoscibilitate et praesentatione, realis relatio intercedet. Patet consequentia, quia fundatur in cognoscibilitate reali et connexione reali ipsius cum hoc signifi-

---

[8] Explained in the Second Preamble above, Article 3, esp. 101/27-102/34, 105/15-109/34.
[9] 138/40-41.

should represent that significate; the relation is not founded on a connection with a cognitive power. Therefore a natural sign will be a substitute for that specific thing and will respect it as the thing signified by a mind-independent relation, although such knowability does not respect a cognitive power independently of mind. For the fact that smoke represents fire rather than water, that the footprint of an ox represents an ox rather than a man, and that the concept of a horse represents a horse rather than a stone, is founded on some mind-independent or physical and intrinsic proportion of those signs with these significates; from a mind-independent proportion and connection with something, however, arises a mind-independent relation. Whence it happens that some thinkers are very much deluded on this point, who, upon seeing that the knowability or apprehensibility of a sign founds the sign-relation, and that this apprehensibility is a mind-dependent relation to a cognitive power, suppose without discussion that the very rationale of a sign is simply a mind-dependent relation. They are greatly deceived in this. The relation of knowability to a cognitive power *precedes and is presupposed for* the rationale of a sign: for it pertains to the rationale common to *any* object or cognizable thing. But for the rationale of a sign it is *further* required that the knowability of the sign be connected and coordinated with another, that is, a thing signified, so that the sign substitutes for and is subordinated and servile to that thing in bringing it to mind. And thus the relation of this knowability of the sign to that of the significate will also be an essentially mind-independent relation, because it is founded on the proportion and greater connection which this knowability has relative to that knowability rather than to some other, so that the sign can substitute for that knowability and be vicegerent, and this is given on the side of physical nature, as is also the exercise of representing to the cognitive power, even though the order and relation to the cognitive power is not mind-independent; for whether the relation of object to power is mind-independent is one question, [but] whether a representation is mind-independent is quite another question again.

Whence St. Thomas says in his *Disputed Questions on Truth*, q. 3, art. 1, reply to obj. 2,[10] that "for a specifying form which is a medium [of awareness], two things are required, namely, a representation of the known thing, which belongs to the specifier according to propinquity to the cognizable, and a spiritual existence, which belongs

cato, ut illud repraesentet, non in connexione cum potentia. Ergo reali relatione erit substitutum illius et respiciet illud ut signatum, licet potentiam talis cognoscibilitas non respiciat realiter. Nam quod fumus repraesentet potius ignem quam aquam, et vestigium bovis potius bovem quam hominem, et conceptus equi potius equum quam lapidem, in aliqua reali proportione et intrinseca istorum signorum cum illis signatis fundatur; ex reali autem proportione et connexione cum aliquo realis relatio innascitur. Unde contingit hic maxime hallucinari aliquos, qui sine discussione, cum videant cognoscibilitatem seu apprehensibilitatem signi fundare relationem signi, et haec apprehensibilitas est relatio rationis ad potentiam, simpliciter ipsam rationem signi relationem esse rationis putant. Ceterum in hoc valde falluntur, quia relatio cognoscibilitatis ad potentiam praecedit et praesupponitur ad rationem signi: pertinet enim ad communem rationem obiecti seu cognoscibilis. Sed ulterius ad rationem signi requiritur, quod cognoscibilitas signi connectatur et coordinetur alteri, id est signato, ita ut substituat pro eo et subordinetur ac serviat ei in deferendo ipsum ad potentiam. Et ita relatio huius cognoscibilitatis signi ad illam signati erit relatio realis et per se, quia fundatur in proportione et maiori connexione, quam habet haec cognoscibilitas ad illam, quam ad aliam, ita ut pro illa possit substituere et vices gerere, et hoc a parte rei datur, et exercitium repraesentandi potentiae etiam a parte rei datur, licet ordo et relatio ad potentiam realis non sit; aliud est enim relatio obiecti ad potentiam an realis sit, aliud an repraesentatio realis sit.

Unde D. Thomas q. 3. de Veritate art. 1. ad 2.[10] inquit, «quod ad speciem, quae est medium, requiruntur duo, scilicet repraesentatio rei cognitae, quae competit ei secundum propinquitatem ad cognoscibile, et esse spirituale, quod competit

[10] *Pa* IX. 54 a.

to the specifier according to the being that it has in one cognizing." I am weighing here particularly these words: "representation, which belongs to a specifying form according to propinquity, etc." Therefore a representation in the case of a natural sign is founded in the propinquity of the sign to the knowable object for which it substitutes and in respect of which it is a medium or means. But this propinquity will be a mind-independent relation in the case of those things which are proportioned and linked independently of mind, because it has in that case a mind-independent fundament.

You may gather from what has been said that **even in the case of stipulated signs the rationale of sign must be explained by a relation to a signified**. But the relation in this case is mind-dependent, yet the sign does not consist only in the extrinsic denomination whereby it is rendered imposed or appointed for signifying by common usage, as some more recent philosophers[11] think, from the fact that, apart from the relation constructed by the understanding, the sign is denominated by the very imposition alone. Yet this imposition is indeed required as the fundament of the relation and rationale of the sign, because it is through this imposition that something is habilitated and appointed to be a stipulated sign, just as it is through some natural sign's being proportioned and connected with a given significate that there is founded a relation of the sign to that significate.

From that extrinsic denomination of stipulation and imposition,[12] thus, a twofold mind-dependent relation arises: The first is one common to every extrinsic denomination, insofar as an extrinsic denomination is conceived by the understanding on the pattern of a form and a denominating relation, as, for example, being seen is conceived relative to the one seeing, being loved relative to the one loving. The other is the particular relation by which one denomination is distinguished from another. For there can be appointment and imposition by the community to various offices, which are not distinguished otherwise than by a relation to those functions for the exercise of which they are appointed, just as someone is appointed and installed as a judge, a president, a teacher, and other things are instituted to be signs or insignia of these offices, and similarly, linguistic expressions are appointed to serve human communication. These offices or functions arise from a distinction of the requirements of public life, which is an extrinsic de-

ei secundum esse, quod habet in cognoscente». Ubi pondero illa verba: «repraesentatio, quae competit ei secundum propinquitatem etc.». Ergo repraesentatio in signo naturali fundatur in propinquitate ipsius ad cognoscibile, pro quo substituit et respectu cuius est medium. Haec autem propinquitas in his, quae realiter proportionantur et coniunguntur, realis relatio erit, cum reale fundamentum habeat.

Ex dictis colliges in signis ad placitum rationem signi etiam per relationem ad signatum explicandam esse. Sed relatio ista rationis est, et non solum consistit signum in extrinseca denominatione, qua redditur impositum seu destinatum a republica ad significandum, ut aliqui recentiores[11] putant, eo quod sine illa fictione intellectus per solam ipsam impositionem denominatur signum. Ceterum haec impositio requiritur quidem tamquam fundamentum relationis et rationis signi, quia per illam habilitatur et destinatur aliquid, ut sit signum, sicut per hoc, quod proportionatur et connectitur aliquod signum naturale cum tali signato, fundat relationem signi ad ipsum.

Itaque ex denominatione illa extrinseca destinationis et impositionis[12] consurgit duplex relatio rationis: *Prima* communis omni extrinsecae denominationi, quatenus concipitur per intellectum ad modum formae et relationis denominantis, ut esse visum ad videntem, esse amatum ad amantem. *Alia* est relatio particularis, qua una denominatio distinguitur ab alia. Destinatio enim et impositio reipublicae ad varia munera esse potest, quae non nisi relatione distinguuntur ad ea, ad quae exercenda destinantur, sicut destinatur aliquis et instituitur, ut sit iudex, praeses, doctor, et aliqua, ut sint signa vel insignia horum munerum, et similiter voces destinantur, ut humanae conversationi deserviant. Haec munera ex distinctione reipublicae oriuntur, quae denom-

[11] In particular, Suarez, *De sacramentis*, disp. 1, par. 6. See Book II below, Question 5, 273/22-275/41.

[12] See the discussion of extrinsic denomination in the First Preamble above, esp. Article 1, 55/7-49 and Article 2, 60/7-44.

nomination. They are further distinguished because a judge is ordered to judging a certain population, a president to governing, a teacher to instructing, etc.: which distinctions are understood through an order to their offices, or to the objects concerning which they are exercised, and they are not explained in any other way than through relations; therefore they are distinguished by the relations to their offices and objects. The same therefore must be said of stipulated signs, even though they are founded by the extrinsic denomination of imposition. And when the relation ceases, these signs are said to remain fundamentally, inasmuch as that appointment of common usage is said to remain morally or virtually.

Resolution of Counter-Arguments

Arguments for proving that the natural sign is something mind-dependently relative can be developed in two ways: either from the aspect in which a sign respects a cognitive power, or from the aspect in which a sign respects a signified.

The argument based on the aspect of the sign which respects the power is a common one, but difficult to resolve: A sign respects a power by a mind-dependent relation. But this relation is intrinsic and essential to a sign, and indeed the more principal one. Therefore a natural sign does not consist precisely in a mind-independent or physical relation.

The major premise in this argument is certain, because between sign and power obtains an order of the same line and rationale as that which exists between object and power. For a sign is a kind of object or substitute for an object, and in this capacity it moves a power objectively, not effectively, and therefore respects the power in the same order as does an object. But it is certain that an object respects a power by a relation constructed by the mind, a mind-dependent relation, because there is not a reciprocal relation between power and object. Therefore from the side of the other extreme [i.e., the object] there is not a mind-independent relation; but not from the side of the power is the case that there no mind-independent relation [i.e., a relation obtaining without having to be itself part of the known object as such], because a power physically respects an object, therefore the relation between power and object will be mind-dependent from the side of the object. Now an instrumental sign in particular cannot manifest anything to a power except as it is known; to be known, however, is something mind-dependent. Therefore an instrumental sign leads to a significate by means of something mind-dependent, i.e., by means of a being known.

The minor premise is proved: First, because a sign is an instrument which the cognitive power uses

inatio extrinseca est. Ceterum distinguuntur, quia iudex ordinatur ad tales subditos iudicandum, praeses ad regendum, doctor ad docendum etc.: quae distinctiones sumuntur per ordinem ad sua officia seu obiecta, circa quae exercentur, et nonnisi per relationes explicantur, et non aliter; ergo relationibus ad sua munera et obiecta distinguuntur. Idem ergo dicendum de signis ad placitum, licet denominatione extrinseca impositionis fundentur. Et cessante relatione dicuntur manere ista fundamentaliter, quatenus illa destinatio reipublicae moraliter dicitur manere aut virtualiter.

Solvuntur argumenta.

Ex duplici capite possunt fieri argumenta ad probandum, quod signum naturale sit relativum rationis: vel qua parte signum respicit potentiam, vel qua parte respicit signatum.

Ex parte, qua respicit potentiam, argumentum est commune, sed difficile: Nam signum respicit potentiam relatione rationis. Sed haec relatio est illi intrinseca et essentialis, imo magis principalis. Ergo signum naturale non consistit praecise in relatione reali.

Maior est certa, quia inter signum et potentiam reperitur ordo eiusdem lineae et rationis, quae est inter obiectum et potentiam. Signum enim quoddam obiectum est seu substitutum obiecti, et ita movet obiective, non effective potentiam, atque adeo in eodem ordine cum obiecto respicit potentiam. Constat autem obiectum respicere potentiam relatione rationis, quia non est relatio mutua inter potentiam et obiectum. Ergo ex parte alterius extremi non est relatio realis; sed non ex parte potentiae, quia haec realiter respicit obiectum, ergo erit rationis ex parte obiecti. Specialiter autem signum instrumentale non potest manifestare aliquid potentiae nisi prout cognitum; esse autem cognitum est aliquid rationis. Ergo signum instrumentale mediante aliquo rationis, id est mediante esse cognitum ducit in signatum.

Minor vero probatur: *Tum*, quia signum est instrumentum, quo potentia uti-

in order to arrive at a thing signified. Second, because the end to which a sign is ordered is a manifestation of the signified to the power itself. Therefore the power itself, or rather, its cognition to which the sign leads, is the end principally intended by the sign, and therefore an order to a power is intrinsic and essential to a sign.

This reasoning is confirmed by the fact that a formal and an instrumental sign differ within the rationale of sign, as we will explain in Book II,[13] yet they do not differ because of a diverse order to the signified, but to a cognitive power. For smoke as an instrumental sign and a concept [i.e., a formal sign] of fire respect the same thing signified, namely, fire; but smoke does so instrumentally, the concept formally. Therefore they differ from diverse orders to a knowing power, and so this order is essential to a sign, inasmuch as a formal sign respects a power as a form of cognition, an instrumental sign as an external stimulus.

The response to this argument[14] is that whether the order of sign to signified and to power is one relation only or two (which will be our next question[15]), in either case, precisely as it is a sign and under this formality, it does not respect a power directly and principally, nor does a sign respect a power as the power's measure, but as a way of access to, and as something leading a power to, that which is the power's object and is manifestable to the power, namely, a significate. Whence power and sign alike respect the signified as a manifestable object by which they are specified and measured—the power indeed as capacity knowing and tending toward that significate, the sign as the way of access and means through which the power is so inclined. But the fact that a sign may also be an object and be known first as such so that through it the power might tend toward the significate, is not that which essentially constitutes a sign insofar as it is a sign; for a formal sign, without being an object known by the power, but being the form rendering the power actually knowing, manifests the signified to it. What pertains essentially to the rationale of a sign, therefore, is that it be something substituting for an object in the representing of that object to a cognitive power, which substitution bespeaks an actual subordination and relation to a signified as to the principal object. This

tur ad deveniendum in signatum. *Tum,* quia finis, ad quem ordinatur signum, est manifestatio signati ad ipsam potentiam. Ergo ipsa potentia seu cognitio eius, ad quam signum ducit, est finis principaliter intentus a signo, atque adeo intrinsecus et essentialis est illi ordo ad potentiam.

Et confirmatur, quia signum formale et instrumentale differunt in ratione signi, ut dicemus in Libro Secundo,[13] et non differunt ex ordine ad signatum, sed ad potentiam. Idem enim signatum respicit fumus ut signum instrumentale, scilicet ignem, et conceptus ignis; sed fumus instrumentaliter, conceptus formaliter. Ergo differunt ex diverso ordine ad potentiam, et ita hic ordo essentialis est signo, quatenus signum formale respicit potentiam ut forma cognitionis, instrumentale ut movens extrinsecum.

Respondetur,[14] quod sive ordo ad signatum et ad potentiam in signo sit unus tantum sive duplex, de quo quaest.[15] seq., tamen ut signum est et stando sub hac formalitate, non respicit potentiam directe et principaliter neque ut mensura eius, sed ut via et ductivum potentiae ad id, quod est obiectum eius et manifestabile ipsi, scil. ad signatum. Unde tam potentia quam signum respiciunt signatum ut obiectum manifestabile, a quo specificantur et mensurantur, potentia quidem ut virtus cognoscens et ad illud tendens, signum ut via et medium, per quod ad illud tenditur. Quod vero signum sit etiam obiectum et prius cognitum, ut per illud tendat potentia ad signatum, non est id, quod essentialiter constituit signum in quantum signum; nam signum formale sine hoc, quod sit obiectum cognitum a potentia, sed forma reddens cognoscentem potentiam, manifestat ei. Quod ergo pertinet per se ad rationem signi, est, quod sit substituens pro obiecto in repraesentando ipsum potentiae, quae substitutio realem subordinationem et relationem dicit ad signatum ut ad principale

[13] In the original Latin: "art."
[14] to 142/21-27
[15] In the original Latin: "art."

is the respect essential to and formally constitutive of the sign, even though indirectly a sign also attains a power, inasmuch as it respects a signified as manifestable to [capable of being known by] a power.

Wherefore the argument may be answered in form as follows: I distinguish the proposition that a sign respects a power by a mind-dependent relation: That a sign formally, insofar as it is a sign, respects a power by a relation direct and of measure to measured, I deny; that a sign respects a power presuppositively and as it is itself a kind of object, I let pass.

To the proof of the major premise[16] it is said: I deny that a sign is in the line and order of an object principally and essentially and as an object is a measure; I grant that a sign is in the line and order of an object as something substituting for and vicegerent of an object. Whence a sign does not respect a cognitive power in the same way that an object does, but directly respects a manifestable object, and indirectly respects a power, just as a habit, for example, which is in the powers, respects the object by which it is specified directly, although in order to assist a power in respect of that object. Nor is the instrumental sign founded on being known as regards the rationale of the sign, but being known is required for the exercise as such of signifying, not for the instrumental sign to be constituted in the being of sign respecting an object as its substitute; for this the sign has prior to being known, because a sign does not consist in actual representation, but in the power of representing.

To the first proof of the minor premise[17] I answer that a sign is said to be an instrument of a cognitive power in the same way that it is said to be an instrument of a signified and its substitute for manifesting itself to a power. For the sign is not an instrument of the power on the side of the elicitation of a cognitive act, as if the power elicits its act by means of the sign, but on the side of the representation of an object, inasmuch as an object is manifested by means of a sign, and so a sign is more principally subordinated to the object as to that for which it is substituted in representing to a power.

To the second proof of the minor[18] I answer that the end of a sign is to manifest a significate to a cognitive power, yet out of a subordination to that very significate as to the principal for which the sign is surrogated and substituted in representing. However, that

obiectum, et hic est respectus essentialis et formaliter constitutivus signi, licet in obliquo etiam potentiam attingat, quatenus respicit signatum ut manifestabile potentiae.

Quare ad argumentum in forma dicitur: Signum respicit potentiam relatione rationis, distinguo: Formaliter, in quantum signum, relatione directa et mensurae ad mensuratum, nego; praesuppositive et ut obiectum quoddam est, transeat.

Et ad probationem[16] dicitur, quod signum est in linea et ordine obiecti principaliter et per se et ut mensura est, nego; ut substituens et vices gerens obiecti, concedo. Unde non eodem modo, quo obiectum, respicit potentiam, sed directe obiectum manifestabile respicit, in obliquo potentiam, sicut etiam habitus, qui est in potentiis, respicit obiectum, a quo specificatur directe, licet in ordine ad adiuvandum potentiam respectu illius. Nec signum instrumentale fundatur in esse cognito quantum ad rationem signi, sed esse cognitum requiritur ad ipsum exercitium significandi, non ut constituatur in esse signi respicientis obiectum ut subsitutum eius; hoc enim habet ante esse cognitum, quia signum non consistit in actuali repraesentatione, sed in potestate repraesentandi.

Ad primam probationem minoris[17] respondetur signum dici instrumentum potentiae eo modo, quo est instrumentum signati et substitutum eius ad manifestandum se potentiae. Nec enim signum est instrumentum potentiae ex parte elicientiae actus, quasi medio signo eliciat, sed ex parte repraesentationis obiecti, quatenus medio signo manifestatur obiectum, et sic principalius subordinatur obiecto tamquam ei, pro quo substituitur in repraesentando potentiae.

Ad secundam probationem[18] respondetur finem signi esse manifestare potentiae signatum, ex subordinatione tamen ad ipsum signatum ut ad principale, pro quo subrogatur et substituitur in repraesen-

[16] 142/28-49.
[17] 142/50-143/1.
[18] 143/1-7.

which, out of a subordination to and substitution for another, respects some end, more principally respects that for which it substitutes and surrogates than it does that in relation to which it stimulates, or the end toward which it tends, because this last it respects as an end-effect, whereas it respects that for which it is substituted as an end-for-the-sake-of-which; for it is out of the subordination to the latter that it respects the former as its effect.

To the confirmation[19] I answer that if the division of signs into formal and instrumental is an essential division (which will be considered in the following Book[20]), it is not taken from the order to a cognitive power precisely, but from diverse orders to a signified.[21] For diverse ways of affecting a power, as an object first known as such or as concept intrinsically informing, redound into diverse rationales of manifesting and representing a significate, because manifestation itself and representation is a kind of movement. And thus the mode of affecting a power, which varies the movement, redounds to a variety of representations. But diverse representations respect a significate under diverse formalities or formal rationales of the representable, because representation and the representable must be proportioned, and vary in function of one another, and it is in this way that signs themselves are rendered formally diversified by reason of the signified and the representable, although materially they may be signs of the same thing signified.

A second argument that a natural sign is something mind-dependently relative can be developed by proving that even from the aspect of sign as respecting a thing signified and in the order to that significate there is not a mind-independent relation. First, there are times when the thing signified does not exist, and yet a sign is no less formally a sign in respect of it, because the sign in question represents that significate in act to the cognitive power in question, and at such times the relation to the nonexistent significate is not mind-independent. Second, there are times when a natural sign represents some mind-dependent being, as, for example, the concept of the Chimera[22] or a statue and image of the mythical Chimera. Third, a relation between a natural sign and its significate is not independent of mind, because a sign-relation differs from an image-relation only in this, that a sign touches the signified

tando. Id autem, quod ex subordinatione ad aliud respicit aliquem finem et ex substitutione pro ipso, principalius respicit id, pro quo substituit et subrogatur, quam id, ad quod movet, seu finem, ad quem tendit, quia hunc respicit ut finem effectum, id autem, pro quo substituitur, ut finem cuius gratia; ex subordinatione enim ad illud respicit talem effectum.

Ad confirmationem[19] respondetur divisionem signi in formale et instrumentale, si est essentialis (de quo seq. liber[20]), non sumi ex ordine ad potentiam praecise, sed ex diverso ordine ad signatum.[21] Diversus enim modus afficiendi potentiam, ut obiectum prius cognitum vel ut conceptus intrinsece informans, refunditur in diversam rationem manifestandi et repraesentandi signatum, quia manifestatio ipsa et repraesentatio quaedam motio est. Et sic modus afficiendi potentiam, qui variat motionem, refunditur in varietatem repraesentationis. Diversa autem repraesentatio respicit signatum sub diversa formalitate seu ratione formali repraesentabilis, quia repraesentatio et repraesentabile proportionari debent, et uno variato variatur et aliud, et ita redditur diversificatum ipsum signum formaliter ratione signati et repraesentabilis, licet materialiter sit idem.

Secundo arguitur probando, quod etiam ex parte signati et in ordine ad illud non sit realis relatio. Primo, quando signatum non existit, et tamen non minus formaliter est signum respectu illius, quia repraesentat illud actu ipsi potentiae, et tunc relatio ad signatum non existens non est realis. Secundo, quando signum repraesentat aliquod ens rationis, ut conceptus chimaerae[22] vel effigies et imago exterior illius. Tertio, quia relatio signi differt a relatione imaginis solum per hoc, quod signum tan-

---

[19] 143/8-20.

[20] In the original Latin: "quaest."

[21] See below, Question 3, 163/12-36, Question 5, 202/19-22 along with 201/28-202/8; and Book II, Question 1, 229/24-38, 238/28-45 with 235/15-25.

[22] The "She-monster" in Greek mythology possessing the head of a lion, the body of a goat, and the tail of a serpent.

as what is to be represented to the cognitive power, whereas an image (a likeness) respects an exemplar as something to be imitated by the image. But in a significate, this being representable to a cognitive power is not something mind-independent or physical, but something mind-dependent and mental, because a thing signified is not ordered to a knowing power by a physical ordination and relation, but [is thus ordered] as something capable of being manifested, and so is like all other objects, which do not respect the power by a mutual relation. Therefore a sign is attained by a significate under a certain mind-dependent formality, and therefore not through a mind-independent relation. Finally, among natural signs the relation of sign to signified is not independent of the human understanding, because the very exercise of signifying or representing places nothing mind-independent in the thing signified. For no change comes about in a signified as the result of its being represented by a sign, but there *is* a physical change in the cognitive power as a result of being stimulated anew by a sign. Therefore, with respect to the signified, the sign-relation is not independent of mind, because the power of signifying cannot be more independent of understanding than the act and exercise of signifying.

The response to the first proof[23] is that when the significate does not exist, the sign does not remain a sign formally, but fundamentally, because the formal and actual rationale of substitution ceases when that for which it substitutes is nonexistent. But the capacity for manifesting itself as well as the signified thus absent remains, because the proportion or connection to that once existent significate, which proportion can found a sign-relation, remains; and by virtue of this proportion or connection representation comes about, not by virtue of the relation by which the sign is formally constituted in the rationale of a substituted thing.

To the second proof[24] I say that the concept of a mind-dependent being, or an image of a chimerical thing, represents the impossible thing in the mode of possible things, as for example the Chimera [of Greek legend] is represented through its parts, which are something physically possible—a lion's head, a goat's body, and a serpent's tail—although their conjunction does not physically exist. And to this very element which in such an object is purely chimerical and a mind-dependent being, there is no mind-independent relation of the natural sign,[25] but there can be a manifestative and represen-

git signatum ut repraesentandum potentiae, imago autem respicit exemplar ut imitandum a se. Sed in signato hoc, quod est esse repraesentabile potentiae, non est aliquid reale, sed rationis, quia ad potentiam cognoscentem non ordinatur signatum reali ordinatione et relatione, sed ut manifestabile, et sic ut cetera obiecta, quae non mutua relatione respiciunt potentiam. Ergo signum attingitur a signato sub formalitate quadam rationis, atque adeo non per relationem realem. Denique, quia ipsum exercitium significandi seu repraesentandi nihil reale ponit in signato. Nec enim mutatio aliqua fit in signato per hoc, quod repraesentatur a signo, fit autem mutatio realis in potentia per hoc, quod moveatur de novo a signo. Ergo respectu signati relatio signi realis non est, quia non potest esse magis realis potestas significandi quam actus et exercitium.

Respondetur ad primam probationem,[23] quod signum non existente signato non manet formaliter signum, sed fundamentaliter, quia deficit formalis et actualis ratio substitutionis non existente eo, pro quo substituit. Sed manet virtus tam manifestandi se quam signatum sic absens, quia manet proportio seu connexio ad ipsum, quae fundare potest talem relationem, et virtute huius fit repraesentatio, non virtute relationis qua formaliter constituitur in ratione substituti.

Ad secundam probationem[24] dicitur, quod conceptus entis rationis vel imago rei chimaericae repraesentat rem impossibilem ad modum rerum possibilium, sicut chimaera repraesentatur per suas partes, quae sunt aliquid reale, ut caput leonis, corpus caprae et cauda serpentis, quorum tamen coniunctio realiter non est. Et ad hoc ipsum, quod in tali obiecto pure chimaericum est et ens rationis, non datur relatio realis signi naturalis,[25] sed dari potest reale manifes-

[23] 145/33-38.

[24] 145/39-42.

[25] See above, Question 1, note 25, bearing in mind also 119/45-48; and below, Question 5, note 21, p. 200.

tative element that has its being independently of being apprehended as an object, namely, the specifying form representing the mental construct on the pattern of mind-independent or physical being; but this mind-independent manifestative element does not require a mind-independent relation, nor does it express the formality of the sign, but the transcendental rationale of something representative.

To the third proof[26] the response is that something signified as an object manifestable to a cognitive power is in itself something mind-independent, even though it is not referred by a reciprocal relation either to the power to which it is representable, or to the sign by means of which it is representable. Indeed, because an object is less dependent in its own order upon a cognitive power than is a cognitive power upon it, it does not have as object a reciprocal relation to the power. Whence, just as knowledge and power respect an object by a mind-independent relation of the third essential type, even though the object does not bear on the power by a mind-independent relation, because it suffices for this type of relation if the terminus exists in the order of mind-independent being and not in the formality of terminus, as was said in article 5 of q. 17[27]: so also the sign-

tativum et repraesentativum, scilicet species ad instar entis realis ens rationis repraesentans; sed hoc manifestativum realem relationem non requirit nec dicit formalitatem signi, sed transcendentalem rationem repraesentativi.

Ad tertiam probationem[26] respondetur, quod signatum ut obiectum manifestabile potentiae aliquid reale est in se, licet non mutua relatione referatur neque ad potentiam, cui est repraesentabile, neque ad signum, per quod repraesentabile est. Imo quia minus dependens est in suo ordine a potentia, quam potentia ab ipso, non habet ut obiectum relationem mutuam ad potentiam. Unde sicut ipsa scientia et potentia reali relatione tertii generis respiciunt obiectum, licet obiectum non reali relatione se habeat ad potentiam, quia sufficit ad hoc realitas termini in esse rei et non in formalitate termini, ut q. 17. art. 5. dictum est[27]: ita

[26] 145/42-146/13.

[27] Logica 2. p. q. 17. art. 5., Reiser ed., 597a41-598a13: "*Probabilius videtur, quod in relativis tertii ordinis non datur terminus formalis correlativus, sed solum fundamentaliter proxime.*

"*. . . Ita tertia sententia supra* [596a27-41] *relata. Et deduci videtur ex D. Thoma, qui saepe docet, quod cointelligitur oppositio in terminis istarum relationum per intellectum et non in re, ut patet in 1. p. q. 13. art. 7., praesertim ad 2. Et in 1. ad Annibaldum dist. 30. art. 1. ad 3.* [*Pa* XXII. 84 b.] *dicit, 'quod cuilibet relationi opponitur alia relatio, quae quandoque est in re, ad quam relatio terminatur, quandoque est in intellectu tantum, non sicut in relato, sed sicut in intelligente aliquid sub relatione'. Constat ergo ex D. Thomas, quod terminus oppositionem dicit relativam, et tamen non semper est ista relatio in re terminante, sed in intellectu, atque adeo non datur terminus formaliter in re.—Et manifeste deducitur ex praecedenti conclusione* [Second Preamble, Article 2, note 21, p.97], *quia formalis ratio termini consistit in oppositione ad suum correlativum; haec oppositio non invenitur formaliter ex parte alterius extremi, quia non habet relationem realem et consequenter neque oppositionem relativam; ergo non est formaliter terminus in re.*

"*Quod vero fundamentaliter proxime sit terminus, probatur, quia denominatur extrinsece talis a relatione existente in altero extremo, sicut Deus dicitur dominus ex relatione servitutis existente in creatura, et Christus secundum D. Thomam 3. p. q. 35. art. 5. et in 3. dist. 8.* [q. 1. art. 5. (*Pa* VII. 103 a.)] *dicitur filius Virginis ob relationem maternitatis existentem in Virgine. Et videri potest in 1. dist. 40. q. 1. art. 1. ad 2.* [*Pa* VI. 328 a.], *ubi inquit: 'In relativis quandoque denominatur aliquid per id, quod in ipso est, sicut pater paternitate, quae est in ipso; quandoque autem denominatur eo, quod solum in altero est, sicut in illis, in quorum alio est relatio secundum rem et in alio secundum rationem tantum.' Quae omnia fundantur in dicto Aristotelis 5. Metaph. textu 20.* [c. 15 (1021 a 29).], *quod saepe repetit S. Thomas, quod mensurabile et scibile dicitur aliquid eo, quod aliquid dicitur ad ipsum, sicut dicitur aliquid scibile, quia de eo datur scientia. Facta autem hac denominatione potest proxime in illa fundari conceptus relationis oppositae, quae importat formalitatem termini.*"—"It seems more probable that in relatives of the third order [i.e., in the case of the nonreciprocal relations of measured to measure] there is no correlative formal term, but only a term proximately correlative after the manner of a fundament.

"Such is the third of the three options outlined above [at 596a27-41]. And it seems to be drawn from St. Thomas, who often teaches that the reciprocal opposition in the termini of these relations is from the understanding and is not in the things related, as is clear in the *Summa theologica*, I, q. 13, art. 7, especially in the reply to objection 2. Also in the first book of the *Commentary on the Sentences Written for Annibald*, dist. 30, art. 1, reply to the third objection, he says, 'that to any relation whatever there is opposed another relation, which sometimes is in the thing at which

relation to that same object as signifiable to a power is mind-independent, because in the order of mind-independent being the signified is mind-independent, even though the relation of the signified to the cognitive power or to the sign itself is not mind-independent.

To the final proof[28] the response is that the exercise of a sign does not posit anything in the thing signified, since the sign rather receives from and depends upon the signified, inasmuch as it is substituting for that signified thing. But if a sign did physically alter the significate, the significate would mind-independently respect the sign by which it was altered. Whence, from the fact that the sign does not physically *alter* the signified, it does not follow that the sign does not mind-independently *respect* the signified, but that the signified does not mind-independently respect the sign, which we freely grant; but the objector needed to prove that the sign was not physically altered by or dependent upon the significate for which it substitutes. In respect of a cognitive power, however, a sign certainly stimulates independently of the mind in an objective way, not by acting productively, as is said below.[29] But such a stimulation belongs to a sign not as a sign formally, but as an object [*which is also a sign*]. To move by substituting for another is the act of [an object which is also] a sign, or to signify; but thus [the stimulus object] implies the relation of a substitute for the significate, and therefore inasmuch as

et relatio signi ad idem obiectum ut significabile potentiae realis est, quia in esse rei signatum est reale, licet relatio signati ad potentiam vel ad ipsum signum realis non sit.

Ad ultimam probationem[28] respondetur, quod exercitium signi non ponit aliquid in signato, cum potius signum a signato recipiat et pendeat, utpote pro ipso substituens. Si autem realiter mutaret signatum, realiter respiceret signum, a quo immutaretur. Unde ex eo, quod non realiter immutat, non sequitur, quod signum realiter non respiciat signatum, sed quod signatum realiter non respiciat signum, quod libenter concedimus; sed oportebat probare, quod signum non realiter immutatur vel pendet a signato, pro quo substituit. Respectu vero potentiae movet quidem signum realiter obiective, non effective agendo, ut infra dicetur.[29] Sed talis motio est signi non ut signum formaliter, sed ut obiectum; movere autem substituendo pro alio est actus signi seu significare, sed sic importat relationem substituti ad signatum, et ideo quatenus signum non

---

the first relation is terminated, sometimes is in the understanding only, not as in a related thing, but as in the understanding of something under the aspect of a relation.' What is certain from this remark by St. Thomas is that a term bespeaks a relative opposition, and yet this relation is not always in the terminating thing, but [can sometimes only be] in the understanding, and in such a case there is no term formally existing in the thing.—And this clearly follows from the preceding conclusion, because the formal character of a term consists in the opposition to its correlative; but this opposition does not have a mind-independent relation, and consequently neither a relative opposition; therefore there is not formally a term in the thing.

"But that there is a term in the thing proximately after the manner of a fundament is proved by the fact that the thing is extrinsically denominated as fundament for a relation by the relation existing in the other extreme, as God, for example, is called Lord from the relation of 'being subject' existing in a creature, or as Christ, according to St. Thomas in the *Summa theologica*, III, q. 35, art. 5, and in his *Commentary on the Sentences of Peter Lombard*, Book 3, dist. 8, question 1, art. 5, is said to be the son of Mary on account of the relation of maternity existing in Mary. Proof of the thesis can also be seen in Book I of St. Thomas's *Commentary on the Sentences of Peter Lombard*, dist. 40, q. 1, art. 1, reply to objection 2, where he says: 'In the case of relative things, sometimes something is denominated by that which is in it, as a father by the paternity which is in him; but sometimes something is denominated by that which is only in the other, as in the case of those relatives in one of which there is a relation according to fact, and in the other of which there is a relation according to the understanding only.' All of which is based on the saying of Aristotle, in the *Metaphysics*, Book 5, chap. 15 [1021 a 29], which St. Thomas often repeats, that something is called measurable and knowable from this, that something is said relative to it, as something is said to be knowable because there is knowledge of it. Given this denomination, however, there can be founded on it proximately the concept of an opposite relation, which imports the formality of a term."

[28] 146/13-24.

[29] Question 5.

it is a sign it does not respect the [stimulated] power directly, but the significate for which it substitutes in stimulating the power.

A third argument: a natural sign and a stipulated sign coincide univocally in the rationale of sign. Therefore the one cannot be mind-independent and the other mind-dependent, because nothing is univocal to mind-independent and mind-dependent relations, nor are both natural and stipulated signs something mind-independent, since a stipulated sign is known to be a mental artifact; therefore both natural and stipulated signs are mind-dependent.

The antecedent is proved: the rationale of an object or knowable thing is univocal in a mind-independent being and in a mind-dependent being, because it pertains to univocal types of systematic knowledge and to the same cognitive power. For Logic, which treats of mind-dependent being, and Metaphysics, which treats of mind-independent being, are univocally sciences [i.e., formally unified object-domains]. Therefore their objects also are univocally objects and systematically knowable things. Similarly, therefore, natural and stipulated signs are univocally signs; if indeed the rationale of sign and signifiable is of the order of an object and knowable thing for which a sign substitutes.

This is confirmed by the oft-repeated argument that because what is common to signs is a determinate species of being or relation, sign must therefore be placed in a determinate category or genus, but cannot abstract from the mind-independent and the mind-dependent. Moreover, even within the [determinate] category or genus of relation [as a possible mode of mind-independent being] it is not clear to which of the three essential types a sign should be determinately assigned. For it is not always in the order of measure and measurable, because sometimes a sign is not perfected by the significate, but vice versa, as when a cause is the sign of the caused—for example, clouds are a sign of rain; nor again is it readily apparent among signs which are effects—how smoke, for example, is measured by fire, or how too in an image the two relations of measure should be distinguished, one in the rationale of image, the other in the rationale of sign, if indeed these rationales are different.

The response to this argument[30] is that it is true that the rationale of something knowable and of an object can be univocal in a mind-independent and in a mind-dependent being; for the divisions of being in the order of physical existence are one thing, while divisions in the order of the knowable are quite another, as Cajetan well teaches in Part I, q. 1, art. 3, of his *Commentary* on the *Summa theologica*.[31]

respicit directe potentiam, sed signatum, pro quo substituit ad movendum potentiam.

Tertio arguitur: Signum naturale et ad placitum conveniunt univoce in ratione signi. Ergo non potest alterum esse reale, alterum rationis, quia ad relationem realem et rationis nihil est univocum, nec utrumque est aliquid reale, cum signum ad placitum constet esse aliquid rationis; ergo utrumque aliquid rationis est.

Antecedens probatur: Ratio obiecti seu cognoscibilis est univoca in ente reali et rationis, quia ad univocas scientias et potentiam eandem pertinet. Logica enim, quae agit de ente rationis, et Metaphysica, quae de ente reali, univoce sunt scientiae. Ergo et obiecta earum univoce sunt obiecta et scibilia. Ergo similiter univoce sunt signa; siquidem ratio signi et significabilis est de genere obiecti et cognoscibilis, pro quo substituit.

Confirmatur illo vulgari argumento, quia signum in communi est determinata species entis seu relationis, ergo debet poni in determinato genere, non vero abstrahere a reali et rationis. Imo in ipsa relatione non apparet, in quo genere determinate ponatur. Nam in genere mensurae et mensurabilis non semper ponitur, cum aliquando signum non perficiatur a signato, sed e contra, sicut quando causa est signum causati, ut nubes est signum pluviae; nec facile etiam apparet inter signa, quae sunt effectus, quomodo fumus mensuretur ab igne, quomodo etiam in imagine distinguatur duplex relatio mensurae, altera in ratione imaginis, altera in ratione signi, siquidem diversae sunt.

RESPONDETUR[30] verum esse, quod ratio cognoscibilis et obiecti in ente reali et rationis potest esse univoca; aliae enim sunt divisiones entis in esse rei, aliae in genere scibilis, ut bene Caietanus docet 1. p. q. 1. art. 3.[31] Et sic ratio

[30] to 149/4-23.

[31] See also the discussion of this in Question 4 below, 187/28-190/23, and note 33 thereto, p. 187; and in Book II, Question 1, 235/36-236/46, Question 5, 270/37-271/21.

And so the rationale of something knowable is not the rationale of being formally, but only presuppositively is it being and consequent upon being; for the true is a coincident property of being, and so formally is not being, but consequent upon being and presuppositively being; but the true is the same as the knowable.[32] Whence it can well be that some being incapable of [mind-independent] existence is capable of truth, not as a subject, but as an object, inasmuch as it does not have in itself the entitative being which as subject founds truth and knowability, but does have that which as object can be known after the pattern of mind-independent being and so exist objectively in the understanding as something

cognoscibilis non est ratio entis formaliter, sed praesuppositive solum est ens et consecutum ad ens; verum enim est passio entis, et sic formaliter non est ens, sed consecutum ad ens et praesuppositive ens; idem est autem verum quod cognoscibile.[32] Unde bene stat, quod aliquod ens incapax existentiae sit capax veritatis, non ut subiectum, sed ut obiectum, quatenus non habet in se entitatem, quae tamquam subiectum fundet veritatem et cognoscibilitatem, sed habet, quod tamquam obiectum possit cognosci ad instar entis realis et sic obiective esse in intellectu tamquam verum. Unde

[32] See Phil. nat. 4. p. q. 6. art. 3., esp. (in the Reiser ed.) III. 186b3-40: "*Et quando instatur, quod omnis unio realis vel est accidentalis vel substantialis,* respondetur, *quod in re ita est, quod omnis talis unio vel identice vel formaliter sit accidentalis vel substantialis, sed non requiritur, quod solum formaliter, sicut passiones entis, ut verum et bonum, non sunt formaliter ens, sed identice, alias non essent passiones entis, sed ens ipsum, cui passiones conveniunt. Unio autem obiectiva intelligibilis datur ratione ipsius veri seu cognoscibilitatis, quae est passio entis. Requiritur tamen ad istam unionem obiectivam praesuppositive vel concomitanter aliqua realis et intima unio, vel in genere causae formalis inhaerentis, sicut nostra species, quae est qualitas, vel in genere causae materialis sustentantis, sicut substantia angeli sustentat intellectum suum et in ratione speciei illi deservit, vel in ratione causae efficientis, sicut Deus operando intra intellectum et dando illi esse per immensitatem etiam in ratione speciei potest illum actuare. Et posita aliqua unione ex istis potest etiam secundo modo seu in genere intelligibili fieri unio, distincta tamen a prima, quia distinctos habet effectus, perficiendo et actuando immaterialiter et faciendo, quod potentia in esse cognoscibili sit obiectum, non tertiam aliquam naturam ex repraesentatione et potentia constituendo, bene tamen potentiam actuatam relinquendo.*"—"And when it is insisted that every real union is either accidental (a subjective modification) or substantial (a subject), the response is that in the mind-independent order it is the case that any given union, *either identically or formally,* is accidental or substantial, but it need not be the case that the union be such *only* formally, just as, for example, the transcendental properties of being, such as true and good, are not formally being, but identically—otherwise they would not be properties of being, but being itself to which the properties belong. But an objective intelligible union is given by reason of the true itself or of knowability, which is a property of being. Yet some real and intimate union is necessary presuppositively or concomitantly to this objective union, either in the order of a formal inhering cause, such as our specifying form, which is a quality, or in the order of a sustaining material cause, as the substance of a pure spirit sustains its self-understanding and serves in the rationale of a specifying form thereto, or in the order of a productive cause, as God, by acting within the understanding and giving it existence through immensity [the divine property of being everywhere present through the creative power], can also actuate it in the rationale of a specifier. And given some union of these factors, there can also come about in a second way or in the intelligible order a union, yet one distinct from the first union [the entitative one], because it has distinct effects, by perfecting and actuating immaterially, and by making the power be in knowable being the object, not by constituting some third nature out of the representation and the power, but indeed by leaving the power actuated."

Powell comments on this as follows. 'Objective union is different from real union because it has different effects. For objective union transcends the difference between the real and unreal. For example, doing Logic, we experience a discipline that treats real and unreal components of science as having necessary functions in scientific theory. Thus the unreal and real elements have the *same logical meaning as elements of theory*. Likewise we experience real signs and unreal stipulated signs as conveying meaning with equal force. For example, smoke as a real sign of fire is no more efficacious than shouting "Fire!" in a crowded theatre (cf. Book I, Question 5, 270/37-271/21). Nevertheless, objective union is real union between the knower and his natural and social environment. But this real union is only presupposed in objective union. Objective union is not *as such* real union. For objective union transcends the difference between the real and the unreal.'

true. Whence, although entitatively mind-independent being and mind-dependent being are analogized, nevertheless, objectively, because the one is represented on the pattern of the other, even beings which are not univocal entitatively can coincide in a univocal rationale of an object,[33] as, for example, God and the creature, substance and accident in the rationale of a metaphysical knowable, or of something understandable by the human mind. Moreover, the rationale of a sign, because it does not consist absolutely in the rationale of an object, but of a substitution for another which is supposed to be the object or thing signified, that it may be represented to a cognitive power, does not pertain to the order of the cognizable absolutely, but relatively and ministerially; and for this role the rationale of a sign takes on something of the entitative order, to wit, as it is a relation and as it draws the order of the knowable to the order of the relative, and for this function a natural sign-relation, which is mind-independent, does not coincide univocally with a stipulated sign-relation, which is mind-dependent.

To the confirmation[34] response has already been made in the preceding question,[35] toward the end.[36] To the difficulty added in the present context concerning the species or type in the category of relation within which the sign is located,[37] the response is that it pertains to the type of measure and measured.[38] For the significate always functions as the principal thing to be represented, and the sign as serving and ministering in this [type of relation or] order, and so a sign respects its principal as an extrinsic measure in the order of what is representable, and through approximation to that measure the sign is the better as it better represents. And thus smoke[39] respects fire as a measure in the rationale of a thing representable, not in the order of being. And an image as an image[40] respects an exemplar as measure in imitation and derivation therefrom as from a principle, but in the rationale of a sign an image respects the exemplar as the measure in the order of something representable and manifestable to a cognitive power, which relations [those of image to exemplar and sign-image to signified] are not the same. Although indeed a respect of cause or effect is found in signs (whether efficient or formal relative to

licet entitative ens reale et ens rationis analogentur, tamen obiective, cum unum ad instar alterius repraesentetur, possunt in ratione univoca obiecti convenire etiam quae entitative univoca non sunt,[33] ut Deus et creatura, substantia et accidens in ratione scibilis metaphysici vel intelligibilis ab intellectu. Ceterum ratio signi cum non consistat in ratione obiecti absolute, sed substitutionis ad alterum, quod supponitur esse obiectum seu signatum, ut repraesentetur potentiae, non pertinet ad genus cognoscibilis absolute, sed relative et ministerialiter; et pro hac parte aliquid entitativi ordinis induit, scilicet ut relatio est et ut trahit genus cognoscibilis ad genus relativi, et pro hac parte non convenit univoce relatio signi naturalis, quae realis est, cum relatione signi ad placitum, quae est rationis.

Ad confirmationem[34] responsum est quaest.[35] praec. circa finem.[36] Quod vero additur de specie, in qua ponitur signum in genere relationis,[37] respondetur pertinere ad genus mensurae et mensurati.[38] Semper enim signatum se habet ut principale repraesentandum, et signum ut deserviens et ministrans in hoc genere, sicque respicit suum principale ut mensuram extrinsecam in genere repraesentabilis et per accessum ad illam magis signum perficitur, quanto melius repraesentat. Et ita fumus[39] respicit ignem ut mensuram in ratione repraesentabilis, non in genere entis. Et imago ut imago[40] respicit exemplar ut mensuram in imitatione et deductione ex ipso ut a principio, a quo derivatur, in ratione vero signi tamquam mensuram in genere repraesentabilis et manifestabilis potentiae, quae relationes diversae sunt. Quod vero in signis invenitur respectus causae vel effectus, sive efficientis sive for-

[33] Cross-references in note 31 above.
[34] 149/24-40.
[35] In the original Latin: "art."
[36] 133/14-134/10, esp. 133/24.
[37] 149/25-28.
[38] 149/28-40.
[39] 149/36-37.
[40] 149/38-40.

the sign's significate[41]), such relations are not formally the sign-relation itself, but something presupposed or concomitant,[42] rendering this sign proportionate to that significate rather than to some other one,[43] but the sign-relation proper is to a significate as a thing representable to a cognitive power, not as an effect or a cause.[44]

malis ad suum signatum,[41] tales relationes non sunt formaliter ipsa relatio signi, sed aliquid praesuppositum aut concomitans,[42] ut hoc signum sit proportionatum illi signato potius quam alteri,[43] propria vero relatio signi est ad signatum ut repraesentabile potentiae non ut effectus vel causa.[44]

---

[41] 149/33-37.

[42] as we pointed out at 135/19-136/11, and again at 137/7, note 4, in the addition made in the 1663 Lyons text.

[43] 135/1-136/29, 138/23-32, 140/21-24.

[44] See 140/21-43.

Question 3

Whether the Relation of Sign to Signified Is the Same as the Relation of Sign to Cognitive Power

Quaestio Tertia

Utrum Sit Eadem Relatio Signi ad Signatum et Potentiam

It is certain that an order to a cognitive power is found in the signs which are external to sense and known first, enabling them to lead to a significate, just as in the case of any other objects known and terminating cognition, because it is clearly apparent that such signs are known as objects are known, as smoke, for example, is first seen as an object, then leads from its own being known to something signified. Whence the respect or order of a sign to a cognitive power in the rationale of an object must be distinct from the order or respect in the rationale of sign, because in this respect of an object a sign coincides with other objects which are not signs, and respects the power objectively in the same way as those other objects do. Considering therefore that an external sign might respect a cognitive power not only purely objectively, but also significatively, it remains to be examined whether that relation whereby a sign respects a significate, and in the order to which it takes on the rationale of a sign, is the very same relation whereby the sign also respects the cognitive power to which this significate is to be manifested by the sign; or whether an external sign has a relation to the signified separate and complete apart from a respect to a cognitive power, which power the sign, in the rationale of an object, respects by a second relation, both of which relations together concur to constitute the rationale of the sign; or even whether there might be found in the very rationale of a sign, over and above the rationale of object, a twofold relation, one to a cognitive power, the other to the significate.

Certum est in signis externis, et quae prius cognoscuntur, ut ducant ad signatum, inveniri ordinem ad potentiam, sicut in reliquis obiectis cognitis et terminantibus cognitionem, cum clare appareat talia signa cognosci ut obiecta, sicut fumus prius videtur ut obiectum, deinde ex cognitione sui ducit in signatum. Unde respectus seu ordo signi ad potentiam in ratione obiecti distinctus debet esse ab ordine seu respectu in ratione signi, cum in hoc respectu obiecti conveniat cum aliis obiectis, quae signa non sunt, et eodem modo atque illa potentiam respicit obiective. Ut ergo non solum pure obiective, sed etiam significative respiciat potentiam, inquirendum restat, an illamet relatio, qua significatum respicit, et in ordine ad quod rationem signi induit, illamet etiam respiciat potentiam, cui signatum hoc manifestandum est a signo; an vero relationem habeat ad signatum purificatam et absolutam a respectu ad potentiam, alia vero relatione respiciat potentiam in ratione obiecti, et utraque concurrat ad rationem signi constituendam, vel etiam in ipsa ratione signi praeter rationem obiecti reperiatur duplex relatio, altera ad potentiam, altera ad signatum.

The reason for the difficulty here arises from the fact that from one side a sign does not respect a significate only in itself, but in an order to a cognitive power, because an order to a power is included in the definition of sign as something manifestative to a cognitive power, etc. If therefore the rationale of a sign bespeaks this respect to a power, either the sign respects both significate and power by one and the same relation, and the difficulties to be touched on below arise from the fact that significate and power are entirely diverse terms, since in respect of a power there is only a mind-dependent relation: in respect of a signified there is [individual-mind-independent] order of measured to measure; in respect of a power, on the contrary, the power is measurable by the [external] sign itself as by a known object. Or the relations of sign to power and to signified are diverse, and so the sign will not be in the category of a relation, because there is in the rationale of sign not just one relation, but a plurality of relations.

The conclusion will nevertheless be: **If power and signified are considered as termini directly attained through a relation, they necessarily require a double relation in the sign, but an external sign considered in this way respects the cognitive power directly as an object, not formally as a sign. But if the power is considered as a terminus indirectly attained, then the significate and the cognitive power are attained by the single sign-relation, and this relation is the proper and formal rationale of the sign.**

In this way one and the same existing relation can be bounded by two termini, one directly, the other indirectly, which is to have simply but one terminus in the formal rationale of terminus.

Many of the more recent proponents of sign theory do not concur in this conclusion. For some are of the opinion that a sign consists in two relations concurring equally, one to what is signified, the other to a cognitive power. Others claim to see in the sign, even as distinguished from an object, the two relations of sign to signified and sign to power, although not equally constituting the rationale of the sign, yet intrinsically and essentially required. But how one of these relations is coupled to the other one, whether as a genus or as a difference or as a property or as a mode, they explain with the greatest difficulty. Still others conflate power and signified as material parts into one integral formal term. Others again deny that a sign as sign respects a cognitive power, and yet others deny that it respects a significate, holding that the entire essence of a sign con-

Et consurgit difficultatis ratio, quia ex una parte signum non respicit solum signatum in se, sed in ordine ad potentiam, cum in definitione signi ordo ad potentiam includatur, scilicet quod sit manifestativum potentiae etc. Si ergo ratio signi respectum istum dicit ad potentiam, vel unica et eadem relatione respicit utrumque, et currunt difficultates infra attingendae, quia sunt termini omnino diversi, cum respectu potentiae sit solum relatio rationis: respectu signati sit ordo mensurati ad mensuram, respectu potentiae e contra potentia sit mensurabilis ab ipso signo ut ab obiecto cognito. Vel est diversa relatio signi ad potentiam et signatum, et sic non erit signum in praedicamento relationis, quia in ratione signi non est unica relatio, sed pluralitas relationum.

Sit nihilominus conclusio: **Si potentia et signatum considerentur ut termini directe attacti per relationem, necessario exigunt duplicem relationem in signo, sed hoc modo signum respicit potentiam directe ut obiectum, non formaliter ut signum. Si vero consideretur potentia ut terminus in obliquo attactus, sic unica relatione signi attingitur signatum et potentia, et haec est propria et formalis ratio signi.**

Itaque potest aliqua relatio una et eadem existens terminari ad duos terminos, alterum in recto, alterum in obliquo, quod est simpliciter habere unum tantum terminum in ratione formali termini.

Non conveniunt in hac conclusione plures ex recentioribus. Aliqui enim existimant signum consistere in duplici relatione ex aequo concurrente, altera ad signatum, altera ad potentiam. Alii vero etiam in signo, ut distinguitur ab obiecto, duplicem relationem agnoscunt, signati et potentiae, licet non ex aequo constituentem rationem signi, intrinsece tamen et essentialiter requisitam. Quomodo autem una istarum relationum comparetur ad aliam, an ut genus vel ut differentia vel ut passio vel ut modus, difficillime explicant. Alii ex potentia et signato conflant unum integrum terminum formalem quasi ex materialibus partibus. Alii negant signum ut signum respicere potentiam, et alii respicere signatum, sed totam essentiam signi con-

sists in a certain apprehensibility by a cognitive power as a means for knowing another. Although these last two opinions are generally rejected on the grounds that the definition of a sign postulates both a significate which is manifested and a cognitive power to which that significate is represented,[1] some nevertheless grant that it is of the intrinsic rationale of a sign only to be able to terminate a power as a means through or in which the signified is known, but that it is not of a sign's intrinsic rationale to be referred to a cognitive power either by a mind-independent or by a transcendental order or by a mind-dependent relation, even though in our way of conceiving, a sign is not apprehended without such an order.

Yet the stated conclusion can be proved.

As regards the first part,[2] that cognitive power and thing signified as termini directly attained postulate a double relation follows from the fact that[3] a cognitive power is not respected directly except by its own object, whether stimulating or terminating; for a power directly respects an object as an object, but a sign does not bespeak directly the rationale of an object, but of something substituting for an object and of a medium between significate and power, therefore a sign directly respects the significate for which it substitutes, insofar as it is a sign. As it directly respects a cognitive power, therefore, a sign needs to be understood in the rationale of an object and not in the rationale of a sign; and thus it directly attains a power by a relation other than the sign-relation, which is to be plurirelative. In sum: A direct relation [of an object] to a power and as directly bearing

sistere in quadam apprehensibilitate a potentia ut medium ad cognoscendum aliud. Quae ultimae opiniones licet communiter reiciantur, quia definitio signi utrumque postulat, et signatum, quod manifestetur, et potentia, cui repraesentetur;[1] tamen aliqui concedunt de intrinseca ratione signi solum esse terminare posse potentiam ut medium, per quod vel in quo cognoscitur signatum, non vero esse de intrinseca ratione eius, quod referatur ad potentiam neque reali aut transcendentali ordine neque relatione rationis, licet ex parte nostri modi concipiendi sine tali ordine non apprehendatur.

Nihilominus conclusio posita probatur.

ET QUOAD PRIMAM PARTEM,[2] quod potentia et signatum ut termini directe attacti postulent duplicem relationem, ex eo constat,[3] quia potentia non respicitur directe nisi a suo obiecto vel movente vel terminante; potentia enim directe respicit obiectum ut obiectum, signum autem non dicit directe rationem obiecti, sed substituentis pro obiecto et medii inter signatum et potentiam, ergo directe respicit signatum, pro quo substituit, in quantum signum est. Ut ergo directe respiciat potentiam, indiget sumi in ratione obiecti et non in ratione signi; et sic alia relatione attinget directe potentiam, quam relatione signi, quod est esse plures relationes. In summa: Relatio ad potentiam in recto et ut directe se habens ad

---

[1] See Question 2 above, 140/22-43; and below, 159/7-22.

[2] 154/21-26.

[3] The 1663 Lyons text at this point reads: ". . . *ex eo constat, quia sic considerati distinguuntur et in esse rei et in ratione formali terminandi. In esse rei, quia signatum est aliquid extra potentiam et ab illa distinctum, sicut ignis cognitus ex fumo, bos ex vestigio. In ratione formali terminandi, quia potentia tantum est terminus, qui directe respicitur, in quantum movetur ab aliquo, vel aliquid terminatur ab ipsa. Nec enim potentia, ut potentia cognoscitiva est, ab aliquo extrinseco directe pendet nisi vel ut movente vel terminante, id est principio vel termino sui actus; quidquid praeter hoc est, non se habet potentia ad illud directe. Sub ratione autem moventis vel terminantis non terminat signatum relationem signi; constat enim, quod signatum neque movetur a signo neque terminatur ad signum, cum non versetur circa signum.*"—". . . follows from the fact that, so considered, power and signified are distinguished both in the order of mind-independent being and in the formal rationale of terminating. In the being of thing, because the signified is something outside the power and distinct from it, as, for example, a fire known from smoke, an ox known from a footprint. In the formal rationale of terminating, because the power is a terminus directly respected only insofar as it is moved by another, or something is terminated by it. For a power, as it is a cognitive power, does not directly depend on anything extrinsic except either as stimulating or terminating, that is, on the principle or the term of its act; whatever is beyond this, the power does not hold itself toward directly. But the significate does not terminate the sign-relation under the rationale of something stimulating or terminating; for it is certain that the significate is neither moved by the sign nor terminated at the sign, since it is not concerned with the sign."

thereto and the relation [of an object] to a sign proceed in opposite ways, because a cognitive power is movable [stimulable] by a sign, for it is moved as by one representing the signified; but the object itself signified is not movable by the sign, but manifestable by the sign, or is that on behalf of which the sign is vicegerent in representation. Therefore, if these relations are taken directly, they respect termini distinct even formally in the rationale of terminus.

And it cannot be said that a sign is something relative to a significate and not to a power, but only terminates a power. For that a sign is referred to a significate is unintelligible, if the sign is unconnected with a cognitive power and conceived without any order thereto, because a sign, insofar as it respects a significate, brings and presents that significate to a cognitive power. Therefore this relation to the significate as what is to be manifested contradicts being unconnected with a cognitive power. But if a sign does not exist absolutely in respect of a cognitive power, but dependently and ordinately thereto, it has consequently a relation thereto.

This is confirmed by the fact that although an object in respect of a power is not constituted essentially in a relation to that power, but rather does the power depend upon the object, nevertheless an external or outward sign, which is vicegerent for an object in representing and exhibiting itself to a cognitive power, necessarily[4] includes this relation; both

potentiam et relatio ad signum opposito modo procedunt, cum potentia sit mobilis a signo, movetur enim ut a repraesentante signatum; ipsum vero signatum non est mobile a signo, sed manifestabile, seu id, pro quo vices gerit signum in repraesentatione. Ergo si istae relationes sumantur in recto, respiciunt distinctos terminos etiam formaliter in ratione termini.

Et non potest dici, quod signum sit relativum ad signatum et non ad potentiam, sed solum terminet potentiam. Repugnat enim intelligere, quod signum referatur ad signatum, si absolvatur a potentia et sine ordine aliquo ad ipsam concipiatur, quia in tantum respicit signatum, in quantum illud defert et praesentat potentiae. Ergo ista relatio ad signatum ut potentiae manifestandum repugnat, quod absolvatur a potentia. Si autem respectu potentiae non absolute se habet, sed dependenter et ordinate ad illam, consequenter relationem habet ad illam.

Confirmatur, quia licet obiectum respectu potentiae non constituatur per se in relatione ad illam, sed potius potentia ab illo dependeat, tamen signum, quod gerit vices obiecti in repraesentando et exhibendo se potentiae, necessario[4] includit hanc relationem; tum

[4] The 1663 Lyons text reads at this point: ". . . *necessario includit hanc relationem; omnis enim repraesentatio est sicut unio sive praesentia unius ad aliud. Omnis autem unio, omnis praesentia et coniunctio involvit intrinsece respectum ad id, cui praesens et coniunctum redditur; omnis enim praesentia et coniunctio respicit extremum, cui coniungitur, nec aliter potest concipi. Ergo licet objectum in ipsa intrinseca ratione obiecti, quod est specificare vel terminare, non includat respectum ad potentiam, tamen repraesentatio obiecti, quae est sicut applicatio et coniunctio eius ad potentiam, intrinsece dicit ordinem ad potentiam, cui fit coniunctio et applicatio. Signum autem subservit obiecto et substituit pro eo in ipsa ratione repraesentandi, non in ratione constitutiva obiecti principalis. Ergo signum intrinsece involvit ordinem ad potentiam, et non solum terminationem ut medium, quia non stat esse medium in vi repraesentationis et applicationis, nisi per ordinem ad terminum cui fit repraesentatio; fit autem potentiae.*"—". . . necessarily includes this relation; for every representation is as a union or presence of one thing to another. But every union, any presence and conjunction, involves intrinsically a respect toward that to which it is rendered present and conjoined; for every presence and conjunction respects the extreme to which it is conjoined, nor can it be conceived otherwise. Therefore, even though an object in the precise intrinsic rationale of object, which is to specify or to terminate [see Question 4 of this Book, p. 166ff. within], does not include a respect to a cognitive power, nevertheless, a representation of an object [see Book II, Questions 2 and 3, pages 240-261, within], which exists as an application and conjunction of it to a cognitive power, does intrinsically express an order to the power relative to which the conjunction and application occurs. But a sign subserves an object and substitutes for it in the very rationale of representing [see Question 1 of Book I and of Book II, p. 116ff. and 223ff.], not in the rationale constitutive of the principal object. Therefore a sign intrinsically involves an order to a cognitive power, and not only the termination as medium or means, because it does not stand in the being of means in virtue of the representation and application except through an order to the term to which the representation occurs; it occurs, however, to a cognitive power ."

because a substitution for anything is always in an order to something, and since a sign substitutes for and functions in the capacity of the thing signified in an order to the office of representing to a cognitive power, a sign must necessarily express an order to a power; and because to represent is to make an object present to a cognitive power, therefore, if a sign is a medium and substitute of the signified in representing, it necessarily involves an order to that to which it represents or makes present; but this [''to which''] is a cognitive power.

The second part of the conclusion[5] is proved as follows: The relation of sign to signified is a relation in the mode of a representation or of its application to a cognitive power. Therefore a sign must respect the signified as the direct terminus ''which'' of its [i.e., of the sign's] respect, which respect also attains a cognitive power indirectly and as a terminus ''to which.'' For in the case of these relations which exist in the mode of substituting and representing, it is impossible that they should respect that whose vicegerent they are, and not that on account of which or in an order to which they substitute, because it is in substituting or functioning in the capacity of another according to some determinate rationale and in an order to some determinate end that one thing is a vicegerent of that other; otherwise that substitution would not be determinate, because a substitution is determined by the end for which it is made. Therefore, if a relation of representing and substituting for some person is determinate, it must needs so respect that person that it also attains that on account of which and in an order to which it substitutes, for it is thence that the substitution is determinate. And so, since a sign is acting in the capacity of and representing a significate and substituting for that signified thing determinately (that it may render an object present to a cognitive power), necessarily, in the very innards and intimate rationale of such a substitution for and representation of a signified, as it is a determinate substitution and representation, some respect toward a cognitive power is involved, because a sign substitutes for this, that it should represent to a cognitive power.

Passing over many and various explanations of how the same relation could be said to attain the significate directly and a cognitive power indirectly, the more adequate explanation seems to be that a sign respects a power indirectly inasmuch as being manifestable to a

quia substitutio pro aliquo semper est in ordine ad aliquid, et cum signum substituat et vices gerat signati in ordine ad munus repraesentandi potentiae, necessario debet dicere ordinem ad potentiam; tum quia repraesentare est praesens facere obiectum potentiae, ergo si signum est medium et substitutum signati in repraesentando, necessario involvit ordinem ad id, cui repraesentat seu praesens facit; hoc autem est potentia.

SECUNDA VERO PARS conclusionis[5] probatur: Relatio signi ad signatum est relatio per modum repraesentationis seu applicationis eius ad potentiam, ergo ita debet respicere signatum ut terminum directum et *quod* sui respectus, quod etiam attingat potentiam in obliquo et ut terminum *cui*. Repugnat enim in istis relationibus, quae per modum substituentis et repraesentantis se habent, quod respiciant id, cuius gerunt vices, et non id, propter quod vel in ordine ad quod substituunt, quia substituens seu gerens vices alicuius secundum aliquam determinatam rationem et in ordine ad aliquem determinatum finem gerit vices illius; alioquin substitutio illa determinata non esset, cum ex fine, propter quem fit, determinetur. Ergo si relatio repraesentantis et substituentis vicem alicuius personae est determinata, oportet, quod ita respiciat illam personam, quod etiam attingat id, propter quod et in ordine ad quod substituit, inde enim determinata substitutio est. Et ita cum signum sit vices gerens et repraesentans signatum substituensque pro illo determinate, ut potentiae reddat praesens obiectum, necessario in ipsis visceribus et intima ratione talis substitutionis et repraesentationis signati, ut determinata est, involvitur respectus aliquis ad potentiam, quia ad hoc substituit, ut potentiae repraesentet.

Quomodo autem eadem relatio dicatur attingere in recto signatum et potentiam in obliquo, omissis multis et variis explicationibus illa adequatior videtur, quod signum respicit potentiam in obliquo, quatenus in ipso signato includitur esse manifestabile

[5] 154/26-30.

power is included within the very thing signified. And so, since the significate is not respected as it is something absolutely in itself or according to some other order, but as manifestable to a cognitive power, the power itself is necessarily touched indirectly by that relation which attains the significate not by resting on it precisely as it is in itself, but as it is manifestable to a cognitive power, and thus in some measure a sign-relation attains a cognitive power in that rationale of something manifestable to another, not by separately attaining the power, but by attaining that which is manifestable to the power, just as, for example, the virtue of religion respects for [its] formal object worship as something to be rendered to God, not that it respects God directly, for thus it would be a theological virtue, but worship directly, and God but indirectly, inasmuch as God is contained in worship as the terminus to which worship is rendered, and religion respects worship as under that terminus, and not absolutely or under some other consideration. The order to good that I will for a friend in friendship is the same; for that order is not terminated at the good willed absolutely, but at a good willed as it is referable to the friend, and the friend as the terminus of that good [willed] for someone terminates the same relation, even though not as the direct object, but as included in the direct object, by the fact that that direct object, the willed good, is respected as relative to this person and not absolutely.

It is indeed true that for a sign to respect a signified in this way, i.e., as something manifestable to a cognitive power, it is essentially presupposed that the sign itself respects the power by some other relation, either as an apprehensible object, if the sign is an instrumental sign, or as a form constituting an apprehension, if it is a formal sign, and thus serves for arriving at an awareness of another as an instrumental or as a formal sign. Yet this relation of sign to power, as we remarked at the beginning of this question, does not belong to the sign as it is formally a sign, but as it is an object or a form; presuppositively, however, this relation to a power is required for an external sign, because an external sign is also an object stimulating a cognitive power, and unless it does this as an object, it will not manifest [function] as a sign. But formally the one relation is distinguished from the other.[6] And although by virtue of the respect to the signified alone, in which is included indirectly the cognitive power to which that signified is manifestable, a sign would not exercise representation

potentiae. Et ita cum signatum non respiciatur, ut est aliquid absolute in se vel secundum alium ordinem, sed ut manifestabile potentiae, necessario ipsa potentia tangitur in obliquo ab illa relatione, quae attingit signatum non sistendo in illo ut in se praecise, sed ut manifestabile potentiae, et sic aliqualiter attingit potentiam in illa ratione manifestabilis alteri, non seorsum attingendo potentiam, sed attingendo id, quod manifestabile est potentiae, sicut religio respicit pro obiecto formali cultum ut exhibendum Deo, non quod Deum respiciat in recto, sic enim esset virtus theologica, sed cultum in recto, Deum vero in obliquo, quatenus Deus continetur in cultu ut terminus, cui exhibetur, et religio respicit cultum, ut subest illi termino, et non absolute vel sub alia consideratione. Et idem est in amicitia ordo ad bonum, quod volo amico; nec enim terminatur ordo ille ad bonum volitum absolute, sed ut est referibile amico, et amicus ut terminus illius boni in aliquo eandem relationem terminat, licet non ut obiectum directum, sed ut inclusum in obiecto directo, eo quod respicitur illud ut ad istud et non absolute.

Verum quidem est, quod, ut signum respiciat signatum hoc modo, id est ut manifestabile potentiae, praesupponitur essentialiter, quod ipsum signum alia relatione respiciat potentiam, vel tamquam obiectum apprehensibile, si sit signum instrumentale, vel tamquam forma constituens apprehensionem, si sit signum formale, et sic deserviat ad deveniendum in notitiam alterius ut signum instrumentale vel formale. Ceterum ista relatio signi ad potentiam, ut diximus in initio articuli, non est signi ut signum formaliter, sed ut obiecti vel formae; praesuppositive autem ad signum requiritur, quia etiam est obiectum movens potentiam, et nisi moveat ut obiectum, non manifestabit ut signum, formaliter autem una relatio distinguitur ab alia.[6] Et licet ex vi solius respectus ad signatum, in quo oblique includitur potentia, cui manifestabile est, non exerceat repraesentationem,

[6] See discussion in note 13 below.

unless a stimulation of the power were adjoined as the sign is a stimulus object, yet it is owing to that respect to the significate that that movement of stimulation is significative, that is to say, vicarious and substituting for the other which it signifies, and is not principally on behalf of [the stimulus object] itself.

From this it can be inferred that the apprehensibility of a sign is not the very rationale founding the sign-relation immediately and formally, because to be apprehensible or knowable is the rationale of an object as object, which is required for the rationale of a sign only presuppositively; but that the fundament [of the sign-relation] is the very rationale of medium or means which the sign has relative to the significate as manifestable to a cognitive power, by substituting for that significate in the rationale of stimulating and representing. Much less does the being known or apprehended in a sign (which some call proximate apprehensibility) found or complete the rationale of the sign, because being known does not pertain to the rationale of a sign, but to its exercise (for when a sign represents in act, it is cognized in act), not as it is capable of representing.

Resolution of Counter-Arguments

It is argued first: the relation of sign to signified is mind-independent among natural signs, but the relation of sign to power among those same signs is mind-dependent, therefore there cannot be a single relation between sign, signified, and cognitive power.

The antecedent for the first part of this argument was established in the preceding question. The antecedent for the second part is proved by the fact that a relation to a cognitive power is a relation of a sign insofar as that sign is apprehensible by a cognitive power. But the relation to a knowing power of something apprehensible or knowable is a mind-dependent relation, even if the something in question is apprehensible as a sign, because being apprehensible or apprehended, whether in a sign or in an object, posits nothing mind-independent in what so exists; for cognition or apprehension really exists only in the cognitive power, but in the thing apprehended, whatever that might be, the apprehension does not posit a physical or mind-independent reality.

The same argument can be made from the diversity in mode and type between the relation [of a sign] to a cognitive power and the relation [of a sign] to the signified: For a relation of sign to signified is one of measured to measure, because the thing signified is the principal for which the sign substitutes and is vicegerent, as has been often said. But a relation of sign to power is conversely a relation of measure to

nisi adiungatur motio potentiae, ut obiectum motivum est, tamen ex respectu illo ad signatum habet, quod illa motio significativa sit, id est vicaria et substituens pro alio, quod significat, non principalis pro se.

Ex quo deducitur apprehensibilitatem signi non esse ipsam rationem fundantem relationem signi immediate et formaliter, cum esse apprehensibile seu cognoscibile sit ratio obiecti ut obiectum, quae solum praesuppositive ad rationem signi requiritur; sed fundamentum esse ipsam rationem medii, quam habet ad significatum ut manifestabile potentiae, substituendo pro ipso in ratione movendi et repraesentandi. Multo minus esse cognitum seu apprehensum in signo, quod aliqui vocant apprehensibilitatem proximam, fundat aut complet rationem signi, quia esse cognitum non pertinet ad rationem signi, sed ad exercitium eius (quando enim actu repraesentat, actu est cognitum), non ut repraesentativum sit.

Solvuntur argumenta.

Primo arguitur: Relatio signi ad signatum in signis naturalibus est realis, ad potentiam vero in eisdem est rationis, ergo non potest esse unica relatio.

Antecedens pro prima parte constat ex praec. art. Pro secunda probatur, quia relatio ad potentiam est relatio signi, in quantum apprehensibile est a potentia. Sed relatio apprehensibilis seu cognoscibilis ad potentiam cognoscentem est relatio rationis, etiamsi sit apprehensibile ut signum, quia esse apprehensibile vel apprehensum, sive in signo sive in obiecto, nihil reale ponit in ipso; cognitio enim seu apprehensio solum est realiter in potentia, in re vero apprehensa, quaecumque illa sit, non ponit realitatem.

Idem argumentum fit ex diverso modo et specie relationis ad potentiam et ad signatum: Nam relatio signi ad signatum est mensurati ad mensuram, quia signatum est principale, pro quo substituit et vices gerit signum, ut saepe dictum est. Signi vero relatio ad potentiam est e converso mensurae ad

measured. For a sign respects a cognitive power by a nonreciprocal relation, because the sign stands on the side of an object representing and does not function as measured by the power, therefore as measuring that power; for a cognitive power does not measure an apprehended thing, but is measured by that thing, because it is perfected by that thing.

The response to this[7] and similar arguments which are multiplied in the same manner is that they prove what we have said from the start, namely, that the relation to a cognitive power from the side of a sign as object of the power, and the relation to the significate, as to direct termini, are not one relation, but multiple. Yet neither of the two is the sign-relation formally. Rather, the relation directly to the cognitive power is an object-relation under the rationale and formality of an object, while the relation directly to the thing signified is in the rationale of a cause, or of an effect, or of some similar rationale; whence the thing which is a sign is determined to be a creature of the signified, and so it represents that significate rather than another.

Moreover, the relation itself of a sign, speaking most formally as it is a sign, respects a knowing power indirectly, not inasmuch as the sign is apprehensible by the power and an object thereof, but inasmuch as the thing itself signified is manifestable to the power. The sign attains the signified or substitutes for it, not absolutely, but as it is manifestable to a cognitive power: in that manner a cognitive power is involved virtually and indirectly. Wherefore, even though the relation of an object or apprehensible thing to a cognitive power understood directly and in the mode of an object is mind-dependent, yet the relation to a significate, even as something manifestable to a cognitive power, can be mind-independent, because in an object being signifiable and representable to a cognitive power is something mind-independent, even though the object does not mind-independently respect the power; for how an object respects a power is one thing, quite another is what being manifestable to a power is in an object. To be manifestable and objectifiable is something independent of mind, and that upon which a cognitive power depends and by which it is specified. Nay rather, it is because an object is thus mind-independent that it does not depend upon a cognitive power by a mind-independent relation. Wherefore, since a sign under the formality of sign does not respect a cognitive power directly (for this is the formality of an object), but respects a thing signifi-

mensuratum. Signum enim respicit potentiam relatione non mutua, cum signum teneat se ex parte obiecti repraesentantis et non se habet ut mensuratum a potentia, ergo ut mensurans illam; potentia enim rem apprehensam non mensurat, sed ab ea mensuratur, quia ab ea perficitur.

Respondetur haec argumenta[7] et similia, quae eodem modo multiplicantur, probare id, quod a principio diximus, scilicet quod relatio ad potentiam ex parte signi, ut obiectum eius est, et ad signatum, ut ad terminos directos, non est una relatio, sed multiplex. Neutra tamen est relatio signi formaliter, sed relatio directe respiciens potentiam est relatio obiecti sub ratione et formalitate obiecti, respiciens vero rem signatam directe est in ratione causae vel effectus aut alterius similis rationis; unde res, quae est signum, determinatur, ut sit aliquid signati, et sic illud potius quam aliud repraesentet.

Ceterum relatio ipsa signi formalissime loquendo ut signum est, respicit potentiam in obliquo, non quatenus signum apprehensibile est a potentia et obiectum illius, sed quatenus ipsum signatum est manifestabile potentiae, et attingendo signatum vel substituendo pro ipso non absolute, sed ut manifestabile est potentiae, ibi virtualiter et in obliquo involvitur potentia. Quare, licet relatio obiecti seu apprehensibilis ad potentiam directe sumptam et per modum obiecti sit rationis, tamen relatio ad signatum, etiam ut manifestabile potentiae, realis esse potest, quia in obiecto esse significabile et repraesentabile potentiae aliquid reale est, licet non realiter respiciat potentiam; aliud enim est quomodo obiectum respiciat potentiam, aliud, quid sit in obiecto esse manifestabile potentiae. Esse manifestabile et obicibile aliquid reale est, et id, a quo dependet potentia et a quo specificatur; imo quia ita reale est, non dependet a potentia reali relatione. Quare cum signum sub formalitate signi non respiciat potentiam directe, hoc enim est formalitatis obiecti, sed respiciat rem signifi-

7 159/25-43.

able or manifestable to a cognitive power, a cognitive power as indirectly included in that manifestable object is attained by a mind-independent sign-relation, because the cognitive power is not respected separately, but as included in that which is mind-independent in the object as something manifestable to a cognitive power; where the whole which is attained in act and formally is mind-independent, and the power whose object it is enters there merely as something connoted and indirectly. For example, a science which treats of colors as they are an object of sight really respects colors as being specificative of itself, although the colors themselves virtually include an order to the cognitive power for which they are the objects, which order is mind-dependent in the colors themselves, but the order of the science to those objects is not mind-dependent. But that respect by which a sign directly respects a cognitive power by stimulating it to cognize the sign itself as well as the significate whose vicegerent the sign is, is a mind-dependent respect, but distinct from the sign-relation by which the sign respects the significate, because it is the respect of an object, not formally the respect of a sign as sign.

Hence it appears that the response to the second argument[8] is that it proceeds from the relation by which a sign directly and formally respects a cognitive power, which is a relation of measure or of object measuring, not from the relation by which a sign respects the significate inasmuch as the significate is an object manifestable to a cognitive power, where the power is attained only indirectly and virtually, not through a mind-dependent respect. And so a sign is not a measure of a cognitive power, but an instrument of the signified in relation to a cognitive power.

A second argument against my thesis: These termini, namely, significate and cognitive power, are distinct even in the formality of terminus, because the one is a terminus as something which is attained directly, while the other is a terminus as something to which; they are distinguished therefore more than materially. For when a sign has several inadequate significates, then it is related to them as to several termini materially diverse, therefore power and signified are distinguished in the rationale of terminus more than materially.

This is confirmed by the fact that signs are specifically distinguished on the basis of an order to a cognitive power, as is clear in the division of signs into formal and instrumental signs, which are diverse

cabilem seu manifestabilem potentiae, sic potentia ut in obliquo inclusa in illo obiecto manifestabili attingitur a reali relatione signi, quia non respicitur potentia seorsum, sed ut inclusa in eo, quod reale est obiecto ut manifestabili potentiae; ubi totum, quod attingitur actu et formaliter reale est, et solum potentia, cuius est obiectum, intrat ibi de connotato et in obliquo. Sicut scientia, quae agit de coloribus, ut sunt obiectum visus, realiter respicit colores, utpote specificativum sui, licet ipsi includant virtualiter ordinem ad potentiam, cuius sunt obiecta, qui ordo est rationis in ipsis coloribus, non ordo scientiae ad ipsa obiecta rationis est. Ille vero respectus, quo signum respicit directe potentiam, movendo eam tam ad cognoscendum se quam signatum, cuius gerit vices, respectus rationis est, sed distinctus a relatione signi, qua respicit signatum, quia est respectus obiecti, non formaliter signi ut signum.

Et hinc patet ad secundum argumentum,[8] quod procedit de relatione, qua signum directe et formaliter respicit potentiam, quae est relatio mensurae seu obiecti mensurantis, non de relatione, qua respicit signatum quatenus obiectum manifestabile potentiae, ubi potentia solum in obliquo et virtualiter attingitur, non per respectum rationis. Et sic signum non est mensura potentiae, sed instrumentum signati ad illam.

Secundo arguitur: Termini isti, scilicet signatum et potentia, sunt distincti etiam in formalitate termini, cum unus sit terminus ut *quod* et directe attactus, alius sit terminus ut *cui*; distinguuntur ergo plus quam materialiter. Quando enim signum habet plura signata inadaequata, tunc se habet ad illa ut ad plures terminos materialiter diversos, ergo plus quam materialiter distinguuntur in ratione terminorum potentia et signatum.

Confirmatur, quia ex ordine ad potentiam distinguuntur specifice signa, ut patet in signo formali et instrumentali,

---

[8] 159/44-160/7.

species within the genus of sign, and are not distinguished on the side of the significate; for a concept of fire, for example, can represent the same thing that smoke does, which is a sign of fire, but a concept of fire and smoke are distinguished in their mode of functioning relative to a cognitive power, to wit, the concept by informing and the smoke by objectifying. Therefore the order to a cognitive power exists directly and not indirectly in a sign, since indeed that order specifies and distinguishes kinds of sign.

This argument can also be stated conversely, because signs can be divided into diverse species or kinds according to the order to the signified when the order to a power remains invariant; this therefore is a sign that there are distinct relations [making up the being proper to the sign, one to a cognitive power and another to a thing signified], for otherwise when the one relation varied the other would vary also. The antecedent is true in fact. For diverse concepts are varied by diverse represented objects while the relation to the cognitive power remains of the same rationale in all.

It is confirmed secondly: The rationale of a sign and the rationale of an image differ in this, that an image does not respect a cognitive power to which it would represent, but the exemplar or idea of which it is an imitation. For even if an image represents to a cognitive power, this is incidental to the fact that it is an image. A sign, however, essentially respects a cognitive power as that to which it would represent. Therefore a relation to a power is intrinsic to a sign and is constitutive of it, since this relation essentially distinguishes a sign from an image.

Finally, a third confirmation comes from the fact that a relation to a cognitive power remains in a sign even after the relation to a thing signified has been destroyed, as is clear when the thing signified does not exist, and yet the sign leads the cognitive power to an awareness of that significate just as before. In such a case the sign respects the cognitive power in the rationale of something conductive and significative just as it did before the significate ceased to exist, and thus the relation to the power remains.

The response to the principal argument[9] is that the signified which is represented, and the power to which the representation is made, are not two termini adequate and distinct in the rationale of terminus, but integrate one terminus established out of something direct and something indirect. Just as, for example, in the practice

quae sunt diversa specie in genere signi, et non distinguuntur ex parte significati; possunt enim idem repraesentare conceptus, v. g. ignis et fumus, qui est signum ignis, sed distinguuntur ex modo se habendi erga potentiam informando vel obiciendo. Ergo ordo ad potentiam habet se in recto et non in obliquo in signo, siquidem illud specificat et distinguit.

Potest etiam e converso fieri hoc argumentum, quia potest signum dividi per diversas species secundum ordinem ad signatum manente invariato ordine ad potentiam; ergo signum est, quod sunt relationes distinctae, alioquin variata una variaretur et alia. *Antecedens* vero constat. Nam diversi conceptus variantur ex diversis obiectis repraesentatis manente relatione ad potentiam eiusdem rationis in omnibus.

Confirmatur secundo: Ratio signi et ratio imaginis in hoc differunt, quod imago non respicit potentiam, cui repraesentet, sed exemplar seu ideam, cuius sit imitatio. Si quid vero repraesentat potentiae, per accidens est ad imaginem. Signum vero per se respicit potentiam, ut cui repraesentet. Ergo relatio ad potentiam signo est intrinseca et de constitutivo eius, cum essentialiter distinguat signum ab imagine.

Denique tertio confirmatur, quia manet relatio ad potentiam in signo destructa relatione ad signatum, ut patet, quando signatum non existit, et tamen signum ducit potentiam ad notitiam illius sicut antea. Ergo respicit potentiam in ratione ductivi et significativi sicut antea, et sic manet relatio ad potentiam.

RESPONDETUR ad principale argumentum,[9] quod signatum, quod repraesentatur, et potentia, cui fit repraesentatio, non sunt duo termini adaequati et distincti in ratione termini, sed unum terminum integrant, qui constat ex directo et ex obliquo. Sicut in religione

[9] 161/35-40.

of the virtue of religion, worship, which is rendered, and God, to whom it is rendered, are not two adequate [i.e., equal and independent] termini, but the one complete term of religion. And to believe in God revealing and to believe in God revealed are not two termini, but the one terminus of faith, inasmuch as thus is attained one terminus, which completes not absolutely and according to itself, but as modified and respectively or connotatively bearing toward something other, just as a thing signified is attained as representable to a cognitive power.

To the first confirmation[10] the response is that the division of signs into formal and instrumental is a division into diverse species or kinds which are directly taken not just from diverse respects to a cognitive power, but from diverse relations to a signified as representable to a cognitive power in diverse ways.[11] For any object is representable by a twofold representative medium or means, namely, a means in which and a means through which.[12] And the first founds a formal representation acting within a cognitive power, the second founds an instrumental representation moving a cognitive power from without. Whence in the representable thing itself signified are distinguished diverse rationales or fundaments for the relations it terminates from these diverse representations or modes of representing in signs, even though the thing represented may be materially the same. And similarly, this division of signs into instrumental and formal presupposes in the signs themselves diverse manners of stimulatively moving and representing to the cognitive power, specifically, as an external object or as an internal form; yet this is related presuppositively to the rationale of sign,[13] whereas the most formal rationale of a sign consists in being something substituted for a significate as representable in this or that way.

cultus, qui exhibetur, et Deus, cui exhibetur, non sunt duo termini adaequati, sed unus terminus integer religionis. Et credere Deo et Deum, non sunt duo termini, sed unus fidei, quatenus sic attingitur unus terminus, quod non absolute et secundum se terminat, sed ut modificatur et respective seu connotative se habet ad aliquid aliud, sicut signatum attingitur ut repraesentabile potentiae.

Ad primam confirmationem[10] respondetur, quod divisio signi in formale et instrumentale est divisio per diversas species, quae directe non sumuntur ex solo diverso respectu ad potentiam, sed ex diversa relatione ad signatum ut diverso modo repraesentabile potentiae.[11] Est enim repraesentabile aliquod obiectum duplici medio repraesentativo, scilicet medio *in quo* et medio *per quod*.[12] Et primum fundat repraesentationem formalem intra potentiam informantem, secundum repraesentationem instrumentalem extra potentiam moventem. Unde in ipso signato repraesentabili invenitur diversa ratio seu fundamentum ad terminandum istas diversas repraesentationes seu modos repraesentandi in signis, licet res repraesentata materialiter sit eadem. Et similiter praesupponit in ipsis signis diversum modum movendi et repraesentandi potentiae, scilicet ut obiectum extra vel ut forma ad intra; hoc tamen praesuppositive se habet ad rationem signi,[13] formalissima vero ratio se habet ut substituti ad signatum, ut tali modo vel tali repraesentabile.

---

10 161/45-162/10.

11 See above, Question 2, 145/10-28, and below, Book II, Question 1, 238/28-45 with 235/15-35.

12 This distinction between a means "in which" and a means "through which" is elsewhere explained by Poinsot (in Book II, Question 1, 224/9-19, 224/29-34) as the difference between a means "in which" that is formal and intrinsic to a cognitive power and a means "in which" that is a material object existing independently of the power and as a sign of something else. Whether it is called a "material and extrinsic means in which" or simply a "means through which," what is in question is the sort of means making cognition mediate as opposed to the sort of means that does not qualify the immediacy of cognition respecting its objective terminus: see Book II, Question 1, 223/16-224/2, 226/35-45, 227/9-228/18, 231/45-233/2; and Question 2, 250/19-39. The point is also explained by Poinsot in his Phil. nat. 4. p. q. 11. art. 2., Reiser ed., III. 358b26-359a11, cited below in Book II, Question 2, note 27, p. 249.

13 The relation of sign to signified, in other words, is necessarily and at once formally distinct from and superordinate to a direct relation of sign to power, by the fact that the former relation is *always* ontological, whereas the latter relation *may be* only transcendental (Book I, Question 1,

And from this it is clear that the response to the converse formulation of the first confirmation[14] is that although the order to a cognitive power may be of the same rationale in diverse significates, yet it is not required that the cognitive power be involved by a distinct relation, because it can well be the case that sign-relations are specifically varied by a diversity of representable objects, even though they may coincide or not differ on the side of the connotation indirectly included, just as, for example, faith and opinion coincide in the mode of obscurity, not in formal specifying character.

To the second confirmation[15] I answer: because a sign respects a signified precisely as representable to a cognitive power, as its vicegerent and consequently subordinate to it, but an image respects its exemplar as something imitable and as the principle from which the image is originated and expressed, and so can be not unequal to that exemplar, for this reason, sign and image have distinct formalities or formal rationales of terminating on the side of that

Et ex hoc patet ad alteram partem argumenti,[14] quod ordo ad potentiam, licet sit eiusdem rationis in diversis signatis, non tamen requiritur, quod distincta relatione attingatur, quia bene stat, quod relationes signi specie varientur ex diversitate obiecti repraesentabilis, licet conveniant seu non differant ex parte connotationis in obliquo inclusae, sicut fides et opinio conveniunt in modo obscuritatis, non in ratione formali specificante.

Ad secundum confirmationem[15] respondetur, quod quia signum respicit signatum praecise ut repraesentabile ad potentiam ut vices eius gerens et consequenter inferius ipso, imago autem respicit suum exemplar ut imitabile et ut principium, a quo originatur et exprimitur, et sic potest illi non inaequalis esse, ideo ex parte ipsius termini, quem directe respiciunt, habent distinctas formalitates seu rationes formales

123/13-25, 126/23-127/6 and 128/9-19, esp. 19). It is precisely this formal superordination that makes possible in the first place signs which are such without being themselves initially cognized objectively in their own right, i.e., signs which relate the knower to external objects immediately (formal signs: cf. Ransdell, 1979, as discussed in Deely, 1980b and 1985). Cf. this Question, 158/1-159/6, with Book I, Question 2, 151/9-14 above. The following diagram, based on a 1975 sketch by the Adlerian psychologist P. Lawrence Belove, is useful here:

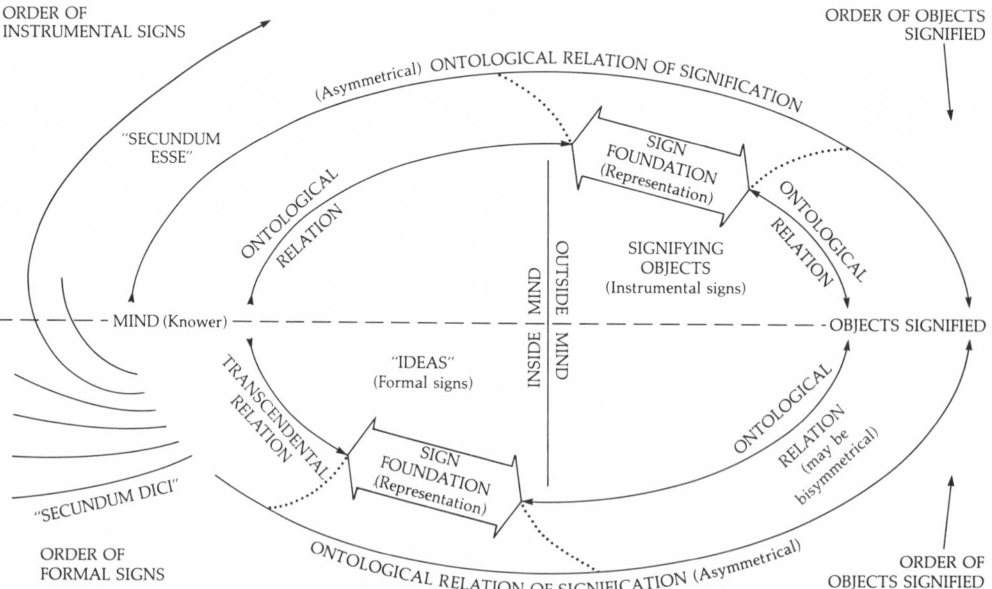

Further to the specifically superordinate character of the constitutive sign relation, refer back to 160/10-21 in this Question, and to Book I, Question 2, esp. the 1663 Lyons variant cited in note 4, p. 137 above.

[14] 162/11-21.

[15] 162/22-32.

very terminus which they directly respect, even though upon the one [i.e., the sign] follows indirectly an order to a cognitive power in the very thing signified, which it concerns, in the other [i.e., the exemplar] not. And so the formal rationale distinguishing in the one case is the rationale of a signified as such, in the other case the rationale of an exemplar as such, and not in either case the cognitive power itself to which representation is made.[16]

To the third confirmation[17] the response is that when the order to a thing signified is destroyed, the order to a cognitive power, which was included in the significate itself indirectly and by connotation, is also destroyed. Yet because this order to the nonexistent thing signified remains in the sign fundamentally and virtually, that order to a cognitive power, which goes with a thing signified, also remains fundamentally.[18] At the same time, the sign can formally retain in itself the rationale of a stimulating object or of a representing form, which rationale is a relation other than the sign-relation, as has been said.

terminandi, licet ad unam sequatur ordo ad potentiam in obliquo in ipso signato, quod tangit, in alia non. Et ita formalis ratio distinguens in utroque est ratio signati ut sic, ratio exemplaris ut sic, non ipsa potentia, cui fit repraesentatio.[16]

Ad tertiam confirmationem[17] respondetur, quod destructo ordine ad signatum destruitur ordo ad potentiam, qui in ipso signato in obliquo et connotato includebatur. Quia tamen remanet fundamentaliter et virtualiter ordo iste in signo ad signatum non existens, remanet etiam fundamentaliter ille ordo ad potentiam, qui cum signato vadit.[18] Formaliter tamen retinere potest signum in se rationem obiecti moventis vel formae repraesentantis, quae est alia relatio a signo, ut dictum est.

---

[16] See above, Question 1, 132/47-133/12, and below, Sequel to Book I, 218/29-48.
[17] 162/33-42.
[18] See Question 1 above, 125/31-39 and note 25 thereon.

Question 4

In What Way Are Objects Divided into Stimulus Objects and Terminative Objects

Quaestio Quarta

Qualiter Dividatur Obiectum in Motivum et Terminativum

The present discussion presupposes the definitions of stimulus and terminative objects given in the *Summulae* books.[1] With those definitions presupposed . . .

Our first conclusion is this: **Object in general, as it abstracts from stimulus and terminus, consists in this, that it be something extrinsic, from which derives and upon which depends the intrinsic rationale and specific character of any power or act; and this is reduced to the category of an extrinsic formal cause not causing existence, but specification.**

To understand this conclusion, advert to the fact pointed out by Cajetan in his *Commentary* on the *Summa theologica*, I, q. 77, art. 3, that some things are entirely absolute, depending in their specification and constitution on nothing extrinsic to themselves, such things as substance, quantity, etc. Other things are entirely relative, those which have their whole content in being toward another and depend upon that other as on a pure terminus. Yet other things are intermediate between these, namely, those things which have in themselves some definable content and an absolute essence, so that they have something other than to respect and to be referred; yet they depend in their constitution and specification on something extrinsic, not for respecting, but for acting or causing or accomplishing something. And it is in this intermediate manner that powers and acts and habits stand with

Supponendae sunt definitiones istorum obiectorum, quas 1. libro Summul.[1] tradidimus. Et illis suppositis.

SIT PRIMA CONCLUSIO: **Obiectum in communi, ut abstrahit a motivo et terminativo, consistit in hoc, quod sit aliquid extrinsecum, a quo sumitur et dependet intrinseca ratio et species alicuius potentiae vel actus; et hoc reducitur ad genus causae formalis extrinsecae non causantis existentiam, sed specificationem.**

Ut conclusio intelligatur, adverte ex Caietano 1. p. q. 77. art. 3., quod *aliquae* res sunt prorsus absolutae, in sui specificatione et constitutione a nullo extrinseco dependentes, ut substantia, quantitas etc. *Aliae* sunt prorsus relativae, quae totum suum esse habent ad aliud et ab illo pendent ut a puro termino. *Aliae* sunt mediae inter istas, quae in se quidem habent quidditatem et essentiam absolutam, ita quod aliquid aliud habent quam respicere et referri; tamen in sui constitutione et specificatione dependent ab aliquo extrinseco, non ad respiciendum, sed ad agendum vel causandum aut aliquid negotiandum. Et sic se habent potentiae et ac-

[1] c. 2., 26/6-20.

respect to the things which they attain, and are said to have a transcendental order to them.

Note well that it is one thing for some thing to be entirely absolute or independent of anything extrinsic in its specification, but quite another thing for it to be such in its existence. For in existing no thing is absolute, i.e., independent of everything external to itself, except God alone, who is from himself, all other things being dependent on God. But for the present we are speaking of the dependence of a thing in its specification upon something extrinsic, and it is in this way that an object stands relative to a power. For an object does not exist relative to a cognitive power or act as effecting or influencing existence; for this does not pertain to an object, but to something producing. Yet the specification of a cognitive act or power by its very nature depends on an object, even abstracting from the object's existence.

Lastly, note that, even though it is an extrinsic formal cause, an object differs from an idea or exemplary cause, both because an idea is that in whose similitude an ideated thing comes to be, but an object is not something in whose likeness a cognitive power or its act exists; and because an idea expresses a cause that is an exemplar by way of origin, but an object is not a principle of origin in respect of a power or an act of a power; and because, finally, an idea is an efficacious exemplary cause, and in this function it also causes existence, for it enters into the formation of an actual singular, and as such the idea belongs to practical understanding extending itself to a work and to the existence of an effect; but an object does not move a power or act as regards exercise or efficacy but only as regards what is formal and as regards a specification.

So understood, therefore, the stated conclusion is derived from St. Thomas's dictum in the *Summa theologica*, I-II, q. 9, art. 1, that "an act is specified according to the rationale of the object," and that an object affects or moves [a power or act] by determining it in the mode of a formal principle through which an action is specified in the order of mind-independent natural things." And in I, q. 77, art. 3, St. Thomas says that "an object is related to a passive power as a principle and moving cause," "but it is related to an active power as a terminus and end." "From these two," he says, "an action receives a specific character, namely, from a principle or from an end, that is, a terminus." Therefore St. Thomas thinks that an object of a passive

tus et habitus circa ea, quae attingunt, dicunturque habere ordinem transcendentalem ad ea.

Et bene nota, quod aliud est rem aliquam esse omnino absolutam ab aliquo extrinseco in *specificatione* sua, aliud in *existentia* sua. In existendo enim nulla res est absoluta ab aliquo extrinseco, nisi solus Deus, qui est a se, reliqua sunt a Deo. At vero in praesenti loquimur de dependentia rei ab aliquo extrinseco in specificatione sua, et sic obiectum se habet ad potentiam. Nec enim ad potentiam vel actum se habet ut efficiens seu influens existentiam; id enim non ad obiectum pertinet, sed ad producens. Ab obiecto autem pendet specificatio actus vel potentiae secundum se, etiam existentia semota.

Denique differt obiectum ab idea seu causa exemplari, etiamsi causa formalis extrinseca sit, *tum* quia idea est, ad cuius similitudinem fit ideatum; obiectum autem non est id, ad cuius similitudinem se habet potentia vel actus eius; *tum* quia idea dicit causam exemplarem per modum originis, obiectum autem non est principium originis respectu potentiae vel actus; *tum* denique quia idea est causa exemplaris efficax, et pro hac parte etiam causat existentiam, influit enim ad formandum rem in actu et in singulari, sicque est in intellectu practico, qui se extendit ad opus et ad existentiam effectus; obiectum autem non movet quoad exercitium seu efficientiam, sed solum quoad formale et quoad specificationem.

Sic ergo conclusio posita sumitur ex D. Thoma 1. 2. q. 9. art. 1. dicente, quod «secundum rationem obiecti specificatur actus», et quod «obiectum movet determinando ad modum principii formalis, a quo in rebus naturalibus specificatur actio». Et. 1. p. q. 77. art. 3. dicit, quod «obiectum ad potentiam passivam comparatur ut principium et causa movens», «ad actum vero potentiae activae comparatur ut terminus et finis». «Ex his autem duobus», inquit, «actio speciem recipit, scilicet ex principio vel fine seu termino». Ergo sentit D. Thomas obiectum passivae et activae

power coincides with an object of an active power in this, that it specifies an act. And finally, in his *Commentary* on Book II of Aristotle's treatise, *On the Soul,* toward the end of reading 6:[2] "It is manifest," he says, "that every object is related to an operation of the soul either as something active or as a terminus; but from both is the operation specified." The word "every" here expresses the universal rationale of an object.

THE REASON FOR THIS is that although active and passive powers are founded on rationales as diverse as are act and potency, because the one is for acting, the other for receiving, as St. Thomas best explains in the *Summa theologica,* I, q. 25, art. 1, yet the objects of both agree in this, that they extrinsically determine or perfect a power or its act. For in respect of a passive power, it is certain that an object functions as something perfecting extrinsically [operating from without], since it reduces that power from potency to act, for it is coupled to that power as a principle of the power's act, which pertains to actuality and perfection; and in respect of an active power, an object is related as terminus and end. But though what is purely a terminus cannot perfect, as, for example, in the case of relatives, owing to the fact that a relation does not adjust or tend by acting productively, but simply by respecting, and though similarly what is simply effect does not perfect but is only perfected, as, for example, creatures in respect of God are effected by God in such a way that his action does not depend in itself on their termination; nevertheless, in created actions termination gives perfection to the acts, because if they were not terminated, they would be neither perfect nor complete, but, as it were, in transition and tendency; they are perfected therefore by that very termination toward which they tend. And so St. Thomas says in his *Disputed Questions on the Power of God,* q. 7, art. 10,[3] that in the effect or reception itself can be perceived a kind of good and perfection of the one exercising a causal influence, as in the case of univocal agents, which perpetuate a specific kind of being through their effects, and in the case of the other agents which move, act, or cause only as they are moved; "for from the very movement that they undergo they are ordered to producing effects. And similarly in all cases where a good of any kind accrues to the cause from the effect." Thus St. Thomas. From this doctrine it is clear how a terminative object can be something perfective of a power or an action.

potentiae convenire in hoc, quod est specificare actum. Ac denique 2. de Anima lect. 6. circa finem:[2] «Manifestum est», inquit, «quod omne obiectum comparatur ad operationem animae vel ut activum vel ut finis; ex utroque autem specificatur operatio». Ubi ly omne universalem rationem obiecti explicat.

ET HUIUS RATIO EST, quia licet potentia activa et passiva fundentur in rationibus ita diversis, sicut sunt actus et potentia, quia una est ad agendum, alia ad recipiendum, ut optime docet S. Thomas 1. p. q. 25. art. 1., tamen utriusque obiectum convenit in hoc, quod est determinare vel perficere extrinsece potentiam vel eius actum. Nam respectu potentiae passivae constat, quod obiectum se habet ut perficiens extrinsece, cum reducat illam de potentia ad actum, comparatur enim ad illam ut principium actus eius, quod pertinet ad actualitatem et perfectionem; ad potentiam autem activam comparatur ut terminus et finis. Licet autem quod est pure terminus, non perficiat, sicut in relativis, eo quod relatio non tendit agendo, sed pure respiciendo, et similiter quod est pure effectus, non perficiat, sed pure perficiatur, sicut creaturae respectu Dei, quae ita efficiuntur a Deo, quod ab earum terminatione eius actio in se non pendet; tamen in actibus creatis terminatio dat perfectionem actibus, quia si terminati non sint, perfecti non sunt nec completi, sed quasi in via et tendentia; perficiuntur ergo determinatione ipsa, ad quam tendunt. Et ita dicit S. Thomas 7. de Potentia art. 10.,[3] quod in ipso effectu seu passione attenditur quoddam bonum et perfectio moventis, sicut in univocis agentibus, quae per suos effectus perpetuant esse speciei, et in aliis, quae mota movent vel agunt vel causant; «nam ex ipso suo motu ordinantur ad effectus producendos. Et similiter in omnibus, quibus quodcumque bonum causae provenit ex effectu». Ita D. Thomas. Ex qua doctrina constat, quomodo obiectum terminativum possit esse perfectivum potentiae vel actionis.

---

[2] *Pa* XX. 55 b.
[3] *Pa* VIII. 165 a.

Second conclusion: **Even as distinguished from a terminative object, the true rationale of an object is preserved in a stimulus object.**

This conclusion is against those who think that the rationale of an object is preserved only in a terminative object, but who exclude a stimulus object from the rationale of an object, on the grounds that it bespeaks production; what belongs to an object as it is an object, however, is not to produce, but to specify.

But a great equivocation is perpetrated in the use of the term ''stimulus'' by applying it only to a productive (an efficient) cause, because it should be applied also to other types of cause, as an end, for example, is said to stimulate or motivate, or as an object proposed by the will stimulates or motivates the will, and an exemplar stimulates relative to its imitation. Following this common usage, therefore, we distinguish between something stimulating through the mode of exercise and through the mode of specification. The first mode pertains to an efficient cause, the second one to a formal object. And this follows from the passages cited from St. Thomas[4] concerning the preceding conclusion. For there St. Thomas perspicuously teaches that a stimulus object specifies a passive power and is related to it as a moving principle, and so is prior to its specificate in the process of defining. Therefore an object in the rationale of a stimulus has the true rationale of an object and not of productive efficiency; for something effecting insofar as it is effecting respects the existence of the thing which it produces, not the specification nor the principles of definition, while St. Thomas nevertheless says, especially in the passage already cited from his *Commentary* on Book II of Aristotle's treatise *On the Soul*, reading 6,[5] that ''objects are prior to the operations of the soul in the way of defining,'' and he had been speaking of terminative and of stimulus objects alike. The rationale of being a stimulus, therefore, does not denote efficiency in an object, but is contained within the limits of an objective form, that is, of something specificative.

Our conclusion is confirmed finally by the fact that a passive power, insofar as it is such, is specifiable by something extrinsic, since indeed a passive power is ordered on the basis of the kind of thing it is to that external specificative, and therefore its specific character, the kind of thing that it is, is not entirely absolute in itself and independent of every extrinsic factor. But whatever is not entirely absolute in itself, but is orderable to another as a consequence of what it is, is specifiable by that other. But

SECUNDA CONCLUSIO: **In obiecto motivo, etiam ut a terminativo distinguitur, salvatur vera ratio obiecti.**

Est contra aliquos, qui existimant rationem obiecti in solo terminativo salvari, excludunt autem motivum a ratione obiecti, quia dicit efficientiam; obiecto autem ut obiecto non convenit efficere, sed specificare.

Ceterum magna aequivocatio committitur in illo termino ,,motivum'' applicando illud solum causae efficienti, cum etiam aliis causis applicetur, sicut finis dicitur movere, et obiectum propositum per voluntatem movet illam, et exemplar movet ad sui imitationem. Sic ergo distinguimus motivum per modum *exercitii* et per modum *specificationis*, et illud primum pertinet ad causam efficientem, hoc secundum ad obiectum formale. Et constat hoc ex D. Thoma locis cit.[4] praec. conclusione. Ibi enim perspicue docet S. Thomas obiectum motivum specificare potentiam passivam et comparari ad ipsam ut principium movens, et sic est prius suo specificato in via definiendi. Ergo in ratione motivi habet veram rationem obiecti et non efficientiae; efficiens enim in quantum efficiens respicit esse rei, quod producit, non specificationem nec definitionis principia, cum tamen D. Thomas specialiter in 2. de Anima lect. 6. cit.[5] dicat, «quod obiecta sunt priora operationibus animae in via definiendi», et locutus fuerat tam de obiectis terminativis quam activis seu motivis. Ratio ergo motivi non efficientiam dicit in obiecto, sed intra limites obiectivae formae, id est specificativae continetur.

Ac denique confirmatur, quia potentia passiva in quantum talis ab aliquo extrinseco specificabilis est, siquidem ex specie sua ordinatur ad illud, atque adeo species eius non est omnino absoluta in se et independens ab omni extrinseco. Quidquid autem non est omnino absolutum in se, sed ex sua specie ordinabile ad aliud, specificabile est ab illo. Sed poten-

[4] at 167/37-168/8.
[5] *Pa* XX. 55 b.

a passive power as such is not related to an extrinsic specificative as to a terminus, but as to a stimulus, because a passive power is in potency to be actuated, not for its actuality to be terminated; for the power in question is a passive, not an active, power. Therefore that which is its stimulus is truly a specificative object.

You might say: at least a stimulus object must concur efficiently with a power in the production of an act; therefore the rationale of stimulus in an object pertains to the order of productive, i.e., efficient, causality.

The response to this is that, in the first place, the conclusion does not hold in respect of every power, but only in the case of a cognitive power, in which case it is more probable that an impressed specifier concurs with the power in the production of the act.[6] But this

tia passiva ut talis non comparatur ad extrinsecum specificativum ut ad terminum, sed ut ad motivum, quia est in potentia, ut actuetur, non ut actualitas eius terminetur; est enim potentia passiva, non activa. Ergo id, quod est motivum eius, est vere obiectum specificativum.

DICES: Saltem obiectum motivum debet efficienter concurrere cum potentia ad actum; ergo ratio motivi in obiecto pertinet ad genus efficientiae.

Respondetur hoc imprimis non currere respectu omnis potentiae, sed tantum in potentia cognoscitiva, in qua est probabilius, quod species in genere efficientis concurrat ad actum cum potentia.[6] Ceterum

[6] Phil. nat. 4. p. q. 6. art. 3., Reiser ed., III. 189b41-190b2: "*Et ratio est, quia cognitio est actus potentiae assimilativus et productivus speciei expressae. Sed potentia sola non est sufficiens principium effectivum huius similitudinis expressae, siquidem non potest ipsi soli assimilari talis effectus. Ergo oportet assignare alterum principium effectivum, cui simul cum potentia assimiletur iste effectus; illud autem principium, cui effectus assimilatur, effectivum est. Non est autem aliud principium, cui assimiletur species expressa ut egrediens a potentia, nisi impressa, quae determinat illam ad tale obiectum. Ergo cum in tali egressione, quae effectiva est, egrediatur a potentia et specie illa cognitio et similitudo, manifestum est, quod non sola potentia est principium effectivum, sed potentia ut determinata per speciem, et consequenter species ipsa effective cooperatur. . . . [D]e concursu vitali dicimus, quod species non est principium concursus vitalis radicale et principale, sed determinativum et specificativum eius, eo quod potentia ista vitalis dependet ab obiecto in suo concursu ut a determinante et specificante. Principium autem concursus vitalis per modum determinantis non oportet, quod sit intrinsecum, sed ab extrinseco potest provenire, sicut habitus, qui supervenit potentiae et cum ipsa concurrit effective, et tamen potest ab extrinseco provenire. Sed est differentia, quod habitus seu lumen determinat potentiam ex parte virtutis et confortando vires eius erga determinatum obiectum, species autem solum repraesentando et uniendo intentionaliter obiectum, et hoc simul cum potentia parit notitiam etiam concurrendo effective, sicut in generatione animalis concurrit active semen viri, quod potest magis ac magis perfici intra lineam suae activitatis et virtutis, sicut potentia per habitum, sed tamen ulterius indiget semine femineo, quod ex coniunctione ad spirituosam virtutem seminis virilis effective influit in productionem foetus.*"—"The reason for this is that cognition is an assimilative action by a power productive of an expressed specification. But the cognitive power alone is not the sufficient productive principle of this expressed similitude, since indeed a given effect cannot be assimilated to itself alone. Another productive principle must therefore be assigned, to which together with the power this effect might be assimilated; but that principle to which an effect is assimilated is a productive principle. But there is no principle to which an expressed specification as issuing from the power might be assimilated other than the impressed specification that determines that power to that effect. Since therefore in such an issuing, which is productive, that cognition and similitude issue from the power and the specification, it is evident that the power alone is not the productive principle, but the power as determined through the specifying form, and consequently the form of the specification itself cooperates productively. . . . [O]f the vital concurrence we say that the specifying form is not the radical and principal principle, but determinative and specificative of it, from the fact that the vital power in question depends upon the object in its concurrence as upon something determining and specifying. Yet the principle determining a vital concurrence need not be intrinsic, but can come from without, just as a habit supervenes upon a power and concurs with it productively, and can nevertheless arise from outside the power. But there is this difference, that a habit or light determines a power on the side of the power by strengthening its energies toward a determinate object, whereas a specifying form determines the power only by representing and intentionally uniting the object, and this object then together with the power gives birth to an awareness by also concurring productively, just as in the generation of an animal the male seed actively concurs, which can be more and more perfected within the line of its own activity and power, like a power by a habit, and yet needs nevertheless the female seed, which from

efficiency is by no means the formal and essential rationale of the specifier, which essentially need only be representative and vicarious of the object on which the cognitive act depends in its specification. But that the act may in fact also depend on the stimulus object effectively as regards existence does not pertain to the object insofar as it is an object, nor does it pertain to the impressed specifying form or stimulus as precisely representative and in the capacity of the object, but because the specifier intrinsically determines and actuates the power, which, thus activated and determined, flows vitally and effectively into an act. For this reason, just as the vitality of the power effectively has an influence, so also do the intrinsic actuality and determination of the object have an influence in eliciting the act in its specification, which depends on the object.

But if you should ask how the rationale of a stimulus should be understood in a case of an objective cause, when it is supposed that an objective cause is not something moving in the mode of a productive cause, the response, based on what has been said, is that it is stimulating or moving as regards specification, not as regards exercise. This is explained by St. Thomas in his *Summa theologica*, I-II, q. 9, art. 1, when he says that "a power or vis of the soul can be in potency in two ways, in one way as regards acting or not acting, in another way as regards acting in this way or that; as the power of sight, for example, sometimes sees, sometimes does not see, and sometimes sees this, say, something white, and sometimes that, say, something black. A power therefore needs something moving and determining as regards these two ways." And determining or moving to act or not to act is said of movement on the side of the subject or of exercise, but moving to acting in this or that way is said of movement and determination on the side of the object. And thus St. Thomas goes on to add that "an object moves by determining an act in the mode of a formal principle." To move in the manner of an agent (or on

haec efficientia non est formalis et per se ratio speciei, quae per se solum dicit, quod sit repraesentativa et vicaria obiecti, a quo dependet actus in specificatione. Quod vero etiam dependeat effective quoad esse, non pertinet ad obiectum quatenus obiectum, nec ad speciem ut praecise repraesentativa et vice obiecti, sed quia intrinsece determinat et actuat potentiam, quae sic actuata et determinata influit vitaliter et effective in actum. Ideo sicut virtus potentiae effective influit, etiam eius actualitas intrinseca et determinatio obiecti influit, ut actum in sua specificatione, quae ab obiecto pendet, eliciat.

Si autem inquiras, quomodo intelligatur ratio motivi in causa obiectiva, supposito quod non est movens per modum efficientis, *respondetur* ex dictis, quod est movens quoad specificationem, non quoad exercitium. Quod explicatur ex Divo Thoma 1. 2. q. 9. art. 1. dicente, «quod potentia seu vis animae potest dupliciter esse in potentia, uno modo quantum ad agere vel non agere, alio modo quantum ad agere hoc vel illud; sicut visus quandoque videt, quandoque non videt, et quandoque videt hoc, puta album, quandoque aliud, puta nigrum. Indiget ergo movente et determinante quantum ad ista duo». Et determinans seu movens ad agere vel non agere dicitur movere ex parte subiecti seu exercitii, movens autem ad agendum hoc vel illud, dicitur movere et determinare ex parte obiecti. Et ita subdit S. Thomas, «quod obiectum movet determinando actum ad modum principii formalis». Distinguitur ergo movere per modum agentis seu

a conjunction with the living energy of the male effectively influxes into the production of a foetus."

See further ibid., 184b8-22: "*Et in hoc differt exemplum vulgare de semine, quod ita est virtus generantis in esse naturali, quod nullo modo participat esse ipsius geniti, sed solum est virtus ad illud. At vero species impressa ita est virtus obiecti ad eliciendam cognitionem et formandum verbum, quod tamen formaliter in se habet esse intentionale, in quo convenit cum obiecto repraesentative, sed non entitative. Et cum specie expressa convenit in eodem esse intentionali, licet non sit ita formatum et expressum sicut in ipso verbo.*"—"An impressed form of specification differs from the common example of seed in this respect. Whereas the male seed is a power of generating in natural being, such that it in no wise shares in the being of the individual generated, but is only a power or energy toward that being, the form of an impressed specification by contrast is a power of the object for eliciting cognition and the forming of a word such that it yet has within itself an intentional existence or being wherein it coincides with the object representatively, but not entitatively. And it coincides with the expressed specification in this same intentional existence, even though it is not as formed and expressed as is the case with the word itself."

the side of a subject and of exercise), which pertains to the order of a producing cause, therefore, is distinguished from a movement in the manner of a stimulus object, which is reduced to the category of an extrinsic formal cause, a cause consisting in nothing but the fact that some power, in order to elicit an act of such or such a kind, needs to be actuated or ordered relative to an extrinsic object, not only in the termination of the act, but also in the elicitation and originating of that act, because even to elicit it, the power is not sufficiently determined to a specific kind of act until it is determined or moved and completed by an object.

From this it follows that even though for it to move de facto, there must sometimes intervene in the case of a stimulus object a production of some thing, which production pertains to the order of an efficient cause, the formal rationale of the stimulus object still does not consist in this production essentially, but the production bears on this formal rationale incidentally or concomitantly. There is the greatest reason for this to happen among the cognitive powers, which cannot be moved by objects unless those objects are impressed on the cognitive powers and specifying forms are effectively produced; but even so, the effective production of specifiers is not the objective causality in the formal rationale of a stimulus object. For to produce specifiers effectively does not pertain to the rationale of an object, as is clear in the case of our understanding and in the case of the intellect of a pure spirit. For in the case of our understanding, it is the agency of the understanding that effectively produces specifying forms, not the object, and in the case of pure spirits God infuses the specifiers, which is to produce them effectively; but objects do not act effectively on the intellect of a pure spirit, according to the opinion of St. Thomas. And theologians agree that in the case of infused knowledge God produces or infuses specifying forms effectively; they are not produced by the objects themselves. The rationale of producing specifiers is therefore preserved independently of the rationale of a specifying object, and conversely. Therefore the formal rationale of a stimulus object specifying does not consist in an efficient production of specifying forms.

It follows secondly that an object which is a stimulus object only is not formally the same as an instrumental sign, nor is an object that is terminative only the same as a secondary object, although these often materially coincide.

The reason why a stimulus object cannot be identified with an instrumental sign is that the rationale of an object which is a stimulus object only, while it acts

ex parte subiecti et exercitii, quod pertinet ad genus causae efficientis, a motione per modum obiecti motivi, quod reducitur ad genus causae formalis extrinsecae, quae non consistit in alio, quam quod aliqua potentia, ut eliciat actum talis vel talis speciei, indigeat actuari seu ordinari ad obiectum extrinsecum, non solum in terminatione actus, sed etiam in elicientia et principio illius, quia etiam ut eliciat, potentia non est sufficienter determinata ad speciem actus, sed determinatur seu movetur et completur ab obiecto.

Ex QUO SEQUITUR, quod licet aliquando in obiecto motivo, ut de facto moveat, intervenire debeat alicuius rei productio, quae ad genus causae efficientis pertinet, non tamen in hoc per se consistit formalis ratio obiecti moventis, sed per accidens aut concomitanter se habet. Quod maxime contingit in potentiis cognoscitivis, quae non possunt moveri ab obiectis, nisi imprimantur in eis et producantur effective species; sed tamen productio effectiva specierum non est causalitas obiectiva in ratione formali obiecti motivi. Nam producere effective species non pertinet ad rationem obiecti, ut patet in nostro intellectu et in angelico. Nam in nobis intellectus agens est, qui effective producit species, non obiectum, et in angelis Deus infundit species, quod est effective eos producere; obiecta vero non agunt effective in intellectum angeli secundum sententiam S. Thomae. Et in omnium sententia constat Deum in scientia infusa producere seu infundere species effective, non ab obiectis ipsis produci. Salvatur ergo ratio efficiendi species sine ratione obiecti specificantis et e contra, ac proinde formalis ratio obiecti motivi specificantis non consistit in efficientia specierum.

Sequitur secundo obiectum motivum tantum non esse formaliter idem quod signum instrumentale, neque obiectum terminativum tantum idem quod obiectum secundarium, licet saepe ista materialiter coincidant.

Primum constat, quia ratio obiecti motivi tantum, licet moveat ad aliud praeter se,

relative to another beyond itself, nevertheless does not directly respect a thing signified which it would represent and of which it would be vicegerent, but directly respects a power as something it is to stimulate or move. Whence it stands in the line of an object coordinated with a power, not in the line of a representation vicegerent for [taking the place of] another and coordinated with the represented thing. The rationale of a stimulus object and the rationale of an instrumental sign are therefore diverse formalities, because they directly respect diverse terms: an object as [an instrumental] sign bespeaks the rationale of a means leading to another; an object as stimulus object bespeaks the rationale of a principle moving a power. Whence [the notion of] a stimulus object does not bespeak something subsidiary to and more imperfect than that relative to which it moves, as, for example, when someone is moved by a mind-independent being to cognizing a mind-dependent being, or when someone is moved by God to a knowledge of creatures, or when through the essence of a pure spirit one comes to know its accidents. But a sign as a sign is always something more imperfect than the thing signified, as being its vicegerent and substituting in its place in the order of the knowable. Thence it is that the rationale of a sign is a categorial relation, as we have said above, but the rationale of a stimulus object is not a categorial relation, because an object does not respect a power, but is respected by it, as being according to the relation of measure and measured, which is not reciprocal.

The reason why a terminative object cannot be identified with a secondary object is clear from an example. Take a case where I know a prototype through an image, or an ox by means of a footprint. In these cases, the prototype and the ox are terminative objects only, as being known from the outward appearances of some other object, and yet they are not secondary objects, but principal ones, as being primarily and essentially intended, whereas the image and the footprint are known as leading to those principal objects.

A final conclusion: **A terminative object also has, in respect both of a cognitive and of an appetitive power, the rationale of an extrinsic formal cause.**

This conclusion is against some more recent authors[7] who think that a terminative object has the rationale of a pure terminus, just as does a terminus in respect of a categorial relation.

But the stated conclusion is taken from the *Summa theologica*, I-II, q. 18, art. 2, reply to obj. 2, where St. Thomas says that "an object is not a matter out of which, but concerning which, and it has in a certain way the rationale of

tamen non directe respicit signatum, quod repraesentet et cuius vices gerat, sed directe respicit potentiam ut a se movendam. Unde habet se in linea obiecti coordinati potentiae, non in linea repraesentationis vices gerentis pro alio et coordinatae rei repraesentatae. Sunt ergo formalitates diversae, quia in recto diversos terminos respiciunt, ut signum dicit rationem medii ductivi ad aliud, ut obiectum motivum rationem principii moventis potentiam. Unde obiectum motivum non dicit, quod sit aliquid inferius et imperfectius eo, ad quod movet, ut cum per ens reale movetur quis ad cognoscendum ens rationis, et per Deum movetur ad cognoscendum creaturas, et per essentiam angeli ad cognoscendum eius accidentia. Signum autem ut signum semper est quid imperfectius re signata, utpote vices eius gerens et loco eius substituens in genere cognoscibili. Et inde est, quod genus signi est relatio praedicamentalis, ut supra diximus, ratio vero obiecti motivi non est relatio praedicamentalis, cum obiectum non respiciat potentiam, sed ab ea respiciatur, utpote secundum relationem mensurae et mensurati, quae non est mutua.

Secundum vero constat, cum per imaginem cognosco prototypum aut per vestigium bovem. Sunt enim obiecta terminativa tantum prototypus et bos, utpote per alterius obiecti species cognita, et tamen non sunt obiecta secundaria, sed principalia, utpote primo et per se intenta, imago autem et vestigium ut deducentia ad illa.

Ultima conclusio: **Obiectum terminativum respectu potentiae cognoscitivae et appetitivae etiam habet rationem causae formalis extrinsecae.**

Est contra aliquos recentiores,[7] qui existimant obiectum terminativum habere rationem puri termini, sicut terminus respectu relationis praedicamentalis.

Sed conclusio posita sumitur ex D. Thoma 1. 2. q. 18. art. 2. ad 2., ubi dicit, «quod obiectum non est materia ex qua, sed circa quam, et habet quodammodo

[7] Principally, again, Francis Suarez: see the *Disputationes Metaphysicae*, disp. 12, sect. 3, par. 17.

a form, inasmuch as it specifies.'' St. Thomas is clearly speaking here of a terminative object: For a matter concerning which is not a principle of an act moving a power to elicit an act, but a principle terminating an act, because the act is engaged with that matter. Therefore a terminative object specifies extrinsically; for a movement takes its specific character from the terminus, as is said in the fifth book of the *Physics*.[8] The conclusion is also taken from the *Commentary on the Sentences of Peter Lombard*, I, dist. 1, q. 2, art. 1, reply to obj. 2,[9] where St. Thomas says that ''the object of an operation terminates and perfects that operation and is its end.'' But anything perfecting functions formally in respect of something perfectible, at least extrinsically, and when it is not something perfecting by effecting, but by terminating, we say that it functions formally extrinsically.

Finally, THE CONCLUSION IS PROVED by the fact that a terminative object does not exist as a pure terminus, as does a terminus in respect of a categorial relation; for a terminative object specifies an active power, which power is not a categorial relation, but respects the object by a transcendental order. Therefore the object is not a pure terminus, otherwise it would terminate only a categorial relation, not a transcendental one. That indeed a terminative object does not terminate and specify in any other order of cause except that of formal cause follows from this: it is not an efficient cause, because it is not a principle but a terminus of action; nor is it a material cause, because it is not a subject receiving or a disposing cause; nor is it an end, because an end is either an end-effect or an end-cause (that is to say, an end-for-the-sake-of-which).[10] An end-effect

rationem formae, in quantum dat speciem». Ubi clare loquitur S. Doctor de obiecto terminativo: Nam materia circa quam non est principium actus movens potentiam ad eliciendum actum, sed terminans actum, quia circa illam versatur actus. Ergo obiectum terminativum extrinsece specificat; nam a termino sumit motus speciem suam, ut dicitur in 5. Phys.[8] Sumitur etiam ex D. Thoma in 1. dist. 1. q. 2. art. 1. ad 2.,[9] ubi inquit, «quod obiectum operationis terminat et perficit ipsam et est finis eius». Omne autem perficiens habet se formaliter respectu perfectibilis, saltem extrinsece, et cum non sit perficiens efficiendo, sed terminando, dicimus, quod se habet formaliter extrinsece.

DEINDE PROBATUR, quia obiectum terminativum non se habet ut purus terminus sicut respectu relationis praedicamentalis; obiectum enim terminativum specificat potentiam activam, quae non est relatio praedicamentalis, sed transcendentali ordine respicit obiectum. Ergo obiectum non est purus terminus, alias solum terminaret relationem praedicamentalem, non transcendentalem. Quod vero non in alio genere causae terminet et specificet, nisi in genere causae formalis, ex eo deducitur, quia non se habet ut causa efficiens, cum non sit principium actionis, sed terminus; nec causa materialis, cum non sit subiectum recipiens aut causa disponens; nec finis, quia finis vel est finis effectus vel finis causa seu id, cuius gratia.[10] Finis effectus ut effectus

---

[8] c. 5. (229 a 25); S. Thom. lect. 8. (*Le* II. 257. n. 6-9. incl.).

[9] *Pa* VI. 13 b.

[10] Poinsot, 1633: Phil. nat. 1. p. q. 13. art. 1., Reiser ed., II. 271b43-44: ''*solum iste est finis causa et condistinguitur a reliquis causis*''—''only the end-for-the-sake-of-which is an end in the sense of a cause and is contradistinguished from the other types of cause.'' Here and in the remarks following Poinsot raises the subject of ''final causality'' not directly in its original context of those natural phenomena which are seen to come about ''regularly and for the most part'' and have nothing to do as such with human intentions (Aristotle, *Physics*, Book II, chap. 8), but in the context primarily of human actions which are governed by the choice of ends and means (Poinsot, 1633: Phil. nat. 1. p. q. 13.; see esp. art. 3, 287a24-b3, also art. 2, 276b46-277a33), yet with an awareness of the prior, fundamental context from which this later, typically renaissance context has been derived (Poinsot, 1633: Phil. nat. 1. p. ''*Summa textus libri secundi Physicorum Aristotelis cap. 8,*'' 169a21-b37; also q. 13, art. 1, 274b17-275a25, 275b40-45, where he distinguishes between ''*apprehensio formalis et ex parte subiecti se tenens*'' and ''*apprehensio radicalis et ex parte obiecti*''). To understand this shift or reversal of primary emphasis and context, two things must be kept in mind. First, the Aristotelian tradition of natural philosophy as it developed in the later Latin age—throughout the Renaissance—became increasingly focused on what we would call in retrospect ''the philosophy of man,'' i.e., the understanding of nature in reference principally to human nature, and of the place of the *animal rationale* in the physical world. Second, the development of this tradition took place, from its beginnings in the twelfth century,

as effect does not specify, because as effect it does not perfect an act or an active power, but is perfected or brought about by an active power, nor as effect does it cause the active power, but is caused by it. But an end as cause does not specify an act terminatively, but

non specificat, quia ut effectus non perficit actum vel potentiam activam, sed perficitur seu fit ab ea, nec causat ipsam ut effectus, sed ab ea causatur. Finis autem ut causa non specificat actum terminative, sed mo-

---

in a theological context completing for these authors even properly philosophical reflection, as we will have occasion to note in the "Editorial Afterword" following the *Treatise* proper, Section III.A., esp. nn. 80-83. On both counts, the most crucial single factor making for difficulty in reading the *Ars Logica* (see discussion in the "Afterword," Section I.B.) is equally and in the same way at work in the reading of the *Philosophia Naturalis* as well, namely, the fact that these later renaissance Latin writers all tend to assume a whole general view or system thoroughly worked out in order to concentrate on and argue about particular points of difficulty within that total view. It is the answering of these particular difficulties or "special questions," rather than the viewpoint of building up from primitive experience a systematic body of interpretation (which was the viewpoint perforce of Aristotle himself) that is the inevitable concern of any grand tradition in its later stages — the reason at once for its maturity and its decline. So much misunderstanding and anthropomorphic distortion have developed around the notion of final causality since Poinsot's day (for a survey of the question in Poinsot's day, see q. 13 of the Phil. nat. 1. p. referred to above, which was anthropocentric without being anthropomorphic, as has been indicated), that it is important to recall the original context of the discussion in the order of observation of events *outside the human sphere of volition entirely*, as witnessed in Aristotle's contention (*Physics*, Book II, chap. 8, 199a20) that "This," i.e., action 'for the sake of' something, "is most obvious in the case of animals other than man," and that (199a23-29) "by gradual advance in this direction," i.e., *away from* the sphere of human volitions, "we come to see clearly that in plants too that is produced which is conducive to the end"—e.g., "it is both by nature and for an end that the swallow makes its nest and the spider its web, and plants . . . send their roots down (not up) for the sake of nourishment . . . ." (See the useful discussions of final "cause" in John Herman Randall, Jr., *Aristotle* [New York: Columbia University Press, 1960], throughout.)

This original context is especially important for the student of semiotic, as is suggested by the fact that the contemporary founder of the discipline, Charles Sanders Peirce, expressly "thought of semiotic as precisely the development of a concept of a final cause process and as a study of such processes" (Ransdell, "Some Leading Ideas of Peirce's Semiotic," *Semiotica* 19:3/4 [1977], 163). Brought up on the modern prejudices and misconceptions of the Latin tradition of natural philosophy, Ransdell remarks, Peirce's would-be commentators seem to have found this fact "an embarrassment, a sort of intellectual club foot that one shouldn't be caught looking at, much less blatantly pointing out to others," which would explain "why the topic of final causation is so strangely absent in criticisms and explanations of Peirce's conception of semiotic and semiosis," despite its centrality in Peirce's own reflections and explanations. The situation is ludicrous, but no more so than the general situation of contemporary historiography vis-à-vis the late Latin age (cf. "Editorial Afterword," Section I.A., and note 129), of which this embarrassed silence of the Peirceians is most likely but a particular manifestation. What we have here in fact is another example, a particularly compelling instance, indeed, of the ways in which semiotic is bound to force a revision of our approaches to the history of philosophy and culture. For it seems that the point of view of the basic analysis of final causality in the tradition Poinsot represented at its culminating stage (see in particular the reconstitution essayed by Benedict Ashley, "Research into the Intrinsic Final Causes of Physical Things," ACPA *Proceedings*, XXVI [1952], 185-194) is very much the point of view adopted spontaneously by Peirce himself (citing from Ransdell 1977: 163): "First of all, Peirce is talking about the overall form of a process, not about the relation of a process to something external to it ["*cum finis quandoque realiter non existat*"—"since the end often enough does not in fact exist" (Poinsot, 1633: 281a19)]. He is talking about the tendency toward an end-state, and the general features of such a tendency in whatever medium the process may be realized." Thus "the final causational form of a process can be realized only through efficient causation, and in that sense presupposes the possibility of a physical explanation as well" (Poinsot, 1633: 282b17-19: "causalitas finis non est ipsa causalitas efficientis formaliter, sed identice"; Thomas Aquinas, c. 1265-1266, q. 5 de Potentia art. 1 [*Pa* VIII. 101 a.]: "finis non est causa, nisi secundum quod movet efficientem ad agendum"). It would be useful to have a detailed comparative analysis of Peirce and Poinsot's tradition of *philosophia naturalis* ("Physics") on this point.

For a brief and philosophically informed historical sketch of the problem—something by no

moves the efficient cause metaphorically,[11] and so does not respect the specification of an action, i.e., its essential content or predicate, but its existence, for it moves relative to that; and therefore as end it is numbered among the circumstances; but as object it can specify,

vet efficientem metaphorice,[11] et sic non respicit specificationem actionis seu essentiale praedicatum eius, sed existentiam, ad illam enim movet; ideoque ut finis inter circumstantias numeratur; ut obiectum vero

---

means easy to come by—see Ashley's two articles, "Final Causality" and "Teleology," in *The New Catholic Encyclopedia* (New York: McGraw-Hill, 1967), Vol. V, pp. 915-919, and Vol. XIII, pp. 979-981, respectively, the first treating primarily of the Greek and Latin periods, the second treating of the modern period. Further discussion in notes 11 and 12 following.

[11] "Aristotle, who gave the first analysis of the notion of teleology,"—a term coined by Christian Wolff (1679-1754) from the Greek τέλος (end, completion, goal) for the doctrine of final causality—"pointed out that a *telos*, or goal, is not a cause in the ordinary sense of that term, but only in an analogical sense (*Gen. et cor.* 324b 16). It does not exert any force of agency, but exists in the agent as a tendency to a determined action. Thus one may say that reproduction is the *telos* of the reproductive system in an animal not in the sense that the offspring (which does not yet exist) exerts any force on these organs, but in the sense that there exists in these organs a natural tendency to produce a new animal.

"Obviously, taken in this sense teleology is something experimentally observable, since it is possible to determine whether such a tendency exists in the organism by observing its regular behavior and by locating this behavior in a particular organ or system. In fact, it is only by observing such effects that it is possible to determine the nature of the agent organs. The question here is not to predict what the organism will do, but to explain what it has been observed to do by discovering the precise agents of this behavior and the steps by which they acted. As Aristotle pointed out (*Part. animal.* 640a 1-9), teleological explanations proceed backward. One begins with the observation of some effect that is observed to recur frequently in nature and then asks: What were the prerequisites of this effect? What matter [material cause], what forces [efficient cause], what structures [formal cause], and what step-by-step processes were necessary to produce this observed effect [final cause]? Hence, for the most part it is precisely the goal that is the best-known and most easily observed feature in man's experience of an event" (Ashley, 1967b: 979-980). Hence, elsewhere (1952: 9 note 20), Ashley calls it "another common delusion about final causality" to suppose "that teleological explanations are tentative and metaphorical in character [in the sense that they] are rendered useless once the exact knowledge of the 'mechanism' has been attained. This fails to see that for a mechanism to be determinate it must be determined by the end and direction of change." "It is this directiveness of natural processes and of the things that produce them, which is not by chance or by strict necessity but to or for a goal, that is final causality in its primary sense" (Ashley, 1967a: 917), so that "philosophy comes to a knowledge of the final causality of particular things by an observation of natural processes, since these for the most part (but not invariably) achieve their goal" (ibid., p. 916). Again (1967b: 981): "Purpose and direction imply a means-end relationship in a structure or a process, but they do not necessarily imply consciousness." Thus (ibid.) "teleological explanations"—properly made and understood—"do not rest on any assumption about the nature of the cosmos or its dependency on God, but only upon the observed difference between random and organized natural structures and processes. Such facts, like all facts, have implications for metaphysics"—such as were the principal concern of the later Latin scholastics (note 10 above)—"but these need not concern natural science" in the contemporary sense.

Ashley imagines the following brief dialogue on this point between a resurrected Aristotle and a modern scientist (1952: 5-6). "If Aristotle were to appear on the scene of research and were to find scientists engaged in the type of study just described, he would certainly declare without equivocation that they are looking for precisely what he meant by the *intrinsic final causes* of physical things. Perhaps the scientist would respond, 'But you are reading something into what we are doing!' To which he might reply, 'But I meant nothing else than this, namely, that things which change naturally (that is, in a manner due to their intrinsic constitution recognizable by us in the *regularity* of these changes) have their changes determined and made definable by the positive result of change.'

"Again we might imagine the modern as objecting, 'We admit that we look for these results, and that we define changes and the things that change by these observed results, but we would never call such products of change its "cause," they are rather *effects*.' To this Aristotle certainly would reply, 'Let us make no difficulty about words. By "cause" you are in the habit of meaning only the *agent* of change. Now of course an agent is a cause only in so far

as is established in the *Summa theologica*, I-II, q. 1, art. 4, where the specification of a moral act is taken from the end, as the end is a good and an object of will. And in q. 18, art. 6, and again in q. 19, art. 2, the end is said to specify insofar as it is the object of the interior or imperating act; but it is a circumstance of the imperated act, which act is for the sake of the end.[12] If therefore an end as end specifies, it takes on the ra-

specificare potest, ut constat 1. 2. q. 1. art. 4., ubi specificatio actus moralis sumitur a fine, ut est bonum et obiectum voluntatis. Et in q. 18. art. 6. et q. 19. art. 2. finis dicitur specificare in quantum obiectum actus interioris seu imperantis; est autem circumstantia actus imperati, qui est gratia finis.[12] Si ergo ut finis specificet, induit ra-

as the change depends upon its activity, and since this change must have a direction (as you constantly observe in your researches on *regular* changes) the agent must itself be determined to produce the very direction of that change, or it could not be an agent at all. But the direction of a change is determined by its *terminus ad quem* [cf. Poinsot, 1633: 276b46-277a4: "*Agens non operatur nisi ut determinatum ad aliquid, quod operetur, alias a casu et per accidens operabitur. Determinatur autem a fine, qui est terminus, in quem tendit agens.*"—"An agent does not act save as determined toward something to be accomplished; otherwise, it will act by chance and incidentally. But it is determined by an outcome, which is the terminus toward which the agent tends."]; hence on the *terminus ad quem* depends the change and even the causality of the agent itself. So if you wish to call the agent a cause, all the more you should be willing to admit that the *terminus ad quem* is a cause (although in a very different way), for the very causality of the agent depends upon it.' The scientist would no doubt still object, 'But how can the result be a cause since it does not even exist when the agent begins to act?' And to this Aristotle would conclude by saying, 'Of course it does not exist as the completed result, but it does exist as a determined tendency in the agent directing its action, and as the very direction of the change itself as it proceeds.' " (Further to this last remark in Ashley, 1967a: 917, bottom right.) Thus the scholastics called the final cause the "cause of causes," in that "a knowledge of the resultants of change is a key to answering all the major types of physical questions."

Finally, as to the consequences of a rejection or confused notion of final causality, Ashley makes the following observation (1952: 12): "Certainly few modern scientists would accept either panpsychism or the doctrine of pure chance, since there is no evidence of consciousness in many of the things they study, and there is wide-spread evidence of innate regularity in these same things, but scientists do waver between the two conceptions. This wavering is the result of a failure to find the correct concept of final causality which precisely mediates between these two extremes and saves a *moderate determinism* in nature, a determinism which far from excluding either chance or free will, includes them as special cases."

On the metaphorical aspect of final causality, see Poinsot, 1633: Phil. nat. 1. p. q. 13. art. 2., "*Quae sit causalitas finis*" ("What constitutes the causality of an end?"), esp. 277a34-278a27, which states the problem and surveys alternative solutions that have been proposed. Poinsot's own position is effectively summarized in the formula (282b2-5; cf. 276a14-18): "*causalitas finis est metaphorice actio, . . . sed non metaphorice est causalitas*" ("the causality of the end is an action in a metaphorical sense, . . . but it is not metaphorically a mode of causality"), because a true ontological dependency is involved. Further discussion in note 12 following.

[12] Phil. nat. 1. p. q. 13. art. 2., Reiser ed. II. 279a27b37: "*Et quidem ille actus seu amor, ut est actus seu operatio causae, respicit ipsam ut efficientia seu actio. Ut vero pendet ab obiecto, adhuc fundat duplicem habitudinem: Aliam specificationis, quae proprie respicit ipsum ut obiectum per modum specificativi et pertinet ad genus causae formalis extrinsecae. Alia est habitudo finalizationis, quatenus actus ille, etiam postquam est specificatus, respicit alterum, cuius intuitu et gratia fiat, vel si intuitu sui fit, in se habet rationem finis distinctam a ratione obiecti. Itaque dependentia actus ab obiecto est communis tam obiecto, qui est finis, quam qui non est finis, et solum consistit in dependentia ab ipso ut determinante speciem actus. At vero finis non constituit speciem, sed movet agens ad exercitium actionis, et quia non potest exercere actionem nisi per aliquam inclinationem, quae generaliter dicitur appetitus, neque inclinatio potest tendere nisi ad aliquid certum, prius necesse est, quod reddatur inclinatio proportionata respectu illius termini, in quem tendit. Et illa proportio seu immutatio reddit inclinationem quasi coniunctam ipsi appetibili.* [Ibid., q. 10. art. 3., 206a33-39: "*Appetibile autem respectu appetitus habet rationem perfecti, et appetitus rationem perfectibilis, quia appetitus fundatur in potentialitate, qua tenditur ad perfectibile*"— it seems the text should read here either *appetibile* or *perfectum*—"*ut ad terminum, in quo appetitus terminatur et perficitur.*"] *Et sic inclinatio ponderosa facta tendit in finem, et quanto plus facit aliquod bonum ponderare in plures actiones, tanto universalior et perfectior finis est, et si facit ponderare in omnes, tunc est ultimus finis et dicitur appeti et diligi toto corde, imo et amari caritate, quia caritas addit super amorem communiter*

tionale of an object, for the rationale of a specifying object is one thing, that of a moving end quite another. And thus specification pertains to the order of an extrinsic formal cause, the "motion" of an end pertains to finalization moving to produce a thing in being: but to move relative to the act of being and existence is outside the order of specification.

From these remarks you can distinguish the other divisions of object, as into primary and secondary,

tionem obiecti, alia est ratio obiecti specificantis, alia finis moventis. Et sic specificatio pertinet ad genus causae formalis extrinsecae, motio finis ad finalizationem moventem ad producendum res in esse, movere autem ad esse et existentiam est extra specificationem.

Ex his distingues alias divisiones obiecti, ut in primarium et secundarium,

---

dictum aestimationem rei voltitae quasi magni et cari pretii, ut dicit S. Thomas 1. 2. q. 26. art. 3. Quare haec immutatio seu pondus appetibilis in voluntate in re per actum amoris fit. Sed quatenus est elicita perfecte a voluntate, dicitur actio voluntatis et effectus finis, quatenus vero est ab appetibili et subordinatur ei ad amandum, est causalitas finis; finis enim est ipsum appetibile, et ab eo causalitas finalis esse debet. Et secundum hanc rationem est ab obiecto proposito et praecedit rationem eius ut est a voluntate elicitive. . . ."—"And indeed that act or love, as it is an act or operation of a cause, respects that cause as an efficiency or action. But as it depends upon an object, it yet founds a twofold relative condition: One of specification, which properly regards the object as object in the mode of a specificative and pertains to the class of an extrinsic formal cause. The other is a relative condition of finalization, inasmuch as that act, even after it is specified, regards something other in consideration of and on account of which it came to be, or, if it comes to be in view of itself, it has in itself the rationale of an end distinct from the rationale of object. Therefore the dependency of an act upon an object is common equally to an object which is an end and to one which is not an end, and consists solely in the dependency upon it as determining the type or species of the act. An end, by contrast, does not constitute the type, but moves the agent toward the exercise of an action, and because it cannot exercise an action save through some inclination, which is generally called an 'appetite,' nor can an inclination tend save toward something definite, it is first necessary that the inclination be rendered proportionate in respect of that terminus into which it tends. And that proportion or proportioning renders the inclination as if united to the appetible object. [Ibid., q. 10. art. 3., 206a33-39: "The appetible in respect of appetite has the rationale of something perfect, while the appetite has the rationale of something perfectible, because appetite is rooted in a potentiality, whereby it is inclined toward the appetible"—reading *appetibile* (*perfectum*) for Reiser's *perfectibile*—"as toward the terminus in which the appetite is terminated and perfected."] And thus an inclination made influential tends toward an end, and by as much as it the more makes something good to weigh or influence in several actions, so much the more universal and perfect is the end, and if it effects an influence on all actions, then it is the final end and is said to be sought and loved with the whole heart, indeed even to be loved by charity, because charity adds, over and above love commonly so called, the estimation of a thing consciously willed as being of great and precious value, as St. Thomas says in the *Summa theologica*, I-II, q. 26, art. 3. Wherefore this proportioning or influence of the object of appetite on the will in fact comes about through an act of love. But insofar as it is fully elicited from the will, it is said to be an action of the will and an effect of the end [an end-effect], while insofar as it is from the appetible [desirable] and subordinated thereto as to something to be loved, we have the causality of the end; for the end is the desirable object itself, and from it must be the final causality. And according to this rationale the causality is from the proposed object and antecedes its rationale as something from the will elicitively. . . ."

Phil. nat. 1. p. q. 13. art. 2., 280a29-36: "*Et ita causalitas eius non debet quaeri in ipsomet fine neque in aliquo motu ab eo egrediente, sed in ipso effectu eius, scilicet in ipso amore, qui est effectus et causalitas finis secundum diversas habitudines et considerationes. . . .*"—"And thus the causality of the end must not be sought in the end itself nor in any movement issuing from it, but in its very effect, that is to say in the love itself, which is the effect and the causality of the end according to different relationships and considerations. . . ."

Ibid., 283a13-18: "*Unde ista attractio et causalitas identice et realiter est ipse actus amoris, formaliter est ordo seu dependentia ipsius ab obiecto appetibili proposito ut ponderante in voluntate.*"—"Whence this attraction and causality identically and physically is the act itself of love, formally it is the order or dependency of the acting upon the proposed desirable object as influencing the will."

All these remarks, as can be seen especially in note 11 above (see also note 10), would extend analogically but properly—as regards the distinctions of dependencies—to the order of development within and among inanimate and noncognitive entities.

formal and material.[13] For that object which essentially or primarily or *formally* specifies, that is to say, that object which is the form and rationale of specifying, is called object essentially or the rationale of object; all other things are said to be an object secondarily or through another and *materially*. And the very rationale

formale et materiale.[13] Id enim, quod per se vel primo aut *formaliter* specificat seu est forma et ratio specificandi, dicitur per se obiectum seu ratio obiecti; reliquum vero dicitur secundario seu per aliud et *materialiter* obiectum. Et ipsa ratio specificandi

[13] In his Phil. nat. 4. p. q. 2. art. 3., Reiser ed. III. 76b37-77b25, Poinsot gives a somewhat more detailed explanation of these distinctions, expressly deriving them from the fundamental doctrine of the univocity of being and non-being in knowledge that is explained by his account of relations and that underlies his doctrine of signs: ". . . *in obiecto aliud est ipsa entitas, quae materialiter in eo consideratur, aliud ipsa formalitas obiecti, secundum quam pertinet ad talem potentiam et actum illumque specificat aut distinguit. Quae formalitas nihil aliud est, quam proportio ipsa seu coaptatio cum tali actu vel potentia; proportio autem respectus est. Et hinc contingit posse plura obiecta entitative et materialiter diversa convenire in una formalitate obiectiva, et e contra posse in una entitate materiali obiecti fundari diversas formalitates obiectivas, sicut manifeste patet exemplis. Videmus enim corpora substantialiter diversa, ut lapis, lignum, homo, convenire in una ratione colorati et proportione movendi visum, et e contra eandem entitatem, v. g. lapidem, fundare formalitatem visibilis ut coloratum, et tangibilis ut frigidum, et intelligibilis ut substantiam, et generalibis ut e materia producibilis, et creabilis ut ex nihilo factibilis. Unde bene dixit Caietanus 1. p. q. 1. art. 3. aliam esse divisionem rei ut res, aliam obiecti ut obiectum. Et scientiae dicuntur secari sicut et res, non quidem in esse rei, sed in esse et formalitate obiecti.*

"*Ex quo colligitur, quid sit obiectum formale, quid materiale, quid adaequatum. Dicitur enim* obiectum adaequatum *illa ratio, quae terminat et complectitur, quidquid potest cadere sub attingentia alicuius potentiae, sive primario sive secundario, tam quoad rationem formalem, sub qua attingitur, quam quoad materiale, quod attingitur.* Obiectum formale *dicitur illa formalitas seu respectus, secundum quem fit proportio et coaptatio inter obiectum et potentiam.* Materiale *dicitur illud, quod tali habitudini seu formalitati substernitur et subiectum eius est.*

"*Sunt autem diversi termini, quibus explicantur rationes istae obiectivae, sicut dicitur ratio formalis sub qua, ratio formalis quae, obiectum quod.* Ratio formalis sub qua *sumitur dupliciter: Uno modo, ut tenet se ex parte potentiae seu habitus, et sic est ipsa ultima ratio virtutis, qua determinatur et proportionatur erga tale obiectum. Alio modo sumitur ex parte ipsius obiecti, et sic est ultima formalitas proportionans et coaptans obiectum potentiae vel actui, sicut in obiecto visibili color non est ultimum, quod proportionat obiectum visui, sed lux, et ideo lux potest dici ratio sub qua ex parte potentiae.* Ratio quae *dicitur solum ex parte obiecti, non ex parte potentiae, et est illa formalitas, quae constituit obiectum attingibile a potentia vel actu, etiamsi non sit ultima formalitas, sicut color est ratio, quae attingitur in corpore, et non solum lucidum. Non tamen repugnat, quod etiam aliquid, quod est ratio sub qua ex parte obiecti, sit etiam ratio, quae attingitur tamquam ultimum, sicut lux attingitur in re visibili. Denique* obiectum quod *est ipsum totum, quod constat ex obiecto materiali et formali; in hoc enim fertur potentia, non tamquam in rationem seu formam attingendi, sed tamquam in rem attactam.*"—"In an object, entitative reality (which is considered therein materially) is one thing, the formality itself of object according to which it pertains to a given power and specifies or distinguishes that act is something else again, which formality is nothing other than the very proportion or adaptation with the given act or power; but a proportion is a respect. And hence it can happen that many objects entitatively and materially diverse can come together or coincide in one objective formality, and conversely diverse objective formalities can be founded on the one material entity of an object, as is manifestly clear from examples. For we see substantially diverse bodies, such as stone, wood, a man, coincide in the one rationale of 'colored' and in the proportion of stimulating sight, and conversely, one same entity, e.g., a stone, founds the formality of 'visible' as colored and of 'tangible' as cold, and of 'intelligible' as a substance, and of 'generable' as something that can be produced from matter, and of 'creatable' as able to be made from nothing. Whence Cajetan well says in his *Commentary* on the *Summa theologica*, I. q. 1, art. 3, that the division of a thing as thing is one division, the division of an object as object quite another. And sciences are said to be distinguished as things are, not indeed in their existence as things, but in the being and formality of an object.

"Whence can be gathered what is a formal object, what a material object, and what an adequate object. For that rationale which terminates and comprises whatever can fall under the attainment of some power, whether primarily or secondarily, as much as regards the formal rationale under which it is attained as regards the material which is attained, is called the *adequate object*. That formality or respect according to which a proportion and adaptation between object and power comes about is called the *formal object*. That which is arranged by such a perspective (habitude) or formality and is its subject is called the *material object*.

of specifying, understood according to itself, is also customarily called the rationale "under which" or the object "by which." But considered as in some thing by affecting it, the thing so effected is called the "rationale which," the material object the "object which." A simple example is the case of a wall colored and lighted in respect of sight.

secundum se sumpta solet etiam dici *ratio sub qua* seu *obiectum quo.* Ut autem consideratur in aliqua re afficiendo ipsam, dicitur res sic effecta *ratio quae*, obiectum vero materiale *obiectum quod.* Exemplum facile est in pariete colorato et lucido respectu visus.

Resolution of Counter-Arguments

The first argument is against our first conclusion. Assuredly the divine intelligence and its power truly and properly have objects; for they are engaged with something primarily and essentially, the intelligence with the divine essence, omnipotence with creatures. And yet they are not specified by these objects; for the divine power is not specified by creatures, otherwise it would have actuality and perfection from them just as it would have species. Nor likewise does the divine essence specify the divine intelligence, for in God extrinsic specificative and specified cannot be distinguished, nor can perfecting and perfectible, actuating and actuable. Therefore the rationale of an object does not consist in specifying extrinsically.

The response to this is that within the divine intelligence and omnipotence the rationale of object is found freed from imperfections, that is to say, from dependence on anything as extrinsically specifying and formally causing. For there is not in God any specific kind or specified thing which is caused, and consequently neither is there the rationale of an object that causes as a formal extrinsic cause. But in the divine acts of intellection and will, there is the rationale of an object as regards that which is of perfection and actuality, in this, that there is a terminus and factor

Solvuntur argumenta.

Primo arguitur contra primam conclusionem. Nam intellectus divinus et eius potentia vere et proprie habent obiecta; versantur enim circa aliquid primo et per se, intellectus circa divinam essentiam, omnipotentia vero circa creaturas. Et tamen non specificantur ab ipsis obiectis; nam divina potentia non specificatur a creaturis, alioquin ab illis haberet actualitatem et perfectionem sicut et speciem. Similiter neque essentia divina specificat intellectum divinum; nec enim ibi potest distingui specificativum et specificatum extrinsecum, sicut nec perficiens et perfectibile, actuans et actuabile. Ergo non consistit in hoc, quod est specificare extrinsece, ratio obiecti.

Respondetur in divinis inveniri rationem obiecti seclusis imperfectionibus, id est dependentia ab aliquo ut ab extrinseco specificante et formaliter causante. Nec enim datur ibi aliqua species seu specificatum, quod sit causatum, et consequenter neque datur ratio obiecti, quod sit causa formalis extrinseca ut causa. Sed in his actibus, quae sunt intelligere et velle, datur ratio obiecti quantum ad id, quod perfec-

"There are, however, different terms by which these objective rationales are explained, such as the 'formal rationale under which,' the 'formal rationale which,' the 'object which.' The *formal rationale under which* is understood in two senses. In one way it is understood as obtaining on the side of the power or habit, and so is the final rationale whereby the ower is determined and proportioned respecting a given object. In another way it is understood on the side of the object itself, and so is the final formality proportioning and adapting the object to the power or to the act, as, for example, color is not the ultimate thing in a visible object that proportions the object to sight, but light is, and therefore light can be called the 'rationale under which' on the side of the object. The *rationale which* is expressed only on the side of the object, not on the side of the power, and is that formality which constitutes the object as attainable by a power or act, even if it is not the final formality, as for example color is the rationale which it attained in a body, and not only illumination. Yet nothing prevents even something that is a rationale under which on the side of the object from being also a rationale which is attained or what is ultimate or final, as light is attained in a visible thing. Finally, the *object which* is that totality which comprises the material and formal object; for a power is borne on this not as on the rationale or form of the attaining, but as in the thing attained."

A slightly less detailed exposition of this same material is given in Poinsot's Logica 2. p. q. 1. art. 3., Reiser ed. I. 266a34-b2. See further discussion in note 33 below.

specificative of the knowledge, since cognition and volition must attain something, though even so the specificative is not distinguished from the specified, nor does the specificative have in relation to the specified the rationale of a cause, but specificative and specified are one and the same owing to their consummate eminence, as is had from St. Thomas, *Summa theologica*, I, q. 14, arts. 2 and 4. Though indeed in respect of the power executive relative to creatures, that is, in respect of omnipotence, there is the rationale of an object insofar as creatures are that with which that executive power of God is engaged as its pure effect, not as perfective of the power, which has every perfection from itself.

A second argument is against the rationale of a stimulus object, which we have explained. For by speaking of a stimulus object formally as it is stimulative, the qualification "stimulus" expresses the rationale either of a productive motion or of a formal one. If the first, it is not an object properly and simply, as we have shown above, because a productive movement does not give specification, but existence. If the second, the rationale of the stimulus object is not distinguished from the rationale of a terminative object, because each has the same mode of causality, namely, the formal mode, and so a stimulus object and a terminative object will specify in the same way. For the fact that a stimulus object has the rationale of a principle does not change in it the rationale of an extrinsic formal cause, and therefore a stimulus object does not possess the rationale of an object insofar as it is a stimulus, but insofar as it coincides with a terminative object in the rationale of specifying extrinsically, not insofar as it has the rationale of a productively moving principle.

This is confirmed by the fact that if a stimulus object insofar as it is a stimulus expresses the proper rationale of an object, then there is no general rationale of object common to both the stimulus and the terminative, in which they coincide. For there cannot be any rationale common to both a stimulus and a terminative object except that of respecting a power as something external to it. But this rationale belongs even to the mere act of a power, which is something distinct from the power and respects it by specifying, yet without being the power's object. Therefore the rationale of an object as such does not consist in respecting a power as something extrinsic specifying.

The response to this argument[14] is that in the expression "stimulus object" the qualification "stimulus"

tionis et actualitatis est, in hoc, quod datur terminus et specificativum cognitionis, eo quod cognitio et volitio aliquid debet attingere, sed tamen specificativum non distinguitur a specificato nec habet in illud rationem causae, sed sunt unum et idem propter summam eminentiam, ut ex D. Thoma habetur 1. p. q. 14. art. 2. et 4. Respectu vero potentiae executivae ad extra seu omnipotentiae datur ratio obiecti, in quantum creaturae sunt id, circa quod versatur potentia illa executiva Dei, ut purus effectus eius, non ut perfectivum potentiae, quae a se habet omnem perfectionem.

Secundo arguitur contra rationem obiecti motivi, quam explicavimus. Nam loquendo de obiecto motivo formaliter ut motivum est, vel ly motivum dicit rationem motionis effectivae vel formalis. Si *primum*, non est proprie et simpliciter obiectum, ut supra ostendimus, quia efficiens motio non dat specificationem, sed existentiam. Si *secundum*, non distinguitur ratio motivi a terminativo, quia utrumque habet eundem modum causalitatis, scilicet formalis, et sic eodem modo specificabit obiectum motivum et terminativum. Quod enim motivum habeat rationem principii, non variat rationem causae formalis extrinsecae, atque adeo rationem obiecti non habet motivum in quantum motivum, sed in quantum convenit cum terminativo in ratione specificandi extrinsece, non in quantum rationem habet principii moventis.

Confirmatur, quia si obiectum motivum in quantum motivum dicit propriam rationem obiecti, sequitur non dari aliquam rationem obiecti in communi, in quo conveniant terminativum et motivum. Nec enim motivo et terminativo potest dari alia ratio communis, nisi respicere potentiam tamquam aliquid extra illam. Hoc autem etiam convenit ipsi actui, qui est distinctum quid a potentia et respicit ipsam specificando, et tamen non est obiectum eius. Ergo ratio obiecti ut sic non consistit in hoc, quod est respicere potentiam ut aliquid extrinsecum specificans.

Respondetur,[14] quod in obiecto motivo ly motivum intelligitur de motione formali

[14] 180/10-24.

is understood of a formal moving in the mode of a principle [of initiation] in respect of a passive power, as was said above, so that the specification of an act, and not only the exercise or existence of that act, depends on such an object, not on the side of termination, but on the side of eliciting and principle.

And when it is insisted that in this a stimulus object coincides with a terminative object, the response is that stimulative and terminative come together in the order of causing specification, but not in the mode nor in the kind of act caused, just as diverse habits and acts are likewise specified in the same general mode of specification, but not by the same specific mode, since they are diverse in kind. But a diversity in modes of specifying and a diversity of specifications is derived, as was said, from this, that an object can function in the mode of a principle or of a terminus, that is to say, an object can be that on which the specification of an act depends either in its being elicited or in its termination, because, as St. Thomas often says, in the *Summa theologica*, I-II, qq. 1 and 18, and elsewhere, the rationale of an act is taken both from its principle or commencement and from its end or termination. And the object functioning in the mode of a principle induces a mode of specifying which is other than that of an object functioning in the mode of a terminus, because an object specifies an active or a passive power, which powers are always diverse powers and have diverse acts.

To the confirmation[15] the response is that just as [the concept of] power in general abstracts from active and passive and joins the two in the rationale of a principle or root of an act, so also ''object in general'' abstracts from stimulus and terminative and expresses the extrinsic specificative of a power on the side of principle or of terminus. An act, however, either is not entirely extrinsic to a power, since it proceeds therefrom, or rather should it be said that in an act in respect of a power two things are considered: there is the rationale of something produced, that is, of an effect, and considered thus as produced the act does not respect the power by specifying it, but by receiving from it existence and specific character and nature; or the rationale of something perfecting the power in acting is considered, inasmuch as an act ultimately consummates the action of a power, and so considered the act does not specify except insofar as it stands on the side of a terminus in which the actuality of the power is consummated, and for this reason it takes on the rationale of a terminating object, just as do other effects in respect of the agents

per modum principii respectu potentiae passivae, ut supra dictum est, ita quod specificatio actus, et non solum exercitium seu esse illius pendent a tali obiecto, non ex parte terminationis, sed ex parte elicientiae et principii.

Et quando instatur, quod in hoc convenit cum terminativo, *respondetur* convenire in genere causandi specificationem, sed non in modo neque in specie actus causata, sicut etiam diversi habitus et actus specificantur eodem modo specificationis in genere, sed non eodem modo specificationis, cum diversae speciei sint. Diversus autem modus specificandi et diversa specificatio sumitur, ut dictum est, ex eo, quod obiectum se habeat per modum principii vel termini, id est a quo dependeat specificatio actus vel in sui elicientia vel in sui terminatione, quia, ut saepe dicit S. Thomas, 1. 2. q. 1. et q. 18. et alibi, a principio et fine sumitur ratio actus. Et habere se per modum principii inducit diversum modum specificandi ab eo, quod est per modum termini, quia specificat potentiam activam vel passivam, quae semper sunt diversae potentiae et diversos actus habent.

Ad confirmationem[15] respondetur, quod sicut potentia in communi abstrahit a potentia activa et passiva et convenit in ratione principii actus, ita obiectum in communi abstrahit a motivo et terminativo et dicit extrinsecum specificativum potentiae ex parte principii vel termini. Actus autem vel non est omnino extrinsecus potentiae, cum procedat ab illa, vel potius dicendum est, quod in actu respectu potentiae considerantur duo, scilicet et ratio producti seu effectus, et sic non respicit potentiam specificando, sed ab ipsa recipiendo esse et speciem et naturam. Vel consideratur ratio perficientis potentiam in agendo, quatenus ultimo consummat actionem, et sic non specificat, nisi in quantum tenet se ex parte termini, in quo consummatur actualitas potentiae, et hac ratione induit rationem obiecti terminantis, sicut alii effectus

[15] 181/35-47.

that produce them, insofar as they perfect and consummate those agents in act.

It is argued thirdly: A given object is a stimulus object from the way in which a power respecting that object is passive; for an object as stimulus corresponds to a passive power as passive. But a cognitive power is passive insofar as it receives a specifying form, in which reception the object does not influx as object, but as effectively producing and impressing. Therefore the rationale of stimulus does not pertain to the object as object, but to the rationale of something effectively producing or impressing specifying forms, since indeed a passive power functions as passive insofar as it undergoes and receives specific determination antecedently to act. But in that prior condition or state in which the power receives a specifying form and is moved, the object is not yet objectified, because it is not then attained [by the power] as object when the forms of specification are impressed.

This is confirmed by the fact that an object as stimulative can specify neither an act nor a power, therefore it specifies nothing.

The antecedent is proved: A stimulus object does not specify an act, because only that which is movable by an object can be specified by that object. But an act is not movable by an object, because it is an effect of the object caused by the power and by the object. Therefore an act cannot be specified by a stimulus object, because a stimulus as stimulus only specifies something movable as movable. Nor can a stimulus object specify a power, because an object does not specify a power except by means of an act, as St. Thomas teaches in the *Summa theologica*, I, q. 77, art. 3. Therefore, if the stimulus object does not specify the cognitive act, neither does it specify the cognitive power.

The response to the main argument[16] is that a cognitive power is passive both in respect of the agent or thing impressing a specifying form, and in respect of the form impressed. But an impressed specifying form has two dimensions or aspects, namely: to inform entitatively or physically, and this pertains to a specifier materially as what it has in common with all other accidents [i.e., determinations of subjectivity]; and to inform intentionally, that is, as the form is representatively one with the object, and in this way the object informs intentionally in the same order as the specifier, that is to say, formally, even though the object is outside and the specifier is inside the cog-

respectu suorum agentium, in quantum perficiunt et consummant illa in actu.

Tertio arguitur: Obiectum eo modo est motivum, quo potentia illud respiciens est passiva; nam obiectum ut motivum correspondet potentiae passivae ut passivae. Sed potentia cognoscitiva in tantum est passiva, in quantum recipit species, in qua receptione obiectum non influit ut obiectum, sed ut efficiens et imprimens. Ergo ratio motivi non pertinet ad obiectum ut obiectum, sed ad rationem efficientis seu imprimentis species, siquidem in tantum se habet potentia passiva ut passiva, in quantum antecedenter ad actum patitur et recipit species. In illo autem priori, quo potentia recipit species et movetur, non obicitur obiectum, quia non attingitur tunc ut obiectum, quando imprimuntur species.

Confirmatur, quia obiectum ut motivum neque potest specificare actum neque potentiam, ergo nihil specificat.

Antecedens probatur: Non specificat actum, quia illud solum est specificabile ab obiecto, quod est mobile ab ipso. Actus autem non est mobilis ab obiecto, cum sit effectus eius causatus a potentia et ab obiecto. Ergo non est specificabilis ab obiecto motivo, quia motivum ut motivum solum specificat mobile ut mobile. Neque potentiam specificare potest, quia obiectum non specificat potentiam, nisi mediante actu, ut docet D. Thomas 1. p. q. 77. art. 3. Ergo si non specificat actum, neque potentiam.

RESPONDETUR,[16] quod potentia est passiva et respectu agentis seu imprimentis species et respectu formae impressae. Forma autem impressa habet duo, scilicet informare entitative seu physice, et hoc materialiter se habet in specie et commune est cum ceteris accidentibus, et informare intentionaliter, id est ut repraesentative est idem cum obiecto, et sic obiectum informat intentionaliter in eo ordine, quo species, scilicet formaliter, licet obiectum extra, species

[16] to 181/15-34.

nitive power.[17] But the impression itself productive of specifying forms is not from the object as causing objectively, but from the thing producing the specifiers, which productive force does not [even materially] always belong to the very thing which is an object, but belongs sometimes to another agent, as, for example, the agency of the understanding in us, or God infusing specifying forms in the pure spirits. Wherefore, the rationale of a stimulus in an object is not the rationale of impressing or producing specifiers, but of objectively actuating and determining a power by means of a

intra potentiam.[17] Ipsa vero impressio effectiva specierum non est ab obiecto ut obiective movente, sed a producente species, quae virtus productiva non semper convenit ipsi rei, quae est obiectum, sed alteri agenti, ut in nobis intellectus agens, in angelis Deus infundens species. Quare ratio motivi in obiecto non est ratio imprimendi vel efficiendi species, sed obiective actuandi et determinandi potentiam mediante specie ut intentionaliter, non ut

---

[17] Phil. nat. 4. p. q. 6. art. 3., Reiser ed. III. 185a26-b36: ". . . *respondetur speciem informare dupliciter potentiam, scilicet entitative seu inhaerendo, intentionaliter autem et vice obiecti perficiendo seu potius transformando potentiam in obiectum.*

"*Et ratio est, quia species inter omnes alias formas hoc habet speciale, quod non solum informat pro se, sed vice alterius, scilicet obiecti, imo propter se non requiritur, sed propter obiectum, a quo perficitur potentia sine hoc, quod cum ipso obiecto constituat naturam aliquam. . . .* [N]*am forma intentionalis entitative considerata dependet in suo esse a subiecto sicut reliquae formae, et actuat subiectum sicut ipsae. At vero obiectum repraesentatum in specie non accipit aliquod esse a subiecto nec constituit cum illo aliquam naturam, sed ita praesentatur potentiae, quod determinat et actuat illam intelligibiliter sine hoc, quod realiter alteret illam et transmutet aut componat aliquod tertium cum illa.* Item *potentia non utitur entitate speciei tamquam principio specificante actus suos, sed obiecto in ea repraesentato utitur tamquam specificativo, sed potentia debet actuari a suo specificativo, in quantum specificativum est. Ergo si ab entitate speciei non specificatur, bene tamen ab obiecto repraesentato, alia unio seu actuatio aut determinatio debet intercedere inter obiectum repraesentatum et potentiam, et haec dicitur unio intelligibilis seu intentionalis, inter entitatem vero speciei et potentiam est unio accidentalis, id est inhaerentiae.* Denique *species inhaeret potentiae, etiam quando actu non cognoscitur obiectum, sed species conservantur in illa per modum reliquorum accidentium. Cum vero potentia actu cognoscit, tunc non solum actuatur entitative ipsa specie, sed actuatur ipso obiecto in ea contento et repraesentato; ab hoc enim non semper actuatur potentia, sed tunc quando actu cognoscit.*"—"A specification informs the cognitive power in a twofold manner, namely, entitatively or by inhering, intentionally, however, and in the stead of the object by perfecting or rather by transforming the power into the object.

"And the reason for this is that a specifying form is unique among all other forms in this, that it informs not only for itself, but in the stead of another, namely, the object—nay rather, it is not needed on its own account, but on account of the object by which the power is perfected without constituting therewith some nature. . . . [F]or an intentional form entitatively considered depends in its being on a subject as do the other forms, and it actuates the subject just as they do. But the object represented in the specifier, by contrast, receives no being from the subject nor does it constitute with that subject some nature, but is presented to the power in such a way that it determines and actuates that power intelligibly without altering and transmuting it in the order of mind-independent being or constituting with it some third thing. *Likewise*, the power does not employ the entitative dimension of the specifying form as a principle specifying its acts, but uses rather the object represented in it as the specificative; but a cognitive power must be actuated by its specificative insofar as it is something specificative. If therefore the power is not specified by the entitative aspect of the specifier, yet indeed by the object represented, another union or actuation or determination must intervene between the object represented and the cognitive power, and this union is called 'intelligible' or 'intentional,' whereas the union between the entitative aspect of the specification and the power is an accidental union, that is, one of inherence [and subjective]. *Finally*, the specifying form inheres in [i.e., subjectively modifies] the power even when the object is not actually cognized, but the specifying forms are preserved there in the manner of other accidents. When, on the other hand, the power actually cognizes, then it is actuated by the specifying form not only entitatively, but it is actuated by the object itself contained and represented therein; for the power is not always actuated by this dimension of the form, but only then while it actually cognizes." Thus the case is somewhat similar to that of the closed book (cf. First Preamble, Article 3, 70/30-71/19; Book I, Question 1, 127/8-131/7; Book II, Question 5, 258/8-28.

Further to this analysis see Phil. nat. 4. p. q. 6. art. 3. *in toto*, but esp. 186b3-40 and 186b42-187a31; Question 5, note 21, p. 201 below; and Book II, Question 2, note 8, p. 243.

specifying form as intentionally, not only as entitatively, informing. And for this reason the stimulus object is preserved in respect of the intellect of a pure spirit, not because the object moves by impressing specifying forms, but because the object determines and actuates that cognitive power formally, not as that object exists in itself entitatively, but intentionally, as represented in the specifier, although it is God that effectively infuses that form.

To the confirmation[18] the response is that a stimulus object specifies a cognitive act by determining or actuating a passive power which is movable by the stimulus object, and by initiating or causing the act as regards specification. For a stimulus object, which specifies a cognitive act, does not respect the act as a subject movable by the stimulus object itself, but as something initiated or principled; but a stimulus object does respect the cognitive power, which it determines, as a movable subject [since it determines the power to a particular act]. Whence we deny that a stimulus object specifies the power as a movable subject, but it specifies the act, whose principle it is, as principled [specifically initiated] by the object itself. For an action, as St. Thomas says in his *Commentary* on Aristotle's treatise *On the Soul*, Book II, reading 6,[19] is specified by a principle or initiation and a terminus; but because it initiates the act by moving and determining the power to elicit this specific cognitive act in particular, an object is called a stimulus object.

A fourth argument is against the rationale of terminative object. For according to my doctrine the rationale of object is to be an extrinsic formal specifier; but a terminus as terminus does not specify an act or a power; therefore a terminative object as terminative is not an object.

The minor premise is proved first, because otherwise the terminus of a categorial relation would be its object, because it specifies by terminating. Second, because something specificative of an act and of a physical power must itself be something mind-independent, because the specifying form given by that specificative thing is independent of mind and dependent on the specificative as on something perfecting and actuating. But it is certain that a terminative object is not always something physical; for the rationale of object is found even in a mind-dependent being, as we said in our introductory question concerning the object of Logic.[20] Third,

entitative tantum informante. Et hac ratione salvatur respectu intellectus angeli obiectum motivum, non quia movet obiectum imprimendo species, sed quia determinat et actuat ipsam potentiam formaliter, non ut in se est entitative, sed intentionaliter, ut repraesentatum in specie, Deus autem effective illam infundit.

Ad confirmationem[18] respondetur obiectum motivum specificare actum determinando seu actuando potentiam passivam, quae est mobilis ab ipso, et principiando seu causando actum quoad specificationem. Nam obiectum motivum, quod specificat actum, non respicit actum ut mobile a se, sed ut principiatum; potentiam vero, quam determinat, respicit ut mobile. Unde negamus, quod obiectum motivum specificet mobile, quod est quasi subiectum, sed specificat actum, cuius est principium, quasi principiatum a se. Actio enim, ut dicit D. Thomas,[19] specificatur a principio et fine; sed quia principiat actum movendo ac determinando potentiam, ut eliciat talem speciem actus, dicitur obiectum motivum.

Quarto arguitur contra rationem obiecti terminativi. Nam obiectum a nobis constituitur in ratione extrinseci specificativi; sed terminus ut terminus non specificat actum vel potentiam; ergo terminativum ut terminativum non est obiectum.

Minor probatur *primo,* quia alias terminus relationis praedicamentalis esset obiectum eius, quia specificat terminando. *Secundo,* quia specificativum actus et potentiae realis debet esse aliquid reale, cum species ab eo data realis sit et ab eo ut a perficiente et actuante dependeat. Constat autem obiectum terminativum non semper esse aliquid reale; invenitur enim ratio obiecti etiam in ente rationis, sicut de obiecto Logicae diximus q. 1. prooemiali.[20] *Tertio,* quia omne specifica-

[18] 183/20-22.
[19] 2. de Anima lect. 6. (*Pa* XX. 55 b).
[20] Logica 2. p. q. 1. art. 3. See also note 35, p. 190 below, with further references therein.

because every specificative is a formal cause at least extrinsically. But every formal cause is a principle giving being; for it is form that determines the existence of a thing. Therefore every object is a principle insofar as it is an object and not a terminus, because it is a formal specifying cause; and so every object will be a stimulus object which specifies in the mode of a principle.

This is confirmed, because a stimulus object and a terminative object participate in the rationale of object analogically, therefore the one is an object simply, the other only in a qualified way, and the rationale of object does not belong to both simply.

The antecedent is proved first because mind-independent and mind-dependent objects alike are stimulus objects and terminative objects; and second because active and passive powers function analogically in the order of power, as is said by St. Thomas in his *Commentary on the Metaphysics of Aristotle* Book IX, lect. 1.[21] Therefore the stimulus and terminative objects corresponding to these powers are also analogues. Whence a stimulus object is an object that actuates and informs simply, and so it is said analogically that both a stimulus and a terminative object specify or have the rationale of a specifying form.

Response is made to the principal argument[22] by denying the minor premise.[23]

To the first proof[24] the response is that the terminus of a relation does not specify precisely as it is a terminus, but as it is subject to a fundament, without which the specific type of relations is not understood, as we have said in our Preamble on Relation[25] and as is established by St. Thomas in his *Commentary on the Sentences of Peter Lombard*, Book I, dist. 26, q. 2, art. 3.[26] By contrast, an object specifies essentially insofar as it is an object.

To the second proof[27] the response is that an intrinsic specificative giving a specific physical character to an act must necessarily be something independent of being itself objectively known in its being, but not an extrinsic specificative, because an extrinsic specificative specifies not by informing and inhering, but by terminating the tendency of another or by determining extrinsically in relation to the eliciting of an act. And thus it suffices for an extrinsic specificative that it should

tivum est causa formalis saltem extrinseca. Omnis autem causa formalis est principium dans esse; forma enim est, quae dat esse rei. Ergo omne obiectum est principium, in quantum obiectum et non terminus, quia est causa formalis specificans; et sic erit obiectum motivum, quod per modum principii specificat.

Confirmatur, quia obiectum motivum et terminativum analogice participant rationem obiecti, ergo alterum simpliciter, alterum secundum quid, et non utrique convenit simpliciter ratio obiecti.

Antecedens probatur, tum quia utrumque tam obiecto reali quam rationis convenit; tum quia potentia activa et passiva analogice se habent in genere potentiae, ut dicitur 9. Metaph. lect. 1. apud D. Thomam.[21] Ergo et obiectum motivum et terminativum illis correspondens analoga sunt. Unde motivum est, quod simpliciter actuat et informat, et sic analogice dicitur utrumque specificare seu habere rationem formae specificantis.

RESPONDETUR ad principale argumentum[22] negando minorem.[23]

Ad primam probationem[24] respondetur, quod terminus relationis non specificat ut praecise terminus est, sed ut subest fundamento, sine quo species relationum non sumitur, ut diximus [in] Praeambulo Secundo,[25] et constat ex D. Thoma in 1. dist. 26. q. 2. art. 3.,[26] obiectum autem per se in quantum obiectum specificat.

Ad secundam probationem[27] respondetur, quod specificativum intrinsecum dans speciem realem actui necessario debet esse aliquid reale, specificativum autem extrinsecum non, quia non informando et inhaerendo specificat, sed tendentiam alterius terminando vel ad elicientiam actus determinando extrinsece. Et ita sufficit, quod media specie reali, quae intrinsece in-

---

21 *Pa* XX. 530 a.

22 185/30-35.

23 185/32-33.

24 185/36-38.

25 In the original Latin: "q. 17." See especially Article 2 of the Second Preamble, 88/8-89/20, 93/1-14; Article 3, 101/2-14, 101/30-102/1. See also Appendix C, 380/10ff.

26 *Pa* VI. 221 b.

27 185/38-47.

determine the power itself to act by means of a specifying form independent of being itself apprehended as object, which form intrinsically informs physically, even if the object itself [the extrinsic specificative] in itself is not mind-independent or does not physically exist.[28]

To the third proof[29] the response is that a terminus has the rationale of a cause or of an effect according to diverse considerations, just as causes are causes one to another. Inasmuch as it precisely terminates in the mode of execution and effect, a terminus does not specify, but rather is specified and given existence. But inasmuch as this terminus is considered as perfecting and consummating in existential fact an act of a power, it gives a specific character by terminating and perfecting, and so is considered as a principle and extrinsic cause determining existence consummatively and finally, not as stimulus and initially; for it is the rationale of the perfection in the act as consummated, not as initiated. And thus St. Thomas says in the *Summa theologica*, I-II, q. 33, art. 4, reply to obj. 2, that "operation causes joy as the efficient cause, but joy perfects the operation as an end." Whence a terminative object does not coincide with a stimulus object; it also precedes in intention, even though in execution as an effect it follows or receives and does not give specification.

To the confirmation[30] I respond by denying the antecedent.[31] To the first proof of the antecedent[32] the response is that whether an object is mind-independent or mind-dependent makes a difference only in the rationale of being, not in the rationale of object and knowable thing. Something can well be an object simply and not be a being simply. For the differences of things in physical existence and being are one matter, differences in the rationale of an object and cognizable thing quite another, as Cajetan well notes in his *Commentary* on the *Summa theologica*, I, q. 1, art. 3. And so many things coincide univocally in the rationale of the knowable, and not in rationale of [entitative] being, or conversely. And similarly can many things coincide specifically in the rationale of the knowable and not in the rationale of being, or conversely, as is more fully discussed in the last question of my discussion of the books of Aristotle's *Posterior Analytics*.[33] For the present purpose, a few examples illustrative of this point will

format realiter, ipsam potentiam determinet ad actum, etiamsi obiectum ipsum in se reale non sit vel realiter non existat.[28]

Ad tertiam probationem[29] respondetur, quod terminus secundum diversam considerationem habet rationem causae vel effectus, sicut causae ad invicem sunt causae. Et quatenus praecise terminat per modum executionis et effectus, non specificat, sed speciem recipit et existentiam. Quatenus vero consideratur iste terminus ut perficiens et consummans in facto esse actum potentiae, dat speciem terminando et perficiendo, et sic consideratur ut principium et causa extrinseca dans esse consummative et finaliter, non motive et initialiter; est enim ratio perfectionis in actu ut consummatae, non ut initiatae. Et ita dicit S. Thomas 1. 2. q. 33. art. 4. ad 2., «quod operatio causat delectationem ut causa efficiens, delectatio autem perficit operationem ut finis». Unde non coincidit cum obiecto motivo; praecedit etiam in intentione, licet in executione ut effectus sequatur seu recipiat, non det specificationem.

Ad confirmationem[30] negatur antecedens.[31] *Ad primam probationem*[32] respondetur, quod obiectum esse reale vel rationis solum facit differentiam in ratione entis, non in ratione obiecti et cognoscibilis. Et stat bene, quod aliquid sit simpliciter obiectum, et simpliciter non sit ens. Aliae enim sunt differentiae rerum in esse rei et entis, aliae in ratione obiecti et cognoscibilis, ut bene advertit Caietanus 1. p. q. 1. art. 3. Et sic univoce conveniunt plura in ratione scibilis et non in ratione entis, vel e contra. Et similiter possunt convenire specifice in ratione scibilis et non in ratione entis, vel e converso, ut plenius dicitur quaest. ult. in libros Posteriorum.[33] Nunc sufficit exemplum ponere

---

[28] See notes 6 and 17 above; and Book I, Question 1, note 25, with further references.

[29] 185/47-186/7.

[30] 186/8-12.

[31] 186/8-10.

[32] 186/13-15.

[33] Logica 2. p. q. 27. art. 1., Reiser ed. 818b24-820a10: "*Est certum, quod scientiae, sicut omnes alii habitus, ex obiecto sumunt suam speciem, ut constat ex 2. de Anima textu 33.* [c. 4. (415 a 20)] *et*

suffice. Logic is a science univocally with the other sciences which treat of mind-independent being, although Logic itself treats of mind-dependent being; and God and a creature coincide univocally in the rationale of a metaphysical object or knowable, but not in the rationale of being; and quantity and substance

in Logica, quae univoce est scientia cum aliis, quae agunt de ente reali, cum ipsa agat de ente rationis; et univoce convenit Deus et creatura in ratione scibilis metaphysici, non in ratione entis; et quantitas et substantia univoce sunt scibilia a

---

determinat D. Thomas 1. p. q. 77. art. 3., et sic semper debent adaequari et conformari unitas et distinctio potentiae vel habitus cum unitate vel distinctione obiecti in ratione obiecti [further at 829a39-b4, 834a40-b3].

"Denique certum est specificationem hanc scientiarum non sumi ex unitate vel distinctione obiecti in esse rei, sed in esse obiecti, id est non ab obiecto considerato materialiter et entitative in se, sed ut conducit vel proportionatur tali habitui vel potentiae [see further 824b30-44, 828a36-b15]. *Ideoque optime monuit Caietanus 1. p. q. 1. art. 3. aliam esse rationem obiecti in ratione seu formalitate obiecti, aliam in esse rei; et alias esse species rerum in esse rei, alias in esse obiecti, ut ipsa exempla clare demonstrant. Nam color in esse qualitatis est quoddam genus, quod dividitur in varias species, et tamen in ratione visibilis habet eandem speciem obiecti visus. Omnia corpora habent eandem speciem in ratione obiecti philosophici, omnia entia in ratione Metaphysicae, licet in ratione entitativa corporis et entis in tam varias species dividantur. E contra vero idem color diverso modo attingitur a visu et ab intellectu, eadem res ut bona a voluntate, ut vera ab intellectu, eadem terra ut rotunda ab astrologo, ut mobilis a physico, et sic de multis aliis. Unde constat aliam esse rationem specificam rei, aliam obiecti in esse et ratione formali obiecti.*

"Quare in praesenti ad hoc devolvitur fere TOTA DIFFICULTAS, *ut investigemus, quae sit illa ratio formalis, quae specifice constituit obiectum in ratione obiecti scientiae et facit ab alio differe in ipsa ratione specifica. Ut autem diximus in quaest. 1. prooemiali art. 3.* [see note 13 above for detailed exposition], *distingui solet in ratione formali obiecti ratio quae et ratio sub qua. Quae distinctio reicienda non est, ut facit Vazquez 1. p. disp. 7. cap. 3. Nam in ipso obiecto, quod attingitur a diversis habitibus vel potentiis, designanda est aliqua ratio, quae specialiter attingitur ab uno et quae specialiter ab alio, et ista ratio, quae specialiter est attacta, dicitur formalis ratio quae, id est quae attingitur ad differentiam materialis obiecti, quod per talem rationem specialem determinatur, ut attingatur. Ratio autem sub qua dicitur formalis illa ratio, quae ceteras actuat et sub se continet, ut attingatur a potentia. Quia enim contingit id, quod est formale respectu unius, esse materiale respectu alterius, ideo ultima formalitas, sub qua ceterae continentur, dicitur formalis ratio sub qua simpliciter. Et sicut ex parte obiecti cognoscibilis consideratur formalitas, quae attingitur, et ratio ultima formalis, sub qua ceterae redduntur attingibiles, quae coincidere solet cum ipsa ratione quae ultima; ita ex parte potentiae correspondet ratio formalis sub qua attingendi obiectum, quod est ipsum lumen seu actualitas, qua potentia redditur ordinata et actuata ad tale obiectum. Exemplum manifestum est in visu. Nam corpus, v. g. paries vel lapis, est materiale, quod videtur, formale autem, quo determinatur ad visum potius quam ad auditum, est color, et est ratio formalis, quae videtur. Rursus vero color actuatur et formatur a luce, et illa est ultima formalitas, qua redditur obiectum visibile et sub qua ceterae rationes ordinantur ad visum, ex parte vero oculi datur lumen, sub quo actuata potentia procedit ad videndum.*

"Similiter ergo applicando haec obiecto scibili et scientiae, obiectum scibile est aliquid complexum constans ex subiecto, de quo proprietas aliqua seu passio demonstratur. Et hoc obiectum, quod est veritas conclusionis illata, illuminari debet per aliquod medium, quod in praemissis ponitur tamquam principium, a quo infertur illa veritas et inferendo illuminatur, et ita definitiones, quae se habent ut principia seu media demonstrandi passiones, debent habere rationem determinandi scibilitatem talis obiecti illati illuminando illud. Unde si quaelibet quidditas adaequate et secundum quod est in se cognosceretur, unaquaeque fundaret distinctam scientiam ab alia respectu suarum passionum [this is the truth which founds the thrust of the insight attributed to Bañez at 824b45-825b35 "*in quo videtur mentem D. Thomae attigisse*"], *sicut probabile est distingui scientiam infusam in Christo secundum distinctionem specierum repraesentantium quidditates, ut significat D. Thomas 3. p. q. 11. art. 6.* [See further 824a39-b44.] *Nunc autem cum intellectus sit unitivus et praecisivus nec quamlibet naturam intelligat, ut est adaequate in se, sed coordinat et coniungit cum alia, et e contra unam et eandem rem diversis modis intelligit, contingit diversas naturas pertinere ad eandem scientiam et eandem naturam in diversis scientiis considerari, et sic oportet assignare aliquam rationem, qua plures naturae uniantur in eadem scientia, vel diversas, quibus diversimode considerentur a diversis*" [see further 825b22-35, 829a20-b19].—"It is certain that the sciences, like all habits, are determined in type by their objects, as is clear from what Aristotle says in Book 2 of his treatise *On the Soul*, chap. 4, 415 a 20, and as St. Thomas establishes in his *Summa theologica*, I. q. 77, art. 3, and so the unity and distinction of a power or habit must always be adequated to and conformed with the unity or distinction of an object in the rationale of object [further at 829a39-b4, 834a40-b3].

are univocally knowable by Mathematics and Physics, just as these sciences are themselves univocally sciences, but quantity and substance are not univocal in rationale of being. For the rationale of the knowable only bespeaks the necessary connection of truth, which connection coincides univocally with any other necessary connection whatever in the rationale of the true, even if they would not coincide in rationale of being. And when it is said that an object perfects a power, the response is that even a mind-depen-

Mathematica et Physica, sicut ipsae scientiae univoce sunt scientiae, non in ratione entis. Ratio enim scibilis solum dicit connexionem necessariam veritatis, quae univoce in ratione veri convenit cum quacumque alia necessaria connexione, etiamsi in ratione entis non conveniant. Et cum dicitur, quod obiectum perficit potentiam, respondetur, quod etiam ens

"Finally, it is certain that this specification of the sciences (the ways of knowing) is not derived from the unity or distinction of the object in the order of physical being, but in objective being, that is to say, not from an object considered materially and in its proper entitative existence, but as it conduces or is proportioned to a given habit or power [see further 824b30-44, 828a36-b15]. And therefore Cajetan wisely points out in his *Commentary* on the *Summa theologica* of St. Thomas, Part I, q. 1, art. 3, that the rationale of an object in the rationale or formality of an object is something quite other than the rationale of an object in the order of physical existence; and that the species or types of things in the order of physical existence are something quite different from the species or types of objective being, as examples clearly show. For color existing as a quality is one kind of thing, which is divided into various species [red, blue, green, etc.], and yet in the rationale of something visible color has the single specific character of the object of sight. All bodies have the same specific type in the rationale of a philosophical object, all beings in the rationale of Metaphysics, although in the entitative rationale of body and of being they are divided into so many [i.e., a great variety of] species or types. Conversely, on the other hand, the same color is attained in a different way by sight and by the understanding, the same thing is differently attained by the will as good and as true by the understanding, the same earth as round by the astronomer, as changeable by the philosopher of nature, and so on with a multitude of other examples. Whence it follows that the specific rationale of a thing is other than that of an object in the being and formal rationale of object.

"Wherefore in the question before us [whence derives the specific unity or diversity of the sciences in the rationale of the knowable] practically the entire difficulty to be investigated comes down to this: what is that formal rationale which specifically constitutes an object in the rationale of an object of one type of knowledge and thanks to that same rationale makes it differ from the object of another type of knowledge [e.g., what makes an object of chemistry, say, differ from an object of psychology, or of mathematics, and so on]. As we have said in our introductory question to Material Logic, art. 3 [see note 13 above for detailed consideration], within the formal rationale of an object, the rationales 'which' and 'under which' are customarily distinguished. Nor should this distinction be rejected, as it is by Vazquez in his *Commentary on and Disputations about the Summa theologica of St. Thomas*, I. p., disp. 7, cap. 3. For in the very object which is attained by diverse habits or powers, some rationale which is specially attained by one rather than another habit or power must be designated, and this specially attained rationale is what is called the 'formal rationale which,' that is, which is attained as differentiating a material object which is determined that it may be attained through such a special rationale [e.g., as noisy, or colored, or hard, etc.]. By contrast, that formal rationale which actuates the others and contains them under itself that a given object may be attained by a power, is called the 'rationale under which.' For it happens that what is formal respecting one rationale is material in respect of another, and for this reason the ultimate formality under which the others are contained is called 'the formal rationale under which' without qualification. And just as the formality which is attained, and the ultimate formal rationale under which others are rendered attainable (which coincides in the customary way of speaking with the ultimate rationale which), must be taken account of on the side of the object, so on the side of the power there corresponds a formal rationale under which of attaining the object, which is the very light or actuality by which the power is rendered ordered and actuated respecting that specific object. The case of seeing provides a clear example. For a body—say, a wall, or a stone—is a material object which is seen, but the formal object by which it is determined to [the power of] sight rather than to hearing is color, and that is the formal rationale which is seen. But again, color is actuated and formed by illumination, and that is the ultimate formality by which the object is rendered visible and under which the other rationales are ordered to sight, while on the side of the eye there is the light under which the actuated power proceeds to the seeing.

dent being perfects, not by reason of itself formally, but by reason of its fundament and of the mind-independent being on whose pattern it is conceived.[34]

And if you should say: the rationale of the knowable is surely transcendent relative to this or that knowable rationale, and therefore is not univocal: *The response is* that the cognizable in general, like the true and the good and the coincident properties of being, is analogous to this or that knowable, in the manner of any essence predicable by a predicability of the second predicable [namely, species] or of the first predicable [namely, genus]; that is to say, it is predicated transcendentally in all univocal categories. Moreover, we say that this or that determinate knowable can be univocal in respect of the subjects or beings to which it belongs denominatively in the manner of the fourth predicable [namely, property] or of the fifth predicable [namely, accident], even though those beings are not univocal entitatively, for the reason that the determinate knowable in question is not consequent on being as it is taken in itself absolutely, but comparatively to a knowing power, and there can be a same way of relating in things not univocally coincident according to themselves and entitatively.[35]

rationis perficit, non ratione sui formaliter sed ratione sui fundamenti et entis realis, ad cuius instar concipitur.[34]

Et si dicas: Nam ista ratio cognoscibilis transcendens est ad istam vel illam rationem cognoscibilis, ergo non univoca: *Respondetur,* quod cognoscibile in communi, sicut verum et bonum et passiones entis, est analogum ad hoc vel illud cognoscibile, per modum cuiusdam quidditatis praedicabilis praedicabilitate secundi praedicabilis vel primi seu transcendentaliter. Ceterum hoc vel illud cognoscibile determinatum dicimus, quod univocum esse potest respectu subiectorum seu entium, quibus convenit denominative per modum quarti vel quinti praedicabilis, licet illa entia univoca non sint entitative, eo quod non consequitur ad ens, ut in se absolute sumitur, sed comparative ad potentiam cognoscentem, et potest esse idem modus comparandi in rebus non univoce convenientibus secundum se et entitative.[35]

"Similarly, therefore, applying this to the case of the knowable object and science, the knowable object is something complex consisting of a subject of which some property or characteristic [some genotypic or phenotypic trait] is demonstrated. And this object, which is the truth of an inferred conclusion, must be illuminated through some medium which is posited in the premises as a principle from which that truth is inferred and by the inferring illuminated, and thus definitions, which stand as the principles or media of demonstrating characteristics, must have the rationale of determining the knowability of such an inferred object by illuminating it. Whence if any knowable essence whatever were cognized adequately and according as it is in itself, each such would found a science distinct from every other in respect of its own characteristics [this is the truth which founds the thrust of the insight attributed to Bañez at 824b45-825b35 "whereby he seems to have gotten the thought of St. Thomas"], in the manner that the infused knowledge in Christ is probably to be distinguished according to a distinction of species representing essences, as St. Thomas signifies in the *Summa theologica,* III, q. 11, art. 6. [See further 824a39-b44.] But now, since the understanding is unitive and precisive, nor does it grasp any nature whatever as it is adequately in itself, but coordinates and conjoins [one nature] with another, and conversely understands one same nature in diverse ways, it happens that diverse natures pertain to the same science and that the same nature is considered in different sciences, and so it is necessary to assign some reason whereby several natures are united in the same science, or diverse reasons whereby the natures are differently considered by the different sciences" [see further 825b22-35, 829a20-b19].

[34] See note 35 below, Question 1 above, 130/44-131/18.

[35] Phil. nat. 4. p. q. 2. art. 3., Reiser ed., III. 77b26-78a46: ". . . *non attendi formaliter in obiecto potentiae realitatem seu entitatem, prout habet esse in se, sed proportionem et coaptationem ad potentiam. Quae quidem proportio, ut subiective existat in re, debet esse realis, sed secundum comparationem ad potentiam non consideratur formaliter, quod sit subiective in ipsa re, sed quod se habet obiective ad talem potentiam, licet aliunde, si potentia ipsa solum respiciat ens reale, etiam in ratione obiecti realitatem petat non prout existentem, sed prout comparatam ad potentiam. Existentia enim semper est in ordine ad se et subiective, ad potentiam autem semper se habet obiective. Unde ens rationis, licet in se subiective non habeat realitatem, potest tamen esse obiectum actus intellectus et specificare illum ratione proportionis obiectivae, quam induit in ordine ad intellectum, quando habet fundamentum reale et ad instar realitatis concipitur. Tunc enim perficere et specificare potest intellectum perfectione reali, non innata sibi aut existente in se, sed emendicata et appropriata ab entitate reali, ad cuius instar obiective concipitur, ut diximus in Logica q. 1.*

To the second proof of the antecedent[36] it is said that St. Thomas, in the text in question, plainly speaks of power as a principle for acting; for it is in this way that a passive and an active power do not coincide univocally, because a passive power does not principle (or initiate) an act except dependently upon an ac-

Ad secundam probationem[36] dicitur, quod D. Thomas aperte loquitur de potentia in ratione principii ad agendum; sic enim non conveniunt univoce potentia passiva et activa, quia passiva non principiat actum, nisi dependenter ab activa, cum de se non sit

---

art. 3. ad 1. Et ita, licet realitas et entitas subiective considerata conveniat enti reali et rationis analogice, et non eodem modo simpliciter, obiective tamen simpliciter et univoce inveniri potest in ente rationis, quia supposita emendicatione ab ente reali et fundamento ipsius, proportio ipsa et coaptatio ad potentiam, quae sola pertinet ad rationem obiectivam, per se invenitur, quia vere et proprie coaptatur, ita ut verum et proprium actum intelligendi terminet sicut alia obiecta.

''*Nec obstat, quod ens rationis habet esse per ipsum actum intellectus; ergo non perficit nec specificat illum, sed perficitur ab illo. Respondetur enim, quod ens rationis habet esse ab intellectu per modum existentiae non realiter, sed denominative, scilicet quantum ad denominationem cogniti, quae consequitur actum intellectus. Et ideo talis denominatio consecuta non est ratio perficiens intellectum, sed ut effecta et consecuta, perficit autem ens rationis intellectum, in quantum antecedenter ad istam denominationem, ratione sui fundamenti induit coaptationem et proportionem obiectivam, qua vere et proprie terminat ut obiectum intellectus, eo quod licet sit ens fictum, non tamen ficte obicitur et intelligitur, sed verum actum terminat vera terminatione, etsi ficta entitate.*''—''In the object of a power the focus of attention is not formally mind-independent or entitative reality, according as the object has being in itself, but the proportion and adaptation to the power. This proportion indeed as it subjectively exists in a thing must be mind-independent; but in terms of the relation to the power, that it exists subjectively in the thing itself is not what is regarded, but rather that it exists *objectively* relative to the power in question—although on other grounds, if the power itself respects only mind-independent being [as the external senses], it will also require a mind-independent being in the object, not as existing, but as related to the power. For existence is always in an order to itself and subjectively, whereas to a power it always pertains objectively. Whence a mind-dependent being, although in itself it has subjectively no reality, can still be the object of an act of understanding and specify that act by reason of an objective proportion which it takes on in an order to the understanding when it has a real fundament and is conceived on the pattern of mind-independent being. For then it can perfect and specify the understanding by a mind-independent perfection, not one innate to itself or existing in itself, but one borrowed and appropriated from mind-independent entity, on whose pattern it is objectively conceived, as we have said in the Logic 2. p. q. 1. art. 3 [Reiser ed., 265b44-266b12]. Thus, even though reality and the character of being belongs to mind-independent and mind-dependent being analogically, and not simply in the same way, nevertheless, objectively it can be found in a mind-dependent being simply in the same way as in a mind-independent being, because, presupposing a borrowing from mind-independent being and from its fundament, the very proportion and adaptation to a cognitive power which alone pertains essentially to an objective rationale is there, for the mind-dependent being is truly and properly coapted, so that it terminates a true and proper act of understanding exactly as do other objects.

''Nor does it matter that the mind-dependent being has existence from the act itself of understanding; therefore it does not perfect and specify that act, but is perfected by it. The answer to this is that the mind-dependent being has existence from the understanding after the manner of an existence not mind-independently, but denominatively, that is to say, as regards the denomination of 'known thing,' which follows upon an act of understanding. And for this reason such a consequent denomination is not a rationale perfecting the understanding, but as one effected and consequent, yet the mind-dependent being does perfect the understanding insofar as, antecedently to this denomination, by reason of its fundament, it takes on an objective adaptation and proportion whereby it truly and properly terminates as an object of understanding, by the fact that, even though it is a constructed or fictive being, it is nevertheless not fictively objectified and understood, but terminates a true act by a true termination, although by a fictive entity.'' And, as we have seen, particularly in Article 3 of the First Preamble, the same basic notions hold for the higher powers of purely sensory life. See also the discussion of this in notes 6 and 13 above; Question 1, note 25 (with further references); Question 2 above, 149/41-151/21; and in Book II, Question 1, 235/36-236/46, Question 5, 270/37-271/21. This, then, is the heart of Poinsot's difference with Suarez introduced in the note at the beginning of the First Preamble, and grounded in their opposed understanding of relative being.

[36] 186/15-20.

tive power, because, of itself, a passive power is not in act. But in the rationale of something specifiable by an extrinsic principle an active and a passive power are related univocally, since they both have the signification of a thing thus dependent. To the added proposition that a stimulus object actuates simply, but not a terminative object, I answer that in specifying extrinsically both objects actuate simply, inasmuch as a power or act depends on both in its action and perfection. For even though that object by which a passive power is moved to elicit an act [i.e., a stimulus object] approaches more in the mode of something moving to the actuation of the intrinsic form, nevertheless, the specification depends simply on both.

in actu. Ceterum in ratione specificabilis ab extrinseco principio univoce se habent passiva et activa potentia, cum utraque significationem sic dependentem habeat. Quod vero additur obiectum motivum simpliciter actuare, non terminativum, respondetur, quod in specificando extrinsece utrumque simpliciter actuat, quatenus ab utroque dependet in sui actione et perfectione potentia vel actus, licet illud, a quo potentia passiva movetur, ut actus eliciatur, magis in modo movendi accedat ad actuationem formae intrinsecae, simpliciter tamen ab utroque dependet specificatio.

Question 5

Whether to Signify, Formally Considered, Is To Cause Something in the Order of Productive Causality

Quaestio Quinta

Utrum Significare Sit Formaliter Causare Aliquid in Genere Efficiendi

That the point of difficulty may be clearly understood, we take it for granted that we are not, in the present context, speaking of sign and signification in terms of the very relation in which a sign formally consists, as we have shown above;[1] for a relation is in no way productive, but purely respective of a terminus, and to respect is not to effect. We are speaking, therefore, of the fundament of a sign and of signification, inasmuch as the fundament represents to a cognitive power something for which the sign substitutes and is vicegerent in representing that something to the power.[2] And we are asking whether this leading and presentation or representation of its significate to a power is some kind of efficient causality, or should be placed in some other order of cause.

In the act itself of signifying or representing, we can distinguish three things which seem to pertain to making an object present in a power; for to represent is nothing other than to make an object present or united to a power.

The first is an emission or production of specifiers which comes about in a power by the agency of an object and external sign.

The second is the excitation of a power to direct attention, which is distinguished from the impression

Ut punctus difficultatis clare intelligatur, SUPPONIMUS nos non loqui in praesenti de signo et significatione pro ipsa relatione, in qua formaliter signum consistit, ut supra[1] ostendimus; nam relatio nullo modo est effectiva, sed pure respectiva ad terminum, respicere autem non est efficere. Loquimur ergo de fundamento signi et significationis, quatenus repraesentat potentiae cognoscitivae aliquid, pro quo substituit et vices gerit in repraesentando ipsum potentiae.[2] ET INQUIRIMUS, an ista deductio et exhibitio seu repraesentatio sui significati ad potentiam sit aliqua effectio, vel in quo genere causae collocari debeat.

Possumus autem in ipso significare seu repraesentare DISTINGUERE tria, quae videntur pertinere ad faciendam praesentiam obiecti in potentia; repraesentare enim non est aliud quam facere obiectum praesens seu unitum potentiae.

Primum est emissio seu productio specierum, quae ab obiecto et signo extrinseco fit in potentiam.

Secundum est excitatio potentiae, ut attendat, quae distinguitur ab ipsa impres-

---

[1] Question 1.

[2] See esp. 201/28-203/32 below and discussion surrounding 380/4-7 in Appendix C.

itself of specifying forms; for even after the specifiers have been received, someone needs to be aroused to attention.

The third is the concurrence [of a sign] with a power to elicit an awareness of a thing signified. To elicit this act, an external sign concurs by means of the intrinsically received specifying form, through which it not only concurs in the formation of an awareness of itself, but also of the significate to which it leads. But this concurrence with a power is not the act of signifying,[3] because this concurrence pertains to the eliciting of knowledge. To elicit knowledge, however, is not to signify, but if the knowledge is of a signified, it is the terminus and end of signifying; for a sign works to this end, that an awareness may be had of the thing signified. On the other hand, if the cognition is of the sign itself, it is presupposed to the actual signifying, because from the fact of being something known, an external sign leads to another or signifies. Nor do we doubt but that this representation of a thing signified and leading of a power to the significate to be attained, since it is some new reality, must have an efficient or productive cause. But we are asking whether this event, precisely as it depends upon the sign, depends in the order of a productive cause in such a way that the sign effects signification and that signifying in second act is a production of an effect; or whether indeed this event is from another cause effectively, but from the sign vice-objectively.

There is only one conclusion: **The act of signifying or representing is in no way effectively produced by a sign, nor is to signify, formally speaking, to produce an effect.**

Therefore this proposition: "A sign effects," is never in the fourth mode of essential predication [agency, "secondness": cf. 1632: 770a40-b6]. This conclusion, which is very common among the more recent Thomists, who are wont to take it up in daily disputations, can be gathered originally FROM ST. THOMAS's *Disputed Questions on Truth*, q. 11, art. 1, reply to obj. 4,[4] where he says that "the proximate cause productive of knowledge is not signs, but reason inferring from principles to a conclusion."

sione specierum; nam etiam post receptas species indiget aliquis excitatione ad attendendum.

Tertium est concursus cum potentia ad eliciendam notitiam rei significatae, ad quem actum eliciendum concurrit signum extrinsecum mediante specie intrinsece recepta, per quam non solum concurrit, ut formetur notitia sui, sed etiam signati, ad quod deducit. Ceterum iste concursus cum potentia non est significare,[3] quia concursus iste pertinet ad elicientiam cognitionis. Elicientia autem cognitionis non est significare, sed si sit cognitio signati, est terminus et finis significandi; ad hoc enim movet signum, ut accipiatur notitia signati. Si vero est cognitio ipsius signi, praesupponitur ad significare, quia ex eo, quod est cognitum, ducit ad aliud seu significat. Nec dubitamus, quin ista repraesentatio signati et deductio potentiae ad ipsum attingendum, cum sit aliquid de novo in rerum natura, aliquam causam efficientem habere debeat. Sed inquirimus, an prout pendet a signo, pendeat in genere causae effectivae ita, quod signum efficiat significationem et significare in actu secundo sit efficere; an vero ab alia causa sit effective, a signo vero vice obiective.

SIT UNICA CONCLUSIO: **Significare seu repraesentare nullo modo est a signo effective, nec significare loquendo formaliter est efficere.**

Itaque haec propositio: «Signum efficit», numquam est in quarto modo per se [agere proprie alterando: cf. 1632: 770a40-b6]. Haec conclusio, quae valde communis est inter recentiores thomistas, qui illam quotidianis disputationibus agitare solent, imprimis colligi potest ex D. Thoma q. 11. de Veritate art. 1. ad. 4.,[4] ubi inquit, «quod proximum effectivum scientiae non sunt signa, sed ratio discurrens a principiis ad conclusionem».

---

[3] The Lyons text of 1663 adds here: "*id est movere potentiam et repraesentare, quod facit signum, sed effectus eius; ex motione quippe signi sequitur cognitio in potentia concurrente obiecto, ad hoc enim movet.*" —"that is to say, it is not the movement of the cognitive power and act of representing which the sign performs, but an effect of it; for indeed a cognition follows in the power from the movement of a sign when an object concurs, for it is relative to this object that the sign moves." See note 21 below.

[4] *Pa* IX. 184 b.

Principally, however, the stated conclusion has its FOUNDATION in two principles:

The first is that an object, insofar as it exercises an objective causality in respect of a power and represents itself, does not do so effectively [that is, productively], but only functions as an extrinsic form which is applied to a cognitive power by some other efficient cause and is rendered present to that power by means of a specifying form. In cases where the very object possesses also an effective force for applying itself to a cognitive power, this active capacity functions materially and incidentally [relative to the object as an extrinsic specificative], just as in the case of natural beings a form manifests its presence in matter, but precisely as derived from the form that presence does not exist effectively but formally, for it is brought about effectively [productively] by the agent applying and uniting the form.

The second principle is that a sign falls under the notion of and is substituted in the place of an object in this very line and order of an objective cause, but not in the rationale of something productively applying nor of something leading a power to a thing signified in the mode of an effective cause. Rather a sign is an objective cause, not the principal objective cause, but a substitutive one, by reason of which a sign is said to be instrumental, not indeed as if it were an instrument of an agent producing a physical effect, but as it is a substitute for an object, not informing as a specifying form, but representing from the outside.

The first principle is explained thus: Because the rationale of an object, as we saw in the preceding question,[5] does not consist in this, that it emit and produce forms representative of itself (specifiers) in a cognitive power, etc. For it is certain that the specifying forms are sometimes infused effectively by God, as in the case of pure spirits and of infused knowledge, when the object [known] is not effectively impressing [does not produce specifying impressions]. And the root reason for this is that the rationale of an object is preserved in this, that something is representable and knowable passively by a power. But to be representable passively does not of itself and as such bespeak [active] capacity for applying and uniting an object to a power, but bespeaks that which is [passively] united and made present; for just as to represent is to make present, so to be represented and representable is to be made present. If therefore the rationale of object is preserved through a thing's being representable, consequently making the representation actively is outside the rationale of object and not required for it; just as if a form consists in being

Praecipue tamen habet suum FUNDAMENTUM in duobus principiis:

Primum est, quod obiectum, in quantum exercet causalitatem obiectivam respectu potentiae et repraesentat se, non effective id facit, sed solum se habet ut forma extrinseca, quae ab alio efficiente applicatur et praesens redditur per species ipsi potentiae. Quodsi ipsum obiectum etiam habet vim effectivam se applicandi, id materialiter et per accidens se habet, sicut in naturalibus forma praesentiam sui exhibet in materia, sed prout a forma non est illa praesentia effective, sed formaliter, effective autem fit ab applicante et uniente formam.

Secundum principium est, quod signum succedit et substituitur loco obiecti in hac ipsa linea et ordine obiectivae causae, non autem in ratione applicantis effective nec deducentis potentiam ad signatum modo effectivo, sed obiectivo, non principali, sed substitutivo, ratione cuius signum dicitur instrumentale, non quidem quasi instrumentum efficientis, sed quasi substitutum obiecti, non informans sicut species, sed ab extrinseco repraesentans.

Primum principium explicatur sic: Quia ratio obiecti, ut vidimus quaest.[5] praec., non consistit in hoc, quod emittat et producat species sui in potentia cognoscitiva etc. Constat enim species aliquando infundi effective a Deo, ut in angelis et scientia infusa, obiecto non imprimente effective. Et radicalis huius ratio est, quia ratio obiecti salvatur in hoc, quod aliquid sit repraesentabile et cognoscibile passive a potentia. Esse autem repraesentabile passive de se et ut sic non dicit virtutem applicantem et unientem obiectum potentiae, sed id, quod unitur et praesens fit; sicut enim repraesentare est praesens facere, ita repraesentari et repraesentabile est praesens fieri. Si ergo ratio obiecti salvatur per hoc, quod sit repraesentabile, consequenter hoc, quod est facere repraesentationem active, extra rationem obiecti est nec requisitum ad rationem obiecti; sicut si forma consistit in hoc, quod sit

[5] In the original Latin: "art."

unitable to matter as informing and by its presence making matter known, the rationale of form cannot consist in effectively applying and uniting itself to matter. Whence an object is compared by St. Thomas to a form or actuality by which a power is rendered actuated and formed. For the understandable [actuated] is the understanding actuated, as he teaches in the *Summa theologica*, I, q. 14, art. 2, and q. 79, art. 2, and in many other places. Therefore to represent or to make present does not pertain to the object itself as it is formally an object, as to the cause effecting or producing this presentation, but as to the form and act which is presented and united to a power.

But from this same reason it follows that to excite effectively does not pertain to the rationale of an object, both because this excitation comes about effectively by the agency of another cause, whether from within by God or from without by a man or some other agency proposing and applying an object to sense; and because in an excitation the object is that which is applied to a power, but it is not required that it be itself the thing effectively producing the application. Finally, for the production of awareness an object placed within a power through a specifying form can effectively concur, not in virtue of the object as it is specifying, but in virtue of the power determined and actuated through the object out of which is constituted conjointly with the power one single principle in act, not that the object itself adds a productive vitality to the power. And this concurrence or production of cognition is not the act of signifying or of representing; for an elicitation of cognition supposes an object represented to a power and stimulating the power to tend toward a consummate cognition and representation of the thing signified. And thus, that cognition of the signified is the terminus and end of a signification; for it moves in an order to knowing.

The second principle is declared by the very rationale proper to a sign as it is a sign, because a sign is substituted for an object in order to bring that object to a power in the way in which the object performs essentially in the rationale of an object. For a sign indeed, if it is instrumental and external, does not represent its significate otherwise than by representing itself as the more known object, and the significate as something virtually contained in itself, that is to say, as something more unknown, to which the sign expresses some relation and connection. Therefore its concurrence for representing

aliquid unibile materiae ut informans et sui praesentia intimans materiam, non potest consistere ratio formae in hoc, quod effective applicet et uniat se materiae. Unde obiectum a D. Thoma comparatur formae seu actualitati, qua potentia redditur actuata et formata. Intelligible enim est actus intellectus, sicut docet 1. p. q. 14. art. 2. et q. 79. art. 2. et multis aliis locis. Igitur repraesentare seu facere praesens non pertinet ad obiectum ipsum, ut formaliter obiectum est, tamquam ad causam efficientem hanc praesentationem, sed ut ad formam et actum qui potentiae praesentatur et unitur.

Ex eadem autem ratione constat, quod ad rationem obiecti non pertinet excitare effective, *tum* quia haec excitatio effective fit ab alia causa, vel interius a Deo vel exterius ab homine aut alio proponente et applicante obiectum sensui; *tum* quia in excitatione obiectum est id, quod applicatur potentiae, non vero requiritur, quod sit ipsum applicans effective. *Denique* ad productionem notitiae obiectum intra potentiam positum per speciem potest effective concurrere, non in vi obiecti, ut specificans est, sed in vi potentiae determinatae et actuatae per obiectum, ex quo et potentia unicum principium constituitur in actu, non ipsum obiectum virtutem addit potentiae effectivam. Et iste concursus seu productio cognitionis non est significare seu repraesentare; elicientia enim cognitionis supponit obiectum repraesentatum potentiae et movens, ut tendat ad consummatam cognitionem et repraesentationem signati. Et ita illa cognitio signati est significationis terminus et finis; movet enim ad cognoscendum.

Secundum principium ex ipsa ratione propria signi, ut signum est, declaratur, quia signum substituitur loco obiecti, ut ducat ipsum ad potentiam eo modo, quo obiectum faceret per se in ratione obiecti. Etenim signum si sit instrumentale et extrinsecum, non aliter repraesentat signatum quam repraesentando se ut obiectum magis notum, et signatum ut aliquid in se virtualiter contentum seu ut ignotius, ad quod dicit habitudinem et connexionem aliquam. Ergo concursus eius ad repraesentandum

the significate to a power is the same as its concurrence for representing itself, because by representing itself it represents also the signified as pertaining to itself. Whence emission of specifying stimuli and excitation of a power pertains to the sign in the same way that it pertains to an object when an object represents itself, to wit, by causing it objectively, not productively, because an instrumental sign does not represent a signified otherwise than by first representing itself as an object, and then further extending the representation of itself to another virtually implicit and contained in itself. Therefore a sign does not represent objectively absolutely, but objectively instrumentally and as serving for another.[6] But if the sign is a formal sign, it is clear that it does not represent productively, but of itself represents formally, as follows from its definition and as is clear in awareness and conception, the subject of Books II and III[7] of this work.

Resolution of Counter-Arguments

The conclusion that signification as such does not involve productive causality can be disputed first from various passages written by St. Thomas. For in the *Summa theologica*, III, q. 62,[8] art. 4, reply to obj. 1, he says that "there is in a person's voice a certain capacity for exciting the mind of another, which is produced in the voice insofar as it proceeds from a conception of the one speaking." But this capacity of which St. Thomas speaks is a physically productive capacity. For St. Thomas says there that the spiritual energy in the sacraments exists in just the way that that excitative energy exists in the voice. But that energy which is in the sacraments is a causally effective energy; therefore so also is the energy of a person's voice for exciting and consequently for signifying, for the excitation comes about by signification.

S i m i l a r l y in the *Disputed Questions on Truth*, q. 11, art. 1, reply to obj. 11,[9] St. Thomas says that "the words of a teacher are more proximate to the causing of knowledge than are the sensible things independent of the mind, insofar as words are the signs of intelligible intentions." Therefore words cause knowledge insofar as they are signs, not by representing objectively, but by leading to the thing signified.

L i k e w i s e in the *Commentary on the Sentences of Peter Lombard*, Book IV, dist. 1, q. 1, art. 1, quaestiunc. 1, reply to obj. 5,[10] he says that "a demonstration that such and such is the case proceeds from a common sign";

signatum potentiae est idem atque ad repraesentandum se, quia repraesentando se repraesentat etiam signatum ut pertinens ad se. Unde emissio specierum et excitatio potentiae eo modo pertinet ad signum sicut ad obiectum quando se repraesentat, scilicet obiective id causando, non effective, quia non aliter signatum repraesentat quam prius se ut obiectum repraesentando, ulterius extendendo repraesentationem sui ad aliud in se virtualiter implicitum et contentum. Et ideo signum non repraesentat obiective absolute, sed obiective instrumentaliter et ut deserviens ad aliud.[6] Si autem sit signum formale, constat, quod non effective, sed seipso formaliter repraesentat, ut ex eius definitione constat et patet in notitia et conceptu, de quo seq. libros.[7]

Solvuntur argumenta.

Primo argui potest ex variis auctoritatibus S. Thomae. Nam in 3. p. q. 62.[8] art. 4. ad 1. dicit, «quod in voce est virtus quaedam ad excitandum animum alterius proveniens in voce, in quantum procedit ex conceptione loquentis». Haec autem virtus, de qua loquitur D. Thomas, est virtus effectiva physice. Dicit enim ibi S. Thomas, quod eo modo se habet vis spiritualis in sacramentis, sicut illa vis excitativa in voce. Illa autem, quae est in sacramentis, vis effectiva est; est ergo et ista, quae est in voce ad excitandum et consequenter ad significandum, significatione enim excitatio fit.

S i m i l i t e r in q. 11. de Veritate art. 1. ad 11.[9] inquit D. Thomas, «quod verba doctoris propinquius se habent ad causandum scientiam, quam sensibilia extra animam, in quantum sunt signa intelligibilium intentionum». Ergo in quantum signa causant scientiam, non obiective repraesentando, sed deducendo ad rem significatam.

I t e m in 4. dist. 1. q. 1. art. 1. quaestiunc. 1. ad 5.[10] inquit, quod «demonstratio quia procedit a signo communi»; de-

[6] See Book I, Question 2, 151/9-14; and cf. Book II, Question 2, note 27, toward the end.
[7] In the original Latin: "seq. quaest."
[8] Correcting the erroneous reference to "q. 64" in the original.
[9] *Pa* IX. 185 a.
[10] *Pa* VII. 455 b.

but a demonstration effectively produces knowledge by reason of the material from which it is established, not by reason of a second intention; therefore a sign, from which a demonstration is established, effectively flows into knowledge.

And finally in his *Treatise on the Unity of the Intellect Against the Averroists*, chap. 3, n. 219,[11] he says that "the action of a mirror, which is to represent, cannot be attributed to the man [reflected in the mirror]," thereby granting that to represent or to signify is at least sometimes an action.

The response to the first citation from St. Thomas[12] is that the excitative energy in a person's voice is not the actual signification itself or the signifying of the voice, since one is aroused rather to attending to the signification of the voice. Rather, the voice's energy is the use itself of the speaker's understanding manifesting his concept through the voice, as Cajetan points out in his *Commentary* on the passage in question. This use [made of the voice] is something besides the signification, because it applies the very voice signifying in order to fix the other's attention. And so that excitation and excitative energy proceeds effectively, as a kind of hidden energy, from the one uttering the voice and using it, whereas the moving representatively and objectively proceeds from the signifying voice. And this excitative energy, i.e., the use of a voice derived from a speaker's understanding, St. Thomas compares to that sanctifying motion by which God moves and uses the sacraments for producing grace, because the sacraments are as it were a kind of sign and voices of God exciting us to grace and producing grace. But this energy is utterly distinct from the signification itself of the sacraments, for it is superadded to that signification in the same way that the use and excitative energy of speech is superadded to the signification of words. For excitation occurs to this end, that we attend to the signification and be moved by that signification. And precisely as resulting from a signifying voice, this signification or representation does not work effectively, but objectively; but as the voice is used by one speaking and stimulating, it has a causally productive energy for exciting, born not of the representation, but of the one propounding and using the voice derivatively signifying, and thus the one speaking functions as applying the signifying voice, while the signifying voice functions as [passively] applied and signifying representatively. Nor need we now dispute whether that energy

monstratio autem effective producit scientiam ratione materiae, ex qua constat, non ratione secundae intentionis; ergo signum, ex quo constat demonstratio, effective influit in scientiam.

Ac denique in opusc. 16. § *Ostenso igitur etc.*[11] dicit, «quod actio speculi, quae est repraesentare, non potest attribui homini»; datur ergo repraesentare seu significare, quod est actio.

Respondetur ad primum locum D. Thomae,[12] quod illa virtus excitativa in voce non est ipsa significatio actualis seu significare vocis, cum potius ad hoc aliquis excitetur, ut ad vocis significationem attendat, sed est usus ipse intellectus loquentis et manifestantis per vocem suum conceptum, ut Caietanus advertit super dictum locum. Qui usus est aliquid praeter significationem, cum vocem ipsam significantem applicet, ut alter attendat. Et sic a proferente vocem et utente illa procedit effective talis excitatio et excitativa vis quasi energia quaedam latens, a voce autem significante repraesentative et obiective movente. Et hanc vim excitativam, i. e. usum vocis ab intellectu loquentis derivatum comparat Divus Thomas virtuoso illi motui, quo Deus movet et utitur sacramentis ad producendam gratiam, eo quod sacramenta sunt sicut quaedam signa et voces Dei excitantis nos ad gratiam ipsamque producentis. Quae vis longe distincta est a significatione ipsa sacramentorum, superadditur enim illi sicut usus vocis et vis excitativa superadditur significationi vocis. Fit enim excitatio ad hoc, ut attendamus ad significationem et moveamur ab ipso. Et significatio seu repraesentatio ista prout a voce significante non est effective, sed obiective; ut autem vox movetur a loquente et excitante, vim habet effectivam excitandi, non a repraesentatione ortam, sed a propenente et movente vocem significantem derivatam, atque ita loquens se habet ut applicans vocem significantem, vox significans ut applicata et significans repraesentative. Nec debemus modo disputare, an illa vis et usus

[11] De unitate intellectus contra Averroistas (*Pa* XVI. 216 b).
[12] 197/20-34.

and use of voice is some physical power superadded to the voice, or something moral.[13] For it suffices for what has been proposed that that excitation, as it functions effectively (whether morally or physically), is not the very act of signifying, and does not proceed effectively from the sign in signifying, unless perchance the signification itself were called morally[14] or metaphorically or rather grammatically an action and productive efficiency.

To the second citation from q. 11 of the *Disputed Questions on Truth*,[15] the response is that St. Thomas says that the words of a teacher are more proximately [closely] related to causing knowledge [than are sensory things], but he does not say that they are related thereto productively, but it suffices for them to be more proximate [closer] representatively or objectively, because a sign is a substitute for the thing signified.

The response to the third citation[16] is that[17] in a demonstration by a sign the actual representing and signifying of the sign is not the effecting of the demonstration or the production of knowledge, but that knowledge proceeds effectively from the understanding moved by the object and the sign objectively, not effectively, representing. And so says St. Thomas himself, in the article cited above from the *Disputed Questions on Truth*, q. 2, art. 1, reply to obj. 4:[18] "signs are not the proximate cause productive of knowledge, but the understanding itself is the proximate productive cause."

The response to the last citation[19] is that the action of a mirror is said to represent presuppositively, as it were, not formally, because through a reflection of light a mirror productively generates an image, which represents.

It is argued secondly: Some rationale of producing effectively is included in the very definition of an instrumental sign, therefore a sign effects (i.e., causes productively) insofar as it is formally a sign.

The antecedent is proved from St. Augustine's commonly accepted definition of a sign: "A sign is something which, beyond the impressions that it conveys to the senses, makes something else come into

vocis sit aliquid physicae virtutis superadditum voci, vel quid morale.[13] Sufficit enim ad propositum, quod illa excitatio, ut effective se habet sive moraliter sive physice, non est ipsum significare, nec a signo in significando procedit effective, nisi forte significatio ipsa moraliter[14] seu metaphorice aut potius grammaticaliter dicatur actio et efficientia.

Ad secundum locum ex q. 11. de Veritate[15] respondetur S. Thomam dicere, quod proximius se habent verba doctoris ad causandum scientiam, sed non dicit, quod effective se habent, sed sufficit, quod repraesentative seu obiective proximius, quia signum est substitutum rei significatae.

Ad tertium locum[16] respondetur, quod[17] in demonstratione a signo ipsum repraesentare et significare signi non est efficere demonstrationem, aut producere scientiam, sed illa procedit effective ab intellectu moto ab obiecto et signo obiective, non effective repraesentante. Et sic dicit ipse D. Thomas q. 2. de Veritate art. 1. sup. cit. ad 4.,[18] «quod proximum effectivum scientiae non sunt signa, sed ipse intellectus».

Ad ultimum locum[19] respondetur, quod repraesentare dicitur actio speculi quasi praesuppositive, non formaliter, quia speculum per refractionem luminis generat effective imaginem, quae repraesentat.

Secundo arguitur: In ipsa definitione signi instrumentalis includitur aliqua ratio efficiendi, ergo signum formaliter in quantum signum efficit.

Antecedens probatur ex illa communi definitione Augustini: «Signum est, quod praeter species, quas ingerit sensibus, aliquid aliud facit in cognitionem venire». Ubi

13 "*quid morale*": i.e., the endurance of cultural stipulations in the habit structures engendered by socialization: cf. Book II, Question 5, note 19 toward the end. Also Deely, 1980a: 215 note 7.

14 Cf. Question 2 above, 142/14, and below, Book II, Question 6, 280/26-36; and references in preceding note.

15 197/35-42.

16 197/43-198/5.

17 The 1663 Lyons text adds: ". . . *quod demonstratio procedens a signo supponit signum cognitum et a fortiori repraesentatum. Et ita ipsum repraesentare etc.*"—". . . that a demonstration proceeding by sign supposes the sign cognized and a fortiori represented. And so the actual representing as such etc."

18 *Pa* IX. 184 b.

19 198/6-11.

knowledge.'' In this definition, ''to convey sense impressions'' and ''to make something else come into knowledge'' both alike import productive causality; for by the same movement and causality by which it conveys sense impressions for representing itself, it leads to the cognition of another. But to convey sense impressions is to effect and produce them, therefore to lead to the cognition of another is likewise to function productively. But this is posited in the definition of a sign; therefore it is essential to a sign to effect [to exercise an efficient causality] insofar as it is a sign, which is to signify. For to effectively represent is nothing other than to produce a representation. But a sign effects sense impressions, which are representations; therefore it represents effectively, i.e., by producing effects.

This is confirmed by the fact that many kinds of productive causality belong to signs insofar as they signify. For the sacraments, which are signs, effect insofar as they signify; therefore to signify in the case of the sacraments is formally to effect, otherwise they would not formally be practical signs, if they did not effect insofar as they signify. Similarly, it belongs to a sign, insofar as it signifies, to excite a power, to emit impressions (specifying stimuli), to influence the inferring of a conclusion, the whole of which belongs to productive causality.

The response to this argument[20] is that the two factors posited in the definition of an instrumental sign, namely, to convey sense impressions and to make something else come into cognition, do not express signification in the mode of efficient causality. For to convey impressions or specifying forms is common to sign and non-sign alike; for even an object which represents itself and does not signify itself, conveys impressions, and the object does not do this effectively insofar as it is an object, as we have proved. Whence the so-called productivity of a signification cannot consist in the conveying of sense impressions. But if external objects effectively impress specifying forms, that efficiency does not constitute the object in the rationale of object, but arises from some power, either an occult power of the celestial spheres, as some think and as St. Thomas suggests in q. 5, art. 8, of his *Disputed Questions on the Power of God*, or from some manifest power, as from light in the case of colors, from refracted air in the case of sounds, etc. But in the second of the two factors, which is to make something else come into cognition, the phrase ''to make'' does not indicate productivity on the part of the sign, but a quasi-objective or vice-objective representation, which does not express

tam ingerere species quam facere aliud in cognitionem venire importat efficientiam; eodem enim motu, et causalitate, qua ingerit species ad repraesentandum se, ducit ad cognitionem alterius. Ingerere autem species est efficere et producere illas, ergo et ducere ad cognitionem alterius est effective se habere. Hoc autem ponitur in definitione signi; ergo essentiale est signo efficere in quantum signum, quod est significare. Nihil enim aliud est effective repraesentare quam efficere repraesentationem. Efficit autem species, quae sunt repraesentationes; ergo repraesentat effective.

Confirmatur, quia signo, in quantum significat, convenit multiplex efficientia. Sacramenta enim, quae sunt signa, efficiunt in quantum significant; ergo formaliter in illis significare est efficere, alioquin formaliter non essent signa practica, si in quantum significant, non efficerent. Similiter convenit signo, in quantum significat, excitare potentiam, species immittere, ad inferendam conclusionem influere, quod totum effectivae causalitatis est.

Respondetur,[20] quod illa duo in definitione signi posita, scilicet ingerere species et facere in cognitionem venire, non dicunt significationem per modum efficientiae. Nam *ingerere species* est commune signo et non signo; nam etiam obiectum, quod se repraesentat et non se significat, ingerit species, et hoc non facit obiectum effective, in quantum obiectum est, ut probavimus. Unde in hoc, quod est ingerere species, non potest consistere efficientia significationis. Quodsi obiecta externa effective imprimunt species, illa efficientia non constituit obiectum in ratione obiecti, sed provenit a virtute aliqua, vel occulta ipsius coeli, ut insinuat S. Thomas q. 5. de Potentia art. 8. et aliqui putant, vel manifesta, ut a luce in coloribus, ab aere refracto in sonis, etc. In secundo autem, quod est *facere in cognitionem venire*, ly facere non dicit efficientiam ex parte signi, sed repraesentationem quasi obiectivam seu vice obiectivam, quae non dicit

---

[20] 199/33-200/15.

a productive concurrence, but the concurrence of an extrinsic formal cause first stimulating representatively to make itself known, and besides this also leading to an awareness of something else.[21]

To the confirmation[22] the response is that each instance of productive efficiency which is enumerated in the argument is extrinsic and superadded to the sign as signifying, nor is it essentially required for signifying that efficiency be added to the sign; whence it is that the proposition, "A sign effects," is never in the fourth mode of essential predication. For that the sacraments effect insofar as they signify is not because the *signification* is formally an effectuation, but because efficiency is adjoined and bound to the signification, either in a moral way, inasmuch as the sacraments are practical and by the command of God and the active will of the minister, proceed to work not precisely by enunciating, but by directing to work. Or else, as another opinion has it, they act in a physical way by receiving the power to produce grace from a command of God. To the added remarks concerning the excitation of a cognitive power and the emission of sense impressions or specifiers, it has already been said that such excitation does not belong to the sign as it is a sign effectively, but objectively or vice-objectively; but objective causality pertains to a formal extrinsic cause, not to an efficient cause.[23]

It is argued thirdly: There can be a formal sign which is denominated such not from the very relation which is most formal in the sign (otherwise every sign would be a formal sign, because every sign expresses relation), but from its fundament, because specifically a sign-relation is founded on something

concursum efficientem, sed causae formalis extrinsecae moventis quidem repraesentative ad sui cognitionem, et praeter hoc etiam ad alterius notitiam.[21]

Ad confirmationem[22] respondetur omnem illam efficientiam, quae in argumento numeratur, esse extrinsecam et superadditam signo ut significanti nec ad significationem per se requiri, ut illia adiungatur; unde numquam est in quarto modo per se ,,signum efficit''. Nam quod sacramenta efficiant, in quantum significant, non est, quia significatio formaliter sit effectio, sed quia significationi adiungitur et alligatur efficientia, vel modo morali, quatenus practica sunt et ab imperio Dei et voluntate practica ministri procedunt non praecise enuntiando, sed ad opus dirigendo, vel etiam modo physico, ex Dei imperio accipiendo virtutem ad producendam gratiam. Quod vero additur de excitatione potentiae et immissione specierum, iam dictum est, quod talis excitatio non convenit signo ut signum est effective, sed obiective seu vice obiective; obiectiva autem causalitas ad formalem extrinsecam pertinet, non ad efficientem.[23]

Tertio arguitur: Potest dari signum formale, quod denominatur tale non ab ipsa relatione, quod formalissimum est in signo, alias omne signum esset formale, quia dicit relationem, sed ab eius fundamento, quia scilicet fundatur relatio signi in aliquo,

---

[21] See Phil. nat. 4. p. q. 6. art. 3., Reiser ed. III. 189a42-b16: "*Species comparata ad obiectum, cuius gerit vices, nullam efficientiam habet circa ipsum, sed nudam repraesentationem, quae non est efficientia erga obiectum, cum plerumque tale obiectum non existat, ut circa illud operari possit, et tamen aeque bene repraesentat. Et sic non pertinet ad speciem efficere aliquid circa obiectum, sed solum loco illius subrogari et reddere illud unitum et praesens potentiae, quod nihil efficientiae dicit, sed tantum imitationem vel similitudinem, quae ad genus causae formalis reducitur, qua redditur obiectum cognoscibile et proxime habile ipsi potentiae, ut ipsi uniatur cognoscibiliter, quod totum pertinet ad genus causae formalis, quae vice obiecti actuat et repraesentat.*"—"Compared to the object of which it is vicegerent, a specifying form has no relation of efficient causality, but bare representation, which is not an efficiency respecting the object, since very often the object in question does not exist for the form to be operative upon, and yet it represents in such a circumstance equally well. Thus it does not pertain to a specifier to effect anything with regard to an object, but only to be surrogated (substituted) in the place of that object and render it united with and present to the cognitive power, which function bespeaks nothing of efficiency, but only imitation or similitude, which is reduced to the order of a formal cause whereby an object is rendered knowable and proximately habilitated to the power itself, that it be united thereto in a knowable way, the whole of which pertains to the order of a formal cause that actuates and represents on behalf of the object."

[22] 200/16-26.

[23] See Question 4 above, 166/4-168/48.

which represents to a cognitive power by informing that power as concept and awareness. Similarly, therefore, because the fundament of an instrumental sign effects, that is to say, emits, specifying forms and excites a cognitive power and unites to it the represented thing, an instrumental sign will be said to signify productively or effectively, just as a formal sign is said to signify formally.

This is confirmed by the fact that a sign is truly called instrumental, and therefore also effective, because an instrumental cause is reduced to an effective cause, not to a formal cause. Nor does it avail to say that an instrumental sign is a logical instrumental cause, not a physical one. For a logical instrument is one that causes by means of some intention of reason. But an instrumental sign, particularly if it is a natural one, does not cause by means of an intention of reason, but by the mind-independent reality of a representation.

The response to this argument[24] is that it is entirely true that a sign is formal or instrumental by reason of the fundament of the sign-relation itself, but not on the part of the relation.[25] Moreover, since this fundament is the very rationale of manifesting another on the side of the object or vice-object it is not impossible for this fundament to function in the order of formal cause from the side of the object; but it is impossible for it to function in the order of efficient cause. For indeed the very rationale of an object as such is to be the act and form of a power; and only incidentally, owing to the fact that it cannot be within the power entitatively, is the object within the power intentionally by means of its signs, which function in the capacity of that object as they are concepts and apprehensions. Whence an extrinsic formal causality belongs to an object essentially. But that it should sometimes be intrinsic, through itself or through its signs conjoined and united with a power, is not contradictory. But that an object should effectively move a power by applying and representing, is outside the line of an objective cause and pertains to another line of causality, not to an object as object, as we have often said. If an object happens *also* to have an effective energy for applying and presenting itself by producing impressions or specifications, that will be incidentally and materially or concomitantly, not essentially formally and in the fourth mode of essential predication.

If you should press the question by asking: What therefore is it to signify and to manifest, if it is neither to excite nor to emit specifying forms nor

quod informando potentiam ei repraesentat, ut conceptus et notitia. Ergo similiter quia fundamentum signi instrumentalis efficit, scilicet immittit species et excitat unitque potentiae rem repraesentatam, poterit dici effective significare, sicut formale signum dicitur significare formaliter.

Confirmatur, quia signum vere dicitur instrumentale, ergo et effectivum, quia causa instrumentalis ad effectivam reducitur, non ad formalem. Nec valet dicere, quod est instrumentalis logica, non physica. Nam instrumentum logicum est, quod mediante aliqua intentione rationis causat. Signum autem praesertim naturale non causat media intentione rationis, sed realitate repraesentationis.

Respondetur[24] verissimum esse, quod signum esse formale vel instrumentale ex ratione fundamenti ipsius relationis signi desumitur, non vero ex parte relationis.[25] Ceterum hoc fundamentum cum sit ratio ipsa manifestandi aliud ex parte obiecti seu vice obiecti, non repugnat, quod in genere causae formalis fiat ex parte obiecti; repugnat autem, quod in genere causae efficientis. Etenim ipsa ratio obiecti de se est actus et forma potentiae et per accidens, quia entitative intra potentiam esse non potest, intentionaliter est per sua signa, quae vices gerunt illius, ut sunt conceptus et notitiae. Unde causalitas formalis extrinseca per se convenit obiecto. Quod vero aliquando sit intrinseca, per se vel per sua signa potentiae coniuncta et unita, non repugnat. At vero, quod effective potentiam moveat applicando et repraesentando obiectum, extra lineam causae obiectivae est et ad aliam lineam causandi pertinet, non ad obiectum ut obiectum, ut saepe diximus. Quodsi obiectum etiam habeat vim effectivam applicandi et praesentandi obiectum efficiendo species, id erit per accidens et materialiter seu concomitanter, non per se formaliter et in quarto modo.

Quodsi instes: Quid est ergo significare et manifestare, si neque est excitare neque emittere species neque producere cogni-

[24] 201/28-202/8.

[25] Cf. Question 2, 145/10-22 above; and below, Book II, Question 1, 229/24-38, 238/28-45.

to produce knowledge effectively? *The response is* that it is to render an object present to a cognitive power in the capacity of the object or thing signified. However, it must be noted that the presence of an object in a power in first or second act depends on many causes: on the cause producing the impressions (the specifying forms) or applying the object effectively; on the cognitive power generating awareness, also effectively; on the object formally presenting itself extrinsically or specificatively; on a sign as substituting in the place of that object in the same order of objective cause, although not as the principal, but as its instrument or substitute, but not effectively.

To the confirmation[26] the response is that a sign is called instrumental objectively, not effectively, that is, in place of (as vicar of) an object, as has been said. And it is well called a logical, not a physical, instrument, not because it works by means of an intention of reason, but because it does not represent nor lead a cognitive power to a significate unless it is first known, and thus it signifies as something known. But that which belongs to a thing as known is said to belong logically, because Logic treats of things as known. But the truth is that this influence of a sign is not effective but objective, or in the capacity and place of an object signified in the same order and line, not in the order of an effective cause, as has been proved. And so this instrument is not reduced to a productive or efficient cause, nor is it an instrument properly speaking, but metaphorically or logically.

tionem effective? *Respondetur,* quod est vice obiecti seu signati reddere obiectum praesens potentiae. Praesentia autem obiecti in actu primo vel secundo in potentia pendet a multis causis: a producente species vel applicante obiectum effective; a potentia generante notitiam, etiam effective; ab obiecto se praesentante formaliter extrinsece seu specificative; a signo ut substituente vice illius in eodem genere causae obiectivae, licet non ut principale, sed ut instrumentum seu substitutum eius, sed non effective.

Ad confirmationem[26] respondetur, quod signum dicitur instrumentale obiective, non effective, id est vice obiecti, ut dictum est. Et bene dicitur instrumentum logicum, non physicum, non quia mediante intentione rationis operetur, sed quia non repraesentat nec ducit potentiam ad significatum, nisi prius cognoscatur, et ita significat ut cognitum. Id autem, quod convenit rei ut cognitae, dicitur logice convenire, quia Logica agit de rebus ut cognitis. Veritas autem est, quod influxus iste signi non est effectivus, sed obiectivus seu vice et loco obiecti significati in eodem ordine et linea, non in genere causae effectivae, ut probatum est. Et ita non reducitur hoc instrumentum ad causam efficientem, nec est instrumentum proprie, sed metaphorice aut logice.

---

[26] 202/9-18.

[685a34-b23]

QUESTION 6

Whether the True Rationale of Sign Is Present in the Behavior of Brute Animals and in the Operation of the External Senses

QUAESTIO SEXTA

Utrum in Brutis et Sensibus Externis Sit Vera Ratio Signi

It is certain that brute animals and external senses do not use signs through the comparison and collation that require discourse. But the difficulty is whether without discourse there can be, properly speaking, a use of signs for knowing signified things. The raising of this question leads most directly to a better understanding of the way in which a sign represents and signifies to a cognitive power.

First conclusion: **Brute animals, properly speaking, make use of signs, both of natural and of customary signs.**

This conclusion is taken from q. 24 of St. Thomas's *Disputed Questions on Truth*, art. 2, reply to obj. 7,[1] where he says that "from a memory of past beatings or kindnesses it comes to pass that brute animals apprehend something as if it were friendly and to be sought, or hostile and to be fled." The observation can also be found in the *Summa theologica*, I-II, q. 40, art. 3. And concerning the use of natural signs, St. Thomas says in the *Disputed Questions on Truth*, q. 9, art. 4, reply to obj. 10,[2] that brute animals express their concepts by natural signs. He also speaks about the use of customary signs in his *Commentary on the Metaphysics of Aristotle*, Book I, reading 1,[3] showing that some animals are capable of learning, that is, able to become accustomed through another's instruction regularly

Certum est bruta et sensus externos non uti signis per comparationem et collationem, quae discursum exigit. SED DIFFICULTAS est, an sine discursu detur proprie usus signorum ad cognoscendum res significatas. Quod utique conducit ad intelligendum modum, quo signum repraesentat et significat potentiae.

PRIMA CONCLUSIO: **Bruta proprie utuntur signis, tam naturalibus quam ex consuetudine.**

Sumitur ex D. Thoma q. 24. de Veritate art. 2. ad 7.,[1] ubi dicit, quod «ex memoria praeteritorum flagellorum vel beneficiorum contingit, ut bruta apprehendant aliquid quasi amicum et prosequendum vel quasi inimicum et fugiendum». Et videri etiam potest 1. 2. q. 40. art. 3. Et de signis naturalibus dicit q. 9. de Veritate art. 4. ad 10.,[2] quod bruta exprimunt suos conceptus signis naturalibus. Et de consuetudine loquitur in 1. Metaph. lect. 1.[3] ostendens, quod aliqua animalia sunt disciplinabilia, ut scilicet per alterius instructionem possint assuescere ad aliquid faci-

[1] *Pa* IX. 354 b.
[2] ibid. 152 a.
[3] *Pa* XX. 249 a.

to do or to avoid doing something; therefore brute animals are able to employ customary signs, i.e., signs resulting from perceived patterns of behavior.

There is a REASON FOR THIS first conclusion over and above the testimony of the daily experience wherein we see animals moved by signs, on one occasion by natural signs, such as a groan or sigh, the bleating of sheep, the song of a bird, etc., on another occasion by associations learned in behavior or customary signs, a dog, for example, moved by custom when called by name, without, for all that, understanding the imposition, but being guided rather by a customary association.[4] Over and above this testimony, I say, we observe that a brute animal, on seeing one thing, directs its course toward some other and quite distinct thing, as in the case where an animal on perceiving a scent bounds along some path, or on seeing a low-hanging branch seeks to avoid it, or circumvents a timber lying across the road, or on hearing the roar of a lion trembles or flees, and six hundred other instances in which an animal does not respond within the limits of that which it perceives by exterior sense, but is led through sensation to something else. Which plainly is to use a sign, that is, to employ a representation of one thing not only for itself, but also for another distinct from itself. And that this employment and use is extended to signs arising from custom is also established from the above remarks, because, since some animals are capable of learning, they do not immediately perceive from the outset some things which they know afterwards when a custom has arisen, as a dog, for example, does not respond the first time he is called by such or such a name, and afterward is moved when a custom has been established. Therefore some brute animals employ signs from custom; for they are not moved as a result of the imposition as such of the name, for that imposition itself, which depends on the will of the one stipulating it, a brute animal does not come to know.[5]

I say secondly: **Not only do internal senses perceive signification and make use of signs, but so do the external senses, both in ourselves and in brute animals**.

And here we are speaking of instrumental signs; for what must be said about formal signs depends on what must be

endum vel vitandum; possunt ergo bruta uti signis ex consuetudine.

RATIO HUIUS praeter quotidianam experientiam, qua videmus bruta moveri signis, tum naturalibus, ut gemitu, balatu, cantu etc., tum ex consuetudine, ut canis vocatus nomine consueto movetur, qui tamen impositionem non intelligit, sed consuetudine ducitur.[4] Praeter hoc, inquam, videmus brutum uno viso in aliud distinctum tendere sicut percepto odore insequitur aliquam viam, vel fugit viso ramo vel ligno transverso in via divertit, audito rugitu leonis tremit aut fugit, et sexcenta alia, in quibus non sistit brutum in eo, quod sensu exteriori percipit, sed per illud in aliud ducitur. Quod plane est uti signo, scilicet repraesentatione unius non solum pro se, sed pro altero distincto a se. Et quod hoc etiam extendatur ad signa ex consuetudine, ex supra dictis constat, quia cum aliqua bruta sint disciplinae capacia, non statim a principio aliqua percipiunt, quae postea consuetudine procedente cognoscunt, ut canis non statim a principio movetur, cum vocatur tali vel tali nomine, et postea movetur habita consuetudine. Ergo utuntur aliqua bruta signis ex consuetudine; nam ex impositione ipsa nominis non moventur, quia non innotescit illis impositio ipsa,[5] quae ex voluntate imponentis dependet.

DICO SECUNDO: **Non solum sensus interni, sed etiam externi in nobis et in brutis percipiunt significationem et utuntur signis.**

Et loquimur de signo instrumentali; nam de signo formali pendet ex dicen-

---

[4] What it means to assert that animals do not perceive the imposition itself involved in customary signs fashioned by men can be gathered from the First Preamble, Article 3, esp. 66/47-71/19, in terms of the difference between mind-dependent beings formed and cognized "materially" and mind-dependent beings formed and cognized "formally": the former type of cognition suffices for customary signs as such, while the latter sort of cognition is required for the apprehension of stipulated elements at play as such within the network of customary associations. See 213/8-20 below; see further my "Modern Logic, Animal Psychology, and Human Discourse," *Revue de l'Université d'Ottowa*, 45 (janvier-mars, 1975), 80-100; "Toward the Origin of Semiotic," in *Sight, Sound, and Sense*, ed. T. A. Sebeok (Bloomington: Indiana University Press, 1978), pp. 1-30, esp. 14 ff.; and "The Nonverbal Inlay in Linguistic Communication," in *The Signifying Animal*, ed. Irmengard Rauch and Gerald F. Carr (Bloomington: Indiana University Press, 1980) pp. 201-217.

[5] See preceding note. Also J. Maritain, "Language and the Theory of Sign," in *Language: An Enquiry into Its Meaning and Function*, ed. R. N. Anshen (New York, 1957), pp. 86-101, esp. 90 ff.

said in Book II as to whether specifying forms or acts of knowing are formal signs, and whether the external senses form some image or idol in the place of a concept.

This second conclusion, therefore, is proved first FROM ST. THOMAS, who teaches that a thing signified through a sign is seen in the very sign, as is clear in the *Disputed Questions on Truth*, q. 8, art. 5:[6] "We know," he says, "Socrates through seeing in two ways, both according as seeing is assimilated to Socrates, and according as it is assimilated to an image of Socrates, and either of these assimilations suffices for knowing Socrates." And further on in the same article: "When external sight sees Hercules in his statue, the cognition does not come about through some other similitude of the statue."[7] This teaching can also be found in the *Summa contra gentiles*, Book III, chap. 49. Since therefore an image and a statue represent their significates to a cognitive power in the mode of a sign, if external vision attains in a statue and an image not only the statue, but also that which the image represents, it cognizes one less known thing through another thing more known, which is to use signs.

THE CONCLUSION IS PROVED secondly: There is no reason to deny that external sense is led from one thing to another without discourse and collation. But for using a sign and signification, nothing more is required, nor is discourse necessary. Therefore the use of signs can be attributed to the external senses.

The major premise is proved by the fact that external sense can discriminate between one object of its knowability and another—for example, sight can discriminate between the color white and the color green, between one carved image which represents, say, Christ, and another which represents his mother; it can also attain through a proper sensible such as color, a common sensible such as movement or a profile, and discriminate between the one and the other. Therefore external sense can in one thing know another or be led to another, because for this it suffices that external sense should know how to discriminate between the one thing and the other, and to know the other thing as it is contained in the first or as it pertains to it. But this suffices for external sense to be led from one thing to another, because if it discriminates between one thing and another and

dis seq. disp., an species vel actus cognoscendi sint signa formalia, et utrum sensus externi forment aliquam imaginem vel idolum loco conceptus.

PROBATUR ergo conclusio primo ex D. Thoma, qui rem significatam per signum docet videri in ipso signo, ut patet q. 8. de Veritate art. 5.:[6] «Cognoscimus», inquit, «Socratem per visum dupliciter, et in quantum visus assimilatur Socrati, et in quantum assimilatur imagini Socratis, et utraque istarum assimilationum sufficit ad cognoscendum Socratem». Et infra: «Cum visus exterior videt Herculem in statua sua, non fit cognitio per aliquam aliam similitudinem statuae.»[7] Videatur etiam in 3. Contra Gent. cap. 49. Cum ergo imago et statua repraesentent potentiae sua significata per modum signi, si visus exterior in statua et imagine non solum statuam attingit, sed etiam id, quod repraesentat imago, cognoscit unum minus notum per aliud notius, quod est uti signis.

Secundo probatur conclusio: Nam non est ulla ratio, cur negetur sensui exteriori, quod deducatur de uno ad aliud sine discursu et collatione. Ad utendum autem signo et significatione non requiritur aliquid amplius nec necessarius est discursus. Ergo usus signi exterioribus sensibus attribui potest.

Maior probatur, quia sensus externus potest discernere inter unum obiectum et aliud suae cognoscibilitatis, v. g. visus inter colorem album et viridem, inter imaginem unam et aliam, v. g. quae repraesentat Christum vel B. Virginem; potest etiam per proprium sensibile, v. g. colorem, attingere sensibile commune, v. g. motum aut figuram, et discernere inter unum et aliud. Ergo potest in uno cognoscere aliud seu deduci ad aliud, quia ad hoc sufficit, ut sciat discernere inter unum et aliud, et cognoscere unum, ut continetur in alio vel ut pertinet ad illud. Hoc autem sufficit, ut deducatur de uno ad aliud, quia si discernit inter unum et aliud

[6] *Pa* IX. 122 a.
[7] ibid.

knows the one as contained in another (for example, a profile as it affects or is affected by color, an image as being in a mirror, Hercules in a statue, a green as distinguished from a white thing), nothing more is required in order that it should know another through one thing and be led from the one to the other.

The minor premise, however, is proved from the fact that a sign calls for nothing in its definition except that it should represent something other than itself and should be a means leading to the other. But that this should come about through discourse or by comparing and knowing the relation of the one thing to the other, the sign does not call for; otherwise, signs could not be found in the internal senses in animals.[8] And if formal discourse were required, a pure spirit would not make use of signs, which is false.

Nevertheless, it should be observed that external sense cannot know the significate apart from the sign and in itself. For a significate is very often absent in this manner, and if it were present and cognized through a sign as something distinct from that sign, this would require a comparison of the one to the other, otherwise how will it be established that this taken distinctly and separately from that is the significate of that? External sense therefore knows a significate as contained in a sign and pertaining to that sign, and, as St. Thomas says, knows Hercules in a statue. Nor is more required for a sign; for a sign represents no more concerning its significate than that it is contained in the sign, and so it is not necessary to know the sign by a fuller and more perfect cognition, by connecting and comparing the signified with the sign as mutually distinct things and by reason of the relation of the one to the other. Nevertheless the significate itself thus contained in the sign is known, just as it is known that this is an image of a man and not of a horse, that that is an image of Peter and not of Paul; which could not be the case if the significate were not known at all.

But you might object: A significate must be known as distinct from a sign. For if it is known as one with the sign, external sense does not reach to a cognition of another from the sign, which is required for the rationale of signification. But through sight a thing signified is not seen as distinct from the sign; for example, when an image of Peter the Apostle is seen, the historical Peter, who is absent, is not attained through the seeing, and that historical person as absent is the thing signified; for whatever is present to the seeing is nothing

et cognoscit unum, ut continetur in alio, sicut figuram, ut afficit vel afficitur colore, imaginem ut in speculo, Herculem in statua, viride ut discernitur ab albo, nihil amplius requiritur, ut per unum cognoscat aliud et deducatur de uno ad aliud.

Minor vero constat, quia signum nihil aliud petit in sua definitione, nisi ut repraesentet aliud a se et sit medium ducens ad aliud. Quod vero fiat per discursum aut comparando et cognoscendo habitudinem unius ad aliud, non petit; alias neque in sensibus internis in brutis posset inveniri.[8] Et si requireretur discursus formalis, neque angelus signis uteretur, quod est falsum.

Est tamen observandum, quod sensus exterior non potest cognoscere signatum seorsum a signo et secundum se. Sic enim plerumque est absens, et si praesens sit et cognoscatur per signum ut ab ipso distinctum, requiret comparationem unius ad aliud, alias quomodo ei constabit, quod hoc distincte et seorsum sumptum ab illo est signatum illius? Cognoscit ergo signatum ut contentum in signo et ad ipsum pertinens, et, ut dicit D. Thomas, Herculem cognoscit in statua. Nec amplius requiritur ad signum; nec enim repraesentat signum de suo signato amplius, quam quod in illo continetur, et sic non est necesse illud cognoscere ampliori et perfectiori cognitione, conferendo et comparando signatum cum signo ut distincta inter se et ratione habitudinis unius ad aliud. Cognoscitur tamen ipsum signatum sic in signo contentum, sicut cognoscitur, quod haec est imago hominis et non equi, illa Petri et non Pauli; quod esse non posset, si signatum omnino ignoraretur.

SED OBICIES: Signatum debet cognosci ut distinctum a signo. Si enim cognoscitur ut idem cum signo, non devenitur in cognitionem alterius a signo, quod requiritur ad rationem significationis. Sed per visum non videtur signatum distinctum a signo, v. g. quando videtur imago D. Petri, non attingitur per visum D. Petrus, qui est absens, et ille ut absens est signatum; quidquid enim est praesens visui, non est nisi

[8] See the First Preamble, Article 3, 73/17-74/4 and 74/39-46.

but the sign and image. Therefore the significate is not attained as distinct from the sign, and so the external sense does not reach from the sign to the significate, but the entire external cognition is absorbed in the sign.

Some are persuaded by this argument to assert that external sense makes use of a sign only when the significate is also present to it, not when the significate is absent.[9] But two considerations stand in the way of this solution.

The first is the fact, cited by St. Thomas, that one who sees a statue of Hercules sees Hercules in the statue; and in chap. 49, n. 3, of Book III of the *Summa contra gentiles,* he says that a man is seen in a mirror through his reflected similitude. Decidedly, however, a man whose reflected image is in a mirror can be in back of the one seeing the reflection and not present to him.

The second consideration is the fact that if both sign and signified are presented to sense, sense is not led to the significate which is separate as a result of the sign, but sees the significate through its proper specifiers as it is present for itself and as it presents itself to sight. Therefore the significate is not then seen through an instrumental sign, nor is the eye led from the sign to the signified, but both sign and significate are manifested from themselves, unless perchance by comparing the sign to the significate it should be seen that this is a sign of that. But this requires an act of comparison knowing a relation under the concept and formality of respecting, and comparatively to the term, which never belongs to external sense.

Wherefore we respond simply that sense cognizes the significate in a sign in the way in which that significate is present in the sign, but not only in the way in which it is the same as the sign. For example, when a proper sensible such as a color is seen, and a common sensible, such as a profile and movement, the profile is not seen as the same as the color, but as conjoined to the color, and rendered visible through that color, nor is the color seen separately and the profile separately; so when a sign is seen and a significate is rendered present in it, the significate is attained there as conjoined to the sign and contained in it, not as existing separately and as absent.

signum et imago. Ergo non attingitur signatum ut distinctum a signo, et sic non devenitur a signo in signatum, sed tota cognitio externa consumitur in signo.

Hoc argumento aliqui convincuntur ad asserendum, quod tunc solum sensus externus utitur signo, cum signatum est etiam ei praesens, non quando est absens.[9] Sed obstant huic solutioni duo:

Primum, quia D. Thomas fatetur, quod qui videt statuam Herculis, videt Herculem in statua, et 3. Contra Gent. cap. 49. dicit, quod homo videtur in speculo per suam similitudinem. Constat autem, quod homo, cuius similitudo est in speculo, potest esse retro videntem et non ei praesens.

Secundum est, quia si utrumque, scilicet signum et signatum, praesentatur sensui, non manuducitur ex signo ad signatum, quod est seorsum, sed signatum videt per species proprias, ut sibi praesens est et ut se praesentat visui. Ergo tunc non videtur signatum per signum nec manuducitur oculus ex signo ad signatum, sed utrumque seipso manifestatur, nisi forte comparando signum ad signatum videatur hoc esse signum illius. Sed hoc exigit actum comparantem et cognoscentem relationem sub conceptu et formalitate respiciendi et comparative ad terminum, quod utique sensui exteriori non convenit.

Quare simpliciter respondemus, quod sensus cognoscit signatum in signo eo modo, quo in signo praesens est, sed non eo solum modo, quo cum signo idem est. Sicut cum videtur sensibile proprium, v. g. color, et sensibile commune, ut figura et motus, non videtur figura ut idem cum colore, sed ut coniuncta colori, et per illum visibilis reddita, nec videtur seorsum color et seorsum figura; sic cum videtur signum et in eo praesens redditur signatum, ibi signatum attingitur ut coniunctum signo et contentum in eo, non ut seorsum se habens et ut absens.

[9] See Book III, Questions 1 and 2, esp. Question 2, 305/34-312/6, for grasping what is at stake for Poinsot in the distinction between the presence and absence of objects to sense.

And if it is insisted: What is that in the significate conjoined to the sign and present in the sign besides the sign itself and its entitative being? *The response is* that it is the very thing signified itself in another existence, just as a thing represented through a specifying form is the very object itself in intentional, not physical, being. And so, just as one who grasps a concept grasps that which is contained in the concept as represented in it, and not merely that which exists as representing,[10] so one who sees an external image sees not only the office or rationale of representing, but also the thing represented as being in that image.[11] But by this very fact, that one also sees the thing represented as being in the image, one sees something distinct from the image, because an image as image is something representing, but it is not the thing represented; one nevertheless sees that represented thing as contained and present in the image, not separately and as absent, and in a word, one sees it as distinct from the image, [but] not as separate and apart from the image.

From the foregoing remarks it can be gathered that a univocal rationale of signs obtains in the case of brute animals and in the case of rational animals, because the rationale of a sign does not depend on the way in which a cognitive power uses it (by discoursing or comparing, or by a simple way of attaining), but on the way in which the sign represents, that is, renders something other than itself present objectively, which is the same whether the power knows in a simple manner or in a discursive one.

Resolution of Counter-Arguments

It is argued first from the written sources. For St. Thomas says, in his *Summa theologica*, II-II, q. 110, art. 1, that "every representation consists in a certain collation, which properly pertains to reason; whence, although brute animals manifest something, yet they do not intend the manifestation." Animals do not, therefore, properly use signs and representation, except quite materially and remotely, inasmuch as they do something from which a manifestation follows, which even inanimate things can do.

Et si instetur: Quid est illud in signato coniunctum signo et praesens in signo praeter ipsum signum et entitatem eius? *Respondetur* esse ipsummet signatum in alio esse, sicut res repraesentata per speciem est ipsummet obiectum in esse intentionali, non reali. Et sic, sicut qui videret conceptum, videret id, quod in conceptu continetur ut repraesentatum in eo, et non solum id, quod se habet ut repraesentans,[10] sic qui videt imaginem externam, videt non solum munus seu rationem repraesentantis, sed etiam repraesentatum prout in ea.[11] Sed hoc ipso, quod videt repraesentatum etiam prout in imagine, videt aliquid distinctum ab imagine, quia imago ut imago repraesentans est, non vero repraesentatum; illud tamen videt ut contentum et praesens in imagine, non seorsum et ut absens, et unico verbo videt ut distinctum ab imagine, non ut separatum et seorsum.

Ex dictis autem colligitur in brutis et in nobis reperiri rationem signi univocam, quia ratio signi non pendet ex modo, quo potentia utitur illo discurrendo vel comparando aut simplici modo attingendo, sed ex modo, quo signum repraesentat, id est reddit praesens aliud a se obiective, quod eodem modo facit, sive potentia simplici modo cognoscat sive discursivo.

Solvuntur argumenta.

Primo arguitur ex auctoritatibus. Nam D. Thomas 2. 2. q. 110. art. 1. inquit, «quod omnis repraesentatio consistit in quadam collatione, quae proprie pertinet ad rationem, unde etsi bruta aliquid manifestant, sed non intendunt manifestationem». Non ergo bruta proprie utuntur signis et repraesentatione, nisi valde materialiter et remote, quatenus aliquid faciunt, unde manifestatio sequitur, quod etiam facere possunt res inanimatae.

---

[10] See Book II, Question 1, 231/46-232/4, and the discussion beginning at 227/1.

[11] See below, 211/29-212/18, and 212/35-213/7. See also, however, Book II, Question 1, 232/32-233/3, for the profound difference between seeing an object "in" an internal versus an external image; also 224/11-19, 224/29-34, and 250/19-39. (Related discussion in Question 4 above, note 33, p. 187.)

Likewise, in the *Disputed Questions on Truth*, q. 9, art. 4, reply to obj. 4,[12] he says that, properly speaking, something cannot be called a sign unless it is something from which a cognition of something else is arrived at as if by discursive reasoning; and on this account he denies signs properly so called to the pure spirits. Therefore signs in the proper sense of the word must with equal reason be denied to brute animals, because they do not use discourse.

The response to this is that, in the first passage,[13] St. Thomas is speaking only of manifestation and representation in the rational mode, not about representation made in a natural mode, concerning which see Cajetan's *Commentary* on this passage. Whence St. Thomas goes on to say that "brute animals do not intend the manifestation, even though they do manifest something." He is therefore of the opinion that they do signify something, even though they do not *deliberately* intend the signification, and so such signification as is deliberately intended calls for collation and discourse, not signification absolutely. Nor are animals said to use signs only because they do something from which signification follows, but because they exercise signification and perceive a significate, which inanimate things do not do.

As regards the second citation[14] the response is that a sign is said to be found properly in discursive knowledge, when speaking of the property of the perfection of signifying, not of the property which would preserve the bare essence of a sign absolutely.[15] To be sure, the rationale of sign is discerned in discursive cognition more expressly and distinctly than in simple cognition, although it is also found in simple cognition, as St. Thomas teaches in other places. And the pure spirits also use signs, because they have discourse eminentially, even though discourse appears more formally in us.

It is argued secondly: knowledge of a sign and of its significance is required for the use of the sign, and likewise a knowledge of sign and signified is required, ordered in such a way that the one knowledge is coordinated to the other and inferred from it: otherwise the definition of an instrumental sign, that it represents something else from a preexistent knowledge of itself, is not preserved. But these two requirements are not preserved without some collative and discursive knowledge. For the signification of something cannot be perceived, unless an order or accord rela-

Item in q. 9. de Veritate art. 4. ad. 4.[12] dicit, quod proprie loquendo signum non potest dici nisi aliquid, ex quo deveniatur in cognitionem alterius quasi discurrendo, et ob id negat huiusmodi signa angelis. Ergo pari ratione negari debent brutis, quia discursu non utuntur.

Respondetur, quod in primo loco[13] solum loquitur D. Thomas de manifestatione et repraesentatione modo rationali, non modo naturali facta, de quo vide ibid. Caietanum. Unde subdit D. Thomas, «quod bruta non intendunt manifestationem, licet aliquid manifestent». Ergo sentit, quod aliquid significent, licet significationem non intendant, et sic talis significatio ut intenta collationem petit et discursum, non significatio absolute. Nec solum dicuntur significare, quia aliquid faciunt, unde significatio sequitur, sed quia significationem exercent et signatum percipiunt, quod non faciunt res inanimatae.

Ad secundum locum[14] respondetur, quod dicitur signum proprie reperiri in cognitione discursiva, loquendo de proprietate perfectionis significandi, non de proprietate, quae salvet essentiam signi absolute.[15] Expressius quippe et distinctius cernitur ratio signi in discursiva cognitione quam in simplici, licet in hac etiam inveniatur, ut aliis locis. S. Thomas docet. Et angeli etiam utuntur signis, quia eminentialiter habent discursum, licet in nobis formalius id appareat.

Secundo arguitur: Ad usum signi requiritur cognitio signi et significationis eius, itemque requiritur cognitio signi et signati ordinata ita, quod una cognitio coordinetur alteri et deducatur ex illa, alias non salvatur definitio, quod ex praeexistenti cognitione sui aliquid aliud repraesentat. Sed ista duo non salvantur sine aliqua cognitione collativa et discursiva. Nam significatio alicuius percipi non potest, nisi percipiatur ordo seu convenien-

[12] *Pa* IX. 151 b.

[13] 209/35-45.

[14] 210/1-9.

[15] See 211/29-39 below; and Book II, Question 1, 226/17-34, 227/1-8.

tive to another is perceived; but to know order is to know a relation and comparison, which the [internal] sense of a brute animal is by no means able to do, much less external sense [whether in brute or in rational animals]. Similarly, if one act of knowledge is coordinated to another and drawn from it in such a way that from the one knowledge the other is arrived at, this is to discourse and to know collatively, which is in no way suited to the senses of brute animals.

This is confirmed by the fact that when some object in which another object is contained is represented or apprehended, that simple apprehension rests solely on the object proposed in an immediate and simple way, otherwise it would not be a simple cognition, if it moved itself by passing from one object to another. Therefore use of an instrumental sign requires a power knowing collatively and comparatively and by more than a simple tendency; but all the senses in brute animals know in a simple manner and not collatively.

And our own experience itself supports the proposition that when we perceive a sign and not its significative force, a collation of the sign with its significate is necessary if we are to elicit from the sign a knowledge of the significate. Therefore, since in brute animals there is no collative power, they cannot perceive the force of a sign naturally unknown to them, and so animals do not advance from custom to understanding of a significate.

The response to this[16] is that a double knowledge is not required for the use of a sign, nor is it required that from one act of knowledge another act of knowledge should be reached, but it suffices that from one known object another known object should be reached. But through one known object to attain another known object is one thing, by one act of knowledge to cause another act of knowledge is quite something else again. For the rationale of signification it suffices to reach from one known object to another, but it is not necessary to pass from one act of knowledge to another.[17] Whence the Philosopher says, in his book *On Memory and Reminiscence*,[18] that a movement toward an image is the same as a movement toward the thing whose image it is, which statement St. Thomas, both in his *Commentary* on this passage (reading 3)[19] and in his *Summa theologica*, III, q. 25, art. 3, explains as referring to movement relative to the image, not as it is a kind of thing, but as image, i.e., as it exercises the office of representing

tia ad alterum; cognoscere autem ordinem est cognoscere relationem et comparationem, quod utique sensus bruti cognoscere non potest, et multo minus sensus externus. *Similiter* si una cognitio coordinatur alteri et ex illa desumitur, ita quod deveniat ex uno ad aliud, hoc est discurrere et collative cognoscere, quod nullo modo sensibus brutorum convenit.

Confirmatur, quia quando repraesentatur vel apprehenditur aliquod obiectum, in quo aliud continetur, illa simplex apprehensio solum sistit in obiecto immediato et simplici modo proposito, alioquin simplex cognitio non esset, si de uno obiecto ad aliud transiret et se moveret. Ergo requirit potentiam cognoscentem collative et comparative et plus quam simplici tendentia; omnes autem sensus in brutis simplici modo cognoscunt et non collative.

Et suffragatur *ipsa experientia* in nobis, quod quando percipimus signum et non vim significativam eius, necessaria est collatio signi ad signatum, ut ex signo eliciamus cognitionem signati. Ergo cum in brutis collativa vis non sit, non poterunt percipere vim signi naturaliter sibi ignoti, et sic non procedent ex consuetudine ad intelligendum signatum.

RESPONDETUR[16] ad usum signi non requiri duplicem cognitionem, nec quod ex una cognitione deveniatur in aliam, sed sufficit, quod ex uno cognito ad aliud cognitum deveniatur. Aliud autem est per unum cognitum attingere alterum, aliud ex una cognitione causare alteram. Ad rationem significationis sufficit, quod de uno cognito deveniatur ad aliud, sed non est necesse, quod de una cognitione ad aliam.[17] Unde dicit Philosophus in libro de Memoria et Reminiscentia,[18] quod idem est motus in imaginem, et in rem, cuius est imago, quod D. Thomas ibi lect. 3.[19] et 3. p. q. 25. art. 3. explicat de motu in imaginem, non ut res quaedam est, sed ut imago, i. e. ut exercet officium reprae-

[16] 210/36-211/19.

[17] Cf. Book II, Question 1, 226/17-34; see also 210/25-35 above, and 212/35-213/7 below.

[18] c. 1. (450 b 20).

[19] *Pa* XX. 204 a.

and leading to another. ''For it is in this sense,'' says St. Thomas, ''that movement toward an image is one and the same as movement toward the thing [imaged].'' Cajetan affords the best interpretation of this in his *Commentary* on the *Summa,* when he gives us to understand that the remarks in question bear on an image considered as image or in the office of a representation, not considered as it is a kind of thing in itself, as if signified in act. And that, from the standpoint of apprehensive movement or knowing, movement toward image and movement toward thing imaged are the same movement, as Cajetan there notes, is the common consensus of all, because in the knowledge of one relative falls the correlative. And so discourse is not necessary, but a simple act of knowledge suffices, in order that when an image or a sign is seen, the thing itself which is contained in the sign and is signified, be attained.

And to that which is said concerning the knowledge of signification,[20] that it is to know some relation and order, the response is that it is not necessary to posit in the brute animals a knowledge of relation formally and comparatively; but it is necessary to posit that animals know its exercise, which founds a relation without comparison and collation,[21] the way an animal knows a distant thing in relation to which it moves, recalls a thing of the past, and has an expectation of future prey, as St. Thomas explains in the *Summa theologica*, I-II, q. 40, art. 3, without knowing the relation of future or past or distance, but the animal knows in exercise that which is distant or future or representing, whereon is founded the relation which the animal does not know formally and comparatively.[22]

To the confirmation[23] the response is that in a simple act of knowledge which does not become discourse or collation, not only can the object which is immediately proposed or apposed to sense be attained, but also that which is contained in that object; just as, for example, external vision sees Hercules in a statue, and just as a specifier [a sense impression] representing a colored thing also represents the profile and movement and other common sensibles there contained and adjoined, yet does not on this account pass beyond simple know-

sentandi et ducendi ad aliud. «Sic enim est unus et idem motus in imaginem cum illo, qui est in rem», inquit S. Thomas. Quod optime Caietanus ibi intelligit de imagine considerata in exercitio imaginis seu officio repraesentationis, non ut res quaedam est in se, quasi in actu signato. Et quod idem sit motus in imaginem et in rem, cuius est imago, ex parte motus apprehensivi seu cognitionis, ut Caietanus ibi advertit, communis est omnium consensus, cum in cognitione unius relativi cadat correlativum. Et sic non est necessarius discursus, sed simplex cognitio sufficit, ut visa imagine seu signo res ipsa, quae in signo continetur et significatur, attingatur.

Et ad id, quod dicitur de cognitione significationis,[20] quod est cognoscere relationem aliquam et ordinem, respondetur, quod non est necesse in brutis ponere cognitionem relationis formaliter et comparative; sed exercitium eius, quod fundat relationem sine comparatione et collatione cognoscunt,[21] sicut brutum cognoscit rem distantem, ad quam se movet, et recordatur rei praeteritae et habet spem praedae futurae, ut docet S. Thomas 1. 2. q. 40. art. 3., sine hoc, quod relationem futuri aut praeteriti vel distantiae cognoscat, sed cognoscit in exercitio id, quod est distans aut futurum aut repraesentans, ubi fundatur relatio, quam formaliter et comparative non cognoscit.[22]

Ad confirmationem[23] respondetur, quod in cognitione simplici sine hoc, quod transeat ad discursum vel collationem, potest attingi non solum obiectum, quod immediate proponitur seu apponitur sensui, sed quod in eo continetur; sicut videt visus externus Herculem in statua et species repraesentans coloratum etiam repraesentat figuram et motum aliaque sensibilia communia ibi contenta et adiuncta, nec tamen ob hoc desinit esse

[20] 210/45-211/4.

[21] See the First Preamble, Article 3, 66/47-76/45, esp. 67/1-19, 69/41-70/2, 73/16-74/9, 74/39-46, for the correct reading of this passage.

[22] See note 4 above. Here again it is a question of mind-dependent objects formed and cognized ''materially'' only: see the references in notes 4 and 21 above.

[23] 211/10-19.

ledge, even though the thing known is not simple, but plural:[24] otherwise, we would not be able to see a plurality of objects by a simple vision. But if we are able to see many objects in a single vision, why not also an ordered plurality and one thing through another, and consequently a significate through a sign and as contained in the sign?[25]

And with respect to our experience of apprehending a sign without apprehending its significative force,[26] it is said that, in the case of signs whose signification we do not know from the outset, we ourselves, no less than brutes, have need of custom. But we accustom ourselves through reason and discourse, whereas animals accustom themselves inasmuch as their memory is fortified by some ordered pluralities heard or known, as, for example, a given name, especially if they are thence affected by some benefit or injury, whence they remember it as something to flee or to seek. And so memory suffices to accustom, and animals which do not have memory do not develop customs. See St. Thomas's *Commentary on the Metaphysics of Aristotle*, Book I, reading 1,[27] and q. 24 of his *Disputed Questions on Truth*, art. 2, reply to obj. 7.[28]

It is argued finally: A sheep, say, on hearing a roar, apprehends the lion only as something harmful, but not as represented by virtue of the roar; therefore, the sheep does not use the roar as a sign.

The consequence is clear from the fact that one cannot use any sign except for that which is represented by virtue of the particular sign. Therefore, if that which one apprehends is represented not by virture of a particular sign, but by virtue of something else, one does not employ that sign as a sign formally speaking. The antecedent is proved by the fact that a sheep apprehends a lion as something harmful by a natural instinct, therefore not from a pre-existing cognition. For that which is known by natural instinct is not attained as a result of pre-existing knowledge; and so the sheep does not apprehend the lion as harmful through a sign. But the sheep does not apprehend the lion other than as something harmful.

simplex cognitio, licet cognitum non sit simplex, sed plura,[24] alioquin non possemus simplici visione plura obiecta videre. Quodsi possumus, cur non etiam ordinata et unum per aliud, et consequenter signatum per signum et ut contentum in signo?[25]

Et ad experientiam illam[26] *dicitur*, quod in signis, quorum significationem a principio non cognoscimus, tam nos quam bruta opus habemus consuetudine. Sed nos assuescimus cum ratione et discursu, illa vero, in quantum eorum memoria roboratur aliquo pluries audito aut cognito, v. g. tali nomine, praesertim si inde afficiuntur aliquo beneficio vel nocumento, unde recordentur ad fugiendum vel prosequendum. Et sic memoria sufficit ad assuetudinem, et bruta, quae non habent memoriam, non assuescunt. Vide D. Thomam 1. Metaph. lect. 1.[27] et q. 24. de Veritate art. 2. ad 7.[28]

Ultimo arguitur: Nam ovis v. g. audito rugitu non apprehendit leonem, nisi ut nocivum, non vero ut repraesentatur ex vi rugitus, ergo non utitur rugitu ut signo.

Consequentia patet, quia non potest uti aliquo signo nisi ad id, quod ex vi talis signi repraesentatur. Ergo si id, quod apprehendit, non ex vi talis signi repraesentatur, sed aliunde, non utitur illo ut signo formaliter loquendo. *Antecedens* vero probatur, quia ovis naturali instinctu apprehendit leonem ut nocivum, ergo non ex praeexistente cognitione. Quod enim naturali instinctu cognoscitur, non ex praeexistente cognitione attingitur; et sic leonem ut nocivum non per signum attingit. Alio autem modo non attingit, quam in quantum nocivum.

[24] See 210/25-35, 211/29-212/18, above; and Book II, Question 1, 226/17-34, below.

[25] Here is the solution to the British empiricists' problem of how to overcome the discrete character of proper sensibles ("sense data") without making all such elaboration of objects a purely mind-dependent construction. In the way indicated by Poinsot, therefore, semiotic provides the solution to the problem of correctly distinguishing within perception the nature and function of a "sensory core." See my "The Doctrine of Signs: Taking Form at Last," *Semiotica*, 18:2 (1976), esp. note 11, pp. 187-188; and "The Nonverbal Inlay in Linguistic Communication," in *The Signifying Animal*, ed. Rauch and Carr (Bloomington: Indiana University Press, 1980), esp. pp. 203-205. See also Book III, Question 1, 292/11-30, Question 2, esp. notes 8 and 9.

[26] 211/20-39.

[27] *Pa* XX. 249 a.

[28] *Pa* IX. 354 b.

This is confirmed, because a sign is essentially a means or medium leading to the cognition of something signified. But means differ in consequence of diverse orders to an end, and therefore signs too differ on this basis. But signs are not ordered to a signified in a univocal way in rational animals and brute animals, because brute animals are not borne toward a signified thing by knowing the order and relation of the sign to that thing in the same way that men are.[29] Therefore, "to signify" in the case of rational and in the case of brute animals is not said univocally, as neither is "to know" or "to be instructed."

The response to this final argument[30] is that a sheep, when it hears a lion's roar, apprehends the lion as something harmful and as harmful in a specific way, for the sheep flees and fears the roar more because it comes from a lion that if it were the howl of a wolf. Whence the sheep discriminates between the one and the other, which would not be the case if it were not led by means of those signs to a lion and to a wolf as different from one another, and harmful in different ways. The fact that the sheep forms the judgment about the lion and the wolf as things to be fled by a natural instinct, does not remove the fact that the sheep does this from a pre-existing knowledge. For some knowledge in external sense must necessarily precede, either a cognition that sees the lion or one that hears his roar, in order for the estimative sense to apprehend and adjudge the lion as an enemy. For brute animals have judgment, but without indifference, and therefore determined to one thing and based on natural instinct, which instinct does not exclude cognition and judgment, but [only liberty of] indifference. Concerning this point St. Thomas's remarks in the *Summa theologica*, I, q. 83, art. 1, and in his *Disputed Questions on Truth*, q. 24, art. 2[31] can be looked at.

To the confirmation[32] the response is that a sign and an act of signifying are taken univocally through the order to the signified as something manifestable to a cognitive power. The fact that this comes about in such or such a way according as the power makes use of the sign does not render the rationale of the sign analogous or equivocal in the order of manifesting, but renders the modes of the cognitive power different in the cognition and use of the sign. Nor is there a parallel between knowing rationally and representing, because "to know rationally" formally bespeaks a cognition according to understanding and con-

Confirmatur, quia signum essentialiter est medium ductivum ad cognitionem signati. Sed media differunt ex diverso ordine ad finem, ergo et signa. Sed in hominibus et in brutis signa non univoco modo ordinantur ad signatum, cum bruta non ferantur ad signatum cognoscendo ordinem et relationem signi ad illud sicut homines.[29] Ergo significare in illis et in brutis non dicitur univoce, sicut nec scire aut disciplinari.

RESPONDETUR,[30] quod ovis audito rugitu apprehendit leonem ut nocivum et ut tale nocivum, magis enim fugit et timet rugitum, quia leonis est, quam clamorem lupi. Unde facit discretionem inter unum et aliud, quod non esset, nisi per illa signa duceretur in leonem et in lupum, ut distinguuntur inter se, et diverso modo nociva. Quod autem naturali instinctu formet iudicium de leone et lupo fugiendo, non tollit, quin id fiat ex praeexistente cognitione. Necessario enim in sensu externo debet praecedere aliqua cognitio, vel quae videat leonem vel audiat eius rugitum, ut aestimativa ipsum ut inimicum apprehendat et iudicet. Habent enim bruta iudicium, sed sine indifferentia, ideoque determinatum ad unum et ex instinctu naturali, qui instinctus cognitionem iudiciumque non excludit, sed indifferentiam. De quo videri potest S. Thomas 1. p. q. 83. art. 1. et q. 24. de Veritate art. 2.[31]

Ad confirmationem[32] respondetur, quod signum et significare desumitur univoce per ordinem ad signatum ut manifestabile potentiae. Quod vero id fiat tali vel tali modo, quo potentia utitur signo, non reddit analogam aut aequivocam rationem signi ex genere manifestandi, sed diversum modum potentiae in cognitione et usu signi. Nec est simile de scire et repraesentare, quia scire formaliter dicit cognitionem secundum rationem et consequentiam, quod bruto non convenit;

---

[29] See the references in note 4 above.

[30] 213/23-40.

[31] *Pa* IX. 354 a.

[32] 214/1-12.

sequence, which is not adapted to brute cognition; but "to represent by signifying" precisely bespeaks the manifestation of one thing through some medium, without determining whether that manifestation be through a consequence or reason [or merely through some association].

repraesentare autem significando praecise dicit manifestationem unius per aliquod medium, non determinando, quod sit per consequentiam seu rationem.

Sequel to Book I[1]

Consectarium Appendix ex Toto Libro[1]

Let us take stock of what we have said in this Book about the nature and rationale of signs. We have established the definition of a sign, the conditions requisite for a sign, and how the rationale of a sign differs from an image and other things manifestative of something besides themselves.

And indeed our general **definition of the sign** is an essential definition. But we have defined sign in general, by abstracting from the formal and the instrumental sign, as: "That which represents something other than itself." For the familiar definition which has been bandied about since Augustine:[2] "A sign is something which, besides the impressions that it conveys to the senses, makes something else come into cognition," treats only of instrumental signs. But the definition we have proposed is handed down from St. Thomas Aquinas in Book IV of his *Commentary on the Sentences of Peter Lombard*, dist. 1, q. 1, art. 1, quaestiunc. 1, reply to obj. 5,[3] where he says, that "a sign imports something manifest with respect to us, by which we are led to a knowledge of some other thing." And in the *Disputed Questions on Truth*, q. 9, art. 4, reply to obj. 4,[4] St. Thomas says that "the sign, speaking generally, is any thing whatever known, in which another thing is known," where the qualification "speaking generally" means the same as "in general."

Colligendo, quae de signi natura et ratione in hac quaestione diximus, constat, qualis sit definitio signi, et quae sint conditiones ad ipsam requisitae, quomodo item ab imagine et aliis manifestativis aliorum differat ratio signi.

Et quidem **definitio signi** in communi essentialis est. Definivimus autem signum in communi abstrahendo a signo formali et instrumentali, scilcet: «Quod repraesentat aliquid aliud a se». Nam illa definitio, quae ex Augustino[2] circumfertur: «Signum est, quod praeter species, quas ingerit sensibus, aliquid aliud facit in cognitionem venire», solum traditur de signo instrumentali. Definitio autem posita traditur a Divo Thoma in 4. dist. 1. q. 1. art. 1. questiunc. 1. ad 5.,[3] ubi inquit, quod «signum importat aliquid manifestum quoad nos, quo manuducimur in alterius cognitionem». Et q. 9. de Veritate art. 4. ad 4.[4] inquit, quod «signum communiter loquendo est quodcumque notum, in quo aliud cognoscitur», ubi ly communiter est idem quod in communi.

[1] In the original Latin: ". . . tota quaestione."
[2] De doctrine christiana II. c. 1. (Migne P. L. XXXIV. 35).
[3] *Pa* VII. 455 b.
[4] *Pa* IX. 151 b.

This definition is essential in the way in which relatives are said to be essentially defined through their fundaments and in an order to a terminus; for an action is specified by a fundament and a terminus. But the rationale of something representative does not consist in a formal categorial relation, because something can be representative even when the [represented] terminus does not exist, as is clear in the case of a dead emperor represented by an image. The rationale of something representative, therefore, remains even when a relation does not exist, and so a representative is not formally a relation, but in a sign the representative is the fundament of the relation, inasmuch as it exists relative to another and founds a representation of another and does not stand in itself. And so the fundament of a sign is treated in terms of genus and difference. For "something representative" is a genus, since indeed it is common [both] to that which represents itself, as an object stimulating a cognition of itself, and to that which represents something other than itself, as a sign; and [from another point of view] it is inferior to being manifestative, because many things manifest and do not represent, such as light, for example, which manifests by illuminating, not by representing, and habit, which is also called a light, and so on for other things which manifest effectively, but not representatively and objectively.

From this you can gather that in the definition of sign, the "represents" is taken strictly and most formally, namely, for that which represents in such a way that it does not manifest in any way other than by representing, that is to say, a sign keeps on the side of a representing object in such a way that only in representing does it serve that object, nor does it manifest in any other way than by representing.

Whence one *excludes* many things which represent something besides themselves and are not signs, and *concludes* that a sign must be more known and more manifest than the significate in the representing, so that in being and in knowable rationale it is dissimilar and [unequal or] subsidiary to that significate.

The first point[5] is clear from the fact that many things manifest things other than themselves by containing those other things or by illuminating or by causing or by inferring, and so not only represent, but illuminate, and manifest in virtue of some connection, not in virtue of a pure representation, that is, in the office of representing and objectifying to a cognitive power in the capacity of another. Thus premises as inferring do

Haec definitio est essentialis eo modo, quo relativa dicuntur essentialiter definiri per sua fundamenta et in ordine ad terminum; a fundamento enim et termino specificatur actio. Ratio autem repraesentativi non consistit in formali relatione praedicamentali, quia datur repraesentativum etiam non existente termino, ut patet cum mortuo imperatore repreaesentatur ab imagine. Ratio ergo repraesentativi manet relatione non existente, et sic formaliter relatio non est, sed in signo est fundamentum relationis, quatenus se habet ad alterum et fundat alterius repraesentationem et non sistit in se. Et sic traditur fundamentum signi per genus et differentiam. Nam ,, repraesentativum '' est genus, siquidem est commune ad id, quod repraesentat se, ut obiectum movens ad sui cognitionem, et id, quod repraesentat aliud a se, ut signum, et est inferius ad esse manifestativum, quia plura manifestant et non repraesentant, ut lux, quae manifestat illustrando, non repraesentando, et habitus, qui etiam dicitur lumen, ac cetera, quae effective manifestant, sed non repraesentative et obiective.

Ex quo colliges, quod in definitione signi ly repraesentat sumitur stricte et formalissime, scilicet pro eo, quod repraesentat ita, quod non alio modo manifestat nisi repraesentando, id est ita ex parte obiecti repraesentantis se tenet, quod solum in repraesentando ei deservit nec alio modo manifestat quam repraesentando.

Unde excludes plura, quae repraesentant aliud a se et non sunt signa, et concludes signum debere esse ita notius et manifestius signato in repraesentando, quod in essendo et in ratione cognoscibili sit illi dissimile et inferius.

P r i m u m[5] p a t e t, quia multa manifestant alia a se continendo illa, aut illuminando aut causando aut inferendo, et sic non solum repraesentant, sed illuminant, et in vi connexionis alicuius ostendunt, non vi purae repraesentationis, id est in officio repraesentandi et obiciendi potentiae vice alterius. Sic praemissae ut in-

[5] 217/36-37.

not signify a conclusion (granted that in some cases a demonstration is inferred from a sign, but in such cases the signifying obtains materially); thus light does not signify colors, but manifests them; thus God does not signify creatures, even though he represents creatures, because he does not contain them purely by representing and portraying their condition, but also as a cause and manifesting by his own light. Wherefore it is impossible that there should be anything manifesting another purely in representing, unless it is subsidiary to and less than that other which is represented, as if substituted for and acting in that other's capacity.

But a sign must be dissimilar [to its significate],[6] because it is more known and more manifest; otherwise, if it is equally manifest, there is no more reason for this to be a sign of one thing rather than a sign of some other thing; but a sign must be inferior to and less than the significate, because, as we have seen, it cannot be equal. But if it is superior, it will contain or cause that significate, but it will not purely represent and function in its capacity. For that which is superior does not represent another unless it causes that other; otherwise, man would represent everything inferior to him, and the highest of the created pure spirits would represent all the things of the world. But if one thing represents another, because it contains in a superior mode and causes that other, it does not purely and precisely represent in the other's capacity, and so is not a sign.

From which you can gather **what conditions are required for something to be a sign.** For the being of a sign essentially consists in an order to a signified as to a distinct thing manifestable to a cognitive power; and so a thing signified and a cognitive power are not among the requisite conditions, but belong to the essential rationale. Similarly, the rationale of something representative is required, but on the side of the fundament, and therefore the representative as such is not a categorial relation, even if it is a representative of another, but a transcendental relation; but in a sign it *founds* a relation of measured to signified, which is categorial.[7]

Besides these, therefore, there are required or follow the three conditions already mentioned: First, that the sign be more known than the signified, not according to nature, but as regards us. Second, that the sign be subsidiary to or more imperfect than the significate. Third, that the sign be dissimilar to that significate.

ferentes non significant conclusionem (licet aliquando ex signo deducatur demonstratio, sed ibi significare materialiter se tenet), sic lux non significat colores, sed manifestat, sic Deus non significat creaturas, licet repraesentet, quia non pure repraesentando et vices earum gerendo, sed etiam ut causa continet et lumine suo manifestans. Quare impossibile est, quod detur aliquid manifestans alterum pure in repraesentando, nisi sit eo inferius et minus illo, quod repraesentatur, quasi substitutum et vices eius gerens.

Dissimile vero esse debet,[6] quia notius et manifestius, alias si aeque manifestum est, non est maior ratio, quod hoc sit signum istius quam hoc alterius; inferius autem et minus, quia aequale, ut vidimus, esse non potest. Si autem sit superius, continebit aut causabit illud, non autem pure repraesentabit et vices eius geret. Id enim, quod superius est, non repraesentat aliud nisi causet illud, alioquin homo repraesentaret omnia sibi inferiora et supremus angelus omnes res mundi. Si autem repraesentat alterum, quia continet superiori modo et causat illud, non pure et praecise repraesentat vice alterius, et sic non est signum.

Ex quo colliges, quae conditiones requirantur ad hoc, ut aliquid sit signum. Essentialiter enim consistit in ordine ad signatum ut ad rem distinctam manifestabilem potentiae; et sic signatum et potentia non sunt ex conditionibus requisitis, sed ex essentiali ratione. Similiter requiritur ratio repraesentativi, sed ex parte fundamenti, ideoque repraesentativum ut sic non est relatio praedicamentalis, etiamsi alterius repraesentativum sit, sed transcendentalis, in signo autem fundat relationem mensurati ad signatum, quae praedicamentalis est.[7]

Requiruntur ergo praeter ista seu consequuntur tres conditiones iam dictae: *Prima*, quod sit notius signato, non secundum naturam, sed quoad nos. *Secunda*, quod sit inferius seu imperfectius signato. *Tertia*, quod sit dissimile ipsi.

---

[6] 217/39-41.

[7] See esp. Book I, Question 1, 123/26-124/18.

Whence it follows that one image is not said to be the sign of another image, nor one sheep of another sheep, and whatever things are the same in kind, *insofar as they are such*, do not function as signs of one another, because each one is equally principal. Nor does it matter that one image was transcribed from another; for that is incidental to the rationale of a sign, even as one man comes from another without being a sign of that other, although he is an image. For in the rationale of signifying each image has the same prototype as essentially represented, although one image can be more excellent than another, because it is older or prior or better made, which is incidental. But one concept can represent another concept, as a reflex concept represents a direct concept, though they differ in kind, because they represent objects different in kind, to wit, the one an external object, the other the very concept within.

But if you should ask, how then does one similar thing represent or manifest another similar thing, the response is that it represents the other as correlative, not as representative, that is, by that general reason whereby one relative expresses an order to its correlative and includes it because correlatives are known simultaneously, not by that special reason whereby one thing is representatively related to another and exercises the function of presenting other objects to a cognitive power.

Finally, from this analysis it becomes clear **how a sign and an image differ**.[8] For in the first place not every image is a sign, nor every sign an image. For an image can be of the same nature as that of which it is an image (for example, a son is of the same nature as a father, even in the divine persons), and yet not be a sign of that imaged thing. Many signs, too, are not images, as smoke of fire, a groan of pain. *The rationale of an image*, therefore, consists in this, that it proceeds from another as from a principle and in a similitude or likeness of that other, as St. Thomas teaches in the *Summa theologica*, I, Qq. 35 and 93, and thus comes to be in imitation of that other and can be so perfectly similar to its principle as to be of the same nature as it and be a propagative image, not only a representative one. But it is not of *the rationale of a sign* that it proceed from another in a similitude, but that it be a means leading that other to a cognitive power and that it substitute for that other in representing as something more imperfect than and dissimilar to it.

Unde sequitur, quod una imago non dicitur signum alterius imaginis nec unum ovum alterius ovi, et quaecumque eiusdem speciei, in quantum in talibus non se habet unum ut signum alterius, quia utrumque est aeque principale. Nec obstat, quod una imago transcribatur ex altera; id enim per accidens est ad rationem signi, sicut etiam unus homo fit ex altero nec est signum illius, licet sit imago. Utraque enim imago in ratione significandi habet idem prototypum ut repraesentatum per se, licet una imago possit haberi ut excellentior altera, quia antiquior vel prior vel melius fabricata, quod per accidens est. Unus autem conceptus potest repraesentare alium, ut reflexus directum, sed differunt specie, cum diversa obiecta specie repraesentent, scilicet unus obiectum extra, alius ipsum conceptum ad intra.

Si autem quaeras, quomodo ergo unum simile repraesentat seu manifestat aliud simile, *respondetur*, quod repraesentat aliud ut correlativum, non ut repraesentativum, id est ea generali ratione, qua unum relativum dicit ordinem ad correlativum illudque includit, quia sunt simul cognitione correlativa, non ea speciali ratione, qua unum repraesentative se habet ad aliud et munus exercet praesentandi alia obiecta potentiae.

Denique innotescit ex dictis, quomodo differant **signum et imago.**[8] Nam imprimis nec omnis imago est signum nec omne signum imago. Potest enim imago esse eiusdem naturae cum eo, cuius est imago, ut filius cum patre etiam in divinis, et tamen non est illius signum. Multa etiam signa non sunt imagines, ut fumus ignis, gemitus doloris. *Ratio ergo imaginis* consistit in hoc, quod procedat ab alio ut a principio et in similitudinem eius, ut docet S. Thomas 1. p. q. 35. et q. 93., et ita fit ad imitationem illius potestque esse ita perfecte similis suo prinicipio, ut sit eiusdem naturae cum ipso et sit imago propagativa, non solum repraesentativa. *De ratione vero signi* non est, quod procedat ab alio in similitudinem, sed quod sit medium ductivum illius ad potentiam et substituat pro illo in repraesentando ut aliquid eo imperfectius et dissimile.

[8] See Book I, Question 1, 132/47-133/12; and Question 3, 164/13-165/8. And Book II, Question 2, note 27, p. 249. Cf. also Book I, Question 1, 116/14-117/17, and 122/17-123/25.

Liber Secundus

DE

DIVISIONIBUS SIGNI*

Book II

CONCERNING THE DIVISIONS OF SIGN*

*In the original Latin: "*Quaestio XXII. De Divisionibus Signi*." Logica 2. p.: "Question 22. Concerning the Divisions of Sign."

Transition to Book II*

The rationale and nature of a sign having been explained, a consideration of its division follows. The division we have proposed for consideration is twofold, one into formal and instrumental signs, the other into natural, stipulated, and customary signs; and we treat of both divisions in this Book.

Transitus Ad Librum Secundum*

Post explicatam rationem et naturam signi, sequitur consideratio de divisione eius, quae duplex est, altera in formale et instrumentale, altera in naturale et ad placitum et ex consuetudine; et de utraque in hac quaestione agendum est.

---

*This passage is not included in Reiser's text, but is found in the Cologne edition of 1638, and may therefore presumably have been either from or approved by Poinsot himself: see "Editorial Afterword," Section III.A. The title for the passage was supplied by the translator.

Question 1

Whether the Division of Signs into Formal and Instrumental Is Univocal and Sound

Quaestio Prima

Utrum Sit Univoca et Bona Divisio Signi in Formale et Instrumentale

No one doubts that an instrumental sign is truly and properly a sign; for nothing is more manifest than the fact that instrumental and exterior signs are truly signs. The whole difficulty is with the formal signs by which a cognitive power is formed and informed for the manifestation and knowledge of an object. The whole difficulty comes down to this: How the rationale of a medium or means leading a cognitive power to a thing signified fits the formal sign, and how the conditions for a sign apply to it, particularly the condition that a sign be more imperfect than its significate, and that a thing is said to be known more imperfectly through a sign than if it were known and represented in itself and immediately.

And the reason for this difficulty is that a formal sign, since it is the awareness itself or concept of a thing, does not add numerically to [does not differ from] the very cognition itself to which it leads the power. It cannot then have the rationale of a means to the end that a power be rendered actually knowing and that from nonmanifest an object should become manifest, since indeed the formal sign is the rationale itself and the form of the knowing; and so the formal sign leads to this, that a concept and awareness be posited in a power and that the power become actually knowing; but not that the concept itself is intermediary to the knowing. On the contrary, *something is said to be known equally immediately when it is known in itself and when it is known by means of a concept* or

De signo instrumentali, quod vere et proprie sit signum, nullus dubitat; nihil enim manifestius quam instrumentalia et exteriora signa vere esse signa. Sed TOTA DIFFICULTAS est circa signa formalia, quibus formatur et informatur potentia cognoscitiva ad manifestationem obiecti eiusque cognitionem. Et tota difficultas devolvitur ad hoc: Quomodo signo formali conveniat ratio medii ductivi potentiae ad signatum, et quomodo conveniant ei conditiones signi, praesertim illa, quod sit imperfectior suo significato, et dicatur res imperfectius cognosci per signum, quam si in seipsa et immediate cognoscatur et repraesentetur.

Et ratio est, quia signum formale, cum sit ipsa notitia vel conceptus rei, non ponit in numero cum ipsamet cognitione, ad quam ducitur potentia. Unde non potest habere rationem medii ad hoc, ut potentia reddatur cognoscens et ut obiectum ex non manifesto fiat manifestum, siquidem est ipsa ratio et forma cognoscendi, et sic signum ad hoc ducit, ut conceptus notitiaque ponatur in potentia fiatque cognoscens; non vero ipse conceptus medium est ad cognoscendum. Imo aeque immediate dicitur aliquid cognosci, quando cognoscitur

awareness; for a concept does not make cognition mediate.

To see how this is so the more briefly and clearly, advert to St. Thomas's teaching in the *Commentary on the Sentences of Peter Lombard*, Book IV, dist. 49, q. 2, art. 1, reply to obj. 15,[1] and in the *Questions at Random*, q. 7, art. 1,[2] that the medium or means in cognition is threefold: the *means under which*, as the light under whose illumination some thing is seen; the *means by which*, namely, the impressed specifying form by which a thing is seen; the *means in which*, namely, that in which another thing is seen, as when I see a man in a mirror. And this means *in which* can yet be twofold:[3] something material and *outside* the cognitive power, namely, that in which there is a similitude or image of another, such as the reflection of a man in a mirror; another formal and *intrinsic* to the power, as is an expressed specifier or mental word, in which a thing understood is cognized. For St. Thomas teaches in his *Disputed Questions on the Power of God*, q. 8, art. 1, and q. 9, art. 5,[4] that the mental word or concept is given as distinct from the act of cognition, and we will ourselves show this to be the case in q. 11[5] in the books *Concerning the Soul*. Moreover, this fact establishes the principal ground for explaining that there is a word in the divine relations, the fact that such a word proceeding through understanding is given in us. But those who deny that there is such a word in us destroy this ground. And *the first means-in-which makes a cognition mediate*, that is, drawn from another known thing or cognition, and it pertains to the instrumental sign, *but the second means-in-which does not* constitute a mediate cognition, *because it does not double the object known nor the cognition*. But indeed it is truly and properly a means representing an object, not as an extrinsic medium, but as one intrinsic and forming the cognitive power. For to represent is nothing other than to render an object present and conjoined to a power in knowable existence, whether as a principle in an impressed specification, which obtains on the side of the principle [of a cognition], because from it and the power cognition must proceed; or on the side

in seipso et quando cognoscitur mediante conceptu vel notitia; conceptus enim non facit cognitionem mediatam.

Ut brevius et clarius res ista percipiatur, adverte ex D. Thoma in 4. dist. 49. q. 2. art. 1. ad 15.[1] et Quodlib. 7. art. 1.,[2] quod medium in cognitione est triplex: *medium sub quo*, ut lumen sub cuius illustratione res aliqua videtur; *medium quo*, scilicet species, qua res videtur; *medium in quo*, scilicet id, in quo alia res videtur, ut in speculo video hominem. Et hoc medium *in quo* potest adhuc esse duplex:[3] quoddam materiale et extra potentiam, scilicet illud, in quo est similitudo seu imago alterius, ut in speculo imago hominis; aliud formale et intrinsecum, sicut species expressa seu verbum mentis, in quo res intellecta cognoscitur. Hoc enim dari ut distinctum ab actu cognitionis docet Divus Thomas q. 8. de Potentia art. 1. et q. 9. art. 5.[4] et nos ostendemus in libris de Anima q. 11.[5] constatque praecipuam rationem explicandi verbum in divinis esse, quia in nobis tale verbum datur procedens per intellectionem. Qui autem negant dari verbum in nobis, evacuant istam rationem. Et primum medium in quo facit cognitionem mediatam, id est ex alio cognito vel cognitione deductam pertinetque ad signum instrumentale, secundum vero medium cognitionem mediatam non constituit, quia non duplicat obiectum cognitum neque cognitionem. Ceterum vere et proprie est medium repraesentans obiectum, non ut medium extrinsecum, sed ut intrinsecum et formans potentiam. Etenim repraesentare non est aliud quam reddere praesens et coniunctum obiectum potentiae in esse cognoscibili, sive per modum principii in specie impressa, quae ex parte principii se tenet, quia ex ipsa et potentia procedere debet cognitio, sive ex

[1] *Pa* VII. 1201 a.

[2] *Pa* IX. 553 a.

[3] See the discussion and references above in Book I, Question 3, note 12, p. 163.

[4] *Pa* VIII. 169 a et 186 a.

[5] In the original Latin: "q. 10," i.e., Phil. nat. 4. p. q. 10, "*De intellectu agente et possibili*" ("On the acting and possible understanding"), which does not fit the context referred to, whereas q. 11, "*De intellectione et conceptu*" ("On the act of understanding and the concept") does, specifically, art. 1, "*Utrum intellectio sit de praedicamento actionis vel qualitatis distinguaturque realiter a verbo mentis*" ("Whether the activity of understanding belongs to the category of action or of quality and whether it should be really distinguished from the mental word").

of the terminus in an expressed specifier, which obtains on the side of the terminus, because in it the object is proposed and presented as cognized and terminating cognition within the power, within which the specifier assumes the rationale of the object. But an object is rendered present or represented to a power not from itself immediately, but by means of a concept or expressed specifier. A concept is therefore a means in representing an object, by which the object is thus rendered represented and conjoined to the cognitive power.

I say therefore first: **In the opinion of St. Thomas, it is more probable that a formal sign is truly and properly a sign, and therefore univocally with an instrumental sign, even though formal signs and instrumental signs greatly differ in mode of specifying.**

In order to make clear the mind of St. Thomas on this question, one must reckon with the fact that sometimes he speaks of a sign precisely as it exercises the office of representing another besides itself, and in this way of speaking he concedes to the formal sign the rationale of a sign simply. At other times St. Thomas speaks of signs which, as things objectified and first known, lead us to something signified, and in this usage he teaches that a sign is principally found in sensible things, not in spiritual things which are less manifest to us, as he says in his *Commentary on the Sentences of Peter Lombard*, Book IV, dist. 1, q. 1, quaestiunc. 2,[6] and in the *Summa theologica*, III, q. 60, art. 4, reply to obj. 1.

That therefore a formal sign is a sign simply and absolutely, is inferred *first* from the *Questions at Random*, q. 4, art. 17,[7] where he says that "a voice is the sign and not the signified; but a concept is sign and signified, just as it is also the thing [known]." But according to St. Thomas, a concept could not be an instrumental sign, as is perfectly clear, since a concept is not an extrinsic stimulating object; therefore he attributes to it the rationale of a sign insofar as it is a formal sign.

Likewise in q. 4 of the *Disputed Questions on Truth*, art. 1, reply to obj. 7,[8] he speaks thus: "The rationale of a sign belongs to an effect before it belongs to a cause by a natural priority when the cause is related to the effect as its cause of being, but not when related to the effect as its cause of signifying. But when an effect has from the cause not only the fact of its existence, but also the fact of its existing as signifying, then, just as the cause is prior to the effect in being, so is it prior in signifying, and therefore the interior word possesses a rationale of

parte termini in specie expressa, quae ex parte termini se tenet, quia in ipsa obiectum proponitur et praesentatur ut cognitum et cognitionem terminans intra potentiam, intra quam induit rationem obiecti. Redditur autem obiectum praesens seu repraesentatur potentiae non seipso immediate, sed mediante conceptu vel specie. Est ergo medium in repraesentando id, quo sic redditur obiectum repraesentatum et coniunctum potentiae.

DICO ERGO PRIMO: **In sententia S. Thomae probabilius est signum formale esse vere et proprie signum, atque adeo univoce cum instrumentali, licet in modo significandi valde differant.**

Et pro mente S. Doctoris declaranda expendendum est, quod aliquando loquitur de signo, ut praecise exercet officium repraesentandi aliud a se, et sic tribuit formali rationem signi simpliciter. Aliquando loquitur S. Thomas de signis, quae tamquam res obiectae et prius cognitae ducunt nos ad aliquod signatum, et in tali acceptione docet signum principaliter inveniri in sensibilibus, non in spiritualibus, quae minus manifesta nobis sunt, ut loquitur in 4. dist. 1. q. 1. art. 1. quaestiunc. 2.[6] et 3. p. q. 60. art. 4. ad 1.

Quod ergo signum formale simpliciter et absolute sit signum, deducitur *primo* ex Quodlib. 4. art. 17.,[7] ubi inquit, «quod vox est signum et non signatum; conceptus autem est signum et signatum, sicut et res». Sed secundum D. Thomam non potuit conceptus esse signum instrumentale, ut de se patet, cum non sit obiectum extrinsecum movens; ergo attribuit ei rationem signi, in quantum signum formale.

Item in q. 4. de Veritate art. 1. ad 7.[8] sic inquit: «Ratio signi per prius convenit effectui quam causae, quando causa est effectui causa essendi, non autem significandi. Sed quando effectus habet a causa non solum, quod sit, sed etiam quod significet, tunc sicut causa est prior quam effectus in essendo, ita in significando, et ideo verbum

[6] *Pa* VII. 455 b.
[7] *Pa* IX. 517 a.
[8] *Pa* IX. 65 a.

signification that is naturally prior to that of the exterior word." Thus St. Thomas, where he speaks absolutely concerning the mental word as such, also attributes to it the rationale of a sign which cannot be an instrumental sign, because a mental word does not exist outside of a cognitive power nor does it stimulate or move, as has been said.

And finally in q. 9 of the *Disputed Questions on Truth*, art. 4, reply to obj. 4,[9] he says that "for us signs are sensible things, because our cognition, as it involves discourse, arises from the senses. But in general we can say that anything whatever known in which another is known is a sign. And according to this usage an intelligible form can be said to be a sign of the thing which is known through it. And so pure spirits know things through signs, and one spirit communicates with another through a sign." Thus when St. Thomas uses the phrase "in general we can say that etc.," he is not using "in general" as a synonym for "improperly and not truly," but is using it in accordance with the rationale of sign that is simultaneously general and true, even though he is not speaking of the usual way in which we employ signs according to our mode of knowing by passing from one thing to another and by forming an imperfect (or, if you will, a discursive) knowledge from sign to signified. And thus as regards the mode of cognizing, the rationale of sign is ascertained with a certain greater propriety in an external and instrumental sign, inasmuch as the act of leading from one thing to another is more manifestly exercised there when the two cognitions exist (first one of the sign, and then one of the signified) than when there is but one cognition, as is found in the leading to another exercised by a formal sign.[10] Whence St. Thomas says finally in q. 9 of the *Disputed Questions on Truth*, art. 4, reply to obj. 5,[11] that "it is not of the rationale of sign properly understood to be prior or posterior by nature, but only to be precognized by us." Whence it happens that for preserving [in anything] the property of [being] a sign, it suffices to verify that [the thing in question] is precognized—known— first—which is accomplished for a formal sign not because it is first known as an object, but as the rationale and form whereby an object is rendered known within a power, and so it is precognized formally, not denominatively and as a thing is cognized.[12]

interius per prius habet rationem significationis quam verbum exterius». Ita D. Thomas, ubi loquitur absolute de quocumque verbo mentis et rationem signi illi attribuit, quod instrumentale esse non potest, cum extra potentiam non sit nec moveat, ut dictum est.

Ac denique in q. 9. de Veritate art. 4. ad 4.[9] inquit, «quod signa in nobis sunt sensibilia, quia nostra cognitio, ut discursiva est, a sensibus oritur. Sed communiter possumus signum dicere quodcumque notum, in quo aliud cognoscatur. Et secundum hoc forma intelligibilis potest dici signum rei, quae per ipsam cognoscitur. Et sic angeli cognoscunt res per signa, et unus angelus per signum alteri loquitur». Ita D. Thomas, ubi quando dicit: « Signum communiter possumus dicere etc.», ly communiter non est idem quod improprie et non vere, sed secundum communem rationem signi, veram tamen, licet non sub ea appropriatione, qua nos utimur signis secundum nostrum modum cognoscendi, deveniendo de uno ad aliud et formando cognitionem imperfectam aut discursivam ex signo ad signatum. Et ita quoad modum cognoscendi cum quadam maiori proprietate invenitur ratio signi in signo externo et instrumentali, quatenus ibi manifestius exercetur ducere de uno ad aliud, duplici existente cognitione, altera signi, altera signati, quam unica solum, sicut in signo formali invenitur.[10] Unde tandem D. Thomas hoc ultimo loco cit. solut. ad 5.[11] dicit, «quod de ratione signi proprie accepta non est, quod sit prius vel posterius natura, sed solummodo, quod sit nobis praecognitum». Ex quo fit, quod ad salvandam proprietatem signi sufficit salvare, quod sit praecognitum, quod in signo formali reperitur, non quia sit praecognitum ut obiectum, sed ut ratio et forma, qua obiectum redditur cognitum intra potentiam, et sic est praecognitum formaliter, non denominative et ut res cognita.[12]

[9] *Pa* IX. 151 b.

[10] See above, Book I, Question 6, 210/25-35, 211/29-39, and 212/15-18.

[11] *Pa* IX. 151 b.

[12] See below, 231/45-232/31; Question 2, 249/13-251/13; Book III, Question 3, 324/7-329/41, and 330/13-332/13, but esp. 325/22-32, 326/35-327/14, 328/40-329/5, and 331/27-35.

And from this is taken the FOUNDATION OF OUR CONCLUSION stated above, because it belongs to a formal sign properly and truly to be representative of another than itself, and it is ordered of its nature to this representation precisely as substituting in the place of the thing or object which it renders present to the understanding; therefore it preserves the essential rationale of a sign.[13]

The consequence is clear, because it substantiates the definition of a sign as a representative of another than itself through the mode of something more known and substituting for another, and therefore not equal to it, but more imperfect and deficient. But the whole of this is found in a formal sign. For the concept, for example, of man, represents another besides itself, namely, human beings; and it is more known, not objectively, but formally, since indeed it renders known and cognized a being who without the concept is unknown and not presented to the understanding; and for the same reason it is something first known formally, that is, it exists as the rationale whereby an object is rendered cognized. But that which is the underlying reason for something's being such, insofar as it is the rationale and form, is prior to that thing in the same way that a form is prior to a formal effect. If therefore a concept is the reason why a thing is known, it is prior by the priority of form to subject and of denominating rationale to denominated thing. Similarly, a concept is not equal to the very object represented, but is subsidiary to and more imperfect than that object, as is clear in the case of created concepts, because created concepts are intentions ordered and subordinated by their nature to substitute for objects and to act in the capacity of those objects (to be their vicegerents) on the side of the terminus represented and of the cognizing [of the object's being known] by a power. Therefore they are subsidiaries of an object precisely as it is the object of those concepts, because an object always exists as the principal and a concept as representing and vicegerent of a principal. And so in intentional being a concept is always subsidiary or inferior, although on other grounds, namely, in the rationale of a spiritual entity, a concept can sometimes be superior to an object. And when we say that an object is more principal and more perfect, we are speaking about the primary and formal object of a concept; for the material and secondary object exists accessorially, nor need it be more perfect than the concept, since the concept does not substitute for that object directly and essentially.

Et ex hoc sumitur FUNDAMENTUM CONCLUSIONIS, quia signo formali convenit proprie et vere esse repraesentativum alterius a se, et ex natura sua ordinatur ad hanc repraesentationem tamquam substituens loco rei seu obiecti, quod reddit praesens intellectui; ergo salvat essentialem rationem signi.[13]

Consequentia patet, quia salvat definitionem traditam signi, quod sit repraesentativum alterius a se per modum alicuius magis noti et substituentis pro alio, atque adeo illi non aequale, sed imperfectius et deficiens. Hoc autem totum invenitur in signo formali. Nam conceptus, v. g. hominis, repraesentat aliud a se, scilicet hominem; et est notior, non obiective, sed formaliter, siquidem hominem reddit notum et cognitum, qui sine conceptu latens est et non praesentatus intellectui; et eadem ratione est prius cognitum formaliter, id est habet se ut ratio, qua obiectum redditur cognitum. Id autem, quod est ratio, ut aliquid sit tale, in quantum ratio et forma, est prius eo, eo modo, quo forma est prior effectu formali. Si ergo conceptus est ratio, ut res sit cognita, prius est prioritate formae ad subiectum et rationis denominantis ad rem denominatam. Similiter non est aequale ipsi obiecto repraesentato, sed inferius et imperfectius illo, ut in conceptibus creatis patet, quia conceptus creati sunt intentiones ex natura sua ordinatae et subordinatae obiectis, ut loco illorum substituant et vices eorum gerant ex parte termini repraesentati et cognoscendi a potentia. Ergo sunt inferiores obiecto, ut obiectum illorum est, quia semper obiectum se habet ut principale et conceptus ut repraesentans et eius gerens vices. Et sic in esse intentionali semper est inferius, licet aliunde in ratione spiritualis entitatis possit aliquando conceptus superare obiectum. Et quando dicimus obiectum esse principalius et perfectius, loquimur de obiecto primario et formali conceptus; nam obiectum materiale et secundarium habet se accessorie, nec est necesse, quod sit perfectius, cum pro illo non directe et per se substituat conceptus.

[13] See Book I, Question 1, 119/28-39; Question 6, 210/25-35.

Finally, it does not matter that a concept does not seem to add numerically to the represented object, since indeed a thing is seen in the concept and not outside of it. For even though in the representative mode one thing may be seen to result from the representing concept and the represented object, yet this unity does not destroy the true and proper representative and significative being. Nay rather, the more a representation is one with the thing represented, the better and more efficacious is the representation. Yet no matter how perfect, a concept in us does not attain to identity with the represented, because it never attains to this, that it represents itself, but [always rather] another than itself, because it always functions as something vicarious in respect of an object; it always retains a distinction, therefore, between the thing signified and itself signifying.[14]

It is otherwise in the Divine Relations. For the Word, because it is a highest representation in pure act, by virtue of so great a representation, attains to identity with the represented divine essence, and thus loses the rationale of a sign,[15] about which see St. Thomas, *Summa theologica*, I, q. 27, art. 1. And for this same reason a concept or expressed specification retains the rationale of a medium or means to an extent sufficient for the rationale of sign. For it possesses the rationale of a means *in which*, because it never represents itself, but another besides itself, as it keeps on the side of a term of the cognition, not on the side of a principle as does an impressed specifier. But because it is not the final terminus, that is to say, because it is not known as the thing, but as servile to a power, that in it the power should apprehend the thing as finally known, therefore it possesses sufficiently the rationale of a means by this very fact, that it is not the final terminus in the knowing.[16] Nor is the concept said to bear toward the thing signified deficiently, as if to say that it represents deficiently and imperfectly; for a deficient and imperfect representation is not of the rationale of a sign, but happens to it. But for a concept to be a sign it is enough that the concept should be of itself subservient to the signified and vicegerent of the represented object and substituting in place of that object, since indeed insofar as it is such it is subsidiary to that for which it substitutes.

Denique non obstat, quod conceptus non videtur ponere in numero cum obiecto repraesentato, siquidem res in conceptu videtur et non extra. Nam licet modo repraesentativo videatur fieri unum ex conceptu repraesentante et obiecto repraesentato, tamen haec unitas non destruit verum et proprium esse repraesentativum et significativum. Imo quanto magis repraesentatio est unum cum re repraesentata, tanto melior et efficacior est repraesentatio. Nec tamen pervenit in nobis conceptus, quantumcumque perfectus, ad identitatem cum repraesentato, quia numquam pervenit ad hoc, quod repraesentet se, sed aliud a se, quia semper se habet ut vicarium quid respectu obiecti; semper ergo retinet distinctionem inter rem significatam et ipsum significans.[14]

Aliud est in Divinis. Verbum enim quia est summa repraesentatio in actu puro, ex vi tantae repraesentationis pervenit ad identitatem cum essentia divina repraesentata, et ita amittit rationem signi,[15] de quo Divus Thomas 1. p. q. 27. art. 1. Et ex hac eadem ratione conceptus seu species expressa retinet rationem medii, quantum sufficit ad rationem signi. Habet enim rationem medii *in quo*, quia numquam se, sed aliud a se repraesentat, ut tenet se ex parte termini cognitionis, non ex parte principii sicut species impressa. Sed quia non est terminus ultimus seu cognitum tamquam res, sed ut deserviens potentiae, ut in eo rem apprehendat tamquam ultimo cognitam, ideo sufficienter habet rationem medii hoc ipso, quod non est terminus ultimus in cognoscendo.[16] Nec dicitur deficienter se habere ad signatum, quasi deficienter et imperfecte repraesentet; deficiens enim repraesentatio et imperfecta non est de ratione signe, sed accidit illi. Sufficit autem, quod ex se sit subserviens signato et vices gerens obiecti repraesentati et loco illius substituens, siquidem in quantum tale est inferius eo, pro quo substituit.

[14] See 233/35-234/5 below.

[15] See below, 233/3-25. And cf. Question 2, 253/4-37.

[16] See below, 231/45-232/31; and Question 2, 249/15-20.

I say secondly: **the division into formal and instrumental signs is essential, univocal, and adequate.**

That it is univocal and essential is inferred from the preceding conclusion, because a formal sign is truly and essentially a sign, as we have shown. But no one doubts that an instrumental sign is truly and essentially a sign. Therefore the division is essential and univocal.

That the division is adequate is established from the fact that the members of the division are reduced to contradictories, and so exhaust the divided whole. For since every sign is a means leading to another, either this means is first known with another's being known as a result, or not [i.e., another's being is known without resulting from the sign's being objectively known]. If it is first known denominatively or objectively, it is an instrumental sign. If it is not first known objectively, and represents another nevertheless, it does so formally, because it is the rationale whereby another is rendered known within a power, not outside as an object known;[17] therefore it is a formal sign.

Finally, that the division is essential, not accidental, is established from the fact that the essential rationale of a sign consists in the representation of a significate, inasmuch as an object is rendered present to a cognitive power and conjoined thereto. But to render another present to a power from one's self formally, and to render another present [to a power] as a thing first known in its own right and as an object of that power, are essentially different modes of representation. Therefore different presences result from a form representing immediately or from an object first known as an object, and consequently there are essentially different representations and different notifications, and therefore essentially different signs.[18]

Resolution of Counter-Arguments

Against the first conclusion arguments can be formed either from certain propositions written by St. Thomas, or by attempting to prove that conditions requisite for the essence of a sign do not fit the case of a formal sign.

From St. Thomas therefore it can be objected first, because in the *Summa theologica*, III, q. 60, art. 4, reply to obj. 1, he says that things which are

Dico secundo: **Divisio in signum formale et instrumentale est essentialis, univoca et adaequata.**

Quod sit univoca et essentialis ex praecedenti conclusione deducitur, quia signum formale vere et essentialiter est signum, ut ostendimus. De instrumentali autem nullus dubitat, quod sit signum. Ergo essentialis et univoca est.

Quod vero sit adaequata, constat, quia divisionis membra reducuntur ad contradictoria, et sic exhauriunt totum divisum. Nam cum omne signum sit medium ductivum ad aliud, vel hoc medium est prius cognitum ad hoc, ut aliud cognoscatur, vel non. Si est prius cognitum denominative seu obiective, est signum instrumentale. Si non est prius cognitum obiective, et tamen repraesentat aliud, id facit formaliter, quia est ratio, qua aliud redditur cognitum intra potentiam, non extra ut obiectum cognitum;[17] ergo est signum formale.

Denique quod divisio essentialis sit, non accidentalis, inde constat, quia essentialis ratio signi consistit in repraesentatione signati, quatenus obiectum redditur praesens potentiae et illi coniungitur. Diversus autem modus repraesentationis est essentialiter in hoc, quod est seipso formaliter reddere alterum praesens potentiae, et in hoc, quod est reddere praesens ut prius cognitum et obiectum potentiae. Ergo fit diversa praesentia per formam repraesentantem immediate vel per obiectum prius cognitum, et consequenter diversa repraesentatio essentialiter est et diversa notificatio, atque adeo diversum signum essentialiter.[18]

Solvuntur argumenta

Contra primam conclusionem formari possunt argumenta vel ex quibusdam auctoritatibus D. Thomae vel intendendo probare, quod non conveniunt signo formali conditiones ad essentiam signi requisitae.

Ex D. Thoma ergo obici potest *primo*, quia 3. p. q. 60. art. 4. ad 1. inquit, quod

---

[17] See Book I, Question 2, 135/6-18 above; and below, Question 2, 249/14-20.

[18] See above, Book I, Question 2, 145/10-28; and below, Book II, Question 2, 238/28-45.

offered to the senses are first and principally called signs, but intelligible effects do not have the rationale of a sign except as they are manifested through some signs. But formal signs are a kind of intelligible effect, as they are concepts and expressed specifying forms; therefore they are not signs, except as they are manifested by something sensible.

Similarly, in Book IV of the *Commentary on the Sentences*, dist. 1, q. 1, art. 1, quaestiunc. 2,[19] he says that "the word 'sign' as regards its first meaning refers to some sensible thing, according as we are led by means of it into a cognition of something hidden." Therefore, since [the expression] "formal signs" does not designate anything sensible leading to something hidden, formal signs are not primarily and essentially signs.

And for the same conclusion, that text will serve which we have cited above from the *Disputed Questions on Truth*, q. 9, art. 4,[20] reply to obj. 4, where he says that a sign is found properly, when cognition passes from one object known to another; nevertheless, it can be said in general that a sign is anything whatever known, in which another is known. The formal sign, therefore, is not properly a sign.

The response[21] is that St. Thomas is speaking in these places about the sign not according to the general rationale of sign, but according as signs are subject to our cognition, insofar as our cognition first needs the external guidance of an object, and only thereafter requires formation through concepts and intelligible forms; and in this latter need our cognition shares with that of pure spirits, but it differs in the first need, and thus it is proper to our cognition to be led by an object externally proposed.[22] In respect of our knowledge, therefore, the proper rationale of a sign is found in a sensible sign leading us to a significate. I say "proper" rationale, not of a sign as such, but "proper" as it is subject to us and first comes into the control or use of our cognition. Whence those things which are spiritual are not subject to our cognition in the mode of a sign [i.e., as objects representing another object] unless they are manifested to us through something sensible. And it is in this way that St. Thomas is speaking in the third part of the *Summa theologica* and in the fourth book of the *Commentary on the Sentences*. But he explains his own mind in the passage cited from q. 9 of the *Disputed Questions on Truth*, where he says that a sign is properly found when cognition passes from one known object to another. "Properly," I say, with respect to ourselves, and as a sign

primo et principaliter dicuntur signa, quae sensibus offeruntur, effectus autem intelligibiles non habent rationem signi, nisi secundum quod sunt manifestati per aliqua signa. Sed signa formalia sunt effectus quidam intelligibiles, sicut conceptus et species expressae; ergo non sunt signa, nisi ut manifestantur aliquo sensibili.

Similiter 4. dist. 1. q. 1. art. 1. quaestiunc. 2.[19] inquit, quod «signum quantum ad primam sui institutionem signat aliquam rem sensibilem, prout per eam manuducimur in cognitionem alicuius occulti». Ergo cum signa formalia non designent aliquid sensibile ducens in occultum, non sunt primo et per se signa.

Et ad idem servit id, quod supra retulimus ex q. 9. de Veritate art. 4. ad 4.,[20] ubi signum proprie dicit reperiri, quando discurritur de uno ad aliud; potest tamen communiter dici signum quodcumque notum, in quo aliud cognoscitur. Non ergo signum formale proprie est signum.

Respondetur[21] D. Thomam in his locis loqui de signo non secundum communem rationem signi, sed prout deservit nostrae cognitioni, quatenus nostra cognitio indiget manuductione externa obiecti, deinde formatione per conceptus et formas intelligibiles; et in hoc convenit cum angelis, sed differt in primo, et ita est proprium nostrae cognitionis deduci ex obiecto externe proposito.[22] Respectu ergo nostri propria ratio signi invenitur in sensibili signo ducente nos ad signatum. Propria, inquam, ratio non signi secundum se, sed propria, ut deservit nobis et venit in usum nostrae cognitionis. Unde ea, quae spiritualia sunt, nisi manifestentur per aliquid sensibile nobis, nostrae cognitioni per modum signi non deserviunt. Et sic loquitur S. Thomas in 3. p. et in 4. Sentent. Explicat autem propriam mentem in q. 9. de Veritate cit., ubi dicit proprie reperiri signum, quando discurritur de uno ad aliud. Proprie, inquam, quoad nos et ut deservit ac-

[19] *Pa* VII. 455 b.

[20] *Pa* IX. 151 b.

[21] to 229/47-230/22.

[22] See Book III, Question 2, esp. 304/10-14 and 305/34-312/6; and Question 3 throughout in the light of 326/23-33.

serves the acquisition of cognition. But he adds that in general anything known in which another is cognized can be called a sign, not by understanding by the term "in general" an improper sign, but the general rationale of a sign, proper indeed according to the way a sign as such has being, but not proper according to the way a sign has being for our mode of acquiring cognition.

It is argued secondly that conditions requisite for a sign are absent from the case of a so-called formal sign. For a formal sign does not have the rationale of medium, but it can have the rationale of terminus of cognition, and consequently is posterior to cognition itself and proceeds therefrom, as is clear in the case of a concept or mental word, which is a terminus of understanding and proceeds from the understanding. Therefore a formal sign is not a medium for the understanding itself. Likewise, a concept does not make a cognition mediate, but immediate; for we understand the objectified thing in itself immediately, albeit we understand by means of a concept and an awareness. But it is against the rationale of a sign to make something known in itself immediately; for when we know a thing in a sign, we know it less perfectly than if we were to know it in itself immediately. Therefore, since a formal sign does not do away with but rather conduces to the knowing of a thing in itself, it does not assume the proper rationale of a sign.

This is confirmed, because we see that a formal rationale "under which" is not called a sign in respect of the objective rationale "which," nor is an impressed specifier called a sign, because it is an intrinsic principle of knowing, as we will say below. Therefore neither will a formal sign be a sign, because it is the very form of an act of knowing, nor does it add numerically to an object in order that that object be rendered known, and it keeps on the side of an intrinsic terminus of cognition, just as an impressed specification keeps on the side of a principle. Therefore, either both impressed and expressed specifiers will be signs, because they are each representative, or both will not be signs, because they are each intrinsic forms of awareness and cognition.

The response to the first part of the argument[23] is that the formal sign, which is a concept, has the rationale of a terminus of knowledge, but not of a final terminus, rather of a terminus ordered to a further terminus, namely, to the thing which is known and rep-

quisitioni cognitionis. Addit autem, quod communiter signum dici potest quodcumque notum, in quo aliud cognoscitur non intelligendo per ly communiter signum improprium, sed communem rationem signi, propriam quidem secundum se, sed non ita propriam pro nostro modo acquirendi cognitionem.

SECUNDO ARGUITUR, quia desunt signo formali conditiones requisitae ad signum. *Nam* signum formale non habet rationem medii, sed potest habere rationem termini cognitionis, et consequenter ipsa cognitione esse posterius et ab illa procedere, ut patet in conceptu seu verbo mentis, quod est terminus intellectionis et procedit ab ipsa. Ergo non est medium ad ipsam intellectionem. *Item* non facit cognitionem mediatam, sed immediatam; rem enim obiectam immediate intelligimus in se, etiamsi mediante conceptu et notitia intelligamus. Est autem contra rationem signi, quod faciat cognitionem rei in se immediate; quando enim cognoscimus rem per signum, minus perfecte cognoscimus, quam si cognosceremus rem in seipsa immediate. Ergo cum signum formale non tollat, sed magis conducat ad cognoscendum rem in se, non induit propriam rationem signi.

Confirmatur, quia videmus rationem formalem *sub qua* non dici signum respectu rationis obiectivae *quae* nec speciem impressam, quia est principium intrinsecum cognoscendi, ut infra dicemus. Ergo neque signum formale erit signum, quia est ipsa forma cognoscendi, nec ponit in numero cum obiecto, ut reddatur cognitum, et tenet se ex parte termini intrinseci cognitionis, sicut species impressa ex parte principii. Ergo vel utrumque erit signum, quia repraesentativum est, vel utrumque non erit signum, quia intrinseca forma notitiae et cognitionis est.

Respondetur *ad primam partem argumenti,*[23] quod signum formale, quod est conceptus, habet rationem termini cognitionis, sed non ultimi, ordinati autem ad ulteriorem terminum scilicet ad rem, quae

[23] 231/9-18.

resented in that [ordered] terminus.[24] But there is nothing antinomic about something's being both a terminus and a medium, when it is not a final terminus, but one respecting and ordered to something outside.

Nor can it be insisted that because the object is not attained according as it is outside, but according as it is contained and rendered understandable within the concept, therefore the concept is not a medium leading to something beyond itself, but one stopping in itself. *This is answered* by distinguishing the antecedent: That the object is not attained according as it is outside the concept is true, if the "according as" expresses the rationale or ground [the intentional mode] of the attaining; if it expresses the thing attained, it is false, for that thing which is outside is truly attained and known, although by the means of an intrinsic cognition and concept, and this suffices for the concept to be a sign or intrinsic means.

To the other part of the argument[25] the response is that it is not necessary for a formal sign to make a cognition mediate by the mediation of an object known, but by the mediation of a form informing and rendering an object present, as we will explain more at length in treating of the word of the mind in the books *Concerning the Soul*, q. 11.[26] And in the same way we confirm that the formal sign is something leading to its significate formally, that is to say, as a form representing and uniting an object to a cognitive power, not instrumentally or as a thing objectively cognized first [known first as an object], and it is also more known formally, not objectively or denominatively.

To the added proposition[27] that it is of the rationale of a sign to make a cognition imperfect and not of the thing as it is in itself, the response is that this proposition pertains only to the instrumental sign, which represents a significate by means of something extraneous, but not to the sign generally speaking, which only expresses something more known in which a less known is manifested, as we have often said in connection with q. 9 of St. Thomas's *Disputed Questions on Truth*, art. 4, reply to obj. 4.[28] And this [general rationale] is preserved in the formal sign, which is more known than the thing signified by the fact that it formally renders the signified known and is also the medium for it formally and representatively, although it is not an imperfect and extraneous representation, but

cognoscitur et in illo termino repraesentatur.[24] Non est autem inconveniens, quod aliquid sit terminus et medium, quando non est terminus ultimus, sed respiciens et ordinatus ad aliquid extra.

Nec potest instari, quia obiectum prout extra non attingitur, sed prout intra conceptum continetur et redditur intelligibile, ergo conceptus non est medium deducens ad aliquid extra se, sed sistens in se. *Respondetur* distinguendo antecedens: Prout extra non attingitur obiectum, si ly prout dicat rationem attingendi, verum est; si dicat rem attactam, est falsum, est enim res vere attacta et cognita illa, quae est extra, licet media intrinseca cognitione et conceptu, et hoc sufficit, ut sit signum seu medium intrinsecum.

Ad aliam partem argumenti[25] respondetur, quod signum formale non est necesse, quod faciat cognitionem mediatam mediatione obiecti cogniti, sed mediatione formae informantis et praesens reddentis obiectum, ut agendo de verbo mentis latius dicemus in libris de Anima q. 11.[26] Et eodem modo verificamus, quod signum formale est manuductivum ad suum signatum formaliter, id est ut forma repraesentans et uniens obiectum potentiae, non instrumentaliter seu ut res prius cognita, et etiam est notius formaliter, non obiective aut denominative.

Quod vero additur[27] esse de ratione signi, quod faciat cognitionem imperfectam et non rei ut est in se, respondetur id solum pertinere ad signum instrumentale, quod per aliquid extraneum repraesentat signatum, non vero ad signum communiter dictum, quod solum dicit aliquid notius, in quo manifestatur minus notum, ut ex D. Thoma saepe diximus quaest. illa 9. de Veritate art. 4. ad 4.[28] Et hoc salvatur in signo formali, quod est notius re significata, quia formaliter illam reddit notam et est medium ad illam etiam formaliter et repraesentative, licet non sit imperfecta et extranea repraesentatio, sed solum repra-

[24] See Question 2 below, 250/7-39, and 251/5-13.
[25] 231/18-29.
[26] Phil. nat. 4. p. q. 11. art. 2.
[27] 231/24-29.
[28] *Pa* IX. 151 b.

only a representation of another than itself, for which other it substitutes and to which it is ordered.

And if you should insist: For the Divine Word is excluded from the rationale of sign for this reason only, because it represents most perfectly the Divine Essence; and similarly the son of Peter, although he is an image of Peter, he is yet not a sign, because he perfectly equals Peter's likeness; and God is not a sign of creatures, although he represents them, because he represents most perfectly. Therefore it is of the rationale of a sign to represent imperfectly. *The response is* that the Divine Word is not a sign of God not only because he represents most perfectly, but because he is consubstantial with and equal to God. And so he is not more known nor substituting for nor servile to God, much less with respect to creatures, to which the Divine Word is not ordered, but rather are creatures ordered to him, and therefore creatures are signs of God, signs which represent God to us as being themselves more known to us. Yet imperfection of the cognition which it generates is not of the rationale of a sign, but substitution on behalf of the significate which the sign represents is. But a man who is the son of his father is not more known than the father, but univocally equal, and therefore does not take on the rationale of a sign.

To the confirmation[29] the response is that a formal rationale "under which"[30] is not a sign because it does not make an object present to a cognitive power, but constitutes the object itself in the being of such or such a kind of object determinately and specifically; but in the rationale of something present to and conjoined with a cognitive power, an object is made present through a formal sign or through an instrumental sign or by something supplying the place of the object.

But to the added proposition[31] that a formal sign does not add numerically to the thing itself signified in order [for that significate] to be made known, the response is that it is true that a formal sign does not add numerically as if there were two things known and represented; but it is not true that a formal sign does not add numerically as one representing and another represented;[32] and so it suffices that there is a sign and a signified, even though in intentional or representative existence the formal sign is said to make one thing with the object, not only as do those things which coincide in one common rationale, but rather because it

sentatio alterius a se, pro quo substituit et ad quod ordinatur.

Et si instes: Nam ideo solum excluditur a ratione signi Verbum Divinum, quia repraesentat perfectissime Divinam Essentiam; et similiter filius Petri licet sit eius imago, sed non signum, quia perfecte adaequat eius similitudinem; et Deus non est signum creaturarum, licet illas repraesentet, quia perfectissime repraesentat. Ergo est de ratione signi imperfecte repraesentare. *Respondetur* Verbum Divinum non esse signum Dei, non solum quia perfectissime repraesentat, sed quia est consubstantiale et aequale ipsi. Et sic non est notius nec substituens pro eo aut deserviens, multo minus respectu creaturarum, ad quas non ordinatur, sed creaturae ad ipsum, et ideo creaturae sunt signa Dei, quae nobis ipsum ut notiora nobis repraesentant. Non tamen est de ratione signi imperfectio cognitionis, quam generat, sed substitutio pro signato, quod repraesentat. Homo autem, qui est filius patris sui, non est eo notior, sed univoce aequalis, et ideo non induit rationem signi.

Ad confirmationem[29] respondetur, quod ratio formalis *sub qua*[30] non est signum quia non facit praesens obiectum potentiae, sed constituit obiectum ipsum in esse talis vel talis obiecti determinate et specifice; in ratione autem praesentis et coniuncti potentiae, id fit per signum formale vel instrumentale aut aliquo supplente vices obiecti.

Quod vero additur[31] signum formale non ponere in numero cum ipsa re signata, ut reddatur cognita, respondetur non ponere in numero quasi duae res cognitae et repraesentatae, verum est; quasi unum repraesentans et alterum repraesentatum, negatur;[32] et sic sufficit, ut sit signum et signatum, licet in esse intentionali seu repraesentativo dicatur facere unum cum obiecto, non solum sicut ea, quae conveniunt in una ratione communi, sed potius

[29] 231/30-44.

[30] Explained above in Book I, Question 4, 178/8-180/7.

[31] 231/35-38.

[32] See above, 228/1-18.

totally contains and represents the numerically same being that is in another. But this fact itself supposes that the representing and the represented are distinct, in such a way that one and the same thing never represents itself; for this identity cancels the rationale of a sign.

Finally, to that which is said[33] concerning the impressed specification or specifying form, namely, that it will be a sign just as is an expressed specifier, this will be treated in Question 3 below.[34] Suffice it to say for now that if the impressed specifier is to be removed from the rationale of sign, the reason is that it does not represent to cognition, but to a cognitive power in order that a cognition might be produced. But an expressed specifier represents both to the power *and* to the cognition, because it is a terminus of the cognition and it is also a form representing to the very cognition. But of this below.

Against the second conclusion it is argued on the grounds that this division of signs into formal and instrumental seems to be neither univocal nor adequate nor essential. Therefore.

The antecedent as regards the first part (that the division is not univocal) is proved by the fact that this division embraces instrumental signs in their entire extent, and so includes natural and stipulated instrumental signs, which do not coincide univocally in the rationale of sign, since the one is mind-independent, the other mind-dependent.

Similarly, the rationale of means is not found univocally in the case of a formal sign and in the case of an instrumental sign, but is found in the one with a priority of nature over the other, and dependently in the case of the exterior sign.[35] Whence St. Thomas says in the *Disputed Questions on Truth*, q. 4, art. 1, reply to obj. 7,[36] that signification is found by priority of nature in the interior rather than in the exterior word, therefore not univocally.

The second part of the antecedent (that the division into formal and instrumental signs is not adequate) is proved by the fact that there seem to be some signs which are neither formal nor instrumental, and also some which can be both at once. An example of the first: Certainly a phantasm is that in which the understanding knows a singular, and yet a phantasm is not a formal sign, since it does not inhere in nor inform the understanding; nor is it an instrumental sign, since it does not lead to a significate from a preexisting cognition, but immediately represents that significate; for the understanding does not

quia totaliter continet idem numero, quod est in alio, et repraesentat illud. Sed hoc ipsum supponit, quod distincta sint repraesentans et repraesentatum, ita ut numquam idem seipsum repraesentet; haec enim identitas evacuat rationem signi.

Denique ad id, quod dicitur[33] de specie impressa, quod erit signum sicut expressa, infra tractabitur, quaest.[34] 3. Sufficit nunc dicere, quod impressa, si removetur a ratione signi, ideo est, quia non repraesentat cognitioni, sed potentiae, ut producatur cognitio. Species autem expressa et potentiae et cognitioni repraesentat, quia terminus cognitionis est et forma repraesentans etiam cognitioni ipsi. Sed de hoc infra.

Contra secundam conclusionem arguitur, quia haec divisio neque videtur univoca neque adaequata neque essentialis. Ergo.

Antecedens quoad primam partem probatur, quia haec divisio comprehendit instrumentale signum in tota sua latitudine, et sic comprehendit instrumentale, naturale et ad placitum, quod univoce non convenit in ratione signi, cum unum sit reale, aliud rationis.

Similiter ratio medii non invenitur univoce in signo formali et instrumentali, sed per prius in uno quam in altero, et dependenter in signo exteriori.[35] Unde dicit D. Thomas 4. de Veritate art. 1. ad 7.,[36] quod significatio per prius invenitur in verbo interiori quam in exteriori, ergo non univoce.

Secunda pars probatur, quia videntur dari aliqua signa, quae non sunt formalia neque instrumentalia, aliqua etiam, quae simul utrumque esse possunt. Exemplum primi: Nam phantasma est id, in quo intellectus cognoscit singulare, et tamen neque est signum formale, cum non inhaereat nec informet intellectum; nec est instrumentale, cum non ex praeexistente cognitione ducat in signatum, sed immediate repraesentet illud; nec enim intellectus indiget ad

[33] 231/40-44.
[34] In the original Latin: "art."
[35] The 1663 Lyons text here adds: "*a signo formali interiori*"—"upon the interior formal sign."
[36] *Pa* IX. 65 a.

need first to know the phantasm as a thing known, in order to have a knowledge of singulars. Similarly, a phantasm of smoke in respect of the understanding is not a formal sign of fire, because it does not inform the understanding; nor is it an instrumental sign, because it is not an effect of the fire itself, as is the mind-independent smoke. Likewise, a preliminary or "nonultimate" concept is a formal sign in respect of a spoken word, and an instrumental sign in respect of the thing signified through the spoken word; and the concept of a man or of a pure spirit is a formal sign for the thinker, yet it is an instrumental sign for the one to whom it is vocally expressed. Therefore the same thing can be an instrumental and a formal sign.

Finally, the third part of the antecedent (that the division of signs into formal and instrumental is not essential) is proved by the fact that the division into instrumental and formal signs is drawn in terms of the order to a power; since indeed a formal sign is one that inheres in a cognitive power, and an instrumental sign is that which is known. But an order to a cognitive power does not pertain to the constitution of a sign directly, but indirectly, as we said in Book I [esp. Question 3]. Therefore it is not an essential division primarily and of itself.

And the antecedent is confirmed by the fact that the same thing cannot be divided by two essential divisions not subalternately posited. But the division of sign into natural and stipulated is an essential division, as will be said below,[37] and is not subordinated to the division into instrumental and formal signs, because the natural sign is also superior to the formal and the instrumental sign, and again the instrumental sign divides into the natural and the stipulated. Therefore these divisions are not essential.

To the first part of the argument (that the division is not univocal)[38] two things can be said:[39] First, that in the division of signs into formal and instrumental, signs are not divided in their entire extent, but only natural signs, because only natural signs are included in both members. And although a stipulated sign too is instrumental, yet it is not an instrumental sign according as instrumental sign is a member opposed to formal sign; for the formal sign is counterposed in this division only to a natural instrumental sign. But a stipulated sign is a sign extrinsically, as it were, and not of itself. But in every division that which is capable

cognitionem singularium prius cognoscere phantasma tamquam rem cognitam. Similiter phantasma fumi respectu intellectus non est formale signum ignis, cum non informet intellectum; nec instrumentale, cum non sit effectus ipsius ignis, sicut fumus a parte rei. Item conceptus non ultimatus est signum formale respectu vocis, et instrumentale respectu rei significatae per vocem; et conceptus hominis vel angeli in ordine ad se est signum formale, et in ordine ad illum, cui loquitur, est instrumentale. Ergo idem potest esse signum instrumentale et formale.

Tertia denique pars, quod non sit essentialis divisio, probatur, quia divisio instrumentalis et formalis sumitur per ordinem ad potentiam; siquidem formale signum est, quod inhaeret potentiae, instrumentale, quod cognoscitur. Ordo autem ad potentiam non pertinet ad constitutionem signi directe, sed in obliquo, ut diximus quaest. praec. Ergo non est divisio essentialis primo et per se.

Et confirmatur, quia non potest idem dividi duplici divisione essentiali non subalternatim posita. Sed divisio signi in naturale et ad placitum est essentialis, ut infra[37] dicetur, et non subordinatur isti divisioni in formale et instrumentale, cum signum naturale etiam sit superius ad formale et instrumentale, et rursus instrumentale in naturale et ad placitum. Ergo istae divisiones non sunt essentiales.

Ad primam partem argumenti[38] dupliciter DICI POTEST.[39] *Primo,* quod in hac divisione non dividitur signum in tota sua latitudine, sed solum signum naturale, eo quod solum signum naturale est capax utriusque membri. Et licet signum ad placitum sit etiam instrumentale, non tamen est instrumentale, secundum quod est membrum oppositum formali; non enim formale contraponitur in hac divisione nisi instrumentali naturali. Signum autem ad placitum est signum quasi ab extrinseco et non per se. In omni autem divisione

[37] Question 5 ("art. 5." in Reiser).
[38] 234/22-36.
[39] Cf. Question 5 below, 269/8-14.

of being included in each of the dividing members must always be accepted as that which is divided. For example, when intellective habit is divided into wisdom and science, the division is univocal; yet the term "wisdom" must not be taken in its full extent, as it includes also uncreated wisdom, for so understood it does not divide habit. And similarly relation is divided univocally into relations of paternity and of similarity; yet paternity must not be understood in its entire extent as including also the divine paternity. So signs are divided into instrumental and formal signs univocally, not in their entire extent on the side of the instrumental sign, but as restricted to the natural sign.

Secondly we answer[40] that the division can be univocal even taking the instrumental sign in its entire extent, as it also includes the stipulated sign, because even though that which is mind-independent and that which is mind-dependent do not coincide univocally in rationale of being, nevertheless in the order and formality of sign they can coincide univocally, inasmuch as a sign pertains to the knowable and objective order. And indeed it can well be the case that a mind-independent and a mind-dependent object coincide univocally in the rationale of object and knowable thing, when they pertain to the same specific power or to sciences univocally agreeing, as, for example, to Logic, which treats of being as it exists dependently upon our objective apprehensions (mind-dependent being), and to Metaphysics, which treats of being as it exists independently of our objective apprehensions (mind-independent being), even though in the rationale of being these objects are analogized. Thus the stipulated and the natural sign, even though they express relations analogically coincident *in rationale of being*, nevertheless, *in the rationale of sign* as pertaining to the order of the knowable, they coincide univocally as means representative of an object. And so when the division of signs is understood precisely in the order and line of the knowable, it can be univocally extended to stipulated signs, but not when the division of signs is understood in the order of mind-independent being or relation.

Through this is explained how formal and instrumental signs coincide univocally in the rationale of a representative medium, inasmuch as both truly and properly serve for representing.[41] But the dependence

semper debet accipi divisum id, quod est capax utriusque membri dividentis. Sicut v. g. quando habitus intellectivus dividitur in sapientiam et scientiam, divisio est univoca; non tamen ly sapientia debet intelligi in tota sua latitudine, ut comprehendit etiam sapientiam increatam, sic enim non dividit habitum. Et similiter relatio dividitur univoce in relationem paternitatis et similitudinis; non tamen debet intelligi paternitas in tota sua latitudine, ut includit etiam divinam. Sic dividitur signum in instrumentale et formale univoce, non pro instrumentali in tota latitudine, sed ut restringitur ad signum naturale.

Secundo[40] respondetur, quod etiam potest esse divisio univoca sumendo signum instrumentale in tota sua latitudine, ut etiam comprehendit signum ad placitum, quia licet in ratione entis non conveniant univoce id, quod est reale et rationis, tamen in ordine et formalitate signi univoce convenire possunt, quatenus signum pertinet ad ordinem cognoscibilem et obiectivum. Bene autem stat, quod in ratione obiecti et cognoscibilis univoce conveniant obiectum reale et rationis, quando pertinent ad eandem specificam potentiam vel ad scientias univoce convenientes, v. g. ad Logicam, quae agit de ente rationis, et Metaphysicam, quae agit de ente reali, licet in ratione entis ista obiecta analogentur. Ita signum ad placitum et naturale, licet dicant relationes analogice convenientes in ratione entis, in ratione tamen signi ut ad genus cognoscibilis pertinentis, ut medium repraesentativum obiecti univoce conveniunt. Et sic intellecta divisione de signo praecise in genere et linea cognoscibilis, potest univoce extendi ad signa ad placitum, non de signo in esse rei seu relationis.

Et per hoc explicatur, quomodo conveniant signum formale et instrumentale univoce in ratione medii repraesentativi, quatenus utrumque vere et proprie deservit ad repraesentandum.[41] Dependentia autem,

[40] to 234/21-36.

[41] This is directly contrary to the common doctrine accepted from Suarez, as indicated above in note 1 to the "Order of the Preamble" on "Mind-Dependent Being." See also the discussions in Book I, Question 2, 149/41-151/21, Question 4, note 13 and 187/28-190/23, above; and below, Question 5, 270/37-271/21.

that is in an instrumental sign in respect of a formal sign, and in a spoken word in respect of a concept,[42] is a physical dependence, not a logical one, that is, it is a dependence in order that one kind of being might be posited physically in exercise, or that some operation of one kind of being can depend on another,[43] somewhat as, for example, a surface depends on a line, a ternary on a binary, a compound on an element, etc. Nevertheless, the dependence is not a logical dependence, that is, it is not a dependence in participating a general rationale, as an accident depends on a substance in the very rationale of being. This last dependency creates analogy, not the first one. This doctrine is common and is expressly propounded by St. Thomas in his *Commentary* on the first book of Aristotle's treatise *On Interpretation*, reading 8, nos. 5-6.[44]

To the second part of the argument (that the division of sign into formal and instrumental is not an adequate division)[45] the response is that the first example is not to the point, because a phantasm of singulars does not serve intellectual knowledge as a sign, but as that from which the agency of the understanding takes specification. And for this reason a universal represents [its object] with some connotation respecting singulars, by reason of which state and connotation the understanding reflecting attains the very singulars, not through the phantasm as through a sign, but through a specifying form abstracted as originated from the phantasm and therefore connoting the singular as a quitted terminus-from-which, not directly representing it, as is explained more at length in q. 1 of my *Physics* and in the books *Concerning the Soul*, q. 10.[46] If, nevertheless, the understanding were to respect the phantasm as a knowable thing and attain the singular by means of it, the understanding would be using the phantasm as a known object manifesting another and consequently as an instrumental sign. But this will be through a reflex cognition upon the entity of the phantasm.

The other examples adduced in the argument[47] are similarly explained, as the one concerning the phantasm of smoke in respect of fire, a preliminary concept in relation to the thing signified, etc. For these examples prove that the same thing can be a formal sign and an instrumental sign in respect of different objects and different modes of representing, not in respect

quae est in signo instrumentali respectu formalis et in voce respectu conceptus,[42] est dependentia physica, non logica, id est ut physice ponatur in exercitio una species, vel aliqua eius operatio potest dependere ab alia,[43] sicut dependet superficies a linea, sicut ternarius a binario, mixtum ab elemento etc. Non tamen est dependentia logica, id est in participando rationem communem, sicut dependet accidens a substantia in ipsa ratione entis; et haec dependentia facit analogiam, non prima. Doctrina haec est communis et traditur expresse a D. Thoma 1. Periherm. lect. 8.[44]

Ad secundam partem argumenti[45] respondetur primum exemplum non esse ad propositum, quia phantasma singularium non deservit ad cognitionem intellectus tamquam signum, sed tamquam id, a quo intellectus agens accipit species. Et ideo repraesentat universale cum aliqua connotatione ad singularia, ratione cuius habitudinis et connotationis reflectens intellectus ipsa singularia attingit, non per phantasma tamquam per signum, sed per speciem abstractam ut originatam a phantasmate et ideo connotantem singulare ut terminum a quo relictum, non directe ipsum repraesentantem, ut latius in 1. quaest. Phys. et in libris de Anima q. 10.[46] dicetur. Si tamen intellectus respiciat phantasma ut rem cognoscibilem et mediante ipso attingat singulare, utetur phantasmate ut obiecto cognito manifestante aliud et consequenter ut signo instrumentali. Sed hoc erit per cognitionem reflexam super entitatem phantasmatis.

Et similiter dicitur ad alia exempla adducta in argumento,[47] ut de phantasmate fumi respectu ignis, conceptus non ultimati ad rem significatam etc. Haec enim probant, quod idem potest esse signum formale et instrumentale respectu diversorum et diversi modi repraesentandi, non re-

[42] 234/29-36.
[43] This same point is expanded by Poinsot in Question 5 below, 271/22-42.
[44] *Le* I. 36. n. 5., 6. See also Question 5 below, 271/22-42.
[45] 234/38-235/14.
[46] Art. 4; correcting the reference in the original Latin to "q. 9."
[47] 234/42-235/14.

of the same [object and mode of representing]; as, for example, the phantasm of smoke is a formal sign in respect of the imagination, and through that representation the imagination formally knows smoke immediately and fire mediately, as contained in the represented smoke, but the external smoke, as known, is an instrumental sign. But if the understanding should reflect upon the phantasm of the smoke as upon a thing known, it would understand in the phantasm as in an instrumental sign the external smoke and the fire which the phantasm signifies. A nonultimate concept likewise represents a significative voice [a spoken word], but it will represent the thing signified and contained in the voice mediately, but formally as two things ordinately represented in the same concept. But in respect of the cognition whereby a nonultimate concept is reflexively known, the preliminary concept will represent both the word or voice and the significate of the word instrumentally, if indeed a concept of a word [a nonultimate concept of a linguistic expression] attains the thing signified by the word in any way, which is not so certain, as we will see below.[48] Finally, in the telephathic communication between spirits, the "speaker's" concept represents formally to the speaker; but to the "listener," who perceives the concept as a thing known and in it a thing represented, it represents instrumentally; but this is in respect of diverse [objects and modes of representing].

To the third contention of the argument (that the division of sign into formal and instrumental is not an essential division)[49] the response is that even though an order to a cognitive power is in a sign consequent upon the order to the thing signified, inasmuch as the sign represents that thing as significate to the power, nevertheless, diverse modes of bringing a thing signified to a cognitive power redound into a formal diversity of the thing signified as it is signified, inasmuch as they respect diverse modes of representability in the thing signified, as they represent that thing to a cognitive power by diverse modes. But a division according to intrinsic modes redounds to or supposes an essential diversity of the things upon which the modes are founded, just as a diversity according to obscurity and clarity diversifies revelations and lights, even though in faith obscurity is an intrinsic mode, not the formal rationale.[50]

To the confirmation[51] the response is that, as we have shown in the *Summulae* books, q. 5, art. 4, reply

spectu eiusdem; sicut phantasma fumi est signum formale respectu phantasiae, et per illam repraesentationem formaliter cognoscit fumum immediate et ignem mediate, ut contentum in fumo repraesentato, fumus autem externus, ut cognitus, est signum instrumentale. Si vero intellectus reflectat supra phantasma fumi tamquam super rem cognitam, intelliget in phantasmate tamquam in signo instrumentali fumum externum et ignem, quem significat. Conceptus etiam non ultimatus repraesentat vocem significativam, rem autem significatam et in voce contentam mediate repraesentabit, sed formaliter sicut duo ordinate repraesentata in eodem conceptu. Respectu autem cognitionis, qua reflexe cognoscitur conceptus non ultimatus, instrumentaliter repraesentabit et vocem et significatum vocis, si tamen conceptus vocis aliquo modo rem significatam attingit, quod non est ita certum, de quo infra.[48] Denique conceptus loquentis angeli formaliter ipsi loquenti repraesentat, audienti autem, qui percipit conceptum ut rem cognitam et in ea rem repraesentatam, instrumentaliter; sed hoc est respectu diversorum.

Ad tertiam partem argumenti[49] respondetur, quod licet ordo ad potentiam sit in signo consequens ordinem ad signatum, quatenus repraesentat illud ut significatum potentiae, tamen diversus modus deducendi signatum ad potentiam redundat in diversitatem formalem signati, ut signatum est, quatenus diversum modum repraesentabilitatis in signato respicit, ut diverso modo illud potentiae repraesentet. Divisio autem penes modos intrinsecos refunditur vel supponit diversitatem essentialem rerum, super quas fundantur, sicut diversitas penes obscuritatem et claritatem diversificat revelationes et lumina, licet in fide obscuritas sit modus intrinsecus, non formalis ratio.[50]

Ad confirmationem[51] respondetur, quod, ut ostendimus in Summulis q.

[48] Book III, Question 4 (correcting Reiser's reference to "art. 6.").
[49] 235/15-25.
[50] See above, Book I, Question 2, 145/8-27, Question 3, 163/12-36.
[51] 235/26-35.

to the second counterargument,[52] where we have proved the point with various examples, nothing prevents the same thing from being divided by several essential divisions, not subalternately, but immediately, as long as each of those divisions is made according to some essential formality inadequately taken, not according to the whole adequately considered. See the examples in the *Summulae*.

5. art. 4. ad 2. arg.,[52] non est inconveniens, quod idem dividatur pluribus essentialibus divisionibus non subalternatim, sed immediate, quando quaelibet illarum fit penes aliquam formalitatem essentialem inadaequate sumptam, non penes totum adaequate consideratum, ubi id ex variis exemplis probavimus. Videatur ibi.

[52] Logica 1. p. q. 5. art. 4. ad 2. arg., Reiser ed. 164a41-165a45.

Question 2

Whether a Concept Is A Formal Sign

Quaestio Secunda

Utrum Conceptus Sit Signum Formale

The question holds as much for a concept of the understanding, which is called an expressed specifier and word, as for an expressed specifier of perception[1] or imagination,[2] which is called an icon or

Procedit quaestio tam de conceptu intellectus, qui vocatur species expressa et verbum, quam de specie expressa phantasiae[1] seu imaginativae,[2] quae dicitur ido-

[1] "... *phantasia (id est cognitio internorum sensuum)* ..." (Phil. nat. 4. p. q. 6. art. 3., Reiser ed., III. 187b32-33)—"... *phantasia* (i.e., the cognition of the internal senses) ...": see the discussion in the following note.

[2] "*phantasia* seu *imaginatio*": *Phantasia* has two distinct uses in scholastic Latin, a broad usage that covers roughly what we express in English by "perception" as contrasted with "sensation," and a narrow usage that is synonymous with imagination as one among several internal senses, i.e., as a name for a distinct cognitive capacity. Since Poinsot is dealing in this Question with the products of all the internal senses, not just of the imagination, as the "second conclusion" below (247/22-24) explicitly tells us, it is clear than *phantasia* should be translated here in the broad sense contrasted with imagination, and not in the narrow sense synonymous with imagination. In other words, *seu* here is employed in the classical disjunctive sense rather than in the conjunctive sense that Poinsot frequently uses (see Book I, Question 1, note 6, above). "Perception" is not the perfect vehicle for this meaning, since the *species expressae phantasiae* would cover the cases of dreams, hallucinations, etc.; but if the reader well understands the point of the contrast here, no difficulties should result from our rendering. In Poinsot's own words (Phil. nat. 4. p. q. 8. art. 2., "*Quid sint phantasia et reliquae potentiae interiores, et in quibus subiectis sint*"—"What is the 'phantasia,' and the other powers of internal sense, and what organisms possess these powers"): "*Phantasia sumitur dupliciter, uno modo communiter pro omni potentia interiori formante obiecta sua et faciente apparere, ad distinctionem sensus communis et sensuum exteriorum, qui non faciunt apparere sua obiecta, sed solum cognoscunt illa, a quibus immutantur. Et sic omnis potentia interior praeter sensum communem habet commune nomen phantasiae, quae ut tradit D. Thomas lect. 6. cit.* [Pa XX. 114 a.] *derivatur a nomine 'phos', quod graece significat idem quod lux, et inde derivatur 'phanos', quod est illuminatio seu apparitio, et 'phantasia', quae est sensus cognoscens et formatus secundum apparitiones, quia necessario supponit obiecta apparuisse in sensu, et exinde formatur alia apparitio. Alio modo sumitur phantasia specialiter pro potentia imaginativa ut distincta ab aestimativa et memoria et appellatur nomine illo generico propter penuriam vocabulorum, praesertim quia ad imaginativam maxime pertinet ipsa apparitio et formatio imaginum, ad aestimativam autem spectat alius actus principalior, qui est intentiones cognoscere et aestimationem facere de rebus secundum convenientiam vel disconvenientiam earum in ordine ad se. ... Itaque phantasiari et sentire distinguuntur*

phantasm.[3] How does the definition of a formal sign, which is a formal awareness and which of it-

lum vel phantasma,[3] quomodo illis conveniat definitio signi formalis, quod sit for-

tamquam duo genera cognoscendi, et definitur unum, ut condistinguitur ab altero. Et sicut sentire in communi dici debet, quod est motus factus a sensibili secundum se, ita phantasiari in communi definitur, quod est motus factus non a sensibili, sed a sensu, id est ab obiecto iam cognito'' (Reiser ed., III. 252b20-253a41).—''*Phantasia* is used in two senses. *In one way* generally for every interior power forming its own objects and making them appear, in contrast with the synthetic or common sense [which coordinates and wholly depends upon the external senses] and the external senses, which likewise do not cause their objects to appear, but cognize only those aspects of things by which they are here and now affected. And so every interior power beyond the common sense has the general or common name of *phantasia*, which, as St. Thomas explains in his *Commentary* on Aristotle's treatise *On the Soul*, Book III, reading 6, is derived from the Greek noun *phos*, which signifies what our word 'light' signifies, and thence is derived *phanos*, which is an illumination or manifestation, and *phantasia*, which is sense knowing and formed according to appearances, because it supposes necessarily objects that have already appeared in sense, and another appearance formed therefrom afterward. *In another way phantasia* is used specifically to designate the power of imagination as distinct from the estimative or evaluative power and the memory, and imagination is called by that generic name on account of the poverty of language, particularly in view of the fact that this manifestation and formation of images pertains especially to the imagination, whereas another act more principally pertains to the estimative power, namely, the activity of cognizing unsensed aspects of things and evaluating them according to their utility or harm to the perceiver. . . . Therefore *phantasiari* [to perceive?] and to sense are distinguished as two types or kinds of knowing, and the one is defined in contrast with the other. And just as that stimulation [of a cognitive power] which is produced by a sensible object according to its own being must be called in general 'sensation,' so that movement [of a cognitive power] which is produced not by the sensible, but by the sense, that is to say, by an object already cognized, is defined in general as *phantasiari* [''perception,'' roughly].'' Further in note 3 following.

For a more thorough discussion of the problematic indicated here, see my ''Animal Intelligence and Concept-Formation,'' *The Thomist*, XXXV (January, 1971), esp. pp. 55-83; and ''Antecedents to Peirce's Notion of Iconic Signs,'' in *Semiotics 1980*, compilation by Michael Herzfeld and Margot D. Lenhart (New York: Plenum, 1982), pp. 109-119.

[3] ''*idolum vel phantasma*'': Corresponding to the broad and the narrow use of *phantasia* as a name, respectively, for all the higher powers of internal sense (that is, those powers able to cognize physically absent or nonexistent objects) or for the one specific power of imagination, as discussed in note 2 above, there is a broad and a narrow use of the term *phantasma* to name the *products*, respectively, of the cognitive activities of all the higher powers of internal sense or of the imagination alone. In the present context again it is the broad usage that is principally at issue.

Synonymous with *phantasma* in this broad sense as the cognitive product of perceptual activity is the term *idolum*, which means a mental image or (roughly) ''percept.'' Although the Oxford English Dictionary does list ''idol'' as an English term meaning ''image,'' the thrust of the term ''idol'' in English is toward an *external* image, and, where it names an internal image, as Poinsot's context strictly requires, it tends to have the sense of a ''false or misleading'' mental image or notion (as in Bacon's early ''idols of the mind''), thus lacking the neutrality toward reality required by Poinsot's formal sign as founding an ontological relation. The same remarks apply to the Oxford Dictionary's listing of ''idolum'' as an English word in use from at least the early 1600s to the late 1800s. The closest English word to Poinsot's use of *idolum* is the term ''icon'' as defined semiotically by C. S. Peirce, c. 1903 (*Collected Papers*, 4.447): ''An icon is a representamen of what it represents and for the mind that interprets it as such, by virtue of its being an immediate image, that is to say by virtue of characters which belong to it in itself as a sensible object, and which it would possess just the same were there no object in nature that it resembled, and though it never were interpreted as a sign. It is of the nature of an appearance, and as such, strictly speaking, exists only in consciousness, although for convenience in ordinary parlance and when extreme precision is not called for, we extend the term icon to the outward objects which excite in consciousness the image itself. . . . A pure icon can convey no positive or factual information; for it affords no assurance that there is any such thing in nature. But it is of the utmost value for enabling its interpreter to study what would be the character of such an object in case any such did exist.'' Cf. Book I, Question 5, note 21 above. Further to iconicity in Peirce and Poinsot, see Ransdell, 1979; Deely, 1980b, 1982, 1985.

self and immediately represents something, apply to these?[4]

But that the uninstructed may grasp a true outline at least of what is a concept, word, expressed specifier, or terminus of understanding (which are all the same), and why it is posited, it is necessary to advert to the fact that, for reasons which we will discuss more at length in the books *Concerning the Soul*,[5] qq. 6, 8, and 11,[6] this terminus of knowledge which is posited within the knowing power is posited for two reasons: either on account of a necessity on the side of the object, or on account of the fecundity on the side of the power.

On account of fecundity indeed because it is from the abundance of the heart[7] that the mouth speaks, and so a concept is called a word, inasmuch as it is expressed and formed by the power for manifesting those things which are known. For the understanding naturally seeks and breaks out in manifestation; and such an expressive manifestation is called an expression or interior discourse, and the word itself is a form of specification or some likeness expressed and spoken.

malis notitia, et quod seipso et immediate aliquid repraesentet.[4]

Ut autem rudi saltem minerva intelligi possit, quid sit conceptus, verbum, species expressa seu terminus intellectionis (quae omnia idem sunt), et propter quid ponatur, advertendum est ex his, quae latius disputabimus in libris de Anima[5] q. 6. 8. et 11.,[6] quod terminus iste cognitionis, qui ponitur intra potentiam cognoscentem, ob duplicem causam ponitur: Vel propter necessitatem ex parte obiecti vel propter fecunditatem ex parte potentiae.

Propter fecunditatem quidem, quia ex abundantia cordis[7] os loquitur, et sic verbum dicitur conceptus, quatenus exprimitur et formatur a potentia ad manifestandum ea, quae cognoscuntur. Naturaliter enim intellectus manifestationem quaerit et in eam prorumpit; et talis manifestatio expressiva vocatur dictio seu locutio interior, et ipsum verbum est species seu similitudo aliqua expressa et dicta.

[4] Thus the notion of the ''expressed form of specification,'' usually called a ''concept'' with reference to understanding and an ''icon,'' ''image,'' or ''phantasm'' with reference to sense perception, is used by Poinsot in a generic way that parallels Locke's use of ''idea'' to cover the products of all of our cognitive powers. But whereas Locke goes on to identify our ideas with the *objects as such* of our awareness (cf. *An Essay concerning Human Understanding* [1690], Introduction, par. 9), Poinsot is careful to show that concepts are only that *on the basis of which* we are related to objects of cognition, and thus avoids the ''idealism'' of both the British empiricists and the Continental rationalists, as of their successors down to contemporary times: see my ''Semiotic and the Controversy over Mental Events,'' ACPA *Proceedings*, LII (1978). Note too that insofar as *species expressa* provides the root notion common to the concept and the icon, one would in semiotic context be justified in extending either specific term to a generic usage, thus speaking of all cognitive products indifferently as ''icons,'' ''concepts,'' or ''ideas,'' i.e., *species expressae*. It is thus generically, for example, that Peirce extends the notion of icon when he says (elided portion of citation in note 3 above): ''A geometrical diagram is a good example of an icon.''

[5] Phil. nat. 4. p.

[6] In the original Latin: ''6. 7. et 10.,'' which would seem to be an error. The reference—namely, what an actively formed terminus of cognition is and under what conditions such an objective terminus must be formed by the cognizing organism—fits q. 6, ''*De obiectis sensuum externorum in communi*'' (''Concerning the objects of the external senses in general''), wherein it is shown, particularly in art. 1. (''*Utrum requiratur necessario, quod obiectum exterius sit praesens, ut sentiri potest*''—''Whether it is necessary that an external object be physically present in order to be sensed'') and art. 4 (''*Utrum sensus externi forment idolum seu speciem expressam, ut cognoscant*''—''Whether the external senses form an icon or expressed specifier in order to cognize'') that there is no actively formed objective terminus at the level of sensation, for want of the conditions requisite for such formation. The reference, however, does not fit q. 7, ''*De obiectis sensuum exteriorum in particulari*'' (''Concerning the objects of each of the external senses in particular''), though it does fit q. 8, ''*De sensibus internis*'' (''On the internal senses''), particularly art. 4, ''*Quae sint species impressae et expressae in sensibus internis*'' (''What are the impressed and expressed forms specifying internal sense''). Finally, the reference does not fit q. 10, though it does fit q. 11, as we have already discussed in this Book, Question 1, note 5, p. 225 above.

[7] ''*abundantia cordis*,'' that is to say, fulfilment of subjectivity: cf. Phil. nat. 4. p. q. II. art. 1. 349a11-28, art. 2. 356a29-357b27.

On account of necessity for an object, on the other hand, the concept is posited so that an object would be rendered united to the power in the rationale of a known terminus and be present to the power. But as St. Thomas teaches in the *Summa contra gentiles*, Book I, chap. 53, there is also a twofold necessity for positing this terminus or object within the knowing power. In the first place, because the object is absent and the knowledge cannot be terminated at it, unless it be rendered present in the rationale of the terminus; and so it is necessary that some similitude or specifier be formed, in which the object is rendered present or represented. For just as it was necessary to posit an impressed specification or form in order for the object to be present and united to a cognitive power in the rationale of a principle concurring in the forming of the power's cognition, so must another similitude or specifier be posited in order for the object to be present in the rationale of the terminus toward which knowledge tends, if the thing objectified is absent. In the second place, it is necessary to posit the concept within the power in order for the things known or objects to be rendered proportioned and conformed to the power itself.[8] For just as

Propter necessitatem autem obiecti ponitur, ut obiectum reddatur unitum potentiae in ratione termini cogniti et ei praesens sit. Ut autem docet S. Thomas 1. Contra Gent. cap. 53., duplex etiam necessitas est ponendi hunc terminum seu obiectum intra potentiam cognoscentem. Vel quia obiectum est absens et non potest terminari cognitio ad ipsum, nisi in ratione termini reddatur praesens; et sic oportet formari aliquam similitudinem seu speciem, in qua praesens seu repraesentatum reddatur. Sicut enim, ut obiectum esset praesens et unitum potentiae in ratione principii concurrentis ad formandam cognitionem, oportuit ponere speciem impressam, ita ut praesens sit in ratione termini, ad quem tendit cognitio, oportet aliam similitudinem seu speciem ponere, si res sit absens. Vel secundo oportet ponere conceptum intra potentiam, ut res cognita seu obiecta reddatur proportionata et conformis ipsi potentiae.[8] Sicut enim obiectum non po-

[8] This second of the reasons why concepts (in the generic sense) are necessary to cognition is by far the more important one from a semiotic point of view, for it applies to *all cases of awareness that exceed bare sensation*, as Poinsot points out (Phil. nat. 4. p. q. 8. art. 4., Reiser ed., III. 265b9-32): ''*Supponimus dari species in sensibus internis, sicut datur cognitio. Quodsi illae potentiae internae sunt altiores in cognoscendo, etiam requirunt altiores species vel saltem altiori modo ordinatas, ut cognitio elevatior elici possit. Specialiter autem quando obiecta repraesentata sunt altioris abstractionis, ut intentiones insensatae, requirere videntur aliquas species perfectiores et elevatiores repraesentantes tales intentiones, sicut odium, inimicitiam, filios, parentes etc. Istae enim formalitates non repraesentantur in sensibus externis, et tamen cognoscuntur ab internis, ergo datur aliquod principium repraesentativum illarum, quod non debet esse ita materiale et imperfectum, quod sistat in ipsis rebus sensatis, sicut sistunt sensus externi; ergo perfectior species debet esse quam species sensus externi, quae solum repraesentat res sensatas.*''—''We suppose that there are specifying forms at work in the internal sense, just as there is cognition there. For if those internal powers are higher in the knowing process [than are the external senses], they also require higher forms of specification, or at least ones ordered in a higher way, in order to bring forth a higher level of awareness. But specifiers of a more perfect and elevated type are seen to be necessary particularly when the objects represented are of a more abstract character [i.e., more removed from the here-and-now immediacy of sensation], as is the case with such perceptible but unsensed characteristics as hatred, hostility, offspring, parents, and so forth. For these formalities are not represented in the external senses, and yet they are known by the internal senses; therefore there exists some principle representative of them, which must not be so material and imperfect as to obtain at the level of the sensed objects as such, at which level the cognitions of external sense are constrained. Therefore it must be a form of specification more perfect than a specification of external sense, which represents only sensed [as contrasted to perceived] things.''

It is here, then, that semiotic accounts for the ''perspectival'' character of all the higher forms of knowledge and apprehension, as for selective perception and ''bias'': ''*Et generaliter est necessaria pro omni cognitione, sive in praesentia sive in absentia rei, eo quod obiectum mediante illa debet concurrere cum potentia ad eliciendam cognitionem. Exigitur tamen, quod etiam obiectum terminet talem cognitionem secundum esse proportionatum ad terminandum illam*'' (Phil. nat. 4. p. q. 8. art. 4, Reiser ed., III. 267b8-17).—''A specifying form is necessary in a general way for all awareness, *whether in the presence or in the absence of a physical thing*, by the fact that the object must concur by means of that form with the power in order to elicit cognition. Yet it is further necessary that the object should terminate the awareness in question *according to a being proportioned to the terminating*'' (see above Book I, Question 4, note 6; and below, note 17). ''. . . *non solum requiri verbum propter absentiam*

an object cannot serve as a terminus for external vision except when it is bathed in visible light, so neither can an object be attained by the understanding unless it is divested of sensibility and is affected and formed by a spiritual light, which is immateriality or abstraction.[9] But an immaterial light is not found outside the intellective power; therefore it must needs be that within the power the object is illuminated and formed by that spirituality as the condition for its being attained; and what has been formed [within the power] in the being of the object is the word or concept, which is not itself the cognition (as we have said above from St. Thomas and as will be said in Question[10] 4 below), because it keeps to the side of the object or terminus known, and its office is not to render formally knowing in the precise way that knowledge is a tendency toward an object, but to render the object present in the mode of a known terminus. Nor does the concept antecede the cognition, as does an impressed form of cognitive specification, because it is formed through the cognition, nor is it given as a principle of cognition, but as a terminus. Nor does this make it necessary that such a word or specifying form be cognized as an object, in the way an exterior image is known, in order for the thing represented in it to be attained, because, since it represents within the understanding and as the form informing the understanding, it does not represent objectively and as something first known, but formally and as the rationale of the process of knowing, as we will explain more at length in the books *Concerning the Soul,*[11] q. 11. Concerning these several points, consult the passage from St. Thomas in the *Summa contra gentiles* referred to above (Book I, chap. 53), also Book IV, chap.

test terminare visionem externam, nisi luce visibili perfundatur, ita nec obiectum potest ab intellectu attingi, nisi a sensibilitate sit denudatum et luce spirituali, quae est immaterialitas seu abstractio[9] affectum et formatum. Immaterialis autem lux non invenitur extra potentiam intellectivam; ergo oportet, quod intra ipsam illuminetur obiectum et formetur illa spiritualitate, ut attingatur; et hoc formatum in esse obiecti est verbum seu conceptus, quod non est ipsa cognitio, ut supra ex D. Thoma diximus et infra quaest.[10] 4. dicetur, quia tenet se ex parte obiecti seu termini cogniti, eiusque officium non est reddere formaliter cognoscentem, ut cognitio est tendentia ad obiectum, sed reddere obiectum praesens per modum termini cogniti. Nec antecedit cognitionem sicut species impressa, quia formatur per cognitionem, nec datur ut principium cognitionis, sed ut terminus. Nec propterea oportet, quod tale verbum seu species cognoscatur ut quod, sicut cognoscitur imago exterior, ut in ea res repraesentata attingatur, quia cum repraesentet intra intellectum et ut forma informans illum, non repraesentat obiective et prius cognitum, sed formaliter et ut ratio cognoscendi, ut latius dicemus in libris de Anima[11] q. 11. De quo plura vide apud D. Thomam loco cit. et 4. Con-

---

physicam obiecti, haec enim non semper invenitur, sed etiam ut obiectum in ratione termini cognitionis reddatur immateriale et intentionale in actu ultimo, ut D. Thomas affirmat 1. Contra Gent. cit. cap. 53. Et ad hoc non sufficit praesentia, quam habet obiectum in specie impressa. . . . Et ita species impressa existit in intellectu, etiam ipso non intelligente per illam; species autem expressa cessante intellectione cessat, quia repraesentat rem ut intellectam in actu'' (Phil. nat. 4. p. q. 11. art. 2., Reiser ed., III. 362a38-47 and 362b21-26).—''A concept is required not only on account of the physical absence of an object, for it is not always the case that a given object is thus absent, but also that the object in the rationale of terminus of the cognition be rendered immaterial and intentional in final act, as St. Thomas affirms in Book I of his *Summa contra gentiles*, chap. 53. And for this the presence that the object has in an impressed form of specification is not sufficient. . . . And so the impressed specifier exists in the understanding even when the individual is not understanding through that form; but an expressed specifier ceases when the activity of understanding ceases, because it represents a thing as actually understood.'' See also Book I, Question 4, note 13.

[9] Here Poinsot uses ''abstraction'' in a common metaphysical sense for an operation performed by the understanding; but in Book III, Questions 1 and 2, he will reduce this classical metaphysical discussion to its experimental ground, where the primary meaning of ''abstraction'' becomes the awareness of an object not physically given as such in the awareness, i.e., removal from the ''here and now'' of external sensation.

[10] In the original Latin: ''art.''

[11] phil. nat. 4. p.

11 of that work, and St. Thomas's *Treatise on the Difference between the Divine and Human Word,*[12] and *Treatise on the Nature of the Word of the Understanding,*[13] together with the many other places where he treats of the mental word.

But if you should ask, through which act does this expression or concept come about, we would say briefly (for this matter looks to the books *Concerning the Soul*) that it comes about in the understanding through the act which substantially is a cognition, but has something more, namely, that it is a fecund cognition, that is, manifestative and speaking or expressive. For the understanding does not know for itself alone, but gives rise also to an impulse for manifesting; and that bursting forth toward something to be manifested is a kind of expression and conception and, indeed, a giving birth by the understanding.

But in sensitive powers, St. Thomas seems to concede that there are two ways of producing these expressed specifying forms, which in these powers are called an idol. First, because the sensitive powers form or produce specifiers actively, as says the *Summa theologica*, I, q. 12, art. 9, reply to obj. 2: "the imagination forms a representation of a golden mountain from previously received specifiers of a mountain and of gold." Second, because the sensitive powers receive the express specifications formed by other causes or powers, concerning which St. Thomas's *Summa contra gentiles*, Book IV, chap. 11, and his *Treatise on the Nature of the Word of the Understanding,*[14] can be seen saying that a form or representation is expressed by sense and terminated in the imagination; and so the principle from which this similitude emanates is one thing, and the principle in which it is terminated another. Although this proposition that the internal senses receive their express forms of specification from the external senses[15] has some probability, it seems yet more probable, as we say in the books *Concerning the Soul*, q. 8, art. 4,[16] that an expressed specifier (or form of specification) is always a living image produced through a vital action by the power which it serves in order that

tra Gent. cap. 11. et opusc. 13.[12] et 14.[13] et multis aliis locis, ubi agit de verbo mentis.

Si autem quaeras, per quem actum fiat haec expressio seu conceptus, breviter dicimus (nam res ista ad libros de Anima spectat) *in intellectu* fieri per actum, qui substantialiter est cognitio, sed aliquid amplius habet, scilicet quod sit cognitio fecunda, id est manifestativa et dicens seu expressiva. Nec enim intellectus sibi soli cognoscit, sed facit etiam impetum ad manifestandum; et illud prorumpere ad manifestandum est expressio quaedam et conceptio ac partus intellectus.

In potentiis autem sensitivis videtur concedere D. Thomas duplicem modum faciendi istas species expressas, quae in ipsis vocantur idolum. Primo, quia ipsae formant eas active aut producunt, sicut dicit 1. p. q. 12. art. 9. ad 2., quod «imaginatio ex praeconceptis speciebus montis et auri format speciem montis aurei». Secundo, quia ab aliis causis seu potentiis formatas recipiunt, de quo videri potest D. Thomas 4. Contra Gent. cap. 11. et opusc. 14.[14] dicens, quod a sensu exprimitur forma seu repraesentatio et terminatur in phantasia; et sic aliud est principium, a quo emanat ista similitudo, et aliud, in quo terminatur. Quod licet probabilitatem habere possit,[15] probabilius tamen videtur, ut dicemus in libris de Anima q. 8. art. 4.,[16] quod species expressa semper est imago viva et producitur per actionem vitalem a potentia, cui deservit, ut per eam cog-

[12] De differentia verbi divini et humani (*Pa* XVI. 177).

[13] De natura verbi intellectus (*Pa* XVI. 179-182).

[14] *Pa* XVI. 179 a.

[15] 245/29-33.

[16] Phil. nat. 4. p. q. 8., "*De sensibus internis*" ("On the internal senses") art. 4., "*Quae sint species impressae et expressae in sensibus internis*" ("Which are the impressed and which the expressed specifiers in the case of the internal senses"), Reiser ed., III. 265b1-271b20, esp. 268b24-269a17 (cited in note 17 below). This corrects the reference in the Reiser Latin to "q. 7. art. 3.," clearly incorrect, since the Phil. nat. 4. p. q. 7. is on the objects of external sense (where for Poinsot there are no expressed specifiers), and art. 3. of that question concerns the nature and subject of sound, containing no mention of *species expressae*. See Appendix B, Part II, below.

the power might know by means of it.[17] But impressed forms of specification are specifiers that are impressed by one power on another and move that other power to cognition and the formation of an icon. And because they are borne by the animal spirits or by the blood, therefore when the blood and animal spirits descend to the organs of sense, they thence arouse the imagination just as if it were moved by the senses, as happens in dreams, and sometimes an excitement of the imagination is procured in this way by a demon or an angel, as St. Thomas teaches in the *Summa theologica*, I, q. 111, art. 3, in the *Disputed Questions on Evil*, q. 16, art. 11,[18] and in other places.

First conclusion. **A concept or specifying form expressed by the understanding is most properly a formal sign.**

This conclusion is taken FROM ST. THOMAS, who often teaches that the [mental] word is a sign and similitude of a thing, as, for example, in the *Questions at Random*, q. 4, art. 17,[19] the *Disputed Questions on Truth*, q. 4, art. 1, reply to obj. 7,[20] and the *Summa contra gentiles*, Book IV, chap.

noscat.[17] Sed species impressae sunt, quae ab una potentia ad aliam imprimuntur et ad cognitionem formationemque idoli movent aliam potentiam. Et quia spiritibus seu sanguine deferuntur, ideo descendente sanguine et spiritibus ad organa sensuum, inde movent phantasiam, perinde ac si a sensibus moveretur, ut accidit in somniis, et aliquando a daemone vel angelo sic procuratur informatio phantasiae, ut docet S. Thomas 1. p. q. 111. art. 3. et q. 16. de Malo art. 11.[18] et aliis locis.

PRIMA CONCLUSIO. **Conceptus seu species expressa ab intellectu propriissime est signum formale.**

Haec conclusio SUMITUR EX DIVO THOMA, qui saepe docet verbum esse signum et similitudinem rei, ut in Quodlib. 4. art. 17.[19] et q. 4. de Veritate art. 1. ad 7. [20] et 4. Contra Gent. cap. 11. Non est autem

---

[17] Phil. nat. 4. p. q. 8. art. 4., Reiser ed. III. 268b24-269a17: "*Ratio autem est, quia species expressa est imago vitalis, quia repraesentat non ut principium cognitionis, sed ut terminus eius, et consequenter non ante vitalem actionem, sed post ipsam et dependenter ab ipsa ut terminus eius, alias non esset expressa species et per modum termini repraesentans ipsi cognitioni. Ergo licet species impressa, quae est principium cognitionis, possit per motum extrinsecum advenire, tamen expressa, quae est terminus cognitionis et operationis immanentis, non potest per extrinsecam operationem, sed per cognitionem vitalem produci. Quod vero talis species expressa non possit formari ab una potentia et deservire alteri, ut in ea tamquam in termino cognoscat, patet, quia quod formatur ab una potentia, non potest esse terminus operationis elicitae ab altera, nec formaliter illi reddere rem cognitam et repraesentatam per modum termini. Sed si species formata ab una potentia repraesentata alteri, solum potest esse movendo illam obiective, siquidem extra illam est, et sic ut tale idolum seu imago repraesentaret et cognosceretur ab alia potentia, deberet emittere speciem sui ad illam, sicut imago exterior, quae obiective movet potentiam, per speciem sui movet illam. Si autem species expressa deberet informare aliam potentiam mediante specie a se emissa, iam non informaret ut terminus cognitionis, sed ut obiectum movens ad extra.*"—"The reason for this is that an expressed specifier is a vital icon or image, but it represents not as the principle of a cognition, but as its terminus, and consequently not prior to a vital action, but after and dependently upon it as its terminus—otherwise, it would not be an *expressed* specifier and one representing to the cognition proper in the mode of a terminus. Therefore, even though an impressed specification, which is the principle or inchoation of a cognition, can arrive [at a cognitive power] through an extrinsic stimulation, yet the expressed specification, which is the terminus of the cognition and immanent operation, cannot come about through an extrinsic activity, but must be produced through the vital cognition. But that such an expressed form of specification cannot be fashioned by one power and function in another so as to be cognized in the other power as in a terminus, is clear from the fact that what is formed by one power cannot be the terminus of an operation elicited from another power, nor can it formally render a thing known and represented in the manner of a terminus for that other power. But if a specifier formed by one power represented to another power, that could only be by stimulating or moving that other power objectively, since by hypothesis it is external to it, and so for such an icon or image to represent to and be known by the other power, it would have to emit a specification of itself to that other power, just as an exterior image stimulating a cognitive power [e.g., just as a statue which stimulates the sense of sight] does so through a specification of itself. But if an expressed specifier must inform another power by means of a specification emitted from itself, already, by that very fact, it would not inform as a terminus of the cognition, but as an object stimulating from outside the power."

[18] *Pa* VIII. 421 b.

[19] *Pa* IX. 517 a.

[20] *Pa* IX. 65 a.

11. But it is not an instrumental sign, because it is not an object first known which leads from a preexisting cognition of itself to a represented thing, but it is a terminus of understanding by which as by an *intrinsic* terminus a thing is rendered known and present to the understanding, as St. Thomas teaches in the places just cited, in his *Treatise on the Difference Between the Divine and Human Word*, and in his *Treatise on the Nature of the Word of the Understanding*.[21] Therefore the word of the mind is a formal sign.

And THE FOUNDATION OF THE CONCLUSION is taken from the fact that an intelligible concept directly represents another than itself to the cognitive power, as, for example, a man or a stone, because it is a natural similitude[22] of those things, and through its information the concept renders the understanding knowing in act by a cognition terminated *by the cognition of itself*, and not from a *preexisting* cognition of itself. Therefore the concept is the formal awareness rendering understanding not in the mode of an act, but in the mode of a terminus or *terminated awareness*.

Second conclusion. **Likewise the icon or sensible form of specification expressed in the interior sense powers is a formal sign in respect of those powers.**

There is no difficulty about this conclusion if these icons are formed by the powers themselves just as a concept is formed in the understanding. But the difficulty is, how can it be maintained that they are formal awarenesses, at least terminatively, if it is true that these expressions can be formed also by an extrinsic principle, as when they are formed by an angel or a demon through an agitation of the animal spirits, or even when they are formed by a descent of the blood to the organs of the senses in persons asleep.

But we say nevertheless that even granting that possibility (whose opposite seems the more likely to be true, as we have said[23]), it would still be the case

signum instrumentale, quia non est obiectum prius cognitum, quod ex praeexistenti sui cognitione ducat ad rem repraesentatam, sed est terminus intellectionis, quo tamquam termino intrinseco res redditur cognita et praesens intellectui, ut eisdem locis docet D. Thomas et opusc. 13. et 14.[21] Ergo est signum formale.

Et ex hoc sumitur FUNDAMENTUM CONCLUSIONIS, quia conceptus intelligibilis directe repraesentat aliud a se potentiae, v. g. hominem vel lapidem, quia est naturalis illorum similitudo,[22] et per sui informationem reddit intellectum cognoscentem in actu cognitione terminata cognitione sui, et non ex praeexistente cognitione sui. Ergo est formalis notitia reddens intelligentem non per modum actus, sed per modum termini seu notitiae terminatae.

SECUNDA CONCLUSIO. **Etiam idolum seu species expressa sensibilis in potentiis interioribus est signum formale respectu talium potentiarum.**

Haec conclusio non habet difficultatem, si ista idola formentur ab ipsis potentiis sicut conceptus in intellectu. SED DIFFICULTAS EST, quomodo salvetur, quod sint formales notitiae, saltem terminative, si verum est, quod possunt istae expressiones formari etiam a principio extrinseco, ut quando formantur ab angelo vel daemone per commotionem spirituum, vel etiam per descensum sanguinis in dormientibus ad organa sensuum.

SED NIHILOMINUS DICITUR, quod etiam illo dato (cuius oppositum verius est, ut diximus[23]) adhuc tales imagines seu idola

---

[21] De differentia verbi divini et humani (*Pa* XVI. 177); De natura verbi intellectus (*Pa* XVI. 179-182).

[22] "*Quod autem species expressa naturaliter repraesentat, non sufficit certificare nobis experimentaliter, quia potest falso repraesentare, ut saepe fit in phantasia. Ergo certitudo experimentalis non potest sistere in intellectu formante verbum neque in phantasia formante idolum, sed debet resolvi in sensum attingentem rem in se sine imagine*" (Phil. nat. 4. p. q. 6. art. 4., Reiser ed., III. 195b6-15).—"The fact that an expressed specifier represents naturally is not enough to give us experimental certitude, because it can represent falsely, as often happens in the imagination. Therefore experimental certitude cannot rest in the understanding forming a word [i.e., concept] nor in the imagination forming an icon, but must be resolved in sense attaining the thing in itself [but see Phil. nat. 4. p. q. 6., Reiser ed., III. 195b21-25, cited in the Second Preamble, Article 1, note 16, p. 86 above] without an image."

See the discussion in notes 2 and 3 above, and of the absence of images in sensation below in Book III, Question 2, esp. notes 1, 9, and 10.

[23] at 245/35-246/1 above, and in note 16 thereto.

that such images or icons are formal signs, because they do not lead the power nor represent to it an object from a prior cognition of themselves as objects, but lead immediately to the very objects represented, because these sensitive powers are not able to reflect upon themselves and upon the expressed specifying forms which they have. Therefore, without these expressed specifiers being objectively known by the sense powers, the things [known] are rendered immediately represented to the powers; therefore this representation comes about formally and not instrumentally, nor from some prior cognition of the image or idol itself. Wherefore for it [i.e., a concept formed by internal sense] to be a formal sign, it suffices that it terminate an act of knowledge, whether it be formed through that very cognition or formed by another cause and united to that cognition in such a way that the act is terminated at that icon; just as if God were by himself alone to unite a concept to the understanding and the act [of the understanding] were terminated at that concept, it would be truly and properly called a formal awareness terminatively, even though it would not emanate from that act of understanding.

sunt signa formalia, quia non ducunt potentiam nec repraesentant illi obiectum ex priori cognitione sui, sed immediate ducunt ad ipsa obiecta repraesentata, quia potentiae istae sensitivae non possunt reflectere supra seipsas et supra species expressas, quas habent. Ergo sine hoc, quod cognoscantur ab illis, immediate res repraesentatae redduntur potentiis; ergo ista repraesentatio fit formaliter et non instrumentaliter, nec ex aliqua priori cognitione ipsius imaginis seu idoli. Quare ut sit formale signum, sufficit, quod terminet actum cognitionis, sive formetur per ipsam sive ab alia causa formetur et illi uniatur ita, ut ad illud actus terminetur; sicut si Deus se solo uniret conceptum intellectui et ad illum terminaretur actus, vere et proprie diceretur formalis notitia terminative, etiamsi ab ipso non emanaret.

Resolution of Counter-Arguments

It is argued first, that a concept represents to a power as an instrumental sign, therefore not as a formal sign.

The antecedent is proved first from St. Thomas's *Questions at Random*, q. 5, art. 9, reply to obj. 1,[24] where he says that "the understanding understands something in two ways: in one way formally, and it is thus that it understands by means of the intelligible specifier whereby it is constituted in act; in another way as by an instrument which is used for understanding something else, and it is in this way that the understanding understands by a word, because it forms a word for this, that it might understand a thing." Therefore according to St. Thomas the understanding does not understand by the word as by a form, but as by an instrument, and for this reason the mental word is not a formal sign, but an instrumental sign.

Then the antecedent is proved by reason, from the fact that a concept represents as something known, therefore as an instrumental sign; for an instrumental sign is something which, when known, leads to a knowledge of another. That the concept as something known leads to the knowledge of another is proved by what St. Thomas says in his *Disputed Questions on Truth*, q. 4, art. 2, reply to obj. 3,[25] that "a conception of the understanding is not only that which is understood, but also that by which a thing is understood, so that in this way that which is understood

Solvuntur argumenta.

Primo arguitur, quia conceptus repraesentat potentiae ut signum instrumentale, ergo non ut formale.

Antecedens probatur primo *ex Divo Thoma* Quodlib. 5. art. 9. ad 1.,[24] ubi inquit, «quod intellectus intelligit aliquid dupliciter, uno modo formaliter, et sic intelligit specie intelligibili, qua fit in actu, alio modo sicut intrumento, quo utitur ad aliud intelligendum, et hoc modo intellectus verbo intelligit, quia format verbum ad hoc, quod intelligat rem». Ergo secundum D. Thomam intellectus non intelligit verbo tamquam forma, sed tamquam instrumento, atque ideo non est signum formale, sed instrumentale.

Deinde probatur *ratione,* quia conceptus repraesentat ut cognitus, ergo ut signum instrumentale; hoc enim est, quod cognitum ducit ad cognitionem alterius. Antecedens probatur, quia dicit D. Thomas in q. 4. de Veritate art. 2. ad 3.,[25] quod «conceptio intellectus non solum est id, quod intellectum est, sed etiam id, quo res intelligitur, ut sic id,

[24] *Pa* IX. 532 b.
[25] *Pa* IX. 66 b.

can be said to be both the thing itself and the conception of the understanding.'' Therefore according to St. Thomas the word is known as that which is known, and so it represents as something known.—The same conclusion follows from the fact that the act of understanding is compared to the word as the act of existence to a being in act, as St. Thomas says in the *Summa theologica,* I, q. 34, art. 1, reply to obj. 2. Therefore the word does not represent except as formed through cognition and as something known, and therefore as an instrumental sign, which is a sign that represents as something known.

We deny the antecedent.[26] To the first proof from the authority of St. Thomas, the response is that St. Thomas calls the mental word an instrument by which the understanding knows something, not as if it were a known medium which is an instrument and *external* means, but as it is an *internal* medium or means in which the understanding understands within itself, and this is to be a formal sign.[27] But ''impressed specifier'' is the name for that form of specification by which the understanding formally understands, *because it obtains on the side of the principle of the action of understanding;* but that which keeps to the side of a

quod intelligitur, possit dici et res ipsa et conceptio intellectus». Ergo secundum D. Thomam verbum est cognitum ut *quod,* et sic tamquam cognitum repraesentat.—Item etiam, quia intelligere comparatur ad verbum sicut esse ad ens actu, ut dicit D. Thomas 1. p. 34. art. 1. ad 2. Ergo verbum non repraesentat, nisi ut formatum per cognitionem et ut cognitum, atque adeo ut signum instrumentale, quod tamquam cognitum repraesentat.

Respondetur negando antecedens.[26] Ad primam probationem ex auctoritate D. Thomae respondetur, quod D. Thomas vocat verbum instrumentum, quo intellectus aliquid cognoscit, non tamquam medium cognitum, quod est instrumentum et medium externum, sed ut medium internum, in quo intellectus intelligit intra se, et hoc est esse signum formale.[27] Species autem impressa dicitur id, quo formaliter intelligit intellectus, quia tenet se ex parte principii intellectionis; quod autem tenet se ex parte principii,

---

[26] 248/24-25.

[27] See Question 1 of Book II above, 224/34-227/8, 231/45-232/31. Cf. Phil. nat. 4. p. q. 11. art. 2., Reiser ed., vol. III, 358b26-359a11: ''*Quodsi inquiras, quomodo ipsum verbum possit deservire ad cognoscendum obiectum, nisi prius cognoscitur tamquam imago repraesentans, cum tamen nullus experiatur se prius videre hanc imaginem, ut in ea videat obiectem; quomodo etiam potest per cognitionem formari, si ipsa cognitio non respicit obiectum nisi in ipso verbo repraesentatum.*

''*Respondetur, quod imago est duplex: Alia exterior et instrumentalis, quae ut cognita ducit in cognitionem obiecti, et talis imago prius debet attingi et cognosci quam obiectum ipsum. Alia est interior et formalis, quae non est obiectum cognitum, sed ipsa est ratio et forma terminans cognitionem, et haec non debet esse cognita obiective, sed solum cognitionem reddere terminatam formaliter respectu obiecti. Debet autem formari per cognitionem ipsum verbum, quia ut dictum est, verbum repraesentat rem ut cognitam et intellectam, et sic intellectione ipsa debet formari. Et vocatur aliquando verbum a D. Thoma instrumentum, quo intellectus utitur ad cognoscendum, ut Quodlib. 5. art. 9. ad 1., sed tamen non sumit instrumentum pro signo instrumentali, quod obiective movet potentiam, sed pro medio intelligendi formali et intrinseco ipsi cognoscenti.*''—''But if you should ask, how can the word serve for knowing the object unless it is itself first known as a representing image, *although no one has the experience of first seeing this image so that in it he sees the object;* how too can it be formed through the cognition, if the cognition itself does not respect the object unless it is represented in the word itself.

''The response to this is that an image is of two sorts: One is exterior and instrumental, which as known leads to a cognition of the object, and an image of this sort must itself be first attained and known as an object. The other is interior and formal, which is not an object known, but is itself the rationale and form terminating the cognition, and this sort of image need not be known objectively, but must only render cognition formally terminated with respect to an object. But the word itself must be formed through the cognition because, as has been said, the word represents a thing as known and understood, and so must be formed by the very activity of understanding. And the word is sometimes called by St. Thomas an instrument which the understanding employs for knowing, as in the *Questions at Random,* 5, art. 9, reply to the first objection, but nevertheless he does not take 'instrument' there for an instrumental sign, but for the medium of understanding formal and intrinsic to the one knowing.''

On the ''interior and formal image,'' see also Book I, Question 1, 132/47-133/12, Question 3, 164/13-165/8; and the First Preamble, Article 3, note 17, p. 73.

principle of acting is called a form. And yet St. Thomas did not say that an impressed specifier formally *signifies* or represents, but that it is that principle *by which* the understanding formally understands; but it is one thing to be a formal sign, and another to be a principle "by which" of understanding.

To the second proof from reason[28] the response is that a concept is not said to represent as something first known in the mode of an extrinsic object, so that the qualification "known" would be an extrinsic denomination; a concept is said to represent as something *intrinsic* known, that is, as the terminus of the knowledge *within* the power. But because it is *not the terminus in which the cognition finally stops*, but one by whose mediation the power is borne to the knowing of an outside object,[29] for this reason a concept has the being of a formal sign, because it is something intrinsic known, that is to say, because it is the intrinsic rationale of the knowing. Whence an instrumental sign is known as something which is known *extrinsically* and as a thing known, *from* the knowledge of which the significate is arrived at; but a concept is known as something which is known, *not* as is an extrinsic known thing, but as that *in which is contained* the thing known *within* the understanding.[30] And so, by the essentially same cognition, concept and thing conceived are attained, but the cognition of the thing conceived is not arrived at *from* the cognition of the concept. And because the concept is that in which the thing or object is rendered proportioned and immaterialized *in the mode of a terminus*, for *this* reason the concept itself is said to be known as something "which"—not as a thing separately known, but as *constituting* the object in the rationale of *known* terminus. But even though an instrumental sign can be attained with the signified by a single act of cognition, it remains true even then that it is *from* the known sign that the significate is arrived at, that the [instrumental] *sign itself* does not *formally* constitute the [signified] thing as known.

To the third proof[31] the response is that the act of understanding, as it is a diction or expression, has for its complement the word itself as terminus. And so St. Thomas, in the *Disputed Questions on Power*, q. 8, art. 1,[32] says that "the act of understanding is completed through the word." But again the word itself in another order is actuated and completed by

vocatur forma. Et tamen non dixit D. Thomas, quod species impressa formaliter significat seu repraesentat, sed quod est id, quo formaliter intellectus intelligit; aliud est autem esse signum formale, aliud principium quo intelligendi.

Ad secondam probationem ex ratione[28] respondetur, quod conceptus non dicitur repraesentare tamquam prius cognitum per modum obiecti extrinseci, ita quod ly cognitum sit denominatio extrinseca, sed tamquam cognitum intrinsecum, id est ut terminus cognitionis intra potentiam. Sed quia non est terminus, in quo ultimate sistit cognitio, sed quo mediante fertur ad cognoscendum obiectum extra,[29] ideo habet esse signum formale, quia est cognitum intrinsecum, id est ratio intrinseca cognoscendi. Unde signum instrumentale est cognitum ut *quod* extrinsece et tamquam res cognita, ex cuius cognitione devenitur in signatum; conceptus autem est cognitum ut *quod*, non tamquam res cognita extrinseca, sed tamquam id, in quo continetur res cognita intra intellectum.[30] Et sic eadem cognitione per se attingitur conceptus et res concepta, non ex cognitione eius devenitur in cognitionem rei conceptae. Et quia est id, in quo res seu obiectum redditur proportionatum et immaterializatum per modum termini, ideo dicitur ipse conceptus cognosci ut quod, non tamquam res seorsum cognita, sed tamquam constituens obiectum in ratione termini cogniti. Licet autem signum instrumentale possit attingi unica cognitione cum signato, tamen etiam tunc ex signo cognito devenitur in signatum, non ipsum signum formaliter constituit rem ut cognitam.

Ad tertiam probationem[31] respondetur, quod intelligere, ut est dictio seu expressio, habet pro complemento ipsum verbum tamquam terminum. Et sic D. Thomas in q. 8. de Potentia art. 1.[32] dicit, quod «intelligere completur per verbum». Rursus vero ipsum verbum in alio genere

---

[28] 248/39-249/4.
[29] See Question 1 above, 226/38-227/22 and 231/45-232/31.
[30] See above, Book I, Question 3, note 12, p. 163.
[31] 249/4-12.
[32] *Pa* VIII. 169 a.

the act of understanding, inasmuch as the act of understanding is the ultimate actuality in the intelligible order, just as the act of being is the ultimate perfection in that [i.e., the entitative] order, as St. Thomas says in the *Summa theologica*, I, q. 14, art. 4. But the fact that the word is rendered known by reason of this actuation does not suffice for the rationale of an instrumental sign, because the word is not known as an object and extrinsic thing, but as the intrinsic terminus of the very action of understanding; for this is to represent within the power by informing it and rendering it actually knowing, and therefore the concept or word is called a formal sign.

It is argued secondly: The word is not a formal awareness, therefore it is not a formal sign.

The consequence is plain from the definition of a formal sign. The antecedent is proved first by the fact that a formal awareness is that which renders a power formally knowing. But a power is rendered formally knowing by an act of cognition, which is the immediate form of the knowing, particularly because to know consists in an action, since it is a vital operation; but a word is not the very operation or action of knowing, but something formed through the cognition and an effect of that action. Therefore it is not the form that constitutes the knowing, but a form that proceeds from and is effected by the knowing; therefore it is not the formal awareness itself of the cognitive power. Whence a word is not constituted by the act of understanding actively, but by being understood passively; therefore neither does it formally constitute the understanding, but formally constitutes the thing understood.

The same antecedent is proved secondly because in the divine relations the Word does not formally produce understanding, because the Father does not understand by a generated wisdom, as St. Thomas, following St. Augustine, teaches in his *Commentary on the Sentences of Peter Lombard*, Book I, dist. 32, q. 2, art. 1.[33] Therefore the mental word does not render [a power] formally understanding from the kind of thing it is.

This is confirmed by the fact that if the word were a formal awareness, without a word the understanding would not be able to be formally knowing, at least not perfectly. But without the formation of a word the understanding does formally know, as is admitted to be probable in the case of the blessed in heaven, and as is manifestly the case in the intellection whereby the Word and the Holy Spirit understand. Therefore.

actuatur et completur per intelligere, quatenus actus intelligendi est ultima actualitas in genere intelligibili, sicut esse est ultima perfectio in eo genere, ut dicit D. Thomas 1. p. q. 14. art. 4. Quod autem ratione huius actuationis verbum redditur cognitum, non sufficit ad rationem signi instrumentalis, quia non est cognitum quasi obiectum et res extrinseca, sed ut terminus intrinsecus ipsius intellectionis; hoc enim est repraesentare intra potentiam informando ipsam et reddendo cognoscentem, ideoque dicitur signum formale.

Secundo arguitur: Verbum non est formalis notitia, ergo non est signum formale.

Consequentia patet ex definitione signi formalis. *Antecedens probatur primo*, quia formalis notitia est illa, quae reddit potentiam formaliter cognoscentem. Redditur autem formaliter cognoscens per actum cognitionis, quae est immediata forma cognoscentis, et praesertim quia cognoscere consistit in actione, cum sit operatio vitalis; verbum autem non est ipsa operatio seu actio cognoscendi, sed aliquid formatum per cognitionem et effectus illius. Ergo non est forma, quae constituit cognoscentem, sed quae procedit et efficitur a cognoscente; ergo non est ipsa formalis notitia potentiae. Unde verbum non constituitur per intelligere active, sed per intelligi passive; ergo nec constituit formaliter intelligentem, sed formaliter constituit rem intellectam.

Secundo probatur idem antecedens, quia in divinis Verbum non facit formaliter intelligentem, quia Pater non intelligit sapientia genita, ut ex Augustino docet D. Thomas in 1. dist. 32. q. 2. art. 1.[33] Ergo ex genere suo verbum non reddit formaliter intelligentem.

Confirmatur, quia si verbum esset formalis notitia, sine verbo non posset intellectus formaliter esse cognoscens saltem perfecte. Sed sine formatione verbi intellectus formaliter cognoscit, ut probabiliter admittitur in Beatis et in intellectione, qua Verbum et Spiritus sanctus intelligunt, manifest constat. Ergo.

[33] *Pa* VI. 261 b.

Response is made to the principal argument by distinguishing the antecedent:[34] That a word is not a formal awareness in the mode of an operation, I grant; that it is not a formal awareness in the mode of a terminus, I deny. And so a word renders the understanding formally understanding, formally *terminatively*, not formally *operatively*. But when[35] it is called a formal sign, which is a formal awareness, this is understood of the formal awareness terminated, not of the very operation of awareness apart from the term, because it is of the rationale of a sign that it be something representative, but an operation as operation does not represent. But that which represents must be something expressed and similar to that which is represented, which pertains to the rationale of an image; but to be something similar and expressed properly belongs to the term issuing forth, which is assimilated to its principle, not to the operation, which is more assimilative than it is a thing [made] similar. But the proposition[36] that an act of understanding consists in an action or operation is true of the formal act itself of understanding. But when the formal sign is called a formal awareness, this is not understood of formal awareness according as it is an operation, but of the formal awareness which is a representation and expression, which belongs only to a terminated formal awareness or to the terminus of the awareness, not to the operation as it is an operation. And when it is said[37] that the word is the effect of the cognition, it is understood that it is an effect of the operation and the way or tendency of the cognition, not of the cognition as terminated. For the word is the form of a cognition as terminated, because the word is cognition's very terminus; but the word is the effect of the cognition as the cognition is an expressive operation and a diction, and so it supposes an act of understanding not terminated and completed, but rather as operating and expressing, and therefore a place is left for the word (or concept) to be a formal awareness formally terminatively, not formally operatively. And for this reason the word is constituted by being understood and not by the act of understanding actively, because it does not pertain to the word insofar as it is a formal sign to be a formal awareness operatively and actively, but terminatively and according to an intrinsic being understood whereby a thing itself is rendered understood and represented intrinsically; but representation,

RESPONDETUR *ad principale argumentum* distinguendo antecedens:[34] Verbum non est formalis notitia per modum operationis, concedo; per modum termini, nego. Et sic reddit intellectum formaliter intelligentem, formaliter terminative, non formaliter operative. Quando autem[35] dicitur signum formale, quod est formalis notitia, intelligitur de formali notitia terminata, non de operatione ipsa notitiae sine termino, quia de ratione signi est, quod sit repraesentativum, operatio autem ut operatio non repraesentat. Sed id, quod repraesentat, debet esse expressum et simile ei, quod repraesentatur, quod pertinet ad rationem imaginis; esse autem simile et expressum, proprie convenit termino procedenti, quod assimilatur suo principio, non operationi, quae magis est assimilativa quam simile. Quod vero dicitur,[36] quod intelligere consistit in actione seu operatione, verum est de ipso actu formali intelligendi. Ceterum quando signum formale dicitur notitia formalis, non intelligitur de notitia formali, prout est operatio, sed de notitia formali, quae est repraesentatio et expressio, quod solum convenit notitiae formali terminatae seu termino notitiae, non operationi, ut operatio est. Et quando dicitur,[37] quod verbum est effectus cognitionis, intelligitur, quod est effectus cognitionis operatio et via seu tendentia, non cognitionis ut terminatae. Cognitionis enim ut terminatae verbum est forma, quia est ipse terminus eius; cognitionis autem, ut operatio expressiva et dictio, verbum est effectus, et ita supponit actum intelligendi non terminatum et completum, sed ut operantem et dicentem, ideoque relinquitur locus, ut sit formalis notitia formaliter terminative, non formaliter operative. Et hac ratione constituitur verbum per intelligi et non per intelligere active, quia non pertinet ad ipsum, in quantum est signum formale, esse formalem notitiam operative et active, sed terminative et secundum intelligi intrinsecum, quo res ipsa redditur intellecta et repraesentata intrinsece; pertinet autem ad ra-

[34] 251/14-15.
[35] 251/17-32.
[36] 251/21-22.
[37] 251/23-25.

not operation, pertains to the rationale of a sign, and to be a formal representative awareness, not an operative one.

To the second proof[38] the response is that the rationale of the Divine Word is not the same as that of a human word, because the Word in the divine relations supposes an essential intellection entirely terminated and complete, since it is a question of pure act in the intelligible order, nor does the Word issue forth that the intellection might be completed essentially, but that it might be spoken and expressed notionally. And so the Divine Word does not render God formally understanding even terminatively, essentially, and in perfect intelligible being, nor does it render God an object understood in act, because the divine essence itself according to its being is in final act understanding *and* understood, because it is pure act in the intelligible order, and it does not possess this condition through the procession of the Word, but rather does the procession of the Word suppose this condition. But in us, because an object is not understood in final act of itself, it is necessary that it be formed within the understanding in the rationale of terminating object; and this comes about through the expression of a word in representative being, and therefore through that word is the understanding rendered formally understanding terminatively.

To the confirmation[39] the response is that there cannot be any cognition without a word, either a word formed by the very one understanding or a word united to the one understanding. Yet it is not always required that the word should proceed from and be formed by the very one understanding. And so in the case of the blessed in heaven the divine essence is united [to their understanding] in the rationale of an expressed specifying form, a point discussed at more length in St. Thomas's *Summa theologica*, I, q. 12,[40] art. 2, and touched on in my books *Concerning the Soul*, q. 11.[41]

tionem signi repraesentatio, non operatio, et esse formalem notitiam repraesentativam, non operativam.

Ad secundam probationem[38] respondetur esse disparem rationem de Verbo Divino, quia Verbum in divinis supponit intellectionem essentialem omnino terminatam et completam, cum sit actus purus in genere intelligibili, nec procedit Verbum, ut compleatur intellectio essentialiter, sed ut dicatur et exprimatur notionaliter. Et ita non reddit formaliter intelligentem Deum etiam terminative, essentialiter et in esse perfecto intelligibili, nec obiectum intellectum in actu, quia ipsa divina essentia secundum se est in actu ultimo intelligens et intellecta, cum sit actus purus in genere intelligibili, et non id habet per processionem Verbi, sed supponit. In nobis autem quia obiectum non est in actu ultimo intellectum per se, oportet, quod formetur intra intellectum in ratione obiecti terminantis; et hoc fit per expressionem verbi in esse repraesentativo, atque adeo per illud redditur intellectus formaliter intelligens terminative.

Ad confirmationem[39] respondetur, quod non potest dari aliqua cognitio sine verbo, vel formato ab ipso intelligente vel illi unito. Non tamen requiritur semper, quod verbum procedat et formetur ab ipso intelligente. Et sic in Beatis divina essentia unitur in ratione speciei expressae, de quo latius 1. p. q. 12.[40] art. 2., et aliquid attingetur in libris de Anima q. 11.[41]

---

[38] 251/33-41.

[39] 251/42-49.

[40] Correcting Reiser's reference to "q. 1."

[41] Correcting the reference to "q. 10" in the original Latin (see the discussion in this Book, Question 1, note 5; and note 6 of this Question, above), since the matter referred to is expressly discussed in Poinsot's Phil. nat. 4. p. q. 11. art. 2., "*Utrum ad omnem intellectionem sit necessaria productio verbi*" ("Whether the production of a word is necessary to every act of understanding"). See esp. 358b37-360a28 of the Reiser edition of the Phil. nat. 4. p.

[707b24-708a10]

Question 3

Whether an Impressed Specification Is a Formal Sign

Quaestio Tertia

Utrum Species Impressa Sit Signum Formale

We suppose that there are impressed specifying forms, which are united to a cognitive power in the capacity of an object for eliciting cognition or awareness, from the fact that cognition is born from a cognitive power and an object. Whence it is necessary that the object be rendered united or present to the power and determine it to an eliciting of cognition. And since the object cannot go into the power and be united thereto of itself, it is necessary for this to come about by means of some form, which is said to be a specifying form, specification, or specifier, which so contains the object itself in an intentional and knowable mode that it can render that object present and united to a cognitive power.[1] And because that form or specifier is instituted by nature for this function, it is said to represent the object to the power, because it presents or renders that object present to a cognitive power.[2] It is also called a natural similitude of the object, because from its very nature it acts as the vicegerent of an object, or rather it is the very object itself in intentional being.[3] This unity or coincidence is said to be a similitude or likeness, and it is said to be such also because it is given for [the] forming [by a cognitive power of] an expressed similitude [of the object].[4] But it is said to be impressed, because it is impressed upon a cognitive power and superadded thereto by an extrinsic principle, but it does

Supponimus dari species impressas, quae vice obiecti uniantur potentiae ad eliciendam cognitionem seu notitiam, eo quod ista paritur a potentia et obiecto. Unde oportet, quod obiectum reddatur unitum seu praesens potentiae illamque determinet ad eliciendam cognitionem. Et cum objectum non possit per seipsum ingredi potentiam illique uniri, oportet hoc fieri media aliqua forma, quae vocatur *species*, quae ita ipsum obiectum continet modo intentionali et cognoscibili, quod potest illud reddere praesens et unitum potentiae.[1] Et quia ad hoc munus illa forma seu species instituta est a natura, dicitur repraesentare obiectum potentiae, quia praesentat seu praesens reddit illud potentiae.[2] Et dicitur etiam *similitudo* obiecti naturalis, quia ex ipsa natura sua gerit vices obiecti, seu est ipsummet obiectum in esse intentionali.[3] Quae unitas seu convenientia similitudo dicitur, et similiter quia datur ad similitudinem expressam formandam.[4] Vocatur autem *impressa*, quia imprimitur potentiae et illi superadditur ab extrinseco prin-

[1] See Book I, Question 4, 169/1-173/38, esp. note 6, p. 170.
[2] See ibid., esp. 183/37-184/1, esp. note 17.
[3] See Book I above, Question 1, esp. note 25, p. 125; Question 5, note 21, p. 201.
[4] See Book I, Question 4, note 6; Book II, Question 2, notes 3, 8, and 22.

not proceed from and is not expressed by that power as is an expressed specifying form. For the impressed specification is given to that power for eliciting cognition, and so it functions in the mode of a principle and concurs with the very power in eliciting an act of knowing, not in the mode of a terminus proceeding from the very power and its act of knowing. These suppositions will be explained at greater length in my three books *Concerning the Soul,*[5] and expositions by St. Thomas can be seen in the *Disputed Questions on the Power of God*, q. 8, art. 1,[6] the *Treatise on the Difference between the Divine and Human Word,*[7] the *Treatise on the Nature of the Word of the Understanding,*[8] the *Treatise on Intelligence and the Intelligible,*[9] the *Questions at Random*, q. 7, art. 1,[10] and in many other places where he explains the nature of impressed forms of specification.

We inquire, therefore, whether this specifier thus representing an object in the mode of a principle of cognition could have the rationale of a formal sign, just as it has [of its very nature] the rationale of something representative [inasmuch as it derives from and so virtually *images* the stimulus object].

There is only one conclusion: **An impressed specifying form is not a formal sign**.

This conclusion is taken in the first place FROM ST. THOMAS, who, speaking of the sign generally expressed, as it has a rationale congruent with a formal [as well as with an instrumental] sign, says in the *Disputed Questions on Truth*, q. 9, art. 4, reply to obj. 4,[11] that a sign is "anything whatever known, in which something is known, and so an intelligible form can be said to be a sign of the thing which is known through it." But an impressed specifying form is not an intelligible form which is something known, in which something [else] is known, because for it to be something known, it would have to be either a thing known or a terminus of the cognition. But an impressed specifier is only that by which a power knows as from a principle, as is established by St. Thomas in the *Questions at Random*, q. 7, art. 1,[12] in the *Summa theologica*, I, q. 85, arts. 2 and 7, and in the *Commentary on the Sentences of Peter Lombard*, Book IV, dist. 49, q. 2, art. 1.[13] Therefore it does not have the rationale of a sign expressed generally and in the mode of an intelligible form, in the sense in which an intelligible form is a formal sign.

cipio, non vero ab ipsa procedit et exprimitur sicut species expressa. Datur enim ipsi potentiae ad eliciendam cognitionem, et sic per modum principii se habet et cum ipsa potentia concurrit ad eliciendam cognitionem, non per modum termini procedentis ab ipsa potentia et cognitione illius. Quod latius dicetur in 3. de Anima[5] et videri potest D. Thomas q. 8. de Potentia art. 1.[6] et opusc. 13.[7] et 14.[8] et 53.[9] et Quodlib. 7. art. 1.[10] et pluribus aliis locis, ubi explicat naturam speciei impressae.

INQUIRIMUS ergo, an species ista sic repraesentans obiectum per modum principii cognitionis habeat rationem signi formalis, sicut habet rationem repraesentativi.

SIT UNICA CONCLUSIO: **Species impressa non est signum formale.**

Haec conclusio sumitur imprimis EX D. THOMA, qui loquens de signo communiter dicto, quale est illud, quod convenit signo formali, dicit q. 9. de Veritate art. 4. ad 4.,[11] quod est «quodcumque notum, in quo aliquid cognoscitur, et sic forma intelligibilis potest dici signum rei, quae per ipsam cognoscitur». Sed species impressa non est forma intelligibilis, quae sit aliquid notum, in quo aliquid cognoscatur, quia ut esset aliquid notum, deberet esse vel res cognita vel terminus cognitionis. Species autem impressa solum est id, quo potentia cognoscit tamquam principio, ut constat ex D. Thoma Quodlib. 7. art. 1.[12] et 1. p. q. 85. art 2. et 7., in 4. dist. 49. q. 2. art. 1.[13] Ergo non habet rationem signi communiter dicti et per modum formae intelligibilis, ut est signum formale.

[5] Phil. nat. 4. p. q. 6. art. 2. et 3.
[6] *Pa* VIII. 169 a.
[7] De differentia verbi divini et humani (*Pa* XVI. 177).
[8] De natura verbi intellectus (*Pa* XVI. 179-182).
[9] De intellectu et intelligibili (*Pa* XVII. 126-127).
[10] *Pa* IX. 553 a.
[11] *Pa* IX. 151 b.
[12] *Pa* IX. 553 a.
[13] *Pa* VII. 1199 a.

The FOUNDATION OF THIS CONCLUSION is the fact that an impressed specifier does not represent an object to a knowing power, or rather, to the cognition of a power, but unites the object to the power in order that that power might know; therefore it is not a formal sign.

The consequence is proved from the very intrinsic rationale of a sign, because the proper and essential work of a sign is to manifest another or to lead a power to something by means of a manifestation. But a specifying form cannot manifest anything to a power antecedently to cognition, because every manifestation supposes or occurs within cognition itself, but a form of impressed specification does not suppose a cognition to which it would manifest, because it is a principle [an inchoative principle] of cognition. But at the time when a cognition has been elicited or posited it is not the impressed specifier itself that manifests, but an expressed specifier, which is a terminus in which the cognition is completed; for cognition neither tends toward the impressed specifying form nor cognizes in that form. Therefore an impressed specification is not a form which manifests an object to cognition formally, but one which produces cognition, in the terminus of which cognition—namely, in an expressed specifying form—the object is rendered manifest. And thus the object concurs in an impressed specifier as a principle of cognition determining a cognitive power for eliciting, not [determining the cognitive power] as an object known, and therefore neither as [an object] manifested; for something is not rendered manifested to a power within that very power, except insofar as it is known. What, therefore, does not manifest something to cognition, does not render an object manifested and consequently neither does it render an object signified.

And this is confirmed by the fact that it can in no way be verified from an impressed specifier that there is a formal awareness which of itself immediately represents. Therefore an impressed specifier is not a formal sign, for such formal awareness is required for the definition of a formal sign.

The antecedent is proved: An impressed specifying form is a principle of formal awareness; for it constitutes an intellect in first act for eliciting a formal awareness. But it is of the rationale of a formal awareness that it proceed from the intellect equally with the terminus of understanding, namely, the word, even though it is not absolutely necessary that a given word proceed from every intelligence understanding by means of that word, but it suffices either that the word be formed by the intellect understanding or that a word formed by another be united to the intellect understanding, as, in the prob-

FUNDAMENTUM EST, quia species impressa non repraesentat obiectum potentiae cognoscenti seu cognitioni potentiae, sed unit obiectum potentiae, ut cognoscat; ergo non est signum formale.

Consequentia probatur ex intrinseca ipsa ratione signi, quia proprium et essentiale munus signi est manifestare alterum seu ducere potentiam mediante manifestatione ad aliquid. Potentiae autem antecedenter ad cognitionem species manifestare non potest aliquid, cum omnis manifestatio cognitionem supponat vel in ipsa cognitione fiat, species autem impressa cognitionem non supponit, cui manifestet, quia est cognitionis principium. Elicita autem seu posita cognitione iam non ipsa species impressam manifestat, sed expressa, quae est terminus, in quo completur cognitio; nec enim cognitio aut tendit ad speciem impressam, aut cognoscit in ipsa. Ergo ipsa non est, quae manifestat cognitioni obiectum formaliter, sed quae cognitionem producit, in cuius cognitionis termino, scilicet in specie expressa, redditur obiectum manifestatum. Itaque in specie impressa obiectum concurrit ut cognitionis principium determinans potentiam ad eliciendum, non ut obiectum cognitum, atque adeo nec manifestatum; nec enim redditur aliquid manifestatum potentiae intra ipsam potentiam, nisi in quantum cognitum. Quod ergo non manifestat cognitioni, non reddit obiectum manifestatum et consequenter neque significatum.

Et confirmatur, quia species impressa nullo modo potest verificari, quod sit formalis notitia, quae seipsa immediate repraesentet. Ergo non est signum formale, hoc enim ad eius definitionem requiritur.

Antecedens probatur: Species impressa est principium notitiae formalis; constituit enim intellectum in actu primo ad eliciendam notitiam formalem. Est autem de ratione formalis notitiae, quod ab intellectu procedat, tam ipsa quam terminus eius, scilicet verbum, licet verbum absolute non sit necesse, quod procedat ab omni intellectu intelligente per illud, sed sufficit, quod vel ab eo formetur vel ab alio formatum ei uniatur, sicut in probabili opinione, quod

able opinion, the divine essence is united to the intellect of the blessed in place of a word. But yet even though the divine essence does not proceed from the intellect of the individual blessed, it is nevertheless united or at least related as the rationale understood intrinsically and as the medium-in-which of knowledge itself and understanding. If therefore "formal awareness" is accepted as standing for the very act of cognition, it is manifest that formal awareness does not coincide with an impressed specifying form, since an impressed specifier is not an act proceeding [from the cognitive power], but a principle of the act and cognition. But if formal awareness is taken for something proceeding from the understanding, not indeed in the mode of an act, but in the mode of a term issuing forth vitally, on this acceptation formal awareness is an expressed specifier, not an impressed one. Therefore nothing proceeding or issuing from the understanding is an impressed specifying form, and consequently an impressed specifier is not in any way a formal awareness, because a formal awareness must proceed from a cognitive power either as an act or as a terminus, because it is something vital, since indeed it has for [its] formal effect to render [a power] vitally and formally knowing. An impressed specifier, therefore, is not a formal awareness, and therefore not a formal sign.

Resolution of Counter-Arguments

It is argued first: Certainly a form of impressed specification is truly and properly representative of an oject and a similitude of that object and substituting in its capacity. And it is not representative objectively nor productively or instrumentally, therefore formally and as a formal sign.

The consequence is clear from the fact that for a specifying form to be representative in the mode of a sign, it suffices that it be representative of another besides itself and in the mode of one substituting for that other which it represents.

The major premise is established by St. Thomas in many places, where he calls an impressed specifier a similitude and representation, as for example in the *Disputed Questions on Truth*, q. 8, art. 1,[14] where he says that that by which one seeing sees either is a similitude of the object seen or its essence. And he adds that the mode of cognition is according to the coincidence of the similarity, which is a coincidence according to representation. But it is certain that that by which one seeing sees is an impressed specifier. And in the book *On Memory and Reminiscence*, reading 3,[15] he says that a kind of sen-

divina essentia loco verbi unitur beatis. Sed tamen licet non procedat ab intellectu beati, unitur tamen vel saltem comparatur ut ratio intellecta intrinsece et ut medium in quo ipsius cognitionis et intelligentiae. Formalis ergo notitia si accipiatur pro ipso cognitionis actu, manifestum est, quod non convenit speciei impressae, cum ipsa non sit actus procedens, sed principium actus et cognitionis. Si autem sumatur pro aliquo procedente ab intellectu, non quidem per modum actus, sed per modum termini procedentis vitaliter, sic est species expressa, non impressa. Ergo nihil procedens ab intellectu est species impressa, et consequenter non est aliquo modo formalis notitia, quia haec procedere debet vel ut actus vel ut terminus, cum sit aliquid vitale, siquidem pro effectu formali habet reddere vitaliter et formaliter cognoscentem. Non ergo species impressa est formalis notitia, atque adeo neque signum formale.

Solvuntur argumenta.

Primo arguitur: Nam species impressa est vere et proprie repraesentativa obiecti et similitudo illius et vice illius substituens. Et non est repraesentativa obiective neque effective aut instrumentaliter, ergo formaliter et ut signum formale.

Consequentia patet, quia ut sit repraesentativa per modum signi, sufficit, quod sit repraesentativa alterius a se et per modum substituentis pro eo, quod repraesentat.

Maior est D. Thomae pluribus in locis, ubi speciem impressam vocat similitudinem et repraesentationem, ut in q. 8. de Veritate art. 1. in c.,[14] ubi inquit, quod id, quo videns videt, vel est similitudo visi vel essentia visi. Et addit, quod modus cognitionis est secundum convenientiam similitudinis, quae est convenientia secundum repraesentationem. Constat autem, quod id, quo videns videt, est species impressa. Et in libro de Memoria et Reminiscentia lect. 3.[15] dicit,

[14] *Pa* IX. 112 a.
[15] *Pa* XX. 202 b.

sible figure, as it were, is impressed on the imagination, which impression remains when the sensible object is absent, just as the figure of a seal is imprinted in wax. But it is certain that the sensible object impresses only an impressed specifying form on the cognitive power. Finally, in the *Summa contra gentiles*, Book I, chap. 53, he says that both, that is, the understood intention and the understandable specifier, are a similitude of the object; and because an understandable specifier, which is a principle of understanding, is a similitude of an exterior thing, it follows that the understanding forms a similar intention of that thing. Here he is most clearly speaking about the impressed specifier as it is distinguished from the expressed specifier.

The minor premise is proved: For in the first place an impressed specifier is constituted in the representative order by the fact that it is in the intentional order. And it does not represent as an object, but as vicegerent of an object, therefore as a medium or means between power and object. Nor does it represent instrumentally, because it does not move [the power] thanks to a pre-existing cognition of itself, for a form of [impressed] specification is not known in order to represent; nor does it represent productively because there is no such thing as a productive representation or signification, as we showed in the preceding Book. Therefore it represents formally, inasmuch as by itself and through a union with the cognitive power it renders that very power similar to the object by an intentional similitude, which is representative.

This is confirmed by the fact that if an impressed specifier is not a formal sign for the reason that it does not represent to cognition, but keeps on the side of the power as a principle of cognition, and yet is truly in the representative order, it is therefore representative as a principle of cognition, therefore it productively represents to the very cognition, and so there is representation or signification productively.

It is responded first to the major premise of the argument[16] that it is true that a form of impressed specification is a representative similitude of an object, but in the mode of a principle of cognition, not in the mode of a formal awareness or of supposing an awareness to which it would represent, and for this reason it is called a *virtual* similitude, because it is a principle *whence arises* a formal similitude and formal awareness. But as a result of this the rationale of a sign is wanting in an impressed specifier, because even though it is a similitude of an object and a representation uniting

quod in phantasia imprimitur quasi quaedam figura sensibilis, quae manet sensibili abeunte, sicut in cera imprimitur figura annuli. Certum est autem, quod sensibile non imprimit in potentia nisi speciem impressam. Denique 1. Contra Gent. cap. 53. dicit, quod utrumque, id est intentio intellecta et species intelligibillis sunt similitudo obiecti; et quia species intelligibilis, quae intelligendi est principium, est similitudo rei exterioris, sequitur, quod formet intellectus intentionem illius rei similem. Ubi clarissime loquitur de specie impressa, ut distinguitur ab expressa.

Minor vero probatur: Nam imprimis species impressa constituitur in genere repraesentativo, quia est in genere intentionali. Et non repraesentat ut obiectum, sed ut vices gerens obiecti, ergo ut medium inter potentiam et obiectum. Neque repraesentat instrumentaliter, quia non ex praeexistenti cognitione sui movet, nec enim cognoscitur species, ut repraesentet; neque effective, quia non datur repraesentatio seu significatio effectiva, ut quaest. praec. ostendimus. Ergo repraesentat formaliter, quatenus seipsa et per unionem ad potentiam reddit ipsam potentiam similem obiecto similitudine intentionali, quae est repraesentativa.

Confirmatur, quia si ideo species impressa non est signum formale, quia non repraesentat cognitioni, sed ex parte potentiae se tenet ut principium cognitionis, et tamen vere est in genere repraesentativo, ergo est repraesentativa ut principium cognitionis, ergo effective repraesentat ipsi cognitioni, et sic datur repraesentatio seu significatio effective.

RESPONDETUR primo ad maiorem argumenti[16] verum esse, quod species impressa sit repraesentativa similitudo obiecti, sed per modum principii cognitionis, non per modum formalis notitiae aut supponentis notitiam, cui repraesentet, et ideo vocatur similitudo virtualis, quia est principium, unde oritur formalis similitudo et formalis notitia. Ex hoc autem deficit in ea ratio signi, quia licet sit similitudo obiecti

[16] 257/28-29, 257/39-258/14.

and making an object present to a cognitive power, it does not posit the object present to cognition, but is a principle of cognition. For representing something to a power and not to cognition, an impressed specifier does not represent by a manifesting in act, because actual manifestation does not occur without an actual cognition, but it represents or unites and makes an object present, in order that the manifestation itself and cognition may be elicited. And it is of this kind of similitude virtual and in the mode of a principle that St. Thomas is speaking [in the passage in question].

And if you should insist that, because it is not said in the definition of sign that a sign should represent to a power as knowing or to the cognition itself, nor that a sign should be a medium or principle of representing, therefore we are arbitrarily adding these requirements to the definition of sign:

The response is that these requirements are not added to the definition but are contained in it, by the fact that a sign essentially must have a representation manifestative of and leading to a significate; but a manifestative representation cannot manifest except to cognition. Whence a representation which unites an object to a cognitive power for that power to be activated to eliciting a cognition, is not a *manifestative* representation, because it is a representation or union and presence of an object to a power not yet knowing. And so when an impressed specifier informs a power it does not inform that power by rendering it knowing as does a formal sign, which is a formal awareness, but by rendering it able to know, and consequently an impressed specification does not render an object manifested in act, but renders an object actuating a cognitive power and determining it to elicit the cognition in which an object is manifested.

To the proof of the minor premise of the principal argument[17] the response is that an impressed specifier is not representative by any of those modes [as an object, as vicegerent of an object, as a medium between power and object, as instrumental sign, as productive agent, or as formal manifestation], because it is not representative by manifesting in act an object, but by actuating and determining a power in the mode of a principle for eliciting cognition, and this formally is what an impressed specifier accomplishes. But this is not formally to be a sign, because it is not to represent by manifesting actually, as is required for the rationale of a sign, whose representation must be manifestative for a knowing power, and not only actuative of the power for eliciting a cognition.

et repraesentatio uniens et ponens obiectum praesens potentiae, sed non cognitioni, est autem principium cognitionis. Repraesentans enim potentiae et non cognitioni, non repraesentat actu manifestando, quia actualis manifestatio non fit sine actuali cognitione, sed repraesentat seu unit et praesens facit obiectum, ut eliciatur ipsa manifestatio et cognitio. Et de isto genere similitudinis virtualis et per modum principii loquitur Divus Thomas.

Et si instes, quia in definitione signi non dicitur, quod signum repraesentet potentiae ut cognoscenti seu ipsi cognitioni, nec ut sit medium vel principium repraesentandi, ergo voluntarie addimus ista omnia definitioni signi:

Respondetur non addi ista, sed contineri, eo quod signum essentialiter debet habere repraesentationem manifestativam et ductivam ad signatum; repraesentatio autem manifestativa non potest manifestare nisi cognitioni. Unde repraesentatio, quae unit obiectum potentiae, ut constituatur determinata ad eliciendam cognitionem, non est repraesentatio manifestativa, quia est repraesentatio seu unio et praesentia obiecti potentiae nondum cognoscenti. Et sic quando species impressa informat potentiam, non informat illam reddendo cognoscentem sicut signum formale, quod est formalis notitia, sed potentem cognoscere, et consequenter non reddit obiectum manifestatum actu, sed actuans potentiam et determinans, ut eliciat cognitionem, in qua manifestatur obiectum.

Ad probationem minoris principalis argumenti[17] respondetur, quod species impressa non est repraesentativa aliquo ex illis modis, quia non est repraesentativa manifestando actu obiectum, sed actuando et determinando potentiam per modum principii ad eliciendam cognitionem, et hoc formaliter facit species impressa. Sed hoc non est formaliter esse signum, quia non est repraesentare manifestando actualiter, sicut requiritur ad rationem signi, cuius repraesentatio debet esse manifestativa et non solum actuativa potentiae ad cognitionem eliciendam.

---

[17] 258/15-30.

To the confirmation[18] the response is that it does not follow that there is such a thing as "to represent" or "to signify productively," especially when speaking of a manifestative representation, because this does not belong to an impressed specifying form actually, but virtually. Nor, moreover, does it belong to any other mode of representing, because an impressed specifier makes representation in the mode of an actuation of a power by informing, not by producing [the representation] in the cognitive power. But the production of an expressed representation indeed comes about productively from an impressed specifier, but this productive effectuation is not the representation, but the production of a representing thing, namely, of the expressed specifying form, from which the actual representation will come about, not productively, but formally [from] within the cognitive power [in the case of a formal sign], or from an exterior sign in the capacity of an object [in the case of an instrumental sign].

It is argued secondly: An impressed specifier has whatever is formally required for the rationale of an image much more than does an exterior image [actually functioning as a sign], therefore it has whatever is required for the rationale of a sign representing in act.

The antecedent is proved by the fact that an impressed specifier has those two conditions which, according to St. Thomas in the *Summa theologica*, I, q. 93, arts. 1 and 2, are required for the rationale of an image, to wit, that it have a similitude with another and an origin from it. But an impressed form of specification is similar to an object, because it has an intentional coincidence with that object, and it is likewise derived from and originated by that object.

The consequence is proved by the fact that that image of the impressed specifying form has an adjoined representation, because it is an intentional similitude, and this suffices for a concept [i.e., an expressed specifier] to be said to have the rationale of a formal sign, notwithstanding the fact that it is a terminus of cognition and not a medium, because it is not the final terminus, but one ordered to an exterior object. Therefore the impressed specifier likewise, even though it has the rationale of a *principle* of representing, still has the rationale of a sign, because it is not the first principle (for this is the cognitive power itself), but mediates between power and object. And thus St. Thomas in the *Commentary on the Sentences of Peter Lombard*, Book IV, dist. 49, q. 2, art. 1, reply to obj. 15,[19] and in the *Questions at Random*, q. 7, art. 1,[20] calls the impressed specifying form a medium of cognition without qualification.

Ad confirmationem[18] respondetur non sequi, quod detur repraesentare vel significare effective, praesertim loquendo de repraesentatione manifestativa, quia haec non convenit actualiter speciei impressae, sed virtualiter. Imo nec alio modo repraesentandi, quia repraesentationem per modum actuationis potentiae facit species impressa informando, non efficiendo in potentia. Productio autem repraesentationis expressae fit quidem effective a specie, sed talis effectio non est repraesentatio, sed productio rei repraesentantis, scilicet speciei expressae, a qua repraesentatio actualis fiet, non effective, sed formaliter intra potentiam, a signo autem exteriori vice obiecti.

Secundo arguitur: Species impressa habet, quidquid requiritur ad rationem imaginis formaliter multo magis, quam imago exterior, ergo habet quidquid requiritur ad rationem signi actu repraesentantis.

Antecedens probatur, quia habet illas duas conditiones, quae requiruntur ad rationem imaginis secundum D. Thomam 1. p. q. 93. art. 1. et 2., scilicet quod habet similitudinem cum aliquo et originem ab illo. Species autem impressa est similis obiecto, quia habet convenientiam intentionalem cum illo, et similiter est deducta et originata ab obiecto.

Consequentia vero probatur, quia illa imago speciei habet adiunctam repraesentationem, cum sit similitudo intentionalis, et hoc sufficit, ut conceptus dicatur habere rationem signi formalis, etiamsi sit terminus cognitionis et non medium, quia non est terminus ultimus, sed ordinatur ad obiectum exterius. Ergo similiter species impressa licet habeat rationem principii repraesentantis, quia tamen non est primum principium, hoc enim est ipsa potentia, sed mediat inter potentiam et obiectum, habebit rationem signi. Et ita D. Thomas in 4. dist. 49. q. 2. art. 1. ad 15.[19] et Quodlib. 7. art. 1.[20] absolute speciem impressam vocat medium cognitionis.

---

[18] 258/31-38.
[19] *Pa* VII. 1201 a.
[20] *Pa* IX. 553 a.

The response to this argument[21] is that in the first place a form of impressed specification is an image only virtually, not formally; for it is without the second condition, namely, that it be expressed, for it is not *expressed* by the object, but *impressed*, just as semen separated from an animal is not an image, because even though it originated from that animal, it is nevertheless not an expressed terminus, but as it were a power impressed for generating. And therefore not just any sort of origin from another constitutes an image, but an origin in the mode of a terminus finally intended.

Second, the consequence[22] is denied because the representation of an impressed specifying form is not a representation in the mode of a manifestative medium, because it does not represent something to the cognition itself, but in the mode of a form determining and actuating the cognitive power *to be able* to know. In this it is far different from a concept, which, although it keeps to the side of a terminus representing an object, yet it represents this object to the cognition itself, and through that representation the cognition is rendered terminated, and so the concept formally represents terminatively to the knowing power in the mode of an actual manifestation. But an impressed specifying form, even though it is indeed not the first principle [of cognition, this being the cognitive power itself[23]], does nevertheless actuate a power *prior* to cognition, and consequently *prior* to an actual manifestation, which is not to be a representative medium manifestatively, but virtually, in the mode of a principle for eliciting manifestation and cognition. Whence not even the instrumental sign itself, which is an extrinsic object, is said to signify and to manifest, except according as it is cognized, not prior to cognition. For it is a condition of an instrumental sign that it first be something known, in order that it signify, and when St. Thomas calls an impressed specifier a medium or means of cognition, he says that it is a means *by which*, not a medium *in which*; but a means by which is a principle of knowing, not something manifestative in act of an object or thing cognized.

Respondetur[21] imprimis speciem impressam non esse imaginem nisi virtualiter, non formaliter; deest enim illi secunda conditio, scilicet quod sit expressa, non enim est expressa ab obiecto, sed impressa, sicut semen decisum ab animali non est imago, quia licet ab illo sit originatum, non tamen tamquam terminus expressus, sed tamquam virtus impressa ad generandum. Et ideo non quaelibet origo ab alio constituit imaginem, sed origo per modum termini ultimo intenti.

Secundo negatur consequentia,[22] quia repraesentatio speciei impressae non est repraesentatio per modum medii manifestativi, quia non repraesentat ipsi cognitioni, sed per modum formae determinantis et actuantis potentiam, ut possit cognoscere. In quo longe differt a conceptu, qui licet teneat se ex parte termini repraesentantis obiectum, tamen repraesentat hoc ipsi cognitioni, et per illam redditur cognitio terminata, et sic formaliter terminative repraesentat potentiae cognoscenti per modum actualis manifestationis. At vero species impressa licet non sit primum principium,[23] tamen actuat potentiam ante cognitionem, et consequenter ante manifestationem actualem, quod est non esse medium repreaesentativum manifestative, sed virtualiter, per modum principii ad eliciendam manifestationem et cognitionem. Unde nec ipsum signum instrumentale, quod est obiectum extrinsecum, signare et manifestare dicitur, nisi prout cognitum, non ante cognitionem. Est enim conditio in signo instrumentali, quod prius sit cognitum, ut significet, et quando Divus Thomas vocat speciem impressam medium cognitionis, dicit esse medium *quo*, non *in quo;* medium autem quo est principium cognoscendi, non actu manifestativum obiecti seu rei cognitae.

---

[21] 260/19-23.
[22] 260/22, 260/32-47.
[23] See 260/42-43.

QUESTION 4

Whether an Act of Cognizing Is a Formal Sign

QUAESTIO QUARTA

Utrum Actus Cognoscendi Sit Signum Formale

We suppose that the act of cognizing is distinguished in the understanding from the object itself cognized, and from the impressed and expressed forms of specification. For, as St. Thomas says in the *Disputed Questions on the Power of God,* q. 8, art. 1,[1] there are four factors which concur in the understanding for cognition, to wit, the thing which is understood, the conception of the understanding, the [impressed] specification by which it is understood, and the very act itself of understanding. And the reason is that there are necessarily acknowledged to be in our understanding some vital operations which proceed from the understanding when it is formed by an impressed specification, since indeed the operation of the understanding and its cognition are born from an object and the power; but an object actuates a power by means of an impressed form of specification. Again, this vital operation cannot formally be the very expressed specifier or word formed by the understanding, because if the word was formed from that [i.e., on the basis of a given] impressed specification, it was formed by some operation, and consequently the operation is distinguished from the expressed specifier in question. And we call the operation "the act of understanding," whereas we call the expressed form of specification "the term or word spoken and expressed by that operation," insofar as it is a mode of expressing or diction.

SUPPONIMUS distingui in intellectu actum cognoscendi ab ipso obiecto cognito et a specie impressa et expressa. Nam, ut dicit D. Thomas q. 8. de Potentia art. 1.,[1] quatuor sunt, quae in intellectu concurrunt ad cognitionem, scilicet res, quae intelligitur, conceptio intellectus, species, qua intelligitur, et ipsum intelligere. Et ratio est, quia necessario fatendum est in nostro intellectu dari aliquam operationem vitalem, quae procedit ab intellectu formato specie, siquidem operatio intellectus et cognitio eius paritur ab obiecto et potentia; obiectum autem media specie actuat potentiam. Rursus haec operatio formaliter non potest esse ipsa species expressa seu verbum formatum ab intellectu, quia si est formatum ab illa, aliqua operatione formatum est, et consequenter operatio distinguitur a tali specie expressa. Et operationem vocamus actum intelligendi, speciem autem expressam terminum seu verbum dictum et expressum ab illa, in quantum dictio est.

---

[1] *Pa* VIII. 168 b.

This is further confirmed by the fact that an act of understanding is considered either as it is an expressing diction, or as a pure act of contemplation and cognition. If as an expression or diction, it is essentially a production of a word, and therefore demands that that word be the terminus of such production. If as a pure act of cognition, it requires that an object be applied and united to that act in an immaterial existence, not only in the mode of a principle by which the cognition is elicited, but also in the mode of a terminus in which the object is attained. But the terminus of a cognition is not the cognition itself, but the cognition is a tendency toward the object known. And because the object is not known and does not terminate a cognition according to a mind-independent and material being outside the act of knowing, but as rendered spiritual and immaterial within the cognitive power, some intelligible form is required in which the object is rendered thus immaterial and spiritual on the side of the terminus. And this is the expressed specifier or word. All of which will be explained more at length in q. 11[2] of the books *Concerning the Soul.*

Seeing therefore that it has been determined, concerning the impressed and the expressed specifiers, whether they are formal signs, it remains to show whether the act itself of the understanding, which is the cognition and tendency toward the object, is a formal sign.

In view of the foregoing distinctions, there is but one conclusion: **The act of understanding thus distinct from the impressed and the expressed specifying forms is not a formal sign, in whatever operation of the understanding it be taken.**

This conclusion is against some more recent authors, including also some Thomists, but nevertheless in favor of it we find Capreolus, in his *Commentary on the Sentences of Peter Lombard,* Book IV, dist. 49, q. 1, and Ferrariensis, in his *Commentary on the Summa contra gentiles,* Book II, chap. 49, toward the end of the paragraph beginning with the words, ''Ex hoc enim . . .'' (''For from this . . .'').

The underlying REASON FOR THIS CONCLUSION is the fact that a sign is essentially something representative, but the act of understanding formally is not a representation, but an operation and tendency toward an object. Whence, since habit is generated as the result of such acts multiplied, an acquired habit is not something representative, but a disposition of the cognitive power for eliciting acts similar to those which formed the habit.

Unde etiam hoc amplius confirmatur, quia intelligere vel consideratur ut est dictio exprimens, vel ut purum contemplari et cognoscere. Si ut dictio, est essentialiter productio verbi, atque adeo petit, quod illud sit terminus talis productionis. Si ut purum cognoscere, requirit, quod obiectum sit illi applicatum et unitum in esse immateriali, non solum per modum principii, quo elicitur cognitio, sed etiam per modum termini, in quo attingitur obiectum. Terminus autem cognitionis non est ipsa cognitio, sed cognitio est tendentia ad obiectum, quod cognoscitur. Et quia non cognoscitur obiectum nec terminat cognitionem secundum esse reale et materiale ad extra, sed ut redditur spirituale et immateriale ad intra, requiritur aliqua forma intelligibilis, in qua reddatur obiectum sic immateriale et spirituale ex parte termini. Et hoc est species expressa seu verbum. Quod totum latius explicabitur in libro de Anima q. 11.[2]

Quia ergo determinatum est de ipsa specie impressa et expressa, an sint signa, restat id videre de actu ipso intellectus, qui est cognitio et tendentia ad obiectum.

SIT ERGO UNICA CONCLUSIO: **Actus intelligendi sic distinctus a specie impressa et expressa non est signum formale, in quacumque operatione intellectus sumatur.**

Haec conclusio est contra aliquos recentiores, etiam ex thomistis, sed tamen pro illa videri potest Capreolus in 4. dist. 49. q. 1., Ferrariensis 2. Contra Gent. cap. 49. § *Ex hoc enim* in fine.

RATIO EST, quia signum essentialiter est repraesentativum, actus autem intelligendi formaliter non est repraesentatio, sed operatio et tendentia ad obiectum. Unde cum per tales actus multiplicatos generatur habitus, habitus genitus non est repraesentativus, sed dispositio potentiae ad eliciendum actus sibi similes.

---

[2] correcting the original reference to ''q. 10.'' For the reasons, see, in this Book, Question 1, note 5, and Question 2, notes 6 and 41.

And thus St. Thomas, denying, in the *Summa theologica,* I, q. 12, art. 2, that there is a specifier representative of God as he is in himself, grants that there exists the light of glory, which is a similitude strenghening the intellect on the side of power, and so he denies to that light or habit the rationale of a representation. Therefore similarly an act of understanding is not a representation, because acts are similar to habits, and if the act of understanding were a representation, much more would the representation coincide with the habit than with the act, because a habit is a kind of permanent thing, whereas an act is a kind of operation.

This is confirmed by considering that if the act of understanding were a representation, it would be a representation either distinct from or the same as the expressed specifier. It cannot be the same as the expressed specifier, because the act of understanding is a thing distinct from the expressed specifier. But if the act of understanding is distinct, either it represents the same object as the word (the expressed specifier), and so one of these two — act or word — is superfluous, or else it represents something distinct, and so the same thing will not be known through the act of cognition and through its terminus which is the word.

Finally, that representation of the act of understanding would be either an impressed similitude or an expressed one, because it does not seem possible for there to be any variable intervening in the order of representation between the expressed and impressed specification of a cognitive act. If the representation in question is an impressed form of specification, it functions in the mode of a principle that is impressed or infused by something extrinsic to the understanding itself. But an act of understanding cannot be imprinted from without, but arises from within the understanding, because it is a vital act. If the representation is a form of expressed specification, then it is the word and functions in the mode of a terminus expressed and produced; but here we are speaking about the act of understanding according as it is distinct from the word.

Resolution of Counter-Arguments

It is argued first: To be a formal sign is to be a formal awareness of some cognitive power in the mode of a representation; but all this belongs to the act of knowing; therefore it is a formal sign.

The minor premise is proved. For certainly it is the case that an act of knowing is a formal awareness, since that act is the very cognition itself which is one with awareness. But that an act of knowing exists in the mode of a representation is proved by the fact that it unites an

Et ita D. Thomas 1. p. q. 12. art. 2. negans dari speciem repraesentativam Dei, ut est in se, concedit dari lumen gloriae, quod est similitudo confortans intellectum ex parte potentiae, et sic negat lumini seu habitui rationem repraesentationis. Ergo similiter actus intelligendi non est repraesentatio, quia actus sunt similes habitibus, et si esset repraesentatio, multo magis id conveniret habitui, quia est res quaedam permanens, quam actui, qui est quaedam operatio.

Et confirmatur, quia si actus esset repraesentatio, vel esset distincta repraesentatio a specie expressa vel eadem. Eadem esse non potest, cum sit res distincta actus intelligendi a specie expressa. Si autem est distincta, vel idem repraesentat, quod verbum, et sic altera illarum superfluit, vel aliquid distinctum, et sic non cognosceretur idem per actum cognitionis et per eius terminum, qui est verbum.

Denique vel illa repraesentatio actus intelligendi esset similitudo impressa vel expressa, quia non videtur posse dari aliquod medium in genere repraesentationis inter expressum et impressum. Si est impressa, habet se per modum principii, quod imprimitur seu infunditur ab extrinseco ipsi intellectui. Actus autem intelligendi non potest ab extrinseco imprimi, sed ab intrinseco intellectus oritur, cum sit actus vitalis. Si est expressa, ergo est verbum et per modum termini expressi et producti se habet; nos autem hic loquimur de actu intelligendi prout distincto a verbo.

Solvuntur argumenta.

Primo arguitur: Signum formale est esse potentiae formalem notitiam alicuius per modum repraesentationis; sed hoc totum convenit actui cognoscendi; ergo est signum formale.

Minor probatur. Nam quod sit formalis notitia, constat, cum sit ipsamet cognitio, quae est idem quod notitia. Quod autem per modum repraesentatio-

object to a cognitive power; for the act of understanding, as St. Thomas says in the *Summa theologica*, I, q. 27, art. 1, reply to obj. 2, consists in this, that it makes the understanding one with the understandable object itself; but this act of uniting is an act of making present to a cognitive power the object which it unites with that power, therefore it is a representation.

And this is confirmed by the fact that an immanent action is not a formal production, but only a virtual one. But formally an act of knowing is an act of the order of a quality, which is engaged with an object by tending toward it, not by operating [having an effect] on it. And yet this tendency unites the object to the cognitive power, even though the respecting does not produce the object, and consequently the act of knowing represents, because to represent is to make present or to unite knowably.

The response to this[3] is that an act of understanding is not a formal sign, because the rationale of representing is wanting to it, as we have said. And to the objection asserting the contrary,[4] the response is that an act of understanding unites an object [to a cognitive power] in the mode of an operation tending toward that object, not in the manner of a form which substitutes for and is a vicegerent on behalf of that object. And therefore an act of understanding does not have a rationale of representing, because a representation is made by containing another as its vicegerent, not by operating. Whence the unitive action [of the act of understanding] is not said to represent, even though it unifies [power and object], and so not every mode of uniting is a mode of representing; just as an impressed specifier too, for example, because it unites [power and object] in the mode of the principle of the cognition, does not unite in the mode of [a specifier] representing formally.

To the confirmation[5] the response is that an act of understanding, though it is a quality, does, nevertheless, not render an object present as a form keeping on the side of the object as if it were a vicegerent of that object, but as a form tending toward and operating with respect to [assimilating] the object from the side of the power. And therefore it is not a representative but an operative union, that is to say, a union in the mode of a second act, not as containing, but as tending toward an object.

It is argued secondly: the awareness of an exterior sense is a formal sign, and yet there there is no word or expressed image, as St. Thomas teaches in the *Disputed Questions on Truth*, q. 8, art. 5,[6] and in the

nis, probatur, quia unit obiectum potentiae; intelligere enim, ut dicit D. Thomas 1. p. q. 27. art. 1. ad 2., consistit in hoc, quod facit unum cum ipso intelligibili; sed hoc unire est praesens facere potentiae obiectum, quod unit, ergo est repraesentatio.

Et confirmatur, quia actio immanens non est formalis productio, sed solum virtualis. Formaliter autem est actus de genere qualitatis, qui versatur circa obiectum tendendo in illud, non operando illud. Ista autem tendentia etsi non producit obiectum, unit obiectum potentiae, et consequenter repraesentat, quia repraesentare est praesens facere seu unire cognoscibiliter.

Respondetur[3] actum intelligendi non esse signum formale, quia deficit ei ratio repraesentandi, ut diximus. Et ad impugnationem in oppositum[4] respondetur, quod actus intelligendi unit obiectum per modum operationis tendentis in illud, non per modum formae, quae substituat et vices gerat pro illa. Et ideo non habet rationem repraesentantis, quia repraesentatio fit continendo alterum tamquam vices eius gerens, non operando. Unde actio unitiva non dicitur repraesentare, licet uniat, et sic non omnis modus uniendi est modus repraesentandi; sicut etiam species impressa, quia unit per modum principii cognitionis, non unit per modum repraesentantis formaliter.

Ad confirmationem[5] respondetur, quod actus intelligendi, licet sit qualitas, non tamen reddit praesens obiectum ut forma ex parte obiecti se tenens quasi vices eius gerens, sed ex parte potentiae tendens et operans circa obiectum. Et ideo non est unio repraesentativa, sed operativa seu per modum actus secundi, non ut continens, sed ut tendens ad obiectum.

Secundo arguitur: Notitia sensus exterioris est signum formale, et tamen ibi non est verbum aut imago expressa, ut docet D. Thomas q. 8. de Veritate art. 5.[6] et

[3] 264/43-265/7.
[4] 264/50-265/7.
[5] 265/8-16.
[6] *Pa* IX. 122 a.

Treatise on the Nature of the Word of the Understanding.[7] Therefore an expressed similitude is not required for the rationale of a formal sign, but an act of knowing suffices.

The major premise is proved by the fact that if the awareness of an exterior sense were not a formal sign, there would not be formal awareness in the external senses, and consequently no formal cognition, because a formal awareness is a formal sign. Indeed, as Master Dominic Soto says in his *Summaries of Logic*, Book I, chap. 3, the awareness of the external senses is a terminus, inasmuch as it derives from the mode of signifying; but it is of the rationale of a terminus to be a sign. Therefore an act of external sense is a sign, and not an instrumental sign, therefore a formal one.

This is confirmed because an act of an external sense is truly an immanent act, therefore it is the final complement and perfection of a power, therefore in it occurs the final and perfect union with an object, therefore also a representation, because there is no other union between external sense and an object than [the one that occurs] by means of the act.

The response to this[8] is that it is true that external sense does not have a word or expressed image in which it could know, because owing to its materiality it does not demand so great a union with the object that the object must be within the power, but rather must sensation be borne to the thing located outside, which is ultimately rendered sensible as it exists independent of sense.[9] And even though the cognition of external sense is an immanent action, yet it is not of necessity a production, nor does it of necessity respect the terminus as altered by itself,[10] but as

opusc. 14.[7] Ergo non requiritur ad rationem signi formalis similitudo expressa, sed sufficit actus cognoscendi.

Maior probatur, quia alias in sensibus externis non daretur notitia formalis, et consequenter neque cognitio formalis, quia notitia formalis est signum formale. Imo, ut dicit Mag. Soto lib. 1. Summul. cap. 3., notitia sensuum exteriorum est terminus, quantum est ex modo significandi; de ratione autem termini est, quod sit signum. Ergo actus sensus externi signum est, et non instrumentale, ergo formale.

Et confirmatur, quia actus sensus externi est vere actus immanens, ergo est ultimum complementum et perfectio potentiae, ergo in ipso fit ultima et perfecta unio cum obiecto, ergo et repraesentatio, cum non sit alia unio inter sensum externum et obiectum quam mediante actu.

RESPONDETUR[8] verum esse, quod sensus externus non habet verbum seu imaginem expressam, in qua cognoscat, quia propter suam materialitatem non petit tantam unionem cum obiecto, ut sit intra potentiam, sed debet ferri in rem extra positam, quae ultimate redditur sensibilis ut est extra sensum.[9] Et licet cognitio sensus externi sit actio immanens, non tamen de necessitate est productio nec respicit terminum ut immutatum a se,[10] sed ut inten-

---

[7] De natura verbi intellectus (*Pa* XVI. 179).

[8] 265/44-266/4.

[9] Cf. Book II, Question 2, notes 2 and 8, but see esp. Book III, Question 2, notes 9 and 10, and the *caveat* in Phil. nat. 4. p. q. 6. art. 4., Reiser ed., III. 195b21-25 (quoted in note 16 to Article 1 of the Second Preamble, p. 86 above).

[10] Phil. nat. 4. p. q. 6. art. 4., Reiser ed., III. 196b31-197a2: "*omnem actionem debere habere terminum, . . . sed non eodem modo. Nam actio immanens ut formaliter immanens solum habet terminum contemplatum aut amatum seu terminum obiectum, non productum, ideoque vocatur actio metaphysica, non physica, id est immutativa termini. Ut autem virtualiter et eminenter transiens habet terminum productum, sed non semper de necessitate, quia in primo, scilicet in termino contemplato, salvatur. Actio autem formaliter transiens semper habet terminum productum seu immutatum, quia est formaliter fieri et tendentia ad terminum.*"—"Every action must have a terminus, but not in the same way. For an immanent action as formally immanent has only a terminus contemplated (apprehended) or loved, that is to say, an objectified, not a produced, terminus; and for this reason it is called a 'metaphysical' action, not a physical action, that is, not an action that leaves its terminus altered. It may indeed have as virtually and eminently transitive a produced terminus, but not as a matter of necessity in every case, because in the first, namely, in a terminus contemplated, the action in question is achieved in what is essential to it. But a formally transitive action always has a terminus produced or altered by its existence, because it formally consists in the becoming and tendency toward the terminus." A clear exposition of this distinction is provided by Yves R. Simon, "An Essay on the Classification of Action and the Understanding of Act," *Revue de l'Université d'Ottawa* 41 (octobre-décembre, 1971), 518-541.

intentionally and objectively united, though it can have a productive energy virtually; just as cognition insofar as it is an expression produces a word, and love insofar as it is a spiration produces an impulse, so external sensation too produces a representation[11] or specifying form, not within itself, but in the internal senses, as St. Thomas teaches in the *Summa contra gentiles*, Book IV, chap. 11, and in the *Treatise on the Nature of the Word of the Understanding.*[12] Nevertheless, of itself an immanent act is not an action in the mode of a movement and of a way of tending toward a further term, but in the mode of a final actuality in which a whole cognition is completed, and for this reason the act of understanding is compared by St. Thomas to the very act of existing, in the *Summa theologica*, I, q. 14, art. 4, and in many other places.

Wherefore to the proof of the argument[13] it is said that in external sense there is a formal awareness in the mode of a cognition which is a tendency of a power toward an object, not in the mode of a representation, which is a form substituting in place of the object in a power. And so even though a formal sign is said to be a formal awareness terminatively, because it is a terminus of cognition, yet not every formal awareness is a formal sign, specifically, the very act of knowing. Nor is the cognition of external sense said by Master Soto to be a terminus unqualifiedly, but qualifiedly, only according as it is a kind of *simple* cognition.

To the confirmation[14] the response is that an act of external sense is a final complement in the mode of second act as counterdistinguished from transient action, because, as St. Thomas says in the *Disputed Questions on Truth*, q. 14, art. 3,[15] the act of a transient operation has [its] complement in a term which is produced outside the agent; but the complement of immanent actions is not derived from that which is produced, but from the mode of the acting, because the act itself is the perfection and actuality of the power. Whence excellence in these powers is not considered according to the best that is made, but according to this, that *the operation* be good. Thus St. Thomas. But, even though the operation of external sense is the final perfection uniting object to power, yet the operation does not accomplish the union representatively, because, as we have often said, it is a union in the mode of a ten-

tionaliter et obiective unitum, virtualiter tamen potest habere vim productionis; sicut cognitio in quantum dictio producit verbum, et amor in quantum spiratio impulsum, et sensatio externa producit repraesentationem[11] seu speciem, non intra se, sed in sensibus internis, ut docet S. Thomas 4. Contra Gent. cap. 11. et opusc. 14.[12] Ex se tamen actus immanens non est actio per modum motus et viae tendentis ad ulteriorem terminum, sed per modum ultimae actualitatis, in qua completur tota cognitio, et ideo comparatur intelligere a Divo Thoma ipsi existere 1. p. q. 14. art. 4. et alibi saepe.

Quare ad probationem[13] argumenti dicitur, quod in sensu externo datur notitia formalis per modum cognitionis, quae est tendentia potentiae ad obiectum, non per modum repraesentationis, quae est forma loco obiecti substituens in potentia. Et sic licet signum formale dicatur notitia formalis terminative, quia est terminus cognitionis, non tamen omnis notitia formalis est signum formale, scilicet ipse actus cognoscendi. Nec dicitur a Mag. Soto terminus cognitio sensus externi absolute, sed secundum quid, solum prout est simplex quaedam cognitio.

Ad confirmationem[14] respondetur, quod actus sensus externi est ultimum complementum per modum actus secundi ad differentiam actionis transeuntis, quia, ut dicit Divus Thomas q. 14. de Veritate art. 3.,[15] actus operationis transeuntis habet complementum in termino, quod fit extra agentem; complementum autem actionum immanentium non sumitur penes id, quod fit, sed penes modum agendi, quia ipse actus est perfectio et actualitas potentiae. Unde virtus in his potentiis non attenditur penes optimum, quod facit, sed penes hoc, quod operatio sit bona. Ita Divus Thomas. Ceterum licet operatio sensus externi sit perfectio ultima uniens obiectum potentiae, non tamen repraesentative id faciat, quia, ut saepe diximus, est unio per modum

[11] The 1663 Lyons text reads here: "*idolum*"—"icon."

[12] *De natura verbi intellectus* (*Pa* XVI. 179).

[13] 266/5-15.

[14] 266/16-22.

[15] *Pa* IX. 232 b.

dency toward the object from the side of the power, not in the mode of a form substituting for the object;[16] but a representation is formally a substitution for that which is represented.

tendentiae ex parte potentiae ad obiectum, non per modum formae substituentis pro obiecto;[16] repraesentatio autem formaliter est substitutio eius, quod repraesentatur.

---

[16] See Book III, Question 2, 309/47-312/6, esp. 311/8-312/6, and 323/13-35, and notes 1, 9, and 10.

Question 5

Whether the Division of Signs into Natural, Stipulated, and Customary[1] *Is a Sound Division*

Quaestio Quinta

Utrum Sit Bona Divisio in Signum Naturale et Ad Placitum et Ex Consuetudine[1]

There is no difficulty about the soundness of this division as regards adequacy, for by these members the whole which is to be divided is exhausted; but there is a difficulty as regards the quality of the division, to wit, how is a stipulated sign truly a sign, and consequently there is a question whether the division is univocal.

The only conclusion is: **If this division of signs into natural and stipulated is considered entitatively and in the order of mind-independent being,[2] it is an analogous division; if it is considered in the order of the representative or knowable, it is a univocal division,[3] and a stipulated sign is truly a sign in the office and capacity of an object, which it exercises.**

The first part of the conclusion is manifest, because, as was established in Book I,[4] a sign is constituted in

Bonitas huius divisionis non habet difficultatem quantum ad adaequationem, exhauritur enim per ista membra totum divisum; sed quantum ad qualitatem, quomodo scilicet signum ad placitum sit vere signum, et consequenter an divisio univoca sit.

Sit unica conclusio: **Si haec divisio signi in naturale et ad placitum entitative et in esse rei[2] consideretur, analoga est; si in genere repraesentativi seu cognoscibilis, univoca est,[3] et signum ad placitum est vere signum in officio et vice obiecti, quam exercet.**

Prima pars conclusionis manifesta est, quia, ut praec. libro[4] tractatum est, signum

---

[1] Here we encounter a structural anomaly in the *Treatise*. Although Poinsot poses this Question in terms of all three of his classes of instrumental sign, in the body of the Question he proceeds in terms of only two of the classes—the stipulated and the natural—reserving the entire next Question to discussing the status of the customary sign vis-à-vis these other two. Implicit in this anomaly is the central novelty of Poinsot's doctrine as it applies to the understanding of how sense perceptible signs function in experience. Here I can only call the reader's attention to the anomaly. Elsewhere I have tried to set forth at length what it implies: see my "Toward the Origin of Semiotic," in *Sight, Sound, and Sense*, ed. T. A. Sebeok (Bloomington: Indiana University Press, 1978), pp. 1-30—with the caveat entered in Deely 1982: 214 (gloss on "1978a").

[2] The 1663 Lyons text reads here: "*materialiter*"—"materially."

[3] See the discussion of Suarez's views in note 1 to the "Order of the Preamble on Mind-Dependent Being," p. 44 above; also Book I, Question 2, 149/41-151/21, Question 4, 187/28-190/23, with notes 13, 33 and 35; and Book II, Question 1, 235/36-236/46, Question 5, 270/37-271/21.

[4] In the original Latin: "quaest."

the category of relation formally speaking. But entitatively speaking, there is nothing univocal to a relation that exists independently of being objectively apprehended (a mind-independent relation) and a relation that depends for its whole existence on being an object of apprehension (a mind-dependent relation), because they cannot be in the same category; but the relation of a natural sign is mind-independent, as we saw in Book I, whereas the relation of a stipulated sign cannot be mind-independent. Therefore there is, entitatively speaking, nothing univocal to these signs.

You might say: It is not certain that the relation of a natural sign is mind-independent, nor that a stipulated sign consists in a mind-dependent relation, but that the extrinsic denomination by which it is said to be imposed by will suffices for a stipulated sign; therefore the foundation for the conclusion that the division entitatively considered is analogous does not hold up.

But this second proposition, that a stipulated sign consists in an extrinsic denomination, does not weaken the foundation of the conclusion that the division of signs into natural and stipulated is analogous in the entitative order, because if a stipulated sign only has the being of a sign from an extrinsic denomination, by this very fact it is a sign in a certain respect and not simply, because an extrinsic denomination is not formally something mind-independent existing in that which is denominated, but it is presuppositively [something independent of being itself apprehended as existing] in the extrinsic subject denominating.[5] *The first proposition*, that the relation of a natural sign to its significate is a mind-independent relation, was explained in the preceding Book, where we show that a natural sign bespeaks something mind-independent in the mode of relation,[6] although some say that the relation is transcendental, not categorial. Yet those who would say that a sign in what is formal to it consists in a mind-dependent relation, must consequently constitute a rationale of sign entitatively univocal in this division of signs into stipulated and natural.

The second part of the conclusion hangs from that distinguished doctrine in Cajetan's *Commentary on the Summa theologica*, I, q. 1, art. 3, that the differences of things *as things* are quite other than the differences of things *as objects* and in the being of an object; and things that differ in kind or more than in kind in the one line, can differ in the other line not at all or not in the same way.[7] And so, seeing that the rationale of a sign pertains to the rationale of the knowable [the line of thing as object], because it substitutes for the object, it will well be the case that in the rationale of object a mind-independent natural sign and a stipulated mind-

constituitur in genere relationis formaliter loquendo. Sed relationi reali et rationis nihil univocum est entitative loquendo, cum non possint esse in eodem praedicamento; relatio autem signi naturalis est realis, ut vidimus ibi, relatio vero signi ad placitum realis esse non potest. Ergo nihil illis univocum est entitative loquendo.

Dices: Non est certum relationem signi naturalis esse realem nec signum ad placitum consistere in relatione rationis, sed sufficit illi denominatio extrinseca, qua dicitur impositum a voluntate; ergo non subsistit fundamentum positum.

Ceterum hoc secundum non enervat illud, quia si solum habet esse signum ex denominatione extrinseca, hoc ipso est secundum quid tale et non simpliciter, quia denominatio extrinseca non est formaliter esse reale existens in eo, quod denominatur, sed praesuppositive in extrinseco denominante.[5] *Primum* vero quaest. praec. explicatum est, ubi ostendimus signum naturale dicere aliquid reale per modum relationis,[6] licet aliqui dicant illam esse transcendentalem, non praedicamentalem. Qui tamen dicerent signum pro formali consistere in relatione rationis, consequenter univocam constituere habent rationem signi entitative in hac divisione signi ad placitum et naturalis.

SECUNDA PARS conclusionis pendet ex illa celebri doctrina apud Caietanum 1. p. q. 1. art. 3., quod aliae sunt differentiae rerum ut res, aliae ut obiectum et in esse obiecti; et quae specie vel plus quam specie differunt in una linea, possunt in alia non differe vel non ita differre.[7] Et sic cum ratio signi pertineat ad rationem cognoscibilis, cum sit vice obiectum, stabit bene, quod in ratione obiecti signum naturale reale et ad placitum rationis sint signa univoca;

[5] As explained in the First Preamble above, Article 1, 55/6-41.
[6] Book I, Question 2.
[7] Cross-references in note 3 above and note 17 below.

dependent sign are univocal signs; just as a mind-independent being and a mind-dependent being assume one rationale in their being as object, since indeed they terminate the same power, namely, the power of understanding, and can be attained by the same habit, namely, by Metaphysics, or at least specify two univocally coincident sciences, as for example, Logic and Physics. Therefore in the being of an object specifying, stipulated and natural signs coincide univocally.

So too a cognitive power is truly and univocally moved and led to a thing signified by means of a stipulated sign and by means of a natural sign. For that we are moved by stipulated signs toward perceiving signified things, experience itself manifests, and that this comes about univocally [i.e., just as if the stipulated signs were mind-independent beings] follows from the fact that a stipulated sign does not signify in a qualified sense and dependently upon a mind-independent natural sign in the very rationale of signifying; for through itself alone an uttered significative sound leads to a signified thing just as do the other instrumental signs that are natural.

Nor does it matter that a sound or name does not signify except by means of a concept, which is a natural sign. For this also holds for a natural instrumental sign, that it does not represent except by means of a concept making it an object of awareness, and yet the natural instrumental sign is not on this account a sign analogically, but truly and univocally.[8] For the fact that [instrumental] signs depend on a concept in representing does not remove the univocal rationale of a sign, since indeed a concept and cognition is that to which the [instrumental] signs represent, not a means by which they represent as by a formal rationale, even though the instrumental signs [if they are stipulated or customary] may be produced from that concept and cognition. For not every dependence of one thing on another constitutes an analogy, but only that which is in an order to participating a general or common rationale; for unless that inequality [i.e., a given dependence] is partly the same [in rationale] and partly different, it does not destroy univocation, as St. Thomas best explains in his *Commentary* on the first book of Aristotle's treatise *On Interpretation*, in the opening paragraphs of the eighth reading.[9]

Finally, this second part of our conclusion is openly taken from St. Thomas. For in the *Summa theologica*, III, q. 60, art. 6, reply to obj. 2, he says that "although words and other sensible things are in different orders so far as pertains to the *nature* of a thing, they nevertheless enter the same order in the rationale of a *signifying* thing, which

sicut ens reale et rationis in esse obiecti induunt unam rationem, siquidem terminant eandem potentiam, scilicet intellectum, et ab eodem habitu possunt attingi, scilicet a Metaphysica, vel saltem duas scientias univoce convenientes specificare, v. g. Logicam et Physicam. Ergo in esse obiecti specificantis univoce conveniunt.

Sic etiam per signum ad placitum et per signum naturale vere et univoce movetur et deducitur potentia ad signatum. Quod enim moveamur a signis ad placitum ad percipienda signata, ipsa experientia manifestat, et quod hoc univoce fiat, constat, cum signum ad placitum non significet secundum quid et dependenter in ipsa ratione significandi a signo naturali; nam per se solum vox significativa prolata deducit ad signatum sicut alia signa naturalia instrumentalia.

Nec obstat, quod vox seu nomen non significat nisi mediante conceptu, qui est signum naturale. Hoc enim etiam signo instrumentali naturali convenit, quod non nisi mediante conceptu et notitia sui repraesentat, et tamen non ob hoc est signum analogice, sed vere et univoce.[8] Quod enim signa in repraesentando dependeant a conceptu, non tollit univocam rationem signi, siquidem conceptus et cognitio est, cui repraesentant, non mediante quo repraesentant tamquam formali ratione, licet effective possint ab eo esse. Non omnis autem dependentia unius ab alio constituit analogiam, sed solum illa, quae est in ordine ad participandam rationem communem; nisi enim illa inaequalis sit et partim eadem, partim diversa, non destruit univocationem, ut optime tradit S. Thomas 1. Periherm. lect. 8. in princ.[9]

Denique haec secunda pars nostrae conclusionis aperte deducitur ex D. Thoma. Nam 3. p. q. 60. art. 6. ad 2. inquit, «quod quamvis verba et aliae res sensibiles sint in diverso genere, quantum pertinet ad naturam rei, conveniunt tamen in ra-

[8] See Question 1 of this Book, 236/46-237/15.

[9] *Le* I. 36. n. 6.

rationale is more perfect in the case of words than in the case of other things. And for this reason a thing that is in a certain way one comes to be from words and things in the case of the sacraments, insofar, to wit, as the signification of the things is perfected through words.'' And in the *Commentary on the Sentences of Peter Lombard*, Book IV, dist. 1, q. 1, art. 1, quaestiunc. 5, reply to obj. 4,[10] he says that ''although the representation which is from the similitude of a natural property imports a certain aptitude for signifying, nevertheless the determination and completion of the signification is from institution.'' St. Thomas therefore feels that the signification in stipulated signs is not signification analogically, since indeed it can actuate and perfect a natural signification and constitute with it the one artificial sign which is the sacrament.

Resolution of Counter-Arguments

First it is argued: A specific rationale cannot remain when the generic rationale is removed; but the generic rationale of a sign, that is, relation, is not found in a stipulated sign except analogically; therefore neither is a specific rationale of sign found there except analogically.

The minor premise of this argument follows from what has been said previously, because the sign-relation in stipulated signs is a mind-dependent relation, which does not coincide univocally with a mind-independent relation in the rationale of relation.

It may be said in response that the argument[11] incontestably shows that a stipulated sign taken in the order of being and categorially is not a sign univocally with a natural sign, but it does not show that it is not univocally a sign in the being of a knowable and representative thing.[12] For just as it is well the case that some things do not coincide univocally in the being of thing, as, for example, quantity and quality and substance, and yet do coincide univocally in the being of object and knowable thing, because they pertain to the same knowledge or cognitive power, so is it also the case that some signs differ in kind in the being of thing and in the rationale of being categorially and do not coincide univocally, yet do coincide univocally in objective or vice-objective rationale, which is the rationale of a representative and significative thing.

And if you should insist: Certainly this very representative genus is relation, or we have unwisely

tione significandi, quae perfectius est in verbis quam in aliis rebus. Et ideo ex verbis et rebus fit quodammodo unum in Sacramentis, in quantum scilicet per verba perficitur significatio rerum». Et in 4. dist. 1. q. 1. art. 1. quaestiunc. 5. ad 4.[10] dicit, quod «etsi repraesentatio, quae est ex similitudine naturalis proprietatis, importet aptitudinem quamdam ad significandum, tamen determinatio et complementum significationis ex institutione est». Sentit ergo D. Thomas in signis ad placitum non esse analogice significationem, siquidem actuare et perficere potest significationem naturalem et cum ea unum signum artificiale constituere, quod est sacramentum.

Solvuntur argumenta

Primo arguitur: Remota ratione generica non potest manere specifica; sed in signo ad placitum non invenitur ratio generica signi, scilicet relatio, nisi analogice; ergo nec specifica ratio signi invenitur nisi analogice.

Minor constat ex dictis, quia relatio signi in signis ad placitum est rationis, quae in ratione relationis non convenit univoce cum relatione reali.

Respondetur argumentum[11] convincere, quod signum ad placitum in genere entis et praedicamentaliter acceptum non sit univoce signum cum signo naturali, non tamen quod in esse cognoscibilis et repraesentativi non sit univoce signum.[12] Sicut enim stat bene, quod aliqua non conveniant univoce in esse rei, ut quantitas et qualitas et substantia, et tamen in esse obiecti et scibilis conveniant univoce, quia pertinent ad eandem scientiam vel potentiam, ita stat bene, quod aliqua signa in esse rei et in ratione entis praedicamentaliter differant genere et non conveniant univoce, in ratione tamen obiectiva seu vice obiectiva, quae est ratio repraesentativi et significativi univoce conveniant.

Et si instes: Nam hoc ipsum genus repraesentativum relatio est, alioquin male

[10] *Pa* VII. 457 a.

[11] 272/19-24.

[12] See esp. Book I, Question 2, 151/1-21, but also the other references in note 3 above and note 15 below; and the Second Preamble, Article 1, note 21, p. 87 above.

said in the preceding Book[13] that a sign in the rationale of sign is posited in the genus or order of [i.e., is a type of] relation.[14] Therefore if a stipulated sign insofar as it is a relation does not coincide univocally with a natural sign, then neither does it coincide univocally with a natural sign in the rationale of a representative thing:

The response is that the significative genus itself is considered in two ways, both in a being of thing and in a being of object or knowable thing, nor can it totally prescind from these rationales, because they are transcendental.[15] And in the rationale of something knowable the significative is only a coincident property of being and presuppositively, not formally, being, while in the rationale of being [formally, i.e., mind-independently] the significative is either a transcendental or a categorial relation. And when we said above[16] that the sign is constitued generically by a relation, we were speaking of signs both formally and categorially,[17] that is, as they exist representatively in the objective order [which order entitatively falls within the *category* of relation whenever the requisite conditions for such relations—92/3-8—are fulfilled.]

It is argued secondly: A stipulated sign is constituted through the very imposition which posits in that sign nothing independent of mind, but only an extrinsic denomination. Therefore a stipulated sign does not consist in a relation the way a natural sign does, nor does it have anything in itself by reason of which it is a representative, but it moves only through another, namely, by reason of the awareness which the understanding has of the very imposition of the vocal sound.

The consequence is proved by the fact that an extrinsic denomination is an effect arising from the denominating form, but the form denominating extrinsically is not a relation, but the act of will of the one imposing. The antecedent, on the other hand, is proved by the fact that if a stipulated sign does not consist in an extrinsic denomination, but in a mind-dependent relation, the sign would not exist in act except when it is actually known, and so writing in a closed book or when not actually considered will not be a sign.

The response to this[18] is that some feel thus in treating of the Sacraments, that the rationale in them of stipulated sign consists in an extrinsic deputation, not in a mind-dependent relation. For example,

diximus [in] libro[13] praec. signum in ratione signi poni in genere relationis.[14] Ergo si in quantum relatio non convenit univoce, nec in ratione repraesentativi convenit univoce:

Respondetur, quod ipsum genus significativum consideratur dupliciter, et in esse rei et in esse obiecti seu cognoscibilis, nec potest ab his rationibus totaliter praescindere, quia transcendentales sunt.[15] Et in ratione cognoscibilis solum est passio entis et praesuppositive ens, non formaliter, in ratione autem entis relatio est vel transcendentalis vel praedicamentalis. Et quando supra diximus[16] signum constitui in genere relationis, locuti sumus de signo formaliter et praedicamentaliter,[17] i.e. repraesentative in genere obiectivo.

Secundo arguitur: Quia signum ad placitum constituitur per ipsam impositionem, quae in eo nihil reale ponit, sed solum extrinsecam denominationem. Ergo non consistit in relatione sicut signum naturale, nec aliquid habet in se, ratione cuius sit repraesentativum, sed solum movet per alterum, nempe ratione notitiae, quam intellectus habet de ipsa impositione vocis.

Consequentia probatur, quia extrinseca denominatio est effectus proveniens a forma denominante, forma autem denominans extrinsece non est relatio, sed actus voluntatis imponentis. *Antecedens* vero probatur, quia si signum ad placitum non consistit in denominatione extrinseca, sed in relatione rationis, non existet actu signum, nisi quando actualiter cognoscitur, et sic scriptura in libro clauso vel quando actualiter non consideratur, non erit signum.

RESPONDETUR[18] aliquos ita sentire agentes de Sacramentis, quod ratio signi ad placitum in illis consistit in extrinseca deputatione, non in relatione rationis, ut

[13] In the original Latin: "quaest. praec."

[14] Book I, Question 1.

[15] See Question 1 of this Book, 235/36-237/14; also Book I, Question 2, 150/1-151/21; and the Phil. nat. 4. p. q. 6. art. 3., esp. 185a26-187a42 of Reiser edition.

[16] Book I, Question 1, esp. 119/10-122/16 and 121/19 ff.

[17] The 1663 Lyons text adds here: "*non fundamentaliter*"—"not fundamentally." Cf. 133/13-134/10, 151/14-21, 235/36-237/15, 270/37-271/42.

[18] 273/22-30.

Suarez, in his treatise *Concerning the Sacraments*, First Disputation, Section 3.[19] But since an imposition of will only serves for determining the function and office of the stipulated sign, not as something absolute, but respectively to a significate to which the voice is not determined from its nature as a thing, it follows that the very deputation of will only does that which in natural signs the nature itself of the thing does, which nature certainly orders a natural sign to its significate from the nature of the thing [which the sign is] and founds the relation in which the very rationale of sign consists. Similarly therefore the imposition appointing the voice for signifying founds the respect of a sign, because the very appointment is in the sign through a respect toward another. But because this respect is founded on some appointment which posits nothing mind-independent in the appointed thing, therefore it is a mind-dependent respect.[20] And besides, the same rationale runs through stipulated and natural signs,

P. Suarez 3. tom. p. 3. disp. 1. sect. 3.[19] Ceterum cum impositio voluntatis solum deserviat ad determinandum munus et officium signi, non tamquam aliquid absolutum, sed respective ad signatum, ad quod ex natura rei vox non est determinata, constat, quod ipsa deputatio voluntatis solum facit id, quod in signis naturalibus ipsa rei natura facit, quae quidem ordinat ex natura rei ad signatum, et sic fundat relationem, in qua consistit ipsa ratio signi. Similiter ergo impositio destinans vocem ad significandum fundat respectum signi, quia destinatio ipsa est in signo per respectum ad alterum. Sed quia iste respectus fundatur in aliqua destinatione, quae nihil reale ponit in re destinata, ideo respectus rationis est.[20] Et praeterea currit in signis ad placitum eadem ratio quae in naturalibus,

---

[19] Francis Suarez, *Opera Omnia* (Paris ed.), vol. XX, Quaestio 60, ''*De Sacramentis*'' (''Concerning the Sacraments''), Disputatio Prima, ''*De Essentia ac Definitione Sacramenti*'' (First Disputation, ''On the Essence and Definition of a Sacrament''), Sectio Tertia, ''*An oporteat sacramentum signum esse sensibile ex institutione*'' (Section 3, ''Whether a sacrament must be a sensible sign from its institution''), p. 21, par. 6: ''. . . *dicendum est, rationem signi, ex impositione significantis, proprie ac formaliter non consistere in relatione, neque reali neque rationis. Primum patet, quia non habet reale fundamentum in re significata; extrinseca enim impositio nullam rem ponit in eo quod ad significandum imponitur. Secundum patet, quia relatio rationis tamdiu est, quamdiu ab intellectu concipitur, seu fingitur. Huiusmodi autem signum postquam impositum est, non pendet ex fictione, vel comparatione intellectus referentis unum ad aliud; sine illa enim seu ante illam, exercet munus signi excitando mentem, ut veniat in rei significatae cognitionem. Haec ergo ratio signi praecise oritur ex impositione, quae re ipsa facta est, quamvis nihil in re ponit physice, nisi denominationem extrinsecam, a reali actu provenientem: moraliter vero et quasi moro humano loquendo, relinquitur in re imposita ad significandum habilitas quaedam, seu aptitudo ad excitandum intellectum, ut rem aliam cognoscat, nam hae denominationes extrinsecae, quatenus manent in memoria et existimatione hominum, multum valent ad huiusmodi actiones morales et humanas, ut facile potest exemplis declarari, in potestate jurisdictionis, in gradu doctoratus; haec enim, et similia, solum per quamdam extrinsecam deputationem et denominationem fiunt.*''—''. . . it must be said that the rationale of a sign signifying by imposition properly and formally does not consist in a relation, neither mind-independent nor mind-dependent. The first is evident from the fact that such a sign has no mind-independent fundament in the signified thing; for an extrinsic imposition posits nothing independent of cognition in that which is imposed for signifying. The second is evident from the fact that a mind-dependent relation exists just so long as it is conceived or constructed by the understanding. But a sign of the sort in question, once it has been stipulated or established, does not depend upon a construction or a comparison of understanding refering one thing to another; for without or before that, it exercises the function of a sign by exciting the mind to come to an awareness of the thing signified. This rationale of sign therefore precisely arises from the imposition which is made from the thing itself, although it puts nothing in the thing physically save the extrinsic denomination arising from the act of cognition existing independently of being itself an object known: yet morally, and speaking as it were in a human way, a certain habilitation or aptitude for exciting the understanding to cognize something else is left in the thing stipulated for signifying, for these extrinsic denominations, to the extent that they endure in the memory and opinion of men, exercise a considerable influence in moral and human actions of this sort, as can be easily shown by such examples as the defining of a jurisdiction, the awarding of a doctorate; for these and similar things come to be only through a kind of extrinsic deputation and denomination.''

[20] See above, Book I, Question 2, 141/12-142/13; and cf. the First Preamble, Article 1, 55/7-49.

since indeed the rationale of a sign is a respective rationale exercising its function in an order to a signified as something substituting. Therefore, if a stipulated sign is a sign and exercises this function, it must take on the rationale of a relation, not a mind-independent one (because it lacks a sufficient foundation[21]), therefore a mind-dependent one.

And to the replication of the argument in the example of a closed book,[22] it is said that writing in a closed book or writing not considered by an understanding is a sign actually fundamentally, not actually formally, because a mind-dependent relation does not have an act of being formally except through the understanding. The writing is nevertheless denominated a sign absolutely and simply, because in these mind-dependent relations the proximate fundament suffices for denominating absolutely, because on the side of the denominable thing whatever is required for such denomination on its part has been posited. But because that relation does not result from a fundament in the way that mind-independent relations do, but depends on an act of cognition, therefore a stipulated sign does not have to wait for the relation itself in order to be denominated a sign absolutely, although it surely does require the relation itself in order to be denominated a being related in act;[23] just as God is absolutely denominated lord and creator, even though the relation of lord and of creation is not known in act; yet God is not denominated related in act to creatures, unless he is so known in act.

But to that which is added — that a stipulated sign does not signify and move through anything which it has in itself, but through another[24] — the response is that a stipulated sign signifies through the imposition which is proper to it, even though that imposition is an extrinsic denomination, and through that imposition as knowable by the understanding the stipulated sign is able to move [a cognitive power] in the way in which it is knowable,[25] although the awareness of such an imposition is required as the condition for and application to exercise of the signification, [but] not for constituting the form [i.e., the formality or rationale] of the sign.

It is argued thirdly: Because some signs are neither stipulated nor natural, therefore the division is not adequate.

siquidem ratio signi est ratio respectiva exercens munus suum in ordine ad signatum per modum substituentis. Ergo si signum ad placitum est signum et exercet hoc munus, rationem relationis debet induere, non realem, quia caret fundamento sufficienti,[21] ergo rationis.

Et ad replicam[22] dicitur, quod scriptura in libro clauso seu non considerata ab intellectu est signum actualiter fundamentaliter, non actualiter formaliter, quia relatio rationis non habet esse formaliter nisi per intellectum. Denominatur tamen absolute et simpliciter signum, quia in istis relationibus rationis sufficit fundamentum proximum ad denominandum absolute, quia ex parte rei denominabilis est positum, quidquid requiritur ad talem denominationem ex parte sui. Sed quia relatio illa non resultat ex fundamento sicut relationes reales, sed pendet ab actu cognitionis, ideo non expectat ipsam relationem, ut denominetur absolute tale, bene tamen, ut denominetur actu esse relatum;[23] sicut Deus absolute denominatur dominus et creator, licet actu non cognoscatur relatio dominii et creationis; non tamen actu denominatur relatus ad creaturas, nisi sic actu cognoscatur.

Ad id vero, quod additur, signum ad placitum non significare et movere per aliquid, quod in se habeat, sed per alterum,[24] respondetur, quod significat per impositionem, quae propria eius est, licet sit denominatio extrinseca, et per illam ut cognoscibilem ab intellectu habet movere eo modo, quo cognoscibilis est,[25] licet requiratur notitia talis impositionis tamquam conditio et applicatio ad exercitium significationis, non ad constituendam formam signi.

Tertio arguitur: Quia sunt aliqua signa nec ad placitum nec naturalia, ergo divisio non est adaequata.

---

[21] See the Second Preamble, Article 2, 91/23-27, and the First Preamble, Article 3, 70/11-71/19.

[22] 273/31-40.

[23] See above, the First Preamble, Article 3, 70/11-71/19, and Book I, Question 1, 127/7-131/18, esp. 127/43-128/6 and 130/10-43, and note 25; also the references in note 20 above.

[24] 273/22-30.

[25] *"eo modo, quo cognoscibilis est"*—"in the way in which it is knowable": see Book I, Question 1, 130/44-131/18, Question 4, 189/8-190/3 and esp. note 34 thereon.

The antecedent is proved: For certainly an image made by a painter of Caesar, for example, with whom the artist was not acquainted, is not a natural sign, because it does not signify from the nature of the thing, but from the free accommodation of the artist; just as there are also many images customarily deputed for such or such a saint, whom they do not signify from propriety [i.e., as historically accurate likenesses]. Nor are they stipulated signs, because they do not signify from an imposition, but in the mode of an image.

Likewise signs which are given by God, such as the rainbow in the clouds for signifying that there will not be another deluge on the scale of the one referred to in *Genesis*, Chapter IX, verses 12-17, and the sign which God placed on Cain, that he should not be slain, were not signs from an imposition, since indeed they were known to all; but stipulated signs are not the same for all, as Aristotle says in the first book of the treatise *On Interpretation*, chap. 1,[26] nor were [the signs given by God] natural signs, otherwise they would have been imposed by God in vain.

Response is made by denying the antecedent.[27] To the first example[28] the response is that a painted image, even though it is a sign made by art, nevertheless represents naturally, to wit, by reason of a similitude which it has physically, and not by reason of the rationale of imposition. But the image is said to be artificial by reason of the efficient cause by which it was produced, not from the side of the formal rationale by which it signifies, which is physical and intrinsic, namely, a similitude to another ordered for representing. But these images do not directly signify the object as it is in itself, but as it is in the idea of the painter, which idea the image directly represents. And because the idea of the artist is sometimes proper in respect of his object, sometimes improper or less proper, therefore the image too does not always represent the object properly as it is in itself, but its idea. But when one image is accommodated to this or that saint from the use of men [i.e., by tradition], such a representation constitutes a customary sign, as we will say in the next Question.[29]

To the second example[30] the response is that many signs are stipulated from divine institution, as is clear in the case of the Sacraments. And such signs do not

Antecedens probatur: Nam imago facta a pictore, v.g. Caesaris, quem non novit, non est signum naturale, quia non significat ex natura rei, sed ex libera accommodatione pictoris; sicut etiam solent multae imagines deputari pro tali vel tali sancto, quem ex proprietate non significant. Neque sunt signa ad placitum, quia non ex impositione significant, sed per modum imaginis.

Item signa, quae sunt data a Deo, ut arcus in nubibus ad significandum diluvium non futurum, ut Gen. IX. 12-17., et signum, quod posuit in Cain, ut non interficeretur, non erant signa ex impositione, siquidem erant omnibus nota; signa autem ad placitum non sunt eadem apud omnes, ut dicit Aristoteles 1. Periherm. cap. 1.,[26] nec erant naturalia, alias frustra imponerentur a Deo.

RESPONDETUR negando antecedens.[27] *Ad primum exemplum*[28] respondetur, quod imago depicta licet sit signum factum ab arte, naturaliter tamen repraesentat, scilicet ratione similitudinis, quam realiter habet, et non ratione impositionis. Dicitur autem imago artificialis ratione causae efficientis, a qua facta est, non ex parte rationis formalis, qua significat, quae realis et intrinseca est, scilicet similitudo ad alterum ordinata ad repraesentandum. Ceterum istae imagines non significant directe obiectum, ut in seipso est, sed ut est in idea pictoris, quam directe imago repraesentat. Et quia idea pictoris aliquando est propria respectu sui obiecti, aliquando impropria vel minus propria, ideo etiam imago non semper repraesentat obiectum proprie, ut est in se, sed ideam suam. Quando autem una imago accommodatur isti vel illi sancto ex hominum usu, talis repraesentatio constituit signum ex consuetudine, ut dicemus seq. quaest.[29]

Ad secundum exemplum[30] respondetur, quod multa signa sunt ad placitum ex institutione divina, sicut patet in Sacramentis. Et talia signa non repraesentant om-

---

26 16 a 5.
27 275/42-43.
28 276/1-11.
29 In the original Latin: "art."
30 276/12-22.

represent for all, but only for the ones knowing the very imposition, and in this way the rainbow signifies that there will not be another deluge by a particular imposition of God. But perhaps the sign placed by God on Cain was something natural, to wit, a certain trembling of the body, as St. Jerome says in his 36th letter,[31] which trembling moved all to compassion, so that they would not slay him. Yet if the sign on Cain was some sign stipulated by a divine institution, it must be said that God inscribed an awareness of it in all who saw Cain, so they would not kill him.

nibus, sed solum impositionem ipsam scientibus, et hoc modo iris significat diluvium non futurum ex particulari Dei impositione. Signum autem positum in Cain fortasse fuit aliquod naturale, scilicet quidam tremor corporis, ut S. Hieronymus ep. 36.[31] dicit, qui tremor movebat omnes ad misericordiam, ne eum interficerent. Si tamen fuit aliquod signum ad placitum ex divina institutione, dicendum est, quod notitiam eius Deus indidit omnibus videntibus Cain, ne illum interficerent.

[31] al. 125. (Migne, P. L. XXII. 453).

[719a16-b11]

Question 6

Whether a Sign Arising from Custom Is truly a Sign

Quaestio Sexta

Utrum Signum ex Consuetudine Sit vere Signum

There is a special difficulty concerning certain signs which are accommodated to signifying something not from any public institution, i.e., not by issuing from a public authority, but from the mere inclination of private individuals to make frequent use of them. Whence, because the whole force of the signifying depends on the very use and frequency, a doubt remains as to whether this use and frequency signifies in a natural mode, or whether indeed by a stipulated signification.

From all that has been said to now, there is but one conclusion: **If custom respects some sign by appointing and proposing it for a sign, such a sign founded on custom will be stipulated. But if custom does not propose or institute something as a sign, but expresses the simple use of the thing, and by reason of that use the thing is taken for a sign, such a sign is reduced to a natural sign.**

Therefore custom either can be the cause of a sign, as, for example, if a people by their customs introduce and propose some sound for signifying; or it can function as an effect which leads us to know its cause, as, for example, a dog frequently seen accompanying someone manifests that that person is its master, and the custom of eating with napkins manifests to us a meal when we see napkins set out, and universally almost every induction [see note 14, p. 64 above] is founded on the frequency and custom whereby we see something often happen.

Specialis difficultas est circa quaedam signa, quae non publica aliqua institutione, i. e. ab auctoritate publica dimanante, sed ex sola voluntate particularium frequenter illis utentium ad aliquid significandum accommodantur. Unde quia tota vis significandi ex ipso usu et frequentia dependet, DUBIUM RESTAT, an iste usus et frequentia modo naturali significet, an vero significatione ad placitum.

SIT ERGO UNICA CONCLUSIO: **Si consuetudo respiciat aliquod signum, destinando illud et proponendo pro signo, tale signum fundatum in consuetudine erit ad placitum. Si vero consuetudo non proponat aliquid vel instituat pro signo, sed dicat simplicem usum alicuius rei et ratione illius assumatur aliquid in signum, tale signum reducitur ad naturale.**

Itaque consuetudo vel potest esse causa signi, sicut si populus consuetudine sua introducat et proponat aliquam vocem ad significandum; vel potest se habere ut effectus, qui nos manuducit ad cognoscendam suam causam, sicut canis frequenter visus comitari aliquem manifestat, quod sit dominus eius, et consuetudo comedendi in mappis manifestat nobis prandium, quando mappas videmus appositas, et in universum fere omnis inductio [vide n. 14, p. 64 supra] fundatur in frequentia et consuetudine, qua videmus aliquid saepe fieri.

The first part of the conclusion, therefore, is proved from St. Thomas's *Summa theologica*, I-II, q. 97, art. 3, where he teaches that custom has the force of law. Therefore a custom introducing something for signifying introduces that thing as a sign by the same authority by which the law itself would introduce it. But if some vocal sound is proposed for a sign by some public law, it is truly a stipulated sign, because it is instituted by a public authority. Therefore custom, which is surrogated in the stead of law and has the authority of law, constitutes a stipulated sign in the same way [as would legislation]. And we see many sounds introduced into common life for signifying in this manner, sounds which formerly did not signify because they were not in use, and many words now do not signify which did signify formerly, because they have now fallen into desuetude. Wherefore, concerning such signs arising from custom, when the "arising from" expresses a productive cause according to the use and consensus of a people, customary signs must be spoken of in the same way that one speaks of stipulated signs.

But the second part of the conclusion is proved from the fact that custom, as it is a kind of effect, leads us to a cognition of its cause in the same way that other effects show their causes; and custom much more than other effects, because the frequency of effecting something heightens the probability that the something in question is the effect of the cause in question. But every effect represents its cause insofar as it proceeds from that cause, and thus has some coincidence and proportion. Therefore signification arising from custom is founded on something natural, to wit, on the procession of an effect from its cause and on its coincidence with that cause. Therefore custom as an effect founding signification is reduced to a natural cause. And thus the Philosopher says that pleasure is the sign of an acquired habit, because we find pleasure in the things to which we are frequently accustomed, on account of a coincidence relative to that of which we have a regular experience.

Resolution of Counter-Arguments

It is argued first that because custom is not a natural effect, but a moral and free one, it therefore cannot found the rationale of a natural sign.

The consequence is established by the fact that a sign cannot be said to be more natural than the cause from which it has being; if therefore

Prima ergo pars conclusionis probatur ex D. Thoma 1. 2. q. 97. art. 3., ubi docet consuetudinem habere vim legis. Ergo consuetudo introducens aliquid ad significandum eadem auctoritate introducit rem illam in signum, qua ipsa lex introduceret. Si autem ex lege publica aliqua vox proponatur in signum, est vere signum ad placitum, quia auctoritate publica instituitur. Ergo consuetudo, quae vice legis subrogatur et auctoritatem legis habet, eodem modo constituit signum ad placitum. Et hoc modo videmus multas voces introductas in republica ad significandum, quae ante non significabant, quia non erant in usu, et multa verba modo non significant, quae olim significabant, quia iam abierunt in desuetudinem. Quare de tali signo ex consuetudine ly ex dicente causam efficientem secundum usum et consensum populi, eodem modo loquendum est sicut de signo ad placitum.

Secunda vero pars conclusionis probatur, quia consuetudo, ut est quidam effectus, ducit nos in cognitionem suae causae eo modo, quo alii effectus suas causas ostendunt; et multo magis consuetudo, quam alii effectus, quia frequentia efficiendi aliquid firmat, quod illud sit effectus talis causae. Sed omnis effectus repraesentat suam causam, in quantum procedit ab illa, et ita habet aliquam convenientiam et proportionem. Ergo talis significatio fundatur in aliquo naturali, scilicet in processu effectus a sua causa et convenientia cum illa. Ergo consuetudo ut effectus fundans significationem reducitur ad causam naturalem. Et ita dicit Philosophus, quod delectatio est signum generati habitus, quia in his, quae frequenter consuescimus, delectamur propter convenientiam ad illud, in quo habemus consuetudinem.

Solvuntur argumenta

Primo arguitur, quia consuetudo non est effectus naturalis, sed moralis et liber, ergo non potest fundare rationem signi naturalis.

Consequentia constat, quia non potest dici signum naturale magis quam eius causa, a qua habet esse; signum ergo si non

a sign is not from a natural cause, neither consequently should it be called a natural sign.

The antecedent is proved by the fact that custom is the same as the mores from which acts are called moral or human, as St. Thomas teaches in the *Summa theologica*, I-II, q. 1, art. 3. Therefore custom among men is not a natural effect but a moral one, and thus a sign which is founded on custom is founded on something moral and free which posits nothing mind-independent in exterior things, but [merely] an extrinsic denomination; but a sign founded on an extrinsic denomination cannot be a natural sign.

The response to this[1] is that, in the first place, custom, generally speaking, is found not only among men, but also among animals operating by natural estimation.[2] Whence St. Thomas shows in his *Commentary on the Metaphysics of Aristotle*, Book I, reading 1,[3] that brute animals are capable of being taught and being accustomed to do or to avoid something through another's instruction, and thus not all custom is a human act, but all custom can found a natural sign, just as the custom of a dog's following someone is a sign that that someone may be the dog's master.

In the second place, when speaking of human custom, even though it proceeds from a free cause and so is denominated a free effect, nevertheless, the formal rationale of signifying is not any free deputation, but the very frequency and repetition of acts, and this signifies naturally, because it is not a moral deputation, that is to say, it is not an extrinsic deputation which denominates only morally, but the intrinsic performance of acts and their frequency and multiplication constitutes the customary sign. Therefore a signification attaches to that sign naturally, even as multiplied free acts generate a habit as a natural and not as a free effect, because the very multiplication of the acts does not function freely relative to generating the habit, so neither to the signifying resulting from the force of the repetition of the acts, even though these acts in themselves [i.e., singly taken] may be free.

It is argued secondly: If a customary sign represents naturally from the fact that it is [the effect of] a frequently repeated act, it follows that any

est a causa naturali, consequenter nec signum naturale dicetur.

Antecedens vero probatur, quia consuetudo est idem, quod mos, a quo actus dicuntur morales seu humani, ut docet D. Thomas 1. 2. q. 1. art. 3. Ergo consuetudo in hominibus non est effectus naturalis, sed moralis, et ita signum, quod fundatur in consuetudine, fundatur in aliquo morali et libero, quod in rebus exterioribus nihil reale ponit, sed extrinsecam denominationem; signum autem fundatum in denominatione extrinseca non potest esse signum naturale.

RESPONDETUR,[1] quod *imprimis* generaliter loquendo consuetudo non solum invenitur in hominibus, sed etiam in brutis naturali instinctu operantibus.[2] Unde D. Thomas 1. Metaph. lect. 1.[3] ostendit, quod bruta possunt esse disciplinabilia et assuescere ad aliquid faciendum vel vitandum per alterius instructionem, et ita non omnis consuetudo est actus humanus et fundare potest signum naturale, sicut consuetudo canis sequentis aliquem est signum, quod sit dominus eius.

Secundo respondetur loquendo de consuetudine humana, quod licet a sua causa libera procedat et sic denominetur effectus liber, tamen ratio formalis significandi non est aliqua libera deputatio, sed ipsa frequentia et repetitio actuum, et haec naturaliter significat, quia non moralis, id est extrinseca deputatio, quae solum moraliter denominat, sed intrinseca processio actuum eorumque frequentatio et multiplicatio constituit signum ex consuetudine. Ergo naturaliter convenit illi significatio, sicut etiam actus liberi multiplicati generant habitum tamquam naturalem effectum et non liberum, quia miltiplicatio ipsa actuum non se habet libere ad generandum habitum, sic neque ad significandum ex vi repetitionis actuum, licet ipsi in se liberi sint.

Secundo arguitur: Si signum ex consuetudine repraesentat naturaliter ex eo, quod est actus saepius repetitus, ergo

---

[1] to 279/46-48.

[2] Detailed discussion in Deely 1971a: 55-83; background framework in Deely 1969; applications to semiotic in Deely 1975a, b, 1978a, 1980a, b, 1982.

[3] *Pa* XX. 249 a.

custom whatever will be a sign of some thing, because every custom is an effect proceeding from repeated acts. But this consequence is contrary to fact, because there are many customs which signify nothing, as, for example, the custom of sleeping at night and eating at noon, approaching a fire in winter, etc., and an infinity of other customs signify nothing. Therefore custom does not signify precisely from the fact that it is the effect of some cause, and so it will not be a natural sign.

This is confirmed by the fact that without undergoing any intrinsic change a sign arising from custom can cease to be a sign, specifically, through desuetude alone or the mere omission of [any community's] using it; therefore it is not a natural sign. The consequence is clear, because a natural sign must be constituted through something intrinsic and natural, therefore something that cannot be lost through the mere suspension of voluntary use, but through some physical reality opposed to it.

The response to this[4] is that for anything to be a customary sign it is required that it should also have those things which concur for the rationale of a sign, namely, being ordered to something which is rendered more known by the very custom, not precisely because custom is an effect, but because it has been frequently repeated. But if a custom either is not taken as a means relative to something else, as napkins relative to a meal, or if something else is not rendered more known by the very frequent repetition, as that someone is the master of the dog by the frequency of [the dog's] following him, then it will not be a customary *sign*, even though it is a custom.

To the confirmation[5] the response is that a sign arising from custom does not perish from a mere suspension removing the institution, but from a suspension removing the multiplication of acts and frequency of use. Thus, because the representation of a customary sign is founded on the very multiplication of acts which constitutes a custom, when such multiplication is removed the fundament of the sign is removed, and so the determination left as consequence of the multiplication is destroyed by means of the opposite privation, just as the habit of a science is lost through being forgotten, especially because something positive always intervenes in a loss of memory or custom, insofar as objects succeed

quaelibet consuetudo erit signum alicuius rei, quia quaelibet consuetudo est effectus procedens ab actibus repetitis. Hoc autem est falsum, quia multae sunt consuetudines, quae nihil significant, sicut consuetudo dormiendi in nocte et prandendi in meridie, accedendi ad ignem in hieme etc., et infinitae aliae consuetudines nihil significant. Non ergo consuetudo ex eo praecise significat, quia effectus alicuius causae est, et sic non erit signum naturale.

Et confirmatur, quia sine aliqua mutatione intrinseca potest aliquod signum ex consuetudine desinere esse signum, scilicet per solam desuetudinem seu omissionem utendi illo; ergo non est signum naturale. *Consequentia* patet, quia signum naturale debet constitui per aliquid intrinsecum et naturale, ergo non potest amitti per solam suspensionem usus voluntarii, sed per aliquid reale oppositum.

RESPONDETUR,[4] quod ut aliquid sit signum ex consuetudine, requiritur, quod etiam habeat ea, quae concurrunt ad rationem signi, scilicet esse ordinatum ad aliquid, quod ipsa consuetudine reddatur notius, non quia praecise effectus est, sed quia frequentatus. Si autem vel non assumatur ut medium ad aliquid aliud, ut mappae ad prandium, vel ipsa frequentatione non reddatur notius, ut quod aliquis sit dominus canis frequentatione sequendi ipsum, non erit signum ex consuetudine, licet consuetudo sit.

Ad confirmationem[5] respondetur, quod signum ex consuetudine non desinit ex sola suspensione tollente institutionem, sed ex suspensione tollente multiplicationem actuum et frequentiam usus. Unde cum repraesentatio signi ex consuetudine fundetur in ipsa multiplicatione actuum, quae consuetudinem constituit, sublata tali multiplicatione tollitur fundamentum signi, et sic destruitur determinatio relicta ex multiplicatione per privationem oppositam, sicut habitus scientiae perditur per oblivionem, praesertim quia semper aliquid positivum intervenit ad perdendum memoriam seu consuetudinem, quatenus alia

[4] to 280/44-281/8.
[5] 281/11-20.

one another in a succession by which the earlier objects gradually slip from memory by disposing toward an opposite act or by impeding the memory itself and custom from becoming rooted.

Finally it is argued: From the will alone, without any multiplication of acts, a customary sign can result; therefore at least then it does not represent as a natural sign.

The antecedent is proved by the fact that from the mere accommodation and designation of men, one statue or image is set up to represent some saint, or likewise an actor represents a king or Caesar not from a decree of the commonwealth nor from a custom of men, but from the bare particular fact of such a man.

This is confirmed, because if the doctrine proposed in this question[6] is true, it follows that spoken words naturally signify that for which they are imposed, because even if the imposition were removed from this sound, "man," it will still continue to represent man to us, because of the custom which we have; therefore it represents naturally from custom.

Finally, that a customary sign does not signify naturally is proved by the fact that a natural sign signifies the same thing for all. But a customary sign does not signify the same thing for all, but only for those knowing the custom, just as a stipulated sign signifies for those knowing the imposition; therefore, a customary sign does not represent naturally.

The response to this argument[7] is that any image whatever, insofar as it is an image, represents only that whose likeness it expresses, namely, its idea, whatever that may be. But if from human usage it is accommodated to representing another object besides its idea, that accommodation or appointement in respect of the object in question constitutes the image in the rationale of a stipulated sign if that appointment comes about from a public authority, or in the rationale of a customary sign if the appointment comes about as a consequence of the use of men. But if someone, through only one act, without a custom, posits something for representing another, such an appointment will be a kind of inchoate custom, and so it will represent to him in the mode of a customary sign or as something stimulating memory. And for this reason an actor is said to represent the king either by a customary signi-

atque alia obiecta succedunt, quibus alia paulatim decidunt a memoria disponendo ad oppositum actum vel impediendo, ne memoria ipsa et consuetudo radicetur.

Ultimo arguitur: Ex sola voluntate, sine aliqua multiplicatione actuum, potest resultare signum ex consuetudine; ergo saltem tunc non repraesentat tamquam signum naturale.

Antecedens probatur, quia ex sola accommodatione et designatione hominum una statua vel imago ponitur ad repraesentandum aliquem sanctum, vel etiam tragaedus repraesentat regem vel Caesarem non ex placito reipublicae nec ex consuetudine hominum, sed ex solo particulari facto talis hominis.

Et confirmatur, quia si doctrina data[6] est vera, sequitur, quod voces naturaliter significent id, ad quod sunt impositae, quia etiamsi tollatur impositio ab hac voce ,,homo'', adhuc propter consuetudinem, quam habemus, repraesentabit nobis hominem; ergo ex consuetudine naturaliter repraesentat.

Denique, quia signum naturale est, quod significat idem apud omnes. Sed signum ex consuetudine non significat idem apud omnes, sed solum apud scientes consuetudinem, sicut signum ad placitum significat apud scientes impositionem; ergo non reprasentat naturaliter.

RESPONDETUR,[7] quod quaecumque imago, in quantum imago est, solum repraesentat id, ad cuius similitudinem est expressa, nempe ideam suam, quaecumque illa sit. Si autem ex usu hominum accommodetur ad repraesentandum aliud obiectum quam suae ideae, illa accommodatio vel destinatio respectu illius obiecti constituet illam imaginem in ratione signi ad placitum, si ex publica auctoritate illa destinatio fiat, vel ex consuetudine, si ex hominum usu id fiat. Quodsi aliquis per unum tantum actum sine consuetudine ponat aliquid ad repraesentandum aliud, talis destinatio erit inchoata quaedam consuetudo, et sic repraesentabit illi ad modum signi ex consuetudine vel ut excitativum memoriae. Et hac ratione etiam tragaedus dicitur repraesentare regem vel significatione ex consuetudine

[6] 278/12-18.
[7] 282/5-15.

fication or as something stimulating memory, because it so happens that when people see an actor who represents such a personage, [the perception] is reduced to a memory of the represented thing; just as from a pact or agreement something can be designated for a sign or a stimulus of memory, the whole of which reductively pertains to a stipulated sign or to a customary sign.

To the confirmation[8] the answer is that essentially spoken words only signify by stipulation, but incidentally from custom, which is to signify naturally not from themselves, but only for those familiar with the custom. Nor is it antinomic that two ways of signifying should attach to the same thing according to distinct formalities. Whence when one mode of signifying is removed the other remains, and so the same sign is never a natural sign and a stipulated sign formally, even though a natural and a stipulated sign may be the same materially, that is, even though a natural and a stipulated mode of signifying may belong to the same subject.

But the proposition[9] that that sign is said to be a natural sign which signifies the same thing for all, is understood of that which is a natural sign simply, because nature is the same for all.[10] But a custom is as a second nature, but not nature itself, and thus it signifies for all to whom it is customary, not for all simply, and so a sign arising from custom is something imperfect in the order of natural sign, just as custom itself is something imperfect in the order of nature.

vel sicut excitativum memoriae, quia ita convenit inter homines, ut viso illo, qui talem personam repraesentat, in memoriam rei repraesentatae reducatur; sicut etiam ex pacto vel convenientia aliquorum potest aliquid designari in signum vel in excitativum memoriae, quod totum reductive pertinet ad signum ad placitum vel ex consuetudine.

Ad confirmationem[8] respondetur, quod voces per se solum significant ad placitum, per accidens autem ex consuetudine, quod est significare naturaliter non ex se, sed solum respectu illorum, apud quos est nota consuetudo. Nec est inconveniens, quod eidem rei conveniant duo modi significandi secundum distinctas formalitates. Unde una sublata altera manet, et sic numquam est idem signum naturale et ad placitum formaliter, licet materialiter sint idem, id est conveniant eidem subiecto.

Quod autem dicitur[9] illud esse signum naturale, quod significat idem apud omnes, intelligitur de eo, quod est signum naturale simpliciter, quia natura est eadem apud omnes.[10] Consuetudo autem est quasi altera natura, sed non natura ipsa, et ita significat omnibus, apud quos est consuetudo, non omnibus simpliciter, et sic est aliquid imperfectius in genere signi naturalis, sicut ipsa consuetudo est aliquid imperfectum in genere naturae.

[8] 282/16-22.

[9] 282/24-30.

[10] One catches here clear echoes of the Greek origins of semiotic in medical tradition particularly: ''Χρὴ εἰδέναι περὶ τῶν τεκμηρίων καὶ τῶν ἄλλων σημείων, ὅτι ἐν παντὶ ἔτει καὶ πάσῃ χώρῃ τά τε κακὰ κακόν τι οημαίνει καὶ τὰ χρηστὰ ἀγαθόν, ἐπεὶ καὶ ἐν Λιβύῃ καὶ ἐν Δήλῳ καὶ ἐν Σκυθίῃ φαίνεται τὰ προγεγραμμένα σημεῖα ἀληθεύοντα. εὖ οὖν χρὴ εἰδέναι, ὅτι ἐν τοῖς αὐτοῖσι χωρίοισιν οὐδὲν δεινὸν τὸ μὴ οὐχὶ τὰ πολλαπλάσια ἐπιτυγχάνειν, ἢν ἐκμαθών τις αὐτὰ κρίνειν τε καὶ ἐκλογιξεσθαι ὀρθῶς ἐπίστηται.'' (Hippocrates, *Prognostic* XXV, c. 415 B.C.: ''One must clearly realize about sure signs and about symptoms generally, that in every year and in every land bad signs indicate something bad, and good signs something favourable, since the symptoms described above prove to have the same significance in Libya, in Delos, and in Scythia. So one must clearly realize that in the same districts it is not strange that one should be right in the vast majority of instances, if one learns them well and knows how to estimate and appreciate them properly.''—English trans. by W.H.S. Jones in *Hippocrates* [New York: G.P. Putnam's Sons, 1923; The Loeb Classical Library], vol. II, p. 55.) Discussion in Sebeok, 1984.

Liber Tertius

DE NOTITIIS ET CONCEPTIBUS*

Book III

CONCERNING MODES OF AWARENESS AND CONCEPTS*

* In the original Latin: "*Quaestio XXIII. De Notitiis et Conceptibus.*" Logica 2 p.: "Question 23. Concerning Modes of Awareness and Concepts."

TRANSITION TO BOOK III[1]

Because the division of terms is made through mental and vocal terms, and mental terms pertain to concepts and awareness,[2] and again because an exact explication of signs depends principally on concepts and awareness,[3] discussion of some of the distinctions concerning concepts and awareness is advisable in connection with their exact explication, particularly as regards those distinctions which pertain to the simple mental terms. But as we have said in the first of the Summulae *books, ch. 3,[4] awareness, which is a simple apprehension or mental term, is divided on the side of cognition into intuitive and abstractive, but on the side of the concept it is divided into preliminary and final, direct and reflex concepts. Therefore we treat in this Book only of these distinctions.*

TRANSITUS AD LIBRUM TERTIUM[1]

Quia terminorum divisio fit, per mentales et vocales, et mentales pertinent ad conceptus et notitias,[2] rursusque exacta signorum explicatio ex conceptibus et notitiis maxime pendet,[3] ad exactam eorum explicationem visum est aliqua disputare de conceptibus et notitiis, praesertim quantum ad ea, quae ad simplices terminos mentales pertinent. Ut autem diximus in 1. libro Summul. cap. 3.,[4] notitia, quae est simplex apprehensio seu terminus mentalis, ex parte cognitionis dividitur in intuitivam et abstractivam, ex parte autem conceptus in conceptum ultimatum et non ultimatum, directum et reflexum. Ideo de istis solum hic agemus.

---

[1] Title of this passage supplied by Translator.
[2] See above, First *Summulae* Book, Chapter 3, 28/1-14.
[3] See above, esp. Book II, Question 1, 236/46-237/6, Question 5, 271/22-42.
[4] 29/7-39.

Question 1

Whether Intuitive and Abstractive Awareness Differ Essentially in the Rationale of Cognition

Quaestio Prima

Utrum Notitia Intuitiva et Abstractiva Differant Essentialiter in Ratione Cognitionis

The traditional definitions of intuitive and abstractive awareness, which we adopted in the first of the *Summulae* books, chap. 3,[1] must be supposed here: intuitive awareness is ''the awareness of a present thing,'' while abstractive awareness is ''the awareness of an absent thing.'' In these definitions presence and absence are not taken in the intentional sense for the very presence or union of object with cognitive power. For it hardly bears noting that there can be no awareness failing this presence, since indeed without an object united and present to a cognitive power no awareness can arise in the power. Accordingly, ''awareness of a present and of an absent thing'' is said, taking ''presence'' and ''absence'' for that which belongs to the thing in itself. Whence St. Thomas says in q. 3 of his *Disputed Questions on Truth*, art. 3, reply to obj. 8,[2] that the knowledge of vision (which is the same as intuitive awareness) adds to simple awareness something which is independent of the order of awareness, namely, the existence of things. Therefore it adds mind-independent physical existence, for an intentional and objective existence is not independent of the order of awareness. And in his *Commentary on the Sentences of Peter Lombard*, Book III, dist. 14, q. 1, art. 2, quaestiunc. 2,[3] he says that ''that object which has an act of being independent of the seeing is apprehended in itself.'' Therefore the existence which intuitive awareness requires must be a mind-independent and physical existence.

Supponenda est definitio notitiae intuitivae et abstractivae, quam tradidimus lib. 1. Summul. cap. 3.,[1] quod notitia intuitiva est ,, notitia rei praesentis'', notitia vero abstractiva est ,,notitia rei absentis''. Ubi praesentia et absentia non sumuntur intentionaliter pro ipsa praesentia seu unione obiecti cum potentia. Constat enim nulli notitiae posse deesse hanc praesentiam, siquidem sine obiecto unito et praesenti potentiae nulla potest oriri notitia in potentia. Igitur dicitur notitia rei praesentis et absentis, sumpta praesentia et absentia pro ea, quae convenit rei in se. Unde dicit D. Thomas in q. 3. de Veritate art. 3. ad 8.,[2] quod scientia visionis (quae est idem, quod notitia intuitiva) addit supra simplicem notitiam aliquid, quod est extra genus notitiae, scilicet existentiam rerum. Ergo addit existentiam realem, nam intentionalis et obiectiva non est extra genus notitiae. Et in 3. dist. 14. q. 1. art. 2. quaestiunc. 2.[3] dicit, quod «illud proprie videtur, quod habet esse extra videntem». Ergo existentia, quam requirit notitia intuitiva, realis et physica esse debet.

[1] 29/13-23.
[2] *Pa* IX. 58 b.
[3] *Pa* VII. 153 a.

Concerning the proposed difficulty, therefore, various positions of authors have gained currency. For some have considered the distinction of these two modes of awareness from the standpoint of initiation, that is to say, of the impressed specifier. And so according to some authors cited by Ferrariensis in Book II, chap. 66 of his *Commentary on the Summa contra gentiles*, that awareness is intuitive which occurs without an intelligible specifier, whereas that awareness is abstractive which comes about by means of some specifier.

This opinion, however, must be entirely rejected, because no awareness at all can be elicited without a specifying form. For every cognition depends upon an object and a cognitive power, and this object, howsoever much it might be present in itself, cannot intentionally inform the power except through a specifying form, unless of course the very object possesses in itself an intentional and spiritual being which is conjoined to the power.

Others say that intuitive cognition is that which knows a thing through proper specifiers, whereas abstractive cognition is that which knows a thing through alien specifiers. It seems that intuitive and abstractive awareness can also be distinguished from the standpoint of evidence, because intuitive awareness is always evident, as being of a thing in itself, whereas abstractive awareness abstracts from obscurity and evidence, and if at any time it has evidence, it is not of a thing in itself immediately, but as contained in some thing else, as, for example, in its causes and principles or the like, or in an image, independently of presence.

Others distinguish intuitive awareness from the standpoint of the terminus or of the object as terminating according to the received definitions, because the one is of an absent thing, the other of a present thing. This point of view is the more common one among the Thomists; for that distinction from the standpoint of the specifying form, that awareness is through a proper specifier or an alien one, [as also the distinction from the standpoint of evidence, that an awareness is of a thing] in itself or in another, obscure or clear: these are not formalities which properly pertain to the rationale of the intuitive or of the abstractive. For the intuitive can be preserved[4] through a mediate cognition, that is to say, a cognition in another; also, the abstractive can be maintained through a cognition of as great an evidence and clarity as the intuitive, and similarly can an abstractive apprehension come about through an immediate cognition and form of specification.

Circa propositam ergo difficultatem VARIA PLACITA AUCTORUM circumferuntur. Quidam enim consideraverunt distinctionem istarum notitiarum ex parte principii, scilicet speciei impressae. Et sic dixerunt aliqui apud Ferrariensem 2. Contra Gent. cap. 66. illam esse notitiam intuitivam, quae fit sine specie intelligibili, illam vero abstractivam, quae fit mediante aliqua specie.

Quae tamen sententia omnino reicienda est, cum nulla notitia sine specie elici possit. Pendet enim omnis cognitio ab obiecto et potentia, et hoc obiectum non potest intentionaliter informare potentiam, quantumcumque in se sit praesens, nisi mediante specie, vel nisi ipsum obiectum in se habeat esse intentionale et spirituale, quod potentiae sit coniunctum.

Alii dicunt intuitivam cognitionem esse illam, quae rem cognoscit per proprias species, abstractivam vero, quae per alienas. Ex parte etiam evidentiae videtur distingui posse notitia intuitiva et abstractiva, quia intuitiva semper est evidens, utpote rei in se, abstractiva vero abstrahit ab obscuritate et evidentia, et si quando evidentiam habet, non est rei in seipsa immediate, sed ut continetur in aliquo alio, v. g. in suis causis et principiis vel aliquo simili aut imagine independenter a praesentia.

Alii distinguunt notitiam intuitivam ex parte termini seu obiecti ut terminantis iuxta definitiones traditas, quia una est de re absente, altera de re praesente. Quae sententia est *communior apud thomistas;* nam distinctio illa ex parte speciei, quod sit per propriam speciem vel per alienam, in se vel in alio, obscura vel clara, non sunt formalitates, quae proprie pertinent ad rationem intuitivi vel abstractivi. Potest enim salvari intuitivum[4] per cognitionem mediatam seu in alio; potest etiam salvari abstractivum per cognitionem tantae evidentiae et claritatis sicut intuitivum, et similiter potest fieri per cognitionem et speciem immediatam.

[4] The 1663 Lyons text adds here: *"per speciem alienam et . . ."*—"by means of an alien specifier and. . . ."

The first part[5] — that the distinction from the standpoint of the specifying form does not express a formality which properly pertains to the rationale of either an intuitive or an abstractive awareness — is manifestly the case, because future creatures are seen in the divine essence as in an alien form of specification, and yet God sees them intuitively. And that cognition is similarly mediate and in another. In like manner, a pure spirit is able, through its proper essence as through a specifying form, to see intuitively the accidents which are in itself; and it can similarly see, by means of a specifier representing another substance, the accidents which are present in that substance. And in the opinion of St. Thomas the human understanding does not have a direct specifier of singulars, and yet it is able to see intuitively singular corporeal things when they are present through the senses. Therefore neither a proper specifier nor an immediate and direct cognition is required for intuitive awareness.

An example of the second point[6] — that the distinction from the standpoint of evidence (clarity and distinctness) does not express a formality proper to the rationale of either intuitive or abstractive awareness — is in the case of God himself, who knows possible creatures abstractively with as great an evidence and clarity from the side of the knowing as if they were present. Similarly, God can infuse in someone a cognition of a possible essence outside of the Word, and then that individual would know that possible thing through a specifier proper to it, and yet that person would know abstractively. Again a pure spirit may have a proper specifier of a future eclipse and [know] of its futurity and existence by means of the proper specifier, and yet the cognition is abstractive; just as we too are able indeed to recollect an absent thing which we have seen through a proper specifier, and even be borne to its existence in the mode of an object, as, for example, when from effects I know that God is present, and yet that cognition is abstractive. Intuitive and abstractive awareness, therefore, are not distinguished on these heads, but it is necessary to recur to the known terminus, namely, that the one cognition attains the object terminating under its own physical presence, the other cognition attains the object terminating under absence.

There remain, then, only two ways of distinguishing these types of awareness, which are also the ways most frequently followed by the Thomists. For some distinguish them essentially according to presence and absence as according to diverse rationales which are represented, and

Prima pars[5] constat manifeste, quia creaturae futurae videntur in divina essentia tamquam in specie aliena, et tamen videt illas intuitive. Et similiter est cognitio illa mediata et in alio. Similiter angelus per propriam essentiam tamquam per speciem potest videre intuitive accidentia, quae in se sunt, et similiter per speciem repraesentantem aliam substantiam potest videre accidentia, quae in ea praesentia sunt. Et in sententia D. Thomae intellectus non habet speciem directam singularium, et tamen potest res singulares corporeas intuitive videre, quando sunt praesentes per sensum. Ergo neque requiritur species propria neque cognitio immediata et directa.

Exemplum secundi[6] est in ipso Deo, qui abstractive cognoscit creaturas possibiles tanta evidentia et claritate ex parte cognoscentis sicut praesentes. Similiter potest alicui infundere cognitionem quidditatis possibilis extra Verbum, et tunc cognoscet rem illam per propriam eius speciem, et tamen abstractive cognoscet. Et angelus habet propriam speciem eclipsis futurae et eius futuritionis et existentiae per propriam speciem, et tamen est cognitio abstractiva; sicut et nos etiam rei absentis, quam vidimus, per propriam speciem possumus recordari, imo et in eius existentiam per modum obiecti ferri, ut quando ex effectibus cognosco Deum esse praesentem et tamen illa cognitio abstractiva est. Non ergo ex istis capitibus distinguuntur intuitiva et abstractiva notitia, sed oportet ad terminum cognitum recurrere, nempe quod una attingat rem sub ipsa praesentia propria et physica terminantem, alia sub absentia.

Quare solum duplex modus restat distinguendi istas notitias, qui etiam apud thomistas frequentes sunt. *Quidam* enim distinguunt illas essentialiter penes praesentiam et absentiam tamquam penes rationes diversas, quae repraesentantur, et consequenter

[5] 288/36-40; 288/19-22.
[6] 288/38-40; 288/22-30.

consequently the very representations differ intrinsically and essentially on account of the diverse represented objects.

Others, however, say that these types of awareness differ incidentally, because they do not require diverse representations formally, but the same thing can be represented in an intuitive awareness and in an abstractive awareness, namely, the thing with its existence and presence signified in act known and represented; but the representations differ only accidentally on account of the diverse exercise of terminating. For if the very object were rendered present in itself and the very presence were represented in the cognition, by this very fact the cognition is rendered intuitive. But if the physical presence of the thing, through which presence the object terminates the cognition, were removed, while all other conditions on the side of the cognition and on the side of the representation remain invariant, the cognition is rendered abstractive. Whence some also say that the intuitive and the abstractive are only extrinsic denominations, arising in the cognition from the very existence or absence of the thing in itself. But others say that the intuitive and the abstractive are modes intrinsic to the very cognition (although not essentially varying the representation itself), because they pertain in truth to the very tendency of the awareness to the object as terminating in this or that mode.

There is therefore but one conclusion: **The formal and proper rationale of the intuitive and the formal and proper rationale of the abstractive are neither of them rationales which essentially and intrinsically change cognition, but are both of them rationales which do so accidentally [and intrinsically]. Incidentally, however, that is to say, through another and by reason of that to which they are conjoined, intuitive and abstractive can import types of awareness different in species or kind.**

The first part of this conclusion is taken FROM THE PASSAGES IN ST. THOMAS cited above from the *Disputed Questions on Truth*, q. 3, art. 3, reply to obj. 8, and from the *Commentary on the Sentences of Peter Lombard*, Book III, dist. 14, q. 1, art. 2, quaestiunc. 2, because specifically the knowledge of vision or intuitive awareness adds to a simple or abstractive awareness something which is independent of the order of awareness, namely, the existence of the thing. He therefore feels that the rationales of intuitive and abstractive awareness do not express essential and intrinsic differences, because these rationales are not independent of the order of cognition, but pertain to the very order of the knowable. But to add something which is independent of the very seeing and independent of the very order of cognition is to add something accidental and extrinsic.

ipsae repraesentationes differunt intrinsece et essentialiter propter diversa obiecta repraesentata.

Alii vero dicunt differre accidentaliter, quia non requirunt diversas repraesentationes formaliter, sed potest idem repraesentari in notitia intuitiva et abstractiva, nempe res cum sua existentia et praesentia in actu signato cognita et repraesentata; solum vero differre accidentaliter propter diversum exercitium terminandi. Si enim obiectum ipsum reddatur praesens in se et ipsa praesentia repraesentetur in cognitione, hoc ipso redditur intuitiva cognitio. Si vero tollatur praesentia physica rei, per quam obiectum terminat cognitionem, reliquis omnibus invariatis ex parte cognitionis et repraesentationis, redditur notitia abstractiva. Unde etiam quidam dicunt intuitivum et abstractivum solum esse denominationes extrinsecas, provenientes in cognitione ex ipsa existentia vel absentia rei in se. Alii vero dicunt esse modos intrinsecos in ipsa notitia (licet non variantes ipsam repraesentationem essentialiter), quia revera pertinent ad ipsam tendentiam notitiae ad obiectum, ut tali vel tali modo terminans.

SIT ERGO UNICA CONCLUSIO. **Formalis et propria ratio intuitivi et abstractivi non sunt rationes essentaliter et intrinsece variantes cognitionem, sed accidentaliter, licet per accidens, id est per aliud et ratione eius, cui coniunguntur, possint diversas specie notitias importare.**

Prima pars sumitur ex locis Divi Thomae supra cit. in q. 3. de Veritate et in 3. dist. 14., quia scilicet scientia visionis seu notitia intuitiva addit supra notitiam simplicem seu abstractivam aliquid, quod est extra genus notitiae, scilicet existentiam rei. Ergo sentit, quod non dicunt differentias essentiales et intrinsecas, quia istae non sunt extra genus notitiae, sed pertinent ad ipsum ordinem cognoscibilis. Addere autem aliquid, quod est extra ipsum videntem et extra genus ipsius cognitionis, est addere aliquid accidentale et extrinsecum.

But THE FOUNDATION OF THIS CONCLUSION is the fact that the intuitive and the abstractive do not import diversity into the formal principle itself of knowability, because the intuitive and the abstractive in awarenesses do not arise out of the very means or stimuli or specifying principles, nor out of a diversity in the immateriality which is the root of cognition, nor out of diverse "which" or "under which" formal rationales[7] of representing. Therefore they do not import specifically distinguishing rationales of themselves and by virtue of their respective formalities.

The antecedent is proved because, as we will show in the following question, presence and absence do not pertain specially to the intuitive and the abstractive as being kinds of things represented, as if they were kinds of definable structures or essences, but only according as they affect and modify the object in itself and render that object coexistent with the cognition or not coexistent. Which is manifestly the case, because specifiers representing the presence itself objectively as a thing represented can be found in an abstractive awareness, as when I know that God is present to me now, or that the soul or the intellect is present to the body, or when we are treating of their presence; and yet we see neither the soul nor God intuitively. And much the same is the case of the specifying forms [the concepts] of pure spirits, which represent things as existent and present before those things exist, and yet the pure spirits do not see the things intuitively, except when the things exist in themselves in act. Therefore presence or absence as represented things essentially and directly do not distinguish the intuitive and the abstractive, but presence as represented can be found in an abstractive cognition. But presence or absence intrinsically vary the knowable order only *as represented* and of themselves knowable or as an object of themselves, not as a modification and accessory of another object, as we will show forthwith. Therefore the formal rationale itself of an intuition is not an essential difference in the order of knowability.

And this is confirmed, because presence and absence constitute the intuitive and the abstractive insofar as the intuitive and the abstractive function as modes of a knowable or represented thing, so that the presence itself does not have the rationale of the object primarily and essentially represented, but only *modifies* the object represented, so that that presence

FUNDAMENTUM vero est, quia intuitivum et abstractivum non important diversitatem in ipso formali principio cognoscibilitatis, quia intuitivum et abstractivum in notitiis non oriuntur ex ipsis mediis seu motivis aut principiis specificantibus, neque ex diversa immaterialitate, quae est radix cognitionis, neque ex diversa ratione formali repraesentandi *quae* nec *sub qua*.[7] Ergo non important rationes specifice distinguentes ex se et vi suae formalitatis.

Antecedens probatur, quia, ut seq. art. ostendemus, praesentia et absentia non pertinent specialiter ad intuitivum et abstractivum prout quaedam res repraesentatae, quasi quaedam quidditates, sed solum prout afficiunt et modificant obiectum in se et reddunt illud coexistens cognitioni vel non coexistens. Quod manifeste patet, quia species repraesentans praesentiam ipsam obiective ut rem repraesentatam, inveniri potest in notitia abstractiva, ut cum modo cognosco Deum esse praesentem mihi, aut animam seu intellectum praesentem esse corpori, vel de eorum praesentia disserimus; et tamen nec animam nec Deum videmus intuitive. Et simile est de speciebus angelicis, quae repraesentant res et existentiam ac praesentiam, antequam sint, et tamen non vident res intuitive, nisi quando actu sunt in se. Ergo praesentia seu absentia ut res repraesentatae, per se et directe non distinguunt intuitivum et abstractivum, sed inveniri potest praesentia ut repraesentata in cognitione abstractiva. Sed praesentia vel absentia solum variant intrinsece genus cognoscibile ut repraesentatae et per se cognoscibiles seu ut obiectum per se, non ut alterius modificatio et accessorium, ut statim ostendemus. Ergo ratio ipsa formalis intuitionis non est differentia essentialis in genere cognoscibili.

Et confirmatur, quia praesentia et absentia in tantum constituunt intuitivum et abstractivum, in quantum se habent ut modi rei cognoscibilis seu repraesentatae, ita quod ipsa praesentia non habeat rationem obiecti primo et per se repraesentati, sed solum modificat obiectum repraesentatum, ita quod facit terminari cognitionem

[7] Explained in Book I, Question 4, 178/8-180/7.

causes the cognition to be terminated at the object inasmuch as that object is present, that is to say, as it [i.e., the physically present object] is rendered coexisting to [i.e., mind-dependently related in its here-and-now physical and perceptible being in act to] the knowing power, not inasmuch as the presence is itself a represented thing. For in this way, as we have said, the existence of the thing in itself can be attained even through an abstractive cognition, because it is represented in the mode of a definable character, which is the mode proper to abstractive cognition. Therefore presence only pertains to the intuitive inasmuch as it modifies the object, not inasmuch as it constitutes the object. Therefore physical presence is not in itself an essential difference, because it does not keep to the side of the specifying principle (which an object or rationale of the representable is) as a rationale "which" or "under which," but it supposes a principal object represented, of which it itself is a mode. For the presence in question modifies the termination of the principal object, it does not constitute the rationale of the stimulus, inasmuch as the presence in question coexists with the rationale terminatively or on the side of the terminus, the whole of which modification varies a cognition accidentally, just as in seeing, the modification of a common sensible in relation to a proper sensible (so that a white thing is seen with or without motion, in this or that position) does not vary the seeing essentially, because it does not keep on the side of the object essentially and formally, but incidentally,[8] just so does the modification of a termination through presence or absence function in respect of awareness.

From which it follows that if modes of awareness differ because one respects presence as directly represented and known, while another does not, such modes could differ essentially on account of objects diverse in the being of representable object, but they would not differ in the rationale of intuitive and abstractive only, but in the rationale of objects diverse in the mode of a definable structure and represented thing.

The second part of the conclusion[9] — namely, the proposition that by reason of something contingent to the rationale of an intuitive or of an abstractive awareness, the intuitive or the abstractive could import a difference in kind [an essential diversity in type of objectification] — is manifestly true, because the intuitive and the abstractive can sometimes be found in cognitions otherwise distinct in kind, either because they represent diverse objects or because they represent under diverse means and specifying lights, as is clear [in the difference between] the

ad obiectum, quatenus praesens, id est ut redditur coexistens potentiae cognoscenti, non quatenus praesentia ipsa res repraesentata est. Sic enim, ut diximus, etiam per abstractivam cognitionem attingi potest, quia per modum quidditatis repraesentatur, quod proprium est cognitionis abstractivae. Ergo praesentia solum pertinet ad intuitivum, quatenus modificativa est obiecti, non quatenus constitutiva obiecti. Ergo per se non est differentia essentialis, quia non ex parte principii specificantis se tenet, quod est obiectum seu ratio repraesentabilis, ut ratio quae vel sub qua, sed supponit obiectum principale repraesentatum, cuius ipsa est modus. Modificat enim terminationem ipsius, non rationem motivam constituit, quatenus illi coexistit terminative seu ex parte termini, quod totum accidentaliter variat cognitionem, sicut in visione modificatio sensibilis communis ad sensibile proprium, ut quod album videatur cum motu vel sine motu, in tali vel tali situ, non variat essentialiter visionem, quia non ex parte obiecti per se et formaliter, sed ex parte obiecti accidentaliter se tenet,[8] sic respectu notitiae se habet modificatio terminationis per praesentiam vel absentiam.

Ex quo sequitur, quod si differunt notitiae, quia una respicit praesentiam ut directe repraesentatam et cognitam, alia non, tales notitiae poterunt differre essentialiter propter diversum obiectum in esse obiecti repraesentabilis, sed non different in ratione intuitivi et abstractivi tantum, sed in ratione diversi obiecti per modum quidditatis et rei repraesentatae.

Secunda vero pars conclusionis[9] manifeste constat, quia potest aliquando intuitivum et abstractivum inveniri in cognitionibus alias specie distinctis, quia vel repraesentant diversa obiecta vel sub diverso medio et lumine specificante, sicut patet in visione intuitiva Dei in se

[8] See Book I, Question 6, above, 212/36-213/7.
[9] 290/32-35.

intuitive vision of God in himself and the abstractive awarenss of him through faith, or [in the difference between] an intuitive cognition of Peter and an abstractive cognition of a horse. But these essential diversities are not taken formally and precisely from the very rationale of the intuitive or of the abstractive, but from other formal rationales which specify these cognitions in the knowable order. Yet the rationale of the intuitive or of the abstractive is added to these other formally specifying rationales as an incidental accompanying rationale, not as the [formally] constitutive rationale [of the essential differences in awareness as such].

But you might ask whether these rationales of the intuitive and the abstractive, granted that they are not of themselves essential differences of awareness, are nevertheless modalities intrinsic to the cognition itself, so that they really modify a cognition; or whether they are only extrinsic denominations born of a physical coexistence; or what finally are they?

The response is that some think that the intuitive and the abstractive consist only in an extrinsic denomination, inasmuch as an object is said to be coexistent with (physically present in cognition to) or not coexistent with the very cognition. And this opinion can be supported by the example of truth and of falsity; for the same cognition is now said to be true, now false, from the mere extrinsic denomination that an object exists or does not exist in itself. Similarly, therefore, since the intuitive bespeaks the physical coexistence of the object and the abstractive negates the same, an awareness is said to be intuitive or abstractive through the mere extrinsic denomination from such a coexistence or noncoexistence. And in the case of God it seems that this must be asserted without doubt, because the numerically same cognition which is of simple understanding in respect of possibles, is rendered intuitive through a mere extrinsic denomination, because specifically the thing itself passes from the possible into the future, that is, to existing, which passage posits nothing in the divine knowledge itself except an extrinsic denomination, as likewise the fact that divine knowledge is a knowledge of approbation is nothing but an extrinsic denomination in the divine knowledge. But St. Thomas, in the *Disputed Questions on Truth*, q. 3, art. 3, reply to obj. 8,[10] equates knowledge of vision with knowledge of approbation as regards this, that it adds something from outside the order of awareness.

This opinion is probable. Nevertheless, it seems *more* probable that the intuitive and the abstractive are

vel abstractiva illius per fidem, in cognitione intuitiva Petri vel abstractiva equi. Ceterum ista diversitas essentialis non sumitur formaliter et praecise ex ipsa ratione intuitivi et abstractivi, sed ex aliis rationibus formalibus, quae in genere cognoscibili specificant istas cognitiones. Quibus tamen adiungitur intuititivum et abstractivum tamquam rationes accidentales consecutae, non constitutivae.

Sed inquires, an ista ratio intuitivi et abstractivi, esto per se non sint essentiales differentiae notitiae, sint tamen modi aliqui intrinseci in ipsa cognitione, ita quod realiter illam immutent; an solum sint extrinsecae denominationes ex physica coexistentia ortae; vel quid tandem sint.

Respondetur aliquos existimare, quod intuitivum et abstractivum solum consistunt in extrinseca denominatione, quatenus obiectum dicitur esse praesens seu coexistens ipsi cognitioni vel non coexistens. Et iuvari potest haec sententia exemplo veritatis et falsitatis; eadem enim cognitio dicitur modo vera, modo falsa ex sola extrinseca denominatione, quod obiectum sit vel non sit in se. Similiter ergo cum intuitivum dicat coexistentiam physicam obiecti et abstractivum neget, per solam extrinsecam denominationem a tali coexistentia vel non coexistentia dicetur notitia intuitiva vel abstractiva. Et in Deo videtur sine dubio hoc asserendum, quia eadem numero cognitio, quae est simplicis intelligentiae respectu possibilium, per solam extrinsecam denominationem redditur intuitiva, quia scilicet res ipsa transit de possibili in futuram seu existentem, quod nihil ponit in ipsa scientia divina, nisi extrinsecam denominationem; sicut etiam quod divina scientia sit approbationis, non est nisi denominatio extrinseca in scientia divina. Aequiparat autem D. Thomas scientiam visionis scientiae approbationis quantum ad hoc, quod est addere aliquid extra genus notitiae, in 3. de Veritate art. 3. ad 8.[10]

Haec sententia est probabilis. *Nihilominus probabilius videtur,* quod intuitivum et abstractivum sint aliquid intrinsecum in ip-

---

[10] *Pa* IX. 58 b.

something intrinsic to awareness itself in its own order. And so when a created awareness passes from intuitive into abstractive and conversely, it is really modified.

The reason is that intuition imports the coexistence of the physical presence of the object with the awareness, coexistence not in any mode whatever, but with the attention and tendency of the very cognition terminated at this specific thing as coexisting with and modifying the object. But a termination of cognition diverse by means of an attention to a coexisting thing posits some intrinsic modification in the very cognition; for an abstractive awareness does not have such an attention to and termination at the coexistence of the presence. *Therein lies the wide difference between the truth or falsity of a cognition and the rationale of the intuitive and of the abstractive,*[11] because truth so consists in conformity to the being or non-being of a thing, that even if one does not attend to the being or non-being of a thing, if just once one yet proffered a judgment when the thing did not exist in *the way* it was judged to be, by this very fact the cognition loses truth, and when the thing exists in the way it is judged to be, the cognition acquires truth without any other variable intervening intrinsically in the cognition. But indeed for someone to see intuitively, it is not enough that while he is knowing something, that something is posited present in itself, but it must needs be that the one knowing *attend* to its presence *as to a presence coexisting* with himself, *and not precisely as* a *represented* presence. If this kind of attention is missing, the intuition is destroyed, even though the thing known be present in itself, because it is not present in the terminating of the attention and awareness; just as God is present in himself to the knowledge which I have of him, and the soul, and those which are in the soul, are present in themselves, yet I do not see them intuitively. An attention, therefore, diverse with such a termination of the object as present and coexisting, is a rationale intrinsic to the cognition, and yet it is not a rationale that varies that cognition essentially, because it is a modification incidental to the object itself, just as the modification of a common sensible in respect of a proper sensible is a modification incidental to the object of the sense and does not vary cognitions essentially, even though it demands a diverse attention and termination. Thus presence as coexisting of itself modifies, not essentially distinguishes, an object, yet it belongs to the act [of knowing] intrinsically on account of a diverse attention.

sis notitiis ex suo genere. Et ita quando notitia creata transit de intuitiva in abstractivam et e contra, realiter mutatur.

Ratio est, quia intuitio importat coexistentiam praesentiae physicae obiecti cum notitia, non quomodocumque, sed cum attentione et tendentia ipsius cognitionis terminatae ad talem rem ut coexistentem et modificantem obiectum. Diversa autem terminatio cognitionis mediante attentione ad rem coexistentem, aliquam intrinsecam mutationem ponit in ipsa cognitione; nec enim talem attentionem et terminationem ad coexistentiam praesentiae habet abstractiva notitia. In quo est latum discrimen inter veritatem seu falsitatem cognitionis et rationem intuitivi et abstractivi,[11] quia veritas ita consistit in conformitate ad esse vel non esse rei, quod etiam, si quis non attendat ad esse vel non esse rei, si tamen semel proferat iudicium, re non existente eo modo, ut iudicat, hoc ipso amittit veritatem, et re ita existente acquirit illam nulla alia mutatione interveniente intrinsece in cognitione. At vero ut aliquis intuitive videat, non sufficit, quod ipso cognoscente aliquid, illud ponatur praesens in se, sed oportet, quod ad eius praesentiam attendat cognoscens ut ad coexistentem sibi, et non ut praecise repraesentatam, quae attentio talis si desit, destruitur intuitio, licet res sit praesens in se, quia non est praesens in terminando attentionem et notitiam; sicut Deus est praesens in se cognitioni, quam habeo de ipso, et anima et ea, quae sunt in anima, sunt in se praesentia, nec tamen intuitive ea video. Diversa ergo attentio cum tali terminatione obiecti ut praesentis et coexistentis est intrinseca ratio in cognitione, et tamen non essentialiter variat ipsam, quia est modificatio accidentalis ipsius obiecti, sicut modificatio sensibilis communis respectu sensibilis proprii, quod non variat essentialiter cognitiones, licet diversam exigat attentionem et terminationem. Sic praesentia ut coexistens modificat obiectum per se, non essentialiter distinguit, propter diversam tamen attentionem intrinsece convenit actui.

---

[11] in response to 293/24-33.

But to the objection concerning the intuitive cognition of God,[12] the response is that just as the same act of God's will, on account of its eminence, is necessary and free through its intrinsic perfection, even though it connotes some mind-dependent respect or extrinsic denomination in respect of the object, so the same divine knowledge, on account of its eminence, is intrinsically abstractive and intuitive and of approbation, and at the same time also practical and speculative, efficacious and inefficacious in respect of diverse objects, even though it connotes some mind-dependent relation or extrinsic denomination in respect of the object. The divine knowledge, nevertheless, does not formally consist in this mind-dependent respect or extrinsic denomination, but without that respect it is not denominated intuitive nor the act of the divine will free. But what one act has in God eminently, several acts have in us on account of the act's limitation.

Resolution of Counter-Arguments

The first argument is drawn from the doctrine of St. Thomas in the *Summa theologica*, I-II, q. 67, art. 5, where he says that the numerically same cognition of faith cannot remain in heaven, because "when the difference of some species is removed, the substance of the genus does not remain the same by number," and so "it cannot be the case that the numerically same awareness which first was enigmatic, should afterwards become a clear vision." From which is formed the argument: St. Thomas denies that the numerically same awareness which was enigmatic can be a clear vision, for when the difference of some species is removed the substance of the genus does not remain the same by number. Therefore St. Thomas supposes that clear vision is a specific difference of awareness; otherwise he could conclude nothing from that reasoning, because if the rationale of intuition or vision adds only an accidental difference, when that difference is removed the whole substance of that cognition can remain.

And this is confirmed, because intuitive awareness and abstractive awareness are opposed formally and expel one another formally from a subject. For they are opposed according to the clear and the obscure concerning the presence of a thing, because the intuitive intrinsically implies evidence and certitude of the presence of the thing, which the abstractive does not import. And by reason of this evidence and certi-

Ad id vero, quod obicitur de cognitione intuitiva Dei,[12] respondetur, quod sicut idem actus voluntatis Dei propter eminentiam suam est necessarius et liber per suam intrinsecam perfectionem, licet connotet respectum aliquem rationis vel denominationem extrinsecam respectu obiecti, ita eadem scientia ob eminentiam suam est intrinsece abstractiva et intuitiva et approbationis, et simul etiam practica et speculativa, efficax et inefficax respectu diversorum, licet connotet respectum aliquem rationis vel extrinsecam denominationem respectu obiecti. In quo tamen formaliter non consistit, sed non sine illo denominatur intuitiva vel libera illa scientia seu actus. Quod vero eminenter in Deo habet unus actus, in nobis habent plures ob sui limitationem.

Solvuntur argumenta

Primo arguitur ex doctrina Divi Thomae 1. 2. q. 67. art. 5., ubi inquit, quod eadem numero cognitio fidei non potest manere in patria, quia «remota differentia alicuius speciei, non remanet substantia generis eadem numero», et ita «non potest esse, quod eadem numero notitia, quae prius aenigmatica erat, postea fiat visio aperta». Ex quo formatur argumentum: Quia ideo negat Divus Thomas, quod eadem numero notitia, quae erat aenigmatica, non potest esse visio aperta, quia remota differentia alicuius speciei non remanet substantia generis eadem numero. Ergo supponit D. Thomas, quod visio aperta est differentia specifica notitiae; alias nihil concluderet illo discursu, quia si ratio intuitionis seu visionis solum addit differentiam accidentalem, potest remota illa manere tota substantia illius cognitionis.

Et confirmatur, quia notitia intuitiva et abstractiva opponuntur formaliter et expellunt se formaliter a subiecto. Opponuntur enim penes clarum et obscurum circa praesentiam rei, quia intuitivum intrinsece importat evidentiam et certitudinem de praesentia rei, quod non importat abstractivum. Et ratione huius evidentiae

[12] 293/33-43.

tude an intuitive awareness expels abstractive awareness; for they are opposed in a subject not only as are two accidents of the same species or kind, otherwise intuitive and abstractive awareness would be no more opposed than two intuitive awarenesses or two abstractive awarenesses are between themselves. Whence too faith is not opposed to the vision of glory otherwise than because it is abstractive and the vision of glory is intuitive.

The response to this[13] is that St. Thomas is speaking about a clear vision and an enigmatic cognition, which are initiated by diverse means and do not only include the mode of the intuitive or the abstractive. But we have already said above that the intuitive and the abstractive, although they are not essential differences of cognition, can nevertheless be consequent upon and presuppose specifically distinct cognitions to which they are conjoined, when, to wit, they are found in cognitions which are constituted through diverse means or lights or through diverse representations. But that in fact an enigmatic cognition and a clear vision differ according to diverse means St. Thomas best explains in his *Commentary on the First Epistle of Paul to the Corinthians*, chap. 13, reading 4.[14]

To the confimation[15] the response is that the intuitive and the abstractive do not always differ according to an evidence (a distinctness) and an indistinctness (a lack of clarity, a certain confusion) essential to the very cognition, which difference, specifically, is derived from the formal rationale itself of the means by which the specific rationale of the cognition is constituted. For there can be an abstractive awareness which is also evident concerning all those objects which the intuitive awareness represents, even though that intuitive awareness would not have the evidence from the very presence as from something coexisting with the awareness itself. But this evidence does not essentially distinguish one awareness from another, because it does not obtain on the side of a formal specifying rationale, but on the side of the coexistence and application of the object. Whence St. Thomas says in his *Commentary on the Sentences of Peter Lombard*, Book III, dist. 14, q. 1, art. 2, quaestiunc. 3,[16] that "clarity of vision results from three sources, either from the efficacy of the cognitive power, as, for example, one who is of stronger vision knows more clearly than one who is of weak vision; or from the efficacy of the light, as, for example, one sees more clearly by sunlight than by moonlight; or finally

et certitudinis intuitiva notitia expellit abstractivam; non enim solum opponuntur in subiecto sicut duo accidentia eiusdem speciei, alias non magis opponerentur notitia intuitiva et abstractiva, quam duae intuitivae et duae abstractivae inter se. Unde et fides non aliter opponitur visioni gloriae, nisi quia illa est abstractiva et ista intuitiva.

Respondetur,[13] quod D. Thomas loquitur de visione aperta et cognitione aenigmatica, quae innituntur diversis mediis et non solum includunt modum intuitivi vel abstractivi. Iam autem supra diximus, quod intuitivum et abstractivum, licet non sint essentiales differentiae cognitionis, possunt tamen consequi et praesupponere cognitiones specie distinctas, quibus coniunguntur, quando scilicet inveniuntur in cognitionibus, quae per diversa media seu lumina aut diversas repraesentationes constituuntur. Quod autem cognitio aenigmatica et visio aperta differant penes diversa media, optime explicat D. Thomas sup. 1. ad Corinth. cap. 13. lect. 4.[14]

Ad confirmationem[15] respondetur, quod intuitivum et abstractivum non semper differunt penes evidentiam et inevidentiam essentialem ipsi cognitioni, quae scilicet desumitur ex ipsa ratione formali medii, qua constituitur specifica ratio cognitionis. Potest enim dari abstractiva notitia etiam evidens circa omnia illa, quae repraesentat notitia intuitiva, licet non habeat evidentiam de ipsa praesentia ut coexistenti sibi. Sed haec evidentia non distinguit essentialiter unam notitiam ab alia, quia non tenet se ex parte rationis formalis specificantis, sed ex parte coexistentiae et applicationis obiecti. Unde dicit D. Thomas 3. dist. 14. q. 1. art. 2. quaestiunc. 3.,[16] quod «claritas visionis contingit ex tribus, vel ex efficacia virtutis cognoscitivae, sicut qui est fortioris visus, clarius cognoscit quam qui est debilis; aut ex efficacia luminis, sicut clarius videt quis in lumine solis quam in lumine lunae; aut denique ex con-

[13] 295/22-41.
[14] *Pa* XIII. 264. sq.
[15] 295/42-296/8.
[16] *Pa* VII. 154 a.

from the conjunction or application of the object, as, for example, things near are seen more clearly than things far away." Therefore the evidence of an intuitive awareness from the precise and formal energy of the intuition arises only from that awareness in this last way.[17] But it is certain that such clarity or evidence is accidental and extrinsic, because it depends solely on the application and coexistence of a presence more or less near.

As regards what is said concerning the opposition of the intuitive and the abstractive in the same subject,[18] the response is that they are indeed mutually opposed formally by a formality incidental to the cognition itself, but essential to the very rationale of intuition; just as it is not essential for a line to be terminated or not terminated by a point, and yet a line cannot have both simultaneously. And the same cognition cannot be simultaneously true and false on account of opposite terminations relative to objects, and yet truth and falsity belong to cognition accidentally. But faith and vision of God in the afterlife differ not only precisely according to the intuitive and the abstractive but also according to a difference of means, because faith is initiated by the testimony of a speaker, vision by the representation of a thing in itself. And in the same way the vision of the divine essence granted to St. Paul and the recollection whereby he called to mind that he had seen it, differed not only according to the abstractive and the intuitive, but according to diverse means of representation, because he saw God immediately in Himself through his representation, but he recollected that he had seen God through a created form of specification representing immediately some created effect, namely, the very vision as regards its having occured in fact.

Secondly it is argued: The intuitive and the abstractive differ according to diverse formal objects and according to diverse things represented; therefore they import essential differences in the order of cognition.

The consequence is clear, because there is no principle for distinguishing cognitions essentially other than according to formal objects, and representations are distinguished according to the diverse things represented. The antecedent is proved, because the intuitive as intuitive respects an object as present to itself formally, and according to this

iunctione seu applicatione obiecti, sicut clarius videntur ea, quae sunt propinqua quam quae sunt remota». Igitur evidentia notitiae intuitivae ex vi praecisa et formali intuitionis solum hoc ultimo modo[17] ab illa provenit. Constat autem, quod talis claritas seu evidentia est accidentalis et extrinseca, quia solum pendet ex applicatione et coexistentia praesentiae magis vel minus propinquae.

Quod vero dicitur *de oppositione intuitivi et abstractivi in eodem subiecto,*[18] respondetur opponi quidem inter se formaliter formalitate accidentali ipsi notitiae, essentiali vero ipsi rationi intuitionis; sicut lineam esse terminatam vel non terminatam per punctum, non est essentiale lineae, et tamen non potest simul utrumque habere. Et eadem cognitio non potest esse simul vera et falsa propter oppositam terminationem ad obiecta, et tamen veritas et falsitas accidentaliter conveniunt cognitioni. Fides autem et visio patriae non solum differunt penes intuitivum et abstractivum praecise, sed etiam penes diversa media, quia fides innititur testimonio dicentis, visio repraesentationi rei in se. Et eodem modo visio divinae essentiae in Divo Paulo et recordatio, qua recordabatur ipsam vidisse, non solum differebant penes abstractivum et intuitivum, sed penes diversa media repraesentationis, quia vidit Deum per repraesentationem eius immediate in se, recordabatur autem se vidisse per speciem creatam repraesentantem immediate aliquem effectum creatum, scilicet ipsam visionem quoad an est.

Secundo arguitur: Intuitivum et abstractivum differunt penes diversa obiecta formalia et penes diversas res repraesentatas; ergo importat differentias essentiales in genere cognitionis.

Consequentia patet, quia non est aliud principium distinguendi essentialiter cognitiones, nisi penes obiecta formalia, et repraesentationes distinguuntur penes diversas res repraesentatas. *Antecedens* probatur, quia intuitivum ut intuitivum respicit obiectum ut praesens sibi formaliter, et penes

[17] 291/35-38.
[18] 295/42-44, 296/2-6.

formality it differs from the abstractive. And in the intuitive awareness the presence itself of the thing is represented, since indeed it is known and attained as a thing known. Nor is it sufficient for the presence to be in the very object, unless that physical presence also is represented in the cognition, as is plain from the case of one who does not advert to a thing which passes before him, and from the other examples brought forward above. Therefore the intuitive does not imply the presence of a thing as purely entitatively and physically independent of the order of awareness, but as represented and attained knowably.

If it were said that that presence is represented exertively and not as the thing directly represented, against this there are two instances: The first is the case of the noun and of the verb, which, as we said in the *Summulae* books, q. 2, art. 3, have in their inflected forms concepts physically, although not categorematically, distinct from the concepts of their uninflected forms, and yet they do not differ according to diverse things represented, but according to diverse exercised connotations of the same represented thing. The second instance is in the formal rationale "under which," through which one cognition is distinguished essentially from another, and yet the rationale in question is not represented nor attained by a direct cognition, for thus it would be a rationale "which" and not "under which."

This is confirmed, because the present and the absent essentially distinguish acts of desire, therefore also acts of cognition.

The consequence is clear from the parity of rationale in the good and the true respecting the present and the absent. The antecedent, on the other hand, is proved by the fact that fear and sadness differ only by reason of an evil absent or present, just as hope and joy differ only by reason of a good absent and present. Therefore, presence and absence alone specifically diversify acts of desire and cognition.

The response to the principal argument[19] is that the intuitive and the abstractive do not differ according to formal objects diverse in the being and formality of something knowable, but in the being and formality of some condition and accidental mode. And that which is formal and essential to the *intuitive* itself is one thing, that which is formal and essential to the *cognition* itself quite another — just as it is essential to white that it differentiate seeing in contrast to black, and yet it is not essential that man be white; and

hanc formalitatem differt ab abstractivo. Et in notitia intuitiva repraesentatur ipsa praesentia rei, siquidem cognoscitur et attingitur ut res cognita, nec sufficit, quod praesentia sit in ipso obiecto, nisi sit etiam repraesentata in cognitione, ut patet in eo, qui non advertit ad rem, quae transit coram se, et in aliis exemplis supra allatis. Ergo intuitivum non importat praesentiam rei, ut pure entitative et physice extra genus notitiae, sed ut repraesentatam et attactam cognoscibiliter.

Si dicatur, quod illa praesentia repraesentatur exercite et non tamquam res directe repraesentata, *contra hoc* est duplex instantia: *Prima* in casibus nominis et verbi, qui, ut diximus in Summul. q. 2. art. 3., habent distinctos conceptus a suis rectis physice, licet non categorematice, et tamen non differunt penes diversas res repraesentatas, sed penes diversam connotationem exercitam eiusdem rei repraesentatae. *Secunda* instantia est in ratione formali sub qua, per quam distinguitur essentialiter una cognitio ab alia, et tamen non repraesentatur nec attingitur directa cognitione, sic enim esset ratio quae et non sub qua.

Confirmatur, quia praesens et absens distinguunt essentialiter actus appetitus, ergo etiam actus cognitionis.

Consequentia patet ex paritate rationis in bono et vero ad praesens et absens. *Antecedens* vero probatur, quia timor et tristitia differunt solum ratione mali absentis vel praesentis, sicut spes et gaudium ratione praesentis et absentis. Ergo sola praesentia et absentia diversificat specie istos actus.

RESPONDETUR *ad principale argumentum,*[19] quod intuitivum et abstractivum non differunt penes diversa obiecta formalia in esse et formalitate cognoscibilis, sed in esse et formalitate alicuius conditionis et modi accidentalis. Et aliud est, quod sit formale et essentiale ipsi intuitivo, aliud, quod sit formale et essentiale ipsi cognitioni, sicut esse disgregativum visus est essentiale albo, ut distinguitur essentialiter a nigro, non ta-

[19] 297/37-41.

similarly, an object as present or as absent, as regards coexistence with the very cognition and application of the object, is essential to the intuitive itself and to the abstractive itself, and yet not to cognition itself. And thus the intuitive and the abstractive *mutually* differ essentially and by definition, just as do white and black, but these differences are accidental *to cognition* itself, because, as has been said, they do not respect the present and the absent as these found knowability and diverse immaterialities, but as they found application to the physical coexistence of the object in terminating cognition.

To what is said about diverse representations,[20] the response is that the intuitive and the abstractive formally and by virtue of themselves do not differ according to diverse things represented. For even an abstractive awareness can *represent* a presence on the side of the thing represented; as, for example, I now think that God is present to me and I know evidently through the effects that a soul is present to me, and yet I see neither God nor the soul intuitively. Wherefore these representations do not differ according to diverse things represented nor according to a connotation or condition relative to a distinct represented thing or according to distinct rationales "under which" essentially conducing to representation, but only according to a diverse termination at the presence of the object as coexistent with the very cognition, as has been stated. Whence not every variation in a representation is an essential variation, unless it could be reduced to diverse rationales "which" or "under which" of the very representation. As also in exterior vision, not any change whatever essentially varies the vision, as, for example, if the variation comes about only according to diverse common sensibles, as when something white is seen with motion or without motion, with this or that position or profile, none of which conditions vary the vision itself essentially, but accidentally, as we have said. Concerning this, see Bañez's *Commentary on the Summa theologica of St. Thomas*, I, q. 78, art. 3, dub. 8. So also presence or absence do not vary cognition essentially, insofar as they imply diverse terminations of cognition at the presence of the object as coexisting with the cognition. But if presence and absence also function as things represented, in this way they can vary modes of awareness as

men est essentiale homini, et similiter obiectum ut praesens vel ut absens, quantum ad coexistentiam cum ipsa cognitione et applicationem obiecti, essentialia sunt ipsi intuitivo et abstractivo, non tamen ipsi cognitioni. Et ita intuitivum et abstractivum essentialiter differunt et definitione inter se sicut album et nigrum, sed istae differentiae sunt accidentales ipsi cognitioni, quia, ut dictum est, non respiciunt praesens et absens, ut fundant cognoscibilitatem et immaterialitatem diversam, sed ut fundant applicationem ad coexistentiam obiecti physicam in terminando cognitionem.

Quod vero dicitur *de diversa repraesentatione,*[20] respondetur intuitivum et abstractivum formaliter et ex vi sua non differre penes diversas res repraesentatas. Potest enim etiam abstractiva notitia repraesentare praesentiam ex parte rei repraesentatae; sicut ego modo cogito Deum mihi praesentem et animam cognosco mihi esse praesentem evidenter per effectus, et tamen nec Deum nec animam intuitive video. Quare non differunt istae repraesentationes penes diversas res repraesentatas nec penes connotationem seu habitudinem ad distinctum repraesentatum vel penes distinctas rationes sub quibus essentialiter conducentibus ad repraesentationem, sed solum penes diversam terminationem ad praesentiam ut coexistentem ipsi cognitioni, ut declaratum est. Unde non omnis variatio in repraesentatione est variatio essentialis, nisi reducatur ad diversam rationem quae vel sub qua ipsius repraesentationis. Sicut etiam in visione exteriori non quaecumque mutatio variat essentialiter visionem, v. g. si solum fiat variatio penes diversum sensibile commune, ut si album videatur cum motu vel sine motu, cum hoc vel illo situ vel figura, quae non variat essentialiter ipsam visionem, sed accidentaliter, ut diximus. De quo videatur Mag. Bañez, 1. p. q. 78. art. 3. dub. 8. Sic etiam praesentia vel absentia non variant essentialiter cognitionem, in quantum important diversam terminationem cognitionis ad praesentiam ut coexistentem sibi. Si autem etiam se habeant ut res repraesentatae, sic variare possunt notitias

[20] 297/42-298/28.

their diverse objects, but not when they function only as a condition pertaining to the coexistence of the presence of an object with the awareness.

From which is also clear the response to the two instances adduced above.[21] For if the diverse cases (i.e., the inflected forms) of nouns distinguish concepts essentially, the reason for this is that they bring to the object some diverse relative condition and connotation to the thing represented, as, for example, to the thing in the mode of an agent or of something possessed, which is [to be represented] in the mode of a "what" or an "of which" or a "to which," relative conditions that are understood to affect the very thing represented and to be founded on it, and that are a fortiori diverse rationales "under which." But the intuitive and the abstractive according to their precise formalities do not bespeak the very presence or absence as they are representable things; for in this way, as we have already said, the presence of a thing can be a thing represented through an abstractive cognition, as when I know abstractively that God is present. But if some abstractive cognition does not represent the presence as a thing represented, while an intuitive cognition does, then those representations would differ essentially not by virtue of the intuitive and the abstractive precisely, but on account of the general reason of representing diverse objects. Standing therefore on the precise formalities of the intuitive and the abstractive, which do not postulate diverse things represented nor diverse relative conditions or connotations founded on the very thing represented, but diverse terminations and applications of the object according to a coexistence relative to the awareness, for this reason the concepts do not vary essentially, as neither does a white thing when it is seen with movement or without movement [vary awareness essentially], or cognition when it is rendered true or false from coexistence relative to the mind-independent being of a thing.

To the confirmation[22] the response is that there are diverse rationales in acts of desire and in acts of cognition, because desire is borne toward good or evil, but the rationale of good or of evil is varied essentially according to diverse conformities or disconformities. But conformity or disconformity depends more than anything else on the presence or absence of a thing, because a present object

tamquam diversa obiecta earum, non autem quando solum gerunt vicem conditionis pertinentis ad coexistentiam praesentiae obiecti cum notitia.

Ex quo etiam patet *ad instantias adductas*.[21] Nam diversi casus nominum si distinguunt conceptus essentialiter, ideo est, quia important in obiecto diversam aliquam habitudinem et connotationem ad rem repraesentatam, v. g. ad rem per modum agentis vel possessae, quod est per modum quid vel cuius vel cui, quae habitudines intelliguntur afficere ipsam rem repraesentatam et in ea fundari, et a fortiori diversa ratio sub qua. At vero intuitivum et abstractivum secundum suam praecisam formalitatem non dicunt ipsam praesentiam vel absentiam ut sunt res repraesentabiles; sic enim, ut iam diximus, potest praesentia rei esse res repraesentata per cognitionem abstractivam, ut cum cognosco Deum esse praesentem abstractive. Quodsi aliqua cognitio abstractiva non repraesentat praesentiam ut rem repraesentatam, intuitiva vero sic, tunc illae repraesentationes different essentialiter non ex vi intuitivi et abstractivi praecise, sed propter generalem rationem repraesentandi diversa obiecta. Stando ergo in praecisa formalitate intuitivi et abstractivi, quae non postulant diversas res repraesentatas nec diversam habitudinem vel connotationem in ipsa re repraesentata fundatam, sed diversam terminationem et applicationem obiecti secundum coexistentiam ad notitiam, ideo non variant essentialiter conceptus, sicut nec album, quando videtur cum motu vel sine motu, vel cognitio, quando redditur vera vel falsa ex coexistentia ad esse rei.

Ad confirmationem[22] respondetur esse diversam rationem in actibus appetitus et in actibus cognitionis, quia appetitus fertur in bonum vel malum, variatur autem essentialiter ratio boni vel mali secundum diversam convenientiam vel disconvenientiam. Maxime autem pendet convenientia vel disconvenientia ex praesentia vel absentia rei, quia obiectum praesens facit quie-

[21] 298/13-28.
[22] 298/29-39.

satisfies desire, but an absent object arouses it, by the fact that desire functions in the mode of an inclination and weight. But a weight behaves in one way when it is at center, and in another way when it is off center, and for this reason the presence or absence of an object to that which functions in the mode of an inclination counts for much in varying the formal rationale of the object. But cognition, by contrast, since it is perfected within the very power by drawing things to itself, is always perfected by the presence of those things in a knowable and intentional existence. Whence, unless such [intentional] presence is varied, no variation occurs in the essential rationale of the cognition, and so what remains beyond that of the physical presence of an object, whether it be coexistent or not coexistent with the awareness, obtains independently of the order of such awareness and is considered incidental, because already it does not pertain to the intentional presence.

Finally it is argued that if the intuitive and the abstractive do not vary awareness essentially, but accidentally, either they are extrinsic denominations or intrinsic ones. They are not extrinsic denominations; for if that were the case the numerically same awareness could be now intuitive, now abstractive, just as the same cognition can be true or false. And if presence and absence are compared in respect of intuitive awareness and abstractive awareness, as is a common sensible in respect of sight, it is clear that they cannot be related as extrinsic denominations; for the tendency toward a common sensible is not an extrinsic denomination in sight. But if the intuitive and the abstractive are intrinsic modes, they cannot be other than the tendency and order toward the object, which essentially varies the cognition. Nor can it be understood how these intrinsic modes would vary a concept accidentally, and not vary the representation itself in the order toward the thing represented.

Rather, there is no division of cognition according to intrinsic modes unless it be also an essential division, just as the distinction according to the clear and the obscure essentially varies cognition, even though obscurity is not a formal rationale, but an intrinsic mode of cognition.

Finally, some examples can be adduced which seem to prove that this distinction is essential, just as the practical and the speculative are essential differences, and yet the practical bespeaks an order to work which is [accomplished] outside of the mind. And good and evil are essential dif-

scere appetitum, absens autem facit moveri, eo quod appetitus se habet per modum inclinationis et ponderis. Pondus autem aliter se habet in centro, aliter extra centrum, et ideo praesentia vel absentia obiecti in eo, quod se habet per modum inclinationis, multum concludit ad variandam formalem rationem obiecti. At vero cognitio cum perficiatur intra ipsam potentiam trahendo res ad se, semper perficitur per praesentiam illarum in esse cognoscibili et intentionali. Unde nisi talis praesentia varietur, non fit variatio in ratione essentiali cognitionis, et ita id, quod restat de praesentia physica obiecti, quod sit coexistens vel non coexistens notitiae, extra genus talis notitiae se tenet et per accidens consideratur, quia iam non pertinet ad praesentiam intentionalem.

Ultimo arguitur, quia intuitivum et abstractivum si non variant essentialiter notitiam, sed accidentaliter, vel sunt denominationes extrinsecae vel intrinsecae. Non extrinsecae; sic enim eadem numero notitia modo posset esse intuitiva, modo abstractiva, sicut potest esse vera vel falsa eadem cognitio. Et si comparatur praesentia et absentia respectu notitiae intuitivae et abstractivae, sicut sensibile commune respectu visionis, clarum est, quod non potest se habere ut denominatio extrinseca; tendentia enim ad sensible commune non est denominatio extrinseca in visione. Si autem intuitivum et abstractivum sunt modi intrinseci, non possunt esse aliud quam tendentia et ordo ad obiectum, quod essentialiter variat cognitionem. Nec intelligi potest, quomodo isti modi intrinseci varient conceptum accidentaliter, et non varient ipsam repraesentationem in ordine ad rem repraesentatam.

Imo neque datur divisio cognitionis penes modos intrinsecos, nisi etiam sit divisio essentialis, sicut distinctio penes clarum et obscurum essentialiter variant cognitionem, licet obscuritas non sit ratio formalis, sed modus intrinsecus cognitionis.

Denique afferri possunt aliqua exempla, quae distinctionem istam essentialem probare videntur, sicut practicum et speculativum sunt differentiae essentiales, et tamen practicum dicit ordinem ad opus, quod est extra rationem. Et bonum et malum sunt differentia essentiales actus humani, et tamen malum

ferences of human acts, and yet evil can be derived from some intrinsic circumstance.

The response to this [23] is that the intuitive and the abstractive are accidental modes which reductively pertain to the order of cognition as modes, not as essential species or kinds, and, as we have said,[24] it is more probable that they are intrinsic modes. And when it is said that they are the very order or tendency toward the object, we say that formally and directly they are not the very order to the object in the rationale of *represented* object, but *modifications* of this order, inasmuch as they make [the awareness] tend toward an object *not only* as represented, but as coexisting [or not coexisting] with the awareness, so that the rationale of being toward the object as represented and known formally constitutes [the specification], but the rationale of being toward the object thus represented as coexisting with the awareness is a *modifying* respect.[25] But when we compare the rationale of the intuitive to the order and respect toward a common sensible, the example holds in this, that a common sensible is not something primarily

potest sumi ex aliqua intrinseca circumstantia.

RESPONDETUR,[23] quod intuitivum et abstractivum sunt modi accidentales, qui reductive pertinent ad genus cognitionis tamquam modi, non tamquam species essentiales, et ut diximus,[24] probabilius est, quod sint modi intrinseci. Et quando dicitur, quod sunt ipse ordo seu tendentia ad obiectum, dicimus, quod formaliter et directe non sunt ipse ordo ad obiectum in ratione obiecti repraesentati, sed modificationes istius ordinis, quatenus faciunt tendere ad obiectum non solum ut repraesentatum, sed ut coexistens notitiae, ita quod ratio ad obiectum, ut repraesentatum et cognitum formaliter constituit, ad obiectum vero sic repraesentatum ut coexistens notitiae est respectus modificans.[25] Quando autem comparamus rationem intuitivi ordini et respectui ad sensibile commune, exemplum tenet in hoc, quod sensibile commune non

---

23 301/20-39.

24 293/48-294/49.

25 291/43-292/30, as anticipating 301/27-36. What constitutes intuition is the tending towards the stimulating object modified by real relation to it as coexisting with the awareness and tendency which the object causally grounds as stimulating (cf. Book I, Question 4). Poinsot has explained in this Question and will further explain in the Question following that this only occurs thanks to understanding an object as partially present in external sensation. For external sensation itself stands upon and consists in a real relation or context of physical interaction (a ''secondness'') in consciously attaining its object by the *further* real relation which first separates the actual semiosis of cognitive life from the virtual semiosis of nature anterior to and supportive of that life, and productive of its sensory specifications (cf. Book I, Question 2, note 4, p. 137 above). The act of sensing takes place through an interaction in which the activity itself as a quality is a transcendental relation categorially related to its object precisely as producing in the sense its specification, as Poinsot best explains in his Phil. nat. 4. p. q. 4. art. 4., Reiser III 126a38-47: ''*Sensus consistit in quadam proportione dupliciter, tum in actu primo, tum in actu secundo. In actu primo quantum ad temperamentum organi et spirituum animalium, qui si dissipantur, impeditur sensatio. In actu secundo est proportio in attingendo obiectum cognoscitive . . . et ideo non potest corrumpi et laedi sensus sola intentionali actione seu repraesentativa, nisi aliqua naturalis alteratio et corruptiva ei adiungatur vel eminenter contineatur in actione intentionali.*'' —''External sensation consists in a certain twofold real proportioning, the one in first act, the other in second act. In first act, it consists in a right proportioning of the organ and of its animal spirits: if these are disrupted, sensation is impeded. In second act, external sensation is real relation in consciously attaining its object . . . and for this reason external sense cannot be destroyed and damaged by an intentional or representative action alone, except in the context of some physical alteration and disruption adjoined to or eminently contained in the intentional action [whereby sensation attains its objects *apprehensively* and not just as effects related *causally* to environmental stimuli].'' The real relation in which external sensation consists immediately involves sign-relations and is inseparable from them (Book I, Question 6, 205/35-215/5, esp. 206/38-207/7, and 211/29-39, etc.), without itself being one (Book I, Question 5) inasmuch as it is the very act of sensing which Poinsot has shown not to be as such a sign (Book II, Question 4). So, inasmuch as understanding ''accidentally'' completes its objectifications by conscious real relation to elements thereof as present in external sensation, *that* understanding *itself* becomes *mind-independently (''realiter'')* either mistaken semiotically or a semiotic intuition of natural being as coexisting with awareness.

represented, but is represented as modifying a color by a modification incidentally bearing on visibility. Thus presence in intuitive knowledge does not function as a thing directly represented, for thus it can also be represented in an abstractive awareness, but as modifying the object represented by an accidental modification, as has been said, yet on the side of coexistence, in which respect the example of the common sensible does not hold.

And when it is said that a division according to intrinsic modes is also an essential division,[26] the response is that modes can be said to be intrinsic, either because they modify the formal constitutive rationale itself, and so are intrinsic to the very constitution; or they can be said to be intrinsic because they do not denominate extrinsically, even though they do not modify the constitution intrinsically. And a division in terms of modes of the first sort is also essential, because a mode cannot be varied without a constitution depending upon it being varied, but a division in terms of modes of the second sort is an accidental division, as has been said.

To the examples,[27] the response is that the practical and the speculative differ essentially, because that order to an external work arises from other principles and means of knowing than the formal rationale of the speculative, but it does not import only a diverse application and coexistence of the object as do the intuitive and the abstractive, but diverse formal principles of knowing an object in a synthetic and an analytic way. But to that which is said concerning the difference of moral evil [from moral good], the response is that there is indeed an essential difference in respect of an act considered within the order of mores, but nevertheless the essential species or kind of an act of moral evil is not derived from circumstance, unless the very circumstance passes into the principal condition of the object, as is said in the *Summa theologica*, I-II, q. 18, art. 10. But the intuitive and the abstractive are always circumstances of cognition, because they pertain to the aforementioned coexistence.

est primario repraesentatum, sed repraesentatur ut modificans colorem modificatione accidentaliter se habente ad visibilitatem. Ita praesentia in intuitivo non se habet ut res directe repraesentata, sic enim etiam in abstractiva notitia repraesentari potest, sed ut modificans obiectum repraesentatum modificatione accidentali, ut dictum est, ex parte tamen coexistentiae, in quo non tenet exemplum de sensibili communi.

Et quando dicitur, quod *divisio penes modos intrinsecos est etiam essentialis*,[26] respondetur, quod modi possunt dici intrinseci, vel quia modificant ipsam formalem rationem constitutivam, et sic intrinseci sunt ipsi constitutioni; vel possunt dici intrinseci, quia non extrinsece denominant, licet nec intrinsece constitutionem modificent. Et divisio per modos primi generis est etiam essentialis, quia non stat variari modum, quin varietur constitutio ab eo dependens, per modos vero secundi generis est accidentalis divisio, ut dictum est.

Ad exempla[27] respondetur, quod practicum et speculativum differunt essentialiter, quia ordo ille ad opus externum oritur ex diversis principiis et mediis cognoscendi, quam sit formalis ratio speculativi, non autem importat solum diversam applicationem et coexistentiam obiecti sicut intuitivum et abstractivum, sed diversa principia formalia cognoscendi obiectum modo compositivo et resolutivo. Quod vero dicitur de differentia mali moralis, respondetur esse quidem differentiam essentialem respectu actus considerati intra genus moris, sed tamen non desumi a circumstantia speciem essentialem actus moralis mali, nisi ipsa circumstantia transeat in principalem obiecti conditionem, ut dicitur 1. 2. q. 18. art. 10. Intuitivum autem et abstractivum semper sunt circumstantiae cognitionis, quia pertinent ad illam coexistentiam.

[26] 301/40-45.
[27] 301/46-302/2.

[732a1-40]

QUESTION 2

Whether there Can Be an Intuitive Cognition, either in the Understanding or in Exterior Sense, of a Thing Physically Absent

QUAESTIO SECUNDA

Utrum Possit Dari Cognitio Intuitiva de Re Physice Absenti, sive in Intellectu sive in Sensu Exteriori

To explain exactly the rationale of the intuitive and the abstractive, it is necessary to see the formal differences which respectively characterize them. Now, there are usually four differences enumerated. The first is on the part of the cause, since intuitive awareness is produced by the presence of the object, while abstractive awareness is brought about by specifications left behind by objects no longer present. The second is on the part of the effect, because intuitive awareness is clearer and more certain than abstractive awareness. The third difference is from the standpoint of priority or order, because intuitive awareness is prior to abstractive awareness; for all our cognition has birth from some external sense by means of an intuitive cognition. The fourth is on the side of the subject, because intuitive awareness can be found in all the cognitive powers, whether sensitive or intellective, but abstractive awareness cannot be found in the external senses.

But these four differences suppose a *principal* difference, which is derived from the thing attained and is explicitly stated in the definitions of these types of awareness, namely, that intuitive awareness is of a thing present physically while abstractive awareness is of an absent thing. And certainly the first three differences are not so intrinsic that they could not sometimes be wanting to these modes of awareness, even though they are differences very often found in our experience. For a specifying form abstractively representing some thing or definable material structure — including indeed even the

Ad exacte explicandum rationem intuitivi et abstractivi oportet videre differentias, quae illis formaliter conveniunt inter se. Solent autem QUATUOR DIFFERENTIAE numerari: *Prima* ex parte causae, quia intuitiva producitur a praesentia obiecti, abstractiva vero a speciebus in absentia obiecti relictis. *Secunda* ex parte effectus, quia intuitiva est clarior et certior quam abstractiva. *Tertia* ex parte ordinis, quia intuitiva est prior quam abstractiva; omnis enim cognitio nostra ortum habet ab aliquo sensu exteriori mediante intuitiva cognitione. *Quarta* est ex parte subiecti, quia intuitiva potest inveniri in omnibus potentiis, sive sensitivis sive intellectivis, abstractiva vero non potest inveniri in sensibus externis.

Istae autem quatuor differentiae supponunt principalem differentiam, quae ex re attacta desumitur et in definitionibus istarum notitiarum explicatur, nempe quod intuitiva sit de re praesenti, abstractiva vero de re absenti. Et quidem tres primae differentiae non sunt ita intrinsecae, quin possint aliquando deficere in istis notitiis, licet plerumque in nobis inveniantur. Potest enim infundi a Deo species repraesentans rem ali-

presence of the thing in the mode of a definable characteristic — can be infused by God *before* any thing is represented intuitively, nor can one attribute less clarity and certitude to the abstractive than to the intuitive awareness, as indeed the Divine Being does not know possible things less clearly than future ones.

Wherefore the principal differences are reduced to these two: namely, one on the side of the object, that intuitive awareness is bound up with the physical presence of a thing; and one on the side of the subject [i.e., the various cognitive powers], in which such awarenesses can obtain, about which there is a question, particularly about the external senses, whether an abstractive awareness can occur in them.

Concerning the first of these two differences, there are a good many who think that the bare objective presence of a thing suffices for an intuitive awareness, and that the physical presence of the thing is not required, that is to say, it suffices that the presence of a thing be known in order for an awareness to be intuitive, but it is not required that the presence be coexistent with the very awareness. From which it follows that there can be an essentially intuitive awareness of a physically absent thing.

And concerning the second difference, some deem it possible for a physically absent thing to be attained by external sense through the power of God, if that thing is represented as present. See the reasoning of the Conimbricenses' *Commentary* on Book II of Aristotle's *Treatise on the Soul*, chap. 3, q. 3, arts. 1 and 2.

Briefly, however (for this matter pertains more to the books *Concerning the Soul*), the response to these opinions is twofold.

The first is: **Intuitive cognition calls not only for the objective presence of its object, but also for the physical presence, and so there is no intuition of the past and the future, unless it be reduced to some measure in which it is present.**

This is the conclusion commonly drawn FROM THE TEACHING OF ST. THOMAS in the *Summa theologica*, I, q. 14, art. 13. And in commenting on that passage, those who have learned from him, in order to posit in God a vision of future events, generally say that future things must be physically present in eternity; for of the future as future there can be no vision. And certainly the argument of St. Thomas in that article necessarily requires the physical presence in eternity of the future. For St. Thomas proves that God knows all future things as present, because he knows them not in their causes, but in themselves, according as each single one of them is in act in itself, and because his cognition is measured

quam seu quidditatem abstractive, imo et praesentiam rei per modum quidditatis, antequam repraesentetur res aliqua intuitive, nec minorem claritatem et certitudinem tribuere notitiae abstractivae quam intuitivae, sicut et ipse Deus non minus clare cognoscit res possibiles quam futuras.

Quare praecipuae differentiae reducuntur ad illas duas: nempe ex parte obiecti, quod intuitiva versetur circa praesentiam rei; et ex parte subiecti, in quo possunt tales notitiae reperiri, praesertim circa sensus externos, an possit in illis reperiri notitia abstractiva.

CIRCA PRIMUM plerique existimant ad notitiam intuitivam solum sufficere praesentiam rei obiectivam, non vero requiri praesentiam rei physicam, id est sufficere, quod praesentia sit cognita, non vero requiri, quod sit coexistens ipsi notitiae. Ex quo sequitur posse essentialiter dari notitiam intuitivam de re physice absenti.

ET CIRCA SECUNDUM aliqui existimant posse per potentiam Dei rem physice absentem attingi a sensu externo, dummodo repraesentetur ut praesens. Videantur Conimbric. 2. de Anima cap. 3. q. 3. art. 1. et 2.

Breviter tamen (quia res ista magis pertinet ad libros de Anima) duplici conclusione respondetur:

PRIMA EST: **Cognitio intuitiva non solum petit praesentiam obiectivam sui obiecti, sed etiam physicam, atque ita de praeterito et futuro nulla datur intuitio, nisi reducatur ad aliquam mensuram, in qua sit praesens.**

Haec conclusio communiter deducitur ex doctrina D. Thomae 1. p. q. 14. art. 13. Et ibi communiter eius discipuli, qui ad ponendam in Deo visionem rerum futurarum dicunt eas debere esse physice praesentes in aeternitate; de futuro enim ut futuro non potest dari aliqua visio. Et certe discursus D. Thomae in illo art. id necessario exigit. Probat enim D. Thomas, quod Deus cognoscit omnia futura ut praesentia, quia non cognoscit ea in suis causis, sed in seipsis, prout unumquodque eorum est in actu in seipso, et quia sua cognitio mensuratur aeternitate, aeternitas autem am-

by eternity, but eternity encompasses the whole of time, so all the things which are in time are present to God by eternity. This argument, if it concerns only objective presence, is completely ineffective, because it would have proved the same through the same, since indeed, when he intends to prove that God sees future things as present in themselves, which is to have their presence in cognition and in an objective mode, he would have proved it on the grounds that they are present in eternity objectively, that is, present to cognition: and so he would have proved that they are present objectively — because they are present objectively!

And THE FOUNDATION OF THIS CONCLUSION is taken from this, that it is agreed by all that an intuitive awareness must respect a [physically] present object. For vision, i.e., seeing, must attain things in themselves, and according as they are independent of the seeing; for an intuitive seeing functions as does an experimental cognition, nay rather, it is the paradigm case of experience. But that there should be an experience of something other than a present thing is unintelligible, for how can the absent as absent fall under experience?[1] But from this fact about seeing

bit totum tempus, omnia autem, quae sunt in tempore, sunt Deo ab aeterno praesentia. Qui discursus si solum procedit de praesentia obiectiva, penitus est inefficax, quia probaret idem per idem, siquidem cum intendat probare, quod Deus videt futura ut in seipsis praesentia, quod est habere earum praesentiam in cognitione et obiective, id probaret, quia sunt in aeternitate obiective praesentia, id est cognitioni praesentia, et sic probaret esse praesentia obiective, quia sunt praesentia obiective.

ET SUMITUR FUNDAMENTUM conclusionis ex hoc, quod apud omnes convenit notitiam intuitivam debere respicere obiectum praesens. Visio enim debet attingere res in seipsis, et secundum quod extra videntem sunt; habet se enim intuitiva visio sicut experimentalis cognitio, imo est ipsamet experientia. Non est autem intelligibile, quod detur experientia nisi de rei praesentia, absens enim ut absens quomodo sub experientia cadere potest?[1] Ex hoc autem,

---

[1] Poinsot, 1632: Logica 2. p. q. 27. art. 1., Reiser ed. I 828a36-b35 (omitting b14-16 only): *"Si res cognoscerentur adaequate prout sunt in se, eadem esset immaterialitas rei in se et ut subest medio cognitionis. Sed quia contingit rem eiusdem immaterialitatis cognosci per diversa media vel secundum diversas connotationes et effectus, qui non eodem modo illuminant et apparere faciunt obiectum, ideo contingit de eadem re immateriali [i.e., de eadem obiecibili realitate formali], non eodem modo et medio immateriali cognita, dari diversas scientias, quia subsunt diversae immaterialitati formali, id est diversis principiis seu mediis sub diversa immaterialitate conclusionem illuminantibus et deducentibus. Sumitur ergo species scientiarum ex diversa immaterialitate obiectiva seu fundamentali, non prout entitative est in ipsa re, sed prout relucet in medio seu principio, quo apparet et demonstratur intellectui.* Similiter *ea, quae in se sunt diversae abstractionis, ut angeli et corpora, possunt uniri in aliqua ratione seu medio superiori utrisque, sicut in ratione entis, quam considerat metaphysicus per unicam abstractionem . . . .*

". . . Etiam in istis scientiis [scil. scientia a priori et a posteriori distinguuntur specie] invenitur diversa abstractio specifica, quia demonstrare per causam et per effectus non est eiusdem immaterialitatis in esse intelligibili, quia dato, quod in esse entis causa et effectus sint eiusdem spiritualitatis, tamen non procedunt istae scientiae a posteriori et quoad an est, nisi quatenus cadunt effectus sub experientia et inductione, a qua originantur. Experimentalis autem cognitio non dicit abstractionem intelligibilem, qua cognoscitur res per suam quidditatem, praesertim quia apud nos experientia semper dependet ab aliquibus sensibilibus. Et sic est diversa abstractio a scientia, quae procedit a priori, quantum est ex se."—"If things were known adequately according to their subjective existence, the immateriality [i.e., the ontological formality] of a thing in its entitative existence and as it is subject to a [channel or] means of cognition would be identical. But since it happens that a thing of one same immateriality is cognized through different channels or according to different connotations and effects which do not illuminate, that is to say, make the object appear, in the same manner, it therefore happens that of one same immaterial thing [i.e., of one same formal reality in its objectifiability] not cognized [and made object] in the same way and by the same immaterial channel, there are [specifically] different sciences, because these sciences are subject to a different formal immateriality, that is to say, to different principles or means illuminating and leading to a conclusion under a different immateriality [a different mode of objective existence]. The specific type of the ways of knowing therefore is taken from the diversity of objective or foundational immateriality, not according as this is entitatively in the thing itself, but according as it reflects in the means or principle by which the thing appears and is presented to the understanding. *In like manner,* those things which in themselves belong to different orders of abstraction, such as pure spirits and

known to all, it manifestly follows that the physical presence of the object is required, nor is the proposal[2] that an objective presence suffices an intelligible proposition.

For indeed the presence of a thing can be known in only two ways, either signified in act as a kind of definable characteristic, or precisely as it is exercised and affects the very thing and renders that thing pres-

quod apud omnes notum est de ipsa visione, deducitur manifeste requiri physicam obiecti praesentiam nec posse intelligi, quod sufficiat obiectiva.[2]

Etenim praesentia rei solum dupliciter cognosci potest, vel in actu signato, ut quidditas quaedam, vel prout exercetur et afficit ipsam rem illamque in se reddit

---

bodies, can be unified in some rationale or medium transcending both, as, for example, in the rationale of being, which the metaphysician considers through one single abstraction. . . .

''. . . Even in the case of knowledge developed a-priori and knowledge developed a-posteriori there is a specifically diverse type of abstraction, because to establish [something] in terms of a cause and to establish [that same thing] through an effect does not belong to the same level of immateriality in the order of intelligible existence, by the fact that, given a cause and effect belonging to the same level of entitative existence, nevertheless these ways of knowing do not proceed a-posteriori and as regards existential fact save insofar as effects fall under an experience and abduction [i.e., in contrast to a deductive or heuristic—''inductive'' or ''*descensus*''—movement: in Deely, 1981, 1982: 67-75, partially cited in note 14, p. 64 above] from which the knowing originates. But an experimental cognition does not express [does not bespeak] an intelligible abstraction whereby a thing is known through its essence, especially seeing that human experience always depends upon surrounding conditions of the physical environment. And thus, so far as it is taken in its own terms, it involves an abstraction heterogeneous to that of a type of knowledge which proceeds a-priori [whether deductively or inductively (*descensive*)]''—namely (Poinsot, 1633: Phil. nat. 1. p. q. 1. art. 3., Reiser ed. II 31a11-20), a negative abstraction ''*qualis etiam potest contingere in sensu, qui accipit unum omisso alio, v.g. colorem in pomo omisso sapore, et in ipso colore possumus videre a longe rationem colorati singularis, non discernendo propriam differentiam talis coloris. Sic in prima cognitione intellectus accipit ens ut concretum quidditati sensibili. . . .*''—*abstractio negativa* ''of the sort that can occur even at the level of sense, which grasps one feature while passing over another—for example, the color in an apple apart from odor, and in the very color we can see from afar the character of a colored individual without discerning the precise hue of the color in question. It is thus that in originative awareness—in primordial apprehension—the understanding grasps being as concretized in a sensible structure. . . .'

See further notes 9 and 10 below, also Book I, Question 4, note 33 and related discussions above.

[2] 305/15-24. Poinsot spells this out at some length in his Phil. nat. 4. p. q. 6., ''*De obiectis sensuum externorum in communi*'' (''General treatment of the objects of external sense''), art. 1, ''*Utrum requiratur necessario, quod obiectum exterius sit praesens, ut sentiri possit*'' (''Whether an external object must be physically present in order to be sensed''), esp. 171b34-172a21 (Reiser ed.): ''*. . . tenendum est implicare scilicet, quod res aliqua physice et realiter absens immediate in se attingatur a sensu externo. Quod vero attingatur in alio, ut res in imagine, non est difficultas in praesenti, quia hoc nihil aliud est quam videri ipsam imaginem, quae praesens est, licet res repraesentata per ipsam in se sit absens. Unde ut tollatur aequivocatio, quando dicimus requiri praesentiam physicam obiecti, loquimur in sensu formali, id est eius, quod proprie et immediate se habet ut obiectum, ita quod bene stat, quod loco alicuius obiecti supponatur aliud, in quod feratur sensus et decipiatur interius iudicium putans esse alterum, tamen sensus externus directe fertur in illud externum, quod sibi supponitur. Similiter potest aliquando ex vehementia imaginationis aliquis decipi aut deludi, putans se vere videre aut sentire exterius rem aliquam, quam tamen non habet praesentem. Sed tunc nec videt nec sentit exterius, sed imaginatur sentire aut videre. Loquimur ergo, quando sensus exterior vere et proprie elicit actum; et de hoc dicimus essentialiter postulare, quod obiectum exterius, in quod fertur, sit praesens physice, in quod talis actus immediate terminetur, nec sufficit, quod species sit in sensu repraesentans aliquid ut praesens, sed requiritur, quod ipsum obiectum praesens sit, ut terminet actum.*''—''It is a contradiction in terms for anything physically and really absent to be immediately attained in itself by an external sense. That it should be attained in another as a thing in an image is not what is at issue here, for this is nothing else than to see the image itself which is present [but as explained in Book II, Question 2, esp. note 27; also the First Preamble, Article 3, note 3], even though the thing represented by that image is in itself absent. Whence to remove equivocation, when we say that the physical presence of the object is necessary, we are speaking in a formal sense, that is, of that which it properly and immediately possesses as object, such that it can well happen that in place of some object another is supposed, on which sense is actually borne, and the interior judgment is deceived thinking it to be another, yet the external sense in spite of this is

ent in itself. The first mode of knowing presence serves abstractively for an awareness, because it is the constitutive property of an abstractive cognition to consider a thing in the mode of a definable characteristic and nature. Thus it considers the presence itself also as a thing and a kind of essence or definable character, and an abstractive cognition is preserved even in respect of a presence considered as it is a kind of thing and as an object of discourse. This appears, for example, when I now understand through discourse or through faith that God is [physically] present and that my soul is [physically] present within me, and yet I see neither God nor the soul intuitively.

For the rationale of the intuitive, therefore, the second mode of knowing presence[3] is required, that is to say, it is required that some thing be attained under presence itself, attained, that is to say, as it is affected by the very presence and as presence is physically exercised in the thing itself. But if presence is attained in this mode, it cannot be attained as it is still within causes and in the mode of something future, nor as it has passed away and has the mode of something past, because neither of these is to see a thing in itself nor to be moved by it, or to be attained except as contained in another. For something future under the rationale of future cannot be understood except in the causes in which it is contained. For a future event or thing is essentially said to be one which is not yet outside causes, but is as yet within those causes which are nevertheless ordered to producing the thing itself. It would therefore involve a contradiction to know something as future except as being within causes or in an order to them; for by this very fact, that it is conceived in itself and apart from causes, it ceases to be conceived as future. Similarly, something past as past cannot be conceived except according to the rationale of a former existence. Therefore it is not conceived as in itself, because in itself it does not have an entitative being and existence. Therefore the past is conceived as divested of [entitative] presence and existence. Whence it cannot be represented except either by means of some effect or trace of itself

praesentem. Et primum deservit abstractivae notitiae, quia proprium est abstractivae cognitionis considerare res per modum quidditatis et naturae, sicque etiam ipsam praesentiam ut rem et quidditatem quamdam considerat, et salvatur abstractiva cognitio etiam respectu praesentiae consideratae, ut res quaedam est et ut obiectum, de quo agatur, ut patet cum modo per discursum vel per fidem intelligo Deum esse praesentem et animam meam esse praesentem in me, et tamen nec Deum nec animam video intuitive.

Requiritur ergo ad rationem intuitivi secundum,[3] scilicet ut res aliqua attingatur sub ipsa praesentia, ut scilicet ab ipsa praesentia afficitur et in ipsa re physice exercetur. Si autem sic attingatur praesentia, non potest attingi ut adhuc est intra causas et per modum futuri, nec ut transivit et habet modum praeteriti, quia neutrum est videre rem in seipsa nec ab ea moveri aut attingi nisi prout in alio. Nam futurum sub ratione futuri non potest intelligi nisi in causis, in quibus continetur. Essentialiter enim futurum dicitur illud, quod nondum est extra causas, sed adhuc est intra illas, quae tamen ordinantur ad producendum rem ipsam. Igitur implicat cognoscere aliquid ut futurum nisi prout intra causas seu in ordine ad ipsas; nam hoc ipso, quod concipitur in se et seorsum a causis, desinit concipi ut futurum. Similiter praeteritum ut praeteritum non potest concipi nisi secundum rationem existentiae amissae. Ergo iam non concipitur ut in se, quia in se entitatem et existentiam non habet, ergo concipitur praeteritum ut denudatum a praesentia et existentia. Unde non potest repraesentari nisi vel mediante aliquo ef-

borne onto *that external thing which is presupposed for sensation.* Similarly, sometimes a person can be deceived or deluded by the force of the imagination into thinking he truly sees or senses outwardly some thing which does not have a present existence. But in such a case the person neither sees nor senses outwardly, but fancies that he senses or sees. We are speaking of the case therefore when external sense truly and properly elicits an act; and of this case we say that the essential postulate is that the exterior object on which sensation bears, in which such an act is immediately terminated, is physically present; nor is it enough for a specifying form to be in the sense representing something as present, but it is necessary that the very object itself be present as terminating the act.''

See esp. Book II, Question 2, notes 2, 8, and 22; and notes 9 and 10 below of this present Question.

[3] 307/7-308/1.

left behind, or by means of the determination of a specifying form to the existence which it had: the whole of which is not to see a thing in itself according to the act of being which it has in itself independently of the seeing, but according as it is contained in another and bespeaks a condition and connotation relative to another.

Since therefore an intuitive seeing or vision is borne on a present thing according as presence affects that thing in itself, and not according as that thing is contained in another or according as the very presence is known as it is a kind of thing and definable character, the manifest conclusion is that intuition is borne on a physical presence as physically obtaining on the side of the object, and not only as the mind-independent presence is objectively present to a cognitive power. For this, which is to be objectively present, is preserved even in an abstractive awareness, which can know presence not as here and now terminating awareness, but as contained in or deduced from some principle, or represented as it is a kind of definable character, as when I now know abstractively that God is present to us.

From which it is gathered that Cajetan, in his *Commentary* on the *Summa theologica*, I, q. 14, art. 9, had best posited the two conditions for anything to be said to be seen of itself and immediately: First, that it be here and now objectified to the one seeing, that is, objectified through a presence not as contained in another, but as affecting the very thing in itself. Second, that the thing seen have an act of being independent of the seeing, a condition which St. Thomas had also posited in his *Commentary on the Sentences of Peter Lombard*, Book III, dist. 14, cited above. This is why it does not suffice for the object of an intuitive awareness to have an act of being within the seeing by means of its intentional representation, but it must also have an act of being independent of the seeing, which is to be a physical object, at which the awareness is terminated.

But if you should ask: Where is the contradiction in supposing that God could infuse in someone's mind a representation of a future thing, as, for example, of the Antichrist, as he is in himself future, and according to an existence distinct from causes, yet with an order and condition relative to causes, just as existing things themselves also bespeak a condition relative to their causes: to this we will respond in the solution of the first counterargument below.[4]

Second conclusion: **It is in no way possible for there to be in exterior sense an abstractive awareness, that is to say, an awareness of an absent thing.**

fectu a se relicto, vel mediante determinatione speciei ad existentiam, quam habuit, quod totum est non videre rem in seipsa secundum esse, quod habet in se extra videntem, sed secundum quod continetur in alio et habitudinem et connotationem dicit ad aliud.

Cum ergo intuitiva visio feratur in rem praesentem, secundum quod praesentia afficit rem illam in se, et non prout in alio continetur vel prout cognoscitur praesentia ipsa ut res quaedam et quidditas est, manifestum relinquitur, quod intuitio fertur in praesentiam physicam, ut physice se tenet ex parte obiecti, et non solum ut obiective est praesens potentiae. Hoc enim, quod est obiective esse praesens, salvatur etiam in notitia abstractiva, quae cognoscere potest praesentiam non ut praesentialiter terminantem notitiam, sed ut contentam vel deductam ex aliquo principio, sive repraesentatam, ut quidditas quaedam est, ut quando modo cognoscimus abstractive Deum esse praesentem nobis.

Ex quo colligitur optime Caietanum 1. p. q. 14. art. 9. posuisse duas conditiones, ut aliquid dicatur visum per se et immediate: *Prima,* quod praesentialiter obiciatur videnti, id est per praesentiam non ut contentam in alio, sed ut afficientem rem ipsam in se. *Secunda,* quod res visa habeat esse extra videntem, quod etiam D. Thomas posuit in 3. dist. 14. supra cit. Hoc est, non sufficit, quod habeat esse intra videntem per intentionalem repraesentationem sui, sed etiam habeat esse extra videntem, quod est esse physicum, ad quod terminetur notitia.

Quodsi petas: Quaenam est implicatio, quod Deus infundat alicui repraesentationem rei futurae, v. g. Antichristi, ut in se futurus est, et secundum esse distinctum a causis, cum ordine tamen et habitudine ad causas, sicut ipase res existentes etiam ad causas suas dicunt habitudinem: ad hoc respondebimus in solutione primi argumenti infra.[4]

Secunda conclusio: **Implicat, quod in sensu exteriori inveniatur notitia abstractiva sive notitia de re absenti.**

[4] 315/22-40.

We treat of this conclusion in the books *Concerning the Soul*, Q. 6, art. 1, and the Conimbricenses mentioned above agree on this, although they differ enormously in the reason given, and deem it possible, speaking absolutely and in terms of a divine influence, for a physically absent thing to be sensed if it is represented as present.

But our conclusion is the more common one among those competent to treat of the question, especially among the Thomistic authors; and St. Thomas's opinion can be seen in the *Summa theologica*, III, q. 76, art. 7, and in his *Commentary on the Sentences of Peter Lombard*, Book IV, dist. 10, q. 1, art. 4, quaestiunc. 1.[5] Certainly it is de facto the case that an absent thing cannot be seen, because the external senses must receive forms of specification from objects. But if the objects are not present to the very senses, they cannot stimulate them and produce specifying forms. Therefore at least for this the physical presence of an object is required.

Then in the senses requiring a physical contact in order to produce sensation, as is the case with touch and taste, it is manifest that the physical presence of the object is essentially required, because a contact is required, through which contact the sensation itself is intrinsically brought about. But a contact essentially requires the presence of the contacting things, because contact cannot take place between distant things; much less, therefore, between absent things, because every thing absent in fact is distant. But if someone touches not the very thing, but something in the place of that thing, then he is not said to touch the thing, but that which is surrogated in its place, just as one who has a tongue infected by a bitter humor tastes that humor rather than the flavor of another thing which seems bitter to him: whence the bitterness, which he senses, is present.

Concerning the rest of the [external] senses it is also proved: First a-posteriori, because every sense cognition is experimental and inductive, since the certitude of understanding is ultimately resolved into that cognition. But it is impossible for an experience to occur engaging an absent thing, because, as long as it is absent, it needs another medium from which its cognition would be taken. Therefore something is yet wanting for experience, because experience rests on the thing itself according as it exists in itself; for thus is a thing subjected to experience, when it is attained in itself.[6] The point is also proved a-priori, because

De hac conclusione agimus in libris de Anima q. 6. art. 1., et in ea conveniunt Conimbric. supra relati, licet valde differant in ratione reddenda et absolute existimant divinitus posse sentiri rem physice absentem, dummodo repraesentetur ut praesens.

Sed nostra conclusio communior est inter auctuores, praesertim thomistas; et videri potest D. Thomas 3. p. q. 76. art. 7. et in 4. dist. 10. q. 1. art. 4. quaestiunc. 1.[5] Et quidem de facto constat non posse videri rem absentem, quia sensus externi debent accipere species ab obiectis. Si autem obiecta praesentia non sint ipsis sensibus, non possunt illos movere et species immittere. Ergo saltem ad hoc requiritur praesentia obiecti physica.

Deinde in sensibus requirentibus physicum contactum ad sensationem, ut tactus et gustus, manifestum est essentialiter requiri physicam praesentiam obiecti, quia requiritur contactus, per quem intrinsece fit ipsa sensatio. Contactus autem essentialiter requirit praesentiam contactorum, quia non potest fieri inter res distantes; ergo multo minus inter absentes, quia omne absens in re est distans. Quodsi aliquis tangat non rem ipsam, sed aliquid loco illius, tunc non dicitur rem illam tangere, sed id, quod loco illius subrogatur, sicut qui habet linguam infectam humore amaro, humorem illum gustat potius quam saporem alterius rei, quae sibi amara videtur, unde amaritudo, quam sentit, praesens est.

De reliquis vero sensibus id etiam probatur: *Tum a posteriori*, quia omnis cognitio sensus est experimentalis et inductiva, cum in illam ultimo resolvatur certitudo intellectus. Repugnat autem, quod experientia fiat circa rem absentem, quia quamdiu absens est, indiget alio medio, quo accipiatur eius cognitio. Ergo adhuc deest aliquid ad experientiam, quia experientia sistit in ipsa re, secundum quod est in seipsa; sic enim experientiae subicitur, quando in seipsa attingitur.[6] *Tum etiam a*

[5] *Pa* VII. 626 b.

[6] See citations in notes 9 and 10 below, and above, Book II, Question 2, notes 2, 3, 4, 8, and 22.

an exterior cognition of sense must necessarily be terminated at some object not as represented within the sense, therefore as situated outside or independent of the sense power.[7] But that which is posited independently of seeing has a physical existence, or, if it does not exist, by this very fact sense will be without a terminating object, and therefore it will not have an object with which it is engaged, which is a contradiction. The minor premise is proved by the fact that the external senses do not form an icon, in order that the cognition might be perfected within the sense itself as in an intrinsic terminus, as must be proved more at length in the books *Concerning the Soul*.[8] The reason for the fact that external sense does not form its own final specification is that the things which are sensed are sensible in final act independently of the power of sense, just as color becomes ultimately visible by means of light, whence sense does not need any expressed specifier in order that in that specifier the object might be rendered formed as sensible in final act. Nor, again, does memory pertain to the external senses, that they may recall absent things as do the interior senses; therefore there is in them no rationale for forming an expressed specifier or word. On this principle, therefore, as in a root, is founded the impossibility of knowing an absent thing through external sense, lest sense should be without a terminating object,[9] supposing that an

priori, quia exterior cognitio sensus necessario debet terminari ad aliquod obiectum, non ut intra se repraesentatum, ergo ut extra se positum.[7] Quod autem ponitur extra videntem, physicam existentiam habet, vel si non existit, hoc ipso sensus carebit obiecto terminante, atque adeo non habebit obiectum, circa quod versetur, quod implicat. Minor vero probatur, quia sensus externi non formant idolum, ut in ipso perficiatur cognitio tamquam in termino intrinseco, ut latius probandum est in libris de Anima.[8] Quod ideo est, quia res, quae sentiuntur, extra ipsum sensum sunt in actu ultimo sensibiles, sicut color per lucem fit ultimate visibilis, unde non indiget aliqua specie expressa, ut in illa reddatur obiectum in actu ultimo sensibili formatum. Nec rursus pertinet ad sensus externos memoria, ut recordentur rerum absentium sicut sensus interiores; ergo nulla est in illis ratio formandi speciem expressam seu verbum. In hoc ergo principio tamquam in radice fundatur impossibilitas cognoscendi rem absentem per sensum externum, ne careat obiecto terminante,[9]

---

[7] See notes 9 and 10 below, and cross-references in preceding note.

[8] Phil. nat. 4. p. q. 6. art. 4 (esp. citation in note 9 below). Poinsot discusses the phenomenon of "after images" ("*simulacra*")—e.g., from looking at a bright light—at 194a23-b20.

[9] Phil. nat. 4. p. q. 6. art. 1., Reiser ed., 172b13-173a30: "*Ratio autem et fundamentum ad hoc reducitur, quia sensus externi ex sua natura sunt infimi in genere cognitionis et immediate continuantur ipsis rebus, a quibus accipiunt species, et magis materiales sunt inter omnes potentias cognoscitivas. Unde quia ex ipsis originatur omnis nostra cognitio et in ipsos resolvitur, oportet, quod moveantur sensus externi ab obiectis accipiendo ab eis species, et rursus quod cognitio terminetur ad res ipsas prout extra sunt. Et licet primum, scilicet moveri ab obiectis et procedere ab ipsis species effective, possit suppleri a Deo infundente vel producente speciem in potentiis loco obiecti, et sic quantum ad productionem speciei non exigat sensus essentialiter praesentiam obiecti, tamen quoad secundum suppleri non potest, quia pertinet ad specificativam rationem sensationis externae quatenus externa est.*

"*Et probatur ex duplici conditione, quam habent sensus externi. Nam debent habere cognitionem experimentalem et in aliquibus eorum, ut in gustu et tactu, exigunt contactum realem neque possunt videre obiectum per reflexionem in seipsis neque in alia potentia interiori vel exteriori, a qua moveantur, quia sunt ultimae potentiae inter omnes cognoscitivas. Ergo immediate debent attingere obiectum in seipso. Quod sit experimentalis cognitio in sensu exteriori patet, quia tunc maxime aliquid experimur, cum ipso sensu exteriori tangimus. Cum autem experientia sit ultimum, in quod resolvitur nostra cognitio, et per quam tamquam per inductionem introducitur in nobis, non potest ultimate resolvi cognitio nisi in ipsum obiectum, ut est realiter in se, quia si in aliquid aliud praeter rem ipsam resolveretur, ut in imaginem vel idolum aut medium aliquod, restaret adhuc istud medium vel idolum conferre cum ipsa re seu obiecto, cuius est, ut constaret, an esset verum necne. Unde semper restaret eadem difficultas conferendi istud medium cum obiecto, cuius est repraesentativum. Quare necesse fuit ad habendam certitudinem et evidentiam experimentalem devenire ad cognitionem, quae ex propria sua ratione tenderet ad res in seipsis, et haec est cognitio sensus exterioris, atque adeo ex ipsa propria ratione cognitionis ultimae et experimentalis exigit obiectum esse praesens et nullo modo absens.*"—"The foundation and basis reduces to this, that external senses of their very nature are the lowest in the order of cognition and are immediately continued by the very things from which they take specification, and they are the more material of all the cognitive powers. Whence, because all our awareness originates from them and is re-

external sense does not form within itself the specification in which [its own] cognition is terminated.[10] But if the object exists in something produced by itself as in an image or effect, it will not be seen immediately, but as contained in the image, while the image itself is that which is seen.

supposito, quod intus non format speciem, in qua cognitio terminetur.[10] Quodsi existat in aliquo sui ut in imagine vel effectu, non immediate videbitur, sed ut contentum in imagine, ipsa vero imago est, quae videtur.

---

solved into them, it is necessary for the external senses to be moved by the objects by receiving from them specifications, and again it is necessary for cognition to be terminated at the things themselves according as they are outside. And even though the first of these functions, namely, to be stimulated by the objects and for the specifications to proceed effectively from them, could be supplied by God infusing or producing a form of specification in the powers in place of an object, and so as regards the production of a specification sense does not essentially require the presence of an object, yet *the second function* cannot be supplied by anything other than the sensible things themselves, because it pertains to the specificative rationale of external sense insofar as the sense is external.

"And this is proved from a twofold condition characterizing the external senses. For they must have an experimental cognition, and in the case of some of them, such as taste and touch, they require physical contact, nor can they see the object through reflexion upon themselves or in some other interior or exterior power by which they are moved, because they are the ultimate or final powers among all the powers of knowing. They must therefore immediately attain the object in itself. That there is an experimental cognition in external sense is clear from the fact that we have the greatest experience of something when we contact it through external sense. But since experience is the final ground into which our awareness is resolved and is the channel through which as through abduction awareness is brought into us, knowledge cannot be finally resolved save into the very object as it is in itself independently of mind, because if it were resolved into anything else besides the thing itself, as for example into an image or icon or some medium, it would yet remain to match this medium or icon with the thing itself or object to which it belongs in order to determine whether it were true or not. *Whence the same difficulty of comparing the medium with the object of which it is the representative always remains*. Wherefore it proves necessary to the having of experimental certainty and evidence to come down to a cognition that of its own proper nature tends toward the things existing in themselves, and this is the cognition of external sense, and therefore it is from the very nature of an ultimate and experimental cognition that an object has to be present and in no way absent." See esp. Book II, Question 2, notes 2, 3, 8, 22, 27.

[10] Phil. nat. 4. p. q. 6. art. 4., Reiser ed., III. 195a5-46: "*. . . sensus externus non format idolum seu speciem expressam, in qua obiectum suum cognoscat; hoc enim praecipue S. Doctor excludit.*

"*Fundamentum est, quia cognitio sensitiva essentialiter est experimentalis, experientia deducta ab ipsis obiectis et ex motione eorum in sensus. De ratione autem talis cognitionis est, ut in illam ultimate resolvatur omnis nostra cognitio utpote ab ipsa inchoata. Ergo necesse est, quod obiectum non attingat in aliqua imagine a se formata, sed immediate in ipsomet obiecto in se.*

"*Patet consequentia, quia si res cognoscitur in imagine formata ex impressione ipsa obiectorum, nondum est experimentalis ipsius rei in se, sed in alio, scilicet in formatione imaginis, in qua res illa repraesentatur. Ergo illa cognitio adhuc est resolubilis secundum comparationem illius imaginis ad ipsam rem, cuius est imago. Unde enim iudicari debet et resolvi, quod illa imago sit talis rei in seipsa, nisi res cognoscatur in se sine imagine tamquam terminus cognitionis? Si enim in alia imagine cognosceretur, de illa rediret eadem difficultas, quomodo deberet ultimate iudicari per experientiam, quod esset imago talis rei, non cognita ipsa re in se sine imagine. Ergo in cognitione desumpta ab ipsis rebus opportet ultimam et experimentalem cognitionem reducere ad aliquam cognitionem, quae fiat sine imagine, sed immediate attingat rem ipsam in se et continuetur seu coordinetur cognitio cum ipsis rebus.*"—"External sense does not form an icon or expressed specification in which it cognizes its object; it is this above all that St. Thomas rules out.

"And the basis for doing so is the fact that sensory cognition is essentially experimental, by an experience drawn from the objects themselves and from their impact on sense. It is of the nature of such awareness that into it all our knowledge is ultimately resolved as being originated therefrom. It is therefore necessarily the case that it does not attain the object in some self-formed image, but attains the object rather immediately in its own being.

"The consequence is clear from the fact that if a thing is known in an image formed from the impression as such of the objects, it is not yet experimental of the thing itself in itself, but in another, namely, in the formation of the image in which that thing is represented. That

Resolution of Counter-Arguments

It is argued first: An intuitive awareness can be sustained without the physical presence of the object, but with only the objective presence; therefore the physical presence is not required.

The antecedent is proved by many examples: First, because God can produce a specifier representing something future (for example, the Antichrist as he is in himself), and with as much evidence and certainty as if he were present. Indeed, it is probable that Christ the Lord saw future things intuitively through infused knowledge. Therefore there can be intuitive cognition which would represent something absent.

The antecedent is proved, on the grounds that such a future thing's being represented does not in itself involve a contradiction any more than a past thing's being represented, yet there is a specifier properly representative of a past thing. Next because that specifier which the Antichrist emits from himself when he will be present can be produced by God independently of the Antichrist; then therefore the Antichrist will be intuitively represented before he exists in himself. And the same argument holds concerning the specifiers [the concepts] of pure spirits, which are infused into them before the things are produced, and represent the things without any intrinsic variation whether the things exist or not; therefore the forms of specification or specifiers in question always represent intuitively. For an intuitive awareness is either the same cognition as an abstractive awareness, or a different cognition. If the same, there will already be an intuitive awareness of an absent thing, because the same awareness continues when the thing is present and when it is absent. If different, the representation in a pure spirit is therefore varied when the spirit sees a thing intuitively and abstractively, while the specification is nevertheless entirely the same.

The second example is in God, who sees future things intuitively, before they exist in themselves, otherwise his awareness would depend for

Solvuntur argumenta

Primo arguitur: Potest salvari notitia intuitiva sine praesentia physica obiecti, sed solum cum obiectiva; ergo non requiritur praesentia physica.

Antecedens probatur multis exemplis: Primo, quia potest Deus producere speciem repraesentantem futurum, v. g. Antichristum sicut est in se, et cum tanta evidentia et certitudine, sicut si esset praesens. Imo probabile est Christum Dominum per scientiam infusam intuitive vidisse futura. Ergo poterit dari intuitiva cognitio, quae repraesentet aliquid absens.

Antecedens probatur, quia nulla est implicatio, quod repraesentetur tale futurum in seipso magis, quam quod repraesentetur praeteritum, cuius tamen datur species proprie repraesentativa praeteriti. *Deinde,* quia illa species, quam Antichristus emittet ex se, quando erit praesens, potest a Deo produci independenter ab Antichristo; ergo tunc repraesentabitur Antichristus intuitive, antequam sit in se. *Et idem est* de speciebus angelicis, quae infunduntur illis, antequam res sint productae, et sine ulla variatione sui repraesentant res, sive existant sive non existant; ergo semper repraesentant intuitive. Nam intuitiva vel est eadem cognitio cum abstractiva vel diversa. Si eadem, iam dabitur intuitiva de re absenti, quia continuatur eadem notitia, quando est praesens et quando absens. Si diversa, ergo variatur repraesentatio in angelo, quando videt rem intuitive et abstractive, cum tamen sit omnino eadem species.

Secundum exemplum est in Deo, qui videt res futuras intuitive, antequam sint in seipsis, alias dependeret notitia eius,

---

cognition therefore is still resolvable in terms of a comparison of that image with the thing itself of which it is the image. For on what grounds must it be judged and decided that that image is of a given thing in itself, unless the thing is known in itself as a terminus of cognition without an image? For if it were known in another image, the same problem would arise again concerning that image—how must it be finally judged through experience that it is the image of a given thing, without knowing the thing itself in itself without an image. It is therefore necessary in the case of knowledge taken from things to reduce the ultimate and experimental level of the knowledge to some awareness that transpires without an image, but attains the very thing in itself so that the cognition is continued by or coordinated with the things themselves."

Thus does a semiotic of sensation enable one to overcome (*überwinden*) the modern heritage of Hume and Kant by reopening for epistemology the way back to the common world of nature and the animals which surrounds and sustains even the most human achievements of our understanding at their origins in sense.

its being intuitive on the physical presence of a thing. Nor can it be said that the [future] things are present [physically] in eternity. First because this is not certain, but the opposite is probable. Further because even if future things do not exist in eternity, they are still seen by God intuitively. Again because future things exist in eternity as in the cause on which their duration in time depends, for they are in an alien act of being and in an alien measure. Therefore for an awareness of a thing to be intuitive the physical existence of the thing in itself is not required, but an existence in another suffices. Finally because things existing only conditionally are seen intuitively, because they are not attained by a simple understanding, and yet they do not have a presence in act, neither in themselves nor in eternity, but they would have that presence if the condition were fulfilled. Therefore an intuitive awareness does not require the actual presence of a thing in itself.

The last example is in our own understanding, which knows things intuitively, and yet does not have a specification representative of the singular thing, and consequently neither of a presence as coexisting, which sort of presence belongs only to the singular thing. Therefore an intuitive cognition does not require the attainment of physical presence.

We answer that in these examples[11] many things are touched on which pertain to theological matters, and for this reason we cannot dwell on them at length.

Briefly, however, the response to the first example[12] is that there cannot be a specifier of a future thing which represents that thing as it is in itself, if the qualification "in itself" expresses the coexistence of the very presence and the termination of the cognition by that very presence immediately, yet there can well be a specifier which represents a future thing as it is in itself, if the qualification "in itself" expresses the proper definable structure of the future thing as it pertains to what is stimulative and specificative of the cognition. Therefore the very essence or definable structure of a future thing can be represented as regards its substance and accidents in the mode of an essence, and this with greater certitude and evidence than if it were seen intuitively, because evidence and certitude are derived from the side of the light and means by which the cognition comes about, not from the side of the termination. Whence a believer is more certain of the mystery of the Incarnation than I am of this paper which I see. Moreover, from the side of the

ut esset intuitiva, a praesentia physica rei. Nec dici potest, quod res sunt praesentes in aeternitate. *Tum* quia hoc non est certum, sed oppositum est probabile. *Tum* quia, etiamsi non essent res in aeternitate, adhuc viderentur intuitive. *Tum* quia res in aeternitate sunt tamquam in causa, a qua dependet duratio earum in tempore, sunt enim in alieno esse et in aliena mensura; ergo non requiritur physica existentia rei in se, sed sufficit in alio esse, ut sit intuitiva. *Tum* denique quia res conditionate tantum existentes videntur intuitive, cum non attingantur per simplicem intelligentiam, et tamen actu non habent praesentiam, nec in se nec in aeternitate, sed haberent illam, si poneretur conditio. Ergo notitia intuitiva non requirit actualem praesentiam rei in se.

Ultimum exemplum est in intellectu nostro, qui cognoscit res intuitive, et tamen non habet speciem repraesentativam rei singularis, et consequenter neque praesentiae ut coexistentis, quae solum convenit rei singulari. Ergo non requirit intuitiva cognitio attingentiam praesentiae physicae.

RESPONDETUR in his exemplis[11] multa tangi, quae pertinent ad materias theologicas, et ideo in illis non possumus ad longum immorari.

Breviter tamen respondetur ad primum exemplum,[12] quod de re futura non potest dari species, quae repraesentet illam, ut est in se, si ly „in se" dicat coexistentiam praesentiae ipsius et terminationem cognitionis per seipsam immediate, bene tamen, si ly „in se" dicat propriam quidditatem rei futurae, ut pertinet ad motivum et specificativum cognitionis. Itaque potest repraesentari ipsa quidditas rei futurae quoad substantiam et accidentia eius per modum quidditatis, et hoc cum maiori certitudine et evidentia, quam si videretur intuitive, quia evidentia et certitudo sumitur ex parte luminis et medii, quo fit cognitio, non ex parte terminationis. Unde fidelis certior est de mysterio Incarnationis quam ego de ista papyro, quam video. Ceterum ex parte modi terminandi

[11] 313/6-314/25.
[12] 313/7-13.

mode of terminating, a future or a past thing can never be known according to presence as it is in itself, but as it is in another, either because it is represented in some similar thing, be it in an image formed of that future thing, or in some cause in which is contained a given future thing, or in some revelation and testimony of a speaker, or in some other such thing. Therefore this mode of cognition, which is to terminate that cognition by the proper presence of the thing, is never found except in an intuitive cognition, howsoever much clearer an abstractive cognition may be on the side of the means and light by which the cognition comes about.

numquam potest futurum vel praeteritum cognosci secundum praesentiam, ut est in se, sed in alio, vel quia repraesentatur in aliquo simili, sive imagine formata de illa re futura, vel in aliqua causa, in qua continetur tale futurum, vel in aliqua revelatione et testimonio dicentis aut in aliquo alio simili. Itaque iste modus cognitionis, qui est terminare illam per propriam praesentiam rei, numquam invenitur nisi in cognitione intuitiva, quantumcumque abstractiva sit clarior ex parte medii et luminis, quo fit cognitio.

Whence appears the response to the proofs adduced in support of this example.[13] For we say of a past thing[14] that there can be a proper representation of the thing in itself, because it has already shown itself and so is able to terminate the representation of itself; but it cannot terminate through itself in the way required for an intuitive awareness, but in something produced by itself, as was said above.

Unde patet ad probationes allatas pro isto exemplo.[13] Dicimus enim, quod de re praeterita[14] potest dari propria repraesentatio rei in se, quia iam extitit et terminare potest repraesentationem sui; sed non potest per seipsam terminare, sicut requiritur ad notitiam intuitivam, sed in aliquo sui, sicut supra dictum est.

To the second proof[15] it is said that that specifier can be produced by God just as it would be produced by the Antichrist as regards the entitative being of the specifier, but it will not be able to have the same exercise of representing the Antichrist as if he were present, as is required for an intuition especially on the side of the termination by physical self-presence. So the cognition can only be able to be terminated at the future thing as in another and by means of another. And for this reason it is impossible that a cognition of the thing as future had by means of such a specifier, would not be varied intrinsically if the thing were rendered present and the cognition became intuitive, on account of the difference between a termination at the thing in itself or in another, and the difference in attention which such a difference in termination requires. Whence a specification immediately representing the Antichrist as a future thing cannot be posited in external sense.

Et ad secundam probationem[15] dicitur, quod species illa potest produci a Deo, sicut produceretur ab *Antichristo*, quantum ad entitatem speciei, sed non poterit habere idem exercitium repraesentandi Antichristum, ac si esset praesens, sicut requiritur ad intuitionem praesertim ex parte terminationis per sui praesentiam, sed solum poterit terminari ad rem futuram, ut in alio et mediante alio. Et ideo impossibile est, quod cognitio habita per talem speciem de re ut futura, si reddatur praesens et fiat intuitiva, non varietur intrinsece, propter diversam terminationem ad rem in se vel in alio, et diversam attentionem, quam exigit. Unde in sensu externo non poterit poni species immediate repraesentans Antichristum ut futurum.

And similarly to the proof concerning the specifiers [or concepts] of pure spirits,[16] it is said that they cannot represent future things by a termination at those things in themselves, but as contained in causes. But future things will then first begin to be represented in themselves when they exist in themselves and cease to be future, which does not require a distinct repre-

Et similiter ad probationem *de speciebus angelicis*[16] dicitur, quod non possunt repraesentare futura per terminationem ad illa in seipsis, sed ut continentur in causis. Sed tunc primo incipiunt repraesentari futura in seipsis, quando in seipsis existunt et desinunt esse futura, quod non requirit distinctam repraesentationem ex parte spe-

[13] 313/14-36.
[14] 313/14-18.
[15] 313/18-22.
[16] 313/22-36.

sentation on the side of the specifier as regards the rationale of representing and the thing represented, but as regards the mode of the terminating of this object, in which termination the similitude of the specifying form is extrinsically completed, as St. Thomas says in the *Summa theologica*, I, q. 57, art. 3, and q. 64, art. 1, reply to obj. 5. Therefore, if future things are contained in causes contingently, a pure spirit cannot, howsoever much it may comprehend their specifying form, know those things as determinately existing, but only indeterminately, because they are not otherwise contained in the cause represented in that specifier, even though the pure spirit would properly know their definable structure. But from this fact, that the cognition of a pure spirit is varied when it is rendered intuitive, it does not follow that its impressed specifier is varied essentially, but only the termination of the represented thing; for the specifier which [now] represents the thing and the presence, also coexists with the present thing.

To the second example[17] the response is that this opinion[18] concerning the physical presence required for an intuition cannot be sustained unless future things are posited as physically coexisting in eternity, in which measure alone can the things coexist physically with the divine cognition before they exist in a proper measure, and for this reason we now suppose this opinion as the more certain, explication of which can be seen in the interpreters of St. Thomas's *Summa theologica*, I, q. 14, art. 13, particularly in the interpretation by Cajetan, and in the *Summa contra gentiles*, Book I, chap. 66. Whence not even Christ the Lord was able to see future things intuitively through infused knowledge, unless that cognition could have been measured by eternity (which, however, does not seem possible to admit), as in the blessed vision which clearly manifests God himself, and consequently his eternity in itself, wherein future things are contained.

And to the proof of this example[19] it is said that things are contained in eternity not only as in an efficient cause, but as in a superior measure measuring the duration of things not yet existing in their own or proper measure, otherwise eternity would not be immutable and indivisible in measuring, if it were actually to measure things only when they mutably exist in

ciei, quantum ad rationem repraesentandi et rem repraesentatam, sed quantum ad modum terminandi istius obiecti, in qua terminatione completur extrinsece similitudo speciei, ut loquitur D. Thomas 1. p. q. 57. art. 3. et q. 64. art. 1. ad 5. Et ideo si futura contingenter continentur in causis, non potest angelus, quantumcumque comprehendat suam speciem, cognoscere illa ut determinate existentia, sed solum indeterminate, quia non aliter continentur in causa repraesentata in illa specie, licet quidditatem eorum proprie cognoscat. Per hoc autem, quod varietur cognitio angeli, quando redditur intuitiva, non sequitur, quod varietur eius species impressa essentialiter, sed solum rei repraesentatae terminatio; species enim, quae repraesentat rem et praesentiam, etiam praesenti coexistit.

Ad secundum exemplum[17] respondetur non posse sustineri istam sententiam[18] de praesentia physica requisita ad intuitionem, nisi ponantur res coexistere physice in aeternitate, in qua solum mensura possunt res coexistere physice cognitioni divinae, antequam sint in propria mensura, et ideo hanc sententiam nunc supponimus ut certiorem, cuius explicatio videri potest apud interpretes D. Thomae 1. p. q. 14. art. 13. et Caietanum ibi, et 1. Contra Gent. cap. 66. Unde neque Christus Dominus per scientiam infusam potuit videre futura intuitive, nisi illa cognitio mensurata fuerit aeternitate, quod tamen non videtur admittendum, sicut in visione beata, quae manifestat clare ipsum Deum, et consequenter eius aeternitatem in se, in qua futura continentur.

Et ad probationem huius exempli[19] dicitur, quod res non continentur in aeternitate solum tamquam in causa efficiente, sed ut mensurante mensura superiori durationem rerum nondum in propria mensura existentium, alias non esset immutabilis et indivisibilis in mensurando, si solum mensuraret actu res, quando mutabiliter exis-

[17] 313/37-314/6.
[18] 305/34-38.
[19] 314/6-11.

themselves, and were not to measure them if they did not so exist, which is against the rationale of the measure of eternity, which measure is immutable and indivisible even in measuring. Wherefore all things are in eternity as in an alien measure, yet in such a way that they are not in it as within causes, but as in themselves, yet not as produced in their own proper measure and according to an illation of reception and mutation, but as attained by an immutable and eternal duration, inasmuch, specifically, as they are attained by the eternal action of God under the aspect of action, not under the aspect of reception. For the action of God is not always conjoined to a reception and the consequence of an effect in a proper mutation, as St. Thomas says in the *Summa theologica*, I, q. 46, art. 1, reply to obj. 10. And nevertheless, in itself the action of God is always an eternal action, and under its eternal aspect respects the term and elevates it to the eternal action's measure in the rationale of action, and respects it not only as being [contained] within causes. But of these distinctions the theologians treat at length.

But to the other proof concerning conditioned future things,[20] the response is that those things are not attained by God intuitively, because truly they are not, but could have been. But they are attained by a simple understanding, not inasmuch as simple understanding excludes a decree of will, but as it excludes intuitively seeing, i.e., vision. For an understanding is said to be simple either because it does not involve anything of the physical presence which pertains to vision, or because it does not involve anything of an order to will, which pertains to decision, as St. Thomas teaches in the *Disputed Questions on Truth*, q. 3, art. 3, reply to obj. 8.[21] And in respect of a conditioned contingent of determinate truth there is a decree determining that truth, not indeed as regards the [unrealized] consequence which, when the condition and the application of the concurrence of God are posited, becomes a proposition of necessary truth. But the decree safeguards the nature of a free subject, which is not sufficiently determined by the mere fulfilling of that condition, but by the decree and will of God. Whence this determination is not attained by a simple understanding, insofar as the qualification "simple" is opposed to an order to will, but it is a simple understanding as opposed to a physical presence in act.

To the last example[22] we answer first that even though our intellect does not have an *impressed* speci-

tunt in seipsis, et si sic non existunt, non mensuraret, quod est contra rationem mensurae aeternitatis, quae etiam in mensurando immutabilis et indivisibilis est. Quare res omnes ita sunt in aeternitate ut in aliena mensura, quod tamen non sunt in ipsa sicut intra causas, sed ut in seipsis, non tamen ut productae in propria mensura et secundum illationem passionis et mutationis, sed ut attactae duratione immutabili et aeterna, quatenus scilicet attinguntur ab actione Dei aeterna sub respectu actionis, non sub respectu passionis. Nec enim actio Dei semper est coniuncta passioni et consecutioni effectus in propria mutatione, ut dicit S. Thomas 1. p. q. 46. art. 1. ad 10. Et tamen in se semper est actio aeterna et sub respectu aeterno terminum respicit et elevat ad suam mensuram in ratione actionis, et non solum eum respicit prout intra causas. Sed de his latius theologi.

Ad aliam vero probationem *de futuris conditionatis*[20] respondetur illa non attingi a Deo intuitive, quia vere non sunt, sed essent. Attinguntur autem per simplicem intelligentiam, non quatenus excludit decretum voluntatis, sed ut excludit visionem. Simplex enim intelligentia dicitur, aut quia non miscet aliquid de praesentia physica, quod pertinet ad visionem, aut quia non miscet aliquid de ordine ad voluntatem, quod pertinet ad decretum, ut docet D. Thomas q. 3. de Veritate art. 3. ad 8.[21] Et respectu conditionati contingentis determinatae veritatis datur decretum determinans illam, non quidem quantum ad consequentiam, quae posita conditione et applicatione concursus Dei est veritatis necessariae, sed attenta natura subiecti liberi, quod per solam positionem conditionis non sufficit determinari, sed per decretum et voluntatem Dei. Unde haec determinatio non attingitur simplici intelligentia, quatenus ly simplex opponitur ordini ad voluntatem, sed est simplex intelligentia, ut opponitur physicae praesentiae actu.

Ad ultimum exemplum[22] respondetur *imprimis*, quod licet intellectus noster

[20] 314/11-18.
[21] *Pa* IX. 58 b.
[22] 314/19-25.

fier directly representing the singular, it nevertheless has as a concomitant, by the order and reflexion toward the phantasm, a concept [or *expressed* specifier] properly[23] representing the singular, as we explain more at length in the books of the *Physics*, Q. 1,[24] and in the books *Concerning the Soul*, Q. 10.[25] This suffices for the understanding to be said to have an intuitive awareness of a present thing, to wit, by means of such a concept.

Or secondly it is said[26] that, from this very fact, [viz.] that the understanding knows with a continuation and dependence upon phantasms, while phantasms are coordinated with the senses (because a phantasm is a movement produced by a sense in act, as is said in Aristotle's treatise *On the Soul*, Book III, chap. 3[27]), it follows that even though the intellectual cognition comes about by a specifier not directly representing the singular, it can nevertheless at least indirectly know that singular by means of this coordination and continuation relative to the senses. This suffices for the understanding to have an intutive awareness in the same way.

It is argued secondly that there can be an abstractive awareness in external sense, because an infidel or a heretic not believing that Christ is made present in the Eucharist by the consecration continues to see and to judge of the bread in the same way as before, and he is assured of the presence of bread in the same way as before, namely, by means of those accidents. But before there was an intuitive awareness not only of the accidents, but also of the bread through the accidents; therefore that intuitive awareness engaging such an object remains just as before. For if it were abstractive, it would be another awareness or judgment, and yet the bread is absent, therefore there is an intuition of an absent thing.

This is confirmed, because in a mirror there is an intuitive awareness of the very thing there represented, since indeed [the reflection] comes about by means of specifying stimuli emitted by the object and reflected from the mirror to the eye. But an awareness that comes about by means of specifiers maintained and emitted by the object itself, is an intuitive cognition. And nevertheless the physical presence of the man is not given in the mirror, because, for example, he can be behind and not in front of the one seeing when he is seen as an ob-

non habeat speciem impressam directe repraesentantem singulare, habet tamen ex adiuncto, ordine et reflexione ad phantasma, conceptum proprie[23] repraesentantem illud, ut latius dicemus in Phys. q. 1.[24] et libris de Anima q. 10.,[25] et hoc sufficit, ut dicatur habere notitiam intuitivam rei praesentis, videlicet mediante tali conceptu.

Vel secundo dicitur,[26] quod hoc ipso quod intellectus cognoscit cum continuatione et dependentia a phantasmatibus, phantasmata autem coordinantur sensibus, quia phantasia est motus factus a sensu in actu, ut dicitur in 3. de Anima,[27] ideo cognitio intellectus licet fiat a specie non repraesentante directe singulare, potest tamen saltem indirecte cognoscere illud mediante ista coordinatione et continuatione ad sensus, et hoc sufficit, ut eodem modo habeat notitiam intuitivam.

Secundo arguitur, quia gentilis vel haereticus non credens in Eucharistia esse Christum facta consecratione eodem modo continuat visionem et iudicium de pane atque antea, et eodem modo certificatur de praesentia panis sicut antea, scilicet mediantibus illis accidentibus. Sed antea erat notitia intuitiva non solum accidentium, sed eitam panis per accidentia; ergo manet illa notitia intuitiva circa tale obiectum sicut antea. Nam si esset abstractiva, esset alia notitia seu iudicium, et tamen panis est absens, ergo datur intuitio de re absenti.

Confirmatur, quia in speculo datur notitia intuitiva de ipsa re ibi repraesentata, siquidem fit per species emissas ab obiecto et reflexas a speculo ad oculum. Quod autem fit per species ab obiecto ipso conservatas et immissas, intuitiva cognitio est. Et tamen in speculo non datur praesentia physica hominis, v. g. quia potest esse retro videntem et non ante, quando videtur in speculo, ideoque panis visus in speculo

[23] The 1663 Lyons text reads here: "*directe*"—"directly."

[24] Phi. nat. 1. p. q. 1. art. 3.

[25] Phil. nat. 4. p. q. 10. art. 4., "*Utrum singulare materiale pro hoc statu sit directe cognoscibile ab intellectu*"—"Whether a material individual is directly knowable as such by human understanding."

[26] in response to 314/19-25.

[27] 428 b 11; S. Thom. lect. 6 (*Pa* XX. 113 a).

ject in the mirror, and for this reason bread seen in a mirror is not apt matter for consecration, because it is not physically present there.

If it were said that the very thing represented is not seen in the mirror, but only its image, there would stand in the way the difficult passage of St. Thomas in the *Disputed Questions on Truth*, q. 2, art. 6,[28] where he says that "by means of the similitude which is received in sight from the mirror, sight is directly borne to a cognition of the mirrored thing, but through a kind of reversion it is borne by means of the same received similitude to the very similitude which is in the mirror." Therefore according to St. Thomas the act of seeing not only sees the similitude in the mirror, but also the very thing represented.

The response to this[29] is that there is in us in respect of consecrated bread a double cognition. One belongs to the exterior eye itself in respect of the object which it sees; the other is a judgment which is made in the understanding concerning the substance of the thing seen. The first cognition remains intuitive just as before, equally for one believing and for one not believing the mystery of the Eucharist, because it remains invariant concerning the primary and essential object, which is something colored. But in respect of the accidental sensible object, which is the substance, that seeing does not remain, because a sense is not acted on by something incidentally sensible, as the Philosopher says in his *Concerning on the Soul*, Book II, chap. 6,[30] and as can be seen in reading 13 of St. Thomas's *Commentary* thereon.[31] Therefore to external sense insofar as it is external, it pertains only to attain intuitively a colored thing according to the outward appearance, but that which is inward, or the very substance of the thing, since it is accidentally seen, is also accidentally attained intuitively by sense. Whence when that substance is removed, it no longer continues to be seen accidentally, but the very act of external vision is not intrinsically varied as a consequence of this fact, because those aspects of things which are incidental [to a given cognition] do not intrinsically vary the cognition. But the judgment of intellect by which the heretic decides that the substance is bread, was never intuitive in itself and immediately, even before the consecration, because the substance of a thing is not seen in itself. Nor is a judgment properly

non est consecrabilis, quia non est praesens.

Si dicatur non videri in speculo rem ipsam repraesentatam, sed tantum eius imaginem, *obstat* difficilis locus D. Thomae q. 2. de Veritate art. 6.,[28] ubi dicit, quod «per similitudinem, quae est in visu a speculo accepta, directe fertur visus in cognitionem rei speculatae, sed per quamdam reversionem fertur per eandem in ipsam similitudinem, quae est in speculo». Ergo secundum Divum Thomam visus non solum videt similitudinem in speculo, sed etiam rem ipsam repraesentatam.

RESPONDETUR,[29] quod in nobis respectu panis consecrati datur duplex cognitio, altera ipsius oculi exterioris respectu obiecti, quod videt; altera est iudicium, quod formatur in intellectu de substantia rei visae. Prima cognitio manet intuitiva sicut antea, tam in credente quam non credente mysterium Eucharistiae, quia manet invariata circa obiectum primarium et per se, quod est coloratum. Respectu vero sensibilis per accidens, quod est substantia, illa visio non manet, quia sensus non patitur a sensibili per accidens, ut dicit Philosophus in 2. de Anima textu 65.[30] et videri potest D. Thomas lect. 13.[31] Et ideo ad sensum externum, in quantum externus est, solum pertinet intuitive attingere coloratum secundum externam superficiem, quod vero intus est, vel ipsa substantia rei, cum per accidens videatur, per accidens etiam attingitur intuitive a sensu. Unde illo remoto non manet amplius visum per accidens, sed non ex hoc variatur intrinsece ipsa visio exterior, quia ea, quae sunt per accidens, non variant intrinsece cognitionem. Iudicium vero intellectus, quo haereticus iudicat esse panis substantiam, numquam fuit intuitivum in se et immediate, etiam ante consecrationem, quia substantia rei in se non videtur. Nec iudicium proprie est in-

---

28 *Pa* IX. 37 b.
29 318/21-34.
30 c. 6. (418 a 23).
31 *Pa* XX. 70.

intuitive or abstractive, except by reason of the extremes from which it is established; for ''intuitive'' is said of simple awareness, not of judicative awareness which formally does not regard a thing as present, but as coincident with (corresponding to) another. the same judgment concerning the substance of bread can therefore be continued before and after consecration, even though the true intuition of bread, whose substance was seen incidentally and not in itself, would be discontinued, because what is only incidentally seen and intuitive does not belong to a cognition intrinsically, but extrinsically, just as does truth or falsity. And just as, if a nude substance could remain when the accidents were removed, its continued cognition in the understanding would not be intuitive, so conversely when the accidents remain but not the substance, its cognition in the intellect is not intuitive, and yet it is the same cognition.

To the confirmation,[32] the response is that in a mirror it is not the [mirrored] thing itself that is seen intuitively, but its image, which is formed in the mirror by the refraction of specifying stimuli and of light. That a mirror image is generated, St. Thomas teaches in the *Commentary on the Sentences of Peter Lombard*, Book IV, dist. 10, q. 1, art. 3, quaestiunc. 3;[33] in the *Summa theologica*, III, q. 76, art. 3; and in his *Commentary on Aristotle's Treatise on Meteorology*, Book III, reading 6, in a kind of digression on the colors of the rainbow, query 4, reply to obj. 2.[34] In the mirror, therefore, by the light refracted together with the specifiers which are borne with that light, the image is generated and results, even as in a cloud opposite the sun result the colors of a rainbow. And that which the eye sees in the mirror is the image formed there, which the eye most definitely sees intuitively; but it sees the mirrored thing only according as that thing is contained in the very mirror-image. Yet the eye is said to see by means of specifying stimuli emitted by the object and refracted, not because it sees formally and immediately by means of the specifiers as emitted by the object, but by means of the specifiers of the very image formed in the mirror by the specifiers which originated from the object, and the other specifiers result through refraction. But when St. Thomas says[35] that the act of seeing is borne directly to a cognition of the thing mirrored by means of the similitude which is received in sight from the mirror, he is not speaking of seeing only

tuitivum vel abstractivum, nisi ratione extremorum, ex quibus constat; intuitivum enim dicitur de simplici notitia, non de iudicativa, quae formaliter non respicit rem ut praesentem, sed ut alteri convenientem. Potest ergo continuari idem iudicium de substantia panis ante et post consecrationem, licet discontinuetur vera intuitio panis, cuius substantia per accidens erat visa et non in se, quia quod solum per accidens est visum et intuitivum, non convenit intrinsece cognitioni, sed extrinsece sicut veritas vel falsitas. Et sicut sublatis accidentibus si substantia nuda maneret, cognitio eius in intellectu continuata non esset intuitiva, ita e contra manentibus accidentibus, sed non substantia, eius cognitio in intellectu intuitiva non est, et tamen est eadem.

Ad confirmationem[32] respondetur, quod in speculo non videtur intuitive res ipsa, sed imago eius, quae per refractionem specierum et luminis formatur in speculo, quam imaginem generari docet D. Thomas in 4. dist. 10. q. 1. art. 3. quaestiunc. 3.[33] et 3. p. q. 76. art. 3. et 3. Meteorolog. lect. 6. in digressione quadem de coloribus iridis circa 4. q. ad 2.[34] Itaque in speculo per lumen refractum simul cum speciebus, quae cum lumine ipso deferuntur, generatur ibi et resultat illa imago, sicut etiam in nube opposita soli resultant colores iridis. Et id, quod videt oculus in speculo, est imago illa ibi formata, quam utique intuitive videt; rem autem speculatam solum videt prout continetur in ipsa imagine speculi. Dicitur autem videre per species ab obiecto immissas et refractas, non quia formaliter et immediate videat per species ut immissas ab obiecto, sed per species ipsius imaginis formatae in speculo a speciebus, quae originatae sunt ab obiecto, et per refractionem aliae resultarunt. Quando vero dicit Divus Thomas,[35] quod visus directe fertur in cognitionem rei speculatae per similitudinem, quae est in visu accepta a speculo, non loquitur de visu pro sola cog-

[32] 318/35-319/3.
[33] *Pa* VII. 624 a.
[34] *Le* III. CII n. 10.
[35] See 319/4-16.

in terms of the exterior sensitive cognition, but in terms of the whole cognition, interior as well as exterior, which is received from the mirror and does not stop at the mirror image itself, but at the mirrored thing to which that image leads, and this whole is named the act of seeing or vision.

Thirdly it is argued: Some specifying form representing an absent thing can be placed in external sense by God or by a pure spirit; that absent thing will therefore then be seen by the eye.

The consequence is clear, because an eye formed by a specifier, particularly when exterior light remains, can produce an act of seeing; for a present object is required for nothing but the supplying of specification to the eye. Therefore, when specifiers are given without the object, the power of vision will elicit an act of seeing.

The antecedent is proved: First, because it is not impossible that God should preserve a specification without the object, because specifying forms depend on that object only in the order of productive cause, which God can supply. Second, because some appearances concerning bodies are often seen when no change is made in the bodies, but in the sense of the one seeing, as is plain when the form of a young man or of flesh appears in the Eucharist, as St. Thomas teaches in the *Summa theologica*, III, q. 76, art. 8. And when Christ was seen by his disciples in another form, as St. Thomas teaches in the same work, q. 54, art. 2, and q. 55, art. 4, which occurs through the production of a similitude in the eye, just as if it were naturally produced, as St. Thomas teaches in the *Commentary on the Sentences of Peter Lombard*, Book IV, dist. 10, q. 1, art. 4, quaestiunc. 2.[36] Moreover, some illusions come about in the same way through the work of demons, when specifying stimuli contact the organs of exterior sense and things are seen as if they were independently present, as St. Thomas teaches in his *Commentary on the Sentences of Peter Lombard*, Book II, dist. 8, q. 1, art. 5, reply to obj. 4.[37]

This is confirmed by the fact that God can elevate a sensible thing so that it could act on something distant, and even act instrumentally on something spiritual. Therefore likewise it is not impossible [for God or a pure spirit] to elevate [external] sense so that it could operate by an immanent act respecting something not present, since the rationale of presence or absence is not outside of its adequate object.

nitione sensitiva exteriori, sed pro tota cognitione, tam interiori quam exteriori, quae accipitur ex speculo et non sistit in ipsa imagine speculi, sed in re speculata, ad quam ducit illa imago, et totum hoc visus nominatur.

Tertio arguitur: Potest in sensu externo poni a Deo vel angelo species aliqua repraesentans rem absentem; ergo tunc videbitur ab oculo.

Consequentia patet, quia oculus formatus specie, praesertim remanente luce exteriori, potest exire in actum; non enim ad aliud requirit obiectum praesens, nisi ut ipsi species subministret. Ergo istis positis sine obiecto visus eliciet actum.

Antecedens vero probatur: *Primo* quia non repugnat, ut Deus conservet species sine obiecto, cum solum pendeant ab illo in genere causae efficientis, quam Deus potest supplere. *Secundo,* quia saepe videntur aliquae apparentiae circa corpora, nulla facta mutatione in corporibus, sed in sensu videntis, ut patet cum apparet forma pueri vel carnis in Eucharistia, ut docet D. Thomas 3. p. q. 76. art. 8. Et quando Christus fuit visus in alia effigie a discipulis, ut docet ibidem q. 54. art. 2. et q. 55. art. 4., quod fit per productionem similitudinis in oculo, perinde ac si naturaliter produceretur, ut docet in 4. dist. 10. q. 1. art. 4. quaestiunc. 2.[36] Imo eodem modo per daemonum operationem fiunt aliqua praestigia, quando species contingunt organa sensus exterioris et videntur res, ac si essent praesentes extra, ut docet D. Thomas in 2. dist. 8. q. 1. art. 5. ad 4.[37]

Et confirmatur, quia Deus potest elevare rem sensibilem, ut operetur circa aliquid distans et etiam instrumentaliter circa aliquid spirituale. Ergo etiam non repugnabit elevare sensum, ut operetur actu immanenti circa non praesens, cum ratio praesentis vel absentis non sit extra adaequatum eius obiectum.

---

[36] *Pa* VII. 626 a.
[37] *Pa* VI. 458 a.

The response to the principal argument[38] is that God can indeed preserve a specification in the eye as regards its entitative being by supplying for the productivity of the object, just as light can be preserved in the air without the sun. But the eye actuated by such a specification cannot tend to the object not present, just as it cannot see without exterior light, because without exterior light or a present object the eye is deprived of the form or terminus of an experimental and external sensation, since indeed no icon is formed within external sense wherein the cognition might be perfected independently of the exterior terminating sensible, as we saw above. Wherefore, it involves a contradiction for a thing to be known by the sensing and experiencing of an external sensation (which differs from an imaginative sensation), except by attaining something external in its external self and not as formed within the sense.

To the second proof[39] it is said that these outward appearances can only come about in two ways, either through the elicitation of an external seeing, or through the elicitation of an imaginative seeing which considers or adjudges itself to see externally, to the entent that specifiers inwardly existing stimulate the organs of sense, whether of the common sense or of the external senses, and moved by those specifiers perception imagines that it sees by an external seeing, because it is moved by the very seeing, that is, by the specifiers stimulating sight. If the appearances come about in the first way, there is always some change in the environment or in some outside body, by a disturbance of the air there and the appearing of color, just as swirling smoke sometimes makes beams look like serpents or vines or the like. And it is not impossible for some apparitions to occur in this way in the Eucharist or concerning the body of Christ, not because a change takes place in the body itself, but in the surrounding environment, yet not because the eye might see something without there being an outward visible thing either apparent or true. The same thing happens whenever visible things are seen multiplied by a refraction of specifying stimuli. In the second way the seeing is not formed by the eye itself, but the imagination is deluded or moved by taking itself to see things which it does not see, just as in drunkards specifying stimuli are doubled for the imagination as

Respondetur *ad principale argumentum,*[38] quod Deus bene potest conservare speciem in oculo quantum ad suam entitatem supplendo efficientiam obiecti, sicut potest lucem conservare in aere sine sole. Ceterum non potest oculus tali specie actuatus tendere in obiectum non praesens, sicut non potest sine luce exteriori videre, quia sine luce exteriori vel obiecto praesenti caret forma vel termino sensationis experimentalis et externae, siquidem non formatur idolum intra sensum externum, ut in eo perficiatur cognitio independenter ab exteriori sensibili terminante, ut supra vidimus. Quare implicat, quod res cognoscatur sentiendo et experiendo sensatione externa, quae differt ab imaginativa, nisi attingendo aliquid externum in seipso et non ut formatum intra se.

Ad secundam probationem[39] dicitur, quod istae apparentiae externae solum possunt fieri dupliciter, aut per elicientiam visionis externae aut per elicientiam imaginativae, quae putat seu iudicat se videre externe, quatenus species intus existentes descendunt circa organa sensuum, sive sensus communis sive sensuum exteriorum, et ab illis mota phantasia putat se videre visu externo, quia ab ipso visu movetur, id est a speciebus descendentibus circa visum. Si primo modo fiat, semper datur aliqua immutatio in medio seu in aliquo corpore extrinseco, ingrossato ibi aere et apparente colore, sicut etiam per aliquem fumum trabes videntur serpentes vel vites aut quid simile. Et hoc modo non repugnat fieri aliquas apparitiones in Eucharistia vel circa corpus Christi, non quia fiat mutatio circa ipsum corpus, sed circa medium circumstans, non tamen quia oculus sine exteriori visibili vel apparenti vel vero aliquid videat. Et idem contingit, quoties per refractionem specierum videntur multiplicari visibilia. Secundo modo non formatur visio ab ipso oculo, sed imaginatio deluditur vel movetur existimando se videre ea, quae non videt, sicut etiam in temulentis ex nimia commotione spirituum duplicantur species

[38] 321/7-22.
[39] 321/22-39.

a consequence of the excessive commotion of the animal spirits, and demons often use them in this way for deluding and deceiving the imagination. But because this comes about through the stimulus of the specifying forms or icons which are in the spirits of the imaginative power, descending all the way down to the external organs, with the result that the imaginative power *seems thence* to be moved, for that reason St. Thomas says that those specifiers contact the organs of external sense, namely, by descending from the head to the senses, that thence they might be thrown up again to the imagination, and so something would *appear* to be seen.

To the confirmation[40] the response is that between agents by a transitive action or whatever productive cause, and a cognition of external sense, there is a disparity of rationale. For a productive cause, the presence of a thing to be acted upon by the agent is only a condition for the acting pertaining to the conjunction of the recipient, not to the formal specification of the acting, and therefore that condition can be supplied preserving the essential rationale of acting. But for the senses, by contrast, the presence of the object does not pertain to the conjunction of a recipient, but to the conjunction of a terminus specifying the action, on which terminus the cognition essentially depends. Just as a transient action depends on the effect produced, so does an immanent action depend on the thing known, even as there cannot be an act of understanding without a word either united or produced; but for the external senses in place of the word is the sensible thing independently present. But if sight were to be strengthened for seeing something far distant which was otherwise absent to it, this is not to be elevated to seeing an absent thing, but that by the sight's strength a thing is rendered present which was not present for the weaker power.

ad imaginativam, et hoc modo saepe utuntur daemones deludendo et decipiendo phantasiam. Sed quia hoc fit per descensum specierum seu idolorum, quae sunt in spiritibus imaginativae, usque ad organa exteriora, ut inde videatur imaginativa moveri, ideo dicit D. Thomas, quod illae species contingunt organa exterioris sensus, scilicet a capite descendendo ad sensus, ut inde iterum eiaculentur in phantasiam, et sic apparet aliquid videri.

Ad confirmationem[40] respondetur esse disparem rationem inter agentia actione transeunte vel quamcumque causam efficientem et cognitionem sensus externi, quod in efficientibus praesentia passi circa agens solum est conditio ad agendum, pertinens ad coniunctionem passi, non ad formalem specificationem agendi, et ideo salva essentiali ratione agendi potest suppleri illa conditio. At vero praesentia obiecti in sensibus non pertinet ad coniunctionem passi, sed ad coniunctionem termini specificantis actionem, a quo termino essentialiter dependet cognitio, sicut actio transiens ab effectu producto, sic immanens a re cognita, sicut etiam intellectio non potest dari sine verbo vel unito vel producto; loco autem verbi in sensibus externis est sensibile extra praesens. Quodsi visus confortetur ad videndum aliquid longe distans, quod alias illi erat absens, hoc non est elevari ad videndam rem absentem, sed quod virtuti eius reddatur praesens, quod virtuti debiliori praesens non erat.

---

[40] 321/41-48.

[741b4-41]

Question 3

How Do Reflexive Concepts Differ from Direct Concepts

Quaestio Tertia

Quomodo Differat Conceptus Reflexus a Directo

Three things cause difficulty in this matter: First, there is the question whether a reflexive concept really is distinguished from a direct concept, and what is the cause of their difference. Second, what is known by means of reflexive concepts, and what sort of objects do they have. Third, whether direct and reflexive concepts differ essentially.

Relative to the first cause of difficulty some are of the opinion that for knowing one's own concepts it is not necessary to form another concept of them, as can be seen in Ferrariensis's *Commentary on the Summa contra gentiles of St. Thomas*, Book I, chap. 53, the paragraph beginning "But when it is objected." But St. Thomas expressly says, in the *Summa theologica*, I, q. 87, art. 3, reply to obj. 2, that "the act by which one understands a stone is one act, the act by which one understands oneself understanding is quite another"; therefore a reflexive concept is also a distinct concept from a direct concept, because distinct acts produce distinct concepts. This is more clearly expressed by St. Thomas in his *Disputed Questions on the Power of God*, q. 9, art. 5,[1] where he says: "In this regard, it makes no difference whether the understanding understands itself or something other than itself. For just as when it understands something other than itself, it forms a concept of that thing (which thing is signified by the voice), so when it understands itself, it forms a word [expressive] of itself, which [expressed mental word or concept] can also be expressed by the voice."

Tria in hoc articulo difficultatem faciunt: *Primum*, an revera conceptus reflexus distinguatur realiter a directo et quae sit huius causa. *Secundum*, quid cognoscatur per conceptum reflexum et quodnam sit eius obiectum. *Tertium*, an essentialiter differant conceptus directus et reflexus.

Ad primum aliqui existimant, quod ad cognoscendum proprium conceptum non oportet formare alium conceptum de illo, ut videri potest in Ferrariensi 1. Contra Gent. cap. 53. § *Cum autem obicitur*. Sed expresse D. Thomas 1. p. q. 87. art. 3. ad 2. dicit, quod «alius est actus, quo quis intelligit lapidem, alius, quo intelligit se intelligere»; ergo et distinctus conceptus est reflexus a directo, quia actus distinctus distinctum conceptum producit. Quod clarius expressit D. Thomas q. 9. de Potentia art. 5.,[1] ubi ait: «Quantum ad hoc non differt, utrum intellectus seipsum intelligat vel aliud a se. Sicut enim cum intelligit aliud a se, format conceptum illius rei, quod voce significatur, ita cum intelligit seipsum, format verbum sui, quod voce etiam potest exprimere».

---

[1] *Pa* VIII. 186 a.

Some authors indeed labor to assign the reason and necessity of this reflexive concept for understanding one's own concepts. But it can be clearly seen to be deducible from the teaching of St. Thomas in the passage cited from the *Summa theologica*, I, q. 87, art. 3, reply to obj. 2. We suppose that only an intellective power (the power of understanding), not a sensitive power, can be reflexive, i.e., able to turn back upon itself, to begin with, because the power of the understanding respects universally every being, and therefore also itself, but a sensitive power in its act is devoid of that which it knows; for example, the act of seeing does not have a color in itself, and so does not attain itself. Again, because one body cannot act upon itself as a whole, but one part always acts on another part; one part of an organ, however, does not suffice for eliciting cognition. On this point St. Thomas's remarks in the *Commentary on the Sentences of Peter Lombard*, Book II, dist. 19, q. 1, art. 1,[2] and Book III, dist. 23, q. 1, art. 2, reply to obj. 3,[3] should be consulted; and what we ourselves say in the books *Concerning the Soul*, Q. 4.[4]

In the intellective power, therefore, that is, in the power of understanding, **the whole rationale of reflexion springs from this, that our understanding and its act are not objectively understandable in this life except dependently upon sensible things, and thus our concepts, even though they are formally present, are nevertheless not present objectively as long as they are not formed on the pattern of a definable sensible structure or "essence," which can only come about by means of a turning back or "reflexion" undertaken from a sensible object.** But in the case of pure spirits and of separated substances such a reflexive concept is not necessary, because pure spirits directly know their own substance and understanding and the things which are in themselves as accidents of their own proper substance, and therefore through the same specifier by which they know themselves they can also attain those accidents. But they do not know themselves reflexively, therefore neither their own concepts, because, when they are produced, concepts of themselves are intelligible to the pure spirit's intelligence no less than is its own substance.

But THE REASON FOR THIS is thus taken from the aforementioned passage of the *Summa*, I, q. 87, art. 3, reply to obj. 2, because each single thing is known according as it is in act. But the final perfection of the

Laborant autem aliqui auctores in reddenda ratione et necessitate huius conceptus reflexi ad intelligendum proprium conceptum. Sed clare videtur deduci posse ex doctrina D. Thomae cit. loco 1. p. q. 87. Et supponimus solum potentiam intellectivam posse reflectere supra se, non sensitivam, tum quia illa respicit universaliter omne ens, atque adeo etiam seipsam, sensitiva vero in suo actu est expers eius, quod cognoscit; v. g. visio non habet in se colorem, et sic non se attingit. Tum quia unum corpus non potest agere in seipsum, sed semper una pars agit in aliam, una autem pars organi non sufficit ad eliciendam cognitionem. De quo videndus est D. Thomas in 2. dist. 19. q. 1. art. 1.[2] et in 3. dist. 23. q. 1. art. 2. ad 3.,[3] et nos dicemus in libris de Anima q. 4.[4]

In potentiis ergo intellectivis tota ratio reflexionis oritur ex eo, quod noster intellectus et eius actus non est obiective intelligibilis pro hac vita, nisi dependenter a sensibilibus, et ita conceptus noster licet formaliter sit praesens, non tamen obiective, quamdiu non formatur ad instar quidditatis sensibilis, quod solum potest fieri per reflexionem ab obiecto sensibili desumptam. In angelis autem et substantiis separatis non est necessarius talis conceptus reflexus, quia directe suam substantiam et intellectum et quae sunt in seipsis, cognoscunt tamquam accidentia suae propriae substantiae, atque adeo per eandem speciem, qua se cognoscunt, etiam accidentia illa possunt attingere. Se autem non cognoscunt reflexe, ergo neque conceptum suum, quia seipso, cum producitur, est intelligibilis suo intellectui non minus quam substantia sua.

RATIO AUTEM HUIUS sic deducitur a D. Thoma praedicto loco 1. p., quia unumquodque cognoscitur, secundum quod est in actu. Ultima autem perfectio in-

[2] *Pa* VI. 554 b.
[3] *Pa* VII. 240 b.
[4] Phil. nat. 4. p. q. 4. art. 4.

intellect is its operation, because through the operation it is not ordered to perfecting another, as is a transient action. Therefore this is the first thing that is understood by the intellect, namely, its own act of understanding, because this is what is most actual in understanding and consequently of itself primarily and maximally intelligible. Nevertheless, this fact is differently realized in different orders of understanding. For there is one intelligence, namely, the divine intelligence, which is itself its own act of understanding, and so for God, to understand himself understanding and to understand his essence are one and the same thing, because his essence is his act of understanding. There is also another intelligence, namely, the purely spiritual or angelic intelligence, which is not its own act of understanding, but nevertheless the first object of its own act of understanding is its own essence. Thus, although for a pure spirit to understand itself understanding, and to understand its essence, are distinct according to rationale, nevertheless a pure spirit understands both at the same time and by the same act, because understanding its own essence is the proper perfection of its essence, but simultaneously and by one act a thing with its perfection is understood. But there is another intelligence, namely, the human understanding, which neither is its own act of understanding, nor is the first object of its act of understanding its own essence, but the first object of human understanding is something extrinsic, namely, the nature of a material thing; and therefore that which is first known by the human understanding is this kind of an object, and the very act by which a material object is known is known secondarily, and through the act is known the intellect itself of which the very act of understanding is the perfection. Thus far the reasoning of St. Thomas.

From this it manifestly follows that *the entire root of* the *reflexion* of a concept upon the act itself and the power of understanding *derives from the objective rationale itself of* [*human*] *understanding,* because even though the concept and the cognition are formally present to the power, they are nevertheless not present objectively; nor does a formal presence suffice for something to be directly knowable,[5] as is best noted by Cajetan in his *Commentary on the summa theologica,* I, q. 87, art. 3, reply to obj. 2. An objective presence is required. But something cannot be objectively present unless it takes on the conditions of an object of a given power. But since the proper object of our understanding is the definable structure or essence of a material thing according to itself, that which is not an essence of a material thing is not

tellectus est eius operatio, quia per operationem non ordinatur ad perficiendum aliud, sicut actio transiens. Igitur hoc est primum, quod intellectu intelligitur, scilicet ipsum eius intelligere, quia hoc est actualissimum in eo, et consequenter se primo et maxime intelligibile. Sed tamen circa hoc diversi intellectus diversimode se habent. Est enim aliquis intellectus, scilicet divinus, qui est ipsum suum intelligere, et sic in Deo idem est, quod intelligat se intelligere, et quod intelligat suam essentiam, quia sua essentia est suum intelligere. Est etiam alius intellectus, scilicet angelicus, qui non est suum intelligere, sed tamen primum obiectum sui intelligere est eius essentia. Unde etsi aliud sit in angelo secundum rationem, quod intelligat se intelligere, et quod intelligat suam essentiam, tamen simul et eodem actu utrumque intelligit, quia hoc, quod est intelligere suam essentiam, est propria perfectio suae essentiae, simul autem et uno actu intelligitur res cum sua perfectione. Est autem alius intellectus, scilicet humanus, qui nec est suum intelligere, nec sui intelligere est obiectum primum ipsa eius essentia, sed aliquid extrinsecum, scilicet natura materialis rei, et ideo quod primo cognoscitur ab intellectu humano, est huiusmodi obiectum, et secundario cognoscitur ipse actus, quo cognoscitur obiectum, et per actum cognoscitur ipse intellectus, cuius est perfectio ipsum intelligere. Hucusque discursus D. Thomae.

Ex quo manifeste deducitur quod tota radix reflexionis conceptus supra ipsum actum et potentiam intelligendi desumitur ex ipsa ratione obiectiva intellectus, quia licet conceptus et cognitio sint formaliter praesentes potentiae, non tamen obiective; nec sufficit formalis praesentia, ut aliquid sit directe cognoscibile,[5] ut optime ibidem notavit Caietanus, sed requiritur obiectiva. Non potest autem aliquid obiective esse praesens, nisi induat conditiones obiecti talis potentiae. Cum autem obiectum proprium nostri intellectus sit quidditas rei materialis secundum se, illud

[5] See Book II above, Questions 1 and 2.

directly present [to our understanding] objectively, and for it to take on such a character it needs a reflexion. And thus our concepts, although they are understandable (intelligible) according to themselves, are nevertheless not understandable according to themselves in the mode of a material structure, and are therefore primarily and directly not present objectively, except as they are taken in the mode of a sensible essence, which mode without exception must be taken from a sensible object. And because they receive this within the power from an exterior object directly known, they are said to be known reflexively, and to be rendered understandable by the intelligibility of a material being. The whole of which does not obtain in the case of pure spirits nor in God, who directly and primarily understand their own essence and whatever is in it.

But if you should ask, What form of impressed specification serves for a reflexive cognition of the concept?, *the response* from St. Thomas in q. 10 of his *Disputed Questions on Truth,* art. 9, reply to objs. 4 and 10,[6] is that those things which are known through reflexive cognition are not known through their own essence nor by means of a proper specifier, but by knowing the object, that is to say, through the specifier of those things with which the act and concept are engaged, from the fact that the concept and act are in need of reflexion inasmuch as they need to be formed on the pattern of a sensible object with which a direct concept is engaged. Therefore reflexive cognition needs the specifying form of such an object in order to be formed on the pattern of that object and known.

Whence St. Thomas says in the *Commentary on the Sentences of Peter Lombard,* Book III, dist. 23, q. 1, art. 2, reply to obj. 3,[7] that "the understanding knows itself just as it knows other things, because of course it knows by means of a specifying form, not indeed of itself, but of the object, which is the form of that from which the intellect knows the nature of its own act, and from the nature of the act the nature of the power, and from the nature of the power the nature of the essence, and consequently of the other powers. Not that the understanding has different similitudes for each of these, but because in its object the understanding knows not only the rationale of the true, but every cognition which is in it, etc." Here St. Thomas clearly teaches how the specifying form of the object serves for the cognition of the act, namely, according as it represents in its object the rationale of

non est directe praesens obiective, quod non est quidditas rei materialis, et ut eam induat, indiget reflexione. Et ita conceptus nostri licet secundum se sint intelligibiles, non tamen secundum se sunt intelligibiles ad modum quidditatis materialis, et ideo primario et directe non sunt praesentes obiective, nisi prout accipiuntur ad modum quidditatis sensibilis, quod utique ab obiecto sensibili accipere debent. Et quia hoc accipiunt intra potentiam ab obiecto exteriori directe cognito, dicuntur reflexe cognosci et reddi intelligibiles intelligibilitate entis materialis. Quod totum non currit in angelis nec in Deo, qui directe et primario intelligunt propriam essentiam et quidquid in ea est.

Quodsi petas, quaenam species impressa deserviat ad cognitionem reflexam conceptus, *respondetur* ex D. Thoma q. 10. de Veritate art. 9. ad 4. et ad 10.,[6] quod ea, quae cognoscuntur per cognitionem reflexam, non cognoscuntur per suam essentiam nec per speciem propriam, sed cognoscendo obiectum seu per speciem eorum, circa quae versatur actus et conceptus, eo quod conceptus et actus in tantum indigent reflexione, in quantum indigent formari ad instar obiecti sensibilis, circa quod conceptus directus versatur, et ideo indiget specie talis obiecti, ut formetur ad instar illius et cognoscatur.

Unde dicit D. Thomas in 3. dist. 23. q. 1. art. 2. ad 3.,[7] quod «intellectus cognoscit seipsum sicut alia, quia scilicet per speciem, non quidem sui, sed obiecti, quae est forma eius, ex qua cognoscit actus sui naturam, et ex natura actus naturam potentiae, et ex natura potentiae naturam essentiae, et per consequens aliarum potentiarum. Non quod habeat de omnibus his diversas similitudines, sed quia in obiecto suo non solum cognoscit rationem veri, sed omnem cognitionem, quae est in eo etc.». Ubi clare D. Thomas docet, quomodo species obiecti deserviat ad cognitionem actus, prout scilicet repraesentat in obiecto suo rationem cogniti. Manet enim in memoria species

[6] *Pa* IX. 173.
[7] *Pa* VII. 241 b.

a known thing. For there remain in memory specifiers not only representing an object, but also representing the fact that it has been known, cognized, and from this relative being of a known thing the understanding turns back toward the very cognition and toward its principles. Whence, too, through such a specification the very form of the specifying can itself be attained reflexively, not immediately in itself, but as it is something of the object known. Yet afterwards it is not contradictory that the understanding should separately form specifiers of the concept and of the power and of other similar things in the same way that it forms other specifiers from previously known forms of specification; for example, by means of the specifiers of a mountain and of gold the imagination forms the specifier of a mountain of gold, as St. Thomas teaches in the *Summa theologica*, I, q. 12, art. 9, reply to obj. 2.

Concerning the second difficulty,[8] there are two things that must be explained:

First, as regards the material object of a reflexive cognition, there is the question of what things reflexive cognition is engaged with. And to this we respond briefly that reflexive awareness concerns all those things which are found in the soul and take on, as a result of the cognition of a material object, the representation and manner of a sensible essence, and so the understanding turns back for knowing not only the concept and the act of knowing, but also habit and specifier and power and the very nature of the soul, as St. Thomas says in the passage recently cited from Book III of his *Commentary on the Sentences of Peter Lombard*, dist. 23, q. 1, art. 2, reply to obj. 3. And when it is said in the definition of a reflexive concept that it is a concept of another concept, it is understood that it is also a concept of all the things which concur within the soul to produce the concept, as we have said in the first of the *Summulae* books, chap. 3.[9] Or it is said that the reflexive concept is a concept of another concept because the first thing that is attained through reflexion is another concept, next the power and soul and so forth.

The second thing which must be explained in connection with the second difficulty pertains to the formal rationale which a reflexive concept respects. And so we also say briefly, from the same text of St. Thomas, that a reflexive concept formally respects the knowing of the nature of that on which it reflects in the way in which that nature can be known through [its sensible] effects or connotatively in the mode of a sensible essence. And although the concepts are present there [in the understanding] physi-

non solum repraesentans obiectum, sed etiam repraesentans, quod fuerit cognitum, et ex hac habitudine cogniti regreditur intellectus ad ipsam cognitionem et ad eius principia. Unde etiam per talem speciem ipsamet species reflexe potest attingi, non immediate in se, sed ut est aliquid obiecti cogniti. Postea tamen non repugnat, quod intellectus formet seorsum species conceptus et potentiae et aliorum similium eo modo, quo ex praeconceptis speciebus format alias, v. g. per speciem montis et auri speciem montis aurei, ut docet D. Thomas 1. p. q. 12. art. 9. ad 2.

Circa secundam difficultatem[8] duo explicari oportet:

PRIMUM quoad obiectum materiale cognitionis reflexae, scilicet circa quae versatur cognitio reflexa. Et ad hoc breviter respondemus, quod sunt omnia illa, quae inveniuntur in anima et ex cognitione obiecti induunt repraesentationem et modum quidditatis sensibilis, et sic regreditur intellectus ad cognoscendum non solum conceptum et actum, sed etiam habitus et species et potentiam et ipsam naturam animae, ut loco nuper cit. ex 3. Sentent. dicit D. Thomas. Et quando dicitur in definitione conceptus reflexi, quod est conceptus alterius conceptus, intelligitur, quod sit etiam omnium, quae intra animam ad conceptum concurrunt, ut diximus 1. lib. Summul. cap. 3.,[9] vel quia primum, quod per reflexionem attingitur, est alter conceptus, deinde potentia et anima etc.

SECUNDUM, quod explicandum est, pertinet ad formalem rationem, quam respicit conceptus reflexus. Et sic etiam breviter dicimus, ex eadem auctoritate D. Thomae, quod formaliter respicit conceptus reflexus cognoscere naturam eius, supra quod reflectit, eo modo, quo cognosci potest per effectus vel connotative ad modum quidditatis sensibilis. Et licet sint ibi praesentes physice, quia tamen

[8] 324/4-5.

[9] 11a6-10 (correcting the erroneous Reiser text reference to "cap. 6").

cally, yet because they are not rendered present objectively by means of themselves, but by means of the similitude and connotation of a sensible structure (which is to attain that presence, as it were, in another and not in itself), we are not said to see our concepts intuitively.[10]

From this it follows that by means of a reflexive concept, inasmuch as it turns back upon a direct concept, that very concept is indeed represented as it is a kind of quality and an image signified in act in the mode of the definable essence of an image. Consequently the thing signified by means of the direct concept is not represented there [i.e., in the reflexive concept] except very remotely and indirectly. And the reason is that in a reflexive concept the very thing signified [by a direct concept] functions as the terminus-from-which reflexion begins; therefore a reflexive concept does not represent that thing as its object and as the terminus-to-which the representation is borne, but only by connoting that thing as the terminus-from-which the reflexion began. And even though a reflexive concept attains a direct concept as the direct concept is a kind of image, and the movement toward an image is also toward the thing imaged, nevertheless, this is understood [to hold true only] when the image is not considered separately and according to itself, but as it exercises the office of leading to its prototype, as the Philosopher teaches in the book *Concerning Memory and Reminiscence,*[11] and as St. Thomas explains in his *Commentary* thereon, reading 3.[12] But in a reflexive concept the movement comes about in the opposite way, that is, from the object to the image; for by knowing an object directly we turn back or reflect in order to know the concept which is the object's image, and therefore the understanding is borne by means of such reflexion toward an image in the mode of a sensible essence and by attaining that image signified in act. Consequently the understanding need not tend through that image toward the thing signified, although indirectly, as we have said, it also attains that significate, inasmuch as the thing signified by the direct concept is the terminus-from-which of this reflexive movement.

Concerning the last difficulty,[13] it is responded briefly that although the qualifications "direct" and "reflexive," according as they signify certain movements of the understanding, would not seem to imply essential differences of cognition, just as knowledge as formed through discursive reasoning

non redduntur per seipsos praesentes obiective, sed mediante similitudine et connotatione quidditatis sensibilis, quod est attingere praesentiam illam quasi in alio et non in seipsa, non dicimur intuitive videre conceptus nostros.[10]

Ex quo deducitur, quod per conceptum reflexum, quatenus regreditur supra conceptum directum, repraesentatur quidem ipse conceptus, ut est qualitas quaedam et imago in actu signato per modum quidditatis imaginis, et per consequens non repraesentatur ibi res significata per conceptum directum, nisi valde remote et in obliquo. *Et ratio est,* quia in conceptu reflexo ipsa res significata habet se ut terminus, a quo reflexio illa incipit; ergo non repraesentat illam tamquam obiectum suum et ut terminum, in quem fertur repraesentatio, sed solum connotando illam ut terminum, a quo incepit reflexio. Et licet conceptus reflexus attingat directum, ut est imago quaedam, et motus in imaginem sit etiam in rem imaginatam, tamen hoc intelligitur, quando non consideratur imago seorsum et secundum se, sed ut exercet officium ducendi ad suum prototypum, ut docet Philosophus in libro de Memoria et Reminiscentia[11] et D. thomas ibi lect. 3.[12] In conceptu autem reflexo fit motus contrario modo, id est ab obiecto ad imaginem; cognoscendo enim obiectum directe reflectimus ad cognoscendum conceptum, qui est eius imago, et ideo per talem reflexionem fertur intellectus ad imaginem per modum quidditatis et in actu signato illam attingendo, et consequenter non oportet per illam tendere ad rem signatam, licet in obliquo, ut diximus, etiam illam attingat, quatenus est terminus a quo huius motus reflexi.

Circa ultimam difficultatem[13] respondetur breviter, quod licet directum et reflexum, secundum quod significant quosdam motus intellectus, non videantur importare essentiales differentias cognitionis, sicut scientia ut formata per discursum et sine

[10] See above, Book II, Question 1, esp. 226/34-227/40, 231/45-233/2; and Question 2, esp. 250/7-39.
[11] c. 1. (450 b 20).
[12] *Pa* XX. 203 b.
[13] 324/6.

and without it, if it is about the same object, does not vary the essential rationale of the knowledge, nevertheless, inasmuch as reflexive and direct concepts import diverse representations and diverse objects represented (because a direct concept is a similitude of an object, whereas a reflexive concept is a similitude of the very concept or of an act or of a power), for this reason, I say, they must differ simply in kind; just as do also other cognitions and representations which are concerned with diverse objects.[14]

discursu, si sit circa idem obiectum, non variat essentialem rationem scientiae, tamen quatenus conceptus reflexus et directus important diversas repraesentationes et diversa obiecta repraesentata, quia directus est similitudo obiecti, reflexus autem est similitudo ipsius conceptus vel actus vel potentiae, ideo simpliciter habent specie differre; sicut etiam aliae cognitiones et repraesentationes, quae versantur circa diversa obiecta.[14]

Resolution of Counter-Arguments

Against our resolution[15] of the first difficulty[16] it is argued first on the grounds that the understanding understands the concept or word and the object represented in that concept by the same act. And similarly the understanding is borne by the same act to the object and to the act [knowing the object], as St. Thomas teaches in the *Commentary on the Sentences of Peter Lombard*, Book I, dist. 10, q. 1, art. 5, reply to obj. 2.[17] Therefore the understanding does not need a reflexive act for discerning the concept and act.

This is confirmed by the fact that the concept and act are much more intimately present and united to the understanding than is the object itself, which is united to the power by means of a given concept. And similarly concept and act are immaterial and understandable in final act, and for that reason the concept is compared to a light whereby the object itself is illuminated, as St. Thomas says in his *Treatise on the Nature of the Word of the Understanding;*[18] but that which is understandable in final act does not need another concept or understandable form in order to be known. Thus light is known by the eye through its essence and not by means of a similitude, which St. Thomas expressly says in his *Commentary on the Sentences of Peter Lombard*, Book II, dist. 23, q. 2, art. 1,[19] where he distinguishes between the way light is seen and the way a stone is seen, saying that light is not seen by the eye by means of some similitude of itself left in the eye, but through its essence informing the eye; but a stone is seen by means of a similitude left in the eye. The same point is made in the *Summa theologica*, I, q. 56, art. 3. The same thing is also usually said of an impressed specifying form (that of itself it is already knowable), a fortiori

Solvuntur argumenta

Contra id, quod resolvimus[15] circa primam difficultatem[16] **arguitur primo,** quia intellectus eodem actu intelligit conceptum seu verbum et obiectum repraesentatum in illo. Et similiter eodem actu fertur in obiectum et in actum, ut docet D. Thomas in 1. dist. 10. q. 1. art. 5. ad 2.[17] Ergo ad agnoscendum conceptum et actum non indiget actu reflexo.

Et confirmatur, quia conceptus et actus sunt intime praesentes et uniti intellectui multo magis quam ipsum obiectum, quod mediante tali conceptu unitur potentiae. Et similiter sunt immateriales et intelligibiles in actu ultimo, ideoque comparatur conceptus luci, qua obiectum ipsum redditur illustratum, ut dicit D. Thomas opusc. 14.;[18] quod autem est in actu ultimo intelligibile, non indiget alio conceptu seu forma intelligibili, ut cognoscatur. Unde lux per suam essentiam et non per similitudinem cognoscitur ab oculo, quod expresse dicit S. Thomas in 2. dist. 23. q. 2. art. 1.,[19] ubi distinguit inter modum, quo videtur lux, et quo videtur lapis, dicens, quod lux non videtur ab oculo per aliquam similitudinem sui in ipso relictam, sed per suam essentiam oculum informans; lapis autem videtur per similitudinem relictam in oculo. Et idem significat 1. p. q. 56. art. 3. Idem etiam dici solet de specie impressa, quod seipsa iam est cognoscibilis, ergo a

[14] Cf. Question 1 above, esp. 290/27-292/38.
[15] 326/35-327/2.
[16] 324/1-4.
[17] *Pa* VI. 94 b.
[18] De natura verbi intellectus (*Pa* XVI. 181 a).
[19] *Pa* VI. 587 a.

therefore a concept (an expressed specifying form), which is more in act than is an impressed specifier.

The response to the principal argument[20] is that the power is borne to the object and to the act by the same act, according as the act is the ground of the knowing, but not according as it is a thing known; for in this mode of being the act needs a reflexive concept. It is in this way that St. Thomas is understood in the text cited by the counterargument: he is speaking about the act of understanding according as it is attained as the ground of knowing the direct object; for it is in this way that the act of understanding is attained by the same act as its object is attained. And the same is true of the concept or word; for the concept and the thing represented are understood by the same act, according as the word is taken as the rationale expressing the object on the side of the terminus. For this reason too the word itself is sometimes said to be known as that which is apprehended when an object is cognized, i.e., because it is known as being on the side of the terminus which is apprehended, and not as being on the side of the principle or as that by which a thing is known.

To the confirmation[21] we answer from St. Thomas's *Disputed Questions on Truth*, q. 10, art. 8, in the reply to obj. 4,[22] and from Cajetan's *Commentary on the Summa theologica*, I, q. 87, art. 3, that the word or concept is present to our understanding formally, but not objectively; for it is the inhering form by which an object is known, yet it is not in itself an object endowed with that intelligibility which is required for our understanding, namely, intelligibility in the mode of a sensible essence, and for that reason a concept is neither understandable nor understood in act by means of itself in respect of our understanding. But in the case of separated substances a concept is of itself understandable formally *and* objectively, because separated substances do not understand only a sensible essence, but whatever is purely spiritual.

And to that which is added about light,[23] we answer from St. Thomas's *Disputed Questions on Truth*, q. 10, art. 8, in the reply given to obj. 10 of the second series of objections,[24] that light is not seen through its essence, except inasmuch as it is a rationale or ground of visibility and a kind of form giving visible being in act. But light according as it is in the sun itself

fortiori conceptus, qui est magis in actu quam species impressa.

Respondetur ad principale argumentum,[20] quod eodem actu fertur potentia in obiectum et in actum, secundum quod actus est ratio cognoscendi, non vero secundum quod est res cognita; sic enim indiget conceptu reflexo. Et sic intelligitur D. Thomas in loco cit. ab argumento, quod loquitur de actu intelligendi, secundum quod attingitur ut ratio cognoscendi obiectum directum; sic enim attingitur eodem actu cum suo obiecto. Et idem est de conceptu seu verbo; intelligitur enim conceptus et res repraesentata eodem actu, secundum quod sumitur verbum ut ratio exprimens obiectum ex parte termini. Qua ratione etiam aliquando dicitur ipsum verbum cognosci ut quod, quando cognoscitur obiectum, id est quia cognoscitur ut tenens se ex parte termini quod, et non ut tenens se ex parte principii seu ut id, quo res cognoscitur.

Ad confirmationem[21] respondetur ex D. Thoma q. 10. de Veritate art. 8. ad 4. secundo loco positum[22] et ex Caietano 1. p. q. 87. art. 3., quod verbum seu conceptus est praesens nostro intellectui formaliter, sed non obiective; est enim forma inhaerens, qua obiectum cognoscitur, non tamen in se est obiectum ea intelligibilitate praeditum, quae requiritur ad intellectum nostrum, scilicet per modum quidditatis sensibilis, et ideo nec est intelligibile nec intellectum in actu per seipsum respectu nostri intellectus. In substantiis autem separatis per seipsum conceptus est intelligibilis formaliter et obiective, quia non intelligunt solum quidditatem sensibilem, sed quodcumque pure spirituale.

Et ad id, quod additur de luce,[23] respondetur ex D. Thoma q. 10. de Veritate art. 8. ad 10. secundo loco positum,[24] quod lux non videtur per essentiam suam, nisi quatenus est ratio visibilitatis et forma quaedam dans esse actu visibile. Lux autem prout est

[20] 330/14-22.
[21] 330/23-331/2.
[22] *Pa* IX. 170 b.
[23] 330/27-45.
[24] *Pa* IX. 171 a.

is not seen except through its similitude in the eye, just as a stone is seen. When therefore St. Thomas says in Book II, dist. 23, q. 2, art. 1, of his *Commentary on the Sentences of Peter Lombard*, that light is seen through its essence, the sense of the statement is that light is the form of visibility through its essence, and precisely as it is such a form giving actual visibility to color, it is not seen by means of a similitude distinct from that which the very color-made-visible emits. But of the impressed specifying form[25] we say that it is knowable through itself as "that by which," but not as "that which" and as a thing known; for in this mode of being [i.e., as a known object] the impressed specifier needs a reflexive concept.

It is argued secondly[26] on the grounds that a spiritual thing — God and pure spirits and whatever is not a material essence — cannot be attained by the [human] understanding, except by taking on the mode of a sensible object, and yet they are not known by a reflexive cognition. Therefore neither our concepts nor our acts are understood reflexively as a consequence of the fact that they are known after the manner of a sensible object. For if they were known as they are in themselves, they would be known directly in the way in which pure spirits know them.

And this is confirmed, because reflexive and direct concepts are formed through distinct forms of specification, since indeed the one is a specifier representing a concept, the other an object, [so reflexive and direct concepts must be different,] just as the [represented] things themselves are also different. Therefore they are not related as a reflexive and a direct movement; for a reflexive movement must necessarily be continuous with a direct movement and arise from the same principle. For if distinct movements proceed from distinct principles, the one is not reflexive in respect of the other.

The response to this[27] is that for the rationale of a reflexive concept it does not suffice to know something on the pattern of another, but it is necessary that that which is known should keep on the side of a principle of knowing. For it is in this way that the regression from the object to the cognition or the principle of the cognition comes about. But when some mind-independent object is clothed [through the construction of our understanding] in the guise of another object, there will be there an order or comparison of the one to the other, but not a reflexion.

To the confirmation[28] the response is that whether or not the concept is known by means of specifiers distinct

in ipso sole, non videtur nisi per similitudinem eius in oculo, sicut videtur lapis. Quando ergo Divus Thomas dicit in 2. Sentent. videri lucem per essentiam suam, sensus est, quod est forma visibilitatis per essentiam suam, et prout talis forma dans esse actu visibile colori, non videtur per similitudinem distinctam ab ea, quam emittit ipse color factus visibilis. De specie autem impressa[25] dicimus, quod est cognoscibilis per seipsam ut quo, non autem ut quod et ut res cognita; sic enim indiget conceptu reflexo.

Secundo arguitur,[26] quia res spiritualis, Deus et angeli et quidquid non est quidditas materialis, non potest attingi ab intellectu, nisi induendo modum obiecti sensibilis, et tamen non cognoscuntur cognitione reflexa. Ergo neque conceptus neque actus nostri intelliguntur reflexe ex eo, quod cognoscuntur ad modum obiecti sensibilis. Si enim cognoscerentur ut sunt in se, cognoscerentur directe eo modo, quo angeli illos cognoscunt.

Et confirmatur, quia conceptus reflexus et directus formantur per distinctas species, siquidem alia species est repraesentans conceptum, alia obiectum, sicut et ipsae res diversae sunt. Ergo non se habent sicut motus reflexus et directus; motus enim reflexus necessario debet continuari cum directo et provenire ab eodem principio. Si enim a distinctis principiis procedant distincti motus, non est unus reflexus respectu alterius.

Respondetur,[27] quod ad rationem conceptus reflexi non sufficit cognoscere aliquid ad instar alterius, sed oportet, quod illud, quod cognoscitur, se teneat ex parte principii cognoscentis. Sic enim fit ab obiecto regressio ad cognitionem vel principium cognitionis. Quando autem aliquod obiectum ad extra induit modum alterius obiecti, erit ibi ordo vel comparatio unius ad alterum, sed non reflexio.

Ad confirmationem[28] respondetur, quod sive conceptus cognoscatur per spe-

[25] 330/43-331/2.
[26] "against our resolution [326/35-327/2] of the first difficulty [324/1-4] . . ."
[27] to 332/14-24.
[28] 332/25-35.

from the specifiers of the object,[29] it is nevertheless said to be known reflexively, because such a movement of cognition has its origin from the object, and from the cognition of the object one is moved to forming a cognition of the concept and of the specifiers by which the object is known. Whence this distinction of the principles[30] does not remove the reflexion [i.e., the reflexive character] of the cognition, but the more conduces to it, because the very principles themselves of the knowing, that is, the specifiers, are formed by that reflexive movement continuous with and derived from the cognition of the object.

cies distinctas a speciebus obiecti, sive non,[29] tamen dicitur cognosci reflexe, quia talis motus cognitionis originem habet ab obiecto, et ab eius cognitione movetur aliquis ad formandam cognitionem conceptus et specierum, quibus cognoscitur. Unde ista discinctio principiorum[30] non tollit reflexionem cognitionis, sed magis conducit, cum ipsamet principia cognoscendi seu species formentur motu illo reflexo continuato et deducto ex congitione obiecti.

[29] cf. 328/9-15.
[30] 332/33-35.

Question 4

What Sort of Distinction Is There between an Ultimate (or "Final") and a Non-Ultimate (or "Preliminary") Concept

Quaestio Quarta

Qualis Sit Distinctio inter Conceptum Ultimatum et Non Ultimatum

The ultimate and the non-ultimate are expressed respectively, as end and means. And so generally any concept whatever can be said to be ultimate, which stands as the terminus and end of another, so that the one concept is ordered to the other; and it is thus that one operation of the understanding is ordered to another operation, that principles are ordered to conclusions, and discursive reasoning to perfect evaluation or judgment. In whatever examples from the line of apprehension, something is found on which the cognition stands, and this is called ultimate; and something else is found through which the cognition is borne toward that final term, and this is called the medium, i.e., the means or non-ultimate term.

Among dialecticians, who deal with names and significative speech, the ultimate and non-ultimate concepts are distinguished through this, that an ultimate concept is engaged with the things signified, whereas a non-ultimate concept is engaged with the very expressions or words signifying. For this way of distinguishing the ultimate and non-ultimate concepts provides an easy way of discerning the object of Logic, because the dialectician does not treat of things themselves as they are things (the way the natural philosopher treats of them), but of the instruments by which things are known, such as most often are significative voices as rightly arranged and ordered.

From the distinction expressed in these terms, it follows that ultimate and non-ultimate are of themselves and formally not essential differences of concepts, because

Ultimatum et non ultimatum dicuntur respective, sicut finis et medium. Et ita generaliter potest dici ultimatus conceptus, quicumque est terminus et finis alterius, ita quod unus ordinatur ad alium; et sic una operatio intellectus ordinatur ad aliam, et principia ordinantur ad conclusiones, et discursus ad iudicium perfectum, et in omnibus istis invenitur aliquid, in quo sistit cognitio, et hoc vocatur ultimum, et aliud, per quod tenditur ad talem terminum, et hoc vocatur medium seu non ultimum.

Ceterum quoad dialecticos, qui agunt de nominibus et vocibus significativis, distinguitur conceptus ultimatus et non ultimatus per hoc, quod ultimatus versatur circa res significatas, non ultimatus autem circa ipsas voces significantes. Hoc enim conducit ad discernendum obiectum Logicae, quia non agit de rebus ipsis, ut res sunt, sicut agit physicus, sed agit de instrumentis, quibus res cognoscuntur, qualia plerumque sunt voces significativae, ut recte dispositae et ordinatae.

Ex quo deducitur, quod ultimatum et non ultimatum per se et formaliter non sunt differentiae essentiales conceptuum, quia non tenent se ex parte ipsius obiecti, ut dicit rationem cognoscibilem, sed tenent se ex

they do not obtain on the side of the very object as expressing the knowable rationale, but they obtain rather on the side of the order of one concept or cognition to another, and so only add to a concept relations or conditions of ''being-toward'' objects, not inasmuch as the objects are knowable and specifying, but inasmuch as they are ordered as means and end. But an essential difference in cognition derives from the object as stimulus and specificative and knowable; all other differences are accompanying relative conditions or connotations. And yet presuppositively, it sometimes happens that these accompanying conditions of being-toward suppose a distinction of objects, even though they do not formally constitute that distinction, and it is in this way that the ultimate and non-ultimate, of which we are speaking in the present context, are exercised between distinct concepts, of which one is engaged with the thing signified, the other with the expression or voice signifying. By this function, because the ultimate concepts and the non-ultimate concepts have different objects with which they are engaged, they are distinct concepts presuppositively, not formally by virtue of being ultimate and non-ultimate.

And it cannot be said that the concept of a significative voice signifies by stipulation the object of the ultimate concept, as some authors teach, not on the grounds that the non-ultimate concept itself is stipulatively established for signifying, but because its object, namely, the expression or voice, signifies a thing by stipulation. But this is impossible, because a concept is the natural similitude of an object in such a way that it does not in any way derive from the object a voluntaristically determined signification, but that very signification of the voice which is stipulated (i.e., voluntaristically determined) the non-ultimate concept itself signifies naturally, to wit, as an image of that [voluntaristically determined] signification; and thus the willfully determined signification of an expresion (or voice) is not the exercise of the signifying of a [non-ultimate] concept [of that voice], but an object signified by [the non-ultimate] concept.

There remains room for doubt in this context of discussion, therefore, whether a non-ultimate concept of a linguistic expression represents only the expression itself, but not its signification, or whether such a concept represents both the expression and its signification.

And almost all agree that some order to the signification is required in order for a concept to have for its object a stipulated sign, i.e., in order for a concept to be non-ultimate. For if the expression voiced is nudely considered as a certain sound made by an animal, it must needs pertain to a concept of a thing signified as an object simply, i.e., to an ultimate concept, because in this way it is con-

parte ordinis unius conceptus seu cognitionis ad aliam, et sic in conceptu solum addunt relationes seu habitudines ad obiecta, non quatenus cognoscibilia et specificantia, sed ut ordinata tamquam medium et terminus. Essentialis autem differentia cognitionis sumitur ex obiecto, ut motivo et specificativo et cognoscibili, reliqua omnia sunt habitudines vel connotationes consecutae. Et tamen praesuppositive aliquando istae habitudines supponunt distinctionem obiectorum, licet formaliter non constituant illam, et sic ultimatum et non ultimatum, de quo in praesenti, exercentur inter distinctos conceptus, quorum unus versatur circa rem significatam, alius circa vocem significantem, et ex hac parte, quia habent diversa obiecta, circa quae versantur, sunt distincti conceptus praesuppositive, non formaliter ex vi ultimati et non ultimati.

Et non potest dici, quod conceptus vocis significativae significat ad placitum obiectum conceptus ultimati, ut aliqui auctores docent, non quia ipse conceptus sit impositus ad significandum, sed quia obiectum eius, scilicet vox, ex impositione rem significat. Sed hoc est impossibile, quia conceptus ita est naturalis similitudo obiecti, quod nullo modo ex obiecto haurit significationem ad placitum, sed illam ipsam significationem vocis, quae ad placitum est, ipse conceptus naturaliter significat, scilicet ut imago illius, et ita significatio vocis ad placitum non est exercitium significandi conceptus, sed obiectum a conceptu significatum.

RESTAT ERGO IN PRAESENTI DUBIUM, an conceptus non ultimatus vocis solum repraesentet ipsam vocem, non vero significationem eius, an vero utrumque.

Et fere omnes conveniunt requiri aliquem ordinem ad significationem, ut conceptus sit non ultimatus. Nam si vox nude consideretur ut quidam sonus est ab animali factus, constat pertinere ad conceptum ultimatum, quia sic

sidered as it is a kind of thing, i.e., in just the way Philosophy treats of that sound.

Yet there are some who say that it is not necessary for the signification of the expression to be represented in a non-ultimate concept (a concept of the spoken word as a stipulated sign), but it suffices for that signification to be exercised or for it to be supposed to be habitually known.

But the more common opinion is the truer one in holding that **the signification itself must also be represented in the non-ultimate concept itself,** because it is said to be non-ultimate insofar as something is conceived in which the cognition does not cease, but which is understood as a means to a further terminus. But only the signification of a voice constitutes that voice in the rationale of a means in respect of a thing signified. Therefore if the signification is not conceived, neither is that conceived through which an expression is constituted in the rationale of a means, that is to say, of something non-ultimate. Nor is it enough to say that the signification in question is exercised, because the case is rather that the voice as represented in a non-ultimate concept does not exercise its stipulated signification.[1] For all that is exercised in that concept is of natural signification; therefore the stipulated signification of the conceived voice is not exercised, but represented, although it is not necessary to attain to the very essence of the stipulated signification and the relation of the imposition, but it suffices to know the signification as regards the fact that it exists. Much less does an habitual awareness of the signification or imposition (stipulation) suffice for an non-ultimate concept, because an habitual awareness is an awareness only in first act; therefore, unless and until that awareness issues forth in second act, it cannot be said to be a concept actually non-ultimate [i.e., an actual concept of a sign], because an actual concept is a representation. Therefore an actual non-ultimate concept cannot be denominated from an habitual awareness of a signification.

But you may object: Surely a peasant, hearing this Latin expression "animal," but without knowing its signification, forms a non-ultimate concept of that utterance, because he does not pass on to the thing signified, and yet he is ignorant of the signification. Therefore a representation of signification is not required for a non-ultimate concept [i.e., for a concept whose object is a stipulated sign as such.].

consideratur, ut quaedam res est, sicut de illo agit Philosophia.

Sed aliqui dicunt non esse necesse, quod significatio vocis repraesentetur in conceptu non ultimato, sed sufficere, quod exerceatur vel quod habitualiter cognita supponatur.

Ceterum verius est, quod etiam ipsa significatio repraesentari debeat in ipso conceptu non ultimato, quia in tantum dicitur non ultimatus, in quantum concipitur aliquid, in quo ultimo non sistitur, sed sumitur ut medium ad ulteriorem terminum. Solum autem significatio vocis constituit illam in ratione medii respectu rei significatae. Ergo si significatio non concipitur, neque concipitur id, per quod constituitur in ratione medii seu non ultimati. Nec sufficit dicere, quod exercetur significatio, quia potius vox prout ibi repraesentata non exercet suam significationem ad placitum.[1] Totum vero, quod exercetur in illo conceptu naturalis significationis est; ergo significatio ad placitum vocis conceptae non exercetur, sed repraesentatur, licet non sit necesse attingere ipsam essentiam significationis ad placitum et relationem impositionis, sed sufficit cognoscere significationem quoad an est. Multo minus sufficit habitualis notitia significationis sive impositionis, quia habitualis notitia solum est notitia in actu primo; ergo nisi illa exeat in actum secundum, non potest dici conceptus actu non ultimatus, quia conceptus actualis repraesentatio est. Ergo ex habituali notitia significationis non potest denominari actualis conceptus non ultimatus.

Sed obicies: Nam rusticus audiens hanc vocem latinam ,, animal'', cuius significationem ignorat, format conceptum illius vocis non ultimatum, quia non transit ad rem significatam, et tamen ignorat significationem. Ergo non requiritur ad conceptum non ultimatum repraesentatio significationis.

---

[1] The 1663 Lyons text here adds: "*sed cognoscitur de illa, quod significativa sit ad placitum*"—"but it is known of it that it is significative in a manner involving stipulation"—stipulation: i.e., the critically controlled element of non-being which in this case the mind-dependent sign relation constitutes when it is apprehended as such and comparatively to the order of mind-independent being.

This objection is confirmed by the fact that a concept signifies the same thing for all, as the Philosopher says in the first Book of the treatise *On Interpretation*, chap. 1.[2] But the significations of voices are not the same for all; therefore non-ultimate concepts do not represent the significations of voices, otherwise they would not signify the same thing for all.

The response to this[3] is that the peasant hearing the Latin expression either knows it to be significative at least as regards the fact, because he sees men using that expression in discourse, even though he does not see what it is that the expression signifies; or else he is in no way aware that the expression is significative. If he apprehends the voice in the first way, i.e., as an element of discourse, he forms a non-ultimate concept, because he truly knows the voice as significative. If in the second way, i.e., if he is totally unaware that the sound is an element of discourse, the concept he forms of it will be an ultimate concept [that is, a concept whose object as it is being apprehended fails to represent anything besides itself], because it only represents the expression or voice as it is a certain sound, not as a sign and a means leading to another. But when he perceives the signification as regards the fact of its being, yet without knowing to what end that signification is intended, the concept in such a case is called non-ultimate, because even though it does not in fact lead to the thing signified as to the ultimate thing in particular, it nevertheless does lead to a thing signified at least in general and in a confusion arising from the deficiency of the subject ignorant of the signification.[4]

To the confirmation[5] we say that concepts signify the same thing for all when they are about the same object and have been formed in the same way; for they are natural similitudes. Thus all non-ultimate concepts representing expressions (or voices) inasmuch as they are significative represent the same thing for all those among whom they are so formed. But if they are not so formed among all hearing them, owing to the fact that not all know the signification of the voices, then the concepts of the voices were not concepts of the same thing, and so will not signify the same thing for all.

It is argued secondly: if a non-ultimate concept (a concept whose object is also a sign) represents the very signification of an expression or voice, then it follows that when a concept represents an equivocal term, either

Et confirmatur, quia conceptus significant idem apud omnes, ut dicit Philosophus 1. Periherm. cap. 1.[2] Sed significationes vocum non sunt eaedem apud omnes; ergo conceptus non ultimati non repraesentant significationes vocum, alias non significarent idem apud omnes.

RESPONDETUR,[3] quod rusticus audiens illam vocem, vel cognoscit esse significativam saltem quoad an est, quia videt homines loqui illa voce, licet ignoret eius significatum, vel nullo modo cognoscit esse significativam. Si primo modo, format conceptum non ultimatum, quia vere cognoscit vocem ut significativam. Si secundo modo, erit conceptus ultimatus, quia solum repraesentat vocem ut quidam sonus est, non ut signum et medium ducens ad aliud. Quando autem percipit significationem quoad an est, nondum tamen cognoscit, ad quid sit imposita illa significatio, talis conceptus dicitur non ultimatus, quia licet de facto non deducat ad rem significatam tamquam ad ultimum in particulari, deducit tamen saltem in communi et in confuso ex defectu subiecti ignorantis significationem.[4]

Ad confirmationem[5] dicitur, quod conceptus significant idem apud omnes, quando sunt circa idem obiectum et eodem modo formati; sunt enim naturales similitudines. Et ita omnes conceptus non ultimati repraesentantes voces quatenus significativas, idem repraesentant apud omnes, apud quos sic formantur. Si autem non sic formantur apud omnes, quia non omnes cognoscunt significationem vocis, sic non erunt iidem conceptus, et sic non significabunt idem apud omnes.

Secundo arguitur: Si conceptus non ultimatus repraesentat ipsam significationem vocis, ergo quando repraesentat

---

[2] 16 a 6.

[3] to 336/38-45.

[4] The Lyons text of 1663 adds here: "*non ex defectu conceptus repraesentantis rem ut de se ductivam ad aliud*"—"not from a deficiency of the concept representing a thing in a way of itself conductive toward another."

[5] 337/1-7.

several concepts are formed of that expression, or only one. If only one, there will be an equivocation in the mind, because the non-ultimate concept signifies the expression with several significations not subordinated. If there are several concepts formed, it follows that there is not in the mind a concept of an equivocal term, because one voice is never represented with several significations, and therefore an equivocal term will not admit of a vocal expression, because the mouth cannot utter save what is conceived by the mind; but in that case, some equivocal term is not conceived, because several concepts are formed of the expression or term in question, each of which concepts has only one signification, and so will be univocal.

The response is that a concept of an equivocal term, as, for example, of ''dog,'' is only one non-ultimate concept, because it represents one expression or voice having several significations, just as a concept which represents a man having several characteristics is one concept; nor does it follow from this that there is an equivocation in that concept, because these several significations are not in the concept formally, but objectively. For the concept in question represents an object which has several significations, namely, the expression or voice in question, but it does so by a single natural similitude representing a single expression affected by several impositions [i.e., by a diversity of accepted stipulated usages]. An equivocation in the mind, however, would follow only when the one concept would have several formal significations, which are natural similitudes; for these cannot be multiplied in one concept. But the fact that one concept should represent the several significations of the one expression or sign as a represented thing is nothing antinomic, because it comes about by a single formal representation.

You will press the point: That non-ultimate concept of the equivocal term is ordered to several ultimate concepts, because it is ordered to several significates, and not by a single ordination, but by several, each of which pertains to the representation of the non-ultimate concept. Therefore, just as there is an equivocation in the expression because of several significations relative to several significates, so the concept of that expression should be called equivocal on account of having several relations to several final concepts.

The response to this is that that non-ultimate concept is ordered to several ultimate ones by one single or-

terminum aequivocum, vel formantur plures conceptus de illa voce vel tantum unus. Si tantum unus, dabitur aequivocatio in mente, quia significat vocem cum pluribus significationibus non subordinatis. Si sunt plures conceptus, sequitur, quod non datur in mente conceptus hominis aequivoci, quia numquam repraesentatur una vox cum pluribus significationibus, atque adeo neque poterit ore proferri, quia non profertur ore, nisi quod concipitur mente; tunc autem non concipitur aliquis terminus aequivocus, quia formantur plures conceptus illius vocis, quorum quilibet habet tantum unam significationem, et ita quilibet erit univocus.

RESPONDETUR conceptum termini aequivoci, v. g. canis, esse tantum unum conceptum non ultimatum, quia repraesentat unam vocem habentem plures significationes, sicut qui repraesentat hominem habentem plura accidentia; nec ex hoc sequitur aequivocatio in illo conceptu, quia illae plures significationes non sunt formaliter in conceptu, sed obiective. Repraesentat enim obiectum, quod habet plures significationes, scilicet vocem illam, sed unica naturali similitudine repraesentante unicam vocem pluribus impositionibus affectam. Aequivocatio autem in mente tunc solum sequeretur, quando unus conceptus haberet plures significationes formales, quae sunt naturales similitudines; has enim repugnat multiplicari in uno conceptu. Quod vero unus conceptus repraesentet plures significationes unius vocis seu signi tamquam rem repraesentatam, nullum inconveniens est, quia unica repraesentatione formali id fit.

Instabis: Ille conceptus non ultimatus termini aequivoci ordinatur ad plures ultimatos, quia ordinatur ad plura significata, et non unica ordinatione, sed pluribus, quae pertinent ad repraesentationem conceptus. Ergo sicut in voce datur aequivocatio propter habitudinem plurium significationum ad plura significata, ita ille conceptus dicetur aequivocus propter plures habitudines ad plures conceptus ultimatos.

Respondetur conceptum illum non ultimatum ordinari ad plures ultimatos unica

dination on the part of the formal representation, but by several ordinations on the part of the object represented. For it represents by a single signification and natural representation an expression ordered to several things signified as the result of several impositions, and thus on the side of its object it represents the several relations belonging to the one expression coinciding with several things and several ultimate concepts, and so the non-ultimate concept in question expresses several relations as represented; but formally it has a single representation of that voice or expression so affected by several relationships.

Lastly it is argued that a non-ultimate concept need not represent the fact of an expression's being significative, because the same non-ultimate concept of a voice, by the mere fact that that voice is cut off from its signification [by falling out of use], will continue as an ultimate concept, because it will [then] signify that voice as a thing in which cognition ultimately rests. Therefore a non-ultimate concept is not distinguished essentially from an ultimate concept, since indeed without any intrinsic change it can be rendered ultimate. Nor can it be said that, because it represents itself, the expression or voice in question will have the capacity of a terminus in respect of itself; for thus any thing whatever representing itself would have a non-ultimate concept, inasmuch as it represents itself.

The response to this is that these concepts do not differ essentially owing precisely to the fact that the one is ultimate while the other is non-ultimate, as has been shown, but owing to the fact that they are presupposed to be of diverse objects, from which the essential difference is derived. Whence in the case of an expression's being deprived of its significance,[6] if the understanding knows that fact and forms a concept of the expression as not signifying, that concept is already distinct from the non-ultimate one which was previously formed of that voice as significative, because it will thus be an ultimate concept of the expression as of a thing, not as of a sign. But if the understanding is unaware that the expression has lost its significance and maintains the concept previously formed of that voice as of a significative sound, that concept remains non-ultimate just as before, although false, and so it will be changed as regards the truth-value, not as regards the essential representation.

And note that the relations of ultimate and non-ultimate, even though they may be distinguished in kind as diverse modes of concepts, nevertheless do not function as specifying the very concepts formally. And so they

ordinatione ex parte repraesentationis formalis, pluribus autem ex parte obiecti repraesentati. Repraesentat enim unica significatione et repraesentatione naturali vocem ordinatam ad plures res significatas per plures impositiones, et ita ex parte sui obiecti plures habitudines repraesentat voci uni convenientes ad plures res et plures conceptus ultimatos, sicque dicit plures habitudines ille conceptus ut repraesentatas; formaliter autem unicam habet repraesentationem illius vocis sic affectae pluribus habitudinibus.

Ultimo arguitur, quia idem conceptus vocis, qui est non ultimatus, per hoc solum, quod vox deponatur a sua significatione, manebit ultimatus, quia significabit illam vocem ut rem, in qua ultimo sistitur. Ergo non distinguitur essentialiter a conceptu ultimato, siquidem sine ulla mutatione intrinseca potest reddi ultimatus. Nec potest dici, quod illa vox habebit vicem termini respectu sui, quia repraesentat se; sic enim quaecumque res se repraesentans haberet conceptum non ultimatum, quatenus seipsam repraesentat.

Respondetur, quod illi conceptus non differunt essentialiter ex eo praecise, quod unus est ultimatus, alter non ultimatus, ut ostensum est, sed ex eo, quod praesupponuntur esse de diversis obiectis, ex quibus essentialis diversitas sumitur. Unde in casu, quo vox deponeretur a sua significatione,[6] si intellectus id cognoscit et format conceptum vocis ut non significantis, iam ille conceptus est distinctus a non ultimato, quem antea formabat de illa voce ut significativa, quia sic erit conceptus ultimatus vocis ut rei, non ut signi. Si autem nescit esse depositam a sua significatione et continuat conceptum antea formatum de ipsa tamquam de significativa, conceptus ille manet non ultimatus sicut antea, licet falsus, et sic mutabitur quoad falsitatem, non quoad essentialem repraesentationem.

Et adverte, quod relationes ultimati et non ultimati, licet specie distinguantur tamquam diversi modi conceptuum, non tamen se habent tamquam specificantes ipsos

[6] 339/16-17.

cause *the modes themselves* to be distinguished in kind (specifically), but *not the intrinsic rationale itself of the concepts*, unless because the concepts, on other grounds, have objects specifically distinct.

conceptus formaliter. Et sic faciunt distingui specifice ipsos modos, non autem ipsam rationem intrinsecam conceptuum, nisi quia alias habent obiecta specie distincta.

APPENDICES

APPENDIX A

Ad Tractatum de Signis:

Exhibens Relationes Quae Se Habent inter Voces, Conceptus, et Obiecta*

APPENDIX A

To the Treatise on Signs:

On the Relations between Words, Ideas, and Objects*

* In the original Latin: Logica 1. p. q. 1. "*De Termino,*" art. 5, "*Utrum Voces Significent per prius Conceptus an Res*"—"Concerning the Term," art. 5, "Whether Vocal Expressions Primarily Signify Concepts or Things."

Appendix A

Whether Vocal Expressions primarily Signify Concepts or Things

We suppose as granted by all that vocal expressions signify formal concepts as much as objective ones, since this is clearly established by the Philosopher in chap. 1, Book I, of his treatise *On Interpretation.*[1] And the fact is manifestly attested to by experience. For when we wish to manifest not only *what* we conceive, but also that *which* we conceive, we do so through the sounds by which we speak. See St. Thomas's *Commentary* on the treatise *On Interpretation*, Book I, reading 2,[2] and his *Disputed Questions on Power*, q. 9, art. 5, where he says that "a spoken word signifies a concept of the understanding, by means of which concept it signifies a thing."[3] In this passage St. Thomas clearly distinguishes between the formal and the objective concept and associates the linguistic sound with both. Again, in his *Summa contra gentiles*, Book IV, chap. 11, he says that "the understood intention is a conceived similitude, which spoken sounds signify."

There can be difficulty therefore on two points: First, do vocal expressions signify concepts and things by the same signification? Second, which of the two do they signify more principally, things or concepts? And the same can be asked of written signs in respect of vocal expressions.

As to the first point of difficulty, some hold that vocal expressions signify things and concepts by a double signi-

Appendix A

Utrum Voces Significent per prius Conceptus an Res

Supponimus tamquam apud omnes certum voces significare conceptus tam formales quam obiectivos, cum id sit aperte statutum a Philosopho in 1. Periherm. cap. 1.[1] Et manifeste attestatur experientia. Cum enim volumus manifestare, non solum *quid* concipiamus, sed etiam *quod* concipimus, id facimus per voces, quibus loquimur. Videatur D. Thomas 1. Periherm. lect. 2.[2] et q. 9. de Potentia art. 5., ubi inquit, «quod vox significat conceptum intellectus, quo mediante significat rem».[3] Ubi aperte distinguit inter conceptum formalem et obiectivum et utrumque attribuit voci. Et in 4. Contra Gent. cap. 11. dicit, «quod intentio intellecta est similitudo concepta, quam voces exteriores significant».

Difficultas ergo potest esse in duobus: *Primum,* an voces eadem significatione significent conceptus et res; *secundum,* quidnam significent principalius, res an conceptus. Et idem potest inquiri de scriptura respectu vocum.

Circa primum aliqui tenent voces significare res et conceptus duplici significa-

---

[1] 16 a 3 - 8.
[2] *Le* I. 11-14.
[3] *Pa* VIII. 186 a.

fication, and they cite Dominic Soto in support of this opinion, but the citation is unwarranted, for Master Soto did not say that a name signifies things and concepts by a double signification, but that the "actual signifying of a name is taken in two ways," either for moving the mind or for expressing a concept; but nevertheless both functions can belong to the same signification.

I say therefore: **Vocal expressions signify things and concepts by one single signification.**

The FOUNDATION FOR THIS statement is that vocal expressions signify both thing and concept by the same imposition, and therefore also by the same signification.

And second, because vocal expressions signify things and concepts not equally immediately, and one separately from the other, but the one by means of the other and as subordinated to the other; therefore the same signification suffices for both.

The consequence is clear from the fact that where several things are subordinated, they are signified by the same signification, just as the name "man," for example, signifies not only human nature, but also the individuals for which it stands, by the same signification. The antecedent is established, first, from St. Thomas's observation in the *Summa theologica*, I, q. 13, art. 1, and in the *Disputed Questions on the Power of God*, q. 9, art. 5, where he says that vocal expressions immediately signify conceptions of the mind and things by means of these conceptions.[4] (The same can be found in his *Commentary* on Aristotle's treatise *On Interpretation*, Book I, reading 2.[5]) Then too, if a spoken expression signified things and concepts by significations so diverse that they were not subordinated relative to one another, every name would be equivocal, and an expression could be deposed from one of the two significations while the other remains, and so it would signify the concept and not the thing, or conversely, which would be absurd.

Notice, however, that the concept itself can be signified in two ways. First as it is in itself a sort of thing explicitly signified and knowable reflexively by means of another concept. And when the concept is referred to in this way it is signified by a special name stipulated for the purpose, such as "concept"; for it is signified in the same way as other things are. In a second way concepts are signified as a kind of interior sign or means of conceiving things, from which interior signs are derived these exterior signs [words and writing or gestures] by which the interior signs are manifested; and in this way con-

tione citantque pro hac sententia Mag. Soto, sed immerito, cum ipse non dixerit, quod nomen significat res et conceptus duplici significatione, sed quod ipsum «significare nominis bifariam accipitur», vel pro movere potentiam vel pro exprimere conceptus; sed tamen utrumque munus convenire potest eidem significationi.

DICO ERGO: **Voces unica significatione significant res et conceptus.**

FUNDAMENTUM est, quia significant utrumque eadem impositione, ergo eadem significatione.

Et secundo, quia significant res et conceptus non aeque immediate, et unum seorsum ab alio, sed unum mediante alio et ut subordinatum alteri; ergo sufficit eadem significatio ad utrumque.

Consequens patet, quia ubi sunt plura subordinata, significantur eadem significatione; sicut nomen homo v. g. non solum significat naturam humanam, sed etiam individua, pro quibus supponit, eadem significatione. *Antecedens* vero constat *tum* ex D. Thoma 1. p. q. 13. art. 1. et q. 9. de Potentia art. 5., ubi dicit, quod voces immediate significant conceptiones mentis et illis mediantibus res[4]. Et idem habet in 1. Periherm. lect. 2.[5] *Tum* etiam, quia si vox diversis significationibus significaret res et conceptus, ita quod non subordinarentur inter se, omne nomen esset aequivocum, et non repugnaret deponi ab una significatione ex illis altera remanente, sicque significaret conceptum et non rem, vel e converso, quod esset absurdum.

Adverte autem, quod ipse conceptus potest significari dupliciter. *Primo* ut in se res quaedam est in actu signato et ut cognoscibilis alio conceptu reflexe. Et hoc modo conceptus significatur speciali nomine ad hoc imposito, ut hoc nomine „conceptus"; significatur enim sicut aliae res. *Alio modo* conceptus significantur tamquam interiora quaedam signa seu media concipiendi res, a quibus haec exteriora signa derivantur, quibus interiora manifestantur; et sic significantur con-

[4] ibid.
[5] *Le* I. 11-14.

cepts are signified by outward expressions as exercising this function [of making things known].

But you might object: There is a double imposition, one for signifying things and one for signifying concepts; therefore there is also a double signification.

The consequence is evident, and the antecedent is proved, because men wished first to communicate their thoughts in general; then they looked for a particular way suited to such communication, which was stipulation of sounds. Therefore, there were two separate acts and accordingly two impositions.

And this is confirmed by the fact that vocal expressions signify the things themselves as "that which [is spoken of]" theoretically, i.e., as that which is signified in the transmission of teachings; but concepts are not signified, but indicated. Whence vocal expressions are said to be substituted for concepts, but to signify things.

I answer that this argument[6] is very deficient, first of all, because it would prove the same thing about the signification of the things themselves alone; for men first wished in general, as it were, to signify things, and then sought a way by which they could signify them by means of a stipulation of vocal sounds. Then too, because to wish or to intend to do something and thereafter (by settling on the necessary means for accomplishing it) to carry out the intention, does not induce a double effect, because in respect of the same effect there must be an intention, selection of means, and execution of the intention through the means chosen. Therefore it does not follow that there was a double imposition, just because they willed by the two acts of intending and of executing.

To the confirmation[7] the response is that everything there noted pertains to one single signification, because everything there mentioned is part of a whole signified by a certain order. For the same signification of a vocal expression has a twofold office, namely, to substitute for the things which the expression manifests, and, second, to substitute for the concepts which signify these very things in a hidden and interior way. The whole of this is brought about by one single signification and imposition, because this sensible sign — the outward expression — is imposed for the purpose of manifesting that interior sign — the concept — as ordered to the things thought about; just as, for example, a minister of the king by his very ministry and office substitutes for the king as for the principal in an order to some affairs to be governed as to an end.

ceptus a vocibus ut exercentes hoc munus.

SED OBICIES: Datur duplex impositio ad significandas res et conceptus, ergo duplex significatio.

Consequentia est nota, et antecedens probatur, quia prius voluerunt homines suos conceptus communicare in communi; deinde investigaverunt modum ad talem communicationem accomodatum, qui fuit impositio vocum. Ergo interfuerunt duo actus atque adeo duae impositiones.

Et confirmatur, quia voces significant res ipsas ,,ut quod'' et doctrinaliter, id est tamquam id, quod significatur in tradendis doctrinis; conceptus vero non significantur, sed indicantur. Unde dicuntur voces substitui pro conceptibus, significare vero res.

Respondetur illud argumentum[6] nimis deficere, *tum* quia idem probaret de significatione ipsarum rerum tantum; nam prius voluerunt homines quasi in communi significare res, deinde investigarunt modum, quo ipsas significarent mediante impositione vocum. *Tum* etiam, quia velle seu intendere aliquid facere, et postea eligendo medium, quo faciendum est, illud exsequi, non inducit duplicem effectum, quia respectu eiusdem effectus debet dari intentio et electio et executio. Ergo non sequitur duplicem impositionem fuisse, quia duplici actu voluerunt intendendo et exsequendo.

Ad confirmationem[7] respondetur, quod illa omnia pertinent ad unicam significationem, quia ordine quodam totum hoc significatur. Nam eadem significatio vocis habet duplex officium, scilicet substituere pro rebus, quas manifestat, et secundo substituere pro conceptibus, qui ipsas res occulte et interius significant. Quod totum fit unica significatione et unica impositione, quia istud signum sensibile imponitur ad manifestandum illud signum interius in ordine ad res cogitatas; sicut minister regis eodem ministerio et officio substituitur regi ut principali in ordine ad res aliquas gubernandas ut ad finem.

---

[6] 346/3-11.

[7] 346/12-18.

You may object secondly: An outward expression cannot signify a concept immediately, and a thing mediately; therefore it is falsely said that such an expression signifies a thing by means of a concept, but the expression must signify that thing immediately, and therefore by a different signification [than the signification whereby the expression signifies the concept].

The antecedent is proved: First, because a concept is not a thing signified reflexively, for this is accomplished by means of this name, "concept"; nor is it the formal rationale of signifying, because the imposition is this rationale; nor is it a condition required for signifying on the side of the thing signified, because things are not signified as conceived, but as existing in themselves. Second, because vocal expressions do not signify by means of a concept of the listener or of the speaker nor of the one who first coined the word, therefore they do not signify by means of any concept. Not of the listener, because the listener is not the one who declares his concepts, but the one to whom the concept of another is declared. Not of the speaker, because even if no one is speaking, as, for example, if voices are formed in the air or by someone sleeping, they still signify; and besides, the concept of the speaker is outside of the listener, therefore is not for the listener a means for knowing the thing. Not of the one who first coined the expression, because we do not remember by means of the voice of the inventor of the expression, nor do we know what sort of concept he had in mind at the time. Moreover, the expression can represent the thing to me better than the originator of the expression himself conceived it; therefore the concept of the one imposing—the one who coined the expression—is not the rationale of the representing.

I answer by denying the antecedent.[8] But it must be noted that to signify one thing by means of another can

Secundo obicies: Vox non potest significare conceptum immediate, et rem mediate; ergo falso dicitur, quod mediante conceptu rem significat, sed immediate debet significare illam, atque adeo diversa significatione.

Antecedens probatur: *Primo*, quia conceptus non est res significata reflexe, id enim fit per hoc nomen ,,conceptus''; neque est ratio formalis significandi, quia haec est impositio; neque est conditio requisita ad significandum ex parte rei significatae, quia non significantur res ut conceptae, sed ut existentes in se. *Secundo*, quia voces non significant medio conceptu audientis neque loquentis neque imponentis, ergo nullo. Non audientis, quia ipse audiens non est, qui declarat suos conceptus, sed cui alterius conceptus declaratur. Non loquentis, quia etiamsi nullus sit loquens, ut si voces formentur in aere vel a dormiente, adhuc significant; et praeterea conceptus loquentis est extra audientem, non ergo est illi medium ad cognoscendam rem. Non imponentis, quia non recordamur per vocem ipsius imponentis neque eius conceptum, qualis fuerit, cognoscimus. Imo potest vox melius mihi repraesentare rem, quam imponens ipse conceperit; ergo conceptus imponentis non est ratio repraesentandi.

Respondetur negando antecedens.[8] Sed est advertendum, quod sig-

---

[8] 347/1-3. The 1663 Lyons text here (based on the 1648 Madrid edition—see "Editorial Afterword," note 78, p. 448 below) reads (Reiser ed., vol. I, 213a35-b19): "*Respondetur: negatur antecedens* [347/1-3]. *Ad probationem conceditur antecedens, quia non omnia adaequate ibi numerantur. Et distinguitur consequens* [347/3-6]: *Ergo vox non significat rem mediante conceptu tamquam ratione formali aut tamquam primario et immediato significato, conceditur consequens; ratio enim formalis significandi in voce est impositio, et in conceptu est similitudo. Mediante conceptu ut principali significante, cuius vox est substitutum et quasi instrumentum, negatur consequens. Vox enim significat conceptum, quia vice eius subrogatur, ut suppleat id, ad quod non potest pertingere conceptus, ut scilicet tam sibi quam aliis manifestet exterius. Et ita vox se habet quasi substitutum, quod repraesentat tam suum principale, cui deservit (quod est verbum mentis, a quo, ut ait S. Thomas q. 4. de Veritate art. 4. ad 7.* [Pa IX. 65 a.] *participat esse et significationem), quam id, ad quod ordinatur, quod est res significata. Et sic voces significant conceptum ut principale significativum, res autem ut significatum directe. Quas quidem repraesentant voces ut conceptas specificative et exercite, seu ly ut dicente conditionem, repraesentantur enim res conceptae; non tamen ly ut reduplicative sumpto pro statu, in quo sunt cognitae. Licet etiam aliquando voces significent res, ut subsunt intentioni et statui, quem habent in mente. Et tunc ipsa intentio est quasi res repraesentata, sicut in intentionibus logicis species, genus etc.*

"*Ad secundam probationem . . . .*" *etc., p. 107a28* [=349/7].—

"The response to this is: I deny the antecedent of the argument [347/1-3]. The proof of the antecedent [347/8-32] I concede, because the list there given is not an adequate enumeration.

be understood in three ways: *In one way* by means of another as by a formal rationale, yet not as by a thing represented, just as a vocal expression is said to signify by means of an imposition, a concept by means of a similitude. *In a second way* by means of another as by a thing represented as primarily and immediately signified, just as "man" is said to signify immediately man in general, and mediately Peter, who is a particular man. *In a third way* by means of another not as the thing signified, but as the signifying principal for which the vocal expression is a substitute and, as it were, an instrument, because it is from the word of the mind itself that the vocal expression participates being and signification, as St. Thomas says in his *Disputed Questions on Truth*, q. 4, art. 1, reply to obj. 7.[9] And it is in this third way that a vocal expression signifies a concept, because it is surrogated in place of [substitutes for] a concept in order to supply that which the concept cannot attain, in order, that is, that the concept should manifest outwardly to oneself as well as to others. And thus a vocal expression exists as something substituted, which represents the principal to which it is servile as well as that to which that principal is ordered, namely, the thing signified.

To the first proof, therefore,[10] the response is that vocal expressions signify concepts not as the thing signified directly, but as the principal significative; they also represent things as conceived, not by taking the qualifier "as conceived" reduplicatively for the state in which they are known, but specificatively and exertively for the condition with which they are rep-

nificare unum mediante alio potest intelligi tripliciter: *Uno modo* mediante alio tamquam ratione formali, non tamen tamquam re repraesentata, sicut vox dicitur significare media impositione, conceptus media similitudine. *Secundo* mediante alio ut re repraesentata tamquam primario et immediato significato, sicut homo dicitur significare immediate hominem in communi, et mediate Petrum, qui est homo in singulari. *Tertio* mediante alio non ut re significata, sed ut principali significante, cuius vox est substitutum et quasi instrumentum, quia ab ipso verbo mentis participat esse et significationem, ut dicit S. Thomas q. 4. de Veritate art. 1. ad 7.[9] Et hoc modo vox significat conceptum, quia vice eius subrogatur, ut suppleat id, ad quod non potest pertingere conceptus, ut scilicet tam sibi quam aliis manifestet exterius. Et ita vox se habet quasi substitutum, quod repraesentat tam suum principale, cui deservit, quam id, ad quod ordinatur, quod est res significata.

Ad primam ergo probationem[10] respondetur voces significare conceptus non ut rem significatam directe, sed ut principale significativum, repraesentare etiam res ut conceptas, non sumendo ly ,,ut conceptas'' reduplicative pro statu, in quo sunt cognitae, sed specificative et exercite pro con-

I distinguish the consequent [347/3-7]: That therefore a spoken word does not signify a thing by means of a concept as by a formal rationale or as by a primary and immediate significate, is the consequent I grant; for the formal rationale of the signifying in the case of an outward expression is a stipulation, and in the case of a concept is a similitude. That an outward expression does not signify a thing by means of a concept as by the principal signifying, for which the spoken word is substituted and, as it were, the instrument, is the consequent I deny. For an outward expression does signify a concept, because it is surrogated in its place in order to supply that which the concept is not able to achieve, namely, outward manifestation to self as well as to others. So a spoken word exists as a kind of substitute, that represents as much its principal to which it is subject (which is the word of the mind, from which, as St. Thomas says in q. 4 of the *Disputed Questions on Truth*, art. 4., reply to the 7th objection [*Pa* IX 65 a.], it participates being and signification), as that to which it is ordered, which is the thing signified. And so spoken words signify a concept as the principal significative, but a thing as signified directly. Which things indeed the spoken words represent as conceived specificatively and exertively, where the 'as' expresses a condition, for things conceived are represented; not however with the 'as' understood reduplicatively [to express] the condition or state in which the things are cognized [that is, as acquiring an intentional being or existence]. Although too words sometimes signify things as they exist in the intention and state that they have in the mind. And then the intention itself is as the thing represented, as in the case of the logical intentions species, genus, etc.

"To the second proof . . . ." as below at 349/7.

[9] *Pa* IX. 65 a.

[10] 347/8-14.

resented, because they are in fact conceived. Yet sometimes too things are signified as they are subject to the intention and state which they have in the mind, and the intention itself is, as it were, a represented thing, as, for example, in the case of the logical intentions, species, genus, etc.

To the second proof[11] it is said that vocal expressions signify from the concept of the one imposing [i.e., of the one who first coined the expression] as from the source whence they get signification and imposition, but they signify the concept of the speaker as that for which they are surrogated; for it is to this end that expressions are imposed or coined, that they might be surrogated [i.e., put to use] by anyone speaking.[12] But when vocal expressions are formed by a non-speaker,[13] those sounds are not speech, but physical sound resembling speech; whence they do not signify from the imposition, but from the custom which we have when we hear similar voices, because the sounds in question are similar to the expressions which are speech. Whence St. Thomas says in his *Summa theologica*, I, q. 51, art. 3, reply to obj. 4, that a sound formed by a pure spirit is not properly a linguistic sound. And supposing that these are truly vocal expressions, i.e., linguistic sounds, and do not signify a concept of a speaker when they are so formed, it does not follow that when they do signify some speaker's concept, they signify the concept and a thing [what the concept is about] by different significations, but by the same signification having the power of signifying both, but not always exercising both; for we do not always advert to the speaker's concepts by distinguishing them from the things [talked about]. And even though the concept of the speaker is outside of the listener, it is nevertheless present to the listener according to itself through the voice, by means of which the concept is rendered sensible.

Concerning the second of the two points of difficulty, to wit, what do **outward expressions more principally signify,** things or concepts, I answer that they more principally signify **things, unless, as may happen, the very thing signified is a concept or its intention.**

The REASON IS that the concept itself is ordered ultimately and principally to representing the thing itself of which it is an intentional similitude. Therefore an outward expression, which is only an instrument of the concept itself in representing and which renders the concept itself sensible, will be ordered more principally to

ditione, cum qua repraesentantur, quia revera conceptae sunt. Aliquando tamen etiam significantur res, ut subsunt intentioni et statui, quem habent in mente, et ipsa intentio est quasi res repraesentata, sicut in intentionibus logicis, species, genus etc.

Ad secundam probationem[11] dicitur, quod voces significant ex conceptu imponentis, ut a quo suscipiunt significationem et impositionem, sed conceptum loquentis tamquam id, pro quo subrogantur; ad hoc enim imponuntur, ut a quolibet loquente subrogari possint.[12] Cum autem voces a non loquente formantur,[13] illae voces non sunt locutio, sed sonus materialis similis locutioni; unde non significant ex impositione, sed ex consuetudine, quam nos habemus, cum similes voces audimus, quia illae similes sunt vocibus, quae sunt locutio. Unde D. Thomas 1. p. q. 51. art. 3. ad 4. dicit, quod vox formata ab angelo non est proprie vox. Et dato, quod istae essent vere voces et non significarent conceptum loquentis, quando sic formantur, non sequitur, quod quando illum significant, diversa significatione significent conceptum et res, sed eadem significatione habente potestatem significandi utrumque, sed non semper utrumque exercente; nec enim semper advertimus ad conceptus loquentis discernendo illos a rebus. Et licet conceptus loquentis sit extra audientem, secundum se est tamen illi praesens per vocem, per quam redditur sensibilis.

Circa secundum punctum huius articuli, scilicet quid voces principalius significent, res an conceptus, **respondetur principalius significare res, nisi forte ipsa res significata sit conceptus vel eius intentio.**

RATIO EST, quia ipse conceptus ordinatur ultimate et principaliter ad repraesentandam ipsam rem, cuius est similitudo intentionalis. Ergo vox, quae solum est instrumentum ipsius conceptus in repraesentando et reddit sensibilem ipsum conceptum, ad easdem res repraesentandas principalius

[11] 347/14-32.
[12] The 1663 Lyons text adds: "*loco sui conceptus*"—"in the place of his concept."
[13] 347/20-22.

representing those same things, because it is for this very task that it serves the concept.[14] And although an instrument would seem to respect more principally the principal by which it is employed as an instrument than the

ordinabitur, quia ad hoc ipsum deservit conceptui.[14] Et licet instrumentum principalius videatur respicere suum principale, a quo movetur, quam effectum, quem facit,

---

[14] From here to the end (from Reiser, 213b37-214a40, but omitting 213b22-36, because it differs from our Latin of 349/37-350/2 only by omission of the two words "huius articuli" at 349/37), the 1663 Lyons text, following the 1648 Madrid edition ("Editorial Afterword," note 78), reads: "*Dices primo: Instrumentum principalius respicit suum principale, a quo movetur, quam effectum, quem facit. Ergo ex eo, quod vox sit instrumentum conceptus, potius infertur, quod principaliter illum significet et minus principaliter rem, quam intelligibilem seu cognoscibilem facit.*

"*Respondetur distinguendo antecedens: Instrumentum consideratum in ratione operandi et agendi, conceditur; in ratione repraesentandi, negatur; quia instrumentum repraesentativum, quale est vox, habet pro principali principio suae repraesentationis conceptum, qui etiam est repraesentativus rei, ad quam repraesentationem manifestandam aliis substituit sibi vocem; et sic praecipuum utriusque significatum est res ipsa. Unde dicit S. Thomas q. 9. de Potentia art. 4.* [*Pa* VIII. 183 a.], *quod 'id formaliter significatur per nomen, ad quod principaliter est impositum, sicut nomen homo ad significandum compositum ex corpore et anima rationali.'*

"*Contra secundo: Verbum divinum principalius repraesentat Patrem, qui est principium exprimens Verbum, quam creaturas, quae sunt res expressae et repraesentatae per ipsum. Ergo etiam verbum exterius seu vox principalius repraesentabit suum principium exprimens, scilicet conceptum, quam rem significatam et expressam.*

"*Respondetur primo: Transeat antecedens et negatur consequens, quia vox non est naturalis expressio sui principii sicut verbum aut conceptus, sed imposita et principaliter ordinata ad significandum id, quod conceptus naturaliter repraesentat, scilicet res; et sic non bene arguitur ex uno ad aliud.*

"*Secundo respondetur, quod conceptus seu verbum principaliter repraesentat suum principale et formale obiectum, quia est expressio sui principii formalis, quod est species impressa repraesentans obiectum, cuius formaliter est species; hoc autem in Divinis est Essentia et Personae. Creaturae autem sunt obiectum secundarium et materiale, et ideo non principaliter repraesentantur a Verbo Divino. Hinc autem non sequitur, quod verbum exterius seu vox principalius repraesentet conceptum, quia non est formale obiectum repraesentatum, sed principale significativum rei.*"—"You may say first: An instrument more principally respects its principal by which it is moved than the effect which it accomplishes. From the fact therefore that a spoken word is an instrument of a concept, it should rather be inferred that the word signifies that concept principally and less principally the thing which it renders intelligible or cognizable.

"I answer by distinguishing the antecedent. That an instrument more principally respects the principal by which it is activated than the effect it accomplishes when considered in the rationale of operating and acting, I grant; when considered in the rationale of representing, however, I deny this; because a representative instrument, such as a spoken word is, has a concept for the principal principle of its representation, which principle is also representative of the thing, and substitutes for itself an outward expression in order to be manifest to others; and so the main significate of both the concept and the word is the thing itself. Whence St. Thomas says in the *Disputed Questions on the Power of God*, q. 9, art. 4 [*Pa* VIII. 183 a.], that 'what a name formally signifies is that for which it is principally stipulated, as the name "man" [is principally coined] to signify the composite of body and rational soul.'

"You may say secondly: The divine Word represents the Father, who is the principle expressing the Word, more principally than creatures, which are the things expressed and represented through the Word. Likewise therefore an exterior spoken word will represent its expressing principle, to wit, a concept, more principally than the thing signified and expressed.

"To this I answer, first: I pass over the antecedent [214a9-13] and deny the consequent [214a13-17], because a spoken word is not a natural expression of its principle in the way that a mental word or concept is, but one stipulated and principally ordered to signifying that which the concept represents naturally, namely, a thing; and so there is no true parallel between the two cases [they are not isomorphic].

"I answer secondly, that a concept or interior word principally represents its principal and formal object because it is an expression of its formal principle, which is the impressed specification representing the object of which it is formally a specifier; but this in the case of the Divinity is the Essence and the Persons. Creatures on the other hand are a secondary and material object, and for this reason are not primarily represented by the divine Word. Whence from this it does not follow that an exterior or spoken word would represent more principally the concept, because the concept is not a formal object represented, but the principal significative of a thing."

effect which it produces, yet this is understood in the rationale of operating and acting [productively]. In the rationale of representing, however, if that which is principal is also something representative of things and substitutes some instrument for itself in order to extend and to manifest to others that very representation, the chief significate of [that which is ultimately signified by] both [principal and instrument] is the thing itself. Whence St. Thomas says, in his *Disputed Questions on the Power of God*, q. 9, art. 4,[15] that "that is formally signified by means of a name, for which the name is principally imposed, as the name 'man' for signifying something composed out of body and rational soul."

And if you should say: A concept or [mental] word does not signify principally the things expressed, but its own expressing principle, as appears in the case of the Divine Word, which more principally represents the Father, to whom it is similar, than creatures; therefore the exterior word also will more principally represent its principle, namely, the concept, than the thing signified and expressed.

I answer that the concept or [mental] word is an expression of its formal principle, which is the impressed specification fecundating the expressing understanding, and this represents the object of which it is formally a specification; and so a concept, by representing its formal principle, represents principally its formal object. But creatures are a secondary and material object [of the Divine Expression or Word], and for this reason are not principally represented by the Divine Word. Whence it does not follow that the exterior word represents more principally the concept [or interior word], because the concept is not the formal object represented, but what is principally significative. Besides which a linguistic sound is not a natural expression of its principle as is a concept, but an expression imposed for and directed to signifying that which is conceived, i.e., that which the concept is of.

tamen hoc intelligitur in ratione operandi et agendi. In ratione tamen repraesentandi, si id quod principale est, etiam est repraesentativum rerum et ad ipsam repraesentationem extendendam et manifestandam aliis substituit sibi aliquod instrumentum, praecipuum utriusque significatum est res ipsa. Unde D. Thomas q. 9. de Potentia art. 4[15] dicit, quod «id formaliter significatur per nomen, ad quod principaliter est impositum, sicut nomen homo ad significandum compositum ex corpore et anima rationali».

Et si dicas: Nam conceptus seu verbum non significat principaliter res expressas, sed suum principium exprimens, ut apparet in Verbo Divino, quod principalius repraesentat Patrem, cui est simile, quam creaturas; ergo etiam verbum exterius principalius repraesentabit suum principium, scilicet conceptum, quam rem significatam et expressam.

Respondetur conceptum seu verbum esse expressionem sui principii formalis, quod est species impressa fecundans intellectum exprimentem, et haec repraesentat obiectum, cuius formaliter est species, et sic conceptus repraesentando suum principium formale repraesentat principaliter suum obiectum formale. Creaturae autem sunt obiectum secundarium et materiale, et ideo non principaliter repraesentatur a Verbo Divino. Unde non sequitur, quod verbum exterius repraesentet principalius conceptum, quia non est formale obiectum repraesentatum, sed principale significativum. Praeterquam quod vox non est naturalis expressio sui principii sicut conceptus, sed imposita et directa ad significandum id, quod conceptus.

[15] *Pa* VIII. 183 a.

APPENDIX B

To the Treatise on Signs:

Synthetic Index and Synoptic Table for Poinsot's Cursus Philosophicus

I. SYNTHETIC INDEX

(Contents)

including pagination of the
1931–1937 Reiser Edition
of the complete Cursus.

IOANNIS A SANCTO THOMA O. P.

IN COMPLUTENSI ACADEMIA PROFESSORIS QUONDAM PRIMARII

CURSUS PHILOSOPHICUS THOMISTICUS

secundum exactam, veram, genuinam Aristotelis et Doctoris Angelici mentem

NOVA EDITIO

a † P. BEATO REISER O. S. B.

IN COLLEGIO INTERNATIONALI SANCTI ANSELMI DE URBE PHILOSOPHIÆ PROFESSORE EXARATA

II Reimpressio revisa.

MARIETTI
Sanctæ Sedis Apostolicæ et Sacræ Rituum Congregationis Typographi

Title page from the Reiser edition of Poinsot's work used in the preparation of this volume.

INDEX SYNTHETICUS

EORUM, QUAE HOC CURSU CONTINENTUR

Reiser Edition, Volume I, Page

PROLOGUS TOTIUS DIALECTICAE.

PRIMA PARS ARTIS LOGICAE.

DE DIALECTICIS INSTITUTIONIBUS, QUAS SUMMULAS VOCANT.

TEXTUS SUMMULARUM.

QUAESTIONES DISPUTANDAE

AD ILLUSTRANDUM DIFFICULTATES ALIQUAS HUIUS TEXTUS.

APPENDIX

AD SECUNDAM PARTEM SUMMULARUM

EXHIBENS TEXTUM EDITIONIS LUGDUNENSIS
PRO IIS ARTICULIS, IN QUIBUS LECTIO SUPRA POSITA AB HAC EDITIONE ALIQUOTIENS RECEDIT.

SECUNDA PARS ARTIS LOGICAE.
DE INSTRUMENTIS LOGICALIBUS EX PARTE MATERIAE.

EXPLICATIO TEXTUS ISAGOGIS PORPHYRII.

LIBER PRAEDICAMENTORUM.

SUPER LIBROS PERIHERMENIAS

CIRCA LIBROS PRIORUM.

IN LIBROS POSTERIORUM.

PRIMA PARS PHILOSOPHIAE NATURALIS.

DE ENTE MOBILI IN COMMUNI.

CIRCA LIBRUM PRIMUM PHYSICORUM.

DE PRINCIPIIS RERUM NATURALIUM.

CIRCA LIBRUM SECUNDUM PHYSICORUM.

DE NATURA ET CAUSIS.

CIRCA LIBRUM TERTIUM PHYSICORUM.

DE MOTU ET INFINITO.

CIRCA LIBRUM QUARTUM PHYSICORUM.

DE LOCO, VACUO ET TEMPORE.

CIRCA LIBRUM QUINTUM PHYSICORUM.

DE DISTINCTIONE, UNITATE ET CONTRARIETATE MOTUS.

CIRCA LIBRUM SEXTUM PHYSICORUM.

DE DIVISIONE MOTUS ET CONTINUI PER PARTES.

CIRCA LIBRUM SEPTIMUM PHYSICORUM.

DE COMPARATIONE MOVENTIUM ET MOBILIUM.

CIRCA LIBRUM OCTAVUM PHYSICORUM.

DE MOTUS AETERNITATE ET REDUCTIONE IN PRIMUM MOTOREM.

SECUNDA PARS PHILOSOPHIAE NATURALIS.

DE ENTE MOBILI INCORRUPTIBILI.
[QUOD NON EXSTAT.]

TERTIA PARS PHILOSOPHIAE NATURALIS.

DE ENTE MOBILI CORRUPTIBILI.

CIRCA LIBRUM PRIMUM DE GENERATIONE ET CORRUPTIONE.

DE ORTU ET INTERITU RERUM IN COMMUNI.

CIRCA LIBRUM SECUNDUM DE GENERATIONE ET CORRUPTIONE.

DE CORPORIBUS GENERABILIBUS.

TRACTATUS DE METEORIS.

AD QUATUOR LIBROS METEOROLOGICORUM ARISTOTELIS.

QUARTA PARS PHILOSOPHIAE NATURALIS.

IN TRES LIBROS DE ANIMA.

DE ENTE MOBILI ANIMATO.

TRACTATUS DE ANIMA INTELLECTIVA.

II. SYNOPTIC TABLE

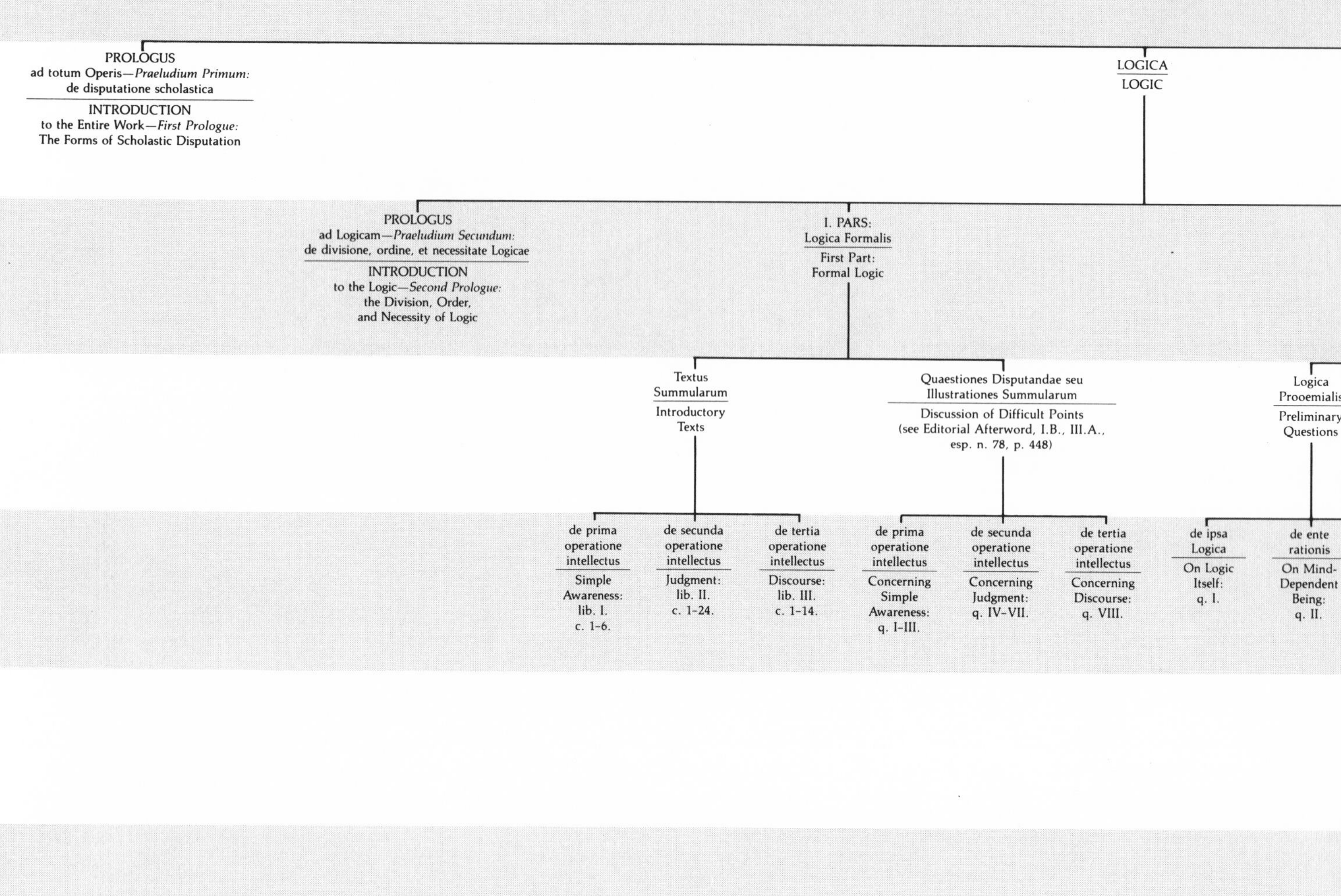

PROLOGUS
ad totum Operis—*Praeludium Primum:*
de disputatione scholastica
INTRODUCTION
to the Entire Work—*First Prologue:*
The Forms of Scholastic Disputation
LOGICA
LOGIC
PROLOGUS
ad Logicam—*Praeludium Secundum:*
de divisione, ordine, et necessitate Logicae
INTRODUCTION
to the Logic—*Second Prologue:*
the Division, Order,
and Necessity of Logic
I. PARS:
Logica Formalis
First Part:
Formal Logic
Textus
Summularum
Introductory
Texts
Quaestiones Disputandae seu
Illustrationes Summularum
Discussion of Difficult Points
(see Editorial Afterword, I.B., III.A.,
esp. n. 78, p. 448)
Logica
Prooemialis
Preliminary
Questions
de prima operatione intellectus
Simple Awareness: lib. I. c. 1-6.
de secunda operatione intellectus
Judgment: lib. II. c. 1-24.
de tertia operatione intellectus
Discourse: lib. III. c. 1-14.
de prima operatione intellectus
Concerning Simple Awareness: q. I-III.
de secunda operatione intellectus
Concerning Judgment: q. IV-VII.
de tertia operatione intellectus
Concerning Discourse: q. VIII.
de ipsa Logica
On Logic Itself: q. I.
de ente rationis
On Mind-Dependent Being: q. II.

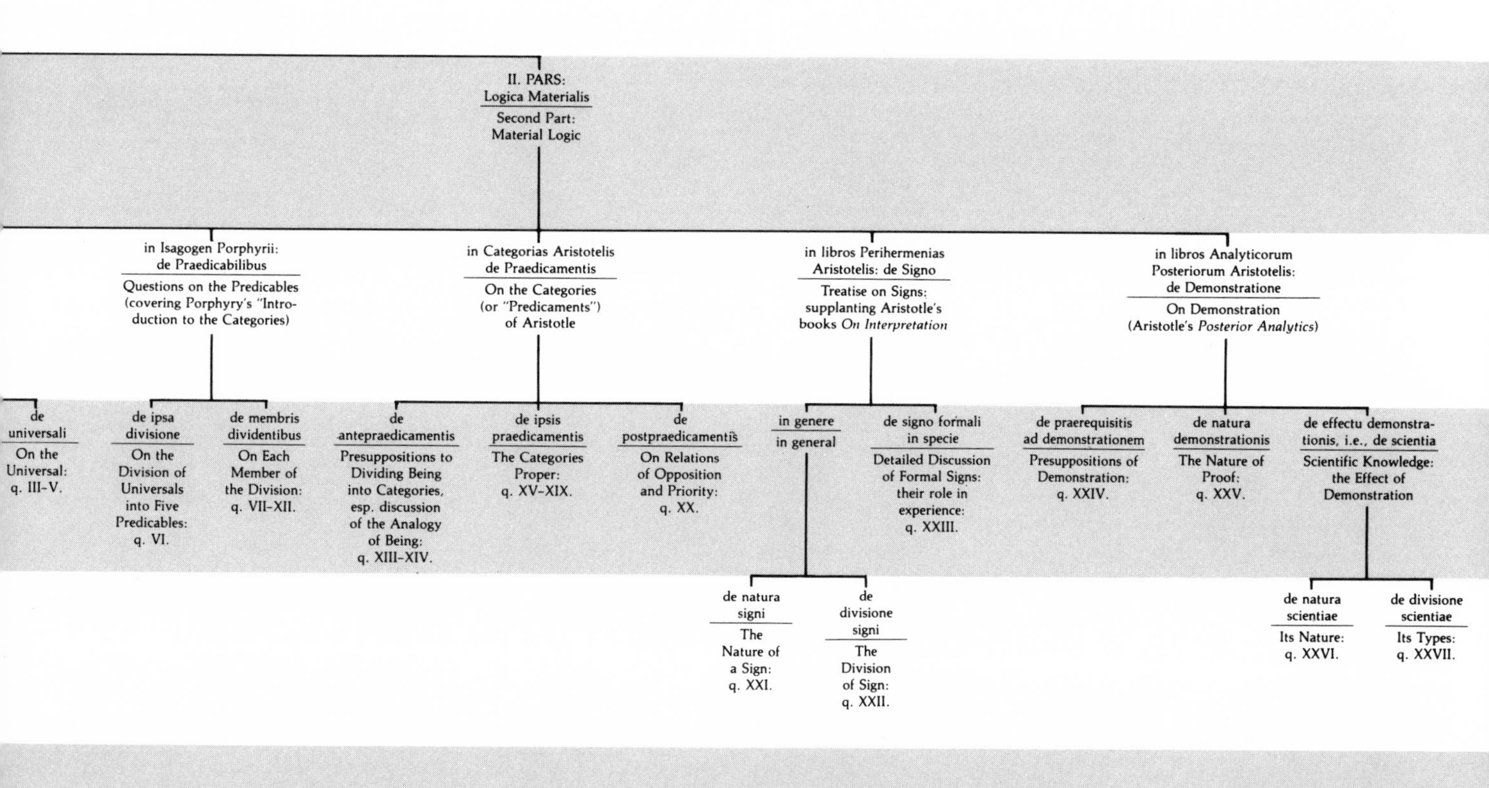

II. PARS:
Logica Materialis
Second Part:
Material Logic
in Isagogen Porphyrii:
de Praedicabilibus
Questions on the Predicables
(covering Porphyry's "Introduction to the Categories)
in Categorias Aristotelis
de Praedicamentis
On the Categories
(or "Predicaments")
of Aristotle
in libros Perihermenias
Aristotelis: de Signo
Treatise on Signs:
supplanting Aristotle's
books On Interpretation
in libros Analyticorum
Posteriorum Aristotelis:
de Demonstratione
On Demonstration
(Aristotle's Posterior Analytics)
de
universali
On the
Universal:
q. III–V.
de ipsa
divisione
On the
Division of
Universals
into Five
Predicables:
q. VI.
de membris
dividentibus
On Each
Member of
the Division:
q. VII–XII.
de
antepraedicamentis
Presuppositions to
Dividing Being
into Categories,
esp. discussion
of the Analogy
of Being:
q. XIII–XIV.
de ipsis
praedicamentis
The Categories
Proper:
q. XV–XIX.
de
postpraedicamentis
On Relations
of Opposition
and Priority:
q. XX.
in genere
in general
de signo formali
in specie
Detailed Discussion
of Formal Signs:
their role in
experience:
q. XXIII.
de praerequisitis
ad demonstrationem
Presuppositions of
Demonstration:
q. XXIV.
de natura
demonstrationis
The Nature of
Proof:
q. XXV.
de effectu demonstrationis, i.e., de scientia
Scientific Knowledge:
the Effect of
Demonstration
de natura
signi
The
Nature of
a Sign:
q. XXI.
de
divisione
signi
The
Division
of Sign:
q. XXII.
de natura
scientiae
Its Nature:
q. XXVI.
de divisione
scientiae
Its Types:
q. XXVII.

The
CURSUS PHILOSOPHICUS
of
John Poinst

- I. PARS: De Ente Mobili in Communi (in libros Physicorum Aristotelis) / FIRST PART: The General Consideration of Being Subject to Chan (the Physics of Aristotle)
  - Prooemium: de Philosophia Naturali / Preliminary Remarks: On Natural Philosophy
    - de eius Obiecto / Its Object: q. I.
    - de eius unitate / Its Integrity: q. I.
    - de primo cognito / Original Awareness: q. I.
  - De Principiis Rerum Naturalium (in 1. librum Physicorum) / The Principles of Natural Things (*Physics*, Book I)
    - in communi / in general: q. X.
    - in particulari / in particular
      - de materia prima / First (or "Prime") Matter: q. III.
      - de forma / Form: q. IV.
      - de privatione / Privation: q. V.
    - de composito / Concerning Complex Wholes
      - substantiali / Substantial
        - de ipso composito substantiali / On Substantial Composites: q. VI.
        - de modis compositionis substantialis / On the Modes of Substantial Composition: q. VII.
      - quantitativo / Quantitative: q. VIII.
  - De Principiis Scientiae Naturalis (in 2. librum Physicorum) / The Principles of Our Philosophical Knowledge of Nature (*Physics*, Book II)
    - de subiecto huius scientiae: de Natura / Nature: the Subject Matter of Such Knowledge: q. IX.
    - de medio demonstrationum: de causis / Causes: the Means of Establishing Its Conclusions
      - in communi / in general: q. II.
      - in particulari / in particular
        - de causa materiali et formali / Material and Formal Causality: q. XI.
        - de causa efficiente / Efficient Causality: q. XII.
        - ca fi / F Cau q.

being similar, being a cause or an effect, and six hundred other relations; and likewise in the same subject (or remote foundation) many different relations can be founded.

We are inquiring, therefore, into two things concerning the unity and specific diversity of relations: First, whether it derives from the fundament alone, or also from the terminus; Second, supposing that it comes from both, how precisely does each one concur in the specifying. Concerning the numerical unity [i.e., the concrete individual identity] of relations, however, we want to determine only whether it is taken from the unity or the plurality of termini, or from the unity of a subject regardless of whether the termini are numerically several.

Concerning the first point, it seems from one point of view that a relation cannot be specified by a terminus: first, because correlatives are simultaneous by nature, therefore one does not exist as prior to the other, therefore neither as its source of specification, because the source of a specification is, as cause, prior to the specification it causes. Second, the terminus is opposed to the relation; but a specific character cannot be taken from an opposite, for it would then have to be a specific character contrary to what it has. Third, a terminus is a pure terminus in respect of a relation, therefore not the relation's source of specific identity; for a *pure* terminus is one which exercises no causality whatever, but simply respects, while to specify is to exercise causality in a certain way. Finally, there is only one relation of a son to the father and to the mother, as St. Thomas explains in his *Summa theologica*, III, q. 35, art. 5; for there is in the child only one birth, and therefore only one sonship which is consequent upon the birth. And yet the relation in question—being the son of—is anchored in terms specifically diverse, to wit, fatherhood and motherhood, which are relations as diverse as are the male and female foundations of the generating. Therefore, being compatible with specifically different terms, the specific unity of a relation cannot be derived from its terminus.

Yet, from another perspective, it would appear that *only* the terminus specifies a relation: First, for the general reason that every thing which has its being with reference to something other than itself is specified by that other relative to which it has being, as is the case, for example, with habits and activities—therefore with greater reason in the case of a relation, which has its entire reality in being toward another than itself, and consequently the whole of its character as something definable and specific. Second, for the reason that the same foundation can give rise to different relations: for the same color white is the ground of a similarity to the dove

relatio similis, causae vel effectus et sexcenta alia; et similiter in eodem subiecto seu fundamento remoto plures relationes possunt fundari.

INQUIRIMUS ergo circa unitatem et diversitatem specificam duo: *Unum*, an sumatur a solo fundamento, an etiam a termino. *Secundum*, dato quod ab utroque, quomodo utrumque concurrat ad specificandum. Circa unitatem autem numericam solum quaeritur, an sumatur ex unitate vel pluralitate terminorum, vel ex unitate subiecti, etiamsi termini numerice sint plures.

Circa primum ex una parte videtur a termino non posse relationem specificari: *Primo* quia correlativa sunt simul natura, ergo unum non se habet ut prius altero, ergo neque ut specificativum, quia specificativum est prius specificatio, utpote causa illius. *Secundo*, terminus est oppositus relationi; ab opposito autem non sumitur species, sumeretur enim species opposita. *Tertio*, terminus est purus terminus respectu relationis, ergo non specificativum illius; ille enim est purus terminus, qui causalitatem nullam exercet, sed pure respicitur; specificare autem quoddam causare est. *Denique* in filio est una tantum relatio ad patrem et matrem, ut S. Thomas docet 3. p. q. 35. art. 5.; est enim in illo una tantum nativitas, atque adeo una filiatio, quae nativitatem sequitur. Et tamen terminatur ad terminos specie diversos, scilicet paternitatem et maternitatem, quae diversae relationes sunt, sicut et fundamenta ad generandum omnino diversa. Ergo unitas relationis specifica stat cum terminis specie diversis et sic non sumitur ex illis.

E contra vero quod solus terminus specificet, probatur: *Tum* in generali ratione, quia omnia, quae sunt ad aliud, specificantur ab illo, ad quod sunt, sicut habitus et actus; ergo multo magis relatio, cuius totum esse est ad aliud, et consequenter tota quidditas et species. *Secundo*, quia idem fundamentum potest servire ad diversas relationes; nam eadem albedo est fundamentum similitudinis ad nivem et

which is white and a dissimilarity to the crow which is black; the same causality of a subordinate cause is the foundation or ground of relations one to the effect and another to the higher cause; and the same sign provides the basis for the [single triadic] relation to the cognizing organism and to the object apprehended by that organism. Therefore relations are differentiated in reality by their termini, not by their fundaments.

dissimilitudinis ad corvum; eadem causalitas causae inferioris est fundamentum relationis ad effectum et ad causam superiorem; et idem signum praebet fundamentum relationi ad potentiam et ad signatum. Ergo relationes distinguuntur ex terminis, non ex fundamentis.

Notwithstanding the apparent antinomy of the foregoing observations, it remains to be said that **both grounds and objectives work together in effecting the specification of any given relation, nor does the one factor exclude the other from the specifying. But a relation has specification from its foundation as from its cause and specifying principle, while it has specification from its term—not as from the cause of the specification, but—as from a factor completing and terminating the rationale of the specifying.**

NIHILOMINUS DICENDUM EST: **Utrumque concurrere ad specificationem relationis, nec unum excludere alterum; sed a fundamento habet relatio specificationem tamquam a causa et principio specificante, a termino autem non ut a causa specificationis, sed ut a complente et terminante rationem specificandi.**

Whence Albert,[5] as Master Soto notes in his *Summulae* text on Relation, Question 1, reply to the eighth objection, well asserts that the being of one relative is not defined through another, but toward another; for the linguistic particle "through" bespeaks a cause, the particle "toward" bespeaks and expresses order. And ST. THOMAS in every case takes the specific identity of the relation under discussion from its foundation or ground, for the reason that, as he says clearly in his *Commentary on the Sentences of Peter Lombard*, Book I, dist. 26, q. 2, art. 2, reply to the fourth objection,[6] it is from its foundation that a relation has its reality: "because a relation has a natural being only owing to a mind-independent foundation, and from this foundation is it established in the category of relation, it follows that the essential differences of relations derive from the differences of other beings, as is clear in the fifth book of Aristotle's *Metaphysics*, where he says that some relations are founded on quantity, some upon action, and so on for others. So it is that according to the order of being on which they are founded derives also the order of the relations." This then is the reason why in so many places St. Thomas takes the specific character of relations from the foundations, as, for example, in the *Summa theologica*, III, q. 35, art. 5, in the *Questions at Random*, q. 1, art. 2,[7] q. 9, art. 4,[8] in the *Compendium theologiae*, ch. 212,[9] and in the *Commentary on the Sentences of Peter Lombard*, Book III, dist. 8, q. 1, art. 5,[10] where too in replying to the fourth objection he points to the difference between

Unde bene dixit Albertus,[5] ut refert Mag. Soto q. 1. de Relatione ad 8., quod unum relativum non definitur per alterum, sed ad alterum; nam ly per dicit causam, ly ad dicit ordinem. Et communiter S. Thomas sumit specificationem relationis ex fundamentis, quia a fundamento dicit habere relationem, quod sit realis, ut patet in 1. dist. 26. q. 2. art. 2. ad 4.,[6] dicens, «quod, quia relatio non habet esse naturale nisi ex hoc, quod habet fundamentum in re, et ex hoc collocatur in genere, inde est, quod differentiae relationum essentiales sumuntur secundum differentias aliorum entium, ut patet ex Philosopho 5. Metaph., ubi dicit, quod quaedam fundantur super quantitatem, quaedam super actionem, et sic de aliis. Inde est, quod secundum ordinem eorum, in quibus fundantur relationes, est etiam ordo relationum». Haec ergo est ratio, cur plerisque locis S. Thomas sumat specificam rationem relationum ex fundamentis, ut in 3. p. q. 35. art. 5. et Quodlib. 1. art. 2.[7] et Quodlib. 9. art. 4.[8] et opusc. 2. cap. 212.[9] et in 3. dist. 8. q. 1. art. 5.,[10] ubi etiam ad 4. ponit differentiam inter

[5] Liber de praedicamentis tract. 4. c. 9.
[6] *Pa* VI. 221 b.
[7] *Pa* IX. 460 a.
[8] *Pa* IX. 589 b.
[9] Compend. Theol. (*Pa* XVI. 59 a).
[10] *Pa* VII. 103 b.

motion and relation with the remark that "every motion is something in the order of mind-independent being, but not every relation. And therefore, although the respects of the relation are multiplied with the terms, it yet need not be the case that relations are multiplied in the order of mind-independent being in the way that motions are multiplied in that order by a diversity of terms." In this passage the learned Teacher consistently reduces the mind-independent being of relations to the foundations,[11] and to the terms with the fundament supposed, yet he does not take this being from the terms alone, as he does in the case of motions. It is in this way that the general rule Aquinas lays down in his *Summa theologica*, I-II, q. 54, art. 2, is to be interpreted, where he says that "all those things which have a being requiring description in terms of another than themselves are distinguished according to the distinction of those things in terms of which the being described requires expression." Whence it is clear that relations also derive their specification from their terms, something Aquinas also asserts in his *Summa theologica*, I, q. 32, art. 2, when he says that "two relations are not specifically different if one relation corresponds to them from the other side," which passage we will consider further below.[12]

THE REASON FOR THESE REMARKS is taken from what has been said, because the whole reality of a relation is from its foundation according to the order to a terminus, since indeed the entire being of a relation is toward another, as the definition of relation says. Whence since a relation essentially requires both foundation and terminus, it ought not to be understood to be from one in any way that precludes its being understood to be from the other also.

But the second part of the conclusion,[13] about the way in which these two work together in effecting the specification, must not be thought to assert that each partially concurs in such a way that the fundament provides a part of the specification and the terminus a part, but must be understood to assert that each provides the entire specification in different orders of causality. Some explain this situation by saying that the fundament concurs by initiating and the terminus by completing, others by saying that the fundament works in the order of an efficient cause and the terminus in the order of an extrinsic formal cause, and others again by saying that the fundament specifies as virtually precontaining within itself the

motum et relationem, «quod omnis motus est aliquid secundum rem, non autem omnis relatio. Et ideo quamvis ex terminis multiplicentur respectus relationis, non tamen oportet, quod multiplicentur relationes secundum rem, sicut motus multiplicantur secundum rem ex diversitate terminorum». Ubi S. Doctor realitatem relationum semper reducit ad fundamenta,[11] et fundamento supposito ad terminos, non tamen ex solis terminis sicut motus. Et sic potest sumi ex generali regula S. Thomae 1. 2. q. 54. art. 2., ubi inquit, «quod omnia, quae dicuntur ad aliquid, distinguuntur secundum distinctionem eorum, ad quae dicuntur». Ergo etiam relationes ex terminis desumunt suam specificationem. Quod etiam expressit in 1. p. q. 32. art. 2., ubi dicit, «quod duae relationes non sunt diversae secundum speciem, si ex opposito una relatio eis correspondeat»; quem locum infra ponderabimus.[12]

Ratio autem istorum ex dictis sumitur, quia tota realitas relationis est ex fundamento secundum ordinem ad terminum, siquidem totum esse relationis est ad aliud, ut dicit eius definitio. Unde cum essentialiter utrumque petat, scilicet fundamentum et terminum, non ita debet sumi praecise ab uno, quod non sumatur etiam ab alio.

SECUNDA VERO PARS conclusionis[13] de modo, quo ista duo concurrunt ad specificandum, non est existimandum, quod ita partialiter concurrant, quod partem specificationis det fundamentum, partem terminus, sed unumquodque dat totam specificationem in diverso genere causae. Quod *aliqui* explicant dicendo, quod fundamentum concurrit initiative et terminus completive. *Alii*, quod fundamentum in genere causae efficientis et terminus in genere causae formalis extrinsecae. *Alii*, quod fundamentum specificat ut virtualiter praehabens in se

---

[11] Since the reality of the relation is not taken from its terminus, it must by implication be taken from its foundation, the only alternative. See the Second Preamble, Article 2, above.

[12] 383/6-33.

[13] 380/13-17.

terminus to which it is proportioned, in this way dissolving the diversity of foundations into the diverse formalities of the termini.

Yet the distinction has to be made between the terminus understood most formally in the rationale of an opposed terminus, and the terminus understood fundamentally on the side of the subjective being founding this rationale of terminating. In the former way a terminus concurs in a specification purely terminatively, but not by causing that specification, because so considered it is a pure terminus and simultaneous by nature and in cognition with the relation; therefore as such it is not a specifying cause, because a cause is not naturally simultaneous with but prior to its effect. If it is considered in the latter way, the terminus stands as an extrinsic formal cause and specifies in the manner of an object, and in this way a single specifying rationale of the relation arises from the foundation and terminus together, inasmuch as the foundation contains the terminus within itself by a proportion and power; for it is not relative to a given terminus unless it is a specific fundament, and conversely. In this way, to the extent that they are mutually proportioned, terminus and foundation together bring about a single rationale specifying a relation which postulates both a specific foundation and a specific terminus corresponding thereto.

From these remarks one can further gather what a formal terminus is in the rationale of something specifying. For although specifically different relations can be anchored to the materially same terminus, yet they cannot be anchored to the *formally* same terminus. But the formal specifying rationale in a terminus is understood in accordance with a correspondence and adequate proportion to its fundament. For example, something white constitutes a formal terminus of a relation of similarity according as it corresponds to an agreement and identity with the fundament, a formal terminus of a relation of dissimilarity as it corresponds to a disagreement with the fundament; of paternity or of filiation as it corresponds to the act of procreation which is its fundament, and so on in other cases. Wherefore, as regards the specifying of any relation, in just the way that the fundament is understood under the final rationale of the grounding of the relation, so the terminus of the relation is understood under the proportion and correspondence of the terminating.

But we have said "corresponding thereto completely or adequately,"[14] because one single complete terminus

terminum, cui proportionatur, et sic diversitas fundamentorum refunditur in diversam formalitatem terminorum.

Sed tamen distinguendum est, quod terminus vel sumitur formalissime in ratione termini oppositi, vel fundamentaliter ex parte absoluti fundantis istam rationem terminandi. Primo modo terminus concurrit pure terminative ad specificationem, non autem causando illam, quia sic est purus terminus et est simul natura et cognitione cum relatione; ergo ut sic non est causa specificans, quia causa non est simul natura, sed prior effectu. Si secundo modo consideratur, habet se ut causa formalis extrinseca et specificat ad modum obiecti, et sic ex fundamento et termino consurgit unica ratio specificandi relationem, quatenus fundamentum continet in se terminum in proportione et virtute; non enim est ad talem terminum, nisi sit tale fundamentum, et e converso. Et sic quatenus inter se proportionantur, conficiunt unam rationem specificandi relationem, quae et tale fundamentum postulat et talem terminum ei correspondentem.

Ex quibus etiam colliges, quid sit formalis terminus in ratione specificantis. Licet enim ad eundem materialem terminum diversae relationes specificae terminari possint, non tamen ad eundem formaliter. Sumitur autem formalis ratio specificans in termino secundum correspondentiam et proportionem adaequatam suo fundamento. V. g. album constituit formalem terminum relationis similitudinis, ut correspondet convenientiae et identitati, dissimilitudinis, ut correspondet disconvenientiae; paternitatis aut filiationis, ut correspondet generationi, et sic de aliis. Quare sicut fundamentum ad specificandum consideratur sub ratione ultima fundandi, sic terminus sub proportione et correspondentia terminandi.

Diximus autem ,,quae complete correspondeat seu adaequate",[14] quia di-

[14] The quotation marks here are not to be taken literally to the words—at 382/32-34—but rather conceptually, i.e., to the idea— e.g., cf. 380/15-17, 383/31-33, 386/30-387/7, etc.

can correspond to relations different in kind, as to the relation of being a son corresponds the relations of being a mother and being a father; for the relation of being a son is caused by that twofold manner of procreation of the father and of the mother, but it springs from the one birth. So St. Thomas teaches in the *Summa theologica*, III, q. 35, art. 5, reply to the third objection. But he seems to say the opposite in the *Summa theologica*, I, q. 32, art. 2, where he says that "two relations are not different in kind when in opposition only one relation corresponds to them." Nor do those who think that the father and mother concur actively in the generating free themselves from this difficulty.[15] For even though they concur actively, they yet do so in ways sufficiently different to found the different relations of fatherhood and motherhood, just as the sun and man concur actively in generation, but in different ways founding different relations of cause [to effect]. Wherefore it must be said in resolution that to a twofold partial relation can correspond one terminus or complete correlative, but not to two total relations. But a father and a mother and many causes of the same order working together to one effect are different virtually only in a partial way, and all together constitute an integral cause and a single complete terminus, even though they are partially several. And St. Thomas in the first passage from the third part of the *Summa*[16] is speaking of several partial relations from the side of the one extreme, to which several partial relations only one single adequate relation can correspond on the side of the other extreme. But in the second passage from the first part of the *Summa*[17] St. Thomas is speaking of relations different adequately and completely.

To the bases of the opinions opposed to our own:[18] The answer to the first[19] is that specification of a relation depends upon its terminus, even though that terminus is simultaneous with its correlative, yet not as on a principle causing the specification but as on something terminating and completing it. In this way

versis specie relationibus potest correspondere unus terminus totalis, sicut filiationi correspondet relatio paternitatis et maternitatis; causatur enim duplici illo modo generationis paternae et maternae, sed unica nativitate egreditur. Et ita docet S. Thomas 3. p. q. 35. art. 5. ad 3. Contrarium autem videtur dicere 1. p. q. 32. art. 2., ubi inquit, «quod duae relationes non sunt specie diversae, si ex opposito una relatio eis correspondeat». Nec ab hac difficultate se liberant, qui putant tam patrem quam matrem concurrere active.[15] Nam etsi concurrant active, diverso tamen modo sufficiente ad fundandam diversam relationem paternitatis et maternitatis, sicut etiam sol et homo concurrunt ad generatinem active, sed diverso modo, qui diversas fundat relationes causae. *Quare respondetur*, quod duplici relationi partiali potest correspondere unus terminus seu correlativum totale, non duplici relationi totali. Pater autem et mater et plures causae eiusdem ordinis ad eundem effectum concurrentes sunt diversae quasi partialiter, et omnes integram causam constituunt et unicum terminum totalem, licet partialiter sint plures. Et D. Thomas primo loco ex 3. p.[16] loquitur de pluribus relationibus partialibus ex parte unius extremi, quibus potest correspondere ex parte alterius extremi unica tantum relatio adaequata. In secundo autem loco ex 1. p.[17] loquitur de diversis relationibus adaequate et complete.

AD FUNDAMENTA PRO SENTENTIIS OPPOSITIS:[18] Ad primum[19] respondetur, quod terminus, licet sit simul cum suo correlativo, tamen ab illo dependet specificatio, non ut a principio causante illam, sed ut a terminante et complente. Et sic tota priori-

[15] According to the view of Aristotle and to medieval biology based on that view, the female was a purely passive matter or "fertile ground" for the male seed, which was alone thought to be active in generation. By Poinsot's day this view was under direct challenge by more enlightened biological views. Poinsot is concerned here strictly to make the point that the question under discussion in the present context is not a biological one. We are dealing rather with a question that belongs—as we will explain below in the Editorial Afterword, Section I.C.—to the realm of *doctrina* rather than to that of *scientia*, and hence with a question that can be neither reduced to the methods of nor resolved by advances in scientific understanding as such. It is, in short, a semiotic question.

[16] 382/48-383/7; cf. 379/29-39, 380/39-40.

[17] 383/8-11; cf. 381/19-23.

[18] 379/15-380/8.

[19] 379/17-21.

the complete priority of the specifying cause obtains on the side of the fundament, indeed it is not through but toward the terminus that the fundament is specified.

To the second opposed opinion[20] the answer is that from a term opposed by a respective opposition can be taken a specification as from something terminating and completing, not as from something causing that specification, because a relative opposition is the least among the forms of opposition; for it does not remove the other extreme, but posits or presupposes it, and so its specification can be ordered to that opposite extreme.

To the third opposed opinion[21] the answer is that a pure terminus under the formality of terminus can specify by terminating and completing, not by causing, and as that *toward which* it is specified, not as that *through which*.

The answer to the final opposed opinion[22] is clear from what has already been said.[23]

To the bases for the second opinion: To the first[24] it has already been answered that termini specify purely by terminating, but foundations by causing. And so the entire being of a relation is toward the terminus as toward something purely terminating.

To the second[25] it is said that the same foundation proximately and formally cannot serve for relations different in kind, as white under the formality of agreement founds similarity, under the formality of disagreement founds dissimilarity. And likewise in the other examples produced, if they are different relations (which I do not dispute), they also have different proximate and formal foundations.

Concerning the second difficulty involved in this article,[26] precisely as it concerns the distinction and individual or numerical unity of a relation: Resolution of this depends upon that celebrated difficulty, whether characteristics are individuated by their subject in suchwise that there could not be two accidents distinct only numerically in one and the same subject. In *the present discussion* no pretension *is* made to treat of this issue in its entirety, but *only to explain whether one single relation can be extended to and anchored on many different termini, each one of which sufficiently*

tas causae specificantis tenet se ex parte fundamenti. Per terminum vero non specificatur, sed ad terminum.

Ad secundum[20] respondetur, quod a termino opposito oppositione respectiva potest sumi specificatio ut a terminante et complente, non ut causante illam, quia oppositio relativa est minima inter omnes oppositiones; neque enim tollit alterum extremum, sed ponit vel supponit, et ita ad illud specificatio eius ordinari potest.

Ad tertium[21] respondetur, quod purus terminus sub formalitate termini specificare potest terminando et complendo, non causando, et tamquam id *ad quod* specificatur, non *per quod*.

Ad ultimum[22] constat ex dictis.[23]

AD FUNDAMENTA PRO SECUNDA SENTENTIA: Ad primum[24] iam responsum est, quod termini specificant pure terminando, fundamenta autem causando. Et sic totum esse relationis est ad terminum ut ad pure terminantem.

Ad secundum[25] dicitur, quod idem fundamentum proxime et formaliter non potest servire ad relationes specie diversas, sicut album sub formalitate convenientiae fundat similitudinem, sub formalitate disconvenientiae dissimilitudinem. Et similiter in aliis exemplis allatis, si sunt diversae relationes (de quo non disputo), etiam dantur diversa fundamenta proxima et formalia.

Circa secundam difficultatem, quae in hoc articulo involvitur,[26] de distinctione et unitate numerica relationis: Pendet quidem ab illa celebri difficultate, utrum accidentia individuentur a subiecto, ita quod non possint duo accidentia solo numero distincta esse in eodem subiecto. Ceterum de hoc in praesenti agendum non est, sed solum explicandum, an possit unica relatio extendi et versari circa plures terminos, quorum quilibet sufficien-

[20] 379/21-24.
[21] 379/24-28.
[22] 379/29-39.
[23] Notably 382/47-383/33.
[24] 379/41-49.
[25] 379/49-380/8.
[26] 378/3, 379/10.

terminates that relation in the way, say, that one father is the father of many different sons. For it seems that this is impossible: First because one and the same effect cannot depend upon many different total causes each belonging to the same order and rationale of causality; but any son whatever is a sufficient and total term of being a father, for the reason that the relation is sufficiently and totally specified to that being of father; therefore the fatherhood in question cannot depend upon a subsequent son. Again too because in respect of the new son there exists a new act of procreation, therefore also a new relation identified with the generation. Nor can the already existing fatherhood be extended, because an extension of this sort is a new increase and addition of a relation and not a part of that already existent, because a relation lacks parts; therefore an additional son gives rise to an additional relation of paternity. Finally because a relation is an indivisible and simple modality;[27] therefore if when one

ter illam terminat, sicut unus pater plures filios. Videtur enim hoc esse impossibile: *Tum* quia non potest idem effectus pendere a pluribus causis totalibus eiusdem ordinis et rationis; quilibet autem filius est sufficiens et totalis terminus paternitatis, quia sufficienter et totaliter ad illam specificatur relatio; ergo non potest a sequenti filio eadem relatio pendere. *Tum* etiam quia respectu novi filii datur nova generatio, ergo et nova relatio, quae cum generatione identificatur. Nec potest de novo extendi, quia extensio ista est novum augmentum et additio relationis et non pars illius, quia relatio caret partibus, ergo nova relatio. *Tum* denique, quia relatio est indivisibilis et simplex modus;[27] ergo si mortuo uno

---

[27] Relation as a mode is ''simple'' in the way that all modes are simple, namely, as having no parts proper to themselves. Thus the ''modal distinction'' is a unique form of mind-independent difference, one which cannot even be treated directly in terms of act and potency, the central concepts of the Aristotelian and scholastic physics (Poinsot, 1632: Logica 2. p. q. 17. art. 4. 593b19-23: ''In quaest. autem 7. de Potentia art. 8. [*Pa* VIII. 161b.] dicit [D. Thomas], quod id, quod attribuitur alteri ut ab eo in aliud procedens, non facit compositionem cum eo, ut actio cum agente''; 1633: Phil. nat. 1. p. q. 4. art. 2. 95b41-96a3: ''*relatio*, ut dimanat a fundamento, non dicitur fieri ab ipso fundamento per eductionem, quia ad relationem non est per se motus, educitur tamen mediate ab ipso agente, a quo productum est illud fundamentum, quia producendo illud virtualiter producit omnes relationes, quae ex tali fundamento possunt consurgere positis terminis''). This is why the sign and semiosic activity as such stand outside the order of efficient and physical causality, as Poinsot notes (*Treatise on Signs*, Book I, Question 5). Nor are sign relations the only modes.

The basic distinction of the *Tractatus de Signis* is that between ontological and transcendental relation, as we have seen. Now a transcendental relation, as we have also seen, is a relative absolute, such as a head vis-a-vis its torso (Second Preamble, Article 2, 90/23-30 [=578b29-38]). A living head is an absolute thing with relativity to its torso ''imbibed into it'' (ibid.). That distinction between the absoluteness of the head and its ''imbibed relativity'' to its torso is a mind-independent or 'real' distinction, though not so great as the distinction between individually separated things, such as two higher organisms. Nor is it so great as a distinction between two relatively absolute but unseparated things, such as the living head and its living torso taken in their separability. Nor is it even so great a distinction as between a substance and its accidental forms inhering in the substance as in their potential subject: e.g., as the accidents quantity and quality inhere in their substantial subject (1632: Logica 2. p. q. 19. art. 1. 624a45-b4). It is called the modal distinction, and it is found in all transcendental relations between the thing as absolute and its imbibed relativity (ibid.: 624b39-47), as well as in all ontological relations between the relation as founded and in its own proper being (and therefore in all signs between the representative element as such and as signifying).

These modes are caused efficiently by the cause of the absolute thing of which they are modes. Such is the case of categorial relations (1633: Phil. nat. 1. p. q. 4. art. 2, Reiser ed. vol. II. 95b41-96a6). A categorial relation is the *imbibed relativity of its fundament* as *determined to a given* ***existing*** *terminus*. Thus the eye of the newborn had been produced in the fetus as transcendentally relative to still-absent light and colors. Once born, the eye's transcendental relativity to the now-present light results in a categorial relation. The new categorial relation is only modally distinct from its transcendental foundation, just as the previous imbibed transcendental relativity was only modally distinct from the absoluteness of the eye as a subjective part. ''*Ex hoc autem explicatur*,'' Poinsot proposes (1632: Logica 2. p. q. 17. art. 4. 594a5-26), ''*quommodo relatio possit fundari etiam in quibuscumque modis, quod non esset, si secundum se esset realitas distincta a fundamento.*

son dies and another survives the respect to the latter endures and that to the former perishes, one and the same entitative character endures and does not endure, because the entitative character of a relation is simple.

St. Thomas holds the contrary opinion in the *Summa Theologica*, III, q. 35, art. 5, and in the first of the *Questions at Random*, art. 2,[28] and in the ninth of the *Questions at Random*, art. 4.[29] And the learned Teacher establishes his opinion in terms not only of the general rationale of subjective characteristics which cannot be multiplied numerically in the same subject, but also in terms of what is unique to the case of relations, the fact namely that the foundation or cause is numerically identical, for example, in a relation of size, the same quantity in respect of all quantities of a given dimension; for one cubit is equal to all cubits by the same quantity; in a relation of paternity, the same generative power in respect of each of the sons, even though that power is modified by different exercises. Then too St. Thomas opts for this view as a way of avoiding the infinite multiplication of relations, as in one subject there are infinite proportions of parts, and in one teacher of a class comprising many students there are not many different teachers but only the one, and in one ruler and king there are not as many masters and relations as there are subjects, since by one same action it is possible to teach and to rule many. Finally, the relation of being a son touches the father and the mother by one single relation, and the many towing a boat are respected by the boat in a single relation. Therefore in like manner **one relation can attain all the termini of its specific character as inadequate terms of its proper extension,**

filio et alio permanente respectus ad unum permanet et ad alterum perit, eadem entitas permanet et non permanet, quia simplex est.

Oppositam sententiam tenet Divus Thomas 3. p. q. 35. art. 5. , Quodlib. 1. art. 2.[28] et Quodlib. 9. art. 4.[29] Et probat S. Doctor non solum propter generalem rationem accidentium, quae non possunt multiplicari numero in eodem subiecto, sed etiam propter specialem in relationibus, quia causa seu fundamentum est idem numero, v. g. in relatione quantitatis eadem quantitas respectu omnium quantitatum eiusdem extensionis; unus enim cubitus eadem quantitate omnibus cubitis aequalis est; eadem potentia generativa respectu omnium filiorum, licet diversis actionibus modificata. *Tum etiam* ne sequatur infinita multiplicatio relationum, sicut in uno subiecto sunt infinitae proportiones partium, et in uno magistro docente plures non sunt plura magisteria, sed unum, et in uno domino et rege non sunt tot dominia et relationes, quot servi, cum eadem actione possint doceri ac regi plures. *Denique* relatio filii tangit patrem ac matrem unica relatione, et plures trahentes navem respiciuntur unica relatione a navi. Ergo similiter potest una relatio attingere omnes terminos suae speciei tamquam inadaequatos suae ex-

Sequitur etiam, quomodo relatio sine mutatione physica dicatur resultare ad positionem termini, quod saepe affirmat ex mente Aristotelis S. Thomas, praesertim 5. Phys. lect. 3 [Le *II. 237. n. 7, et. 8*] *et in 1. dist. 26. q. 2. art. 1. ad 3.* [Pa *VI. 220 a.*], *ubi dicit relationem cessare nulla facta mutatione in re ipsa, quae refertur, hoc enim intelligitur fieri sine mutatione physica et entitativa, solum per novi modi resultantiam, quam D. Thomas non negat, sed manifeste ponit loco cit. ex 5. Phys. dicens, quod de novo determinatur radix relationis, quae est in aliquo, quando ponitur relatio ad istum vel illum, licet nihil de novo adveniat.*''—''In these terms is explicable how a relation can be founded even upon the various other modes which are not relations, which could not be explained if relation in its proper being exercised an existence distinct [i.e., in this context, separable] from its fundament independently of mind. In these terms too is explicable how a relation should be said to radiate toward a posited terminus, something often affirmed by St. Thomas as being in the line of the thinking of Aristotle, notably in the *Commentary* on the fifth book of the *Physics*, lect. 3 [*Le* II. 237. n. 7. et 8.] and in the *Commentary* on the first book of the *Sentences of Peter Lombard*, q. 2, dist. 26, art. 1, reply to the third objection [*Pa* VI. 220 a.], where Aquinas says that a relation ceases to be without any change being wrought in the thing which is referred, for this is understood to be without any physical and entitative change, only the result of a new modality, something Aquinas not only does not deny, but openly asserts in the passage cited from the *Commentary* on the fifth book of the *Physics* where he says that the root of a relation which has existence on the basis of another is determined anew when the relation is posited toward this or that, even though nothing new happens in the root itself.''

[28] *Pa* IX. 460 a.

[29] *Pa* IX. 589 b.96

even though each single terminus would suffice by itself for the existence of the relation in question; and so even though **this relation** would respect numerically this term in a determinate way, yet it would not do so adequately, but **would respect adequately all those termini in which there is the formality of term of this determinate character or given kind.**

To the foundations of the opposed views[30] the answer is: To the first[31] we say that one effect cannot depend on many different total and adequate causes formally; but if these causes are several only materially, the effect can well depend upon them inasmuch as they are coincident in some one way of causing or terminating. If for example ten men are enough to haul a certain stone, it can yet be hauled by twenty men who are only materially many more, but formally coincident in the single rationale of the hauling. In this way, the relation of being a father is sufficiently terminated at one son, yet if there are several offspring, this relation will also be terminated at each of the offspring coinciding in the same rationale of terminating the one same generative power modified by the different acts of procreation; for in that power thus modified is grounded the relation of parenthood in question, as we said in our explanation of St. Thomas in Article Three of the Second Preamble above.[32]

Finally, this resolution of the present difficulty may be clarified by a series of examples selected to show that when some one effect is produced by a single sufficient cause, if another sufficient cause joins in the production, that concurring cause does not produce the effect in question all over again, but is active respecting it in a new modality or way. In just this way, an alteration produces a quality, but if that altering process becomes suddenly more vigorous, the intensification of the action does not produce the quality in question but establishes and attains it in a new way, even if the amount of the increase would have been sufficient by itself to produce the quality in the first place. And in the case of the transsubstantiation of the Eucharist, even though the action of consecration is sufficient to produce the body of Christ, yet since it falls on something already existent, it does not produce it anew but establishes it in a new way. In the same way, even though one son sufficiently terminates the relation of being a father, yet if a new son is added to the existent relationship, that new son does not terminate a new relationship but extends the existing fatherhood as something now pertaining to himself as well. In the light of the opinion of St. Thomas that there is only

tensioni, licet quilibet sufficiat ad suam existentiam; et sic licet haec relatio numero respiciat determinate hunc terminum, non tamen adaequate, sed omnes illos, in quibus est formalitas talis termini.

Ad fundamenta opposita[30] respondetur: Ad primum[31] dicimus, quod unus effectus non potest pendere a pluribus causis totalibus et adaequatis formaliter; si tamen sint plures solum materialiter, bene potest ab illis pendere effectus, quatenus in uno modo causandi vel terminandi conveniunt. Sicut si tractio lapidis sufficienter fit a decem hominibus, potest nihilominus fieri a viginti, qui materialiter solum sunt plures, sed formaliter conveniunt in una ratione causandi. Sic relatio patris sufficienter terminatur ad unum filium, si tamen sint plures, etiam terminabitur ad illos tamquam convenientes in eadem ratione terminandi unicam potentiam generativam diversis actionibus modificatam; in ea enim sic modificata fundatur ista relatio, ut art. 3. ex D. Thoma diximus.[32]

Denique explicatur hoc diversis exemplis, quibus videmus unum effectum, quando est productus ab una causa sufficiente, si alia causa sufficiens superveniat, non de novo producit illum, sed novo modo versatur circa illum. Sicut alteratio producit qualitatem, intensio vero, quae de novo advenit, non producit illam, sed novo modo applicat et attingit, licet sufficiens esset producere qualitatem. Et transubstantiatio in Eucharistia licet sit sufficiens producere substantiam corporis Christi, tamen quia invenit productam, non de novo producit, sed novo modo applicat. Sic unus filius licet sufficienter terminet relationem patris, tamen si novus filius relationi productae superveniat, non terminat novam relationem, sed eandem ut ad se pertinentem extendit. In sententia Divi Thomae, quod in toto composito est

[30] 385/2-386/4.
[31] 385/3-9.
[32] 110/33-112/35, esp. 111/25-112/35.

one act of existence in a complex natural whole, an example more to the point can be found in the *Summa Theologica*, III, q. 17, art. 2. If an existing whole loses one of its parts, say, a hand or a foot, and afterward acquires a new one, a new existence is not produced in that individual, but the individual existence of the whole is applied to the new part as to something pertaining to the whole itself; and we say the same of the basic principles[33] of a science extended to many different conclusions without the addition of a new type of knowledge; and an intense quality is more firmly rooted without the addition of a new quality.

To the second contrary view[34] I say that even though a new act of generation is posited respecting the new son, by the fact that it occurs in a different time and matter (for otherwise there can well be several sons born of the same act of generation), yet the relation of being a father is not identified with nor founded in the act of generation except insofar as that action determines the generative power, as we explained above, and this power is one. Whence just as the relation of being a father can only be one relation in the case of twins or triplets, because it results from a single sexual act, so too when sons are produced through several different copulations; for it is only incidental whether several different actions or a single action of a given power modify that power respecting a relation of one specific rationale and character. Nor does this extension of a relation to different termini come about through the addition of a new relation, but through further deployment of the already existing relation, inasmuch as that relation of itself respects all termini proceding from the same fundament. But it is deployed in act when an action either founds or at least posits in fact a new terminus, as St. Thomas says in his *Commentary on the Physics of Aristotle*, Book V, lect. 3,[35] of the relation which springs from the root of the fundament to a newly posited term, where the terminus in question was virtually precontained.[36] And that a new relation should issue from a fundament or that a relation already in existence should be expanded or applied to that new terminus as pertaining to the existent relation is something intrinsic to the being proper to relation, namely, to tend and to be determined in act toward that in respect to which the relation was already tending virtually, and only for want of an existent terminus was not anchored. This serves to explain how

tantum una existentia, est accomodatius exemplum 3. p. q. 17. art. 2., quod si existente toto illi desit una pars, v. g. manus vel pes, si postea adveniat, non producitur in illo nova existentia, sed existentia totius illi applicatur tamquam rei ad se pertinenti; et idem dicimus de simplici habitu[33] scientiae se extendente ad plures conclusiones sine additione novi habitus; et radiocatur qualitas intensa sine additione novae qualitatis.

Ad secundum[34] dicitur, quod licet ponatur nova generatio respectu novi filii, eo quod diverso tempore et ex diversa materia fit (alias enim bene possint eadem generatione plures filii nasci), tamen relatio non identificatur cum actione nec fundatur in illa, nisi quatenus determinat potentiam generativam, ut supra diximus, et haec unica est. Unde sicut quando plures filii nascuntur ex eodem partu, relatio patris non potest esse nisi unica, quia in eadem actione fundatur, ita etiam quando per plures actiones producuntur; per accidens enim se habet, quod plures actiones vel unica actio eiusdem potentiae eam modificent ad relationem eiusdem rationis. Nec extensio ista relationis ad diversos terminos fit per additionem relationis novae, sed per explicationem praeexistentis, quatenus ipsa de se respicit omnes terminos procedentes ex eodem fundamento; explicatur vero in actu, quando actio vel fundat vel saltem ponit de facto novum terminum, sicut D. Thomas 5. Phys. lect. 3.[35] declarat de resultantia relationis ad positionem termini ex radice fundamenti, ubi praehabebatur.[36] Et quod e fundamento emittatur de novo relatio vel iam emissa explicetur aut applicetur ad illum novum terminum ut ad se pertinentem, ipsi relationi intrinsecum est, scilicet tendere et determinari in actu ad id, ad quod de se tendebat virtualiter, et solum defectu existentiae termini non dabatur. Servit hoc

33 Reiser's text reads ''habitus''.
34 385/10-16.
35 *Le* II. 237. n. 7. et 8.
36 Cf. 381/40-382/26.

the ideas of pure spirits, without any change in the representative character of the ideas, can represent a new object which formerly did not exist and now begins to exist.[37]

To the third view[38] I answer that a relation is entitatively simple but terminatively multiple, which is to be divisible respectively, indivisible entitatively; and so when one among a given relation's materially several termini perishes, the relation perishes as regards its being anchored at and extended to that terminus, but it does not perish simply and in its proper being. The situation is similar to what we find in a science which is extended to new conclusions and can fail to reach some particular conclusion without failing in respect of the others nor entitatively in itself; and in the existence of a whole communicated to different parts, and in one angelic idea attaining some existing objects but not the non-existing ones. All of which cases will be examined in their proper place.

ad explicandum, quomodo species angeli sine mutatione repraesentationis novum obiectum repraesentent, quod ante non existebat et nunc incipit existere.[37]

Ad tertium[38] respondetur, quod relatio entitative est simplex, sed terminative multiplex, quod est respective esse divisibilem, entitative indivisibilem; et ita pereunte uno ex terminis materialiter ibi repertis, perit relatio quoad applicationem et extensionem ad illum, non simpliciter et in se. Simile quid invenitur in habitu simplici scientiae, qui extenditur ad novas conclusiones, et potest deficere una conclusio, non deficiendo quoad alias nec entitative in se; et in existentia totius communicata ad diversas partes, et in una specie angelica attingente aliqua obiecta existentia, non vero non existentia. Quae omnia suis locis examinabuntur.

[37] Detailed exposition in Poinsot 1643b: disp. 42. art. 2., esp. par. 30, p. 646.
[38] 385/17-386/4.

EDITORIAL AFTERWORD

CVRSVS PHILOSOPHICI

THOMISTICI,

SECVNDVM EXACTAM, VERAM ET GENVINAM ARISTOTELIS ET DOCTORIS ANGELICI MENTEM,

Monrij PARS PRIMA. Reichenbace

CONTINENS EA QVÆ AD ARTEM LOGICAM SPECTANT, TRACTATVM DE DIALECTICIS INSTITVTIONIBVS QVAS SVMMVLAS VOCANT, IN ISAGOGEN PORPHYRII, ARISTOTELIS CATHEGORIAS, ET LIBROS POSTERIORVM.

Auctore

Admodum Reuerendo & Eximio

P. F. IOANNE à SANCTO THOMA, OLISIPPONENSI, Ordinis Prædicatorum S. T. M. quondam in alma Complutensi Vniuersitate; nunc verò Salmaticensi Theologicæ Cathedræ vespertinæ Moderatore; ibidemq; Collegiorum eiusdem Ordinis Regente, Supremi Consilij, sanctæ generalis Inquisitionis in causis fidei, Censore.

Nunc primùm in Germania excusus, à multis mendis vindicatus, & ex eiusdem Magistri doctrina illustratus,

Per A. R. P. F. THOMAM DE SARRIA, Compostellanum, Ord. Prædicatorum, S. T. M. Conuentus sanctæ Crucis Regentem, ac in Coloniensi Vniuersitate publicum & ordinarium Professorem.

COLONIÆ AGRIPPINÆ,
Sumptibus CONSTANTINI MüNICH Bibliopolæ,
ANNO M. DC. XXXVIII.

Cum speciali Gratia & Priuil. S. Cæs. Maiest.

Title page from the 1638 Cologne edition of the *Cursus Philosophicus* issued by Thomas of Sarria. See discussion below, pp. 446–448, esp. p. 447 note 76. Photograph courtesy of Achim Eschbach.

EDITORIAL AFTERWORD: CONTENTS

I.

The Project of John Poinsot and the Text of the Treatise on Signs

The text of the *Treatise on Signs*, just presented integrally for the first time in autonomous form, is the latest in a series of editions of Poinsot's writings that began within Poinsot's own lifetime and have continued at intervals down to the present day.

The project expressed by these writings, taken in their entirety, is nothing less than a judicious assessment of the philosophical and theological thought of the Latin West, taken in its historical totality as synthesizing influences of ancient Greece, Rome, Byzantium (Constantinople), and Islam.

Poinsot devoted the full energies of his mature life, with a literally religious fervor, to this monumental undertaking, leaving behind at the time of his death a complete edition of his proposed university *Cursus Philosophicus*, and a partially completed edition of a much larger *Cursus Theologicus*, the remaining manuscripts for which were posthumously edited and published in a series of volumes completed only in 1667, a full twenty-three years after the death of their author.[1] These two *Cursus*, taken together, constitute in its integrity

[1] One of the main lines separating modern from medieval times is the transition from manuscript copies to printed texts. By this criterion, Poinsot, a renaissance Latin by intellectual tradition, belongs firmly on the modern side of the line. The *manuscript traditions* which wind so tortuously across the centuries transmitting the major Latin writers down to the era of published texts, and which make for such difficulty in researching the Latin origins of modern times, play no role whatever in the study of Poinsot's work, not only because the greater part of his writing was brought to press under his own direction, but because not so much as a fragment of the original manuscripts for either *Cursus* is known to have survived beyond the 1667 publication of the final tome of his theological writings (Reiser, 1930: XII-XIII; Solesmes, 1931: xxx-xxxj). The Solesmes editors conjecture from this fact (ibid.) that Poinsot's posthumous editors may simply have followed his own example in treating the original manuscripts as things of little or no value once they had been set into type. (*''Quo ex exemplo conjicere fas est auctoris nostri autographa, ubi primum typis fuerunt excusa, quasi res nullius valoris neglecta atque destructa esse. Manuscriptis ergo prorsus deficientibus, reliquum erat ut ad edita volumina converteremur.''*)

the major project of Poinsot's intellectual life.[2] The truly extraordinary scale of this enterprise was in many respects typical of the spirit of medieval and renaissance scholasticism, which reached its final, most exotic bloom in the university world of the Iberian peninsula. Since our *Treatise* originally appeared as an integrated part of this much vaster enterprise, it is useful to begin with some appreciation of the scale of the original whole. To this end, the following chart of the various editions, partial and total, during and after their author's lifetime, of Poinsot's main writings may be of some assistance:

[2] Our author also wrote in Spanish some minor works of an ascetical and devotional nature, which have also had an impressive publication history.

1) *Explicación de la doctrina christiana y la obligación de los fieles en creer y obrar, ofrecida a la santisima Virgen del Rosario señora neustra*, Madrid, 1640. A fifth edition of this work was prepared by Poinsot in the final months of his life, which was published at Alcalá in 1645. A sixth edition appeared this same year at Saragossa, a seventh at Antwerp in 1651. After these seven Spanish editions, Henricus Hechtermans translated the work into Latin and published it at Brussels in 1658 under the title, *Compendium totius doctrinae christianae*. An Italian translation, *Catechismo ò vero explicatione della Dottrina cristiana*, by Joseph Bonfilio, was published at Rome in 1633. A French translation by Antoine du Prat Chassagny, *Catéchisme du R.P. Jean de S. Thomas, de l'ordre des Frères Prêcheurs*, published at Lyons in 1675, lists on its elaborate title page two additional translations, without assigning them a date, one into Irish by a du Rosaire, and one into Polish by Jean-Baptiste Gabriesquy; but the Solesmes editors (1931: XV) consider it uncertain whether these last two translations ever went to press. Further discussion of this work can be found in Reiser's "Editoris Praefatio" (1930: IX-X).

2) *Practica y consideración para ayudar a bien morir*, first published along with the preceding work at Alcalá in 1645, and again in 1645 at Saragossa. Hechtermans translated it into Latin and published it along with his 1658 Brussels Latin edition of the preceding work. Raymond Knilling made an independent Latin translation, *Praxis adjuvandi infirmos, ad bene feliciterque moriendum*, which he published at Prague, c. 1663, along with his Latin translation of the *Promptuario de materias morales* written in Spanish by Simone de Salazar (see Solesmes "Praefatio," 1931: XV note 4). An Italian translation entitled *Prattica e considerazioni per ajutare e per disporsi a ben morire* was published at Florence in 1674. Another Latin translation appeared in Venice in 1693: *Aurea praxis adiuvandi infirmos ad bene feliciterque moriendum, simulque tractatus duo, alter ecclesiasticas censuras omnes atque cunctarum propositionum damnatarum notitiam complectens, alter confessionem regis generalem, et ut singularis persona et ut rex est edocens.*

3) *Breve tratado y muy importante, que por mandato de su Majesdad escribibió el R. P. Fr. Juan de S. Tomas para saber hacer una confesion general*, Madrid, 1644, 1692. In Latin translation, this work was published along with the preceding work at Venice in 1693.

4) The 1692 Madrid edition of the preceding *Breve tratado* is bound along with another work, *Mysterios del Santisimo Rosario y modo ofrecerle*, which Reiser ("Praefatio," 1930: X) ascribes to Poinsot, but which the Solesmes editors (1931: xvj note 1) consider doubtful ("Quod enim una cum genuino opusculo in uno volumine compactum invenitur, non est nisi valde debile de ejus origine indicium").

CURSUS PHILOSOPHICUS

	Artis Logicae Ia Pars	IIa Pars	Naturalis Philosophiae Ia Pars	IIIa Pars	IVa Pars
1631	Alcalá				
1632		Alcalá			
1633			Madrid		
1634	Alcalá			Alcalá	
1635	Douai				Alcalá
1637					
1637-1638	Rome	Rome	Rome	Rome	Rome
1638	Cologne	Cologne	Cologne	Cologne	Cologne
1640		Madrid			
1643					
1644			Saragossa †		
1645					
1648	Madrid				
1649					
1654	Cologne	Cologne	Cologne	Cologne	Cologne
1656					
1658					
1663	Lyons	Lyons	Lyons	Lyons	Lyons
1667					
1674					
1678	Lyons	Lyons	Lyons	Lyons	Lyons
1684	Bologna	Bologna	Bologna	Bologna	Bologna
1694	Ferrara	Ferrara			
1711					
1883-1886	Paris	Paris	Paris	Paris	Paris
1928					
1930	Turin	Turin			
1931					
1933			Turin	Turin	
1934					
1937					Turin
1946					
1947					
1948					
1949					
1951					
1952					
1953					
1954					
1955		Chicago[4e]			
1962	Milwaukee[4e]				
1964					
1985		The Semiotic: *Tractatus de Signis*			

1e Partial, Latin
2e Partial, Spanish
3e Partial, French
4e Partial, English

†Death of Poinsot

CURSUS THEOLOGICUS

POINSOT, *Joannes ("a sancto Thoma,"* with variants, in the late Latin period, and after)

Tomus Primus	Secundus	Tertius	Quartus	Quintus	Sextus	Septimus	Octavus
Alcalá							
	Lyons	Lyons					
			Madrid	Madrid			
					Madrid		
Genoa							
						Madrid	
Cologne[1e]							
Lyons	Lyons	Lyons	Lyons	Lyons	Lyons	Lyons	
							Paris
							Lyons
Cologne	Cologne	Cologne	Cologne	Cologne	Cologne	Cologne	Cologne
Paris I, II	Paris III	Paris IV	Paris V	Paris VI	Paris VII	Paris VIII	Paris IX
Paris[3e]							
				Paris[3e]			
Solesmes I							
Solesmes II							
	Solesmes III						
		Solesmes IV					
Laval[1e]					Laval[1e]		
				Madrid[2e]; Laval[1e]			
			Laval[1e]				
				New York[4e]			
			Laval[1e]				
					Laval(bis)[1e]		
				Laval[1e]			
				Laval[1e]			
			Solesmes V				

The story of the *Cursus Theologicus* in particular is an involved tale interspersed with disasters, too intricate to be directly recounted here.[3] Suffice to say that it is only in our own century, beginning with the first Solesmes volume of 1931, that a definitive editing of this work as a whole is being achieved,[4] with the four final volumes yet to apear as of this writing.

Fortunately for our purposes, the story of the text of the *Cursus Philosophicus*, whence our *Treatise* derives, is much less involved, inasmuch as its several parts

---

[3] The interested reader, however, will find much of the story indirectly told in the following series of notes, and is referred to the "Editorum Solesmensium Praefatio" of 1931, Caput Secundum, pp. xvij-xxv, where the story is told in full directly. (This fantastic document—the Solesmes "Praefatio" in its entirety, i.e., along with its eighteen Appendices, Epilogue, Index Materiarum, and Index Onomasticus Virorum, Locorum, atque Operum—is the most indispensable single piece of historical scholarship relative to Poinsot's life and works that one could imagine.) For the relation of the Solesmes' edition of Poinsot's *Cursus Theologicus* to the earlier editions, see ibid., Caput Quartum, pp. xxx-xxxiv, esp. p. xxxiij, par. 3; also the "Solesmensium Editorum Praefatio in Tomum Secundum," 1934, pp. i-v, esp. p. i, pars. 2-4, and the table, "Omnium Editionum Concordia," p. iii (the Solesmes editors reprint this concordance in the front of each of their next two volumes); "Solesmensium Editorum Praefatio in Tomum Quartum," 1953, esp. pp. iv-vi, pars. 8-15; and "Solesmensium Editorum Praefatio in Tomum Quintum," 1964, esp. p. vi, pars. 2-3.

The contents of the original eight volumes in terms of the *Summa theologiae* of Thomas Aquinas can be briefly gathered from this table, taken from Lavaud (1926: 414), who in turn takes it from Quetif-Echard, 1721:

"*Cursus Theologicus*. Éditions Partielles.

T. I. *Tres Tractatus ad theologiae tyrones praemissi: Primus* in Universum textum Magistri sententiarum in ordinem redigit; *Secundus*, omnium quaestionum D. Thomae et materiarum in sua summa ordinem explicat; *Tertius*, vindicias D. Thomae pro doctrinae ejus puritate probitate et singulari approbatione offert. *In Iam Partem, de Deo, qq. 1-14*, et tractatus de opere sex dierum, Alcalá (Ant. Vasquez), 1637; Gênes (Ben. Guaschi), 1654.

T. II. *In Iam Partem, de Deo, qq. 15-26*, Lyon (Pierre Prost), 1643.

T. III. *In Iam Partem, de Trinitate et Angelis*, ibid.

Ces 3 volumes furent édités par Jean de Saint-Thomas lui-même.

T. IV. *In Iam IIae, de Ultimo fine et de actibus humanis, qq. 1-20*, Madrid (M. de Quiñonez), 1645.

T. V. *In Iam IIae, qq. 21-70 et 109-114*, Madrid (M. de Quiñonez), 1645.

T. VI. *In IIam IIae, qq. 1-23, 64, 81, 82* [inserting the correction of Simonin, 1930: 147 note 1], *83, 88.—VIII Quaest. Quodlibetales*, Madrid (M. de Quiñonez), 1649.

T. VII. *In IIIam Partem, de Incarnatione, qq. 1-26*, Madrid (typis regiis), 1656.

Ces trois volumes furent publiés par Diego Ramirez.

T. VIII. *In IIIam Partem, de Sacramentis in genere, de Eucharistia, de Poenitentia*, Paris (Ant. Berthier), 1667; Lyons (Cl. Langloys), 1674.

Ce volume fut publié par les PP. Combefis et Quetif."

The contents of this table are reviewed in narrative form by Lavaud, 1928: 424-435, in a very insightful survey.

[4] Solesmes, 1931: xxx: "*Quodsi igitur* critica *tibi audiat editio quaecumque monumentis diligenter scrutatis, testimoniis undique collectis et attente ponderatis, originalem textum eruere studet, eique, nisi aperte corrupto sancte adhaeret, arbitrio privato mutationem concedens nullam, omnibus interim annotatis lectionibus variis unde aliquid commodi speretur: et si quando conjecturalis correctio sit introducenda, numquam reticens quid praeferant testes antiqui: hujusmodi criticam editionem elaborasse nobis in votis fuit.*" —"If therefore by a *critical* edition one understands an original text established by a careful investigation of the literary remains in the light of evidence gathered from wherever possible and considered attentively, a text religiously adhered to save where it has been unmistakably corrupted, with no changes made from private judgment, but with annotation of all variant readings whence some profit might be hoped for: a text where whenever a conjectural correction needs to be introduced, the old readings are never concealed: it is to this sort of a critical edition that we have committed ourselves." (Within the limits afforded by the Reiser text, I may add, as the reader of Sections I.B.D. and III.A.B.C. below can learn, these are the standards and principles that have been applied to the establishment of our edition of the *Tractatus de signis*.)

were brought to completed publication within their author's lifetime and under his own editorial guidance.[5] Nonetheless, there are anomalies and one striking lacuna in this *Cursus* that bear closer examination for those seeking to appreciate in its historical origins the *Treatise on Signs* that is our central concern in this work.

In the intellectual traditions of Latin scholasticism to which Poinsot was heir, philosophical study was considered to include the entire life of reason or human understanding with the resources proper to it, and to provide the necessary foundation for and preamble to theological study as the enhancement of human understanding made possible by Christian faith. As such, Poinsot's *Cursus Philosophicus* demands to be understood on its own ground and in its own terms, and it is to this task that we now turn.

A. The Structure of the *Cursus Philosophicus*

> *L'ouvrage de Jean de St.-Thomas se presente donc comme un ouvrage de transition; c'est là la marque de son originalité. . . . Aussi n'est-ce pas sans émotion que l'on voit Jean de St.-Thomas s'essayer à faire la synthèse de l'inconciliable. D'un côté il n'entend laisser perdre aucune des acquisitions nouvelles, et profiter des derniers développements d'une scolastique qui s'épuise elle même à force de raffinements, mais d'autre part il entend, davantage encore, rester un homme du passé et disposer l'ensemble de son oeuvre selon le plan ancien et les anciennes méthodes. Il y fallait évidemment le coup d'oeil et la main d'un artiste exceptionnel, et, quelque sympathie que l'on puisse avoir pour la tentative, il semble bien qu'elle n'était pas appelée à se développer et à s'épanouir normalement. . . . Ainsi comprise et située à sa place dans l'ensemble d'une evolution, l'oeuvre de Jean de St.-Thomas prend une signification spéciale, et peut-être un intérêt notable en un moment où l'on retrouve le goût du style ancien.*
>
> Simonin, 1930: 145-146
>
> *The work of Poinsot reveals itself as a work of transition; that is the mark of its author's originality. . . . It is not without feeling that one watches Poinsot attempt a synthesis of irreconcilables. On the one hand, he is determined to let no new achievements be lost, and to profit from the final developments of a Scholasticism which has exhausted itself in the plentitude of its refinements; but on the*

[5] The general title of "Cursus Philosophicus" for the volumes Poinsot himself edited, first appears in the first general edition of all the parts, the 1637-38 Rome edition—but applied only to the volumes of Natural Philosophy (Solesmes, 1931: xiv note 2). Whether this title was affixed by Poinsot himself or only by the Roman publisher is not known (Reiser, "Editoris in Secundum Volumen Praefatio," 1933: V; cf. Reiser, "Editoris Praefatio," 1930: XII and XVI). The general title Reiser himself uses for his edition, "Cursus Philosophicus Thomisticus," does not appear until the Cologne edition of 1638 edited by Thomas of Sarria, and was perhaps only of Sarria's, not of Poinsot's, devising. This fact, coupled with the lesser authority of the Cologne edition (Reiser "Praefatio," 1930: XIV, XVI), leads me to prefer the earlier general title, which may well have been given the work by Poinsot himself, and which the better parallels the general title unquestionably chosen by Poinsot himself for his subsequent theological volumes. Following the custom since at least 1638, I also extend this title to include the logic. See the discussion in note 10 below.

> *other hand, he is determined further still to remain a man of the past and to arrange his work in its totality according to the pattern and methods of long-standing tradition. One sees there quite clearly the eye and hand of an exceptional artist, and, whatever sympathy one may have for the attempt, it seems equally clear that it was not destined to develop and fulfill itself normally. . . . Thus understood and given its place in the development of history, the work of Poinsot acquires a particular significance, and perhaps an especial interest at a time when one rediscovers the flavor of an ancient style.*

The *Cursus Philosophicus* has two main parts, Logic and Natural Philosophy.[6] Poinsot's presentation of both parts, but in very different ways, is a revolutionary departure from the traditions to which he was heir. So as to wind up at the point of principal interest to us, let us look first at the revolutionary aspect in his discussion of the philosophy of nature.

As originally projected by its author, the *Philosophia Naturalis* was to have four parts: I. a general study of material being (''de ente mobili in communi''); II. a study of the material being thought to be impervious to growth and decay, namely, the celestial bodies (''de ente mobili incorruptibili, quod est coelum''); III. a study of the various ways in which material being is subjected to growth and decay (''de ente mobili corruptibili''); and finally, IV. a study of the living world in particular (''de ente mobili animato'').

To appreciate the thoroughly traditional character of this fourfold division, the reader needs to know something about integral Latin Aristotelianism, which had its origin in the mid-twelfth-century translations of the entire body of Aristotle's writings along with the extensive *Commentaries* thereon developed by Islamic philosophers. The beginnings of this movement in the thirteenth century in the writings of such men as Albertus Magnus (c. 1200-1280), Thomas Aquinas (1225-1274), and Roger Bacon (1214-1292), and its influence in the fourteenth century on such men as Duns Scotus (1265-1308), William of Ockham (1280-1349), and John Buridan (c. 1300-1358), are a well-known and standard part of the current academic presentation of ''medieval philosophy.''

Not so well-known or appreciated is the fact that the work of these ''medieval'' and early renaissance Latin Aristotelians formed but the first wave of a philosophical movement that became the backbone of the development of European academic and university life for the next four hundred years. The best of its writers tried to envision nothing less than a complete integration and synthesis in the life of reason of all the achievements of the ancient Greeks and Romans as of the civilizations of Christianity and Islam. The heterogeneous currents of this broad movement in many ways reached their fullest expression in the vast compendia worked out in Iberia by the Jesuit Aristotelians of Coimbra (the so-called *Conimbricenses*, sixteenth-seventeenth centuries), and by the Carmelite Aristotelians of Alcalá (the *Complutenses*, late sixteenth-early seventeenth centuries) and of Salamanca (the *Salmanticenses*, seventeenth century);

---

[6] For the then-traditional way of understanding these parts, the reader is referred to Poinsot's ''Prooemium'' (1633) to phil. nat. 1. p. (Reiser ed. Vol. II, pp. 3-4); and to the remarks of Reiser, 1930: XII (cited in note 83, page 450 below) on the treatment of metaphysics and ethics in Poinsot's writings. See also Lavaud, 1928: 413-421.

but the way was prepared and the movement developed through the works of more individual thinkers as diverse as John Capreolus (c. 1380-1444), Sylvester Ferrariensis (c. 1474-1528), Pietro Pomponazzi (1462-1524), Thomas de vio Cajetan (1469-1534), Francis Vitoria (1483-1546), Domingo Bañez (1582-1604), Louis Molina (1535-1600), the towering Francis Suarez (1548-1617), and our own John Poinsot (1589-1644), to name only a few.

Compared to the work and influence of this mainstream Aristotelianism, such popularly studied renaissance figures as Nicholas of Cusa (1401-1464), Marsilius Ficino (1433-1499), Petrus Ramus (1515-1572), and others of comparative modern fame, were in many respects (Kristeller, 1961a: 42-44) side currents, eddies in the general development dominated by the writings of Aristotle. The controversies of mainstream Aristotelianism aimed, at their best, to deepen our grasp of the world, if all too often succeeding only (and this is the aspect of the period alone emphasized in the conventionalized modern stereotype of "the scholastics") in confounding constructs of reason with natural structures and substituting dialectical domination for philosophical understanding.

This is not the place to clear away at a stroke the hoary prejudices that have grown up since the time of Descartes to obscure and distort the age and achievements of Latin Aristotelianism. Suffice here to observe only that the want of a *proper outline* of the intellectual currents providing the connecting links is a large part of the reason why "the transition from the thirteenth to the seventeenth centuries, when modern philosophy is conventionally supposed to have begun," is, as Randall (1962: vi-viii) well says, the "least known period in the history of Western philosophy." As Kristeller, virtually alone among modern historians, has enabled us to see (1961b: 114-116 *passim*; see also 99-100, 111, 119; 161a: 34; 1961b: 134):

> . . . Renaissance Aristotelianism continued the medieval scholastic tradition without any visible break. It preserved a firm hold on the university chairs of logic, natural philosophy, and metaphysics, whereas even the humanist professors of moral philospphy continued to base their lectures on Aristotle. The literary activity of these Aristotelian philosophers . . . is difficult of access and arduous to read, but rich in philosophical problems and doctrines. It represents the bulk and kernel of the philosophical thought of the period, but it has been badly neglected by modern historians. . . . Consequently, most modern scholars have condemned the Aristotelian philosophers of the Renaissance without a hearing. . . . If we want to judge the merits and limitations of Renaissance Aristotelianism we will have to proceed to a new direct investigation of the source materials, instead of repeating antiquated judgments.

The last of these cited comments is the key one: what is needed before all else is a *return to sources*, of which this present edition is one. For, in simple fact, there is no name or place in the conventionalized history of philosophy as settled, in particular, by the careful German-trained historians of the late nineteenth and early twentieth centuries (e.g., Höffding, 1900; Windelband, 1901), for the epoch of "philosophia naturalis" that culminates in the *Cursus Philosophicus* of John Poinsot and other like syntheses of the period. Fascinated by the rise of experimental science and taken in by the concomitant rhetoric

of the early modern philosophers against the Latin tradition, these historians lacked the means to interpret or appreciate the medieval Aristotelian heritage, let alone its maturation through the renaissance. Even the great revival of medieval studies after Gilson (d. 1978) carried no further than the fourteenth century (cf. Kristeller, 1961a: 34; 1961b: 114-115; and note 130 below), while the pioneering studies of Giacon (1944, 1946, 1950) can be regarded as no more than partial and preliminary. Yet the "Middle Ages" from Augustine (354-430) and Boethius (c. 480-525) to Abelard (1079-1142) and John of Salisbury (1115-1180) are one thing; the development after the new translations of Aristotle (post-c. 1150) culminating in the syntheses of Suarez and Poinsot at the dawn of "modern philosophy" with the work particularly of Descartes (1596-1650) and Locke (1632-1704) is something else again. This period, c. 1150-1650, was the age of the philosophy of nature (Kristeller, 1961a, b, c; J. Maritain, 1922, 1932a, 1935a, b) rooted in the conviction that human understanding could attain a grasp of what exists independently of human understanding, *as* it thus exists, a conviction that was weakened and eventually lost in modern times as the focus of philosophical understanding shifted from being to discourse as the process and product of that very understanding.

In any event, it is to this tradition of natural philosophy that Poinsot's *Cursus Philosophicus* firmly belongs, and it is the mainstream of *this* development as it had taken form over the two and a half centuries or so before him that Poinsot consciously and deliberately expressed in the fourfold division projected for his *philosophia naturalis*.

But when it comes to the publication of his lecture courses, a remarkable lacuna appears under the author's own control, without any word of explanation or apology of any kind.[7]

Beginning in 1631, and in each subsequent year, Poinsot publishes a new part of his *Cursus Philosophicus*. But immediately following the 1633 publication of the *Philosophiae Naturalis Prima Pars* (the general study of material being), Poinsot suppresses or omits the traditional "astronomy" (as a study of bodies impervious to development or decline, subject only to change of position in space), or *Secunda Pars*, and proceeds immediately to publish directly in 1634 the *Tertia Pars*, or study of the ways in which material being is subject

[7] The Solesmes editors (1953: iv-vj, pars. 8-15) relate a similar (and not unrelated) lacuna caused by Poinsot in the publication of the manuscripts for his theological courses, namely, his suppression of his treatise on the creation of the world (*Tractatus de opere sex dierum*), but with the difference that, in this case (unlike the one we are considering above), the manuscript itself did not disappear, and was posthumously published at the end of Vol. I of the criminal 1663 Lyons edition that Père Combefis went so far as to attempt to have juridically suppressed (Solesmes, 1931: xxj-xxiv, Art. III, and Appendix XVII, xc-xciij; 1953: v par. 13; see notes 8 and 64 below), a place where—fittingly enough, given the editors—it completely disrupts the proper order of the *Cursus* (Solesmes, 1931: xxxiij, number 3). Hence the Solesmes editors, under the direction of Dom Boissard, relocate this tractate in its doctrinally proper place, after the treatment of angels (*Tomus Quartus Cursus Theologici*, Solesmes ed. 1946, 1953: 837 ad finem tomi), but set in a lesser typeface than the *Cursus tractates* (*seu "disputationes"*) authorized by Poinsot for publication, *"veluti opusculum quoddam origine quidem genuinum, at fructu sententiarumque pondere certe inferius"* (Solesmes 1953: v par. 14: "so as to indicate a lesser work of undoubtedly genuine origin, but one whose results and opinions are certainly of a lesser order"). See further discussion in note 55 below.

to generation and corruption. As if to heighten perplexity on the point, in his ''Preface'' or ''Word to the Reader'' (''Lectori'') opening this *tertia pars*, Poinsot, entirely silent on the matter of the *secunda pars*, devotes himself to explaining the *direct* connection of the third part (that is, the detailed treatment of the modes of alteration to which material being is subject) to the first part (namely, the general treatment of the principles which render material being subject to change) of the philosophy of nature! By coincidence at least, 1634 is of course the year of the famous condemnation in Rome of Galileo. It is also the year in which the traditional treatment of astronomy (''de caelo'') was tentatively adjudged irrelevant to the essential principles and proper understanding of the Aristotelian philosophy of nature by the professor principally charged at that time with the development of the curriculum of Arts at the major university of Alcalá de Henares, second only to Salamanca in Spain of the period.

I say ''tentatively,'' because Poinsot never took the further step of suppressing the then-traditional fourfold division itself in favor of a tri-partite structure (though his posthumous editors took the liberty of doing that for him[8]). None-

---

[8] Reiser details these posthumous attempts ''to cover and obliterate'' (''*oblinere et oblitterare*'') Poinsot's original partition of the Natural Philosophy in his ''Prefaces'' of 1930: XIV-XV and 1933: V-VI. Already with the 1654 Cologne edition (Reiser, 1933: V note 4), early editors had supplanted Poinsot's original fourfold division with a tripartite structure. The 1663 Lyons editors did the same, and then, through the inexcusable device of unacknowledged alterations in Poinsot's 1634 ''Prooemium'' to his *Tertia Pars Naturalis Philosophiae* (Reiser ed., 1933: 536a1-5 and note 1), presented their work as though it were Poinsot's own (this was the same group of greedy and unscrupulous bookdealers—''*ab his suspectae fidei bibliopolis*,'' as the Solesmes editors later summarized, 1953: iv—responsible for the crime of the 1663 Lyons general edition of the *Cursus Theologicus* related in appalling detail in Solesmes, 1931, 1953, as cited in note 7 above, which edition set theological scholarship in this area back for a full three centuries). In 1721: 538, Quetif-Echard, in order ''to remove major inconveniences and achieve a smooth-flowing division,'' Reiser conjectures (1930: VII), so misrepresented the content of Poinsot's fourfold division as to disguise the fact that one part had in fact been suppressed by its author. From that time onward—''one writer copies another without so much as a look at or reading of the actual works,'' Reiser says with perhaps a touch of scorn (1930: XV: ''*alius alium transcripsit, quin viderit aut legerit ipsa opera*'')—this convenient manner of ''exposition'' became commonplace (e.g., J. M. Ramirez, 1924: 804; Lavaud, 1926: 413, 1928: 414), thus making unwitting forfeiture of one of the most pregnant of historical clues to the significance of Poinsot's *Cursus Philosophicus* and perpetuating the myth that he clung to the discredited empirical beliefs of the ancients (Lavaud, 1928: 416-417) and knew nothing of the works of Galileo and Descartes (Simon, 1955: xix). On the contrary, silence in the case of Poinsot does not automatically mean nescience (see the discussion below of the Index Personarum in Section III.B.3), and such allegations seem simply incompatible with the circumstances of Poinsot's life, the education he received, and the offices he was called on to fill (see Section II below). Indeed, to the partisans of Poinsot's philosophical work from within Iberia, it could only seem that his ''Cursus Omnium Artium,'' as his first biographer, Didacus Ramirez, called it (1645: in Solesmes, 1931: xxxvij), bid fair to establish itself and renew the university traditions through the whole of Europe: ''fere totam peragravit Europam, omnibus sic applaudentibus, et tanta aviditate inhiantibus ut repetitas ipse in Italia, Gallia, Germania, et Belgio adhuc vivens viderit impressiones, superstitibus adhuc protestantibus Cartis quibus progredi eum suppliciter Universitates exposcunt in exarandis doctrinae Thomisticae Commentariis, quibus veritati Adversantium tela diluerunt.''

It is also worth noting, with Kristeller (1961b: 118; see also 1961a: 45-46), that if the progress during the sixteenth century enabling mathematics and astronomy to assume increasing importance in practical affairs and in the curricula of the schools and universities ''did not immediately affect philosophy, this was due not to the stupidity or inertia of contemporary philosophers, but to the fact that physics or natural philosophy was considered as a part of philosophy and that there was almost no traditional link between the mathematical sciences and philosophy.''

See further note 55 below.

theless, the quiet dropping of the traditional treatment of astronomy as something alien and extraneous to the implicit consequences of the general structure of material being is something of a revolution, if one views Poinsot's work retrospectively vis-à-vis the Latin Aristotelian mainstream. In effect, Poinsot is suggesting that the entire development of the *Quaestiones de caelo et mundo* after Aristotle in the Latin translations of Averroes (1126-1198) and Avicenna (980-1037), in the works of Albertus Magnus, Thomas Aquinas, Peter of Auvergne (d. 1302), Aegidius Romanus (c. 1247-1316), Buridan (c. 1300-1358), and the "steady series of Expositions and Problems" (Moody, 1942: xviii) after Buridan down to Galileo's time, has been parasitic upon and detrimental to the true philosophical understanding of the material world in what is proper to it.

This construction of Poinsot's omission of this traditional treatise is supported by Poinsot's letter of 3 July 1635 to Nicolaus Ridolfi,[9] where, "having before his eyes the publication of the first part of the Logic from 1631, of the second part from 1632, of the first part of the Natural Philosophy from 1633, the third part from 1634, and the fourth part from 1635," Poinsot described his *Cursus Philosophicus* as a "corpus artium finitum seu perfectum" ("cuerpo de Artes acabado")[10]—a finished curriculum of Arts.

Thus Poinsot's handling of the traditional philosophy of nature is revolutionary in a negative way, by deletion. His handling of the logical tradition, by contrast, to which we now turn, is revolutionary in a positive way, and indeed, it would seem, in an absolutely foundational way that, while clearly envisioned to some extent by its author, was so skillfully balanced and qualified by his artistic integration of it into the traditional treatment of logic that its deep tendency escaped the notice of his contemporary readers, however active and influential it doubless remained in his own thought (and throughout the *Cursus Theologicus* as well) and as it was destined to enter the history of these questions anew in our own time.

B. The Novel Status of the *Tractatus de Signis* within the *Cursus Philosophicus*

Here we must in effect resume and gather into a more compressed form the insights that are woven into the reading of Poinsot's own text over the

[9] Published in Reiser, 1933: VI-VII.

[10] Reiser, 1933: VII, commenting on the letter in question, notes, among others, the following points, from which the translated quotations above are excerpted:

"a) Prae oculis habeatur primam publicationem prioris partis Artis Logicae factam esse 1631, alterius partis 1632, primae partis Philosophiae Naturalis 1633, tertiae 1634, quartae 1635.

"b) Auctor loquitur de 'Corpore artium (cuerpo de Artes).' Atqui 'corpus' non significat membrum vel partem, sed totum. Ergo auctor loquitur de toto Cursu Philosophico, non solummodo de aliquo volumine huius Cursus.

"c) Certum est termino 'artes' in plurali secundum usum illius aetatis non Logicam significari, sed Philosophiam. Logica quidem dicitur 'ars' (ars logicalis), sed non artes.

"Ergo 'corpus artium' idem est ac Cursus Philosophicus.

"d) Hoc corpus artium dicitur 'finitum seu perfectum (acabado).' Auctor igitur Superiori suo, Reverendissimo Patri Generali, noluit transmittere unam vel alteram partem Cursus Philosophici, quod aliquid imperfectum fuisset, sed totum Cursum, opus completum et perfectum. Neque Cursu feliciter ad finem perducto auctor per longius tempus exspectasse, sed paulo post opus perfectum Reverendissimo Patri Generali transmisisse putandus est."

several opening pages of this edition, through the device of the Semiotic Markers. By that device, we were able to show how the editorial artifices deployed to present the above work as an autonomous unit derive their integrity from the express intentions and philosophical views of Poinsot, not from imaginings of the present editor.

The following remarks cover this same ground. That is, they are intended to show directly what readers familiar with the opening parts of this edition will have already seen for themselves, namely, that an entirely independent edition of Poinsot's doctrine of signs does not violate the context within which Poinsot conceived and drafted the work, even though he did not ever himself edit such a presentation apart from the larger project of the *Ars Logica* within the *Cursus Philosophicus*. (Since the texts cited from Poinsot in this section all are taken from the Latin texts produced in the above edition, there is no need to separately footnote them here.) As we shall see (again, in a different mode of presentation), it has been not only Poinsot's own intention, but also his philosophical views that have governed the contours of the editing: the organization of the *Treatise* is determined internally by the requirements of the doctrine Poinsot proposes, for those requirements[11] provide the entire warrant for what has been included and what has been excluded from the *Cursus Philosophicus* as a whole in preparing this first independent edition of the treatise *de signis*, the first to appear as such, therefore, in any language. Having shown this much, we will then be in a position to consider more directly what is revolutionary about Poinsot's doctrine, no longer as a part merely, integrated within a traditional presentation (i.e., not only in spite of itself), but in itself and in its direct implications, even for the Latin tradition, as a new starting point for the whole of philosophy, transcending the opposition between being and discourse which, in a general way, divides modern and contemporary philosophy from the philosophical traditions of ancient, medieval, and renaissance times. In a word, having shown how Poinsot's *Treatise* is revolutionary within his philosophical tradition, we will look directly at how it is revolutionary within our own time as semiotic, the first such according to the definition proposed by Locke and Peirce and the movement that has developed around the possibilities of such a point of view only in the most recent decades.

As we have said, the first of the two main parts of the *Cursus Philosophicus* is the Logic, titled by Poinsot *Ars Logica*. It is from the *Ars Logica* that the whole of the *Treatise on Signs* derives. *Ars Logica* therefore is the collective name for the first two of the five parts of Poinsot's *Cursus Philosophicus*. The *Prima Pars Artis Logicae*, published in 1631 at Alcalá,[12] Spain, consists of an introductory

---

[11] I am referring to the theoretical demands the work places particularly on the *Ars Logica* as a whole in order to be fully intelligible in its own right.

[12] No exemplar of this very first edition of the *Textus Summularum* is known to have survived to the present day. Nonetheless, there is little room to doubt of its at least former existence, for which indirect evidence is conclusive. See Solesmes, 1931: xiij note 4: "Hanc editionem non vidimus neque bibliothecam ullam novimus quae eam possideat. Indubium tamen est revera exstitisse, tum Echardi testimonio [Quetif-Echard, 1721: 538b], tum quia in 2 editione (1634) invenimus facultatem Provincialis datam die 29 augusti 1631, censuram vero P. Joannis Ponce de Leon 4 junii 1631." A second and even stronger line of evidence is drawn in the following note

logic text for beginners—called *Summulae* books, according to the custom of the times[13]—followed by a series of eight ''Quaestiones Disputandae'' or exercises designed to illustrate some difficulties incident to the *Summulae* books,[14] and to ease transition to the ''major'' questions.

The *Secunda Pars Artis Logicae* was published at Alcalá in 1632, and is of an altogether different character, dealing primarily with questions raised by the imperfect interrelations of truth and logical form.[15] Whereas Part I was intended for beginning students, Part II is intended for advanced students, and indeed for the author's peers. More philosophical than logical, by modern standards, the task of Part II is ''to explain—leisurely, patiently, thoroughly, and with unique skill in the selection and multiplication of standpoints—a restricted number of wonderful questions'' (Simon, 1955: xx). The readers of this Part, in Poinsot's milieu, could all be assumed to be familiar with the *Organon* (the logical works) of Aristotle and with the major Latin writings related

---

(ibid., note 5), where, after citing the title page of the 1635 Douai edition, which claims to be ''secunda,'' the Solesmes editors comment: ''Quae editio reapse tertia fuit; quod autem *secunda* nuncupatur, satis indicat in Belgio tunc adhuc ignotam fuisse editionem Complutensem 1634. *Duocensis igitur editio principem (Compluti 1631) editionem imitatur* . . .'' (final emphasis added). Reiser takes for granted the reality of the 1631 exemplar in his reflections on Poinsot's letter of 3 July 1635 (''Praefatio,'' 1933: VII—see note 10 above).

On the textual problems created by the variety of the editions of Poinsot's philosophical volumes, particularly the Logic, note Solesmes, 1931: xxxj, text and note 4; and see discussion in note 78 below.

[13] Simonin, 1930: 148, comments on this aspect of Reiser's edition: ''il ne semble pas que Dom R.'' paraît ''connaitre le texte qui sert de base à la partie de la Logique intitulée: '*Summulae*,' alors qu'il s'agit d'une interprétation, assez libre d'ailleurs, des '*Summulae logicales*' de *Petrus Hispanus*. Il y avait là toute une série de citations plus ou moins explicites à identifier.''

[14] Of this first part of the *Ars Logica*, the *Summulae* books (but not the ''*Quaestiones Disputandae*,'' the ''*Praeludium Primum*,'' or the ''*Lectori*'' of 1631) have been translated into English by Francis C. Wade under the title, *Outlines of Formal Logic* (Milwaukee: Marquette University Press, 1955). Thus, Wade's work includes the following sections from the present edition of the *Treatise on Signs*: from the ''Introduction to the Entire Work,'' the ''Second Prologue'' (Wade, pp. 25-27); and from the *Summulae Texts*, Chapters 1-3 (Wade, pp. 29-33).

Simon (1955: xx) reports, in this connection, that ''much of the doctrine'' contained in Poinsot's *Summulae* formal logic ''is available in the *Formal Logic* of Jacques Maritain,'' Imelda Choquette's translation (New York: Sheed and Ward, 1937, 1946) of *Eléments de philosophie: II. L'ordre des concepts—Petite logique (logique formelle)* (Paris: Tequi, 1923).

[15] Of this second part of the *Ars Logica*, about three fifths of the whole has been translated into English by Yves R. Simon, John J. Glanville, and G. Donald Hollenhorst under the title, *The Material Logic of John of St. Thomas* (Chicago: University of Chicago Press, 1955). This work includes the following sections from the present edition of the *Tractatus de Signis*: from the ''First Preamble,'' Articles 1 and 2 (Simon, pp. 59-76); from the ''Second Preamble,'' Articles 1, 2, and 3 (Simon, pp. 306-335); from Book I, Question 1 (Simon, pp. 388-404); from Book III, Questions 1, 3, and 4 (Simon, pp. 405-435). It should be noted that this translation can be used in the study of Poinsot's doctrine only with the greatest caution, since from the point of view neither of style and terminology—see Section III.C.1., esp. notes 92 and 93, and III.C.2.(a). below—nor of doctrinal interpretation of the origins and point of departure of Poinsot's account of signs—see Book I, Question 1, note 6 of *Treatise*—can it be said to achieve semiotic clarity, i.e., clarity in the principal matter-at-issue at this node of doctrinal reticulation. Nonetheless, in view of the scarcity of works in this area and the difficulty of the problems involved in their mastery, this pioneering effort of Simon and his collaborators is an indispensable mine of scholastic lore in Simon's ''Notes'' and ''Foreword'' to the text. Simon's vignettes of reflection on the distinction between formal and material logic in the scholastic context (pp. ix-xviii) bear particular mention in this regard.

Related discussion in notes 92 and 93 below.

thereto; and it must be said that, taken as a whole, the series of twenty-seven questions comprising Part II of the *Ars Logica* acquires continuity and completeness only when set explicitly in relation to the Latin translations of Aristotle's texts together with the major Latin discussions sparked by those texts all the way back to Boethius in the sixth century. This makes for enormous difficulty in reading Poinsot, because it means that eleven hundred years of Latin discussions of logical and philosophical questions are resumed and at issue at each point of Poinsot's work. In the particular case of the discussion of signs, fortunately, this difficulty is minimized, owing to the originality of Poinsot's standpoint, and to his conscious intention in giving it expression.[16]

---

[16] What is especially true of the *Treatise on Signs* as a part—in a paradigm way, we might say—is nonetheless *also* true of other parts of the *Cursus* as well, as Simonin (1930: 144-145) has so wonderfully explained: "*Quant au genre littéraire de Jean de Saint-Thomas, à son procédé général de composition, Dom R. note justement qu'il suit l'ordre des traités d'Aristote (comme il suit l'ordre de la Somme dans le* Cursus theologicus), *mais sans s'astreindre à un commentaire littéral suivi: 'Quod attinet viam et rationem procedendi* in genere *dicendum est magistrum nostrum seriem quidem et ordinem operum Aristotelis, non tamen litteram more commentatoris secutum esse' (p. XV). Cela est exactement dit, un peu brièvement peut-être, car il est facile d'envisager les raisons historiques qui engagèrent Jean de St-Thomas à agir de la sorte et de situer son travail dans l'ensemble des productions analogues. Certes l'oeuvre de Jean de St-Thomas ne constitue plus un commentaire littéral des traités d'Aristote à la manière de ceux des XIII*[e] *et XIV*[e] *siècles, dans lesquels le texte du Philosophe était exposé et expliqué, cette exégèse étant coupée, çà et là, à l'occasion de passages traditionnels, par des* questiones *plus développées qui prenaient les allures de dissertations indépendantes. Par contre, le* Cursus Philosophicus *n'est pas non plus un traité didactique, organisé par exemple à la manière des* 'Disputationes Metaphysicae' *de Suarez, selon un plan établi par l'auteur lui-même, et parfaitement indépendant des oeuvres de Stagirite. Jean de St-Thomas, et ceci fait honneur à son sens de la tradition, conserve le cadre habituel de l'enseignement philosophique, tel qu'il a été fixé au XIII*[e] *siècle, il suit l'ordre convenu des écrits d'Aristote, préfacés par les* 'Summulae' *et par Porphyre, en ce qui concerne la logique. Mais à l'intérieur de l'ancien édifice, dont il conserve le cadre hiératique, abrité sous ces voûtes solennelles, notre théologien construit, sur un plan logique, et selon les exigences de la matière, une série de petits traités indépendants. L'ouvrage de Jean de St-Thomas se présente donc comme un ouvrage de transition; c'est là la marque de son originalité. D'une part il est l'aboutissant naturel de toute une lente évolution subie par le genre classique des commentaires, au terme de laquelle la* quaestio *s'est complètement substituée à l'exégèse littérale dans laquelle elle était autrefois enchâssée; désormais elle subsiste seule et s'organise de plus en plus selon les exigences d'un moderne traité. D'autre part l'ordre même dans lequel ces* quaestiones *se présentent reste encore celui des anciens commentateurs; nous n'avons pas encore le traité moderne, tel que cependant Suarez l'a déjà réalisé. Le* Cursus *de Jean de St-Thomas fait songer à une ancienne cathédrale gothique entièrement décorée et aménagée par un artiste de la fin de la Renaissance.*"—"As regards the literary genre of Poinsot's work, the general manner of his composition, Reiser accurately notes that he follows the order of the treatises of Aristotle (even as he follows the order of the *Summa* of St. Thomas in the *Cursus Theologicus*), but without tying himself down to a literal commentary: 'In general, it must be said that our author follows the sequence indeed and the order of the works of Aristotle' (Reiser, 1930: XV). That is exactly stated, but perhaps a bit too briefly, for it is not hard to contemplate the historical pressures which urge Poinsot to proceed in that way and to situate his work in the totality of analogous undertakings. Certainly the work of Poinsot no longer constitutes a literal commentary on the treatises of Aristotle in the manner of works of the thirteenth and fourteenth centuries, during which the text of Aristotle was expounded and explained— that exegesis being interrupted, here and there, at the occasion of traditional passages, by some more developed *questions* which take on the appearance of independent treatments. On the other hand, neither is the *Cursus Philosophicus* a didactic treatise organized, say, in the manner of the *Metaphysical Disputations* of Suarez, according to a plan determined by the author himself, and perfectly independent of the works of the Stagirite. Poinsot—and this does credit to his sense of tradition—preserves the accustomed framework of philosophical teaching as it had been settled in the thirteenth century; he follows the conventional order of Aristotle's writings, prefaced by the *Summulae* [in Part 1] and by the *Isagoge* of Porphyry [in Part 2] in what concerns Logic. But within the ancient edifice, of which he conserves the hieratic framework, under the shelter

At the very beginning of the *Ars Logica*, in the "Word to the Reader,"[17] Poinsot draws particular attention to the originality in his handling of signs:

> We have taken care to cut out [of the introductory text] an immense forest of intractable questions and a thorny thicket of sophisms. . . . The metaphysical and other difficulties from the books *On the Soul* which break out in the very beginning of the *Summulae* books from the ardor of disputants, we have removed to their proper place, and we have set forth the tractate on signs and notices in Logic in relation to the *Perihermenias* books.

Why does Poinsot regard the discussion of Aristotle's *Perihermenias* books as the proper context for considering the nature and function of signs? Not because of the actual content of the traditional books so named, he will explain (in his "Remarks Concerning the Books *Perihermenias*"[18]), but because of the *name itself, perihermenias*, which means, in Latin, "on or concerning interpretation" (*de interpretatione*).

In writing his books on this subject, Aristotle (and subsequently his commentators) restricted the consideration of interpretation to the logical elements of discourse, with the result that the subject of interpretation has been (as of Poinsot's time) neither foundationally nor adequately treated. For *interpretation*, being an activity coextensive with awareness in its entirety, is far more universal than logical analysis, and indeed, being based on signs, it includes the logicians' instruments along with the many other instruments by which sense is made out of the world. Thus, if the "theory of interpretation" is to become transparent to itself and grounded in principle, Poinsot is saying, it must not restrict itself to logical elements as such (as in the older Aristotelian tradition), but must extend itself to include a consideration of signs taken *in their entire amplitude*. It is the recognition of this fact that leads Poinsot to say that in setting his discussion of signs in relation to the *Perihermenias* books, he has at the same time found the proper place for inserting a *Treatise on Signs* into the philosophical tradition of the Latin West. Hence the distinctive cast of Poinsot's *Treatise*: it introduces a revolutionary viewpoint, but it does so in a conservative way. Nothing of the old tradition is lost, but it is yet made to surpass itself in the direction of its foundations.

Thus, the *Summulae* books, which open the *Ars Logica* and the *Cursus Philosophicus*, begin with a chapter defining what a term is, followed by a chapter

---

of its solemn vaults, our theologian constructs, according to a logical plan and following the requirements of the material, a series of lesser independent treatises. The work of Poinsot reveals itself therefore as a work of transition. That is the index of its originality. On the one hand, it is the natural outcome of a whole slow evolution undergone by the classical genre of commentaries, at the term of which the *question* is completely substituted for the literal exegesis in which it was formerly embedded; henceforward it subsists on its own and organizes itself more and more according to the exigencies of a modern treatise. On the other hand, the very order within which these *questions* present themselves continues to be that of the bygone commentators; we do not yet have the modern treatise, such as had meanwhile already been realized by Suarez. The *Cursus* of John Poinsot makes one think of an old gothic cathedral entirely reclaimed and decorated by an artist of the twilight of the Renaissance."

[17] The presumption is that this segment of text too, certainly extant as of 1634, belongs equally to the lost exemplar of 1631: see note 12 above.

[18] "Super libros perihermenias"—see note 1 on this text as it occurs in the *Treatise*, p. 38 above.

on the definition and division of signs, and a third chapter dividing terms in various ways. These initial three *Summulae* chapters, each less than two pages in length, are pregnant with all the metaphysical and psychological difficulties which Poinsot considers susceptible of a systematically unified treatment such as they have heretofore not received, and which he thinks he has "removed to their proper place" by dealing with them (as befits "uncommon difficulties") in Part II rather than in Part I of the *Ars Logica*, and in particular by relating them to the discussion of interpretation (*perihermenias*). These initial three Summulae chapters, therefore, are included in this edition of the *Treatise on Signs*, according to an order dictated by the historical arrangement of the Books of the *Treatise*, as explained by Poinsot in the subsequent "Remarks Concerning the Books *On Interpretation*" ("super libros perihermenias") in Part II of the *Ars Logica*. There one finds, together with the already-discussed statement of Poinsot's reason for thinking this the proper place to develop his doctrine of signs, a statement of the order which that development presupposes — in the earlier discussions of mind-dependent being (Question 2 of Part II of the *Ars Logica*) and relation (Question 17 of Part II) that form the "Preambles" to our *Treatise*—and will follow over the next hundred pages or so (Questions 21-23 of Part II) that form the substance, i.e., the three main "Books," of his treatment of signs. Poinsot himself, in the special "Preface" added to the 1640 Madrid edition of Part II of the *Ars Logica*, made a particular point of emphasizing this special autonomy he accorded to his discussion of signs within the *Ars Logica* as a whole:

> Our promise to resolve in the first part of Logic the several questions customarily treated there has now been fulfilled, except that, for just reasons, we have decided to publish separately the treatise on signs—swarming with many and uncommon difficulties—in place of a commentary on the *Perihermenias* books, and together with some questions on the books of the *Posterior Analytics*; and for the more convenient use of the work we have separated the treatise on signs from the treatment of the *Categories*.

This "special autonomy" involves a good deal more than the susceptibility for being edited separately we have so far emphasized. It is a special autonomy within the very heart of the speculative order proper to philosophy as a mode of understanding, for in the doctrine of signs are *united*, in a unique standpoint, the traditionally opposed orders of discourse (*non ens*, or "ens rationis") and being (*esse*, or "ens reale").

To see how this is so, two passages from Poinsot's text are particularly helpful. The first occurs among Poinsot's opening remarks to Book I of the *Treatise*, where he observes (117/28-118/6 [=*646b25-33*]) that a principal problem to be solved at the outset by any doctrine of signs is that posed by the fact that signs involve equally the being of nature ("ens reale") and the being that results from the activities of our own minds ("ens rationis"),[19] so that any standpoint

[19] Thomas Aquinas earlier had expressed this classical division as follows (c. 1269-1271: *In IV Met.*, lect. 4, n. 574): ". . . *ens est duplex: ens scilicet rationis et ens naturae. Ens autem rationis dicitur proprie de illis intentionibus, quas ratio adinvenit in rebus consideratis; sicut intentio generis, speciei*

proportioned preclusively to the apprehension of the one (e.g., traditional *philosophia naturalis*) or the other (e.g., traditional *logica*[20]) will be *ipso facto* inadequate to the study of signifying. For this study, an entirely new standpoint must be adopted, one that straddles or bridges the two orders without being restricted to or preoccupied with either taken separately.

The second passage occurs in Poinsot's 1631 Word to the Reader (''Lectori'') already referred to, where he remarks that the intrusion into the introductory logic texts of ''metaphysical and other difficulties'' properly handled traditionally in the fourth part of natural philosophy (the *de anima*), can *also* be handled properly as they directly impinge on discourse by incorporating them into the new standpoint demanded if one wishes to treat of signs (''de interpretatione'') in what is proper to them according to their unique way of being.

Thus, if one glances at the Synthetic Index to and Synoptic Table of the entire *Cursus Philosophicus* provided in Appendix B above, and compares in particular the contents of Books II and III of the *Treatise* (*Ars Logica*, Qq. XXII-XXIII) with the contents of Questions IV-IX and Question XI of the fourth part of the *Philosophia Naturalis*, one can discover that *the very same material* covered from a semiotic point of view under the rubric of ''signum formale'' and ''notitia'' is *also* covered from an ontological point of view (the point of view of the then-traditional natural philosophy and metaphysics) under the rubric of sensation and intellection. (See III.B.4. below.)

In this way, it can be seen concretely how the theoretical requirement that semiotic develop from a standpoint superior to the classical division of being into *ens reale* and *ens rationis* is realized in the development of Poinsot's *Tractatus*: not only does the *Treatise on Signs* return to the beginnings of Logic and reconceptualize the foundations proper to discourse in its entirety, but it incorporates into that new beginning and reaches in its own way results that

---

et similium, quae quidem non inveniuntur in rerum natura, sed considerationem rationis consequuntur. Et huiusmodi, scilicet ens rationis, est proprie subiectum logicae. Huiusmodi autem intentiones intelligibiles, entibus naturae aequiparantur, eo quod omnia entia naturae sub consideratione rationis cadunt. Et ideo subiectum logicae ad omnia se extendit, de quibus ens naturae praedicatur. Unde concludit, quod subiectum logicae aequiparatur subiecto philosophiae, quod est ens naturae. Philosophus igitur ex principiis ipsius procedit ad probandum ea quae sunt consideranda circa huiusmodi communia accidentia entis. Dialecticus autem procedit ad ea consideranda ex intentionibus rationis, quae sunt extranea a natura rerum. Et ideo dicitur, quod dialectica est tentativa, quia tentare proprium est ex principiis extraneis procedere.''—''Being is of two kinds: specifically, of the mind [mind-dependent being] and of nature [mind-independent being]. Those intentions that reason introduces into considered things are properly called mind-dependent being, such intentions as that of a genus, a species, and the like, which sorts of intentions are not found in the nature of the things, but are consequent upon the mind's consideration. And being of this sort, specifically, mind-dependent being, is properly the subject of logic. Yet intelligible intentions of this sort are coextensive with the beings of nature, from the fact that all beings of nature fall under the consideration of reason. And therefore the subject of logic covers all those things of which mind-independent being is predicated. Whence Aristotle concludes that the subject of logic [which is mind-dependent being] is coextensive with the subject of philosophy, which is mind-independent being. A philosopher therefore proceeds from his principles to demonstrate those things which must be considered regarding the common characteristics of mind-independent being. But the logician proceeds to those things which must be considered from intentions of the mind, which are extraneous to the nature of things. And this is why it is said that a logical proof is provisional or tentative, because it is proper to a provisional scheme to proceed from extraneous principles.''

[20] See the passage cited in the preceding note.

were *also* reached in traditional philosophy through the ontological analysis of living beings as capable of perception and concept formation. It is not just the beginnings but also the conclusions of the traditional *Cursus Philosophicus* that are transcended in the point of view proper to the *doctrina signorum*. It is the whole of philosophy that is embryonic to the semiotic point of view.

C. The *Treatise on Signs* as Semiotic

Since the term ''semiotic'' was never used by Poinsot, some explanation is called for by our use of it in the subtitle to this edition of his *tractatus de signis*.

''Semiotic'' is an adaptation or ''normal development,'' Romeo would say, of the Greek term σημιωτική, which appears to have been a neologism devised by John Locke for the purpose of designating the key component in his suggestion for a new distribution of human knowledge, at the close of his *Essay Concerning Human Understanding*, specifically, Book IV, Chapter XXI.[21]

Leading up to the term, he opens this concluding chapter of his *Essay* with the following observation:

> All that can fall within the compass of Humane Understanding, being either *First*, the Nature of Things, as they are in themselves, their Relations, and their manner of Operation: Or, *Secondly*, That which Man himself ought to do, as a rational and voluntary Agent, for the Attainment of any End, especially Happiness: or, *Thirdly*, The ways and means, whereby the Knowledge of both the one and the other of these, are attained and communicated; I think, *Science* may be divided properly into these *Three* sorts:

whence he goes on to designate three branches corresponding to the above partition, namely, *physica* or natural philosophy, *practica* or ethics, and a third branch which he called

> Σημιωτική, or *the Doctrine of Signs*; the most usual whereof being Words, it is aptly enough termed also Λογική, Logick; the business whereof, is to consider the Nature of Signs, the Mind makes use of for the understanding of Things, or conveying its Knowledge to others.

Locke then introduces the familiar distinction between ideas in the mind and articulate sounds as the broadest and most convenient but not the only class of outward manifestations of the mind's workings, after discussing which he concludes:

---

[21] Such is the picture that emerges from the researches so far of Luigi Romeo, 1977: 37-49. In particular, Romeo establishes (p. 38) that ''Locke 1690: 361 introduces the term 'σημιωτική' (not 'σημειωτική') into the discipline (note also 'Σημιωτική' in the 'contents,' third line from the bottom).'' ''Semeiotic,'' the variant spelling which Peirce came to prefer, quasi-transliterates the Greek term σημειωτική, which is the spelling customarily used in later editions of Locke's *Essay* (e.g., Fraser, 1894: 461; Nidditch, 1975: 720/25). The first known appearance of Locke's original espelling as such is in the 1572 *Thesaurus Graecae Linguae* of Henricus Stephanus, seemingly (cf. Romeo, pp. 41-42, 43) as a faulty variant of σημειωτικός, a term associated since ancient times with a part of medicine (''symptomatology,'' or the reading of organic signs). These facts suggest to Romeo (p. 45) that ''the term 'σημειωτική' and Locke's 'σημιωτική' have been borrowed from classical philology, not from medical or musical sources in post-Renaissance times,'' as earlier researchers (L. J. Russell, 1939; Sebeok, 1971) had conjectured.

> The Consideration, then, of *Ideas* and *Words* as the great instruments of Knowledge, makes no despicable part of their Contemplation who would take a view of humane Knowledge in the whole Extent of it. *And, perhaps, if they were distinctly weighed, and duly considered, they would afford us with another sort of Logick and Critick, than what we have been hitherto acquainted with*. [Concluding emphasis added.]

The "logic and critic" with which Locke was familiar was generically "scholastic," but of the sort taught in the English universities of his day, which by all accounts was an exceedingly decadent vestige of the medieval heritage. It is curious to wonder what course Locke's thinking might have taken had he been acquainted with the richer Latin traditions of logic still living in Iberia, and in particular with the course of logic taught at Alcalá and first published in the very year of Locke's birth by our John Poinsot. Curious, but a line of wonderment impossible to resolve.

What is certain is that Locke had no inkling of the fact that his prophecy had already been proved true by Poinsot's *Tractatus*. In the medieval tradition, Augustine's definition of the sign, enshrined in the *Sentences* (c. 1150) of Peter Lombard, was assumed as a matter of course in the theological discussions of sacrament. That definition, laid down in the opening chapter of Book II of Augustine's *On Christian Doctrine* (c. 397-426), made being sense perceptible an essential element of the sign, and it was in taking exception to this generally assumed point that Poinsot was led to his decisive interpretation of the distinction between signs which make present in awareness something other than themselves before being themselves objects of possible apprehension in their own right—which he called, from the point of view of his treatise on signs, *formal signs*, but which he called *concepts or ideas* from the point of view of his natural philosophy—and signs which indicate something else precisely and only by virtue of their being themselves apprehended objectively, which he called *instrumental* signs, according to the usage of the time (Romeo, 1979; Deely, 1981, 1982, 1983).

This distinction, Poinsot went on to show, was required in order to account for the relation between words and ideas, as the former function in communication and the latter in the structuring of experience. In short, he showed that a semiotic approach to "words and ideas" systematically pursued—"distinctly weighed and duly considered"—leads not only to "a different sort of logic and critic" from what has hitherto been found in philosophy, but as well to an understanding of "ideas" incompatible with their definition as direct objects of our apprehension, such as Locke, Descartes, and the main moderns after them had led themselves to accept, with such solipsistic consequences as the history of modern thought gives us to know (Deely, 1978c).

Moreover, as we have already had occasion to note, Poinsot's doctrine of signs bridges the distinction between what is independent of man and what comes about through human action in exactly the way proposed by Locke for semiotic. In short, we call Poinsot's *Tractatus de Signis* his *semiotic*, because his doctrine of signs fits exactly the definition and function proposed for semiotic by John Locke as something *new* in philosophy.

The importance of appreciating this point cannot be overstressed. In pub-

lishing a work from the seventeenth century, the powerful expectation is that a modern editor's goals are historical. But the purpose of this edition of the *Treatise* is to achieve something else, quite different, and in fact presupposed for the genuine fruitfulness of any purely historical inquiry—namely, an understanding of the *intrinsic structure* of Poinsot's doctrine of signs, taken in itself and as an account of the phenomenon of signifying ("semeiosis") as it structures experience. Only when and if a theory is understood in its own terms can it *also* be related to, and *further understood* in light of, its predecessors and successors. Otherwise, of course, what is it that we should be seeking forerunners of and successors to? It is this point, I should think, that Maritain had in mind when he observed (1955: vi) that thinkers of Poinsot's caliber "set such an example of exacting respect" for genuine thought in works they consider "that their guidance is a most effective protection against the risk of ignoring the historical evolution of problems."

There can be no question of the value of a work approaching Poinsot's work historically (cf. Romeo, 1979; Herculano de Carvalho, 1970), tracing precisely in his forebears (such as the Conimbricenses, Complutenses, and other more individualized thinkers) views and controversies on the subject of signs which, as Poinsot mentions in the course of his *Treatise* (Book I, Question 5, 194/39-40 [=*680a38-39*]) had by his time become matters of "almost daily dispute" in the schools. What is central to the present presentation of the work, however, is rather Poinsot's *own understanding* of the relation of his treatment of signs to the *Summulae Logicales* tradition of medieval origin, of which Poinsot's *Artis Logicae Prima Pars* was consciously a continuation. Few thinkers of any age have been more conscious or respectful of tradition than was John Poinsot ("Novarum rerum et singularium opinionum aeque inimicus," says Reiser, 1930: VIII—hardly the description of a neoteric). This gives all the more weight to his explicit identification, on more than one occasion, of his systematic treatment of signs precisely as novel and without formal precedent in the work of forebears. In this regard, Poinsot's *doctrina signorum* precisely fits the definition of the prospective "science" of semiotic limned by Locke, knowing nothing of Poinsot, as in 1690 something *to be accomplished*, i.e., without precedent—exactly as Poinsot saw his own work in formal terms. This was precisely the understanding of semiotic taken up by Peirce in our own time and made the rallying point of the international movement that has taken shape particularly since the end of the last war (Sebeok, 1974; 1975a). Hence, it is in relation to *this* idea and movement that the first edition of Poinsot's *Treatise* is conceived, not primarily as one more item in the newly interesting history of logic and philosophy between 1400 and 1650. Indeed, what first strikes one about Poinsot's doctrine viewed retrospectively is precisely its stepping outside, as it were, of the previous history of logic (details in Deely, 1981, 1982). (There is also the point that it is not in the tradition of Logic as such that Poinsot locates the roots of his account, but in the metaphysics of relation and in the epistemological thesis appropriated from Cajetan—and anticipatory of Hegel—asserting the univocity of being and non-being in the order of knowledge.) Its retrospective significance as a glimpse into the past—indeed, as a new point of entry into the lost centuries of renaissance Latin Aristotelianism and natural philosophy—is

there to be developed; but the dominant interest of the work remains the prospective significance of semiotic as a wave of the future. Poinsot's is primarily a *seminal treatment*, not a culminating one respecting former ages; it illuminates *prospectively* the possibilities for a future age. Thus, the study of the *Tractatus de signis* should best begin as quickly as possible with the *text itself* (which is why these editorial explanations have been placed behind rather than before the *Tractatus* proper). It harbingers a revolution against modern philosophy, to be sure, but it is likewise revolutionary in the way it looks back toward the medieval and classical times.

In short, we may say that the principal interest of the first edition of Poinsot's semiotic is not historical, but doctrinal, in a very precise sense.

I have used the terms ''theory'' and ''science'' above in connection with Poinsot's work only with the greatest reluctance and reservations. Careful semantics here can be of considerable help in conceptually clarifying what semiotic promises. Sebeok (1976a: ix and following) was the first to remark that Locke's designation of this could-be discipline as a ''doctrine,'' rather than a ''science'' (even though Locke speaks, in context, of the ''division of the *sciences*''), was particularly fortunate. This is true in a number of ways, but especially, perhaps, against the Latin background of the seventeenth-century usage of terms. For the Latin *doctrina*, whence Locke's English ''doctrine'' comes, was a crucial theoretical concept of scholasticism, expressing, we can say in light of historical developments since then, a level or type of knowledge critically distinct from scientific knowledge or *science* (''scientia'') in the modern sense that that term has inexorably taken on.

A ''doctrine,'' in Latin or English, refers first of all to a ''teaching,'' i.e., to *what* some person or persons even unknown assert to be the case respecting this or that. Thus, *doctrina* may concern natural or social reality, or any web and admixture of the two. But, in the systematic context of Latin scholasticism, as illustrated, for example (c. 1266), in the Question opening the *Summa theologiae* of Thomas Aquinas,[22] *doctrina* referred to a body of thought sensitive to its own implications and striving for consistency throughout, while achieving explanations at a level beyond what can be empirically circumscribed in unambiguous ways. Thus, the notion of *doctrina* is one of the avenues to realizing the differing ways in which the sensory core of experience is relied upon in dominant moods of thought that are typically ''scientific'' as contrasted with those that tend more to typically ''philosophic'' analysis (cf. Simon, 1943; Cahalan, 1981, 1985).

In the former case, crucial theoretical claims are considered established in a satisfactory way only when they have been successfully correlated with an empirically accessible instantiation of consequence that is *as thus accessible*

---

22 ''*De sacra doctrina, qualis sit, et ad quae se extendat*'' (''Concerning sacred doctrine, what it is and what it extends to''), the first article of which queries, ''*Utrum sit necessarium, praeter philosophicas disciplinas, aliam doctrinam haberi*'' (''Whether there is need for another doctrine over and above that provided by the disciplines of philosophy''—logic, natural philosophy, metaphysics, ethics, etc.)—whence it is clear that philosophy itself is for Aquinas a mode or type of *doctrine*. (We may note that Poinsot has a lengthy commentary on this question: see Joannis a Sancto Thoma, 1637: *Cursus Theologici Tomus Primus*, Solesmes ed. 1931: 305-410, esp., for the present context, Disp. II, Arts. 1, 3, and 5-11). See Deely 1982: 127-130, ''On the Notion 'Doctrine of Signs.' ''

unambiguously circumscribed—for example, the requirement of Einstein's equations that light passing in its propagation close by a star be bent in its path to a degree proportioned to known physical properties of the star; or the Michelson-Morley requirements for the presence of ether. In the mood of thought proper to *scientia*, everything—principles, conclusions, theory, and method—is but an instruments subservient to discovery of new data of experience and expanding its reach.

But inasmuch as empirical ambiguity surrounds in principle the structure or structures demanded by some concern of theoretical understanding (requiring thereby the environment of a natural language for progress in the explication of its concepts), we are in the realm of philosophical reason and the field proper to the development of *doctrina*—for example, the requirement of Aristotle's natural philosophy that there be principles of being neither existent in their own right nor accessible to perception (not "empirically accessible," not isolable as sensory variables), two in number, and constitutive of individuality at its base as something subject to alteration and exercising an existence independently of perception and conception; or the requirement of the Kantian account of reason that the objects of our experience be conformed to our concepts insofar as they are phenomena, rather than the other way around. Data of experience, in this mood of thinking, are studied for the sake of understanding the conclusions they imply.

Put in the perspective and terms of our *Treatise* text above (especially Book III, Questions 1 and 2): both *scientia* and *doctrina* ultimately derive their legitimated assertions exclusively from intuition of what is physically present in sensation. But what is intuited leads *scientia* to seek *principally* for their own sake *only* further intuitions of what is physically present in external sense, whereas it leads *doctrina* to seek *principally* for its own sake *rather* what the intuited necessarily implies at the level of understanding in its own right.

Semiotic, thus, as *doctrina*, is a department of knowledge belonging to the order of what is not as opposed to what is susceptible of critical resolution at the empirical level. It is an objective discipline ruled by intrinsic demands indifferent to subjectivity in its individual (though not in its social) dimensions, and grounded in the *signifying* whereby the here and now acquires coherence of structure, and what may be absent or non-existent becomes a part of the texture of present experience—whereby, in a word, the transcendence of the given distinguishing cognitive life from merely assimilative and physically bound processes of material individuality is established. Precisely because of its explicit grasp of the possibility of uncovering these foundations, first surveyed by Poinsot, what Sebeok (1976a: ix) dubs "the semiotic tradition of Locke and Peirce" exhibits itself on the contemporary scene as the increasingly dominant one in the growing literature on signs.[23]

---

[23] "In contrast to what might be called the 'Locke-Peirce-Morris pattern'," Sebeok writes (1971: 53), "that prevails generally in America, as it does, too, in both Northern and Eastern Europe, there exists quite another tradition, widespread throughout the Romance areas, but not confined to them, since reflexes of it occur in English, particularly British. This tradition, that I shall refer to as the 'Saussure pattern,' actually has two different sources: originally, Greek medicine [whence principally "sem*e*iotic," as in Italian today]; then, superimposed much later, the direct heritage of Ferdinand de Saussure (1857-1913) [whence principally "semi*ology*"]. Syn-

This foundational doctrine we may distinguish from the much larger, and, in one very important sense, limitless *field* of "semiotics": that is, the development of attempts to isolate and pursue the implications of specifically signifying *aspects* and elements of phenomena, natural or socio-cultural, that are studied in their own right by the range of traditional specialized pursuits (music, architecture, ethology, etc.) now becoming sensitized to the semiotic *dimension* that permeates all things.[24] This new "field" of semiotics in turn can be conceptualized prospectively as a discipline in its own right, "an ancient discipline, stemming from a pre-Socratic clinical tradition, which then led to the development of three fundamental semiotic traditions—the musical, the philosophical [but so understood as to include religious thought, and particularly theology[25]], and the linguistic—that have thoroughly intermingled at various periods in

---

chronically, we are dealing here with the simultaneous multilingual interplay of polysemy (involving several connected meanings)." And, a little later (ibid., 56): "Even in the narrow sense, excluding, that is, their medical uses, semiotic, semiotics, semiology, to mention only the three most common English congeners, are by no means wholly interchangeable. While every contributor to *Semiotica* . . . may indulge his personal taste when attaching a label to the theory of signs, his terminology within the same piece of discourse will not oscillate *ad libitum*, for his initial selection will have signalled to his sophisticated readership whether he has chosen to align himself with the Locke-Peirce-Morris tradition [perhaps better termed "the Poinsot-Locke-Peirce tradition"], the Mead variation [i.e., "semiotics": see Mead, 1964: 275], or the Saussurean pattern of thought and action."

[24] This brings into focus the inherently transdisciplinary ramifications of the development of a unified doctrine of signs—the practically unlimited range of implications and applications. Up until now, "interdisciplinary programs," so essential to compensating for the myopic tendencies of specialization in modern academe, have always required *ad hoc* contrivances for their development and, as a consequence, have never attained more than a tenuous status vis-à-vis the specialties. Within semiotic perspective, the situation changes radically for the better. No longer is an interdisciplinary outlook something contrived or tenuous. On the contrary, it is something built-in to semiotics, simply by virtue of the universal role of signs as the vehicle of communication—within and between specialties, as everywhere else, wherever there is cognition, mutual or unilateral.

[25] The middle ages and renaissance were filled with writings and discussions pregnant with import for semiotics, not only on the level of logic and language (e.g., Ashworth, 1974; Bursill-Hall, 1971; Pinborg, 1967; Kneale and Kneale, 1962; and countless others), but even more on the level of the theological discourse itself which properly expressed the dominant mood of medieval speculation. Men of that time, as Jones (1969: II, xix) has remarked, "conceived this world to be but the visible sign of an invisible reality, a world thoroughly impregnated with the energy, purpose, and love of its Creator, who dwells in it as He dwells in the bread and wine on the altar." The most formal conceptualization of this outlook naturally took place in the theology of the sacraments, the principal means of communion between God and men. St. Augustine's semiotic analysis in his *De doctrina christiana* in particular, as we noted already in another context, became the focal point for the extraordinary development in medieval writings of sacramental theology. Moreover, not only among the scholastic theologians of the late Latin period, but universally among the so-called Church Fathers, Greek and Latin, the sacraments of Christian faith were from the beginning understood as *signs* divine in origin and of a unique efficacy, the key to the life of man with God. Thus we should have to distinguish in medieval thought, as it were, a *high* and a *low* semiotics, the former to be traced in the theology of the sacraments and unique to the Christian era, the latter to be found in the traditions of logic, grammar, and dialectic developed in the world of Latin Christendom but also having counterparts in the pagan eras of Greece and Rome, in the linguistic and logical discussions of Plato, Aristotle, the Stoics, Epicureans, and the neo-Platonists of the last phase of Roman antiquity. Poinsot in particular (1667) has some decisive contributions to the Latin tradition of high semiotics in the concluding volume of his *Cursus Theologicus, De Sacramentis*, where he introduces divisions of the sign apropos of discussing the sacraments that are not mentioned at all in the text of his semiotic proper, the present *Treatise*.

Western intellectual history, although there have been times when they strove for autonomy'' (Sebeok, 1976b: 1). The interdisciplinary—or, rather, transdisciplinary—field of semiotics, thus, may be entered from an infinite variety of disciplinary standpoints, but it is the attempt in principle to totalize these possibilities, as it were, that sets the enterprise of semiotics apart from the merely specialized pursuit. The example of Peirce comes readily to mind (c.1897: 1.7): ''My philosophy may be described as the attempt of a physicist to make such conjecture as to the constitution of the universe as the methods of science permit, with the aid of all that had been done by previous philosophers.''

At the foundational level of semiotic strictly so-called, Poinsot, distinguished in his own time by an intimate familiarity with the entire tradition of the Latin West, brought his thorough understanding to bear on the subject of signs at the very point when the sacramental outlook of earlier Christian times was effectively dissolving in favor of a more general interest in signs as the universal instrument whereby *any* communication, sacred or secular, is effected. Fully cognizant of the importance of *signum* in the theology of patristic and medieval times, but also aware of the new focus *signum* was acquiring in modern times (indeed, since the fourteenth century, and as it would soon eventuate in Locke's call for ''semiotic'' as the general study of ''the nature of signs, the mind makes use of for the understanding of things, or conveying its knowledge to others''), Poinsot, in authoring his *Treatise*—one of the earliest known and possibly the actual first fully systematized attempt to thematize philosophically the being proper to signs as the universal means of communication (not only between God and man, according to the classical religious understanding achieved in the sacramental notions of the saints and fathers, but also between persons, and between men and the beings of nature)—took up a uniquely important position of liaison between the world of Christian theology, philosophical Latinity, and modern intellectual concerns.

D. The Method and Literary Forms of the *Treatise on Signs*

The first of Poinsot's two ''Prologues'' which opened the original volume of the entire *Cursus Philosophicus* also open this first edition of the *Treatise on Signs*. In these pages, Poinsot himself explains fully the traditional forms and styles of arguing according to scholastic standards of the time embodied in the *Cursus*, and therefore in our *Treatise* as a part thereof. In more general terms, following the stylized scholastic forms of that age, Poinsot defines in these pages the respective tasks that fall in any age to one who proposes an argument, to one who responds to the argument, and to one who adjudicates the exchange.

It is not their general historical character as ''scholastic forms'' that holds the chief interest for purposes of this edition, however, but rather their appropriation by Poinsot as vehicles for the literary forms *proper and peculiar* to his own text (cf. Lavaud, 1928: 414-416). These are what I wish to bring out in the remarks that follow.

Thus, besides providing us with a trenchant and remarkably full yet succinct account of the forms of disputation characteristic of late Latin scholasticism (forms which become elemental *literary* forms in the scholastic writings), the

pages of the First Prologue just mentioned, read in conjunction with the "Lectori" of 1631, explain the logical and *dialectical ideal* which Poinsot set himself to realize in his philosophical writing. They comprise, as it were, Poinsot's *Discours de la méthode*. The reader who takes the trouble to remember the points and distinctions Poinsot there lays down will find himself well along the way to mastering the peculiarly abstract and elliptical style that results from Poinsot's effort to subordinate clashes of authors and texts to the "wrestling of truth" (*luctae veritatis*)[26] within the orbit of human understanding.

Over and above the exclusively dialectical and philosophical ideal of rendering publicly competing views relative to truth, however, Poinsot (as we shall see in relating the events of his life) entertained the belief that the first principles of understanding—namely, those intellectual intuitions in which the functional capacity characterizing understanding *in its distinction* from perception and sense becomes transparent to itself—have been indicated by St. Thomas Aquinas in an order conformed to the real and thereby disposed to actively develop and assimilate the infinity of future truths to be gleaned in the experience of mankind. A judicious reading of St. Thomas's texts, Poinsot held, can be made to illustrate the grounds and validity of this belief in particular cases.

Accordingly, in addition to the stylized incorporation into his writing of the respective roles played by the partisans in philosophical controversy, Poinsot included in stylized form a device for calling explicit attention to the continuity of principle underlying his own thought and that of Thomas Aquinas. Since the contemporary reader is likely to be without grounds for sharing or particularly interesting himself in Poinsot's belief on this point, it is important to be aware of the stylized device or *literary form* which is used to isolate, as it were, this quasi-subjective element in its play against the objective elements of dialectical purity and philosophical truth.[27] The "mood of conquering vitality" and "quiet ardor of intellectual life" which distinguish Poinsot's work (Maritain,

---

[26] See the "Word to the Reader" ("*Lectori*") of 1631, pp. 4-5 above, concluding paragraph. See also the discussion in Section III.B.3. below of the Index Personarum, and the express discussion of problems relating to Poinsot's style in III.C.1. below.

[27] I say "quasi-subjective," because it was not from the point of view of *persona* that Poinsot principally regarded St. Thomas, but from that of *doctrina*, so that he considered that in the work of St. Thomas, something much greater than an individual person is at stake ("*non est solius privatae personae vindicatio*"). And this is certainly true. Moreover, the secret of Poinsot's respect for tradition and the reason for his constant focus on its sound development taking precedence over winning personal fame by promoting one's own opinions for their novelty ("*non quaeritur propriae opinionis plausus et novitas*"), must be sought first of all in this dimension of his interior and intellectual life, i.e., his respect for doctrine over the person propounding it. While Poinsot's "Thomism" is not the sort of thing that is as such a foreground concern to the readers of his semiotic, therefore, neither is it something without semiotic interest to be lightly dismissed or superficially accounted for. It was in this way that Poinsot sought to come to terms reflectively with nothing less than the overwhelming historicity of man, according to his own lights and with all the considerable resources of information and analysis at his disposal. Fortunately, he has left us a partial record at least of his contemplation in this particular, which cannot in my opinion be summarized or abbreviated or taken out of context without fatal distortion and inevitable misunderstanding, namely, his *Tractatus de Approbatione et Auctoritate Doctrinae D. Thomae*, in his *Cursus Theologici Tomus Primus* (1637), Solesmes ed., 1931: 221-301. See also Lavaud, 1928: 424-425 and 436-444. And particularly the *circumstances of its composition*, in Solesmes' note on pp. 223-224 of their edition of Poinsot 1637.

1955: vii, viii) nowhere better left their mark than in the purity of these literary forms at play in his writing.

With a few exceptions (most notably, Article 2 of the First Preamble, and Book II, Question 1), the organization of the text of Book I, Question 1, is typical of the organization of each of the Questions in each of the Books of our *Treatise*. A Question opens with a statement of presupposed definitions or propositions, followed by a summary of the opposed opinions extant within the framework of the discussion, and a succinct statement of the point or points that must be decided in order to adjudicate conflicts.

Poinsot then makes a formal statement of his own point of view, i.e., the thesis he will defend. After whatever clarification of terms he deems necessary to stave off ambiguity in the reading of the thesis, he sets himself to establish the thesis in two distinct and notably different senses.

First, he sets himself to show the consonance between his own views and the view that an informed reader would find himself or herself inclined to ascribe to St. Thomas. Then he sets himself to show the rational necessities implicit in his thesis, along with, often, consonances with sensory experience.[28]

Stylistically, the first "proof" is introduced by the expression "Ex D. Thoma" or some variant of this expression. The second or properly philosophical attempt to establish the thesis is then introduced by the expression "fundamentum huius" or "ratio huius." This *ex Thoma/fundamentum huius* distinction of literary forms runs throughout the *Treatise*, and will be found in the paragraphs following most of the formal conclusions or "theses" Poinsot sets himself to defend. The reader should note this distinction well, because the sense of the citation of texts, whether from St. Thomas or anyone else, is determined by the literary form dominating the passage in which the citation occurs.

Finally, after the preliminary establishment of his own position, Poinsot devotes the remainder of his discussion—usually about half the treatment of the particular question under investigation—to the formal entertainment of arguments against his own position. This section of each question is introduced by the title, "Resolution of Counter-Arguments" (*Solvuntur Argumenta*). In this section, Poinsot first sets out at length and then responds step by step to various and often enormously sophisticated alternative positions that might seem available within the framework of the question being discussed. These "resolution of counter-arguments" sections are undoubtedly the most difficult for the modern reader of Poinsot to follow, because not only is it necessary to have in mind the literary form determining the condition and mood of the "speaker" of any given lines, but it is further necessary to explicitly recur to the *particular step* in the objector's argument that Poinsot is responding to in a given passage. The attentive reader will soon enough find within the counterarguments section minor stylistic clues that will help him to find his way, but in addition to

[28] Reiser, 1930: XV, describes the procedure thus: "Unaquaequae thesis duplici fere semper argumento probatur: Prius desumitur ex auctioritate Aristotelis, D. Thomae nobiliorumque scholae thomisticae doctorum, quo mens Philosophi et Doctoris Angelici patet, i.e., non tam scitur rem ita esse, sed scholam aristotelico-thomisticam per continuitatem successionem ita docuisse; ceterum his et via panditur ad ipsa argumenta philosophica. Alterum enim argumentum ex ratione desumptum est vere philosophicum faciens scire."

the stylized forms of the seventeenth-century text, I have introduced in footnotes to the counterarguments a reference back to the lines containing the exact part of the argument Poinsot is answering in any given paragraph of his "resolution" of a counterargument.

Such, then, are the main literary forms under which the questions forming the books of the *Treatise on Signs* are discussed: each Question is divided into *two parts,* a first part wherein Poinsot sets forth his own position, and a second part wherein he answers arguments against his own view. Each of these main parts is in turn divided into further parts, *the first* into an assessment of the state of the question, formal statement of a position, and an establishment of the truth of that position first in terms of its traditional roots ("*ex Thoma*") and then in terms of philosophical truth ("*fundamentum seu ratio huius*"); *the second* into a statement of counterarguments together with their resolution, one by one, part by part, according to the structure of formal argument and definition of technical terms explained in the "First Prologue" to the *Ars Logica* and *Cursus Philosophicus* as a whole.

II.

The Author of the Treatise on Signs

It is not often that a special discussion has to be devoted to the name of the author of a given work, though indeed such a problem is far from unheard-of. There are a number of considerations that make such a discussion useful in the present case. Accordingly, I will proceed to identify the author of our text in two steps: First, by explaining why I have settled on "John Poinsot" as the most appropriate for our purpose of the several variant names he might be and has been called by; Second, by recounting the events of his life in the context of European history of the time.

A. The Name and National Origin of our Author

Joanni a S. Thoma id propemodum accidisse quod olim inclyto Homero, multis gentibus ut eum sibi vindicarent jurgantibus, jam advertebat Quetivius. Quae contentio nondum sopita est; immo major hodie confusio, non solis Hispanio, Belgis, Gallis, Austriis Lusitanisque (quos recensebat Quetivius) suae patriae Joannis ortum adjudicantibus, sed in concertationem ingredientibus Hungaris et Burgundionibus, septenariumque litigatorum numerum complentibus.

Solesmes "Preface," 1931: lxxxvi

Quetif early remarked [1667] *that what happened to the celebrated Homer in ancient times happened likewise to Poinsot, namely, that many peoples claimed him as one of their own. This dispute has not yet been laid to rest. Indeed, the confusion today has increased, with not only the Spaniards, Belgians, French, Austrians, and Portuguese mentioned by Quetif claiming theirs as his land of origin, but also Hungarians and Burgundians entering the fray, bringing the complement of disputants to the full seven* [*i.e., to equal the number of cities that claimed Homer for their own*].

The principal posthumous editors of Poinsot's works—Reiser in the case of the *Cursus Philosophicus*, the Solesmes editors in the case of the *Cursus Theologicus*—use for their author's name the Latin form "Joannes a Sancto Thoma" ("John of Saint Thomas"). It was this name in this form that Poinsot himself attached to the first three volumes he himself edited of his *Cursus Theologicus*.

Nonetheless, the following three posthumous volumes of the *Cursus Theologicus* revert to the variant, "Joannes de Sancto Thoma," which is also the form used on the early editions of the volumes of the *Cursus Philosophicus*—one time, in the 1635 Douai edition of the *Artis Logicae Prima Pars*, with the spelling "Johannes . . . ."[29]

In personal correspondence, our author often wrote and signed in the vernacular of Spain, "Juan de S. Thoma" (or "Thomas," "Toma," "Tomás").

The Solesmes editors seem to think that use of the Latin "de" form arose in this case from assimilation to the Spanish version of the Latin "a Sancto Thoma," to wit, "de Santo Thoma" (and "de Sancto Thoma" is not incorrect Latin in any case), but that it was "a Sancto Thoma" that was the form Poinsot actually received in religious life.[30]

The surname "Poinsot" certainly belonged to our author by birth, but its etymological connotations create yet other problems in the present case, since to modern ears it is unmistakably French in flavor, though our author's father came from Austria while his mother (Maria Garcez) was Portuguese, and he himself was educated in Portugal and Belgium, after which he entered for the rest of his life the heartland of Spain, where he studied, taught, and labored, ending his days in the Council of the King.[31] Living at the time just prior to the emergence of the nation states as we think of them today, Poinsot belongs to no "nationality" in the usual sense.

Portuguese by maternal blood, Viennese and French (Burgundian) by paternal blood, Portuguese, Belgian, and Spanish by education, it is very difficult to say how such a man identified himself in the civil order. How would he think of himself? Certainly, no modern category would be the likely answer to that question.[32]

---

[29] A full description of the original title pages of the various editions is given in the Solesmes "Praefatio" (1931), Caput I, Art. III, "De operibus Joannis a Sancto Thoma," p. xiij and following.

[30] Solesmes, 1931: vij, par. 12 and note 3: "Ab hac die," scil., 18 July 1610, the day of Poinsot's religious profession (see II.B.2., below), "relicto quo in saeculo audierat nomine non jam Joannes *Poinsot* vocari voluit, sed Joannes a Sancto Thoma." "Triplex invenitur hujus nominis forma.—Prima, vernaculâ hispanorum lingua: *Juan de Santo Thoma* [Reiser, 1933: XII, reproduces a letter of this signature from 3 July 1635 ending Thomas] (vel: *Toma*, vel *Tomás*).—Secunda: *Joannes de Sancto Thoma*, quae, utpote primae similior, saepius usurpatur et ab ipso Joanne, et ab huius temporis Hispanis.—Tertia, *Joannes a Sancto Thoma*, reperitur . . . in fronte hujusce tomi (inde a prima editione) . . . ; quam igitur formam universali jam usu receptam, retinendam esse duximus."

Conspicuously absent from this account, the most definitive we have on the subject, is the variant, "*João de Santo Thomaz*," which appears nowhere in principal editions of Poinsot's work, but which some sciolist who decides how card catalogues for modern libraries should read for the United States had somehow settled upon for the principal listing! (The British Museum is a letter better: see note 33 following.)

[31] See Section II.B.2. below.

[32] Though "Spanish" would probably come closest. The Solesmes editors observe (1931:

Nonetheless, the complexity of our author's situation in the twilight of the Latin era and dawn of modern times helps account for the perplexity of our contemporary situation, where upward of a "baker's dozen" different versions of our author's name must be used to locate in scholarly sources what has been written about him in recent times![33]

---

lxxxvi, par. 4) that "Hispanum *fuisse Joannem a Sancto Thoma non dixerunt nisi pauci, aut historiae parum gnari, aut ad regimen politicum externave locorum, institutionum disciplinarumque adjuncta, quibus excolitur ingenium, magis attendentes quam ad sanguinem ac progeniem; si etenim ingenii culturam, si civitatis jura, si erga regem regnumque summam fidelitatem spectas, non ambiguum est Philippi IV Confessarium legitime Hispanis accenseri posse.*"—"Some have called Poinsot a Spaniard for want of historical knowledge. But some [e.g., Simonin, 1930: 140] have called him such not through ignorance, but because they gave greater weight to affairs of state or to the environmental conditions of the places, customs, and traditions of learning by which the mind is cultivated, than to blood and family ancestry. For if one looks to the culture in which his mind was nurtured, to the political rights he enjoyed, or to the king and kingdom that laid highest claim to his loyalty, it is clear that the Confessor to Philip IV can be rightly counted a Spaniard."

It is true that Poinsot refers in his treatise on creation (*Tractatus de Opere Sex Dierum*, in the Solesmes ed. of Poinsot 1645a: 878) to the Portuguese adventurers who had at that time explored previously unknown African lands as "*our* adventurers" ("*ut ex nostrorum peregrinationibus hoc tempore constat*"). But this should not be taken to imply, as the later Solesmes editors suggest (1935: v note 1), that Poinsot is here making a principal identification of himself as a Portuguese. On the contrary, when one considers that at the time of Poinsot's birth Portugal had come under the rule of the Spanish king, that the household of Poinsot's father had as its principal patron the Spanish king's delegate for the rule of Portugal, that Poinsot in no wise sided against the Spanish crown when Portugal revolted in 1640, and that he died at the king of Spain's side on a battlefield to restore unquestioned Spanish sovereignty over Catalonia, the far more probable inference is that in referring to the Portuguese adventurers of the time as "our own," he was rather identifying the Portuguese as a part of greater Iberia, i.e., the rule of the Spanish king, than he was identifying himself as a Portuguese vis-à-vis the Spaniards. Yet the situation is complex, and it remains that no modern nationalistic category—yet still, I think, Portuguese less than Spanish—fits this extraordinary case: By birth and upbringing he was identified with Portugal; by education and family ties with larger Europe; by vocation and personal choice with Spain; by his writings with the Latin world of an earlier, universal Christendom.

[33] From notes taken in preparing this edition, I give the following list, without trying to ensure its completeness. (1) "*Jean de Saint-Thomas*": J. M. Ramirez, 1924: 803 ff.; Lavaud, 1926: 387; Gardeil, 1927: XVIII; R. Maritain, 1930; Ghoos, 1951; Moreny, 1951; Dandenault, 1966; Abel, 1970. (2) "*João de São Tomé*": Marías, 1967: 206-207. (3) "*Juan de Santo Tomás*": Belisario, 1954; Rodriguez, 1954; Rodriguez and Camino, 1954; Blanes, 1956; Moreno, 1959, 1963; Prieto del Rey, 1963; Gambra, 1973: 175. (4) "*John of St. Thomas*": Oesterle, 1944; Glanville, Hollenhorst, and Simon, 1949, 1955; Thomas, 1950; Veatch, 1950; Hughes, 1951; Doyle, 1953; Wade, 1955; J. Maritain, 1959a: esp. 387ff.; Kane, 1959; Ehr, 1961; Makonski, 1962; Bondi, 1966; Masson, 1966; Bourke, 1967: 284. (5) "*Joâo de Sâo Tomás*": Bellerate, 1955; Gonçalves, 1955a, b; Herculano de Carvalho, 1969. (6) "*Giovanni di San Tommaso*": Degl'Innocenti, 1969; Alonso, 1957: 770. (7) "Jean de S. Thomas": Wojtkiewicz, 1961. (8) "*Joannes a Sancto Thoma*": D. Ramirez, 1645; Reiser, 1930; Solesmes, 1931; Mathieu and Gagné: 1947, 1948, 1949, 1952, 1953a, b, 1954, 1955. Crépeault, 1961; Coseriu, 1969: 135f. (9) "*Johannes a Sancto Thoma*": Quetif-Echard, 1721: 538. (10) "*Jean Poinsot*": Lavaud, 1926: 388, Deely, 1974, 1975b; Sebeok, 1979. (11) "*John Poinsot*": Simon, 1955: xviii; Glanville, 1958. (12) "*Juan Poinsot*": Ashworth, 1974: 286. (13) "*João de S. Tomás*": Bellerate, 1958. (14) "*Juan de Santo Toma*": Trapiello, 1889. (15) "*John of Saint Thomas*": Wolicka, 1979: 96 ff. (16) "*Poinsot (Joannes)*": *British Museum. General Catalogue of Printed Books*, vol. 192, p. 67, cross-referring for all entries to (17) "*Juan* [*Poinsot*], *a Sancto Thoma*" (a puzzling hybridization of the Spanish and Latin forms—see note 30 above); (18) "*João de Santo Thomaz*": entry for the Lilly Library 1637 holding, as for the Library of Congress *National Union Catalog* prior to 1982.

The variations in this list range from the trivial to the significant, but their cumulative effect is to import the desirability within semiotics of as simple and accurate a standard designation for this author as is possible. Personally, it seems clear to me that "*Joannes a Sancto Thoma*" is the proper Latin name for our author, but that outside the Latin language the best hope for eliminating confusion is to recur to his family name of "Poinsot," which would be invariant

On all the verions, *John* is the English form of our author's first name. That his family surname was *Poinsot* is equally certain. Hence, for our English edition of his semiotic, the first such in any language, we thus nominally identify our author.

Reverting to his family name, instead of continuing with some version of the name substituted for it in religious life—"de" or "a Sancto Thoma"—has a number of advantages for our purposes in addition to its simplicity. In the first place, the peculiar religious and cultural circumstances which gave meaning to such a substitution in Poinsot's age no longer prevail and are not so easily understood—indeed, are more likely to generate misunderstandings—in the English-speaking world of today. In the second place, apart from the inelegance of using our author's most proper Latin name for presenting an English edition, "Joannes a Sancto Thoma" was the very name adopted by two other illustrious figures living in Poinsot's time—Daniel Rindtfleisch ("Buccretius") and one Sarasatenus. This circumstance has in the past led to confusion over the authorship of certain writings (Reiser, 1930: VII).

In the third place, and finally, among those few modern writers acquainted with Poinsot's work even by way of his Latin religious name,[34] there are none who demonstrate an awareness of the unique, pre-eminent, we might almost say *governing*, position that the treatment of signs held in Poinsot's own mind in the generation of the *Cursus Philosophicus*, the "first offspring born of John's genius," as the Solesmes editors say (1931: xiij). Poinsot's doctrine of signs, no longer controlled, balanced, qualified, and restricted by the total concerns of Latin tradition ("tironum captui quaestiones istae de signis disproportionatae sunt," in Poinsot's terms: cf. 38/21-22 [=*642a22-24*]), but free now to exhibit its deep tendency as a beginning in its own right and to enter history on its own terms, is for the first time achieved with this edition. It is just as well that it comes to all readers for the first time under a name which harbors no illusions of familiarity.

B. The Historical Period and Life of Our Author

Unde Gallia, Lusitania Austriaque sanguinem, Lusitania iterum, Belgio et Hispania scientiam virtutesque ministrantibus, melius elucet quanta veritate pronuntiaverit quondam Ramirezius, ut in

---

across all the national language lines, unlike the multiple possibilities of rendering opened up by "de" or "a Sancto Thoma." Moreover, there is no other writer of this surname writing on our Poinsot's topics. I continue this argument in the text above.

[34] Poinsot under any name, for example, is entirely absent from the Kneale's *The Development of Logic* (Oxford, 1962) from ancient times to the present. Or again, the very Latin itself of Poinsot's first name has led to minor confusions of its own. Thus Sebeok (1975a: 152) reports him "commonly known as Joannis . . . ," i.e., "of John," since "Joannis" is the possessive form of the name "Joannes," which is no doubt all that Sebeok meant. Yet I have been asked "why they sometimes spell his name with an 'e', other times with an 'i';" and, as a final note on the confusion, the Latin interchangeability of "i" with "j" leads some editors (e.g., Reiser) to spell John "Ioannes," while other editors (e.g., Solesmes) spell it "Joannes" (and I myself have been systematically faithful to Reiser's "i" preference only in the main *Treatise* texts as such, not in the notes or this "Afterword").

supremum unum *sapientiae probitatisque exemplar tanta merita* congerentur, celebriores Europae partes adjuvasse.

Solesmes "Preface," 1931: lxxxvij

Seeing that France, Portugal, and Austria supplied his blood, while Portugal again, Belgium, and Spain contributed his learning and character, the better shows how much truth there was in the pronouncement [1645] of his biographer Ramirez, that the more famous lands of Europe helped bring together so many qualities of insight and integrity in one supreme exemplar.

Considerably scholarly effort has been expended in search of the origin of Poinsot's family line.[35] The best opinion on the question holds that his father, Peter Poinsot, himself born of noble blood in Austria, was descended from the family of Jean Poinsot de Chatenois, ennobled on March 11, 1457, by letters of Philip the Good, Duke of Burgundy, which letters gave to the daughters of the family the rare privilege of ennobling bourgeoisie whom they wed. Members of this family, thus, by serving the inheritors of the Burgundian lands, were serving the lines of the German emperors and the Spanish kings through the fifteenth and sixteenth centuries.[36]

Peter Poinsot was the companion and secretary of the Archduke Albert VI of Austria, who was the son of the Emperor Maximilian II, erstwhile cardinal pro-King of Portugal, and later Prince of the Spanish Netherlands (Belgium) and husband of Isabel, daughter of King Philip II of Spain. Peter Poinsot's service to the Archduke took him around the year 1570 from Austria to Spain, thence to Portugal in 1583, and finally to Belgium in 1598. It was in Lisbon, Portugal, some time after 1583,[37] that Peter Poinsot met and married Maria

---

[35] See "De Joannis a S. Thoma Gente et Stirpe," Appendix XV to the Solesmes "Preface," 1931, pp. 1xxxvi-1xxxvij.

[36] Ibid., p. 1xxxvij, par. 9: ". . . frequentior fuit toto saeculo XVI hujusmodi familiarum fortuna ex Burgundiae Comitatu ad Belgium, Hispaniam, Austriamve transeuntium, cunctis istis regionibus tunc ad idem pertinentibus, Caesareaeque Domus principibus libenter ex Burgundionibus, ob perspectam gentis fidem, viros assumentibus quibus magnam aut etiam summam in re publica crederent potestatem: inter quos clarissimi refulsere Nicolaus Perrenot, Caroli V. Cancellarius, ejusque filius Cardinalis Granvelle. Dum igitur reperta non fuerit nobilis quaepiam Poinsotiorum stirps quae reapse ex Austria originem sumat, satis tuto judicio adscribi poterit Joannes a S. Thoma illi ex Burgundiae Comitatu veteri prosapiae, paternique seminis titulo inter Burgundiones computari." "Ceterum," they add (ibid., note 3), "ut vidimus, rationibus omnino concinunt documenta ex archivis desumpta."

Ibid., note 2, cites the following instructive passage from Courchetet d'Esnans, *Histoire du Cardinal de Granvelle* (Paris, 1761), p. 24: "Il est remarquable même, que de toutes les Nations qui furent soumises à Charles-Quint, il n'y en eut pas une seule qui ne se révoltat sous son règne, si l'on en excepte la Franche-Comté, toujours féconde en Noblesse et en Peuples guerriers, et toujours fidelle à ses Maîtres. Aussi Charles-Quint la distingua parmi toutes ses Provinces, et il répandit sur elle ses grâces les plus signalées. Sa Noblesse occupa de grands Gouvernements, et les premières Charges de la Maison de l'Empereur; l'Histoire la nomme dans toutes les guerres et dans toutes les grandes entreprises du tems. Ses magistrats dans le Ministère, dans les Ambassades de France, d'Allemagne, d'Angleterre, et dans le Conseil d'Etat des Pays-Bas. Plusieurs Evêques furent choisis dans l'Ordre Ecclesiastique de la Province, et pour donner à la Nation une preuve de la confiance qu'il avait en sa fidélité, Charles-Quint lui confia la garde de sa personne."

See in this same line Simonin, 1930: 141-142.

[37] The Solesmes editors, 1931: vj, say simply: "verisimile est nonnisi post annum 1583 obtigisse."

Garcez, daughter of an old established Lisbon family. At least two children were born of this union, our John and his elder brother Louis.[38]

Not a great deal is known about John Poinsot's life, and what little is known is so bound up with his studies that it seems best for our purposes to give simply a bare chronology of the outward events of his life based on the best available scholarly sources, together with a chronology of parallel events in the history of science and culture of the time sufficient to situate Poinsot's life and work in the context of European events more likely to be familiar to the reader's mind.

I precede this chronology with a brief account of the main political events that determined the context of Poinsot's public life in Spain, those events minimally requisite for seeing the historical connections between the titles, personages, and places that occur prominently in the events of Poinsot's life.

1. The Political Formation of Poinsot's Lebenswelt

In seeking for a global understanding of a philosopher's thought, it is helpful to have enough facts at hand to enable one to get some feel for the context of life within his period and region. Being children of the French Revolution and heirs of the English common-law traditions, we are accustomed to look back in time from the perspective of the world that *began* in 1492, a world almost entirely outside the peninsula of Iberia, rather than trouble ourselves to make the effort of relating the data of our common European heritage along the quite other patterns of probability and custom which had to be assessed and confronted by anyone living within the Iberian peninsula in the seventeenth century and participating in its public life. Any serious appreciation of Poinsot's life and work in a global way requires an imaginative and sustained effort along lines of vision that are not habitual to our eyes, but that afford a strikingly new opening into "that least known period in the history of Western philosophy, the transition from the thirteenth to the seventeenth centuries."[39]

I have tried to gather here that minimum of facts which allows one to see continuous lines of historical connection between the principal titles, individuals, and places that will be mentioned in the chronology of events in Poinsot's life. I find that this minimum can be provided by tracing the lines of political and social power at the time as they pass through the kings of Spain in direct relation to the careers in public life of both Peter and John Poinsot. Since it was the Holy Roman Emperor Charles V who established Philip II on the Spanish

---

[38] Louis received his Bachelor's degree from the University of Coimbra the same year as his brother, 1605, and took up the study of law at Coimbra in the fall of that same year. In 1610 Louis professed vows in the "Trinitarian Order for Redemption of Captives," where he turned to the study of theology. Louis later became a respected Professor of Theology at Coimbra, holding at different times the chair of Durandus and of Scotus. He died in 1655. See Solesmes, 1931: vj-vij, pars. 6-7.

[39] Randall, 1962: I, vii-viii. In the particular case of Poinsot, the angle of vision afforded into this lost period, involving the "mature" bloom of the medieval institutions of censorship and inquisition, has a singular speculative and empirical value in our present-day search for ways to pattern humane civilization that can transcend national and racial bounds. As I have said elsewhere (1977c: 16) the detailed historical reconstruction and study of Poinsot's *Lebenswelt* is bound to come, and the sooner the better for modern prejudices all around! See references in note 53 below.

throne and who provides the political connection as well as the blood connection between Peter Poinsot's patron (the Archduke Albert) and Philip II, which connections eventually led Peter Poinsot to Portugal and the arms of Maria Garcez, our John's mother, I will begin my minimal reconstruction of the formation of Poinsot's *Lebenswelt* along political lines with the famous abdication by Charles of his royal titles. Beginning here gives us the added advantage of making our preliminary entry into the unfamiliar world of Poinsot's Iberia in terms of an extremely well known landmark figure for more familiar aspects of European history.

Reserving to himself his other title as Charles V, Holy Roman Emperor, in 1555 Charles I of Spain transferred to his son Philip sovereignty over the seventeen Netherlands provinces (which included at that period most of what we still call the "Low Countries," all of Belgium as well as Holland), and in the following year he transferred his sovereignty over Spain as well, making his son King Philip II.

Charles himself, born and raised in Flanders, came to Spain as the offspring of a marriage in 1496 between Juana (Joan), the seemingly half-mad daughter of Ferdinand and Isabella, and Philip the Handsome, son of the Austrian Holy Roman Emperor Maximilian I, regent of the Netherlands from 1494. On the death of his father in 1506, Charles became heir to the Netherlands (though he would not be declared "of age" to rule until 1515, his own fifteenth year).

In 1516, when Ferdinand followed Isabella to the grave, he left Cardinal Ximenes, who had been Queen Isabella's chaplain and confessor since 1492, Archbishop of Toledo and Primate of Spain since 1495, to act as Regent in Castile, until such time as Charles should journey from Flanders to claim the throne of Spain. This Charles did in September of 1517. Ximenes died within three months, aged 81, willing his great personal fortune to the University of Alcalá, which he had himself founded in 1508.

When, therefore, Charles I handed to his son Philip II the Spanish crown, he handed him what was then—thanks principally to the long and skillful reign of Ferdinand and Isabella—the largest empire and one of the three most unified states in Europe. In 1492, Columbus had opened the New World for Spain. But of far greater importance to the people of the time was the fall of Granada in that year to the armies of Ferdinand, ending seven hundred and eighty-one years of Islamic presence in Spain. Already in 1483, Ferdinand and Isabella had managed to persuade Pope Sixtus IV to grant to the civil government of Spain power to name all successors to the office of Inquisitor General, at the same time that the Pope appointed Torquemada, the Dominican friar nominated by Ferdinand, to first hold the post. With Torquemada installed, the Supreme Council of the Inquisition was established in the same year (1483) as a governmental agency in Spain. With this instrument for molding together the political and religious unity of Spain already in place, it is not surprising, perhaps, that the fall of Granada (where Francis Suarez would be born in 1548) in 1492 inspired the Spanish sovereigns to complete the unity of their Christian polity by issuing in that same year an edict of exile for all unconverted Jews, followed within seven years by a similar decree by Isabella (at Cardinal Ximenes's urging) against all unconverted followers of Islam (1499).

Unlike his father who had grown up among the Netherlands' nobles, Philip II was entirely a son of Spain. Not understanding or appreciating the long traditions of independent and republican rule in the Low Countries, Philip's promotion of the Inquisition in the Netherlands and other demands brought about armed and bloody revolt in those provinces. This revolt was headed principally by William of Nassau, Prince of Orange. Brought up to age eleven as a Lutheran, then (for inheritance reasons) as a Catholic, not until 1572 did he decide to become a Calvinist and to declare himself such (in part for reasons of state, as it seems). This revolt developed through many complex, murderous stages under a succession of regents appointed by Philip from distant Spain.

Having given Spain and its dependencies to his son in 1555-56, Charles V soon abdicated his imperial title also, transferring the emperor's crown to his brother Ferdinand in Austria, who became, in 1558, Ferdinand I. In 1564 Ferdinand died, and the electors transmitted the imperial crown to Ferdinand's son, who thus became Emperor Maximilian II. Among Maximilian's sons was the Archduke Albert VI. It was this Albert, first cousin once removed of the reigning king of Spain (Philip II), who was the employer and patron in Vienna of Peter Poinsot, and who received in 1570 a summons to come to Spain for reasons of the Spanish king. The Archduke Albert spent presumably the next twelve years with Peter Poinsot in Philip's Spain, receiving from the Pope during this period a cardinal's hat and a title to the see of Toledo (Ximenes' old domain), even though he was not a priest.

In 1493, during the reign of Ferdinand and Isabella, the judicious intervention of Pope Alexander VI with a "line of demarcation" separating the New World claims of Portugal from those of Spain had averted a war between the peninsular powers. By 1580, however, the last heir of the royal Aviz dynasty (which had ruled Portugal since John I's defeat of the armies of Castile in 1385) died without issue, and Philip II, as grandson of King Manuel of Portugal (1495-1521), claimed the Portugese throne. The Cortes of Lisbon recognized Philip's claim against other contenders, and, in 1581, Philip II of Spain marched his armies into Lisbon as Philip I of Portugal. Thus, the papal division of the New World was for a time rendered nugatory, and the whole of Iberia (except for Navarre) came under one rule. In 1583, Philip I of Portugal installed the Cardinal Archduke Albert (again accompanied by Peter Poinsot) in Lisbon as pro-King of Portugal, while he himself returned to Madrid as Philip II.

In February of 1592, Philip's regent in the Netherlands since 1579, the skillful Duke of Parma, died. In the fourteen years of his regency, Parma had not succeeded in entirely quelling the rebellion and hatreds made so implacable during the murderous regency of the Duke of Alva (1567-1573), who even the Catholic clergy had warned Philip was ruining the state. But by 1585 Parma had turned the near-total Spanish collapse of 1576 into a firm reassertion of control over the ten southern provinces, confining the rebel factions in their control to the seven northern provinces.

To succeed Parma, Philip II appointed as his regent in the Netherlands Archduke Ernest of Austria, who neither lived long nor affected the status quo. Philip II, now nearing death, conceived of a different strategy for reconciling the northern and southern provinces. At the King's suggestion, and with the Pope's

permission, the Cardinal Archduke Albert resigned his cardinalate, then married Isabel, Philip II's daughter. The King then (1598) bestowed upon the couple full sovereignty in the Netherlands, with the proviso that the sovereignty would revert to Spain if the couple died without an heir. Peter Poinsot accompanied the new royal couple to their new lands, where Albert too proved unable to subdue the north, but established in the south a civilized and humane regime under which learning and the arts flourished. (At Antwerp, for example, in 1609, Albert appointed Rubens Court Painter.) In 1621, Albert, Prince of the Netherlands, died childless. Sovereignty reverted to Spain, but so did war with the northern provinces, which Spain did not acknowledge free until the signing in 1648 of the Treaty of Westphalia.

Shortly after establishing his now son-in-law Albert and his daughter on a throne in the Spanish Netherlands, Philip II died. His crown passed, on September 13, 1598, to his twenty-year-old son, Philip III, a pious soul, timid and weak, who promptly turned over management of his government to the Duke of Lerma. Philip II had conceived during his reign a plan to endow theological Chairs for the teaching of the thought of St. Thomas Aquinas at the principal Iberian universities of Castile and Coimbra, and perhaps also at the universities of Aragon and Andalusia (Beltran de Heredia, 1916: 268-269). In August of 1611, acting with the authority of Philip II's son, the reigning Philip III, the Duke of Lerma began negotiations for the establishment of such a Morning and an Evening Chair at Alcalá, to be held in perpetuity by the Dominican Order (ibid., 269). By September of 1613, a papal bull confirmed the establishment of the Chairs (ibid., 272). Seventeen years later, our John Poinsot would become the fourth holder of this Evening Chair at Alcalá (ibid., 294), and twenty-eight years later he would become the fifth holder of the Morning Chair (ibid., 286).

In the meantime, the Spanish Crown would pass by death to Philip III's son, crowned Philip IV. From 1621 to 1642, Philip IV entrusted the management of his kingdom to the Count of Olivares, known in European history for the countergame he played with Richelieu of France for hegemony of Europe. In late January of 1643 Philip IV dismissed Olivares, and also the royal confessor, Antonius de Sotomayor. In February he called upon John Poinsot to leave his university chair and undertake to counsel and assist the King in reforming and reorganizing the affairs of the Spanish Crown. Poinsot, according to the report,[40] put to the King one condition of his service, "whether, namely, the King is willing to hear and to follow the truth in all affairs; for if not, he will not by any means undertake to guide Philip's conscience." An unusual way to speak to a Hapsburg King. But it was not to politics that Poinsot had chosen to order his life, and he did not relish the role his King was forcing upon him. The imposition would not last long. Within eighteen months of his first summons by the King, the author of our *Treatise on Signs* would be dead.

[40] Solesmes, 1931: x, par. 25: "D. Ludovico de Haro qui cum eo regis consilium communicabat, respondit Joannes unum antea regi deliberandum: an scilicet vellet veritatem in omnibus audire et sequi; sin minus, nequaquam se Philippi conscientiam regendam suscipere potest."

2. Chronology of Events

	EVENTS OF POINSOT'S LIFE	PARALLEL EVENTS IN THE HISTORY OF IBERIA AND EUROPE:
1588:	Embryogenesis.	Thomas Hobbes is born at Westport in England. The "Spanish Armada" of Philip II is sunk in the seas off England. Kepler obtains a B.A. from the University of Tübingen.
1589:	July 9: Born to Maria and Peter Poinsot in Lisbon, Portugal.	Francis Bacon begins teaching at the school of law in London. In the year and place of Poinsot's birth, Luis de Molina publishes his famous work, *Concordia liberi arbitrii cum gratiae donis, divina praescientia, providentia, praedestinatione et reprobatione*, soon the principal focus of the classic theological controversy concerning free will and grace.
1596:		Kepler publishes his work advocating the Copernican system, *Mysterium Cosmographicum*; Galileo writes him a letter of praise and encouragement. March 31: Birth of Descartes in France.
1597:		Francis Suarez is appointed *Professor Primarius* at the University of Coimbra by Philip II. In this same year Suarez publishes his celebrated *Disputationes Metaphysicae*. The first extended independent treatise in scholastic metaphysics, this work includes a dialectical survey and assessment of opinions covering the preceding 400 years of Latin scholasticism, and was destined to become for more than a century the main philosophical textbook in use throughout both the Catholic and the Protestant countries of Europe, the *philosophia recepta* so far as concerned the Latin heritage of the parts of Europe where modern thought was being born in the national languages. Suarez thus became the almost exclusive principal channel by which

"Thomism" and Latin Aristotelianism in general influenced the circles of Descartes and Leibniz and eventually (through Christian Wolff) of Kant, a fact of special interest, because Poinsot's theory of signs and relations is opposed to the influence of Suarez, with whose work Poinsot shows detailed familiarity, at every structural point.[41]

1598: The Archduke Albert receives from Philip II sovereignty over the Netherlands. Albert and Peter Poinsot move to Belgium. September 13: Philip III accedes to the throne on his father's death, and entrusts his government to the Duke of Lerma.

1600: Kepler joins Tycho Brahe in Prague.

1601: October 24: Brahe dies.

1603: Hobbes enters Magdalen Hall, Oxford.

1604: Around this time, Poinsot is studying under professors involved in the Conimbricenses group writing a treatise *De Signo* as the first chapter of their commentary on Aristotle's *Perihermenias* (cf. Doyle 1984).

Descartes enters the Jesuit College at La Flèche.

Kepler discovers that the orbit of Mars is not circular but elliptical.

---

[41] Reiser, 1930: XI: "Quibus omnibus diligentissime observatis Ioannes discipulus S. Thomae maxime egregius manifestatur, et cum Cajetanus doctrinam Angelici Doctoris commentariis profundis illustraret, Capreolus contra Scotum, Bañez contra Molinam defenderet, Ioannes a Sancto Thoma eam evolvit disputans contra Vazquez et praesertim Suarez, sine ulla tamen violentia aut acerbitate. In qua concertatione virum nobilem et superiorem se praebuit ad unguem perficiens, quae veritatis defensorem perficere in fine praenominati tractatus [cf. note 27 above, *in finem*] expostulavit."

Comparing this work of Suarez to the more tradition-honoring plan of Poinsot's *Cursus* (see note 16 above), Simonin (1930: 145) says with a hint of wistfulness:

"Au contraire Suarez a mis à bas résolument le vieil édifice, il tente de le reconstruire à neuf, sur de nouveaux plans, en fonction du nouveau décor. Cette formule plus logique et plus simple devait nécessairement l'emporter. Avec Suarez le traité de philosophie, genre dans lequel s'illustreront un Leibnitz, un Spinoza et un Kant, est entré de facon définitive dans les moeurs nouvelles; ce procédé n'est évidemment possible qu'avec le triomphe du préjugé moderne selon lequel chaque philosophe doit nécessairement construire sa vue personnelle du monde et concevoir son système propre. Les Anciens, plus modestes, mais faisant preuve d'une mentalité peut-être plus scientifique, préféraient demeurer à l'abri de l'ancienne cathédrale dont l'ombre leur était familière et propice."

1605: March 11: Poinsot, age 16, receives his Bachelor of Arts degree from the University of Coimbra in Portugal. (This Coimbra degree was elsewhere in Europe called a Master of Arts degree.)[42]

October 14: Poinsot begins studying theology at Coimbra.

Suarez is at this period a member of the faculty and *Doctor Eximius* at Coimbra, but was away through most of the years of Poinsot's studies. The Solesmes editors conclude (1931: vij note 1) that Poinsot probably "saw but did not hear" Suarez in the course of his studies.

In England, Francis Bacon publishes *The Advancement of Learning*.

1606: May 8: Last mention of Poinsot in the Coimbra University archives as "having attended the first-year theological lectures."

c. June: Poinsot, age 17, goes to Belgium (the southern or "Spanish" Netherlands) for the purpose of continuing his studies at the University of Louvain (see entry under 1608: February 12: below).

c. October: Poinsot attends lectures given from the theological chair in the public auditoriums of the University of Louvain by Thomas de Torres, a Dominican friar from the convent of Our Lady of Atocha in Madrid (Spanish capital since 1561). Impressed, Poinsot comes strongly under the influence of de Torres,[43] and over the next two years conducts an independent study of the writings of Thomas Aquinas under de Torres' direction.

1607: Cornelius Jansen receives the Biblical Bachelor degree from Louvain. Less than forty years hence, the Louvain faculty itself would become a center of resistance to the papal

---

[42] See Solesmes, 1931: vj note 1.

[43] Reiser, 1930: VIII, describes the association thus: "Quibus annis apud Louvanienses sacram scientiam docuit Thomas de Torres y Jibaja. Quocum viro scientiae et virtutis laude aeque praecellenti Joannem amicitia sancta conjunxit, quae ex communi magistri et discipuli desiderio exorta est, in dies profundiores radices mittere in doctrina S. Thomae, non ut argutias dialecticas jactarent, sed rerum divinarum contemplationem in fide et caritate fundatam magis magisque intenderunt. Ita mirum non est, quod in corde adolescentis propositum maturuit vitam religiosam in familia Fratrum Praedicatorum amplecti."

Thomas de Torres himself would remain at Louvain until 1614, when he returned to Spain. In 1620, he was sent to Paraguay in the New World as a bishop, was transferred six years later to Tucuman, and finally, in 1530, while attending a provincial council in Lima, Peru, was struck by an illness and died, at the age of 66 (Lavaud, 1926: 390 note 1).

condemnation (1643) of Jansen's book *Augustinus*, and would appeal to Poinsot to intervene in the affair which pitted Jansenists against Molinists within the University (see entry for 1644 below).

1608: February 9: Poinsot responds under Master Samuel of the Louvain faculty, as part of his *Baccalaureus* examinations, to questions on "Divine concurrence in human freedom." (In 1607, a special Roman Congregation *de auxiliis* had closed its nine-year review of the question by declaring all existing opinions in the Molina-Bañez controversy inadequate to the exigencies of the question, with a subsequent moratorium imposed on continued public debate.[44])

February 12: Poinsot, age 19, completes under Master Samuel the requirements for and receives the theological degree of Biblical Bachelor (*Baccalaureus biblicus*).

(By the statutes of the University of Louvain,[45] reception of this required having followed theological lectures for about three years after the Master of Arts degree: hence the inference that Poinsot came to Louvain toward the middle of 1606.)

Thomas Hobbes enters the service of William Cavendish, Earl of Devonshire. The Cavendish family will become lifelong patrons of Hobbes.

[44] This event of Poinsot's youth was to leave its mark years later on the structure of his *Cursus Theologicus*.

Poinsot "s'attarde relativement peu sur la grace actuelle," Lavaud observes (1928: 430); et "sans doute, la raison principale d'une attitude qui n'est pas propre à notre auteur, [est qu'] il était interdit alors de publier des livres sur les questions débattues naguère devant la congrégation *de Auxiliis*, sans les avoir au préalable soumis à la sainte Inquisition." "Paul V," Lavaud further explains (ibid., note 1), "pour mettre fin aux controverses trop ardent, s'était d'abord contenté d'interdire les qualifications injurieuses entre thomistes et molinistes (lettre du 5 Sept. 1607, *Denz.* 1090). Plus tard il avait defendu de publier des livres *in materia de auxiliis etiam sub praetextu commentandi S. Thomam . . . quin prius S. Inquisitioni propositi fuissent* (décret du 1er déc. 1611). Urbain VI avait aggravé cette defense en la sanctionnant par des peines rigoreuses (décrets du 22 mai 1625 et du 1er août 1641, *Denzinger*, p. 339-340, note 3). Ces ordannances, qui tombèrent peu à peu en désuétude, étaient alors en pleine vigeur. Les théologiens de ce temps traitent très brièvement de la grace actuelle, ou plutôt transportent ailleurs généralement à propos de la science et de la volonté divines, ce qu'ils ont en dire. C'est ce que fait Jean de Saint-Thomas." See, therefore, esp. *Cursus Theologicus*, Vol. 3 (1643) of Solesmes ed., 1937: disp. 27-30, pp. 329-357, for Poinsot's views on this matter.

We may also note that the central philosophical issue at play here, namely, the understanding of human freedom to originate actions responsibly, has been taken up, renewed, and extended in the express context of Poinsot's work by his modern student J. Maritain, 1966a, 1959b, 1948 (to a lesser extent: see the reservations in 1966a: 32-43), and elsewhere.

[45] See Solesmes, 1931: vij, par. 9 and note 2.

1609: Poinsot decides in his twentieth year to become a Dominican friar and to begin a lifelong study and explication of the philosophical and theological thought of Thomas Aquinas.

The long and bloody revolt of the northern Netherlands provinces under William of Nassau, Prince of Orange, against Spanish sovereignty, not healed with the arrival of the Archduke Albert as Philip II's chosen ruler of this low-countries region, had severely disrupted regularity of life in the Belgian (i.e., southern Netherlands) Dominican houses, and studies there were in a state of comparative disarray.

On these grounds, Friar Thomas de Torres urged young Poinsot to join a house of the Order in Spain proper. This Poinsot did on July 17, spending the next year at the Dominican Convent of Our Lady of Atocha in Madrid, de Torres's own house, in order to consider well the implications of his resolve.

The Archduke Albert appoints Rubens Court Painter at Antwerp.

Descartes, age 13, begins his philosophical and theological courses under the Jesuits at La Flèche, and begins to wonder that nothing to date "more lofty" has been erected on such firm foundations as mathematics alone among the sciences has.

Galileo Galilei applies the newly invented telescope to use in astronomy.

Kepler publishes his *Astronomia Nova* in Prague, the first work to suggest—as a consequence of postulating elliptical orbits for the planets—that *neither* the sun *nor* the earth lies at the center of things.

1610: July 17: Poinsot, age 21, professes religious vows as a Dominican brother in the Order of Friars Preachers. Following the ancient religious custom of choosing a new name to signify newness of life in the spirit, Poinsot chooses to be known in his new way of life by the name of "Joannes a Sancto Thoma."[46]

Following this profession, notwithstanding his earlier studies at Coimbra and Louvain, Poinsot is required to take at Atocha the entire curriculum of studies for students in the Order, excepting only the courses of introductory ("Summulae") and advanced Logic. These studies, omitting the Logic, probably covered three years of Philosophy and four of Theology.[47]

Galileo publishes the *Sidereus Nuncius* ("Celestial Messenger") in Italy, announcing his first telescopic discoveries and providing a Copernican line of rational interpretation for these observations.

Thomas Hobbes visits France and Italy.

---

[46] See Section II.A. above, esp. notes 30 and 33. Also note 27, p. 418 above. An attempt at a sympathetic reconstruction of the religious and personal dimension of Poinsot's life and work is attempted by Lavaud, 1926.

[47] Solesmes, 1931: viij, note 2: "Si ratio studiorum, a Magistro Sixto Fabri anno 1585 promulgata, etiam tum vigebat, integrum curriculum duobus Logicae, Philosophiae tribus, Theologiae quattuor annis absolvebatur. Joannes itaque, a Summulis Logicaque tantum immunis, septem annos Philosophiae ac Theologiae auditor adhuc fuisset: quod vix credibile arbitramur."

1611: August: The Duke of Lerma, acting with the authority of the King of Spain, begins negotiations for founding at the University of Alcalá Morning and Evening Chairs for the thought of St. Thomas Aquinas. (Similar Chairs were founded at Salamanca and other principal Iberian universities.)[48]

1612: Descartes leaves La Flèche.

1613: Galileo publishes his *Letters on Sunspots*.

September 26: A papal bull is issued confirming the foundation of the two theological chairs for the teaching of St. Thomas at Alcalá.

1615: Cervantes finishes *Don Quixote* at Alcalá.

1616: Cervantes dies.

March 5: The Holy Office publicly issues from Rome a condemnation of Copernicus and Copernicanism, privately warning Galileo to take this as a sign that he should moderate the course of his public statements.

1617: Poinsot is made Lecturer in Arts (philosophy) in the school of the Atocha convent, and soon after also the Student Master. (This date is conjectured upon the probable course of his studies at Atocha: see entry under 1610: above.) It may be from this period, then, that the beginnings of the *Treatise on Signs* date.

Francis Suarez dies at Coimbra.

1618: Descartes graduates from the University of Poitiers with degrees in civil and canon law. To the amazement of friends, he enlists in the army of Maurice of Nassau, Prince of Orange, leader of the Netherlands revolt

[48] See Beltran de Heredia, 1916.

		against Philip II which is now being carried on against the Archduke Albert, patron and friend of Poinsot's father. At Breda, Descartes meets Isaac Beeckman, who "returns his mind to science and worthier occupations" than military engineering: together the two discuss ways of rendering physical problems susceptible of mathematical treatment.
1619:		Descartes, having left the military service of the Netherlands' rebel Prince, joins the army of Maximilian of Bavaria, and is stationed at Neuberg, near Ulm. At Ulm, Germany, on November 10, he dreams of the reduction of physics to geometry. Kepler publishes *The Harmony of the World*, containing his third law of planetary motion.
1620:	Poinsot is sent to Plascencia in southwestern Spain as Lecturer in theology at the Dominican priory.[49]	Francis Bacon publishes his *Novum Organum* in England. Beginning of the Thirty Years War.
1621:		The Archduke Albert dies childless, and Netherlands sovereignty reverts to Spain. Philip III dies; his son Philip IV accedes to the throne, and appoints Don Gaspar de Guzman, Count of Olivares, as his chief minister caring for the affairs of state.
1622:		Descartes sells his estate at Poitou in order to free himself for travel and leisure pursuits.
1623:		Jacob Boehme publishes his *Mysterium Magnum* in Germany. June 19: Birth of Pascal.

[49] See Solesmes, 1931: p. viij, par. 14; Appendix IV, "Exerpta e Calatogo Religiosorum Atochensis Conventus," p. lv, par. 4; and Appendix VI, "Excerpta ex Historia Atochensi Gabrielis de Cepeda, O.P.," p. lxj, par. 4.

This corrects the chronology given by J. M. Ramirez, 1924: 804.

1624: Galileo seeks to have the 1616 decree of condemnation against Copernicus revoked.

Isabel of the Netherlands, widow of the Archduke Albert, persuades Philip IV to ennoble the painter Rubens.

1625: Poinsot is made Regent of the College of St. Thomas at the University of Alcalá, along with Salamanca and Coimbra one of the greatest centers of learning in Iberia of the time.

Poinsot becomes fast friends here with another friar, Peter of Tapia, who had come to Alcalá two years previously as third holder of the "Evening Chair" of theology founded by the Duke of Lerma.

1627: Already Poinsot's reputation for learning is spread throughout Spain, and he is called upon in connection with difficult cases in the capacity of a Qualificator both for the Supreme Council of the Spanish Inquisition and for the Inquisition at Coimbra.[50]

Poinsot is elected about this time to the Evening Chair at the University of Salamanca, considered to be Spain's greatest university center, but he declines to accept.[51]

Francis Bacon publishes his plan for organizing scientific research, *New Atlantis*.

1628: Descartes returns to Holland and takes up permanent residence.

Harvey publishes his work on the circulation of blood.

1629: Descartes publishes his *Rules for the Direction of the Mind*, and begins work on his treatise *On the World*.

---

[50] Solesmes, 1931: ix par. 20 and notes 2-4, with further references given therein. It is mentioned that Poinsot was given the thankless task of editing either the sixth (1632) or the seventh (1640) edition of the *Index* of forbidden books. See note 53 below.

[51] This accolade was printed by Thomas of Sarria on the title page of his 1638 Cologne edition of the *Cursus Philosophicus* as though Poinsot had accepted the election, which was not the case. See Solesmes, 1931: xiv, text at note 3; also p. ix par. 19bis, and Appendix VI, the "Excerpta ex Historia Atochensi Gabrielis de Cepeda, O.P.," p. lxj no. 5.

		Hobbes publishes his translation of Thucydides to instruct his countrymen on the dangers of democracy.
1630:	October: Poinsot, now 41 years of age, gives his first public lectures at Alcalá, after having been appointed as fourth one to hold the Evening Chair at the University. This chair had become vacant in July upon the promotion of Poinsot's friend, Peter of Tapia, to the principal or Morning chair. Poinsot immediately arranges for the publication of his *Cursus Philosophicus*.	November 15: Kepler dies.
1631:	Poinsot begins the publication of his philosophical writings, which he has now been laboring over for about 20 years,[52] with the publication of Part I of his *Ars Logica* at Alcalá.	
1632:	Poinsot publishes at Alcalá Part II of his *Ars Logica*, containing the revolutionary doctrine of signs.	John Locke is born in England, Spinoza in Amsterdam. Galileo publishes his Copernican *Dialogue Concerning the Two Chief World Systems*.
1633:	Part I of Poinsot's *Philosophia Naturalis* (*De Ente Mobili in Communi*) is published at Madrid. Poinsot receives the title "Doctor of Theology," a degree consequent upon holding the Evening Chair for two years, and considered the highest academic honor in Spain.[54]	February: Galileo is summoned to Rome for trial by the Inquisition. June 21: Galileo is condemned.[53] Descartes completes his Copernican treatise *On the World* (*Le Monde*), but, immediately on learning from Mersenne of Galileo's condemnation, stops its publication in order to avoid conflict with Rome.

---

[52] Hence the expression of the Solesmes editors to describe this event (1931: viij): "Ab anno 1631 coepit Joannes in lucem dare *Cursum Philosophicum*." It is to this period also (post-1631) that the Solesmes editors assign the probable composition of the *Tractatus de Approbatione et Auctoritate Doctrinae D. Thomae* discussed in note 27 above (see *Cursus Theologici Tomus Primus* (1637), Solesmes ed. 1931: 224 note 1).

[53] This whole affair and related matter has been interestingly reviewed recently by a student of Poinsot's thought, J. Maritain, 1970: 257-361, esp. "Que penser de l'Inquisition," 303 ff., and "La condamnation de Galilée," 345 ff. (pp. 176-199 and 200-211, respectively, in 1973 English trans.: see References).

[54] Solesmes, 1931: ix par. 21: "supremus magisterii gradus."

1634: Part III of Poinsot's *Philosophia Naturalis* (*De Ente Mobili Corruptibili*) is published at Alcalá. Part II of this part of the *Cursus Philosophicus, De Ente Mobili Incorruptibili, Quod Est Coelum* (i.e., the tract on astronomy), though Poinsot includes a place for it in the outlines of his work, is not published nor has any manuscript of this section been found to this day.[55] This missing part of Poinsot's *Cursus* has been a mystery to scholars (see the solution proposed in Section I.A. above).

1635: The last part of Poinsot's *Philosophia Naturalis* (*De Ente Mobili Animato*) is published at Alcalá. Poinsot turns to the preparation for publication of his theological writing.

---

[55] Reiser, 1933: V-VI, argues from four explicit references and one ambiguous reference within other parts of the *Cursus Philosophicus* that such a manuscript must have existed at some time prior to 1634, concluding simply:

''Libellum a Ioanne pro praelectionibus manu scriptum in bibliotheca alicuius conventus vel capituli Hispaniae sepultum esse possibile est; ex quo sepulchro an futura sit resuscitatio, quis audet dicere?'' (See note 1 above, however, on Poinsot's manuscripts.)

The one trace I have been able to find in Poinsot's work of the celebrated astronomical controversies of the early seventeenth century is a passing reference (in an article on projectile motion) to, without comment upon, Paul V's condemnation of the opinion of Copernicus ''et aliorum de motu naturali terrae per modum gyrationis,'' adding, as condemned by Gregory XV, ''etiam librationis'': phil. nat. 1. p. q. 23. art. 2, Reiser ed. vol. II, 474b19-32. Yet it is impossible not to relate Poinsot's suppression of this manuscript from the publication of his *Cursus Philosophicus* to misgivings on his part concerning the current state of scientific knowledge of the heavens—as indeed St. Thomas long before (c. 1272-1273) had warned concerning the Ptolemaic astronomy (*In I de caelo*, lect. 7, n. 77, and lect. 17, n. 451, as discussed in Deely 1973: 45-46, and 1969: 261-264ff. and 252 note 154), just as the Solesmes editors relate Poinsot's suppression of his manuscript *Treatise on the Work of the Six Days* (i.e., the creation of the world by God) to reservations perhaps weighing in the author's mind concerning Biblical criticism and the current state of exegesis (Solesmes, 1953: v par. 14: ''quia videbatur ab auctore scienter consultoque in Cursu suo Theologico non admissus, fortasse quod magis ad exegesim et biblicam expositionem pertineret quam ad theologicam disquisitionem''). No doubt these (the traditional tracts on astronomy and creation) were two of the areas Poinsot had in mind when he reflected, in closing his treatment of Logic (1632: q. 27. art. 2., 839a8-b10): ''*In fine huius articuli nota, quod cum in scientiis, ut modo apud nos sunt, non solum inveniantur demonstrationes, sed etiam multae opiniones, quoad ea, quae sub opinione cadunt, non deservit habitus scientificus, quia revera tales opiniones ad scientiam non pertinent quantum ad assensum scientificum, licet quia versantur circa eandem materiam scientiae, tractentur in eadem scientia, sed distinctum habitum generant.*''—''Note finally that since, in the present state of the sciences, there are not only genuine points of certainty, but many uncertain opinions as well, as regards those matters which are subject to opinion, scientific confidence is inappropriate, for in truth such matters of opinion do not pertain to science as regards the assent proper to it, even though, by the fact that the opinions bear on the same objects a science is concerned to understand, they must be weighed within that science, yet they create a different state of mind.''

Further discussion in notes 7 and 8 above, pp. 402 and 403.

1637:	Poinsot publishes the first volume of his *Cursus Theologicus* at Alcalá.	Descartes publishes in Leyden his *Discourse on Method* (*Discours de la Méthode de bien conduire sa raison et chercher la vérité dans les sciences*).
1637-38:	The first complete simultaneous edition of Poinsot's philosophical works—i.e., the works published between 1631 and 1635—is issued at Rome with the title *Cursus Philosophicus* added to the volumes of the Natural Philosophy.	
1638:	The second complete edition of the *Cursus Philosophicus* is issued at Cologne with "*Thomisticus*" added to the title, and the general title extended to the volumes of Logic as well as of Natural Philosophy.[56] One of Poinsot's earliest biographers (Quetif, 1667) has left us this portrait of Poinsot as a teacher at this period: "He was never seen to exasperate or shun anyone with the stern pompous arrogance of the professor."[57]	Galileo publishes his *Mathematical Discourses and Demonstrations Concerning Two New Sciences* at Leyden.
1640:	Poinsot adds a special "Preface" to the new edition (Madrid) of his *Artis Logicae Secunda Pars*, directing particular attention to the position, autonomy, and utility of his *Treatise on Signs* within the whole.	Hobbes privately circulates *The Elements of Law, Natural and Politic*, in England. Portugal and Catalonia rebel against the Spanish Crown.
1641:	Poinsot, age 52, is promoted to the Morning Chair at Alcalá, vacated by Peter of Tapia on his being appointed Bishop of Segovia by Philip IV. He is the fifth to hold the Chair since Lerma's foundation.	Descartes publishes his *Meditations on First Philosophy*.
1642:		January 8: Galileo dies.

[56] See notes 5 and 10 above, pp. 399 and 404.

[57] "Nullum lacessere, nullum aspernari vel austero tumidoque Magisterii supercilio dedignari visus est: sed nec aliorum forte disputando verbis impetitus procacioribus accendebatur aut reponebat, solus si modo ipse premeretur, non veritas."—from the "Synopsis Vitae Joannis a Sancto Thoma Auctore Jacobo Quetif" (anno 1667 in limine tomi de Sacramentis primum vulgatum), Appendix III to Solesmes, 1931: xlix no. 32.

Hobbes publishes *De cive* in Paris.

Antoine Arnauld, brother of Mère Angélique, Abbess of Port-Royal, and future author with Pierre Nicole of *La Logique ou l'art de penser* (the celebrated *Port-Royal Logic,* 1662), receives his Ph.D. at the Sorbonne. Arnauld will shortly begin his written defenses of Jansen's book *Augustinus*, a controversy that will eventually occasion Pascal's famous *Provincial Letters*.

1643: Late February: Philip summons Poinsot to Madrid and proposes that he become the royal Confessor. Poinsot asks the King to first consider whether he is willing "to hear and to follow the truth in all affairs; for if not, he will not by any means undertake to guide Philip's conscience."[58] The King allows Poinsot to return to Alcalá, setting Palm Sunday (March 29 that year) as the date for further discussing the matter, which date, however, seems not to have been held to.[59]

Condemnation of Jansen's work.

The Apostolic Nuncio for Spain, learning of Philip's intention, directly holds a meeting with Poinsot to remind him of the interests of the Apostolic See in the Spanish kingdom. Poinsot informs him that nothing has been settled yet,[60] and returns to his teaching at Alcalá, secretly in the hope, it would seem, of somehow managing to avoid the new role proposed for him.[61]

May 20: The King sends a letter peremptorily summoning Poinsot to return to Madrid and assume the duties of counselor and con-

---

[58] "D. Ludovico de Haro qui cum eo regis consilium communicabat, respondit Joannes unum antea regi deliberandum: an scilicet vellet veritatem in omnibus audire et sequi; sin minus, nequaquam se Philippi conscientiam regendam suscipere posse."—Solesmes, 1931: x par. 25, with further references.

[59] See Solesmes, 1931: x note 1.

[60] Solesmes, 1931: x par. 26 and Appendix XIII, "Excerpta e Litteris Apostolici Nuntii," lxxxiij nos. 5, 7, and 9.

[61] Solesmes, 1931: x par. 27: "Complutum igitur regressus . . . fortasse et ipsi Joanni adhuc remanserat spes importunum onus evadendi." See also xij note 1 *in finem*. Simonin (1930: esp. 142) remarks "la vive répugnance manifestée par Jean de St-Thomas lorsqu'il fut nommé à ces nouvelles fonctions. . . ."

fessor to the King. Didacus Ramirez, friend and first biographer of Poinsot (1645), reports the event as follows: ''He read the letter in silence. His lips paled, his tongue and eyes thrashed, and, with consternation in his heart, he broke out in the words: 'Fathers, my life is ended, I am dead; pray for me'. ''[62]

July 10: Poinsot accompanies Philip to visit Maria of Agreda, a renowned Franciscan mystic and later spiritual writer (*The Mystical City of God*, published 1670) in Spain of the period. Poinsot attests to the authenticity of her spiritual life and gifts,[63] and so begins a relationship the King will continue, through visits and letters, until Maria's death in 1665.

Volumes II and III of Poinsot's *Cursus Theologicus* are published at Lyons.[64]

1643-44: History records that, after ousting Olivares in January of 1643 and taking Poinsot among his counselors shortly thereafter, Philip IV for a time took a direct and responsible hand in the affairs of his kingdom, as he had not done since ascending the throne. This change may largely have been due to the influence of Poinsot.[65]

---

[62] From the ''Vita Joannis a Sancto Thoma Didaco Ramirez O.P. Auctore'' (initio tomi IV *Cursus Theologici* Matriti 1645), reproduced as Appendix I to Solesmes 1931: xxxvij-xxxviij nos. 25-26: ''Ex alta ergo illa Complutensi Turri, Omnium Litterarum Specula, Scientiarumque munitissima arce: ex praeeminenti virtutum culmine, cui alte repositus assistebat, in Confessarium eligitur, Regiae, et Regni curae destinatur, et cum coram Fratribus Epistolam Matritum avocantem silentio perlegisset, toto pallens ore, lingua et oculis conturbatus, totoque consernatus pectore in hanc erupit vocem *Actum est Patres de vita mea: Mortuus sum, Orate pro me*, nihil amplius edicens pluries interrogatus, donec eventus rem manifestavit.''

[63] See ''Joannis a S. Thoma de Maria Agreda Judicium,'' Appendix XII to Solesmes, 1931: lxxxij. Also Solesmes, 1931: xj par. 32.

[64] Solesmes, 1931: xviij, conjecture that Poinsot went to a publisher outside Spain at this point in order to achieve more easily a wide distribution for his works.

Apparently (Lavaud, 1926: 393), Poinsot realized considerable sums from the publication of his writings, which, like his stipend for being a counsel to the king (Solesmes, 1931: x par. 28), he disposed of entirely in favor of the poor, the College of St. Thomas at Alcalá, or his convent in Madrid. Indeed, it was no doubt just the anticipation of such sums that inspired the action of the Lyons booksellers to secure the royal monopoly for their irresponsible 1663 edition of Poinsot's works, mentioned in note 8 above.

[65] See Solesmes, 1931: x-xij pars. 23-39, esp. pars. 29-30. Poinsot's friend, Didacus Ramirez, describes the quick ascendancy of Poinsot among the king's counselors in exuberant terms: ''So armed with truth and religious integrity, when it came to solving problems concerning war and

1644: In the early months of this year, partisans of Jansen on the Louvain faculty write to Poinsot seeking his assistance in maintaining their refusal, under protection of the Spanish Crown, to accept the papal bull *In Eminenti* (1643) condemning Jansen's work. Other members of the Louvain faculty write to Poinsot vindicating the rightness of the bull, a view urged on Poinsot also by the Apostolic Nuncio. Poinsot, however, does not feel himself sufficiently apprised of the situation, and writes to the Governor of Belgium demanding fuller and fully accurate information. Poinsot will be dead before the dispute can be resolved one way or the other.[66]

Descartes publishes his *Principles of Philosophy*.

With the King on the Catalan expedition, during the seige of Lerida, Poinsot retires with Philip to Fraga. There he is stricken by fever and dies on the 17th of June, 1644, not yet 55 years of age: "a man worthy of a longer life, but already mature for immortality."[67]

On this journey with the King, Poinsot has taken with him, and continued to correct, copy for a new edition of the first part of his *Philosophia Naturalis* and the yet-unpublished

---

peace, Faith and human rights in a Christian polity (as befits the King and our Kingdom), at the highest levels of affairs and of government almost he alone came to be heard. With the consummate flexibility of his mind, he perceived rapidly things that he had never heard before, and things which, even if often heard, seemed scarcely soluble, disposing as he did of the key of truth, virtue, and divine zeal." Ramirez, 1645: reprinted as Appendix I to Solesmes, 1931: xxxix no. 44: "*Sic veritate, ac vere religiosa integritate munitus, ut inter suprema tot negociorum, ac Gravissimorum Assistentium Conclavia, tum Jurio, tum Politicae Christianitatis (ut regem decet, et Regnum Nostrum) dubiis resolvendis, quasi Ipse solus ab Omnibus exaudiendus veniret, brevi momento quae nunquam audivit, nec saepius audita de facili videbantur expendenda, summa ingenii dexteritate percipiens, veritatisque, virtutis ac divini zeli clavo disponens.*"

[66] Solesmes, 1931: xij par. 37, and Appendix VIII: "Decerpta e Monumentis Lovaniensis Universitatis," lxvj-lxviij.

[67] Quoted anonymously from a Spanish hagiographer by Getino, 1916: 435: "*hombre, dici un historiador, digno de una vida más larga, pero y maduro para la immortalidad.*" Solesmes, 1931: xii, par. 39, has this description of Poinsot's deathbed: "Generali praemunitus confessione, religionis habitus indutus, sacram Eucharistiam humi genuflexus adorare voluit atque in conspectu Dei sui magna voce protestatus 'numquam triginta annorum spatio aut scripsisse aut docuisse quod veritati consonum, atque Angelico Doctori conforme non judicaret . . . numquam regi quidquam consuluisse quod non in majus Dei obsequium, reipublicae commodum et Principio beneficium credidisset,' laetus in pace Domini exspiravit, die 17 junii 1644, quinquagesimo quinto aetatis anno nondum plene exacto." (Cf. Reiser, 1930: IX no. 6.)

"Quoi qu'il en soit la cause immédiate de cette mort," observes Lavaud (1926: 412), "à un âge ou Jean semblait devoir fournir une longue carrière, en expédition, loin de son couvent et de ses frères, on ne peut se refuser d'y voir un dernier trait touchant de ressemblance avec saint Thomas."

fifth volume of his *Cursus Theologicus*.[68] This last section of his *Cursus Theologicus* that Poinsot corrected in his own hand while journeying with the King has come to be recognized as a classical theological treatise on the nature of mysticism and spiritual experience.[69]

1645: In the years immediately following Poinsot's death, the publication of his theological writings continued under the direction of his intimate friend and associate, Didacus Ramirez.[70] Ramirez attached to the first posthumous volume of these writings (volume IV of the *Cursus Theologicus*) the first biography of Poinsot, which makes a fitting epigraphic comment on our author: "One in person, many in role, serving God, the King, and the World: his spirit to God, his life to the King, his pen to the World."[71]

1646: Birth of Leibniz.

---

[68] "Res prope incredibilis!" exclaim the Solesmes editors (1964: vj), "ut serenis theologiae contemplationibus destiterit incumbere," in view of the circumstances: "Mediis in castris, dum Catalonicum bellum paratur et peragitur, editionem [quartam] curat Naturalis suae Philosophiae [primae partis]; posteriorem tomum in Primam-Secundae recognoscit et corrigit (cum jam priorem typis paratum, a censoribus Ordinis anno 1643 examinatum et probatum, Matriti reliquisset), atque cum perducit usque ad perfectum de Donis Spiritus Sancti," i.e., disp. 18 of what would appear in 1645 as the fifth volume (*tomus quintus*) of the *Cursus Theologicus* (vol. 6 of the 1883 Paris Vivès edition and of the Solesmes edition). Reiser, 1930: XII, remarks likewise: "Quam firmiter coelestibus adhaerere et quam familiariter cum Deo conversari oportuit eum, qui inter arma in castris sublimem illum de donis Spiritus Sancti tractatum scripsit, attestante nota in fine tractatus opposita: 'Ad honorem Domini nostri Iesu Christi crucifixi, Beatissimae Virginis, Beati Dominici et Thomae, 21 Aprilis 1644, cum essemus Caesaragustae in expeditione Catalanica.' "

[69] "En cette matière," J. M. Ramirez says simply (1924: 807), "on peut dire qu'il est le theologien classique"—echoing in so saying the judgment of several centuries: "M. Johannes a S. Thoma," wrote the *Salmanticenses* (1644), Tractatus XVIII, "De Spe Theologica," disp. IV, dub. 4 (Palmé ed., 1879: vol. 11, p. 564, col. 2 *in fine*), "*de hac materia tam docte, tam profunde et luculenter agit ut palmam aliis immo et sibi alia scribenti praeripere videatur*"—"John of St. Thomas has treated of this matter with such wisdom, depth and clarity, that he surpasses all others, and indeed even himself, making it seem impossible for anyone to write after him."

Within the Iberian world, many regard Menendez-Rigada's translation of this work, with commentary (1948) as the classic rendition. Outside Iberia, two independent national-language editions have appeared, one in French (R. Maritain, 1930), and a later one—which, however, curiously takes no notice of the earlier interpretations—in English (D. Hughes, 1951). Both are introduced by distinguished Dominican theologians of their period, the former by Garrigou-Lagrange and the latter by Walter Farrell.

[70] Didacus Ramirez brought out Volumes IV and V of the *Cursus Theologicus* in 1645, Volume VI in 1649, at which point he was elected to govern the Regal Convent of Our Lady of Atocha in Madrid, which slowed down his work of editing. Volume VII did not appear until 1656. Before completing the last volume, however, Ramirez died in late August of 1662. By unknown channels, the manuscript materials for this volume were transmitted to a convent of the Friars Preachers in Paris, France, where finally it was published under the editorship of Francis Combefis in 1667. Thus, the work which Poinsot carried to his deathbed was brought to completion by his brethren within twenty-three years. See Solesmes, 1931: esp. xviij-xx and xxj-xxiv.

[71] Ramirez, 1645: "Vita Joannis," in Solesmes, 1931: xl no. 4: "*unus persona, multus officio, Deo, Regi, et Orbi deserviens, mente Deo, Vita Regi, Calamo Orbi.*"

III.

The Translation

In works of this kind, it is often more important to know what has not been done than to know what has been. To achieve what it is capable of, a source-edition translation must not only serve to be intelligible in itself, but must also be expected to provide a firm base for further researches of various kinds. It is essential therefore to be as clear as possible about the exact relations between this bi-lingual edition of the *Treatise on Signs* and the Latin edition of the *Cursus Philosophicus* from which it is derived.[72]

A. The Bi-Lingual Text: Overall Structure

To begin with the main title of our presentation, *Tractatus de Signis*, it is the designation chosen by Poinsot himself to refer to this part of his work in

[72] This demand arises directly from the purpose for which Reiser (1930: XVI) expressly provided his text:

''Amicis libenter acquiescens opus perfeci et hunc finem assequi studeo:

''a) ut legentes doctrinam scholae thomisticae ab eo potius percipiant, qui morte imminente coram SS. Sacramento adiuravit se nihil per triginta totos annos aut scripsisse aut docuisse, quod non iudicaret et veritati consonum et doctrinae S. Thomae conforme, quique ab omnibus doctrinae thomisticae magister et defensor est habitus, quam ab iis, qui semper in eo sunt, ut rationes quaerant, quibus excusati doctrinam S. Thomae possint subterfugere.

''b) ut legentes clare cognoscant, quomodo Ioannes a S. Thoma propositiones suas ex auctoritatibus optimis scholae thomisticae, et praesertim ex operibus S. Thomae confirmaverit et defenderit, et ut legentes tali magistro ducente ad ipsos fontes genuinos et principales perveniant, ex quibus doctrina thomistica fluere dicitur, ita ut ipsi iam ex se ipsis nemine cogente decidere possint, utrum ex illis fontibus originem ducat necne. Nolo ergo hac editione ego per me doctrinam thomisticam defendere, sed legentes conducere ad fontes, ut ipsi legant et videant.

''c) ut legentes diiudicare et discernere possint, in quantum opiniones physicae illius aetatis in explicandum et confirmandum systema thomisticum influxerint.

''*Nova ergo hac editione Historiae philosophiae non minus quam speculationi philosophicae inservire desidero*.'' (Emphasis added.)

his 1640 "Word to the Reader" of the Second Part of his Logic, as also in his more general "Word to the Reader" of 1631 introducing the whole of the Logic (see text, pp. 34-36 and 4-6, respectively, above).

The text and translation presented here have been based on the 1932 emended second impression of the edition and text of the complete *Ars Logica* published in 1930 at Turin, Italy, by Marietti, edited by B. Reiser. Though it was not yet a complete critical edition (e.g., see note 90 below, p. 455), H.-D. Simonin (1930: 147, 148) nevertheless did not hesitate to call Reiser's text "the classical edition" of Poinsot's work. For the first part of the *Ars Logica*—the part whence the materials of 1631 ("Lectori," "Prologus Totius," and "Summulae") for this edition of the *Treatise on Signs* are taken—Reiser used the text of the 1637 Rome edition, citing, in footnotes and an Appendix, variant texts from the first Lyons edition of 1663, "insofar as they seemed to be useful for clarifying Poinsot's position."[73] For the second part of the *Ars Logica*—the part whence are taken for presentation the *Tractatus* proper of 1632, with its "Preambles," and the 1640 "Word to the Reader" ("Lectori") of the second part—Reiser used the 1640 Madrid text, noting again, this time in footnotes only, 1663 Lyons variants when these seemed to illustrate some important aspect of Poinsot's thought.[74] Reiser explains that his reason for choosing the 1637 Rome text for Part One and the 1640 Madrid text for Part Two was simply that these were the last and most reliable editions of the respective parts that appeared within their author's lifetime and went under the exercise of their author's own hand.[75]

There is, however, one short passage in our *Treatise*—the so-called "Transition to Book II"—that is not included in Reiser's edition of the *Ars Logica*, but which I have included in this edition of the semiotic, from the text of the 1638 Cologne edition made by Thomas of Sarria, a professor of Poinsot's Order at

[73] "In priore parte Logicae, scilicet in textu Summularum et quaestionibus disputandis huic textui annexis secuti sumus ed. Romanam 1637. . . . Omnium utilitati consulere desiderantes lectiones discrepantes, quae ad magistri sententiam illustrandam aliquid conferre videbantur, ex ed. Lugdunensi (Parisiensi [i.e., the 1883 Paris edition, which only reproduces the Lyons text, but with added corruptions]), in notis apposuimus, imo 'Illustrationes' Summularum, in quantum cum 'Quaestionibus disputandis' in textu nostro ex ed. Romana positis non concordant, in modum appendicis parti priori Logicae addimus" (Reiser, 1930: XVI). On this last point, see the observations in Solesmes, 1931: xxxj note 4, and note 78 below.

[74] "In altera parte Logicae, scilicet in Logica materiali secuti sumus ed. Matritensem 1640, addentes sicut in parte priore lectiones discrepantes ex ed. Lugd. 1663, in quantum ad Magistri sententiam illustrandam alicuius momenti esse videbantur" (Reiser, 1930: XVII).

[75] "*Quoad textum,* hanc regulam semper observamus: Praeeligatur semper textus eius editionis, cui ultima ipsius auctoris manus accessit" (Reiser, 1930: XVI).

Which raises a question concerning our *Textus Summularum,* for while Reiser tells us (1930: XVI) that "In priore parte Logicae . . . secuti sumus ed. Romanam 1637" (which, by the way, can be seen in what concerns the *Treatise on Signs* in the Lilly Library of Indiana University at Bloomington), he has earlier (XIII) told us that the 1634 Alcalá edition (available in the University of Madrid Library) is the "ultima ab auctore edita." Since the Rome publishers claim their edition of the Logic to be the third edition authenticated by the author ("ab auctore recognita"—Reiser, 1930: XIV), and these same publishers were unaware of the 1635 Douai edition (Solesmes, 1931: xiij note 5—discussion in note 12, pp. 405-406 above), this would seem to imply that the Roman text follows that of the 1634 Alcalá edition (see Solesmes, 1931: xxxj note 4), in which case Reiser's rule might be preserved. But this is a curious slip in so careful an editor.

Fortunately for our purposes, there is no such problem regarding the main text of the *Treatise* itself. The 1640 Madrid text (available in the National Library in Paris and in Madrid), which Reiser followed, is the authoritative and final one Poinsot edited.

the University of Cologne.[76] Professor Sarria, according to his ''Preface'' to his Cologne edition, had made some additions to the text of the *Cursus Philosophicus* taken from ''certain writings of Poinsot himself'' (''quaedam ex magistri scriptis''). For his purposes, Reiser felt obliged to lay Sarria's edition aside, because of the impossibility of determining whether its textual additions were indeed authorized by Poinsot himself, as Sarria claimed.[77] Nonetheless, for our

[76] By the sheerest luck, in a 1974 visit to an old Jesuit library in the walled city of Amberg, Germany, I chanced upon a 1638 edition of Poinsot's *Cursus Philosophicus*. Not being under leisurely circumstances at the time, I turned quickly to the section on signs, and was amazed to see how much more an impression of independence the *Tractatus* there presented made simply by virtue of its typographical layout. I was more amazed still to find the passage above mentioned, which is exceedingly valuable to the text on signs but is nowhere mentioned in Reiser's work. I hastily copied it out on an envelope and had to leave. Subsequent reading in Reiser, 1930, and Solesmes, 1931, led me to assume that the text I held in hand must have been that of Sarria (as it bore the imprint of Cologne and the date of 1638) but rebound in a single large volume, as both Reiser and Solesmes report the original publication to have been in three volumes. Thanks to Achim Eschbach, who generously had the pertinent sections of the Amberg volume photographed and mailed to me in the summer of 1983, I was able to confirm it as indeed Sarria's edition. Photocopy sent me in this same summer by Michael Dodds from Fribourg revealed this same brief text as appearing on p. 295 even in the 1663 Lyons edition, which makes Reiser's silence on this text, discussed in the following note, the more inexplicable. One day I would like to check the text of the *Treatise* against all the earlier editions, and publish a ''*Variorum*'' appendix to this work. Yet I doubt that any so striking as the one chanced on so haphazardly in Amberg are awaiting discovery among the old tomes!

[77] ''Coloniensem 1638 seposuimus propter additamenta a Thoma Sarria facta, quae an ad mentem auctoris fuerint, nescimus'' (Reiser, 1930: XVI).

I have already cited in full (notes 73 and 74 above, the ellipsis in note 73 being the statement just cited in this note) Reiser's statements about his textual-variant footnotes, which, as we have seen, refer basically to the 1663 Lyons text. Nonetheless, Simonin, in his review (1930: 147), reports in this particular: ''En plus du texte qui lui sert de base, l'éditeur ajoute en note les additions de Cologne et de Lyons . . . pour autant que ces additions peuvent servir à éclairer le texte.'' And inded, at the front of each of Reiser's three volumes, in his list of Abbreviations, we find the entry, ''*Col* = ed. Coloniensis 1638.'' But an actual check of the three volumes reveals that, while the notes are sprinkled with Lyons variants throughout, in the entire 2,152 pages of Poinsot's text in Reiser's edition, there are but two variants entered under ''*Col*,'' one of seven lines in the Log. II p. q. 1. art. 5. (I, 278 note 1), the other of one word in phil. nat. 1. q. 7. art. 2 (II, 155 note 1). It is hard to believe, in view of Reiser's remarks and Sarria's own ''Preface,'' that these are indeed the only ''additamenta.'' It may be that, while Reiser's scrutiny of Lyons 1663 was thorough, what scrutiny he made of the Cologne text was more casual. Yet it seems puzzling that Reiser should evince an apparently much keener interest in a text whose variants (with the exception indicated in the note following) quite likely did not come from Poinsot, than in a text whose variants are alleged to have come from Poinsot's own manuscripts (''quaedam ex magistri scriptis'': Sarria's *Praefatio* to the 1638 Cologne ed., cited in Reiser 1930: XIV), particularly when the former text is celebrated for its corruptness and the want of integrity in its sponsors (Solesmes 1931: xxi-xxiv; Reiser, 1930: XIV: ''Harum trium editionem igitur Lugdunensis est peior, melior Romana, Coloniensi medium tenente''). Or again, from quite another approach, in his well-known ''Sign and Symbol'' essay (see Section IV below, opening paragraph and note 129), Maritain quotes extensively from the texts of Poinsot's *Treatise on Signs* in the *Ars Logica*. Using, as he himself describes it (1959a: xviii), ''the rather off-hand manner which is customary among French authors . . . quoting texts,'' no indication is given as to which edition of Poinsot's *Artis Logicae Secunda Pars* Maritain had before him; but in 1943: 270, note 3, he cites a passage which would be, in Reiser's edition, 669b26-45. Reiser notes no variant readings on this passage, which creates a presumption, but no full assurance, that Maritain had in hand neither Lyons 1663, Rome 1637-38, nor Cologne 1638; and yet, in Maritain's citation, the punctuation differs from 669b26-39, at which point the very wording diverges (Reiser, 669b39-40: ''. . . in obliquo in ipso signato, quod tangit, in alia non''; Maritain citation: ''. . .in obliquo, aut etiam praesupponatur, in alia non''), and again at the end (Reiser, 669b44-45: ''non ipsa potentia, cui fit repraesentatio''; Maritain citation: ''non ipsa potentia directe attacta''). Perhaps the text of the *Treatise on Signs* is exactly the point where a full-scale critical edition of Poinsot's philosophical texts might begin.

purposes of presenting the *Treatise on Signs* independently, the particular passage in question fits in nicely, and its parallel to the paragraph of text similarly introducing Book III of our *Treatise*, which is unquestionably from Poinsot's own hand, creates an impression of its authenticity sufficiently strong to warrant its inclusion here.

The three Appendices included in this edition are quite different in character. Appendix A, "On the Relations between Words, Ideas, and Objects," treats of a perennial question in philosophy, resolving it from the point of view of Poinsot's doctrine—the question, namely, of what it is that the marks and sounds of language refer to, and how it is that they perform this function. The relevance of this matter to the doctrine of signs is so transparent as to hardly warrant specific discussion of the rationale of its inclusion. The text of this Appendix is from the "Quaestiones Disputandae" designed to illustrate and develop difficulties incident to the *Summulae* or introductory texts, in this case particularly with reference to Chapter 1.[78]

Appendix B is a research tool of two parts, designed to give the reader first a detailed prospectus of the intricacies of the entire system Poinsot envisaged in his *Cursus Philosophicus*, and second a comprehensive overview of that system. The former is achieved by the simple expedient of reproducing in full Reiser's *Index Syntheticus* or "Table of Contents" of each of the parts of the entire *Cursus Philosophicus*, along with the page numbers in his edition for each entry. The latter has been achieved as follows.

At the beginning of each of the various Parts of the *Cursus Philosophicus*, Reiser has taken the trouble to draw up a "synoptic table" providing at a glance a view of the overall organization of the materials covered in that Part,[79] except that, for reasons undisclosed, he omitted from his *Tabulae* for the Third Part of the Natural Philosophy (p. 539) the "Tractate on Meteorology" with

---

[78] The 1663 Lyons variant readings of the text in this Appendix derive from the 1648 Madrid edition of the *Artis Logicae Prima Pars*, which was the edition used by the Lyons editors as the basis for this part of their edition (Reiser, 1930: XIV). These variants Reiser incorporates in his own edition as an Appendix to the *Prima Pars*, specifically, Vol. I, pp. 213a28-214a40 (see text and note 73 above). This posthumous Madrid edition was the first and last entirely separate publication of the First Part of the Logic (excepting the partial English edition of 1962), and differs from all editions that appeared in Poinsot's lifetime not so much in the *Summulae* books themselves as in the "Quaestiones Disputandae" which follow the *Summulae* and prepare the way, as it were, for the beginning student to pass on to the more difficult materials of the so-called "major logic," i.e., the *Artis Logicae Secunda Pars*. (Reiser, 1930: XV, "prius proponit textum institutionum dein annectit 'quaestiones disputandas' ad difficultates circa hunc textum vigentes enodandas et ad ipsum textum profundius penetrandum. Quibus via iam sternitur ad alteram partem Logicae, quae est de materia operationum intellectus et quaecumque sunt difficiliora et subtiliora modo rigide scientifice tractat.") In the Madrid edition, as accordingly in the subsequent general editions which incorporate it (Lyons, Paris), the "Quaestiones Disputandae" are called rather "Illustrationes" and differ from the earlier "Quaestiones" principally in having been rigidly reduced to the form of scholastic disputation (see the Second Prologue of main text, p. 14ff. above, and Section I.D. of this Afterword; also Reiser, 1930: XVII: "Discrepantia fere unice in eo deprehenditur, quod in 'Illustrationibus' omnia magis in rigidam formam scholasticam redacta sunt quam in 'Quaestionibus disputandis' "). The Solesmes editors (1931: xxxj note 4) are of the opinion that these particular variants were probably based on manuscript changes proposed by Poinsot himself, since this 1648 edition was prepared by Poinsot's brethren at the Royal Convent of Atocha in Madrid, where Poinsot's friend, literary heir, and first posthumous editor, Didacus Ramirez, had taken the manuscripts in his charge.

[79] See 1930: XXVII; 1933: XVII, XVIII, and 539; 1937: XV.

which Poinsot concludes that Part (*Tractatus de Meteoris*, pp. 797-888). What I have done is to take Reiser's series of five little tables, add thereto some minor details and a complete outline of the previously omitted discussion of environmental phenomena (''de Meteoris'') just mentioned, and rework these materials into a single whole within a format of my own designed to bring out the literary and cultural genre of Poinsot's work taken in its entirety, as described by Simonin, 1930: 144-145 (cited in note 16 above). The result provides for the first time a synoptic view of the philosophical system *as a whole*, comparable perhaps to the breathtaking view Stace provides of the Hegelian system (1924, foldout Diagram inside back cover of 1954 reprint)—with important differences. Hegel always proceeds from the whole and works down to the particulars systematically, so that a pretension to completeness is present in principle in the work in the unfolding of each of its parts. Through the method of the dialectic, the intelligible progressively concretizes itself in the particulars. With Poinsot, the method of the work does not intrinsically require completeness, but treats phenomena piecemeal. The general principles by no means determine in advance or contain within themselves the means of determining the particular instances that may be found in experience *in their particularity*. The way is open to novelty, contingence, the unpredictable (cf. Deely, 1969). Gaps in the system—such as the missing Astronomy—are possible without embarrassment, as indicators of the need for new and further data. Understanding has no priority to experience, but only illumines in what is experienced its necessary features, which are not its whole. Here, dialectic bridges experiential gaps at its own peril, since it has to rely in such instances on principles extrinsic to the order of what is purportedly accounted for (see Sections I.B. and C. above), so that the notion of ''system'' is veritably equivocal as it applies to Stace's ''Diagram'' and to our ''Synoptic Table.'' In any event, here at a glance is the entire refined world-view of five centuries of Latin Aristotelianism, though one must always remember, of course, that in that scheme of things, philosophical reflection was but the groundwork and seed for the yet vaster syntheses of theological understanding; and indeed, Poinsot's *Cursus Philosophicus*, considerable as it is, is rather brief by comparison with the edifice of his *Cursus Theologicus*, and is moreover in certain respects intrinsically completed thereby, as Reiser tells us (1930: XII):

> The fact that our author does not provide a specific dissertation on Metaphysics and especially on Ethics within the compass of his *Cursus Philosophicus*, while unfortunate from our point of view, should not lead anyone to think that Poinsot has written little or nothing on these matters in other places. Matters pertaining to natural theology and to ethics were left for thematic treatment in the *Cursus Theologicus*, according to the custom of that age, and, specifically, the matters of natural theology to the Commentary on the First Part [Poinsot, 1637, 1643], those of Ethics[80] to the Commentary on the Second Part [Poinsot, 1645, 1649] of the *Summa Theologica* of St. Thomas, where all these matters are found treated at great length.[81]

[80] In particular, Lavaud, 1928: 429-430, mentions that Poinsot (1645; Vivès ed., vol. 6, pp. 194-234) provides a classic summary of the scholastic view of the life of the feelings, a subject usually neglected in their treatises, even up to the present time.

[81] Latin in note 83 below.

Moreover, while a superficial inspection of the Synthetic Index and Synoptic Table of our Appendix B might seem to reveal little or nothing of Poinsot's metaphysical stance,

> anyone who not only looks at the index of questions and articles, but who also reads the text attentively in its entirety, will find that practically everything expounded by modern authors under the title of Ontology can be found in Poinsot under his treatment of material Logic and under his treatment of causes and the ground of motion in the Natural Philosophy. Likewise for the fundamentals of Criteriology,[82] which can be found treated in the Second Part of the Logic in the questions on foreknowledge and premises, demonstration and scientific knowledge.[83]

With these restrictions in mind, readers of this *Treatise* should find this second Appendix a useful tool particularly in the planning of strategies for research into the larger implications of semiotic for the reinterpretation of the history of philosophy and culture in general in its historical ("seinsgeschichtliches") dimension as a *semiotic web,* to borrow a particularly felicitous title from Sebeok (1975a). This Appendix will also serve the purpose of enabling the student of the discipline to get a very concrete notion of the comprehensive environment in which the doctrine of signs was gestated, and of the historical stratum in which its seemingly first thematic expression was embedded.

Appendix C is related to this larger question of research strategies, but in a very specific way. It is provided to ground in Poinsot's text the Peircean idea of extending semiotic understanding beyond the sphere of cognitive phenomena to the whole of nature itself as a network virtually semiosic in character: see, for example, Sebeok 1963, 1976a: 59-69, 95-130, Krampen 1981, Deely 1982a, and Section IV of this Afterword, below. The discussion in this Third Appendix, more specifically, extends and completes the discussion of objective causality in Book I, Question 4, of the *Treatise on Signs*.

So much for the overall structures. Now for the details.

---

[82] Lalande, *Vocabulaire technique et critique de la philosophie* (5th ed.; 1947), p. 188: "*Critériologie*—Partie de la Logique qui concerne les critères. Neologisme, particulièrement dans l'Ecole de Louvain," and following entry: "*Critérium* ou *Critère*—A. Signe apparent qui permet de reconnaître une chose ou une notion; B. Caractère ou propriété d'un objet (personne ou chose) d'après lequel on porte sur lui un jugement d'appréciation. En particulier, on appele *Critérium de la vérité* un signe extrinsèque ou un caractère intrinsèque permettant de reconnaître la vérité et de la distinguer sûrement de l'erreur (Stoïcens, Descartes, etc.)."

[83] Reiser, 1930: XII: "Titulis demonstrantibus agit de Logica et de Philosophia naturali. Ex professo neque Metaphysicam neque Ethicam tractat, quare obiter inspicienti de his rebus nihil vel prope nihil dixisse facile videtur. *Qui quidem non tantum indicem quaestionum et articulorum, sed ipsum textum eumque totum attente perlegerit, inveniet paene omnia, quae a recentioribus in Ontologia exponuntur, apud ipsum in Logica totum tractatum de causis et de prima motore in Philosophia haberi. Imo et fundamenta Criteriologiae* [see note 82 above] *in secunda parte Logicae, in quaestionibus de praecognitis et praemissis, de demonstratione et scientia tangit. Quod auctor de Metaphysica et praesertim de Ethica intra ambitum Cursus philosophici propriis dissertationibus non egit, quamvis dolendum sit, nemini tamen persuadere licet ipsum nihil vel pauca solummodo de his materiis aliis locis scripsisse. Quae ad Theologiam naturalem et ad Ethicam spectant, ad morem illius aetatis ad Cursum theologicum ex professo tractanda remittit, et quidem quae sunt Theologiae naturalis ad primam* [Poinsot, 1637, 1643], *quae sunt Ethicae ad secundam partem Summae theologicae* [Poinsot, 1645, 1649], *ubi haec omnia plene evoluta inveniuntur.*" (Italics represent the English citation on p. 449 at note 81 as well as at note 83 above.)

B. Mechanical Aspects: 1. Format, 2. Page Design, 3. Indices, 4. Footnotes, 5. Typographical Devices

1. Format. Given Poinsot's own identification of Questions 21-23 of the *Ars Logica* as an independent *tractatus de signis*, and the inelegance of beginning an actually independent edition of that *tractatus* with "Question 21 . . . ," it was decided to renumber the main parts of Poinsot's tractate to begin with one (I) rather than with twenty-one (XXI), as in the original text. The further decision to call the main parts "Books" rather than "Questions," with the internal divisions called "Questions" rather than "Articles" (except in the two Preambles, where "Article" is retained as the name of the main subdivisions), was made simply on the grounds that this format seemed better suited to the autonomous status the *Treatise on Signs* is here given, while it is at the same time a format well suited to the appearance in English of a seventeenth-century philosophical work, owing to customs established by major writings of that period.

2. Page Design. The double-column page design—a column of Latin of the approximate size of Reiser's text, a facing column in English, with the width (the line-length) of each column determined on the given page by the requirements of the two columns being identical in length and beginning and ending in a common sentence, and with a vertical column of numbers between the language columns at every fifth line—was chosen over a facing page format for the two languages for three reasons.

First, it helps make unmistakable the *source* character of our edition, and the *genre* to which our presentation in English belongs. Specifically, it is the kind of translation in which each line is a commentary and not really usable *except* as a commentary (see III.C.I. of this Section below).

Second, it makes possible a single set of footnotes for both languages located appropriately at the bottom of the same page on which the superscript appears. I will explain the system of these notes more fully below.

Third, by this simple device, the reader of any given entry in the indices (e.g., "287/14-18") is immediately informed of the page (287) and lines (14-18) where the entry may be found *either* (exactly) in the English interpretation *or* (approximately) in the Latin original (=, in this case, *722b39-45* of Reiser).

The Reiser pagination has been provided in the running head for the ease of readers who will also do further work with the original.

3. Indices. The indices to this edition are derived from the extraordinary, detailed indices Reiser constructed for his Latin text of Poinsot's *Cursus Philosophicus*. These indices appeared in 1937 at the end of the third and last volume of Reiser's own edition of the complete *Cursus*. They are of five different kinds: an *Index Biblicus*, or Index of Biblical Citations; an *Index Aristotelicus*, or Index of Aristotelian Passages; an *Index Thomisticus*, or Index of Passages from St. Thomas; an *Index Personarum*, or Index of Persons Mentioned by Name in Poinsot's *Cursus*; and an *Index Rerum*, or Index of Terms and Propositions.

Stripped of all the references to pages in the *Ars Logica* or the other parts of the *Cursus Philosophicus* that fall outside the boundaries which establish this English edition of Poinsot's *Treatise* as an independent whole, the first of these

five indices (the *Index Biblicus*) entirely disappears,[84] and the remaining four indices are reduced in size by roughly 93 percent. (The *Treatise on Signs* with its ''Preambles,'' quantitatively considered, takes up less than 1/6—about 16.6 percent—of the *Ars Logica*, and just over 1/14—or 7.1 percent—of the *Cursus Philosophicus* as a whole in Reiser's edition.) Of these remaining four indices, then, it is to be noted that they refer to the text itself of the *Treatise*.

Except for the *Index Rerum*, which I will discuss separately, these proportionally reduced indices are otherwise reproduced here just as they appear in Reiser's edition, with only minor corrections or additions, and translated where appropriate (i.e., wherever properly philosophical or purely biographical details or instructions were concerned). Accordingly, they may be described in order as follows.

The *Index Aristotelicus* and the *Index Thomisticus* are both twofold indices. First, there is a table listing all and only the works of Aristotle and St. Thomas to which Poinsot makes reference in the course of his *Treatise*; and in respect of each single one of these works referred to, indication is made as to whether it is genuine or spurious,[85] when it was composed, and in which editions and where it may be found. Then follows an index of the passages in which Poinsot refers to a given work according to title, chapter, question, etc.[86]

The *Index Personarum*, except in the case of individual authors regarded by Reiser as most celebrated and widely known, includes very brief biographical notices followed by the titles of the works of the given author to which Poinsot refers his readers; the editions named are the editions which Reiser used in collating the references. In addition, a list of the propositions for which a

---

[84] There was no point in maintaining an entire index for the sake of just three references, one direct (276/15, 277/2-3 [=*718b11-12, 719a3-5*]), and two indirect (242/14-15 [=*702b20*]; and 276/16-17, 277/4-11 [=*718b12-13, 719a6-15*]).

[85] In this regard, much has sometimes been made, from the point of view of the narrower tradition of Thomistic commentary, and by critics hostile to Poinsot's general position of eminence in that school, of the fact that Poinsot sometimes refers to the authority of certain works—notably, as regards the *Treatise on Signs* (cf. Simon, 1955: xxvii), the *Summa totius logicae Aristotelis*, and the commentary on Lombard's Sentences *ad Annibaldum*—as being ''of St. Thomas'' which the critical apparatus of nineteenth-century and later scholarship has been able to definitively establish as spurious. Since, as has already been said (Section I.D. above, esp. note 27), this was not a foreground concern of this edition, nothing touching this matter has been included in the notes on the text itself of the *Treatise*. Here I wish only to make two general points. The first is to remark simply that while the techniques and sensitivities of critical historical textual scholarship were not yet wholly appreciated or consequently highly developed in the seventeenth century, Poinsot was capable of displaying considerable skill in sorting out the intricacy of such matters when he felt it necessary (cf. 1637: Solesmes ed. pp. 228-239 and 255-260; see also the remarks of Simonin, 1930: 143, and Solesmes, 1931: xxxij). The second is to observe with Solesmes, 1931: xxxij, that, to the extent Poinsot is deficient in this area by the standards of contemporary criticism, his mistakes are those of his age more than they are of his own (''*Qui tamen errores istius saeculi sunt, non unius hominis*''). Whence the appropriateness of the general heading under which the Solesmes editors take up this matter: ''Minutiora quaedam notantur.'' It should be noted that it has not yet even been established which of the manuscript-based editions of St. Thomas Poinsot habitually relied on for his own work (see Simonin, 1930: 142-143).

[86] Reiser, 1937: IX: ''Index Aristotelicus et Thomisticus *hoc modo compositi sunt, ut prius tabula ponatur, in qua non omnia, sed ea sola opera Aristotelis et S. Thomae inveniuntur, ad quae auctor recurrit. Dein respectu uniuscuiusque operis indicatur, utrum sit genuinum an spurium, quo tempore sit compositum, in quibus editionibus et ubi inveniatur. Postea sequitur index locorum secundum seriem operum, librorum, capitum, quaestionum etc.*''

given author is cited by Poinsot in his *Treatise* is provided, along with the page and line number of the citation.[87]

The value of Reiser's work in this particular can hardly be overestimated, as can be gathered from Ashworth's description of the scholastic customs of the period (1974: XI): ''Authors not only used each other's work without acknowledgement, but they also criticized each other's work without giving more specific references than 'a certain doctor said'. '' Though this would hardly describe Suarez, it does have some application to the case of Poinsot.

The reader should be aware, therefore, with respect to this *Index Personarum*, that its value for determining the range of Poinsot's awareness of contemporary developments, as, for example, the fashions in the empirical and mathematical sciences of the extra-Iberian Europe of his day, is sharply limited, owing to the extreme discipline with which Poinsot chooses to execute his expositions according to a style which eschews without remorse all the trappings of learned or scholarly display, as he explained in his ''Word to the Reader'' of 1631:

> In referring to the position of various authors, whether to impugn or to follow them, it will be our policy generally to abstain from lengthy citations and lists of names. For we publish our position without yielding to contention or jealous rivalry, but giving ourselves to the pursuit of truth, which concerns doctrine and not persons.

No one understood better than Poinsot that, in philosophical discourse above all, ''if universality is attained,''—*pace* Chomsky—''it will not be through a universal language that would go back prior to the diversity of languages to provide us with the foundations of all possible languages'' (Merleau-Ponty, 1960; as per McCleary, 1964: 87). Indeed, as Jacques Maritain suggests (1955: vi-vii), Poinsot may well be without peer in the entire Western tradition for the internal freedom his thought attains from contradiction and inconsistency in the order of its material expression, while at the same time reconciling itself throughout with a view of experience as providing in its sensory elements a naturally determined identity at the base of objectivity in being. But this makes for difficulty for those who like to reduce philosophy so far as possible to a matter of ''sources'' and ''influences.''[88]

This brings us to the last of the indices, the *Index Rerum* or Index of Terms and Propositions. For this index the proportionally reduced *Index Rerum* from

---

[87] Ibid.: ''Index personarum *apud singulos auctores (exceptis celeberrimis et notissimis) continet brevissimas notas biographicas necnon nomina eorum operum, ad quae Ioannes a S. Thoma lectores remittit; et quidem eae editiones nominantur, quibuscum loci ab editore collati sunt. Praeterea fons ille adducitur, ex quo notae adiectae sunt haustae et in quo lectores plura, si desiderant, reperire possunt. Dispositio denique in articulis longioribus (Caietanus, Suarez etc.) servata nonnisi utilitati quaerentium consulere intendit, quin statuatur quidquam per modum thesis de ordine systematico Philosophiae.''*

See further discussion in note 90 below.

[88] Thus Thomas Deman (1936: 480) is led to conjecture that ''de saint Thomas à son commentateur de XVIIe siècle, il n'est pas sûr qu'il y ait une tradition d'école sans rupture ni mélange,'' largely on the grounds that ''Le thomisme du célèbre commentateur fut . . . perméable aux influences de son milieu et son temps,'' and ''il le commente, en fonction d'un milieu doctrinal déterminé, où lui-même evolue''—as if a philosopher could do otherwise! This same misapprehension of the nature of philosophical truth and its relation to traditions is exhibited in other otherwise highly insightful studies, notably that of Krempel, 1952 (mentioned in notes 119 and 139 below).

Reiser's edition served as both base and model. ''In the index of terms and propositions,'' Reiser writes, ''are included not only those things which pertain strictly to Philosophy, but whatever items of information are useful or delightful and able to satisfy the tastes of anyone's erudition, studiousness, or indeed scientific curiosity. In particular, all examples and explanations which are drawn from theological matters are included.'' Under each entry are listed one or more propositions in a numbered and roughly systematic sequence, followed by a list of cross-references to treatments of the same ideas from other angles.[89]

This base provided from Reiser's *Index Rerum* I have greatly expanded upon, being careful to draw from the text for inclusion in the index only those propositions properly ascribable to Poinsot himself. That is to say, the propositional index is entirely derived in a manner conformed to the literary forms which distinguish throughout his text Poinsot's own positions from those of other persons (see Section I.D. above). This index as expanded now is, I believe, virtually exhaustive of the ideas and propositions—key and curious alike—laced throughout Poinsot's *Treatise*, and should serve whatever research-standpoint a reader might have in mind in turning to the semiotical elements of Poinsot's work.

Selby-Bigge (1896: v) felt it necessary to apologize or at least show cause for the length of the Index he attached to his edition of Hume's *Treatise*. Besides serving the purpose of a critical introduction to a complex author, he remarked, a long index, if well devised, ''should point, not loudly but unmmistakably, to any contradictions or inconsequences, and, if the work be systematic, to any omissions which are of importance''; and this he declared to be ''the aim'' of his index to Hume's *Treatise*. In the case of Poinsot's *Treatise*, however, a well-devised index has the opposite effect of quietly and unmistakably pointing up the consistency and rigor that uniquely distinguish Poinsot's work even within the tradition he made his own:

> Progress in the philosophic sciences is normally effected not by the substitution of one system for another system, but by the accomplishment of greater profundity and comprehensiveness within one and the same continuously living body of truth. Yet history offers few examples of processes conforming to such a pattern. . . . But, if we compare the work of John of St. Thomas—latest of the great commentators—with that of St. Thomas himself, all important changes can be interpreted in terms of pure development [J. Maritain, 1955: vii].

4. Footnotes. As regards footnotes, the following rule has been observed throughout: foreign language quotations are set in italics when accompanied by an English translation, otherwise not.

---

[89] Reiser, 1937: IX-X: ''*In* Indice rerum *non tantum ponuntur ea, quae stricte ad Philosophiam pertinent, sed quaecumque scitu utilia vel iucunda sunt et eruditioni, studiositati, immo scientificae cuidam curiositati satisfacere possunt. Praeprimis adducuntur omnia exempla omnesque explicationes, quae de materiis theologicis afferuntur. In omni articulo prius ponuntur singulae materiae, in quantum fieri potuit, systematice ordinatae, et numeris arabicis insignitae. Dein sub 'Vide' ii articuli adnectuntur, in quibus de eadem materia quaedam dicta sunt; et quidem nomini articuli additur numerus arabicus, sub quo desiderata quam celerrime inveniuntur.*''

In the Afterword, foreign language citations in the notes which are closely paraphrased by the main text to which the note is appended are also italicized.

In the bilingual text of the *Treatise on Signs* proper, the footnotes are identically numbered in both the Latin and English columns, and are of about ten different sorts, in addition to the sort of footnote already described above (pp. 419-420) in connection with the literary forms of the *Solvuntur Argumenta* sections of Poinsot's text (I.D. of this Afterword).

First of all, I have retained all of Reiser's own footnotes. Where these consist of editorial comments, a translation is provided. Where these consist of a citation of the actual sources referred to in Poinsot's text and checked out by Reiser, I have retained the exact abbreviations, punctuation, capitalization, and spacing of the Reiser original. By their style, therefore, the careful reader will soon be able to recognize them at once, without any need for an intrusive indexical sign of identification. In particular, Reiser has cited Aristotle according to the text of the 1831 Berlin edition, providing in the first part of the *Index Aristotelicus* a concordance with the Paris (Didot) edition. Reiser has cited St. Thomas according to the incomplete critical Leonine edition where available, otherwise according to the complete Parma edition of 1852-1873. All other authors are noted in the *Index Personarum*, wherein are described the editions according to which Reiser made check of Poinsot's references.[90]

The only group of Reiser footnotes that I have recast in my own form are the variant readings introduced into the text posthumously by the 1663 Lyons editors, or cross-references internal to the *Treatise* where Questions become Books or Articles become Questions, as explained in III.B.1., p. 451 above.

In notes entirely my own added to the text will be found: 1) discussions of terminology; 2) occasional comments of philosophical or historical nature; 3) internal cross-references on important or obscure points of the doctrine of signs being propounded; 4) a record of *all* changes introduced into Poinsot's Latin according to the pattern explained above whereby Questions XXI-XXIII of the *Ars Logica* become Books I-III of the *Treatise on Signs*, Questions II and XVII become the "Preambles" to the *Treatise* (these changes involve a few words only, and the wording of the original is given in the note in each case); 5) identification, sometimes with citation and commentary, of Poinsot's veiled references to the celebrated Suarez, the older contemporary with whom Poinsot was in conscious opposition (note 41 above) in all that pertained to his doctrine of signs, who dominated philosophy in all that concerned the survival and transmission of the Latin tradition within the schools of Europe for the subsequent two centuries, and who is therefore the single most important figure of study for exploring via Poinsot the late stages of Latin Aristotelianism as they bear on our understanding of modern and contemporary philosophy; 6) a

---

[90] Reiser, 1930: XVII: "Specialis labor isque summe spinosus erat, ea quae ex aliis auctoribus desumpta et relata inveniebantur, *cum ipsis fontibus conferre* ad probandum, an recte sint relata. Quod a nulla hucusque editione factum videtur, cum fere apud omnes iidem inveniantur errores, qui a generatione in generationem haereditate quadam traditi deprehenduntur. . . . Alii auctores [praeter Aristotelem et S. Thomam] omnes in indice personarum in fine tertii voluminis annexo notantur, ubi et editiones describuntur, secundum quas a nobis collatio est facta."

Simonin, 1930: 148, seems to enter a caveat: "Il ne semble pas que Dom R. ait vérifié les nombreux renvois aux commentaires logiques de D. Soto et à la logique de Bañez."

few notes on Cajetan in the context of texts of his that were influential in shaping one of the central ideas of Poinsot's semiotic, to wit, the univocity of being and non-being in semiosis; 7) incorporation from other parts of the *Cursus Philophicus* (esp. the phil. nat. 4. p.: see Section I.B. above, concluding paragraphs) of Poinsot's treatment in traditional perspective of the very materials treated in the discussion of signs from the new, semiotic point of view; or 8) the incorporation of passages from other parts of the *Cursus Philosophicus* of texts that amplify or explain some point or distinction Poinsot assumes in his exposition of semiotic; 9) occasional corrections of Reiser's text, where the original wording and reasons for the suggested correction are unfailingly given in the notes (e.g., Second Preamble, Article 2, note 19; Book II, Question 2, notes 16 and 40; Book II, Question 4, note 2; Book III, Question 3, note 9).

5. Typographical Devices. As regards typographical devices, I have left those employed in *Reiser's Latin original* unchanged. But I have not hesitated to put these devices in *the translation text* (as distinguished from the Notes, as just discussed, p. 454ff., above) to a use largely of my own devising, as follows.

I have used *italics*, conventionally, for the names of books and for conceptual emphases in the wording of the translation, according to my own judgment. The "thesis" Poinsot sets himself to propound in any given Question or Article I have set in **bold-face** type, reserving the use of SMALL CAPITALS to indicate the *ex Thoma/fundamentum huius* distinction explained above (Section I.D., pp. 418-419) in discussing the literary forms of the *Treatise*. The beginning of any paragraph of an argument being developed *to the contrary of what Poinsot himself holds* I have set off by the use of w i d e - s p a c i n g for the letters of the words in the opening phrase.

Thus, italics are used for emphasizing conceptual points or nodes in an argument *regardless* of whether that argument is subscribed to by Poinsot or not; but boldface type is used *only* in connection with propositions Poinsot holds as expressing his own mind, and wide-spacing of type is used *only* to introduce arguments Poinsot does *not* accept as his own, whether not at all or at least not without qualification.

The conventions just outlined for the use of typographical devices, I repeat, are my own and apply as outlined only to the *English* text, *not* to the Latin, which is as Reiser presented it according to a use of typographical devices which does not seem to me to relate to the substance of the *Tractatus* so much as to that of the *traditional Cursus*, and hence to the literary complexities of a given Article as these may vary (by increase or decrease) in a *formal* way relatively independent of *what* is being asserted or denied in the course of the discussion, or "controversy."[91] Without denying the aesthetic elegance and utility of employing typographical devices in this way, where translation is involved, or perhaps rather, *interpreting*, it seems to me *more* helpful if such devices are conventionally related in a systematic way to the opposition of philosophical judgments that distinguish the text in the order of internal subtlety, and this

[91] Reiser, 1930: VII: "Docentium et discentium commodo aeque providentes editionem hanc nostram ita confecimus, ut *argumentum et structura* uniuscuiusque articuli primo aspectu quam clarissime appareat. . . ."

is what I have tried to effect in the English, to wit, the *autonomy* of the tractate vis-à-vis the traditional books.

Parentheses are used in the translation wherever they occur in the Latin, and occasionally for parenthetical clauses Poinsot set off only by commas: but always in the main text for Poinsot's own thought. Square brackets in that text, in sharp contrast, are used always and only to indicate the translator's own explanations or comments: and they are used extremely sparingly.

C. Conceptual Aspects: Principles and Terminology

> *''La chose se supporte en son latin assez spécial; il y a conformité entre la langue qu'il s'est faite et son mode de penser; ce serait moins supportable dans une traduction française. . . . Il n'était pas non plus aisé de mettre en français courant un exposé scolastique, qui contient bien des termes techniques difficiles à rendre dans une autre langue.''*
>
> Garrigou-Lagrange, 1930: XIV
>
> *''The matter is supported by this rather peculiar Latin; there is a conformity between the language its author creates and his way of thinking; it would be less supportable in a modern translation. . . . Having to put into current language a scholastic treatise filled with technical terms difficult to render in another tongue did not make the task any easier.''*

Here must be explained the principles that were adopted in generating our English text and the reasons why they were adopted. Here too we must show concretely how these principles apply in the actual rendering of our text, first from the point of view of the key terms considered simply as semantic elements, and then, in a separate section, from the point of view of their function as doctrinal vehicles.

1. Principles. There are three basic principles underlying this translation. The *first and overriding principle* is that the translation is dictated throughout by the doctrine of signs Poinsot was setting forth. The translation, like the editing, is made entirely in light of the intelligible content and scheme of the Latin text, and aims before all else at fidelity to that scheme, conceptual by definition. Thus, the first objective is to render expressions in function of the doctrine of signs Poinsot proposes, aiming to convey the basic concepts exactly (even when this requires lengthy English statements for concise Latin ones), and with terminological consistency.

It is impossible to exaggerate the importance of this first principle in the generation of our English text. It is this principle integrally understood that requires the presence in this edition of Poinsot's original Latin. For the control factor over interpretation and translation alike is always *the original text*, for which in either case there is in the final arbitration no substitute. That is why, in presenting a fundamentally new doctrine to the reader—making an interpretation, if you like: see note 106 below—it is essential if at all possible that that reader be given access at the same time *to the original*, the sole and only means by which the reader can at will resolve the perplexities of translation

for him or her self; and this we have provided in the present edition, as consolation to the readers for asking them to take seriously in philosophy so startlingly unheard-of and novel a tale ("verba plane inaudita," as Solesmes put it) as the English presentation of the *Treatise on Signs* has to tell. It is from this principle that the remaining two fundamental principles follow.

The *second of the three principles* is: to retain the literary quality of the original, specifically by duplicating in the English so far as possible the style and syntax of the original, particularly as regards the use of subordinate clauses and parallel grammatical structures to convey theoretical niceties in the development of the thought.[92] The alternative of attempting to improve upon Poinsot's style (for example, by breaking up the complex syntax with simple units in the transla-

---

[92] The writing style of our author has been the occasion of much comment, puzzlement, and indeed consternation over the centuries among his readers, friendly and hostile. In fact, it is part and parcel of the unique genius of his doctrine, and one tampers with its idiosyncratic elements at the peril of deceiving oneself as to the content of that doctrine, as the examples of such attempts sufficiently attest (see notes 93 and 95 below). The most judicious appraisal of his style so far offered, not surprisingly, is to be found in the remarkable document we have drawn on so heavily in this work, the "Editorum Solesmensium Praefatio" of 1931, where an entire chapter is given over to the question ("Caput Tertium. De stilo Joannis a Sancto Thoma," pp. xxvj-xxix). In this style they see first of all yet one more illustration of how vitally our author made the traditions of the historically structured world of his time live according to his own proper genius, and beyond that, how he pressed those customs into the service of the doctrine he set himself to develop: "Recall the customs which flourished in the theological schools of the period," they counsel. "Adapting himself to those customs, John in his lectures was concerned little or not at all with the literary purity of his speech, since indeed the Spaniards of the time unanimously sought in the theological schools doctrine, not words," whence "they took pains to achieve simplicity and perspicuity at the expense of elegance." As a result, "he made little use of the skill which he had in the Latin language, except for his Prefaces and Prologues"—such as particularly, in our text, the "Lectori" of 1631 and 1640—"and at times when he was attacking adversaries: then he preserved a more accurate and ornate style. Aside from those contexts, he always employed a manner of expression rough indeed and unpolished, yet clear and wanting neither force nor strength, one eminently suited to the most refined points of metaphysics—a style of the sort that all were accustomed to use in the schools." These general remarks form the heart of the First Article of their "Caput Tertium."

In a Second Article, they examine the more personal idiosyncrasies of his style, under three headings. 1) *New or strange words:* "That John of St. Thomas uses rare or simply unheard-of words is evident to anyone reading him: many such, it is true, he takes from the use of the scholastics, but many seem to be the work of his own proper genius" ("*plura tamen propria minerva fabricasse videtur*"). 2) *Words that are employed in an unusual sense*: following the centuries-old practice of the philosophers, John sometimes twists words away from their proper sense (cf. also p. xxxiij, no. 2, "De interpunctione et orthographia"). 3) *Unwonted verbal constructions:* (a) "There is a rule of the grammarians that when two clauses are opposed as parallels, what is actually said in the one can be understood in the other; in the case of our author, it is not usually the exact same words that are to be understood, but somewhat dissimilar ones by which the opposition of the clauses is increased"; (b) often negatives accumulate to a degree disruptive of the sentence, which accumulation yet lends colorfulness and force to the discourse; (c) "not rarely" does John shift constructions within a sentence so as to create syntactical inconsistencies (anacoluthons); (d) thus he sometimes fails to match the case of subjects and predicates; (e) often our author indulges redundancies; (f) at other times excessive brevity on his part creates some obscurity, though Solesmes suspects that most of these cases are owing to slips of the early typographers.

This summary of the Solesmes stylistic analysis may serve as the basis for the otherwise sometimes harsh-seeming remarks in notes 93 and 95 below, as well as amply to justify the adoption of this second principle for the generation of the translation presented above, and perhaps to recommend adoption of this principle by anyone seeking to create a national-language version of Poinsot's Latin.

tion[93]) is not really feasible, not only because of the inevitable loss of important nuances cumulatively conveyed by the original semantic and grammatical structures (refinements the more important, usually, the longer the stretch of text being considered),[94] but also in view of the actual disasters into which such attempts at "improvement" have led earlier editors and translators of Poinsot's work.[95] Since the Latin of Poinsot's thought depends for many of its nuances on compound-complex sentence structures and the use of subordinate clauses, in sum, faithful conveyance of that syntactical structure is the only appropriate course.[96]

---

[93] This was the course attempted by Simon and his collaborators (1955: xxi): "John of St. Thomas is capable of sharpness and beauty in expression, but he often writes in the uninhibited style of a teacher who depends confidently upon friendly communication with eager scholars. In many cases, we have had [sic: yet *chosen* is the correct expression here] to reshape clauses, to divide exceedingly long sentences, to modify the order of phrases, and effect other changes, on the same minor scale, for the sake of better readability. We believe that accuracy has never suffered in the process"—a belief that, at least as concerns the doctrine of signs (see note 15 in this Afterword and Book I, Question 1, note 6, p. 117), is certainly illusory. In fact, for the reasons given in the text as it continues above ("not only because of . . .") and amplified in the discussion and notes following, changes of the sort Simon and his colleagues effected can seldom be accurately said to be of a "minor scale" in the rendering of Poinsot's thought, except where it is a question of comparatively short passages translated in isolation and therefore supported in the main point by the surrounding narrative of the one using the translation, which narrative in that case can supply for the syntactical balance subtly but essentially supplied the passage in its original environment.

[94] My point here has also been nicely made by Simonin (1930: 144), who reports as follows: "*Du point de vue plus extérieur de la forme littéraire, Dom R. loue la facilité, la clarté et la limpidité du style, mais il ne peut se retenir de deplorer les nombreuses incorrectious qui le déparent (p. XII).*"—"Reiser (p. XII) lauds the effortlessness, clarity and serenity of Poinsot's style, but he cannot refrain from bemoaning the numerous solecisms which mar it from the purely external point of view of literary form." Simonin then goes on to politely demur from the suggestion that these material flaws are counterproductive to Poinsot's formal aim of doctrinal clarity (ibid.): "*Et cependant ces phrases longues, coupées d'incidentes, alourdies par des redites, nous apportent souvent des formules définitives, sagement equilibrées et dont le caractère lumineux nous éblouit. On chemine d'abord dans une épaisse forêt, mais tout à coup, dans une éclaircie, l'ombre cesse, le jour paraît dans tout son éclat et l'on peut sans peine apprecier le chemin parcouru et contrôler les résultats acquis.*"—"For when all is said and done, these long phrases, crisscrossed with difficulties, weighed down with repetitions, often convey to the reader some conclusive formulae, judiciously balanced, of a dazzling luminosity. One starts out in a dense forest, but suddenly, in a clearing, the shadow disappears, day shines in all its splendor, and one can without difficulty appreciate the path covered and control the acquired results."

[95] The editors of the 1663 Lyons publication of Poinsot's *Cursus* claimed on their cover pages to have "much improved" the text ("*ab innumeris expurgatum esse mendis*"). In the sections of that text examined by the Solesmes editors, however (1931: xxij), "the truth is that the Lyons editors applied so much diligence that the style of Poinsot, frequently primitive and careless of rules, they undertook to correct, in many cases uselessly, occasionally with some success, too often obtusely, so that by this clumsy industry they did more harm than good"—"*Revera id tantum diligentiae contulerunt Lugdunenses, ut Joannis a S. Thoma stilum saepe agrestem regulasque parvipendentem corrigere studuerint, in multis inutiliter, aliquando felicius, stolide nonnumquam, ita ut inscita hoc sedulitate, plus etiam nocuerint quam profuerint.*" As we have already noted, the same fate befell the like undertaking of Simon and his collaborators (note 93 above, with references), as it awaits, I suspect, all future such attempts sustained over a sufficient length of Poinsot's text, for the reasons that have been explained.

[96] One last remark on the style of Poinsot, showing particularly why a bi-lingual format is appropriate to the case of Poinsot's work far more than in most cases of translation, may be cited here. "Poinsot—to use the terminology of Pseudo-Dionysius preserved by St. Thomas (*Summa theologica*, II-II, q. 180, art. 6)—had a 'circular contemplation' which, in contrast with an ascensive movement, whether direct or indirect, returns constantly to the same things, describ-

The *third principle* adopted in this translation is to make use of the full historical resources of the English language in our selection of terms. Since the audience for Poinsot's own writings (as distinguished, perhaps, from his doctrine of signs) will never be a popular but always a relatively specialized and usually philosophically sophisticated one, and since the work I had undertaken to translate came from the crucial period of transition from Latin to the national languages as the medium of philosophical writing, there seemed no compelling reason to overly strive for currency of usage in the terms of the translation, especially as the ideas at play in the Latin original are by and large anything but current notions. Therefore it seemed wisest within limits to avail ourselves of older as well as current English vocabulary in the effort to remain faithful to the Latin text.

The first criterion for the acceptable range of terms has been the *Oxford English Dictionary*. Not that a word would be used without further ado if only it appeared in the OED; but if an uncommon or obsolete word occurred there that better and more exactly fitted the Latin thought than anything in current or more common usage—e.g., "ordinately," "fundament," "fictive," "significate"—its unfamiliarity or obsolescence would not necessarily rule it out. I have, in short, not tried to disguise the fact that Poinsot's is a doctrine conceived and expressed in an earlier century, by automatically shying away from uncommon or older forms of English usage. Accuracy within the resources of the language, the affording of the patient reader with maximum access to a work of another age and linguistic community, the making available of this work in a precise and conceptually reliable form: this was the essential task, and my only final objective throughout.

In this regard, the difficulty of the concepts and conceptual architecture

---

ing the same circle several times without tiring, the better to see and review all the aspects and all the riches of a higher truth. So the eagle, having soared to lofty heights by a direct or spiral movement, is content to describe the same circle several times, then to hover motionless while searching the horizon with its powerful gaze. These circular recursions to the same points can tire readers who have not attained to a viewpoint so simple and lofty, who have not the same joy as Poinsot in 'restating the same thing without ever repeating it'; they see the material repetition, and not enough the formal continuity of the gaze of understanding. . . .

"This is said in defense of our noble author, recognizing the while that he sometimes seems to love a little too much the circle on which he returns. . . . He can for that reason appear to be diffuse. The matter is supported by his peculiar enough Latin; there is a conformity between the language that he creates and his way of thinking; it would be less supportable in a French translation."—Garrigou-Lagrange, 1930: XIII-XIV: "*Jean de Saint-Thomas avait, pour employer la terminologie de Denys, conservée par saint Thomas* [*Summa theologica*, II-II, q. 180, art. 6], *la 'contemplation circulaire,' qui, par opposition au mouvement ascensionnel, soit droit, soit oblique, revient constamment sur les mêmes choses, en décrivant plusiers fois le méme cercle, sans se lasser, pour mieux voir et revoir tous les aspects et toutes les richesses d'une vérité superieure. Ainsi l'aigle, après s'être élevé très haut par un mouvement droit ou par un mouvement en spirale, se plaît à décrire plusieurs fois le même cercle, puis à planer comme immobile, en scrutant l'horizon de son puissant regard. Ces retours circulaires sur les mêmes choses peuvent fatiguer les lecteurs qui ne sont pas parvenus à une vue si simple et si haute, qui n'ont pas la même joie que Jean de Saint-Thomas à 'redire la même chose sans la répéter jamais'; ils voient la répétition matérielle, et pas assez la continuité formelle du regard intelligent. . . .*

"*Ceci dit pour défendre le noble Jean de Saint-Thomas, tout en reconnaissant qu'il paraît quelque-fois un peu trop aimer le cercle sur lequel il revient, et qui n'est encore qu'une image lointaine de Dieu. Il peut à cause de cela paraître diffus; la chose se supporte en son latin assez spécial; il y a conformité entre la langue qu'il s'est faite et son mode de penser; ce serait moins supportable dans une traduction francaise.*"

of Poinsot's original Latin should not be underestimated. In the end, I would hazard, difficulty in following the translation traces first to that source, and it is not likely that an easy-to-follow English could succeed at this point in time in conveying the meaning of this dense and elliptical Latin author whose content as regards this "theory" of the sign has virtually eluded the best even of Latin readers (e.g. J. Gredt, 1961[97]) except for Jacques Maritain in our own time. And even Maritain, that unique philosophical genius and incomparable student of Poinsot, still did not get clear about the foundations in relative being of the doctrine of formal signs applied so fruitfully in his epistemological writings (see discussion in Deely, 1978a: 22 note 10; and note 129 below, p. 490).

So, the third principle has been to achieve maximum readability and intelligibility for the non-Latin-speaking public (which today means practically everyone), on condition that the readers be willing to draw upon the historical resources of their own tongue and forsake for a time the superficial pleasures of accustomed and up-to-date literary qualities where the forging of new understandings is called for.

Within the boundaries defined by these three principles, what has been attempted is the improbable goal of a translation so constituted that a reader with reasonable linguistic competence and a key to the conventions of the text (in this case, especially that provided by the double-column format together with the *Index Rerum*) would be able to *retranslate* the new version into the very words of the original,[98] according to the maxim of Augustine: "we do not clearly see what the actual thought is which the several translators endeavor to express, each according to his or her own ability and judgment, unless we examine it in the language which they translate."[99]

Let us now consider these principles further, first at the level of individual terms (III.C.2.), and then at the level of an understanding of the whole (III.D.).

---

[97] The learned Benedictine philosopher-scientist, Joseph Gredt (1863-1940), undertook on the basis of Poinsot's *Cursus Philosophicus* to write in Latin a two-volume text entitled *Elementa Philosophiae Aristotelico-Thomisticae*, which would follow exactly the doctrine and order of Poinsot's Logic and Natural Philosophy, but updating particularly the latter in terms of modern developments in psychology, biology, and physics, and addressing the problems under more current headings (see the discussion of Appendix B in III.A. of this Afterword). This project, which Gredt worked at and refined through many editions (twelve within his lifetime), is one of the most extraordinary episodes in the Poinsot story, "an extremely exact and conscientious work," as J. Maritain says (1966b: 202), "a precious repository of information," but precisely one adhering entirely to what I have called the *traditional* perspective ("ce genre de philosophie thomiste," as Maritain says) of Logic and Natural Philosophy (towards *ens rationis secundae intentionis* and *ens reale*, respectively) as opposed to the *semiotic* viewpoint of the *Tractatus*. Thus, if one compares the contents of the last edition of Gredt (1961) with the *Index Syntheticus* to Poinsot's *Cursus* (Appendix B.I., pp. 353-370 above), everything is there, newly decorated by an artist of the late modern instead of the late renaissance era—except that the *tractatus de signis* has disappeared as such, having been reabsorbed into and redistributed throughout the purely traditional perspectives which otherwise dominate Poinsot's *Cursus* and characterize the philosophical traditions of Latin Aristotelianism and neoscholasticism alike.

[98] That is, I have set myself to realize in this edition the ideal of philosophical translation rightly described but not striven for (of course, for the famous "practical reasons") by Macquarrie and Robinson (1962:13), the translators of *Being and Time*.

[99] St. Augustine, *De Doctrina Christiana*, liber 2, cap. 13, in P.L., vol. 34, p. 43: ". . . *quoniam et quae sit ipsa sententia, quam plures interpretes pro sua quisque facultate atque judicio conantur eloqui, non apparet, nisi in ea lingua inspiciatur quam interpretantur.*"

2. Terms. Six terms in particular may be singled out from our text for lexicographic consideration.[100]

(a) The first of these is *relatio secundum dici*. In Poinsot's text, as in other Latin writings from the renaissance and medieval periods, this term regularly appears in juxtaposition with and contrast to *relatio secundum esse*. The only major historical study that has been made of these terms (Krempel, 1952: esp. Chap. XVIII) is not encouraging, since its author found it impossible to arrive at a satisfactory rendering (p. 394). Fortunately, it is only *Poinsot's* use of these terms that concerns us, and here a consistent interpretation is possible. For this, it is first necessary to get beyond the superficial opposition in the two phrases of *esse* (''existence'') to *dici* (''discourse,'' or ''being spoken''), as if the former were a simple matter of reality, the latter a simple matter of language. In the Latin of Poinsot's philosophical tradition, the ''esse'' of ''*relatio secundum esse*'' denotes not the *existence* of relations, but their peculiar *way* of existing, that is, their *essential* structure or essence.[101] Similarly, ''dici'' in ''*relatio secundum dici*'' denotes not the *expression* of a relation, but the realization in the order of expression of an obligation imposed on that order from the side of the mind-independent nature of *whatever it is* that is being or to be talked about.[102] ''*Relatio secundum dici*'' is the name for a requirement inscribed in the intelligibility of things which imposes itself *if and when and insofar as* they come to be understood.

Thus, the opposition of relation *secundum esse* and *secundum dici* at the start of Poinsot's discussion of signs (Book I, Question 1, fifth paragraph) is far from any convenient opposition between ''relations according to existence'' and ''relations according to expression,'' as Simon would have it (1955: 314; 609 note 9; 389) and others have suggested. There is no simple opposition here of the ''order or plane of existence'' to the ''order or plane of expression,'' superficially plausible as such an interpretation might seem. It is much rather a question of what, in the order of existence, makes the order of expression possible in the first place (which for Poinsot turns out to be the essential being peculiar to relation); and he begins his *Treatise* from this opposition because prior analysis (our ''Second Preamble'' to the *Treatise* proper) has revealed that everything in the physical universe is relative in one of these two ways, and therefore the very first question to be settled about signs as relative beings is the question of what sort of relative beings are they precisely as signs?[103] And the answer

[100] I wish to express thanks here particularly to Fr. Joseph Owens and Fr. Armand Maurer of the Pontifical Institute of Mediaeval Studies, Toronto, acting for the DeRance Publication Fund, whose exacting demands and probing questions about the translation text in general and the terminology that I am here about to discuss in particular not only reflected their years of scholarly familiarity with the Latin age of Western philosophy, but also brought the text to a level of clarity and relative readability greater than it would have otherwise had.

[101] The following texts at the base of Poinsot's tradition may be profitably consulted: St. Thomas, 1252-1256: *In I Sent.* d. 33, q. 1, art. 1, ad 1; d. 8, q. 4, art. 3; d. 26, q. 2, art. 1; d. 33, q. 1, art. 1, ad 3; c. 1266: *Summa Theologiae*, I, q. 28, art. 2; c. 1265-1266: *de Potentia*, q. 3, art. 5; q. 7, art. 10, ad 11.

[102] Consult, along with the texts just cited (note 101), *In V Met.* (Aquinas, c. 1269-1272), lect. 17, nn. 1003, 1004, 1026, 1027-1029; also Cajetan, 1498: *Commentaria in Praedicamenta Aristotelis* (1939 Rome ed.: Angelicum), pp. 114-115.

[103] In these terms, the theoretical importance and historical uniqueness of Poinsot's approach to the subject of signs can be briefly stated. From ancient Greek times to the present, all who

to this question must be, by the terms of the prior analysis, either relative "secundum esse" or relative "secundum dici."

Here, with the notion of the relative "secundum dici," as much as anywhere else in the entire *Treatise*, we are dealing with a notion that, "at the time when [or in the places rather *where*] modern philosophic languages were formed," was, like other concepts of Latin Aristotelianism (Simon, 1955: 611 note 5), "absent from philosophic thought." (Cf. McKeon, 1929: xvi-xviii.) To translate "secundum dici" as *transcendental*, on the ground that Poinsot expressly equates "relatio transcendentalis" with the problematic "relatio secundum dici," is convenient nominally, but of course it leaves the conceptual difficulties exactly where they were.[104]

I leave the final clarification of this matter to the following section (III.D.I.).

(b) To parallel the use of "transcendental" as a synonym for "secundum dici," in the case of "relatio secundum dici," I have introduced the term "ontological" in a somewhat new sense to supply a one-word equivalent in English for the "secundum esse" of "relatio secundum esse." The two cases are not parallel, however, in the very important particular that neither Poinsot nor any other Latin writer suggests a one-word equivalent for "secundum esse" in the sense that Poinsot speaks of "relatio secundum esse." Here then we confront a peculiarity of the translation that reflects a linguistic lacuna in the tradition out of which Poinsot works, a lacuna indexical of the novelty and strict originality of his semiotic.

As has already been indicated and will be discussed more at length in the doctrinal section to follow, *relatio secundum esse* versus *relatio secundum dici* is the key theoretical couplet in the *Treatise*. Both these terms require strict interpretation rather than simple translation in order to make any sense in a modern language, with the unfortunate consequence of demanding cumbersome render-

---

have treated signs agree that a sign, as such, is something relative—*aliquid ad aliquid*. Hence, if the understanding of signs is to be grounded in principle, the first thing to be settled is the question of what exactly constitutes the relativity peculiar to and characteristic of signs as such. It is from this standpoint that Poinsot's *Treatise* is written, and all the many considerations advanced in the *Treatise* are developed in this light. Hence, Poinsot's work not only considers various kinds and divisions of signs, but seeks to uncover a foundation common to all possible kinds and divisions of signs. This foundational drive of the *Treatise* is its principal merit, and gives it its importance for the modern context, as has been pointed out above (Section I.B. and C.) and will be further discussed in D. of this section below. See also Deely, 1977a.

[104] Here may be recorded the characteristically thoughtful comment communicated to me in correspondence about these questions by R. J. LaPlante (letter of 18 January 1972): "Strictly speaking," he writes, but looking exclusively from the perspective of traditional "realism," it is possible to place a difference "between the divisions of relation into *relatio secundum esse* and *secundum dici*, and predicamental and transcendental relations. (a) The division into *secundum esse* and *secundum dici* hinges on whether the one in the formal reason of relation (in general), i.e., the order of one to another, is relative or absolute. (b) The division into predicamental and transcendental hinges on whether the one in the formal reason of relation (in general), i.e., the order of one to another, remains in the specific predicament [category] of relation or transcends this, attaining the other predicaments (quantity, quality, measure), or attaining substance or even the order of being. Thus the division into *relatio secundum esse* and *secundum dici* considers the relative and the absolute simply; but the division into predicamental and transcendental relation considers the way or the how the absolute departs from the relative. This is the sense of 'significat absolutum respective.' 'Respective' is an adverb of manner. If we look at the fact that it is an adverb, we have the 'relatio secundum dici'; in the manner, we have the transcendental relation."

ings.[105] Fortunately, as we have just noted, Poinsot expressly equates *secundum dici* with *transcendentalis*, which lends itself readily to a one-word rendering. It would be nice if he had provided us with an equally manageable one-

---

[105] Here I may note, with reference especially to the doctrinal account below (III.D.) of the rendering of this distinction in our English *Treatise*, that a striking independent verification of the appropriateness of the rendering settled upon was provided in correspondence with Dr. John C. Cahalan. We have here a subject matter of the sort Poinsot describes (1632: Logica 2. p. q. 27. art. 1., 822b23-28) as calling for diverse ways of speaking which yet say the same thing, but by bringing to light unexpected dimensions of that "sameness"—"*nec tamen diversum sensum habent, sed eandem rem explicant, quae uno solum modo explicari non potest.*"

It will be recalled that one of the first problems posed for the understanding of Poinsot's semiotic (see Section I.B. above) was the problem of deciding which other parts of the *Ars Logica* were essential to the intelligibility of the problematic and text of the *Treatise on Signs*. Q. XVII of the Logic, "On the Category of Relation" ("*De praedicamento relationis*") comprises seven articles, only the first three of which proved necessary for the justification of the rendering finally arrived at in English of *secundum esse/secundum dici*. Other possible ways of construing the distinction seemed to require more than this on the side of the Latin text, as appears in the following exchange (Cahalan, letter of 29 October 1975): "Would it cause any difficulty to your presentation to admit that transcendental relations must always be defined with reference to something else? I see dialectical difficulties only, not doctrinal difficulties. The manner of distinguishing transcendental relations from predicamental relations may become more cumbersome or subtle, but nothing prevents the distinction from being made. On this hypothesis, both transcendental relations and predicamental relations must be defined with reference to something else, a term. But in the case of predicamental relations the term is required as nothing but an opposing term, while in the case of transcendental relations the term is required as cause or effect (which is precisely the point you make in saying that from 'an *explanatory* perspective concerned with the conditions of actual existence . . . the relativity of the relative absolute forces itself to the fore'). This method of making the distinction is accurate just as yours is. But *using this method would require going into the subtleties of Articles 5 and 6* of Poinsot's question on relations" (final emphasis added).

Further remarks of Cahalan's likely to be of interest to those interested in these problems of terminology can also be included here: "In Article 2, by the way, Poinsot refrains from classifying all terms of transcendental relations as causes or effects; in addition he mentions objects (p. 314 of the 1955 Simon translation). Perhaps I am failing to comprehend something, but since objects—at least necessary objects, which are the only ones under consideration in a discussion of transcendental relations—are causes in the order of specification, why not say that all terms of transcendental relations are either causes or effects of the transcendental relation? This would bolster your account of transcendental relations as requiring to be expressed relatively when viewed from the perspective of the explanation of existence. Of course, predicamental relations must be caused to exist also, but that is not the *reason why* their definition requires reference to a term. I cannot think of any transcendental relations whose terms are not either their causes or their effects if 'cause' and 'effect' are understood broadly enough.

"This suggests another way of making the distinction. Could one say that predicamental relations are relative in the order of specification while transcendental relations are relative only in the order of exercise? The very form of a predicamental relation requires a reference to a term and in addition there is the reference to a term required by the postulation in existence of this form. In the case of the transcendental relation a reference to a term is required only for the postulation in existence of the form, not by the form considered in itself. This method of formulation would only be in *apparent* contradiction to Poinsot's statement (p. 314) that transcendental relations 'ground the relation rather than exercise it actually.' (See the similar usage in Simon's note 10, p. 609). What Poinsot means here by exercising a relation, or being a relation according to *existence*, is precisely what I mean by being a relation in the order of specification. In other words relations according to existence could also be called things whose essence is to be relations, and transcendental relations are things whose essence is not that of relations but which are related to other things either because their essence requires these things in order to exist or because the postulation of their essence in existence brings about the existence of some other thing. Again, there is nothing doctrinally wrong with these formulas, but their apparent contradiction to standard formulas may make their use disadvantageous from a pragmatic point of view."

word equivalent for the cumbersome rendering required to express *secundum esse*. Unfortunately, he did not; there is no Latin one-word equivalent for the cumbersome demands of *secundum esse* to parallel the *transcendentalis* = *secundum dici* usage. Moreover, because the demands of rendering *secundum esse* are quite cumbersome, some such short equivalent is sorely needed. "Ontological" I have settled upon as the most viable candidate. It is a term already coined in the period from which the *Treatise* comes to us, even though it did not attain wide usage until Wolff's time (1679-1754). In addition, it suggests itself from the Poinsot-based work of Jacques Maritain, especially *Creative Intuition in Art and Poetry* (1953; see also Hanke, 1973). There is no exact or perfect term in any language, so far as I know, for the unique role Poinsot assigns the *relatio secundum esse* in his explanation of signifying. I have settled upon "ontological" *faute de mieux*.

(c) A third term that bears scrutiny is *ens reale*. The obvious (and fairly standard) rendering of this expression is *real being*. This actually is quite unsatisfactory, despite its widespread adoption, for a number of reasons. First of all, *ens reale* in the Latin writings always implies a juxtaposition with and contrast to *ens rationis*. We have here a couplet that ought to be rendered correlatively. Yet the standard translation of *ens reale* as "real being" obscures the fact that *ens reale—ens rationis* is a distinction of two sorts of being, *each* having some "reality," though of very different kinds, the former having existence independently of being apprehended in cognition, while the latter owes its existence precisely to being thus apprehended. It is a problem of drawing a contrast between two sorts of being both of which are "real"—members of a class R possessing and not possessing property P, as it were; so no "translation" that obscures or avoids this problem should be accepted.

The prevalence of this poor translation in English writings is all the more astonishing in view of the fact that there is no doubt as to the signification of *ens reale*: what exists independently of being known by a finite mind.[106] *Mind-*

[106] It might thus be objected, as Fr. Owens did in fact suggest (letter of 1 June 1977), that what I am proposing here "is not a translation but an interpretation." There is a valid point here, but in the case of the present work it is a weak one. First of all, the line between translation and interpretation is hard and fast only in cases where there clearly exist in two languages semantic units so governed by established conventions and rules of usage that no understanding beyond straightforward linguistic competence in the two tongues is required to see their comparative synonymy. Where this is not the case, then translation without interpretation degenerates to transliteration or to a greater or lesser degree of sheer guesswork. Where interpretation becomes necessary, then, to guide the work of translation through a problem passage, the question is not whether interpretation is involved, but whether it is correct or not; and no simple appeal to the distinction between translation and interpretation can resolve the problem-situation, though it remains the case that translation and interpretation should indeed be kept as separate as the established conventions governing the respective languages allow. Second, in the case of philosophical writers generally, and all the more so in the case of one as original and little known as Poinsot, new ground is always being broken that is simply not covered by patterns of usage prejacent to the writer's thought, as has been made abundantly clear in the matter of Poinsot's writing ("maxima semper libertate usus est Joannis a S. Thoma" is a remark from Solesmes, 1931: xxxij, that we could well apply here; see also note 92 above), so that interpretation is normally necessary in philosophical translation to a greater extent than in most literary genres. He who does not understand an author cannot be a reliable guide to the establishment of that author's text in a second language. Third, as has been said above concerning the first principle for the generation of our English text of this edition, to which principle I would again refer the reader here, the control factor over interpretation and translation alike, in their imperfect but real separability and interweave, can only be *the original text*, and this has been provided in the present edition.

independent being at once suggests itself as a shorthand rendering of this notion. The correlative rendering for *ens rationis* in that case would be *mind-dependent being,*[107] with the caveat that this rendering is open to misunderstanding in a number of ways, for, as our author observes in the "First Preamble" to the *Treatise* (at 48/1-22 [=*285a19-43*]), there are several senses in which something can be said to be "dependent upon the mind," and only one of these strictly speaking answers to the notion of *ens rationis*, namely, that of being entirely dependent *as an object* upon cognitive activity for existing.

Technically, then, "*cognition*-independent being" and "*cognition*-dependent being" might be the most exact shorthand rendering for *ens reale* and *ens rationis;*

---

[107] As good a defense of this choice as could be wished has been made by Prof. Rulon Wells, who himself (owing to what I regard as an inadequate grasp of the role the correlative *entia rationis* play in semiosis as Poinsot discloses it) would wish nonetheless to accept the "real being" of neoscholasticism for *ens reale,* Poinsot's included. Professor Wells, in a communication dated 8 August 1979, remarks that there is a good side and a bad side to this rendering. "The good features are that (i) the two modifiers are obviously correlative and complementary, which was not obvious with their Latin originals; (ii) 'mind-dependent' is an adjective, so that an adverb can be formed from it, which was not true of *rationis* nor of the traditional translation thereof, 'of reason.' In actual discussion of these matters, feature (ii) proves to be a great convenience. On the other hand," he continues, on the bad side, "the phrases 'mind-independent, mind-dependent' are uncouth mouthfillers." Yet in the context of conveying an author who by all accounts uses a rough and primitive style, filled with "verba nova aut barbara . . . quae aures latinas offenderent" (see note 92 above and Solesmes, 1931: xxvij), this does not constitute a serious objection.

Fr. Joseph Owens, in a letter of 1 June 1977, advanced the following considerations on this point of terminology. "The force of the adjectival 'real' here," i.e., in the expression 'real being' for *ens reale,* "is that they [i.e., 'real' beings] exist in themselves (*in re: in se*), whereas *entia rationis* have to be produced by reason. Except for the vagueness in 'mind,' instead of the more specific 'reason,' 'mind-dependent' may pass as a translation of *ens rationis,* but the required parallelism is in that case 'mind' and 'thing,' not 'dependent' and 'independent'. " Fr. Owens therefore would suggest "thing-dependent being" for the translation of *ens reale.* But this revives the same objection telling against the common rendering as "real being" examined above, namely, that of a "distinction" one member of which includes the other member to which it is supposed to be set in contrast; for there is no getting around the fact that, in the context of Latin philosophy (e.g., see Poinsot, 1632: 594a1-2: "*res est de transcendentalibus . . .*"), "thing" is a transcendental, whence "thing-dependent being" does not provide a contrast to but includes as well "mind-dependent being." I note too that the comparative vagueness of "mind" instead of the more specific "reason" is for the case of our author not a disadvantage but something required by the theoretical point that, for Poinsot, animals without reason ("animalia bruta") as well as men form "entia rationis" in semiotic exchanges (see Deely, 1978a: 1-30 for an extended account; also 1975a), which point I will discuss in D.2.(b) of this Section, below. (And, whereas Fr. Owens accepts "mind-dependent" for *ens rationis,* objecting only to "mind-independent" for *ens reale,* in a communication from the well-known medievalist Fr. James Weisheipl early in 1977 is the suggestion that while "mind-independent being" seems perhaps right for *ens reale,* "mind-dependent being" for *ens rationis* will never do!) Wells' proposal (loc. cit.) of "mind-made" for *ens rationis* strikes me as being at least as awkward and uncultivated as "mind-dependent," if not more so, while in addition it precludes the possibility of a correlative complement for *ens reale,* which is the whole point of the couplet as it functions in our *Treatise on Signs.* Clearly we are at a point of considerable theoretical and linguistic sensitivity here, and the shop-worn "real being" is not likely to contribute needed clarity at this point. By contrast, the lively response from all quarters to the correlative rendering settled upon—mind-dependent and mind-independent—is an excellent indication that it touches all the right nerves. Hence it is my gamble that the rendering adopted in our text above is the best one for the circumstances; and I will wager further that it will eventually supplant the current renderings and become common, which is also the opinion of John Cahalan.

yet somehow the expressions using ''mind'' have more the flavor of the seventeenth century, and seem more likely to become generally adopted.[108]

I leave further clarification of this matter to the following section (III.D.), where we will also consider serious theoretical difficulties, in the context of semiotic, to the standard English rendering of *ens rationis* as ''being of reason.''

(d) Poinsot writes of *signa ex consuetudine* and *signa ad placitum*, which I have rendered, respectively, ''customary signs'' and ''stipulated signs.'' Dr. Joseph Owens, a particularly learned and distinguished scholar in Aristotelian and scholastic studies, remarked in a private communication (September 20, 1976) that '' 'customary' and 'stipulated' are correct, but seem somewhat strange and forced in the context, where 'conventional' would be the translation expected.'' This seems to me an excellent example, in line with our discussion above of the third principle of this translation, of the fact that reliance on current or familiar notions in the reading of Poinsot is almost certain to result in a missing of what is essential to his doctrine of signs.

Nothing is more standard and familiar in works of modern and contemporary philosophy than the distinction between ''conventional'' and ''natural'' signs. However, a main theoretical point of Poinsot's analysis is that such a dichotomy will not do in accounting for the way natural and artificial beings interpenetrate in the process of semeiosis and order of signification. Natural and stipulated signs in fact have a kind of common ground in custom, which is also a common ground in the experience of human and other animals; and the interplay of *ens reale* and *ens rationis* in the sign as Poinsot exhibits it has no counterpart known to me in the philosophical tradition apart from the analysis of being and non-being essayed by Hegel at the beginning of his *Logic* (1812), where it is asserted that in becoming, the two are somehow one. I believe it is the same insight that is at the foundation of both works. Be this as it may, it can be shown (see Deely, 1978a, and, to a lesser extent, 1980a) that to translate Poinsot's *signa ad placitum* and *signa ex consuetudine* alike as ''conventional signs'' would have been to blur one of the major theoretical contributions of the *Treatise* as a whole.

(e) In one of the lengthiest and (to modern ears) strangest of the questions of our *Treatise* (Book I, Question 4), Poinsot dwells on the distinction between *objectum motivum* and *objectum terminativum*. How to render ''motivum''? I finally settled on ''stimulus,'' after several experiments with ''motive object,'' ''moving object,'' even the ludicrous ''motor object.'' In the case of this and all related expressions, it is clear in the *Treatise* that an arousal or stimulation of a cognitive power is what is at issue, but usually in the context of objective, not efficient, specificative, not executive, causality. This is not a context for which

[108] My reasons for so thinking are admittedly vague, as the ''yet somehow . . .'' above openly implies. A good enough linguist could probably explain the impression that I can only report, namely, that in the course of making this translation, I found consistently that wherever there was a choice of English words to render the Latin where one option led to an Anglo-Saxon root while the other back to a Latin root, the latter choice seemed on the surface a better ''fit,'' and yet somehow seemed ''soft'' or ''mushy,'' whereas the term of Anglo-Saxon origin had a phenomenological solidity or ''punch'' and ''felt'' more correct in an indefinable way. It was Dr. Powell who directed my attention to the respective etymological backgrounds invariably accompanying this quasi-experiential difference in possible renderings.

modern philosophical languages have developed anything like a sophisticated usage, and hence there is no expression that of itself adequately carries Poinsot's discussions beyond the Latin. Still, it seemed that "stimulus" and related expressions came the *closest*, and would succeed in the end for a careful reader sufficiently attentive to context.

(f) The final lexical item I single out for discussion and as transition to our doctrinal résumé of the entire work, is the term *ratio* as it functions in the main contexts of our *Treatise*. Originally, following the suggestion of Yves Simon (1955), I tried rendering the term as "notion," experimenting subsequently with several standard alternatives—"nature," "character," etc. Finally "rationale" was suggested by Dr. Ralph Powell, and it seemed right in all the main theoretical contexts, though "nature" and "character" fit better in some sub-contexts.[109] I would like to report here Dr. Powell's explanation of why "rationale" is the correct rendering, by citing at length from his memorandum to me of July 30, 1977. This account will also serve as the transition to our discussion of terms as doctrinal vehicles within Poinsot's *Treatise*.

"A basic presupposition has guided this translation of the *Treatise on Signs*. It is that three novelties in the understanding of reality and of knowing underlie the *Treatise*. The three novelties are intimately connected with the primary meaning of *ratio* in the crucial texts.

"The novel understanding of reality consists in reducing all created reality into two categories, each of which can be directly experienced: namely, the categories of relation *secundum dici* and predicamental relation ('Second Preamble,' 82/7-18 [=*574b21-32*]):

> Relations *secundum dici* have absolute being and their whole being is not relation to another. Relations of reason exist only in the intellect apprehending by which they have objective being. But without any intellect considering, some things are found having no being except relation to another. Therefore these latter are real relations that are not relations *secundum dici* but constitute a separate category of real being.

"Thanks to this exhaustive division of created reality, substance is included under relation *secundum dici* (ibid., 86/14-20 [=*577a17-25*]). Pre-Aristotelian philosophers recognized only relations *secundum dici*. According to this it follows

---

[109] In a letter dated 9 September 1975 discussing this problem, John Cahalan wrote as follows: "when suggesting a footnote explaining why you chose 'rationale,' I was thinking of an explanation which would include a statement to the effect that you are translating a Latin term for which there is really no English equivalent. If one is not directly commenting on a statement by a Latin author using *ratio* in the scholastic sense, it is best to avoid the term altogether. As you know, many terms are adequate substitutes for it in certain contexts. 'Intelligible structure,' 'formal intelligibility,' 'objective concept,' 'essence,' 'formal type,' 'essential type,' 'definable type,' 'intelligibility,' can all serve in some contexts, as can 'meaning,' despite the abuses of that term in analytic philosophy. But in other contexts only circumlocutions will do.

"I can think of one good argument, however, for consistently translating *ratio* as 'rationale.' The meaning of 'rationale' as an explanation for something or the reason for something is, of course, one important aspect of *ratio* as used by the scholastics. For the essence of a thing, whether a real essence or an 'essence' of reason, is the reason for its properties. And to explain a thing's properties is to know the reason for them, that is, to know its essence. Hence the proper *ratio* of any mode of being is the rationale of the properties of that mode of being."

that even substance is a relative. Except for substance, all remaining created reality consists of accidents: accidents being either relations *secundum dici* or predicamental relations. Now all accidents are knowable in experience (ibid., 86/19-20 [=*577a23-25*]):

> We need no greater experience to recognize the existence of relations than for any other kind of accidental form in which we experience their effects but not their distinction from substance.

''*Since we do not experience the distinction of substance from accidents, substance is not known by experience as a distinct reality*. But since all accidents are either relations *secundum dici* or predicamental ones, and since all accidents are knowable in experience, then both kinds of accidents are knowable in experience. Hence the two categories that include all created reality can be directly experienced. Experience gives these categories only in what *will be called accidents* once substance has been rationally distinguished as a distinct category or reality. Experience itself gives only, e.g., this white object, that sound, etc.

''The second novelty is to reduce real sign relations and unreal sign relations to univocity *as known*. Signs as such are something apt to be known. Real and unreal sign relations are univocal *in esse objecti* because the real and the unreal are univocal objects of the same power of intellect or of the same habit of science, metaphysics (Book II, Question 5, 270/43-271/9 [=*715b45-716a12*]). More proximate to the point, we *experience* this univocity of meaning between natural signs and *ad placitum* signs (ibid., 271/12-15 [=*716a16-19*]). But natural signs are real sign relations (Book I, Question 2, 137/9-14 [=*656b20-26*]); and *ad placitum* signs are unreal sign relations (ibid., 140/44-142/13 [*658b11-659a40*]). Real and unreal relations are called relations *secundum esse*. From the beginning of the *Treatise*, the first thing shown is that the 'formalis ratio signi' *consists* in relations *secundum esse*. Thus, the relation *secundum esse* as the *formalis ratio signi* is the proper subject of the *Treatise*. The univocity as known of the real and unreal sign relations determines *how this proper subject exists as known*.

''The third novelty is to reduce unfree real sign relations experienced in special habits to intelligible unity with experienced free unreal relations. This reduction is achieved thanks to the doctrine that the real sign relation is *univocal as known* with the unreal sign relation that has only objective being. A people's custom is a natural sign because it manifests (even more than other effects) its cause, namely, the people's habits (Book II, Question 6, 279/24-38 [=*719b37-720a6*]). However, a people's custom becomes a natural sign only when its frequent observance is publicly taken as notification of something less manifest (ibid., 281/21-34 [=*721a7-21*]). Hence the customary sign is always an object of frequent experience. Now we experience language as a customary sign, it being an effect of the habits of speech of a people. As manifesting the causal effect of habit, language is not a free sign but is reduced to natural sign as an imperfect species thereof—being imperfect because it is not perceptible to the whole human race, but only to that language group whose custom it is (ibid., 283/26-32 [=*722a29-37*]). Inasmuch as language is used with moral freedom it is an *ad placitum* sign (ibid., 280/26-43 [=*720b5-26*]). Thus the single

experiential fact of language manifests both the natural real sign relation and the *ad placitum unreal sign relation under different formalities* (ibid., 283/13-22 [=*722a16-24*]). And both kinds of relation have the same univocal meaning as experienced. Thus in the experience of language, real relations in a people's customary signs and unreal relations in the free *ad placitum* signs are reduced to common intelligibility thanks to the univocity as known of the two kinds of signs.

"The real sign relation becomes for Poinsot the proximate means whereby concepts actually connect with the *existing* object world (Book I, Question 2, 139/39-140/15 [=*658a3-25*]). The concept as similitude is a mere transcendental relation to the object which may exist or not (Book I, Question 1, 122/17-36 [=*649a11-35*]). The concept as similitude is a transcendental relation that founds the real predicamental relation to the existing object (ibid., 132/16-133/12 [=*654b3-655a8*]). But the concept as similitude is but a remote connection with the existing object.

"Now the univocity of real and unreal relations as known is essential to Poinsot's doctrine that all signs are relations. Otherwise, the meaning in public language of natural customary signs and free signs would not be univocally the same. And that is contrary to experience. But the univocity of real and unreal sign relations is ultimately grounded in Poinsot's doctrine of the *primum cognitum* of the intellect. For him, what the intellect first knows is *the reality* of concrete singulars in which it cannot yet distinguish substance from accidents. Thus intellectual knowledge is not yet abstract, but concerns these sensible singulars themselves as real (Phil. nat. 1. p., Reiser ed., Vol. II, 24a42-25a43). This original experience is readily understood in Poinsot's terms. A concrete experience is really related to the concrete singulars experienced just as a bovine footprint is really related to an ox (Book III, Questions 1 and 2). This original experience is the paradigm for all other knowledge of existing objects. All other signs and objects must be univocal *as known* to this original experience under pain of not being conformed to reality, the proper object of the one power of intellect (Book II, Question 5, 271/1-9 [=*716a3-12*]).

"Thanks to these innovations Poinsot can be seen as a bridge for a philosophy of realism between medieval philosophy of real individual substance and modern philosophers of empiricism and of social world. Empiricism is satisfied in terms of realism by making transcendental relations and predicamental relations the empirical origin of realism in philosophy. Social world is made intelligible in terms of realism by the univocity *as known* of real and unreal relations in language as customary social signs.

"Now the basic use of *ratio* in this *Treatise* is *ratio* as used in the phrase *formalis ratio signi*. Commanding the whole *Treatise* is the question: *Quaerimus ergo, an formalis ista ratio signi consistat in relatione secundum esse primo et per se, an in relatione secundum dici* (Book I, Question 1, 117/18-22 [=*646b16-19*]). The answer to the question determines that the *formalis ratio signi* is the *relatio secundum esse*. This is the principle whence he will conclude to the experienced univocity *as known* of real and unreal sign relations. By this conclusion the whole *Treatise* is virtually completed, as I have indicated.

"The most obvious translation of *ratio* is 'reason.' The translation 'reason'

comes recommended by the whole medieval usage in the meaning of 'notion' or 'aspect' derived from the Greek *logos*, and it has the theological overtones applied to God as *ratio divina* or *ratio Dei*. But it is precisely this history and these theological overtones that render it inapt as a translation in the crucial texts that govern the *Treatise* (our usage is mixed in other contexts). 'Reason' cannot capture the meaning of *ratio* in Poinsot's phrase, *formalis ratio signi*.

"For our translation must capture what is historically unique in Poinsot's concept *formalis ratio signi*. He wrote many purely traditional treatises as well as this one, but this *Treatise* contains in the concept *formalis ratio signi* a moment when medieval realism of individual substance was passing into modern philosophies of empiricism and social world. We do not claim that Poinsot's concept of the *formalis ratio signi* is the only such moment. But the 'formalis ratio signi' *defined* as *relatio secundum esse* expresses both the 'realist reason' of medieval substance philosophy and the 'subjective empiricist reason' of modern philosophies. Our translation of *ratio* must capture this meaning.

"According to the *Oxford English Dictionary*, contemporary English usage has five generic meanings of 'reason' and twenty-three specific ones, eight of which latter are obsolete. Number 9 of the specific meanings (qualified as 'obsolete') is 'rationale.' Illustrating the obsolete meaning of 'ratio' as 'rationale,' the OED cites Gale, writing in 1678: 'The formal reason or nature of Sin consists in its being a deordination or transgression of the Divine law.' (*Cont. Gentiles*, III, 7.) Hence, according to the OED, what we mean by 'rationale' today was expressed by 'formal reason or nature' in a 17th century writer. Moreover, this writer is speaking of 'the formal reason or nature' just as Poinsot had written *formalis ratio signi*. Hence, according to the OED we must translate 'formal reason' or 'nature' of 17th century English by the contemporary term 'rationale.' So likewise we must translate Poinsot's term *formalis ratio signi* by 'the formal rationale of the sign.'

"According to the OED the contemporary word 'rationale' has only two meanings: '1. A reasoned exposition of principles; an explanation or statement of reasons. 2. The fundamental reason, the logical or rational basis (of anything).' Here we have that realist and subjective meaning of *ratio* that we are seeking. The first meaning clearly expresses a *subjective meaning* of reason: 'a reasonable exposition of principles.' The second meaning carries a *realist meaning* of reason. The OED cites examples under the second meaning: '1791. Paine, *Rights of Man* (4th edition, p. 161): "He sees the rationale of the whole system, its origin and its operation." 1894, H. Drummond, *Ascent of Man*, p. 3: "To discover the rationale of social progress is the ambition of this age."' Thus our contemporary use of the word 'rationale' expresses both the subjective and the realist meanings of 'reason' as found in Gale's 17th century English: 'the formal reason [subjective meaning] or the nature [realist meaning].'

"Therefore, 'the formal rationale of a sign' is the correct English translation of Poinsot's *formalis ratio signi*."

D. Doctrinal Résumé

Here we take up all the fundamental questions of terminology and translation, but now exclusively from the point of view of our first and governing

principle of translation, where the questions are resolved, not lexically and historically, but (so far as possible) purely doctrinally. We are at the heart of the *Treatise on Signs*, so far as it is a creation of contemporary understanding.

1. The Secundum Dici-Secundum Esse Couplet: The Fundamental Architecture of the Treatise on Signs.

So far as there is any one key to the understanding of Poinsot's doctrine of signs, the distinction between what is relative *secundum dici* and what is relative *secundum esse* is that key. The contrast may be explained as follows (and, of course, in other ways as well: see note 105 above).

According to the view of Aristotelian metaphysics, the natural world is made up of "a many, each of which is itself one,"[110] and subject to change in time. The "ones" or fundamental natural units in this scheme Aristotle called *substance*, and the various ways in which the being of a substance could be affected without losing its basic self-identity Aristotle called *accidents*, of which he himself enumerated nine. Substance and the nine accidents make up the traditional list of Aristotelian "categories." Though the number of categories that ought to be listed was sometimes argued over among the important figures in the Latin West, by the time of the high middle ages, there was general agreement among them as to the purpose for which the Aristotelian categorial scheme had been devised, a consensus well expressed by Poinsot in the following passage:

> The distinction of the categories was introduced for this, that the orders and classes of diverse natures might be set forth, to which all the things which participate some nature might be reduced, and on this basis the first thing that must be excluded from *every* category is mind-dependent being, because being which depends for its being on being cognized (mind-dependent being) has not a nature nor a true entity, but a constructed one, and therefore must be relegated not to a true category, but to a constructed one. Whence St. Thomas says (in q. 7, art. 9 of his *Disputed Questions on the Power of God*) that only a thing independent of the soul pertains to the categories.[111]

Substance and its accidents thus were understood by our author in the traditional sense as constituting the categories of mind-independent ways of being. Aristotle was of the opinion that a category of "the relative" ought to be in-

---

[110] Aristotle, *Metaphysics*, Book III, Chapter 4, 1001b5-6: "all things are either one or many, and of the many each is one": ἅπαντα δὲ τὰ ὄντα ἢ ἓν ἢ πολλά, ὧν ἓν ἕκαστον.

[111] *Ars Logica* (Reiser ed.), Part II, Q. XIV, Art. 1, "*Quid sit praedicamentum et quid requiratur ut aliquid sit in praedicamento*" ("What Would a Category Be and What Would Be Required for Something To Be in a Category"), 500b36-501a2: "*Et quia praedicamentorum distinctio ad hoc introducta est, ut diversarum naturarum ordines et classes proponerentur, ad quae omnia, quae naturam aliquam participant, reducerentur, ideo imprimis secludendum est ab omni praedicamento ens rationis, quia non habet naturam neque entitatem veram, sed fictam, ideoque neque ad praedicamentum verum, sed fictum reici debet. Unde D. Thomas q. 7. de Potentia art. 9. tantum res extra animam dicit pertinere ad praedicamenta.*"

cluded in the list of categorial accidents, and his first suggestion for the definition of this category was as follows:

> Those things are called relative which, being either said to be *of* something else or *related to* something else, are explained by reference to that other thing.[112]

Although this definition of the category of relation seemed sound to Aristotle,[113] he conceded that it presented some difficulty from the point of view of constituting a *distinct* category within the substance-accident scheme:

> Indeed, if our definition of that which is relative was complete, it is very difficult, if not impossible, to prove that no substance is relative. If, however, our definition was not complete, if those things only are properly called relative in the case of which relation to an external object is a necessary condition of existence, perhaps some explanation of the dilemma may be found.
>
> The former definition does indeed apply to all relatives, but the fact that a thing is *explained* with reference to something else does not make it *essentially* relative.[114]

---

[112] Aristotle, *Categories*, chap. 7, 6a36-39: Πρός τι δὲ τὰ τοιαῦτα λέγεται, ὅσα αὐτὰ ἅπερ ἐστὶν ἑτέρων εἶναι λέγεται, ἢ ὁπωσοῦν ἄλλως πρὸς ἕτερον, οἷον τὸ μεῖζον τοῦθ' ὅπερ ἐστὶν ἑτέρου λέγεται· τινὸς γὰρ λέγεται μεῖζον·

I have cited the translation by E. M. Edghill in *The Basic Works of Aristotle*, ed. Richard McKeon (New York: Random House, 1941), p. 17. Cf. the translation by J. L. Ackrill, *Aristotle's Categories and De Interpretatione* (Oxford: Clarendon, 1963), p. 17: "We call *relatives* all such things as are said to be just what they are, *of* or *than* other things, or in some other way in relation *to* something else."

[113] For example, he explicitly reaffirms it ibid., 6b6-9: πρός τι οὖν ἐστὶν ὅσα αὐτὰ ἅπερ ἐστὶν ἑτέρων εἶναι λέγεται, ἢ ὁπωσοῦν ἄλλως πρὸς ἕτερον, οἷον ὄρος μέγα λέγεται πρὸς ἕτερον·

[114] *Categories*, chap. 7, 8a28-34: εἰ μὲν οὖν ἱκανῶς ὁ τῶν πρός τι ὁρισμὸς ἀποδέδοται, ἢ τῶν πάνυ χαλεπῶν ἢ τῶν ἀδυνάτων ἐστὶ τὸ δεῖξαι ὡς οὐδεμία οὐσία τῶν πρός τι λέγεται· εἰ δὲ μὴ ἱκανῶς, ἀλλ' ἔστι τὰ πρός τι οἷς τὸ εἶναι ταὐτόν ἐστι τῷ πρός τί πως ἔχειν, ἴσως ἂν ῥηθείη τι πρὸς αὐτά. ὁ δὲ πρότερος ὁρισμὸς παρακολουθεῖ μὲν πᾶσι τοῖς πρός τι, οὐ μὴν ταὐτόν γέ ἐστι τῷ πρός τι αὐτοῖς εἶναι τὸ αὐτὰ ἅπερ ἐστὶν ἑτέρων λέγεσθαι.

Edghill trans. (see note 112 above), p. 22. Whatever else is to be said of this translation, in this passage and in the next one I shall quote, Edghill's rendering at least conveys in English the Greek-Latin parallel between λέγεται and *dicuntur* ("Dans le texte grec comme dans la version latine," notes Krempel, 1952: 398, "l'ancienne définition est dominée par un double λέγεται, *dicuntur,* la nouvelle, par εἶναι, *esse*"). This contrast, everywhere discussed in the Latin West for over a thousand years, is much obscured, for example, in Ackrill's rendering (reference in note 112 above), pp. 22-23: "Now if the definition of relatives which was given above was adequate, it is either exceedingly difficult or impossible to reach the solution that no substance is spoken of as a relative. But if it was not adequate, and if those things are relatives for which *being is the same as being somehow related to something,* then perhaps some answer may be found. The previous definition does, indeed, apply to all relatives, yet this—their being called what they are, of other things—is not what their being relatives is."

What seems to take place in Ackrill's rendering is a repetition of the now long-forgotten (in the modern languages) attenuation of the Aristotelian conception of the categories introduced into the sixth-century Latin West by Boethius under the Platonic construction of the categorial scheme at work in Alexander of Aphrodisias, Plotinus, and Porphyry, according to the description of Krempel: "C'est ce qui amenait déjà Alexandre d'Aphrodise (200 avant J.C., à Athènes), et plus tard Plotin, à opposer trop brutalement λέγεται ετ εἶναι. *Pour Aristote,* λέγεται n'est jamais un simple: on dit. Si, par principe, il commence par le mot, il finit par la chose. Les prédicaments sont pour lui l'écho de la réalité. Boèce semble avoir perdu ce fait de vue quand, sous l'influence de ses prédécesseurs, il accentuait outre mesure dicuntur *et* esse." This description by Krempel

This distinction between what must be *explained* by reference to something else without having itself to be a relation, and what is *essentially* a reference to something other than that on which it is founded or based, is the classical germ of the Latin distinction within the order of relation between what is relative *secundum dici* and what is relative *secundum esse*. Relativity in the first sense characterizes not only what falls under the category of relation in Aristotle's scheme, but what falls under the ''absolute'' categories of substance, quantity, and quality as well (categories called ''absolute'' from the fact that they are defined subjectively, in terms of themselves, without including an essential relation to something else). Outside the mind, a substance and its accidents other than relations—a subject of existence in its subjective determinations, let us say—constitute the order of ''absolute'' and mind-independent being. Absolute beings in this sense, though they can be *defined* without reference to anything else, cannot be *accounted for* except by reference to something else, namely, their principles and causes; and in this sense they are relative according to the way their being must be *expressed* in discourse, even though they are not relative according to the way they essentially *have* being. Such relativity, found as it is in each of the absolute categories, is called by Poinsot *transcendental,*[115] in line with the medieval custom of calling properties of being which are not restricted to any one category ''transcendental,'' i.e., transcending the categorial divisions of the substance-accident scheme.[116]

Opposed to what is relative only according to the way its being must be expressed in discourse (*secundum dici*), or to the *transcendental* notion of relation, there is the second kind of relativity, the relativity which affects a thing according to the way it exercises existence and is *essentially* a reference toward another. Beings relative in *this* sense are the constitutent structures of ontological *inter*subjectivity, and can be neither defined nor accounted for save in terms

---

would seem to be confirmed by Gilson's evaluation (1952b: 141) of Boethius' rendering of Aristotle: ''La logique de Boèce est un commentaire de celle d'Aristote, où perce fréquemment le désir de l'interpréter selon la philosophie de Platon. Ce fait s'explique parce que Boèce suit de près un commentaire de Porphyre (J. Bidez), et il explique à son tour le pullulements des opinions contraires qui s'affronteront au XIIe siècle sur l'objet de la doctrine d'Aristote, car tous les professeurs commenteront le texte de Boèce, mais alors que les uns en retiendront ce qu'il avait gardé d'Aristote, les autres s'y attacheront au contraire à ce que son auteur y avait introduit de Platon.''

In any event, there is no question in Poinsot that the *secundum dici* involves, in principle, being according to its own exigencies for understanding, and not merely a question of being spoken of in an entirely contingent or dialectical fashion. It is precisely because the categories are ''l'écho de la réalité'' that Poinsot's contrast between *dici* and *esse* establishes in principle the ground of the categorial interconnections. Cf. Heidegger, 1927: p. 3, number 1, partially quoted in notes 118 and 175 below.

[115] *Ars Logica* (Reiser ed.), 590b48-591a5: Relationes ''transcendentales non sunt aliquid distinctum a re absoluta, sed vere sunt absolutae entitates; neque enim habent speciale praedicamentum, sed per omnia vagantur et sic ex sua transcendentia habent imbibi in ipsa re absoluta, non distingui.''

[116] E.g., Poinsot notes (*Ars Logica*, 594a43-b6) that St. Thomas ''docet in 1. dist. 2, q. 1. art. 5. ad 2., quod res est de transcendentalibus et ideo se habet communiter ad absoluta et relativa. Ibi enim sumit rem transcendentaliter, prout est communis ad entitatem et modum.'' (See also note 139 below, and note 27 in Appendix C above, p. 385.) Cahalan remarks (letter of 9 September 1975), ''to say that transcendental relations are relative but not relations seems to be precisely the kind of paradox that the imperfect abstraction of analogical concepts accounts for.'' Cf. Cahalan, ''Analogy and the Disrepute of Metaphysics,'' *The Thomist*, XXXIV (July, 1970), 387-422.

of what they themselves are not, namely, subjects or subjective determinations of being.

The question concerning the relative raised by Aristotle in seeking to clarify the divisions of his categorial scheme thus became, in the Latin West, the question of whether there ought to be admitted among the categories of mind-independent ways of being a category of external relation between subjects (hence *categorial* relation); or ought it to be said rather that relation in a pure form, i.e., as essentially toward another according to the way it *has* being, exists only thanks to the powers of sense perception and understanding?

According to many of the Latin Aristotelians, most notably, perhaps, William of Ockham in the fourteenth century and the nominalist movement after him,[117] in the order of mind-independent being as such, there are *only* absolute subjects with their individual determinations. Relativity in the precise sense of something wholly *essentially* relative arises among these subjects only as a result of our perceptions and attempts to explain things. This order of being—the order of being which does not depend for its existence on being cognized: the *mind-independent* order of being—reveals itself as relative according to the way it must be expressed in discourse; but apart from the work of perception and discourse, there is nothing of relative being in a way that extends beyond subjectivity. The relative, on this view, is divided between what Poinsot calls transcendental relations, which are not truly relations according to their way of being independently of the mind, and mental relations, which are truly relations but as such are in no way independent of the mind: there is a mode of being which is a relation according to the way it has being, but this mode is given existence only by the mind. Relation according to the way it has being belongs exclusively to the order of mind-dependent being.

For the tradition of Latin Aristotelianism represented by Poinsot, however, there are relations given according to the way they have being independently of our cognition as well as dependently upon it. Relation according to the way relation has being is both a category of mind-independent being in the strictest Aristotelian sense of category, with its instances called *categorial* relations, and something that is found existing sometimes entirely dependently upon the mind. On this view, the relative includes not only transcendental relations, which are mind-independent but not as relations, but also categorial relations, which are mind-independent in their very existence as relations; and finally mental or mind-dependent relations.

Relation according to the way relation has being thus provides the only ontological rationale in Aristotle's categorial scheme which embraces both the mind-independent and the mind-dependent orders of being. Not that mental relations can be said to belong to the *category* of relation—which would be a contradiction in terms—but that mental relations are relative according to the way they have being, just as are categorial relations:

---

[117] See Etienne Gilson, *History of Christian Philosophy in the Middle Ages*, 1955: 487-494, esp. note 17, p. 787. Also, by the same author, *La philosophie au moyen age*, 1952b: 638-686; *The Unity of Philosophical Experience*, 1937: 61-91.

> Any unreal object whatever conceived as being a subject or subjective modification of being is the mind-dependent being which is called *negation,* yet it *will not be a mind-dependent substance,* because substance itself is not conceived as a mind-dependent being patterned after some mind-independent being: rather, negations or non-beings are conceived on the pattern of substance and quantity.
>
> *But in the case of* relatives, not only is there indeed *some non-being conceived on the pattern of relation,* but also the very relative itself conceived, on the part of *the respect towards,* while it does not exist in the mind-independent order, it is conceived or formed on the pattern of a mind-independent relation, and so that which *is formed,* as well as the pattern on which it is formed [the template for its formation], is a relation: and for this reason there are in fact mind-dependent relations, but not mind-dependent substances [''Second Preamble,'' Article 2, 96/21-31 (=*581b47-582a16*)].

Relation in this sense, relation as *indifferent* to realization according to its proper being in the opposed orders of what is mind-independent and what is mind-dependent, is also called *ontological relation* in our translation of Poinsot's *Treatise,* but this, as remarked above [III.C.2.(b), pp. 463-465], is an *invented* term, i.e., having no medieval or renaissance counterpart in the national languages until *well after* the turn of the seventeenth century.

With this much background, we are in a position to grasp the conceptual architecture of Poinsot's *Treatise.* The difficulty and originality of Poinsot's work alike derive from his recognition that *the first concern* of anyone who would seek to explain signs, the universal means of communication, must be to pay heed ''to Aristotle's *problem of the unity of Being* [as that which is experientially first in human understanding] as over against the multiplicity of 'categories' applicable to things.''[118] The experience of signs and of the escape from the subjectivity of the here and now is as fundamental in its own way as is the experience of things in terms of the data which provide experimental justification for the scheme of the categories, as is clear from the fact (''Second Preamble,'' Article 1, 86/9-22 [=*577a9-28*]) that the derivation of the categories from experience is itself a function of the use we make of signs in developed discourse.

The sign, as the medium of communication, functions by *distinguishing connections* within experience, and so is not only presupposed to any system of categories, but is also the instrument of their establishment. The analysis of the sign, therefore, must be precisely *fundamental* to any *categorial ontology,* that is to say, it must explain how it is that signs so function as to make possible the eventual assimilation of experience to a categorial scheme of *whatever* kind (further in Deely, 1977a: 47-48).

The genius of Poinsot's *Treatise* was to see in the distinction between what is relative *secundum dici* and what is relative *secundum esse* the resources for explaining the ontological status of signs according to their peculiar indifference to the presence and absence, the being or non-being, of what they signify.

---

[118] Martin Heidegger, 1927: 3: ''. . . *er das von Aristoteles schon gestellte Problem der Einheit des Seins gegenüber der Mannigfaltigkeit der sachhaltigen 'Kategorien' aus der Hand gibt.*'' Fuller text in note 175 below. Cf. discussion in note 114 above.

Consider the question with which Poinsot opens his *Treatise*: Whether a sign is in the order of relation. This question is answered affirmatively in the very definition of the sign as that which makes present for cognition something other than itself, but not without ambiguity: for something can be in the order of relation either *transcendentally*—i.e., simply according to the way its being *must be expressed* in discourse (*secundum dici*); or *ontologically*—i.e., according to the way it *has* being (*secundum esse*). In which way does the sign pertain to the order of the relative? Hence when Poinsot comes to express precisely the import of Book I, Question 1, he does so in these terms. ''We are asking,'' he writes (117/18-23 [=*646a16-21*]), ''whether the formal rationale of a sign consists, primarily and essentially, in a relation *secundum esse* or in a relation *secundum dici*.''

By posing the question in these terms, Poinsot allows his inquiry the broadest possible scope. In the first place, these two ways exhaust the possibilities of anything's pertaining to the order of relation (''Second Preamble,'' Article 1). In the second place, by opposing ontological relation to transcendental relation, Poinsot has made room for stipulated signs which as such are mind-dependent, without thereby foreclosing the possibility of signs whose relation to what they signify is given independently of mind (Book I, Question 1, 117/28-118/18 [=*646b26-45*]). In short, he has posed the question in terms that enable him to bring together in the sign the opposed orders of mind-dependent and mind-independent being (Book I, Question 2, 151/9-21 [=*663a28-41*]) just as they are found together in our direct experience of the world (''First Preamble,'' Article 3, 66/47-51 [=*301b33-38*], 71/20-29 [=*304a6-14*], 75/1-16 [=*305b30-45*]).

Now, it does not take Poinsot long to resolve the pertinence of signs to the order of relation in favor of relation according to the way it *has* being. Signs, without exception, are constituted formally by ontological relations. But ontological relations, for Poinsot, are both categorial and mental. This puts him in a position to root his theory of the sign in mind-independent nature by arguing that some signs are as such physically related to what they signify (Book I, Question 2), and to show at the same time how initially stipulated or mind-dependent signs can become through custom assimilated to the world of what is natural (for a given community) and possessed in their turn of a relatively mind-independent significance (Book II, Questions 5 and 6, especially 283/9-22 [=*722a10-24*], 282/31-283/8 [=*721b27-722a9*]; Deely, 1978a; and cf. Sebeok, 1975b).

Thus, the distinction between what is relative *secundum esse* and what is so only *secundum dici* is the first and most fundamental analytical couplet of Poinsot's *Treatise*. Since, moreover, the relative *secundum esse* unites under one (ontological) rationale the distinct orders of mind-independent and mind-dependent being, and so includes implicitly (analytically) the second fundamental couplet of the *Treatise* (*ens reale/ens rationis*), it does not seem too much to say that the systematic contrast of these two terms determines the conceptual architecture of the *Treatise on Signs* as a whole: eleven hundred years of Latin philosophizing are summarized and rendered *aufgehoben* in this application.[119] Nor

[119] A. Krempel traces the origin of these two expressions in the Latin West all the way back to Boethius' sixth-century translation of and commentaries upon Aristotle's *Categories*. From that

does it seem too much to say that Poinsot's *Treatise* is the first successful attempt in any language to construe in a systematic way the intricate network of contrasts that oppose these notions and give them unrestricted scope. For between them, they divide the order of subjectivity taken in all its possible determinations (transcendental relation), from the order of intersubjectivity and public life (ontological relation) where truth and history are given among men. For Poinsot, successful communication, whenever it occurs, and whether it transpires between men and animals without human understanding, or between men and the physical world: wherever there is a "communing" between things, it occurs because and only because a pure relation—*a relation according to the way relation has being*—has arisen and serves as the medium of the communion.[120] Unlike the subjects brought into union by such a relationship, the relationship as such is an intersubjective reality: regardless of its subjective cause—mind or nature—its positive content remains unchanged. It extends the

---

time until the seventeenth century, Krempel finds, "le couple au nom si étrange préoccupait tous les scolastiques": *La doctrine de la relation chez St. Thomas* (Paris: J. Vrin, 1952), Chapitre XVIII, "Le relativum secundum dici et le relativum secundum esse," p. 394. This chapter in particular paradigmatically illustrates the strange character of Krempel's massive and remarkable volume as a whole: a most careful and exhaustive compilation of texts on the subject of relation drawn from the entire period of Latin schoolmen, combined with a flatly unsuccessful attempt to interpret the import of the compilation philosophically. Nowhere is the philosophical barrenness of this impeccable (and invaluable) scholarly study more clearly in evidence than in Krempel's conclusion concerning the secundum esse-secundum dici couplet. "Impossible," he writes (p. 394), "de trouver une traduction satisfaisante pour les deux termes." It is hardly to be wondered at, in light of this failure, that Krempel, when he comes to interpret Poinsot (p. 412), finds (or thinks he finds, for a whole nest of misconstructions in his work come together on this point) that "à ce moment la tradition est rompue." What has actually transpired is something quite different and of another order. At this moment, the latent possibilities of the tradition in the distinction in question are freed of long-standing confusions and rendered actual in their proper scope. It is not a matter of something *rompue*, but of something *aufgehoben*. And it must be said that in whatever respects his interpretation falls short, it was conceived in the effort to elaborate discursively a profoundly true intuition of the scope of the difficulty: "s'il y a des cas où l'on doit remonter à l'origine et à l'original, c'est bien ici" (Krempel, p. 397).

120 The following diagram, taken from Deely 1978b: 168-171, "situating semiotics in the context of communication phenomena," may be useful here:

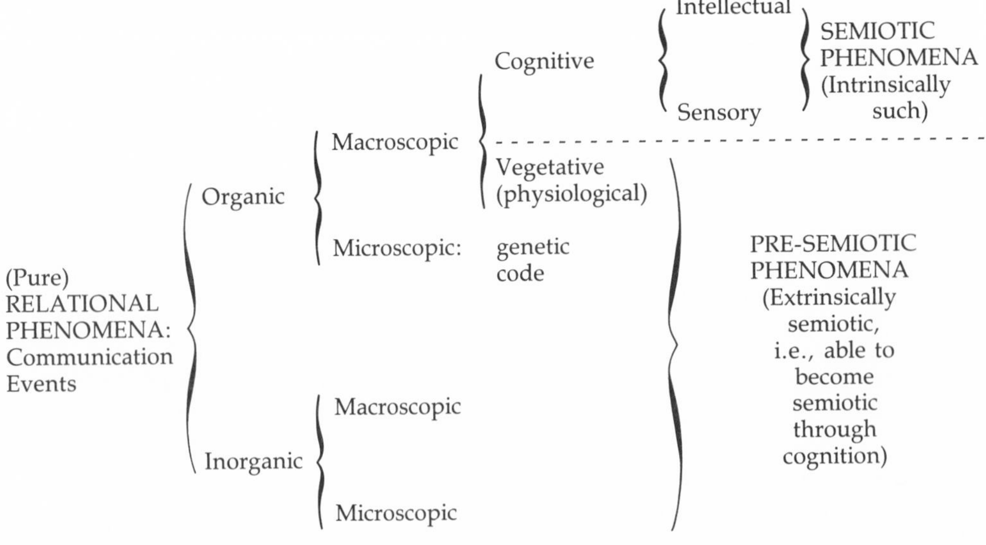

boundaries of existence over and beyond the boundaries of the subjective here and now, mediating (in the case of real existents) a transsubjective contact and union between otherwise isolated members of the material world. And because of the ontological indifference relation enjoys toward its subjective ground, this extension beyond subjectivity takes place sometimes along lines drawn by nature, sometimes along lines drawn by the customs of a community, and sometimes along lines creatively drawn by the free exercise of genius—a pattern which may in its turn become *naturalized* by customs to contribute to the historical achievement of humanity expressed in a privileged line of transmission, a *traditio* in the highest sense.

2. Other Terminology

All the terminology that plays an architectural role in Poinsot's *Treatise* is governed by the fundamental discovery in the order of relation of an ontological rationale which at once *divides* the intersubjective from the subjective (the distinction of ontological from transcendental relation, *secundum esse* from *secundum dici*) and *unites* within the intersubjective the opposed orders of being existing now independently of and now dependently upon human (or animal) awareness; for it is this discovery that enables Poinsot to explain how signs enable us to transcend the sensory here and now by reason of their indifference to the mind-independent existence or nonexistence of what they signify, itself a consequence of the functional equivalence in cognition of "real" or mind-independent and "unreal" or mind-dependent relations, which springs from the indifference of relation in its proper rationale to the subjective cause or ground whence it exercises existence. If this is well understood by the reader of the *Treatise*, the rest of Poinsot's terminology will soon begin to take care of itself. The process has been well described before (J. Maritain, 1955: viii): In reading Poinsot, "a beginner who refuses to be discouraged by initial difficulties will soon notice that things are no longer so hard, and by that time he has already learned a great deal."

Nonetheless, the reader of this difficult work today is likely to appreciate some assistance in mastering the complex of detail in the working out of this extended and slippery contrast as it is verified in differing ways through application to the variety of signs considered from various points of view. Accordingly, I will attempt in this section to provide a summary glimpse of what seem to me the ways in which Poinsot's two main divisions of signs depend for being rightly understood on being seen fundamentally in terms of the *secundum dici-secundum esse* contrast.

(a) The Subordinate Status of the Formale-Instrumentale Couplet under the Secundum Esse-Secundum Dici Contrast

From the standpoint of their mode of functioning in cognition and discourse, Poinsot says, signs may be divided according as their foundations or "vehicles" are first of all themselves objects of conscious awareness (objectified signs) or as they are not—and indeed cannot be—first of all objects of conscious awareness (unobjectified signs). Signs of the former sort he calls *instrumental* signs,

signs of the latter sort he calls *formal* signs. Now all signs are instrumental respecting their principal objects. Since as relations they draw cognition to the order of being which is naturally determined, signs are naturally determined instruments of their principal objects (Book I, Question 2, 151/9-18 [=*663a28-38*]):

> The rationale of a sign, since it does not consist in the rationale of an object absolutely, but of a substitution for another which is supposed to be the object or significate representable to a cognitive power, does not pertain to the order of the cognizable absolutely, but relatively and ministerially; and for this function the rationale of a sign takes on something of the entitative order, specifically, as it is a relation and as it draws the order of the cognizable to the order of the relative.

Thus signs are instrumental objects determined as such to their principal objects. The principal objects are transcendental relations absolutely determining mental acts to their extrinsic formal specification (see Book I, Question 4). Thus principal objects are the extrinsic specification of subjectivity, being but the relativity of the ''absolute'' act as a subject distinct from other transcendental relations similarly fixed in their subjectivity. But the sign instruments of objects are relations indifferently mind-independent or mind-dependent, i.e., ontological relations. Therefore the naturally determined sign, as instrumentally containing the object in relations indifferently real or unreal, frees the object from relation either to one's own subjectivity or to that of others, since mind-dependent relations can refer either to self or to others. Now both unobjectified formal signs within awareness and objectified instrumental signs are univocally ontological relations (Book II, Question 1). Therefore, it is clear that the *formale-instrumentale* couplet functions in Poinsot's thought in a manner subordinate to and derived from the contrast between the transcendentally (*secundum dici*) and the ontologically (*secundum esse*) relative.

But moreover, the very possibility of conceiving formal signs as subjective means of knowing able to present objects other than themselves without first having to be themselves fundamentally objectified, depends for its intelligibility on the fact that signs as such do not pertain to the conizable order directly, but ministerially (Book I, Question 2, 151/9-15 [=*663a28-34*]; Question 3, esp. 163/12-36 [=*669a34-b12*]). That is to say, the distinction between the subjective means of objectification intrinsic to a cognizing power as signs that need not themselves be cognized in order to function in awareness, and the objective means of communication extrinsic to a cognitive power as signs that must be themselves cognized in order to function in awareness, is a distinction based in its proper intelligibility on the fact that since the ontological relation constitutive of signifying respects the signified object directly and a cognitive power only indirectly, the *direct* relation of sign to cognitive power *can be* merely transcendental, i.e., can be entirely intrinsic to the cognitive power and the subjectivity of the knower, without the signifying as such (the formal rationale whereby the sign functions to present another than itself) being in any way affected (Book I, Question 3). It is owing to this fact that a concept, a ''quality'' and ''inhering accident,'' as such bound up with the subjectivity of the knower, can yet serve as such to found an ontological relation to an object out-

side of the subject, by which relation the external object is made present in cognition even though the foundation of that relation itself remains unobjectified in that same cognition and intrinsic to it. "A sign is formal or instrumental," i.e., intrinsic or extrinsic, unconscious or conscious for its immediate user, Poinsot says simply, "by reason of the fundament of the sign-relation itself, but not on the part of the relation" (Book I, Question 5, 202/19-22 [=*684b10-14*]). On the part of the relation itself, the sign is simply ontological; and so it is that Poinsot is able to reconcile (in the being proper to signs whereby they "draw the order of the cognizable to the order of the relative") the subjectivity of our means of knowing with the intersubjective character of our objects of knowledge, by showing that these subjective means do not interpose themselves between conscious awareness and being, provided we understand "being" as it includes mind-dependent as well as mind-independent patterns of actuality (*praedicamenta vera et ficta*) ("Order of the First Preamble," 44/2-7 [=*284b46-50*]), and provided we understand that both the signs that *need not* themselves be cognized and *cannot* be observed under any circumstances except in their effects on the sensible patterns in perception (formal signs) and the signs that are objects first of all (instrumental signs) can function as natural signs even when what they signify is itself unreal, by virtue of the principal object's character as transcendental relation of the subject founding ontological relations indifferently real or unreal—or, put the other way round, by virtue of the signs' foundations in a subject for the rationale of the relative indifferent in its positive content to the source of its exercise (that is, the rationale of the ontological, not of the transcendental, relative).[121]

It is only because all signs as such are ontologically relative that they are able to function in cognition and communication without of themselves blocking or interfering with the public character of objectivity as indifferent to the subjective rationales whence it derives existence—in part from the mind alone and in part from nature and mind simultaneously—in the order of exercise, and indifferent as well to the physical presence or absence of individual objects signified. It is this contention that makes room in Poinsot's theory for knowability as a mind-independent property of objects despite the fact that all objects as actually known depend in their being such on elements subjective to the knower (Book I, Question 2, 138/38-140/42 [=*657a38-658b10*]), in the same way that it makes room for mind-independent relations to enter as such into the structures of objectivity through formal and instrumental signs alike (e.g., Book I, Question 2, 140/15-43 [=*658a25-b10*]; Question 3, 160/45-161/23 [=*667b45-668a41*]; etc.).

(b) The Role of the Secundum Dici-Secundum Esse Couplet in Developing the Division of Signs into Natural, Stipulated, and Customary

To understand the influence of the *secundum dici-secundum esse* contrast over Poinsot's other main division of signs it is first necessary to get clear about Poinsot's understanding of the distinction between *ens reale* and *ens rationis*, for it

[121] For the case of instrumental signs, see (*inter alia*) the *Treatise on Signs*, Book I, Question 1, 126/1-22 (=*651a15-41*), and Book III, Question 4, 335/29-39 (=*747a41-b2*); and for the case of formal signs, Book I, Question 1, note 25 with references, pp. 125-126; Question 4, 186/35-187/5 (=*678a18-32*). See also "Second Preamble," Art. 2, etc.

is his application of this distinction as an architectural couplet subordinate to the *secundum dici-secundum esse* couplet that provides his principal way of explaining and justifying the division of signs into natural, stipulated, and customary.

The distinction between *ens reale* and *ens rationis,* just because it is almost universally familiar to philosophers, presents in many ways probable cause of misunderstanding among latter-day readers of Poinsot; for it is certain that Poinsot's understanding and use of this analytical couplet is by no means a commonly received one among contemporary philosophers. For example, the commonest translation of *ens reale* and *ens rationis* is perhaps "real being" and "being of reason," with the latter term often further identified in more or less vague ways as comprising mainly "second intentions." Quite apart from the objection that even a being of reason is something real in its own way, and so is united more fundamentally than it is opposed to real being (which is an objection not devoid of sophistry), it is certain that this translation is unworkable within the framework of Poinsot's doctrine, for according to that doctrine, animals other than men—other animals than the ones possessed of *reason* or human understanding—form *entia rationis.*[122] A deepened understanding on all counts is called for in point of "received interpretations" of these matters.

As explained in the very "First Preamble," and as key passages elsewhere illustrate, what is opposed in this couplet throughout is the order of being as it exists independently of being known (being as cut up by the *praedicamenta vera*) and being as it exists dependently upon being known (being as cut up according to *praedicamenta ficta*). The shortest expression I was able to devise that still seemed to express virtually the entire extent of this opposition was *mind-independent being* (sometimes "cognition-independent being") for *ens reale* and *mind-dependent being* (or "cognition-dependent being") for *ens rationis,* it being well understood that these shorthand expressions would sometimes be misleading if the long equivalent expressions were not substituted. For example, the concept or "formal sign" in Poinsot's theory is produced in and by an act of cognition, and so considered, it is certainly something mind-dependent, but it is not mind-dependent in the way that would constitute it an *ens rationis.* To be an *ens rationis,* a being must be something objectively cognized here and now (an actual object of direct awareness), even though it is something here and now nonexistent relative to what is physically *as well as* objectively given within the cognition, "inside" or "outside" the organism cognizing.

In short, *entia rationis* or mind-dependent beings are not mind-dependent in a *psychological* sense. Psychological attitudes and states, psychological properties and characteristics of any kind, are, in Poinsot's framework, as much a part of the order of *ens reale* and *relatio transcendentalis* as the physical dispositions and attributes of material bodies ("First Preamble," Article 1, 48/6-16 [=*285a25-36*]). Only the objective order, the order of what exists in awareness, harbors what Poinsot terms "mind-dependent being" (*ens rationis*).

Once this understanding of the term is secure, the reader is not surprised

---

[122] "Materially," in Poinsot's terms: see the *Treatise on Signs,* "First Preamble," Article 3, 66/47-68/34 (=*301b33-302b9*), and 73/17-74/4 (=*305a14-29*); and the last of the semiotic markers in the above edition of the *Treatise,* pp. 46-47.

that Poinsot finds mind-dependent beings (*entia rationis*) present wherever cognition organizes sensation within perceptual and conceptual wholes, and sees in their formation a process common to men and all higher animals alike. Thus, all perception involves a network of relations not entirely given as such in the order of being as it exists here and now in a physical way independent in its being of actually being cognized. The network as such derives its formally unified character from the mind, but it is not for this reason entirely structured in mind-dependent ways. It is in its structural elements a fusion and confusion of being (*ens reale*) and non-being (*ens rationis*).[123]

The peculiar work of human understanding, according to Poinsot, comes to light in the attempt to sort out and control in a critical way the mind-dependent and mind-independent elements of objectivity as they relate among themselves and to us as physical individuals. (What distinguishes the ''objective'' observer *engagé*, for example, is not the absence of subjective influences on the structures of reportable objectivity, but the limited *critical control* consciously and however imperfectly exercised over the presence of such influences.) Such limited critical access to the element of non-being in awareness is accounted for in Poinsot's theory in terms of the *stipulated element* in signs, which as stipulated introduces conscious deliberation into semiosis in a way expressly recognizable (''structured'') as not given independently of the individual mind. But any stipulation systematically adhered to in discourse, by the very repetition in which its use consists, generates a habit of usage or *custom* among those who frequently employ the term, and through this custom the stipulated sign becomes itself ''naturalized'' among its users in the form of habitual patterns whereby regular associations and connotations increment and alter the force of the sign across time as it becomes an element increasingly assimilated to an *Umwelt* or (culturated) life-world (*Lebenswelt*), through the observable actual patterns of behavior, i.e., as it becomes a *customary sign*. In this way, the order of mind-independent being becomes itself permeated and transformed by the regular influx of non-being into the habits and institutions of a people, as new patterns and possibilities are envisioned for and communicated to the materials of the physical world (cf. Book II, Question 6; Deely 1978a, 1980a). Mud huts become universities, observatories, and cathedrals; while cries and signals become explanations, hypotheses, and ''likely stories.'' Thus successful stipulation, though it arises formally in the order of non-being, soon takes the form of custom, and through signs made customary becomes transposed, as it were, into the order of being, where it is materially accessible (in behavior and perception) to animals without human understanding as well as to men (Book II, Question 6, 280/14-25 [=*720a39-b4*]). But the stipulation as such, or, more generally, *the element of non-being among signs formally distinguished and recognized as such in its opposition* to mind-independent being—this is found only where the true and the false come to be consciously played off and set in thematic contrast, that is to say, in the orbit of human understanding.

[123] Cf. Poinsot's discussion (1633: phil. nat. 1. p.) of the *primum cognitum* in Vol. II of Reiser's edition of the *Cursus Philosophicus*, Q. 1, Art. 2, 20a1-33b38, esp. 22a6-30 and 24a42-27a28. And Deely, 1975a: esp. 96-99.

With this, one begins to see the import and amplitude of the *reale-rationis* couplet for the *Treatise on Signs*, according to Poinsot's way of understanding the distinction. First of all, it is a couplet that applies to being in the order of objectivity as expressible in signs, not to the order of mere subjectivity of transcendental relations of acts to their objects. But more importantly, it is a distinction based on experience through explicit recognition of the difference in objects signified by natural signs of external sense respecting physical presence (*idem apud omnes*) and things known by stipulated and customary signs based ultimately on the former, as this difference relates to the order of physical existence.[124] Thus the order of *ens rationis* is distinguished by a thoroughgoing relativity in its contrast at any point with the order of *ens reale*. Whereas "being relative" is only one of the several ways in which mind-independent being can be known to exist, mind-dependent being cannot become consciously known to exist as such at all except as a condition relative to mind-independent being ("First Preamble," Article 3). And it need not become so known in any given case.

The identity in rationale of mind-dependent and mind-independent being in the order of the strictly relative is what enables Poinsot to account for the indifference of signs to the mind-independent being or non-being of what they signify: for whether the relation the sign consists in is mind-independent (as in the case of a concept whose object exists actually or aspectually in the order of mind-independent being as well as objectively) or entirely mind-dependent (as in the case of a concept whose object is given only objectively, i.e., only in the order of being existing here and now dependently upn cognition), its positive content and rationale of being (though not its cause of existence) is unaffected. Thus, the same concept which (as itself an *ens reale* and quality inhering in a subject) both guides the apprehensive tendency of the cognitive act and founds in its own right a relation in the order of mind-independent being to its object as long as that object exists ("Second Preamble," Article 2, 91/30-92/2 [=*579a37-b6*]), continues to guide the apprehensive tendency according to the same rationale and in exactly the same way (and so "founds" a relation only in the order of mind-dependent being) when that object no longer exists and so cannot terminate a mind-independent relation (Book I, Question 1, 124/42-127/6 [=*650b11-651b15*], text and notes).

The same remarks apply when the sign in question is itself also an object (an "instrumental" sign) existing independently of cognition, instead of a concept (a "formal" sign): it suffices that a foundation be given in that object whence *would result* (under appropriate physical conditions) a mind-independent relation, in order for that object perceived in terms of that foundation to function as a *natural* (or "naturalized") *sign* even when what it signifies no longer exists (or never did exist as such) in nature (see references in note 121 above, p. 481). As Poinsot summarily puts it (126/3-4 [=*651a18-19*]), "it suffices to be virtually a sign in order to actually signify," for the vitality of the mind can supply for the deficiency of a fundament in respect of the physical conditions required for categorial relation, by *itself alone* causing the exercise of relativity according

[124] On this last point, see *Treatise on Signs*, "First Preamble," Article 1, 51/8-28 (=*286b23-44*).

to the very rationale whence *would* result from the foundation a mind-independent exercise of relativity given physical conditions appropriately other than those prevailing here and now.

With this scheme, Poinsot draws not only logical discourse under the rubric of *ens rationis*, as in the common understanding of this traditional term, but also society and culture (see Book I, Question 2, 141/12-142/13 [=*658b30-659a39*]; "First Preamble," Article 2, 60/15-25 [=*291b9-21*]), inasmuch as what is *formally* constitutive of them (namely, a mind-dependent and objective pattern) pertains first of all to the order of non-being from the point of view of what is given independently of human understanding. Yet, at the same time, by showing how this order of non-being itself and the *praedicamenta ficta* penetrate and structure in time the order of *ens reale* in the guise of custom and habit and *social institutions* generally, Poinsot lays bare the ground of Dasein as a *seinsgeschichtliches Wesen*, that is, of "the dependence in which the human spirit finds itself regarding age-old traditions, cultural environment, and, in general, the weight of history."[125]

(c) The Couplets in Book III of the Treatise on Signs

Book III of Poinsot's *Treatise* introduces three further analytical couplets, the distinction between knowledge of a present object and knowledge of an absent object (what Poinsot calls "intuitive" and "abstractive" cognition), the distinction between direct and reflexive concepts, and the distinction between concepts whose objects do not function de facto in a given case as instrumental signs (so-called "ultimate" or "final" concepts) and concepts whose objects as such are instrumental signs (so-called "nonultimate" or "intermediate" concepts). But there is this great difference between this book and the preceding two: whereas the definition of Book I and the divisions of Book II are considered by Poinsot to be essential to signs as such, the couplets of Book III do not of themselves express essential differences in signs as signs, and moreover they concern accidental conditions pertaining principally to the order of formal signs. Nonetheless, the issues faced in Book III have been implicit throughout the discussions of the previous two Books, which are as it were put to the test of experience in Book III.

The difference between knowing a present object (intuition) and an absent one (abstraction), Poinsot argues (Book III, Questions 1 and 2), is not of itself an essential difference in cognitions, since it is *the same* object made present by the concept in both cases; and yet it is an *intrinsic* difference that really modifies the cognition. What does this mean? It means, in the simplest terms, that mind-independent or "physical" things *as such* are objectified aspectually, according to Poinsot, when they are within range of our sensory powers and we advert to them in our perception. Thus, the discussion of intuitive and abstractive cognition is in many respects a spelling out in detail of the assertion that mind-independent being, and not only mind-dependent being, belongs as such to the objective order. But it is also in this discussion that Poinsot un-

---

[125] "*. . . la dépendence dans laquelle se trouve l'esprit humain à l'égard des traditions séculaires, du milieu culturel, et, généralement parlant, du poids de l'histoire*" (Jacques Maritain, 1966b: 121).

folds the meaning, for him, of the ancient and commonly accepted maxim that 'there is nothing in the understanding that is not first in the senses' (see also the discussion in the "Second Preamble," p. 67 note 3 above). Knowledge in presence, or intuitive knowledge, is precisely knowledge of something given in sensation here and now. Such cognition, Poinsot argues, is ineluctably tied to the order of mind-independent being in an objective and non-inferential way, which provides the base upon which all "abstractive" cognition—all knowledge, that is, which transcends the sensory immediate in what it attains—must ultimately rest.

This doctrine sets Poinsot apart in the scholastic world from Ockham and Suarez, who did not tie the objective element in intuitive knowledge to the order of what has being independently of cognition. It also clearly follows from Poinsot's doctrine that all concepts are signs and all signs are relations: for all relations are intrinsically modified by their term (presence and absence of the term makes the difference between a mind-independent and a mind-dependent relation: whereas the sameness of the object in each case is fixed by the transcendental relation of acts to that determinate principal object). Thus, just as the ontological status of signs as relations explains the indifference of discourse to being and nonbeing, so it explains why cognition is intrinsically and mind-independently—though not essentially—modified by the physical presence or absence of its objects, that is, modified from within in a way that does not depend on the truth of our judgment as to what the object physically present through sensation is in itself, though it does depend on our conscious attention to the physically present object (see especially Book III, Question 1, 294/14-49 [=*726b14-727a6*]).

Here again it is the *secundum esse-secundum dici* contrast that provides the controlling framework, but now the doctrine of signs it controls is being applied to the origins of our knowledge in experience and external sense. The same doctrine of experience as rooted willy-nilly in mind-independent being (through the sensory core of perception) that follows from Poinsot's definition of the difference between objectification (which is as such transcendentally relative) and signification (which is as such ontologically relative) sets him in opposition not only to Suarez and Ockham before him, but also to the common doctrine that will come after him in the writings of Hobbes, Locke, Berkeley, Hume, Descartes, Leibniz, and Kant, as we shall examine in Section IV below. A wholly different doctrine of sense and of the relation of understanding to experience thus comes to light as soon as Poinsot applies his theory of the sign as an ontological relation to the foundations of experience in sensory change. It is not too much to say that Poinsot's discussion of intuitive and abstractive cognition, which occupies well over half of Book III, traces back to its experimental ground the great medieval controversies over particulars and universals that were carried on heretofore on principally metaphysical grounds.[126]

---

[126] "On a longtemps parlé de la philosophie médiévale comme si elle avait porté presque entière sur le problème des universaux," writes Gilson (1952b: 141-142). "En fait, le problème des universaux est un champ de bataille sur lequel les adversaires n'engageaient le combat que munis déjà de toutes leurs armes. Des métaphysiques adverses ont mesuré leurs forces en concourant à qui saurait mieux le résoudre, mais elles ne sont pas nées des solutions qu'elles en proposaient." (See also Gilson, 1955: 96). With Poinsot, this whole situation is changed, "stood on its head."

From this point of view Poinsot's treatment of the difference between intuitive and abstractive awareness can be regarded as subordinate only to the secundum esse/secundum dici-ens reale/ens rationis distinctions as a key to his semiotic, for it is here that he applies his doctrine to the explanation of human experience in its most concrete form—to wit, as here and now circumscribed by physically constraining and objectively stimulating objects experienced as such apprehensively. Particularly in Question 1 of this third Book, Poinsot is turning over new ground in his treatment of previous tradition. Here, external sensation is viewed not only as originative of human knowledge, but as *constantly terminative* of it in the "secondness" of physical interaction. Thus, the senses are treated—rather than as a distinct level of apprehension (the strictly traditional perspective, largely resumed by Poinsot in Question 2 of Book III)—as a modifying aspect of understanding itself whereby the intellectual and thoroughly semiotic superstructure of understanding is tied by real relations to the surrounding bodies it interprets objectively in the building up of experience (*Umwelt* alone in the case of *animalia bruta, Lebenswelt* in the case of the *animalia rationalia*).

Hence it is not the objects as such of external sense which determine experiential knowing, still less some imagined mind-independence of the thoroughly relative qualities of sense whereby these objects are manifested (despite the slip of 310/33-35 [*734b28-31*]: see the Second Preamble, Article 1, note 16 [p. 86] with references), but the fact that the act of external sensation exists through and consists in real relations to its object (its *terminus cognoscitivus qua talis,* let us say) as physically present interactively here and now; so that what Poinsot calls intuitive awareness is achieved at the level of understanding only when and insofar as the act of understanding finds its object accidentally modified from within the very act of awareness by real relation to objective elements given as coexisting with the awareness itself as anchoring it to an existent order of things which, while known aspectually, are also independent of the knowing in the intuitive elements constituting that knowing as here and now circumscribed or modified environmentally in objective but physical ways.

This doctrine of Book III, which is established in the perspective of Poinsot's doctrine of signs in Question 1 and refined in more traditional ways in Question 2 (a Question which directly addresses what were to become for Hume the final grounds of skepticism—but with opposite results for Poinsot owing to the more sophisticated treatment of ideas required by the perspective of semiotic), carries over directly into Poinsot's treatment of our awareness of interior cognitive states in Question 3 of Book III.

The distinction between direct and reflexive concepts has a long history of discussion, but in Poinsot's framework it derives from the central fact that concepts as formal signs make objects present without themselves having been objectified. This at once raises the question of how we ever come to know of concepts' existence in the first place? From their sensible effects—the presence of objects in perception[127]—Poinsot answers, we can come to know them reflex-

[127] In phil. nat. 4. p., 1635 (Reiser ed., vol. III, 185a41-45), Poinsot cryptically writes: "haec unio obiectiva non debet reputari intelligibilis [i.e., 178b13-14: ponitur "in potentia ut res cognitae . . ."], sed maxime ad intelligendum conducens, et ex ipsis effectibus manifeste colligitur debere eam poni."

ively and connotatively (analogously) by construing them on the pattern of what of being is given directly in experience. Thus the distinction between direct and reflexive concepts too appears in Poinsot's *Treatise* in a way directly tied to the doctrine of signs as ontologically relative, since, as we have seen, it was this doctrine that gave in the first place the notion of the pure or formal sign a grounding in principle. Poinsot is to some extent in agreement with Locke: "The Understanding, like the Eye, whilst it makes us see and perceive all other Things, takes no notice of it self; and it requires Art and Pains to set it at a distance, and make it its own Object."[128] The former point Poinsot explains by the formal sign (unlike Locke, who remarks it without explanation). The latter requirement he meets by reflexive concepts.

Poinsot's position that we have no *intuitive* awareness of our interior cognitive states save analogously to the sensory objects made present in direct experience of the environment merits being singled out for comment. The results of experimental psychology in the last hundred years have tended to reject as scientifically unreliable data arrived at by the method of introspection. The doctrine of formal signs explains precisely why data arrived at in this fashion lack the precision of what is understood in external sensation, as "methodological behaviorism" has cogently argued, while at the same time avoiding the *petitio principii* of substantive behaviorism which uses the observer to explain the observer away. I reflect on the table or person as known and ponder it in absence only on the analogy of the table or person as experienced intuitively as the secondness of experience modifies thirdness and grounds its hypotheses 'inductively' (*descensive*).

This brings Poinsot to the last major question he treats of (Book III, Question 3), namely, the distinction between what were then called "ultimate" and "non-ultimate" concepts, a distinction in the order of formal signs parallelling the contemporary discussion in the order of instrumental signs of "language" and "metalanguage". Thus, Poinsot brings his *Treatise* to a close (Book III, Question 4) with a discussion of our experience at the level of linguistic interchange of the difference between signs as such and objects, or, perhaps better, between objects given in sensation which are experienced as signs and other such objects experienced as not yet signifying or as not signifying in one or another way for us what they are experienced as signifying for others apprehending them here and now. The controlling point in this discussion appears at 335/29 (=*747a41*), where Poinsot shows why even a concept which has as its object a formally mind-dependent non-being nonetheless signifies that object in a naturally determined way. He has in mind here a controversy developed among the Latins at least since the time of Pierre d'Ailly (1350-1420). D'Ailly argued, in his *Treatise on Concepts* (1372: pars. 16-20), that "the same mental term improperly so called ["a concept of an utterance, or of an inscription synonymous with such an utterance" (par. 16), a "non-ultimate" concept or "conceptus vocis significativae" in Poinsot's vocabulary] is significative naturally and by convention" (par. 17), because it signifies one and the same thing "both naturally, properly and adequately, and by convention ultimately inadequately" (par. 20).

---

[128] John Locke, *An Essay concerning Human Understanding*, ed. P. H. Nidditch (Oxford: Clarendon Press, 1975), "Introduction," par. 1, p. 43/4-7.

It is clear thus that notwithstanding the shift in Book III to ''accidental'' differences among signs, the essential notions of Books I and II derived directly from the elements of the *secundum dici-secundum esse* contrast (especially as underlying the notion of ''formal'' signs) continue at play, and do so under the governance of that relative ground. This suffices to demonstrate the philosophical unity underlying the artistic unity Poinsot creates in his selection for Book III of traditional but current (in his milieu) and long-standing controversies to be resolved on the basis of a right understanding of the ontological status proper to signs.

For present concerns this suffices, though it by no means explores fully the connection of Book III to the rest of the *Treatise*. To fully explain this connection would be to show how the concerns of the *Treatise on Signs* remain subordinated, as they do, even in their independence, to the larger concerns of the *Cursus Philosophicus* as a whole—a project which goes well beyond the compass of the present work, but which is anticipated here by our inclusion of Appendices B and C. Suffice it to say that in this respect the *Treatise* forever bears the mark of its origin as a part—albeit the privileged and most vital part—of a vast ontological synthesis that ambitioned to know the world in its proper possibilities, and as it includes the power of human understanding.

But Poinsot's semiotic reduction of Aristotle's interpretive list of the traditional ten categories of mind-independent being to the two experiential categories of transcendental and categorial relation has important consequences for any future ontological synthesis, consequences for which Poinsot was content to lay the foundations, as one link in a work belonging to all the generations. After a long gestation, the actual work of new construction, of refashioning a synthesis as superior to idealism (which in Poinsot's day had only begun to establish itself as the peculiar modern development) as it must also be to the ancient realism of the *Cursus* proper (and as Poinsot clearly indicated in the sixth paragraph opening his *Treatise on Signs*), seems to be finally underway—with what results, as Saussure said, as shall have to be seen.

IV.

Situating Semiotic

Hume (1776: 4) remarked of his *Treatise of Human Nature* that "it fell dead-born from the press." The same could be said of Poinsot's *Treatise on Signs*, with even greater justification, in view of the subsequent history of the respective works. Not until 1938, a full 306 years after its first publication, did any leading ideas from Poinsot's semiotic surface in the national-language traditions of modern times. In that year, roughly simultaneously in French and in an English version in the *Journal of the Warburg Institute* (1937-1938), Jacques Maritain sketched out under the title of "Sign and Symbol" the project for "a treatise on the sign and on the symbol" such as he hoped "may some day be written." Yet even that remarkable essay, taking over its definitions and preliminary distinctions entirely from Poinsot, and adding an Appendix of Latin extracts from Poinsot's work, remained unclear about the foundations of semiotic (the doctrine of signs) in the account of relative being.[129]

---

[129] This first and most fundamental point about Poinsot's doctrine Maritain treats in a single sentence (1943: 192). After remarking that "each sign is constituted as such by the typical relationship of notification of another," he states: "Taken precisely as such, this relationship does not belong to the class of transcendental relationships (*relatio secundum dici*), but to that of relationship as a special entity (*relatio secundum esse*)," whereupon he cites in his Notes (number 2, p. 268) from Book I, Question 1, of our *Treatise*. "And in the case of the natural sign," he continues, it is a *real* relationship," concluding: "This realist idea of the natural sign definitively rests upon a metaphysics for which intelligibility is consubstantial with being (*ens et verum convertuntur*)." How closely Maritain is taking his lead from Poinsot in this area appears from Maritain's series of textual footnotes to his essay, which notes follow in general sequence Poinsot's order of exposition in his 1632 and 1667 discussions of signifying (i.e., the *tractatus de signis*, esp. Qq. XXI and XXII, from the *Cursus Philosophicus*—notes 1-8, pp. 268-273—and the *de sacramentis*, esp. disputatio 22, from the *Cursus Theologicus*—notes 10-16, pp. 273-276).

The other fundamental point about Poinsot's doctrine of signs, namely, that it constitutes a new beginning for the whole of philosophy (see Section I.C. above), is implicated by Maritain's opening sentences (p. 191). "The sign," he says, "is in the human world a universal

This situation makes it difficult to situate historically Poinsot's semiotic, owing both to the originality of the doctrine (a difficulty we may expect to diminish largely in proportion as a study of renaissance philosophy in its actual sources proceeds to replace the prejudices and myths of modern "histories" of philosophy),[130] and to the absence until recently of any direct influences. To overcome the difficulty, at least partly, I have settled on the following strategy, which presupposes only an understanding of the basics of Poinsot's doctrine of signs in its own terms, i.e., the Text of 1632.

Readers of the *Treatise* know that its doctrine presupposes that there are in the world relations among individuals, which relations obtain independently of sensation, perception, or conception. If this proposition be denied, the way to Poinsot's account of signs—or rather, Poinsot would argue, to *any* finally coherent account of signs (see Book I, Question 1, 117/28-118/8 [=*646b26-35*])—is closed.

Now, though Poinsot's doctrine proper transcends its sources (the "influences": see Delgado, 1972), and has no immediate successors, this proposition about external relations it presupposes is both simple (hence comparatively easy to identify in the views of a philosopher, however complex otherwise) and expressive of a position commonly accepted or rejected by all the major figures throughout the medieval, renaissance, and modern periods alike. Hence this proposition can be used *heuristically*, as it were, as a vehicle for situating Poinsot *historically* by the terms of the central *doctrinal presupposition*, as it were, of his account of signs. The entire section to follow, therefore, is structured around this strategic theoretical proposition, set off by the foil of a preliminary *excursus* to contrast the twilight of modern thought in our own time with its dawning in the time of Poinsot.

---

instrument, just as is movement in the physical world." That seems like an innocent enough, almost passing remark, unless one realizes that, in the tradition of philosophical analysis of nature Maritain considered his own, motion in the physical world is the first and most universal feature of being and element of experience, from the ontological analysis of which Natural Philosophy ("physics" in the Aristotelian sense) takes its origin (cf. Ashley, 1973). Thus, to say that the sign is to the human world what motion is to the world of nature, is to say that it is the *key* to the philosophical understanding of the world of human experience in what is proper to it (*animal rationale* as *Dasein*), as it *transcends* (but all the while including *formaliter eminenter*: a *Lebenswelt* is an *Umwelt* first of all) the physical order in *its* own way of being.

[130] This situation, already mentioned in the opening Section of this essay (I.A. above), may be appropriately referred to again here. The Aristotelian tradition exhibited in the writings of Aquinas and others of the High Middle Ages, "though exposed to attacks and subject to transformation, continued strongly and vigorously to the end of the sixteenth century and even later" (Kristeller, 1961a: 33-34). Throughout this period, in contrast to the standard modern presentations, and "in contrast to the humanists and to the Platonists" of renaissance times, "the Aristotelians represent the solid professional tradition" (Kristeller, 1961c: 134). Failure to appreciate this fact, Kristeller suggests (1961a: 34), is owing to a simple triumph of fashion over the hard work necessary to master the sources! By and large, he observes, "historians of thought have been sympathetic to the opponents of Aristotelianism in the Renaissance, whereas most of the defenders of medieval philosophy have limited their efforts to its earlier phases before the end of the thirteenth century, and have sacrificed the late scholastics to the critique of their contemporary and modern adversaries" (1961a: 34; see also 1961b: 114-115). Whatever its causes, we have a situation here that does not do credit to the capacities of modern scholarship, a situation which it may be hoped the present work, opening as it does a new perspective on the late Latin stages of medieval and renaissance times, will help to change in the direction of study of the sources, to be sure, but more than that, of far more general perception of the *rationale* required of source materials as a mode of presentation and of advancing in philosophy.

In the English-speaking world, no name is more closely associated with the theory of signs than the name of Charles S. Peirce (1839-1914), and for the best of reasons, since he was the first philosopher who sought not only to work out the fundamental principles of a doctrine of signs, as did Poinsot, but also to work out in detail the applications and implications of these principles for the entire range of philosophical thought—a project Poinsot glimpsed but never attempted, confining himself strictly to the establishment of a sound foundation in relation to past tradition, leaving future philosophy to care for itself. Thus Peirce, though second to Poinsot as the first systematizer of semiotic foundations,[131] was nonetheless the first to make of the vision of semiotic suggested by Locke a beacon and guideline for actually developing a new direction and general path for future philosophizing (c.1906: 5.488):

> I am, as far as I know, a pioneer, or rather, a backwoodsman, in the work of clearing and opening up what I call *semiotic*, that is, the doctrine of the essential nature and fundamental varieties of possible semiosis [or signifying]; and I find the field too vast, the labor too great, for a first-comer.[132]

Beginning with his "New List of Categories" in 1867, and continuing until his death in 1914, semiotic provided the underlying thrust and unity for the whole of Peirce's philosophy, something which came to be realized only gradually by later students of his thought (coming to it, as they generally did, from some pre-established perspective—such as realism, idealism, pragmatism, etc.), and which has the effect of relegating all of the earlier publications concerning Peirce—including notably the *Collected Papers*—to the status of provisional enterprises (cf. esp. Fisch, Ketner, and Kloesel 1979; Ransdell 1984).

Indeed, even in the "New List of Categories" as originally drafted, it is fair to say that Peirce labored overly under the influence of Kant as Master of

---

[131] As late as 1974 (p. 220), Sebeok could still consider that Peirce "was heir to the entire tradition of philosophical analysis of signs." Considering that Sebeok's knowledge—as Steiner observed at the time (1975: vii)—"of the whole range of current language studies may well be unrivalled," few remarks would better illustrate the oblivion into which Poinsot's seventeenth century work on signs fell. Poinsot is a classic example, as I have argued elsewhere (Deely 1983: 115 ff.), of how writing the history of semiotic "must inevitably take the form also of a *rewriting* of the entire history of ideas and of philosophy," and of how we find in the course of this writing "that figures known secondarily or not at all (quite forgotten) in the currently established histories"—figures neglected "almost *because of* their importance for a discipline and doctrinal point of view whose time had not yet come"—"must be reckoned as primary sources and pioneers of the first importance for the history of semiotic."

[132] "Like Aristotle," writes T. A. Goudge, *The Thought of C. S. Peirce* (Toronto: University of Toronto Press, 1950), p. 137, Peirce "saw that symbols are the medium through which the rationality in the universe must be expressed and communicated." The facts making this so "prior to Peirce's day," Goudge hazards, "had never been systematically investigated," and Peirce "was thus forced to become the founder of a new discipline."

Charles Morris, in his book, *Signs, Language, and Behavior* (New York: George Braziller, 1955), p. 287, states flatly that "Peirce was the heir of the whole historical philosophical analysis of signs."

"Many thinkers—most notably C. S. Peirce—have supposed," writes William P. Alston in the article, "Sign and Symbol," for Edwards' *Encyclopedia of Philosophy* (New York: Free Press, 1967), Vol. 7, p. 438, that all the different kinds of signs "are species of a single genus, for which the term 'sign' can be employed."

Writing in the same volume of the *Encyclopedia* on "Semantics, History of," p. 395, Norman Kretzman asserts that Peirce "went much further than anyone before him had tried to go toward the development of a completely general theory of signs."

the Moderns—that is to say, between the horns of the dilemma set by the (false) dichotomy of the realism vs. idealism controversy, a controversy which semiotic in principle begins by transcending (see Poinsot 1632: 117/28ff. [=*646b26-45*]; Deely 1977a, 1982; Williams 1985 throughout). This I suggest is why Peirce is so hard to classify in realist-idealist terms, and why he had such a time of it classifying himself. Assuming naturally the terms of the controversy as it had developed over the course of modern thought, he only gradually came to critical terms with the fact that semiotic as such is a form neither of realism nor idealism, but beyond both.

As a disciple of Kant in early life, Peirce labored at the impossible task of establishing the complete autonomy of the ideal/mental from what is individually existent in nature. In late life, he concluded that this erroneous quest had vitiated modern philosophy (1903a: 1.19-21). Significant of this evolution of his thought is the fact that in Peirce's later philosophy his supreme category of Thirdness changed from representation in 1867 to triadic relation—which is common to both representations and to laws existent in nature (c.1899: 1.565).

By his Lowell Lectures of 1903, and even already in his c.1890 "Guess at the Riddle," it is clear that Peirce is well on the way to taking his categories of semiosis properly in hand, and is marking out a course of future development for philosophy (as semiotic) that is nothing less than a new age, as different in its characteristics as is the realism of Greek and Latin times from the idealism of modern times in the national languages, especially German, French, and English.

In Peirce's "Minute Logic" (c.1902: 1.204-272) we have a lengthy analysis of what he calls "ideal" or "final" causality. He assimilates these two terms as descriptions of the same general type of causality (ibid.: 1.211, 227). But, in successive analyses (ibid.: 1.211, 214, 227, 231; and similarly in 1903a: 1.26), it emerges that *causality by ideas* constitutes the more general form of this sort of explanation, inasmuch as final causality, being concerned with mind, purpose, or quasi-purpose, is restricted to psychology and biology (c.1902: 1.269), while ideal causality in its general type requires as such neither purpose (1.211) nor mind or soul (1.216).

Close examination of Peirce's texts on "ideal" causality reveals it to be what is in Poinsot's text extrinsic formal causality, particularly that extrinsic formal causality peculiar to real relations (*Treatise on Signs*, Second Preamble, esp. Article 2; Book I, Question 4; and—particularly—Appendix C). Now philosophy of science, so dear to Peirce (c.1897: 1.7), has a great stake in the difference between extrinsic formal causality and final causality. Only substantial natures, in the perspective of Aristotelian physics, can have *natural* final causes. But, as Peirce so well pointed out (c.1896: 1.493), our science for a long time has been centrally concerned with natural phenomena lacking substantial unity, such phenomena as waves, foci of light, etc. Phenomena of this sort, indeed, are typical of the concerns of modern physics, in sharp contrast to the ancient or Aristotelian and scholastic "physics", and admit of explanation of terms of extrinsic formal causality, but they cannot be explained by *natural final causality* because the "subjects" or infrastructure of such phenomena are not substances as such. Since a substance alone has a *nature* it alone can relate to some things as favorable and to some as unfavorable to the natural unity in which it consists. Hence

substance alone is subject to *natural* final causality. Artifacts are subject to a kind of final causality, to be sure, but this ''final causality'' is not only extrinsic but precisely mind-dependent and *not part of nature* in its prior being.

What Peirce calls ''ideal'' causality gives a ''general character'' to the effect of the efficient cause (c.1902: 1.211 and 1903a: 1.26). Moreover, the ideal cause is the ''potential regularity'' required by the efficient cause (ibid.: 1.213). Hence Peirce's ''ideal cause'' corresponds to Poinsot's late scholastic notion of ''objective'' or ''extrinsic formal'' causality.

Now Peirce identifies this ideal causality with his category of Thirdness, the central element of his semiotic (ibid.: 1.26). Thirdness consists of triadic relations (c.1899: 1.565). In these triadic relations the foundations specify the several relations in different ways, so that one relation is specified, e.g., as ''lover of'' and another as ''loved by'' (1897: 3.466). Hence Peirce's ''ideal'' causality functions in his semiotic as do Poinsot's foundations of sign relations, to wit, as their extrinsic formal cause.

So Peirce's semiotic, similarly to that of Poinsot (Book I, Question 3 above, pp. 153ff.), rests on the triadic specification of relations. Thanks to their specification, triadic relations have a certain generality (c.1902: 2.92; 1903b: 1.26). Signs constitute one general class of triadic relations, and the laws of nature constitute the other general class (c.1896: 1.480). Signs themselves are either genuine or degenerate. Genuine signs concern existential relations between interacting bodies, and need an interpretant to be fully specified as signs (c.1902: 2.92). For the genuine triadic sign relation is a mind-dependent similarity relation[133] between the object of the existential relation and the existential relation itself as object for the interpretant (1904: 8.332). For example, words need an interpretant to be fully specified as signs. Triadic sign relations degenerate in the first degree concern existential relations between interacting bodies, but require no interpretant to make them fully specified as signs; a rap on the door means a visitor, with no explanation needed. Triadic sign relations degenerate in the second degree concern mind-dependent relations specified by the intrinsic possibility of the objects with which they are concerned because these relations cannot vary between truth and falsity whatever any group of single men may think: for example, mathematics, logic, ethics, esthetics, psychology, and poetry (1903b: 5.125; 1908: 6.455; c.1909: 6.328).

---

[133] The expression ''mind-dependent relation,'' it will be remembered, is our rendering of the Latin ''relatio rationis,'' which has previously been rendered generally ''relation of reason,'' as discussed above in this Afterword (text and note 107). Since this expression, with its correlate ''mind-independent,'' is not typical of the Peirce literature, some textual justification for use of the expression in the context even of this passing exposition is called for. The following quote from ''A Guess at the Riddle'' (c.1890: 1.365) may suffice here: ''. . . besides genuine Secondness, there is a degenerate sort which does not exist as such, but is only so conceived. The medieval logicians (following a hint of Aristotle) distinguished between real relations and relations of reason. A real relation subsists in virtue of a fact which would be totally impossible were either of the related objects destroyed; while a relation of reason subsists in virtue of two facts, one only of which would disappear on the annihilation of either of the relates. . . . This brings us to consider a[nother] sort of degenerate Secondness that does not fulfill the definition of a relation of reason. Identity is the relation that everything bears to itself: Lucullus dines with Lucullus. . . . But the relations of reason and these self-relations are alike in this, that they arise from the mind setting one part of a notion into relation to another.'' (For Poinsot, of course, what Peirce here terms ''self-relations'' were a paradigm of *relatio rationis*.)

The second class of triadic relations concerns the laws of nature. All laws of nature are genuine triadic relations (c.1896: 1.480). They concern existential relations as specified by their foundations. Laws of nature are of two kinds. The specifying foundations of some laws are such subjects of existential relations as remain intact in an identical existent individual despite interactions with environment. These individuals are substances (c.1896: 1.461, 488, 493). Other laws of nature concern existential relations similarly specified from different substantial subjects: for example, the existential relations involved in a wave or a focus of light do not get specified from any single substantial particle.

Peirce's semiotic is built around his system of categories. Triadic relations comprising signs and laws of nature constitute Peirce's category of Thirdness (c.1896: 1.480). Existential relations and mind-dependent relations comprise his category of Secondness—the existential ones being genuine, and mind-dependent ones being degenerate Secondness (c. 1890: 1.365). The merely intrinsically possible objects such as those of mathematics and poetry comprise the category of Firstness (1908: 6.455).

Truth revealed by any signs degenerate in the second degree—such as truths of mathematics, logic, ethics, esthetics, and psychology—derive ultimately from existential relations. For sciences based on signs of this type derive from instincts honed by evolution in the existential relations involved in eating and procreation (1878: 6.418; 1898: 5.586; 1903a: 5.591; c.1910: 6.491).

Therefore Peirce's semiotic concerns specification of triadic relations. For any triadic relation "*consists* in the fact that future facts of Secondness will take on a determinate general character" (1903: 1.26, Peirce's own emphasis). Sign relations, one great genus of triadic relations, derive their specification from their *representamens*. For the representamen of a sign relation is its *subject* which, because it is its subject, has the *power* to specify innumerable interpreting thoughts to that same object (1903a: 1.540-542; c.1902: 2.274-276). Triadic relations of the other great genus are the laws of nature. They possess only the conditional necessity of a *habit* (c.1890: 1.409-411). "Habits are understood to apply to man, animal, plant, crystallizable chemical substance or to anything else" (c.1902: 5.538). Habits account for conformity to the laws of nature—i.e., habits specify the permanent relations observed, for example, in the laws of mass, momentum, and energy (ibid.: 1.409, 1.415), within the framework of which conformity most events in nature occur by chance (1868: 5.342; c.1890: 1.406; 1901: 8.146).

Peirce's semiotic of triadic relations as specified, thus, strikingly resembles the semiotic of Poinsot. In Poinsot, the identity of specification/meaning between the mind-dependent and existential relation is the necessary core of a doctrine of signs, as we have seen. Moreover, both relations derive specification from the foundation of the categorial or "real" relation, which foundation Poinsot calls the transcendental relation specifying the categorial relation (1632: Logica 2. p. q. 16. art. 7. 607a36ff.: "Concurrit enim fundamentum ut specificans per modum principii et causae, cum ordine tamen ad terminum, in quo completur et terminatur specificatio.") Likewise in Peirce, the specification of the existential relation in its existent foundation traces back through the genuine sign relation to all other known relations, at least thanks to the

evolutionary formation of man himself. For Peirce, too, truth is conformity of the sign to the interacting object (c.1905a: 5.554): "Truth is the conformity of a representamen to *its* object. . . . There must be an action of the object upon the sign to make the latter true." Perhaps the most important and certainly the most striking, point is that, for Poinsot as for Peirce, the 'objects' which the sciences isolate in experience as essential units subject to distinctive laws of nature *need not be substances*. Such essential units subject to determinate natural laws may merely be *systems of real relations specified by a single extrinsic formal cause*. Poinsot's examples are units of composition such as a house, or a successive order over a time span of many years such as a river (1632: Logica 2. p. q. 16. art. 2.).[134] The parallel examples in Peirce are a wave and a focus of light (c.1896: 1.493).

---

[134] Reiser ed. Vol. I, 560b44-561a11: ". . . *ex pluribus entibus in actu non fit unum per se unitate formae, bene tamen unitate ordinis et mensurae, sicut fit ex pluribus entibus in actu unum artefactum et unum sacramentum et unum convivium. Habent enim ista unitatem per se, quatenus opponitur unitati per accidens, quae sumitur a multitudine et non ab aliquo uno, sive forma sive compositione sive ordine, ut vidimus ex S. Thoma, 7. Metaph. lect. ult.*"—". . . many actual entities cannot be essentially unified by a unity of form, but they can well become so unified by a unity of order and of measure, as one artifact and one sacrament and one banquet comes to be from many actual entities. For these have an essential unity insofar as essential unity is opposed to the accidental unity taken from a multitude and not from any one source, be it a form or a composition or an order, as we saw from the final lesson in St. Thomas's *Commentary* on Book VII of Aristotle's *Metaphysics*"

Here Poinsot is referring back to his discussion at 557a38-b7: "*Quod autem hoc sufficiat, ut numerus sit unum simpliciter et non per accidens, sumitur ex doctrina S. Thomae 7. Metaph. lect. ult. super textum 60., ubi reddit rationem distinguendi inter compositionem ex multis, quae facit unum simpliciter, et quae facit unum secundum quid. 'Huius', inquit, 'diversitatis ratio est, quia compositum quandoque sortitur speciem ab aliquo uno, quod est vel forma, ut patet in corpore mixto, vel compositio, ut patet in domo, vel ordo, ut patet in syllaba et numero; et tunc oportet, quod totum compositum sit unum simpliciter. Quandoque vero compositum speciem sortitur ab ipsa multitudine partium collectarum, ut patet in acervo et populo et aliis huiusmodi. Et in talibus totum compositum non est unum simpliciter, sed solum secundum quid.' Quae doctrina valde observanda est ad discernendum varios modos unitatis simpliciter et per accidens; nec enim omnia ista dicuntur uno modo unum, sed sunt diversi gradus. Perfectiori enim modo est unum angelus et coelum, qui nullam varietatem recipiunt, quam animalia seu viventia, quae continuo incremento et decremento transeunt, et quam fluvius, qui nec in materia nec in forma est idem, qui modo fluit, ab illo, qui fluebat a viginti annis, sed solum ratione loci, per quem fluit, et similiter artefacta sunt unum solum ex parte formae artificialis. Et tamen haec omnia includuntur sub ratione unitatis simpliciter ex illa regula S. Thomae, quod ea sunt unum simpliciter, quae sumunt speciem ab uno, sive illud unum sit forma sive compositio sive ordo; solum autem sunt unum secundum quid, quae non ab uno sumunt speciem, sed a multitudine.*"—"But that [the order of many things as a] specific number should suffice for a unity simply speaking rather than being merely an accidental unity is the teaching of St. Thomas in his *Commentary on the Metaphysics*, Book VII, the last reading, par. 60. There he gives the rationale for distinguishing from an accidental unity a composite of many things which constitutes a unity simply speaking. The reason for this diversity, he says, is that sometimes a composite is allotted its specification by some one thing which is either a form, as in a chemical compound, or is a structure, such as a house, or is an order, as is manifest in a syllable and a number. And then the total composite must be a unity simply speaking. But sometimes a composed whole takes its specific character from the very multitude of the collected parts, as can be seen in the case of a heap and a population and in other such cases. In all such cases the composed whole is not one thing simply speaking but only from some accident of contiguity [i.e., it is something unified not from any single principle internal to itself but externally and in the conception of some observer].' This doctrine can be effectively employed to discriminate the various modes of essential and accidental unity; nor are these various modes all said to be one in a single way, for units of diverse levels or grades form alike within the orders of that which is essentially and that which is accidentally one. For a pure spirit or a celestial body which suffers no variation is unified in a more perfect manner than are animals or plants which endure dependently upon continual processes of growth and decay, or than is a river,

In sum, while it is unfortunate Peirce did not know that his was not the first attempt to overcome the ''beastlike superficiality and lack of generalizing thought [that] spreads like a pall over the writings of the scholastic masters of logic'' in the early Latin phrase of the modern period (c.1905b: 1.560; cf. Ashworth 1964: XI), yet the situation is not without some redeeming value. We

---

which is the same river flowing now as flowed twenty years ago neither in manner nor in form but only thanks to the place through which it flows; and artifacts likewise are one only owing to an artificial form. And yet all these diverse types of unity are included under the rationale of a unity simply speaking [i.e., absolutely, from the standpoint of the thing itself unified taken in its own being independent of being observed] according to the rule of St. Thomas that those things which derive their specific character from one source are one simply speaking, whether that one source be a form or a composition or an ordering; whereas only those things are relatively one which derive their specific character not from one source but from a multitude.'' Poinsot adds, a little further on (563a32-48): ''*Si autem formalitas determinata sit, sed materialis designatio sit indeterminata, simpliciter datur species determinata in re, sicut datur unitas fluvii in re, licet materialiter aqua non sit eadem, sed modo ista, modo illa; quia tamen fluit sub eadem habitudine et successione ad alveum, manet idem fluvius. Et similiter est de unitate loci succedentibus diversis superficiebus in eadem distantia. Sic diversae unitates possunt succedere per designationem intellectus in eadem ratione ultimae, et sic habent unitatem in re formaliter, licet non materialiter.*''—''Now if the formality is determined, although the material designation of its many parts is not, a specific unity nevertheless exists in the order of mind-independent being. Thus, for example, a river has a natural unity, notwithstanding the fact that its water is not the same water materially at one time and at another time. The river remains one same river because it flows in a channel according to a determinate pattern of relationships in space and time. And the case of a unity of place is similar: it obtains in spite of the diverse succession of bodily surfaces over a given distance. Thus unities diverse in type can be seen, through the designation of the understanding, to fall under or enter into the same ultimate rationale, and thus have a unity in the order of natural being formally, although not materially.''

Throughout these texts, Poinsot consistently distinguishes between two types of organization or order—that which suffices to constitute an essential or ''absolute'' (subjective) unity, and that which does not suffice for a unit of being in the order of what is able to obtain independently of the conceptions of a here and now observer. The former is an order of specification or *specifying order* (''ordo specificationis''), the latter an order obaining only through relations diversely founded absent any single source subordinating the diversity as such (''ordo relationis''). The situation may be summarized thus:

unitas ordinis {
- *sumitur ab uno* (557b33): having a single source of natural specification
- *sumitur a pluralitate* (563a2-3): a criss-cross of relations lacking a single center of now-mind-independent unity

''*Et sic distinguitur unitas ordinis in numero ab unitate exercitus vel civitatis, quae sunt entia per accidens, eo quod in istis solum invenitur ordo relationis, qui non sufficit ad unitatem per se. Nam relatio formaliter versatur inter plura extrema, et ideo unitas ordinis sumitur potius a pluralitate, quando tantum est relativa. At vero unitas ordinis* [*e.g.*] *quantitativi seu extensionis in numero, non est solum unitas relationis, sed distinctio quantitum divisarum sub una ultima unitate, sub qua ceterae ordinantur et clauduntur, ut induentes novum mensurandi modum in ipsa extensione et quantitate discreta*'' (562b42-563a11).—''In this way the unity of order in a number is distinguished from the unity of an armed force or of a city, which unities are accidental beings by the fact that only an order of relation obtains within them, of the sort which does not suffice for an essential unity. For a relation obtains formally among or between several extremes, and for this reason a unity of order derives rather from the several when the unity is only relative. By contrast, the unity of a quantitative order or of extension in a number is not solely the order of a relation, but a distinction of diverse quantities subordinated to one ultimate unity, under which unity the others are ordered and fall as taking on a new mode of measuring in the very extension and discretion of quantity.'' ''*Et habet se unitas numeri sicut unitas loci. Sicut enim plures superficies transeunt in una distantia et cum superficiebus plures relationes ad polos mundi, manet tamen idem locus formaliter respectu huius termini fixi, quem respicit, licet materialiter sint plura, ut in 4. Phys. dicetur* [*c. 4. (212 a 19); S. Thom. lect. 6.* (Le *II. 164. n. 14-17). Cf. Phil. nat. 1. p. q. 16. art. 1.*]; *sic in numero datur ratio ultimae unitatis ceteras terminantis*'' (Ibid.: 556b12-22).—''And the unity of a number obtains in the way that unity

have in the doctrinal convergence of these two disparate but profound thinkers, for one thing, a remarkable testimony to the objective character of semiotic as a possible doctrine having, as Saussure is reported to have put it (1916: 33), "a right to existence, its place . . . marked out in advance"; and, for another, the uniqueness (not to say idiosyncracy) of Poinsot's historical situation respecting semiotic foundations gives the philosophical view expressed in the *Treatise on Signs* a unique heuristic value for interpreting the history of philosophy both before and after the crucial seventeenth century—including Peirce's effort to re-establish a systematic view of signifying and erect upon its sound foundations a new era of philosophical understanding.

What seems to me to be called for first of all is a clarification in terms of the development of philosophy between Poinsot and the present, of the *fundamental option* which Poinsot poses at the very beginning of his *Treatise*, the need for a choice between regarding signs as primarily and essentially relative only according to the way their being must be cognized or expressed (transcendentally), or according to the way they *have* the being proper to them as signs (ontologically) and therefore (sometimes) independently of expression.

Yet, as Poinsot shows, this choice itself depends for its recognition and possibility on a prior decision concerning the nature and reality of the relative as it belongs to the order of mind-independent being. In this, Poinsot advances the issue a step beyond his later contemporary, John Locke, who, having set himself "to examine the Extent and Certainty of our Knowledge," soon enough "found it had so near a connexion with Words, that unless their force and manner of Signification were first well observed, there could be very little said clearly and pertinently concerning Knowledge."[135] Thus Locke had already uncovered for modern thought the decisive connection between signs and *knowledge*, and no insight was to exercise greater influence over the immediate development of philosophical thought both in England and in Europe; but it was the privilege of Poinsot to see in exactly what way the connection between knowledge and *being* is *also* decisively at stake in the explanation of signifying, though this insight of Poinsot's is traceable after Locke mostly by its neglect or absence.

We begin our attempt to historically situate the philosophical substance of Poinsot's *Treatise*, therefore, with a sketch of the history in the Latin West of the discussion of whether there are pure relations in the world, existing as such dependently upon but supraordinate to and really distinct from their foundations in material subjects. It was in the discussion of this question, according to the terms of Poinsot's theory, that the way was prepared at the dawn of modern times for the split between being and intelligibility that received its classic systematic formulation in Kant and which has perpetuated itself down to

---

of location obtains. For just as a plurality of bodily surfaces and therewith several relations to the poles of the earth traverse a given distance and yet the location remains formally the same in respect of this fixed term which the location respects, even though these comprising surfaces are plural, as is said in Book IV of the *Physics* [c. 4. (212 a 19); S. Thom. lect. 6. (*Le* II. 164. n. 14-17). Cf. Phil. nat. 1. p. q. 16. art. 1.]; so in the case of number is there the rationale of an ultimate unity terminating the others."

[135] John Locke, *An Essay concerning Human Understanding*, Book III, Chap. IX, par. 21 (Nidditch ed. p. 488/20-24).

our own times as the characteristic heritage of philosophy after Locke and Descartes, but which is already implicit in any view of signs (and therefore of concepts) as primarily relative in a transcendental rather than in an ontological way. Poinsot's theory of the sign is the unique remedy for this split. At stake in the contrast between the relative *secundum esse* (or ontologically relative) and the relative *secundum dici* (or transcendentally relative) as Poinsot makes it the foundation of his *Treatise* is nothing less than the classical medieval thesis, *ens et verum convertuntur*. It is a question of being able to explain the apparent intersubjectivity of objects in discourse (whereby they are referable indifferently to the self and to others) and their partial coincidence in experience with mind-independent beings, or having to explain all this away.

A. The Discussion of Mind-Independent Relation in the Latin West up to Poinsot.

As Krempel has shown, the question of whether there are in nature relations given as such independently of mind was commonly discussed in the West, beginning with Boethius's sixth-century translation of and commentaries upon the book of Aristotle's *Categories*; and with a few exceptions, the question was resolved in the affirmative. Thus, well before the end of the thirteenth century, there was a general consensus in the West that there are relations in the world, existing as such dependently upon but supraordinate to and really distinct from their subjective foundations in things.

This consensus was first challenged effectively in the work of William of Ockham (c. 1300-1350), which gave rise to a movement called *nominalism*—"a term which does not at all serve to define it"[136]—whose partisans were also known as "terminists" (*terministae*) and "moderns" (*moderni*).[137] Complex as the movement was, it was united in its denial of the mind-independent reality of relations,[138] a denial to which Suarez had attached by Poinsot's day the weight and influence of his *Disputationes Metaphysicae*. Thus, by the time of Poinsot's publication in 1632 of his *Ars Logica*, Part II, the medieval consensus in this matter had given way to a clear opposition within the ranks of the Latin Aristotelians:

> Those at one extreme think that relations are not distinguished on the side of mind-independent being from their fundaments, but only by the mind. This position is traditionally ascribed to the Nominalists, against whom we argued in [the *Treatise on Signs*, First Preamble,] Article 1. Others, how-

---

[136] "Nous pénétrons ici," writes Gilson (1952b: 657), "sur un terrain doctrinal mal connu, extrêmement complexe et dont on sait du moins déjà ceci, que le terme de nominalisme ne suffit aucunement à le définir."

[137] Ibid., pp. 656-657.

[138] "Les noms dont on désignait au XIVe siècle les partisans des anciennes et ceux de la nouvelle doctrine, supposent que l'on traçait entre eux une ligne de démarcation extrêmement nette," writes Gilson (ibid., p. 656). This is the most fundamental such line suggested by Poinsot's *Treatise*, and one that, in the context of present considerations, gives an entirely new dimension to Jacques Maritain's contention (1959a: 1) that "a deep vice besets the philosophers of our day, whether they be neo-Kantians, neo-positivists, idealists, Bergsonians, logisticians, pragmatists, neo-Spinozists, or neo-mystics. It is the ancient error of the *nominalists*"—or, as Peirce put it some years earlier (1903a: 1.19): "all modern philosophy of every sect has been nominalistic."

> ever, who admit categorial relations against those Nominalists, follow this opinion concerning a mind-independent distinction from the fundament. Thus Suarez in his *Disputationes Metaphysicae*, disp. 47, sec. 2. And others at the opposite extreme distinguish all categorial relations from their fundaments mind-independently, which the Thomists generally follow, although some distinguish the relation from the fundament as a thing from a thing, others only as a mode.[139]

Outside what Poinsot here calls the "Thomist" line, the position of Ockham and Suarez was universally adopted by the figures who exercised the controlling influence over the transition in the seventeenth and eighteenth centuries from Latin philosophizing to philosophical discourse in the new national languages. Whether we look to the work of Hobbes, Locke, Berkeley, and Hume in England, or to the work of Descartes, Leibniz, and Kant on the Continent, we find the unanimous adoption of the view of Suarez and Ockham denying the reality in nature of mind-independent relations as such.

B. The Semiotic of Poinsot as Watershed of the Philosophical Tradition

This puts into a strikingly new perspective what Randall (1962: vii-viii) well calls—despite his own work embodying the results of several decades of research in the area—"that least known period in the history of Western philosophy, the transition from the thirteenth to the seventeenth centuries, when modern philosophy is conventionally supposed to have begun." The "essential continuity between medieval and modern philosophy" that increasingly impressed Randall "ever since the early studies of Gilson on Descartes" is in reality superficial. It does not at all obtain at the level of ultimate philosophical understanding of the foundations in the order of the relative for the medieval theory of knowledge and of truth as convertible with being. For Poinsot's theory of signs precisely extends to the *means* of knowledge—the instruments whereby objectivity is structured in cognition, let us say—St. Thomas's use (c. 1256-1259) of the ontological rationale of the relative to explain truth as a "property" of being, i.e., the convertibility of *ens* and *verum*.[140]

---

[139] Poinsot, *Ars Logica*, Part II (1632), Q. 17, Art. 4, "*Utrum relatio distinguatur a parte rei a suo fundamento*" ("Whether a Relation Is Mind-Independently Distinct from Its Fundament"), 591a6-23: "*Circa hanc ergo difficultatem divisi sunt auctores. Quidam in uno extremo existimant relationes non distingui a parte rei a suis fundamentis, sed solum ratione; quod Nominalibus tribui solet, contra quos egimus art. 1.* [i.e., the *Treatise on Signs*, First Preamble, Article 1]. *Aliqui tamen, qui contra illos admittunt relationes praedicamentales, sententiam istam sequuntur de distinctione rationis a fundamento. Ita P. Suarez disp. 47. Metaph. sec. 2. Et alii in alio extremo omnes relationes praedicamentales realiter distinguunt a suo fundamento, quod communiter thomistae sequuntur, licet aliqui distinguunt relationem a fundamento ut rem a re, alii solum ut modum.*"

Here Poinsot clearly identifies modal distinction as *a type of real distinction*. Here then is clear proof of the unreliability of Krempel's study of relation so far as it concerns Poinsot; for Krempel (1952: 270) writes: "Sous l'influence de saint Albert et surtout de Boèce, la plupart des thomistes primitifs, tel Hervé de Nédellec et Nicolas Trivet, rejetèrent la distinction réele entre la relation accidentelle et son fondement absolu. De même Gilles de Rome, les nominalistes, Suarez, et Jean de saint Thomas." See further Appendix C, esp. note 27, p. 385, and note 116, p. 474, above.

[140] See Thomas Aquinas, c. 1256-1259: *Quaestiones disputatae de veritate*, Q. 1, art. 1; Poinsot, 1643a: disp. II (Solesmes ed. 1953: disp. XXII, pp. 589-638), "De veritate transcendentali et formali."

This extension is impossible within the confines of the modern tradition. Having only the transcendental rationale of the relative with which to explain the connection of being and truth, in the terms of Poinsot's theory, the modern tradition is without resources for explaining the possibility of even the most limited escape from the basic condition of subjectivity as something closed upon itself.[141] The ontological relative does allow for intersubjectivity as a rationale of being equiprimordial with subjectivity, and, as realized in the particular case of signs actually manifesting in cognition what they signify, does explain the intersubjective character of discourse and the public character of objects both real and unreal. Discourse is intersubjective and objects of awareness are public, in principle because the means or instruments of discourse and objectification are *ontologically* relative as signs, not transcendentally relative, and so "do not pertain to the order of the cognizable absolutely, but relatively and ministerially,"[142] i.e., in such a way as to be able to manifest otherwise than in terms of their objective selves alone,[143] and otherwise than in terms of the physical presence or absence of objects signified. If signs are not ontologically relative, however, they do not pertain to the order of the cognizable in a ministerial capacity first of all, but in an objective capacity. The grounds for Poinsot's distinction, first, between formal and instrumental signs, and second, between instrumental signs which are founded in nature and instrumental signs which are founded in custom or stipulation, are entirely removed. Being transcendentally relative, concepts, even as signs, would be determinative of rather than specified by and subordinate to their objects; nor would they be mind-independently distinct from the subjective being of the knower as closed upon itself. There could be no formal signs in Poinsot's sense, for being cognized would pertain to the rationale as well as to the exercise of a sign; being formed by the mind and being constituted in objective existence would be everywhere and at all points the same.[144] There would still be signs founded on custom and stipulation; but no signs founded on nature as something knowable in itself given with and by the objects of experience. Whatever necessity human understanding might think it discerns among objects would perforce be the result either of custom alone, or of custom together with some hidden mechanisms of understanding which determine thought along lines inscribed in and prescribed by an order of "things-in-themselves" which are *absolutely* other than the objects presented in consciousness by our concepts or discussed with our fellows through signs.[145]

---

[141] On the view that only transcendental relation is common to the two orders of mind-independent and mind-dependent being, for example, even though mind-dependent being further contains genuine relations, it does not contain them in a fully intersubjective way, for it does not contain them as enjoying an indifference to their subjective ground. For this, mental relation must be itself but a mind-dependent instance of something which is also given in its positive content independently of the mind. Further in Deely, 1974, and esp. 1977a.

[142] *Treatise on Signs*, Book I, Question 2, 151/13-15 (*663a32-34*).

[143] See the *Treatise on Signs*, Book II, Question 1, esp. 227/1-228/47 (=*695b5-696b16*); and Jacques Maritain, 1959a:119-120.

[144] Just as it became for each one of the British empiricists and Continental rationalists. See, in particular, John Locke's *Essay concerning Human Understanding*, Introduction, par. 8 (Nidditch ed. p. 47/24-33).

[145] This line of thought, it seems clear, is what is at stake in Chomsky's well-known study, *Cartesian Linguistics* (New York: Harper and Row, 1966), which is much rather a "Kantian Linguis-

In the choice between signs as ontologically relative or signs as transcendentally relative, one chooses between the acceptance or denial of being and truth as convertible; but in choosing to deny the mind-independent reality of relation as distinct from and superordinate to its fundament, one perforce excludes the very notion of an ontological relative in the sense required to reconcile the medieval doctrine of transcendental truth with the dependence of objects in their cognized being on means of objectification rooted in the subjectivity of the being who knows.

Among those in the modern tradition conscious of the consequences of excluding relation as an ontological rationale realized independently of human understanding, few were more conscious than William of Ockham himself. And it is useful to conjecture that the structure of Book III of Poinsot's *Treatise* may have been conceived in part as a philosophical counter to what Gilson (1937: 68) called "Ockham's master stroke," namely, the perception that the problem of removing *entirely* the character of relation as an ontological rationale "could not be solved unless a new classification of the various types of knowledge was first substituted for the old one," specifically, a classification beginning with our experience of the difference between cognition of things present and absent to sense. "Hence his division of knowledge into abstractive and intuitive, terms that had already been used before him, but to which he gave a new turn and was to use in a new way." (See also Gilson, 1955: 489-491).

This last remark I apply to Poinsot as well as Ockham; for Poinsot did not simply restore this division of knowledge to its foundation in Scotus's pre-Ockhamite usage.[146] Rather, he rethought the experience on which it is based, entirely in terms of the systematic implications of the identification of signs as ontologically relative in rationale. It is because concepts as signs are ontologically relative that they are able to mediate between the transcendental relations of objects to the order of mind-independent being (on the one side) and to the order of what depends on cognition for its being (on the other side), and to unite in the object the divisions relative to both orders—the order of *praedicamenta vera et ficta simul*.

Poinsot shows that the foundations for the prior possibility of critical truth as the *conformitas intellectus ad rem* lies in the ontological peculiarity of the relative as something realizable as such in the order of mind-independent existence.[147] With his two divisions, one of natural signs into formal and instru-

tics," hardly *Cartesian*, which was essentially a philosophy of inner *experience* of consciousness, not of an a-priori mapping mechanism not only hidden but wholly distinct from the intelligence (Chomsky, 1968).

[146] For Poinsot and Scotus alike, intuitive knowledge requires physical presence on the part of the object apprehended as such. But for Scotus, abstractive knowledge prescinds from the existence or nonexistence of its object, whereas for Poinsot abstractive awareness prescinds only from physical presence, not necessarily from existence. These remarks may suffice here, but a detailed comparison of Scotus and Poinsot on these points should eventually be made.

[147] Thus Poinsot's theory at once answers Heidegger's central question in *Vom Wesen der Wahrheit* (1943), namely, what is the basis for the *prior possibility* of truth as a 'correspondence' or 'agreement' between thought and what is independent of thought, and provides the foundations in ancient ontology required to ground in principle Heidegger's anticonstructivist view (1927: 62) that "im Sichrichten auf . . . und Erfassen geht das Dasein nicht etwa erst aus seiner Innensphäre hinaus, in die es zunächst verkapselt ist, sondern es ist seiner primären Seinsart nach immer schon 'draussen' bei einem begegnenden Seienden der je schon entdeckten Welt."

mental, and one of instrumental signs into natural, stipulated, and customary, both founded on the contrast between the ontologically and the merely transcendentally relative as explaining the presence of non-being in cognition and the mediating role of custom in structuring the apprehensive relations between human understanding and mind-independent being, Poinsot may be said to have provided, for the first time, and at the very end of a tradition founded on an eleven-hundred-year-old consensus on the reality of relation as an intersubjective union, a metaphysical apparatus for analysis sufficiently refined and delicate (''ens minimum, scilicet, relatio''[148]) to accommodate transcendental truth to history. At the very time when the medieval consensus entirely gave way in modern thought to the nominalist or Ockhamite tradition on the non-reality of relation (as transmitted through the work of Suarez, Hobbes, and Descartes *within Poinsot's very lifetime*, and as removing the foundation of truth in the order of mind-independent being as such), Poinsot was achieving in the older tradition the first entirely systematic clarification of the ontological foundations in relation for the possibility of truth as a conformity known in the structures of objectivity between thought and things.

C. The Modern Tradition up to Kant.

Hobbes spoke for the fundamentally new (and Ockhamite) way philosophy was to take in England, we may say, when he wrote in his *Philosophia Prima*: ''De Relatione autem non ita censendum est, tamquam ea esset accidens aliquod diversum ab aliis Relati accidentibus, sed unum ex illis, nempe, illud ipsum secundum quod fit comparatio.''[149] The implications of this view for the grounds of knowledge and the understanding of signs were early put to work systematically in the national language traditions of philosophy, it seems, with the appearance in 1690 of John Locke's *Essay concerning Human Understanding*. Here, all the consequences of choosing the transcendental alternative to Poinsot's answer concerning the rationale constitutive of signs begin to come into the open, for here for the first time a systematic work appears devoted to exploring the structures of signs and cognition on the supposition that ''Ideas *of Modes and Relations, are* Originals, and *Archetypes*; are not Copies, nor made after the Pattern of any real Existence, to which the Mind intends them to be conformable, and exactly to answer.''[150]

Now there is no doubt that we experience things as connected with one another in various ways. But if there are no true relations save those our mind makes, on what grounds do we experience these connections? Locke, it must

---

[148] Thomas Aquinas, c. 1252-1256: *In I Sent.* dist. 26, q. 2 ad 2. As Maritain remarks (1963: 217): le problème ''le plus important de tous les problèmes de la noetique . . . ne peut être traité comme il faut qu'en mettant en oeuvre l'outillage métaphysique le plus affine. . . .'' (English in 1959a: 112.)

[149] Thomas Hobbes, ''Philosophia Prima,'' in *Opera Philosophica, Quae Latine Scripsit, Omnia* (Amsterdam: Joannes Blaev, 1668), Vol. I, Caput 11, par. 6, p. 71: ''Concerning relation, however, it must not be thought to exist in such a way as to be diverse from the other accidents of the related thing, but as one of them, namely, that very one according to which a comparison is made.'' Cf. the *Treatise on Signs*, Second Preamble, Article 1, 80/22-81/5 (=*573b44-574a7*).

[150] John Locke, *An Essay concerning Human Understanding*, Book II, Chap. XXXI, par. 14 (Nidditch ed. pp. 383/35-384/3).

be said, failed to face this question in a fully consistent way, and introduced as a result many inconsistencies into his *Essay*.

It was left for Hume to remove these inconsistencies, by giving, in 1739 with his *Treatise of Human Nature*, the first of the two possible answers (within the confines of the modern tradition) to why we connect objects in our experience:

> Nature, by an absolute and uncontroulable necessity, has determin'd us to judge as well as to breathe and feel; nor can we any more forbear viewing certain objects in a stronger and fuller light, upon account of their customary connexion with a present impression, than we can hinder ourselves from thinking as long as we are awake, or seeing surrounding bodies, when we turn our eyes towards them in broad sunshine.[151]

This certainly improves upon Locke's contention "there is nothing more required" than that relations have reality "only in the minds of men."[152]

To Poinsot's question: "How does understanding form pure respects if it has only absolute things (i.e., transcendental relations) as the pattern on which to form them?,"[153] Hume can now answer: If anything further be required, as Locke doubted, the intervention of customs in our perceptions supplies that requirement.

Poinsot has no doubt of the correctness of Hume's contention that custom intervenes to structure the relations we directly perceive in objects. In simple awareness, he writes, "we apprehend many things not through proper concepts but through connotative ones."[154] Indeed, it is on this ground that he explains the incorporation into nature of patterns of non-being through the transformation of free creations into customary institutions through the use men make of them in everyday life.[155] It is on this ground too that he explains how language in use becomes a *Lebensform*, wherein stipulation, which belongs to the order of non-being according to its foundation or *direct* ground in subjectivity, is sensibly transformed into custom, whereby the element of stipulated non-being is indirectly naturalized and made perceptible in the order of instrumental signs.[156] But, in Poinsot's scheme, the formal recognition of mind-dependent relations as such by human understanding, whereby stipulation itself first becomes possible,[157] also provides the resources for *critically distinguishing* among customary associations those which are *also* connections realized independently of custom (and so of human understanding) and those which are only

---

[151] David Hume, *A Treatise of Human Nature*, 2nd ed. by L.A. Selby-Bigge with notes by P.H. Nidditch (Oxford: Clarendon, 1978), Book I, Part IV, Section 1, p. 183.

[152] John Locke, *An Essay concerning Human Understanding*, Book II, Chap. XXX, par. 4 (Nidditch ed. p. 373/26-29): "*Mixed Modes and Relations*, having no other *reality*, but what they have in the Minds of Men, there is nothing more required to those kinds of *Ideas*, to make them *real*, but that they be so framed . . . ."

[153] See the *Treatise on Signs*, Second Preamble, Article 1, 83/9-16 (=*575a25-32*).

[154] *Treatise on Signs*, First Preamble, Article 3, 75/12-13 (=*305b41-43*).

[155] See the *Treatise on Signs*, Book II, Question 6, esp. 282/32-42 (=*721b27-40*).

[156] Cf. *Treatise on Signs*, Book II, Question 6, 279/4-23 (=*719b15-36*) and 283/10-22 (=*722a11-24*), with Ludwig Wittgenstein, *Philosophical Investigations*, trans. G. E. M. Anscombe, 3rd ed. (New York: Macmillan, 1958), p. 88, pars. 240-242, esp. 241.

[157] Cf. *Treatise on Signs*, First Preamble, Article 3, 74/39-45 (*305b19-25*); Book I, Question 6, 205/9-11 (=*685b29-32*).

connections realized through custom; because, for Poinsot, the discrimination of the mind-dependent element in objective relations presupposes that relation in the ontological sense, i.e., as including mind-independent relations cognized as such before being recognized as such in their contrast to mind-dependent relations, has *already* been given in the line of being as first known (*ens ut primum cognitum*). There is room thus in Poinsot's theory for the further difference between customary signs, i.e., signs naturalized in experience, and natural signs simply speaking, i.e., signs connected with what they signify antecedently to and independently of their appearance as associated within human experience.[158]

Poinsot's theory achieves in this way a connection and *commercium* between mind-dependent and mind-independent elements of objective structure knowable as such, because his theory of signs as relations enables *any* given sign to "take on something of the entitative order,"[159] even though only *some* signs have this entitative dimension immediately from the fact that cognizability itself is something mind-independent in the order of the relative (*ens ut verum fundamentaliter*).

But such discrimination is impossible for Hume, because it contradicts the premise that relations as such have their being entirely from the work of human understanding. Consequently, where Poinsot explains the discrimination between natural and customary elements on the grounds of the ontological rationale proper to relation whereby non-being becomes a functional and structural element in our direct experience of objects, Hume is obliged to explain this discrimination away as a natural illusion:

> 'Tis natural for men, in their common and careless way of thinking, to imagine they perceive a connection betwixt such objects as they have constantly found united together; and because custom has render'd it difficult to separate the ideas, they are apt to fancy such a separation to be in itself impossible and absurd. But philosophers, who abstract from the effects of custom, and compare the ideas of objects, immediately perceive the falsehood of these vulgar sentiments, and discover that there is no known connexion among objects.[160]

Thus, by the middle of the eighteenth century in England, the denial by Hobbes and Locke of the mind-independent character and ontological rationale of relations has led directly to a theory according to which all objective structures are the free work of the mind, moderated or stayed, so far as can be known, only by custom, the warrant available to man for his seeing things as related in various ways.

The reduction of all connections among objects to custom is disastrous for the theory of the sciences, which, since the time of Aristotle, had thought to uncover *necessary* connections among things. This reduction was not acceptable to Kant. Agreeing with Locke and Hume that all relations as such are the work

---

[158] See the *Treatise on Signs*, Book II, Question 6, 278/27-29 (=*719b8-11*) and 279/24-43 (=*719b37-720a11*).

[159] *Treatise on Signs*, Book I, Question 2, 151/15-16 (=*663a34-36*).

[160] David Hume, *A Treatise of Human Nature*, Book I, Part IV, Section 3, p. 223 of Selby-Bigge/Nidditch ed.

of mind, Kant thought to restore true necessity among objective connections by adding to the customary connections admitted by Hume, relations which the mind forms by an a-priori necessity of its manner of operations.

Moreover, unlike Locke and Hume, who began to treat of human thought and handled the question of relations along the way, Kant's critical reflections are distinguished by beginning exactly as Poinsot's begin, with the problem of the relative in being explicitly envisaged as such as the determining ground for any problematic involving concepts.

For this reason, within the modern tradition as it took form in the national languages, Kant, writing nearly a hundred and fifty years after Poinsot, emerges as the only figure whose work stands to the foundations of the modern tradition in a position comparable to the position Poinsot's work occupies within the older tradition. With Kant, for the first time in the national languages, we have an entirely systematic work which not only (as with Locke and Hume) explores the structures of signs and cognition, but does so from the first under the guidance of the notion of relation. Just as Poinsot's *Treatise* is an attempt to think through the affirmation of relation as an ontological rationale as this bears on the order of human understanding and its possible objects, so the enterprise of Kant's *Critique* can be viewed as an attempt to think through the denial of relation as an ontological rationale as this bears on the order of human understanding and its possible objects. Gilson (1952a: 122) considers that Hume's influence on Kant was, in this respect, as direct as could be:

> ''There are two principles I cannot render consistent,'' Hume says in the Appendix of his *Treatise of Human Nature*,[161] ''nor is it in my power to renounce either of them, namely, *that all our distinct perceptions are distinct existences*, and *that the mind never perceives any real connection among distinct existences*.'' We do not know with certainty what, exactly, Kant had read of Hume, but there is little doubt that this sentence was the very one that aroused Kant from his dogmatic slumber.

Kant's *Critique* is a systematic attempt to go to the very foundations of the modern ''way of ideas'' as only transcendentally relative in founding the structures of objectivity, and to do so in a way revelatory of the nature of truth in connection with objective being. Since the possible conformity of concepts to mind-independent objects given in experience requires relation as an ontological rationale indifferent in its positive content to its subjective ground, from within the modern tradition premised on the denial of such a rationale, the most consistent pursuit would indeed be to ''make trial whether we may not have more success in the tasks of metaphysics, if we suppose that objects must conform to our knowledge.''[162]

It is instructive, with the contrast between the ontologically and the transcendentally relative expressly in mind, to re-read the paragraphs in which Kant

---

[161] p. 636 of the Selby-Bigge/Nidditch ed.

[162] Immanuel Kant, *Critique of Pure Reason*, trans. Norman Kemp Smith (London: Macmillan, 1963), ''Preface to Second Edition'' (1787), p. 22. Kant's *Gesammelte Schriften*, herausgegeben von der Königlich Preussischen Akademie der Wissenschaften (Berlin: Reimer, 1911), Band III, p. 12: ''*Man versuche es daher einmal, ob wir nicht in den Aufgaben der Metaphysik damit besser fortkommen, dass wir annehmen, die Gegenstände mussen sich nach unserem Erkenntnis richten.*''

explains the revolution he wishes to effect in philosophy by bringing its assumptions concerning the relation between objectivity and truth in knowledge into conformity with the fact that relation is not an ontological rationale—the passages in which he celebrates his proposal by comparing it to the method of Copernicus:

> Failing of satisfactory progress in explaining the movements of the heavenly bodies on the supposition that they all revolved around the spectator, he tried whether he might not have better success if he made the spectator to revolve and the stars to remain at rest.[163]

For Poinsot, this reduces the Copernican hypothesis down to a question of alternate suppositions concerning which was the primarily real and which the primarily unreal relation, and well illustrates the functional equivalence of the two types of relation within an objective scheme. Kant continues:

> A similar experiment can be tried in metaphysics as regards the *intuition* of objects. If intuition must conform to the constitution of the objects, I do not see how we could know anything of the latter *a priori* [i.e., how there could be necessity in certain connections between objects—in certain *objective structures*, let us say—not reducible to the merely apparent necessity of customary association alone postulated by Hume]; but if the object (as object of the senses) must conform to the constitution of our faculty of intuition, I have no difficulty in conceiving such a possibility.[164]

So far, Poinsot still has no quarrel with Kant. The objects of our senses must indeed conform to the constitution of the sense faculties: objects can affect the eye primarily only as colored, and so on for each sense. Moreover, there is a sense for Poinsot in which an external sense is in a privileged way called a "faculty of intuition," since its operation alone requires the here-and-now presence in physical being of its adequate object.[165] This is but to say, in Poinsot's terms, that powers are transcendentally related to their objects, and that, in the case of sensation, physical interaction by itself alone suffices to explain the objective union attendant upon the physical influence (categorial relation) here and now of a physical object upon a passive sensory organ.[166] But here,

---

163 Ibid.: "*Nachdem es mit der Erklärung der Himmelsbewegungen nicht gut fort wollte, wenn er annahm, das ganze Sternenheer drehe sich um den Zuschauer, versuchte, ob es nicht besser gelingen mochte, wenn er den Zuschauer sich drehen und dagegen die Sterne in Ruhe liess.*"

164 Ibid.: "*In der Metaphysik kann man nun, was die Anschauung der Gegenstände betrifft, es auf ähnliche Weise versuchen. Wenn die Anschauung sich nach der Beschaffenheit der Gegenstände richten müsste, so sehe ich nicht ein, wie man a priori von ihr etwas wissen könne; richtet sich aber der Gegenstand (als Objekt der Sinne) nach der Beschaffenheit unseres Anschauungsvermögens, so kann ich mir diese Möglichkeit ganz wohl vorstellen.*"

165 *Treatise on Signs*, Book III, Question 2, 309/47-312/6 (= *734a37-735a36*); *Summulae* text, Book I, chap. 3, 29/7-23 (=*10b22-40*).

166 For Poinsot, sense knowledge, analytically distinguished as such at the foundation and core of experience, differs from all other cognition in this, that of itself it gives rise to no ontological relation of signification over and above the categorial relation in the order of cause to effect and effect to cause resulting from the action of the sensible object on the sense. Hence sensory apprehension, inasmuch as it bears on the proper sensibles directly, enjoys none of the indifference to the being of its object exhibited by imagination, memory, and understanding, though it does involve real relations between such so-called "proper" sensibles as color or sound and such so-called "common" sensibles as movement and shape, and so does not

possible agreement ends. For as cognition develops out of the passivity of sense through the active formation of concepts by internal sense (imagination, memory, natural instinct of various kinds), the transcendental relation of power to object is superseded in Poinsot's scheme by an ontological relation of sign (concept as formal sign) to signified (object as made naturally present in cognition as extrinsic specifier). This reversal and subordination of the internal subjective means of objectification to external specifications initially introduced through the senses in not possible from within the modern tradition, for it can only come about through the intervention of relation as an ontological rationale mediating the connection between concepts and their objects in perception and understanding. Hence Kant makes the decisive determination constitutive of his Copernican revolution: he extends the primacy of transcendental relation over the means of knowing not only into the active process of concept formation, but into the actual function concepts perform as *means* of objectification: if sensory intuitions are to become known, "*I* cannot rest in these intuitions . . . but *must relate them as representations* to something as their object, and determine this latter through them."[167]

Kant may be said to be the first in the modern tradition concerning the difference between a relation and its subjective foundation to have seen, with a clarify and depth comparable to that found in Poinsot's *Treatise,* the true requirements of the problem:

> Either I must assume that the *concepts,* by means of which I obtain this determination [of what has been given in intuition], conform to the object [in which case the concept as it functions in cognition is ontologically relative], or else I assume that the objects, or what is the same thing, that the *experience* in which alone, as given objects, they can be known, conform to the concepts [in which case the concept, even as it functions formally as a pure *means of cognition,* is only transcendentally relative].[168]

To the question "whether the formal rationale constitutive of a sign as such consists, primarily and essentially, in an ontological or in a transcendental rela-

---

have an "atomic" or isolated character, but immediately reveals objects as mind-independently *structured* within sensation according to size and distance, shape and movement, etc. See esp. Book I, Question 6, of the *Treatise on Signs,* and Deely, 1976: 187 note 11, 1980a: 203-207, 1982: 107-123. Also J. Gredt, 1924. Whereas for Locke and Hume (as later for Russell), the sense-data were regarded as bare effects within my subjectivity directly known and supposedly caused by unknown things, sense-data for Poinsot are effects indeed, but such effects as presuppose *and exhibit* the *here-and-now* action of the cause as object, and hence effects which, as transcendental relations, are *pure means by which* (*principia quo*) their causes are cognized under the aspect of being noisy, colored, shaped, in motion, etc., and present in awareness in themselves here and now. Thus Poinsot's view of sense experience comes much closer to the view of T. H. Green (1836-1882), except that with Green even the primitive relations of sense perception remain wholly the achievement of mind.

[167] Immanuel Kant, *Critique of Pure Reason,* "Preface to Second Edition" (1787), p. 22, emphasis added. *Kant's Gesammelte Schriften* (note 162 above), p. 12: "*Weil ich aber bei diesen Anschauungen, wenn sie Erkentnisse werden sollen, nicht stehen bleiben kann, sondern sie als Vorstellungen auf irgend etwas als Gegenstand beziehen und diesen durch jene bestimmen muss.*"

[168] Ibid.: "*So kann ich entweder annehmen, die Begriffe, wodurch ich diese Bestimmung zu Stande bringe, richten sich auch nach dem Gegenstände, . . . oder ich nehme an, die Gegenstände oder, welches einerlei ist, die Erfahrung, in welcher sie allein (als gegebene Gegenstände) erkannt werden, richte sich nach diesen Begriffen.*"

tion,"[169] we have only two systematically conceived answers. One, published by a professor at Alcalá, in Iberia, in the year 1632, according to which concepts (being natural signs formal in type) as they function in cognition are *ontologically* relative, and so sustain the convertibility of being with truth: this is Poinsot's *Treatise on Signs*. The other, published by a professor at Königsberg, Germany, in 1781, according to which concepts even as functioning in actual cognition remain primarily transcendental in their relative being, and so compromise the transcendental character of truth (i.e., the character of truth as mind-independently founded) and its convertibility with being.

Poinsot and Kant are, each in his own way, the culmination of two radically opposed traditions concerning the connection between being and truth. These two traditions overlap in their Latin development for about 300 years (1350-1650), at which point the older tradition that Poinsot represents is effectively terminated for the time, and the initial formation of the modern tradition in the national languages takes place entirely under the influence of the modern and nominalistic position concerning the relative which underlies the standpoint of the great Kantian critiques. The doctrine of intuition which Poinsot introduces in Book I, Question 6, and develops in terms of formal signs throughout most of Book III, clearly expresses the consequences of construing concepts and the means of knowing generally as signs and ontologically rather than transcendentally relative. As such, these pages serve to oppose Poinsot's notions of intuition and experience as well to those of Kant after him as to those of Ockham and the nominalists before him in what proved to be indeed the early modern period.

D. The Twilight of Modern Times.

From the viewpoint of its foundations in the being proper to relation, the modern tradition as found in the national languages is perfectly continuous up to Kant, who, as we have said, brings into systematic play the innermost possibilities of that tradition concerning concepts (the formal signs of understanding) much as Poinsot does for the older tradition. This unity of the formative stage of the modern philosophical mind was clearly perceived by Hegel, who wrote (in 1802): "Hume's and Locke's reflective way of philosophizing, more thoroughly and systematically worked out on German ground and soil, becomes German philosophy."[170]

Hegel also brings the unity to an end. He becomes the first figure of stature to challenge and deny the all but universal assumption that every relation existing as a relation is the work of the human mind.

I do not wish to say a great deal about Hegel here, beyond this: first, he certainly seems to recognize, with his "absolute relation," essentially the same

[169] *Treatise on Signs*, Book I, Question 1, 117/18-23 (=*646b16-21*).

[170] Hume's and Locke's "*Reflexionswesen, auf deutschem Grund und Boden weitläufiger und systematischer ausgesponnen, deutsche . . . Philosophie gennant wird*" (G. W. F. Hegel, "Glauben und Wissen oder die Reflexionsphilosophie der Subjektivität," *Journal der Philosophie*, Band II, Stück 2 [1802], as reprinted in *Sämtliche Werke* [Stuttgart: Frommann, 1964], Vol. I, p. 374).

notion of the relative termed "transcendental relation" by Poinsot;[171] second, he certainly recognizes mind-dependent relations;[172] and third, he seems also to recognize the equivalent of what Poinsot terms mind-independent or categorial relations.[173] Thus, at least in a tacit and confused way, there would be operative in Hegel's thought the notion of relation as the ontological rationale whereby Poinsot accounts for the presence of being and non-being alike in the objects of our experience and awareness. The univocity of being and non-being in cognition is a fundamental principle for Poinsot's *Treatise*. It would not seem entirely unrelated to the famous text at the opening of Hegel's *Logic*: "Being, the immediate indeterminate, is in fact nothing."[174]

But it does not seem to me that Hegel ever works out in a clear way the reduction of mind-independent and mind-dependent relations to their common ground, or their functional interrelation in knowledge. It seems to me that Heidegger's critique in passing of Hegel is probably sound: "when Hegel at last defines 'Being' as the 'indeterminate immediate' and makes this definition basic for all the further categorial explications of his 'logic,' *he keeps looking in the same direction as ancient ontology*,"[175] whereas with signs it is the question of the prior possibility of a categorial scheme of any kind that is posed for settlement in a fundamental way. The first problem is not to derive one categorial scheme as superior to some other, but to lay bare the possibility of deriving categorial schemes from experience and of distinguishing within experience the mind-dependent and mind-independent elements of objectivity.[176]

Be that as it may, if we look at modern philosophy from its national-language beginnings in the seventeenth century up to its culmination in Kant's *Critiques*, Hegel by comparison marks a perhaps confused but decidedly new beginning. For the first time in almost two hundred years, the common assumption of modern times underlying and necessitating its constant proclivity toward solipsism and subjectivism is put into question. Without anywhere gaining clarity as to its principles, the influence of Hegelian thought is pervasive throughout the nineteenth century, and has begun to wax again in recent times; but the confusion in Hegelianism nowhere demonstrates itself more effectively, perhaps, than in the failure of the Hegelians to isolate and develop the consequences of categorial relation with its ontological rationale.

---

[171] "Das Nothwendige ist in sich absolutes Verhältniss. . . ." (*System der Philosophie, Erster Teil: Die Wissenschaft der Logik* [1830a], SW, Vol. 8, p. 337).

[172] ". . . der Gedanke ist die Sache; einfache Identität des subjectiven und Objektiven" (*System der Philosophie, Dritter Teil: Die Philosophie des Geistes* [1830b], SW, Vol. 10, p. 359).

[173] ". . . das Verhältniss des Kindes im Mutter Leibe,—ein Verhältniss, das weder bloss leiblich noch bloss geistig, sondern psychisch ist,—ein Verhältniss der Seele" (Ibid., p. 158).

[174] "*Das Seyn, das unbestimmte das Immittelbare ist in der that Nichts, und nicht mehr noch weniger als Nichts*" (*Wissenschaft der Logik* [1812], Erster Teil, Erstes Abschnitt, Bestimmtheit, Erstes Kapitel, Seyn, par. A, *Sämtliche Werke*, Vol. 4, p. 88).

[175] "*Und wenn schliesslich* Hegel *das 'Sein' bestimmt als das 'unbestimmte Unmittelbare' und diese Bestimmung allen weiteren kategorialen Explikationen seiner 'Logik' zugrunde legt, so hält er sich in derselben Blickrichtung wie die antike Ontologie, nur dass er das von Aristoteles schon gestellte Problem der Einheit des Seins gegenüber der Mannigfaltigkeit der sachhaltigen 'Kategorien' aus der Hand gibt*" (Martin Heidegger, *Sein und Zeit*, p. 3, emphasis added in English rendition).

[176] See Section III.D.1. above.

After Hegel, there are at least two developments of particular interest in the light of Poinsot's notion of the ontologically relative.[177] The first is introduced by Franz Brentano (1838-1917), the second by Bertrand Russell (1872-1970).

Brentano is celebrated for having introduced into modern discussions the notion of *intentionality*, and for having inspired with this notion the founder of phenomenology, Edmund Husserl (1859-1938). With his doctrine of intentionality, Brentano originally set himself to explain the difference between mental and physical phenomena precisely in terms of relation. This attempt foundered in Brentano's inability to explain how a mental phenomenon could be truly related or referred to an unreal object. Failing to get clear about the ontological peculiarity of the relative whereby precisely it introduces into discourse its own characteristic indifference to physical reality, Brentano eventually abandoned his view of mental phenomena as truly relative in structure (*etwas Relatives*) and fell back upon a notion of it as after all only what Poinsot would call transcendentally relative (*etwas Relativliches*: see Deely, 1972; 1975b; 1978c).

Husserl sustained and developed Brentano's original idea of intentionality as the thoroughly relational structure of consciousness, but in Husserl there can be no question of relation as an ontological rationale in Poinsot's sense. For this requires the explicit contrast between and comparison of natural and mind-dependent elements in objects, a distinction within objectivity precluded by Husserl's dogmatic adherence to what Heidegger (1927: 61) well terms the "constructivist standpoint" regarding the being of objectivity. With Husserl, there is no possible ground for introducing the contrast between mind-dependent and mind-independent being in Poinsot's sense, and hence no possibility for developing the notion of an ontological rationale whereby the Husserlian ego might slip out of its "transcendental subjectivity." Husserl reverts entirely, but in highly suggestive and idiosyncratic ways comparable to those of Kant in their obsessive power, to the modern and nominalistic tradition uniting the mainstream of British empiricism and Continental rationalism[178] in its denial of relation as a properly ontological rationale capable of bringing together knowing and being through the instrument of signs.

In the English tradition, it is Bertrand Russell who, more than any other single figure, has brought the notion of relation in recent years to the foreground

---

[177] I pass over the developments in England from Green, Caird, Wallace, etc., to Bradley, developments to which Russell is in his origins largely a reaction, because, despite Bradley's clear metaphysical superiority to anything that comes after him—not only to Russell, but even more to Ayer and Ryle—he remains wholly within the confines of the modern assumption concerning the categorial relative, and continues—under the opposition of appearance and reality—the ineluctably consequent split between being and the intelligible. At the same time, it must be noted that Bradley's thought on the relative is essentially unfinished, as his *ex professo* treatment of relation was interrupted by his death in September of 1924. See F. H. Bradley, 1935.

[178] According to Herbert Spiegelberg, *The Phenomenological Movement*, 2nd ed. (The Hague: Martinus Nijhoff, 1965), Vol. I, pp. 92-93, "the British empiricists from Locke to Hume were Husserl's introductory readings in philosophy and remained of basic importance to him all through his later development. . . . He even kept recommending them to his students . . . as one of the best approaches to phenomenology."

On the side of Continental rationalism, it suffices merely to recall the title and content of Husserl's late work (1931), the *Cartesian Meditations*.

of discussion in British and American circles. In 1965, Weinberg could still write that "we owe to Russell, more than to any single philosopher, a clear understanding of the nature and importance of relations."[179] From his earliest studies of Leibniz, and in opposition to Leibniz, Russell developed a lively sense of the independent reality of relations and of their importance for any theory of knowledge and truth.[180] Yet, from Poinsot's standpoint, Russell consistently mistakes what is proper to relation *as conceivable* for what is proper to relation *as susceptible of existence.*[181] Because relation is *conceivable* as indifferent to physical or mental existence, Russell argued that relation as such *exists* in neither the mental nor the physical realm. But the notion of *ontological* relation derives from what is peculiar to relation not as something *conceivable*, but as something *susceptible as such of existing in nature* independently of perception and conception, though not of subjective being *tout court*. It is perhaps not surprising, therefore, that Russell repudiated Brentano's early views without correcting them,[182] and spent most of his speculative time with relations in an effort to construct a logic that would enable the sufficiently informed observer to correct, in principle at least, the supposed defect (directly consequent upon the very nature of signs as ontologically relative) whereby language can be used to speak of what does not "in fact" exist.[183]

On the exclusively American scene, John Dewey built an elaborate doctrine of experience and nature around the notion of relation.[184] But this theory nowhere shows a clear awareness of its foundations or of the alternatives concerning relation that the history of thought has made available.

E. Conclusion.

No matter where we look in modern times, we find far-reaching and detailed differences, both dialectical and philosophical, directly related to the effective termination with Poinsot's *Treatise* of the influence of the older medieval tradition concerning relation as far as concerns the epistemological and critical reflections of modern times. Given the date of publication of the part of Poinsot's *Cursus Philosophicus* containing the *tractatus de signis*, it is no longer possible to accept Whitehead's famous summation of our intellectual situation as the twentieth century entered its second quarter: "a brief, but sufficiently accurate,

---

[179] Julius R. Weinberg, *Abstraction, Relation, and Induction* (Madison: University of Wisconsin Press, 1965), p. 117.

[180] E.g., see Bertrand Russell, *A Critical Exposition of the Philosophy of Leibniz*, 2nd ed. (London: Allen and Unwin, 1937), pp. 14-15, et alibi.

[181] E.g., compare the *Treatise on Signs*, Second Preamble, Article 1, 97/1-98/39 (=*582a17-b36*), with Russell's remarks in *The Problems of Philosophy* (1912), pp. 90 ff.

[182] See "Recent Criticisms of Consciousness," chap. 1 of Russell's *The Analysis of Mind* (1921), pp. 9-40.

[183] I am thinking, of course, of Russell's celebrated 1905 "theory of descriptions," apparently inspired by a passing comment of Frege's (in *Über Sinn und Bedeutung*, 1892), which became a fundamental part (specifically, the third introductory chapter) of Russell and Whitehead's *Principia Mathematica* and a principal inspiration to a whole generation of American logicians. See my "Reference to the Non-Existent" (1975b), esp. pp. 258-270.

[184] In particular, see his *Human Nature and Conduct* (1922), esp. Parts I and III; and his *Logic: The Theory of Inquiry* (1938).

description of the intellectual life of the European races during the succeeding two centuries and a quarter up to our own times is that they have been living upon the accumulated capital of ideas provided for them by the genius of the seventeenth century."[185]

If we except the remarkable studies of Jacques Maritain (1882-1973) and his school,[186] and some of the logical investigations conducted by Henry Veatch,[187] we can say that Poinsot's work in philosophy remains in its entirety to be considered in modern times. It does not seem too much to expect that at last it will be considered, and that the oldest Western tradition concerning truth and the relative, lost at the very period when the concepts and philosophical vocabulary of modern thought were being formed in the national languages during the seventeenth and eighteenth centuries, will once again become familiar in the world of learning and a civilizing force in the culture of the West, restoring to a yet richer unity and continuity man's understanding of himself and of his being in the world. For, as the sole figure in modern times who achieved an adequate grasp of Poinsot's properly philosophical thought has observed, "the sign involves the whole extent of moral and human life; it is in the human world a universal instrument, just as is movement in the physical world."[188] When we consider, as a consequence, that "there are no more complex problems, no problems of wider bearing on psychology and on culture than those pertaining to the sign,"[189] we can perhaps appreciate just how radical and revolutionary in principle was Poinsot's return to the beginnings of his *Cursus Philosophicus* in his *Treatise on Signs*. For the first time in the history of the West, the world of society and culture and history generally was brought in principle and in a thematic way into the orbit of philosophical understanding, along with the subjectivity of the knower whereby he becomes inserted through his experience into a definite epoch and historical

---

[185] Alfred North Whitehead, *Science and the Modern World* (New York: 1925), p. 39.

[186] Particularly Maritain, 1924, 1932a (=1963 *infra*), 1937-8, 1938, 1943, 1957, and 1963: esp. pp. 769-819, and 231 par. 24-263 *fin*.

[187] In particular, his book, *Intentional Logic* (Yale: 1952), where he says explicitly (p. ix): "I have relied heavily on the very rich but sadly neglected *Ars Logica* of John of St. Thomas. Needless to say, I make no pretense of having exhausted or even adequately understood this massive work." But also Francis H. Parker and Henry Veatch, *Logic as a Human Instrument* (1959), which relies on Poinsot's doctrine of the formal sign (without, however, explicitly envisioning its dependence on the *secundum dici-secundum esse* contrast); and Henry Veatch and Theodore Young, "Metaphysics and the Paradoxes," *The Review of Metaphysics*, VI (December, 1952), 199-218. Veatch's later study, *Two Logics* (Evanston: Northwestern, 1969), does not directly rely on Poinsot, but continues to develop in lively and trenchant ways the contrasts between mathematical logic and the philosophical logic of the Aristotelian tradition.

Ironically, Veatch was originally directed to Poinsot by John Wild, who himself, though he drew on Poinsot's doctrine of signs (e.g., "An Introduction to the Phenomenology of Signs," *Philosophy and Phenomenological Research*, VIII [December, 1947], 217-244), shows, by his review of Simon's 1955 translation (in *Philosophy and Phenomenological Research*, XVII [June, 1956], p. 558) wherein he expresses puzzlement as to why Poinsot thinks categorial relations exist as mind-independently distinct from their fundament, that his grasp of Poinsot's doctrine was never grounded in principle. From the standpoint of Poinsot's *Treatise*, Wild, while professing realism, develops in spite of himself in the direction of nominalism and subjectivism.

Further comments in Deely, 1978a: 22 note 10.

[188] Maritain, 1943: 191. See discussion in note 129, p. 490 above.

[189] Ibid.

world,[190] without thereby losing the privilege of intelligence whereby it is able to grasp truths about things as they are ''in themselves,'' and to speak languages ''other than its own.''

When we consider the radical nature of the semiotic enterprise, and see something of its possible scope in the doctrinal confluence of Poinsot's *Tractatus* with the contemporary Peircean enterprise for philosophy commented on above (pp. 491-498), it seems indeed that we are entering upon a new age. Whether this future thought will no longer be called philosophy, as Heidegger predicted,[191] is beside the point. The point is to achieve an understanding of nature and culture expressing all that was sound in the ancient realisms and modern idealisms, but at the level of a synthesis beyond both. Semiotic reveals itself from the outset in the transcendental guise of *ens ut verum,* just as semiosis reveals in its structuring of experience the formula Hegel tried in vain to teach the moderns, *ens et verum convertuntur*. The conclusion to our reflections at this point may be put in the words of the learned Benedictine, Eleuthère Winance (1983: 515): ''It is in the tradition of Peirce, Locke, and Poinsot that Logic becomes semiotic, able to assimilate the whole of epistemology and natural philosophy as well.''[192]

[190] A preliminary account of this fact (after Heidegger) is given in Deely, *The Tradition via Heidegger* (The Hague: Martinus Nijhoff, 1971), chap. VII, ''Dasein as the Intentional Life of Man,'' pp. 88-110.

[191] ''Das künftige Denken ist nicht mehr Philosophie, weil es ursprünglicher denkt als die Metaphysik, welcher Name das gleiche Sagt'': Martin Heidegger, *Platons Lehre von der Wahrheit, mit einem Brief über den Humanismus* (Bern: Francke, 1947), p. 119.

[192] *''Sommaire: c'est dans la tradition de Peirce, Locke, et Jean de Saint-Thomas que la logique peut devenir une sémiotique qui absorberait l'épistémologie et même la philosophie de la nature.''*

INDICES

GENERAL KEY to the INDICES:

Abbreviations specific to any given index will be indicated at the beginning of that index. The following abbreviations are those general to all the indices:

IFP = Introduction to the Entire Work, First Prologue

ISP = Introduction to the Entire Work, Second Prologue

S = Summulae Texts

FP = First Preamble

SP = Second Preamble

I = Book I

II = Book II

III = Book III

A = Appendix A

C = Appendix C

EA = Editorial Afterword

n. = footnote

≐ signifies rough equivalence or synonymy

In the first four indices, page and line references are to the English column of our bi-lingual *Treatise* text. These are followed in italicized parentheses by the equivalent page, column, and line number in Reiser's edition. Where the reference is in a footnote citing other parts of Poinsot's *Cursus Philosophicus*, the year is usually added within the parentheses, to help the reader to identify exactly the part of Reiser's text from outside the *Treatise* being referred to (following the ''Abbreviations'', p. xii above).

I.
INDEX ARISTOTELICUS:
PASSAGES FROM ARISTOTLE

A. TABLE SHOWING ALL THE WORKS OF ARISTOTLE MENTIONED IN THE *TREATISE ON SIGNS*

NOMINA OPERUM	ORIGO B.C.	EDITIO BEROLINENSI	EDITIO PARISIENSI (DIDOT)
1. *Logica:*			
Categoriae seu de Praedicamentis	c.360	1	I 1
Perihermenias seu de Interpretatione	c.330	16	I 24
Analytica Priora	c.348-347	24	I 39
Analytica Posteriora	c.348-347	71	I 121
2. *Physica:*			
De Naturali Auscultatione seu Libri Physicorum seu Physica	i.353-347	184	II 248
De Anima	c.330	402	III 431
De Memoria et Reminiscentia	c.330	449	III 494
3. *Metpahysica:*			
De Prima Philosophia seu Libri Metaphysicorum seu Metaphysica	i.348-330	980	II 468
4. *Aesthetica:*			
De Arte Rhetorica	c.335-334	1354	I 310

B) LOCI

CATEGORIAE seu DE PRAEDICAMENTIS:
c. 7: **I**, 80/9, 81/7 *(=573b30, 584a8)*.

PERIHERMENIAS:
liber 1:
c. 1: **A**, 343/4 *(=104b40)*; **II**, 271/41 *(=716b1)*; **III**, 337/3 *(=748a21)*.
c. 5: **S**, 23/25 *(=8a23)*.

ANALYTICA PRIORA:
liber I:
c. 1: **S**, 23/9 *(=8a2)*.

ANALYTICA POSTERIORA: in genere: **ISP**, 14/1-17/20 *(=5a10-6b34)*, espec. 17/9 *(=6b18)*.

PHYSICA seu DE NATURALI AUSCULTATIONE:
liber II:
c. 8: **I**, 174 n. 10 *(=1633: 169a21)*.
liber V:
c. 5: **I**, 174/8 *(=674a19)*.

DE ANIMA:
liber II:
c. 4: **I**, 187 n. 33 *(=1632: 818b27)*;
c. 6: **III**, 319/30 *(=739a10)*.

DE MEMORIA ET REMINISCENTIA:
c. 1: **I**, 211/39 *(=689b1)*; **III**, 329/27 *(=744b7)*.

METAPHYSICA:
liber 2:
c. 2: **SP**, 104/5 *(=585b27)*.
liber 5: **C**, 380/34 *(=602a9)*;
c. 7: **FP**, 75/40 *(=306a29)*;
c. 15: **SP**, 81/7, 101/14, 106/17, 109/5 *(=574a9, 584a8, 587a10, 588b17)*; **I**, 147-148 n. 27 *(=1632: 598a4)*.

RHETORICA:
liber 1:
c. 4: **S**, 22/14 *(=7b1)*

II.
INDEX THOMISTICUS:
PASSAGES FROM ST. THOMAS

A. TABLE SHOWING THOSE WORKS OF ST. THOMAS OF WHICH MENTION IS MADE IN THE *TREATISE ON SIGNS*

NOMINA OPERUM	AUTH.	ORIGO	ED. PARMA	ED. VIVES	ED. LEONINA	ED. MANDONNET
1. *Commentaria:*						
a) in Sacram Scripturam						
Expositio in 1. epistolam ad Cor. . .	+	1259-1265	XIII 1	XX 377		
b) in Aristotelem:						
In libros Perihermenias expositio . .	+	1269-1272	XVIII 1	XXII 1	I 5	
In octo libros Physicorum.	+	ca. 1265	XVIII 226	XXII 292	II 3	
In libros Meteorologicorum	+	1269-1271	XIX 300	XXIII 387	III 385	
In libros de Anima	+	1270-1272	XX 1	XXIV 1		
In librum de Memoria et Reminiscentia	+	ca. 1266	XX 197	XXIV 269		
In libros Metaphysicorum.	+	ca. 1268-1272	XX 245	XXIV 333		
c) Commentum super 4 libros Sententiarum Mag. Petri Lombardi .	+	1254-1256	VI-VII	VII-X		tria vol.[2]
d) Scriptum aliud in IV. Libros Sententiarum, ad Annibaldum Cardinalem	–	ca. 1258-1260	XXII 1			
2. *Magna opera systematica:*						
Summa contra Gentiles.	+	1258-ca. 1264	V	XII	XIII et XIV	
Summa theologiae.	+	1266-1273	I-IV	I-IV	IV-XII	
3. *Quaestiones*						
a) Disputatae:						
De Veritate	+	1256-1259	IX 1	XIV 315		
De Potentia	+	1265-1266(67)	VIII 1	XIII 1		
De Malo	+	1263-1268	VIII 219	XIII 320		
b) Quodlibetales:						
Quodlibetum 4, 5.	+	1269-1272	IX 459	XV 357		vol. un.[3]
Quodlibetum 7.	+	1256-1259				
4. *Opuscula:*						
op. 2. Compendium theologiae . . .	+	1272-1273	XVI 1	XXVII 1		opusc. II 1
op. 13. De differentia verbi divini et humani	+	?	XVI 177	XXVII 266		opusc. V 365
op. 14. De natura verbi intellectus . .	+	?	XVI 179	XXVII 268		opusc. V 368
op. 16. De unitate intellectus contra Averroistas	+	1270	XVI 208	XXVII 311		opusc. I 33
op. 30. De ente et essentia	+	1254-1256	XVI 330	XXVII 468		opusc. I 145
op. 42. De natura generis.	+	?	XVII 8	XXVIII 5		opusc. V 221
op. 48. Summa totius Logicae Aristotelis	–		XVII 54	XXVIII 68		opusc. V 1
op. 53. De intellectu et intelligibili . .	–		XVII 126	XXVIII 170		opusc. V 376

1) Signum + indicat opus genuinum, – opus spurium. Vide Ueberweg I21 53-77. Quae opera sint genuina, quae spuria, docent praesertim *M. Grabmann* (Die Werke des hl. Thomas von Aquin, ed. 2., Meunster 1931), *P. Mandonnet* (Les écrits authentique de Saint Thomas d'Aquin, ed. 2., Friburgii Helvet. 1910), *A. Bacic* (Introductio compendiosa in opera S. Thomae Aquinatis, Romae apud «Angelicum» 1925), *G. Manser* (Das Wesen des Thomismus, ed. 2., Friburgii Helvet. 1935, ubi quasi totam bibliographicam invenies).

2) Scriptum super Libros Sententiarum Magistri Petri Lombardi, vol. 1. et 2. a P. Mandonnet ed., Parisiis, Lethielleux 1929; vol. 3.: Scriptum super Sententiis..., a P. Moos ed., Parisiis, Lethielleux 1933.

3) Parisiis, Lethielleux 1926.

B) LOCI

III.
INDEX PERSONARUM

INDEX OF OTHER AUTHORS CITED BY POINSOT AND OF SOME CONTEMPORARIES

The following abbreviations are used for the works usually referred to in this index:

EA: Editorial Afterword, pp. 391-514 of the present volume.

EI: *Enciclopedia italiana* (Istituto Giovanni Treccani 1930).

EU: *Enciclopedia universal illustrada Europeo-Americana* (Barcelona, España).

H: Hurter Hugo, *Nomenclator Litterarius* (3rd ed.; Innsbruck, 1906-1910).

NA: Nicolaus Antonius, *Bibliotheca Hispana Nova*, 2 vols. (Romae 1672).

QE: Quetif et Echard, *Scriptores Ordinis Praedicatorum Recensiti Notisque Historicis et Criticis Illustrati*, 2 vols. (Lutetiae Parisiorum 1719).

Ue: Ueberweg, *Grundriss der Geschichte der Philosophie* (12th ed.; Berlin, 1926).

Capitalization of titles of works in the entries comprising this index follow Reiser.

— A —

ALBERTUS MAGNUS, Doctor of the Church, O.Pr., 1193-1280, principal teacher and good friend of Thomas Aquinas.

Works: *Opera Omnia* (Paris: Vivès, 1890-1899).

A relative is not defined through another, but toward another: C, 380/18 *(=601b40)*.

ANNIBALD OF ANNIBALD, Romanus, O.P.: Taught at Paris (1260-1261), friend of Thomas Aquinas, was made a cardinal in 1263. Died 1272. QE, I, 261a.

Works: *Commentaria in 4 libros Sententiarum*, published among the works of St. Thomas in vol. 22 of the Parma edition.

On the mind-independent status of relations: SP, 82/36 *(=575a7)*;—What is relation: SP, 88/28 *(=577b43)*;—A mind-dependent relation lacks a mind-independent fundament: SP, 91/27 *(=579a33)*;—Relation can be either physical (mind-independent) or mental (mind-dependent): SP, 95/5 *(=581a24)*;—On the nature of relation: I, 120/9 *(=647b34)*.

AUGUSTINE, Saint (Aurelius Augustinus): Father and Doctor of the Church, 354-430.

Definition of sign: I, 116/10, 199/37, 216/12 *(=646a24, 683a31, 691a38)*.

— B —

BAÑEZ, Dominicus, O.P.: Counted among the most outstanding theologians, from about the middle of the sixteenth century until the beginning of the seventeenth, he greatly advanced the Thomistic school by the light of his erudition and wisdom; taught at Salamanca. Died 1604. QE, II, 352a.

Works: *Institutiones minoris Dialecticae, quas Summulas vocant* [''which they call *Summulae* books''] (Salamanca, 1599); *In Aristotelis Dialecticam* (Cologne, 1618); *De Generatione, et Corruptione* (Cologne, 1616); *Scholastica Commentaria in primam partem Angelici Doctoris S. Thomae*, 2 vols. (Douay, 1614).

Not every change whatever essentially varies seeing: I, 299/42 *(=729b42)*;—On the ultimate ground of diversity among the sciences (''in which he seems to have attained the mind of St. Thomas''): I, 188-190 n. 33 *(=1635: 825a1-2)*.

— C —

CABERO, Chrysostomus, Ord. Cist.: theological Doctor of the ''Complutenses'' group of Carmelite professors (founded by Cardinal Ximenes in 1489 and later associated with the University of Alcalá). Died 1653. Seems for the most part to be cited by Poinsot not because of the importance of his doctrine, but because he taught in the same Alcalán Academy in which Poinsot taught. NA, I, 194a; EU, X, 114a.

Works: *Brevis Summularum recapitulatio succinctaque totius Logicae evisceratio* (Valladolid, 1623); *Commentaria in octos libros Physicorum* (Alcalá, 1628); *In duos libros de Ortu et Interitu* (Alcalá, 1636).

On the division of mind-dependent being: FP, 52/17 *(=287a48)*.

CAJETAN, Thomas de Vio, O.P.: 1468-1534. QE, II, 14a. Renaissance Cardinal and Thomistic Commentator; met

with Luther at Augsburg in 1518 as the Pope's representative; author of a celebrated *Commentary* on the *Summa theologiae* which is reprinted in the Leonine edition of the works of Thomas Aquinas.

Works: *Commentaria in Summam theologicam S. Thomae* (in the Leonine edition of the works of St. Thomas); *Super Praedicabilia Porphyrii et Aristotelis Praedicamenta ac Posteriorum Analyticorum libros* (Venice, 1554), nova editio by Isnardo M. Marega, O.P. (Rome, 1934); *Super tres libros de Anima* (Florence, 1509, "Romae anno salutis 1509. 25. Februarium aetatis suae anno 41. inchoante . . ."); *Opuscula*, 3 vols. (Venice, 1588); *De nominum analogia. De conceptu entis*, nova ed. by P. N. Zammit (Rome, 1934); *In Ecclesiasten commentarii simul cum commentariis in parabolas Salomonis in uno volumine* (Rome, 1542; at the conclusion of this volume the author wrote: "Romae, die 23. Iunii 1534., anno autem aetatis meae sexagesimo sexto. Deo gratias. Amen.").

Mind-dependent beings do not result from the will: FP, 65/9 *(=301a19)*;—The divisions of being in the order of physical existence are one thing, while the divisions in the order of the knowable are quite another thing: I, 149/46, 179 n. 13 *(=663a1, 1635: 77a17)*;—Distinguishes things entirely relative, entirely absolute, and intermediate between these: I, 166/12 *(=670a31)*;—The differences of things in physical being and existence are one matter, differences in the rationale of object and knowable thing quite another: I, 187/35, 188 n. 33 *(=678b24, 1632: 818b42)*;— What is actual signification in a voice: I, 198/18 *(=682a44)*;—On the rationale of an image: I, 212/4 *(=689b12, 19)*;—The sense in which Aristotle defined relation: I, 81/35 *(=574a43)*;—A mind-dependent relation is a true relation, not by the truth of an entity and of an informing form, but by the truth of an objective and positive tendency toward a term: I, 95/37 *(=581b14)*;—The differences of things as things are quite other than the differences of things as objects and in the being of object: II, 270/38 *(=715b38)*;—Posits two conditions for something to be said to be cognized intuitively: III, 309/22 *(=734a11)*;—For anything to be directly cognizable, a formal presence does not suffice, but objective presence is required: III, 326/42 *(=743a3)*;—A word [i.e., a concept] is present to our understanding formally, but not objectively: III, 331/26 *(=745b19)*;—Future things are seen by God in his eternity: III, 316/32 *(=737a37)*.

CAPREOLUS, Joannes, O. P.: 1380-1444. Titled "Prince of the Thomists." QE, I, 795b.

Works: *Libri defensionum*, new ed. by Paban and Peques, 7 vols. (Toulouse, 1900-1908).

The act of understanding is not a formal sign: II, 263/35 *(=712b43)*.

CARMELITANI (Carrmelites): The generic name for the two groups of Professors at the Carmelite Colleges associated respectively with the University of Alcalá and the University of Salamanca.

1) The professors of the Alcalán College of St. Cyril of the Discalced Brothers of the Order of Our Lady of Mount Carmel, referred to collectively as the **Complutenses** (late 16th-early 17th century), authors of the following works: *In Aristotelis Dialecticam et Philosophiam naturalem* (Lyons, 1651); *in duos libros de Generatione et Corruptione* (Lyons, 1651); *in tres libros de Anima* (Lyons, 1651).

2) The professors of the Salamancan College of the Discalced Brothers of the Order of Our Lady of Mount Carmel, known collectively as the **Salmanticenses** (17th century), who authored a celebrated *Cursus theologicus* (new. ed. Paris: Victor Palmé, 1870ff.).

COMPLUTENSES: See Carmelitani, 1.

CONIMBRICENSES: School of commentary formed by Jesuit Professors of the College of Coimbra, 16th-17th centuries, under the original leadership of Petrus Fonsecus (Pedro da Fonseca). Teachers of Poinsot (see Doyle 1984).

Works: *Commentarii in universam Dialecticam Aristotelis* (written *inter* 1592-1606: Lyons 1606; Venice, 1616); *in octos libros Physicorum* (Lyons, 1610); *in duos libros de Generatione et Corruptione* (Lyons, 1613); *in tres libros de Anima* (Lyons, 1612).

The definitive rationale of a sign: I, 136/14 *(=656a7)*;—Whether by the absolute power of God a physically absent thing could be attained by external sense: III, 305/28 *(=732b21)*.

— D —

DURANDUS OF SAINT-POURCAIN, O.P.: Called "the most resolute doctor". Died 1334. QE, I, 586a.

Works: *In Petri Lombardi Sententias theologicas commentariorum libri quattuor* (Venice, 1571).

On mind-dependent being: FP, 49/29 *(=285b36)*.

— E —

EUCLID: *floruit* c. 300 B.C., taught at Alexandria. Called the "Father of Geometry".

Works: *Elementorum libri XV* (Paris, 1573).

Definition of proportionality: SP, 103/8 *(=585a19)*.

— F —

FERRARIENSIS: Francis Sylvester of Sylvester, known by the cognomen "Ferrariensis". Taught at Bologna, c.1474-1528. QE, II, 59b.

Works: *Commentaria in libros Sanctae Thomae Contra Gentes* (in the Leonine edition of the works of St. Thomas, vol. XIII and XIV).

On the distinction between intuitive and abstractive awareness: III, 288/6 *(=723a12)*;—The act of understanding is not a formal sign: II, 263/37 *(=712b44)*;—Whether it is necessary to form another concept of our own concept in order to cognize it: III, 324/10 *(=741b24)*.

— G —

GARCEZ, Maria: Mother of Louis and John Poinsot. EA, 425-426.

— H —

HENRICUS, GANDAVINUS (Henry of Ghent): taught at Paris, "the Solemn Doctor", ca. 1217-1293. Ue II 498.

Works: *Quodlibeta* (Paris, 1518; Venice, 1608-1613); *Summa Theologiae* (Ghent, 1520; Ferrara, 1647). Mentioned by Suarez: FP, 44-45 n. 1.

HERVAEUS NATALIS (Hervé Nédélec), O.Pr.: Doctor and Professor at Paris, Master General of the Dominican Order, the first to vigorously oppose the doctrine of St. Thomas to positions of Scotus, mayhap more with vigor than insight. Died 1323. QE, I, 533 b. Cited by Suarez: FP, 44-45 n. 1.

— J —

JEROME (Eusebius Hieronymus), Saint: Father and Doctor of the Church, 331-429.

On the sign placed by God on Cain: II, 277/6 *(=719a9)*.

— L —

LOMBARD, Peter: "Master of the Sentences", died 1160.

Works: *Libri quatuor Sententiarum*, edited by the Professors of the College of St. Bonaventure, in two volumes (Clear Waters [Quaracchi], near Florence, 1916).

— M —

MARTINEZ, John Gonzalez M.: From Burgos, but a professor at Alcalá three times assigned the course of arts, he both taught and wrote. Martinez seems to be referred to by Poinsot because he too taught at Alcalá, and especially because Martinez was a vehement and mordant enemy of the Thomists and of Thomistic teaching. Died 1656. NA, II, 563; P. Beltran de Heredia, "La enseñanza de Sto. Tomas en Alcalá," *La Ciencia Tomista*, XIII (1915), 407-408.

Works: *Fabrica Syllogistica Aristotelis* (Alcalá, 1628, 1632); *Aristotelis Stagiritae Physica* (Alcalá, 1622); *Aristotelis Stagiritae de Generatione et Corruptione libri duo* (Alcalá, 1623).

On the division of mind-dependent being: FP, 52/26 *(=287b9)*.

MERINERO, John, O.F.M., of Madrid: Formerly a celebrated reader of theology in the convent of St. Mary of Jesus at Alcalá, a provincial minister in the province of Castille, afterwards minister general of the whole Franciscan Order, finally Bishop of Valladolid. Died 1663. NA, I, 568a.

Works: *Commentarii in universam Aristotelis Dialecticam juxta subtilis Doctoris Joannis Duns Scoti mentem* (Alcalá, 1629).

On the division of mind-dependent being: FP, 52/18 *(=287b1)*.

— N —

NOMINALISTS: SP, 80/19 *(=573b39)*; EA, 499ff.

— O —

OCKHAM (also spelled "Occam" and "Ocham"), William of, O.F.M.: Called in the schools "venerabilis inceptor" ["distinguished innovator"] and "auctor invincibilis". Prince of the Nominalists. Died 1349. Ue, II, 572; EA, III.C. and IV., *passim*.

Works: *Quaestiones in libros Physicorum; Quaestiones in 4 libros Sententiarum; Quodlibeta.*

— P —

St. PAUL THE APOSTLE:

On the beatific vision: III, 297/27 *(=728b7)*.

— R —

RAMIREZ, Didacus, O.P.: Friend and first biographer of Poinsot. Died 1660. EU, LXIX, 516b. EA, 444.

— S —

SALMANTICENSES: See Carmelitani, 2.

SCOTUS, John Duns, O.F.M.: "The subtle doctor", 1266-1308.

Works: *Opera omnia* (Paris, 1891-1895); *Commentaria Oxoniensa ad IV Libros Magistri Sententiarum*, ed. Marianus Fernandez Garcia, O.F.M. (Clear Waters [Quaracchi], 1912-1914 [in the Vatican edition of Scotus' work begun in 1950 this work is referred to as the *Ordinatio*]).

Mind-dependent beings also result from the will: FP, 65/8, 10 *(=301a18, 20)*;—On the conditions for a categorial relation: SP, 92/8 *(=579b12)*;—That upon one categorial relation can be founded another such relation: SP, 102/39 *(=584b42)*;—Relations of the first and third type are also categorial: SP, 106/22 *(=587a16)*;—Action cannot be the fundament of a relation: SP, 109/40 *(=589a14)*.

SERNA, Peter: Prefect and later general definitor for the Conception province of the Discalced (from 1608 on) Order [originally] for the Ransom of [i.e., exchange of self for] Captives [taken by the Moslems].

Works: *Commentaria in Logicam Aristotelis* (Seville, 1624).

On the division of mind-dependent being: FP, 52/16 *(=287a46)*.

SONCINAS, Paul, O.P. Died 1494. QE, I, 879b.

Works: *Quaestiones Metaphysicae* (Lyons, 1579).

Cited by Suarez against the idea of any univocity between mind-independent and mind-dependent being: 44-45 n. 1.

SOTO, Dominic, O.P.: Taught at Salamanca, 1494-1560. QE, II, 181a.

Works: *Summulae* (Salamanca, 1571); *In Dialecticam Aristotelis commentaria* (Salamanca, 1580); *Super octos libros Physicorum* (Venice, 1582).

What voices signify: A, 345/1 *(=105a24)*;—In what sense the cognition of external sense is said to be a term: II, 267/27 *(=714b37)*;—how relatives are to be defined according to Albert the Great: C, 380/18 *(=601b41)*.

SUAREZ, Francis, S.J., from Granada: 1548-1617. Taught philosophy at Segovia, theology at Avila, Segovia, Valladolid, Rome (1580-1585), Alcalá, Salamanca, Coimbra.

Works: *Opera omnia* (Paris, 1856).

On extrinsic denomination: FP, 55/15 *(=289a14)*;—A relation is founded neither on action nor on a proximate power, but on the radical power, i.e., on substance itself: SP, 110/5 *(=589a25)*;—What the rationale of the stipulated sign consists in, in the case of the sacraments: II, 274/1 *(=717b21)*. On mind-dependent being: FP, 44-45 n. 2.

— V —

VAZQUEZ, Gabriel, S.J.: Taught principally at Alcalá and Rome between about 1551 and 1604. H, III, 385.

Works: *Commentariorum ac disputationum in primam partem S. Thomae*, 2 vols.; *in primam secundae*, 2 vols.; *in tertiam partem*, 4 vols. (Lyons, 1631).

On extrinsic denomination: FP, 55/9 *(=289a8)*;— Rejects the distinction of rationales "which" and "under which" within the formal rationale of object: I, 188-189 n. 33 *(=1632: 819a30)*.

IV.
INDEX RERUM
TERMS AND PROPOSITIONS

Roughhewn, by comparison with the other indices, the following index of terms and propositions propriate to the semiotic we present is in some ways the most useful. The index proper is alphabetized according a series of English terms derived from the text of the *Treatise,* with propositions numerically listed under these terminological entries. Since the *Treatise* text is not English, however, it is necessary first to identify the Latin terms which conceptually underlie the alphabetized English entries used to organize the propositions of the index proper. The following list provides this identification, and is not intended as a dictionary. The Latin base terms are listed below in their own alphabetical order, with the derivative English Index entries set opposite (and therefore out of the order in which they organize the Index proper). The Index proper is placed after the list.

A) ALPHABETIZED LIST OF LATIN BASE TERMS

Absens: Absent
Absentia: Absence
Abstractio: Abstraction
Accidens: Accident, Subjective Determination
Actio: Action
Actio Immanens, Actus Immanens: Immanent Action
Actio Transiens, Actus Transiens: Transient Action
Actus: Act
Actus Cognoscendi: Act of Cognizing, Cognitive Act
Actus Cognoscitivus: Cognitive Act
Actus Comparativus: Comparative Act
Actus Intellectus: Act of Understanding
Actus Moralis: Moral Act
Ad Placitum: Stipulation, Imposition
Aeternitas: Eternity
Amicitia: Friendship
Analogia: Analogy
Analogum: Analogue
Analytica: Analytics
Angelus, Angeli: Pure Spirits, Angel, Angels
Animalia: Animals
Antecedens: Antecedent
Antichristus: Antichrist
Apparitiones: Apparitions
Appetitus: Appetite, Desire
Applicans: Applying
Applicatio: Application
Apprehensibilitas: Apprehensibility
Apprehensio: Awareness
Argumentum: Argument
Ascensus: Ascent
Bruta: Brute Animals
Cain: Cain
Casus: Cases
Causa: Cause
Causa Finalis: Final Cause
Causa Formalis Extrinseca: Extrinsic Formal Cause
Character: Character
Christus: Christ
Claritas et Evidens: Clarity and Distinctness in Knowledge
Cognitio: Cognition, Knowledge
Cognito Reflexiva: Reflexion
Cognoscibilitas: Cognizability
Color: Color
Comparatio: Comparison
Conceptus: Concept
Conceptus Connotativus: Connotative Concepts
Conditionatum Contingens: Conditioned Contingent
Connotatio: Connotation
Consequens: Consequent
Consequentia: Consequence
Consuetudo: Custom
Contactus: Contact
Contiguum: Contiguous

Creatura: Creature
Cultus: Worship
Daemon: Demon
Denominatio: Denomination
Denominatio Extrinseca: Extrinsic Denomination
Descensus: Descent
Deus: God
Dictio: Diction
Discursus: Discourse
Disputatio: Disputation
Disputatio Dialectica: Dialectical Disputation
Divisio: Division
Doctor: Teacher
Doctrina: Teaching
Ens: Being
Ens Praedicamentale: Categorial Being, Mind-Independent Being
Ens Rationis: Mind-Dependent Being
Ens Reale: Mind-Independent Being, Real Being
Enthymema: Enthymeme
Esse: Being, Copula signifying existence
Esse Cognitum: Being Cognized
Eucharistia: Eucharist
Exemplar: Exemplar
Existentia: Existence
Experientia, Experimentum: Experience, Experimental Contact, i.e., Grounded in Physical Interaction
Expressio: Expression
Facere Cognoscere: Making Cognizant
Falsitas: Falsity
Fides: Faith
Finis: End
Finis Causa: Final Cause
Finis Cuius Gratia: Final Cause
Forma: Forma
Fundamentum: Fundament (also: Basis, Ground, Foundation, Subject Term)
Futura: Future
Futura Conditionata: Conditioned Future Things
Gratia: Grace
Habitus: Habit
Idea: Idea
Idealismus (Reiser Neologism): Idealism
Idolum: Icon
Illation: Illation
Imaginatio: Imagination
Imago: Image
Impositio: Imposition, Stipulation
Independentia: Independence
Indifferentia: Indifference
Individuatio: Individuation
Individuum: Individual
Inductio: Induction
Inductio per Ascensum: Abduction
Inductio per Descensum: Induction
Instinctus: Instinct
Instrumentum: Instrument
Intellectus: Human Understanding, Intellect, Intelligence, Understanding
Intentio: Intention
Intentio Prima: First Intention
Intentio Secunda: Second Intention
Intuitio: Intuition
Judicium: Judgment
Liber Clausus: Closed Book
Libertas: Liberty
Locutio Interior: Interior Discourse
Logica: Logic
Lumen: Light
Lux: Light
Manifestatio: Manifestation
Manifestativum: Manifestative
Materia: Matter
Medium: Means, Medium
Mensura: Measure
Metaphora: Metaphor
Minor: Minor
Motio: Motion, Movement
Motivum: Stimulation, Stimulus
Movere Obiective, Movere Potentiam Cognoscitivam: Stimulate
Mutatio: Change, Mutation
Natura: Nature
Negatio: Negation
Nomina: Names
Nominales, Nominalistae: Nominalists
Non Ens: Mind-Dependent Being, Non-Being
Notitia: Awareness
Notitia Abstractiva: Abstractive Awareness
Notitia Experimentalis: Experimental Knowledge
Notitia Formalis: Formal Awareness
Notitia Intuitiva: Intuitive Awareness
Notitia Simplex: Simple Awareness
Obiective Esse Praesens: Objective Presence
Obiectum: Object
Obiectum Physicum: Physical Object
Operatio Immanens: Immanent Action
Operatio Transiens: Transient Action
Opinio: Opinion
Phantasia: Imagination
Phantasma, Species Expressa Sensus Interioris: Phantasm
Potentia: Power
Potentia Cognitiva: Cognitive Power
Potentia Cognoscitiva: Cognitive Power
Praecognitum: First Cognized, Known First Objectively
Praedicamentum: Category
Praesentia: Presence
Praesentia Obiectiva: Objective Presence
Praeteritum: Past
Principium: Principle
Processus in Infinitum: Infinite Regress
Proprium Sensibile: Proper Sensible
Qualitas: Quality
Ratio: Human Understanding, Rationale, Reason, Understanding
Ratiocinatio: Reasoning
Realitas: Real Being, Reality
Reddere Praesens: Making Present
Reflexio: Reflexion

Refractio: Refraction
Regressus: Regress
Relatio: Relation
Relatio Praedicamentalis: Categorial Relation, Mind-Independent Relation
Relatio Rationis: Mind-Dependent Relation
Relatio Realis: Mind-Independent Relation, Physical Relation
Relatio Secundum Dici: Relation According to the Way Being Must Be Expressed in Discourse
Relatio Secundum Esse: Relation According to the Way Relation Has Being
Relatio Transcendentalis: Transcendental Relation
Religio: Religion
Repraesentabile: Representable
Repraesentans: Representing
Repraesentatio: Representation
Repraesentativum: Representative
Res Absoluta: Subjectivity, Existing as or in a Subject Simply
Sacramenta: Sacraments
Scibile: Knowable
Scibilitas: Knowability
Scientia: Knowledge
Scientia Visionis: Knowledge of Vision
Scriptura: Writing
Sensatio: Sensation
Sensibile: Sense Datum
Sensibile Commune: Common Sensible
Sensus: Sense
Sensus Externus: External Sense
Sensus Internus: Internal Sense, Perception
Signans: Signifying
Signatum: Significate
Significare: Signifying
Significatio: Signification
Signum: Sign
Signum Formale: Formal Sign
Signum Instrumentale: Instrumental Sign
Signum Naturale: Natural Sign
Signum ad Placitum: Stipulated Sign
Signum ex Consuetudine: Customary Sign
Simplex Apprehensio: Simple Awareness
Singulare: Singular
Species: Specification, Specifier, Specifying Form
Species Expressa: Expressed Specifier
Species Impressa: Impressed Specifier
Specificatio: Specification
Specificativum: Specificative
Speculum: Mirror
Spiritus: Spirit
Spiritus Animalium: Animal Spirits
Subiectum: Subject
Substantia: Substance
Terminus: Term, Terminus
Transcendentalia, Transcendentia: Transcendentals
Trinitas: Trinity
Ultimatus et Nonultimatus: Ultimate and Non-Ultimate
Unio Obiectiva: Objective Union
Unitas: Unity
Universale: Universal
Universalitas: Universality
Univocum: Univocal
Usus: Use
Usus Vocis: Linguistic Usage
Verbum: Word
Veritas: Truth
Verum: The True (something true)
Virtus: Virtue
Visio, Visus: Act of Seeing, Seeing, Vision
Voluntas: Will
Vox: Voice
Vox Significans ut Applicata: Linguistic Usage
Vox Significativa: Linguistic Expression

B) INDEX OF TERMS AND PROPOSITIONS

— A —

ABDUCTION (*Inductio per Ascensum*): Induction is divided through ascent from singulars to universals and descent from universals to singulars: FP, 64/11 *(=293b42)*—i.e., into abduction and induction: FP, 64 note 14.

SEE: Induction

ABSENCE (*Absentia*):

SEE: Intuition
Presence
Sense

ABSENT (*Absens*): It is in no way possible for there to be in external sense an awareness of a physically absent thing: III, 306/13, 309/47, 310/37, 311/23 *(=733a13, 734a37, 734b26, 734b35)*.

SEE: Intuition
Presence
Sense
Sign

ABSTRACTION (*Abstractio*): Just as an object cannot terminate external vision except when it is bathed in visible light, so neither can an object be attained by the understanding unless it is divested of sensibility and is affected and formed by a spiritual light, which is immateriality or abstraction: II, 243/22-244/5 *(=703a9)*.

ABSTRACTIVE AWARENESS (*Notitia Abstractiva*):
SEE: Awareness
God
Intuition
Objective Presence
Presence
Truth

ACCIDENT, SUBJECTIVE DETERMINATION (*Accidens*): We experience the effects of accidental forms but we do not experience their distinction from substance: SP, 86/20 *(=577b25)*.
SEE: Sense 22
Subjectivity

ACT (*Actus*):
SEE: Action

ACT OF COGNIZING (*Actus Cognoscendi*):
SEE: Act of Understanding
Cognitive Act
Power 3
Specificative
Specifier
Stimulus

ACT OF SEEING (*Visio, Visus*):
SEE: Common Sensible
Intuition
Vision

ACT OF UNDERSTANDING (*Actus Intellectus, Actus Intelligendi*):

1. An act of understanding, though it is a quality, does, nevertheless, not render an object present as a form keeping on the side of the object as if it were a vicegerent of that object, but as a form tending toward and operating with respect to—that is, assimilating—the object from the side of the power; it is therefore not a representative but an operative union, that is, a union in the mode of a second act, not as containing but as tending toward an object: II, 265/2 *(=714a2)*.

2. Of itself an immanent act is not an action in the mode of a movement and of a way of tending toward a further term, but in the mode of a final actuality in which a whole cognition is completed; and for this reason St. Thomas compares the act of understanding to the very act of existing: 267/9 *(=714b17)*.

3. The act of understanding is the ultimate actuality in the intelligible order, just as the act of being is the ultimate perfection in the entitative order: II, 251/1 *(=706a14)*.

SEE: Cognition
Cognitive Act
Making Cognizant
Quality
Relation

ACTION (*Actio*): Difference between transitive and immanent action: II, 267/34 *(=715a2)*.
SEE: Cause
Existence
Immanent Action
Mind-Dependent Being 42
Movement
Transient Action

ANALOGY, ANALOGUE (*Analogia, Analogum*):

1. A logical dependence, that is, a dependence in participating a general rationale, creates an analogy, but a physical dependence in being and exercise does not create analogy: II, 236/46-237/1 *(=701a17, 30)*.

2. Not every dependence of one thing on another makes for an analogy, but only that which is in an order to participating a general or common rationale; for unless a given dependence is partly the same in rationale and partly different, it does not destroy univocation: II, 271/35 *(=716a41)*

3. Nothing prevents less universal things from being clothed in an analogous concept and divided in a manner analogical to, although more restricted than, more universal things: I, 133/28 *(=655a25)*.

4. According as analogues of a more restricted analogy are referred to a more universal analogous concept, they are not located under a determinate and univocal member of a division of the more universal in the restricted analogy but relate in varying ways both among themselves in the restricted analogy and to the members of the more universal analogy: I, 133/32 *(=655a30)*.

5. The cognizable in general, like the true and the good and the coincident properties of being, is analogous to this or that cognizable: I, 190/7 *(=679a10)*.

SEE: Division
Object
Transcendentals
Univocal

ANALYTICS (*Analytica*): Logic is called 'analytics' by Aristotle because it is resolutory: S, 22/14 *(=7b1)*.

ANGEL, ANGELS (*Angelus, Angeli*):

1. Objects do not act effectively on the intellect of a pure spirit: I, 172/34 *(=673a32)*.

2. How the stimulus object is preserved in respect of the intellect of a pure spirit: I, 185/2 *(=677a21)*.

3. The specifiers [or concepts] which pure spirits have of the future cannot represent things by a termination at those things in themselves, but as contained in causes: III, 315/41 *(=736b43)*.

4. Although for a pure spirit, understanding itself understanding and understanding its own essence are distinct in rationale, nevertheless, the first object of its own act of understanding is its own essence, and for this reason it understands both itself and its own essence at once and by the same act: III, 326/13 *(=742b13)*.

5. Pure spirits use signs because they have discourse eminentially: I, 210/33 *(=688b33)*.

6. In the case of pure spirits and of separated substances reflexive concepts are not necessary: III, 325/32 *(=742a26)*.

7. How a pure spirit cognizes its own subjective modifications and how it cognizes those of another substance: III, 289/8 *(=723b19)*.

SEE: Demon
Future

ANIMAL SPIRITS (*Spiritus Animalium*): Why apparitions can be produced in the imagination by a disturbance of the animal spirits: II, 246/4 *(=704a1)*; III, 322/44 *(=741a5)*.

ANIMALS (*Animalia*):

1. Animals have a judgment, but without indifference, and therefore determined to one thing and based on natural instinct: I, 246/4 *(=690b42)*.

2. Animals are able to represent in perception that on whose pattern some fictive entity is formed: FP, 66/47 *(=301b33)*.

3. Animals apprehend non-being objectively but not comparatively to the difference between being and non-being: FP, 67/1 *(=301b39)*.

4. Animals attain to the sensible *perception* of the condition relative to non-being which an object has without reflecting the formal element of its indifference to such a condition, and therefore as if it were not a condition relative to non-being: FP, 67/21 *(=302a11)*.

5. Higher animals form and know mind-dependent beings without recognizing the mind-dependent elements as such in what they objectively apprehend: FP, 66/47 *(=301b33)*; cf. 205/23 *(=685b44)*.

6. Customs are both learned by and formed by animals: II, 280/14 *(=720a44)*.
7. Animals make use of signs: I, 204/9 *(=685b4)*.
SEE: Brute Animals
Custom
Imagination
Mind-Dependent Being
Perception
Sensation
Sign

ANTECEDENT (*Antecedens*): The first of the two propositions contained in an enthymeme: 10/18 *(=3a29)*.

ANTICHRIST (*Antichristus*): How God could produce a specifier [concept] representing the future antichrist just as he will be in himself: III, 315/22 *(=736b22)*.

APPARITIONS (*Apparitiones*): How apparitions observed in the Eucharist or concerning the body of Christ might be explained: III, 322/20 *(=740b23)*.
SEE: Awareness
Imagination
Intuition
Animal Spirits

APPETITE (*Appetitus*):
SEE: Awareness

APPLICATION, APPLYING (*Applicatio, Applicans*):
SEE: Making cognizant
Stimulus
Use

APPREHENSIBILITY (*Apprehensibilitas*):
SEE: Cognizability

APPREHENSION (*Apprehensio*):
SEE: Awareness
Term
Truth 14
Word

ARGUMENT (*Argumentum*):
SEE: Disputation

ASCENT (*Ascensus*): Ascent and descent in argumentation: FP, 64/11 *(=293b42)* and n. 14.
SEE: Descent
Induction

AWARENESS (*Notitia*):
1. Awareness ≅ simple apprehension ≅ mental term ≅ concept: 28/2, 29/7 *(=10a35, 10b22)*.
2. No awareness at all can be elicited without a specifying form: III, 288/12 *(=723a18)*.
3. Intuitive and abstractive awareness defined: III, 287/1 *(=722b24)*; S, 29/13, 21 *(=10b31,38)*.
4. Four differences between intuitive and abstractive cognition are assigned: III, 304/3 *(=732a12)*.
5. The principal difference between an intuitive and an abstractive awareness: III, 304/19 *(=732a30)*.
6. Intuitive awareness demands not only an intentional but also the physical presence of the object, and abstractive awareness demands the physical absence of the object: III, 287/5 *(=722b29)*.
7. Intuitive awareness can be preserved through a mediate cognition, that is to say, a cognition in another: III, 288/42, 289/1 *(=723b7, 14)*.
8. Formal awareness and the proper rationales of the intuitive and the abstractive are not rationales essentially and intrinsically altering cognition: III, 290/27 *(=724b3)*.
9. Presence and absence as represented things essentially and directly do not distinguish the intuitive and the abstractive: III, 291/31, 299/14, 307/5 *(=725a12, 729b9, 733a35)*.
10. Presence pertains to the intuitive only inasmuch as it is modificative of the object, not inasmuch as it is constitutive of it: III, 292/11 *(=725a44)*.
11. The intuitive and the abstractive differ from one another essentially and by definition, but these differences are accidental to the cognition itself [subjectively considered]: III, 299/5 *(=729a47)*.
12. The intuitive and the abstractive do not differ according to formal objects diverse in the being and formality of the cognizable, but in the being and formality of some condition and accidental mode: III, 298/40 *(=729a30)*.
13. Incidentally, i.e., through another to which they are conjoined (or: by reason of a concomitant attribute) the intuitive and the abstractive can import types of awareness different in kind: III, 290/32, 296/13 *(=724b7, 727b31)*. Examples: 292/48 *(=725b37)*.
14. The intuitive and the abstractive are something intrinsic to the very awareness in their own order as awareness: III, 293/49 *(=726a43)*.
15. When created awareness passes from intuitive to abstractive and conversely, it is really modified: III, 294/2 *(=726a46)*.
16. Not every variation in a representation is an essential variation, unless it is reduced to diverse rationales 'which' or 'under which' of the very representation: III, 299/31 *(=729b29)*.
17. Why the physical presence and absence of an object essentially distinguish acts of desire, but not acts of cognition: III, 300/41 *(=730a47)*.
18. The intuitive and the abstractive are accidental (incidental) modes which pertain reductively to the order of cognition as modes, not as essential kinds: III, 302/3 *(=731a25)*.
19. The intuitive and the abstractive do not essentially vary awareness because they are circumstances of awareness and always remain such: III, 303/41 *(=731b47)*.
20. A past or a future "thing as such" cannot terminate an intuitive cognition: III, 305/36 *(=732b28)*.
21. An abstractive awareness, that is to say, an awareness of a physically absent thing, is in no way possible for exterior sense: III, 309/47 *(=734a37)*.
22. Intuitive seeing or vision bears on a present thing according as presence affects that thing in itself, and not according as that thing is attained in another or according as presence is cognized as a kind of definable character: III, 309/7 *(=733b41)*.
23. Reflexive awareness concerns all those things which are found in the soul and take on as the result of the cognition of a material object the representation and manner of a sensible essence: III, 328/22 *(=743b47)*.
SEE: Formal Awareness
Intuition
Presence
Simple Awareness

— B —

BASIS (*Fundamentum*):
SEE: Extrinsic Formal Cause
Foundation, Fundament
Non-Being
Relation
Specifier

BEING (*Ens*): Being is denominated from the act of being and in terms of an order to existence: FP, 49/21 *(=285b25)*.
SEE: Object
Mind-Dependent Being
Mind-Independent Being
Presence

BEING (*Esse*):
SEE: Act of Understanding
Existence
Intuition
Mind-Independent Being
Presence

BEING COGNIZED (*Esse Cognitum*):
1. "Being cognized" is an extrinsic denomination: FP, 49/31 *(=285b34)*.
2. Being cognized is opposed to being cognizable as that which follows upon to that which antecedes the activity of a cognitive power: I, 138/44 *(=657a45)*.
3. Being cognized does not pertain to the rationale of a sign, but to its exercise: I, 159/19 *(=667a22)*.
4. Being seen or cognized provenates from a cognition existing in a cognizing subject, just as every extrinsic denomination provenates from some real (i.e., independent of being itself apprehended) form existing in another subject: SP, 83/20 *(=575a37)*.
5. When the concept is said to be "that which is cognized" by one and the same cognition as that by which the thing signified by the concept is attained, because the concept is attained only *formally* while the thing is attained *objectively*, the "being that which is cognized" is an extrinsic denomination only with respect to the thing; with respect to the concept, the qualification "cognized" designates only the real form which founds that denomination: II, 250/8 *(=705b14)*; cf. I, 202/19 *(=684b10)*.
6. "Being cognized" is a denomination that can fall upon mind-dependent and mind-independent beings alike: FP, 49/42 *(=286a1)*.
7. Things denominated "cognized" on the pattern of another are not ipso facto denominated as mind-dependent beings: FP, 51/21 *(=286b37)*.
8. Things denominated cognized by way of an alien nature (on the pattern of another), rather than by way of their proper being, receive thence in their cognized being a connotation relative to that on whose pattern they are cognized: FP, 51/15 *(=286b31)*.
SEE: Cognizable
Concept 27, 28
Intuition
Mind-Dependent Being
Presence

BRUTE ANIMALS (*Bruta*): Animals which lack sufficient grounds for thematizing concern for the order of the true inasmuch as its formal being is relative [editors' definition]: cf. FP, 67/14, 74/39, etc. *(=302a4, 305b19)*.
SEE: Animals
Cognition
Custom
Experience
Instinct
Mind-Dependent Being esp. 45-48
Perception
Sense

— C —

CAIN: What sort of sign might have been placed on Cain by God: II, 277/4 *(=719a6)*.

CASES (*Casus*): Why the cases of names distinguish concepts essentially in an inflected language: III, 300/5 *(=730a6)*.

CATEGORIAL RELATION (*Relatio Praedicamentalis*):
SEE: Relation

CATEGORY (*Praedicamentum*) [see the discussion of categories in FP page 86 n. 16, and in EA pages 472-479, 489]:
1. The distinction of the categories was introduced for this, that the diverse orders of natures and classes to which all the things which participate some nature might be reduced should be set out; for this reason, the first thing that must be excluded from any category is mind-dependent being because it does not have a nature or true entity, but a constructed or fictive one. Whence St. Thomas says that only things outside the soul pertain to the categories: I, 118 n. 10; EA, 472 n. 111 *(=500b36-501a12)*.
2. There is no less necessity for positing this category of a relative entity or rationale of being than there is for positing the category of quantity or quality. For it is from perceiving the effects of quantity and quality that we gather that there are such forms. So in the same way it is from perceiving this efffect—namely, some things ordered and having a condition relative to other things (such as similitude, paternity, priority, etc.)—not mixed with a subjective rationale, but entirely consisting in a respect: thence we best gather that this type of relative entity is given, just as we gather that there are subjective or absolute entities from subjective effects. Nor is greater experience necessary for this than in the cases of other accidental forms (determinations of subjective being) in which we experience the effects indeed, but not their distinction from substance: SP, 86/6 *(=577a7)*.
SEE: Mind-Dependent Being
Mind-Independent Being
Relation

CAUSE (*Causa*):
1. Actions leave on the side of a cause some determination to the past effect, whether through habit or through disposition or right or anything similar: SP, 111/28 *(=590a17)*.
2. A created cause, when an action is over and an effect produced, respects this effect otherwise than it had formerly respected it: SP, 111/34 *(=590a26)*; And so some determination or change or ordination to the produced effect is left in the cause, by reason of which it is ordered to that effect as to something produced and no longer as to something possible: SP, 111/46 *(=590a41)*.
3. A progression to infinity in causes must be rejected, because if, for one effect, infinite concourses or causalities are required,

2. Cognizability does not follow on being in itself considered absolutely, but on being as relative to a cognitive power: I, 190/19 *(=679a24)*.

3. Being cognizable or apprehensible is the rationale of an object as object: I, 159/7 *(=667a6)*.

4. Absolutely and in itself, cognizability is something mind-independent in mind-independent things, but relatively to a cognitive power it is something mind-dependent: I, 139/27, 37 *(=657b35, 47)*.

5. That an object or cognizable thing respects a cognitive power by a mind-dependent rather than by a mind-independent relation proves that cognizability is something mind-independent: I, 139/5; cf. 147/13 *(=657b9; 662a5)*.

6. That there is greater intelligibility or cognizability in one thing than in another does not derive from the mind-dependent relation to a power which is found in every object, but a greater force and efficacy of stimulating and manifesting, which in itself is something mind-independent: I, 139/30 *(=657b38)*.

7. The rationale of the cognizable is not the rationale of being formally, but presuppositively: I, 150/1 *(=663a2)*.

8. The cognizable or knowable does not follow on being as taken in itself absolutely, but comparatively to a cognitive power: I, 190/19 *(=679a23)*.

9. The cognizable is the same as the true: I, 150/6 text *(=663a8)* and note 32 *(=1635: 186b3-40)*.

10. The rationale of cognizable can be univocal in the case of a mind-dependent and of a mind-independent object: I, 149/41 *(=662b44)*.

11. Whether an object is mind-independent or mind-dependent makes a difference only in the rationale of being, not in the rationale of cognizability: I, 187/28 *(=678b15)*.

12. The differences of things in the order of physical existence and being are one matter, differences in the order of objective existence and cognizability quite another: I, 149/44, 187/32 *(=662b47, 678b20)*; II, 270/39 *(=715b39)*.

13. The rationale of the knowable bespeaks only a nesessary connection of truth, which is univocally congruent with any other necessary connection whatever in the rationale of the true, even if the connections in question are not congruent in the rationale of being: I, 189/4 *(=678b42)*.

14. Non-mind-independent beings are cognizable not immediately and by reason of themselves, but mediately and through another, and so suppose a cognizability borrowed from mind-independent beings: I, 131/12, 189/8 *(=653b41, 679a2)*.

15. The cognizable in general, like the true and the good and the coincident properties of being, is analogous to this or that cognizable, that is to say, it is predicated transcendentally in all univocal categories: I, 190/7 *(=679a10)*.

SEE: Analogy
Mind-Dependent Being
Sign
Transcendentals
Truth

COLOR (*Color*):
SEE: Light

COMMON SENSIBLE (*Sensibile Commune*): The common sensibles are attained through the proper sensibles by a sign relationship: I, 206/38, 208/38 *(=686b15, 687b30)*.
SEE: Sense
Sign esp. 14, 15, 18, 19, 91, 94, 97, 108, 109

COMPARATIVE ACT (*Actus Comparativus*): By the phrase "a comparative act" is understood any cognition whatever that conceives its object with a connotation of and an ordering to another: FP, 69/41 *(=303a21)*.
SEE: Connotation
Mind-Dependent Being

COMPARISON (*Comparatio*): Some constitute relations formally not in a respect but in a comparison, and therefore entirely in the order of cognition-dependent being: SP, 80/23 *(=573b44)*.
SEE: Comparative Act
Relation
Sign

CONCEPT (*Conceptus*):

1. Concept ≡ mental word ≡ expressed specifier ≡ expressed specifying form ≡ expressed specification: II, 242/4 *(=702b6)*.

2. Concepts tend toward their objects by an entirely natural similitude or representation: III, 335/29 *(=747a41)*.

3. A concept is a natural expression of its principle: A, 351/36 *(=108a30)*.

4. The concept in one mode is formal, in another mode objective: FP, 58/21 *(=291a5)*; A, 344/1 *(=104b37)*.

5. A precise statement of how a concept is a formal sign: II, 227/14 *(=695b21)*.

6. A concept or awareness as an informative quality is the fundament of a relation, as objectively signifying it is a formal sign and an instance of relation: I, 132/48 *(=654b43)*; thus a concept and an awareness are qualities which signify informatively, not objectively, but they found the relation constitutive of a formal sign, that is, the relation of the sign whose representation and exercise of signifying is brought about by the fact that it is informing: I, 133/8 *(=655a3)*—see diagram in note 13, page 164.

7. Concept and thing conceived are attained by essentially the same cognition, but the cognition of the thing conceived is not arrived at *from* the cognition of the concept, because the concept is that in which the thing is rendered proportioned to the knower and formally constituted in the rationale of cognized term; when a cognition of one thing is arrived at *from* the cognition of another, however, the one from which the other is cognized is not the *formal* constitutive of the other as cognized: II, 250/25 *(=705b35)*.

8. A concept is cognized as something *which* is known, not as an extrinsic cognized thing, but as that in which the thing cognized is contained within the understanding: II, 250/22 *(=705b31)*; III, 331/13 *(=745b4)*.

9. Because the concept is that in which the thing or object is rendered proportioned and immaterialized in the mode of a terminus, it is said to be itself that *which* is cognized, not as a separate object, but as constituting the object cognized in the rationale of that which is cognized: II, 250/29 *(=705b39)*.

10. A concept is cognized as the rationale and form whereby an object is rendered cognized within a power, and so is precognized formally, not denominatively and as the thing is cognized: II, 226/38, 232/20 *(=695a43, 698b10)*.

11. A concept is cognized formally, not objectively or denominatively: II, 227/16, 232/30 *(=695b23, 698b22)*; III, 331/27 *(=745b20)*.

12. The concept does not add numerically to the very cognition itself to which it leads the power: II, 223/15 *(=693b16)*.

13. The concept is not itself intermediary to the cognizing; on the contrary, a thing is said to be cognized equally immediately when it is cognized in itself and when it is cognized by means of a concept: II, 223/27 *(=693b29)*.

14. A concept does not make a cognition mediate: II, 224/1 *(=693b33)*.

15. A concept does not constitute a cognition as mediate, because it does not double the object cognized or the cognition: II, 224/32, 233/35 *(=694a20, 699a36)*.

16. In intentional being a concept is always inferior or "subsidiary" to its object, although on other grounds, to wit, in entitative being, a concept can sometimes be superior to the object: II, 227/40, 227/28, 41 *(=696a4, 695b38, 696a5)*.

17. The concept is said to be identified with the object in intentional being not only as are those things which coincide in one common rationale, but rather because it totally contains the same content as is in the other, and represents that object. But this identity itself supposes that the representing and the represented are distinct, so that the same concept never represents itself: II, 233/43 *(=699a43)*.

18. A speaker's concept, whether the speaker be a pure spirit or a human being, represents formally to the speaker, but to the listener who perceives the concept as a thing cognized and in it a represented thing, it represents instrumentally: II, 238/23 *(=702a1)*, as response to 235/11-14 *(=700a16-20)*; in the case of human discourse in particular, even though the speaker's concept is outside the listener, it yet is present to the listener according to itself through the voice, by means of which voice the concept is rendered sensible: A, 349/32 *(=107b11)*.

19. Concepts must be posited within a cognitive power for one or both of two reasons: on account of a necessity on the side of the object, or on account of a necessity on the side of the subject: II, 242/9 *(=702b12)*.

20. Concepts are posited on account of the subject, inasmuch as a concept is expressed and formed by a cognitive power for manifesting the things which are cognized: II, 242/16 *(=702b21)*.

21. Concepts are posited on account of a twofold necessity on the side of the object: either because the object is absent and cognition cannot be terminated at it unless it be rendered present in the rationale of terminus, i.e., to supply presence; or because the object must be proportioned and conformed to the power: II, 243/5 *(=702b36)*.

22. The role of the concept is not to render formally cognizing in the way cognition is a tendency toward an object, but to render the object present in the mode of a cognized terminus: II, 244/14 *(=703a26)*; cf. 223/19 *(=693b20-29)*.

23. Since a concept represents within the understanding and as the form informing the understanding, it does not represent objectively and as something first cognized, but formally and as the rationale of the cognizing: II, 244/24 *(=703a39)*.

24. The most probable opinion is that a concept is always a living image produced by the vital action of the power which it serves in cognizing: II, 245/35 *(=703b37)*: but see God 15.

25. All and only the products of cognitive powers are concepts, and all concepts are what are called formal signs: II, 246/13, 247/22 *(=704a11, a42)*.

26. A concept is called an instrument by which the understanding cognizes something, not as if it were the cognized means which an instrument and external means is, but as it is the internal means in which the understanding understands within itself, and this is to be a formal sign: II, 249/14 *(=705a42)*.

27. A concept has the rationale of a formal sign because it is not the terminus in which cognition finally stops, but is rather a 'terminus' by means of which cognition is borne to the cognizing of an *object* outside the power—i.e., it is rather a *term* which serves to *found*—i.e., a subject term—than one which *anchors* a relation ("term" as terminus): II, 250/13, 232/10 *(=705b21, 698a46)*.

28. A concept, considered as the term of a cognition within a power, is not the *terminus* in which the cognition rests: II, 250/11, 252/28 *(=705b20, 707a9)*.

29. A concept is not said to represent as something first cognized in the mode of an extrinsic object, so that "cognized" would be an extrinsic denomination; it is said rather "to represent" as something intrinsic cognized, that is, as a term of cognition *within* the power *at* which the cognition does not rest save as on the power foundation or fundament of a relation: II, 250/8 *(=705b14)*, I, 202/19 *(=684b10)*; cf. II, 232/5 *(=698a41)*.

30. When it is said that the concept or word is an effect of cognition, it is understood that it is an effect of the operation and way or tendency, not of the cognition as terminated: II, 252/28 *(=707a9)*.

31. The concept is the form of the cognition as terminated, but it is the effect of the cognition as an expressive operation and diction: II, 252/32 *(=707a13)*.

32. Ultimate and non-ultimate concepts: S, 29/24 *(=10b41)*; III, 334/1 *(=746b24)*.

33. Any concept to which another concept is ordered as to a terminus can be said to be an ultimate concept: III, 334/2 *(=746b26)*.

34. Among dialecticians, however, ultimate and non-ultimate concepts are distinguished as being, respectively, concepts of things signified by words, and concepts of the words themselves: III, 334/15 *(=746b39)*.

35. Dialecticians prefer this way of distinguishing ultimate from non-ultimate concepts because it provides a facile way of discriminating the object of Logic, which, as including dialectic, is concerned not with things as such, but with the instruments by which things are cognized: III, 334/20 *(=746b45)*.

36. Ultimate from non-ultimate are of themselves and formally not essential differences of concepts, because they do not obtain on the side of the object itself as expressing the cognizable rationale, but on the side of the order of one concept or cognition to another: III, 334/27 *(=747a3)*.

37. Being ultimate or non-ultimate adds to a concept only relations or conditions of being-toward objects, not inasmuch as the objects are cognizable and specifying, but inasmuch as they are ordered as means and end: III, 335/4 *(=747a10)*.

38. It sometimes happens that the connotations accompanying a cognition presuppose a distinction of objects even though they do not constitute the distinction, and it is in this way that the ultimate and the non-ultimate as presently considered are exercised between distinct concepts, of which one is engaged with a thing signified, the other with the expression signifying: III, 335/10 *(=747a20)*.

39. Presuppositively, therefore, because they are engaged with different objects, not formally by virtue of being ultimate and non-ultimate, ultimate and non-ultimate concepts are distinct from one another: III, 335/18 *(=747a28)*.

40. The stipulated signification of a linguistic expression is the object naturally signified by a non-ultimate concept: III, 335/32 *(=747a44)*.

41. Some order to the signification of a linguistic expression

is required in order for a concept of that expression to be non-ultimate, because a concept is said to be non-ultimate only insofar as the object conceived is *itself* conceived to be a means to a *further* terminus: III, 335/45, 336/8 *(=747b8, 23)*.

42. A non-ultimate concept of a voice not only represents the voice, but also its signification, because only the signification of a voice constitutes it as a means in respect of a thing signified: III, 336/13 *(=747b29)*.

43. The signification of an expression conceived by a non-ultimate concept is a signification represented but not exercised: III, 336/18, 22 *(=747b35, 40)*.

44. A non-ultimate concept must signify the signification of an expression at least as regards the fact of its existence: III, 336/23, 337/8, 337/23 *(=747b41, 748a27, 748a40)*.

45. Habitual awareness of a signification does not suffice for a non-ultimate concept: III, 336/28 *(=747b47)*.

46. Even a non-ultimate concept represents a significative voice, but it will represent the thing signified and contained in the voice mediately, but formally as two things ordinately represented in the same concept: II, 238/11 *(=701b34)*.

47. In respect of the cognition whereby a non-ultimate concept is reflexively cognized, the non-ultimate concept will represent both the voice and the significate of the voice instrumentally, if indeed a concept of a voice (a non-ultimate concept of a linguistic expression) attains the thing signified by the voice in any way, which is not always the case: II, 238/15 *(=701b40)*.

48. If one is ignorant of the fact that a voice is significant, the concept of that voice in the mind of the ignorant one will be an ultimate concept: III, 337/17 *(=748a36)*.

49. Concepts signify the same for all only when they are about the same object and formed in the same way: III, 337/31 *(=748b3)*.

50. All non-ultimate concepts represent the same thing for all those among whom the represented expressions are in common use; otherwise not: III, 337/34 *(=748b7)*.

51. A concept of an equivocal term is only one non-ultimate concept: III, 338/16 *(=748b39)*.

52. That non-ultimate concept of an equivocal term represents by a single signification and natural representation the expression ordered to several things signified by several impositions: III, 339/3 *(=749a35)*.

53. Ultimate and non-ultimate concepts do not differ essentially owing to the fact that one is ultimate while the other is non-ultimate, but sometimes owing to the fact that they are of diverse objects whence an essential difference derives: III, 339/28 *(=749b15)*.

54. How things stand with regard to the ultimate and non-ultimate in a case where an expression has lost its significance: III, 339/33*(=749b21)*.

55. Of themselves, the relations of ultimate and non-ultimate specifically distinguish only modes of concepts, not the intrinsic rationale of concepts: III, 339/46 *(=749b38)*.

56. Reflex and direct concepts defined: S, 29/32 *(=11a5)*.

57. Our concepts, even though they are formally present, are nevertheless not present objectively as long as they are not formed on the pattern of a definable sensible structure or "essence": III, 325/26 *(=742a21)*.

58. Even though concept and cognition are formally present to the cognitive power, they are nevertheless not present objectively: III, 326/38 *(=742b43)*.

59. A formal presence does not suffice for something to be directly cognizable, but an objective presence is required: III, 326/40 *(=742b46)*; and so our concepts, even though they are intelliglble according to themselves, are yet not intelligible according to the mode of a material structure, and therefore primarily and directly they are not present to us objectively: III, 327/3 *(=743a12)*.

60. One concept can represent another concept; for example, a reflexive concept represents a direct concept, but these concepts differ in kind, because they represent objects different in kind, to wit, the one an external object, the other the internal concept itself: I, 219/14 *(=692b41)*.

61. Concept and act of cognition are in need of reflexion inasmuch as they need to be formed on the pattern of a sensible object with which a direct concept is engaged: III, 327/26 *(=743a39)*.

63. When it is said in the definition of a reflexive concept that it is a concept of another concept, this is because the first thing that is attained through reflexion is another concept, then all the things which concur in the soul to produce the concept: III, 328/32 *(=744a3)*.

64. A reflexive concept formally respects the cognizing of the nature of that on which it reflects in the way in which that nature can be cognized through [sensible] effects or connotatively in the mode of a sensible essence: III, 328/43 *(=744a16)*.

65. Even though concepts are present in the understanding physically, yet because they are not rendered present by means of themselves, but by means of a similitude and connotation of a sensible structure, we are not said to see our concepts intuitively: III, 328/47 *(=744a21)*.

66. A direct concept is represented by a reflexive concept as it is a kind of quality and image signified in act in the mode of the definable essence of an image: III, 329/6 *(=744a30)*.

67. In a reflexive concept, the object signified by a direct concept functions as the term-from-which reflexion begins; therefore a reflexive concept does not represent that object except by connotation: III, 329/14 *(=744a40)*.

68. Direct and reflex concepts differ in kind: III, 330/3 *(=744b32)*; cf. I, 219/14 *(=692b41)*—entry 60 above.

69. Because our understanding and its act are not objectively understandable except dependently upon sensible things, our concepts, even though they are formally present, are nevertheless not present objectively as long as they are not formed on the pattern of a definable sensible structure, which can only come about through a reflexion undertaken from a sensible object: III, 325/22 *(=742a16)*.

70. A concept is an inhering form by which an object is cognized, yet is not in itself endowed with that understandability which is required for our understanding, namely, understandability in the mode of a sensible essence, and, for that reason, a concept is neither understandable nor understood by means of itself in respect of our understanding: III, 331/29 *(=745b22)*.

71. For the rationale of a reflexive concept it does not suffice to cognize something on the pattern of another, but it is necessary that that which is cognized should keep on the side of a principle of the cognizing: III, 332/36 *(=746a38)*.

72. The concept itself can be signified in two ways: A, 345/38 *(=105b21)*.

73. The concept itself is ordered ultimately and principally to representing the thing itself of which it is an intentional similitude: A, 349/42 *(=107b21)*.

74. A concept is an expression of its formal principle, which is the impressed specification fecundating the expressing under-

standing, and thus represents the principle of which it is formally a specfification; and so the concept, by representing its formal principle, represents principally its formal object: A, 351/23 (=108a13).

75. How unity and distinction are possessed in a created concept with respect to the represented object: III, 228/4 (=696a19).

76. A concept or expressed specifier retains the rationale of a means to an extent sufficient for the rationale of a sign: II, 228/25 (=696a43).

77. Because our concepts receive the guise of a sensible essence within the understanding from an exterior object directly cognized, they are said to be cognized reflexively, and to be rendered understandable by the understandability of a material being: III, 327/10 (=743a20).

78. We do not always advert to a speaker's concepts by contrasting them with the things talked about, which shows that, even though the signification of linguistic expressions has the power of signifying both concept and thing conceived, this double signification is not always exercised: A, 349/25 (=107b2).

79. A linguistic expression refers to a concept not as a thing signified but as the signifying principal for which the vocal or written expression is substitute and instrument, because it is from the word of the mind that the outer word participates being and signification: A, 348/9 (=106b46).

80. In what sense the concept itself is said to be "that which" is known: II, 250/29 (=705b39).

81. Whence the name "concept": A, 345/41 (=105b25).

SEE: Angel
Awareness
Equivocal
Expression
Formal Awareness
Formal Sign
Idea
Image
Linguistic Expression
Means
Quality
Reflexion
Representation
Simple Awareness
Sign
Specifier
Term
Ultimate/Non-ultimate
Voice
Word

CONDITIONED CONTINGENT (*Conditionatum Contingens*): How a determining divine decree is given in respect of the decree itself: III, 317/34 (=737b48).

CONDITIONED FUTURE THINGS (*Futura Conditionata*): How they are known by God: III, 317/22 (=737b34).

CONNOTATION, CONNOTATIVE CONCEPTS (*Connotatio, Conceptus Connotativus*): We apprehend many things not through proper concepts, but connotative ones: FP, 75/12 (=305b41); as when I conceive Rome after the pattern of Toledo, I conceive Rome comparatively and not absolutely, because connotatively and respectively to another: FP, 69/27 (=303a6).

SEE: Analogy
Concept
Experience 2, 3, 4, 11
Mind-Dependent Being
Past
Reflexion
Relation

CONSEQUENCE (*Consequentia*):

1. What it is: IFP, 10/16 (=3a26).

2. The consequence is valid or invalid, not true or false: IFP, 11/41 (=4a20).

SEE: Illation

CONSEQUENT (*Consequens*): What it is: IFP, 10/14, 19 (=3a24, 30).

CONTACT (*Contactus*):
SEE: Sense 3, 4, 19

CONTIGUOUS (*Contiguum*):
SEE: Experience 5, 6, 7
Sense 3, 4, 19

CREATURE (*Creatura*):

1. Creatures are effected by God in such a way that his action does not in itself depend on their termination: I, 168/28 (=671a42).

2. Creatures are signs of God which represent him to us as being themselves the more known to us: II, 233/18 (=699a16).

CUSTOM (*Consuetudo*):

1. If custom respects a sign by appointing and proposing it as a sign, such a sign founded on custom will be stipulated: III, 278/12 (=719a35).

2. If "custom" expresses the simple use of a thing by reason of which it can be taken as a sign, such a sign will be a natural sign: III, 278/14 (=719a39).

3. Custom can function as an effect which leads us to cognize its cause: III, 278/21 (=719b1).

4. Almost every induction is founded on the frequency and custom whereby we see something often happen: III, 278/27(=719b8).

5. Concerning signs arising from custom, when the "arising from" expresses the productive cause in terms of the use and consensus of a people, customary signs must be spoken of in the same way that one speaks of stipulated signs: III, 279/18 (=719b32).

6. Animals are able to form and use customary signs: I, 204/9, 204/21, 205/8, 205/23 (=685b4, b18, b28, b45); III, 280/15 (=720a40).

7. Custom as it is a kind of effect leads us to a cognition of its cause in the same way that any other effects show their causes: III, 279/25 (=719b38); therefore signification arising from custom is founded on something natural: III, 279/33 (=720a1).

8. The intrinsic progression of acts and their frequency and multiplication constitutes a customary sign: III, 280/34 (=720b14).

9. Not all custom is a human act, but all custom can found a natural sign relation: III, 280/21 (=720a48).

10. As multiplication of acts does not function freely relative to the generation of habit, so neither does it function freely relative to the generation of a customary significance: III, 280/36 (=720b19).

11. If a custom is not taken as a means relative to something else, or if something else is not rendered more known by the frequent repetition itself, then it will not be a customary sign, even though it will be a custom: III, 281/27 (=721a14).

12. A sign arising from custom perishes from a suspension removing the multiplication of acts and the frequency of use: III, 281/35 *(=721a23)*.

13. Because the representation of a customary sign is founded on the very multiplication of acts which constitutes the custom, when such multilplication is removed, the fundament of the sign is removed: III, 281/39 *(=721a27)*.

14. Something positive always intervenes in the loss of a custom: III, 281/47 *(=721a36)*.

15. If someone through only one act without a custom posits something for representing another, such an appointment will be a kind of inchoate custom: III, 282/42 *(=721b40)*.

16. Linguistic expressions essentially signify from stipulation, but incidentally from custom, which is to signify naturally not from themselves, but only in respect of those among whom the custom is known: III, 283/9 *(=722a11)*.

17. A custom is as a second nature, but not nature itself, and so it signifies for all to whom it is a custom, not for all simply: III, 283/27 *(=722a25)*.

18. A sign arising from custom is something imperfect in the order of natural sign, just as custom itself is something imperfect in the order of nature: II, 283/29 *(=722a34)*.

SEE: Animals
Brute Animals
Experience
Instinct
Mind-Dependent Being
Perception

CUSTOMARY SIGN (*Signum Ex Consuetudine*):
SEE: Animal
Custom
Sign

— D —

DEMON (*Daemon*):

1. How an excitement of the imagination might be procured by a demon or an angel: II, 246/10 *(=704a7)*.

2. How apparitions might be caused by demons in the imagination: III, 323/2 *(=741a12)*.

SEE: Angels
Animal Spirits
Future

DENOMINATION (*Denominatio*):
SEE: Extrinsic Denomination

DESCENT (*Descensus*): Descent in argumentation: FP, 64/11 *(=293b42)*, text and note 14.
SEE: Abduction
Ascent
Induction

DESIRE (*Appetitus*):
SEE: Awareness 17

DIALECTICAL DISPUTATION (*Disputatio Dialectica*):
SEE: Disputation

DICTION (*Dictio*):
SEE: Expression
Linguistic Expression
Term

DISCOURSE (*Discursus*):
SEE: Angel
Sign

DISPUTATION (*Disputatio*):

1. The argument: IFP, 10/7 *(=3a16)*.

2. The task of the one presenting the argument (the argumentator): IFP, 10/6, 12/31 *(=3a15, 4b14)*.

3. The task of the one responding: IFP, 11/1 *(=3b9)*.

4. The task of the Moderator: IFP, 13/1 *(=4b40)*.

DIVISION (*Divisio*):

1. In every division, that which is capable of being included in each of the dividing members must always be accepted as that which is divided; illustrated by examples: II, 235/47 *(=700b10)*.

2. Whether it is possible for something to be divided by several essential divisions: II, 239/2 *(=702a28)*.

3. Divisions in the two orders of being: I, 149/44, 187/32 *(=662b47, 678b20)*; II, 270/39 *(=715b39)*.

SEE: Analogy 4
Object

— E —

END (*Finis*):

1. An end is either an end-effect or an end-cause: I, 174/32 *(=674b1)*.

2. An end-effect as effect does not specify: I, 174/33 *(=674b3)*.

3. Only the end-for-the-sake-of-which is an end in the sense of a cause and is counterdistinguished from the other types of cause: I, 174 note 10 *(=1633: 271b43-44)*.

4. An end-cause as cause does not respect the specification of an action, but its existence, for relative to existence it ''moves'' the efficient cause *metaphorically*: I, 175/4 *(=674b8)*.

5. An end-cause as end is counted among the circumstances of an action, but as an object it can also specify: I, 176/4 *(=674b14)*; if, therefore, an end specifies, it does so neither in the rationale of cause nor of effect, but by taking on the rationale of an end-object: I, 177/8 *(=674b24)*.

6. The rationale of a specifying object is one thing, that of a moving end quite another: I, 178/1 *(=674b26)*.

7. The ''motion'' of an end-cause cause pertains to finalization moving to produce a thing in being: but to move relative to the act of being and existence is outside the order of specification: I, 178/4*(=674b29)*.

SEE: Idea
Object
Specification

ENTHYMEME (*Enthymema*): Described in IFP, 10/17 *(=3a27)*.

''ESSE'': Copula which signifies existence: FP, 50/16 *(=286a29)*.

ETERNITY (*Aeternitas*): How things are contained in eternity: III, 316/42 *(=737a48)*.

EUCHARIST (*Eucharistia*): What sort of cognition we have in respect of consecrated bread: III, 319/17 *(=738b40)*.

EXEMPLAR (*Exemplar*):
SEE: Act of Understanding
Cognizability
Idea
Image
Intuition
Movement
Object
Presence
Relation

EXISTENCE (*Existentia*):

1. It can well be that some being incapable of existence is capable of truth: I, 150/7 *(=663a9)*.

2. The existence of things which is independent of the order of awareness is physical, not objective, existence: III, 287/15 *(=722b41)*.

SEE: Act of Understanding
Cognizability
Intuition
Mind-Dependent Being
Mind-Independent Being
Object
Presence
Relation

EXPERIENCE (*Experientia, Experimentum*):

1. The paradigm case of experience is the intuitive seeing of physically present things as they are in themselves independent of the seeing: III, 306/16 *(=733a16)*.

2. Such mind-independent beings as lie outside our own experience are conceived by us on the pattern of the physical beings of which we have had experience: FP, 51/11 *(=286b26)*.

3. Such mind-independent beings as lie outside our own direct experience and are so conceived by us do not have the rationale of being attributed to them from the process of cognition but from the supposition of their having a mind-independent act of being: FP, 51/15 *(=286b31)*.

4. Such mind-independent beings as are conceived but not experienced are denominated cognized by way of an alien nature rather than by way of their proper being, and they receive in their cognized being a connotation relative to that on whose pattern they are cognized, but this connotation does not suffice for denominating them beings formed simply by the mind in the rationale of being: FP, 51/21 *(=286b37)*.

5. That there should be an experience of something other than a present thing is unintelligible, for the absent as absent cannot enter experience: III, 306/20 *(=733a21)*.

6. Cognition by external sense must as such be experimental: root of this proposition: III, 311/23 *(=735a26)*.

7. Every cognition of sense is experimental and inductive, since into that cognition certitude of the understanding is resolved: III, 310/38 *(=734b35)*.

8. We experience the effects of accidental forms but we do not experience their distinction from substance: SP, 86/20, text *(=577b25)* and note 16.

9. It repugns for there to be an experience engaging an absent thing, because, as long as it is absent, it needs another medium from which its cognition would be derived: III, 310/41 *(=734b38)*.

10. Experience rests on the thing in itself according as it exists in itself; for a thing is subjected to experience when it is attained in itself: III, 310/45 *(=734b44)*; but see SP, 86 note 16.

11. All cognition has its birth in experience from some external sense by way of an intuitive apprehension: III, 304/12 *(=732a21)*.

12. It involves a contradiction for a thing to be cognized by experiencing an external sensation, which differs from an imaginative sensation, except by attaining something external in its external self and not as formed within the sense: III, 322/14 *(=740b17)*.

13. The physical presence of an object is required for that object to be experienced: III, 307/1 *(=733a27)*.

SEE: Common Sensible
Connotation
Formal Awareness 4
God 17
Intuition
Objective Presence
Perception
Presence
Relation
Sense

EXPERIMENTAL KNOWLEGE (*Notitia Experimentalis*):

SEE: Experience
Intuition Perception
Presence
Sense
Sensation

EXPRESSED SPECIFIER (*Species Expressa*):

SEE: Awareness
Concept
Icon
Image
Mirror
Object
Phantasm
Quality
Representation
Sense
Specifier
Understanding
Word

EXPRESSION (*Expressio*):

1. The act of understnading, as it is a diction or expression, has for its completion the word itself as term: II, 250/40 *(=706a6)*.

2. The concept or mental word is the effect of cognition as an expressive operation and diction: II, 252/34 *(=707a16)*.

SEE: Concept
Linguistic Expression
Specifier
Term
Understanding
Word
Voice

EXTERNAL SENSE (*Sensus Externus*):

SEE: Experience
Intuition
Intuitive Awareness
Perception
Presence
Sense

EXTRINSIC DENOMINATION (*Denominatio Extrinseca*):

1. Extrinsic denomination is not coextensive with mind-dependent being: FP, 49/36 *(=285b41)*.

2. In an extrinsic denomination a factor dependent in its

being on being objectively cognized concurs with a factor independent of being itself cognized for its being: FP, 55/16 *(=289a16)*.

3. The mind-dependent factor in an extrinsic denomination is a relation: FP, 55/42 *(=289a44)*.

4. Second intentions suppose the extrinsic denomination of a thing cognized and abstracted, but they are not themselves extrinsic denominations: FP, 61/19 *(=292a20)*.

5. Every extrinsic denomination provenates from some real (i.e., independent of being itself apprehended) form existing in another subject, just as being seen or being cognized provenates from the cognition existing in a cognizing subject: SP, 83/20 *(=575a37)*.

6. In itself an extrinsic denomination is a mind-independent form (i.e., a form existing independently of being itself objectively cognized), but it does not mind-independently exist in that which it denominates: FP, 55/35 *(=289a36)*.

7. By reason of its non-existence in that which it denominates, an extrinsic denomination is taken as a mind-dependent being; yet by reason of its pre-existence in another from which it respects the denominated thing, it is said to denominate prior to the operation whereby it is objectified by the understanding: FP, 55/37 *(=289a38)*.

8. Extrinsic denomination, when it is conceived as a mind-dependent being, pertains to relation because it is not conceived as affecting by negating and removing a form, but by ordering and depending on that whence the denomination is taken, or on that toward which it is imposed and destined through cognition: FP, 55/42 *(=289a44)*.

SEE: Being Cognized
Mind-Dependent Being 11, 52, 58
Relation
Intuitive Awareness
Nominalists
Non-Being
Relation 8

EXTRINSIC FORMAL CAUSE (*Causa Formalis Extrinseca*):

1. An extrinsic formal cause consists in nothing but the fact that some power, in order to elicit an act of such or such a kind, needs to be actuated or ordered relative to an extrinsic object, not only in the termination of the act, but also in the elicitation and originating of that act, because even to elicit it, the power is not sufficiently determined to a specific kind of act until it is determined or moved and completed by an object: I, 172/4 *(=672b46)*; cf. C, 382/15 *(=603a1)*.

2. Distinction must be made between the terminus of a relation understood most formally in the rationale of opposed terminus, and the terminus understood fundamentally on the side of subjectivity as founding this rationale of terminating: C, 382/4 *(=602b33)*; in the latter sense, the terminus of a relation functions as the extrinsic formal cause of the relation specifying it in the manner of an object: C, 382/14 *(=602b45)*.

SEE: Movement
Object
Relation
Specificative
Specifier
Terminus

— F —

FAITH (*Fides*):

1. Obscurity is an intrinsic mode but not the formal rationale of faith: II, 238/44 *(=702a24)*.

2. Faith and opinion coincide in the rationale of obscurity (insufficiency of evidence) as in a generic rationale, but they differ in kind on account of a difference in means: I, 164/11 *(=669b23)*.

3. Believing in God revealing and believing in God revealed are not two terms of faith, but one: I, 163/4 *(=669a24)*.

4. The difference between faith and clear vision in the homeland is a difference in part between abstractive and intuitive awareness and in part a difference in the means of awareness: III, 297/21 *(=728a48)*.

FALSITY (*Falsitas*): How falsity and truth differ from the rationale of cognition as intuitive or abstractive: III, 294/14 *(=726b14)*.
SEE: Truth

FINAL CAUSE (*Finis Cuius Gratia, Causa Finalis*):
SEE: End

FIRST COGNIZED (*Prius Cognitum, Praecognitum*):
SEE: Concept
Sign

FIRST INTENTION (*Intentio Prima*):
SEE: Intention

FORM (*Forma*): That which keeps to the side of a principle of action is called a form: II, 249/24 *(=705b5)*.
SEE: Object
Quality
Relation
Specifier

FORMAL AWARENESS (*Notitia Formalis*):

1. A formal awareness must proceed from a cognitive power either as an act or as a term, because it is something vital: II, 257/20 *(=709b2)*.

2. A formal awareness is something vital, because it has for formal effect to render vitally and formally cognizing: II, 257/22 *(=709b4)*.

3. Even though a formal sign is said to be a formal awareness terminatively, because it is a terminus of cognition, yet not every formal awareness is a formal sign, namely, the act itself of cognizing: II, 267/22 *(=714b32)*.

4. It pertains to the rationale of a sign to be a formal representative awareness, not an operative one: II, 253/1 *(=707a33)*; the concept or formal sign is a formal awareness formally terminatively, not formally operatively: II, 252/39 *(=707a20)*.

5. In external sense there is formal awareness in the mode of the cognition which is the tendency of the power toward an object, not in the mode of the representation which is a form substituting in the power in the place of an object as terminus: II, 267/18 *(=714b26)*.

6. When the formal sign is called a formal awareness, this is not understood of formal awareness according as it is an operation, but of the formal awareness which is a representation and expression, which belongs only to a terminated formal awareness or to rather the terminus of the awareness, not to the operation as it is an operation producing the concept: II, 252/22 *(=707a1)*.

SEE: Act of Understanding
Awareness
Cognitive Act
Concept

Quality
Sense 7, 24
Sign 52
Simple Awareness
Specifier
Stimulus

FORMAL SIGN (*Signum Formale*):

1. A formal sign is that sign whose representation and exercise of signifying is brought about by the fact that it is informing: I, 133/10 *(=655a5)*. See diagram on page 164 note 13.

2. A sign is formal or instrumental by reason of the fundament of the sign-relation itself, but not on the part of the relation: I, 202/19 *(=684b11)*; Since this fundament is the very rationale of manifesting another on the side of the object or in the role of object [if the sign is instrumental], it is not impossible for this fundament to function in the order of formal cause from the side of the object, but it is impossible for it to function in the order of efficient cause: I, 202/22 *(=684b14)*.

SEE: Concept
Formal Awareness
Icon
Image
Quality
Representation
Sign
Specifier
Word

FOUNDATION, FUNDAMENT (*Fundamentum*):

1. The principle points of difficulty concerning the fundaments of relations reduce to three: whether one relation can found another; whether each of the three essential fundaments found mind-independent ontological relations, and what is the proximate foundation for cause and effect relations: SP, 102/22 *(=584b24)*.

2. A concept and an awareness are qualities which signify informatively, not objectively, but they *found* the relation constitutive of a formal sign, that is, the relation of the sign whose representing and exercise of signifying is brought about by the fact that it is informing: I, 133/8 *(=655a3)*.

3. A sign is formal or instrumental by reason of the foundation (the fundament) of the sign-relation itself, but not on the part of the relation: I, 202/11 *(=684b11)*; Since this fundament is the very rationale of manifesting another on the side of the object or in the role of object [if the sign is instrumental], it is not impossible for this foundation, as basis or ground of signifying, to function in the order of formal cause from the side of the object, but it is impossible for it to function in the order of an efficient cause: I, 202/22 *(=684b14)*.

4. A relation's terminus *as such* does not specify the relation; a relation's terminus specifies the relation rather *as it is subordinated existentially* to its foundation: I, 186/27 *(=678a10)*; An intrinsic specificative giving a specific physical character to an act must needs be independent of being itself as such cognized objectively, *but not an extrinsic specificative*, because an extrinsic specificative plays its role not by informing and inhering, but by terminating the tendency of another or by determining extrinsically relative to the elicitation of an act in the first place: I, 186/35 *(=678a19)*; So is it that it suffices for an extrinsic specificative to determine the cognitive power to act by means of a specifying form independent of being itself apprehended as object—an informing, not an objective, form—intrinsically informing physically (whether in the mode of an impression, or expressly), *even if the object itself in itself* is either not in its totality as such mind-independent, *or does not physically exist at all*: I, 186/42 *(=678a19)*.

SEE: Extrinsic Formal Cause
Formal Sign
Mind-Dependent Being
Non-Being
Relation
Representation
Sign
Specifier

FRIENDSHIP (*Amicitia*): In friendship there is an order to the good which I will the friend; the order is to the good directly, to the friend indirectly; the good is the terminus *which*, the friend the terminus *to which*: I, 158/20 *(=666b13)*.

FUTURE (*Futura*):

1. The future under the rationale of future cannot be understood except in the causes in which it is contained: III, 308/26 *(=733b12)*.

2. In what sense there can be a concept of a future thing representing that thing as it is in itself: III, 314/30 *(=736a27)*.

3. It would involve a contradiction to cognize something future except as being within causes or in an order to causes, for by the very fact that something is conceived in itself and apart from causes, it ceases to be conceived as future: III, 308/30 *(=733b19)*.

4. Cognition will only be able to be terminated at a future thing as in another and by means of another: III, 315/29 *(=736b31)*.

5. If future things are contained in causes contingently, a pure spirit, howsoevermuch it may comprehend their specifying form, cannot cognize those things as determinately existing, but only indeterminately, because they are not otherwise contained in the cause represented in that specifier, even though the pure spirit would properly cognize their definable structure: III, 316/7 *(=737a9)*.

SEE: Awareness
Experience
God 10, 11
Intuition
Past
Presence

— G —

GOD (*Deus*):

1. Between God and creature there is no reciprocal relation: SP, 100/20 *(=583b33)*.

2. God and creature univocally come together in the rationale of a metaphysical knowable, not in the rationale of being: I, 151/4, 188/4 *(=663a25, 678b35)*.

3. In what sense God is lord: I, 139/21 *(=657b28)*.

4. The free act in God: I, 139/23 *(=657b30)*.

5. How the rationale of object is found in the divine intelligence and power: I, 180/25 *(=675a26)*.

6. The action of God is not always conjoined to a reception and the consequence of an effect in a proper mutation: III, 317/12 *(=737b23)*.

7. God is absolutely denominated lord and creator, even though the relation of lord and of creation is not cognized in act: II, 275/25 *(=718a24)*.

8. In the case of God, to understand himself understanding and to understand his essence are the same: III, 326/10 *(=742b10)*.

9. God sees future things intuitively insofar as they are posited as coexisting in eternity: I, 316/22 *(=737a25).*

10. How God attains future conditioned things: III, 317/22 *(=737b34).*

11. How God has an intuitive cognition of future things: III, 305/41 *(=732b34).*

12. Just as the same act of God's will is on account of its eminence necessary and free, so the same knowledge on account of its eminence is intrinsically abstractive and intuitive, and at the same time also practical and speculative, efficacious and inefficacious, in respect of diverse things: III, 295/2 *(=727a9).*

13. How there is given the rationale of an object in respect of the divine omnipotence: I, 181/8 *(=675a47).*

14. God seen manifests creatures to those seeing: I, 117/7, 119/25 *(=646b3, 647a44).*

15. What if God were by himself alone to unite a concept or expressed specifier to the understanding: II, 248/17 *(=704b35).*

16. How God would be able to produce a specifier representing a future thing just as it is in itself, and how not: III, 314/30 *(=736a27).*

17. God can preserve a sensible specification in the absence of an object by supplying the efficiency of that object, but he cannot supply the elicitation of a cognition by that specifying form in the external sense concerning the absent object: III, 322/2 *(=740b2).*

18. God uses the sacraments as a kind of sign and also to produce grace: I, 198/29 *(=682b10).*

SEE: Accident
Existence
Faith
Relation
Sacrament
Sign
Trinity
Virtue

GRACE (*Gratia*):
SEE: Light 5

GROUND (*Fundamentum*):
SEE: Foundation, Fundament

— H —

HABIT (*Habitus*): Since habit is generated as the result of specific acts multiplied, an acquired habit is not something representative, but a disposition of the power toward eliciting acts similar to those which formed the habit: II, 263/45 *(=713a5).*
SEE: Concept
Custom

HUMAN UNDERSTANDING (*Intellectus, Ratio*):
SEE: Reflexion
Understanding

— I —

ICON (*Idolum*) [discussion of translation term in II, page 241 note 3]:

1. The concept or expressed specifier formed in the higher or internal sensory powers is called an icon: II, 245/19 *(=703b21).*

2. St. Thomas apparently concedes that there are two ways in which icons are produced: II, 245/17 *(=703b18)*; but this opinion has little probability to recommend it: II, 245/35 *(=703b36).*

SEE: Concept
Idea
Image
Quality
Representation
Specifier
Word

IDEA (*Idea*):

1. An idea or exemplary cause is that in whose similitude an ideated thing comes to be: I, 167/22 *(=670b23).*

2. An idea expresses a cause that is an exemplar by way of origin: I, 167/25 *(=670b27).*

3. An idea is an efficacious exemplary cause, and in this capacity it also causes existence, for it influxes into the formation of an actual singular, and as such belongs to practical understanding extending itself to work and to the existence of an effect: I, 167/28 *(=670b31).*

4. By each of the above points, an idea is set in systematic contrast with an object: I, 167/20 *(=670b21).*

5. An image (a statue or a painting) does not directly signify an object as it is in itself, but as it is in the idea of the artist, which idea the image directly represents: II, 276/33 *(=718b32).*

6. Because the idea of the artist is sometimes proper in respect of his object, sometimes improper or less proper, therefore the image too does not always represent the object properly as it is in itself, but his idea: II, 276/35 *(=718b36).*

7. Any image whatever made by art, insofar as it is an image, represents only that in whose similitude it was expressed, namely, its idea, whatever that may be: II, 282/31 *(=721b27).*

8. If from the use of men a painting or statue is accomodated to represent another object besides its idea, that accomodation in respect of that object constitutes the image in the rationale sometimes of a stipulated sign, sometimes of a customary sign: II, 282/34 *(=721b31).*

SEE: Concept
Icon
Image
Phantasm
Quality
Representation

IDEALISM (*Idealismus*): Note the distinction opposing idealism and semi-idealism: The proposition that an object is not attained according as it is outside (or independent of) a concept must be distinguished: if the qualification ''according as'' expresses the rationale or ground of the attaining, it must be granted; but if the qualification ''according as'' expresses the thing attained as object, it must be denied: II, 232/5 *(=698a41).*

ILLATION (*Illatio*):

1. An illation is the logical connection itself between the premises of a syllogism or the parts of an enthymeme: IFP, 10/16, 10/19, 11/41 *(=3a26, 3a30, 4b20).*

2. ''Illation'' is a synonym for ''consequence'': IFP, 10/16, 11/41 *(=3a26, 4b20).*

3. The particle ''therefore'' is the note or sign of illation: IFP, 10/15 *(=3a24).*

SEE: Consequence
Disputation

IMAGE (*Imago*):

1. An awareness and concept have the rationale of a quality as they are an act or image of an object upon which likeness is founded the relation of formal sign, in which relation the sign essentially consists insofar as it is through it that awareness and concepts substitute for the object: I, 132/48 *(=654b43)*; cf. 202/19 *(=684b10).*

INSTINCT (*Instinctus*):

1. Instinct does not exclude cognition and judgment, but indifference: I, 214/31 *(=690b45)*.

2. Customs arise not only among humans acting by reason but also among animals acting by natural estimation or 'instinct': 280/15 *(=720a40)*.

INSTRUMENT (*Instrumentum*):

1. An audible or visual expression is an instrument of the concept in representing which renders the concept itself sensible: A, 349/44 *(=107b24)*.

2. Although an instrument would seem to respect more principally the principal by which it is employed as an instrument than the effect which it produces, yet this is understood in the rationale of something operating and acting productively. In the rationale of representing, however, if that which is principal is also something representative of things and substitutes some instrument for itself in order to extend and to manifest to others that very representation, the chief significate of both principal (the concept) and instrument (a perceptible expression) is the thing itself which is the object of the concept: A, 350/2 *(=107b30)*.

3. A verbal sign is called a logical, not a physical, instrument, not because it works by means of an intention of reason, but because it does not represent nor lead to a significate unless it is first cognized, and thus it signifies as something cognized, and that which belongs to a thing as cognized is said to belong logically: I, 203/18 *(=685a16)*.

4. A logical instrument is not reduced to a productive cause, nor is it an instrument properly speaking, but metaphorically or logically: I, 203/29 *(=685a30)*.

5. A perceptible sign is said to be an instrument, not as if it were an instrument of an agent producing a physical effect, but as it is a substitute for an object, not informing as a specifying form, but representing from outside a cognitive power: I, 195/25 *(=680b25)*.

6. The word of the mind or concept is sometimes called by St. Thomas an instrument which the understanding employs for knowing, but he does not take "instrument" there for an instrumental sign, but for the medium of understanding formal and intrinsic to the one knowing: II, 249 note 27 *(=1635: 359a3)*.

7. St. Thomas calls the mental word an instrument by which the understanding cognizes something, not as if it were a cognized medium which is an instrument and *external* means, but as it is an *internal* medium or means in which the understanding understands within itself; and this is to be a formal sign: II, 249/15 *(=705a42)*.

SEE: Concept 26
Linguistic Expression
Sign
Voice

INSTRUMENTAL SIGN (*Signum Instrumentale*):

1. An instrumental sign is that sign whose representation and exercise of signifying is brought about by the fact that it is itself apprehended as an object associated with some other object: S, 27/14 *(=10a7) et passim*; such signs, whether natural or social, exercise signification by reason of their fundaments, and hence can signify what does not exist: I, 130/17-25 *(=653a40-65)*.

2. Even though an instrumental sign can be attained with the signified by a single act of cognition, it remains true even then that it is *from* the known sign as object that the significate is reached, that the instrumental *sign itself* does not formally constitute the object signified as known: 250/34 *(=705b46)*.

SEE: Formal Sign 2
Linguistic Expression
Movement
Object
Perception
Sense
Sign
Voice

INTELLECT, INTELLIGENCE (*Intellectus*):

SEE: Act of Understanding
Perception
Simple Awareness
Understanding

INTENTION (*Intentio*):

1. "Intention" as standing for an act or concept of the understanding is different from "intention"as standing for an act of desire or will: FP, 58/14 *(=290b45)*; cf. A, 346/24 *(=106a19, 24)*.

2. An act or concept of the understanding is called an "intention" on the grounds that it tends toward another, namely, toward the object of a cognition: FP, 58/17 *(=291a1)*.

3. A formal intention is distinct from an objective intention, just as a formal concept is distinct from an objective one: FP, 58/21 *(=291a5)*.

4. An objective intention is a mind-dependent cognized relation which is attributed to a cognized thing: FP, 59/2 *(=291a9)*.

5. A formal intention is the very concept by which an objective intention is formed: FP, 59/4 *(=291a11)*.

6. A formal intention, as distinguished against an objective intention, is other than the formality of a second intention as obtaining on the side of an object: FP, 59/11 *(=291a19)*.

7. The formality of a second intention is always something dependent for its being on being cognized, but a formal intention is an act independent of being itself cognized for its being: A, 59/14 *(=291a23)*.

8. Distiction between first and second intentions: FP, 59/19 *(=291a26, 40)*; fn. to 58/14 *(=1631: 12b49)*.

9. Why Logic of itself considers second intentions: FP, 60/3 *(=291a44)*.

10. Not every mind-dependent relation is a second intention, but every second intention is a mind-dependent relation: FP, 60/7 *(=291b2)*.

11. A second is predicated of a first intention in the concrete, not in the abstract: FP: 62/44 *(=293a13)*.

12. One second intention can be founded on another second intention: FP, 61/37 *(=292a40)*.

13. How second intentions are divided and how many kinds there are: FP, 63/9 *(=293a31)*.

14. A second does not respect a first intention as correlative in the mode of a terminus, but in the mode of a subject on which it is founded: FP, 62/29 *(=292b41)*.

15. Second intentions consist in relations founded on natures which have been abstracted and conceived in the manner of a unity: FP, 57/40 *(=290b10)*.

16. A second intention is a mind-dependent relation, not a negation like unity, and yet it belongs to a thing abstracted and one: FP, 57/46 *(=290b18)*.

17. Second intentions belong to things as being cognized by the understanding; they are therefore not mind-independent objective forms, but mind-dependent ones: FP, 60/47 *(=292a1)*.

18. Second intentions suppose cognition not only as regards

themselves formally considered, but also as regards the aptness of the subjects which they denominate: FP, 60/15, 60/26, 60/39 *(=291b9, 291b22, 291b40)*.

19. Second intentions are properties belonging to things as a result of their having being in understanding: FP, 60/1, 60/47 *(=291a42, 292a1)*.

20. Second intention supposes the extrinsic denomination of a thing cognized and abstracted, but that extrinsic denomination is not itself the second intention formally, only fundamentally: FP, 61/19 *(=292a20)*.

21. A first intention absolutely taken must be something belonging to something in a state of being independent of objective apprehension: FP, 61/31 *(=292a34)*.

22. Since the understanding is reflexive upon its own acts, it can reflexively cognize the very second intention and found upon that cognized intention another second intention: FP, 61/43 *(=292b1)*; in which case this founded second intention denominates the founding second intention as prior or relatively first: FP, 62/1 *(=292b10)*.

23. It frequently happens among second intentions that one of them is of itself formally of a certain type and denominatively as cognized it is of another type; yet both founding and founded second intentions are still called "second," and not "third," "fourth,"etc., because they all belong to the object according to its cognized being, which is a second state of things: FP, 62/5 *(=292b15)*.

24. Second intentions suppose for their fundament cognized being: FP, 61/15 *(=292a15)*.

25. The act itself of understanding is not an objective second intention, but the formal intention from which the objective intention results: FP, 61/26 *(=292a27)*.

26. Because the fundament of a second intention is a thing as cognized and as subjected to the state of apprehension, the division of second intention is drawn not only in terms of the proximate fundaments or rationales of founding, just as any other division of relations, but also according to the diverse orders of the cognized for whose ordination the second intention is formed: FP, 63/16 *(=293a39)*; illustrations: FP, 63/22-64/14 *(=293b1-45)*.

27. All second intentions are formed by some comparing or relating act: FP, 69/10 *(=302b34)*.

28. When a proposition is formed there is not yet the second intention of the proposition formally, but fundamentally proximately, just as when a universal nature is abstracted from singulars there is not yet an intention of universality, but its fundament: FP, 76/4 *(=306a41)*.

SEE: Extrinsic Denomination
Logic
Mind-Dependent Being 38, 39
Relation
Universal

INTERIOR DISCOURSE (*Locutio Interior*): Interior discourse is an expressive manifestation of things as understood: II, 242/20 *(=702b46)*.

SEE: Concept
Reflexion

INTERNAL SENSE (*Sensus Internus*):

SEE: Animals
Brute Animals
Custom
Experience
Mind-Dependent Being
Perception

INTUITION, INTUITIVE AWARENESS (*Intuitio, Notitia Intuitiva*):

1. The awareness which is a simple apprehension or mental term can be divided into intuitive awareness and abstractive awareness: S, 29/7 *(=10b22)*.

2. This division embraces the awareness of the external senses, which is always intuitive, of the internal senses, which is sometimes intuitive and sometimes abstractive, and of the understanding, which is also sometimes intuitive and sometimes abstractive: S, 29/9 *(=10b25)*.

3. An intuitive awareness is the awareness of a thing physically present to the cognitive power: S, 29/13 *(=10b31)*; III, 287/25 *(=723a3)*.

4. Note the difference between saying that a given awareness is "of a thing physically present" and saying merely that it is "of a thing presented to a given cognitive power": "to be physically present" pertains to a thing *in itself*, as it is independently of the power; "to be presented" pertains to a thing *as objectified* to the very power, and is common to every awareness: S, 29/14 *(=10b32)*.

5. Intuitive awareness is understood by way of opposition to abstractive awareness, which accordingly is awareness of a thing not physically given with and by the object here and now apprehended: S, 29/21 *(=10b38)*.

6. In the definition of intuitive and abstractive awareness, therefore, "awareness of a present thing and awareness of an absent thing" is said, taking "presence" and "absence" for that which belongs to the object in itself: III, 287/11 *(=722b36)*.

7. "Knowledge of vision," which is another name for intuitive awareness, is defined by St. Thomas as adding to simple awareness something which is independent of the order of awareness, namely, the existence of things: therefore physical or mind-independent existence is meant, for an intentional and objective existence is not independent of the order of awareness: III, 287/14, 290/41 *(=722b40, 724b14)*.

8. Some ill-conceived attempts have been made to distinguish intuitive and abstractive awareness according to formalities which are not proper to the two modes of awareness in question: III, 288/36 *(=723b2)*.

9. The understanding is able to see singular corporeal things when they are present through the senses: III, 289/14 *(=723b26)*.

10. An intuitive and an abstractive awareness can be on a par in point of clarity and distinctness (evidence): III, 288/44, 296/24, 305/3 *(=723b9, 727b46, 732a44)*.

11. To properly distinguish intuitive from abstractive awareness it is necessary to recur to the terminus cognized objectively: the former cognition attains a thing terminating under its own physical presence, the latter not: III, 289/40 *(=724a8)*.

12. The rationales of the intuitive and the abstractive do not of themselves express essential intrinsic differences, because they pertain on the side of the subject to the very order of the cognizable and are not independent of the order of cognition, while insofar as the intuitive adds something to awareness on the side of the object, what it adds is independent of the order of cognition and therefore incidental and extrinsic to awareness *qua* awareness: III, 290/44, 292/31 *(=724b19, 725b20)*.

13. Why the intuitive and the abstrative do not import a diversity into the formal principle itself of cognizability: III, 291/2 *(=724b27)*.

14. Presence and absence pertain specially to the intuitive and the abstractive only according as they affect and modify the object in itself and render that object coexistent or not coexistent with the cognition: III, 291/13 *(=724b41)*.

15. Presence or absence as represented things essentially and directly do not distinguish the intuitive and the abstractive: III, 291/31 *(=725a12)*.

16. Presence or absence intrinsically vary the cognizable order only as represented and of themselves cognizable, or as objects essentially, not as a modification and accessory of another object: therefore the formal rationale of intuition is not an essential difference in the cognizable order: III, 291/35 *(=725a18)*; cf. entries 19 and 34 below.

17. In differentiating intuitive from abstractive awareness, the physical presence itself does not have the rationale of the object primarily and essentially represented, but only *modifies* the object represented, so that the presence makes the cognition be terminated at the object inasmuch as that object is as object physically present and coexistent with the power, not inasmuch as the presence is itself a represented thing: III, 291/43 *(=725a27)*.

18. Physical presence modifies the termination of the principal object in an intuitive awareness, it does not constitute the rationale of the stimulus, inasmuch as it coexists with that rationale terminatively, and hence it varies the cognition not essentially, but incidentally: III, 292/18 *(=725b4)*.

19. The intuitive and the abstractive can sometimes be found in cognitions otherwise distinct in kind: III, 292/44 *(=725b32)*; in such cases, the rationale of intuitive or of abstrative is added to the other formally specifying rationales as an incidental accompanying rationale: III, 293/8 *(=725b46)*.

20. The opinion that the intuitive and the abstractive consist only in an extrinsic denomination is probable: III, 293/48 *(=726a42)*; but the opinion that the intuitive and the abstractive are intrinsic to awareness itself in its own order is more probable: III, 293/48 *(=726a43)*.

21. When our awareness passes from intuitive into abstractive and conversely it is really modified: III, 294/2 *(=726a46)*; because intuition imports the coexistence of the physical presence of the object with the attention and tendency of the very cognition terminated at this specific thing as coexisting with and modifying the object, and a termination of cognition diverse by means of an attention to a coexisting thing posists some intrinsic modification in the very cognition: III, 294/4 *(=726b1)*.

22. What the difference is between the truth or falsity of a cognition and the rationale of the intuitive and of the abstractive: III, 294/14 *(=726b14)*.

23. For anyone to see intuitively, it does not suffice that while he is cognizing something that something is posited present in itself, but it must needs be that the one cognizing attend to its presence as to a presence coexisting with himself, and not as precisely a represented presence; which attention, if it is missing, the intuition is destroyed, even though the thing be present in itself: III, 294/25 *(=726b26)*.

24. The intuitive and the abstractive, although they are not essential differences of cognition, can nevertheless be consequent upon and presuppose specifically distinct cognitions to which they are conjoined, when, to wit, they are found in cognitions which are constituted through diverse means or lights or representations: III, 296/13 *(=727b32)*.

25. Clarity and distinctness do not distinguish one awareness from another essentially, because they do not obtain on the side of the formal specifying rationale, but on the side of the coexistence and application of the object: III, 296/36 *(=728a8)*.

26. Clarity of vision results from three sources: III, 296/42 *(=728a15)*.

27. The evidence (clarity and distinctness) of an intuitive awareness *from the precise and formal energy of the intuition* only provenates from that awareness owing to the conjunction or application of the object from more or less close at hand: but this is accidental and extrinsic: III, 297/3 *(=728a26)*.

28. The intuitive and abstractive in the same subject are opposed by a formality incidental to the cognition itself, but essential to the very rationale of intuition: III, 297/10 *(=728a34)*.

29. Faith and the direct vision of God differ by more than the difference between abstractive and intuitive awareness: III, 297/21 *(=728a48)*.

30. The intuitive and the abstractive do not differ according to formal objects diverse in the being and formality of something cognizable, but in the being and formality of some condition and accidental mode: III, 298/41 *(=729a30)*.

31. That which is formal and essential to the intuitive itself is one thing, that which is formal and essential to cognition itself quite another: III, 298/44 *(=729a35)*.

32. The intuitive and the abstractive mutually differ essentially and by definition, but these differences are accidental to cognition itself, because they do not respect the present and the absent as these found cognizability and diverse immaterialities, but as they found application to the mind-independent coexsistence of the object in terminating cognition: III, 299/5 *(=729a47)*.

33. The intuitive and the abstractive formally and by virtue of themselves do not differ acording to diverse things represented, for even an abstractive awareness can *represent* a presence on the side of the thing represented: III, 299/15 *(=729b9)*; nor do they differ according to a connotation or condition relative to a distinct represented thing or according to distinct ''rationales under which'' essentially conducing to representation, but only according to a diverse termination at presence as coexistent with the very cognition: III, 299/23 *(=729b19)*.

34. If some abstractive cognition does not represent the present physical existence of its object as a thing represented while an intuitive cognition of that same object does so represent its presence, then those cognitions would differ essentially, not by virtue of the intuitive and the abstrative precisely, but for the general reason of representing diverse objects: III, 300/22 *(=730a25)*.

35. The intuitive and the abstractive are accidental modes which reductively pertain to the order of cognition as modes, not as essential species or kinds, and it is more probable that they are intrinsic modes: III, 302/3 *(=731a25)*.

36. Formally and directly, the intuitive and the abstractive are not the very order or tendency toward the object in the rationale of represented object, but modifications of this order, inamuch as they make awareness tend toward an object not only as represented, but as coexisting or not with the awareness: III, 302/9 *(=731a33)*.

37. The rationale of being toward an object as represented and cognized formally constitutes an awareness, but the rationale of being toward the object thus represented as physically coexisting within the awareness is a modifying respect constituting the awareness as intuitive: III, 302/15 *(=731a40)*.

38. The physical presence of the object in intuitive awareness does not function as a thing directly represented, for thus it can

also be represented in an abstractive awareness, but as modifying the object represented by an accidental modification: III, 303/3 *(=731b2)*.

39. Modes can be said to be intrinsic either because they modify the formal constitutive rationale itself, and so, being intrinsic to the very constitution, make an essential difference therein; or because they do not extrinsically denominate, even though they do not essentially modify the constitution: and it is in the latter way that the intuitive and the abstractive are modes of awareness: III, 303/12 *(=731b13)*.

40. The intuitive and the abstractive are always circumstances of cognition: III, 303/41 *(=731b47)*.

41. Four differences are usually enumerated as formally differentiating intuitive and abstractive awareness: III, 304/3 *(=732a12)*; But these four presuppose a principal difference derived from the thing attained and explicitly stated in the definitions of the types of awareness in question: III, 304/19 *(=732a29)*.

42. The principal differences between intuition and abstractive awareness reduce to two, one on the side of the object, and one on the side of the subject: III, 305/7 *(=732a49)*.

43. There can be no intuition of the past and the future, unless the past or the future is reduced to some measure in which it is present: III, 305/36 *(=732b29)*.

44. Intuitive seeing functions as an experimental cognition, and is indeed the paradigm case of experience: III, 306/18 *(=733a19)*.

45. The proposition that an objective presence of itself suffices to make a cognition intuitive is unintelligible: III, 307/2 *(=733a28)*

46. For the rationale of the intuitive it is required that an object be attained under presence itself, that is, attained as it is affected by the very presence and as it exercises that presence mind-independently: III, 308/14 *(=733b1)*; Presence attained in this mode cannot be attained as it is still within causes (something future) nor as it has passed away (something past): III, 308/19 *(=733b5)*.

47. The two conditions for anything to be said to be seen of itself and immediately, i.e., in an intuition: III, 309/24 *(=734a12)*.

48. It does not suffice for the object of an intuitive awareness to have an act of being within the seeing by means of its intentional representation, but it must also have an act of being independent of the seeing, which is to be a physical object at which an awareness is terminated: III, 309/32, 309/7 *(=734a21, 733b41)*.

49. Awareness in the exterior senses is always and necessarily intuitive: III, 309/47 *(=734a37)*; Proof: III, 310/14, 310/20, 310/38, 310/48 *(=734b5, b13, b35, b47)*.

50. That mode of cognition which is to be terminated by the proper presence of a thing is never found outside intuition, howsoever clear an abstractive cognition might become: III, 315/8 *(=736b6)*.

51. It is impossible for a cognition of a thing as future not to be varied intrinsically if the thing is rendered present suchwise that the cognition became intuitive, on account of the difference between a termination at a thing in itself or in another, and the difference in attention such a difference in termination requires: III, 315/31 *(=736b33)*.

52. From the fact that a cognition is intrinsically varied when it is rendered intuitive, it does not follow that its impressed specifier is varied essentially, but only the termination of the represented thing; for the specifier which represents the thing and the presence also coexists with the present thing: III, 316/15 *(=737a17)*.

53. If God has an intuitive vision of future things, then future things must be present in eternity physically; for of the future as future there can be no vision: III, 305/41, 316/22 *(=732b35, 737a26)*.

54. Past things can be known intuitively only in their traces, i.e., indirectly, even if known properly, because physical self-presence of an object as terminating is required for intuitive awareness: III, 315/15 *(=736b15)*.

55. Even though our understanding does not have an impressed specifier *directly* representing the singular, it nevertheless has from adjunction, by the order and reflexion toward the phantasm, a concept *properly* representing the singular, and this suffices for the understanding to be said to have, through such a concept, an intuitive awareness of a present thing: III, 317/47 *(=738a16)*.

56. By the fact that the understanding cognizes with a continuation and dependence upon phantasms, while phantasms are co-ordinated with the senses (because a phantasm is a movement produced by a sense in act), it follows that even though the cognition of the understanding comes about by a specifier not directly representing the singular, it can nevertheless at least indirectly cognize that singular by means of this co-ordination and continuation relative to the senses; and this suffices for the understanding to have in the same way an intuitive awareness: III, 318/9 *(=738a27)*.

57. Intuitive awareness is prior to abstractive awareness, for all our cognition has birth from some external sense by means of an intuitive cognition: III, 304/11 *(=732a20)*.

58. There is a great difference between the presence of a thing to be acted upon by an agent (i.e., the presence of a recipient of another's action) and the presence of the object in an intuitive cognition, between causes producing effects by transitive action and the cognition of external sense: III, 323/13 *(=741a24)*.

59. Not even by divine intervention can an awareness of external sense be borne to an absent object: III, 309/47, 315/22, 322/2 *(=734a37, 736b22, 740b2)*.

60. Intuition is borne on a physical presence as physically obtaining on the side of the object, and not only as the mind-independent presence is objectively present to the cognitive power: III, 309/12 *(=733b47)*.

61. Intuitive awareness can be found in all the cognitive powers, whether sensitive or intellective, but abstractive awareness cannot be found in the external senses: III, 304/15 *(=732a25)*.

62. Why we can have no objective intuition of our own concepts: III, 328/47, 326/44, 331/27 *(=744a21, 743a4, 745b20)*.

SEE: Awareness 1-22
Experience
Perception
Judgment
Presence
Sense
Understanding

— J —

JUDGMENT (*Judicium*): Judgment properly speaking is neither intuitive nor abstractive except by reason of the extremes from which it is established; for "intuitive" is said of simple awareness, not of judicative awareness, which does not formally respect a thing as present, but as belonging to or agreeing or coinciding with another: III, 319/47 *(=739a29)*.

SEE: Animals 1
Instinct

Sense 13
Truth

— K —

KNOWABILITY, KNOWABLE (*Scibilitas, Cognoscibilitas, Scibile*):
SEE: Cognizability

KNOWLEDGE (*Scientia*):
SEE: Cognition
Experience
Intuition
Perception
Sense

KNOWLEDGE OF VISION (*Scientia Visionis*): is the same as intuitive awareness: III, 287/15 *(=722b41)*.
SEE: Intuition 7

— L —

LIBERTY (*Libertas*):
SEE: God 4

LIGHT (*Lumen, Lux*):

1. Without exterior light or a physically present object the eye is deprived of the form or of the terminus of an experimental and external sensation: III, 322/8 *(=740b10)*.

2. Light is seen through its essence only inasmuch as its essence is to be the rationale or ground of visibililty and a kind of form giving visible being in act to the objects of sense: III, 331/43 *(=745b39)*.

3. Light is the form of the visibility of sensible things through its essence: III, 332/5 *(=746a3)*.

4. Precisely as it is the form giving actual visibility to color, light is not seen by means of a similitude distinct from that which the very color-made-visible emits: III, 332/6 *(=746a4)*.

5. The light of glory does not have the rationale of a representation: II, 264/1 *(=713a8)*.

6. Color becomes ultimately visible by means of light: III, 311/16 *(=735a17)*.

SEE: Abstraction
Mirror 1, 2, 3
Sense

LINGUISTIC EXPRESSION (*Vox Significativa*):

1. The term "linguistic expression" here applies to any sense-perceptible mark, sound, or movement intended to express a conception of the understanding: cf. A, 344/21 *(=105a19)*.

2. Linguistic expressions signify both formal and objective concepts: A, 344/1 *(=104a37)*.

3. Linguistic expressions signify formal concepts as *what* we conceive, objective concepts as that *which* we conceive: A, 344/5, 344/12 *(=104a41, 105a7)*.

4. A linguistic expression signifies object and concept by the same imposition and signification: A, 345/8 *(=105a33)*; this is because the outward expression is imposed for the purpose of manifesting the concept as ordered to or sign of certain things thought about: A, 346/40 *(=106a37)*.

5. Linguistic expressions do not signify objects and concepts with equal immediacy, nor do they signify objects and concepts separately, but objects by means of concepts and concepts as subordinated to objects: A, 345/13 *(=105a38)*.

6. If linguistic expressions signified objects and concepts by different and relatively unsubordinated significations, every name would be equivocal, which is absurd: A, 345/30 *(=105b12)*.

7. Concepts are signified by linguistic expressions as exercising the function of making things cognized: A, 345/48 *(=105b34)*.

8. Linguistic expressions signify by participating in the signification of concepts: A, 348/12 *(=106b49)*.

9. Linguistic expressions as instruments render concepts sensible to the extent that they express what the concepts signify: A, 349/44, 349/32 *(=107b24; 107b11)*. See entry 17 below.

10. One and the same signification of a linguistic expression has a double function, to wit, to substitute for the objects which the expression manifests, and to substitute for the concepts which signify these objects in an interior and imperceptible way: A, 346/36 *(=106a32)*; and because this comes about through a single signification and convention—346/40 *(=106a37)*—either reference can be exercised separately: 349/28 *(=107b7)*. See entry 14 below.

11. A linguistic expression signifies a concept not as that which is signified, but as that which signifies principally and as that for which the expression is a substitute and instrument of representation: A, 346/36 *(=106a2)*.

12. A linguistic expression as such participates in the being and signification of the mental word or concept: A, 348/12 *(=106b49)*; Thus linguistic expressions exist as substitutes representing a principal to which they are servile as well as by representing the objects to which that principal is ordered, namely, the things signified: A, 348/21 *(=107a7)*.

13. Linguistic expressions signify concepts immediately, but not directly as object signified; rather, they represent concepts as the principal significative by the medium of which objects are directly signified: A, 345/26, 348/26 *(=105b8, 107a13)*.

14. Linguistic expressions can represent things conceived in two different ways: in one way, where the qualification "as conceived" is taken specificatively and exertively for the condition with which they are represented; in another way, where the qualification "as conceived" is taken reduplicatively for the state in which the things are cognized, i.e., as signifying not the mere fact of the things' being conceived, but the things conceived precisely as subject to the intention and state which they have in the mind, that state itself being explicitly represented as such: A, 348/28 *(=107a16)*.

15. Linguistic expressions are created in such a way that anyone may subsequently make use of them; therefore they signify by the concept of their creator as from the source of their linguistic status and signification, but they signify the concept of an actual speaker here and now as that for which they are surrogated: A, 349/7 *(=107a29)*.

16. Linguistic expressions formed by a non-speaker [let us say, a recording device on playback, a computer, or a robot] signify by custom: A, 349/14 *(=107a35)*.

17. Even though the speaker's concept is external to the listener, it is yet present to the listener according to its own being through the linguistic expression, by means of which it is rendered sensible: A, 349/32 *(=107b11)*.

18. Linguistic expressions have the power of signifying both concept and object, but this twofold signifying is not always exercised, for example, when the expression is produced by a non-speaker, or when a speaker's concepts are not adverted to by the listener's in their distinction from the objects spoken about: A, 349/28 *(=107b5)*.

19. Linguistic expressions signify the objects of concepts more principally than they signify concepts, because it is to those objects that the concepts themselves, which the speech expresses, are themselves ordered in representing: A, 349/42 *(=107b21)*.

material and outside the cognitive power, or formal and within the power: II, 224/13, 249 note 27 *(=693b45, 1635: 358b26).*

3. A means-in-which outside the power makes a cognition mediate; a means-in-which inside the power does not: II, 224/29 *(=694a16).*

SEE: Instrument
Sign
Specifier

MEASURE (*Mensura*):
SEE: Relation
Sign

MEDIUM (*Medium*):
SEE: Means

METAPHOR (*Metaphora*):
SEE: End 4

MIND-DEPENDENT BEING (*Ens Rationis, Non Ens*):

1. Mind-dependent being (i.e., being as it exists dependently upon apprehension), precisely as it is opposed to mind-independent being (i.e., being as existing independently of apprehension), pertains to Metaphysics: FP, 44/4 *(=284b47).*

2. Mind-dependent being, i.e., dependence upon apprehension, as common only to second intentions, pertains to Logic: FP, 44/8 *(=284b50).*

3. Taken in the fullest extent of its signification, ''mind-dependent being'' expresses that which depends on the mind in any way: FP, 48/1 *(=285a19).*

4. Something can depend on the mind in two ways, either as an effect upon a cause, or as an object upon some organism cognizing: FP, 48/3 *(=285a22).*

5. That which depends upon the mind as an effect upon a cause has a true and physical existence though one dependent upon mind: FP, 48/12 *(=285a32).*

6. That which depends upon the mind as an object is most properly called a mind-dependent being, because it has no existence apart from the mind, and so is opposed to mind-independent or physical being without qualification: FP, 48/17 *(=285a37).*

7. Direct experience sufficiently proves that there is such a thing as being whose entire existence depends upon the mind: FP, 49/1 *(=285b4).*

8. Mind-dependent being in the most proper sense can be defined as ''being having existence objectively in apprehension, to which no being existing independently in the physical world corresponds'': FP, 49/9 *(=285b12).*

9. That being is called mind-dependent or mental which, while it posits nothing in the physical world and in itself is not a being, is nevertheless formed or understood as a being in the mind: FP, 49/16 *(=285b20).*

10. Since being is denominated from the act of being and in terms of an order to existence, just as mind-independent being is defined in terms of the order to the existence it has truly and in the world of physical nature, so mind-dependent being, which is opposed to physical being, must be explicated in an opposite way, namely, as that which does not have an existence in the world of physical nature and does have existence in cognition objectively: FP, 49/21 *(=285b25).*

11. The proposition that mind-dependent being universally speaking consists as such in the sole extrinsic denomination of ''something cognized'' is false: FP, 49/36 *(=285b41).*

12. That extrinsic denomination cannot be the constitutive form of mind-dependent being is proved by the fact that such denomination can also fall upon mind-independent beings which are denominated ''cognized'' without thereby being formed into mind-dependent beings, because they are not rendered constructs or fictions: FP, 49/41 *(=285b47).*

13. Considered as that which receives the formation of a mind-dependent being, an extrinsic denomination (such as ''being cognized'') is apprehended as a mind-dependent being, but so also are other non-beings as well: FP, 49/46 *(=286a6).*

14. The formation of a proposition concerning an object that does not have a physical existence in the world of nature is a sign that the object in question is grasped by the understanding in the way a being is grasped: FP, 50/12 *(=286a25).*

15. An act of understanding attaining an object that does not exist extramentally as if it did so exist has two aspects: FP, 50/18 *(=286a31).*

16. A mind-dependent being is produced whenever the understanding attempts to apprehend that which is not as if it were a being: FP, 50/28, 72/4 *(=286a42, 304a42).*

17. A mind-dependent being results as a consequence of a manner of understanding reality that exists independently of the human mind: FP, 50/33 *(=286b1).*

18. A mind-dependent being does not have a formally constructed or objective being from the fact that it is rendered cognized as *that which* is cognized, for thus it already presupposes having a being or some rationale upon which the denomination ''cognized'' falls: FP, 50/42, 71/30 *(=286b9, 304a15).*

19. That act which respects a non-being under the rationale and guise of a being is said to construct or form the mind-dependent being, and not just to denominate: FP, 50/46 *(=286b15).*

20. The having of objective being exclusively in the understanding consists in this, that that which is not a being is apprehensively constructed as a being by the very method of the cognizing: FP, 51/2 *(=286b18).*

21. The proposition that every object conceived by the understanding otherwise than as it is in the physical world is a mind-dependent being is false: FP, 51/8 *(=286b23)*; because the fact of something's being cognized on the pattern of another does not suffice for its being denominated a being formed absolutely by the mind in the rationale of being: FP, 51/15 *(=286b31)*; for we apprehend many things not through proper concepts, but connotative ones: FP, 75/12 *(=305b41).*

22. The task of exhaustively dividing mind-dependent being does not fall to the logician, but to the metaphysician: FP, 44/7, 51/31 *(=284b9, 287a1).*

23. Mind-dependent being in its fullest extent can be exhaustively divided into relations and negations, where negation is understood as including also privation: FP, 51/39 *(=287a10).*

24. This division of mind-dependent being into negations and relations is the only one based on the formal element that is attained in mind-dependent being, namely, an object which, though it does not exist in the physical world, is cognized in the way a physical being is cognized: FP, 53/8, 53/16 *(=287b44, 288a5).*

25. We can consider three elements in a mind-dependent being, namely, the subject to which it is attributed, the rationale conceived and attributed, and that on whose pattern the mind-dependent being is conceived: FP, 52/35 *(=287b17).*

26. The division of mind-dependent being into that which has a foundation in mind-independent being (a so-called *reasoned*

mind-dependent being) and that which does not (a so-called *mind-dependent being of reasoning*) is based on the subject to which a mental construct is attributed, not on what is formal to the construct as such: FP, 52/41 *(=287b24)*.

27. Thus other divisions of mind-dependent being besides the division into negations and relations can be admitted, but as based on various conditions of mind-dependent being rather than on mind-dependent being itself: FP, 53/18 *(=288a8)*.

28. Why the division of mind-dependent being into negations and relations is exhaustive: FP, 53/21 *(=288a13)*.

29. Every positive absolute is conceived in terms of itself, either as a subject or a subjective determination; wherefore no positive absolute can be understood as a mind-dependent being: FP, 53/29, 32 *(=288a20, 25)*.

30. Relation alone has in its proper and positive conception (as a being toward another) an indifference to subjective being, and so does not repugn being found positively in apprehension alone and not in physical reality—when, specifically, it so bears toward another that it does not inhere in anything; and so relation provides the only positive form of mind-dependent being: FP, 52/1, 53/29, 53/36 *(=287a27, 288a20, 288a29)*; SP, 95/18, 96/28 *(=581a38, 582a6)*.

31. Negation is called a mind-dependent being, not because it is given on the side of mind-independent being negatively, but because it is understood by the mind after the manner of a being while in the physical world it is not a being: FP, 54/32 *(=288b26)*.

32. A negation, being a deficiency or lack in a subject, is not properly a formal effect, nor is to remove a form some form; but the deficiency is taken by the understanding in the manner of a formal effect inasmuch as it is understood in the mode of a form, and consequently after the pattern of a formal effect, while in fact the deficiency or lack in question is not a formal effect, but the ablation of that effect: FP, 54/37 *(=288b32)*.

33. Every non-physical apprehended thing is something mind-dependent: FP, 55/26 *(=289a28)*.

34. From the side of the cause producing or causing mind-dependent being, a unity that is only mental is taken from the unity of a concept, and a mind-dependent or mental distinction is taken from a plurality of concepts: FP, 56/30 *(=289b39)*.

35. From the side of the object, a mind-dependent unity pertains formally to negation or privation, because it is nothing other than a segregation of that in which there is coincidence from the several making the difference: FP, 56/38 *(=289b46)*.

36. A mind-dependent distinction is formally a purely objective relation, the very relation itself of the distinguished terms: FP, 57/6 *(=290a14)*.

37. The purely objective relation formally constituting a mind-dependent distinction is founded on the virtual plurality that obtains on the side of the object as subjected to a plurality of concepts: FP, 57/13 *(=290a23)*.

38. That on whose pattern something is conceived is not said to be a mind-dependent being, but that object which, while in itself it is not a being, is conceived after the pattern of a being: FP, 57/26 *(=290a39)*; SP, 96/7 *(=581b30)*.

39. In a universal which expresses only a nature abstracted and conceived in the manner of a unity there is already found something mind-dependent, namely, the unity or aptitude or non-repugnance for being in many that belongs to the nature represented or cognized owing to the abstraction: FP, 57/31 *(=290b45)*.

40. Though every mind-dependent relation results from cognition, yet not every such relation denominates a thing only in the state of cognized being, which is a second state, but some also do so in the state of an existence independent of cognition: FP, 60/15 *(=291b9)*.

41. Even though cognition is the cause from which results a mind-dependent relation (as it is the cause of all mind-dependent being), and thus, as a mind-dependent relation belongs to and denominates some subject, it necessarily requires cognition; yet cognition does not always render the object itself apt for and coincidentally receptive of such denomination, so that the denomination belongs to that object *only* in cognized being; for this happens only in second intentions: FP, 60/26 *(=291b22)*. See Relation 60, 62.

42. Mind-dependent relations can be divided according as the cognition causing them also presupposes or does not presuppose cognition as the cause rendering the subject of the relations apt for being denominated by them: FP, 60/26, 35, 39 *(=291b22, b34, b40)*.

43. The powers by which objective mind-dependent being is produced must be powers that work immanently, i.e., completing their operation within themselves, not transitively, i.e., completing their operation in the production of an external physical effect: FP, 65/1 *(=301a9)*.

44. Neither the will nor the external senses produce mind-dependent beings, because both alike presuppose their object as formed outside themselves: FP, 66/21 *(=301b4)*.

45. Materially, to cognize a mind-dependent being is to attain the very appearance of a being physically real without discriminating between that which is of the mind and that which is of the physical world: FP, 67/5 *(=301b43)*; In this sense, the internal senses form mind-dependent beings: FP, 66/48 *(=301b35, b48)*.

46. The fact of anything's being regarded as a constructed or fictive being (a mind-dependent being) *formally*, consists in this: that it is known to have nothing of entitative reality even though it is attained on the pattern of a physical entity; otherwise, no discrimination is made between mind-independent being and constructed or fictive being, but only that is attained on whose pattern mind-dependent being is formed, which, when it is something sensible, does not repugn being cognized by sense: FP, 68/1 *(=302a17)*.

47. To sense it pertains only to attain that which is of sensibility in an object, whereas a condition relative to non-being in whose place the object is surrogated and whence it fictively has being does not pertain to sense, and therefore sense does not differentiate fictive being under the formal rationale of fiction from true being: FP, 67/13, 68/11 *(=302a1, a23)*.

48. That sense is able to cognize fictive being materially is manifestly the case, because internal sense synthesizes many things which outside itself in no way are or can be, although the fiction itself sense does not apprehend, but only that which offers itself in the fiction as sensible: FP, 68/18 *(=302a35)*.

49. The understanding needs some comparative act in order that mind-dependent beings might be formed and said to exist formally and not only fundamentally ("materially"): FP, 68/35 *(=302b9)*.

50. Every mind-dependent being is either a relation or some negation: if a relation, it must be apprehended relatively to some terminus; if a negation, it must be conceived positively on the pattern of being, which is to be conceived comparatively to another: FP, 69/14 *(=302b39)*).

51. The fundament of a mind-dependent relation does not require being conceived in a comparative act: FP, 70/14 *(=303a44)*.

52. In the case of mind-dependent relations, there comes about a denomination even before the relation itself is cognized in act through a comparison owing only to this: that the fundament is posited: FP, 70/24 *(=303b8)*.

53. How mind-dependent relations differ from mind-independent relations: FP, 70/35 *(=303b22)*.

54. The actual existence of mind-dependent relations consists in actually being cognized objectively, which does not provenate from the fundament and terminus, but from the understanding: FP, 70/43 *(=303b29)*.

55. Mind-dependent being is formed by or results from that direct cognition which denominates the non-mind-independent being itself cognized on the pattern of a mind-independent being: FP, 71/20, 72/11 *(=304a6, 304b2)*.

56. A cognition whereby a mind-dependent being is denominated cognized reflexively supposes the being as already formed; therefore the reflexive cognition does not initially form mind-dependent being: FP, 71/30 *(=304a15)*.

57. When anyone understands mind-dependent intentions by examining their nature, the intentions examined are not then formed, but others are founded upon them, inasmuch as they are cognized in general or by way of predication, etc.: FP, 71/46 *(=304a34)*.

58. The extrinsic denomination that results from an act of appetite or will is a mind-dependent being fundamentally, but not formally until and unless it is cognized in act on the pattern of a mind-independent relation: FP, 73/1 *(=304b43)*.

59. Internal sense so compares or relates one thing to another by forming a proposition and discourse that the very ordination of predicate and of subject and of antecedent to consequent the sense does not formally cognize by distinguishing the fictive from physical relation: FP, 73/17 *(=305a14)*.

60. Simple apprehension does not compare one thing to another by affirming or denying, but it does indeed compare by differentiating one thing from another and by attaining the order of one thing to another; whence simple apprehension at the level of human understanding has enough of comparison for forming a mind-dependent being formally: FP, 74/27 *(=305b6)*.

61. We do not deny that internal sense formally forms a mind-dependent being on the grounds of lack of comparison, but on the grounds of the absence of a cognizing of the more universal rationales distinguishing true being from fictive being: FP, 74/39 *(=305b19)*.

62. Simple apprehension is not a construction in the way of an enuntiation affirming or denying, but it can well be a construction in the way of formation, by apprehending something which is not apart from the apprehension: FP, 75/1 *(=305b30)*.

63. Simple apprehension does not always apprehend a thing as it is in itself, in the sense of never apprehending one thing on the pattern of another, because we apprehend many things not through proper concepts but through connotative ones, but only in the sense of not *formally* judging of that which is apprehended: FP, 75/9 *(=305b39)*.

64. When a mind-dependent being is cognized reflexively it exists objectively as denominated extrinsically in cognized being, not as initially formed: FP, 76/18 *(=306b14)*.

65. When mind-depedent being is cognized in general, it is not said to be formed, because it is supposed as formed already; but the very universality or community under which it is cognized is formed: FP, 76/28 *(=306b25)*.

66. There is no such thing, properly speaking, as a mind-dependent substance or quantity, etc., because even though some non-being may be conceived on the pattern of a substance, yet neither substance itself nor any rationale of subjectivity is conceived by the understanding and formed in being on the pattern of some other mind-independent being: SP, 96/11 *(=581b35)*.

67. From that content by which a relation is considered toward a terminus, it both exists positively and is not determinately a mind-independent form, but is indifferent to the exercise of a mind-independent or a mind-dependent act of existence: SP, 94/37 *(=581a11)*.

68. Relation has this peculiarity, that for it to exist dependently upon the mind is not a condition diminishing its rationale, because that relation which is mind-dependent is a true relation: SP, 93/44, 95/34 *(=580b9, 581b11)*.

69. The rationale of something cognizable and of an object can be univocal in a mind-independent and in a mind-dependent being: I, 149/41 *(=662b45)*.

70. Although entitatively mind-independent being and mind-dependent being are analogized, nevertheless, objectively, because the one is represented on the pattern of the other, even beings which are not univocal entitatively can coincide in a univocal rationale of object: I, 151/1 *(=663a19)*.

71. It can well be that some being incapable of mind-independent existence is capable of truth, not as a subject, but as an object, inasmuch as it does not have in itself the entitative being which as subject founds truth and cognizability, but does have that which as object can be cognized on the pattern of mind-independent being and so exist objectively in the understanding as something true: I, 150/7 *(=663a9)*.

72. Whether an object is mind-independent or mind-dependent makes a difference only in the rationale of being, not in the rationale of object and cognizable thing: I, 187/28 *(=678b15)*.

73. Even a mind-dependent object perfects a cognitive power, not by reason of itself formally, but by reason of its fundament and of the mind-independent being on whose pattern it is conceived: I, 189/8, 186/35 *(=679a3, 678a19)*.

74. Mind-independent and mind-dependent being assume in the being of object a single rationale: II, 271/1 *(=716a3)*.

75. All non-mind-independent (or ''unreal'') beings are cognizable not immediately and by reason of themselves but mediately and through another, and in the way, supposing a borrowed cognizability, they take on the rationale of stimulating and representing: I, 131/11 *(=653b41)*.

76. Even though some non-being may be conceived on the pattern of a substance, yet neither substance itself nor any rationale of subjectivity is conceived by the understanding and formed on the pattern of some other cognition-independent being; and for this reason—since that non-mind-independent being which is conceived on the pattern of a cognition-independent being is called mind-dependent being—a non-being conceived on the pattern of substance is properly called a mind-dependent *being*, but it cannot properly be called a mind-dependent *substance*; rather, all non-mind-independent beings conceived according to any rationale of subjectivity are called *negations*: SP, 96/7 *(=581b30)*.

77. When that on whose pattern mind-dependent being is formed is something sensible, it can be cognized by internal sense, i.e., perceived: FP, 68/9 *(=302a25)*.

78. The fact of anything's being regarded as a constructed,

purely objective, or fictive being formally consists in this, that it is known to have nothing of entitative reality in the physical world, and yet is attained or grasped cognitively on the pattern of a physical being; *otherwise*, no discrimination is made between mind-independent and constructed or fictive [purely objective: mind-dependent] being, but *only that is cognized on whose pattern a mind-dependent being could be formed*, and when this object is something sensible, nothing prevents its being known by sense, which is to know mind-dependent being fundamentally and materially: 68/1, 68/27 *(=302a17, 302a45)*.

SEE: Cognizability
Intention
Logic
Mind-Independent Being
Object
Relation
Stipulated Sign
Stipulation
Truth
Understanding

MIND-DEPENDENT RELATION (*Relatio Rationis*):
SEE: Mind-Dependent Being
Relation

MIND-INDEPENDENENT BEING (*Ens Praedicamentale, Ens Reale*):

1. Mind-independent being is defined in terms of the order to existence that being has truly and in the world of physical nature: FP, 49/23 *(=285b26)*.

2. Things which depend on the mind as on an efficient cause (works of art and technology) or as on a material cause (as the cognitive powers are the subject in which acts and habits exist) nevertheless pertain to the order of mind-independent being as well, because what has being dependent upon the mind in either of these two ways has a true existence which does not depend for its being upon being actually cognized and objectified by the mind: FP, 48/6 *(=285a25)*.

3. Such mind-independent beings as lie outside our own experience are conceived by us after the pattern of the physical beings of which we have had experience: FP, 51/11 *(=286b26)*.

4. Such mind-independent beings as lie outside our direct experience and are conceived by us as supposed to exist in fact do not have the rationale of being attributed to them from the process of cognition, but from the supposition of their having an act of mind-independent being: FP, 51/15 *(=286b31)*.

5. Such mind-independent beings as are conceived by us but not experienced in themselves are denominated cognized by way of an alien nature, not by way of their proper being, and they receive from that on whose pattern they are cognized a relative connotation in their cognized being which connotation yet does not suffice for them to be denominated beings formed *absolutely* by the mind in the rationale of being: FP, 51/19 *(=286b35)*.

6. Whatever exists independently of being itself cognized objectively is said to pertain to the order of mind-independent being, even if on other grounds it can be said to depend upon the mind for its being: FP, 48/6, 55/19, 61/26 *(=285a25, 289a21, 292a27)*.

7. Mind-independent and mind-dependent being assume in the being of object a single rationale: II, 271/1 *(=716a3)*.

SEE: Connotation
Cognizability
Intuition
Mind-Dependent Being
Relation
Object
Sense
Truth

MIND-INDEPENDENT RELATION (*Relatio Praedicamentalis, Relatio Realis*):
SEE: Mind-Independent Being
Relation

MINOR (*Minor*): The second premise of a syllogism: IFP, 10/13 *(=3a23)*.

MIRROR (*Speculum*):

1. The action of a mirror is said to represent presuppositively, as it were, not formally, because through the refraction of light a mirror productively generates an image which represents: I, 199/29 *(=683a21)*.

2. It is not the thing itself that is seen intuitively in a mirror, but its image, formed in the mirror by the refraction of specifying stimuli and of light: III, 320/19 *(=739b9)*.

3. In a mirror, by refracted light together with specifiers borne with the light, an image is generated and results: III, 320/29 *(=739b18)*; that which the eye sees in the mirror is that image, which it sees intuitively; and it sees the mirrored thing only as contained in that image: III, 320/33 *(=739b23)*.

4. When St. Thomas says that the act of seeing is borne directly to a cognition of the thing mirrored by means of the similitude received in sight from the mirror, he is not speaking of seeing in terms only of the exterior sensitive cognition, but in terms of the whole cognition, interior as well as exterior, which is received from the mirror and does not stop at the mirror image itself, but at the mirrored thing to which that image leads, and this whole is named the act of seeing or vision: II, 320/44 *(=739b36)*.

5. The eye is said to see in a mirror by means of specifying stimuli emitted by the object and refracted, not because it sees formally and immediately by means of the specifiers as emitted by the object but by means of the specifiers of the very image formed in the mirror by the specifiers which originated from the subject objectified, and through the refraction other specifiers result: III, 320/37 *(=739b28)*.

MORAL ACT (*Actus Moralis*): To speak of a sign being in act "morally" is to employ a mitigating particle: I, 130/1-9 *(=653a21-30)*, cf. 130/38-43, 198/45 *(=653b20-26, 682b30-44)*; for an extrinsic deputation denominates only morally: II, 280/26-36, esp. 32-34 *(=720b5-17, esp. 12-14)*, cf. I, 142/8-13, 198/45-199/9 *(=659a32-39, 682b30-44)*.

MOTION, MOVEMENT (*Motio, Motus*): Movement in the manner of an agent, that is, on the side of subject and exercise, which pertains to the order of a producing cause, is distinct from motion in the manner of a stimulus object, which reduces to the order of an extrinsic formal cause, since even in eliciting its act a power is not sufficiently determined to a specific act until it is determined or moved and completed by an object: 171/38 *(=672b41)*.

SEE: End
Intention
Object
Relation
Sign
Stimulus

MUTATION (*Mutatio*):
SEE: Cause
Change
Motion

— N —

NAMES (*Nomina*):

1. If inflected forms of names distinguish concepts essentially, it is because they import into the object some diverse relative condition and connotation to the thing represented, which conditions are understood to affect the very thing represented and to be founded on it, and which a-fortiori are diverse "rationales under which": III, 300/5 *(=730a6)*.

2. An animal called by name is moved by custom, yet without understanding the imposition (stipulation), but being guided rather by a customary association: I, 205/9 *(=685b29)*.

SEE: Custom
Linguistic Expression
Means
Object
Sign
Stipulated Sign
Stipulation
Term

NATURAL SIGN (*Signum Naturale*): Because the rationale or character of sign pertains to the rationale of the knowable [the line of thing as object, *ens ut verum*], since a sign substitutes for an object by way of representation, it will of needs happen that in the character of object a mind-independent natural sign and a mind-dependent stipulated sign will come together univocally, just as do other natural and cultural forms of being in human experience: II, 270/43; see I, 151/9-21 *(=715b45; vide 663a28-41)*.

SEE: Mind-Dependent Being
Object
Sign

NATURE (*Natura*):

SEE: Image
Intuition
Mind-Independent Being
Presence
Representation
Sign

NEGATION (*Negatio*):

1. What a negation is: FP, 51/47, 53/27 *(=287a23, 288a17)*.

2. In what way a negation is given in the order of mind-independent being: FP, 54/29 *(=288b23)*.

SEE: Mind-Dependent Being 27-28, 31-32, 35, 50, 76

NOMINALISTS (*Nominales, Nominalistae*):

1. Nominalists teach that relations are only extrinsic denominations or something mind-dependent: SP, 80/16 *(=573b36)*.

2. Nominalists hold, along with others, that relations are not distinguished from their fundaments in the order of mind-independent being, but only by the mind: SP, 80/19 *(=573b39)*.

NON-BEING (*Ens Rationis, Non Ens*):

SEE: Experience
Mind-Dependent Being
Object
Perception
Relation 57, and throughout
Representation 6

— O —

OBJECT (*Obiectum*):

1. Mind-independent and mind-dependent being take on one rationale in the existence of an object, and so can coincide univocally in objective existence: I, 149/41, 187/36 text and note 33 *(=662b45, 678b25)*; II, 271/1, 272/35 *(=716a3, 717a2)*.

2. Whether something is mind-independent or mind-dependent makes a difference only in the rationale of being, not in the rationale of object and cognizable; and hence something can well be simply an object, and simply not a being: I, 187/28 *(=678b15)*.

3. Just as the notion of power in general abstracts from active and passive and joins the two in the rationale of a principle or root of an act, so too object in general abstracts from stimulus and terminative and bespeaks the extrinsic specificative of a power on the side of principle or of terminus: I, 182/29 *(=676a30)*; in specifying extrinsically both objects actuate simply, inasmuch as a power or act depends on both in its action and perfection: I, 192/7 *(=679a44)*; but though the stimulative and the terminative come together in the line of causing specification, they do not coincide in the mode nor in the kind of act caused: I, 182/9 *(=676a6)*; the object functioning in the mode of a principle induces a mode of specifying which is other than that of an object functioning in the mode of a terminus, because an object specifies an active or a passive power, which powers are always diverse powers and have diverse acts: I, 182/23 *(=676a22)*.

4. What an object in general consists in, and to what order of causality it is reduced: I, 166/4 *(=670a21)*.

5. How an object differs from an idea: I, 167/20 *(=670b21)*.

6. The object of a passive power coincides with the object of an active power in this, that it specifies an act: I, 167/51, 168/9, 182/32 *(=671a9, a19, 676a33)*; but not in the mode nor in the kind of act caused: I, 182/9, 182/23 *(=676a6, 676a22)*.

7. An object functions in respect of a passive power as a principle of the power's act, but it is related to an active power as a terminus and end: I, 168/15 *(=671a28)*.

8. How it is that a terminative object can perfect a power or action even though a terminus purely as such does not perfect: I, 168/22 *(=671a37)*.

9. The true rationale of an object is found in a stimulus object: I, 169/1 *(=671b20)*.

10. What belongs to an object as it is an object is not to produce, but to specify: I, 169/8 *(=671b27)*; that is, to extrinsically determine or perfect a power: 168/13 *(=671a25)*.

11. We distinguish between what is a stimulus in the way of exercise and what is a stimulus in the way of specification, and predicate the latter of a formal object: I, 169/17 *(=671b37)*.

12. A stimulus object specifies a passive power and is related thereto as a moving principle, and so it is prior to its specificate in the process of defining: I, 169/23 *(=671b44)*; therefore an object in the rationale of a stimulus has the true rationale of an object: I, 169/26 *(=672a1)*.

13. The rationale of stimulus as applicable to an object is contained within the limits of an objective form: I, 169/36, 172/13 *(=672a12, 673a10)*.

14. How powers and their acts and habits exist relative to their objects, and are said to have a transcendental order to them: I, 166/26 *(=670a47)*.

15. That a cognitive act may in fact also depend on a stimulus object productively as regards existence does not pertain to the object insofar as it is an object: I, 171/4, 172/13 *(=672b3, 673a10)*.

16. A stimulus object as such is stimulating or moving as regards specification, not as regards exercise: I, 171/21 *(=672b20)*.

17. Determining or moving to act or not to act is said of move-

ment on the side of the subject or of exercise, but moving to acting in this way or that is said of movement and determination on the side of the object: I, 171/32 *(=672b33)*.

18. An extrinsic formal cause consists in nothing but the fact that some power, in order to elicit an act of such or such a kind, needs to be actuated or ordered relative to an extrinsic object, not only in the termination of the act, but also in the elicitation and originating of that act, because even to elicit it, the power is not sufficiently determined to a specific kind of act until it is determined or moved and completed by an object: I, 172/5 *(=672b46)*.

19. Why a stimulus object cannot be formally identified with an instrumental sign: I, 172/49 *(=673b1)*.

20. Why a terminative object cannot be formally identified with a secondary object: I, 173/29 *(=673b36)*.

21. A terminative object does not exist as a pure terminus, for a terminative object specifies an active power, which power is not an ontological relation, but a transcendental one; but a pure terminus terminates only a categorial relation: I, 174/19 *(=674a30)*; see further entry 32 below.

22. Proof that a terminative object does not specify in any order of cause other than that of formal cause: I, 174/25 *(=674a40)*.

23. Explanation of the division of objects into primary and secondary, formal and material: I, 178/8 *(=674b34)*.

24. Formal rationale *under which* and *which*; object *by which* and object *which*: I, 179/6 *(=674b43)*.

25. Within the divine intelligence and omnipotence the rationale of object is free of the imperfection of dependence upon anything as upon something extrinsic specifying and formally causing: I, 180/25 *(=675a26)*; though in the divine acts of intellection and will there is the rationale of an object as regards that which is of perfection and actuality, in this, that there is a terminus and specificative: I, 180/32 *(=675a35)*.

26. In the expression, ''stimulus object,'' the qualification ''stimulus'' is understood of a formal moving in the mode of a principle in respect of a passive power, so that the specification of an act, and not only the exercise or existence of that act, depends on such an object, not on the side of termination, but on the side of elicitation and commencement: I, 181/48 *(=675b45)*.

27. In what way an act of cognition can be considered as taking on the rationale of a terminative object: I, 182/42, 187/11 *(=676a45, 678a40)*.

28. How an object which is outside a cognitive power informs intentionally in the same order as the specifying form which is inside the power: I, 183/40, 183/45 *(=676b47, 677a1)*.

29. The rationale of a stimulus object is not the rationale of impressing or producing specifiers, but of objectively actuating and determining a power by means of a specifying form as intentionally, not only entitatively, informing: I, 184/8 *(=677a15)*.

30. A stimulus object which specifies a cognitive act respects the power as a subject movable by itself, but it respects the act only as principled by itself: I, 185/14 *(=677a36)*.

31. An object is called a stimulus object because it principles an act by moving the cognitive power to elicit this specific cognitive act in particular: I, 185/26 *(=677b1)*.

32. The terminus of a relation does not specify except as it is subject to a fundament: I, 186/27 *(=678a10)*; but an object specifies essentially insofar as it is an object: I, 186/34 *(=678a15)*; see entry 21 above.

33. An object or extrinsic specificative need not have a mind-independent being, because it specifies not by informing and inhering, but by terminating the tendency of another: I, 186/38 *(=678a22)*.

34. A mind-dependent object perfects a cognitive power not by reason of itself formally, but by reason of its fundament and of the mind-independent being on whose pattern it is conceived: I, 189/9 *(=679a3)*.

35. In specifying extrinsically, all objects , whether stimulative or terminative, actuate simply, inasmuch as a power or act depends on both in its action and perfection: I, 192/7 *(=679a44)*.

36. How an extrinsic formal cause differs from an exemplary cause: I, 167/20 *(=670b21)*.

37. An object, insofar as it exercises an objective causality in respect of a power and represents itself, does not do so effectively, that is, productively, but only functions as an extrinsic form which is applied to a cognitive power by some other efficient cause and is rendered present to that power by means of a specifying form: I, 195/3 *(=680b1)*.

38. An object is not understood in final act of itself, but must be formed within the understanding in the rationale of terminating object: II, 253/20 *(=707b5)*.

39. An object is a thing which stimulates or toward which a cognition tends: IFP, 25/19 *(=9a28)*; Accordingly, any given object is either stimulative only: IFP, 26/8 *(=9a40)*; terminative only: IFP, 26/13 *(=9a44)*; or both stimulative and terminative at once: IFP, 26/16 *(=9b3)*.

40. An object ''by which'' is the same as a rationale of specifying ''under which''; a material object is sometimes called the ''object which'': 180/2 *(=674b3)*.

41. The rationale of a sign can, but the rationale of a stimulus object cannot, consist in a categorial relation, because an object does not respect but is respected by a power according to a non-reciprocal relation of measured to measure: I, 173/23 *(=673b27)*.

42. The rationale of stimulating or moving in an objective cause is a matter of moving as regards specification, not as regards exercise: I, 171/17 *(=672b16)*.

43. Although sometimes the production of some thing must intervene in the causality of a stimulus object, nevertheless, the formal rationale of the stimulating object does not consist in this production: I, 172/13 *(=673a10)*.

44. There is the greatest reason for an intervention of productive causality incidental to the rationale of a stimulus object in the case of the cognitive powers, since those powers cannot be moved by objects unless the objects are impressed on the powers and specifying forms are effectively produced in the powers; yet the effective production of specifiers remains other than the objective causality exercised by the stimulus object in the formal rationale of object: I, 172/20 *(=673a17)*.

45. A stimulus object specifies an act by determining or actuating a passive power which is movable by the object: I, 185/10 *(=677a30)*.

46. A terminative object is a principle and extrinsic cause giving being consummatively and finally, not stimulatively and initially: I, 187/15 *(=678a44)*.

47. The first object of human understanding is something extrinsic, namely, the nature of a material thing, and therefore that which is first cognized by human understanding is this kind of an object, and the act itself by which the material object is cognized is cognized secondarily: III, 326/26 *(=742b29)*.

48. The rationale of an object is preserved in this, that something is representable and cognizable passively by a power, which does not of itself and as such bespeak a power for ap-

plying and uniting an object to a power, but that which is united and made present: I, 195/38 *(=680b39)*.

49. Since the rationale of an object is preserved through a thing's being representable, consequently making the representation actively is outside the rationale of an object and not required for it: I, 195/45 *(=681a2)*.

50. To represent or to make present does not pertain to the object itself as it is formally an object as to the cause effecting this presentation, but as to the form and act which is presented and united to a power: I, 196/9 *(=681a19)*.

51. To excite effectively does not pertain to the rationale of an object for two reasons: I, 196/15 *(=681a27)*.

52. The presence of an object in a power in first or second act depends on many causes: I, 203/4 *(=684b49)*; four such are enumerated including the sign: I, 203/6 *(=685a2)*.

SEE: Cognizability
Concept
Extrinsic Formal Cause
Induction
Instrumental Sign
Making Present
Mind-Dependent Being
Mind-Independent Being
Reflexion
Relation
Sense
Sign
Specifier
Stimulus
Truth
Univocal
Word

OBJECTIVE PRESENCE (*Obiective Esse Praesens, Praesentia Obiectiva*):

1. Something cannot be objectively present unless it takes on the conditions of an object of a specific kind of cognitive power: III, 326/44 *(=743a4)*.

2. The presence of a thing can be known in only two ways, either signified in act as a kind of definable character—objective presence as such—or precisely as it is exercised and affects the very thing made object, rendering it present in itself as coexistent with the very awareness had of it objectively; and the first mode of knowing presence suffices for abstractive awareness, but the second is further required for an awareness to be intuitive: III, 307/1, 5 *(=733a25, 31)*; see further III, 291/43 *(=725a27)*.

SEE: Object
Presence
Sense
Understanding

OBJECTIVE UNION (*Unio Obiectiva*): There exists such a thing as objective union by reason of the true itself, that is to say, by virtue of knowability as a property of being; yet some physical union is presupposed or concomitant to an objective union, normally, as far as concerns direct human experience, in the order of a formal inhering cause, such as our expressed specifying form, which is a quality; yet the objective union remains distinct from this other union prerequired, because it has effects irreducibly distinct: I, 150 note 32 *(=1635: 186b3-40)*.

SEE: Act of Understanding
Formal Sign
Immanent Action

ONTOLOGICAL RELATION (*Relatio Secundum Esse*):

SEE: Editorial Afterword III.C.2.(b)., page 463ff.
Relation

OPINION (*Opinio*):

SEE: Faith 2

— P —

PAST (*Praeteritum*):

1. The past as past cannot be conceived except according to the rationale of a lost existence: III, 308/34 *(=733b24)*.

2. In what sense there can be a representation of a past thing in itself: III, 315/15 *(=736b15)*.

3. The past cannot be represented except either by means of some effect or trace of itself left behind, or by means of the determination of a specifying form to the existence which it had, the whole of which is not to see a thing in itself according to an act of being that it has in itself independently of the seeing, but according as it is contained in and expresses a condition and connotation relative to another: III, 308/38, 315/15 *(=733b29, 736b15)*.

SEE: Awareness
Future
Intuition
Memory
Mind-Dependent Being
Objective Presence
Presence

PERCEPTION (*Sensus Internus*):

1. Perception does not necessarily attain the fact that some elements among its objects have a condition relative to non-being, owing to which they are said to be constructs, fictive, mind-dependent, or purely objective: FP, 67/14 *(=302a4)*.

2. The fact that that which is represented as sensible in perception happens to be existentially opposed to physical being does not pertain to perception to discriminate: FP, 67/20 *(=302a11)*.

3. Perception can well include non-being within its object, because internal sense can well represent what is on the pattern of what is not now: FP, 67/20, 68/9, 68/18, 73/22 *(=302a11, 302a25, 302a35, 305a21)*.

4. How perception is altered by the formal apprehension of non-being among its objects: FP, 74/27 *(=305b6)*.

5. Perception puts together many things which outside perception in no way are or can be: FP, 68/24 *(=302a43)*.

6. Perception of the sensible includes non-being which offers itself as sensible and as if it were being: FP, 67/13, 68/8, 68/29 *(=302a1, 302a24, 302b1)*.

7. The change in colors of perceived objects as lighting conditions change is an effect of the lighting, not of the senses: FP, 68/21 *(=302a40)*.

SEE: Animals
Experience
Mind-Dependent Being
Object
Objective Presence
Sense
Sign

PHANTASM (*Phantasma*) [see discussion in Book II, Question 2, notes 1-4, pages 240-242 above]:

1. A specifier expressed and produced by the internal sense powers is sometimes called a "phantasm": II, 240/3 *(=702a48)*.

2. A phantasm of singulars does not serve for a cognition of the understanding as a sign, but as that from which the agency of the understanding takes specification: II, 237/20 *(=701a37)*.

SEE: Animal Spirits
Concept
Icon
Idea
Imagination
Quality
Representation
Sense
Sign
Specifier

PHYSICAL OBJECT (*Obiectum Physicum*):

SEE: Intuition 17, 48, 54, 60
Mind-Independent Being
Object
Objective Presence
Presence
Sense 3, 4, 14, 15, 17, 18, 19, 21

POWER (*Potentia*):

1. The notion of power in general abstracts from active and passive and joins the two in the rationale of a principle of action: I, 182/29 *(=676a30)*.

2. Some things are intermediate between entirely absolute things (things whose constitution is entirely specified internally) and entirely relative things (things whose constitution is entirely specified externally), namely, those things which have in themselves some definable content and absolute essence (so that they have something besides respecting or being referred) and yet depend in their constitution and specification on something outside themselves in order to act: and it is in this intermediate manner that powers (and acts and habits) exist with regard to their objects, whence powers are said to be transcendentally related to objects: I, 166/19 *(=670a38)*.

3. Whatever is not entirely absolute in itself, but is orderable to another as a consequence of its own nature, is specifiable by that other: I, 169/46, 166/19 *(=672a23, 670a38)*; It is in this way that powers and acts and habits exist relative to their objects, and are said to have a transcendental order to them: I, 166/26 *(=670a47)*.

4. In an act in respect of a power two things are considered: there is the rationale of something produced, that is, of an effect, and considered thus as produced the act does not respect the power by specifying it, but by receiving from it existence and specific character and nature; or the rationale of something perfecting the power in acting is considered, inasmuch as an act ultimately consummates the action of a power, and so considered the act does not specify except insofar as it stands on the side of a terminus in which the actuality of the power is consummated, and for this reason it takes on the rationale of a terminating object, just as do other effects in respect of the agents that produce them, insofar as they perfect and consummate those agents in act: I, 182/37 *(=676a40)*.

5. A passive power as such is not compared to an extrinsic specificative as to a term, but as to a stimulus, because a passive power is in potency to be actuated, not for its actuality to be terminated: I, 170/1 *(=672a27)*.

6. A cognitive power is passive both in respect of the agent impressing a specification and in respect of the form impressed: I, 183/37 *(=676b44)*.

7. How an active and a passive power do and do not compare univocally: I, 191/1 *(=679a30)*.

SEE: Mind-Dependent Being
Object
Reflexion
Relation
Sign
Specifier
Stimulus

PRESENCE (*Praesentia*):

1. The presence of a thing can only be cognized in two ways: either signified in act (as a kind of definable character) or precisely as it is exercised and affects the very thing cognized so as to render it physically present in its mind-independent existence: III, 307/5 *(=733a31)*.

2. The presence of a thing signified in act serves for abstractive cognition: III, 308/1 *(=733a36)*.

3. The presence of a thing exercised in act is further required for intuitive cognition: III, 308/14 *(=733b1)*.

4. ''Presence'' taken in an intentional sense stands for the very union of an object with a cognitive power: III, 287/6 *(=722b30)*.

5. Without presence in the intentional sense there can be no awareness whatever, for without an object united and present to a cognitive power no awareness can arise in the power: III, 287/8 *(=722b32)*.

6. Presence or absence intrinsically vary the cognizable order only as represented and of themselves cognizable or as objects essentially, not as a modification and accessory of another object: III, 291/35 *(=725a18)*. Cf. entry 11 below.

7. Inasmuch as physical presence is *represented,* even an abstractive cognition can attain to the existence of a thing in itself: III, 292/6 *(=725a40)*.

8. Presence on the side of the object pertains specially to intuition only inasmuch as it is a presence modificative of the object, not constitutive of it: III, 292/11 *(=725a44)*.

9. Physical presence is not of itself an essential difference in a cognition because it does not obtain on the side of the specifying principle as a rationale ''which''or ''under which'', but supposes a principal represented object of which it itself is a mode: III, 292/13 *(=725a48)*.

10. Physical presence as coexisting with and objectively present within cognition as modificative of the cognized term is an intrinsic rationale in the cognition on account of a diverse attention, yet it is not a rationale that essentially varies that cognition, because it is an incidental modification of the object itself as term of the cognition: III, 294/37 *(=726b40)*.

11. Physical presence or absence of the object does not vary the cognition of that object essentially insofar as these import diverse terminations of cognition to presence as coexisting with the cognition; but if presence and absence *also* function as things represented, in this way they can vary awarenesses as their diverse objects; but not when they only function as a condition pertaining to the coexistence of the presence of the object with the awareness: III, 299/44 *(=729b44)*.

12. Cognition, since it is always perfected within the cognitive power by drawing things to itself, is always perfected by the presence of those things in a cognizable and intentional existence; whence, unless such intentional presence is varied, no variation occurs in the essential rationale of the cognition, and so what

remains beyond that intentional presence of the physical presence of the object, whether it be coexistent or not coexistent with the awareness, obtains independently of the order of such awareness and is considered incidental, because already it does not pertain to the intentional presence: III, 301/8 *(=730b17)*.

13. On what causes including the sign, the presence of an object in a power depends: I, 203/4 *(=684b49)*.

SEE: Awareness
Cognition
Intuition
Objective Presence
Representation
Sense
Sign
Singular

PRINCIPLE (*Principium*): Principles manifest the conclusions which depend upon them: I, 117/6 *(=646b2)*.

SEE: Form
Object
Specifier

PROPER SENSIBLE (*Proprium Sensibile*):

SEE: Common Sensible

PURE SPIRITS (*Angelus, Angeli*):

SEE: Angel
Demon
Future 5

— Q —

QUALITY (*Qualitas*):

1. A concept and an awareness are qualities which signify informatively, not objectively, but they found the relation constitutive of a formal sign, that is, the relation of the sign whose representing and exercise of signifying is brought about by the fact that it is informing: I, 133/8 *(=655a3)*.

2. A sacramental character in itself is a quality founding a sign relation: I, 133/7 *(=655a1)*; For this reason, St. Thomas calls the quality constituting a sacrament a sign fundamentally: I, 133/5 *(=654b49)*; And the sacramental character consists in this quality superadded to the essence of the soul *antecedently* [by a logical, not a temporal, priority] to the relation constitutive of the sign formally as sign: I, 120/38 *(=648a18)*.

SEE: Formal Sign
Reflection 7
Sacrament
Understanding

— R —

RATIONALE (*Ratio*):

1. Rationale of specifying or rationale under which: I, 179/6 *(=674b43)*.

2. Rationale which: I, 180/3 *(=674b47)*.

SEE: Editorial Afterword III.C.2.(f)., pp. 468-471

REAL BEING, REALITY (*Ens Reale, Realitas*):

SEE: Category
Mind-Independent Being
Subjectivity

REASON (*Ratio*):

SEE: Understanding

REASONING (*Ratiocinatio*):

SEE: Disputation

REFLEXION (*Reflexio, Cognitio Reflexiva*):

1. An intellective power can be reflexive, i.e., able fully to turn back on itself, but not a sensitive power: III, 325/6 *(=741b48)*.

2. The whole rationale or need for reflexion arises from this, that the human understanding and its acts are not objectively understandable except dependently upon sensible things: III, 325/22 *(=742a16, b40)*.

3. Since the proper object of our understanding is the definable structure of a material thing according to itself, that which is not an essence of a material thing is not directly present to us objectively, and for it to become so a reflexion so constructing it is required: III, 326/35 *(=743a6)*.

4. Which are the impressed specifiers that serve for a reflexive cognition of concepts: III, 327/17 *(=743a29)*.

5. The "material object" of reflexive cognition (what it is engaged with) includes all those things which are found in the soul and take on as a result of the cognition of a material object the representation and manner of a sensible essence—concept and act, habit and specifier, power and the nature of the soul: III, 328/23 *(=743b40)*.

6. The formal rationale which reflexive cognition respects is the cognizing of the nature of that on which it reflects in the way in which that nature can be cognized through effects or connotatively in the manner of a sensible essence: III, 328/40 *(=744a12)*.

7. Through a reflexive concept is represented the direct concept itself signified in act as it is a kind of quality and image, but the object signified through the direct concept is represented only very remotely and obliquely: III, 329/6 *(=744a30)*.

8. In reflexion a material thing signified by a direct concept functions as the term-from-which the reflexion begins, and therefore it is connoted only in the reflexive concept: III, 329/14 *(=744a40)*.

9. In what sense the maxim "a cognitive movement toward an image is also toward the thing imaged" applies to the direct concept as attained objectively in reflexion: III, 329/20 *(=744a47)*.

10. Why it is that direct cognition and reflexive cognition differ in kind: III, 329/43 *(=744b24)*.

11. By the same act the cognitive power is borne to the object and the act according as the act is the rationale or ground of the cognizing, and to the concept or word expressing the object, but not according as the act and concept are things cognized objectively: III, 331/4 *(=745a37)*.

12. For an impressed specifier to be cognized as that which and as a thing is cognized, reflexion is required: I, 332/9 *(=746a8)*.

13. In reflexion, i.e., for the rationale of a reflexive concept, a regression toward cognition or a principle of cognition always comes about and is necessary: III, 332/36 *(=746a38)*.

SEE: Concept
Experience
Mind-Dependent Being

REFRACTION (*Refractio*):

SEE: Mirror 1-3, 5

REGRESS (*Regressus*):

SEE: Infinite Regress
Relation

RELATION (*Relatio*):

1. If relation and the relative are defined according to the requirements of expressing being in discourse, any being whatever that is expressed with a dependence on and comparison to another is relative, including substance: SP, 81/12 *(=574a15)*.

ing to the way relation has being is itself nothing but a relation: SP, 89/47 *(=578b4)*.

32. A transcendental relation is the same as a relation according to the way being must be expressed in discourse: SP, 90/16, 29 *(=578b19, b36)*.

33. An ontological relation is the same as a relation according to the way relation has being: By convention of the translator: EA, III. C. 2. (b)., p. 463ff.; for textual grounding, cf. SP, 92/4 *(=579b8)*; I, 117/28-118/18 *(=646b25-45), et passim*.

34. A transcendental relation is not a form advenient to a subject or absolute thing, but one assimilated to it, yet connoting something extrinsic upon which the subject depends or with which it is engaged: SP, 90/23 *(=578b29)*.

35. A transcendental relation is in the absolute entity itself and does not differ from its subjective being, and so its whole being is not toward another, as is required for an ontological relation, i.e., a relation according to the way relation has being: SP, 90/33 *(=578b41)*.

36. Relations according to the way relation has being (ontological relations) are divided into mind-independent relations and mind-dependent relations: SP, 90/41 *(=579a5)*.

37. Five conditions are required for a mind-independent relation: SP, 91/3 *(=579a10)*.

38. Formally and principally the whole difference between a mind-independent relation and a mind-dependent one comes down to this, that a mind-independent relation has a mind-independent fundament with a coexistent terminus, while a mind-dependent relation lacks such a fundament: SP, 91/23 *(=579a28)*.

39. A categorial relation must be, first, ontological (that is, a relation according to the way it has being), second, physical (that is, mind-independent), and third, finite: SP, 92/3 *(=579b6)*; the first of these conditions excludes all transcendental relations, the second all purely objective (mind-dependent) relations, the third all divine relations: SP, 92/19 *(=579b27)*.

40. In the case of a relation that is categorial and mind-independent, it is required that the extremes of the relation—i.e., the subject and the terminus—be mind-independently distinct formally as well as materially, i.e., it is required that they be distinct on the part of the rationale of the founding, so that the proximate fundament of the relation is also mind-independently distinct from the relation: SP, 92/26 *(=579b35, 579b44)*.

41. In the case of ontological relatives that are reciprocal, the material extremes are referred because the very rationales of the founding are referred: SP, 93/2 *(=580a14)*.

42. Only in the case of the things which are a being toward something are instances found conformed both to the order of mind-independent being and to the order of mind-dependent being: SP, 93/19 *(=580a34)*. See cross-references in I, 118 note 12.

43. Ontological relation in its entire latitude abstracts from the division into mind-dependent and mind-independent, and exhibits a peculiarity in its positive structure: SP, 94/25 *(=580b47)*.

44. The peculiarity in the positive character of relation consists in this, that from that content by which a relation is considered toward a terminus, i.e., considered in terms of its proper content, it not only exists positively (for this is true of all other kinds of being susceptible of mind-independence), but it also (and this is not true of any other modification of being susceptible of realization in the mind-independent world) is not determinately a mind-independent form, but permits being either mind-independent or mind-dependent: SP, 94/37 *(=581a11)*.

45. Relation, even though it can have a mind-independent existence *in* its being-toward a terminus, nevertheless it does not have such an existence *from* its being-toward: SP, 95/2 *(=581a21)*; see entries 48-50 below.

46. Relation can be considered in two ways, from the point of view of the rationale proper to it (in which case it is indifferent to dependence upon or independence of mind), or from the point of view of inherence in a subject (in which case it belongs determinately to the order of mind-independent being): SP, 95/7 *(=581a25)*.

47. How indifference to realization dependently upon or independently of cognition is unique and peculiar to relation in a way not found in any other kind of being is explicable in terms of the fact that all other aspects of mind-independent being have a proper and most formal rationale that cannot be understood positively unless it is also understood entitatively, because their positive rationale is toward themselves only and subjective: SP, 95/18 *(=581a38)*.

48. The unique and peculiar status of relation vis-a-vis the orders of mind-independent and mind-dependent existence derives from the fact that only relation has to be a being toward as well as a being, and though it exists positively from its content as toward being, yet it does not have thence the rationale of being mind-independent: SP, 95/25 *(=581b1)*; see entry 45 above.

49. Mind-independent existence provenates to relation from one place, namely, from a mind-independent fundament, the positive rationale of toward from elsewhere, namely, from the terminus, from which the relation does not have its existence as *being* but *toward* being (although that *toward* is truly mind-independent when it is founded): SP, 95/28 *(=581b5)*.

50. That something can be considered positively, even if it does not exist entitatively independently of cognition, is peculiar to relation: SP, 95/34 *(=581b11)*.

51. A cognition-dependent relation is a true relation, not by the truth of an entity and of an informing form, but by the truth of a positive tendency toward a terminus: SP, 95/39 *(=581b15)*.

52. In the case of a categorial relation, the toward is itself truly instantiated independently of cognition: SP, 95/42 *(=581b20)*.

53. In the case of relatives, not only is there some non-being conceived on the pattern of relation, but also, the very relation conceived on the part of the respect toward, while it does not exist in the mind-independent order, is conceived or formed on the pattern of a mind-independent relation, and so that which is formed in being, and not only that on whose pattern it is formed, is a relation: and by reason of this there are in fact cognition-dependent relations, but not cognition-dependent subjects: SP, 96/28 *(=582a7)*.

54. A transcendental relation is not primarily and essentially toward another in the way a categorial relation is, because, even though the entire specific rationale and essence of transcendental relations derives from or depends upon another, it is nevertheless not toward another: SP, 99/6, 32 *(=583a8, a38)*.

55. Categorial relation respects a terminus purely, that is, only as toward another, not as from another or concerning another or by any other mode of causality whatever, just as the transcendental relation respects a terminus not purely but by reason of some mode of causality: SP, 99/15, 17 *(=583a18, a21)*.

56. The fact that a categorial relation exists in a subject does

not take away from the fact that its whole being—that is, the being proper and peculiar to itself, in which it differs from other absolute categories (subjective kinds of being)—is toward another: SP, 99/23 *(=583a26)*.

57. Why a transcendental relation can in its own way concern what might but in fact does not exist: SP, 99/36 *(=583a42)*.

58. Mind-dependent or purely objective relations differ from mind-independent or physical relations in this, that in the case of mind-dependent relations there comes about a denomination when the fundament is posited even before the relation itself is cognized in act through a comparison, but mind-independent relations do not denominate unless they exist in act: FP, 70/35, 70/24 *(=303b22, b8)*; the reason for which difference is that, in the case of mind-dependent relations, their actual existence consists in actually being cognized objectively, which is something that does not provenate from the fundament and the terminus, but from the understanding: whence many things could be said of a subject by reason of the fundament without the resultance of a relation, because this does not follow upon the fundament itself and the terminus, but upon cognition; in the case of mind-independent relations, by contrast, since the relation naturally results from the fundament and the terminus, nothing belongs in an order to a terminus by virtue of a fundament, except by the medium of a relation, so that when the relations do not exist their fundaments in no way denominate in an order to a terminus: FP, 70/42, 71/15 *(=303b28, 304a2)*.

59. Relation alone has in its proper and positive conception an indifference to existing subjects, and so does not repugn being found positively in apprehension alone and not in physical reality, when, specifically, it so bears toward another that it does not inhere in anything: FP, 52/1, 53/29, 53/36 *(=287a27, 288a20, 288a29)*.

60. Though every mind-dependent relation results from cognition, yet not every such relation denominates a thing only in the state of cognized being, but some do so in the state of existence independent of cognition: FP, 60/15 *(=291b9)*.

61. Even though cognition is the cause from which a mind-dependent relation results, and thus the mind-dependent relation necessarily requires cognition as it belongs to and denominates some subject, yet it is not always cognition that renders the object itself apt for and coincidentally receptive of such denomination, so that the denomination belongs to that object in cognized being: FP, 60/26 *(=291b22)*.

62. Mind-dependent relations can be divided according as the cognition causing them also presupposes or does not presuppose cognition as the cause of the subject's aptness for being denominated by the relations: FP, 60/26, 35, 39 *(=291b22, b34, b40)*.

63. Mind-dependent relations do not require being conceived in a comparative act in order to be fundamentally, but they do require being so conceived in order to be formally: FP, 70/12 *(=303a42)*.

64. How mind-dependent relations differ from mind-independent relations in respect of their fundaments: FP, 70/35 *(=303b22)*. See entry 58 above.

65. The actual existence of mind-dependent relations consists in actually being cognized objectively, which does not provenate from the fundament and terminus, but from the understanding: FP, 70/43 *(=303b29)*.

66. Relation has this peculiarity, that for it to exist dependently upon cognition is not a condition diminishing its rationale, because that relation which is cognition-dependent is a true relation: SP, 93/44, 95/18 *(=580b9, 581a37)*.

67. Relations can be divided either on the basis of conditions incidental to relation, or on the basis of specific and essential differences: SP, 100/1 *(=583b10)*.

68. In terms of incidental conditions relations can be divided into reciprocal and non-reciprocal, and reciprocal relatons can be further divided into symmetrical and asymmetrical: SP, 100/5 *(=583b15)*.

69. Reciprocal relations defined: SP, 100/8 *(=583b20)*.

70. Non-reciprocal rlations defined: SP, 100/18 *(=583b30)*.

71. Symmetrical relations defined: SP, 100/22 *(=583b35)*.

72. Asymmetrical relatons defined: SP, 100/26 *(=583b40)*.

73. The divisions into reciprocal and non-reciprocal, and symmetrical and asymmetrical, are not essential divisions because relations so divided are not understood directly according to their fundaments and termini but as consequent upon their mode of touching a given terminus and fundament: SP, 101/2 *(=583b45)*.

74. Relations divide into essential types according to their fundaments, to which fundaments must also correspond diverse formal termini: SP, 101/11 *(=584a3)*.

75. Although every subjective category of mind-independent being can be the subject of a relation as materially receiving and denominated by the given relation, yet only those characteristics of subjects which have the rationale of ordering one subject to another can have the rationale of a fundament: SP, 101/30 *(=584a24)*.

76. Those things alone which induce a rationale of ordering one thing to another will be foundatons (fundaments) for relations: SP, 101/33 *(=584a42)*; But every thing which is ordered to another is ordered either according to being (measured to measure), or according to operation or power to operate (action and reception), or according to unity and number (quantity): SP, 102/1 *(=584a44)*; There is no fourth rationale habilitating and ordering one thing to another which cannot be reduced to one of these three: SP, 102/13 *(=584b15)*; Therefore there are three fundaments by which relation in general is divided essentially: SP, 101/16 *(=584a9)*.

77. If one thing is ordered to another according to being, it is a fundament for relations of measure and measurable, because those things are measured which receive being and specification dependently from another; if according to operation and power, it is a fundament according to action and reception (cause and effect); if according to unity or number (quantity), it is a foundation for relations of similarity and dissimilarity, agreement and disagreement: SP, 102/4, 101/17-26 *(=584b3, 584a11-20)*.

78. The principal points of difficulty concerning the fundaments of relations reduce to three: whether one relation can found another; whether each of the three essential fundaments found mind-independent ontological relations, and what is the proximate foundation for cause and effect relations: SP, 102/22 *(=584b24)*.

79. If one relation could be the fundament for another relation, a progression into infinity would follow: SP, 103/16 *(=585a27)*; But in causes with respect to effects there cannot be a progression into infinity, because the infinite is not traversible, neither by motion nor by causality: SP, 103/31 *(=585b2)*; But the fundaments of mind-independent relations are the causes from which the relations result: therefore there is not an infinite regress in them—i.e., one relaton cannot found another relation in the order of mind-independent being: SP, 103/36, 86/1 *(=585b8, 577a1)*.

80. In the order of mind-dependent being, however, one relation can be founded on another relation, because in this order of being it is not the fundaments of the relations but acts of cognition which give to the relations their actual being: FP, 61/37 *(=292a40)*. See entry 93 below.

81. Relations of the same type indeed have a similarity that is quasi-transcendental, but not a categorial relative, for otherwise an infinite regress would result: SP, 104/37 *(=586a21)*.

82. A further reason why one relation cannot serve mind-independently as fundament for another relation is owing to the debility of relation, which has so minimal a rationale of entitative being that it is not sufficient to found a mind-independent relation, because every fundament must be more perfect than that which is founded: thus, since all relations are equal in the mode of being relative, one cannot be the fundament of another (just as one accident cannot substand another by sustaining that other): SP, 104/42 *(=586a27)*.

83. Relations of the first and third type, i.e., relations founded on quantity and on measurable being, no less than relations of the second type, i.e., relations founded on causal action, are categorial, because all the factors required for a categorial relation concur in the case of each of these fundaments: SP, 106/19, 23 *(=587a13, a18)*.

84. In relations of the third type (measured to measure), the fundament is the mind-independent dependence in specification upon an object, just as in relations of the second type the physical foundation of the relations is the dependence of effect upon cause: SP, 106/33 *(=587a31)*.

85. The fundament of relations of the third type (measured to measure) is distinct from the relation itself of the second type (whether of cause to effect or effect to cause), because the fundament of the third type of relation is the commensuration to the specifying object, not a proportion or unity, as in the first type, or an action and efficiency, as in the second: SP, 106/39 *(=587a36)*.

86. A mind-dependent distinction is required between the extremes of a categorial relation, but not necessarily between the subject and the rationale of founding: SP, 107/13 *(=587b14)*.

87. Nothing prevents there being mind-independent relations of coexistence and distance any more than anything prevents there being such relations of similiarity and difference: SP, 108/29 *(=588a40)*.

88. A categorial relation is frequently founded on a transcendental relation, as in the case of the relation to a cause founded on an effect: SP, 108/41 *(=588b9)*; when a categorial relation is founded on a transcendental relation and the terminus is destroyed, the transcendental order remains, but not the categorial one: SP, 109/1 *(=588b12)*.

89. The reason why relations of the third type (measured to measure) are not reciprocal is that the extremes are not of the same order, but the one depends upon and is subordinated to the other, not conversely; whence they are not ordered reciprocally, but only the measured is ordered categorially to the measure: SP, 109/17 *(=588b30)*.

90. Action and reception are required generally as a condition for any and every relation, because a new relation cannnot arise in anything independently of cognition except through a movement, specifically, one mediately terminated at the very relation, immediately at the fundament or terminus: SP, 110/35 *(=589b15)*; therefore relations of the second type (cause and effect) must be founded upon action and reception as on the proper fundament, and not only as a requisite condition: SP, 110/33 *(=589b11)*.

91. Actions are not said to found relations according as actions are in the order of becoming, but according as they have accomplished something in fact: SP, 111/25 *(=590a14)*.

92. The unity which is the fundament of a relation is not the unity of indivision, but of agreement and conformity of the termini: SP, 107/44 *(=588a1)*.

93. The relation in the case of a mind-dependent relation does not result from the positing of the fundament, but through cognition: SP, 70/43 *(=303b29)*.

94. Being able to determine the identity of relations depends upon our understanding of how one thing is specified by another and of how characteristics are distinctive of individuals: C, 378/1-5 *(=600b31)*.

95. Powers and acts are specified by objects formally, not materially, taken: C, 378/6-13 *(=600b37)*.

96. A relation depends upon a fundament and a terminus for the same reason that objects are said to specify: C, 378/14 *(=601a1)*.

97. Many different relations can terminate at the materially same terminus, just as the materially same subject can found many different relations: C, 378/22 *(=601a10)*.

98. The same sign provides the basis for its relation to the cognitive power on the one hand and to the object signified on the other: C, 380/4 *(=601b26)*; These entitatively several relations in nature are reduced to a single triadic relation in the being proper to the sign: I, 154/21 *(=664a41)*.

99. Foundations and termini of relations work together in determining the specific character of the relations, the foundations as originating causal ground and the term as completing: C, 380/10 *(=601b31)*; They do this according to a mutual proportioning whereby is completed one single rationale of specifying: C, 382/22 *(=603a10)*.

100. One relative is defined *toward* rather than *by* or *through* another: C, 380/20 *(=601b42)*.

101. Why, though respects of a relation are multiplied from its terms, yet the being of relations is not taken from these terms alone, wherein relation differs from motion: C, 381/3 *(=602a23)*.

102. How motion and relation differ: C, 381/1 *(=602a23)*.

103. Since the whole reality of relation derives from its fundament according to an order to a terminus, the relation in its specific identity or character must not be understood to be from one in any way that precludes its being understood as from the other as well: C, 381/26 *(=602b5)*.

104. Foundation and terminus concur in the giving of specific identity to relations not each partially, but each wholly in diverse orders of causality: C, 381/34 *(=602b15)*.

105. Distinction must be made between a terminus understood most formally in the rationale of opposed terminus, and a terminus understood fundamentally on the side of subjectivity as founding this rationale of terminating: C, 382/4 *(=602b33)*; in the former sense a terminus concurs in but does not cause specification, while in the latter sense it functions as an extrinsic formal cause specifying in the manner of an object: C, 382/8, 383/39 *(=602b38, 603b33)*; and it is in this way that a single specifying rationale of a relation arises from foundation and terminus together: C, 382/16 *(=603a3)*.

106. Terminus and foundation together bring about a single rationale specifying a relation to the extent that they are mutually proportioned: C, 382/22 *(=603a10)*.

107. What a formal terminus is in the rationale of something specifying: C, 382/27 *(=603a15)*.

108. In just the way that a fundament is understood under the determinate aspect of grounding a relation, so the terminus of the relation is understood under the proportion and correspondence of completing: C, 382/41 *(=603a31)*.

109. A single complete terminus can correspond to relations partially different in kind: C, 382/43, 383/19 *(=603a36, 603b8)*.

110. How relation is a simple mode: C, 385 note 27.

111. Why one single relation can be extended to and anchored on many different termini, each one of which sufficiently terminates the relation: C, 386/8-387/7 *(=604b16-605a3)*.

112. One effect can well depend upon many materially different causes: 387/10 *(=605a8)*; But many causes of the same order working together to one effect are different virtually only in a partial way: C, 383/21 *(=603a12-18)*.

113. When some one effect is being produced by a sufficient cause, if another sufficient cause joins in the production, that concurring cause adds to the being of the given effect a further modality: 387/27 *(=605a28)*; in the same way, a new term extends further an existing relationship: C, 387/42 *(=605a43)*.

114. It is only incidental whether several different actions or a single action of a given power modify that power respecting a relation of one specific rationale and character: C, 388/25 *(=605b30)*.

115. That an already existent relation should expand to a newly posited terminus as pertaining to the existent relation is intrinsic to the being proper to relation: C, 388/40 *(=605b46)*.

116. A relation is entitatively simple but terminatively multiple: C, 389/5 *(=606a13)*.

117. A relation is indivisible entitatively but divisible respectively: C, 389/7 *(=606a15)*.

118. When one among a given relation's materially several termini perishes, the relation perishes only as regards its being anchored at and extended to that terminus, but it does not perish in its proper being: C, 389/8 *(=606a17)*.

SEE: Existence
Extrinsic Denomination
God
Linguistic Expression
Mind-Dependent Being
Mind-Independent Being
Nominalists
Object 32
Sign
Term
Trinity

RELATION ACCORDING TO THE WAY BEING MUST BE EXPRESSED IN DISCOURSE (*Relatio Secundum Dici*):
SEE: Relation

RELATION ACCORDING TO THE WAY RELATION HAS BEING (*Relatio Secundum Esse*):
SEE: Relation

RELIGION (*Religio*): Religion respects worship directly, God indirectly: I, 158/12, 162/48 *(=666b4, 669a21)*.

REPRESENTABLE (*Repraesentabile*):
SEE: Cognizable
Object
Representation

REPRESENTATION, REPRESENTATIVE, REPRESENTING (*Repraesentatio, Repraesentativum, Repraesentans*):

1. To represent is said of each cause whereby anything is made present to a power, and so is said in three ways—objectively (of an object representing itself), formally (as awareness represents an object), and instrumentally (as a perceptible sign represents its significate): S, 26/39 *(=9b30)*; cf. I, 193/17, 203/4 *(=679b32, 684b49)*.

2. To represent is nothing other then to render an object present and conjoined to a power in cognizable existence, whether on the side of the principle in the mode of an impressed specification, or on the side of the terminus in the mode of an expressed specification: II, 224/37 *(=694a27)*; I, 193/17, 202/46, 203/1 *(=679b36, 684b43, 684b47)*.

3. An object is rendered present or represented to a power not from itself immediately, but by means of a concept, an expressed specifier: II, 225/5 *(=694a40)*.

4. To represent something to the mind is accomplished only by rendering it present in cognizable fashion, which is but for the mind to contain a similitude of the represented: 122/21 *(=649a16)*.

5. Just as to represent is to make present, so to be represented and representable is to be made present: I, 195/44 *(=680b46)*.

6. The representation of an object within cognition, since it is a new reality, must have an efficient or productive cause, but this cause is other than the actual representing itself: I, 194/20, 31 *(=680a18, a31)*.

7. Representation can be conserved and exercised even when what is represented does not exist: I, 122/32, 217/5 *(=649a30, 691b15)*. See also page 125 note 25, *(=1635: 191a4-25)*.

8. To represent and to manifest do not consist in an ontological relation: I, 122/46 *(=649a46)*.

9. How representation (or manifestation) differs from signification: I, 122/17 *(=649a11)*.

10. Many things represent something besides themselves and are not signs: I, 217/36, 217/42, 116/23 *(=692a3, 692a9, 646a39)*.

11. What manifests in virtue of a pure representation functions in the office of representing and objectifying to a cognitive power in the capacity of another: I, 217/47 *(=692a15)*.

12. It is impossible that there should be anything manifesting another purely in representing, unless it is subsidiary to and less than that other which is represented, as if substituted for and acting in that other's capacity: I, 218/9, 19, 25 *(=692a27, a39, a46)*.

13. That which is superior does not represent another unless it causes that other: I, 218/21 *(=692a42)*.

14. The representative as such is not a categorial relation, even if it is a representative of another, but a transcendental relation, which, if it is in a sign, founds a relation of measured to signified which is categorial: I, 218/37 *(=692b10)*.

15. One similar thing represents or manifests another similar thing as correlative, not as representative, that is to say, by that general reason whereby one relative expresses an order to its correlative and includes it because correlatives are cognized simultaneously, not by that special reason whereby one thing is representatively related to another and exercises the function of presenting other objects to a cognitive power: I, 219/19 *(=692b47)*.

16. Not every variation in a representation is an essential variation, unless it could be reduced to diverse rationales "which" or "under which" of the very representation: III, 299/31 *(=729b29)*.

17. In the act of representing we can distinguish three things: I, 193/17 *(=679b32)*.

18. Not every mode of uniting is a mode of representing formally: II, 265/30 *(=713b46)*.

19. Representing in relation to making cognizant and to signifying: S, 26/21 *(=9b7)*.

20. How the representative element in a sign differs from a representation simply: I, 117/12, 217/12, 217/17 *(=646b9, 691b21, 691b26)*.

21. The representative is a genus common both to that which represents itself as an object and to that which represents something other than itself as a sign: I, 217/17 *(=691b26)*.

22. Being representative is inferior to being manifestative, because many things manifest without representing, that is, because the manifestative can work effectively as well as representatively and objectively: I, 217/21, 42 *(=691b31, 692a9)*.

23. The representative element in a sign manifests in no other way than by representing: I, 217/28 *(=691b39)*.

24. A representation is formally a substitution for that which is represented: 268/3 *(=715a19)*.

SEE: Formal Sign
Manifestation
Manifestative
Object
Quality
Sign

— S —

SACRAMENTS (*Sacramenta*):

1. The sacraments are stipulated signs by divine institution: II, 276/44*(=718b47)*.

2. That the sacraments effect insofar as they signify is not because the signification is formally an effectuation, but because efficiency is adjoined and bound to the signification: I, 201/11 *(=684a12)*.

3. A sign imports a relation founded on something, and since the sign-relation of the sacramental character cannot be founded immediately on the essence of the soul, it must be founded on some superadded quality, and the sacramental character consists in this quality antecedently to the relation of sign: I, 120/34 *(=648a13)*.

SEE: God
Quality 2
Use 2

SECOND INTENTION (*Intentio Secunda*):

SEE: Intention 6-20, 22-28
Mind-Dependent Being 57
Understanding 5
Universal 1-6
Word 14-16, 18-19

SEEING (*Visus, Visio*):

SEE: Awareness
Experience
Intuition
Perception
Sense
Vision

SENSATION (*Sensatio*): An external sensation differs from an imaginative sensation: III, 322/15 *(=740b19)*.

SEE: Common Sensible
Experience
Intuition
Perception
Sense
Vision

SENSE (*Sensus*):

1. All our cognition has birth from some external sense by means of an intuitive cognition: III, 304/11 *(=732a20)*; and the certitude of understanding is resolved into the experimental and inductive cognition of sense: III, 310/38 *(=734b36)*.

2. Abstractive awareness cannot be found in the external senses: III, 304/17 *(=732a27)*.

3. An exterior cognition of sense must be terminated at some object not as present within the sense but as posited outside and independent of sense power, failing which, sense will be by that very fact deprived of a terminating object: III, 311/1 *(=734b48)*.

4. External sense does not have a word or expressed image in which it cognizes because, owing to its materiality, it does not demand so great a union with the object that the object must be within the power, but rather must sensation be borne to the thing posited outside, which is ultimately rendered sensible in its being independent of sense: II, 266/23 *(=714a41)*.

5. Even though the cognition of external sense is an immanent action, yet it is not of necessity a production nor does it of necessity respect the terminus as altered by itself, but as intentionally and objectively united, though it can have a productive energy virtually: II, 266/29 *(=714b3)*.

6. External sensation produces a representation or specifying form, not within itself, but in the internal senses: II, 267/4 *(=714b12)*.

7. Although the cognition of external sense is an immanent action, it is yet not of necessity a production, nor does it of necessity respect the terminus as altered by but as intentionally and objectively united to itself, though it can have a productive energy virtually: II, 266/29 (=714b3).

8. The internal and external senses alike cognize signification and make use of instrumental signs: I, 205/35 *(=686a13)*.

9. External sense is led from one thing to another without discourse and collation I, 206/26 *(=686b1)*; Proof: I, 206/32 *(=686b9)*.

10. External sense cannot cognize a significate apart from a sign and in itself: I, 207/18, 208/34 *(=686b46, 687b28)*.

11. An act of comparison cognizing a relation under the concept and formality of respecting and comparatively to the terminus does not belong to external sense at any time: I, 208/30 *(=687b21)*.

12. External sense cognizes the significate in a sign in the way in which that significate is present in the sign, but not only in the way in which it is the same as the sign: I, 208/34, 209/7, 207/26 *(=687b28, 687b50, 687a9)*.

13. Some cognition in external sense must necessarily precede an instinctive judgment in animals: I, 214/25 *(=690b37)*.

14. The external senses do not form an icon in order that their cognition might be perfected within the sense power itself as in an intrinsic terminus: III, 311/9 *(=735a10)*; The reason for this is that the things which are sensed are sensible in final act independently of the power of sense, whence sense does not need any expressed specifier in order that in that specifier the object

might be rendered formed as sensible in final act: III, 311/13 *(=735a14)*, 311 note 9, *(=1635: 172b13-173a30)*.

15. In this principle as in a root is founded the impossibility of cognizing an absent thing through external sense: lest sense should be without a terminating object, supposing that an external sense does not form within itself the specification in which the cognition is terminated: III, 311/23 *(=735a26)*, 311 note 9.

16. There is no rationale for the formation of an expressed specifier or word at the level of external sensation: III, 311/13 *(=735a14)*.

17. Without exterior light or a present object the eye is deprived of the form or terminus of an experimental and external sensation, since indeed no icon is formed within external sense wherein cognition might be perfected independently of the exterior terminating sensible: III, 322/8 *(=740b10)*.

18. It involves a contradiction for a thing to be cognized by the sensing and experiencing of an external sensation (which differs from an imaginative sensation) except by attaining something external in its external self and not as formed within the sense: III, 322/14 *(=740b17)*.

19. The external senses require the physical presence of their objects on two grounds: first, that the objects might stimulate and impress on the sense their forms of specification: III, 310/15 *(=734b6)*; second, for the cognition of external sense to have a terminative object: III, 311/23, 322/8, 322/14 *(=735a26, 740b10, 740b17)*, 311 note 9; and the power of God can supply for the first of these reasons, but not even the divine power can supplant the second, for this would involve a contradiction: III, 322/2, 309/47; also 315/22-40 *(=740b2, 734a37; etiam 736b22-42)*. On this last point, see entry 25 below.

20. It pertains to external sense insofar as it is external to attain a thing only according to its outward appearance; but that which is inward, or the very substance of the thing, is attained by sense only incidentally: III, 319/32 *(=739a12)*.

21. There cannot be an act of understanding without a word (a concept) either united to or produced by the understanding: but for external sense, in the place of the word there is the sensible thing independently present: III, 323/27 *(=741a42)*.

22. External sense cognition, on account of its imperfection and materiality, can attain neither itself nor even the accidents that are independent of sensation, save as they characterize objects as here and now physically acting upon the sense: SP, 86 note 16 *(=1635: 195b21)*.

23. External sense necessarily respects its terminus as intentionally and objectively united to itself, but not necessarily as altered by itself: II, 266/30 text and note 10 *(=714b2, 1635: 196b31)*.

24. Although the operation of external sense is the final perfection uniting object to power, yet the operation does not accomplish the union representatively, because it is a union in the mode of a tendency toward the object from the side of the power, not in the mode of a form substituting for the object, whereas a representation formally is a substitution for that which is represented: II, 267/42 *(=715a12)*.

25. Between agents by a transitive action or whatever productive cause, and a cognition of external sense, there is a disparity of rationale: for a productive cause, the presence of the thing to be acted upon is only a condition for the action pertaining to the conjunction of the recipient, not to the formal specification of the acting, and can therefore be supplied while preserving the essential rationale of the acting; but for the senses, in contrast, the presence of the object does not pertain to the conjunction of a recipient, but to the conjunction of the terminus specifying the action—that is, to the conjunction of a terminus on which the cognition *esentially* depends: III, 323/13 *(=741a25)*.

26. An act of external sense is a final complement in the mode of second act as counterdistinguished from transient action, because the act of a transient operation finds its completion in the production of a terminus external to the agent, while the completion of immanent actions is not derived from what is produced but from the manner of the acting, because the act itself is the perfection and actuality of the power: II, 267/30 *(=714b42)*.

SEE: Awareness
Common Sensible
Experience
Formal Awareness 4
God 17
Imagination
Intuition
Mind-Dependent Being
Mind-Independent Being
Objective Presence
Perception
Presence
Reflexion
Sign esp. 14, 15, 18, 19, 91, 94, 97, 108, 109
Singular
Specifier

SENSE DATUM (*Sensibile*):
SEE: Common Sensible

SIGN (*Signum*):

1. Sign defined: S, 25/11 *(=9a18)*; I, 116/3 *(=646a16)*.

2. The definition of the sign is an essential definition: I, 216/7 *(=691a32)*; it is essential in the way in which relatives are said to be essentially defined through their fundaments and in an order to a terminus: 217/1 *(=691b8)*.

3. The sign is defined in its entire extent: I, 116/4 *(=646a18)*.

4. Two factors concur in the rationale of the sign: I, 116/14 *(=646a29)*.

5. The manifestative as such and the manifestative element of a sign: I, 116/23, 117/12, 122/17, 217/42 *(=646a39, 646b9, 649a11, 692a9)*.

6. The conditions for anything's being a sign: I, 218/29 *(=692b1)*.

7. The special property of the sign: I, 121/21, 143/42, 217/36, 218/8 *(=648b1, 660a31, 692a3, 692a27)*.

8. The rationale of sign to signified is a rationale of measured to measure: I, 121/21 *(=648b1)*.

9. The relation of sign to signified is superordinate to whatever relations of cause and effect or of similarity may also be present in a sign: I, Lyons addition to 137/7 given in note 4 *(=656b19 note 2)*.

10. The rationale and office of a sign ceases if the thing is manifested from itself: I, 121/38 *(=648b24)*.

11. An order to a cognitive power is in a sign consequent upon the order to the signified: II, 238/30 *(=702a8)*.

12. The proper rationale of a sign expressed: I, 196/40 *(=681b7)*.

13. How a sign and an image differ: I, 164/14, 219/29 *(=669b27, 693a9)*.

14. The rationale of the sign is found univocally in the behavior of men and of animals: I, 209/23 *(=688a18)*.

15. How animals and man develop signs through custom: I, 213/10 *(=690a21)*.

16. The rationale of a sign is discerned more expressly in discursive cognition than in simple cognition: I, 210/29 *(=688b28)*.

17. For the rationale of an instrumental sign it is required that from one cognized *object* another *object* should be reached, but it is not required that from one *cognition* another *cognition* should be reached: I, 211/29 *(=689a36)*.

18. For cognizing a sign it is not required to cognize relation formally and comparatively, but its exercise: I, 212/21 *(=689b34)*; for a sign represents no more concerning its significate than that it is contained in the sign, and so it is [possible at the level of understanding but] not necessary [at the level of social interaction] to know the sign by a fuller and more perfect cognition, by connecting and comparing the signified with the sign as mutually distinct things and by reason of the relation of the one to the other: I, 207/29 *(=687a13)*.

19. In respect of our cognition, the proper rationale of the sign, not as such, but as it first falls under our control and use in experience, is found in a sensible sign leading us to a significate: I, 230/31 *(=697b11)*.

20. The formal rationale of a sign does not consist in a relation according to the way being must be expressed in discourse (a transcendental relation), but in a relation according to the way relation has being (an ontological relation): I, 119/10 *(=647a30)*.

21. The formal rationale of a sign does not consist only in representing another: I, 119/21 *(=647a39)*.

22. A sign adds something beyond representing, and formally expresses representing another dependently upon the thing signified and as functioning in the capacity of that thing: I, 119/28 *(=647b1)*.

23. A sign respects a signified by a relation according to the way being must be expressed in discourse (a transcendental relation) and by a relation according to the way relation has being (an ontological relation): I, 121/48 *(=648b37)*. See entry 50 below.

24. The distinction between the rationale of the manifestative (representative) and the rationale of the significative: I, 122/17 *(=649a11)*.

25. A sign does not respect its significate in the way that a cognitive power and knowledge respect their objects: I, 122/17, 123/1 *(=649a11, b1)*. See entry 38 below.

26. For an instrumental sign to signify in act, it suffices for it to be a sign virtually, just as for a cause to cause in act, it suffices that it should exist virtually: I, 126/3 *(=651a18)*.

27. The representative is not the genus of sign, but the fundament: I, 132/16 *(=654b3)*.

28. A sign begins to consist in a substitutive relation to a significate: I, 132/42 *(=654b36)*.

29. There are several relations which can concur in a sign besides the formal sign-relation (the relation constitutive of the sign as such): I, 135/1, 137 note 4 *(=655b16, 656 note 2)*.

30. In a sign both the capacity for moving a cognitive power and the order of substituting for that on whose behalf it moves are considered; and the first is a transcendental relation, the second the categorial relation in which the rationale of the sign consists: I, 128/14 *(=652a30)*.

31. The fundament of a sign does not constitute the sign formally as regards substitution, but as regards the capacity for moving: I, 128/31 *(=652b2)*.

32. How a sign in a closed book could perfectly signify: I, 129/18, answered at 130/10 *(=652b35, responsum est ad 653a31-654a3)*; II, 275/8 *(=718a6)*.

33. Without a cognized relation a stipulated sign remains a sign morally and fundamentally and (as it were) metaphysically, i.e., in an order to the effect of representing, not formally and (as it were) logically or as regards the intention of the relation: I, 130/38 *(=653b19)*.

34. Presupposing the environmental conditions requisite to physical relations, the relation of a natural sign to its significate, by which the sign is constituted in the being of a sign, does not depend for its being on being itself objectively cognized: I, 137/9 *(=656b20)*.

35. A sign is anything more known whereby is represented and manifested something more unknown: I, 138/18 *(=657a15)*.

36. Both sign and cognitive power respect the significate as a manifestable object by which they are specified and measured: I, 143/30 *(=660a16)*.

37. The cognitive power respects the significate as the capacity cognizing and tending toward the significate, the sign as the way of access and means through which the power tends toward that significate: I, 143/32 *(=660a20)*.

38. A sign does not respect a cognitive power in the same way as an object does, i.e., directly; rather, a sign directly respects a manifestable object, indirectly a power: I, 144/17 *(=660b3)*; that is to say, the sign-relation as such is triadic: see I, Ques. 3, 153-165 *(=663b29-670a8)*; EA, 494ff.; see entries 42, 47, 54, 90, and 111.

39. How a sign respects both a cognitive power and its significate as ends, but the significate more principally: I, 144/44 *(=660b36)*.

40. An instrumental sign does not remain a sign formally but fundamentally when its significate does not exist: I, 146/25 *(=661b15)*. See also 125 note 25 *(=1635: 191a4-25)*.

41. In the case of a concept of a mind-dependent being, there is given a mind-independent manifestative element, yet not the cognition-independent relation of a natural sign, nor does this manifestative element express the formality of the sign, but the transcendental relation of something representative: I, 146/37 *(=661b29)*.

42. The relation of a natural sign to an object signified is cognition-independent, even though the relation of the signified to the cognitive power or to the sign itself is not cognition-independent: I, 147/22 *(=662a16)*.

43. The exercise of a sign does not posit anything in the significate; otherwise, the significate would depend upon the sign: I, 148/6 *(=662a23)*.

44. An instrumental sign exercises a twofold motion or stimulation, one in the being of sign, another in the being of object: I, 148/19 *(=662a37)*. See entry 46 below.

45. A sign as an instance of relation is in the determinate type of measure and measured: I, 151/24 *(=663a44)*.

46. The respect of an instrumental sign to a cognitive power in the being of an object is distinct from that by which it respects that power as it is a sign: I, 153/8 *(=663b43)*.

47. If cognitive power and thing signified are considered as termini directly attained by means of a relation, they necessarily require two relations in the sign; but if the power is considered as a terminus indirectly attained, in this way the significate and the power are attained by one single relation: I, 154/21 *(=664a41)*.

48. An istrumental sign respects its significate as the terminus *which*, but a cognitive power as the terminus *to which*: I, 157/15 *(=666a1)*.

49. The relation of sign to signified presupposes essentially another relation of sign to power: I, 158/29 *(=666b24)*; and this relation (of sign to power) need not be ontological, i.e., a relation according to the way it exercises mind-independent existence, but can be only transcendental or according to the way being must be expressed in discourse: I, 158/34, 128/9-34 *(=666b31, 652a24-b7)*. See entry for "Significate" below.

50. The relation of sign to signified is ontological as well as transcendental: I, 121/48 *(=648b37)*; but the relation of sign to power can be only transcendental: I, 123/13, 126/32, 128/9 *(=649b15, 651b2, 652a24)*. See entry for "Significate" below.

51. The apprehensability of a sign is not the rationale founding the sign-relation: I, 159/7 *(=667a6)*.

52. "Being cognized" does not pertain to the rationale of a sign, but to its exercise: I, 159/19 *(=667a22)*. See entry 105 below.

53. An instrumental sign under the formality of sign does not directly respect a cognitive power, but the thing signifiable to a power: in this way, the cognitive power is attained by the cognition-independent relation constituting a natural sign as indirectly included in the significate: I, 160/46 *(=668a12)*.

54. Significate and cognitive power are not two adequate termini, but one adequate terminus integrated out of the direct and the indirect: I, 162/43 *(=669a15)*. See entry for "Significate" below.

55. The divisions of signs: S, 27/7 *(=9b42)*, with cross references to Books I and II in note 13, page 27.

56. Preliminary description of a formal sign: S, 27/12 *(=10a4)*; an instrumental sign: S, 27/15 *(=10a7)*; a natural sign: S, 27/19 *(=10a12)*; a stipulated sign: S, 27/23 *(=10a16)*; a customary sign: S, 27/26 *(=10a20)*.

57. Clarification of the rationale of the division of signs into formal and instrumental: I, 163/13 *(=669a34)*. See entry 55 above.

58. A sign is formal or instrumental by reason of the fundament of the sign-relation, not by reason of the relation itself: I, 202/20 *(=684b11)*.

59. Sign-relations can well be varied by a diversity of representable objects, even though they do not differ on the side of the indirectly included connotation toward a cognitive power: I, 164/6 *(=669b18)*.

60. The division of signs into formal and instrumental is essential, univocal, and exhaustive: I, 229/1 *(=696b17)*.

61. How the division of signs into formal and instrumental can be a univocal division even taking the notion of instrumental sign in its entire extent as including both natural and stipulated signs: II, 236/15 *(=700b29)*.

62. How formal and instrumental signs coincide univocally in the rationale of a representative means: II, 236/43 *(=701a12)*.

63. The basic difficulty in the notion of a formal sign: II, 223/7 *(=693b6)*.

64. In the opinion of St. Thomas it is more probable that a formal sign is truly and properly a sign univocally with an instrumental sign: II, 225/11 *(=694b1)*.

65. How a formal sign is more known, first cognized, subsidiary to, and more imperfect than its significate: II, 227/13 *(=695b19)*.

66. A formal sign has the rationale of a terminus, but not of a final terminus: II, 228/32, 231/46 *(=696b1, 698a31)*.

67. A formal sign does not make a cognition mediate by the mediation of an object cognized, but by the mediation of an informing form: II, 232/20 *(=698b10)*. See Specifier 39, 40.

68. A formal sign does not add numerically to the thing signified as a second object cognized, but it does indeed add numerically as one thing representing and another thing represented: II, 233/38, 228/11 *(=699a39, 696a27)*; it always retains the distinction therefore between the thing signified and itself signifying: 228/16 *(=696a33)*.

69. A sign is said to be instrumental objectively, not effectively: I, 203/15 *(=685a13)*; it is a logical, not a physical, instrument: I, 203/18 *(=685a15)*.

70. The dependency of an instrumental sign in respect of the formal sign is a physical dependency, not a logical dependency: II, 236/46, 271/28 *(=701a17, 716a34)*.

71. An instrumental sign does not exercise its signification except by means of a concept: II, 271/22 *(=716a27)*.

72. The absolute priority of the formal sign consists in this, that no signs exercise their signification in act except within an actual cognition: II, 261/33, 256/11, 259/3, 271/22 *(=712a3, 708b25, 710b1, 716a27)*.

73. The same sign can be a formal sign and an instrumental sign in respect of diverse objects but not in respect of the same object (illustrated by examples): II, 237/42 *(=701b18)*.

74. The division of signs into natural and stipulated, entitatively considered, is analogous; but considered in the order of the representative and cognizable it is a univocal division: II, 236/33, 269/8 *(=701a1, 715a39)*.

75. A consideration of the division of signs into formal and instrumental as restricted to the signs which are natural (i.e., to the exclusion of stipulated signs): II, 235/40 *(=700a47)*.

76. One must distinguish between the natural sign simply, which is founded on nature itself, and a more imperfect natural sign founded on a certain aspect of nature, namely, custom (which results naturally from a repetition of acts), which is as a second nature: II, 283/23 *(=722a25)*.

77. A natural instrumental sign is in itself a thing mind-independently cognizable: II, 138/43 *(=657a43)*; a mind-independent relation also intervenes in respect of the other for which the sign substitutes: I, 139/41 *(=658a5)*.

78. A stipulated sign, if viewed in the perspective of natural being, appears as if it were, so to say, a sign extrinsically rather than of itself: II, 235/45 *(=700b7)*.

79. The rationale of the sign must be explained in terms of a relation to a significate even in the case of stipulated signs, but the relation in this case is one dependent upon cognition: II, 141/12 *(=658b30)*.

80. A double mind-dependent relation arises from the imposition as from a fundament, in the case of stipulated signs: II, 141/28 *(=659a1)*.

81. The deputation itself of the will does in the case of stipulated signs nothing more than what the nature of a thing does in the case of natural signs: II, 274/7 *(=717b28)*.

82. Awareness of the imposition in stipulated signs is the condition for the application to exercise of the signification as stipulated, but it is not required for constituting the form of the sign: II, 275/38 *(=718a38)*. See entry 84.

83. Signs stipulated from a divine institution: II, 276/44 *(=718b47)*.

84. A stipulated sign moves a cognitive power immediately by reason of the imposition, not as something cognizable immediately and by reason of itself, but mediately and through another, just as do any other non-mind-independent beings: I, 131/12 *(=653b40)*. See entry 82.

85. A stipulated sign is truly a sign functioning in the office and capacity which it exercises of the object: II, 269/13 *(=715a44)*.

86. Custom can be the cause of a sign, or it can function as an effect founding signification; in the first case the result is a stipulated sign, in the second, a natural sign: II, 278/12, 278/19, 279/37 *(=719a35, 719a45, 720a4).*

87. A customary sign does not cease to be such from only a suspension removing institution, but from a suspension removing the multiplication of acts and the frequency of use: II, 281/35 *(=721a23).*

88. A sign essentially stipulated can be accidentally customary: II, 283/19 *(=722a11).*

89. It is not antinomic for a customary exercise of signification and a stipulated exercise of signification to come together in the same sign according to diverse formalities: II, 283/13 *(=722a16).*

90. When the order to a signified is destroyed, the order to a cognitive power is also destroyed, even though both orders may remain virtually when the significate is destroyed: I, 165/9 *(=669b46).*

91. How it is that the conveying of sense impressions and the making another come into cognition does not bespeak an efficiency (a productive causality) in a sign: I, 200/27 *(=683b19).*

92. Whether without discourse there can be properly speaking a use of signs for cognizing the things signified: I, 204/3 *(=685a44).*

93. For a sign it is required that it should lead from one thing to another, for which result discourse is not indispensable: I, 206/25 *(=686b1).*

94. The external senses also use signs respecting a signified that is not physically present to them: I, 208/6ff. *(=687a44)*; but then—in this situation—the signified is attained as conjoined to and contained in the sign, not as existing separately and *as* absent: I, 208/44 *(=687b40).*

95. There are many things which represent another than themselves without being signs: I, 217/42 *(=692a9).*

96. How a sign must be dissimilar to its significate and inferior (subsidiary) to it: I, 218/13 *(=692a33).*

97. The rationale of a sign does not depend on the way in which a cognitive power uses it—by discursive comparison or by a simple way of attaining—but only on the way in which the sign represents, that is, renders something other than itself present objectively, which is the same whether the power cognizes in a simple manner or in a discursive one: I, 209/25 *(=688a20).*

98. Because the rationale of a sign does not consist in the rationale of an object absolutely, but of a substitution for another which is suppposed to be the object or thing signified (in order that this object might be represented to a cognitive power), a sign does not pertain to the order of the cognizable absolutely, but relatively and ministerially: I, 151/9 *(=663a28).*

99. In order to function as pertaining to the cogizable order relatively and ministerially, rather than simply in the rationale of an object, a sign takes on in its very rationale something of the entitative order, specifically, as it is a relation and draws the order of the cognizable to the order of the relative; and for this function (considered in this light), a natural sign-relation, which is independent of itself being cognized, does not come together univocally with a stipulated sign-relation, which depends for its being on being itself cognized: I, 151/15 *(=663a34).*

100. The significate always functions as the principal thing to be represented, and the sign as serving and ministering in the order of something measured relative to its measure; and so a sign respects its principal as an extrinsic measure in the order of the representable, and through accession to that measure a sign is the better by as much as it the better represents: I, 151/27 *(=663a47).*

101. Since a sign pertains in its rationale to the rationale of the cognizable (the line of thing as object) inasmuch as a sign is substitutionary of an object, it will well be the case that in the rationale of object a mind-independent natural sign and a mind-dependent stipulated sign are univocally signs, just as cognition-independent and cognition-dependent being assume one rationale in the being of object; therefore stipulated and natural signs coincide univocally in the being of a specifying object: II, 270/43 *(=715b45).*

102. It is one thing to be a formal sign, quite another to be a principle by which (*principium quo*) of understanding: II, 250/4 *(=705b10).* See entries 7, 8, 9, 47-60 under "Specifier", and entry 106 below.

103. How the qualifier "first cognized" applies differently according as a sign functions in a given cognition as an intrinsic or an extrinsic rationale of the cognition of the signified: II, 250/8 *(=705b14).*

104. The proper and essential work of a sign is to manifest another or to lead a power to something by means of a manifestation: II, 256/7 *(=708b19).*

105. That a sign should represent to a cognitive power *as cognizing* and should be a means of representing are requirements attaching to a sign from the fact that a sign must have a representation manifestative of and leading to a significate: II, 259/12-23 *(=710b11-24).* See entry 52 above.

106. A representation in the rationale of a sign must be manifestative for a cognizing power, and not only actuative of a power for eliciting a cognition: II, 259/44 *(=710b49).* See entry 102 above.

107. Not even an instrumental sign itself, which is an extrinsic object, is said to signify and to manifest, except according as it is cognized, not prior to cognition: II, 261/33 *(=712a3).* See entries 49 and 70-72 above.

108. A sign is said to be found properly in discursive cognition by speaking of the property of the perfection of the signifying, not of the property which secures the essence of a sign absolutely: I, 210/25 *(=688b24).*

109. The rationale of a sign is discerned more expressly and distinctly in discursive than in simple cognition, although it is also found in simple cognition: I, 210/29, 212/35 *(=688b28, 690a1).* See entry 97 above.

110. Contrast of the ways in which formal and instrumental signs are said to be known: II, 250/8-39 *(=705b14-706a4).*

111. The same sign provides the basis for its relation to the cognitive power on the one hand and to the object signified on the other: C, 380/4 *(=601b26)*; These entitatively several relations in nature are reduced to a single triadic relation in the being proper to the sign: I, 154/21 *(=664a41).*

SEE: Common Sensible
Concept
Creature
Experience
God
Imposition
Moral Act
Perception
Quality
Representation
Sense
Linguistic Expression
Mind-Dependent Being
Object 41

SPECIFIER, SPECIFICATION, SPECIFYING FORM (*Species, Specificatio*):

1. Specification pertains to the order of an extrinsic formal cause: I, 178/3 (=*674b27*).

2. A specifying form essentially is representative and vicarious of the object on which a cognitive power depends in its specification: I, 171/1 (=*672a47*).

3. Basis of the distinction between cognitive power and specifying form: I, 124/19 (=*650a33*).

4. The relation between objects and the effective production of specifiers: I, 172/13 (=*673a10*).

5. The properties characteristic of impressed forms of specification: II, 254/1ff., 249/20 (=*707b31ff., 705b2*); A, 351/24 (=*108a15*).

6. The characteristics and function of impressed specifiers: II, 254/1 (=*707b31*).

7. An impressed specification unites power and object in the mode of a principle of cognition, not in the mode of representing formally: II, 265/31 (=*713b47*).

8. An impressed specifier actuates a power prior to cognition: II, 261/25, 259/27 (=*711b41, 710b31*).

9. An impressed specifier is a means *by which* of cognition, not a means *in which*: II, 261/38 (=*712a9*).

10. An impressed specifier does not represent an object in a productive way: II, 260/1 (=*711a6*).

11. An impressed specifier is not an image formally, but only virtually: II, 261/2, 260/3 (=*711b13, 711a8*).

12. How an impressed form of specification functions and why it is not a formal sign: II, 259/23 (=*710b24*).

13. Why an impressed specifier is called a virtual similitude: II, 258/40 (=*710a38*); how it follows from this that an impressed specification is not a formal sign: II, 258/47 (=*710a45*).

14. An impressed specifier does not suppose a cognition to which it manifests, because it is a principle of a cognition: II, 256/12 (=*708b27*).

15. An impressed specifier is not a sign because it represents not to cognition, but to a cognitive power that cognition might be produced: II, 234/9 (=*699b10*).

16. An impressed specifier is not a formal sign: II, 255/22 (=*708a30*).

17. The interrelation of impressed and expressed specifiers: A, 351/23 (=*108a13*).

18. What an expressed specifier is: A, 351/23 (=*108a13*).

19. The expressed specifier (or concept) is posited either on account of fecundity of the side of the subjective power, or on account of a necessity on the side of the object: II, 242/9 (=*702b12*).

20. How an expressed specifier or word and an act of understanding are related: II, 250/40 (=*706a5*).

21. An expressed specifier or word renders the understanding formally understanding in a terminative, not in an operative, way: II, 252/2 (=*706b25*).

22. There can be no cognition without an expressed specifier or word, whether it be formed by the understanding itself or united thereto: II, 253/27 (=*707b14*).

23. How an expressed specifier is both a form and an effect of cognition: II, 252/32 (=*707a13*).

24. In what sense an expressed specifier can be called an "instrument" of cognition, in what sense not: II, 249/13 (=*705a42*), text and note 27, (=*1635: 358b26*).

25. An instrumental sign is cognized as that which is known extrinsically and as a thing is known, but an expressed specifier is cognized as that which is known not as an extrinsic cognized thing, but as that in which the cognized thing is contained within the understanding: II, 250/19 (=*705b27*).

26. By which act an expressed specifier is brought about in the understanding and in the sensitive powers: II, 245/5, 252/34 (=*703b6, 707b16*).

27. Impressed specifiers concur effectively in the production of a cognitive act not precisely as they are specifying, but as and because they intrinsically determine and actuate a power which, thus activated and determined, influxes vitally and effectively into a cognitive act: I, 171/4 (=*672b3*).

28. Just as the vitality of the power effectively influxes, so also does its intrinsic actuality and the determination of the object [i.e., the specifying stimulus or impressed form] influx in eliciting the act in its specification, which depends on the object: I, 171/13 (=*672b11*).

29. Cognitive powers cannot be moved by objects unless those objects are impressed on the powers and forms of specification are effectively produced: I, 172/21 (=*673a19*).

30. An impressed specifying form has two dimensions or aspects, namely, to inform entitatively or physically, and this pertains to a specifier materially as what it has in common with all other determinations of a subject; and to inform intentionally, that is, as the form is representatively one with the object: I, 183/40 (=*676b47*).

31. The impression itself productive of specifying forms is not from the object as moving objectively, but from the thing producing the specifiers, which productive force often belongs to an agent materially as well as formally distinct from the object as such: I, 184/1 (=*677a8*).

32. An expressed specifier of the understanding is called a concept and a word; an expressed specifier of the internal senses (i.e., of perception) is called an icon or phantasm: II, 240/1 (=*702a44*). See Book II, Question 2, notes 3 and 4, pages 241-242.

33. Just as it is necessary to posit an impressed specifier in order that the object be present and united to the cognitive power in the rationale of a principle concurring in forming the power's cognition, so is it necessary to posit an expressed specifier in order to explain the *proportional* presence of the object to the power in the rationale of terminus whenever it is a case of more than simple sensation: II, 243/12, 263/13 (=*702b45, 712b20*).

34. The office of an expressed specifier is not to render formally cognizing in the precise way that cognition is a tendency toward an object, but to render the object present in the mode of a terminus cognized; whence an expressed specifier, unlike the impressed one, does not antecede cognition, but is formed through cognition: II, 244/14 (=*703a26*).

35. An expressed specifier represents within the cognitive power and as the form informing the power, and for this reason it does not represent as something first cognized objectively, but formally and as the rationale of the cognizing: II, 244/24 (=*703a39*).

36. An expressed specifier is, in all probability, an image living and produced through a vital action by the cognitive power it serves for cognizing by means of it: II, 245/35 (=*703b37*).

37. A specification expressed by the understanding is most properly a formal sign: II, 246/13 (=*704a11*); specifications expressed by sensory powers are likewise formal signs in respect of those powers: II, 247/22 (=*704a42*). See entry 32 above.

38. An expressed specifier directly represents another than itself to the cognitive power: II, 247/12 (=*704a30*).

39. It is true of all expressed specifiers of perception without exception that, in respect of the cognitive power which forms them, they do not lead the power nor represent an object to it from a prior cognition of themselves as objects, but they lead immediately to the very objects represented: II, 247/37 *(=704b15)*.

40. Without their expressed specifiers being objectively cognized by the sense powers, things are rendered immediately represented to the powers; therefore this representation comes about formally and not instrumentally, nor from some prior cognition of the image or icon itself: wherefore for an expressed specifier to be a formal sign, it suffices that it terminate an act of cognition: II, 248/6 *(=704b24)*.

41. We infer that there are impressed spcifying forms (specifiers) which are united to the cognitive power in the capacity of the object for eliciting cognition or awareness, from the fact that cognition is born of the cognitive power *and* the object: II, 254/1 *(=707b31)*.

42. Since an object cannot of itself enter a power and be united thereto, it must needs be that this comes about through some form, which is said to be a *specifying* form, *specification*, or *specifier*, which so contains the object in itself in an intentional and cognizable mode that it can render that object present and united to a cognitive power: II, 254/7 *(=707b38)*.

43. A specifier is called a "natural" similitude of the object, because from its very nature it acts as the vicegerent of the object, or rather, it is the very object itself in intentional being: II, 254/16 *(=707a50)*.

44. An impressed specifier is said to be "of the object" because it is given for the forming by the cognitive power of an expressed similitude: II, 254/20 *(=708a4)*.

45. A specifier is said to be an *impressed* specifier because it is superadded to a given cognitive power by an extrinsic principle, and does not proceed from and is not expressed by that power: II, 254/23 *(=708a7)*.

46. An impressed specification is given to a power that the power might elicit a cognition, and so an impressed specifier functions in the mode of a principle and concurs with the very power in eliciting the cognition, not in the mode of a terminus proceeding from the power itself and its cognition: II, 255/2 *(=708a12)*.

47. An impressed specifying form has the rationale of something virtually representative: II, 258/40 *(=710a38)*; It does not have the rationale of a formal sign: II, 258/47 *(=710a45)*.

48. An impressed specifying form is not the intelligible form which is something known, for otherwise it would not belong on the side of the principle of a given cognition, but on the side of its terminus: II, 255/31 *(=708b40)*.

49. A specifying form cannot manifest anything to a power antecedently to cognition, because every manifestation supposes or occurs within cognition itself: II, 256/9 *(=708b23)*.

50. An impressed specification is not a form which manifests an object to cognition formally, but one which produces cognition, in the terminus of which cognition—namely, in an expressed specification—the object is rendered manifest: II, 256/20 *(=708b36)*.

51. An object concurs in an impressed specifier as a principle of cognition determining a cognitive power for eliciting, not as an object cognized: II, 256/25 *(=708b41)*.

52. If "formal awareness" is accepted as standing for the act itself of cognition, it is evident that formal awareness does not coincide with an impressed specifier because such a specifier is not the proceeding act, but a principle of the act and cognition; but if "formal awareness" is taken for something proceeding from the understanding, not indeed in the mode of an act, but in the mode of a terminus issuing forth vitally, on this acceptation a formal awareness is an *expressed* specifier: II, 257/7 *(=709a36)*.

53. A form of impressed specification is a representative similitude of an object, but in the mode of a principle of cognition, not in the mode of a formal awareness or of supposing an awareness to which it would represent; and for this reason it is called a *virtual* similitude, because it is a principle whence arises a formal similitude and a formal awareness: II, 258/40 *(=710a38)*.

54. When an impressed specifier informs a power, it does not inform that power by rendering it cognizing, as does a formal sign (which is a formal awareness), but by rendering it *able* to cognize; and consequently an impressed specifier does not render an object manifested in act, but does render an object actuating a cognitive power and determining it to elicit a cognition in which the object is manifested: II, 259/27 *(=710b31)*.

55. An impressed specifier is representative neither as an object, nor as a vicegerent of an object, nor as a medium between power and object, nor as an instrumental sign, nor as a productive agent, nor as a formal manifestation, because it is not representative by actually manifesting an object, but by actuating and determining a power in the mode of a principle for eliciting cognition, and this formally is what an impressed specifier does, but this is not formally to be a sign: II, 259/36 *(=710b42)*.

56. A manifestative representation does not belong to an impressed specifying form actually, but virtually: II, 260/3 *(=711a9)*.

57. The production of an expressed representation comes about effectively from an impressed specifier, but this productive effectuation is not the representation, but the production of a representing thing, namely, the expressed specifier, from which expressed specifier the actual representation will come about, not productively, but formally: II, 260/10 *(=711a16)*.

58. A form of impressed specification is an image only virtually, not formally: II, 261/2 *(=711b13)*.

59. The representation of an impressed specifying form is not a representation in the mode of a manifestative medium, but in the mode of a form determining and actuating a cognitive power to be able to cognize: II, 261/14 *(=711b28)*; In this it differs from the representation of an expressed specifier, which represents an object in cognition itself: II, 261/19 *(=711b34)*.

60. An impressed specifier actuates a power prior to cognition, and consequently prior to an actual manifestation, which is not to be a representative medium manifestatively, but virtually, in the mode of a principle for eliciting manifestation and cognition: II, 261/28 *(=711b43)*.

61. If an expressed specifier is formed from an impressed specifier, it is formed by some operation, and consequently the operation is distinguished from such an expressed specifier: II, 262/19 *(=712a42)*.

62. Every cognition depends upon an object and a cognitive power, and this object, howsoevermuch it might be present in itself, cannot intentionally inform the power except through a specifying form: III, 288/13 *(=723a19)*.

63. External sense does not need any expressed specifier in order that the object might be rendered in that specifier formed as sensible in final act: III, 311/17 *(=735a18)*.

64. Of the impressed specifier we say that it is cognizable of itself as "that by which" but not as "that which" and as a thing

cognized; for in this mode of being—i.e., as an object cognized—the impressed specifier needs a reflexive concept: III, 332/9 (=746a8).

65. To convey sense impressions or specifying forms is common to material objects regardless of whether those objects also function as signs: I, 200/31 (=683b24).

66. The excitation of a cognitive power to attend is distinguished from the impression itself of specifying forms; for even after specifiers have been received one needs an excitation for attending: I, 193/25 (=679b42).

67. An expressed specifier is an expression of its formal principle, which is the impressed specifier fecundating the understanding expressing, and this represents the object of which it is formally a specification; and so a concept, by representing its formal principle, represents principally its formal object: A, 351/23 (=108a13).

68. Efficient (effective) concurrence with a cognitive power in the production of a cognitive act is by no means the formal and essential rationale of a specifier, which essentially need only be representative and vicarious of the object on which the cognitive act depends in its specification: I, 170/16 (=672a46).

69. The specification of a cognitive act or power by its very nature depends on an object, even be that object nonexistent: I, 167/16 (=670b17).

SEE: Movement
Object
Specificative
Stimulus
Terminus

SPIRIT (*Angelus; Spiritus Animalium*):
SEE: Angel
Animal Spirits
Concept
Demon

STIMULATE, STIMULATION (*Motivum*):
SEE: Stimulus

STIMULUS (*Motivum*):

1. A great equivocation is perpetrated in the use of the term "stimulus" by applying it only to a productive (an efficient) cause, because it should be applied also to other types of cause: I, 169/10 (=671b29).

2. We distinguish between something stimulating in the mode of exercise and in the mode of specification; and the former pertains to an efficient cause, the latter to a formal object: I, 169/17 (=671b37).

3. An object in the rationale of a stimulus has the true rationale of an object and not of productive efficiency; for something effecting insofar as it is effecting respects the existence of what it produces, not the specification nor the principles of definition: I, 169/26 (=672a1).

4. The rationale of being a stimulus does not bespeak efficiency in an object, but is contained within the limits of an objective form, that is, of something specificative: I, 169/36 (=672a12).

5. That which is the stimulus of a passive power is truly a specificative object: I, 170/6 (=672a33).

6. The rationale of stimulus in the case of an objective cause is understood in terms of specification, not in terms of exercise: I, 171/17 (=672b16).

7. To stimulate or move in the mode of an agent, i.e., on the side of the subject and of exercise, pertains to the order of a producing cause and is distinguished from movement in the mode of a stimulus object, which is reduced to the category of an extrinsic formal cause, a cause consisting in nothing but the fact that some power, in order to elicit an act of such or such a kind, needs to be actuated or ordered relative to an extrinsic object not only in the termination of the act, but also in the elicitation and originating of that act, because even to elicit it the power is not sufficiently determined to a specific kind of act until it is determined or moved and completed by an object: I, 171/38 (=672b41).

8. The qualifier "stimulus" in the phrase "stimulus object" is understood of a formal moving in the mode of a principle in respect of a passive power, so that the *specification* of an act, and not only the exercise or existence of that act, depends on such an object—not on the side of termination, but on the side of elicitation and commencement or principle: I, 181/48 (=675b45).

9. A stimulus object coincides with a terminative object in the order of causing specification, but not in the mode nor in the kind of act caused: I, 182/7 (=676a4).

10. The rationale of a stimulus in an object is not the rationale of impressing or producing specifiers, but of objectively actuating and determining a power by means of a specifying form as intentionally, not only as entitatively, informing: I, 184/8 (=677a15).

11. Why the rationale of a stimulus object obtains even in respect of the intellect of a pure spirit: I, 185/2 (=677a21).

12. The rationale of producing specifiers can obtain independently of the rationale of a specifying object, and conversely; therefore the formal rationale of a stimulus object specifying does not consist in the *production* of specifying forms: I, 172/39 (=673a38).

13. An object does not move a power or act as regards exercise or efficiency but only as regards what is formal and as regards specification: I, 167/33 (=670b38).

14. Why a stimulus object cannot be identified with an instrumental sign: I, 172/49 (=673a43).

SEE: Extrinsic Formal Cause
Movement
Object
Specificative
Sense 14, 24, 25
Specifier

STIPULATED SIGN (*Signum ad Placitum*):

1. Just as a natural instrumental sign exercises signification by reason of its fundament even when it does not have a relation in act to what is signified owing to the fact of that particular significate's not existing, so a stipulated sign signifies and represents by reason of the imposition once made even when the relation is not conceived in act and consequently does not exist by means of a concept: I, 130/17 (=653a40).

2. Because a mind-dependent relation does not result from the fundament as do mind-independent relations, but depends on an act of cognition, therefore a stipulated sign does not have to wait for the relation itself in order to be denominated a sign absolutely, although it does indeed require the relation itself in order to be denominated a being related in act: II, 275/19 (=718a18).

3. A stipulated sign signifies through the imposition which is proper to it even though that imposition is an extrinsic denomination; and through that imposition as cognizable by the understanding a stipulated sign is able to move a cognitive power in the way in which it is cognizable: II, 275/33 (=718a34).

4. It is always true of stipulated signs that they are something produced by the mind—something mind-dependent—that is, strictly but solely objective: I, 131/10 *(=653b39)*.

5. A stipulated sign moves by reason of the imposition not as cognizable immediately and by reason of itself, but mediately and through another, just like any other unreal being; and so we say, presupposing its cognizability is got by borrowing, that a stipulated sign takes on the rationale of something moving and representing, just as it also takes on the rationale of something cognizable: I, 131/11 *(=653b41)*.

6. Just as a natural sign exercises signification by reason of its fundament, even when it does not have a relation in act to what is signified owing to the nonexistence of that particular significate, so a stipulated sign, even when the relation is not conceived in act and consequently does not exist by means of a concept, still signifies and represents by reason of the imposition once made, which imposition does not create the sign formally, but fundamentally and proximately: I, 130/17 *(=653a40)*. Full explanation at II, 275/9 *(=718a6)*.

7. A stipulated sign without a cognized relation continues to be a sign morally and fundamentally and quasi-metaphysically—that is to say, it remains in an order to the effect of representing; but it does not continue to be a sign formally and quasi-logically, or as regards the intention of the relation: I, 130/38 *(=653b20)*.

8. Even in the case of stipulated signs the rationale of the sign must be explained by a relation to a signified: I, 141/12 *(=658b30)*.

SEE: Custom
Extrinsic Denomination
Idea
Linguistic Expression
Sign
Stipulation
Terminus
Use
Voice
Writing

STIPULATION (*Impositio, Ad Placitum*):

1. The imposition or stipulation of something to be a sign of such or such a thing is only the fundament of the relation of the sign (just as the abstraction of a nature is the fundament of universality), because it gives to the sign a connection with a given thing and a surrogation for it to the end of signifyig not naturally but according to the objective of the one imposing: I, 130/10 *(=653a32)*; Whence an imposition does not create a sign formally, but fundamentally and proximately: I, 130/25 *(=653b4)*.

2. Awareness of a given imposition is required as the condition for and application to exercise of the signification of a stipulated sign, not for constituting the form of the sign: II, 275/38 *(=718a38)*.

3. The extrinsic denomination whereby a stipulated sign is rendered imposed or appointed for signifying by common usage is required as the fundament of the relation and rationale of the sign, because it is through this imposition that something is habilitated and appointed to be a stipulated sign, just as it is through the fact of some natural sign's being proportioned and connected with a given significate that there is founded a relation of the sign to that significate: I, 141/14, 141/21 *(=658b34, 658b41)*.

4. From the extrinsic denomination of imposition and stipulation a twofold mind-dependent relation arises: I, 141/28 *(=659a1)*.

5. An appointment and imposition in common life can be to various offices, which are not distinguished otherwise than by a relation to those functions for the exercise of which they are established: I, 141/37 *(=659a11)*.

SEE: Closed Book
Custom
Extrinsic Denomination
Idea
Name
Sign
Stipulated Sign
Voice
Word
Writing

SUBJECT (*Subiectum*):

SEE: Mind-Dependent Being
Relation
Subjectivity

SUBJECTIVE DETERMINATION (*Accidens*):

SEE: Accident
Mind-Dependent Being
Subjectivity

SUBJECTIVITY (*Res Absoluta*): There is no such thing, properly speaking, as a mind-dependent substance or quantity, etc., because even though some non-being may be conceived on the pattern of a substance, yet neither substance itself nor any rationale of subjectivity is conceived by the understanding and formed in being on the pattern of some other mind-independent being: SP, 96/1 *(=581b35)*.

SEE: Mind-Dependent Being
Truth

SUBSTANCE (*Substantia*):

SEE: Category
Mind-Dependent Being
Relation
Subjectivity

— T —

TEACHER, TEACHING (*Doctor, Doctrina*): The words of a teacher are representatvely or objectively more proximately related to causing knowledge than are the sensible things independent of mind, because a sign is a substitute of the thing signified, which is more closely bound to the order of understanding in the former than in the latter case: I, 199/11 *(=683a1)*.

TERM (*Terminus*):

1. It behooves one to recognize which among the diverse respects or offices that can be considered in a discussion of terms more suitably expresses the nature of a term for purposes of present discussion: S, 22/10 *(=7a18)*.

2. Since our minds proceed analytically in matters of knowledge there must needs be a designatably final element or term of this analysis, beyond which resolution by logical art cannot proceed (otherwise the reslolution would proceed to infinity): S, 22/13 *(=7a20)*.

3. Because the term of an analysis and the starting point of synthesis are the same, that which will be the last element into which logical composites are resolved or analyzed will also be

said to be the first element out of which the others are composed: S, 22/22 *(=7b10)*.

4. Our concern in the present discussion is with the term understood as the last element in which every resolution of a logical composite—even of a proposition itself and a statement—is terminated: S, 23/3 *(=7b17)*.

5. Terms considered according as they serve for syllogistic construction are considered restrictively, and not in their entire extent: S, 23/8 *(=8a2)*.

6. A more universal rationale of term appears when names and verbs are considered as they alike take on the order of composing an enuntiation: S, 23/17 *(=8a13)*; This more universal rationale of term as restricted to elements of spoken language is called by Aristotle "vocal expression" (*vox significativa*): S, 24/5 *(=8b9)*.

7. One division of terms is into mental, vocal, and written: S, 28/1 *(=10a34)*.

8. A mental term logically considered is the awareness or concept from which a simple proposition is made: S, 28/2 *(=10a35)*.

9. A vocal term logically considered is a sound which signifies by stipulation: S, 24/8 *(=8b14)*.

10. A written term is a mark signifying by stipulation: S, 28/4 *(=10a39)*.

11. Mental terms are essentially diverse acording to the objects from which the differences in kinds of awareness derive: S, 28/7 *(=10a42)*; and so in the discussions of Book III we treat only of certain general conditions of apprehensions or of concepts whereby various ways of knowing are distinguished, and not of divisions essential to the term as an element of language: 28/10 *(=10a45)*.

SEE: Concept
Object
Power
Relation
Sign
Simple Awareness
Specificative
Specifier
Voice
Word

TERMINUS (*Terminus*):

1. The terminus of an ontological relation understood fundamentally on the side of the subject founding the rationale of the terminus as formally opposed to the subject, obtains as an extrinsic formal cause specifying in the manner of an object, and so the single specifying rationale of an ontological relation arises from the foundation and terminus together: C, 382/15 *(=602b45)*.

2. The terminus of a relation does not specify precisely as it is a terminus, but as it is subject to a fundament, without which the specific type of relations is not understood: I, 186/27 *(=678a10)*.

SEE: Object
Relation
Specificative
Specifier

TRANSCENDENTAL RELATION (*Relatio Transcendentalis*):

SEE: EA, III.C.2.(a). pages 462-463, and III.D.1. pages 472-479
Relation

TRANSCENDENTALS (*Transcendentalia, Transcendentia*):

1. St. Thomas teaches that "thing" is of the transcendentals, and for this reason pertains commonly to absolutes and relatives: Poinsot 1632: 594a43-b6, set out in EA, III.D.1. page 474 text and notes 115, 116. See also C, 385 n. 27.

2. The making precise of analogates and of the transcendentals does not occur through abstraction from diverse things but according to diverse explications or indeed the confusion of one and the same conception: Poinsot, 1632: 494b18 (*ibid.*: 494b39: ". . . . transcendentia, ut ens, quia dicunt rationem, quae in ipsis differentiis et modis imbibitur, quia omnia entia sunt, ideo non potest separari conceptus entis in communi ab aliquo, quod enti sit extraneum, sicut segregatur animal a rationali ut ab extraneo sibi, in quantum animal est, sed separatur conceptus entis a suis contrahentibus per hoc, quod in confuso et non explicite cognoscuntur ea, quae divisa sunt in inferioribus. Et haec est doctrina D. Thomae . . . .").

SEE: Analogy
Relation
Truth 1, 2, 7

TRANSIENT ACTION (*Operatio Transiens, Actio Transiens*):

SEE: Action
Cause
Immanent Action
Movement
Sense 6, 25, 26

TRINITY (*Trinitas*):

1. Concerning relations in God: SP, 82/39, 83/42 *(=575a9, 575b12)*.

2. Why there is no ontological relation of similarity and equality between the divine persons independently of our minds: SP, 92/42 *(=580a5)*.

SEE: Object
Relation

TRUTH, THE TRUE (*Veritas, Verum*):

1. The true is the same as the cognizable: I, 150/6 *(=663a8)*; Thus the rationale of the cognizable is not the rationale of being formally, but presuppositively only is it being and consequent upon being, for the true is a coincident property of being: I, 150/1 *(=663a2)*. See also 150 note 32 *(=1635: 186b3)*.

2. It can well be that some being incapable of mind-independent existence is capable of truth, not as a subject, but as an object, inasmuch as it does not have in itself the entitative being which as subject founds truth and cognizability, but does have that which as object can be cognized on the pattern of mind-independent being and so exist objectively in the understanding as something true: I, 150/7 *(=663a9)*.

3. The difference between the rationale of a cognition as true or false, and the rationale of a cognition as intuitive or abstractive, explained: III, 294/14 *(=726b14)*.

4. The same cognition cannot be simultaneously true and false on account of opposite terminations relative to objects, and yet truth and falsity belong to cognition incidentally: III, 297/18 *(=728a43)*.

5. Truth so consists in conformity to the being or non-being of a thing, that even if one does not attend to the being or non-being of the thing, if one yet but a single time proferred a judgment when the thing did not exist in the way it was judged to be, by this very fact the cognition loses truth, and when the thing exists in the way it is judged to be the cognition acquires truth without any other variable intervening in cognition: III 294/16 *(=726b17)*.

6. Formal truth or falsity consists in a judgment or enunciation: FP, 75/17 (=305b47).

7. The rationale of the knowable bespeaks only the necessary connection of truth, which connection coincides univocally with any other necessary connection whatever in the rationale of the true, even if they would not coincide in the rationale of being: I, 189/4 (=678b42).

SEE: Existence
Mind-Dependent Being
Object
Transcendentals

— U —

ULTIMATE AND NON-ULTIMATE (*Ultimatus et Non-Ultimatus*):

1. General rationale of this distinction explained: III, 334/1 (=746b24).

2. Ultimate and non-ultimate concepts: III, 334/15 (=746b39).

3. The ultimate and non-ultimate of themselves and formally are not essential differences of concepts: III, 334/27 (=747a3).

SEE: Concept

UNDERSTANDING (*Intellectus, Ratio*):

1. An understanding is said to be simple *either* because it does not involve anything of the physical presence which pertains to vision, *or* because it does not involve anything of an order to will, which pertains to decision: III, 317/28 (=737b41).

2. Human understanding is neither its own act of understanding, nor is its own essence the first object of its act of understanding, but the first object of human understanding is something extrinsic, namely, the nature of a material thing: III, 326/23 (=742b26).

3. The direct object of human understanding is something extrinsic, namely, the nature of a material thing, and therefore that which is first cognized by human understanding is this kind of an object: III, 326/26 (=742b29).

4. That which is first cognized by human understanding is an external material object, and the very act by which the material object is cognized, is cognized secondarily; and through the act is cognized the understanding itself of which the very act of understanding is the perfection: III, 326/29 (=742b32).

5. The act of understanding is the formal intention from which an objective second intention results: FP, 61/26 (=292a27).

6. The act of cognizing is distinguished in the understanding from the object itself cognized, and from the impressed and expressed forms of specification: II, 262/1 (=712a24).

7. Four factors concur in the understanding to produce cognition, to wit, the thing which is understood (the object), the conception of the understanding, the impressed specifier by which it is understood, and the act itself of understanding: II, 262/5 (=712a28); Proof that these four factors are to be mutually distinguished: II, 262/10, 263/1 (=712a33, 712b4).

8. The act of understanding can be considered either as it is an expressing diction, or as a pure act of contemplation and cognition: II, 263/1 (=712b5); As it is a diction or expression, it has for its complement the concept as a terminus: 250/40 (=706a6), that is, it is essentially a production: II, 263/4, 252/28 (=712b8, 707a9); But as it is a cognition, the concept is constituted not by the act of understanding actively but passively, i.e., by being understood, because it does not pertain to the concept insofar as it is a formal sign to be a formal awareness operatively and actively, but terminatively and according to an intrinsic being understood whereby a thing itself is rendered understood and represented: II, 252/38 (=707a20).

9. The act of understanding is completed through producing a word; but in another order the word itself is actuated and completed through the act of understanding, inasmuch as the act of understanding is the ultimate actuality in the intelligible order: II, 250/44 (=706a11). See preceding entry.

10. The act of understanding unites object to cognitive power in the mode of an operation tending toward that object, not in the manner of a form which substitutes and is vicegerent on behalf of that object: II, 265/20 (=713b36); Therefore an act as such of cognition is not a formal sign: II, 265/17 (=713b32).

11. An act of understanding is not a formal sign: II, 263/29, 265/17 (=712b36, 713b32); A sign is essentially something representative, but the act of understanding formally is not a representation, it is an operation and tendency toward an object: 263/42 (=712b47).

12. The understanding cognizes through signs: S, 25/4 (=9a9).

13. An act of understanding is not formally a representation, but an operation and tendency toward an object: II, 263/43 (=712b48); This is confirmed by considering that if the act of understanding were a representation, it would be a representation either *distinct from* or *the same as* the expressed specifier: since it is not the same, it must be distinct; but if distinct, it represents either the same object or a different one: if the same, it is superfluous, but if different, it will not make the *same* thing known, and so will be a sign in a completely different—an equivocal—sense [q.e.d.]: II, 264/13 (=713a21).

14. Different intellects are related to their own act of understanding according to different circumstances of existence, namely, that of God at one extreme, that of pure spirits in the middle, and that of human beings: II, 326/7 (=742b6).

15. The act of understanding is a quality and is an operative, not a representative, union, i.e., a union not containing but tending toward a given object: II, 265/35 (=714a2).

16. The understanding does not cognize for itself alone, but gives rise also to an impulse for manifesting; and that bursting forth toward manifestation is a kind of expression and conception and indeed a giving birth by the understanding: II, 245/11 (=703b12). See 242 note 7.

17. The act of understanding is the ultimate actuality in the intelligible order [i.e., the order of intentional as supraordinate to entitative union: I, 150 note 32 (=1635: 186b3); cf. Ramirez 1924: 807-808], just as the act of being is the ultimate perfection in the entitative order: II, 251/1 (=706a14).

SEE: Act of Understanding
Experience
Mind-Dependent Being
Object
Perception
Phantasm
Rationale
Reflexion
Representing
Representation
Sense
Singular
Specifier
Universal

UNITY (*Unitas*):

1. A mind-dependent unity pertains in what is formal to it to negation: FP, 56/38 *(=289b46)*.

2. A unitive action is not said to represent, even though it unifies, and thus not every mode of uniting is a mode of representing: II, 265/28 *(=713b44)*; the impressed specifier is another example of the point: II, 265/31 *(=713b47)*.

SEE: Mind-Dependent Being
Relation
Universal 1-2, 6

UNIVERSAL, UNIVERSALITY (*Universale, Universalitas*):

1. A metaphysical universal expresses only a nature abstracted and conceived in the manner of a unity: FP, 57/31 *(=290a45)*; The universal thus abstracted is called metaphysical, not logical, because not every mind-dependent being formally and directly pertains to Logic: FP, 57/41 *(=290b12)*.

2. In a metaphysical universal there is already found something mind-dependent, namely, that which, owing to an abstracting, belongs to the nature represented or cognized, namely, the unity or aptitude or non-repugnance to being in many: FP, 57/31 *(=290a45)*.

3. A metaphysical universal is the fundament for a logical universal, just as a formal apprehension of a mind-dependent being—a 'non-existent' object—supposes a comparative act as its fundament: FP, 70/11 *(=303a42)*.

4. A nature is denominated universal by the very fact that it is abstracted, even before it is actually related or compared: FP, 70/28 *(=303b13)*.

5. When a universal nature is abstracted from singulars, there is not yet an intention of universality, but its fundament [i.e., an expressed specifier]: FP, 76/7 *(=306a44)*.

6. The rationale of genus and of species and *of any other formal universals* consists in a relation of superiors to inferiors: FP, 61/9 *(=292a9)*; These relations cannot be mind-independent, because otherwise there would be given a universal formally existing in the order of mind-independent being, and because these relations suppose a cognized being for their fundament: FP, 61/12 *(=292a12)*.

SEE: Mind-Dependent Being
Relation

UNIVOCAL (*Univocum*):

1. Even though mind-independent and mind-dependent being are analogized, nevertheless, objectively, in the rationale of an object can coincide univocally even things which are not univocal entitatively: I, 151/1 *(=663a19)*.

2. Many things can come together univocally in the rationale of the knowable and not in the rationale of being, and conversely: I, 187/37 *(=678b25)*.

3. Mind-independent and mind-dependent being take on one rationale in the existence of an object and can specify two sciences coming together univocally: II, 271/1, 271/6 *(=716a3, 716a8)*.

4. This or that determinate cognizable can be univocal in respect of the subjects or beings to which it belongs denominatively, even though those beings are not univocal entitatively, for the reason that the determinate cognizable in question is not consequent on being as being is taken in itself absolutely, but as it is taken comparatively to a cognizing power, and the same mode of comparing can be in things not univocally coincident according to themselves and entitatively: I, 190/13 *(=679a17)*.

SEE: Analogy
Object
Mind-Dependent Being
Transcendentals

USE (*Usus*):

1. The excitive energy in a person's voice is not itself the actual signification or signifying of the voice, but it is rather the use itself of the understanding of the one speaking and manifesting his concept through the voice: I, 198/13 *(=682a37)*.

2. The use of words is something besides their signification, since it applies signifying expressions to fix the attention of another: I, 198/19 *(=682a45)*; The use and excitative energy of speech is superadded to this signification of words in just the way that the sanctifying movement of sacraments is utterly distinct from and superadded to their signification: 198/27, 198/34 *(=682b7, 17)*.

3. As the voice is used by a speaker, it has a causally productive energy for exciting, born not of representation, but of the one propounding and using the voice derivatively signifying; and thus the one speaking functions as applying the signifying voice, while the signifying voice functions as something applied and signifying representatively: I, 198/41 *(=682b25)*.

4. The use made of an expression, as it functions effectively (whether morally or physically), is not the act itself of signifying, and does not proceed effectively from the sign in signifying—unless, perchance, the signification itself were metaphorically, or rather, grammatically, called an action and productive efficiency: I, 199/3 *(=682b37)*.

5. Expressions are coined that they might be used by some speaker: A, 349/12 *(=107a33)*.

6. The extrinsic denomination whereby a stipulated sign is rendered imposed or appointed for signifying by common usage is required as the fundament of the relation and rationale of the sign, because it is through this imposition that something is habilitated and appointed to be a stipulated sign: I, 141/15, 21 *(=658b34, 41)*.

SEE: Custom
Linguistic Expression
Stimulus
Voice
Writing

— V —

VIRTUE (*Virtus*): A theological virtue respects God directly: I, 158/15 *(=666b7)*.

VISION (*Visus, Visio*):

1. Knowledge of vision is the same as intuitive awareness: III, 287/15 *(=722b41)*.

2. Vision must attain things as they are in themselves, and according as they exist independent of the seeing, for intuitive seeing functions as does an experimental cognition: III, 306/16 *(=733a16)*.

SEE: Experience
Intuition
Mirror
Presence
Sense

VOICE (*Vox*):

1. Non-signficative voices are not terms: S, 24/14, 19 *(=8b19, 24)*.

of a word in representative being, and for this reason the understanding is rendered through that word formally understanding terminatively: II, 253/11 (=707b45).

17. There cannot be any cognition without a word either formed by or united to the one understanding: II, 253/27 (=707b14).

18. Why the Divine Word loses the rationale of a sign: II, 228/19, 233/12 (=696a36, 699a9).

19. Creatures are a secondary and material object of, and for this reason are not represented by, the Divine Word: A, 351/29 (=108a21).

20. An exterior word does not represent the interior word more principally than it represents the thing signified by the interior word, because the interior word is not the formal object represented but the principal significative: A, 351/32 (=108a25).

21. Concept [word] and thing represented are understood by the same act according as the word is taken as the rationale expressing the object on the side of the terminus, for which reason the word itself is sometimes said to be cognized as that which is apprehended when an object is cognized, that is, because it is cognized as keeping on the side of the terminus which is apprehended, and not as keeping on the side of the principle or as that by which the thing is cognized: III, 331/13 (=745b4).

22. The word or concept is present to our understanding formally, but not objectively; for it is the inhering form by which an object is cognized, yet it is not in itself an object endowed with that understandability which is required for our understanding, namely, understandability in the mode of a sensible structure: III, 331/27 (=745b20).

SEE: Act of Understanding
Concept
Formal Awareness
Linguistic Expression
Phantasm
Quality
Reflexion
Representation
Sense
Sign
Specifier
Stipulated Sign
Term
Understanding
Use
Voice
Writing

WORSHIP (*Cultus*):
SEE: Religion

WRITING (*Scriptura*):

1. The same questions as can be raised of vocal expressions in respect of concepts can be asked of written expressions: A, 344/21 (=105a19); nor is it particularly puzzling that, in the case of these mind-dependent relatives of discourse, when the actual cognition of some pattern ceases, the formal existence of that pattern and the formal denomination originating from such an existence should also cease, and arise again when there is another actual cognition, so long as the fundamental denomination remains constant; so a linguistic element without a cognized relation continues to be a sign fundamentally and, as it were, metaphysically—that is to say, it remains in an order to the effect of representing, it does not continue to be a sign formally as regards the intention of the relation: I, 130/27 (=653b8).

2. The writing in a closed book is a sign actually fundamentally, not actually formally: I, 130/22 (=653b1); II, 275/8 (=718a5).

SEE: Closed Book
Instrumental Sign
Linguistic Expression
Relation
Sign
Term
Use
Voice

V.
INDEX ONOMASTICUS EDITORIALIS:
EDITORIAL INDEX

The following Index was not discussed in the Editorial Afterword, since it is not an index to Poinsot's work but only to the editorial materials which have been developed for the purpose of presenting this edition of the *Treatise on Signs*.

It covers, therefore, the front materials and the Semiotic Markers, the footnotes added to the Reiser text, and the whole of the Editorial Afterword itself. (Reiser's original notes to our text and the contents of citations drawn from other parts of the *Cursus Philosophicus* and added as notes to our text have already been incorporated into the previous indices).

It does not cover the References concluding the volume, which complete the editorial materials. No systematic attempt has been made to include in this Index the names of works referred to only by year in preceding editorial materials. A few sources will be found by name therefore only in the References at the end of this volume.

The term according to which entries in this Index have been alphabetized is in capitals for ease of reference. The reader is asked to keep in mind that, logically, a ''term'' of language may be either *simple* (a single ''word'' in the dictionary sense) or *complex* (more than one word but short of a ''complete thought''—short, that is, of a 'dicent' or *saying sign*. Thus—e.g.—''DE CIVE'' is alphabetized under ''dec . . .'', whereas ''De CIVE'' would be under ''civ . . .'', etc.

Under the entry ''REISER'' I have included a complete list of the corrections, alterations, and additions made to Reiser's text, and of the locus of cross-references made to other parts of Poinsot's *Cursus Philosophicus* in the form of citations from those Parts appended as footnotes to the *Treatise*.

Under the entry ''LYONS'' will be found a complete listing of the textual additions made to the *Treatise on Signs* in the 1663 Lyons publication of the *Cursus Philosophicus*, as well as indication of discussion of this infamous publishing event.

Finally, it may be noted that the main theological *Summa* of St. Thomas Aquinas, to offer some hint and flavor of the difference between contemporary and older usages, has been referred to in the editorial materials as *theologiae*, while in the translation materials as *theologica*.

REFERENCES

REFERENCES IN EDITORIAL MATERIALS

with Some Annotations

(The references in the following Bibliography cover the editorial materials of the present work in their entirety, i.e., the opening "To the Reader," the Semiotic Markers, the notes to the text of the Treatise, and the "Editorial Afterword." They are listed alphabetically by author in the customary fashion, with entries under authors historically layered so far as practical.)

ABEL, Jean.

1970. *L'Influence de la charité sur les actes moraux dans une controverse posttridentine* (Louvain: Faculté de Théologie).

d'AILLY, Pierre.

c.1372. *Concepts and Insolubles*, an annotated translation by Paul Vincent Spade (Dordrecht, Holland: D. Reidel Publishing Company, 1980).

a.1396. *Destructiones Modorum Significandi (secundum viam nominalium)*, nach Inkunabelausgaben in einer Vorläufigen Fassung neu Zusammengestellt und mit Anmerkungen Versehen von Ludger Kaczmarek (Münster: Münsteraner Arbeitskreis für Semiotik, 1980).

ALONSO, A. Muñoz.

1957. "Giovanni di San Tommaso," *Enciclopedia Filosofica* (Rome: Istituto per la Collaborazione Culturale), Vol. II, p. 770.

ALSTON, William P.

1967. "Sign and Symbol," in *The Encyclopedia of Philosophy*, ed. Paul Edwards (New York: Macmillan), Vol. 7, pp. 437-441.

AQUINAS, St. Thomas.

c.1252-1256. *Scriptum super libros sententiarum magistri Petri Lombardi*, in 4 volumes; Vols. 1 and 2 ed. R. P. Mandonnet (Paris: Lethielleux, 1929); Vols. 3 and 4 ed. R. P. Maria Fabianus Moos (Paris: Lethielleux, 1939, 1947).

c.1256-1259. *Quaestiones disputatae de veritate*, in *Quaestiones disputatae*, Vol. I, 9th ed. rev. by R. Spiazzi (Turin: Marietti, 1953).

c.1265-1266. *Quaestiones disputatae de potentia*, ed. R. P. Pauli M. Pession, in *Quaestiones disputatae*, Vol. II, 9th ed. rev. by P. Bazzi, M. Calcaterra, T. S. Centi, E. Odetto, and P. M. Pession (Turin: Marietti, 1953), pp. 7-276.

c.1266. *Summa theologiae prima pars*, ed. P. Carmello cum textu ex recensione leonina (Turin: Marietti, 1952).

c.1268. *In octo libros Physicorum Aristotelis expositio*, cura et studio P. M. Maggiolo (Rome: Marietti, 1954).

c.1269-1272. *In duodecim libros metaphysicorum Aristotelis expositio*, ed. M. R. Cathala et R. M. Spiazzi (Turin: Marietti, 1950).

c.1269-1273. *In Aristotelis librum de anima commentarium*, 3rd ed. by P. F. A. M. Pirotta (Turin: Marietti, 1948).

c.1272-1273. *In Aristotelis libros de caelo et mundo expositio*, ed. R.M. Spiazzi cum textu ex recensione leonina, and bound together with the commentaries on *De generatione et corruptione* and *Meteorologica* (Turin: Marietti, 1953), pp. 1-311.

ARISTOTLE.

c.335-322B.C. *Categories*. In the present work, the English translations of J. F. Ackrill, *Aristotle's Categories and De Interpretatione* (Oxford: Clarendon, 1963), and E. M. Edghill in *The Basic Works of Aristotle*, ed. R. McKeon (New York: Random House, 1941), pp. 3-37, were used.

c.348-330B.C. *Metaphysics*. In the present work, the English translation of W. D. Ross in *The Basic Works of Aristotle*, ed. R. McKeon (New York: Random House, 1941), pp. 681-926, was used.

ASHLEY, Benedict M.

1952. ''Research into the Intrinsic Final Causes of Physical Things,'' ACPA *Proceedings*, XXVI (1952), 185-194.

1967a. ''Final Causality,'' in *The New Catholic Encyclopedia* (New York: McGraw-Hill), Vol. V, pp. 915-919.

1967b. ''Teleology,'' in *The New Catholic Encyclopedia* (New York: McGraw-Hill), Vol. XIII, pp. 979-981.

1973. ''Change and Process,'' in *The Problem of Evolution*, ed. John N. Deely and Raymond J. Nogar (Indianapolis, Ind.: Hackett Publishing Co.), pp. 265-294.

ASHWORTH, E. J.

1974. *Language and Logic in the Post-Medieval Period* (Dordrecht, Holland: Reidel).

Saint AUGUSTINE of Hippo.

c.397-426. *De doctrina christiana libri quattuor* (''Of'' or ''Concerning Christian Doctrine''), in *Patrologiae Cursus Completus*, ed. J. P. Migne, *Series Latina* (P.L.), Vol. 34, cols. 15-122.

BELISARIO, D. Tello.

1954. ''El ente de razón según Juan de Santo Thomás,'' *Philosophia* (Mendoza) 11, no. 19, pp. 43-50.

BELLERATE, Bruno.

1955. ''Principais contributos de Frei João de São Tomás à doutrina de analogia do Cardeal Caetano,'' *Revista Portuguesa di Filosofia* (Lisbon), 11, nos. 3-4, pp. 344-351 [Actas do I Congresso Nacional de Filosofia].

1958. ''Conceito de existência em João de S. Tomás'' (Tradução de António Mateus Areias), *Filosofia L.* (5), 154-169.

BELTRAN DE HEREDIA, V.

1916. ''La Enseñanza de Santo Tomás en la Universidad de Alcalá. Fundación de dos cátedras de Teología de Santo Tomás por el Duque de Lerma para la Orden de Predicatores,'' *La Ciencia Tomista*, XIV, 267-297.

BLANES, Guil (Francisco).

1956. ''Las raíces de la doctrina de Juan de Santo Tomás acerca del universal lógico,'' *Estudios Filosóficos. Las Caldas de Besaya* (Santander) (17), 418-421.

BOCHENSKI, I. M.

1961. *A History of Formal Logic*, translated and edited ''with the author's full concurrence'' by Ivo Thomas from *Formale Logik* (Freiburg: Verlag Karl Alber, 1956) (Notre Dame, Indiana: University of Notre Dame Press).

BONDI, Eugene.

1966. "Predication: A Study Based in the *Ars Logica* of John of St. Thomas," *The Thomist*, XXX, 260-294.

BOURKE, Vernon J.

1967. "John of St. Thomas," in *The Encyclopedia of Philosophy*, ed. Paul Edwards (New York: Macmillan), Vol. 4, p. 284.

BRADLEY, F. H.

1935. "Relations," in *Collected Essays* (Oxford: Clarendon), Vol. II, pp. 628-676.

BRENTANO, Franz.

1874, 1911. *Psychologie vom empirischen Standpunkt*, ed. by Oskar Kraus, trans. into English under the title *Psychology from an Empirical Standpoint* (New York: Humanities) by Antos C. Rancurello, D. B. Terrell and Linda L. McAlister, this last translator being also editor for the English edition.

BURSILL-HALL, Geoffrey L.

1971. *Speculative Grammars of the Middle Ages. The Doctrine of Partes Orationis of the Modistae* (The Hague: Mouton).

CAHALAN, John C.

1970. "Analogy and the Disrepute of Metaphysics," *The Thomist*, XXXIV (July), 387-422.

1975. See "Editorial Afterword," notes 105, 107, 109, 116.

1981. "Maritain's View on the Philosophy of Nature," in *Selected Papers from the Conference-Seminar on The Degrees of Knowledge*, ed. Robert J. Henle, Marion Cordes, and Jeanne Vatterott (Saint Louis: The American Maritain Association), pp. 185-218.

1985. *Causal Realism: An essay on philosophical method and the foundations of knowledge* (Washington, D.C.: University Press of America).

CAJETAN, Thomas de Vio.

1498. *Commentaria in Praedicamenta Aristotelis* (Pavia, Jan. 9). The ed. of M.-H. Laurent (Rome: Angelicum, 1939) was used in preparing the present work.

1507. *Commentaria in summam theologicam. Prima pars.* (Rome: May 2). Reprinted in the Leonine edition of the *Sancti Thomae Aquinatis Doctoris Angelici Opera Omnia*, vols. 4 and 5 (Rome, 1888-1889), used in preparing the present work.

CHOMSKY, Noam.

1966. *Cartesian Linguistics* (New York: Harper & Row).

1968. *Language and Mind* (New York: Harcourt, Brace & World).

COSERIU, Eugenio.

1969. *Die Geschichte der Sprachphilosophie von der Antike bis zur Gegenwart. Eine Übersicht. Teil I: Von der Antike bis Leibniz* (Stuttgart: Vogt KG).

COURCHETET D'ESNANS.

1761. *Histoire du Cardinal de Granvelle* (Paris).

CREPEAULT, P.-E.

1961. *De essentia gratiae habitualis. Utrum possit dici secundum Joannem a Sancto Thoma Divinae Naturae univoca participatio* (Québec: Les Presses Universitaires Laval).

DANDENAULT, Germain.

1966. *De la supériorité de la justice légale sur la religion d'après Cajetan et Jean de Saint-Thomas* (Rome: Tip. San Pio X).

DEELY, John N.

1969. "The Philosophical Dimensions of the Origin of Species," *The Thomist*, XXXIII (January and April), I, 75-149; II, 251-342.

1971a. "Animal Intelligence and Concept-Formation," *The Thomist*, XXXV (January), 43-93.

1971b. *The Tradition via Heidegger* (The Hague: Martinus Nijhoff).

1972. "The Ontological Status of Intentionality," *The New Scholasticism*, XLVI, 220-233.

1973. "The Impact of Evolution on Scientific Method," in *The Problem of Evolution*, ed. John N. Deely and Raymond J. Nogar (New York: Appleton-Century-Crofts; Indianapolis, Ind.: Hackett Publishing Co.), pp. 3-82.

1974. "The Two Approaches to Language: Philosophical and Historical Reflections on the Point of Departure of Jean Poinsot's Semiotic," *The Thomist*, XXXVII, 4 (October), 856-907.

1975a. "Modern Logic, Animal Psychology, and Human Discourse," *Revue de l'Université d'Ottawa* 45, 1 (janvier-mars), 80-100.

1975b. "Reference to the Non-Existent," *The Thomist*, XXXIX, 2 (April), 253-308.

1976. "The Doctrine of Signs: Taking Form at Last," *Semiotica*, 18:2, 171-193.

1977a. " 'Semiotic' as the Doctrine of Signs," *Ars Semeiotica* 1/3, 41-68.

1977b. "Metaphysics, Modern Thought, and 'Thomism,' " in *Notes et Documents de l'Institut International "Jacques Maritain,"* 8 (juillet-septembre), 12-18. (The reader must be warned that proofs were not supplied for this text, and it is filled with printer's errors—some quite substantial.)

1978a. "Toward the Origin of Semiotic," in *Sight, Sound, and Sense*, ed. Thomas A. Sebeok (Bloomington: Indiana University Press), pp. 1-30. This work erroneously conjectures (p. 7) that the explicit thematization and appellation of the division of signs into formal and instrumental "may well have been original with Poinsot." Romeo (1979), working from Herculano de Carvalho, 1970 (q.v.), shows that while Poinsot's thematization in Book II, Question 2, of the *Treatise* was indeed original, the appellation of this contrast was already in use with Petrus Fonsecus' *Institutionum dialecticarum libri octo* (1564), a work with which Poinsot was certainly familiar. See Romeo, 1979: 194-195, for a translation of Fonseca's summary remarks "about formal and instrumental signs." Follow-up in Deely, 1981, 1982; Doyle, 1984.

1978b. "What's in a Name," *Semiotica*, 22:1/2, 151-181.

1978c. "Semiotic and the Controversy over Mental Events," ACPA *Proceedings*, LII: 16-27.

1980a. "The Nonverbal Inlay in Linguistic Communication," in *The Signifying Animal*, ed. Irmengard Rauch and Gerald F. Carr (Bloomington: Indiana University Press), pp. 201-217. This essay is incorporated in revised form under the title "Experience" as Part II, Section 3 (pp. 107-123) of the 1982 entry below.

1980b. "Antecedents to Peirce's Notion of Iconic Signs," in *Semiotics 1980* (Proceedings of the Semiotic Society of America, Fifth Annual Meeting), ed. Margot D. Lenhart and Michael Herzfeld (New York: Plenum), pp. 109-120.

1981. "The Relation of Logic to Semiotics," *Semiotica* 35—3/4: 193-265. This essay is incorporated in its entirety, with revisions and expansions, as Part I (pp. 5-84) of the 1982 entry following.

1982a. "On the Notion of Phytosemiotics," in *Semiotics 1982*, ed. John N. Deely and Margot D. Lenhart (New York: Plenum, 1985).

1982. *Introducing Semiotic. Its History and Doctrine* (Bloomington: Indiana University Press).

1983a. "Neglected Figures in the History of Semiotic Inquiry: John Poinsot," in *History of Semiotics*, edited by Achim Eschbach and Jürgen Trabant (Amsterdam: John Benjamins Publishing Company), pp. 115-126.

1983b. ''Pierre d'Ailly as Piece in a Puzzle,'' presentation at the eighth Annual Meeting of the Semiotic Society of America, Snowbird, Utah; October.
1985. ''Idolum: Archeology and Ontology of the Iconic Sign,'' in *Iconicity. Essays on the Nature of Culture*, ed. Paul Bouissac, Michael Herzfeld and Roland Posner (The Hague: Mouton).

DEGL'INNOCENTI, Umberto.
1969. ''Il principio d'individuazione dei corpi e Giovanni di S. Tommaso,'' *Aquinas* 12: 55-99.

DELGADO, V. Muñoz.
1972. *Lógica Hispana-Portuguesa hasta 1600* (Salamanca).

DEMAN, Thomas.
1936. ''Probabalisme,'' *Dictionnaire de théologie catholique* (Paris: Librairie Letouzey et Ané), Vol. 13, première partie, cols. 417-619.

DEWEY, John.
1922. *Human Nature and Conduct* (New York: Holt).
1938. *Logic: The Theory of Inquiry* (New York: Holt).

DOYLE, John J.
1953. ''John of St. Thomas and Mathematical Logic,'' *The New Scholasticism*, XXVII, 3-38.

DOYLE, John P.
1983. ''Suarez on Truth and Mind-Dependent Beings: Implication for a Unified Semiotic,'' in *Semiotics 1983*, ed. John N. Deely and Margot D. Lenhart (in preparation).
1984. ''The *Conimbricenses* on the Relations Involved in Signs,'' in *Semiotics 1984*, ed. John N. Deely (Washington: University Press of America). Breakthrough presentation of research into Poinsot's immediate semiotic predecessors.

DU CANGE, Carolus du Fresne.
1883-1887. *Glossarium Mediae et Infimae Latinitatis* (Graz, Austria: Akademische Druck- u. Verlagsanstalt, 1954 republication).

ECO, Umberto.
1976. *A Theory of Semiotics* (Bloomington: Indiana University Press). Reviewed in Deely 1976.

EHR, Donaldo J.
1961. *The Purpose of the Creator and of Creatures* (Techny, Ill.: Divine Word Publications).

FARRELL, Walter.
1951. ''Foreword'' to Hughes, 1951, q.v., pp. v-vii.

FISCH, Max H., KETNER, Kenneth Laine, and KLOESEL, Christian J. W.
1979. ''The New Tools of Peirce Scholarship, with Particular Reference to Semiotic,'' in *Studies in Peirce's Semiotic*, ed. Kenneth Laine Ketner and Joseph M. Ransdell, *Peirce Studies* no. 1 (Lubbock, Texas: Institute for Studies in Pragmaticism), pp. 1-17.

FREGE, G.
1892. ''Über Sinn und Bedeutung,'' *Zeitschrift für Philosophie und philosophische Kritik* 100: 25-50.

GAGNÉ, Hervé.
See under "MATHIEU, Armand and . . ."

GAMBRA, Rafael.
1973. *Historia Sencilla de la Filosofía*, 7th ed. (Madrid: Ediciones Rialp).

GARDEIL, A.
1927. *La Structure de l'âme et l'expérience mystique*, 2 vols. (Paris: Victor Lecoffre). Gardeil's "Introduction," vol. I, pp. XVIII-XXI, has an extended series of remarks on Poinsot.

GARRIGOU-LAGRANGE, Reginald.
1930. "Preface" to Maritain, Raïssa, 1930, q.v., pp. VII-XV.

GETINO, Luis G. Alonso.
1916. "Domínicos Españoles Confessores de Reyes," *La Ciencia Tomista*, XIV, 374-451.

GHOOS, J.
1951. "L'Acte à double effet: Étude de théologie positive [Navarrus, Medina, Vazquez, Jean de Saint-Thomas]," *Ephemerides Theologiae Lovaniensis* 27: 30-52.

GIACON, Carlo.
1944-1950. *La Seconda Scolastica*, in 3 Vols.:
1944. *I Grandi Commentatori di San Tommaso* [Cajetan, d. 1534; Ferrariensis, d. c. 1528; Vitoria, d. 1546] (Milan: Fratelli Bocca).
1946. *Precedenza Teoretiche ai Problemi Giuridici Toledo, Pereira, Fonseca, Molina, Suarez* (Milan: Fratelli Bocca).
1950. *I Problemi Giuridico-Politici Suarez, Bellarmino, Mariana* (Milan: Fratelli Bocca).

GILSON, Étienne.
1937. *The Unity of Philosophical Experience* (New York: Scribner's).
1952a. *Being and Some Philosophers*, 2nd ed. corrected and enlarged (Toronto: Pontifical Institute of Mediaeval Studies).
1952b. *La philosophie au moyen âge: Des origines patristiques à la fin du XIVe siècle*, 2ème ed. rev. et aug. (Paris: Payot).
1955. *History of Christian Philosophy in the Middle Ages* (New York: Random House).

GLANVILLE, John J. See also "SIMON, Yves R., and . . ."
1958. "Zabarella and Poinsot on the Object and Nature of Logic," in *Readings in Logic*, ed. Roland Houde (Dubuque: William C. Brown), pp. 204-226.

GONÇALVES, António Manuel.
1955a. "O tomismo indefectível de Frei João de São Tomás," *Filosofia* (Lisbon), 2 (April): 45-51.
1955b. "Actualidade de Frei João de São Tomás," *Revista Portuguesa di Filosofia* 11: 586-594 [Actas do I Congresso Nacional de Filosofia].

GOUDGE, T. A.
1950. *The Thought of C. S. Peirce* (Toronto: University of Toronto Press).

GREDT, Josephus.
1924. *De Cognitione Sensuum Externorum Inquisitio Psychologico-Criteriologica circa Realismum Criticum et Objectivitatem Qualitatum Sensibilium* (ed. altera, aucta et emendata; Rome: Desclée).
1961. *Elementa Philosophiae Aristotelico-Thomisticae*, 13th ed. recognita et aucta ab Euchario Zenzen, O.S.B. (Barcelona: Herder), 2 Vols.

GREEN, Theodore Hill.
1886. ''General Introduction to the First Volume'' of *The Philosophical Works of Hume*, ed. Theodore Hill Green and Thomas Hodge Grose (Aalen: Scientia Verlag reprint, 1964), pp. 1-299.

HANKE, John W.
1973. *Maritain's Ontology of the Work of Art* (The Hague: Martinus Nijhoff).

HEGEL, G. W. F.
1802. ''Glauben und Wissen oder die Reflexionsphilosophie der Subjektivität,'' from the *Journal der Philosophie*, Band II, Stück 1, as reprinted in the *Sämtliche Werke*, ed. Hermann Glockner (Stuttgart: Frommann, 1958), Vol. I, pp. 278-433.
1812. *Wissenschaft der Logik. Erster Teil: Die Objektive Logik*, in *Sämtliche Werke*, Vol. 4 (Stuttgart: Frommann, 1958).
1830a. *Die Logik*, being the *Erster Teil* of *System der Philosophie*, in *Sämtliche Werke*, Vol. 8 (Stuttgart: Frommann, 1964), i.e., Part I of the 3rd edition of *Enzyklopädie der philosophischen Wissenschaften*, first published in 1816.
1830b. *Die Philosophie des Geistes*, being the *Dritter Teil* of *System der Philosophie*, in *Sämtliche Werke*, Vol. 10 (Stuttgart: Frommann, 1958), i.e., Part III of *Enzyklopädie der philosophischen Wissenschaften*, first published in 1816.

HEIDEGGER, Martin.
1927. *Sein und Zeit*, originally published in the *Jahrbuch für Phänomenologie und phänomenologische Forschung*, ed. E. Husserl. Page references in the present work are to the 10th edition (Tübingen: Niemeyer, 1963).
1929. *Vom Wesen des Grundes* (Frankfurt: Klostermann, 1955).
1943. *Vom Wesen der Wahrheit* (Frankfurt: Klostermann, 1954; actual composition 1930). The English translation by R. F. C. Hull and Alan Crick, ''On the Essence of Truth,'' in *Existence and Being*, ed. Werner Brock (Chicago: Gateway, 1949), pp. 292-324, was particularly consulted in preparing the present work.
1947. *Platons Lehre von der Wahrheit, mit einem Brief über den Humanismus* (Bern: Francke).

HERCULANO DE CARVALHO, José G.
1969. ''Segno e significazione in João de São Tomás,'' in *Estudos Linguísticos*, Vol. 2 (Coimbra: Atlântida Editora). Pp. 129-153 are exposition; 154-168 reproduce selected passages of Latin text. This careful essay, a most important piece of work on our author's semiotic, stands along with the essay of Maritain, 1938, 1943, as a firsthand presentation of Poinsot's views on the subject of signs.
1970. *Teoria da linguagem. Natureza do fenómeno linguístico e a análise das línguas* (reprint with additions of 1967 work of same title, and now as ''Tomo I'' with a second volume of the same name published in 1973; Coimbra: Atlântida). ''Rarely acknowledged in the English-speaking world'' (Romeo, 1979: 188-189), several chapters of this work form ''a basic introduction to general semiotics'' (in particular, Chs. 5-8 ''should be required reading as a challenging and fresh outlook on language analysis within semiotics'') written ''on the basis of and stemming from a wide view of the science of language within the western tradition of studies on the sign,'' and containing ''considerations on both human and non-human communication.'' This richly learned study was a singularly fruitful result, according to Romeo, of the establishment in 1957 of a chair for linguistics within the Faculty of Letters at the University of Coimbra. ''Should Herculano de Carvalho's *Teoria* be translated one

day,'' Romeo muses (1979: 189), ''crossing either the Channel or the Atlantic, doubtless it will have an impact on a younger generation understandably tired of being led by the nose by those astero-linguists who try to reinvent the wheel each time a Ph.D. dissertation is 'published.' Let us hope his work will not have to wait half a century for a Baskin.''

HIPPOCRATES.

c.415B.C. *Prognostic*, in *The Loeb Classical Library Hippocrates*, Vol. II, ed. by E. Capps, T. E. Page, W. H. D. Rouse, with an English translation by W. H. S. Jones (New York: G. P. Putnam's Sons, 1923), pp. 6-54.

HOBBES, Thomas.

1668. *Opera Philosophica, Quae Latine Scripsit, Omnia* (Amsterdam: Joannes Blaev, 1668), 2 Vols.

HÖFFDING, Harald.

1900. *A History of Modern Philosophy*, trans. from the German by E. E. Meyer (New York: Macmillan), 2 Vols. Dover republication 1955.

HOLLENHORST, G. Donald. See under ''SIMON, Yves R., and . . .''

HUGHES, Dominic, trans.

1951. *The Gifts of the Holy Ghost* (New York: Sheed and Ward), translation of Poinsot's ''De Donis Spiritus Sancti,'' from the *Tomus Quintus Cursus Theologici* (1645), disp. 18 (Vol. VI of the Vivès edition, Paris, 1885: 572-715.)

HUME, David.

1739-1740. *A Treatise of Human Nature*, ed. Selby-Bigge (1896), second ed. with text rev. and variant readings by P. H. Nidditch (Oxford: Clarendon, 1978).

1776 (April 18). ''My Own Life,'' Hume's autobiography, reprinted in *An Enquiry Concerning Human Understanding*, ed. and intro. by Charles W. Hendel (New York: Bobbs-Merrill, 1955), pp. 3-11.

HUSSERL, Edmund H.

1931. *Cartesianische Meditationen*. The English translation by Dorian Cairns, *Cartesian Meditations* (The Hague: Martinus Nijhoff, 1960), was consulted in preparing the present work.

JONES, W. T.

1969. *The Medieval Mind*. Vol. II of the five-volume *History of Western Philosophy*, 2nd ed. rev. (New York: Harcourt, Brace & World).

KANE, Declan.

1959. ''The Subject of Predicamental Action according to John of St. Thomas,'' *The Thomist*, XXII, 366-388.

KANT, Immanuel.

1781, 1787. *Kritik der reinen Vernunft* (Riga). References in the present work are to the N.K. Smith translation, *Kant's Critique of Pure Reason* (New York: St. Martin's Press, 1963), and to *Kant's Gesammelte Schriften*, issued by the Königlich Preussischen Akademie der Wissenschaften, Band III, *Kritik der reinen Vernunft*, 2nd ed. (1787) (Berlin: Druck und Verlag von Georg Reimer, 1911).

KEMP SMITH, Norman.

1963. Translation of and preface and notes to Kant, 1781, 1787 (q.v.).

KNEALE, William and Martha.
1962. *The Development of Logic* (Oxford).

KRAMPEN, Martin.
1981. "Phytosemiotics," *Semiotica* 36: 3-4, 187-209.

KREMPEL, A.
1952. *La Doctrine de la relation chez St. Thomas* (Paris: Vrin).

KRETZMAN, Norman.
1967. "Semantics, History of," in *The Encyclopedia of Philosophy*, ed. Paul Edwards (New York: Macmillan), Vol. 7, pp. 358-406.

KRISTELLER, Paul Oskar.
1961a. "The Aristotelian Tradition," in his *Renaissance Thought* (New York: Harper), pp. 24-47.
1961b. "Humanism and Scholasticism in the Italian Renaissance," ibid., pp. 92-119.
1961c. "The Philosophy of Man in the Italian Renaissance," ibid., pp. 120-139.

LALANDE, André.
1947. *Vocabulaire technique et critique de la philosophie*, 5th ed. aug. (Paris: Presses Universitaires de France).

LA PLANTE, Robert J.
1972. See "Editorial Afterword," note 104.

LAVAL. See under "MATHIEU, Armand, and GAGNÉ, Hervé, eds."

LAVAUD, M.-Benoît.
1926. "Les maîtres et modèles: Jean de Saint-Thomas (1589-1644)," *La Vie spirituelle* (juillet-août), 387-415.
1928. "Jean de Saint-Thomas, l'homme et l'oeuvre," Appendix II to *Introduction à la théologie de saint Thomas*, being Lavaud's French translation of Poinsot's "Isagoge ad D. Thomae Theologiam" (in the *Tomus Primus Cursus Theologici* [1637], Solesmes ed., 1931: 142-219) (Paris: André Blot), pp. 411-446.

LOCKE, John.
1690. *An Essay concerning Human Understanding*, ed. P. H. Nidditch (Oxford: Clarendon Press, 1975). The edition of Alexander Campbell Fraser (Oxford, 1894; Dover reprint 1959) was also consulted.

LOMBARD, Peter.
c.1150. *Libri quattuor sententiarum* ("The Four Books of the Sentences"), in *Patrologiae Cursus Completus*, ed. J. P. Migne, *Series Latina* (P.L.), vol. 192, cols. 522-963. (One of the very earliest printed editions of this formerly ubiquitous work appeared in Venice: Vandelin Spire, 1477.)

MACQUARRIE, John, and ROBINSON, Edward.
1962. "Translator's Preface" to Martin Heidegger's *Being and Time* (New York: Harper & Row), pp. 13-16.

MAKONSKI, Thomas J.
1962. *The Radical Interiority of Liberty according to the Principles of John of St. Thomas* (Rome: Officium libri catholici).

MARÍAS, Julián.
1967. *History of Philosophy*, trans. from the 22nd Spanish ed. by Stanley Applebaum and Clarence C. Stowbridge (New York: Dover).

MARITAIN, Jacques.

1922. ''De quelques conditions de la renaissance thomiste,'' in *Antimoderne* (Paris: Éditions de la Revue des Jeunes), pp. 121-167.

1923. *Éléments de philosophie: II. L'ordre des concepts—Petite logique (Logique formelle)* (Paris: Tequi), translation by Imelda Choquette titled *Formal Logic* (New York: Sheed and Ward, 1937, 1946). See ''Editorial Afterword,'' note 14, p. 406 above.

1924. *Réflexions sur l'intelligence et sur sa vie propre*, 2nd ed. (Paris: Nouvelle Librarie Nationale, 1926).

1932a. *Distinguer pour unir: ou les degrés du savoir* (Paris: Desclée). See also entries for 1959a and 1963.

1932b. *Le Songe de Descartes* (Paris: Corrêa).

1935a. *La Philosophie de la nature, essai critique sur ses frontières et son objet* (Paris: Tequi). The English translation by Imelda C. Byrne, *Philosophy of Nature* (New York: Philosophical Library, 1951), was also consulted in preparing the present work.

1935b. ''La Philosophie de la nature,'' in *Science et sagesse* (Paris: Labergerie), trans. Bernard Wall as ''The Philosophy of Nature,'' in *Science and Wisdom* (New York: Scribner's, 1940), pp. 34-69, which translation was used in preparing the present work.

1937-38. ''Sign and Symbol,'' trans. Mary Morris in *Journal of the Warburg Institute*, I, pp. 1-11. See also entries for 1938 and 1943.

1938. ''Signe et symbole,'' *Revue Thomiste*, XLIV (avril), 299-330.

1941. ''The Conflict of Methods at the End of the Middle Ages,'' *The Thomist*, III (October), 527-538.

1943. ''Sign and Symbol,'' English trans. of 1938 entry above (q.v.) by H. L. Binsse in *Redeeming the Time* (London: Geoffrey Bles), text pp. 191-224, Latin notes pp. 268-276.

1948. *Existence and the Existent*, trans. Lewis Galantiere and Gerald B. Phelan (New York: Pantheon, 1948). Original French publication 1947.

1953. *Creative Intuition in Art and Poetry* (New York: Pantheon).

1955. ''Preface'' to *The Material Logic of John of St. Thomas*, ed. and trans. Yves R. Simon, John J. Glanville, and G. Donald Hollenhorst (Chicago: University of Chicago Press), pp. v-viii.

1957. ''Language and the Theory of Sign,'' in *Language: An Enquiry into Its Meaning and Function*, ed. Ruth Nanda Anshen (New York: Harper), pp. 86-101.

1959a. *The Degrees of Knowledge*, trans. of the 4th French ed. (see entry for 1932a) supervised by Gerald Phelan (New York: Scribner's).

1959b. *The Sin of the Angel*, trans. William Rossner (Westminster, Maryland: Newman).

1963. *Distinguer pour unir, ou Les degrés du savoir*, 7th ed. rev. et aug. (Paris: Desclée de Brouwer).

1966a. *God and the Permission of Evil*, trans. Joseph W. Evans (Milwaukee: Bruce).

1966b. *Le paysan de la Garonne* (Paris: Desclée).

1970. *De l'Église du Christ* (Paris: Desclée, 1970). The English trans. by Joseph W. Evans, *On the Church of Christ* (Notre Dame, 1973), was also consulted.

MARITAIN, Raïssa, translator and editor.

1930. *Les Dons du Saint Esprit* (Paris: Editions du Cerf). Translation into French of Poinsot's ''De Donis Spiritus Sancti,'' from the *Tomus Quintus Cursus Theologici* (1637), disp. 18 (Vol. VI of the Vivès edition, Paris, 1885: 572-715).

MASSON, Reginald.
1966. "Duns Scotus according to John of St. Thomas: An Appraisal," in *De Doctrina Joannis Duns Scoti* (Acta Congressus Scotistici Internationalis Oxonii et Edinburgi, 11-17 Sept. 1966 celebrati), Vol. IV, pp. 517-534.

MATHIEU, Armand, and GAGNÉ, Hervé, eds. Joannis a Sancto Thoma *Cursus Theologici* (CT) secundum principium sic dictum: "textum correximus ex interna comparatione et meditatione" (cf. "Editorial Afterword," note 4 page 398), Collectio Lavallensis, Sectio theologica (Québec: Presses Universitaires Laval).
1947. *De certitudine principiorum theologiae; De auctoritate summi Pontificis. Theologiae dogmaticae communia.*
1948. *CT in Iam IIae De Donis Spiritus Sancti.*
1949. *CT in Iam IIae De Habitibus.*
1952. *CT in Iam IIae De Virtutibus.*
1953a. *CT in IIam IIae De Caritate.*
1953b. *CT in IIam IIae De Spe.*
1954. *CT in Iam IIae De Gratia.*
1955. *CT in Iam IIae De Effectibus Gratiae.*

McCLEARY, Richard C., trans.
1964. Translation of Merleau-Ponty's 1960 work *Signes* (q.v.), titled *Signs* (Evanston: Northwestern University Press).

McKEON, Richard
1929. "General Introduction" to his *Selections from Medieval Philosophers* (New York: Scribner's), Vol. I, pp. ix-xx.

MEAD, Margaret.
1964. Remarks in "Discussion Session on Linguistics" and "Vicissitudes of the Total Communication Process," *Approaches to Semiotics*, ed. Thomas A. Sebeok, Alfred S. Hayes, and Mary Catherine Bateson (The Hague: Mouton), pp. 265-287.

MENÉNDEZ-RIGADA, Ignacio.
1948. *Los Dones del Espíritu Santo y la Perfección Christiana*, with notes and commentary (Madrid: Consejo Superior de Investigaciones Scientíficas).

MERLEAU-PONTY, Maurice.
1960. *Signes* (Paris). Translated as *Signs* (Evanston: Northwestern University Press, 1964) by Richard McCleary (q.v.), the sole source consulted for the present edition.

MOODY, Ernest Addison.
1942. "Introduction" to *Johannis Buridani Quaestiones Super Libris Quattuor de Caelo et Mundo* (pre-1358), ed. Ernest Addison Moody (Cambridge, Mass.: The Mediaeval Academy of America).

MORENO, Alberto.
1959. "Implicación material en Juan de Santo Tomás," *Sapientia* 14: 188-191.
1963. "Lógica proposicional en Juan de Santo Tomás," *Sapientia* 18: 86-107.

MORENY, Robert.
1951. "L'Action transitive [Jean de Saint-Thomas]," *Sciences ecclésiastiques* (Montréal) 4: 55-64.

MORRIS, Charles.
1955. *Signs, Language, and Behavior* (New York: George Braziller).

OESTERLE, John A.
1944. "Another Approach to the Problem of Meaning," *The Thomist*, VII, 233-263. (An analysis of key distinctions in Poinsot, concluding with a point-by-point comparison between Poinsot and Ogden and Richards, *The Meaning of Meaning*.)

OWENS, Joseph.
1977. See "Editorial Afterword," notes 100, 106, 107.

PARKER, Francis H. and VEATCH, Henry B.
1959. *Logic as a Human Instrument* (New York: Harper & Row).

PEIRCE, Charles Sanders. Our references to Peirce are exclusively from the eight-volume *Collected Papers of Charles Sanders Peirce*, Vols. I-VI ed. Charles Hartshorne and Paul Weiss (Cambridge, Massachusetts: Harvard University Press, 1931-1935); Vols. VII and VIII ed. Arthur W. Burks (Cambridge, Massachusetts: Harvard University Press, 1958). We have chronologized our references to the *Collected Papers* (CP) exclusively on the basis of the "Bibliography" provided by Arthur W. Burks on pp. 249-330 in CP 8.
1867. "On a New List of Categories," CP 1.545-559: Burks p. 261.
1868. "Grounds of Validity of the Laws of Logic: Further Consequences of Four Incapacities," CP 5.318-357: Burks p. 262.
1878. "Illustrations of the Logic of Science," CP 6.395-426: Burks p. 265.
c.1890. "A Guess at the Riddle," CP 1.354-416: Burks p. 276.
c.1896. "The Logic of Mathematics; An Attempt to Develop My Categories from Within," CP 1.417-520: Burks p. 287.
1897. "The Logic of Relatives," CP 3.456-552: Burks p. 287.
c.1897. A fragment of biographical comments, CP 1.3-7: Burks p. 287.
1898. "The First Rule of Logic," CP 5.574-589: Burks p. 288.
c.1899. Insert covering CP 1.564-567 into the c.1895 essay "That Categorical and Hypothetical Propositions Are One in Essence, with some connected matters": Burks p. 286.
1901. "Pearson's Grammar of Science, Annotations on the First Three Chapters," CP 8.132-156: Burks p. 290.
c.1902. "Minute Logic," cited passages are in CP 1.204-276, 2.92, 5.538: Burks pp. 293-294.
c.1903. "On Existential Graphs, Euler's Diagrams, and Logical Algebra," in CP 4.418-509 from 'Logical Tracts, No. 2': Burks p. 296.
1903a. Lowell Lectures (at Harvard) given under the general title "Some Topics of Logic Bearing on Questions Now Vexed". Citations are from Lecture IIIa entitled "Lessons from the History of Philosophy" in CP 1.15-26, from draft 3 of Lecture III entitled "Degenerate Cases" in 1.521-544, and from Lecture VIII, "How to Theorize," in CP 5.590-604: Burks p. 295.
1903b. "Lectures on Pragmatism," citation is from Lecture V, "The Three Kinds of Goodness," in CP 5.120-150: Burks pp. 204-205.
1904. "On Signs and the Categories," from a letter to Lady Welby dated 12 October, in CP 8.327-341: Burks p. 321.
c.1905a. "Basis of Pragmaticism," CP 5.549-573: Burks p. 298.
c.1905b. "Pragmatism," comments on "A New List of Categories," CP, 1.560-562: Burks p. 280.

c.1906. From "Pragmatism (Editor [3])," citation from CP 5.488: Burks p. 299.
1908. "A Neglected Argument for the Reality of God," CP 6.452-485: Burks p. 300.
c.1909. "Some Amazing Mazes, Fourth Curiosity," CP, 6.318-348: Burks p. 300.
c.1910. "Additament" to 1908 above, CP 6.486-491: Burks p. 301.

PETER OF SPAIN (Petrus Hispanus).
c.1245. *Summulae Logicales*, ed. I. M. Bochenski (Rome: Marietti, 1947).

PINBORG, Jan.
1967. *Die Entwicklung der Sprachtheorie im Mittelalter* (Copenhagen: Verlag Arne Frost-Hansen).

POINSOT, John (Joannes a Sancto Thoma).
1631. *Artis Logicae Prima Pars* (Alcalá, Spain). The Reiser edition of this work (Vol. I; Turin: Marietti, 1930: pp. 1-247), was used in this work and is the basis for all page, column, and line references beyond the confines of the *Treatise on Signs* text.
1632. *Artis Logicae Secunda Pars* (Alcalá, Spain). The Reiser edition of this work (Vol. I; Turin: Marietti, 1930: pp. 249-839) was used in this work and is the basis for all page, column, and line references beyond the confines of the *Treatise on Signs* text.
1632. *Tractatus de Signis* ("Treatise on Signs"), appearing within the *Artis Logicae Secunda Pars* (entry immediately preceding), as explained in the "Editorial Afterword," Section I.B.
1633. *Naturalis Philosophiae Prima Pars* (Madrid, Spain). The Reiser edition of this work (Vol. II; Turin: Marietti, 1933: pp. 1-529) was used in preparing the present work and is the basis for all page, column, and line references in the present work.
1634. *Naturalis Philosophiae Tertia Pars* (Alcalá, Spain). The Reiser edition of this work (Vol. II; Turin: Marietti, 1933: pp. 533-888) was used in preparing the present work and is the basis for all page, column, and line references.
1635. *Naturalis Philosophiae Quarta Pars: De Ente Mobili Animato* (Alcalá, Spain). The Reiser edition of this work (Vol. III; Turin: Marietti, 1937: pp. 1-425) was used in preparing the present work and is the basis for all page, column, and line references.
1637. *Tomus Primus Cursus Theologici* (Alcalá, Spain). The Solesmes edition of this work (Vol. I and Vol. II to p. 529; Paris: Desclée, 1931 and 1934) was used in preparing the present work.
1640. "Lectori," Preface added to the 4th edition (Madrid) of the Second Part of the *Ars Logica*, calling attention to the uniqueness, position, and utility of the text of the *Treatise on Signs* within the *Ars Logica* and *Cursus Philosophicus*. Included in the 1930 Reiser ed., p. 249.
1640a. *Explicación de la doctrina christiana y la obligación de los fieles en creer y obrar* (Madrid). Full information in "Editorial Afterword," note 2.
1643a. *Tomus Secundus Cursus Theologici* (Lyons). The Solesmes edition of this work (Vol. II p. 531-end and Vol. III; Paris: Desclée, 1934 and 1937) was used in preparing the present work.
1643b. *Tomus Tertius Cursus Theologici*. The Solesmes edition of this work (Vol. IV; Paris: Desclée, 1946) was used in preparing the present work.
1644. *Breve tratado y muy importante, que por mandato de su Majesdad escribibió el R.P. Fr. Juan de S. Tomás para saber hacer una confesión general* (Madrid). Full information in "Editorial Afterword," note 2.
1645a (posthumous). *Tomus Quartus Cursus Theologici*, ed. Didacus Ramirez (Madrid). The Solesmes edition of this work (Vol. V; Matiscone: Protat Frères, 1946, 1953) was used in preparing the present work.

1645b (posthumous). *Tomus Quintus Cursus Theologici,* ed. Didacus Ramirez (Madrid). The Vivès edition of this work (Vol. VI; Paris, 1885) was used in preparing the present work.

1645c (posthumous). *Practica y consideración para ayudar a bien morir* (Alcalá, Spain). Full information in "Editorial Afterword," note 2.

1649 (posthumous). *Tomus Sextus Cursus Theologici,* ed. Didacus Ramirez (Madrid). The Vivès edition of this work (Vol. VII; Paris, 1885) was used in preparing the present work.

1656 (posthumous). *Tomus Septimus Cursus Theologici,* ed. Didacus Ramirez (Madrid). The Vivès edition of this work (Vol. VIII; Paris, 1885) was used in preparing the present work.

1667 (posthumous). *Tomus Octavus Cursus Theologici,* ed. Franciscus Combefis (Paris). The Vivès edition of this work (Vol. IX; Paris, 1885) was used in preparing the present work.

POWELL, Ralph Austin.

1983. *Freely Chosen Reality* (Washington: University Press of America).

PORPHYRY.

c.271. *Porphyrii Isagoge et in Aristotelis Categorias Commentarium* (Greek text), ed. A. Busse (Berlin, 1887), English trans. by Edward W. Warren, *Porphyry the Phoenician: Isagoge* (Toronto: Pontifical Institute of Mediaeval Studies, 1975).

PRIETO DEL RAY, Maurilio.

1963-1965. "Significación y sentido ultimado: La noción de 'suppositio' en la lógica de Juan de Santo Tomás," *Convivium,* 15-16 (1963), 33-73 (part 1); 19-20 (1965), 45-72 (part 2).

QUETIF, Jacobus.

1667. "Synopsis Vitae Joannis a Sancto Thoma," in the 1667 *Tomus Octavus Cursus Theologici,* immediately after the "Praefatio" of Franciscus Combefis, the editor of the volume; reprinted as Appendix III to Solesmes, 1931: xlvj-liij.

QUETIF-ECHARD (Jacobus Quetif and Jacobus Echard).

1719. *Scriptores Ordinis Praedicatorum Tomus Primus* (Paris).

1721. *Scriptores Ordinis Praedicatorum Tomus Secundus* (Paris).

RAMIREZ, Didacus.

1645. "Vita Rmi P. Joannis a Sto Thoma," earliest biography of Poinsot, originally published at the beginning of the first posthumous volume, i.e., *Tomus Quartus,* of the *Cursus Theologicus;* reprinted as Appendix I to Solesmes, 1931: xxv-xliij.

RAMIREZ, J. M.

1924. "Jean de St. Thomas," *Dictionnaire de théologie catholique* (Paris: Letouzey), Vol. 8, 803-808. (Note: This work is not reliable for chronology. See Reiser, 1930: XV, par. c.) "Comme particularité de la doctrine de Jean de Saint-Thomas, il faut noter encore qu'il place le constitutif formel de la deité dans l'intellection actuelle de Dieu par lui-même" (cols. 807-808).

RANDALL, Jr., John Herman.

1960. *Aristotle* (New York: Columbia University Press).

1962. *The Career of Philosophy*. Vol. 1: *From the Middle Ages to the Enlightenment* (New York: Columbia University Press).

RANSDELL, Joseph.
1977. "Some Leading Ideas of Peirce's Semiotic," *Semiotica* 19: 157-178.
1979. "The Epistemic Function of Iconicity in Perception," in *Studies in Peirce's Semiotic*, ed. Kenneth Laine Ketner and Joseph M. Ransdell, *Peirce Studies* no. 1 (Lubbock, Texas: Institute for Studies in Pragmaticism), pp. 51-66.
1985(?). "Peircean Semiotic," in preparation for *Semiotica* (complete in draft; awaiting author's final revisions for production).

REISER, B.
1930. "Editoris Praefatio" to Ioannes a Sancto Thoma (Poinsot), *Ars Logica* (1631-1632), nova editio a Reiser (Turin: Marietti), pp. VII-XVIII.
1933. "Editoris in Secundum Volumen Praefatio" to Ioannes a Sancto Thoma, *Naturalis Philosophiae I. et III. Pars* (1633-1634), nova editio a Reiser (Turin: Marietti), pp. V-VIII.
1937. "Editoris in Tertium et Ultimum Volumen Praefatio" to Ioannes a Sancto Thoma, *Naturalis Philosophiae IV. Pars* (1635), nova editio a Reiser (Turin: Marietti), IX-X.

ROBINSON, Edward. See under "MACQUARRIE, John, and . . ."

RODRIGUEZ, Leopoldo Eulogio Palacios.
1954. "Juan de Santo Tomás en la coyuntura de nuestro tiempo y la naturaleza de la ciencia moral," *Anales de la Real Academia de Ciencias Morales y Políticas*, 6, no. 1, 7-20.

RODRIGUEZ, Leopoldo Eulogio Palacios, and CAMINO, Marcial Solana G.
1954. *Discursos leídos en la Junta pública del martes 9 de nov. de 1954 para inaugurar el curso academico 1954-1955 (Real Academia de Ciencias Morales y Politicas). Temas: Juan de Santo Tomás en la coyuntura de nuestro tiempo y la naturaleza de la ciencia moral.—Existencia y caracteres distintivos de la filosofía española según Menéndez Pelayo* (Madrid: C. Bermejo, 1954), 56 pp.

ROMEO, Luigi.
1977. "The Derivation of 'Semiotics' through the History of the Discipline," in *Semiosis* 6, ed. M. Bense, G. Deledalle, and E. Walther, Heft 2, 37-49.
1979. "Pedro da Fonseca in Renaissance Semiotics: A Segmental History of Footnotes," *Ars Semeiotica* II:2, 187-204.

RUSSELL, Bertrand. See also "WHITEHEAD, Alfred North, and . . ."
1905. "On Denoting," *Mind*, XIV: 479-493.
1912. *The Problems of Philosophy* (Oxford).
1921. "Recent Criticisms of Consciousness," chap. 1 of Russell's *The Analysis of Mind* (London: Allen and Unwin), pp. 9-40.
1937. *A Critical Exposition of the Philosophy of Leibniz*, 2nd ed. (London: Allen and Unwin).

RUSSELL, L. J.
1939. "Note on the Term ΣΗΜΕΙΩΤΙΚΗ [sic] in Locke," *Mind* 48:405-406.

SALMANTICENSES.
1644. "De Spe (a quaestione 17 II-II)" (actual author: Fr. Dominic of St. Theresa), Vol. 11, Tractatus 18 (Paris: Palmé éd., 1879), pp. 440-619.

de SAUSSURE, Ferdinand.
1916 (posthumous). *Cours de Linguistique Generale*, publié par Charles Bally et Albert Sechehaye avec la collaboration d'Albert Riedlinger, edition critique preparée par Tullio de Mauro (Paris: Payot, 1972).

SEBEOK, Thomas A.

1963. ''Communication among Social Bees; Porpoises and Sonar; Man and Dolphin'' (review article), *Language* 39, 448-466.

1971. (Original draft). '' 'Semiotics' and Its Congeners,'' reprinted in Sebeok, 1976a: 47-58, q.v. Page references in the present work are to the 1976 reprint.

1974. ''Semiotics: A Survey of the State of the Art,'' in *Linguistics and Adjacent Arts and Sciences,* Vol. 12 of the Current Trends in Linguistics Series, ed. by Sebeok (The Hague: Mouton), pp. 211-264.

1975a. ''The Semiotic Web: A Chronicle of Prejudices,'' *Bulletin of Literary Semiotics* 2: 1-63; reprinted in Sebeok, 1976: 149-188, q.v. Page references in the present work are to the 1976 reprint.

1975b. ''Zoosemiotics: At the Intersection of Nature and Culture,'' in *The Tell-Tale Sign,* ed. Sebeok (Lisse, Netherlands: Peter de Ridder Press), pp. 85-95.

1976a. *Contributions to the Doctrine of Signs* (Lisse, Netherlands: Peter de Ridder Press).

1976b. ''Final Report: Narrative'' for the National Endowment for the Humanities on the Pilot Program in Semiotics in the Humanities at Indiana University, Bloomington, August 1, 1975-July 31, 1976 (June 1, 1976: Research Center for Language and Semiotic Studies, Indiana University, Bloomington), 14 pp.; subsequently published as ''Appendix III. Teaching Semiotics: Report on a Pilot Program,'' in Sebeok 1979: 272-279.

1979. *The Sign & Its Masters* (Austin: University of Texas Press).

1984. ''Symptom,'' Chapter 10 of *New Directions in Linguistics and Semiotics,* ed. James E. Copeland (Houston: Rice University Studies), pp. 212-230.

SELBY-BIGGE, L. A.

1896. ''Editor's Preface'' to the Selby-Bigge edition of David Hume, *A Treatise of Human Nature,* 2nd ed. rev. by P. H. Nidditch (Oxford: Clarendon, 1978), p. v.

SIMON, Yves R.

1943. ''Maritain's Philosophy of the Sciences,'' *The Thomist,* V, 85-102.

1955. ''Foreword'' and ''Notes'' to *The Material Logic of John of St. Thomas,* trans. Yves R. Simon, John J. Glanville, and G. Donald Hollenhorst (Chicago: University of Chicago Press), pp. ix-xxiii and 587-625.

1971. ''An Essay on the Classification of Action and the Understanding of Act,'' *Revue de l'Université d'Ottawa,* 41 (octobre-décembre), 518-541.

SIMON, Yves R., GLANVILLE, John J., and HOLLENHORST, G. Donald, trans. and eds.

1949. ''John of St. Thomas, 'Entia Rationis and Second Intentions,' trans. from *Ars Logica,* Part II, Q. II, Art. 1,'' *The New Scholasticism,* XXIII, 395-413.

1955. *The Material Logic of John of St. Thomas,* partial translation of Poinsot, 1632, corresponding to pp. 250-300, 313a18-342, 475b17-521b10, 523-621a29, 646-655b7, 722b17-731, 741b5-749, 752b39-773a20, 791b27-839b10, of the 1930 Reiser edition of the *Ars Logica* (Chicago: University of Chicago Press). See ''Editorial Afterword,'' note 15, p. 406 above.

SIMONIN, H.-D.

1930. ''Review'' of the 1930 Reiser edition of Poinsot, 1631 and 1632, in *Bulletin Thomiste* (septembre), 140-148.

SOLESMES.

1931. ''Editorum Solesmensium Praefatio'' to Joannes a Sancto Thoma (Poinsot, 1637) *Cursus Theologici Tomus Primus* (Paris: Desclée), i-cviij.

1934. ''Solesmensium Editorum Praefatio in Tomum Secundum'' *Cursus Theologici* Joannis a Sancto Thoma (Poinsot, 1643a) (Paris: Desclée), i-vj.

1937. ''Solesmensium Editorum Praefatio in Tomum Tertium'' *Cursus Theologici* Joannis a Sancto Thoma (Poinsot, 1643b) (Paris: Desclée), i-vj.
1953. ''Solesmensium Editorum Praefatio in Tomum Quartum'' *Cursus Theologici* Joannis a Sancto Thoma (Poinsot, 1645a) (Paris: Desclée, 1946), iii-x.
1964. ''Solesmensium Editorum Praefatio in Tomum Quintum'' *Cursus Theologici* Joannis a Sancto Thoma (Poinsot, 1645b) (Matiscone: Protat Frères), iv-xv.

SPIAZZI, Raymond.
1955. ''Introductio Editoris'' to St. Thomas Aquinas, *In Aristotelis Libros Peri Hermeneias et Posteriorum Analyticorum Expositio,* cum textu ex recensione leonina, ed. R. M. Spiazzi, pp. v-xvii.

SPIEGELBERG, Herbert H.
1965. *The Phenomenological Movement*, 2nd ed. (The Hague: M. Nijhoff), 2 Vols.

STACE, W. T.
1924. *The Philosophy of Hegel* (London: Macmillan). Reprinted 1955 by Dover Publications.

STEINER, George.
1975. *After Babel: Aspects of Language in Translation* (Oxford).

STEPHANUS, Henricus.
1572-1573. *Thesaurus Graecae Linguae,* 6 Vols. (Geneva: excudebat H. Stephanus). Paris edition of 1831-1865, *Thesaurus Graecae linguae ab Henrico Stephano constructus. Post editionem Anglicam novis additamentis auctum ordineque alphabetico tertio ediderunt,* ed. C. B. Case and others, reprinted in Graz, Austria, by Akademische Druck- u. Verlagsanstalt, 1954-1955.

SUAREZ, Francis.
1597. *Disputationes Metaphysicae* (Salamanca: Renaut Fratres). Vols. 25 and 26 of the *Opera Omnia*, editio nova a Carolo Berton (Paris: Vivès, 1861), were used in preparing the present work.
1605. *De Sacramentis* (Venice: Apud Societatem Minimam). Vol. 20 of the *Opera Omnia*, editio nova a Carolo Berton (Paris: Vivès, 1860), was used in preparing the present work.

THOMAS, Ivo.
1950. ''Material Implication in John of St. Thomas,'' *Dominican Studies* 3: 180.

TRAPIELLO.
1889. *Juan de Santo Toma* (Oviedo).

VEATCH, Henry B.
1950. ''Aristotelian and Mathematical Logic,'' *The Thomist*, XIII, 50-96.
1952. *Intentional Logic* (New Haven: Yale University Press).
1969. *Two Logics* (Evanston: Northwestern University Press).

VEATCH, Henry B. and PARKER, Francis H. See under ''PARKER, Francis H., and . . .''

VEATCH, Henry B. and YOUNG, Theodore.
1952. ''Metaphysics and the Paradoxes,'' *The Review of Metaphysics*, VI (December), 199-218.

WADE, Francis C.
1955. *Outlines of Formal Logic,* partial trans. of Poinsot, 1631, corresponding to

pp. 5a5-83b36 of 1930 Reiser edition of the *Ars Logica* (Milwaukee: Marquette University Press). See the "Editorial Afterword," note 14, p. 406 above.

WEINBERG, Julius R.
1965. "The Concept of Relation: Some Observations on Its History," in *Abstraction, Relation, and Induction* (Madison: University of Wisconsin Press), pp. 61-119.

WEISHEIPL, James A.
1977. See "Editorial Afterword," note 107, page 466.

WELLS, Rulon.
1979. See "Editorial Afterword," note 107, page 466.

WHITEHEAD, Alfred North.
1925. *Science and the Modern World* (New York: Free Press).

WHITEHEAD, Alfred North, and RUSSELL, Bertrand.
1910. "Incomplete Symbols," chap. 3 of *Principia Mathematica* (London: Cambridge University Press), pp. 66-84.

WILD, John.
1947. "An Introduction to the Phenomenology of Signs," *Philosophy and Phenomenological Research*, VIII (December), 217-244.
1956. "Review" of *The Material Logic of John of St. Thomas* as edited and trans. by Yves R. Simon, G. Donald Hollenhorst, and John J. Glanville, in *Philosophy and Phenomenological Research*, XVII (June), 558.

WILLIAMS, Brooke.
1985. "What Has History To Do with Semiotic?", *Semiotica* 54 (in press). Also available with index, and bibliography layered historically, under the title *History and Semiotic* (Victoria University: Toronto Semiotic Circle Monograph, Summer 1985).

WINANCE, Eleuthère.
1983. "Review" of *Introducing Semiotic* (Deely 1982), *Revue Thomiste*, LXXX (juillet-août), 514-516.
1985. "Echo de la querrelle du psychologisme et de l'antipsychologisme dans l'Ars Logica de Jean Poinsot," *Semiotica* (in press).

WINDELBAND, Wilhelm.
1901. *A History of Philosophy*, authorized trans. by James H. Tufts, 2nd ed. rev. and enlarged (New York: Macmillan).

WITTGENSTEIN, Ludwig.
1958. *Philosophical Investigations*, 3rd ed. G. E. M. Anscombe (New York: Macmillan).

WOJTKIEWICZ, C.
1961. "L'Objet de la logique chez Jean de S. Thomas" (en polonais avec résumé en français), *Roczniki filozoficzne* 9, no. 1.

WOLICKA, Elżbieta.
1979. "Notion of Truth in the Epistemology of John of St. Thomas," *The New Scholasticism*, LIII (Winter), 96-106.

YOUNG, Theodore.
See under "VEATCH, Henry, and . . ."

ZIGLIARA, Thomas M.
1882. Synopses and Annotations to the Tomus Primus of the leonine *Opera omnia sancti Thomae Aquinatis*, containing St. Thomas' uncompleted commentary *In Aristotelis libros perihermenias expositio*, composed c. 1269-1274.

Colophon

It is a time-honored habit in publishing books, when space permits, to comment on the "making of a book". Since our signatures in this book have broken in a way that allows such space, we wish here to share with our readers the more salient aspects of the process of getting the type onto paper.

This book began in 1969 as an idea for a simple translation of a Latin text. The one principle operative at that stage was that this book be a translation, as distinct from a transliteration of any sort. When, however, it took three years to reach an intelligible rendering of the key terms of the *Treatise* ("secundum esse/secundum dici"), and seeing that this rendering took seventeen English words (two terms of seven and ten words, respectively) to convey the point of the bare four Latin words, it also became clear that the translation should not be presented apart from the original text.

Once the commitment was made to a bilingual presentation, the rest of the design was dictated by the objective of making the languages interplay as exactly as possible, a demand enhanced by the plan to generate a detailed set of indices. Originally, the plan was to key the indices to the Latin text, rendered photographically from the Reiser edition. Eventually, however, it became clear that the Latin would have to be set afresh for reasons of aesthetics.

The decision to reset the Latin suggested a further possibility: perfectly matched columns of Latin and English, perhaps the most exact bilingual presentation in the history of right-justified printing, with line numbers between the columns to key the indices. The process of executing this plan gradually imposed the realization that, for all its fundamentality, the Latin text in this edition was nonetheless framed and carried by the English language, and final keying of the indices was made accordingly.

A major problem from the outset was the selection and arrangement of the segments of Latin text required to read Poinsot's questions on semiotic as a whole unto themselves. The first attempt at solution caused a disruption of the pagination sequence of the texts as they appear in the *Ars Logica,* and had the further disadvantage of making the text proper accessible only by way of a lengthy and tedious "Translator's Introduction".

The second solution was the series of "semiotic markers". This device at a stroke restored the pagination sequence of Poinsot's original presentation, and removed from the reader's path the obstacle of a ponderous Introduction.

The conception and basic editorial design of the work was now complete. There remained only the matter of execution. For this, several vendors were invited to respond to the task. One response—that of Mr. Bud MacFarlane, Manager of Composition Specialists—stood out from all the others in that he

alone was able to produce complete sample pages with matched columns and notes without any "cut and paste", from his Compugraphic 8400 phototypesetter.

There was also Mr. MacFarlane's attitude. "I want this job," he told me. "It's my chance to produce a masterpiece." Chet Grycz, as Production and Design Manager of the University of California Press, after some lengthy discussion with Bud, confirmed the estimate. We had in Bud, Chet said, "some sort of typesetting genius; grab him."

The manuscript pages of Latin and English were marked every third to fifth word with numbered slashes, enabling the typesetter to know exactly where he was in both languages at all times. Two devices were then employed to secure the identical length with opening and closing line match for the columns: subtle variations in set-size (i.e., letter-width), combined with, especially, a floating margin between the columns, making of each page, in effect, a composition unto itself. "There is no photocomposing machine built," Grycz once wrote, "that can easily generate pages of such complexity as these. To look at Bud's accomplished pages with even a little knowledge of the typographic art is immediately to understand that a human being made numberless small judgments and decisions on each page; and made slight compromises here and there, all with the purpose of bringing the text more clearly to the reader's eye. To do so, is a mark of a craftsman. To do so with elegance, the mark of an artist."

It is Bud MacFarlane's masterpiece, and we are pleased to thank him openly for it, in this colophon.

The typeface, chosen for the particular openness that makes it legible even in reduced point sizes (see especially the Indices), is Palacio, a face derived from the Palatino type designed in 1948 by the German-born calligrapher/designer (1918–) Hermann Zapf based upon an oldstyle typeface from the late 15th century and first issued by Mergenthaler Linotype, 1955. The text is set throughout in two image sizes, a 40 pica line for bilingual matter in a point size of 10.5 on a leading of 12, and a 32 pica line set 11 on 13, with the notes on pages 44–45, which are set 8.5 on 9.1 in order to fit on the pages with the text they accompany). To describe the agony of finding an appropriate typographical vehicle to convey the various sorts of information inherent in a complicated set of indices would defy our space limits: suffice to say that the indices are predominantly set 8 on 10, but with some further internal variations, especially in the Index Personarum. (We only hope that the readers who turn to the indices in the course of studying this work will experience an ease of use and utility that is the result of our efforts.) Design coordination of the display text for title pages throughout and for the gatefold and other charts is by Mark Ong. The book is printed on acid-free paper manufactured by the Glatfelter Paper Mill in Spring Grove, Pennsylvania. It was printed by Malloy Lithographing in Ann Arbor, Michigan. The sheets were folded and bound by John Dekker and Sons bindery in Grand Rapids, Michigan.

C.J.G.
J.D.
Berkeley, California
7 May 1985